Charisma
UNDER PRESSURE

"*Deep water is what I am wont to swim in, it all has become a second nature to me*"
—Joseph Smith, Sep. 1, 1842

UNDER PRESSURE

JOSEPH SMITH | AMERICAN PROPHET | 1831–1839

DAN VOGEL

SIGNATURE BOOKS | 2023 | SALT LAKE CITY

To my brother and sister, Larry and Donna

Design by Jason Francis.

Frontispiece image: detail from "The two martyrs, Joseph & Hyrum Smith. Murdered at Carthage, Ill. June 27th 1844," undated. Courtesy of Yale University Library.

FIRST EDITION | 2023

LIBRARY OF CONGRESS CONTROL NUMBER: 2023931707

Hardback ISBN: 978-1-56085-460-9
Ebook ISBN: 978-1-56085-439-5

Contents

Introduction

Behold, that seer will the Lord bless; and they that seek to destroy him, shall be confounded ... And his name shall be called after me; and it shall be after the name of his father. And he shall be like unto me; for the thing which the Lord shall bring forth by his hand, by the power of the Lord shall bring my people unto salvation; yea, thus prophesied Joseph.
  —*Lehi*, Book of Mormon, *1830 ed., 66–67 [2 Ne 3:4, 14–15]*

His early followers called him Joseph—the Seer. It must have been comforting for them to be in the presence of someone in direct contact with God. One needed no longer guess as to what God wanted his children to believe and do. The veil had been parted. The only thing that remained was to be obedient and mindful of the prophet's guidance—for one's salvation depended upon it, both spiritually and physically. Joseph Smith announced that the end of the world was near, that Christ's second coming was imminent, and that he had been called by God to establish a New Jerusalem near the western border of the United States, where believers would gather to escape the wars and plagues about to sweep the wicked from the earth and live God's law in perfect harmony and peace. The Book of Mormon and several revelations had proclaimed it, but success depended on Smith's ability to win and maintain influence over his people.

While historian Jan Shipps has suggested, "The mystery of Mormonism cannot be solved until we solve the mystery of Joseph Smith,"[1] it may also be said that the mystery of Joseph Smith cannot be solved until we understand better the larger mystery of the attraction of the charismatic leader and the devotion of the true believer. When one understands more fully the symbiosis of leader and follower, then perhaps Smith will seem less a puzzle

---

1. Shipps, "The Prophet Puzzle," 43.

and more like a person fulfilling his own needs through his followers. Shamans, prophets, heroes, and charismatic leaders are in important ways *social constructs*,[2] because they mirror back to their followers what is demanded of them. Cultural anthropologist Ernest Becker describes the interdependence between leaders and followers, each looking to the other to fulfill their needs. This is not without cost. Summarizing Wilfred R. Bion's work in group psychology, Becker observes that "the leader is as much a creature of the group as they of him and that he loses his 'individual distinctiveness' by being the leader, as they do by being followers. He has no more freedom to be himself than any other member of the group, precisely because he has to be a reflex of their assumptions in order to qualify for leadership in the first place."[3] For this reason, I suspect, the "real" Joseph Smith will always remain elusive.

There are, in fact, many possible constructions of Joseph Smith, and depending on how one assesses the evidence for his truth-claims, a completely different Joseph Smith emerges. But this is probably as Smith wanted it. Both as a treasure seer and as a prophet, his claims demanded belief or skepticism. There was seemingly no middle ground. But is the search for a middle ground itself antithetical to the essence of Smith's personality and message? In his provocative essay, "A Joseph Smith for the Twenty-first Century," Smith biographer Richard L. Bushman worried that the growing "tolerance" of non-Mormon scholars would bring "a blurring of the real issues," and asked: "Wouldn't believing biographers [among whom Bushman counted himself] prefer to have the question of authenticity laid squarely before our readers, even at the cost of having the revelations disputed? Do we want Joseph Smith's challenge to the world to be lost in a haze of a patronizing kindness?"[4]

This worry applies to the academy of religion, which brackets truth-claims for other reasons than "patronizing kindness"—scholarship simply lacks the tools necessary to make the kinds of determinations Bushman calls for. Strictly speaking, scholars cannot answer questions such as: "Was Joseph Smith a *true* prophet?" "Is the Book of Mormon *inspired*?" However, I suggest that there are more interpretive choices than some would have us believe, for while Smith's truth-claims are beyond the scope of scholarship, the Book

---

2. I use "social construction" in a local and limited sense and differentiate it from *universal constructionism*, or linguistic idealism. See Hacking, *The Social Construction of What?*, 24–25. On the theory of social construction, see, for example, Berger and Luckmann, *The Social Construction of Reality*. On the social construction of prophetic charisma, see Wallis, "The Social Construction of Charisma"; Blasi, *Making Charisma*.

3. Becker, *The Denial of Death*, 136.

4. Bushman, *Believing History*, 269.

of Mormon's historical status is another matter. I believe that historians are free to conclude the Book of Mormon is not historical and to revise or adjust Smith's biography accordingly. In other words, a non-historical Book of Mormon presents scholars with a different interpretive paradigm(s) from which to consider Smith.

To some apologetic traditionalists, Joseph Smith cannot be a true prophet if the Book of Mormon is not real history, for, they argue, God and prophets do not engage in deception. Brigham Young University professor William J. Hamblin, for example, stressed: "The issue is: if the Book of Mormon is fiction, then Joseph Smith could not be a true prophet, a point tacitly accepted by most of those who reject historicity, since all of their accounts include serious equivocation or redefinition of the key concepts [of] revelation, inspiration, and prophet."[5] A non-historical Book of Mormon might be a challenge to some believers, but the consequences of that proposition are not as clear as Hamblin represented. It is not as if these terms have not already been redefined by traditionalists themselves to accommodate textual changes Smith made in subsequent editions of the Book of Mormon and early revelations, as well as "corrections" he made in the Bible. Without equivocation, it would be difficult to explain the various historical and literary anachronisms that appear in the Book of Mormon. So, in principle, traditionalists have already equivocated on fundamental definitions of key terms like *translation* and *revelation*. Clearly, there are other ways to construe the evidence, even for traditionalists. To accommodate parallels in the Book of Mormon to the nineteenth century within a traditionalist paradigm, LDS scholar Blake Ostler, for example, has suggested Smith made inspired textual "expansions" to an ancient text.[6]

Nevertheless, there are significant interpretive consequences for historians, especially biographers of Smith, who have concluded there is no historical basis for the Book of Mormon's ancient narrative. If the history described in the Book of Mormon is fictitious, then there were no ancient Nephites to make gold plates or to appear to Smith many centuries later. It therefore follows that Smith constructed the plates, probably out of tin, which he then placed in a box or wrapped in a cloth and allowed others to handle.[7] While the construction of the plates was part of a conscious

---

5. Hamblin, "'There Really Is a God,'" 81.

6. Ostler, "The Book of Mormon as a Modern Expansion of an Ancient Source."

7. In addition to three and eight witnesses to the Book of Mormon, Joseph Smith allowed others to handle the plates while concealed in a box or wrapped in a cloth, and there is significant evidence that their experiences with the plates were a combination of physical handling and spiritual sight. See Vogel, "The Validity of the Witnesses' Testimonies."

deception,[8] one does not necessarily have to conclude that Smith thought of himself as a fraudulent prophet. As I have previously suggested, interpreters of Smith's life would do well to move beyond the simplistic prophet-or-charlatan paradigm and explore the possibility that he considered himself an inspired prophet, despite his occasional use of deception.[9] Perhaps we should attempt to understand him on his own terms. What did he believe about himself? What were his definitions of truth, revelation, and prophet? Did he believe God sometimes inspires deception?

When Moroni—the last prophet in the Book of Mormon—exhorts readers to "ask God ... if these things are not true" and promises that "he will manifest the truth of it unto you," the text points to a specific kind of truth.[10] Previously, Moroni quoted God as saying: "For because of my spirit, he [that believeth] shall know that these things are true; for it persuadeth men to do good; and whatsoever thing persuadeth men to do good, is of me: for good cometh of none, save it be of me. I am the same that leadeth men to all good."[11] Similarly, Mormon reasoned: "I shew unto you the way to judge: for every thing which inviteth to do good, and to persuade to believe in Christ, is sent forth by the power and gift of Christ; wherefore ye may know with a perfect knowledge, it is of God."[12] In other words, since all good comes from God, and the Book of Mormon tries to persuade humankind to do and be good—be righteous and believe in Christ—it is therefore true and inspired even if, in the final analysis, it is not historical.

This concept of inspiration ties in well with Smith's definition of prophet. In a letter published in the *Elders' Journal* in July 1838, Smith responded to the question: "Do you believe Joseph Smith, Jr., to be a prophet?" His answer was: "Yes, and every other man who has the testimony of Jesus." He then quoted Revelation 19:10: "For the testimony of Jesus, is the spirit of

---

8. Ann Taves suggests that although Smith constructed the plates himself, possibly out of tin, the plates nevertheless "might have become *real* for Smith as well as his followers" in the same way that the elements of the Eucharist transubstantiate into the body and blood of Christ for Catholics. In this way, Taves hoped to resolve the charge of conscious deception and preserve for his current followers a belief in his complete sincerity. Taves, "History and the Claims of Revelation." Taves proposed this model despite Smith's rejection of the doctrine of transubstantiation (Moro. 4 and 5; D&C 27:4). In my view, such an explanation resolves nothing since the plates were at the center of a web of interrelated deceptions. Ultimately, it is an unnecessary hypothesis since, as I explain here, Smith's construction of fake plates would not make him a fraudulent prophet in his own mind.

9. Vogel, "'The Prophet Puzzle' Revisited"; Vogel, *Joseph Smith*, viii–xxi.

10. Book of Mormon, 1830 ed., 586 [Moro. 10:4].

11. Book of Mormon, 1830 ed., 546–47 [Ether 4:11–12].

12. Book of Mormon, 1830 ed., 578 [Moro. 7:16]. Cf. 1 John 4:2: "Hereby know ye the Spirit of God: Every spirit that confesseth that Jesus Christ is come in the flesh is of God."

prophecy."[13] To return to the either/or definition of prophet, Smith *could* believe himself to be an inspired prophet and the Book of Mormon a true revelation even if it were not ancient history so long as he had a testimony of Jesus and viewed the book as an extension of that testimony.

Religious forgery has a long history. From the fake discovery of the Book of Deuteronomy in the ruins of the temple in the seventh century BCE (2 Kgs. 22), to the many pseudepigraphic (or pseudonymous) writings—like the Assumption of Moses, the Book of Enoch, and the Ascension of Isaiah—generally dating from 200 BCE to CE 200, to the forged letters of the apostles Peter and Paul within the present New Testament canon,[14] to the many forgeries of medieval monks and clerics,[15] and finally, as I suggest, to the Book of Mormon and the Book of Abraham. The motivation of these pseudonymous authors, explains New Testament scholar Bart Ehrman, was to give their own religious views—often deemed heretical by the dominant group of believers—respectability and authority that otherwise would not be given an obscure author.[16] Likewise, few people outside his own family and small circle of friends would have wanted to read a theological book written by Joseph the money-digging farmer—that is, if he could get it published.

In my 1998 essay, "'The Prophet Puzzle' Revisited,"[17] I suggested Smith was what has long been termed a "pious fraud" or "sincere charlatan" and drew on his own writings to explain how he may have rationalized the ethical conflict of using deception in God's name. A revelation Smith dictated in March 1830, for example, declared that the terms "eternal punishment" and "endless punishment" are synonyms for "God's punishment," and that punishment is not eternal after all, but God uses those terms to mislead and

---

13. Joseph Smith, Questions and Answers, May 8, 1838, in *Elders' Journal*, July 1838, 43 (*JSP*, D6:141).

14. Letters traditionally assigned to Paul but now thought to be pseudepigraphic by most scholars are: 1 and 2 Timothy, Titus, and Ephesians. Colossians and 2 Thessalonians are also doubted by many scholars. See Ehrman, *Forgery and Counter-Forgery*, and Ehrman, *Forged*, which examine the motivation and function behind early Christian forgeries.

15. Hiatt, *The Making of Medieval Forgeries*.

16. Ehrman, *Forged*, 8–9; Ehrman, *Forgery and Counter-Forgery*, 150. While the Book of Mormon is a pseudonymous work, it is not strictly speaking a forgery since it did not use the authority of *known* prophets, except when Lehi quotes the lost writings of the ancient patriarch Joseph concerning the great seer of the latter days named Joseph (2 Ne. 3:6, 15). Given the New World setting of his scripture, Joseph Smith had to create his own authorities. While the Book of Mormon did not draw on the authority of known prophets in the Bible, it did attempt to align itself with the lost books of the Bible—not with writings mentioned in the Old Testament like the book of Nathan the prophet or visions of Iddo the seer (2 Chron. 9:29), but with the writings of the prophet Zenos and Zenock recorded on Lehi's brass plates (1 Ne. 19:10).

17. Vogel, "'The Prophet Puzzle' Revisited."

frighten his children into repenting, that "it might work upon the hearts of the children of men, altogether for my name's glory."[18] Despite the decided anti-Universalist stance of the Book of Mormon, the revelation also disclosed that Smith was secretly a believer in universal salvation and therefore would not have feared punishment for his pious deception, especially if he also believed God had authorized him to do so.[19]

Another example comes from the Book of Mormon, when the spirit of the Lord commands Nephi to kill the drunken and defenseless Laban, but Nephi hesitates and argues: "Never at any time have I shed the blood of man." The Spirit reissues the command: "The Lord slayeth the wicked to bring forth his righteous purposes. It is better that one man should perish than that a nation should dwindle and perish in unbelief."[20] I suggest that the story of Nephi reflects Smith's own struggle to accept the moral and ethical compromise necessary to deceive in God's name, but was finally convinced that it was the best way to accomplish a greater good and that he had God's approval. "That which is wrong under one circumstance, may be and often is, right under another," Smith dictated privately in 1842. "Whatever God requires is right, no matter what it is, although we may not see the reason thereof till long after the events transpire ... even things which may be considered abominable to all who do not understand the order of heaven."[21] My conclusion in 1998 was modest, I thought: "We may never know exactly Smith's reasoning, but we can at least say that if he wrote the Book of Mormon, became a prophet, and founded the church as a pious deception, it is evident that he had the psychological means of justifying such acts."[22]

Since I introduced the term "pious fraud" into Joseph Smith and early Mormon studies, it has been criticized on both sides of the interpretive gap. However, as I explained then, "fraud" does not refer to Smith's self-perception, but rather to some of his activities, such as constructing a set of plates as a faith-promoting object. Critics of Smith, on the other hand, argue

18. BC XVI:8 [D&C 19:7] (*JSP*, D1:89).

19. BC XVI:7–12, 22–23 [D&C 19:6–12, 21–22] (*JSP*, D1:89–90). On the Book of Mormon's anti-Universalist stance, see Vogel, "Anti-Universalist Rhetoric in the Book of Mormon."

20. Book of Mormon, 1830 ed., 12 [1 Ne. 4:10, 12–13]. Cf. John 11:50.

21. Joseph Smith, Letter to [Nancy Rigdon, ca. mid-Apr. 1842], in *Sangamo Journal*, Aug. 19, 1842, [2] (*JSP*, D9:417). Gerrit J. Dirkmaat has questioned Joseph Smith's authorship of the letter to Nancy Rigdon. Dirkmaat, "Searching for 'Happiness.'" However, I find his arguments unconvincing. He also failed to consider Devery S. Anderson's textual evidence supporting Joseph Smith's authorship: "'I Could Love Them All': Nauvoo Polygamy in the Marriage of Willard and Jennetta Richards," *Sunstone*, June 2013, 23–26.

22. Vogel, "'Prophet Puzzle' Revisited," 62.

that Smith was anything but pious. To them, he was little more than a malignant narcissist who cared only about himself and the acquisition of wealth, power, and sexual conquest. Of course, I would not argue that Smith *was* pious. He never made that claim himself. "I dont want you to think I am very righteous. for I am not very righteous," he confessed in 1843.[23] My argument is that his motive, or, at least, his chief motive, for producing the Book of Mormon and founding a church, was pious. People generally have more than one motive for doing things, and having other motives (like the acquisition of power and wealth) would not necessarily negate pious intentions. Indeed, the acquisition of power and wealth may be necessary to better promote the intended good, especially if that good included being the leader of a communal society—of which there were many examples in the nineteenth century.

As a biographer of Joseph Smith, I eschew binary caricatures of him. My purpose is to present a more complete, holistic way of viewing Smith. I allow that Smith may have had more than one motive, and that his motives were fluid over time. As historiographer David Hackett Fischer notes, "In the realm of consciousness, a man who does something does it for every reason he can think of, and a few unthinkable reasons as well." Fischer also speaks of "motivational pluralism" and mentions psychologist Abraham Maslow's "hierarchies" of motivation.[24] Robert Jones Shafer, in his *Guide to Historical Method*, warns: "Psychology has not agreed on a single theory of human personality. It gives us insights, but not answers. Historians thus will be cautious about blanket assignment of human motivation to self-interest, the will to dominate, or altruism."[25] Motive is difficult to ascertain, to be sure. As Fischer explains, "There can be no primary, direct evidence of any past motive. But there is a tacit logic of inference which can attain a high degree of probable accuracy."[26]

Charismatic Leadership

To his followers, Joseph Smith was a man of great charisma, who exuded a magnetic energy and had a commanding presence. In his classic study of political and religious charisma, German sociologist Max Weber (1864–1920) described charisma as "a certain quality of an individual personality, by virtue of which he is set apart from ordinary men and treated as endowed with

---

23. Smith, Journal, May 21, 1843 (*JSP*, J3:20).
24. Fischer, *Historians' Fallacies*, 214.
25. Shafer, *A Guide to Historical Method*, 31.
26. Fischer, *Historians' Fallacies*, 215.

supernatural, superhuman, or at least specifically exceptional powers or qualities. These are such as are not accessible to the ordinary person, but are regarded as of divine origin or as exemplary, and on the basis of them the individual concerned is treated as a leader."[27] Thus, charismatic authority (as opposed to institutional authority) is a particular kind of authority that rests "on devotion to the exceptional sanctity, heroism or exemplary character of an individual person, and of the normative patterns or order revealed or ordained" by that individual.[28] While Weber focused on charisma as a quality of the would-be leader's personality, he also discussed the essential role of the "followers" or "disciples" in "recognizing" their leader and in accepting their moral "duty" to respond to his call:

> The holder of Charisma seizes the task ... and demands obedience and a following by virtue of his mission. His success determines whether he finds them. His charismatic claim breaks down if his mission is not recognized by those to whom he feels he has been sent. If they recognize him, he is their master—so long as he knows how to maintain recognition through "proving" himself. But he does not derive his "right" from their will, in the manner of an election. Rather, the reverse holds: it is the *duty* of those to whom he addresses his mission to recognize him as their charismatically qualified leader.[29]

According to Weber, "Recognition on the part of those subject to authority ... is decisive for the validity of charisma. ... Psychologically this 'recognition' is a matter of complete personal devotion to the possessor of the quality, arising out of enthusiasm, or of despair and hope." Such allegiance to the leader "is freely given and guaranteed by what is held to be a 'sign' or proof, originally always a miracle, and consists in devotion to the corresponding revelation, hero worship, or absolute trust in the leader." Charisma itself is not the basis for legitimacy, Weber states, but "legitimacy ... lies rather in the conception that it is the duty of those who have been called to a charismatic mission to recognize its quality and to act accordingly."[30]

Weber specifically mentioned Joseph Smith as an example of a charismatic leader who "proved himself to be charismatically qualified" through his production of the Book of Mormon.[31] First-generation Mormon de-

---

27. Eisenstadt, *Max Weber on Charisma and Institution Building*, 48.
28. Eisenstadt, 46.
29. Eisenstadt, 20.
30. Eisenstadt, 49.
31. Eisenstadt, 19.

scriptions of their prophet support Weber's definition of a charismatic leader. "My impression on beholding the Prophet and shaking hands with him was, that I stood face to face with the greatest man on earth," recalled John M. Chidester.[32] Elias Cox, who met Smith in 1842, remembered that "he was a very handsome man, with blue eyes, and a countenance gleaming with beauty from his pure thoughts and enlightened work."[33] Oliver B. Huntington said: "All the time he was delivering the word of the Lord his face shone as if there was a light within him and his flesh was translucent."[34] In recounting her first encounter with the prophet, Jane S. Richards said she "recognized him from a dream" and that "he had such [an] angelic countenance as I never saw before."[35] Lyman O. Littlefield remarked that Smith's "conversation and public teaching" were "attended by a power truly Godlike."[36] Remembering her first impressions of Smith, Bathsheba W. Smith said she believed "he was an extraordinary man—a man of great penetration; was different from any other man I ever saw: had the most heavenly countenance, was genial, affable and kind."[37] Mercy R. Thompson, whose husband was the private secretary to Smith, remembered: "I have seen him as if carried away by the power of God beyond all mortal conception, when speaking to the Saints in their public gatherings; and ... I have heard him explaining ... the glorious principles of the gospel, as no man could, except by prophetic power."[38] Emmeline B. Wells, who later became prominent as president of the women's Relief Society in Utah, gave a most remarkable account of meeting Smith after her boat landed at the Mormon capital of Nauvoo, Illinois, in 1844. "When he took my hand," she remembered, "I was simply electrified,—thrilled through and through to the tips of my fingers, and every part of my body, as if some magic elixir had given me new life and vitality. ... I was overwhelmed with indefinable emotion."[39]

---

32. John M. Chidester, "Recollections of the Prophet Joseph Smith," *Juvenile Instructor* (Salt Lake City), Mar. 1, 1892, 151.

33. Elias Cox, "Joseph Smith, the Prophet," *Young Woman's Journal* (Salt Lake City), Dec. 1906, 544.

34. Oliver B. Huntington, "Words and Incidents of the Prophet Joseph's Life," *Young Woman's Journal*, Dec. 1890, 124–25.

35. Richards, "Reminiscences," 11.

36. Lyman O. Littlefield, "Recollections of the Prophet Joseph Smith," *Juvenile Instructor*, Jan. 15, 1892, 64–65.

37. Bathsheba W. Smith, "Recollections of the Prophet Joseph Smith," *Juvenile Instructor*, June 1, 1892, 344.

38. Mercy R. Thompson, "Recollections of the Prophet Joseph Smith," *Juvenile Instructor*, July 1, 1892, 398.

39. Emmeline B. Wells, "Joseph Smith, the Prophet," *Young Woman's Journal*, Dec. 1905, 554–56.

Such descriptions of the Mormon leader often reveal more about the psychology of the true believer than they do about Joseph Smith. Much has been learned about the leader-follower dynamic since the early twentieth century when Weber wrote about charisma. Sociologists have come to view charisma as more of a social phenomenon than a character trait. Sociologist Kojiro Miyahara, for example, has observed: "The charisma of a leader … is a product of the followers. It is essentially an illusion. The actual personality of a leader has little to do with charisma. This assertion does not deny the existence of remarkably innovative individuals. Rather, the point is that innovativeness of an individual as such is just one of many factors that facilitate the imputation of charisma."[40] According to Miyahara, the charisma of a leader may be considered "a social phenomenon in which people (followers) impute a superior quality to a leader," although "it is apprehended by the followers as a gift of grace, i.e., something that is coming from superhuman sources. Yet, the extraordinary quality of the leader remains, in actuality, the product of the followers' perception that there exists a certain alien power … behind the leader's expressed words and deeds."[41]

Sociologist Anthony J. Blasi has similarly observed: "The individual who has a charisma is not only a person but a personage, a public character in a public drama who receives and imparts legitimacy. That public drama is a process rather than an entity. It not only takes a processual form such as narrative, lending itself to reenactment, imitation, and recitation, but also is a process in the sense of itself having to be constituted and reconstituted in history."[42] Since charisma is socially constructed and may be "constituted and reconstituted," then it is possible according to Blasi for "any one person's charisma, if it is to last more than a short time, [to] be constructed anew for each generation." Moreover, says Blasi, "if a given personage's charisma has survived over an extended period of time, it has probably done so by changing with the times. The changes in question do not imply that the individual has shifted with every fashion but that the public has remade its impression of the personage several times."[43]

This has already happened for Joseph Smith. Even now Smith's image is being reconstituted for the next generation, spurred on by the internet and the publication of a multi-volume scholarly edition of the *Joseph*

---

40. Miyahara, "Charisma," 383.
41. Miyahara, 382.
42. Blasi, *Making Charisma*, 5–6.
43. Blasi, 6.

Smith Papers. The first reconstitution of Smith's charisma happened in 1834 and 1835, when he enhanced his image, with the help of colleague Oliver Cowdery, as a charismatic personage and imparted legitimacy by introducing a new narrative of angelic ordinations. He did this while at the same time establishing a hierarchy under him that stratified and centralized authority. This was a major step in a process that began almost immediately after Smith organized his church in April 1830. This process, which Weber called the "routinization" or *institutionalization* of charisma, inevitably happens as the founder stabilizes the erratic aspects of charisma, thwarts challengers, and ensures the perpetuation of the community.

A second reconstitution occurred in 1838, when Smith began to create an official history of his life and the church he founded. In this history, which he began publishing in 1842 in the Mormon periodical *Times and Seasons,* Smith obfuscated the true nature of his early activity as a treasure seer, suppressed the folk-magic and treasure-seeking context of his 1823, 1824, and 1827 encounters with the "spirit" in charge of the gold plates, and inserted anachronistic elements such as the terms "angel" and "Urim and Thummim" (instead of "spirit" and "spectacles"), all of which gave this narrative a more mainstream Christian flavoring. In so doing, Smith was not only defending his reputation, he was reconstituting his charisma through a story that would be more appealing to the wider culture, thus attracting more converts and thereby expanding his charismatic authority.

Prophetic Call

Just who was this Joseph Smith who captivated so many of his generation? Many contemporaries saw nothing especially extraordinary in the farm boy who was twenty-four years old when he published the Book of Mormon and founded the Church of Christ. What did they miss?

Adding to the inaccurate assessment of Smith was the role in which he cast himself—the unlearned prophet confounding the professional educated clergy. To accentuate the miracle of the Book of Mormon, Smith actively downplayed his intelligence. He and his siblings were "deprived of the bennifit of an education," he said in an 1832 history. "Suffice it to say I was mearly instructid in reading and writing and the ground rules of Arithmatic which const[it]uted my whole literary acquirements."[44] Although this was an exaggeration, there was an element of truth in that his grammar was

---

44. JS History, 1832, JS Letterbook 1, 1 (*JSP*, H1:11).

poor and he was plain spoken. Sarah Pratt, Apostle Orson Pratt's estranged first wife, said Smith would play up his lack of education as a fulfillment of scripture.[45] Yet he possessed something a school could not give him—intelligence. Smith's lawyer in Missouri, Peter H. Burnett, observed that although Sidney Rigdon, a counselor in the church's presidency with Smith and a former Campbellite minister, "was a man of superior education, [and] an eloquent speaker, ... he did not posses the native intellect of Smith, and lacked his determined will."[46] Kirtland, Ohio, resident Christopher Crary, who had business dealings with both Smith and Rigdon, similarly observed: "I considered [Smith] far superior to the educated Rigdon in intellectual ability."[47]

Smith's inability to write well was amply compensated by his gift of moving people emotionally through his words, although as a public speaker he could be awkward. Dictating his text to scribes was suited to his slow deliberative style of producing text. Although Smith had some experience in his youth delivering what Methodists called the "exhortation" following the minister's sermon, he nevertheless appointed more fluent orators such as Oliver Cowdery and Sidney Rigdon to speak for him.[48] Because of this self-consciousness as a public speaker, Smith included a prophecy in his book that the Lord would raise up a great seer in the last days by the name of Joseph, who would write revelations and translate a record but would not be "mighty in speaking" and that another man would be appointed as his "spokesman."[49] Although Smith grew more comfortable as a public speaker and could captivate audiences, he would never become a great orator in the strict sense of what nineteenth-century audiences expected. He had a power with words that was unconventional but effective. As if describing himself, Smith had Nephi declare, "neither am I mighty in writing, like unto speaking: for when a man speaketh by the power of the Holy Ghost, the power of the Holy Ghost carrieth it unto the hearts of the children of men."[50]

---

45. Sarah Pratt, Interview, Mar.–May 1885, in Wyl, *Mormon Portraits*, 25.

46. Burnett, *Recollections and Opinions of an Old Pioneer*, 67.

47. Crary, *Pioneer and Personal Reminiscences*, 21.

48. Former Palmyra resident Orsamus Turner, who often visited the village between 1822 and 1828, said that the young Joseph, "after catching a spark of Methodism in the camp meeting, away down in the woods, on the Vienna road," became a "very passable exhorter in evening meetings." Turner, *History of the Pioneer Settlement of Phelps and Gorham's Purchase*, 214 (*EMD*, 3:50). The Methodists did not acquire their property in the woods on the Vienna Road until July 1821. See Walters, "A Reply to Dr. Bushman," 99. Former Palmyra resident Daniel Hendrix said, "He was a good talker, and would have made a fine stump speaker, if he had the training." *San Francisco Chronicle*, May 14, 1893, 12 (*EMD*, 3:211).

49. Book of Mormon, 1830 ed., 66–67 [2 Ne. 3:14–18].

50. Book of Mormon, 1830 ed., 121 [2 Ne. 33:1].

There are no verbatim texts of Smith's sermons, but those who heard him preach describe his style as unpolished but sincere, energetic, forceful, and extremely compelling. Referring to a June 1831 conference held in Kirtland, Jared Carter wrote: "Brother Joseph, not withstanding he is not naturally talented for a speaker yet he was filled with the power of the Holy Ghost so that he spoke as I never heard man speak for God."[51] Burnett said that in "conversation he was slow, and used too many words to express ideas, and would not generally go directly to the point," but that as a sermonizer he was an "awkward but vehement speaker."[52] According to Crary, "His language, so far as I was qualified to judge, was correct, forcible, and right to the point and convincing."[53] Wandle Mace thought Smith was "very interesting and eloquent in speech," while Job Smith said he was "powerful in invective and occasionally sarcastic."[54] One visitor to Nauvoo remarked that "the Prophet spoke very fluently, but ungrammatically, like an uneducated man; but he possessed the gift of a rough eloquence, and could be most persuasive when he tried," and that on one occasion Smith "exhorted with rude eloquence from the Scripture text."[55] Joseph Lee Robinson said Smith's "voice … is like the voise of the mighty thunders of Heaven yet his Language is meek and instructive, Edefieth much, but there is a power and magesty that attends his words and Preaching that we never beheld in any man before."[56] Howard Coray, who became one of Smith's scribes in Nauvoo, recalled: "I sat and listened to his preaching at the stand in Nauvoo a great many times when I have been completely carried away with his indescribable eloquence—power of expression—speaking as I have never heard any other man speak."[57] Rachel Ridgeway Grant simply said, "When he was preaching you could feel the power and influence."[58] Parley P. Pratt, a former Campbellite missionary, said:

> [Smith's] language abounded in original eloquence peculiar to himself— not polished—not studied—not smoothed and softened by education and refined by art; but flowing forth in its own native simplicity, and profusely abounding in variety of subject and manner. He interested and edified, while, at the same time, he amused and entertained his audience; and none

51. Carter, Journal, 17.
52. Burnett, *Recollections and Opinions of an Old Pioneer*, 66.
53. Crary, *Pioneer and Personal Reminiscences*, 21.
54. Mace, "Autobiography," 37; Job Smith, "Diary," 6.
55. de Leon, *Thirty Years of My Life on Three Continents*, 57, 62.
56. Robinson, Autobiography and Journal, 22.
57. Coray, Letter to Martha Jane Lewis, Aug. 2, 1889, 4.
58. Rachel Ridgeway Grant, "Joseph Smith, the Prophet," *Young Woman's Journal,* Dec. 1905, 550.

listened to him that were ever weary with his discourse. I have even known him to retain a congregation of willing and anxious listeners for many hours together, in the midst of cold or sunshine, rain or wind, while they were laughing at one moment and weeping the next.[59]

The content of Smith's sermons more than made up for the unpolished delivery. "We soon felt and knew we were listening to one that had not been taught of men—so different were all his thoughts and language," wrote William Rowley.[60] He could make the gospel "so plain to the understanding," said James Palmer, "that on reflection one would be apt to think you allways known it."[61] Early convert from Colesville, New York, Newel Knight, said: "His words were meat & Drink for us for with wisdom & edification Did he Speak to us & made plain the way of life & Salvation & made the glories of the kingdom Shine with a more briliant lusture than before."[62] Lorenzo Snow, who heard Smith speak in 1836 and later joined his church, said Smith "was not, at that time, what would be called a fluent speaker. His remarks were confined principally to his own experiences, especially the visitation of the holy angel, giving a strong and powerful testimony in regard to these marvelous manifestations. ... At first he seemed a little diffident and spoke in rather a low voice, but as he proceeded he became very strong and powerful, and seemed to affect the whole audience with the feeling that he was honest and sincere."[63]

On April 6, 1837, Wilford Woodruff, who became an apostle and later president of the church in Utah, heard the Prophet speak for three hours "clothed with the power, spirit, & image of GOD. ... He presented many things of vast importance to the minds of the Elders of Israel. O that they might be written upon our hearts with an iron pen to remain forever."[64] Three days later he saw Smith stand before an audience "like a lion of the tribe of Judah. ... His mind like Enochs swells wide as eternity. Nothing short of a God can comprehend his soul."[65] George Laub, an English convert, said Smith spoke "with great power and much ashurance" and expounded the scriptures in a way that "it could not be missunderstood for plainness ... My Soul found

59. Pratt, *Autobiography*, 47.
60. William Rowley, Autobiography, Nov. 12, 1843.
61. Palmer, Reminiscences, 69.
62. Knight, Autobiography and Journal, ca. Mar.–Apr. 1838.
63. Lorenzo Snow, "The Grand Destiny of Man," *Deseret Evening News* (Salt Lake City), July 20, 1901, 22.
64. Woodruff, Journal, Apr. 6, 1837 (Vogel, ed., *Wilford Woodruff Journals*, 1:112–13).
65. Woodruff, Journal, Apr. 9, 1837 (Vogel, ed., *Wilford Woodruff Journals*, 1:115).

food, as a hungary mans body."[66] Emmeline B. Wells, who was sixteen when Smith died, captured the power of Smith's delivery, especially when heard by a true believer, when she wrote: "His expression was mild and almost child-like in repose; and when addressing the people, the glory of his countenance was beyond description. At other times the great power of his manner, more than of his voice (which was sublimely eloquent to me) seemed to shake the place on which we stood and penetrate the inmost soul of his hearers. ... I always listened spellbound to his every utterance."[67]

Enhancing this verbal charisma were Smith's physical attributes and what might be described as hyper-masculine behavior. Six feet in height, about 200 pounds, and athletically built, Smith loved to show off his physical prowess by wrestling and pulling sticks. Lucy Morley Allen, the wife of one of Smith's bodyguards in Nauvoo, remembered: "I've seen the Prophet wrestle, and run, and jump, but have never seen him beaten. In all that he did he was manly and almost godlike."[68] Wandle Mace recalled, "Often when we met and shook hands [Smith] would pull me to him for a wrestle," but Mace would always decline.[69]

Smith was also known to lose his temper occasionally and get into physical altercations. Luke Johnson, who was converted in Kirtland, remembered that a Baptist minister who had known Smith in New York came and stayed the night in the prophet's home, but after breakfast he "called Joseph a hypocrite, a liar imposter, and a false prophet, and called upon him to repent." According to Johnson, "Joseph boxed his ears with both hands, and turning his face towards the door, kicked him into the street."[70] On one occasion, Smith confessed to Allen J. Stout that "whenever he had laid his hand in anger on a fellow creature it gave him sorrow and a feeling of shame."[71]

Most of the time, however, Smith was good-natured, relaxed, and sociable. Jonathan Crosby, who met Smith in 1834, commented that Smith was not what he expected of a prophet but said, "I found him to be a friendly cheerful pleasant agreable man. I could not help likeing him."[72] Jacob Jones remembered that the prophet "was always jovial and could crack a joke. He

66. Laub, Reminiscences and journal, 19–20.
67. Emmeline B. Wells, "Joseph Smith, the Prophet," *Young Woman's Journal*, Dec. 1905, 556.
68. Lucy Diantha Morley Allen, "Joseph Smith, the Prophet," *Young Woman's Journal*, Dec. 1906, 537–38.
69. Mace, "Autobiography," 92–93.
70. Historian's Office, "History of Luke Johnson," 5–6.
71. Stout, Statement.
72. Crosby, Autobiographical Sketch, 13.

could sing well and loved music, loved to dance and would leave a meal at any time to wrestle with anyone. He was nimble as a cat and he was fond of us boys and would often play with us. Anyone could not help but love him and he loved everybody."[73] William Taylor said: "He was always the most companionable and lovable of men—cheerful and jovial! ... Much has been said of his geniality and personal magnetism. I was a witness of this—people, old or young, loved him and trusted him instinctively."[74]

Others were troubled by Smith's personality. Ezra Booth, who quickly became disillusioned with Smith, wrote Bishop Edward Partridge in September 1831: "Have you not frequently observed in Joseph, a want of that sobriety, prudence and stability, which are some of the most prominent traits in the christian character? Have you not often discovered in him, a spirit of lightness and levity, a temper easily irritated, and an habitual proneness to jesting and joking? Have you not often proven to your satisfaction that he says he knows things to be so by the spirit, when they are not so? You most certainly have."[75] Booth knew his words were likely to fall on deaf ears, for Rigdon had argued that Smith's revelations would still be true even if his wickedness rose to the level of King David, who had committed adultery and murder, and that "many others concurred with him in sentiment."[76] Such was the strength of his charisma. Wells, a poet and women's rights advocate in later life, wrote most insightfully regarding Smith's ability to foster loyalty in his followers. "In the Prophet Joseph Smith," she wrote, was a miraculous combination of "that strong comradeship that made such a bond of brotherliness with those who were his companions in civil and military life" and "the innate refinement that one finds in the born poet."[77]

Smith possessed another quality that drew followers to him, a trait that goes hand-in-hand with charisma—narcissism. Who better to display unshakeable self-confidence and voice their opinions with absolute certainty than a narcissist?

Psychiatrist Robert D. Anderson has written at length on Smith's narcissism, concluding that Smith was a malignant narcissist—the worst possible kind.[78] According to the *Diagnostic and Statistical Manual of Mental Disor-*

---

73. Jones, "Testimony."

74. William Taylor, "Joseph Smith, the Prophet," *Young Woman's Journal*, Dec. 1906, 547–48.

75. Ezra Booth, Letter to Ira Eddy, Nov. 21, 1831, in "Mormonism—No. VII," *Ohio Star* (Ravenna, OH), Nov. 24, 1831, [1].

76. Booth, [1].

77. Emmeline B. Wells, "Joseph Smith, the Prophet," *Young Woman's Journal*, Dec. 1905, 556.

78. Anderson, *Inside the Mind of Joseph Smith*. On Joseph Smith's narcissism, see Foster, "The Psychology of Prophetic Charisma"; and Foster, "Why the Prophet is a Puzzle."

ders (DSM-V), those who suffer from narcissistic personality disorder display the following traits: "a grandiose sense of self-importance"; "requires excessive admiration"; "a sense of entitlement"; "a lack of empathy"; tends to be exploitative, manipulative, and arrogant.[79] Personally, I am skeptical of any specific diagnosis. Not only is it speculative, but it is also unnecessary. It is possible to have narcissistic traits without having the disorder. The distinction may be only a matter of degree.[80] What interests me is how Smith's narcissism may have contributed to his charisma and made him appealing to others as a leader.

For evidence of Smith's grandiosity, one need only look at his failed attempt to establish his New Jerusalem theocracy in the wilderness of Missouri. Can a more grandiose, delusional project be imagined? I believe there can be no better example of how Smith was "preoccupied with fantasies of unlimited success, power, brilliance, beauty, or ideal love,"[81] than his vision of a utopian Zion, where the "pure in heart" shall dwell.[82]

Smith's grandiosity shows up clearly in his Nauvoo sermons, where he becomes the main topic of his discourse. Even in his famous King Follett funeral sermon, one of the most theologically important discourses Smith delivered shortly before his untimely death, he proclaimed his spiritual superiority: "I know more than all the world put tog[ethe]r. & If the h[oly]. G[host]. in me com[municates]: more than all the world I will associate with it."[83] Charlotte Haven, who visited Nauvoo in 1843, noticed that Smith "talked incessantly about himself, what he had done and could do more than other mortals, and remarked that he was 'a giant, physically and mentally.' In fact, he seemed to forget that he was a man."[84] This may have been a lifelong character trait as Samantha Payne, who attended school with Smith in Manchester, New York, recalled that even then he had a reputation as a "braggadocio."[85]

79. DSM-V, 670–71.

80. The current edition of the *Diagnostic and Statistical Manual of Mental Disorders* (DSM-V) cautions: "Many highly successful individuals display personality traits that might be considered narcissistic. Only when those traits are inflexible, maladaptive, and persisting, and cause significant functional impairment or subjective distress do they constitute narcissistic personality disorder" (672).

81. DSM-V.

82. Revelation Book 2, 63 [D&C 97:21] (*JSP*, D3:202). For an analysis of Joseph Smith's increasing narcissism and grandiosity in his final years, which may have led to his early death, see Bergera, "Joseph Smith and the Hazards of Charismatic Leadership." Bergera discusses a dozen examples of where Smith's controversial actions seem to suggest "the tenuousness of the grasp he may have held, at times, on reality." Bergera, 241.

83. Joseph Smith, Discourse, Apr. 7, 1844, in Ehat and Cook, *The Words of Joseph Smith*, 351.

84. Charlotte Haven, Letter to her mother, Feb. 19, 1843, in "A Girl's Letters from Nauvoo," *Overland Monthly* (San Francisco, CA), Dec. 1890, 623.

85. As quoted in Braden and Kelley, *Public Discussion of the Issues*, 350 (*EMD*, 3:173).

Smith's self-promotion is evident in the Book of Mormon, where as he neared the end of his dictation in June 1829, the character Lehi referenced a pseudepigraphic writing of the ancient patriarch Joseph, who had prophesied that in the last days "a choice seer" would appear from his lineage who would write a companion volume to the Bible.[86] Lest there be any mistake about the identity of this "choice seer," Lehi prophesied that his name would be Joseph, the son of Joseph, who would be "mighty ... both in word and in deed, being an instrument in the hands of God, with exceeding faith, to work mighty wonders, and do that thing which is great in the sight of God."[87] Smith had previously said that the title "seer" pertained to those who possessed special stones and that the use of such stones was the greatest gift a human can possess "except he should possess the power of God."[88]

The charismatic leader's enthusiasm and dedication to his mission are essential to his success in attracting followers, but when coupled with narcissism may lead to exploitation. As the DSM-V states, "This sense of entitlement, combined with a lack of sensitivity to the wants and needs of others, may result in the conscious or unconscious exploitation of others. They expect to be given whatever they may want or feel they need, no matter what it might mean to others. For example, these individuals may expect great dedication from others and may overwork them without regard to the impact on their lives."[89]

Some of Smith's behavior may be interpreted as exhibiting a "lack of empathy" for others, at times appearing exploitative and manipulative—either to further his ambitions or gratify personal needs. Smith expected loyalty and sacrifice from his followers, no matter the inconvenience. He sent many of them on missions despite their ill health or the hardship it caused their families. Probably the clearest evidence of Smith's lack of empathy and willingness to exploit his followers is his polygamous marriages to more than thirty women in Nauvoo. Particularly disturbing is his apparent disregard for the disruption and emotional pain that his actions would cause when he married at least fourteen women who were already married to other men.[90] Only a few months after her marriage to Henry Jacobs, twenty-year-old Zina D. Huntington was approached by her older brother Dimick with a

---

86. Book of Mormon, 1830 ed., 66–67 [2 Ne. 3:7–12].

87. Book of Mormon, 1830 ed., 66, 68 [2 Ne. 3:15, 24].

88. Book of Mormon, 1830 ed., 66, 173 [2 Ne. 3:7; Mos. 8:13, 16].

89. DSM-V, 670–71.

90. On Joseph Smith's polygamous and polyandrous wives, see Compton, *In Sacred Loneliness*; and Compton, "A Trajectory of Plurality."

message from Smith: "Tell Zina, I put it off and put it off till an angel with a drawn sword stood by me and told me if I did not establish that principle upon the earth I would lose my position and my life.'"[91] After several months of spiritual turmoil and contemplation, a pregnant Zina married the thirty-five-year old Smith on October 27, 1841.

The narcissist's grandiosity masks an underlying vulnerability in self-esteem, which, according to the DSM-V, makes them "very sensitive to 'injury' from criticism or defeat. ... They may react with disdain, rage, or defiant counterattack. ... Though overweening ambition and confidence may lead to high achievement, performance may be disrupted because of intolerance of criticism or defeat."[92] One of Smith's close friends, Benjamin F. Johnson, said that although Smith could be "Social and Eaven Convivial at times He would alow no arogance or undue liberties—and criticisms Even by his associates was Rarely acceptable & Contradiction would Rouse in him the Lion at once." Continuing, Johnson recalled, "For by no one of his Fellows would he be Superseeded, or disputed, and in the Early days at Kirtland & Elsewhare ware [more] than once for their Impudence helped from the Congregation by his foot."[93]

What is it about the followers that attract them to the narcissistic charismatic leader? Recent studies show that many people are attracted to the narcissist's projection of grandiose self-confidence, power, enthusiasm, and lack of self-doubt, at least initially.[94] In the 1970s Austrian-American psychoanalyst Heinz Kohut and others began studying narcissism and found that a symbiosis existed between charismatic leaders and followers, that both were attempting to alleviate deep-seated feelings of inadequacy—the leader by attracting adulation for his false persona and the followers by attempting to draw strength from an idealized powerful figure.[95] This relationship was not unlike what Sigmund Freud called *transference*. He noticed that his patients were developing an intense attachment to him and that much like the early stages of a love affair they idealized and overestimated his qualities. Freud hypothesized that his patients were regressing to a mental-emotional state

---

91. Zina Huntington Young et al., "Joseph, the Prophet, His Life and Mission as Viewed by Intimate Acquaintances," *Salt Lake Herald Church and Farm Supplement*, Jan. 12, 1895, 212.

92. DSM-V, 671.

93. Johnson, Letter to George S. Gibbs, Apr.–Oct. 1903, 7–8.

94. Holtzman and Strube, "Narcissism and Attractiveness."

95. Kohut, *The Analysis of the Self*, 317; Kohut, "Reflections on *Advances in Self-psychology*," 393, 493; Kohut, *Self-psychology and the Humanities*, 219.

experienced as a child, where the parents were the all-powerful all-knowing gods and the child was helpless and submissive but felt buoyant and safe.[96]

Jerrold M. Post, formerly a professor of psychiatry and director of the political psychology program at George Washington University, described the symbiosis of charismatic leaders and their followers, stating that a charismatic leader "requires a continuing flow of admiration from his audience in order to nourish his famished self." To attract these admiring followers, he must "convey a sense of grandeur, omnipotence, and strength." Followers, on the other hand, "are consumed by doubt and uncertainty" and "can only feel whole when in relationship with, when attached to, when merged with this idealized other. The charismatic leader comes to the psychological rescue of the ideal hungry followers. Taking on heroic proportions and representing what the followers wish to be, he protects them from confronting themselves and their fundamental inadequacy and alienation." Post knows he is generalizing and cautions that the "phenomenon of the charismatic leader-follower is surely too complex to lend itself to a single overarching psychodynamic personality model." Nevertheless, he believes "elements of the narcissistic transferences … are present in all charismatic leader-follower relationships, and in some charismatic leader-follower relationships are critical determinants."[97]

In *Prophetic Charisma,* New Zealand psychologist Len Oakes similarly warns that "charismatic appeal is too widespread and varied a phenomenon to be reduced to a simple explanation such as that people follow charismatic leaders because of economic distress or personal deficiencies." Nevertheless, Oakes describes the charismatic leader-follower relationship as a "symbiosis or codependence, perhaps even of mutual exploitation." Through a process of projection, "the followers come to see the prophet as the embodiment of their ultimate concerns." Oakes observes that "the inflated testimonies of the followers"—such as I have previously quoted for Smith's followers—"demonstrate" they "love the prophet as a symbol of [their] ultimate concerns" and that they are "blind to his actual person."[98] In such case, neither the charismatic leader nor the followers experience true love since they merely love their own distorted and idealized projections.

---

96. Kohut, *Self-psychology and the Humanities,* 47; Becker, *The Denial of Death,* 128–20.
97. Post, "Narcissism and the Charismatic Leader-Follower Relationship," 679–80, 684.
98. Oakes, *Prophetic Charisma,* 126, 129, 160.

Mission[99]

The attraction to a charismatic leader, according to Weber, "may involve a subjective or internal reorientation born out of suffering, conflicts or enthusiasm," and that this seems to occur "in times of psychic, physical, economic, ethical, religious, political distress."[100] Post also recognized that historical situations can be conducive to the rise of charismatic leadership: "At moments of societal crisis, otherwise mature and psychologically healthy individuals may temporarily come to feel overwhelmed and in need of a strong and self-assured leader."[101] Indeed, an understanding of the sociopolitical situation surrounding Smith in western New York, prior to his moves to Ohio and Missouri, not only explains his initial success but also the willingness of his followers to accept his mission of building a utopian New Jerusalem in the American wilderness.

Smith began his career just as it seemed to some in America that their nation had turned away from God and was ripe for destruction. When Smith sat down with scribe Martin Harris in April 1828 to dictate the history of a "fallen people,"[102] the United States was in the midst of an election in which the future of the nation seemed to be held in the balance. By the time he finished dictating his history of ancient America in late June 1829, General Andrew Jackson, hero of the War of 1812 from Tennessee, had been elected president and had occupied the office for less than two months. Religious conservatives worried that Jackson's views on the separation of church and state would further incur divine displeasure on the United States.[103] On January 11, 1828, the *Wayne Sentinel,* a newspaper published near the Smith residence in Manchester, New York, reported that some believed that Jackson's election would be one of "the harbingers of ruin, and the indication of the early downfall of this great republic." On July 11 the *Sentinel* reported that the opponents of Jackson were declaring that "the crisis has arrived, and that the elevation of Jackson to the presidency is only the first step—the *entering-wedge* to the dissolution of the Union."

When it was discovered that Jackson had served as grand master of the

---

99. What follows is a brief summary of what I have previously written regarding the Book of Mormon's general anti-Masonic and anti-Jackson stance. For more details, see Vogel, "Mormonism's 'Anti-Masonick Bible.'"

100. Eisenstadt, *Max Weber on Charisma and Institution Building,* 53, 18.

101. Post, "Narcissism and the Charismatic Leader-Follower Relationship," 683.

102. D&C 20:9; see also 3:18.

103. On the Jacksonian insistence on the complete separation of church and state, or the principle of religious nonintervention, see Schlesinger, *The Age of Jackson,* 350–60.

Grand Lodge of Tennessee (1822–24), supporters of John Quincy Adams in New York quickly exploited the situation by attempting to draw the Masonic issue along factional lines. This strategy proved especially potent in western New York, where William Morgan, a stonemason from Batavia, mysteriously disappeared in 1826 and was believed to have been assassinated by the Masons for attempting to publish their secret rituals.[104] Thurlow Weed, who had established the *Anti-Masonic Enquirer* at Rochester, New York, consistently associated the Jacksonians with Masonry.[105] When supporters of Jackson in Wayne County met for a convention, the *Wayne Sentinel* reported on August 15, 1828, that conservatives were spreading the false rumor that it "was a Masonic meeting, and designed for the benefit and promotion of masons." On October 31, 1828, the *Susquehanna Register*, a paper published in Montrose, Pennsylvania, about twenty miles south of Smith's residence in Harmony, printed a letter written by "A Young Politician," which defended Jackson against insinuations that "the whole Masonic Fraternity in the Union are acting in concert to elevate Gen. Jackson to the presidency on his masonic merits." The writer complained that some of Adams's supporters "in the eastern part of the county are so much heated with enthusiasm that they insinuate to the people that Jacksonianism and Freemasonry are synonimous." The union of the politically powerful Jacksonians and their militaristic leader with the murderous "secret combination" of Masonry must have become for at least some New York conservatives the ultimate possible danger to their liberties and freedoms.

Jackson's election had anti-Masons worried that the fraternity had placed a Masonic king in the nation's highest office. The Reverend Lebbeus Armstrong warned in 1830: "Let masonry prevail and prosper, and the deplorable results may be looked for, of a Masonic Monarchy for our form of government. … Then might be written with tears and blood, America is fallen!"[106] Through publication of his 1827 book, *An Inquiry into the Nature and Tendency of Speculative Free-Masonry*, John G. Stearns, according to historian William Preston Vaughn, "led the way in expounding the theory that

---

104. Morgan's book was published posthumously in 1826 under the title *Illustrations of Masonry: By One of the Fraternity Who Has Devoted Thirty Years to the Subject* (Batavia, NY: David C. Miller, 1826).

105. Weed later admitted that his perception was that "the Masons generally, without reference to their political antecedents, sought refuge in the Jackson or Democratic party. Most of the anti-Masonic leaders had been Clintonians and were supporters of Mr. Adams' administration." Weed, *Autobiography of Thurlow Weed*, 302. On the Freemasonry issue in the campaign of 1828, see Remini, *The Election of Andrew Jackson*, 135–43.

106. Armstrong, *Masonry Proved to Be a Work of Darkness*, 24.

Masonry was a state within a state and that one day Masons would over-throw the democratic government of the United States and would crown one of their 'grand kings' as ruler of this nation."[107] With the election of Jackson the following year, Stearns's worst fears had been realized.

Thus the Book of Mormon appeared at a time when the stress of transition was acutely felt in America and in many ways it echoed the fears of the anti-Jacksons and anti-Masons. When the book came off the press in March 1830, it not only described the entire destruction of two ancient American civilizations by "secret combinations" but contained ominous and foreboding predictions concerning latter-day America's own national calamity. Moroni, who predicted that his record would come forth "in a day ... of secret com-binations,"[108] spoke directly to his American readers and warned them to repent and "suffer not that these murderous combinations shall get above you, which are built up to get [political] power and [economic] gain" lest "the work of destruction come upon you; yea, even the sword of the justice of the eternal God, shall fall upon you, to your overthrow and destruction."[109] Moroni further warned: "Whatsoever nation shall uphold such secret com-binations, to get power and gain, until they shall spread over the nation, behold, they shall be destroyed."[110] Significantly, Moroni's warning of "secret combinations" switches to the singular: "Wherefore, the Lord commandeth you, when ye shall see these things come among you, that ye shall awake to a sense of your awful situation, because of *this* secret combination which shall be among you, or wo be unto *it*, because of the blood of them who have been slain; for they cry from the dust for vengeance upon *it*, and also upon those who build *it* up."[111] The Book of Mormon also warns that God has decreed that America is a land of promise, and "whatsoever nation shall possess it, shall serve God, or they shall be swept off."[112]

When Smith wanted to motivate his followers in New York to move to Ohio, he dictated a revelation on January 2, 1831, that tapped into the widespread apprehension following Jackson's election: "Behold the enemy is combined & now I shew unto you a Mystery a thing which is had in seecret Chambers to bring to pass even your destruction in process of time

---

107. Vaughn, *The Antimasonic Party in the United States*, 20. See Stearns, *An Inquiry Into the Nature and Tendency of Speculative Free-masonry.*

108. Book of Mormon, 1830 ed., 534 [Morm. 8:27].

109. Book of Mormon, 1830 ed., 554 [Ether 8:23].

110. Book of Mormon, 1830 ed., 554 [Ether 8:22].

111. Book of Mormon, 1830 ed., 554 [Ether 8:24]; emphasis added.

112. Book of Mormon, 1830 ed., 541 [Ether 2:9].

& ye knew it not ... & again I say unto you that the Enemy in the Seecret Chambers seek[e]th your lives[.] ye hear of wars in far Countries & you say in your hearts that there will soon be great wars in far Countries but ye know not the hearts of they in your own Land ... Wherefore for this cause I gave unto you The commandment that ye should go to the Ohio."[113] Later that spring three major waves of Mormons moved to northern Ohio totaling nearly 200 people.[114]

To those who could not accept the outcome of the 1828 election and believed America was on the high road to destruction, Smith held out the option of establishing a western theocracy as a refuge for God's children. This was a radical and revolutionary plan, to be sure, but charismatic leadership tends to be such a force. As Weber observed: "The bearer of charisma enjoys loyalty and authority by virtue of a mission believed to be embodied in him: this mission has not necessarily and not always been revolutionary, but in its most charismatic forms, it has inverted all value hierarchies and overthrown custom, law and tradition."[115]

Smith's New Jerusalem was intended to fill the entire earth, eventually. In June 1833, a month before the Mormons were driven out of Jackson County, Smith and church leaders in Ohio sent Bishop Edward Partridge and other officials in Missouri a master plan for the city of Zion to be built in Independence, which included a one-square-mile grid, and declared: "Where this square is thus laid off and supplied lay off another in the same way and so fill up the world in these last days and let every man live in the City for this is the City of Zion."[116] Smith's vision could not be any bigger, or any more impractical.

From the start, Smith was on a collision course with reality. Responding to scholars who have noted that "failure is inevitable, both for prophets and for charismatic leaders generally," Oakes remarks: "Granted that no prophet has yet ushered in the kingdom of heaven, nevertheless quite a few have led successful movements and died with their integrity intact."[117] Smith is one of those prophets who survived failure. "The inevitable fate of all millenarian movements is failure and collapse," observes historian John G. Gager. "They either—and the majority would certainly fall into this class—disintegrate

---

113. Revelation, Jan. 2, 1830, Revelation Book 1, 50, 51–52 [D&C 38:12–13, 28–29, 32] (*JSP*, D1:231, 232).

114. Porter, "'Ye Shall Go to the Ohio,'" 1–25.

115. Weber, *Economy and Society*, 1117.

116. Plat and Explanation of the City of Zion, ca. early June–June 25, 1833, [1] (*JSP*, D3:128).

117. Oakes, *Prophetic Charisma*, 182.

and disappear when their millennial expectations remain unfulfilled or— and here I think of both Christianity and Mormonism—they cease to be millenarian in the strict sense." Gager argues that "those movements which survive the trauma of non-fulfillment usually do so in rather predictable ways" and lists four approaches to adjustment which can apply to Mormonism: (1) "they generate a series of rational explanations for the non-arrival of the millennium"; (2) "they reach out and seek to persuade others of the truth of their religion"; (3) "they redirect their energies away from preparing for the End and toward the development of institutional structures"; and (4) "as an essential part of this reorientation, they either forget or suppress the memory of their millenarian origins, for it is precisely in the transformation of millennial energies into other forms of action that we can locate the key to survival and success, on the one hand, or disintegration and collapse on the other."[118] The brilliance with which Joseph Smith utilized all these strategies is the reason we still talk about him two centuries later.

Sources and Acknowledgments

In quoting from manuscript or holograph sources, I have not used editorial marks to indicate cancellations or interlinear insertions, but have given the final form of the texts as intended by their authors at or near the time of composition. Superscript (1st) has been lowered to the line (1st), and I have also taken the liberty to silently capitalize or lower case the first letter depending on its syntactical context. Wherever possible I have cited original documents and have provided references to published versions, such as the *Joseph Smith Papers* and *Early Mormon Documents*, within parentheses. In labeling and dating sources, I have generally followed the *Joseph Smith Papers*.

I extend my thanks to Margie Dresser-Vogel for her love and support, to my friends and colleagues for their knowledge and advice, especially H. Michael Marquardt, and to the Smith-Pettit Foundation, for making the research and writing of this work possible. Of course, I am alone responsible for any errors of interpretation and transcription of sources.

---

118. Gager, "Early Mormonism and Early Christianity," 56–57. See also Gager's *Kingdom and Community*, esp. 37–49; and Festinger et al., *When Prophecy Fails*.

PART ONE

Stabilizing Charisma

Arrival in Ohio

*Thou art the man which an angel saith in a vision, Thou shalt re-
ceive; therefore go with me into my house, and I will impart unto
thee of my food; and I know that thou will be a blessing unto me and
my house.*
—Amulek to Alma, Book of Mormon, *1830 ed., 244 [Alma 8:20]*

Upon arriving in Kirtland, Ohio, on February 4, 1831,[1] Joseph Smith
jumped from the sleigh and walked briskly into the local store, extended his
hand over the counter, and mysteriously exclaimed to the astonished proprietor: "Newel K. Whitney, thou art the man"! Whitney, who would turn
thirty-six the next day, was used to seeing unfamiliar faces in his store, but
none who could call him by name. When he protested that he did not know
this stranger, Smith confidently said, "I am Joseph the Prophet; you prayed
me here, now what do you want of me?"[2]

While this would have probably been true of any of Smith's Ohio followers anxiously anticipating his arrival,[3] to Whitney's grandson, Orson F.
Whitney, this implied that the prophet had referred to "a vision in which he
had seen the merchant and his wife praying for his coming to Kirtland."[4]
Despite the prescience with which Whitney family folklore has endowed

---

1. The *Painesville (OH) Telegraph* reported that Rigdon arrived on the first of February and
that Smith arrived three days later. [Matthew S. Clapp], "Mormonism," *Painesville Telegraph*, Feb.
15, 1831, [1]–[2].

2. Orson F. Whitney, "Newel K. Whitney," *Contributor* (Salt Lake City), Jan. 1885, 125; and
[Elizabeth Ann Whitney], "A Leaf from an Autobiography," *Woman's Exponent* (Salt Lake City),
Sep. 1, 1878, 51.

3. "Joseph Smith and all his forces are to be on here soon to take possession of the promised
land." *Painesville Telegraph*, Jan. 18, 1831, 3.

4. Orson F. Whitney, "Newel K. Whitney," *Contributor*, Jan. 1885, 125.

this story, it is more likely that Smith had learned of Whitney from Sidney Rigdon and Edward Partridge.

Whitney's "white store" was located on the northeast corner of the busy intersection of Chardon and Chester roads. Chester road ran north and south through Kirtland, connecting with the southern town of Chester and continuing on for more than 200 miles to Chillicothe, a major town in southwestern Ohio. Whitney sent Smith across the road to his old "red store," now occupied by Algernon Sidney Gilbert, Whitney's business partner, and his family, to inquire about lodging.[5] While Smith was inside engaged in conversation with Gilbert, the wagon carrying a pregnant Emma had difficulty negotiating the steep and icy road leading down to the "Kirtland Flats" from the north and flipped, throwing Emma and two or three unidentified children into the snow. This scene was witnessed by Gilbert's fourteen-year-old nephew James Henry Rollins, who ran into the house to get Smith and his uncle. "Joseph ran to assist them without his hat," Rollins recalled. "My first impression was, that if any of the occupants were hurt seriously that Joseph could heal them, but none of them were hurt."[6]

After Emma had recovered from her spill and warmed up in the Gilbert residence, Rollins reported that the Smiths determined that "none of our rooms suited them," so "they found other quarters."[7] Joseph and Emma ended up staying in the Whitney home, opposite the Red Store to the north. The Whitneys lived in a modest home with a half-level upper story where they slept, leaving a small room on the main floor for Joseph and Emma.[8] In his history, Smith would later state that he and Emma lived with the Whitneys for "several weeks," recalling that they "received every kindness and attention, which could be expected, and especially from sister Whitney."[9] Elizabeth Ann Whitney, Newel's thirty-year-old wife, recalled that at the time she had "a babe in arms and two older children living," but that "Joseph

---

5. On Whitney's extensive business ventures in the Kirtland area, see Staker, "'Thou Art the Man,'" 75–95.

6. Rollins, Reminiscences, 1.

7. Rollins, "The History of James Henry Rollins," 3; Cf. Rollins, Reminiscences, 3.

8. After visiting Kirtland in 1870, Horace Whitney wrote his mother and described their former residence: "Your old 'East Room,'—where Joseph & Emma lived on their first arrival from York State in December [February] 1831,—looks quite natural." Horace Whitney, Letter to Elizabeth Ann Whitney, Feb. 16, 1870.

9. JS History, vol. A-1, 93. Composed in 1842. Vogel, *History of Joseph Smith*, 1:lxxxiv. Newel K. Whitney's unbelieving brother, Samuel F., reported that "Jo Smith stopped with my brother, N. K. Whitney, some weeks, when he moved his family to Kirtland, where I became acquainted with him." Samuel F. Whitney, "Statement of Rev. S. F. Whitney on Mormonism," *Naked Truths about Mormonism* (Oakland, CA), Jan. 1888, 3.

and Emma were very dear to me, and with my own hands I ministered to them, feeling it a privilege and an honor to do so."[10]

A Bishop

Elizabeth Ann also boasted that "during the time they resided with us, and under our roof, were many of the revelations given which are recorded in the Book of Doctrine and Covenants."[11] While Elizabeth Ann apparently included the time when the Smiths subsequently occupied the upper level of the White Store, Smith did indeed dictate a revelation on the day he arrived in Kirtland. It called for thirty-seven-year-old Edward Partridge to "be appointed by the voice of the Church & be ordained a bishop unto the Church & leave his merchandise [business] & spend all his time in the labours of the Church & see to all things as it shall be appointed in my Laws in the day that I shall give them."[12] Smith chose Partridge, but Sidney Rigdon had previously been a bishop in Alexander Campbell's organization.[13] As the office of bishop had yet to be defined in Smith's new church, it is likely, as historian Mark Staker has observed, that Partridge and many Ohio converts, as former Campbellites, "would have understood the office as leading a single congregation—the description of the position that they had developed among the Disciples of Christ."[14] The revelation explained that Partridge was chosen as the first bishop "because his heart is pure before me for he is like unto Nathaniel of old in whome there is no guile."[15] Apparently Partridge was expected to sell his hat business in Painesville, Ohio, and other assets to serve as a full-time official of the church, which he eventually did at a great financial loss.[16]

An early copy of this revelation includes a heading that explains the circumstances of its dictation. The revelation had been given in response to a generous offer by a man named Leman Copley, who owned a large farm in Thompson Township, located about sixteen miles northeast of Kirtland. "Copl[e]y ... had requested Brother Joseph & Sidney to live with him & he would furnish them [with] houses & provisions &c." Apparently Smith

---

10. [Whitney], "Leaf from an Autobiography," 51.

11. Whitney, 51.

12. Revelation, Feb. 4, 1831, Revelation Book 1, 62 [D&C 41:9] (*JSP*, D1:244).

13. Prince, *Power from on High*, 63.

14. Staker, *Hearken, O Ye People*, 227.

15. Revelation, Feb. 4, 1831, Revelation Book 1, 62 [D&C 41:11] (*JSP*, D1:245). For Nathanael, see John 1:43–47.

16. Partridge, "Edward Partridge in Painesville, Ohio"; *JSP*, D1:244–45n32.

did not want to accept Copley's offer. At this time, he needed to stay near his new converts and deal with problems associated with religious excesses and communal living. After all, that is why he moved to Ohio. Instead, the revelation directed the church to provide for Smith's and Rigdon's housing needs: "It is meet that my servant Joseph should have a house built in which to live & translate & again it is meet that my Servant Sidney should have a comfortable Room to live in."[17]

The Law

Five days after his arrival, Smith held a meeting in Kirtland and in the presence of twelve elders dictated a revelation containing the law of the Lord to his church, including the law of consecration of property.[18] Even before Smith left New York, a revelation promised: "There [in Ohio] I will give unto you my law."[19] On the day he arrived, a revelation said: "By the prayer of your faith ye shall receive my law that ye may know how to govern my Church."[20] John Whitmer, one of the Book of Mormon's eight witnesses who would soon be called as a church historian, wrote that in preparation for this revelation "the Elders were called together, and united in mighty prayer, and were agreed as touching the reception of the Law."[21]

What were known as "The Laws of the Church of Christ" consist of responses to questions in eight parts, the last three being dictated on February 23, 1831. To the question of whether or not the church should begin to gather, the revelation directed that missionaries be sent out two by two and that churches be built up in place "untill the time shall come when it Shall be revealed unto you from on high & the City of the New Jerusalam Shall be prepared that ye may be gathered in one that ye may be my people & I will be your God."[22]

The bulk of the revelation reviewed various commandments, especially those punishable by excommunication—murder, stealing, lying, adultery— followed by a long passage about the law of consecration and how it was to be administered. This was apparently in response to Isaac Morley's "common stock" farm not far from the Whitney store, which had for two years

---

17. Revelation, Feb. 4, 1831, Revelation Book 1, 62 [D&C 41:7] (*JSP*, D1:245).

18. Revelation, Feb. 9, 1831, "The Laws of the Church of Christ," Revelations Collection [D&C 42:1–72] (*JSP*, D1: 245–56).

19. Revelation, Jan. 2, 1830, Revelation Book 1, 52 [D&C 38:32] (*JSP*, D1:232).

20. Revelation, Feb. 4, 1831, Revelation Book 1, 61 [D&C 41:3] (*JSP*, D1:245).

21. John Whitmer, History, 12 (*JSP*, H2:24).

22. Revelation, Feb. 9, 1831, "The Laws of the Church of Christ," [1]–[2], Revelations Collection [D&C 42:4–9] (*JSP*, D1:250).

held all things in common but was experiencing disharmony. John Whitmer, who visited the "Morley Family," wrote, "The disciples had all things common, and were going to destruction very fast as to temporal things: for they considered from reading the scripture that what belonged to a brother belonged to any of the brethren, therefore they would take each others clothes and other property and use it without leave: which brought on confusion and disappointments: for they did not understand the scripture."[23] In establishing communal orders in Mentor and Kirtland, Rigdon and Morley were influenced by the secular socialism of Robert Owen, a wealthy Scottish reformer and deist who advocated the abolition of private property and founded his own communal order in New Harmony, Indiana, in 1825.[24]

Smith's revelation encouraged them to abandon "the family" for his "more perfect law of the Lord."[25] The plan was to consecrate all properties and then receive a stewardship from the bishop, with the surplus being kept in a storehouse for the poor and for "purchaseing Land & building up of the New Jerusalem which is here after to be revealed." Once the consecration of property was made, there was no retrieving one's former holdings should there be a loss of faith—"Behold thou shalt conscrate all thy properties that which thou hast unto me with a covena[n]t and Deed which cannot be broken & they Shall be laid before the Bishop of my church ... & it shall come to pass that the Bishop of my church after that he has received the properties of my church that it cannot be taken from you."[26]

Concerning the families of missionaries, the revelation instructed that "the Bishop ... is to see that their families are supported out of the property which is consecrated to the Lord."[27] In dealing with "the world," the revelation stipulated: "Thou Shalt contract no debts with them & again the Elders & Bishop shall Council together & they shall do by the directions of the spirit as it must be necessary."[28] Regarding the anticipated arrival of the New York converts, the revelation ordered the bishop to assist them "in obtaining places that they may be together as much as can be & is directed by the holy Spirit & every family Shall have places that they may live by themselves & every Church Shall be organized in as close bodies as they can be in consequence of

---

23. Whitmer, History, 11 (*JSP*, H2:22–23).

24. [Owen], *Robert Owen's Opening Speech*, 38–39.

25. JS History, vol. A-1, 93 (DHC 1:146–47).

26. Revelation, Feb. 9, 1831, [3], Revelations Collection [D&C 42:30–35] (*JSP*, D1:251–52).

27. Revelation, [5] [D&C 42:70–72] (*JSP*, D1:255).

28. Revelation, [6] [BC XLIV:55] (*JSP*, D1:255). This and next passage were omitted when printed in the 1835 Doctrine and Covenants.

the enemy!"[29] Two weeks after this revelation was dictated, Smith asked Martin Harris to come to Ohio "as soon as you can" ahead of the migration of the New York members "in order to choose a place which may be best adapted to the circumstances of yourself and breatheren in the east to settle on," adding that "you may chose any place which may best suit yourselves any where in this part of the country so as to be as compact as possable."[30]

John Whitmer later recorded that "Bishop Edward Partridge visited the church in is its several branches, there were some that would not receive the Law." Apparently some members stumbled over the dissolution of Morley's "Common Stock" and the implementation of Smith's new law of consecration and stewardship. "There were some of the disciples," Whitmer wrote, "who were flattered into this church because they thought that all things were to be common, therefore they thought to glut themselves upon the labors of others."[31] They may also have rejected the mandatory handing over of all their property into the hands of the bishop with an irrevocable deed.

It was understood that those who participated in the law of consecration "are to hold no property should they leave the community."[32] The Reverend Joshua V. Himes warned prospective converts that once they put their money into the general fund "they can never draw back again, should they get sick of Mormonism, and wish to return home to their friends."[33] On March 9, 1831, the *Palmyra Reflector* reported that "two of the most responsible *Mormonites*, as it respects property, in that vicinity, have *demurred* to the divine command, through Jo Smith, requiring them to sell their property and put it into the common *fund*, and repair with all convenient speed to the New Jerusalem."

William E. McLellin, who joined in August 1831 but later had misgivings, revealed possible reasons some members hesitated in supporting Smith's economic system. He objected that New Testament bishops were spiritual overseers, not the administrators of temporal affairs (1 Tim. 3:1–7; Titus 1:5–9).[34] "The disciples on both continents had their goods in common stock, but [Joseph Smith's] system was entirely different from that. ...

---

29. Revelation, [6] [BC XLIV:56–57] (*JSP*, D1:255–56).

30. Joseph Smith, Letter to Martin Harris, Feb. 22, 1831, [1], JS Collection (*JSP*, D1:262–63).

31. Whitmer, History, 17–18 (*JSP*, H2:29).

32. *Ohio Atlas and Lorain County Gazette* (Elyria, OH), Dec. 6, 1832.

33. "The Mormonites," *Christian Watchman* (Boston), Sep. 7, 1832.

34. In fact, as Charles R. Harrell has observed: "The New Testament terms 'elder,' 'presbyter,' 'overseer,' 'pastor,' and 'bishop' are all descriptive titles for the same function of overseer." Harrell, *"This Is My Doctrine,"* 379.

It was the most mixed up law or system that I ever contemplated. It had no parallel in all past time."[35] McLellin distinguished between everyone owning everything in a cooperative—which seemed to him mandated by the New Testament and Book of Mormon—and the bishop owning everything and distributing the property and money according to what he determined was everyone's need and holding the rest in a storehouse (see Acts 2:44–45; 4:32–37; 3 Ne. 26:19; 4 Ne. 3).

Others in Smith's time—including Alexander Campbell—rejected the notion that believers were required to have "all things common" simply because it was practiced among early Christians. Since the New Testament mentions collections being taken for the poor (1 Cor. 16:1; Rom. 15:26.), Bible commentator Adam Clarke argued that "it was something that was done at this time, on this occasion, through some *local necessity*, which the circumstances of the infant Church at Jerusalem might render expedient for that *place* and on that *occasion* only." Clarke reasoned, "If everyone, on entering the Church, gave up all his goods to the common stock, there could have been no such *distinction* as *rich* and *poor*."[36] Smith apparently did not submit his own land in Harmony, Pennsylvania, to the Law of Consecration. Prior to leaving Harmony, Smith made the final payment for the property to Isaac Hale, his father-in-law, by borrowing money from George H. Noble & Co. for $190.95. This debt was satisfied before June 3, 1831, but it is unknown where Smith got the funds. Sometime before June 1833, Smith sold the Harmony land to Joseph McKune for $300. What happened to this money is also unknown.[37]

In mid-February Smith received another challenge to his leadership similar to what he had experienced in Fayette with new member Hiram Page's revelations, which he claimed to have received through a seer stone.[38] This challenge came from a woman known in Mormon history only by her last name Hubble who, as John Whitmer explained, "professed to be a prophetess of the Lord" and "professed to have many revelations," insisting at the same time that "she should become a teacher in the Church of Christ."[39] The seriousness of

35. McLellin, Notebook, ca. 1880, 27, 29, in "Reasons Why I am Not a 'Mormon,'" Larson and Passey, eds., *The William E. McLellin Papers*, 409, 411.

36. Clarke, *The Holy Bible*, Acts 2:44. On Campbell's objections, see Van Wagoner, *Sidney Rigdon*, 54.

37. For a discussion of the various transactions dealing with this property, see *EMD*, 4:424–27; and *JSP*, D3:159–60.

38. JS History, vol. A-1, 54 (*EMD*, 1:133; *JSP*, H1:436).

39. Whitmer, History, 18 (*JSP*, H2:29).

Hubble's challenge was reported by Ezra Booth, a Methodist minister from Portage County who had recently joined the Mormons but would become a critic by September 1831. Booth reported that Hubble "so ingratiated herself into the esteem and favor of some of the Elders, that they received her, as a person commissioned to act a conspicuous part in Mormonizing the world." Booth added, "Rigdon, and some others, gave her the right hand of fellowship, and literally saluted her with what they called the kiss of charity. But Smith viewing her as encroaching upon his sacred premises, declared her an impostor, and she returned to the place from whence she came."[40] The revelation that Smith dictated declared that "there is none other appointed unto you to receive commandments & Revelations" except Smith "untill he be taken if he abide in me." Should Smith transgress and be no longer worthy to exercise his gift, the revelation informed his followers that "none else shall be appointed unto this gift except it be through him for if it be taken from him he shall not have power except to appoint another in his stead." It is hard to imagine how that would work, mostly because it never did, although some would call for it in later years. The revelation reiterated this principle: "This shall be a law unto you that ye receive not the teachings of any that shall Come before you as Revelations or commandments & this I give unto you that you may not be deceived, that you may know they are not of me for Verily I say unto you that he that is ordained of me shall come in at the gate & be ordained."[41]

Although the revelation dictated in September 1830 concerning Hiram Page clearly stated that "no one shall be appointed to Receive commandments & Revelations in this Church excepting my Servant Joseph," it had to be repeated with more clarity perhaps because Hubble had not written her revelations down. The previous revelation had given Oliver Cowdery permission to "speak or teach … by way of Commandment unto the Church … But thou shalt not write by way of Commandment."[42] Nevertheless, Booth ridiculed the idea that Smith was given sole authority to receive revelations for the church, including authority to replace himself should he fall. "Never was there a despot more jealous of his prerogative than Smith," Booth scoffed.[43]

---

40. Ezra Booth, Letter to Ira Eddy, Nov. 29, 1831, in "Mormonism—Nos. VIII–IX," *Ohio Star* (Ravenna, OH), Dec. 8, 1831, [1]. The Joseph Smith Papers editors suggest Mrs. Hubble was "likely 'Mrs. Louisa Hubbell,' who had converted from the Disciples of Christ and later rejoined the Disciples in May 1831." Hayden, *Early History of the Disciples in the Western Reserve*, 472; *JSP*, D1:257n95; see also Staker, *Hearken, O Ye People*, 79–80, 111–14.

41. Revelation, Feb. 1831-A, Revelation Book 1, 67–68 [D&C 43:3–7] (*JSP*, D1:258).

42. Revelation, Sep. 1830, Revelation Book 1, 40–41 [D&C 28:2, 4–5] (*JSP*, D1:185).

43. Booth, Letter to Ira Eddy, Nov. 29, 1831, "Mormonism—Nos. VIII–IX," *Ohio Star*, Dec. 8, 1831, [1].

The revelation repeated earlier instructions for the church to provide for Smith's temporal needs: "I say unto you that if you desire the mysteries of the Kingdom provide for him food & raiment & whatsoever thing he needeth to accomplish the work which I have commanded him."[44] It also alluded to a promised endowment of power, enjoining the elders to "bind yourselves to act in all holiness before me ... purge ye out the iniquity which is among you Sanctify yourselves before me ... & ye shall be endowed with power from on high."[45] The remainder of the revelation dealt with preaching to the world before the Lord came to destroy the wicked and reign with his saints during the Millennium.

According to John Whitmer, "After this commandment was receivd, the saints came to understanding on this subject, and unity and harmony prevailed throughout the church of God: and the Saints began to learn wisdom, and treasure up knowledge which they learned from the word of God, and by experiance as they advanced in the way of eternal life."[46] Whitmer also mentioned that Smith continued to work on his revision of the King James Bible, reviewing and revising the Old Testament with Rigdon as his scribe.[47]

About this time Smith dictated another revelation calling the elders together for a special conference: "It is expedient in me that the Elders of my Church should be called to gether from the East & from the West & from the North & from the South by letter or some other way & it shall come to pass that I will pour out my Spirit upon them in the day that they assemble themselves together."[48] John Whitmer later recorded that "the elders were sent for according to the ... Revelation."[49] On February 22 Smith wrote to Martin Harris in Palmyra, New York, instructing him to "inform the Elders which are there that all of them who can be spared will come here without delay if possable this by Commandment of the Lord."[50] This conference occurred in early June.

In his letter to Harris, Smith asked him to come as soon as possible to

44. Revelation, Feb. 1831-A, Revelation Book 1, 68 [D&C 43:13] (*JSP*, D1:258). See also Revelation, July 1830-A, Revelation Book 1, 32 [D&C 24:3] (*JSP*, D1:158); and Revelation, Feb. 4, 1831, Revelation Book 1, 62 [D&C 41:7] (*JSP*, D1:244).

45. Revelation, Feb. 1831-A, Revelation Book 1, 68–69 [D&C 43:9, 11, 16] (*JSP*, D1:258–59). In the original, the words "from on high" are canceled to avoid an awkward repetition.

46. Whitmer, History, 21 (*JSP*, H2:32).

47. Whitmer, 21 (*JSP*, H2:33); and Faulring et al., eds., *Joseph Smith's New Translation of the Bible*, 4.

48. Revelation, Feb. 1831-B, Revelation Book 1, 70 [D&C 44:1–2] (*JSP*, D1:261).

49. Whitmer, History, 21 (*JSP*, H2:33).

50. Smith, Letter to Martin Harris, Feb. 22, 1831, [1], JS Collection (*JSP*, D1:263).

help settle the Mormon immigrants. He also requested Harris to "bring or cause to be brought all the books [of Mormon], as the work is here breaking forth on the east west north and south," and ordered: "You will not sell the books for less than 10 Shillings."[51] This was equal to $1.25, which was 50 cents lower than the original price. At twice the amount a common laborer earned per day, the sale of books was slow even at a discounted price.[52] Moreover, due to an agreement with the Smith family on January 16, 1830, Harris was only entitled to half of the proceeds from sales until his debt to the publisher, Egbert B. Grandin, was paid off, which meant that Harris would not recoup his original $3,000 investment until the entire print run of 5,000 copies was sold.[53] According to Henry Harris, the original price for the Book of Mormon was set by revelation and Martin told him that another revelation reduced the price.[54]

On February 23 Smith and seven elders met at Kirtland to determine "how the Elders of the church of Christ are to act upon the points of the Law," and Smith dictated three more sections to add to the five sections of "The Law" previously dictated on February 9.[55] The heading on the earliest copy of this revelation states that it contains additional points of the law "as agreed upon by Seven Elders ... according to the commandment of God."[56] The February 4 revelation had directed them to "assemble yourselves to gether to agree upon my word," and another given only days before the present one implied that establishing the law was an ongoing process: "I give unto you a commandment that when ye are assembled yourselves together ye shall note with a Pen how to act ... upon the points of my law ... & thus it shall become a law unto you."[57] Smith's church was founded not only on the rock of revelation but also on the consent of the governed.

Mormon anthropologist Rex Eugene Cooper has noted that the methods Smith followed to organize a church "had close affinity to Congregationalist

---

51. Smith, Letter to Harris (*JSP*, D1:263–64).

52. *JSP*, D1:264n133.

53. Joseph Smith [Jr./Sr.?], Agreement with Martin Harris, Jan. 16, 1830, Simon Gratz Autograph Collection, Historical Society of Pennsylvania, Philadelphia, PA (*EMD*, 3:485; *JSP*, D1:108 and n. 429).

54. Henry Harris, Statement, ca. Nov. 1833, in Howe, *Mormonism Unvailed*, 251–52.

55. Revelation, Feb. 23, 1831, "The rules and regulations of the Law," [6]–[8], Revelations Collection [D&C 42:74–93] (*JSP*, D1:266).

56. Revelation, [6].

57. Revelation, Feb. 4, 1831, Revelation Book 1, 61 [D&C 41:2] (*JSP*, D1:244); Revelation, Feb. 1831-A, Revelation Book 1, 68 [D&C 43:8–9] (*JSP*, D1:258).

concepts of church government."[58] Congregational polity is characterized by a lack of hierarchy but is administered by local control, held together by the consent of the congregation. Cooper observed that the church's organizational meeting was held on April 6, 1830, according to Smith's history, and that Smith and Cowdery "call[ed] on our brethren to know whether they accepted us as their teachers in the things of the Kingdom of God," to which they "consented by an unanimous vote."[59] A July 1830 revelation declared that "all things must be done in order & by Common consent in the Church," which, as Cooper observed, became "basic to the Mormon notion of Church government."[60] Cooper also recognized that with the development of a hierarchy in the mid-1830s "the Congregational-like procedure of sustaining ecclesiastical officers became essentially a formality."[61]

With the calling together of the elders in February 1831 and assigning them the responsibility of formulating new laws for the church, Smith seemed to be moving toward a presbyteral form of church governance. Presbyterian polity is marked by the rule of a council of elders or presbyters. The first new section merely rewords the first commandment of the February 9 revelation dealing with the command for the elders to go on missions and establish churches.

The second section reviews church laws requiring punishment given in the previous revelation but adds details about church discipline. In cases of adultery, for example, the offender "shall be tried before two Elders of the Church or more and every word shall be established against him by two witnesses of the Church and not of the world ... and the Elders shall lay the case before the Church and the Church shall lift up their hands against them ... and if it can be [arranged] it is necessary that the Bishop is present also and thus ye shall do in all cases which shall come before you."[62] The law for reconciling disputes followed New Testament practice: "If thy Brother offend thee, thou shalt take him between him and thee alone and if he confess thou shalt be reconciled and if he confess not thou shalt take another with thee and then if he confess not thou Shalt deliver him up unto the Church not to the members but to the Elders and it shall be done in a meeting and that not before the world and if thy Brother offend many he shall be chas-

---

58. Cooper, "The Promises Made to the Fathers," 1:121.
59. JS History, vol. A-1, 37 (*JSP*, H1:366).
60. Revelation, Sep. 1830, Revelation Book 1, 41 [D&C 28:2] (*JSP*, D1:186).
61. Cooper, "The Promises Made to the Fathers," 1:122.
62. Revelation, Feb. 23, 1831, [7] [D&C 42:80–83] (*JSP*, D1:266).

tened before many and if any one offend openly he shall be rebuked openly that he may be ashamed."[63]

Section three deals with how the church is to "act in cases of Adultery," as indicated by a brief heading in the manuscript copies. The wording of this section is awkward, but it seems to describe specific kinds of adultery related to divorce or spousal abandonment. The first instance was simply a reiteration of Matthew 5:32: "Whatsoever person among you having put away their companion for the cause of fornication or in otherwords if he shall testify before you in all Lowliness of heart that this is the case ye shall not cast them out."[64] Thus the only legitimate ground for divorce was unfaithfulness on the part of the former spouse. In April 1833 Smith's older brother, Hyrum, recorded an instance of this in his diary: "Went to Brother Roundays there we met with Brother morse we questioned him on the Subject of his Situation of his life he Being a man that has had two wifes he living with his Seccond wife the first Being yet a live But She was Put away for the Cause of fornication he Being innonent She the offender He testified in all loliness of Heart and Sett free."[65]

In the second case, anyone who has "left their companion for the sake of adultery and they themselves are the offender and their companions are living they shall be cast out." In other words, if a person divorces their spouse to pursue an adulterous relationship, they commit sin whether or not they remarry. The elders are instructed to "be watchful and careful with all inquiry that ye receive none such among you if they are married and if they are not married they shall repent of all their sins or ye shall not receive them."[66]

It is perhaps significant that this last section of the Law dealing with adultery is textually different from the preceding portion and may not have been part of the text that had been worked out on February 23. The previous two sections are numbered, the last is not. It is the only section with a heading and written in the divine first-person. Section two had already described how cases of adultery were to be handled.[67] The singling

---

63. Revelation, [7] [D&C 42:88–91] (*JSP*, D1:267). See Matt. 18:15–17; and 1 Tim. 5:20.

64. Revelation, [8] [D&C 42:74]. "Whosoever shall put away his wife, saving for the cause of fornication, causeth her to commit adultery: and whosoever shall marry her that is divorced committeth adultery" (Matt. 5:32).

65. Hyrum Smith, Diary, Apr. 4, 1833.

66. Revelation, Feb. 23, 1831, [8] [D&C 42:75–77] (*JSP*, D1:267).

67. The February 23, 1831, additions to the Law were not transcribed by John Whitmer into Revelation Book 1. However, the last paragraph was copied by Oliver Cowdery on a separate slip of paper and attached at the end of the February 9, 1831, revelation containing the first part of the Law. Revelation Book 1, 67 (*JSP*, MRB:107).

out of adultery in the last section for further comment may have been due to Smith's discovery of beliefs or perhaps even activities among members of Morley's communal family. Henry Carroll, who lived on the land bordering the Morley farm, recalled that those who lived there "claimed all things were common, even to free love, among the Mormons in Kirtland."[68] George A. Smith, who arrived at Kirtland in 1833, apparently referred to this early period of false spirits and religious enthusiasm when he remarked that in the early days of the church, there were "Persons who professed to have revelations on every subject and who were ready to banish every moral principle under the guidance of these false spirits."[69] Lucia Goldsmith seemed to describe a belief similar to the "spiritual wifery" espoused by Jacob Cochran and his followers in Maine in 1818–19 when she recalled: "Any male member could have a 'revelation' that he could take another wife … [until] the prophet called a 'council of Elders' and it was decided that only Smith, Rigdon, and Oliver Cowdery, could have 'revelations.' This put a stop to much of the trouble."[70]

Concerning these accounts, Mark Staker has observed: "Because no records from insiders have survived about their beliefs as part of the Family, it is not easy to tell if outsiders projected their own assumptions about Owenite communities onto Kirtland or if the Family organization in Kirtland had indeed not only adopted Owenite views on property but also those on abolition, marriage, and other subjects as well."[71] Robert Owen advocated a sort of open marriage system. "The artificial bands of indissoluble marriage, and the single family arrangements, to which marriage leads, are much more calculated to destroy than to promote affection," he argued. "In the new state of existence, that which experience has proved to be really beneficial in marriage, or single family arrangements, will be retained; while all that is injurious and contrary to nature will be dismissed."[72] If the charges of "free love" stemmed from some of the members of the Family changing partners, we might have an explanation for Joseph Smith's addition to the Law explicitly forbidding such practice.

---

68. Henry Carroll, "Statement," in *Naked Truths about Mormonism*, Apr. 1888, 3.

69. George A. Smith, Sermon, Nov. 15, 1864, 32, George D. Watt Papers, CHL, in Staker, *Hearken, O Ye People*, 592.

70. Lucia Goldsmith, "Sidney Rigdon, The First Mormon Elder," n.p., n.d., Lucia A. Goldsmith Papers, Western Reserve Historical Society, Cleveland, OH, as quoted in Staker, *Hearken, O Ye People*, 105. On the Cochranites, see Ridlon, *Saco Valley Settlements and Families*, 269–80.

71. Staker, *Hearken, O Ye People*, 46, 105.

72. [Owen], *Robert Owen's Opening Speech, and His Reply to the Rev. Alex. Campbell*, 40.

Move to the Morley Farm

After staying with the Whitneys a few weeks, Joseph and Emma moved into Isaac Morley's home, located on the Chillicothe Turnpike, a mile east of the Whitney store. According to Morley's daughter, "Father [Morley] took [Smith] into his own home, and he lived with us throughout the winter. In the Spring they put him up a small frame house to live in while he stayed there."[73] Morley's communal farm consisted of 130 acres on the north side of the turnpike and included a housing complex near the road and a school house.[74] Kirtland resident Josiah Jones estimated that Morley's Family "consisted of perhaps 50 or 60, old and young."[75] Morley's commune provided a central location from which to regulate church affairs as well as a place to hold meetings.

On March 1 Smith wrote to Oliver Cowdery in Jackson County, Missouri, in response to a letter Cowdery had written to his Ohio converts, dated January 29, and informed Cowdery of his move to Ohio.[76] Cowdery's letter announced that he and the other missionaries had arrived "a few days since" at Independence, which was the nearest white settlement to Indian Territory.[77] "Two of our number now commenced work as tailors in the village of Independence," wrote Parley P. Pratt, "while the others crossed the frontier line and commenced a mission among the Lamanites." After visiting the Shawnees briefly, the travelers "crossed the Kansas River and entered among the Delawares."[78]

Two days later Smith wrote to his brother Hyrum in Colesville, New York, informing him of recent activities in Kirtland and requesting him to bring their father from Fayette to Kirtland. Orson Pratt and Samuel Harrison Smith had arrived in Kirtland with news that David Jackways of Palmyra was planning to have Joseph Smith Sr. arrested for an unpaid debt. "Come in a one horse wagon if you Can," Smith Jr. advised, "do not Come threw Buffalo for th[e]y will lie in wait for you God protect you." Smith informed Hyrum: "I hav[e] been ingageed in regulating the Churches here as the deciples are numerous and the devil had made many attempts to over throw

---

73. Cox, "Brief History of Patriarch Isaac Morley and Family," 1.

74. See Staker, *Hearken, O Ye People*, 44, 156.

75. Josiah Jones, "History of the Mormonites," *Evangelist* (Carthage, OH), June 1, 1841, 132.

76. This letter from Joseph Smith and others in Kirtland, Ohio, dated March 1, 1831, is no longer extant but is mentioned in Cowdery, Letter to "My dearly beloved brethren & sisters in the Lord," Apr. 8, 1831, JS Letterbook 1, 10 (*JSP*, D1:291).

77. Cowdery's Jan. 29, 1831, letter is no longer extant but was quoted in Joseph Smith, Letter to Hyrum Smith, Mar. 3–4, 1831, JS Collection (*JSP*, D1:272).

78. Pratt, *Autobiography*, 53.

them"—referring to his efforts to rein in religious enthusiasm and spiritual excesses. "It has been a Serious job," Joseph wrote, "but the Lord is with us and we have overcome and have all things regular." He excitedly reported: "The work is brakeing forth on the right hand and on the left and there is a great Call for Elders in this place."[79]

On the following day, Smith finished his letter to Hyrum and related that he had cast a devil out of a woman that morning. "After being Colled out of my bed in the night to go a small distance," Smith recounted. "I went and had and an awful strugle with satan but being armed with the power of God he was cast out and the woman is Clothed in hir right mind the Lord worketh wonders in this land."[80] Smith had moved into the neighborhood where most of the extravagant and wild expressions of religious enthusiasm had occurred before his arrival. What Smith interpreted as a manifestation worthy of exorcism likely involved facial and bodily contortions or convulsions as described in E. D. Howe's 1831 account that some converts were seen to "roll upon the floor" and "exhibited all the apish actions imaginable, making grimaces both horrid and ridiculous."[81] As with Newel Knight's exorcism in Colesville, New York, ten months earlier, Smith's followers called on him for help. At that time, Smith took Knight by the hand and rebuked the devil, commanding him "in the name of Jesus Christ" to depart. It worked for Knight and evidently it worked in this case as well.[82] Not long after this, Philo Dibble said he heard Smith declare: "God has sent me here, and the devil must leave here, or I will."[83] Of course, Joseph Smith had no intention of leaving.

---

79. Smith, Letter to Hyrum Smith, Mar. 3–4, 1831, 1, 3, JS Collection (*JSP*, D1:270, 273).

80. Smith, 2. Cf. Mark 5:15.

81. *Painesville Telegraph*, Nov. 1, 1831, 3.

82. Newel Knight's exorcism is recounted in JS History, vol. A-1, 39–41 (*EMD*, 1:101–105; *JSP*, H1:382–87). See also Vogel, *Joseph Smith*, 496–99.

83. Philo Dibble, "Recollections of the Prophet Joseph Smith," *Juvenile Instructor*, Jan. 1, 1892, 23.

2

Fixing the Bible

FEBRUARY–MARCH 1831

I believe the bible, as it ought to be as it came from the pen of the original writers.

—*Joseph Smith, Oct. 15, 1843*[1]

Shortly after they arrived in Ohio in early February 1831, Joseph Smith and Sidney Rigdon continued their revision of the Bible, reaching Genesis chapter 24 by March 7. This work was referred to in Smith's revelations as a "translation," which implied that it was a restoration of the corrupted text to its original reading. In reality, it was creative responses to perceived problems existing in the English text along with occasional imaginative/inspired expansions.

The Book of Mormon had claimed that sectarian division and strife were due to the Bible's being altered by the Roman Catholic Church, that "many plain and precious things which have been taken out of the book."[2] While the body of textual evidence for both testaments has grown since Smith's day, nothing has surfaced to support the wholesale alteration of the Bible. However, the texts that Smith copied from the King James Version (KJV), such as twenty-one chapters from Isaiah, two from Malachi, and three from Matthew, were altered by *him* with changes that were artificial and anachronistic. In his study of the Isaiah chapters in the Book of Mormon, Hebrew scholar David Wright concluded that the Book of Mormon's use of "Isaiah derives directly from the KJV text with some secondary modifications by Smith and that it does not derive from an ancient text through translation."[3] He also noted that the variant readings "can be explained as modifications of the KJV text, especially where there are italics," and that Smith's alterations of these

---

1. Smith, Journal, Oct. 15, 1843 (*JSP*, J3:113).
2. Book of Mormon, 1830 ed., 30 [1 Ne. 13:29].
3. Wright, "Isaiah in the Book of Mormon," 209.

italicized words often produced "incomplete and conceptually difficult or impossible readings" that were "incompatible with the Hebrew text" of Isaiah.[4] New Testament scholar Stan Larson, in his study of the Sermon on the Mount in 3 Nephi 12–14, similarly concluded that the Book of Mormon's text "originated in the nineteenth century, derived from unacknowledged plagiarism of the KJV," which "Smith copied [from] the KJV blindly, not showing awareness of translation problems and errors in the KJV."[5] Larson also noted that some alterations were made to italicized words, but that "the Book of Mormon fails to revise places where the KJV text ought to have been printed in italics but is not."[6] Wright observed that the character of the alterations Smith made in his Bible revision are the same as what has been found in the Book of Mormon and that Smith's 1829 efforts could be considered a "training ground" for his subsequent work on the Bible.[7]

Similar to what was found in the Book of Mormon, Kevin Barney demonstrated that the "majority of ... changes" in Smith's inspired "translation" of the Bible "lack ancient textual support" but are instances where Smith "solves a problem created by the English translation in the KJV."[8] Smith may have become aware of problems in the biblical text from skeptical and deistical writings, as well as Bible commentaries such as Methodist Adam Clarke's multi-volume *Holy Bible, Containing the Old and New Testaments*, which went through many editions and was widely known to Smith's contemporaries, although there is no direct evidence of this.[9] Barney also noted that the Joseph Smith Translation (JST) "is almost entirely comprised of additions to the KJV" and that "the most common deliberate scribal corruptions were additions to the [Bible] text, not deletions," which puts Smith in the same category as the ancient editors. "Therefore, the tendency of the

---

4. Wright, 164, 165, 181.

5. Larson, "The Historicity of the Matthean Sermon on the Mount in 3 Nephi," 132.

6. Larson, 131.

7. Wright, "Isaiah in the Book of Mormon," 209–10.

8. Barney, "The Joseph Smith Translation and Ancient Texts of the Bible," 157.

9. In 2017 BYU professor of ancient scripture Thomas Wayment and research assistant Haley Wilson announced that they "uncovered evidence that Smith and his associates used a readily available Bible commentary while compiling a new Bible translation." Wilson and Wayment, "A Recently Recovered Source." Three years later, Wayment and Wilson-Lemmon reported that they had found that there were hundreds of "direct parallels between Smith's translation and Adam Clarke's biblical commentary," which they argued "demonstrate Smith's open reliance upon Clarke and establish that he was inclined to lean on Clarke's commentary for matters of history, textual questions, clarification of wording, and theological nuance." Wayment and Wilson-Lemmon, "A Recovered Resource"; see also Wayment, "Joseph Smith, Adam Clarke, and the Making of a Bible Revision." For criticism that Wayment and Wilson-Lemmon have overstated their evidence, see Jackson, "Some Notes on Joseph Smith and Adam Clarke."

JST to expand the KJV text by adding material," Barney observes, "is the opposite of what we should expect in a textual restoration based on what has been learned since the nineteenth century."[10]

In their attempt to rescue the Book of Mormon's historicity from evidence of anachronisms, both in its use of the KJV and in parallels to various aspects of nineteenth-century American culture, some apologetic writers have attempted to broaden the definition of "translation" to include what they speculate was Smith's rewording and expansion of the original text, ignoring his claim to have merely read the words from his seer stone. Some apologetic writers point to Smith's Bible revision, which he called a "translation," as evidence that he used a non-standard definition. However, the rarefied definition comes from what the apologetic writers believe is needed to escape problems encountered in the texts, rather than from what Smith said he was doing. In 1843 he declared: "I believe the bible, as it ought to be, as it came from the pen of the original writers." He then gave an example of a problematic text that was resolved in his revision of the Old Testament, implying that he had corrected the text to its original reading.[11]

Apologetic writers, therefore, have things backward. Rather than redefining "translation" to accommodate the anachronisms and problems and thereby create a vicious circularity—a question-begging definition—the anachronisms should tell us that Smith was not translating as he claimed. If Smith felt inspired to correct perceived problems in the Bible and produce pseudepigraphic additions to the text, he also believed himself justified in presenting his work as a "translation," implying that he was restoring the original text. It had the same effect as when he claimed to "read" the God-given text of the Book of Mormon directly from his seer stone, when he was actually working the words out in his mind (D&C 9). Both were misdirections intended to increase faith in what he believed were inspired works. In revising and expanding the Bible, Smith's procedure was similar to that of an ancient pseudepigraphist who, in the words of one Bible scholar, "created something new, an imaginary Sacred Past, the way it *should* have been."[12]

Old Testament

Smith began working on his revision of the Bible in June 1830, dictating to

---

10. Barney, "The Joseph Smith Translation and Ancient Texts of the Bible," 145.

11. Smith, Journal, Oct. 15, 1843 (*JSP*, J3:113). The text Joseph Smith used as an example was Genesis 6:6, which states that "it repented the LORD that he had made man on the earth, and it grieved him at his heart" (Gen. 6:6). See below for a discussion of Smith's revision of this text.

12. Price, "Joseph Smith," 324.

Oliver Cowdery what might be called a preface to Genesis, which explains the circumstances of Moses's receiving a revelation regarding the creation of the heavens and earth. In Smith's addition, Moses gazes upon God and his creations with his "spiritual eyes," for as he states, "My natural eyes could not have beheld for I should have withered & died in his presence."[13] This was an explanation for the subsequent passage in Exodus 33:20, where God declares: "Thou canst not see my face: for there shall no man see me, and live." A few verses before this in Exodus 33:11, it confusingly states: "And the LORD spake unto Moses face to face, as a man speaketh unto his friend." Commentators had long noted the apparent contradiction, which Smith later resolved by modifying the statement in Exodus 33:20 to read:

> And he said unto Moses, Thou canst not see my face *at this time, lest mine anger be kindled against thee also, and I destroy thee, and thy people;* for there shall no man *among them* see me *at this time* and live, *for they are exceeding sinful, and no sinful man hath at any time, neither shall there be any sinful man at any time that shall see my face and live.*[14]

With so many examples of theophany in Christian literature,[15] little wonder many of Smith's contemporaries resolved the Bible's ambiguity by similarly making a distinction between "spiritual" and "natural" eyes.[16] Methodist founder John Wesley had likewise declared: "No man hath seen God—With bodily eyes: yet believers see him with the eye of faith."[17] During the following year, Smith will claim an early vision of Jesus and will soon encourage theophany among his followers.

After the vision closes, Satan appears to tempt Moses, saying: "Moses, Son of man, worship me." But—much as Smith had done at Newel Knight's exorcism in April 1830—Moses commands: "Get thee hence Satan deceive me not." Instead of departing, "Satan cried with a loud [voice and] went upon the Ear[th] & commanded [Moses] saying I am the only

---

13. Old Testament Revision 1, 1 [Moses 1:11] (Faulring et al., eds., *Joseph Smith's New Translation of the Bible*, 84). Composed in June 1830, and redacted in Old Testament Revision 2, 1, shortly after it was created between March 8 and April 1831. Faulring et al., 57–58. At that time, Smith clarified the text by having Rigdon insert the words "spiritual" and "natural" above the line. Faulring et al., 592.

14. Old Testament Revision 2, 1 [Ex. 33:20] (Faulring et al., 701); emphasis added. Joseph Smith's revision of Exodus dates between July 1832 and July 1833. Faulring et al., 59.

15. Lambert and Cracroft, "Literary Form and Historical Understanding."

16. Juster, *Doomsayers*, 114–17.

17. John Wesley, "John Wesley's Notes on the Bible," as quoted in Harrell, *"This Is My Doctrine,"* 137.

begotten worship me." Calling upon God for strength, Moses declares: "In the name of the Jesus Christ depart hence Satan."[18] With a screech and a howl, Satan vanishes.

When God reappears, he tells Moses: "Worlds without number have I created."[19] This reflects prevalent nineteenth-century speculation that the sun, moon, and stars were inhabited by God's other children, a theme that Smith will develop further in subsequent revelations.[20] God then informs Moses that he wishes to speak "concerning this Earth upon which thou standest," and instructs him to "write the things which I shall speak."[21] At this point, Smith began to revise the opening lines of Genesis. Although his revisions were minimal, they attempted to bring Genesis into conformity with New Testament and Book of Mormon teaching that Jesus is the Creator (John 1:1–4, 14; Heb. 1:1–3; Ether 3:14–16; Hel. 14:12):

God said, Let us make man in our image, after our likeness … So God created man in his own image, in the image of God created he him. (Gen. 1:26–27)	*I* God said *unto mine only begotten which was with me from the beginning* Let us make man in our image after our likeness … So *I* God created man in *mine* own image in the image of *mine only begotten* created *I* him.[22]

By inserting the Son into Genesis, Smith was only making explicit what most Trinitarian Christians already assumed about the text. The additional wording was likely inspired by the main proof text for Jesus being the Creator in the Gospel of John, which declares Jesus is the Word that was with God "in the beginning" and that "all things were made by him" and in process of time "the Word was made flesh, and dwelt among us, (and we beheld his glory, the glory as of the only begotten of the Father,) full of grace and truth" (John 1:1, 2, 14). The three major Bible commentaries at the time interpreted the passage as describing agreement among the persons of the

---

18. Old Testament Revision 1, 1–2 [Moses 1:12, 16, 19, 21] (Faulring et al., eds., *Joseph Smith's New Translation of the Bible*, 84).

19. Old Testament Revision 1, 2 [Moses 1:33] (Faulring et al., 85). Cf. Heb. 1:2.

20. See, for example, D&C 76 and 88. For a discussion of this topic, see Vogel and Metcalfe, "Joseph Smith's Scriptural Cosmology."

21. Old Testament Revision 1, 1–2 [Moses 1:40] (Faulring et al., eds., *Joseph Smith's New Translation of the Bible*, 86).

22. Old Testament Revision 1, 4 [Moses 2:26–27] (Faulring et al., eds., *Joseph Smith's New Translation of the Bible*, 88).

Godhead,[23] but other Christian theologians were more specific: "St. Paul says, That the Son is the Image of the invisible God, and the express Image of his Person [Col. 1:15; Heb. 1:3]; which is not said of the highest Angels, nor of the Holy Spirit himself; and is therefore a strong Proof, that God spake to his Son, when he said, Let us make Man in our Image."[24] Some Mormon interpreters have argued that Smith's insertion of the Son into the creation account in Genesis is proof that he believed the Father and Son were distinct persons and therefore he was not a modalist as the Book of Mormon seems to indicate when it refers to Jesus as both Father and Son, but this is no more true for Smith than for the Trinitarians.[25]

Another important change in Genesis occurs when Smith tried to reconcile the two stories of creation, which deists and skeptics believed demonstrated multiple authorship.[26] Many puzzled over the incongruity of the declaration in Genesis 2:1 that "the heavens and the earth were finished, and all the host of them," and the statement in verse 5 that "there was not a man to till the ground," so God in verse 7 "formed man of the dust of the ground, and breathed into his nostrils the breath of life; and man became a living soul." Smith resolved this problem by inserting the words: "For I the Lord God created all things of which I have spoken spiritually before they were naturally upon the face of the Earth. ... For in Heaven created I them & there was not yet flesh upon the earth neither in the water neither in

---

23. See Clarke, *The Holy Bible ... With a Commentary and Critical Notes*, Gen. 1:26; Henry, *Exposition of the Old and New Testament*, 1:6; Scott, *The Holy Bible, Containing the Old and New Testaments*, 1:31.

24. Anon., *An Enquiry into the Meaning of that Text Genesis i. 26*, 26. In his 1824 notes on *The Book of Common Prayer*, English theologian John Bayley commented on Genesis 1:26: "In the Epistle of St. Barnabas, and in the Apostolical Constitutions, the words are considered as addressed by God the Father to God the Son." Then he quoted one Constitution as saying, "The Holy Scripture witnesseth that God said to the only begotten Christ, Let us make man." Bayley, *The Book of Common Prayer*, 502.

25. Bickmore, "Does the Book of Mormon Teach Mainstream Trinitarianism or Modalism?"; Bruening and Paulsen, "The Development of the Mormon Understanding of God," 118–20. However, the book of Moses never states that the "Only Begotten" is a separate personage from the Father, but rather equates that title with the "word of my power" (Moses 1:32; 2:1, 5; see also D&C 29:30–31). Notice also that the ambiguity in Genesis where the plural ("our image") changes to singular ("his own image"), which Smith retained. See Vogel, "The Earliest Mormon Concept of God."

26. English skeptic Robert Cooper, for example, asserted: "With respect to the book of Genesis in particular, it is quite evident it must have been written by two different historians, at least, and therefore could not be the work of Moses ... There are two different stories of this event [of creation], so opposite to each 'other, in style and fact, that no one individual but a lunatic, without memory, could write them. ... From all these considerations, therefore, we are warranted in affirming that the Pentateuch could not have been written until after the Babylonish captivity." Cooper, *The Infidel's Text-book*, 80–81.

the air."[27] This echoes a revelation Smith had dictated in September 1830, in which God declares: "For by the Power of my Spirit created I them yea all things both Spiritual & Temporally first spiritual secondly temporally."[28] It remains unclear whether Smith meant to describe a spiritual creation in the sense of a premortal existence of the spirits of humankind, as he would later teach, or an "ideal" creation or what has been described as a "conceptual blue-print" that existed in God's foreknowledge.[29] Either way, there was precedent among Smith's contemporaries.

In his popular 1805 book *A Treatise on the Atonement*, Unitarian Hosea Ballou suggested that in the first account of creation "man stood in his created character, which is Christ, the heavenly man" and that in the second account "God *formed* (not created) man of the dust of the ground."[30] Another of Smith's contemporaries argued that when God formed man out of the ground and "breathed into his nostrils the breath of life," he "infused into the earthly man that same intellectual spirit, before created and blessed; so that the animal and spiritual nature of man, both became mystically incorporated together, as one living soul or man."[31]

The next important change expanded Genesis 3 to explain the origin of Satan and how he influenced the serpent that beguiled Eve in the Garden of Eden. Similar to Lehi's description of Satan as a fallen angel (2 Ne. 2:17–18), Smith had God state:

> Satan ... came before me saying Behold [here am] I send me I will be thy Son & I will redeem all mankind that one soul shall not be lost & surely I will do it Wherefore give me thine honour But behold my beloved Son ... saith unto me Father thy will be done & the glory be thine forever Wherefore because that Satan rebelled against me & sought to destroy the agency of man which I the Lord God had given him & also that I should give unto him mine own power by the power of mine only

---

27. Old Testament Revision 1, 5 [Moses 1:40] (Faulring et al., eds., *Joseph Smith's New Translation of the Bible*, 88–89).

28. Revelation, Sep. 1830-A, Revelation Book 1, 38–39 [D&C 29:31–32] (*JSP*, D1:181).

29. See Ostler, "The Idea of Pre-Existence in the Development of Mormon Thought," 59–61; and Ostler, "Earliest Pre-Existence Allusion?" While Ostler suggests that Smith introduced the concept of human pre-existence in 1833 (D&C 93:32–34), Anthony Hutchinson believes that Smith's revision of Genesis "triggered an insight or speculation about human pre-mortal existence." Hutchinson, "A Mormon Midrash?" 37. Charles Harrell argues that while pre-existence is absent in the Book of Mormon, it is present in the Book of Moses (Moses 3:1–7; 5:24; 6:36, 51, 63) and other early revelations (D&C 29:30–32; 49:17; 77:2). Harrell, *"This Is My Doctrine,"* 208.

30. Ballou, *A Treatise on Atonement*, 30.

31. Ferriss, *The Plain Restitutionist*, 16.

begotten I caused that he should be cast down ... [And] Satan ... spake by the mouth of the Serpent.[32]

Interestingly, Satan's competing plan of salvation was particularly meaningful to Smith's followers in Colesville, for, similar to the Universalists, Satan wanted to save all humanity. However, this proposal is said to conflict with God's plan, which ironically requires not only free will but also temptation, which Satan provides.

The insertion of Satan into Genesis is anachronistic, and the idea that Satan spoke through the serpent is foreign to the Bible. Smith also linked Satan and the angel that fell from heaven in Isaiah 14:12, which in poetic language describes Lucifer's fall from heaven (cf. 2 Ne. 24:12; D&C 76:25–26). However, the identification of Lucifer with Satan or the devil is also post-biblical. The passage in Isaiah is embedded in a taunt parable predicting the fall of Nebuchadnezzar, king of Babylon (Isa. 14:4–21). The ancient prophet draws on the Canaanite myth regarding the "Day Star" (Vulgate, "Lucifer") wanting to rise above all other stars, only to be cast down to hell by the sun. Jesus uses Isaiah's imagery to describe both the fall of the city of Capernaum and the devil (Luke 10:15, 18), but nowhere in the New Testament is Lucifer a synonym for Satan or the devil. Adam Clarke complained about this common misinterpretation of Isaiah 14:12: "Although the context speaks explicitly concerning Nebuchadnezzar, yet this has been, I know not why, applied to the chief of the fallen angels, who is most incongruously denominated *Lucifer*, (the bringer of light!) ... But the truth is, the text speaks nothing at all concerning *Satan* nor his *fall*, nor the *occasion* of that fall, which many divines have with great confidence deduced from this text."[33]

The insertion about Satan appears in Cowdery's handwriting in the manuscript of the Old Testament and therefore dates to sometime after June and before Cowdery's departure from New York about October 17, 1830. In September, Smith dictated a revelation that not only touched on spiritual and physical creation but also on the origin of the devil: "Behold the Devil was before Adam for he rebelled against me saying give me thine honour which is my Power & also a third part of the host of Heaven turned he away from me Because of their agency & they were thrust down & thus came the Devil & his Angels."[34]

---

32. Old Testament Revision 1, 6 [Moses 4:1–3, 6, 7] (Faulring et al., eds., *Joseph Smith's New Translation of the Bible*, 90).

33. Clarke, *The Holy Bible*, Isa. 14:12.

34. Revelation, Sep. 1830-A, Revelation Book 1, 39 [D&C 29:36–37] (*JSP*, D1:181).

This time Smith used Revelation 12:3–4 to describe the premortal fall of the devil and his angels, where he is described as "a great red dragon" that draws a "third part of the stars" with its tail and casts them down to Earth. While some of Smith's contemporaries interpreted this as occurring at the creation, most commentators interpreted it as a future event, since Revelation itself states that John was to be shown "things which must shortly come to pass" (Rev. 1:1).[35]

Between Genesis 3 and 4, Smith added fifteen verses to describe events following Adam and Eve's exile from the garden. This material claims not only that Cain and Abel had older siblings, but consistent with the Book of Mormon's descriptions of pre-Christian Christianity, Adam and his children are commanded to sacrifice "the firstlings of their flocks … [in] similitude of the sacrifice of the only begotten of the Father." Then Satan appears to Adam's children, declaring himself to be a "son of God" and causing many to sin. Through the Holy Ghost, God commands Adam's children to repent or be damned, and, in words full of meaning for Universalists, the new text states: "The words went forth out of the mouth of God in a firm decree Wherefore they must be fulfilled."[36]

In revising the story of Cain's murder of Abel, Smith revisited the subject of "secret combinations," which plays a significant role in the Book of Mormon's narrative. In the book of Ether, Akish administers an oath which was "handed down even from Cain, who was a murderer from the beginning" (Ether 8:14–15; see also Hel. 6:27). Thus Smith had Satan say to Abel: "Swear unto me by thy throat & if thou tell it thou shalt die & swear thy brethren by their heads & by the living God that they tell it not for if they tell it they shall surely die." While the term "secret combination" is not used here, another term is utilized which is just as revealing. After entering into an oath with Satan, Cain exclaims: "Truly I am Mahon the master of this great secret that I may murder & get gain Wherefore Cain was called Master Mahon & he gloried in his wickedness."[37] Many scholars have commented on the play between "Master Mahon" and "Master Mason," the name given to third-degree Masons.[38]

---

35. Harrell, *"This Is My Doctrine,"* 220.

36. Old Testament Revision 1, 8 [Moses 5:5, 7, 13, 15] (Faulring et al., eds., *Joseph Smith's New Translation of the Bible*, 93). See also 2 Ne. 9:9.

37. Old Testament Revision 1, 9 [Moses 5:29, 31] (Faulring et al., eds., 94).

38. Historian D. Michael Quinn suggests that "Mahon" may be linked to one of Satan's names, "Mahoun," pronounced "Mahan," in use during the early nineteenth century. Quinn, *Early Mormonism and the Magic World View*, 208–209. This is certainly a possibility, but the full term that Smith uses, "*Master* Mahon," is closer to the Masonic usage.

Following Cowdery's departure to Missouri in mid-October 1830, John Whitmer and Emma Smith became the scribes for five pages. Whitmer began on October 21; then Emma wrote three pages on December 1, followed by a brief entry by Whitmer. In Whitmer's last contribution, God teaches Adam the gospel and plan of salvation, and then Adam is baptized by a magical power of levitation.[39] God also tells Adam, "Thou art after the order of him who was without beginning of days or end of years from all eternity to all eternity."[40] This refers to the high priesthood mentioned in Alma 13, described as "the order of the Son of the only begotten of the Father, which is without beginning of days or end of years"—which order Smith would reveal to his followers in Kirtland in June 1831.[41]

In Alma 13 Smith attempted to establish the existence of high priests and a high priesthood among the ancient patriarchs, a subject upon which the Bible is completely silent. This not only explained how non-Levitical priests could arise among the Nephites but also justified a continuance of the high priesthood among Smith's followers. Smith's approach was to expand the story of Abraham paying tithes to Melchizedek, priest of Salem, in Genesis 14, while at the same time anachronistically incorporating interpretations from Hebrews 7.

The author of Hebrews explains how Jesus is the "Apostle and High Priest of our profession" (Heb. 3:1), whose priesthood is superior to that of the Levitical and Aaronic priests, by arguing that while Jesus was not from the priestly tribe of Levi, he was nevertheless a priest "after the order of Melchizedek" (Heb. 7:1–4, 11–14). As proof, the writer of Hebrews repeatedly quotes Psalm 110:4—"The Lord hath sworn, and will not repent, Thou art a priest for ever after the order of Melchizedek" (5:6, 10; 6:20; 7:17, 21; cf. Alma 13:9, 14). Originally intended as a statement about Israelite rulers who were seen as kingly priests, Psalm 110 had taken on messianic meaning by New Testament times (e.g., Matt. 22:41–46). Hebrews does not assert that Jesus held the same priesthood as Melchizedek, but that he held a priesthood that was similar to the ancient king-priest's: one that was neither lineal nor responsible for administering the Law of Moses. Taking advantage of a lack of biographical data in Genesis 14, the writer of Hebrews argues that Melchizedek, as a type of Christ, was "without father, without

---

39. Old Testament Revision 1, 14–15 [Moses 6:52–66] (Faulring et al., eds., *Joseph Smith's New Translation of the Bible*, 101–103).

40. Old Testament Revision 1, 15 [Moses 6:67] (Faulring et al., 103).

41. Book of Mormon, 1830 ed., 259 [Alma 13:9].

mother, without descent, having neither beginning of days, nor end of life; but made like unto the Son of God; [and] abideth a priest continually" (Heb. 7:3). Unlike Levitical priests, Melchizedek and Jesus were said to be immortal and therefore not in need of successors; hence, their priesthoods were superior to that of the Levites.

However, Alma 13 destroys the analogy Hebrews made between a parentless Melchizedek and the immortal Jesus. Whereas Hebrews calls Jesus a priest "after the order of Melchizedek" (Heb. 7:11, 17, 21), Alma calls Melchizedek a priest "after the order of the Son." This reversal resolved a troubling aspect of Hebrews, one that placed Melchizedek in a position that was superior to Jesus, but it also allowed for an order of priests to exist before Melchizedek. As Alma explains, this priesthood became associated with Melchizedek because of his prominence, that "there were many before [Melchizedek], and also there were many afterwards, but none were greater; therefore of him they have more particularly made mention." Rather than Melchizedek being without father and mother, Alma applies the description to the high priesthood: "This High Priesthood being after the order of his Son, which order was from the foundation of the world; or in other words, being without beginning of days or end of years, being prepared from eternity to all eternity." At the same time, Alma removes centuries of speculation about Melchizedek's lack of parentage by stating that the king of Salem "did reign under his father."[42]

In Alma 13, Smith added an important element not mentioned in either Genesis or Hebrews, which is repeated in his revision of Genesis—that the high priesthood included the power of physical translation and of entering into the presence of the Lord. As Alma explained, "There were many which were ordained and became High Priests of God; ... and were sanctified, and their garments were washed white, through the blood of the Lamb. ... And there were many, exceeding great many, which were made pure, and entered into the rest of the Lord their God."[43] Becoming pure and entering into the rest of the Lord will become a major theme of Smith's early teachings and revelations, and reception of the high priesthood was an essential step in that process.

In a revelation that Smith would dictate in September 1832, it will be explained that without the high priesthood "no man can see the face of God even the father and live," and that when the children of Israel rebelled

---

42. Book of Mormon, 1830 ed., 259–60 [Alma 13:7, 9, 14, 18, 19]. See also Alma 13:8–9.
43. Book of Mormon, 1830 ed., 259–60 [Alma 13:10–12].

against Moses, "the Lord in his wrath ... swore that they should not enter into his rest, which rest is the fulness of his glory while in the wilderness."[44] Where Moses failed, Smith would succeed in bringing his followers into the rest of the Lord in the New Jerusalem, where Jesus promised in 3 Nephi that "the powers of heaven shall be in the midst of this people; yea, even I will be in the midst of you."[45]

After Rigdon arrived in New York in early December 1830, a revelation instructed that he "write for him [Joseph Smith] & the scriptures shall be given even as they are in mine own bosom."[46] At this time, according to John Whitmer, Smith dictated a long addition to Genesis known as the "prophecy of Enoch the seventh from Adam."[47] Rigdon's handwriting begins on page 15 of the Old Testament manuscript (Moses 7:2) with an expansion of Genesis 5:22–24, which mentions that "Enoch walked with God: and he was not: for God took him." Smith expanded the account in Genesis to include Enoch's founding of a city named Zion, which was so powerful that it was feared by the armies of the nations. Like some of Rigdon's followers in Ohio, Enoch's Zion was a utopian communal organization: "And the Lord called his people Zion because they were of one heart and one mind and dwelt in righteousness and there was no poor among them." In Smith's expansion of Genesis, the Lord not only took Enoch into heaven but also his entire city: "Enoch ... built a City that was called the City of Holiness even Zion ... [And] the Lord said unto Enock Zion hath I bless'd but the residue of the people have I cursed[.] and it came to pass that the Lord shewed unto Enock all the inhabitants of the earth and he beheld and lo! Zion in process of time was taken up into heaven ... and from thence went forth the saying Zion is fled."[48]

Next, God tells Enoch about the establishment of a latter-day Zion: "Truth will I cause to sweep the earth as with a flood to gether out mine elect from the four quarters of the earth unto a place which I shall prepare an holy City that my people may gird up their loins and be looking fourth for the time of my coming for there shall be my tabernicle and it shall be called Zion a New Jerusalem." Though not clearly stated in his Bible revision, Smith envisioned the rapture or levitation of the earthly Zion at Jesus's return and

---

44. Revelation, Sep. 22–23, 1832, [1], Newel K. Whitney Papers [D&C 84:22, 24] (*JSP*, D2:295–96).

45. Book of Mormon, 1830 ed., 297 [3 Ne. 20:22]. See also 3 Ne. 21:25.

46. Revelation, Dec. 7, 1830, Revelation Book 1, 47 [D&C 35:20] (*JSP*, D1:223).

47. John Whitmer, History, 4 (*JSP*, H2:17).

48. Old Testament Revision 1, 16, 19 [Moses 7:13, 18–21, 69] (Faulring et al., eds., *Joseph Smith's New Translation of the Bible*, 104–105, 110). Composed before March 7, 1831. Faulring et al., 57.

union of the two Zions above the earth. As God tells Enoch, "Then shalt thou and all thy City meet them there and we will receive them into our bosom and they shall see us and we will fall upon their necks and they shall fall upon our necks and we will kiss each other and there shall be mine abode and it shall be Zion ... and for the space of a thousand years the earth shall [res]t."[49] According to Smith, Enoch and his city will be among the heavenly hosts returning with Jesus at his Second Advent, when "the Son of man shall come in his glory, and all the holy angels with him" (Matt. 25:31).[50]

Smith and Rigdon continued to work on the Bible revision in Ohio, expanding the account of Noah to include the claim that "the Lord ordained Noah after his own order and commanded him that he should go forth and declare His Gospel unto the children of m[en] even as it was given unto Enoch."[51] After inserting several verses where Noah preaches about Jesus Christ, repentance and baptism, and warns his generation of the impending Flood, Smith even incorporated Jesus's statement in the New Testament that "in the days that were before the flood they were eating and drinking, marrying and giving in marriage, until the day that Noe entered into the ark" (Matt. 24:38; cf. Moses 8:21).

Smith also took occasion to fix a troubling passage in Genesis 6:6, which states that "it repented the LORD that he had made man on the earth, and it grieved him at his heart" (Gen. 6:6). In light of the statement in Numbers 23:19 that "God [is] not a man, that he should lie; neither the son of man, that he should repent," some of Smith's contemporaries wondered how God could repent.[52] Smith therefore corrected this to read: "It repented Noah and his heart was pained that the Lord had made man on the earth and it grieved him at his heart."[53] However clever Smith's revision, it was unneces-

---

49. Old Testament Revision 1, 19 [Moses 7:62–64] (Faulring et al., 109).

50. In the record of Joseph Smith and Sidney Rigdon's vision of three heavens, it is declared that Jesus would return "in the clouds of heaven" with "an innumerable company of Angels" that would include "the general assembly and church of Enoch and of the first born," and that those who are "gathered with the saints" will "be caught up unto the church of the first born and received into the cloud." "The Vision," Feb. 16, 1832, Revelation Book 2, 6, 9 [D&C 76:63, 67, 102] (*JSP*, D2:188–89, 191). See also Heb. 12:22–23.

51. Old Testament Revision 1, 20 [Moses 8:19] (Faulring et al., eds., *Joseph Smith's New Translation of the Bible*, 111).

52. Universalist John Murray listed several instances where the Bible says God repented (e.g., Gen. 6:6–7; Ex. 32:14; Judg. 2:18; 1 Sam. 15:35; 2 Sam. 24:16) and wondered if they were the result of mistranslation but concluded that it might be a matter "beyond my comprehension." Murray, *Letters, and Sketches of Sermons*, 3:92–94.

53. Old Testament Revision 1, 20 [Moses 8:24–25] (Faulring et al., eds., *Joseph Smith's New Translation of the Bible*, 111–12).

sary since, as Kevin Barney observed, the Hebrew verb *nicham* that the KJV translates as "repented" is better translated as "grieved," which is the reading in modern Bible translations. Clearly, as Barney states, Smith's revision merely "solves a problem created by the English translation in the KJV" and in no way can it be considered a restoration or "translation" of the original text.[54] Smith also reworded several other Bible passages that speak of God repenting with similar results (Ex. 32:12, 14; 1 Sam. 15:11; 1 Chron. 21:15; Jer. 26:19; Amos 7:3, 6).

Smith also expanded the covenant God made with Noah following the Flood, symbolized by the rainbow, to include a promise "that when men should keep all my commandments Zion should again come on the earth the City of Enock which I have caught up unto myself. … And the general assembly of the church of the first born shall come down out of heaven and possess the earth and shall have place untill the end come and this is mine everlasting covenant which I made with thy father Enock."[55]

Another expansion of Genesis involves Smith's account of Melchizedek's childhood and his being "ordained a high Priest after the order of the covenant which God made with Enock." Drawing on the insight of Alma 13, it is explained that Melchizedek had been ordained "after the order of the Son of God which order came not by man nor the will of man neither by father nor Mother neither by begining of days nor end of years of God." Smith also inserted a unique description of the powers of the high priesthood: "Every one being ordained after this order and calling should have power by faith … to put at defience the armies of nations to divide the earth to break every band to stand in the preasence of God to do all things according to his will according to his command subdue principalities and powers."[56] This description of the powers of the high priesthood inspired Smith's followers and prepared them for the great and dangerous work that lay ahead.

Smith envisioned righteous people being added to Enoch's city after it had been taken into heaven and that this ability was tied to the high priesthood—"And men having this faith coming up unto this order of God were translated and taken up into heaven. And now Melchizedeck was a Priest of this order … and his people wraught righteousness and obtained heaven and

---

54. Barney, "The Joseph Smith Translation," 144.

55. Old Testament Revision 1, 25 [I.V. Gen. 9:21, 23] (Faulring et al., eds., *Joseph Smith's New Translation of the Bible*, 117).

56. Old Testament Revision 1, 33–34 [I.V. Gen. 14:27, 28, 30–31] (Faulring et al., 127). Composed before April 5, 1831. Faulring et al., 58.

sought for the City of Enock which God had before taken seperating it from the earth having reserved it unto the latter days or the end of the world."[57]

In Alma 13 Smith took Melchizedek's title "King of Salem, *which is, King of peace*" in Hebrews 7:2 (without parallel in Genesis 14) and expanded it into a historical event, explaining that "Melchizedek was a king over the land of Salem" and that he had succeeded in calling his people to repentance insomuch that "Melchizedek did establish peace in the land in his days; therefore he was called the Prince of Peace, for he was the king of Salem."[58] This passage became the basis for Smith's 1831 revision of Genesis 14: "And now Melchizedek was a Priest of this order therefore he obtained peace in Salem and was called the prince of peace." Referring to Melchizedek as a "prince of peace" instead of the "King of peace" alludes to Isaiah 9:6, which is usually interpreted by Christians as a messianic prophecy fulfilled in Jesus. In so doing, Smith tightened the connection between Jesus and Melchizedek, a connection made only in Hebrews. Smith also expanded the account of Abraham paying tithes to Melchizedek in Genesis 14:20, adding that Melchizedek—like Bishop Edward Partridge—was "the keeper of the store house of God ... to receive tithes for the poor."[59]

When Smith came to the introduction of circumcision as a token of God's covenant with Abraham in Genesis 17, he added a passage condemning infant baptism. God tells Abraham: "My people have gone astray from my precepts ... and taken unto themselves the washing of children, ... and have not known wherein [children] are accountable before me ... And I will establish a covenant of circumcision with thee ... that thou mayest know for ever that children are not accountable before me till eight years old."[60] Previous revelations had mentioned baptizing children when they reach the age of accountability (D&C 18:42; 20:71; 29:47), but the exact age will not be given until the following November (D&C 68:25, 27). The link between infant sprinkling and circumcision is also made in the Book of Mormon (Moro. 8:1–23), which is an anachronism for the Nephites as well as Abraham. Catholics, Anglicans, and Presbyterians practiced infant baptism; Seekers, Anabaptists, Baptists, and Alexander Campbell's Reformed Baptists rejected it. Under the Puritan system, children were included in their parents' covenant and were said to have been "born in the covenant." Puritan infants were baptized, not for the remission of

---

57. Old Testament Revision 1, 34 [I.V. Gen. 14:32–34] (Faulring et al., 127–28).
58. Book of Mormon, 1830 ed., 260 [Alma 13:17–18].
59. Old Testament Revision 1, 34 [I.V. Gen. 14:33, 38–40] (Faulring et al., 127–28).
60. Old Testament Revision 1, 34 [I.V. Gen. 17:4–7, 11] (Faulring et al., 132).

sins, but as a "seal" of the covenant which they inherited from their believing parents. Nevertheless, some argued that the baptism of infants was justified on grounds that it replaced the circumcision of infants under the old law and was necessary to counter the effects of Adam's original sin.[61]

New Testament

On March 7, 1831, Smith dictated a long revelation to "the people of my Church & ye Elders" about the great and urgent work they were called to perform in preparation for the end of the world. The revelation reviewed various Bible prophecies about the end times, including Matthew 24, in which Jesus prophesied about the obliteration of Jerusalem and its temple, the scattering of the Jews, and the calamities and destruction that would precede his coming. Smith's followers were called to "be a light to the world & to be a standard for my people & for the gentiles to seek to it And to be a mesinger before my face to prepare the way before me."[62]

Matthew 24 mentions that before the end of the world the gospel would be preached to all nations and that angels would be sent out to gather the elect (Matt. 24:14, 31), but Smith added three references to the "times of the Gentiles" being fulfilled before the Second Coming, which he took from the parallel version of Jesus's sermon in Luke 21:24 (D&C 45:25, 28, 30). He also added an elliptical comment that "my Deciples shall stand in Holy places & shall not be moved" while the wicked are destroyed by an "overflowing scourge" and continual wars. These additions were meant to be restorations to Matthew as Smith's revelation concludes the section with the statement that "when I the Lord had spoken these words unto my Deciples, they were troubled."[63]

The purpose of reviewing these prophecies was to motivate Smith's followers about their mission to establish the New Jerusalem as a means of escaping the "great tribulation" of the last days—"Not many years hence ye Shall hear of wars in your own lands wherefore I the Lord have said gether ye out from the Eastern lands [and] assemble ye yourselves together."[64] The revelation began by referencing "Enoch & his Brethren who were separated from the Earth ... which was sought for by all Holy men & they found it

---

61. See, e.g., Dickinson, *Remarks*, 41, 43, 51–56; and Morgan, *The Portsmouth disputation examined*, 10, 42, 47.

62. Revelation, ca. Mar. 7, 1831, Revelation Book 1, 71 [D&C 45:6, 9] (*JSP*, D2:275–76). Compare D&C 45:16–59 with Matt. 24:1–35.

63. Revelation, 71, 73 [D&C 45:6, 9, 31, 33, 34] (*JSP*, D2:275–77).

64. Revelation, 75 [D&C 45:63–64] (*JSP*, D2:279). Cf. Matt. 24:6.

not Because of wickedness & abominations"; and near the end instructed the Saints to "gether up your riches that you may purchase an inheritance" in the soon-to-be-revealed Zion.[65]

> It shall be called the New Jerusalem a land of peace a City of refuge a place of safety for the saints of The most high God & the glory of the Lord shall be there ... [And] evry man that will not take his sword against his Neighbour must needs flee unto Zion for safety & there shall be getherd unto it out of evry Nation under Heaven & it shall be the only people that shall not be at war one with another & it shall be said among the wicked let us not go up to battle against Zion for the inhabitants of Zion are terible wherefore we cannot stand.[66]

Here Smith deepened the analogy between Enoch's Zion and the latter-day Zion. Of the former, it was said that when "their enemies came to battle against them ... and the roar of the Lions was heard out of the wilderness and all nations feared greatly."[67] Of Melchizedek, it was said that his priesthood gave him "power by faith ... to put at defience the armies of nations to divide the earth to break every band to stand in the preasence of God to do all things according to his will according to his command subdue principalities and powers."[68]

Finally, the revelation commanded Smith to discontinue revising the Old Testament and to begin translating the New (D&C 45:6, 60–62). At the top of the first page of the New Testament manuscript, Rigdon wrote: "A Translation of the New Testament translated by the power of God."[69] Later, John Whitmer added: "March 8th 1831." Over the next month, Smith revised Matthew up to at least chapter 9.[70]

For those who wondered how an incarnated God would behave as a child, Smith added three verses explaining that "Jesus ... served under his father, and he spake not as other men, neither could he be taught; for he needed not that any man should teach him."[71]

---

65. Revelation, 72, 75–76 [D&C 45:11–12, 65] (*JSP*, D1:276, 280).

66. Revelation, 75–76 [D&C 45:66–70] (*JSP*, D1:280).

67. Old Testament Revision 1, 16 [Moses 7:13] (Faulring et al., eds., *Joseph Smith's New Translation of the Bible*, 104).

68. Old Testament Revision 1, 34 [I.V. Gen. 14:30–31] (Faulring et al., 127). Composed before April 5, 1831. Faulring et al., 58.

69. New Testament Revision 1, 1 (Faulring et al., 159).

70. John Whitmer copied New Testament Revision 1 into New Testament Revision 2 up to Matthew 9:1 and then wrote on New Testament Revision 1, page 21, line 2: "Thus far Transscribed April 7th 1831." Faulring et al., 178.

71. New Testament Revision 1, 4 [I.V. Matt. 3:24–25] (Faulring et al., eds., 162–63). Composed between Mar. 8–Apr. 7, 1831. Faulring et al., 58.

To the Beatitudes in the Sermon on the Mount, Smith added two verses from the parallel passage in 3 Nephi 12:1–2, where Jesus tells his disciples: "Blessed are they who shall believe on me, and again more blessed are they who shall believe on your words when ye shall testify that ye have seen me and that I am."[72] In making this addition in 3 Nephi and Matthew 5, Smith may have been inspired by the story of Thomas, who after doubting the word of the other apostles was permitted to see the risen Jesus, who declared: "Because thou hast seen me, thou hast believed: blessed are they that have not seen, and yet have believed" (John 20:29). As noted, Smith made changes in the Sermon on the Mount in 3 Nephi which were carried over into his Bible revision and which were responses to the English of the KJV.[73]

Discerning Spirits

On March 8, 1831, Smith dictated a revelation about the manner of holding public meetings and regulating the gifts of the spirit.[74] His followers in Ohio had previous to this revelation excluded non-members from their sacrament meetings. Jesse J. Moss, a Campbellite who taught school in Kirtland, described the early Mormon practice of closed communion: "They partook of the Lords supper at night with darkened windows & excluded from the room all but their own till they got through & then they opened the doors & called [in] the outsiders."[75]

When John Whitmer introduced this revelation in his history he explained: "In the beginning of the church, while yet in her infancy, the disciples used to exclude unbelievers, which caused some to marvel, and converse about this matter because of the things that were written in the Book of Mormon."[76] Indeed, the Book of Mormon had declared: "And behold, ye shall meet together oft, and ye shall not forbid any man from coming unto you when ye shall meet together, but suffer them that they may come unto you, and forbid them not."[77] Thus the revelation Smith dictated on this occasion states: "Ye are commanded never to cast any one out from your publick meetings which are held before the world."[78]

The revelation also addressed the issue of spiritual gifts, listing those that have a biblical basis—speaking in tongues, healing, prophecy, discernment,

---

72. New Testament Revision 1, 8 [I.V. Matt. 5:3] (Faulring et al., 166).
73. Larson, "The Historicity of the Matthean Sermon on the Mount in 3 Nephi," 132.
74. Revelation, ca. Mar. 8, 1831-A, Revelation Book 1, 76–78 [D&C 46] (*JSP*, D1:280–83).
75. J. J. Moss, Letter to J. T. Cobb, Dec. 17, 1878.
76. Whitmer, History, 23 (*JSP*, H2:34).
77. Book of Mormon, 1830 ed., 492 [3 Ne. 18:22].
78. Revelation, ca. Mar. 8, 1831-A, Revelation Book 1, 76–77 [D&C 46:3] (*JSP*, D1:282).

etc.—in language borrowed from Paul's words on the "diversities of gifts" in 1 Corinthians 12:8–11 and its parallel in Moroni 10:8–18.[79] Not wishing to stifle spiritual gifts, the revelation nevertheless warned Smith's followers to be circumspect and prayerful, "that ye may not be seduced by evil spirits or doctrines of Devils or the commandments of men for some are of men & others of Devils Wherefore beware lest ye are deceived & that ye may not be deceived seek ye earnestly the best gifts."[80] The Morley farm had been the scene of much of the wild religious excitement involving bodily agitations thought to be spiritual manifestations.

Not long after Oliver Cowdery, Parley Pratt, Ziba Peterson, and Peter Whitmer Jr. left Kirtland to continue their journey to Missouri in mid-November 1830 the area was set ablaze by an uncontrollable fire of religious enthusiasm. "Many improprieties and visionary notions crept into the church, which tried the feelings of the more sound minded," John Corrill recalled. As one of the more sober onlookers, Corrill reported:

> Many young persons became very visionary, and had divers operations of the spirit, as they supposed. They saw wonderful lights in the air and on the ground, and would relate many great and marvellous things which they saw in their visions. They conducted themselves in a strange manner, sometimes imitating Indians in their manoeuvres, sometimes running out into the fields, getting on stumps of trees and there preaching as though surrounded by a congregation,—all the while so completely absorbed in visions as to be apparently insensible to all that was passing around them. I would here remark, however, that it was but a very few of the Church who were exercised in that way, The more substantial minded looked upon it with astonishment, and were suspicious that it was from an evil source.[81]

Early Mormon historian John Whitmer, who had arrived at Kirtland sometime during the week following January 9, 1831, from New York,[82] described how easily this group of about 300 followers of charismatic authority could be led astray. Satan, according to Whitmer, "took a notion to blind the minds of some of the weaker ones, and made them think that an angel of the Lord appeared to them and showed them writings on the outside cover of the Bible, and on parchment, which flew through the air, and on the

---

79. Revelation, 77–78 [D&C 46:8–30] (*JSP*, D1:282–83).

80. Revelation, 77 [D&C 46:7–8] (*JSP*, D1:282).

81. Corrill, *Brief History*, 16–17 (*JSP*, H2:143).

82. On January 18, 1831, the *Painesville Telegraph* reported that John Whitmer arrived the previous week (Jan. 9–15, 1831).

back of their hands, and many such foolish and vain things—others lost their strength, and some slid on the floor, and such like maneuvers, which proved greatly to the injury of the cause."[83] Newspaperman Eber D. Howe scoffed when he reported these events: "A scene of the wildest enthusiasm was exhibited ... They would fall, as without strength, roll upon the floor, ... [and] exhibited all the apish actions imaginable, making grimaces both horrid and ridiculous. ... At other times they are taken with a fit of jabbering which they neither understand themselves nor any body else, and this they call speaking foreign languages by divine inspiration."[84]

Levi Hancock, who participated in the religious excitement but later regretted it, recalled: "Those elders ran into all manner of doings Receiving Revelations seeing Angels falling down frothing at the mouth."[85] Former Methodist preacher Ezra Booth wrote in 1831 that such charismatic manifestations stood "as the principal foundation of the faith of several hundred of the members of their church." He reported that commissions to preach had been received from heaven, written on the palms of hands and the lids of Bibles. "These commissions, when transcribed upon a piece of paper, were read to the church, and the persons who had received them, were ordained to the Elder's office, and sent out into the world to preach."[86]

In 1842 Smith explained that the true gifts of the spirit were somewhere between two common extremes. "Some people have been in the habit of calling every supernatural manifestation, the effects of the spirit of God, whilst there are others that think their [sic] is no manifestation connected with it at all," he said. The Latter-day Saints believe in the gifts of the Holy Ghost but believe in them "rationally, reasonably, consistently, and scripturally, and not according to the wild vagaries, foolish, notions and traditions of men."[87] This meant that they believed in such scriptural gifts of the spirit as tongues, interpretation of tongues, discernment, prophesy, and healing but rejected such excesses as "jerking" and "barking."

This position was not unlike that of moderate revivalists such as Jonathan

---

83. Whitmer, History, 10 (*JSP*, H2:22).

84. *Painesville Telegraph*, Nov. 1, 1831, [3].

85. Hancock, Autobiography, 77.

86. Howe, *Mormonism Unvailed*, 183, 185. See also Whitmer, History, 10 (*JSP*, H2:22). Thomas Campbell, father of Alexander, spent the winter of 1830–31 in Mentor, Ohio, and on February 4 wrote a letter to Sidney Rigdon, complaining that Mormon claims to authority based on charismatic displays of spiritual revival were "in no wise superior to the pretentions of the first quakers, of the French Prophets, of the Shakers, of Jemima Wilkinson, &c." Howe, *Mormonism Unvailed*, 121–22.

87. Joseph Smith, "Gift of the Holy Ghost," *Times and Seasons*, June 15, 1842, 823.

Edwards who advised that "gifts [of the spirit] were to be exercised with prudence, because God was not the author of confusion but of peace."[88] The wild scenes of religious enthusiasm experienced by early Mormon converts in Ohio were not unlike what was experienced at the revivals during the eighteenth and early nineteenth centuries, both in America and England. In May 1741, Edwards attended a meeting where "the whole room was full of nothing but outcries, faintings, and such like." The phenomena soon attracted others to the meeting who, as Edwards recorded, "were overpowered in like manner: and it continued thus for some hours." Edwards later reflected on the scene: "It was a very frequent thing to see an house full of outcries, faintings, convulsions and such like, both with distress, and also with admiration and joy. ... There were some that were so affected, and their bodies so overcome, that they could not go home, but were obliged to stay all night at the house where they were."[89] While many revivalists viewed the physical phenomena as an outward manifestation of the inward working of the Spirit, others disagreed. John Williamson Nevin, a German Reformed professor of theology at Mercersburg Seminary, wrote a 150-page attack on revivalism in 1843 entitled *The Anxious Bench*. Nevin charged that revivalistic phenomena were the result of "wild fanatical influences" and did not "proceed from the Holy Ghost."[90]

One aspect of the Ohio manifestations that Smith found most threatening was likely those that were accompanied by competing revelations. The previous month Smith dictated a revelation that dealt specifically with the revelations produced by a woman named Hubble.[91] The religious excesses produced other revelators such as Heman Basset, whom Levi Hancock recalled received a revelation from an angel.[92] A former slave named "Black Pete," according to George A. Smith, claimed to receive heavenly messages written on objects floating across the sky and fell down an embankment on the Morley farm trying to capture one of them. Smith also named Wycom Clark, who founded the "Pure Church of Christ" with five others, after he "got a revelation that he was to be the prophet."[93]

---

88. Jonathan Edwards, *The Great Awakening*, in John E. Smith, ed., *The Works of Jonathan Edwards*, 4:108.

89. Edwards, in Smith, 546, 547.

90. Nevin, *The Anxious Bench*, 4, 7.

91. Revelation, Feb. 1831-A [D&C 43:3–7], Revelation Book 1, 67–68 (*JSP*, D1:258).

92. Hancock, Autobiography, 77.

93. George A. Smith, "Historical Discourse," Nov. 15, 1864, *Journal of Discourses*, 11:3–4; also Joseph Smith, "Try the Spirits," *Times and Seasons*, Apr. 1, 1842, 747 (*JSP*, D9:335–36).

Smith worried that uncontrolled charisma was incompatible with the institution he was attempting to organize, which eventually would include the founding of a New Jerusalem theocracy. "By its very nature," German sociologist Max Weber noted, "the existence of charismatic authority is specifically unstable."[94] In his study of early Mormon charisma, Catholic sociologist Thomas O'Dea observed:

> Since the new church had been founded upon the claims of contemporary revelation, such revelation remained the basis of all its ecclesiastical authority. This meant that there were two possible paths of development open for the church. It could permit unrestrained prophecy and thereby splinter into smaller and smaller groups, finally breaking up into a Babel of private revelation. On the other hand, it could restrain prophetic gifts, restricting revelation and prophecy to one man, and develop a centrally directed organization about that one leader. Compromises between the two positions were, of course, possible but were likely to be unstable, at least until original enthusiasm had dissipated itself. If more than one strong prophetic figure claimed revelation, it is hard to see how schism could have been avoided.[95]

Weber observed that charismatic-based authority must evolve and become more stable if it is to survive. If such groups are to "take on the character of a permanent relationship forming a stable community of disciples or a band of followers or party organization or any sort of political or hierocratic organization, it is necessary for the character of charismatic authority to become radically changed." In time, states Weber, charisma must be "routinized" or institutionalized; that is, less reliant on the personality of the leader, who must constantly prove he possesses such authority, and more dependent on the authority derived from legal ordination and office within an institution that increasingly defines authority in legal-rational terms.[96] The goal is not to destroy charisma, but to harness its creative energy within the institution.

By the time of this revelation, Smith had already accomplished much by way of bringing order to the church. As he told Hyrum in his March 4 letter, "I hav[e] been ingageed in regulating the Churches here as ... the devil had made many attempts to over throw them it has been a Serious job but the Lord is with us and we have overcome and have all things regular."[97] Yet he felt a revelation was needed. In dealing with charismatic challengers

---

94. Eisenstadt, ed., *Max Weber on Charisma*, 22.

95. O'Dea, *The Mormons*, 156.

96. Eisenstadt, ed., *Max Weber on Charisma*, 54.

97. Joseph Smith, Letter to Hyrum Smith, Mar. 3–4, 1831, JS Collection (*JSP*, D1:273).

like Cowdery, Page, and Hubble, he drew on his charisma either to declare the supremacy of his revelations or to denounce their revelations as Satan-inspired. In this instance, because the threats were ongoing, he relegated church discipline to other officers. Thus the revelation stated: "Unto the Bishop of the Church & unto such as God shall appoint & ordain to watch over the Church & to be the Elders unto the Church are to have it given unto [them] to decern all those gifts lest there shall be any among you prophecying & yet not be of God."[98]

Record Keeping

On the same day, Smith dictated another revelation calling John Whitmer as Church Historian and Recorder.[99] Whitmer had served as scribe for Smith's Bible revision, but when Smith told him "you must also keep the Church history," he demurred: "I would rather not do it but observed that the will of the Lord be done, and if he desires it, I desire that he would manifest it through Joseph the Seer."[100] The revelation commanded: "Behold it is expedient that my servant John should write & keep a regular [regular] history & assist my servant Joseph in Transcribing all things which shall be given him." Then, addressing Whitmer directly, the Lord explained: "I say unto you that it shall be appointed unto you to Keep the Church Record & History continually for Oliver [Cowdery] I have appointed to an other office."[101]

Cowdery had served as scribe and church recorder in New York before leaving on his mission to Missouri in mid-late October 1830. While Cowdery had not begun to write a history, Whitmer apparently assumed he did and wrote as if he were continuing Cowdery's work, which he began writing on June 12, 1831, commencing with Cowdery's departure from New York with Parley P. Pratt, Ziba Peterson, and Peter Whitmer Jr.[102] On April 9, 1831, John Whitmer acted as a clerk at "a special meeting of the Elders of the Church of Christ," which was probably attended by Joseph Smith. No details are given except that "agreeable to a commandment received March 8, 1831, John Whitmer was appointed to keep the Church record & History by the voice of ten Elders."[103] Yet Whitmer delayed beginning his history for another three months.

---

98. Revelation, ca. Mar. 8, 1831-A, Revelation Book 1, 78 [D&C 46:27] (*JSP*, D1:283).
99. Revelation, Mar. 8, 1831-B, Revelation Book 1, 79–80 [D&C 47] (*JSP*, D1:284–86).
100. Whitmer, History, 24 (*JSP*, H2:36).
101. Revelation, Mar. 8, 1831-B, Revelation Book 1, 79–80 [D&C 47:1, 3] (*JSP*, D1:286).
102. Whitmer, History, 1, 25 (*JSP*, H2:12, 36); see also Historical Introduction in *JSP*, H2:8.
103. Minutes, Apr. 9, 1831, Minute Book 2, 3 (Cannon and Cook, *Far West Record*, 5).

About the same time, Whitmer began transcribing Smith's revelations into a bound volume entitled "A Book of Commandments and Revelations of the Lord Given to Joseph the Seer and Others by the Inspiration of God and Gift and Power of the Holy Ghost Which Beareth Re[c]ord of the Father and Son and Holy Ghost Which Is One God Infinite and Eternal World without End Amen."[104] In November 1831, Whitmer and Oliver Cowdery would carry the partly filled volume to Independence, Missouri, where it would serve as the main text for typesetting and publishing Smith's revelations in the Mormon periodical *The Evening and Morning Star* and the 1833 Book of Commandments.

---

104. See *JSP*, MRB, 9.

3

Gathering in Ohio

MARCH–MAY 1831

A commandment I give unto the Church that it is expedient in me that they should assemble together at the Ohio.
—*Revelation, Dec. 30, 1830, Revelation Book 1, 49 [D&C 37:3]*

As spring 1831 approached, Joseph Smith and his followers in Ohio began to think about the arrival of more than a hundred believers from New York. There were many practical considerations to prepare for such an event, but the most crucial was where to have them settle.

The question of the settlement of the Mormon migrants was raised within days of Smith's arrival in Kirtland, and on February 9, 1831, he dictated a revelation stating that individuals should be appointed to assist Bishop Partridge in "obtaining places" for the New York believers and advised that members cluster together, with "every Church … organized in as close bodies as they can be in consequence of the enemy."[1] In a February 22 letter, Smith had requested Martin Harris to come to Kirtland "as soon as you can in order to choose a place which may be best adapted to the circumstances of yourself and breatheren in the east to settle on" and to settle "as compact as possable."[2] By March 10, Harris had not yet arrived, and, as John Whitmer recorded, "no preparation [had been] made for the reception of the Saints," which made Partridge "anxious to know something concerning the matter" of settling the caravan of migrants.[3] Naturally, he looked to Smith for guidance.

In his introduction to the revelation, Whitmer mentioned that some believers in Ohio had supposed that the New York Saints were coming to settle

---

1. Revelation, Feb. 9, 1831, [6], Revelations Collection [BC XLIV:57] (*JSP*, D1:255–56). Deleted in D&C, 1835 ed.
2. Joseph Smith, Letter to Martin Harris, Feb. 22, 1831, JS Collection (*JSP*, D1:262–63).
3. Whitmer, History, 23 (*JSP*, H2:35).

in the Kirtland area because "it was the place of gathering even the place of the New Jerusalam spoken of in the Book of Mormon."[4] Even though Smith's revelations had located the New Jerusalem in or near Missouri,[5] Sidney Rigdon saw the "land of promise" as encompassing the entire vast territory west of New York. While preaching in the Waterloo courthouse prior to leaving New York in late January, Rigdon declared that Kirtland was situated "just within the east bounds of this new land of promise, which extends from thence to the Pacific Ocean, embracing a territory of 1500 miles in extent, from north to south."[6] Ohio convert Ezra Booth wrote in December 1831 that while in New York, Rigdon had received visions of "Kirtland with the surrounding country, consecrated as the promised land, and the churches in the state of N.Y. expected to receive their everlasting inheritance in the state of Ohio."[7] Confirming Booth's account is a letter Rigdon wrote on January 4, 1831, from New York to the believers in Ohio: "You are living on the land of promise, and that there is the place of gathering, and from that place to the Pacific Ocean, God has dedicated to himself, not only in time, but through eternity, and he has given it to us and our children. ... Therefore, be it known to you, brethren, that you are dwelling on your eternal inheritance ... for our God hath in visions shown it unto me."[8] Rigdon's pronouncements may have contributed to the confusion about the location of the New Jerusalem, but by the time Booth wrote in December of that year, Rigdon's New York visions were "considered by the church as entitled to no credit, and laid aside as mere rubbish."[9]

The revelation Smith dictated instructed Partridge and the church to "save all the money that ye can (& that ye obtain all that ye can) that in time ye may be enabled to purchase lands for an inheritance (even the City) the place is not yet to be revealed but after your Brethren come from the East there are to be certain men to be appointed & to them it shall be given to

---

4. Whitmer, 23.

5. As early as the fall of 1830, it was known that Zion was to be built somewhere near Missouri's western border. Revelation, Sep. 1830-B, Revelation Book 1, 41 [D&C 28:9] (*JSP*, D1:185–86).

6. *Palmyra (NY) Reflector,* Feb. 1, 1831, 95 (*EMD*, 2:244).

7. Ezra Booth, Letter to Ira Eddy, Dec. 6, 1831, "Mormonism—Nos. VIII—IX," *Ohio Star* (Ravenna, OH), Dec. 8, 1831, [1] (*EMD*, 5:310).

8. Sidney Rigdon, Letter to the Ohio Saints, Jan. 4, 1831, in Howe, *Mormonism Unvailed,* 111 (*EMD*, 5:306). The date of Rigdon's letter is surmised from his reference to the January 2, 1831, revelation (D&C 38) as "one of the commandments, received day before yesterday."

9. Booth, Letter to Ira Eddy, Dec. 6, 1831, "Mormonism—Nos. VIII—IX," *Ohio Star*, Dec. 8, 1831, [1] (*EMD*, 5:310).

know the place as to them it shall be revealed."[10] In other words, the location of the New Jerusalem will be revealed after the New York converts settle in Ohio, but Smith was unable to name a location until he and other men could personally inspect the region near Missouri's western border.

In time, according to the revelation, Partridge and other elders "shall be appointed to purchase the lands & to make a commencement to lay the foundation of the City & then ye shall begin to be gethered with your families evry man according to his family according to his circumstances & as is appointed to them by the Bishop & Elders of the Church according to the laws & commandments which ye have received & which ye shall hereafter receive."[11] This refers to appointing inheritances according to the law of consecration, as explained in the February 9 revelation.[12]

Meanwhile, the revelation directed the Ohio Mormons: "Inasmuch as ye [have] lands ye shall impart to the Eastern Brethren & in as much as ye have not lands let them buy for the present time in those regions round about as seemeth them good for it must needs be nessessary that they have places to live for the present time."[13] Until the New Jerusalem can be located the New York Saints will settle in Ohio for an unknown length of time.

Harris finally arrived in Kirtland on March 12, 1831, presumably delivering the Books of Mormon Smith requested.[14] Little is known about Harris's activities during his brief stay, but he may have discussed the issue of settlement with Leman Copley, on whose land in Thompson Township the Colesville church would eventually settle. Harris soon returned to Palmyra to prepare for the move.

Faith Healing

On the evening of March 29 twenty-nine-year-old Warner Doty, a zealous Mormon missionary, died after being blessed by Joseph Smith. According to the *Painesville Telegraph*, "So fully did he believe in the divinity of Smith, that he had been made to have full faith that he should live a thousand years—this he confessed to a near relative some four weeks before his decease." When he was suddenly attacked with a typhoid-like illness, "no

---

10. Revelation, Mar. 10, 1831, Revelation Book 1, 79 [D&C 48:4–5] (*JSP*, D1:287–88).

11. Revelation, 79 [D&C 48:6] (*JSP*, D1:288).

12. Revelation, Feb. 9, 1831, "The Laws of the Church of Christ," Revelations Collection [D&C 42:1–72]; see also Revelation Book 1, 62–67 (*JSP*, D1: 245–56).

13. Revelation, Mar. 10, 1831, Revelation Book 1, 79 [D&C 48:2–3] (*JSP*, D1:287).

14. According to the *Painesville Telegraph*, Harris arrived in Ohio "last Saturday from the bible *quarry* in New-York." *Painesville [OH] Telegraph*, Mar. 15, 1831, [3]; italics in original; and Smith, Letter to Martin Harris, Feb. 22, 1831 (*JSP*, D1:263).

persuasion could induce the young man to have a physician called, so strong was he impressed with the supernatural powers of Smith." Smith at first refused to give him a blessing, saying on the way to Doty's house that "he received a command not to go to Doty's and 'cast his pearl before swine.'" However, two days later Smith blessed Doty, promised he would get well, and advised against calling a physician. When Doty's condition worsened and death appeared imminent, Doty's relatives sent for a Dr. Brainard, who "pronounced his disease past remedy, and told the mormon doctors that their superstitions had probably been the means of the young man's death." According to report, Doty said to an old Mormon, "You are a friend to every body—I must shake hands with you—this is a lesson that I have learnt by actual experience, by which you ought to profit, but with me it is too late."[15]

According to Samuel F. Whitney, the non-believing brother of Newel K. Whitney, the Reverend Elijah Ward preached Doty's funeral sermon from Job 36:18: "Because there is wrath, beware lest he take thee away with his stroke; then a great ransom cannot deliver thee." The text was meant to indict Smith and Rigdon, who were present. Whitney claimed that the two Mormon leaders "writhed under the sermon." Whitney also reported: "I heard Oliver Cowdery say the saints would live one thousand years. They all claimed it. Jo and Rigdon claimed they could heal all diseases and perform miracles, cast out devils and raise the dead."[16] Whitmer probably alluded to Doty's death when he mentioned in his history that there was "a tradition among some of the disciples, that those who obeyed the covenant in the last days, would never die: but by experience they have learned to the contrary."[17]

When Cowdery and the other missionaries arrived in the Kirtland area in November 1830, they claimed the restoration of spiritual gifts. The Book of Mormon concluded with an exhortation to its readers to "deny not the gifts of God," including tongues, prophecy, and healing.[18] A July 1830 revelation instructed Cowdery to "require not Miracles except I shall command you except casting [out] Devils healing the sick … & these things ye shall not do except it be required of you by them who desire it."[19] In a December

---

15. "Fanaticism," *Painesville Telegraph*, Apr. 5, 1831, [3]. The *Telegraph* reports, "We have our information from a relative of the disceased, who was present during the last 18 hours of his life."

16. Samuel F. Whitney, "Statement of Rev. S. F. Whitney on Mormonism," *Naked Truths about Mormonism* (Oakland, CA), Jan. 1888, 3.

17. Whitmer, History, 22 (*JSP*, H2:33).

18. Book of Mormon, 1830 ed., 586 [Moro. 10:8–18].

19. Revelation, July 1830-A, Revelation Book 1, 33 [D&C 24:13] (*JSP*, D1:159).

1830 revelation, Rigdon was told: "I am God … I will shew miricles, signs & wonders unto all those who believe on my name."[20]

Concerning the preaching of Cowdery and the other missionaries in the Kirtland area, the *Painesville Telegraph* reported in December 1830 that "these newly commissioned disciples have totally failed thus far in their attempts to heal."[21] Two months later the *Palmyra Reflector* summarized information obtained from a Painesville correspondent, stating that "they pretend to heal the sick and work miracles, and had made a number of unsuccessful attempts to do so."[22] According to the *Telegraph*, "Mr. R[igdon]. now blames Cowdery for *attempting* to work miracles, and says it was not intended to be confirmed in that way."[23] As Smith's March 8, 1831, revelation declared: "To some it is given to have faith to be healed & to others it is given to have faith to heal" and that such gifts were to benefit the faithful "& not for a sign that he may consume it upon his lusts."[24]

In time, Mormon faith healers will move past their initial failure and begin to collect faith-promoting accounts of miraculous healing. Like any faith healer who claims to heal the sick or the dying, early Mormons explained away the failures as a lack of faith and announced the few successes from the housetops. Notably, there are no Mormon sources for the Doty debacle.

Much has been learned about the variableness of illness and the placebo effect since Smith's day. Yet belief in the efficacy of prayer, faith healing, and faith healers persists to the present aided by wishful thinking, selective validation, and anecdotal evidence.[25] Statistically, people recover or die at the same rate with or without attempted faith healing.[26] In many cases, the sick are not terminal or are misdiagnosed as terminal and would have eventually recovered without a faith healing. Some serious illnesses like cancer, rheumatoid arthritis, and multiple sclerosis can have spontaneous remissions or take years to subside, making it difficult to determine even the efficacy of a specific medical treatment.[27]

---

20. Revelation, Dec. 7, 1830, Revelation Book 1, 46–47 [D&C 35:8] (*JSP*, D1:221).

21. "The Book of Mormon," *Painesville Telegraph*, Dec. 7, 1830, [3].

22. *Palmyra Reflector*, Feb. 14, 1831.

23. "Mormonism," *Painesville Telegraph*, Feb. 15, 1831, [1]; emphasis in original.

24. Revelation, Mar. 8, 1831-B, Revelation Book 1, 77, 78 [D&C 47:9, 19–20] (*JSP*, D1:282, 283). Cf. James 4:1.

25. See discussion in Schick and Vaughn, *How to Think about Weird Things*, 198–211.

26. J. Witmer and M. Zimmerman, "Intercessory Prayer as Medical Treatment? An Inquiry," *Skeptical Inquirer*, Winter 1991, 177–80; Gary Posner, "God in the CCU? A Critique of the San Francisco Hospital Study on Intercessory Prayer and Healing," *Free Inquiry*, Spring 1990, 44–45; Courcey, "Medical Claims for Intercessory Prayer Remain Elusive."

27. Nickell, *Looking For a Miracle*, 134.

About one-third of patients respond to placebos or fake treatments, although the symptoms in many cases eventually return.[28] The placebo effect can be facilitated by the patient's belief in an authority figure such as a physician, hypnotist, or faith healer.[29] New medications are routinely tested against a control group using placebos, and if there are no significant differences, new medications are rejected—but the placebo does appear to work in some cases.

We know that some ailments are psychogenic or psychosomatic and manifest symptoms of illness without an underlying physical cause. Two psychological disorders—Somatization Disorder (or Somatic Symptom Disorder) and Conversion Disorder (or Functional Neurological Symptom Disorder)—can manifest as physical ailments, including paralysis or localized weakness, inability to speak, blindness, deafness, seizures or convulsions, numbness, tremors, difficulty walking, even hallucinations, and are difficult to distinguish from real physiological ailments.[30] To help matters, one study has demonstrated that "conversion patients were significantly more responsive to hypnotic suggestions than control patients."[31] This makes them susceptible to suggestion.

In late March 1831,[32] Smith performed a dramatic faith healing that helped to increase his charisma among followers. Fifty-three-year-old John Johnson and his wife, Elsa, a well-to-do couple from Hiram, a town located about twenty-five miles south of Kirtland, visited Smith. They were joined by their minister Ezra Booth and his wife, Dorcas, neighbors Symonds and Mehitable Ryder, and a Dr. Right of Windham. During this visit, Smith appeared to heal Elsa's rheumatic arm. From reading the Book of Mormon, Elsa

---

28. Brody, *Placebos and the Philosophy of Medicine*, 8–24; J. E. Dodes, "The Mysterious Placebo," *Skeptical Inquirer*, Jan./Feb. 1997, 44–45.

29. Nickell, *Looking For a Miracle*, 134.

30. *Diagnostic and Statistical Manual of Mental Disorders-IV-TR* (Washington, DC: American Psychiatric Ass., 2000), see under 300.81 for Somatization Disorder and 300.11 for Conversion Disorder (486–97). The DSM-V removes the requirement for a psychological trigger or stressor to be present. Somatization Disorder has been reported in 0.2 to 2 percent of women and less than 0.2 percent of men. For Conversion Disorder, the rate varies between 11 and 500 in 100,000 in the general population, but between 1 percent and 14 percent among general and surgical inpatients (487, 496).

31. Karin Roelofs et al., "Hypnotic Susceptibility in Patients with Conversion Disorder."

32. Mark Staker dates Elsa Johnson's healing to "late March." *Hearken, O Ye People*, 284. He cites the statement of her daughter Marinda Nancy that her parents went to Kirtland to visit Joseph Smith and were baptized while there and that she was baptized "in April following." Marinda Nancy Johnson Hyde, Autobiography, in Tullidge, *The Women of Mormondom*, 404; Staker, *Hearken, O Ye People*, 291n53.

became convinced that Smith could heal her.[33] Philo Dibble, who talked with Right and members of the Johnson family soon afterward, wrote in 1882:

> [Elsa] persuaded her husband … to take her to Kirtland to get her arm healed. … She went to Joseph and requested him to heal her. Joseph asked her if she believed the Lord was able to make him an instrument in healing her arm. She said she believed the Lord was able to heal her arm. Joseph put her off till the next morning, when he met her at Brother Whitney's house. There were eight persons present, one a Methodist preacher, and one doctor. Joseph took her by the hand, prayed in silence a moment, pronounced her arm whole, in the name of Jesus Christ, and turned and left the room. The preacher asked her if her arm was whole, and she straightened it out and replied: "It is as good as the other." The question was then asked if it would remain whole. Joseph hearing this, answered and said: "It is as good as the other, and as liable to accident as the other."[34]

While in his 1882 account Dibble said the arm was "crocked," he told Oliver B. Huntington in 1891 that it had been merely "stiff a long time" and afterward that she "immediately stretched out her arm straight."[35] According to their son Luke, Elsa had been suffering "under an attack of chronic rheumatism in the shoulder, so that she could not raise her hand to her head for about two years."[36] In another account, Huntington reported that Elsa "had a stiff arm and had not combed her hair nor put food to her mouth with it for a very long time. Everybody that knew her, knew that she was a cripple."[37] Dibble also told Huntingdon that Right came to his house the next day and tried to explain away the miracle—"When Joseph pronounced the arm whole in the name of Jesus Christ it scared her so bad that it threw her in a heavy perspiration and relaxed the cords, and the result was that she could straighten her arm."[38] The fact that this physician could offer a naturalistic explanation means that the arm was otherwise normal and therefore highly probable that Elsa suffered from something like rheumatism, tendinitis, or even a psychosomatic illness. A photograph of Elsa shows her apparently "holding her right arm in position," prompting historian Mark Staker to

---

33. Luke Johnson, "The History of Luke Johnson," *LDS Millennial Star* (Liverpool, Eng.), Dec. 31, 1864, 834–36.

34. Dibble, "Philo Dibble's Narrative," 79–80.

35. Oliver B. Huntington, "To the Editor," *Young Woman's Journal* (Salt Lake City), Feb. 1891, 225–26.

36. Luke Johnson, "The History of Luke Johnson," *LDS Millennial Star*, Dec. 31, 1864, 834.

37. Oliver B. Huntington, "Early Miracles," *Young Woman's Journal*, June 1891, 411–12.

38. Oliver B. Huntington, "To the Editor," *Young Woman's Journal*, Feb. 1891, 226.

suggest that "her ailment may have returned in later years."[39] While Elsa's husband and some of her children later left Smith's church following the failure of Kirtland Bank in 1837, it is unknown if her feelings about Smith and the church had likewise changed.

Before they returned to Hiram, John and Elsa were baptized.[40] Ezra and Dorcas Booth were also converted by the exhibition of Smith's apparent healing power. Reflecting on his conversion to Mormonism, Booth did not mention Elsa's healing but described his emotions: "When I embraced Mormonism, I conscientiously believed it to be of God. The impressions of my mind were deep and powerful, and my feelings were excited to a degree to which I had been a stranger. Like a ghost, it haunted me by night and by day, until I was mysteriously hurried, as it were, by a kind of necessity, into the vortex of delusion."[41]

The Johnsons were naturally excited to share their newfound faith with neighbors and friends in Portage County and invited Smith and Rigdon to their home in Hiram, which the Mormon leaders accepted. Smith's official history is silent about Elsa's healing as well as what transpired during his stay in Portage County, but other sources document Smith and Rigdon preaching several times at a schoolhouse located about a mile east of the Johnsons' home.[42] With the help of Booth, formerly a Methodist minister in the area, and eyewitness accounts of Elsa's healing, many baptisms followed, and in a few months a sizable branch was established in Hiram. Campbellite historian Amos Sutton Hayden remarked: "Perhaps in no place, except Kirtland, did the doctrine of the 'Latter Day Saints' gain a more permanent footing than in Hiram. It entrenched itself there so strongly that its leaders felt assured of the capture of the town. Rigdon's former popularity in that region gave wings to their appeal, and many people, not avowed converts, were under a spell of wonder at the strange things sounded in their ears."[43]

Report from Missouri

In late April 1831, Smith and the Ohio Mormons received a letter from Cowdery in Jackson County, Missouri, reporting on the progress of the

---

39. Staker, *Hearken, O Ye People*, 271.

40. Marinda Nancy Johnson Hyde said her parents "were convinced and baptized before they returned." Tullidge, *The Women of Mormondom*, 404.

41. Booth, Letter to Ira Eddy, Sep. 12, 1831, *Ohio Star*, Oct. 13, 1831, [3].

42. Symonds Ryder to Amos Sutton Hayden, Feb. 1, 1868, in Hayden, *Early History of the Disciples in the Western Reserve*, 220.

43. Ryder, Letter to Hayden.

four missionaries in the area. Cowdery had been called to preach the gospel to the Lamanites and "rear up a pillar as a witness where the Temple of God shall be built, in the glorious New-Jerusalem."[44] He had left New York on foot the previous October with Parley Pratt, Ziba Peterson, and Peter Whitmer Jr. Along the way, they made a fateful stopover in the Kirtland-Mentor area of northern Ohio, where they converted Sidney Rigdon, the majority of his congregation, and many others over the next three weeks. The missionaries left Kirtland about mid-November, accompanied by new convert Frederick G. Williams, and after walking more than 800 miles through snow and ice arrived in Independence, Missouri, in mid-January.[45] Whitmer began working as a tailor and Peterson as a teacher to support the mission, while Cowdery, Pratt, and Williams crossed into Indian Territory and attempted to fulfill Book of Mormon prophecy about the conversion of the Lamanites in the last days prior to their participation in building the New Jerusalem.[46]

Concerning the object of their mission of converting the Indians, Cowdery disclosed that federal Indian agent Richard W. Cummins was "very strict with us and we think some what strenuous respecting our having liberty to visit our brethren the Lamanites," and that Cummins says that he "must have a recommend or security before he can give a permit for any stranger or foreigner to go among them to teach or preach."[47] Cowdery said that they were awaiting the return of Parley P. Pratt, who had left Missouri on February 14 to consult with church leaders in Ohio with a stopover in St. Louis to obtain a permit to preach to the Indians from William Clark, superintendent of Indian affairs. Cowdery was unaware that Pratt had been delayed by illness and had not yet reached Ohio.

---

44. Covenant of Oliver Cowdery and Others, Oct. 17, 1830, in Ezra Booth, Letter to Ira Eddy, Nov. 29, 1831, "Mormonism—Nos. VIII–IX," *Ohio Star* (Ravenna, OH), Dec. 8, 1831, [1] (*JSP*, D1:204; *EMD*, 3:505–506).

45. Cowdery and the other missionaries probably left Kirtland "no later than 22 November 1830." See *JSP*, D1:268–70n155. Cowdery and Whitmer reported that Williams accompanied them to Missouri. Cowdery, Letter to "Dearly Beloved Brethren & Sisters," Apr. 8, 1831, in JS Letterbook 1, 11; Whitmer, Journal, Dec. 1831, [1]. Whitmer was apparently off by a month when he recorded: "we came to independance in the twelfth month on the 13 d[ay] of the month." See *JSP*, D2:6n23. In a letter dated January 29, 1831, Cowdery wrote that they had arrived "a few days since." Cowdery's letter was copied in Joseph Smith, Kirtland, OH, to Hyrum Smith, Harpursville, NY, 3–4 Mar. 1831, JS Collection, CHL (*JSP*, D1:270–73).

46. See 3 Ne. 20:15–22; 21:1, 22–25; Ether 13:4–10.

47. Oliver Cowdery, Letter to "My dearly beloved brethren & Sister in the Lord" [Newel K. Whitney and other church members, including Joseph Smith], Apr. 8, 1831, JS Letterbook 1, 11–12 (*JSP*, D1:293).

Before February 14 Cowdery and companions were preaching to the Shawnee and Delaware Indians in the territory just over Missouri's western border and were planning to open a school among the Delaware until Cummins ordered them to leave. Isaac McCoy, a Baptist missionary to the Indians, recalled in 1833: "The Mormons, as I suppose from information, came here so ignorant of laws, regulating intercourse with the Indian tribes, that they expected to pass on into the Indian Territory, procure lands of the Indians, aid them in adopting habits of civilization, and attach them to their party. At the western line of Missouri, they were arrested by the proper authorities of government."[48] Consequently, on February 14 Cowdery wrote to Superintendent Clark requesting permission to "have free intercourse with the several tribes in establishing schools for the instruction of their children and also teaching them the Christian religion."[49] Presumably Pratt took Cowdery's letter with him, but when he reached St. Louis he found that Clark was out of town and so he continued on to Kirtland, arriving sometime in April.

Unable to enter Indian Territory, the missionaries preached to the white settlers. "We have traveld about in this country considerable and proclaimed repentence and very many are very anxious serious & honest," Cowdery wrote. "Yesterday we held a meeting and proclaimed the word of the Lord," he optimistically reported, "and one sister thank the Lord obeyed the truth and at evening we held another meeting when another sister obeyed also and trust that the time is not far distant when more will follow." Cowdery recounted that at one baptismal meeting he stood on a large rock, and it felt as though "I stood in spirit upon a rock that was broader then the heavens and in full assurance that the gospel was commited to me to proclaim [and] the lord gave his spirit and sinners were pricke[d] in there hearts."[50]

Cowdery reported that on the same day he wrote his letter he had a conversation with a man named James Pool. Employed as a blacksmith for the Delaware, Shawnee, and Seneca tribes of Indians, Pool informed Cowdery that he intended to join the church. According to Pool, the tribes had been stirred up by the preaching of Cowdery and the other missionaries, who were no doubt confirmed in their faith when Pool told them that "evry [Indian] Nation have now the name of Nephy who is the son of Nephi

---

48. Isaac McCoy, "The Disturbances in Jackson County," *Missouri Republican* (St. Louis), Dec. 20, 1833, [2].

49. Oliver Cowdery, Letter to William Clark, Feb. 14, 1831.

50. Cowdery, Letter to "My dearly beloved brethren & sisters in the Lord," Apr. 8, 1831, JS Letterbook 1, 10 (*JSP*, D1:291–92).

& handed down to this very generation." Pool also told Cowdery that "the principl[e] chief says he believes evry word of the Book [of Mormon] & there are many more in the Nation who believes & we understand there are many among the Shawnees who also believe & we trust that when the Lord shall open our way we shall have glorious times."[51] Pool evidently referred to Kikthawenund, the chief of the Delaware also known as William Anderson. Pool never joined the church; his report was no doubt a hoax.

About two weeks later, Smith and the Ohio Mormons received another letter from Cowdery, which is no longer extant, and about two weeks after that another letter describing missionary work among the white settlers.[52] "I have nothing particular to write as concerning the Lamanites," Cowdery wrote. This was the case because Pratt had not returned with the permit to proselytize among the Indians, and would not for some time. Cowdery mentions that he had received a letter from Pratt, who was still in St. Louis, which no doubt carried the disappointing news that Superintendent Clark was away. By the time Cowdery's letter reached Kirtland, Smith had already learned about the situation from Pratt himself.

Emma's Twins

On April 30 Emma Smith gave birth to twins, a son and daughter, who lived only three hours. Samuel F. Whitney remembered years later that Emma had a "hard labor and the blood went to her head which became black," and that Joseph "became frightened and sent to Willoughby for Dr. Card, and told the messenger to run his horse." When the doctor came to Emma's bedside, "he bled her" and then delivered the twins.[53] Whitney said that afterward he saw the doctor on his way home, and that in conversation he "laughed heartily about Jo's revelation that the Mormons should not employ physicians." The doctor apparently was familiar with the law of the church dictated by Smith the previous February, which directed that the sick were to "be nourished in all tenderness with herbs and mild food & that not of the world & the Elders of the church two or more Shall be called & shall pray for and lay their hands upon them in my name & if they die they shall

---

51. Cowdery, 10–11 (*JSP*, D1:292).

52. Oliver Cowdery, Letter to Newel K. Whitney and Others (Including Joseph Smith), May 7, 1831, JS Letterbook 1, 12–13 (*JSP*, D1:294–97). This letter mentions a no longer extant letter, dated April 16, having been sent.

53. Bloodletting for therapeutic reasons has an ancient origin and was a common practice in America until the late nineteenth century. See Carter, *The Decline of Therapeutic Bloodletting and the Collapse of Traditional Medicine.*

die unto me."[54] This seeming indifference to death appeared to the doctor to give way to self-preservation when put to the test. This was a trial to some of Smith's followers, for, according to Whitney, "One of their mid-wives, old Mrs. Birdsley, told me of Jo's inconsistency in calling Dr. Card, and came near leaving them for it."[55] Smith had not yet begun keeping a journal, but the burial of the twins, later identified in family records as Thaddeus and Louisa, must have brought solemn thoughts to his mind. In less than three years, the Smiths had lost three children shortly after a difficult birth. No doubt his enemies interpreted such events as signs of God's displeasure.

Isaac Morley's two daughters assisted Emma while she convalesced in the small frame home their father had recently built.[56] By a remarkable coincidence, John Murdock's wife, Julia, gave birth the same day to boy-and-girl twins, Joseph and Julia. Sadly, the mother died after lingering for six hours.[57] Nine days later, Murdock, who had been called on a mission and needed to leave his children in the care of others, gave the twins to Emma to nurse and raise as her own.[58]

Shakers

As the time neared for the arrival of his followers from New York, Smith began to think of places of settlement. It was determined that the Colesville branch would settle on a large tract of land in Thompson owned by Leman Copley. In making these arrangements, Smith became aware that Copley, a former Shaker who had recently joined the church, "was anxious that some of the elders should go to his former brethren and preach the gospel."[59] Accordingly, Smith dictated a revelation on May 7 calling Sidney Rigdon, Parley P. Pratt, who had recently arrived from Missouri, and Leman Copley on a mission to the Shakers in North Union, a communal society located near Cleveland. According to Smith's official history, the revelation was necessary because Copley "still retained ideas that the Shakers were right in some particulars of their faith."[60] In addition to calling the three missionaries, the

---

54. Revelation, Feb. 9, 1831, "The Laws of the Church of Christ," [4], Revelations Collection [D&C 42:43–44] (*JSP*, D1: 252).

55. Samuel F. Whitney, "Statement of Rev. S. F. Whitney on Mormonism," *Naked Truths about Mormonism*, Jan. 1888, 3. Whitney confused the birth of the twins on the Morley farm with the birth of Joseph Smith III above the Whitney store the following year.

56. Lucy Diantha Morley Allen, "Joseph Smith, the Prophet," *Young Woman's Journal*, Dec. 1906, 537.

57. John Murdock, Autobiography, 2.

58. JS History, vol. A-1, 204 (DHC 1:260).

59. Whitmer, History, 26 (*JSP*, H2:38).

60. JS History, vol. A-1, 112 (DHC 1:167).

revelation denounced celibacy, the main tenet of the Shakers, as well as their teaching that Ann Lee, who had founded the Shakers in the eighteenth-century in England, was "Christ's Second Appearance."[61]

Smith sent two of his most able theologians and preachers to the Shaker village no doubt to firm up Copley's faith in Mormonism since his land was crucial to settling the New York Saints and for the growth of the fledgling church in the area. The mission, however, would prove a failure and eventually lead to Copley's disaffection. Rigdon and Copley left immediately after Smith called them, arriving at North Union the same evening, with Pratt arriving the following day.

Presiding elder Ashbel Kitchell gave an account of the contentious exchange between his people and the Mormon missionaries, recording that Copley "had been among us; but not likeing the cross any to[o] well" (a reference to celibacy) "had taken up with Mormonism as the easier plan and had been appointed by them as one of the missionaries to convert us." In the course of the evening, Kitchell wrote, "the doctrines of the cross and the Mormon faith were both investigated; and we found that the life of self-denial corresponded better with the life of Christ, than Mormonism." According to Kitchell, Rigdon "frankly acknowledged" the correctness of the celibacy principle, "but said he did not bear that cross, and did not expect to." To which the Shaker elder responded that he "could not look on him as a Christian."[62]

In the morning, Kitchell instructed Rigdon and Copley not to disrupt his community and urged that neither they nor the Shakers "force their doctrine on the other at this time." Shortly, Pratt arrived, and learned that Kitchell "had bound them to silence, and nothing could be done." Parley, according to Kitchell, "told them to pay no attention to me, for they had come with the authority of the Lord Jesus Christ, and the people must hear it." Pratt and the others attended Sabbath meeting with the Shaker community, sitting quietly until its conclusion when Rigdon arose and announced that he had "a message from the Lord Jesus Christ to this people." He then read the revelation that denounced Ann Lee and the principle of celibacy.

Of course, the Shakers were offended. Kitchell denounced the revelation as inspired by the devil, and the congregation began to disperse. According

---

61. Revelation, May 7, 1831, Revelation Book 1, 80–82 [D&C 49] (*JSP*, D1:297–303).

62. My account of the exchange between the Mormon missionaries and the Shakers relies on Ashbel Kitchell, Reminiscences, copied in 1856 by Elisha D. Blakeman. See Blakeman, "A Mormon Interview."

to Kitchell, "Parley Pratt arose and commenced shakeing his coattail; he said he shook the dust from his garments as a testimony against us, that we had rejected the word of the Lord Jesus."[63] Facing off with Pratt, Kitchell declared: "You filthy Beast, dare you presume to come in here, and try to imitate a man of God by shaking your filthy tail; confess your sins and purge your soul from your lusts, and your other abominations before you ever presume to do the like again." Kitchell said Pratt "settled trembling into his seat, and covered his face." The Shaker elder then castigated a weeping Copley, "You hypocrite, you knew better;—you knew where the living work of God was; but for the sake of indulgence, you could consent to deceive yourself and them, but you shall reap the fruit of your own doings."

At this, Pratt mounted his horse and rode off. Kitchell said Rigdon remained for supper, during which he "acknowledged that we were the purest people he had ever been acquainted with but he was not prepared to live such a life." Copley remained all night and left in the morning—his faith in Mormonism shaken.

New York Arrivals

Meanwhile, three groups of Mormon migrants had started to make their way to Ohio, leaving Colesville and Fayette and rendezvousing at Buffalo. One group consisting of about sixty-eight people headed by thirty-year-old Newel Knight left Colesville, Broome County, on April 21 and reached Buffalo on May 1.[64] The Fayette branch in Seneca County was organized into two groups—one company of about fifty headed by Lucy Smith and another of about thirty headed by Thomas B. Marsh, which departed from Waterloo on canal boats on May 3 or 4. Using the Cayuga, Seneca, and Erie Canals, the Fayette branch reached Buffalo about May 7 or 8.[65]

When the ice finally broke on May 8, the Mormon migrants continued their journey on Lake Erie and arrived at Fairport, Ohio, on May 14. A group headed by Jared Carter had already left Buffalo by land to Dunkirk, New York, then by steamboat to Fairport. About this time, a fourth group of

---

63. Shaking the dust from the feet was a form of cursing those who rejected the Mormon gospel, which was based on Jesus's instructions in the New Testament but no longer practiced (Matt. 10:14; Mark 6:11; Luke 9:5; 10:10–12; see also Acts 13:51–52: D&C 24:15; 60:15; 75:20). See Weber, "'Shake Off the Dust of Thy Feet.'"

64. Newel Knight said he left Colesville in early April 1831. Newel Knight, Journal, 29 (*EMD*, 4:44). However, a brief chronology sketched on the back of a land Indenture made out in Joseph Knight's name gives the date of departure: "Colesville April 21 1831 on thursday Setout we arived at ithica on Saturday the next [April 23]." Joseph Knight, Sr., Land Indenture, Apr. 14, 1826, CHL.

65. For the migration of the New York Mormons, see Porter, "'Ye Shall Go to the Ohio,'" 15–18.

56

approximately fifty people headed by Martin Harris left Palmyra and would not arrive at Kirtland, Ohio, until late May or early June.[66]

When Lucy's group landed at Fairport, Joseph and Samuel Smith greeted her. "We met in tears of joy," she remembered. Samuel told her that he was "warned of God in a dream to come immidiately to this place to meet the company from Waterloo and I was afraid that some dreadful thing had befallen you indeed I feared that you was dead and that I should only meet your corpse."[67] No doubt the dream was triggered by the fact that Lucy's company was three days late, but Samuel was relieved to learn that his premonition was mistaken.

Joseph took his mother and some of the other women to Partridge's home in Painesville, where they ate and refreshed themselves. After a short carriage ride and visit with Joseph Kingsbury, Smith took Lucy to the Morley farm in Kirtland, where she was reunited with her husband. In the evening, Lucy saw the Murdock twins, who she said "was given to [Emma] a few days before ... to supply the places of a pair of twins which she had lost."[68] Joseph Sr. and Lucy stayed with Morley for two weeks, then moved about a mile south on the Chillicothe Road onto a farm located a little south of the cemetery owned by Frederick G. Williams, who was still in Missouri with Cowdery and the others.

The two-week delay in the crowded Morley home was necessary because there was some trouble procuring access to the Williams property. Williams had not completed exchanging his property in Warrensville, Ohio, for the Kirtland property and still owed $500 when he joined the Mormons and then left for Missouri. In Williams's absence, Isaac Moore, a Campbellite, continued to live on the property and was refusing to vacate, but as Williams acknowledged in a recently-received letter from Missouri, which included instructions to his wife, Rebecca, nothing could be done until the August term of the county court.[69]

Unwilling to wait until August to settle the dispute with Moore, Smith dictated a revelation on May 15 directing Joseph Sr. to occupy the farm owned by Williams and that forty-year-old Ezra Thayer and his family

---

66. On May 27 the *Wayne Sentinel* reported that Martin Harris and several other families "took up their march from this town [Palmyra] last week for the 'promised land.'" News Item, *Wayne Sentinel* (Palmyra, NY), May 27, 1831, [3]. See Porter, "'Ye Shall Go to the Ohio,'" 19.

67. Lucy Mack Smith, History, 1844–45, bk. 12, [5] (Anderson, ed., *Lucy's Book*, 537).

68. Lucy Mack Smith, [6] (Anderson, *Lucy's Book*, 537–38).

69. Cowdery, Letter to "My dearly beloved brethren & sisters in the Lord," Apr. 8, 1831, JS Letterbook 1, 12 (*JSP*, D1:293).

should board with him until a house could be built for them. The revelation, which was not published among Smith's other revelations, commanded: "Let the bargain stand that ye have made concerning these farms untill it be so fulfilled … pay no more money for the present time untill the contract be fulfilled." Apparently, someone—possibly Thayer—paid Moore $100, but the threat of withholding the remainder probably forced Moore to vacate the property and remove to Warrensville, whereupon Joseph Sr. and Lucy moved into the house, which, according to the revelation, needed to be "repaired."[70] Lucy later wrote that "on this farm my family were all established with this arrangement that we were to cultivate the farm and the produce was to be applied to the suport of our families and the use of persons who were came to the place and had no acquaintances there."[71]

Smith directed the Colesville Branch to settle in Thompson Township, located about twenty miles northeast of Kirtland, on the 759-acre farm of Leman Copley.[72] Newel Knight, who was appointed as branch president, later wrote that upon their arrival "it was advised that the Coalesville Branch remain together and go to [a] neigboring town called Thompson as a man by the name [Leman] Copley owned a considerabl[e] tract of land there which he offered to let the Brethren occuppy."[73] Newel's father, Joseph Knight Sr., remembered that they "all went to work and made fence[s] and planted and sowed the fields."[74]

On May 20 Smith dictated a revelation that commanded Partridge to organize the Colesville branch at Thompson into an economic cooperative. Compliance was mandatory, for the revelation commanded obedience to the law of consecration and threatened "otherwise they will be cut off."[75] Orson Pratt, who was present when Smith dictated the revelation, remembered that "no great noise or physical manifestation was made; Joseph was as calm as the morning sun," although "his face was exceedingly white, and seemed to shine."[76]

Because Copley apparently lacked a clear title to the land, the revelation instructed Partridge to "go & obtain a deed or Article of this land." Joseph

---

70. Revelation, May 15, 1831, Revelation Book 1, 85 [uncanonized] (*JSP*, D1:309–14). The remaining $400 was raised by Philo Dibble in April 1832. Dibble, Reminiscences, [4].

71. Lucy Mack Smith, History, 1844–45, bk. 12, [6] (Anderson, *Lucy's Book*, 537–38).

72. Geauga County tax records from 1832 indicate Copley owned 759 acres in Thompson Township. Geauga Co., OH, Duplicate Tax Records, 1832–33, 282.

73. Newel Knight, Autobiography and Journal, 29–30.

74. Joseph Knight, Reminiscences, 9.

75. Revelation, May 20, 1831, Revelation Book 1, 86 [D&C 51:2] (*JSP*, D1:315).

76. Orson Pratt, Discourse, June 28, 1874, Brigham City, UT, *LDS Millennial Star*, Aug. 11, 1874, 498.

Knight Sr. later wrote that one of Smith's revelations gave instruction "to purchase a thousand acres of Land which was Claimed By Leman Copley and not paid for."[77] The deed for Copley's land would be obtained with funds gathered from the members of the Colesville branch, either in money or by signing the deeds to their New York properties over to the bishop. As the revelation commanded: "Let my Servent Edward receive the properties of this People ... & let my Servent Edward receive the money as it shall be laid before him according to the covenant."[78] Knight confirmed that he and others from New York "were Cald upon to Consecrate our properties."[79]

Still, this method was evidently not sufficient to pay for the land, probably because the deeds could not be easily converted into cash. Ezra Booth remembered that Smith ordered Partridge to borrow the money, contrary to the laws of the church about contracting debts with the world.[80] According to Booth, "A thousand acres of land in the town of Thompson could be purchased for one half its value, and [Partridge] was commanded to secure it; and in order to do it, he was under the necessity to contract a debt to the world. He hesitated, but the command was repeated, 'you must secure the land.' ... He saw the impropriety, and it shook his faith."[81] The law regarding debt, which was probably designed to pressure members to give more of their substance, proved to be impractical in the face of the large-scale demands of running a church. When the revelation was published in the 1833 Book of Commandments, it was changed to read: "Thou shalt contract no debts with the world, *except thou art commanded*."[82] In the 1835 Doctrine and Covenants, the revelation was deleted altogether. In the end, however, it became unnecessary to contract the debt because Copley refused to consecrate his property, renounced Mormonism, and returned to the Shakers.[83]

The non-Mormons in the area were no doubt alarmed at the sudden influx of an alien religion. On May 17 the *Painesville Telegraph* reported:

77. Joseph Knight, Reminiscences, 9.

78. Revelation, May 20, 1831, Revelation Book 1, 86 [D&C 51] (*JSP*, D1:315–16). Portions of this revelation were deleted when it was published as section XXIII in D&C, 1835 ed., 150–51.

79. Joseph Knight, Reminiscences, 9.

80. "Thou Shalt contract no debts with them," that is, "the wo[r]ld." Revelation, Feb. 9, 1831, [6]; see also Revelation Book 1, 67 [D&C 42] (*JSP*, D1: 255).

81. Booth, Letter to Ira Eddy, Nov. 21, 1831, "Mormonism—No. VII," *Ohio Star*, Nov. 24, 1831, [1].

82. Revelation, Feb. 9, 1831, BC XLIV:55; emphasis added. In Revelation Book 1, 67, the phrase "except thou art commanded" is inserted above the line in Oliver Cowdery's handwriting (*JSP*, MRB:105).

83. Joseph Knight reported that "Brother Copley would not Consecrate his property therefore he was Cut of[f] from the Church." Knight, Reminiscences, 9.

"About two hundred men, women and children, of the deluded followers of Jo Smith's Bible speculation have arrived on our coast during the last week, from the State of New York, & are about seating themselves down upon the 'promised land' in this county."[84] By amassing his followers in northern Ohio, Smith would soon wield considerable economic and political power.

---

84. "Mormon Emigration," *Painesville Telegraph*, May 17, 1831.

4

Power from on High

Ye should go to the Ohio ... & there you shall be endowed with power from on high.

—Revelation, Jan., 1831, Revelation Book 1, 51–52 [D&C 38:32–33]

Mary Rollins Lightner remembered that when she was thirteen, her mother took her to the Morley farm to meet the newly arrived Smith family. A small group had gathered in a room when Joseph Smith walked in with Martin Harris and called for an impromptu meeting. After singing and prayer, Smith stood before the group. "As he began to speak very solemnly and very earnestly," Lightner recalled, "all at once his countenance changed and he stood mute. Those who looked at him that day said there was a search light within him, over every part of his body. I never saw anything like it on the earth. I could not take my eyes off him; he got so white that anyone who saw him would have thought he was transparent. ... He stood some moments. He looked over the congregation as if to pierce every heart. He said, 'Do you know who has been in your midst?'"

Someone ventured a guess, "An angel of the Lord"? Martin Harris, who was sitting on a small box at Smith's feet, said, "It was our Lord and Savior, Jesus Christ." Smith, putting his hand down on Harris, said: "God revealed that to you."

Smith electrified the group: "Brethren and sisters, the Spirit of God has been here. The Savior has been in your midst this night and I want you to remember it. There is a veil over your eyes for you could not endure to look upon Him. You must be fed with milk, not with strong meat. I want you to remember this as if it were the last thing that escaped my lips. He has given all of you to me and has sealed you up to everlasting life that where he is, you may be also. And if you are tempted of Satan say, 'Get behind me, Satan.'"

Smith then knelt and prayed. "I have never heard anything like it before or since," Lightner recalled. "I felt that he was talking to the Lord and that power rested down upon the congregation. Every soul felt it. The spirit rested upon us in every fiber of our bodies, and we received a sermon from the lips of the representative of God."[1]

The fourth general conference of the church was held in Kirtland on June 3–4. About fifty elders convened in the log schoolhouse located on the hill just above the Morley settlement.[2] On the second day of the conference, the long-awaited endowment of "power from on high" was fulfilled in the form of ordinations to the high priesthood.[3] In addition to fulfilling the January 2 revelation, John Whitmer said the meeting also fulfilled a February revelation in which the Lord had declared that "the Elders of my Church should be called to gether from the East & from the West & from the North & from the South," and "I will pour out my Spirit upon them in the day that they assemble themselves together."[4] Before conference, according to Ezra Booth, several church members expected spiritual manifestations and declared that they were "perfectly assured, that the work of miracles would commence at the ensuing conference." Booth further reported, "Smith, the day before the conference, professing to be filled with the spirit of prophecy, declared, that 'not three days should pass away, before some should see their Savior, face to face.'"[5] According to Whitmer, Smith also "Prophecied the day Previous that the man of Sin should be revealed."[6] There was great anticipation among the attendees. Smith did not disappoint.

After the men had seated themselves on the slab benches of the one-room schoolhouse, the meeting commenced with a song and prayer, after which Smith stepped forward and spoke. Jared Carter, a member of the

---

1. Lightner, Address at Brigham Young University, Apr. 14, 1905, 1–3; see also Mary E. Rollins Lightner, "Testimony," *Young Woman's Journal*, Dec. 1905, 556–57. Lightner dates the event to "the next night after [the Smiths] came to Kirtland." However, the Smith family arrived on May 14, but Martin Harris did not arrive until the end of May or beginning of June.

2. On the location of the conference, see Levi Hancock, Autobiography, ca. 1854, 90. John Corrill said: "About fifty elders met, which was about all the elders that then belonged to the church." Corrill, *A Brief History*, 18 (*JSP*, H2:145). The conference minutes identify sixty-two participants—forty-three elders, nine priests, and ten teachers. Minutes, June 3, 1831, Minute Book 2, 3 (*JSP*, D1:324–26).

3. Revelation, Jan. 2, 1831, Revelation Book 1, 52 [D&C 38:32] (*JSP*, D1:232). On the probable dating of the ordinations, see discussion in *JSP*, D1:317–18.

4. Whitmer, History, 27 (*JSP*, H2:39); Revelation, Feb. 1831-B, Revelation Book 1, 70 [D&C 44:1–2] (*JSP*, D1:261).

5. Ezra Booth, Letter, Nelson, OH, to Ira Eddy, Oct. 31, 1831, "Mormonism—No. IV," *Ohio Star*, Nov. 3, 1831, [3].

6. Whitmer, History, 28–29 (*JSP*, H2:40).

Colesville branch, remarked that "Brother Joseph, not withstanding he is not naturally talented for a speaker yet he was filled with the power of the Holy Ghost so that he spoke as I never heard man speak for God, … and marvelous was the display of the power of the spirit among the elders present."[7]

The minutes mention exhortations by Smith and Rigdon but give no content. Hancock remembered that among other things Smith said the apostle "John was to tarry until Christ come," and that "he is now with the ten tribes a preaching and when we can get ready for them they will come."[8] Whitmer wrote that "the Spirit of the Lord fell upon Joseph in an unusual manner" and that he prophesied "that John the Revelator was then among the ten tribes of Israel … to prepare them for their return" and "many more things … that I have not written."[9] This was probably part of Smith's discussion of the powers of the high priesthood, which included the power of physical translation and of entering into God's presence as discussed in Alma 13.[10]

Among other things, according to Levi Hancock, Smith "said that the kingdom of Christ that he spoke of that was like a grain of musterd seed was now before him and some should see it put forth its branches And the angels of heaven would some day come like Birds to its branches just as the Saviour said."[11] One purpose of the gathering and bestowal of additional authority was to energize the missionary force Smith was about to send out.

Booth, who published the earliest account of the conference, reported that "Smith arose to harangue the conference. He reminded those present of the prophecy, which he said 'was given by the spirit yesterday.' He wished them not to be overcome with surprise, when that event ushered in. He continued, until by long speaking, himself and some others became much excited."[12] As if taking the lead in a visionary exercise, Smith astonished the congregation, declaring dramatically, "I now see God and Jesus Christ at his right hand," and exclaimed, "Let them kill me I should not feel death [in such a state] as I am now."[13]

Looking at Lyman Wight, a former Campbellite who had been ordained

---

7. Jared Carter, Journal, 17.

8. Hancock, Autobiography, 90. See 3 Ne. 28:6–9; BC VI [D&C 7].

9. Whitmer, History, 27 (JSP, H2:39).

10. As Alma explains, "There were many which were ordained and became High Priests of God … and were sanctified, and their garments were washed white, through the blood of the Lamb. … And there were many, exceeding great many, which were made pure, and entered into the rest of the Lord their God" (Book of Mormon, 1830 ed., 259 [Alma 13:10–12]).

11. Hancock, Autobiography, 90. Cf. Matt. 13:31–32.

12. Booth, Letter to Ira Eddy, Oct. 31, 1831, "Mormonism—No. IV," Ohio Star, Nov. 3, 1831, [3].

13. Hancock, Autobiography, 90.

an elder by Oliver Cowdery and was then living on the Morley farm, Smith announced: "You shall see the Lord." Approaching Wight, who was sitting in the corner of the room, he laid his hands upon his head, ordained him to the high priesthood, and "blessed him with the visions of heaven."[14] Booth added that Smith also set him apart "for the service of the Indians, and was ordained to the gift of tongues, healing the sick, casting out devils, and discerning spirits." Smith then invited Wight to speak. According to Booth, "Wight arose, and presented a pale countenance, a fierce look, with his arms extended, and his hands cramped back, the whole system agitated, and a very unpleasant object to look upon. He ... called upon those around him 'if you want to see a sign, look at me.' He then stepped upon a bench, and declared with a loud voice, he saw the Savior."[15]

Whitmer also said Wight "saw the hevans opened, and the Son of man sitting on the right hand of the Father," but gave more details about what Wight had said, reporting that he prophesied that "there were some in this congregation that should live until the Savior shoud decend from heaven, with a Shout, with all the holy angels with him. ... Yea, he will appear in his brightness, and consume all before him. ... And some of my brethren shall suffer marterdom, for the sake of the religion of Jesus Christ. and seal the testimony of Jesus with their blood."[16]

Smith then put his hands on Harvey Whitlock, a recent convert who lived near the Johnson family in Hiram, and ordained him to the high priesthood. Instantly, according to Hancock and Booth, Whitlock experienced uncontrollable bodily contortions and was unable to speak, which was interpreted as a sign of demonic possession.[17]

Smith's brother Hyrum, the former Presbyterian, said, "Joseph that is not of God." Joseph, who had been a Methodist exhorter in his youth, said, "Do not speak against this." Hyrum responded, "I will not believe ... unless you inquire of God and [he] owns it." Joseph bowed his head a short time and then walked over to Whitlock, laid his hands on his head, and commanded Satan to leave.[18]

14. Hancock, 90.

15. Booth, Letter to Ira Eddy, Oct. 31, 1831, "Mormonism—No. IV," *Ohio Star*, Nov. 3, 1831, [3].

16. Whitmer, 28 (*JSP*, H2:40). Hancock remembered that Joseph Smith said "some of you shall live to see it come with great glory," but "some of you must die for the testimony of this work." Hancock, Autobiography, 90. While Whitmer is more likely correct, writing closer to the event, it is possible that Smith and Wight said the same thing.

17. Hancock, Autobiography, 90; Booth, Letter to Ira Eddy, Oct. 31, 1831, "Mormonism—No. IV," *Ohio Star*, Nov. 3, 1831, [3].

18. Hancock, Autobiography, 90.

This seemed to trigger other suggestive elders, for immediately former Shaker Leman Copley, who was sitting on a window sill, somersaulted into the room and landed on one of the benches. "The evil spirit left him," Hancock said, "and as quick as lightning Harv[e]y Green fell bound and screamed like a Panther." When "satan was cast out of him," it "amediately entered another" person. This "continued all day and the greatest part of the knight," Hancock recalled.[19]

Parley P. Pratt reported that during the conference there "were some strange manifestations of false spirits, which were immediately rebuked."[20] Corrill wrote that the religious enthusiasm that Smith had rebuked in February reappeared at the conference and that "the same visionary and marvellous spirits ... got hold of some of the elders; it threw one from his seat to the floor; it bound another, so that for some time he could not use his limbs nor speak; and some other curious effects were experienced, but, by a mighty exertion, in the name of the Lord, it was exposed and shown to be from an evil source."[21] Whitmer wrote that "Joseph the Seer ... commanded the devil in the name of Christ and he departed to our Joy and comfort."[22]

During this display of wild religious enthusiasm, Smith tried to heal John Murdock's crippled hand. At age seventeen, Murdock said he "fell on a scythe and became a cripple by a severe wound in my wrist, having cut two of the main leaders I came near bleeding to death."[23] According to Booth, Smith was unable to heal Murdock's hand as well as the leg of another elder who had come to the meeting with a crutch.[24] These events went unreported in the surviving accounts of those who remained believers in Smith's prophetic calling.

The meeting and ordinations to the high priesthood continued despite the occasional exorcism. Intermingled with demonic possession were heavenly manifestations as well. Lyman Wight recounted that he had witnessed "the visible manifestations of the power of God as plain as could have been on the day of pentecost," including "the heeling of the sick, casting out devils, speaking in unknown tongues, discerning of spirits, and prophesying with mighty power."[25] None of this was mentioned in the official minutes.[26]

---

19. Hancock, 91.
20. Pratt, *Autobiography*, 72.
21. Corrill, *Brief History*, 1839, 18 (*JSP*, H2:145).
22. Whitmer, History, 29 (*JSP*, H2:40–41).
23. Murdock, Autobiography, 3–4.
24. Booth, Letter to Ira Eddy, Oct. 31, 1831, "Mormonism—No. IV," *Ohio Star*, Nov. 3, 1831, [3].
25. Wight, Letter to Wilford Woodruff, Aug. 24, 1857, 5–6; see also Smith and Smith, *History of The Reorganized Church*, 1:193.
26. Minutes, June 3–[4], 1831, Minute Book 2, 3–4 (*JSP*, D1:324–27).

Finally, Wight ordained Smith and Rigdon to the high priesthood. In all, twenty-two elders and one priest were ordained to the high priesthood. At this time, these ordinations were not understood as bestowing a new office of high priest, but rather it was the introduction of a new priesthood. Thus the minutes of meetings over the next four months continued to list those ordained to the high priesthood under "Elders present," meaning they were considered elders with additional authority.[27] But on October 25, 1831, the minutes list elders separately from the "Names of those ordained to the Highpriesthood," which implies that the high priesthood was by then recognized as a distinct office in the church.[28] Indeed, the high priesthood is referred to as an "office" in the minutes of meetings held on October 26, although on November 1 and 8 both high priests and elders are listed under the heading "Elders Present."[29] The minutes for January 28, 1832, list the "Names of Elders Present who were ordained to the H[igh]. P[riest]. H[ood]." and the "Names of Elders who were not ordained to the H[igh]. P[riest]. H[ood]."[30] Uncertainty about the nature of the high priesthood seems to have been resolved by April 26, 1832, when Smith was sustained in Missouri as president of the high priesthood and the minutes of the meeting list "High Priests" and "Elders" separately.[31]

Before June 1831, the only major division of authority was between elders—the charismatic leaders—and all others: that is, priests, teachers, and deacons (see D&C 20:38–45). However, it is important to note that while these men held different offices and callings, they had no concept that there were two priesthoods in the church until the introduction of the high priesthood. Thus Corrill remarked in his 1839 account of the event: "The Malchisedec [Melchizedek] priesthood was then for the first time introduced, and conferred on several of the elders."[32] Smith's official history similarly asserted: "The authority of the Melchisedec priesthood was manifested and conferred, for the first time, upon several of the elders."[33]

---

27. This is the case for meetings held between August 4 and October 21, 1831. See *JSP*, D2:22–23, 58, 61, 68, 71, 75, 77.

28. Minutes, Oct. 25–26, 1831, Minute Book 2, 10 (*JSP*, D2:80).

29. Minutes, 15, 16 (*JSP*, D2:86, 97, 123).

30. Oliver Cowdery, Letter to Joseph Smith, Jan. 28, 1832, [1], JS Collection (*JSP*, D2:165).

31. Minutes, Apr. 26–27, 1832, Minute Book 2, 24 (*JSP*, D2:231).

32. Corrill, *Brief History*, 18 (*JSP*, H2:145).

33. JS History, vol. A-1, 118 (DHC 1:175–76). Originally scribed by W. W. Phelps between June and November 1842. See Vogel, ed., *History of Joseph Smith*, 1:lxxxiv. This passage was later emended by Willard Richards to read: "the authority of the Melchisedec <priesthood> was manifested and <I> conferred, <the high priesthood> for the first time, upon several of the elders."

At this point, nothing had been said about Smith and Cowdery having been ordained by angels; and nothing about Aaronic and Melchizedek priesthoods. This would come later. The understanding in 1831 was that Smith and Cowdery had ordained one another elders in response to a divine command Smith had received while working on the translation of the Book of Mormon at the home of Peter Whitmer Sr. in Fayette, New York, in June 1829. As Smith's official history would later state: "We had not long been engaged in solemn and fervent prayer, when the word of the Lord, came unto us in the Chamber, commanding us; that I should ordain Oliver Cowdery to be an Elder in the Church of Jesus Christ, and that he also should ordain me to the same office."[34] In an 1842 epistle to the church, Smith mentioned this event as "the voice of God in the chamber of old Father [Peter] Whitmerss in Fayette, Senneca County [New York]."[35] Thus, with the introduction of the high priesthood, there were now two priesthoods in the church with separate origins—both authorized by revelation.

In endowing the elders with "power from on high" before sending them out on missions, Smith was following the New Testament pattern, where Jesus tells his apostles: "I send the promise of my Father upon you: but tarry ye in the city of Jerusalem, until ye be endued with power from on high" (Luke 24:49). In Acts, Luke reminds Theophilus that Christ had appeared to the Twelve and commanded them not to depart Jerusalem until they had received "power, after that the Holy Ghost is come upon you: and ye shall be witnesses unto me both in Jerusalem, and in all Judaea, and in Samaria, and unto the uttermost part of the earth" (Acts 1:8).

It was not clear to those who received the high priesthood at the June conference why additional authority was needed. Levi Hancock later recalled a conversation he had in January 1832 with Lyman Wight about the new priesthood, but confessed "neither of us understood what it was." He said, "I did not understand it, and he [Wight] could give me no light."[36] Neither man was at the October 25 meeting when Smith and Rigdon attempted to explain the powers of the high priesthood, but it is noteworthy that at least

---

See Vogel, 127n5. The wording had to be modified to make it harmonize with the previous account in the narrative of the introduction of the eldership by the "word of the Lord" in June 1829 (DHC 1:60), which was later associated with the Melchizedek priesthood in September 1832 (D&C 84:29).

34. JS History, vol. A-1, 27 (*JSP*, H1:326; DHC 1:60–61).

35. Joseph Smith, Letter to "the Church of Jesus Christ of Latter Day Saints," Sep. 7, 1842, 7, Revelations Collection (*JSP*, D11:67). Cf. D&C 128:21.

36. Mosiah Lyman Hancock, "Autobiography of Levi Ward Hancock," 43.

two of the participants in the June conference remained uncertain about what it all meant and that much remained to be explained.

Missionaries by the Pair

Levi Hancock wrote that on Sunday, June 5, "a larg[e] Concourse of people Collected" in a field on the hill near the schoolhouse on the Morley farm, and that Lyman Wight and Joseph Smith spoke. Smith said, "From that time the Elders would have large Congregations to speak to and they must soon take there departure into the Reagions west."[37] On the following evening, Smith dictated a revelation that organized the elders into fourteen pairs and commanded them to proselyte en route to Missouri for the next conference to be held in early August.[38]

The main purpose of the trip to Missouri was to locate the spot where the city of Zion and its temple would be built, a task that unexpectedly required Smith's presence. In 1835 Smith said he "received, by a heavenly vision, a commandment, in June following, to take my journey to the western boundaries of the State of Missouri, and there designate the very spot, which was to be the central spot, for the commencement of the gathering."[39] While a September 1830 revelation had declared the New Jerusalem would be built "among the Lamanites," the revelation Smith dictated on June 6, 1831, hinted that it was among the white settlers instead, instructing that Smith and the other elders "assemble yourselves together to rejoice upon the land of your inheritance which is now the land of your enemies but behold I the lord will hasten the City in its time."[40]

The revelation also directed: "Let my Servant Joseph & Sidney & Edward take with them a recomend from the Church & let there be one obtained for my Servant Oliver [Cowdery]."[41] While not entirely clear, this probably refers to the permit needed from General William Clark in St. Louis to enter Indian Territory, which Parley P. Pratt had been unsuccessful in obtaining.[42]

Hancock, who was commanded in the revelation to pair with Zebedee

---

37. Levi Hancock, Autobiography, 92–93.

38. Revelation, June 6, 1831, Revelation Book 1, 87–89 [D&C 52] (*JSP*, D1:327–32).

39. Joseph Smith, Letter to "the Elders of the Church of Latter Day Saints," Oct. 2, 1835, *LDS Messenger and Advocate*, Sep. 1835, 179 (*JSP*, D5:7).

40. Revelation, Sep. 1830-B, Revelation Book 1, 41 [D&C 28:9] (*JSP*, D1:186); Revelation, June 6, 1831, Revelation Book 1, 89 [D&C 52:42–43] (*JSP*, D1:332).

41. Revelation, June 6, 1831, Revelation Book 1, 89 [D&C 52:41] (*JSP*, D1:332).

42. Oliver Cowdery, Letter to "My dearly beloved brethren & sisters in the Lord," Apr. 8, 1831, JS Letterbook 1, 11 (*JSP*, D1:293); see also License for Edward Partridge, ca. Aug. 4, 1831–ca. Jan. 5, 1832, JS Collection; and discussion in *JSP*, D1:332n465.

Coltrin, wrote that it was a great sacrifice to drop all worldly affairs and leave on his mission, but as he reflected on the supernatural manifestations at the conference, he felt bound to follow Smith to Missouri. He therefore concluded to "let all other things go" and "do as I am told in the Revelation."[43]

Two days later, Smith dictated another revelation calling Algernon Sidney Gilbert, Newel K. Whitney's business partner, "to be an agent unto this Church" and instructing him to accompany Smith and Rigdon to Missouri.[44] Gilbert's appointment fulfilled a previous revelation that called for the selection of an agent to assist Bishop Partridge, who would "take the money to provide food & raiment according to the wants of this people."[45] What this entailed exactly would be given in a revelation that Smith later dictated in Missouri.

Colesville Branch Troubles

Following his exorcism at the June conference, Leman Copley found his faith in Smith beginning to falter. According to Joseph Knight Sr., Copley struggled with the law of consecration. "Brother Copley would not Consecrate his property," Knight remembered, "therefore he was Cut of[f] from the Church."[46] It may be that Copley was not convinced that the bodily agitations experienced at the June conference, particularly his flip from the window sill, were the result of demonic possession. This may have been what Smith referred to when he said in his official history that Copley "still retained ideas that the Shakers were right in some particulars of their faith."[47]

Shaker leader Ashbel Kitchell, who had confronted Parley P. Pratt and Sidney Rigdon when Copley brought them to North Union in early May, later wrote that Copley "came back to us and begged for union." Kitchell accompanied Copley to his Thompson property, whereupon he "held a meeting in the dooryard, among the Mormons," who reportedly scattered out of hearing range. "They appeared to be struck with terror and fear lest some of them might get converted," Kitchell remarked. In the morning, Kitchell talked with Newel Knight, the branch president. Newel's father, Joseph, became angry and started yelling at the Shaker elder "at the top of his voice, and wound up by informing me that unless I repented I should go to Hell!" Kitchell said his words carried no weight since he was not a man of

---

43. Hancock, Autobiography, 94–95.
44. Revelation, June 8, 1831, Revelation Book 1, 89–90 [D&C 53] (*JSP*, D1:332–34).
45. Revelation, May 20, 1831, Revelation Book 1, 86 [D&C 51:8] (*JSP*, D1:316).
46. Knight, Reminiscences, 9.
47. JS History, vol. A-1, 112 (DHC 1:167).

God but "a man that lived in his lusts," meaning not celibate. "I then gave him a lecture on the subject of the cross [that is, celibacy], and a life of self denyal." After further conversation, Joseph Knight stormed out the door. During the day, Kitchell helped to settle the affair between Copley and the Colesville branch, creating legal documents and initiating efforts to remove the Mormons.[48]

Concerning the eviction from Copley's land, Joseph Knight explained that "we sold out what we Could But Copley took the advantege of us, and we Could not git any thing for what we had done so we left," meaning they were not paid for improvements they had made.[49] Joseph Knight Jr. recalled, "We had to leave [Copley's] farm and pay sixty dollars damage," adding sarcastically that the payment was for "fitting up his houses and planting his ground."[50]

Copley's disaffection only hastened the inevitable move to Missouri. The May 20 revelation had made it clear that their stay on Copley's land was temporary: "I consecrate unto them this land for a little season untill I the Lord shall provide for them otherwise & command them to go hence."[51] The time for the command had arrived sooner than anyone anticipated, even God apparently. John Whitmer recalled that "the rebellion of Leman Copley ... confused the whole church."[52]

Distraught and perplexed, Newel Knight went to Kirtland to consult Smith. On June 10 Smith dictated a revelation to Knight about the difficulties the branch at Thompson was experiencing. The revelation commanded Knight to "stand fast in the office wherewith I have appointed you & if your Brethren desire to escape their enemies let them repent of all their sins & become truly humble before me & contrite." Because Copley had broken the covenant, "it hath become void & of none affect" and therefore the branch was released from fulfilling it. Instead, the branch was commanded to "flee the land lest your enemies come upon you And take your Journey ... into the regions westward unto Missorie unto the borders of the Lamanites."[53]

Shortly after William W. Phelps arrived at Kirtland from New York, Smith dictated a revelation for him. The soon-to-be-baptized Phelps had

48. Blakeman, "A Mormon Interview."

49. Knight, Reminiscences, 9.

50. Joseph Knight Jr., Autobiographical Sketch, 2–3. According to a newspaper report, some Colesville saints were forced to "leave their spring crops all upon the ground." *Painesville Telegraph*, June 28, 1831, [3].

51. Revelation, May 20, 1831, Revelation Book 1, 87 [D&C 51:16] (*JSP*, D1:316–17).

52. Whitmer, History, 29 (*JSP*, H2:41–42).

53. Revelation, June 10, 1831, Revelation Book 1, 90–91 [D&C 54] (*JSP*, D1:334–36).

come with gifts Smith wanted to utilize immediately. Phelps had been the editor of the anti-Masonic newspaper *Ontario Phoenix*, printed at Canandaigua, New York, so it is not surprising that Smith's revelation not only called him to preach but to be "ordained to assist my servent Oliver [Cowdery] to do the work of Printing & of Selecting & writing Books for Schools in this Church that little Children also may receive instruction before me." Phelps was therefore commanded to "Journey with my servents Joseph & Sidney [Rigdon] that thou mayest be planted in the land of thine inheritance to do this work."[54]

On June 15 Smith dictated a revelation that altered the June 6 revelation concerning the pairs of missionaries that were to go to Missouri.[55] John Whitmer wrote that the revelation came because "some of those who had been commanded to take their Journey speedily … had denied the faith, and turned from the truth. And the church at Thompson Ohio, had not done according to the will of the [Lord]."[56] Of the fourteen pairs of missionaries, two pairs—Edson Fuller and Jacob Scott, and Wheeler Baldwin and William Carter—evidently did not go, and two were subsequently disciplined.[57]

While the June 6 revelation had paired Thomas B. Marsh with Ezra Thayer, this revelation reassigned Marsh to be a companion with Selah Griffin. Griffin had been paired with Newel Knight, who now was assigned to lead the Colesville branch, which is what branch members wanted anyway.[58] Similar to the revelation to Newel Knight five days earlier, this revelation also addressed the problem of God changing his commands, as if he had lost his power of foreknowledge. Thus the revelation declared: "Wherefore I the lord command & revoke as it seemeth me good & all this to be answered upon the heads of the rebelious saith the Lord. … For behold I revoke the commandment which was given to my servents Sealy [Selah] & Newel in consequence of the stiffneckedness of my people which are in Thompson &

---

54. Revelation, June 14, 1831, Revelation Book 1, 91 [D&C 55] (*JSP*, D1:336–39).

55. Revelation, June 15, 1831, Revelation Book 1, 91–93 [D&C 56] (*JSP*, D1:339–42).

56. Whitmer, History, 30 (*JSP*, H2:42, 43).

57. On September 1, 1831, Edson Fuller and William Carter were "silenced from holding office of Elders." Minutes, Sep. 1, 1831, Minute Book 2, 5 (*JSP*, D2:59).

58. Revelation, June 6, 1831, Revelation Book 1, 88 [D&C 52:22, 32] (*JSP*, D1:330); Revelation, June 15, 1831, Revelation Book 1, 88 [D&C 56:5–6] (*JSP*, D1:341). According to the compiler of Newel Knight's history, the Saints at Thompson were "grieved at the thought of brother Knight leaving them, for he had been with them from their first acquaintanc with the Church, and they leaned on him, as their guide and appointed him as their leader, from Thompson to Missouri. This reached the prophet Joseph's ears, and in a revelation … brother Newel's mission was revoked, and he was sustaind in leading them." Newel Knight, History, ca. 1871, 310a–310b, private possession, copy at CHL, as quoted in *JSP*, D1:340n513.

their rebelions Wherefore let my servent Newel remain with them."[59] Thus, by necessity, Smith moved away from the traditional view that God is omniscient, which seemed to contradict the Book of Mormon's teaching that "the decrees of God are unalterable."[60]

Marsh indicated that his change of missionary companion resulted from "Ezra Thayre delaying so much."[61] Thayer's hesitation was apparently due to his interest in the Frederick G. Williams property. A previous revelation had directed Thayer to board with the Joseph Smith Sr. family on Williams's property until a house could be built for him and his family.[62] This revelation commanded Thayer to "repent of his pride & his selfishness & obey the former commandment which I have given him concerning the place upon which he lives." Thayer's "selfishness" probably referred to his request to have a title drawn up for a portion of the land in exchange for the money he had paid to previous owner Isaac Moore. The revelation rejected that idea, stating that "there shall no divisions be made upon the land." The command for Thayer to go to Missouri was reissued, "otherwise he shall receive the money which he has paid & shall leave the place & shall be cut off out of my Church saith the Lord god of host."[63] Thayer did not go and, though not cut off, was reprimanded by a conference of elders on October 10.[64]

Smith began his journey to Missouri on Sunday, June 19, but the first group of Colesville believers led by Newel Knight did not embark on their month-long trip until June 28. Another group left the next day. Whitmer wrote: "The Church at Thompson made all possible haste to leav[e] for Missouri, and left and none of their enemies harmed them."[65] Joseph Knight Sr. remembered: "We left Copleys in June, and moved our things to wellsvill[e] on the ohio river which was about ninety miles" southeast of Kirtland.[66] Each group consisted of twelve wagons. Emily Coburn, sister-in-law to Newel Knight, remarked: "People all along the road stared at us as they would at a circus or a caravan, and our appearance did not deceive the public eye. We

---

59. Revelation, June 15, 1831, Revelation Book 1, 92 [D&C 56:5–7] (*JSP*, D1:341).

60. Book of Mormon, 1830 ed., 337 [Alma 41:8]. See also 303 [Alma 29:4], where it is declared that God "decreeth ... decrees which are unalterable." These words were inexplicably dropped from all editions after the first until it was restored in 1981.

61. Marsh, History and Autobiography, 3.

62. Revelation, May 15, 1831, Revelation Book 1, 85 [uncanonized] (*JSP*, D1:309–14).

63. Revelation, June 15, 1831, Revelation Book 1, 92 [D&C 56:8–10] (*JSP*, D1:341–42). See also discussion in *JSP*, D1:340.

64. Minutes, Oct. 10, 1831, Minute Book 2, 7–8 (Cannon and Cook, *Far West Record*, 15–16).

65. Whitmer, History, 30 (*JSP*, H2:43).

66. Knight, Reminiscences, 9.

most truly were a band of pilgrims, started out to seek a better country."[67] The two groups arrived at Wellsville on the Ohio River, where they boarded a steamer on July 3, changing boats at St. Louis and landing at Independence, Missouri, on July 26—two weeks after Smith.[68]

67. Austin, *Mormonism*, 63.

68. Knight, Reminiscences, 9. See also Porter, "The Colesville Branch in Kaw Township, Jackson County, Missouri, 1831–1833," 286–87.

5

Zion Found

*Please also, instead of some Recreation, when you can spare the time,
to give me your Reasons why the Heart of America may not be the
seat of the New-Jerusalem.*
                                    —*Samuel Sewell to Cotton Mather, Dec. 1684*[1]

On Sunday, June 19, Joseph Smith, accompanied by Sidney Rigdon, Martin
Harris, Edward Partridge, W. W. Phelps, Joseph Coe, Algernon Sidney Gilbert, and his wife Elisabeth, started for Jackson County, Missouri, traveling
by wagon, canal boats, and stages to Cincinnati, where Rigdon introduced
the Mormon prophet to the Reverend Walter Scott, one of the leading ministers in the Campbellite movement. The two men soon clashed over the
subject of spiritual gifts existing in the latter-day church. In his official history, Smith recalled: "Before the close of our interview, he manifested one of
the bitterest spirits against the doctrine of the New Testament, ('that these
signs shall follow them that believe,' as recorded in the 16th chapter of the
gospel, according to St. Mark,) that I ever witnessed among men."[2]

Of course, Mark 16:17—"And these signs shall follow them that believe;
In my name shall they cast out devils; they shall speak with new tongues;
they shall take up serpents; and if they drink any deadly thing, it shall not
hurt them: they shall lay hands on the sick, and they shall recover"—was
oft-quoted by the believers in charismatic Christianity, and it was a passage
Smith had placed in Moroni's mouth in the Book of Mormon (Mormon
9:24), but the words come from the forged ending to the gospel of Mark.[3]

---

1. In *Collections of the Massachusetts Historical Society*, series 5, vol. 1 (Boston: Massachusetts Historical Society, 1878), 58.
2. JS History, vol. A-1, 126 (DHC 1:188). This entry is in the handwriting of Phelps, who evidently witnessed the encounter between Smith and Scott and may have been responsible for the wording of this passage. See Vogel, ed., *History of Joseph Smith*, 1:134.
3. Ehrman, *Misquoting Jesus*, 65–68.

In 1841 Rev. Scott recalled his conversation with "the impostor himself ... on the wharf at Cincinnati," wherein Joseph Smith gave an account of "his experience," meaning his conversion experience or his reception of saving grace. "When we heard it," Scott said, "we could not refrain from telling him in answer, that there was not an old Methodist lady in the community, who would not, if put to the proof, tell a better story."[4] Scott's response implies that Smith's account was typical and unremarkable. The following summer, Smith would reveal in a history that remained unpublished during his lifetime that as a young man he had a vision of Jesus. Prior to this time, however, he had only claimed that previous to his 1823 vision of the angel and discovery of the gold plates "it truly was manifested unto ... [him] that he had received remission of his sins."[5]

Smith and company left Cincinnati on a steamer and reached Louisville, Kentucky, on June 25, where after a three-day stopover they boarded another steamer for St. Louis. Phelps wrote that while in Louisville, they "viewed the Grand Canal round the Falls of Ohio—a magnificent display of human skill, which cost $900,000. Three superb locks of hewn stone, the largest of which, for high water, is 60 feet wide, 43 feet deep, and 300 feet long. Saw the Franklin, a boat of the largest size, mount through in a kind of 'dreadful splendor.' On the 27th, [we] left for St. Louis in the Steam-boat Don Juan."[6]

Phelps reported that the company arrived at St. Louis on July 1, remarking that it was "quite a city, with the small pox in it."[7] At this point, Rigdon, Gilbert, and Gilbert's wife decided to continue by water, while Smith and the others traveled the remaining 240 miles by foot, arriving at Independence on July 14, followed by Rigdon and company a week later.[8] Phelps wrote: "I passed through patches of timber, and fields of prairies till I arrived at Independence, 12 miles from the west line of the United States, containing the last, or outside post-office."[9] Smith said that the 900-mile trip had been "a long and tedious journey," during which he had suffered "many privations and hardships."[10] Nevertheless, according to Smith's history, his meeting with

---

4. [Walter Scott], "Mormon Bible—No. III," *Evangelist*, Mar. 1, 1841, [1].

5. Articles and Covenants, ca. Apr. 1830 [D&C 20:5], as published in "The Mormon Creed," *Painesville (OH) Telegraph*, Apr. 19, 1831, [4] (*JSP*, D1:121).

6. [William W. Phelps], "Extract of a Letter from the Late Editor," *Ontario Phoenix* (Canandaigua, NY), Sep. 7, 1831, [2].

7. Phelps, [2].

8. JS History, vol. A-1, 126 (DHC 1:188). See also discussion in *JSP*, D2:3, 6.

9. [Phelps], "Extract of a Letter from the Late Editor," *Ontario Phoenix*, Sep. 7, 1831, [2].

10. Joseph Smith, Letter to "the Elders of the Church of Latter Day Saints," Oct. 2, 1835, *LDS Messenger and Advocate*, Sep. 1835, 179 (*JSP*, D5:7–8).

Oliver Cowdery, Frederick G. Williams, and Ziba Peterson, "who had long waited our arrival, was a glorious one and moistened with many tears."[11]

Smith soon became acquainted with the small village of Independence, later described by Ezra Booth as containing only "two or three merchant stores, and fifteen or twenty dwelling houses, built mostly of logs hewed on both sides."[12] Charles Latrobe, who traveled through Independence with famed writer Washington Irving in 1832, described the village as "full of promise" but containing "nothing but a ragged congeries of five or six rough log huts, two or three clapboard houses, two or three so-called hotels, alias grogshops; [and] a few stores."[13] In March 1834 John K. Townsend estimated that there were about fifty houses in Independence, which "are very much scattered, composed of logs and clay, and are low and inconvenient," and that there were "six to eight stores here, two taverns, and a few tipling houses."[14] The village was situated on gently rolling bluffs on the southern side of the Missouri River. At the center of the village was a public square, which at the time of Smith's visit hosted a two-story brick courthouse in the final stages of construction.[15] Early traveler Josiah Gregg described Independence as well situated on the Missouri River to serve as "a point of convenient access" to the prairies and "port of embarkation" for "Santa Fé caravans, most Rocky Mountain traders and trappers, as well as emigrants to Oregon," making the town "a place of much bustle and active business."[16]

The arrival of Smith's company probably aroused the suspicions of the county's inhabitants, many of whom had migrated there from southern states, whereas Smith and his company (as well as the Colesville branch who were about to arrive) were from the Northeast, with different accents, manners, and especially attitudes about slavery. As Phelps explained in a July 1831 letter, Jackson County residents were "emigrants from Tennessee, Kentucky, Virginia, and the Carolinas, &c., with customs, manners, modes of living and a climate entirely different from the northerners."[17]

In addition to the cultural differences, the inhabitants of Jackson County tended to be rough, unruly, and occasionally violent. Three years earlier, a

---

11. JS History, vol. A-1, 127 (DHC 1:189).

12. Ezra Booth, Letter to Ira Eddy, Nov. 14, 1831, "Mormonism—No VI," *Ohio Star*, Nov. 17, 1831, [3].

13. Latrobe, *The Rambler in North America*, 104.

14. Townsend, *Narrative of a Journey*, 22.

15. Parkin, "The Courthouse Mentioned in the Revelation on Zion."

16. Gregg, *Commerce of the Prairies*, 1:33–34.

17. [Phelps], "Extract of a Letter from the Late Editor," *Ontario Phoenix*, Sep. 7, 1831, [2].

missionary from the American Home Missionary Society assigned to Jackson County, described it as "a godless place, filled with so many profane swearers ... [who] make a mild profession of Christian religion, but it is mere words, not manifested in Christian living." This missionary reported the prevalence of public drunkenness, gambling, fighting, and prostitution. Of the "few so-called ministers of the Gospel" he encountered, he wrote that "they are a sad lot of churchmen, untrained, uncouth, given to imbibing spirituous liquors, and indulging, as participants, in the gambling which accompanies horseracing, and cock fighting." The village had little need for a church building, because "Christian Sabbath observance here appears to be unknown. It is a day for merchandising, jollity, drinking, gambling, and general anti-Christian conduct."[18]

Smith's history describes the cultural shock he experienced on his arrival at Independence: "But our reflections were great: coming as we had from a highly cultivated state of society in the east, and standing now upon the confines or western limits of the united states, and looking into the vast wilderness of those that sat in darkness, how natural it was to observe the degradation, leanness of intellect, ferocity and jealousy of a people that were nearly a century behind the times."[19]

Indian Territory

On Sunday morning, July 17, despite not being able to obtain a permit to preach to the Indians, Smith, accompanied by Cowdery, Phelps, Martin Harris, Joseph Coe, Ziba Peterson, and Joshua Lewis, a convert from Jackson County, crossed over the western boundary line into Indian Territory. According to Phelps, the men "united their hearts in prayer, in a private place, to inquire of the Lord who should preach the first sermon to the remnants of the Lamanites and Nephites, and the people of that Section, that should assemble that day, in the Indian Country, to hear the gospel and the revelations according to the Book of Mormon."[20] As a result, Smith dictated

---

18. American Home Missionary Society, Correspondence, Amistad Research Center, Tulane University, New Orleans, quoted in Lyon, "Independence, Missouri, and the Mormons," 16.

19. JS History, vol. A-1, 127 (DHC 1:189). This part of the history was written in the handwriting of Phelps, no doubt with Smith's oversight. See Vogel, ed., *History of Joseph Smith*, 1:lxxi.

20. There are two copies of the revelation, both in the handwriting of Phelps and apparently written about the same time in 1861. One is a draft of the revelation written on scrap paper that once served as a draft for a letter. The text bears the marks of editing and includes the same introductory and concluding explanatory statements as the second copy. At the end of the revelation's text is written "Reported by W. W. P.," instead of "transcribed by" or "copied by." The second copy is a letter from Phelps to Young, Aug. 12, 1861. Both are in the same folder in Revelations Collection.

a revelation that was not recorded at the time that assigned Phelps to deliver the sermon and called Peterson and Coe to bear testimony. In an 1861 letter to Brigham Young, Phelps recorded what he said was the 573-word revelation, evidently from memory.[21] Phelps's transcription contained the following curious passage:

> Verily I say unto you that the wisdom of man in his fallen state, knoweth not the purposes and the privileges of my holy priesthood. but ye shall know when ye receive a fulness by reason of the anointing: For it is my will, that in time, ye should take unto you wives of the Lamanites and Nephites, that their posterity may become white, delightsome and Just, for even now their females are more virtuous than the gentiles.

Phelps interpreted this passage as an early reference to polygamy, explaining to Young: "About three years after this was given, I asked brother Joseph privately, how 'we,' that were mentioned in the revelation could take wives from the 'natives'—as we were all married men? He replied instantly 'In th[e] same manner that Abraham took Hagar and Katurah; and Jacob took Rachel Bilhah and Zilpah: by revelation—the saints of the Lord are always directed by revelation.'" Phelps makes it clear that at the time the revelation was supposed to have been dictated, it was not interpreted as a reference to polygamy. Rather, according to Phelps, it was an interpretation applied by Smith near the time of his own first plural marriage (to Fanny Alger). Smith's subsequent interpretation, however, is likely responsible for the anachronistic wording of the passage. Indeed, Phelps reflects later understandings of polygamy when he links marriages to Indian women with one of "the privileges of my holy priesthood" and the future reception of "a fulness by reason of the anointing."[22]

---

21. Phelps's transcription of the revelation contains several significant anachronisms. The first paragraph alludes to the loss of Zion in 1833 as "a trial of your faith," and that "the zion of God shall be built up in the last days, when it is redeemed." Writing four months after the beginning of the Civil War, Phelps was influenced by Joseph Smith's December 25, 1832, prophecy on war (D&C 87; see also *JSP*, D2:328–31). Phelps's text declares: "Even so shall rebellion follow after speedily, with hatred for war until the consumption decreed hath made a full end of all the kingdoms and nations" (cf. D&C 87:1, 6). Another passage makes several allusions to the 1832 revelation: "The day of *vexation* and vengeance is nigh at the doors of this nation, when wicked, ungodly and daring men will *rise up* in wrath and might, and go forth in *anger*, … and they will be the means of the destruction of the government, and cause the *death and misery of man[y] souls*, but the faithful among my people shall be preserved in *holy places*, during all these tribulations" (cf. D&C 87:1, 4, 5, 8; emphasis added).

22. See D&C 132:41, where sealing in marriage is called "the holy anointing," and D&C 131:2, where the "new and everlasting covenant of marriage" is referred to as an "order of the priesthood."

The changing of the Natives' skin color through intermarriage also reflects later thinking. The Book of Mormon predicted the Lamanites would become "white and delightsome" by the power of God, not through interracial marriage, and there is no other instance where Smith expressed such an idea.[23] On the other hand, Brigham Young and other church leaders following Smith's death in 1844 did encourage Mormon men to marry Indian women as a means of fulfilling the Book of Mormon's prediction.[24]

At the time of the revelation, therefore, it was probably interpreted as a general directive to form a matrimonial alliance with Indigenous people as a means of circumventing the Indian agents, and not as an endorsement of polygamy. As Ezra Booth reported, "It has been made known by revelation, that it will be pleasing to the Lord, should they form a matrimonial alliance with the Natives; and by this means the Elders, who comply with the thing so pleasing to the Lord, and for which the Lord has promised to bless those who do it abundantly, gain a residence in the Indian territory, independent of the agent." According to Booth, Martin Harris believed he was "entirely free from his wife, and he is at pleasure to take him a wife from among the Lamanites. ... But before this contemplated marriage can be carried into effect, he must return to the State of New York and settle his business, for fear, should he return after that affair had taken place, the civil authority would apprehend him as a criminal."[25] Booth's subsequent comment about Harris makes it clear that polygamy was not intended. LDS historian David J. Whittaker correctly observes, "Ezra Booth confirms early talk about marrying Indians, but the reasons for doing so probably did not include polygamy or even changing skin color, but rather facilitating entrance into the reservation for missionary work."[26] No marriages between the Mormons and Natives are known to have occurred at this time.

---

23. The Book of Mormon predicts the latter-day conversion of the Lamanites, declaring that "their scales of darkness shall begin to fall from their eyes; and many generations shall not pass away among them, save they shall be a white and delightsome people" (Book of Mormon, 1830 ed., 117 [2 Ne. 30:6]).

24. Hall, *The Abominations of Mormonism Exposed*, 58–59; Stenhouse, *The Rocky Mountain Saints*, 657–59; Hyde, *Mormonism*, 109–110.

25. Booth, Letter to Ira Eddy, Nov. 29, 1831, "Mormonism—Nos. VIII–IX," *Ohio Star*, Dec. 8, 1831, [1]. At a council meeting held on February 27, 1845, Phelps said "6 or 8. went over the boundaries of the U.S. to preach—Jos. went to prayer—he then commenced a revelation that Martin was to marry among the Laminites—& that I was to preach that day—&c &c it was a long revelation." "Council Meeting Minutes," Jan. 10–Mar. 24, 1845, 5, CHL, quoted in Hales, *Joseph Smith's Polygamy*, 1:86.

26. See Whittaker, "Mormons and Native Americans," 35; and Van Wagoner, *Mormon Polygamy*, 12–13.

Smith's history reports that "brother W W Phelps preached to a western audience, over the boundary of the United States, wherein were present specimens of 'all the families of the earth:' for there were several of the Indians, quite a respectable number of Negroes; and the balance was made up of citizens of the surrounding country, and fully represented themselves as pioneers of the west. At this meeting, two were baptized, who had previously believed in the fulness of the gospel."[27]

Locating the City of Zion

Three days later, Smith dictated a revelation designating Independence as the site for the city of Zion and the location for the construction of a temple. In this revelation, the Lord declared: "Missorie ... is the Land which I, have appointed & consecrated for the gethering of the Saints. Wherefore, this is the land of promise & the place for the City of Zion. ... Behold the place which is now called Independence is the centre place, & the spot for the Temple is lying westward upon a lot which is not far from the court-house."[28] Booth wrote that the temple spot was "one half of a mile out of the Town" on "a rise of ground, a short distance south of the road."[29]

According to Smith's history, the revelation came while he was pondering the deplorable state of the Indians on the other side of the border.[30] In another account, Smith said, "After viewing the country, seeking diligently at the hand of God, he manifested himself unto me, and designated to me and others, the very spot upon which he designed to commence the work of the gathering, and the upbuilding of an 'Holy City,' which should be called Zion."[31] Apparently, Smith's inspection was necessary before he could receive a revelation identifying the location of Zion and its temple.

Smith had to be careful. His charismatic authority was already in jeopardy since his original plan of building the city of Zion "among the Lamanites" had proved unworkable. A September 1830 revelation had commanded Cowdery to "go unto the Lamanites & Preach my Gospel unto them & cause my Church to be established among them," and also that "no man

---

27. JS History, vol. A-1, 129 (DHC 1:190–91). This passage was composed and edited by Phelps. See Vogel, *History of Joseph Smith*, 1:lxxi, 136.

28. Revelation, July 20, 1831, Revelation Book 1, 93 [D&C 57:1–3] (*JSP*, D2:7–8). This revelation was not included in the Book of Commandments in 1833 but was first published in the 1835 Doctrine and Covenants.

29. Booth, Letter to Eddy, Nov. 14, 1831, "Mormonism—No. VI," *Ohio Star*, Nov. 17, 1831, [3].

30. JS History, Book A-1, 127 (DHC 1:189).

31. Joseph Smith, Letter to "the Elders of the Church of Latter Day Saints," Oct. 2, 1835, *LDS Messenger and Advocate*, Sep. 1835, 179 (*JSP*, D5:8).

knoweth where the City shall be built But ... I say unto you that it shall be among the Lamanites."[32] Since neither of these things happened, this passage was later emended in 1833 and 1835. The first part was emended in 1835 to read: "You shall go unto the Lamanites and preach my gospel unto them; and *inasmuch as they receive thy teachings, thou shalt* cause my church to be established among them." And the second part was changed in the manuscript revelation book by Rigdon before being printed in the 1833 Book of Commandments to read: "No man knoweth where the city shall be built, but ... I say unto you, that it shall be *on the borders by the* Lamanites."[33] Smith's change did not escape Booth, who shortly afterward observed: "As a City and a Temple must be built, as every avenue leading to the Indians was closed against the Mormonites, it was thought that they should be built among the Gentiles, which is in direct opposition to the original plan."[34]

Smith's confidence prevented him from appreciating the possibility of failure. The only thing that lay ahead was planning and building—turning his utopian vision into reality. As Smith's history explained, with the identification of Independence as the "centre place" of the latter-day Zion, "'the land of Zion' was now the most important temporal object in view."[35] Once Smith designated the exact location of Zion by revelation, he forever linked that spot of ground with prophecy and the legitimacy of his mission. If something went wrong, it was no longer a simple matter of choosing another spot. Revelation had endowed the spot with cosmic significance; letting go of that vision would not be easy. Ironically, Smith's prophetic gifts gave him no warning of what his people were about to endure at the hands of their Jackson County neighbors.

The revelation also directed that "the land should be purchased by the saints & also every tract lying westward even unto the line runing directly betwen Jew & gentile," meaning between the Indians and the white settlers. "And also every tract bordering by the Prairies in as much as my Deciples are enabled to buy lands Behold this is wisdom that they may obtain it for an everlasting inheritance."[36] The commandment to purchase additional tracts along the border was apparently intended to facilitate preaching to the Indians. By the end of the year Bishop Partridge will purchase a 63.27-acre

32. Revelation, Sep. 1830-B, Revelation Book 1, 41 [D&C 28:8, 9] (*JSP*, D1:185–86).

33. Revelation, 41 [D&C 28:9] (*JSP*, MRB:53); Cf. BC XXX:9.

34. Booth, Letter to Eddy, Nov. 29, 1831, "Mormonism—Nos. VII–IX," *Ohio Star*, Dec. 8, 1831, [1].

35. JS History, vol. A-1, 146 (DHC 1:207).

36. Revelation, July 20, 1831, Revelation Book 1, 93 [D&C 57:4–5] (*JSP*, D2:8–10).

parcel of land from Jones H. Flournoy, a prominent business owner, for $130.00, which included the spot of land designated for the temple.[37]

The revelation commanded Sidney Gilbert, who had accompanied Smith to Missouri, to settle in Independence and assist Partridge with the church's temporal affairs by keeping a store and acting as a land agent. Partridge was commanded to "stand in the office which I have appointed him to divide unto the saints their inheritance even as I have commanded & also them whom he has appointed to assist him."[38]

This revelation suggested a scheme for proselytizing the Natives, instructing Gilbert to apply for a license to trade or "send goods also unto the Lamanites ... and thus the gospel may be preached unto them."[39] Booth wrote about the scheme four months later: "Another method has been invented, in order to remove obstacles which hitherto have proved insurmountable. 'The Lord's store-house,' is to be furnished with goods suited to the Indian trade, and persons are to obtain license from the government to dispose of them to the Indians in their own territory; at the same time, they are to disseminate the principles of Mormonism among them. From this smug[g]ling method of preaching to the Indians, they anticipate a favorable result."[40]

When this plan failed, the wording of the revelation was later changed to conceal that fact, instructing Gilbert to "send goods also unto the *people*" instead of the "Lamanites" and replacing "and thus the gospel may be preached unto them" with "and thus *provide for my saints, that my* gospel may be preached unto *those who sit in darkness and in the region and shadow of death*."[41] For obvious reasons, this revelation was not published in the 1833 Book of Commandments in accordance with a note in the handwriting of John Whitmer in the manuscript revelation book: "Not be printed at present."[42]

Phelps, who had come to Independence with Smith to join Cowdery in the printing business, was again told: "Let my servant William also be

---

37. Richard P. Howard, "The Spot for the Temple," *Saints' Herald*, June 1987, 9–10; Romig, *Early Independence, Missouri*, 15–18; and Addams, "The History and Acquisition of the Original Temple Lot," 39–44.

38. Revelation, July 20, 1831, Revelation Book 1, 93 [D&C 57:6–8] (*JSP*, D2:11).

39. Revelation, 94 [D&C 57:9] (*JSP*, D2:11).

40. Booth, Letter to Ira Eddy, Dec. 6, 1831, "Mormonism—Nos. VIII–IX," *Ohio Star,* Dec. 8, 1831, [3].

41. Doctrine and Covenants, 1835 ed., XXVII:4 [D&C 57:10]. The change was made in the handwriting of W. W. Phelps in Revelation Book 1, 94 (*JSP*, MRB:161); emphasis added.

42. Revelation, July 20, 1831, Revelation Book 1, 93 (*JSP*, MRB:159).

planted in this place & be established as a Printer unto the Church."[43] In addition to typesetting the revelations for the Book of Commandments, Phelps began editing *The Evening and the Morning Star* in June 1832, which was "devoted to the great concerns of eternal things and the gathering of the saints."[44] Instead of serving the interests of the broader community, Phelps proclaimed the Mormon gospel and reported various calamities as harbingers of the nearness of Christ's Second Advent, alienating and angering non-Mormons.[45]

Arrival of the Colesville Branch

The Colesville branch—recently evicted by Leman Copley from their temporary settlement in Thompson, Ohio—arrived in Jackson County on July 26, 1831. Within days the group of about sixty men, women, and children settled twelve miles west of Independence in Kaw Township, which bordered the Indian Territory.[46]

Some of those arriving in Jackson County were disappointed at the situation they found. Booth said that he and the other elders "expected to find a large Church, which Smith said, was revealed to him in a vision, Oliver had raised up there."[47] Instead, they found a congregation consisting of no more than seven individuals.[48] According to Booth, some elders concluded that "*prophecy* and *vision* had failed, or rather had proved false.—The fact was so notorious, and the evidence so clear, that no one could mistake it—so much so, that Mr. Rigdon himself said, that 'Joseph's *vision* was a bad thing.' This was glossed over, apparently, to the satisfaction of most persons present; but not fully to my own."[49]

Responding to this disappointment, Smith on August 1 dictated a revelation that Eber D. Howe, editor of the *Painesville Telegraph*, described "as a specimen of the manner in which the Prophet governs and rebukes

---

43. Revelation, 94 [D&C 57:11] (*JSP*, D2:11). See Revelation, June 14, 1831 [D&C 55:4] (*JSP*, D1:339).

44. "To Man," *The Evening and the Morning Star*, June 1832, [6].

45. Romig and Siebert, "First Impressions," 58–59.

46. Knight, Autobiography and Journal, 30–31; Parley P. Pratt et al., "'The Mormons' So Called," *The Evening and the Morning Star* (Kirtland, OH), Extra, Feb. 1834, [1]–[2]; see also Porter, "Colesville Branch in Kaw Township," 286–87.

47. Booth, Letter to Ira Eddy, Nov. 7, 1831, "Mormonism—No. V," *Ohio Star*, Nov. 10, 1831, [3]. In 1834 Smith confirmed that his trip to Missouri had been preceded by a "heavenly vision," but he said very little about its content. Joseph Smith, "To the Elders of the Church of Latter Day Saints," (Oct. 2, 1835), *LDS Messenger and Advocate*, Sep. 1835, 179 (*JSP*, D5:7).

48. Peter Whitmer, Jr., Journal, [1] (Dec. 1831).

49. Booth, Letter to Ira Eddy, Sep. 12, 1831, "Mormonism—No. I," *Ohio Star*, Oct. 13, 1831, [3].

his dupes."[50] After preliminary remarks to the elders about enduring tribulations, the revelation rebuked Partridge: "I have Sent you hither & have
Selected my Servent Edward & appointed him his mission in this land but
if he repent not of his sins which is unbelief & blindness of heart let him
take heed lest he fall."[51] It was apparent to the other elders that Partridge's
faith in Smith was faltering. A few days after this revelation was dictated,
Partridge wrote a letter to his wife, Lydia, expressing uncertainty about fulfilling his appointment as bishop "to the acceptance of my hevenly father"
and requesting her to "pray for me that I may not fall."[52]

Partridge was surprised when the revelation instructed him to remain in
Missouri as the presiding authority—"Now as I spoke concerning my Servent Edward this land is the land of his residence" and "[he] is appointed to
be a Judge in Israel like as it was in ancient days to divide the lands of the
heritage of God unto his children & to Judge his people by the testimony of
the Just & by the assistance of his councillors according to the laws of the
kingdom which are given by the Prophets of God for verily I say unto you
my laws shall be kept on this land."[53] Partridge had not anticipated that he
would be commanded to remain in Missouri, as he explained in the letter to
his wife—"When I left Painesville I told people I was coming back & bid
none a farewell but for a short time."[54]

Partridge would be responsible for enforcing church law, which, together
with his control of land through the law of consecration, placed him in a
powerful position. Those called to stand trial before him and his counselors
not only risked their memberships but were also subject to being evicted
from their homes and banished from the community.

One passage of the revelation attempted to defend Smith's charismatic
authority and claim to revelation, responding to questions about unfulfilled
promises and last-minute changes in the assignment of missionary companions. The revelation declared: "Who am I saith the Lord that have promised
& have not fulfilled[?] I command & a man obeys not[.] I revoke & they
receive not the blessing[.] then they say in their hearts this is not the work
of the Lord for his promises are not fulfilled but wo unto such for their
reward lurketh beneath & not from above."[55] This passage hints at some

---

50. Howe, *Mormonism Unvailed*, 221.
51. Revelation, Aug. 1, 1831, Revelation Book 1, 95 [D&C 58:14–15] (*JSP*, D2:15).
52. Edward Partridge, Letter to Lydia Partridge, Aug. 5–7, 1831, [2].
53. Revelation, Aug. 1, 1831, Revelation Book 1, 95–96 [D&C 58:24, 16–19] (*JSP*, D2:15).
54. Edward Partridge to Lydia Partridge, Aug. 5–7, 1831, [2].
55. Revelation, Aug. 1, 1831, Revelation Book 1, 96 [D&C 58:31–33] (*JSP*, D2:17).

rumblings of discontent that will soon erupt into open criticism and challenge of Smith's leadership.

Smith was anxious to break ground on his Zion project, but first he needed to acquire the ground. So he tapped a reliable source, Martin Harris. "It is wisdom in me," the revelation declared, "that my servent Martin should be an example unto the church in laying his money before the bishop of the Church."[56] Harris's son, Martin Jr., claimed in 1875 that his father gave $1,200 to Partridge to purchase land in Missouri, but it is uncertain where the money would have come from.[57] Harris may have served as an example, but consecrating one's money and property was mandatory. As the revelation directed, "This is a law unto every man that cometh unto the Land to receive an inheritance and he shall do with his moneys according as the law directs." Besides the obvious purchase of the temple lot, the revelation directed Partridge to purchase "lands ... in Independence for the place of the storehouse & also for the house of the Printing."[58] The next week, Partridge purchased a lot in Independence for the printing office for $50, and six months later purchased another lot containing the old courthouse for $371 for the bishop's storehouse.[59]

Because Sidney Gilbert was now permanently stationed in Missouri, the revelation directed that a new agent be appointed "by the voice of the Church" in Kirtland.[60] Shortly after returning to Ohio, Smith dictated a revelation naming Newel K. Whitney as the new agent.[61]

The revelation commanded Rigdon to do several things. First, he was to "write a discription of the Land of Zion & a statement of the will of God as it shall be made known by the spirit unto him." Smith's official history recounts that "we sought for all the information necessary" to compose "a description of the land of Zion."[62] However, the description that Rigdon composed was rejected, and he was forced to submit a second draft.[63] Next,

56. Revelation, 96 [D&C 58:35] (*JSP*, D2:17).

57. Obituary for Martin Harris, *Ogden Junction* (Utah Territory), July 16, 1875, [2]. See discussion in *JSP*, D2:17n81.

58. Revelation, Aug. 1, 1831, Revelation Book 1, 96 [D&C 58:36–37] (*JSP*, D2:17).

59. Jackson Co., MO, Deed Records, 1827–1909, vol. A, 114–15, Aug. 8, 1831; vol. B, 32–33, Feb. 20, 1832, microfilm 1,017,978, U.S. and Canada Record Collection, FHL.

60. Revelation, Aug. 1, 1831, Revelation Book 1, 97 [D&C 58:49] (*JSP*, D2:19). Doctrine and Covenants, 1835 ed., 139 [XVIII:10], added the phrase "unto the church in Ohio, to receive moneys to purchase lands in Zion" for clarification.

61. Revelation, Aug. 30, 1831, [2], Newel K. Whitney Papers [D&C 63:42–45] (*JSP*, D2:52–53).

62. JS History, vol. A-1, 137 (DHC 1:197).

63. Revelation, Aug. 30, 1831, [2], Newel K. Whitney Papers [D&C 63:55–56]; Rigdon, Letter to "the Saints," Aug. 31, 1831.

he was assigned to write "an Epistle & subscription to be presented unto all the Churches to obtain money to be put into the hands of the Bishop to purchase lands ... or the agent ... even to purchase this whole region of country as soon as time will permit." Finally, he was told to "consecrate & dedicate this land & the spot of the temple unto the Lord," which will be fulfilled in the next two days.[64]

Smith and Rigdon were also commanded to hold "a conference meeting," after which they were to return to Ohio, taking Cowdery with them. Once in Ohio, they are to finish "the residue of the work which I have appointed unto them," meaning the revision of the Bible.[65]

The revelation rebuked Ziba Peterson, who had traveled to Missouri with Cowdery and the others—"Let that which has been bestowed upon Ziba be taken from him & let him stand as a member in the Church & labour with his own hands with the brethren untill he is sufficiently chastened for all his sins for he confeseth them not & he thinketh to hide them."[66] Church records do not indicate why Peterson lost his standing in the church, but Booth learned that it was similar to Cowdery's transgression, about which church records are equally silent. Booth wrote that Whitmer and Frederick G. Williams had "divulged a secret respecting Oliver, which placed his conduct on a parallel with Ziba's." That conduct occurred in late 1830 while Cowdery and his missionary companions were in Ohio on their way to Missouri and consisted of his courting a woman there while being engaged to seventeen-year-old Elizabeth Ann Whitmer in New York. According to Booth, Cowdery "enters into a matrimonial contract with a young lady [Whitmer], and obtains the consent of her parents; but as soon as his back is turned upon her, he violates his engagements, and prostitutes his honor by becoming the gallant of another, and resolved in his heart, and expresses resolutions to marry her."[67]

Peterson confessed his "transgressions" at the August 4 conference, which was accepted by "unanimous vote."[68] A week later he married Rebecca Hopper of Lafayette County, Missouri.[69] Cowdery would not be censured by

---

64. Revelation, Aug. 1, 1831, Revelation Book 1, 97 [D&C 58:50–52, 57] (*JSP*, D2:19–20).

65. Revelation, 98 [D&C 58:58] (*JSP*, D2:21).

66. Revelation, 97 [D&C 58:60] (*JSP*, D2:19).

67. Booth, Letter to Ira Eddy, Nov. 21, 1831, "Mormonism—No. VII," *Ohio Star*, Nov. 24, 1831, [1].

68. Minutes, Aug. 4, 1831, Minute Book 2, 5 (*JSP*, D2:23).

69. Lafayette Co., MO, Marriage Records, 1821–73, vol. B, 21, microfilm, 959,414, U.S. and Canada Record Collection, FHL.

church leaders for "transgression ... in the fall of 1830 in the Township of Mayfield Cuyahoga County State of Ohio" until May 26, 1832, and on the following December 18 he finally married Whitmer.[70] However, in 1831 Booth remarked about what seemed like Cowdery's preferential treatment—"Ziba was deprived of his Elder and Apostleship ... while Oliver the scribe, also an Apostle [elder], who had been guilty of similar conduct, is set on high, to prepare work for the press; and no commandment touches him, only to exalt him higher." According to Booth, Whitmer and Williams told him that "had they known previous to their journey to Missouri, what they then knew, they never should have accompanied Oliver thither."[71] When finally a church council addressed Cowdery's behavior, it excused the delay in dealing with Cowdery by explaining that "some of the Elders supposed that the affair had been adjusted last year when brother Oliver made his confession to the individuals injured & received their forgiveness."[72]

An offhanded remark near the close of the revelation was seized on by some of the faithful as a confirmation of Smith's gift—"Let the residue of the Elders of this Church which are coming to this land some of whom are exceedingly blessed even above measure also hold a conference."[73] When some of the missionaries arrived and reported they had baptized people on their way to Missouri, the baptisms were interpreted as the blessing mentioned in the revelation. Levi Hancock, one of the elders who had recently arrived in Missouri, reported that Sister Elizabeth Gilbert showed him a copy of this revelation and said: "That means you brother Levi, Zebedee [Coltrin], Simeon [Carter], and Solomon [Humphrey]! Joseph gave this when you were seven hundred miles away." Prior to this, "she said some were tried when these words came and their faith almost failed them because they had heard that nothing was done many had appostatized." However, "as soon as the news had come that Solomon and Simeon had baptized between twenty and thirty it revived their drooping Spirits and as soon as they heard that zebedee and Levi had baptized upwards of a hundred; Sidney Rigdon gave

70. Minutes, May 26, 1832, Minute Book 2, 27 (Cannon and Cook, *Far West Record*, 49); Oliver Cowdery and Elizabeth Ann Whitmer, Kaw Township, Jackson Co., MO, Dec. 18, 1832, Jackson Co., MO, Marriage Record, 1827–60, vol. 1, 20, Naturalization and Court Records, 1800–1991, Missouri State Archives, Jefferson City, microfilm 7,425,094, U.S. and Canada Record Collection, FHL.

71. Booth, Letter to Ira Eddy, Nov. 21, 1831, "Mormonism—No. VII," *Ohio Star*, Nov. 24, 1831, [1]. Apostleship is used here, not as a church office, but as a function of the office of elder, as explained in the Article and Covenants (D&C 20:38). See also *JSP*, D2:22.

72. Minutes, May 26, 1832, Minute Book 2, 27 (Cannon and Cook, *Far West Record*, 49).

73. Revelation, Aug. 1, 1831, Revelation Book 1, 98 [D&C 58:61] (*JSP*, D2:21).

glory to the God of Heaven and said I did not know what those revelations meant before."[74] The account provides another glimpse into troubles Smith was encountering with some of his followers in Missouri and how Smith's charisma was bolstered by carefully choosing among and subjectively interpreting his inspired utterances.

The closing words of this revelation instructed the elders to "return [to Ohio] preaching by the way," for "the sound must go forth from this place into all the world & unto the uttermost parts of the Earth the gospel must be preached unto every creature with signs following them that believe & behold the son of man cometh."[75] Regarding these words, Booth reported that Rigdon declared: "The Lord has set us our *stint*; no matter how soon we perform it—for when this is done, he will make his second appearance."[76] The promise of Jesus's return depended on how fast the elders could perform their missions, and their missions were not only to make converts but to funnel them into Smith's Zion—a program that would no doubt increase Smith's political power.

On August 2 Smith assisted the Colesville branch in laying the first log of the first house in Kaw Township.[77] They settled on an 80-acre tract of land purchased by Partridge.[78] Booth said that the laying of the log "was attended with considerable parade, and an ostentatious display of talents, both by Rigdon and Cowdery." As the revelation of the previous day instructed, "Rigdon consecrated the ground, by an address in the first place to the God whom the Mormonites profess to worship; and then making some remarks respecting the extraordinary purpose for which we were assembled, prepared the way for administering the oath of allegiance, to those who, were then to receive their 'everlasting inheritance' in that City. He laid them under the most solemn obligations, to constantly obey all the commandments of Smith."[79] Whitmer similarly reported that Rigdon asked the Saints, "Do you pledge yourselves to keep the laws of God on this land, which you have never have kept in your own land?" After the

---

74. Hancock, "Autobiography of Levi Ward Hancock," 40–41.

75. Revelation, Aug. 1, 1831, Revelation Book 1, 98 [D&C 58:64] (*JSP*, D2:21).

76. Booth, Letter to Ira Eddy, Sep. 12, 1831, "Mormonism—No. I," *Ohio Star*, Oct. 13, 1831, [3]; emphasis in original.

77. JS History, vol. A-1, 138 (DHC 1:196).

78. Jackson Co., MO, Land and Property Records, 1832–57, "Record of Original Entries to Lands in Jackson County Missouri," Dec. 20, 1898, Township 49 North, Range 33 West, [16], microfilm, 1,019,781, U.S. and Canada Record Collection, FHL; Berrett, *Sacred Places*, 4:110n12.

79. Booth, Letter to Ira Eddy, Nov. 14, 1831, "Mormonism—No. VI," *Ohio Star*, Nov. 17, 1831, [3].

congregation said, "We do," Rigdon knelt in prayer and then arose to pronounce the land "consecrated and dedicated to the Lord for a possession and inheritance for the Saints."[80]

Twelve men including Smith, representing the twelve tribes, carried a log and laid it in place. Cowdery carried a large stone to the spot, removed some of the earth, and placed the stone in the small depression as a cornerstone. Cowdery afterward "displayed his oratorical power, in delivering an address, suited to the important occasion."[81]

Dedicating the Temple Lot

On August 3, 1831, eight elders and a few others gathered on a wooded lot located about a half-mile west of the village of Independence to dedicate the ground for the construction of the New Jerusalem temple.[82] Smith may have previously gained access to the property from Jones H. Flournoy, who had obtained squatter's rights to large tracts of land in the area with a view of selling them.[83] The meeting began by reading Psalm 87, which among other things declares: "The Lord loveth the gates of Zion more than all the dwellings of Jacob."

Whitmer later recorded Cowdery's report that Rigdon "dedicated the ground where the city is to Stand: and Joseph Smith Jr. laid a stone at the North east corner of the contemplated Temple in the name of the Lord Jesus of Nazareth." Rigdon then "pronounced this Spot of ground wholly dedicated unto the Lord forever."[84] Phelps stated in 1864 that the stone was laid "at the southeast corner of the ten acres for the first temple."[85] According to Booth, the spot was also marked by "means of a sappling, distinguished from others by the bark being taken off on the north and on the east side.— On the south side of the sappling will be found the letter, T, which stands for Temple; and on the east side ZOM for Zomar; which Smith says is the original word for Zion. Near the foot of the sappling, they will find a small

---

80. Whitmer, History, 31–32 (*JSP*, H2:44–45).

81. Booth, Letter to Ira Eddy, Nov. 14, 1831, "Mormonism—No. VI," *Ohio Star*, Nov. 17, 1831, [3].

82. The dedication of the temple lot is best described in Addams, "The History and Acquisition of the Original Temple Lot," 33–38. Orson Pratt described the lot as "a wilderness, with large trees." Pratt, "Exhortation from Isaiah," Salt Lake City, Oct. 26, 1879, *Journal of Discourses*, 24:24.

83. See discussion in Addams, 38–44.

84. Whitmer, History, 32 (*JSP*, H2:45). Cowdery's report is otherwise not extant. Smith's history incorrectly states that Smith, not Rigdon, dedicated the temple spot. JS History, vol. A-1, 139 (DHC 1:199).

85. Phelps, Reminiscence ["Short History"], 1864, [1].

stone, covered over with bushes, which were cut for that purpose. This is the corner-stone for the Temple."[86]

The next day, Smith conducted the first conference of the church in Missouri at the home of Joshua and Margaret Kelsey Lewis in Kaw Township, about eight miles west of Independence, where the Colesville branch had settled. According to the minutes, fourteen elders and about thirty-one members were present at the meeting held by a "special commandment of the Lord." During this conference, Ziba Peterson confessed and was forgiven for his inappropriate dealings with a woman whom he would later marry, although he would not be re-ordained an elder until October 1832. Smith exhorted members to perform "acts of righteousness and keeping the commandments of the Lord with [a] promise of blessings." The minutes also hint at a growing rift between Smith and Partridge when Cowdery as clerk recorded that Rigdon delivered an "Exhortation to obedience to the requisition of Heaven by delivering a charge in the name of Christ to the Bishop, Rulers & Members."[87]

Prior to the conference, according to Booth, Partridge complained about the poor quality of the land Smith and Cowdery had selected for purchase and reported that Smith became enraged and displayed "violent passions, bordering on madness." Partridge not only complained about Smith's abuse but angrily remarked, "I wish you not to tell us any more, that you know these by the spirit when you do not; you told us, that Oliver has raised up a large church here, and there is no such thing." Smith responded: "I see it, and it will be so."[88]

From subsequent sources, it appears the matter was considered resolved during this conference. In March 1832, a conference in Missouri dismissed some of the charges against Partridge, because the misbehavior had "transpired previous to a Conference held on this land at which our brs. Edward and Sidney were present face to face when confessions were made by several

---

86. Booth, Letter to Ira Eddy, Nov. 14, 1831, "Mormonism—No. VI," *Ohio Star*, Nov. 17, 1831, [3].

87. Minutes, Aug. 4, 1831, Minute Book 2, 4–5 (*JSP*, D2:22–24). The commandment to assemble in Missouri probably refers to D&C 52:2 and 57:1. On Peterson's re-ordination, see Minutes, Oct. 2, 1832, Minute Book 2, 31 (Cannon and Cook, *Far West Record*, 56).

88. Booth, Letter to Ira Eddy, Nov. 21, 1831, "Mormonism—No. VII," *Ohio Star*, Nov. 24, 1831, [1]. According to one early resident of Independence, "Nearly all the best land had been entered" at the claims office before the arrival of the Mormons in Jackson County and that "the worst portions only were entered by their bishop, Partridge, and settled upon by them." J. C. M. [John Calvin McCoy], "The Other Side: An Old Settler Gives the Gentile Version of the Mormon Troubles," *Kansas City Daily Journal*, Apr. 24, 1881.

brethren & by br. Edward in particular, to our joy and thanksgiving to our God we can truly say his spirit was there also, we cannot consider them justifiable." However, problems between Partridge and Smith persisted.

An aspect of Partridge's disagreement with Smith that most concerned the Mormon prophet was revealed when Rigdon accused Partridge of "having insulted the Lord's prophet in particular & assumed authority over him in open violation of the Laws of God."[89] Partridge took his calling from God seriously and resisted what he perceived as interference from Smith. Concerning Partridge's resistance to Smith's control, LDS historian Matthew Godfrey has observed: "If he was familiar with Alexander Campbell's definition of bishops as 'those who have the presidency or oversight of one congregation,' he may have also believed that, as bishop, it was his prerogative to administer the Church in Missouri as he thought best."[90] Historian Kenneth Winn has similarly remarked: "Partridge apparently held a highly decentralized view of church authority, giving the Missouri church virtually complete authority over its own affairs. … While Smith thought Partridge disrespectful of his prophetic authority, Partridge was concerned about creeping authoritarianism."[91] This view was held by other leaders in the Missouri church as well, and it would become the source of continuing conflict. On August 7 Partridge wrote to his wife, expressing trepidation concerning his calling: "You know I stand in an important station & as I am accasionally chastised I sometimes feel as though I must fall, not to give up the cause, but I fear my station is above what I can perform to the acceptance of my hevenly Father."[92]

Smith cut his stay in Missouri short, deciding not to await the arrival of all the elders to hold another conference as he had planned.[93] On August 6 Partridge reported to his wife: "Last thursday we had a conference & a number are to start back immediately when the rest arrive here we are to hold another conference."[94] Even during the conference preparations were being

89. Minutes, Mar. 10, 1832, Minute Book 2, 22 (Cannon and Cook, *Far West Record*, 40–41).

90. Godfrey, "'Seeking after Monarchal Power and Authority,'" 20. On Alexander Campbell's view of the bishop's duties, see "Extracts of Letters," *Christian Baptist*, June 2, 1828, 452; "A Restoration of the Ancient Order of Things. No. XXXII. Official Names and Titles," *Christian Observer*, Sep. 7, 1829, 585–86.

91. Winn, "'Such Republicanism as This,'" 50.

92. Partridge, Letter to Lydia Partridge, Aug. 5–7, 1831, [2].

93. Several elders appointed to travel to Missouri, including Hyrum Smith, John Murdock, David Whitmer, and Harvey Whitlock, had not yet arrived. Revelation, June 6, 1831, Revelation Book 1, 87–89 [D&C 52] (*JSP*, D1:327–32).

94. Partridge, Letter to Lydia Partridge, Aug. 5–7, 1831, [2].

made for Smith's departure. In a November 1831 letter, Booth reported: "We expected to assemble together in conference according to commandment, and the Lord would signally display his power, for the confirmation of our faith; but we commenced our journey home, before most of the Elders arrived. It is true, a conference was held, but it was considered so unimportant, that myself and another man were permitted to be absent, for the purpose of procuring the means of conveyance down the river."[95]

On the morning of August 7, Polly Knight, the fifty-seven-year-old wife of Joseph Knight Sr. from Colesville, died in the home where the conference had been held. Later the same day, Smith dictated a revelation that declared: "Behold blessed saith the Lord are they who have come up unto this land with an eye single to my glory according to my Commandments for them that live shall inherit the earth and them that die shall rest from all their labours & their works shall follow them they shall receive a crown in the mansions of my Father which I have prepared for them." The revelation was also about Sabbath observance: "And that thou mayest more fully keep thyself unspotted from the world thou shalt go to the house of prayer & offer up thy sacraments upon my holy day for verily this is a day appointed unto you to rest from your labours & to pay thy devotions unto the most high."[96] Three years earlier a Christian missionary reported that Sabbath observance in Jackson County was "unknown" and instead of going to church the inhabitants engaged in "merchandising, jollity, drinking, gambling, and general anti-Christian conduct."[97] Strict Sabbath observance would therefore be a distinguishing feature of the growing Mormon community in Jackson County.

On Monday, August 8, Smith and Rigdon attended Polly Knight's funeral.[98] Later the same day, Smith dictated another revelation instructing "some of the Elders" who had traveled to Missouri to return to Ohio, preaching along the way.[99] "Finding but little or no business for us to accomplish," Booth wrote, "most of us became anxious to return home."[100] According to

---

95. Booth, Letter to Ira Eddy, Nov. 7, 1831, "Mormonism—No. V," *Ohio Star*, Nov. 10, 1831, [3].

96. Revelation, Aug. 7, 1831, [1], Newel K. Whitney Papers [D&C 59:1–2, 9–10] (*JSP*, D2:32–33).

97. American Home Missionary Society, Correspondence, Amistad Research Center, Tulane University, New Orleans, quoted in Lyon, "Independence, Missouri, and the Mormons," 16.

98. Knight, Reminiscences, 11, dates her death to August 7 and her funeral to the 8th. Partridge's letter to his wife also dates her death to the morning of the 7th. Partridge, Letter to Lydia Partridge, Aug. 5–7, 1831, [2]. JS History, vol. A-1, 139 (DHC 1:199), dates the funeral to August 7.

99. Revelation, Aug. 8, 1831, Revelation Book 1, 100–101 [D&C 60] (*JSP*, D2:35–37).

100. Ezra Booth, Letter to Ira Eddy, Nov. 14, 1831, "Mormonism—No. VI," *Ohio Star*, Nov. 17, 1831, [3].

Smith's history, the elders inquired of their prophet "what they were to do," and in response he dictated a short revelation.[101] Among other things, the Lord rebuked some of the elders "for they will not open their mouths but hide the tallent which I have given unto them because of the fear of man."[102] Booth later confirmed: "For more than two weeks, while I remained there [in Missouri], the disposition of the Elders appeared to be averse to preaching."[103]

Regarding Smith's departure, the revelation commanded: "Let there be a craft made or bout [boat] as seemeth you good it mattereth not unto me & take your Journey speedily for the place which is called St. Lewis. & from thence let my Servent Sidney & Joseph & Oliver take their Journey for Cincinnati & in this place let them lift up their voice & declare my word with loud voices. … Let the residue take their Journey from St. Lowis two by two & preach the word not in haste among the congregations of the wicked untill they return to the churches from whence they came."[104]

The revelation also instructed Partridge to use church funds to aid some of the elders in their return to Ohio, for which Partridge was later called to account. One of the charges investigated by the March 1832 conference involved Partridge's "handing over money to brs. Joseph Oliver & Sidney for their expense to Ohio." To which Partridge responded that "he had no disposition to defraud or deceive his brethren in that case … [and] he now asks their forgiveness as well as the forgiveness of the Lord."[105]

Finally, the revelation instructed missionaries to "shake off the dust of thy feet against those who receive thee not[.] not in their presence lest thou provoke them but in secret & wash thy feet as a testimony against them in the day of Judgement."[106] The same instruction had been given in a July 1830 revelation, and although based on Jesus's instruction to his disciples in the New Testament, it is not known if others of Smith's contemporaries practiced this form of cursing their enemies (Matt. 10:14; Mark 6:11; Luke 10:10–11).[107] While traveling in Upper Canada in July 1835, Brigham Young and William E. McLellin asked a tavern keeper to feed them

---

101. JS History, vol. A-1, 141 (DHC 1:201).

102. Revelation, Aug. 8, 1831, Revelation Book 1, 100 [D&C 60:2] (*JSP*, D2:36).

103. Booth, Letter to Ira Eddy, Nov. 7, 1831, "Mormonism—No. V," *Ohio Star*, Nov. 10, 1831, [3].

104. Revelation, Aug. 8, 1831, Revelation Book 1, 100 [D&C 60:5–6, 8] (*JSP*, D2:36–37).

105. Revelation, 100 [D&C 60:10–11] (*JSP*, D2:36); Minutes, Mar. 10, 1832, Minute Book 2, 22 (Cannon and Cook, *Far West Record*, 41).

106. Revelation, Aug. 8, 1831, Revelation Book 1, 100 [D&C 60:15] (*JSP*, D2:37).

107. See Revelation, July 1830-A, Revelation Book 1, 33 [D&C 24:15] (*JSP*, D1:159).

breakfast as they were preachers traveling without purse or scrip. The man refused and called them impostors. Young later recorded in his journal: "We left him and went on our way we washed our feet in testamoney aganest him."[108] On another occasion following rejection from a Methodist minister, Young recorded that he and his missionary companion "shook the dust of[f] our feet as a testamony aganst them and when wee cam to Pure watter we whashed our feet and bore witness unto the Father."[109] While foot washing has fallen into disuse today, its practice among early missionaries shows both how closely they adhered to biblical precedent and how seriously they took their callings.[110]

On the same day that he was told to defray the traveling expenses of the departing elders, Partridge paid $50 to purchase a lot in Independence from James Gray for the printing office.[111] On the following day, Tuesday, August 9, Smith and ten elders, including Rigdon, Cowdery, and Whitmer, left Independence on canoes headed down the Missouri River toward St. Louis. The first day they traveled about forty miles, stopping for the night at Fort Osage.[112]

The next morning, shortly after the group had set out in their canoes, according to Booth, a "spirit of animosity and discord" was manifested wherein Cowdery became displeased with the reckless conduct of some of the elders and uttered a dire warning: "As the Lord God liveth, if you do not behave better, some accident will befall you." Cowdery's indignation was not appreciated but "increased the irritation of the crew," Booth remembered.[113] Cowdery may have felt some validation when on the third day of the trip the canoe in which Smith and Rigdon were riding hit debris in the river and nearly capsized. Shaken, Smith ordered the group to exit the river. The eleven men set up camp on the banks of the Missouri River at McIlwaine's Bend, about a hundred miles downstream from Independence, which no longer exists because the river has changed its course.[114] Not long after,

---

108. Brigham Young, Journal, July 4, 1835.

109. Young, June 1, 1836.

110. Belnap, "'Those Who Receive You Not.'"

111. Jackson Co., MO, Deed Records, 1827–1909, vol. A, 114–15, Aug. 8, 1831, microfilm 1,017,978, U.S. and Canada Record Collection, FHL.

112. Smith History, vol. A-1, 142, 146 (DHC 1:202–203).

113. Booth, Letter to Ira Eddy, Nov. 21, 1831, "Mormonism—No. VII," *Ohio Star*, Nov. 24, 1831, [1].

114. Berrett, *Sacred Places*, 4:138–39. According to Reynolds Cahoon, the group had traveled a hundred miles before leaving the river. Cahoon, Diary, Aug. 9, 1831, [10].

Phelps announced that he had a vision of "the Destroyer in his most horrible power" riding on the river.[115]

During the evening, Booth recalled, some of the elders accused Smith and Cowdery of being "highly imperious and quite dictatorial," and reprimanded Smith and Rigdon for their "extensive cowardice." When Smith began to chastise them in his customary prophetic manner, someone retorted, "None of your threats," which caused Smith to stop short. Booth said he had drifted off to sleep only to be awoken at a "late hour" to observe "a reconciliation between the parties."[116]

On the following day, August 12, Smith explained why he was going to St. Louis by land contrary to the instructions given in his previous revelation. Instead of traveling on the river to "Journey speedily for the place which is called St. Lewis," Smith dictated a new revelation that instructed: "It is not needfull for this whole company of mine Elders to be moveing swiftly upon the waters whilst the Inhabitants on either sides are perishing in unbelief nevertheless I suffered it that ye might bear record."[117] Playing on Phelps's vision, the revelation declared: "I the Lord hath decreed & the destroyer rideth upon the face thereof & I revoke not the decree."[118] The Lord may not have revoked the decree concerning "the destroyer," but he did revoke the command to travel by river: "Now concerning my servents Sidney Joseph & Oliver let them come not again upon the waters save it be upon the canal while Journeying unto their homes."[119] Smith may have feared canoeing in the rough and treacherous currents of the Missouri River—which he referred to as the "river of Destruction"—but he was more comfortable with using the canal system in Ohio and gave himself permission to do so.[120]

To continue their journey by land would require additional money since

---

115. JS History, vol. A-1, 142 (DHC 1:203). Neither Booth nor Reynolds Cahoon mentioned Phelps's vision in their contemporary accounts of the journey. The information about the vision likely came from Phelps, who helped prepare this section of Smith's history. See Booth, Letter to Ira Eddy, Nov. 21, 1831, "Mormonism—No. VII," *Ohio Star*, Nov. 24, 1831, [1]; Cahoon, Diary, Aug. 9, 1831; see also Vogel, *History of Joseph Smith*, 1:lxxi, 144.

116. Booth, Letter to Ira Eddy, Nov. 21, 1831, "Mormonism—No. VII," *Ohio Star*, Nov. 24, 1831, [1].

117. Revelation, Aug. 8, 1831, Revelation Book 1, 100 [D&C 60:5] (*JSP*, D2:36); Revelation, Aug. 12, 1831, Revelation Book 1, 101 [D&C 61:3–4] (*JSP*, D2:40).

118. Revelation, Aug. 12, 1831, Revelation Book 1, 102 [D&C 61:19] (*JSP*, D2:41).

119. Revelation, 102 [D&C 61:23] (*JSP*, D2:41).

120. Ezra Booth mentioned the naming of the river in Booth, Letter to Ira Eddy, Nov. 21, 1831, "Mormonism—No. VII," *Ohio Star*, Nov. 24, 1831, [1]. The heading of the revelation in John Whitmer's handwriting locates its reception "on the Banks of the River Destruction (or Missorie)." Revelation Book 1, 101 [D&C 61] (*JSP*, D2:39).

Smith, Rigdon, and Cowdery insisted on traveling by stage. When the others objected, according to Booth, Rigdon retorted: "The Lord don't care how much money it takes to get us home." Booth recalled that the money they had received from Partridge was insufficient, so the three leaders pressured the others to hand over their money, telling them, "You can beg your passage on foot, but as we are to travel in the stage, we must have money."[121] They may have had a legitimate need for a speedy return to Kirtland, which Booth neglected to mention.

Smith, Rigdon, and Cowdery traveled about forty miles eastward to Chariton and crossed to the north side of the river, where they met two pairs of missionaries on their way from Kirtland to Independence: Hyrum Smith and John Murdock, who were accompanied by David Whitmer (John's older brother) and Harvey Whitlock. At this time, Smith dictated an encouraging revelation instructing those elders to continue to Zion, to hold a meeting there, and then return to their homes. When the Mormons in Jackson County saw a copy of this revelation, it apparently "tried" their faith because it seemed to imply the missionaries had been "blessed" with converts while preaching on their way to Missouri, which seemed to contradict what they were hearing from the missionaries themselves. Elizabeth Gilbert, wife of Algernon Sidney Gilbert, told Levi Hancock, "Their faith almost failed them because they had heard that nothing was done" and "many had apostatized." Later that fall, other missionaries arrived at Independence with news that they had baptized over a hundred people, which "revived" the Saints' "drooping Spirits."[122]

From Chariton, Smith traveled eastward to Fayette, where he, Rigdon, and Cowdery took the stage to St. Louis. At St. Louis, they "overtook" Phelps and Sidney Gilbert, and then continued by stage to Cincinnati.[123] Booth later discovered that the three men ran out of funds when they reached Cincinnati and were "under the necessity of pawning their trunk, in order to continue their journey home." They quickly left the city without preaching, which Booth found troubling. Upon further inquiry concerning the matter, he was disappointed to hear them explain that "the Lord made it known to them, that they should go on." From this, Booth concluded: "They

---

121. Booth, Letter to Ira Eddy, Nov. 21, 1831, "Mormonism—No. VII," *Ohio Star*, Nov. 24, 1831, [1].

122. Hancock, "Autobiography of Levi Ward Hancock," ca. 1896, 40–41; see also Smith and Smith, *History of the Reorganized Church*, 1:195.

123. JS History, vol. A-1, 146 (DHC 1:206). Reynolds Cahoon mentions that Smith, Rigdon, and Cowdery took the stage at Fayette. Cahoon, Diary, [11].

can at any time obtain a commandment suited to their desires, and as their desires fluctuate and become reversed, they get a new one to supercede the other, and hence the contradictions which abound in this species of revelation." Booth further reported that after Smith, Rigdon, and Cowdery had left the group, he and three others ignored Smith's revelation and continued canoeing down the river without incident, which Booth concluded proved that the "great dangers" existed only in Smith's "imagination."[124]

124. Booth, Letter to Ira Eddy, Nov. 21, 1831, "Mormonism—No. VII," *Ohio Star*, Nov. 24, 1831, [1].

6

Move to Hiram

AUGUST–OCTOBER 1831

*He was only twenty-five years of age and was not, at that time,
what would be called a fluent speaker.*
—LeRoi C. Snow, *"How Lorenzo Snow Found
God,"* Improvement Era, *Feb. 1937, 82*

Upon his return to Kirtland on Saturday, August 27, 1831, Joseph Smith discovered that "in the absence of the Elders many [had] apostitized," requiring them to give "much exortation" to the congregations in and around the Kirtland.[1] "We could not help beholding," Smith's history recounts, "the exertions of Satan to blind the eyes of the people so as to hide the true light that lights every man that comes into the world."[2] In an October 1831 conference in Orange, Cuyahoga County, Ohio, Simeon Carter said that he "Mourned because of the falling away" that had transpired "since he took his journey to the Land of Zion."[3] Consequently, Smith would participate in several disciplinary councils in early September 1831.[4] Eventually the elders succeeded in bringing many back into the fold, aided by the performance of faith healings. John Whitmer, for example, mentioned that "many mighty miracles were wrought by the Elders," and described the healing by three Kirtland elders of an old woman who had been bedridden for eight years because of an "infirmity."[5]

Oliver Cowdery's return to Kirtland was no doubt accompanied by celebration since many of those in the Kirtland area owed their conversions to him. On the day following Smith's arrival, a meeting was held at which

---

1. JS History, vol. A-1, 146 (DHC 1:206); Whitmer, History, 33 (*JSP*, H2:45).
2. JS History, vol. A-1, 146 (DHC 1:206).
3. Minutes, Oct. 25–26, 1831, Minute Book 2, 12 (*JSP*, D2:83).
4. See Minutes, Sep. 1, 6, 12, 1831, Minute Book 2, 5–6 (*JSP*, D2:56–61, 67–68).
5. Whitmer, History, 33 (*JSP*, H2:45–46).

Cowdery was ordained to the high priesthood by Sidney Rigdon. The record of the ordination, by John Whitmer, states that Cowdery was ordained "by the voice of the Church & command of the Lord."[6] Cowdery, who was in Missouri during the June 1831 conference, was singled out for immediate elevation for the leadership role he was about to assume.

Two days after he had returned to his family residing on the Isaac Morley farm, Smith dictated a revelation about the gathering of believers to Missouri, the purchase of land, and preparing for Christ's coming.[7] As Rigdon wrote the next day, the revelation told the faithful how to "escape … the day of tribulation which is coming on the earth" by building the Missouri Zion.[8] However, it began by alluding to the troubled state of affairs in which Smith found the church. Thus the Lord warned: "There are those among you who seeketh signs … But behold faith cometh not by signs but signs follow those that believe. … God is angry … wherefore unto such he sheweth no signs only in wrath unto their condemnation." Apparently referring to some of Smith's followers who had not been properly divorced from their first spouse, or perhaps practicing a form of polygamy, the revelation further warned: "There were among you adulterers & adulteresses some of whom have turned away from you & others remain with you that hereafter shall be revealed let such be aware & repent speedily lest judgements shall come upon them as a snare & their folly shall be made manifest."[9]

Concerning the gathering to Zion, the revelation instructed that the Saints to do so "not in haste lest there should be confusion which bringeth pestilence." They were further commanded to "purchase the lands that you may have advantage of the world that you may have claim on the world that they may not be stired up unto anger for satan putteth it into their hearts to anger & to the shedding of blood." In other words, do not simply squat on the land and claim God has given it to you but obtain legal title to it. The revelation labored to persuade members that purchasing the land and avoiding conflict with non-Mormons was the best course of action. "Wherefore the land of Zion shall not be obtained but by purchase or by blood otherwise

---

6. Minutes, Aug. 28, 1831, Minute Book 2, 5 (Cannon and Cook, *Far West Record*, 10).

7. Revelation, Aug. 30, 1831, Newel K. Whitney Papers [D&C 63] (*JSP*, D2:48–55). A reference in this revelation to "this farm" (D&C 63:38) indicated that Joseph Smith dictated it on the Isaac Morley farm, where he had left his family in June. Backman, *Heavens Resound,* 70; Staker, *Hearken, O Ye People,* 309–310.

8. Rigdon, Letter to "the Saints," Aug. 31, 1831, [2].

9. Revelation, Aug. 30, 1831, [1], Newel K. Whitney Papers [D&C 63: 8–9, 11, 14–15] (*JSP*, D2:50).

there is none inheritance for you." There are only two ways to obtain the land: legally or by force: "If by purchased behold you are blessed & if by blood as ye are forbidden to shed blood lo your enemies are upon you & ye shall be scourged from city to city & from Synagogue to synagogue & but few shall stand to receive an inheritance."[10] Smith was trying to temper some of the militancy and zeal he saw in his followers.

The revelation directed Titus Billings to sell the Morley farm and prepare to move to Missouri in the spring.[11] Billings had been given power of attorney over the farm before his brother-in-law Isaac Morley left for Missouri in June 1831 and finalized the sale of approximately eighty acres of Morley's farm in October.[12] The revelation further directed that "all the moneys which can be spared (it mattereth not unto me whether it be little or much) sent up unto the land of Zion unto them whom I have appointed to receive."[13]

A revelation dictated in early August indicated that migration to Missouri would proceed in an orderly fashion and that conferences of elders would regulate who moved to Zion.[14] This revelation declared: "Behold I the Lord will give unto my servant Joseph power that he shall be enabled to descern by the spirit those who shall go up unto the land of Zion & those of my Desiples that shall tarry."[15] On the following day, Smith dictated another short revelation "by the voice of the Spirit" directing that John Burk, David Elliott, and Erastus Babbitt "Journey this fall to the land of Zion."[16]

The revelation told Newel K. Whitney to "retain his store ... for a little season nevertheless let him impart all the money which he can impart to be sent up unto the land of Zion." Whitney was also called to serve as the church's agent in Ohio to replace Sidney Gilbert who had moved to Missouri.[17] Two days later at a conference in Kirtland, Whitney was ordained by Cowdery as an "agent unto the Disciples" in Ohio with the responsibility, along with Cowdery, of collecting money to send to Missouri.[18] The

10. Revelation, [1] [D&C 63:24, 27–31] (*JSP*, D2:51).

11. Revelation, [2] [D&C 63:38–39] (*JSP*, D2:52).

12. Geauga Co., OH, Deed Records, vol. 14, 583–84; vol. 15, 492–94. See also Minutes, Oct. 25–26, 1831, Minute Book 2, 10–15 (*JSP*, D2:78–87); and Partridge, Letter to Lydia Partridge, Aug. 5–7, 1831.

13. Revelation, Aug. 30, 1831, [2], Newel K. Whitney Papers [D&C 63:40] (*JSP*, D2:52).

14. Revelation, Aug. 1, 1831, Revelation Book 1, 97 [D&C 58:44] (*JSP*, D2:20).

15. Revelation, Aug. 30, 1831, [2], Newel K. Whitney Papers [D&C 63:41] (*JSP*, D2:52).

16. Revelation, Aug. 31, 1831, Jameson Family Collection, 1825–1938, CHL [uncanonized] (*JSP*, D2:55–56).

17. Revelation, Aug. 30, 1831, [2], Newel K. Whitney Papers [D&C 63:42–46] (*JSP*, D2:53).

18. Minutes, Sep. 1, 1831, Minute Book 2, 5 (*JSP*, D2:56–59).

revelation directed Whitney to "speedily ... visit the churches expounding these things unto them with my servant Oliver ... obtaining moneys even as I have directed. ... He that sendeth up treasures unto the land of Zion shall receive an inheritance in this world."[19] On the same day, Rigdon wrote an epistle introducing Whitney and Cowdery and exhorting members to donate the "means for purchasing this land of our inheritance that we may escape in the day of tribulation which is coming on the earth."[20] Whitmer later recorded that "the disciples truly opened their hearts" and purses to Cowdery and Whitney "for the purpose of buying lands for the Saints according to commandments."[21]

The revelation singled out Rigdon for rebuke: "I the Lord am not pleased with my servant Sidney he exaulted himself in his heart & received not counsel but grieved the spirit Wherefore his writing is not acceptable unto the Lord & he shall make another & if the Lord receive it not behold he standeth no longer in the office which he hath appointed him."[22] According to Booth, Rigdon had overstated the quality of the land in his first description of Zion, which an early August 1831 revelation had commanded him to write.[23] He composed a second draft immediately, which was accepted and taken with Cowdery and Whitney on their tour of the churches.[24]

Since this revelation instructed Morley to sell his farm, it closed by telling Smith and Rigdon to seek another home.[25] Within two weeks the two men will move their families to the Johnson farm located about twenty-five miles southeast of Kirtland in Hiram. Before leaving, Smith participated in disciplinary councils on September 1, 6, and 12, wherein several elders and priests were silenced, including Ezra Booth, who had grown increasingly critical of Smith. After arriving in Ohio on September 1, Booth said he "had several interviews with Messrs. Smith, Rigdon, and Cowdery," wherein he became dismayed at the "various shifts and turns, to which they resorted in order to obviate objections and difficulties, [which] produced in my mind additional evidence, that there was nothing else than a deeply laid plan of craft and

---

19. Revelation, Aug. 30, 1831, [2], Newel K. Whitney Papers [D&C 63:46] (*JSP*, D2:53).

20. Whitmer, History, 37 (*JSP*, H2:48).

21. Whitmer, History, 36–37 (*JSP*, H2:48–49).

22. Revelation, Aug. 30, 1831, [2], Newel K. Whitney Papers [D&C 63:55–56] (*JSP*, D2:54).

23. Ezra Booth, Letter to Ira Eddy, Nov. 21, 1831, "Mormonism—No. VII," *Ohio Star* (Ravenna, OH), Nov. 24, 1831, [1]; Revelation, Aug. 1, 1831, Revelation Book 1, 97 [D&C 58:50] (*JSP*, D2:19).

24. Rigdon, Letter to "the Saints," Aug. 31, 1831; see also Whitmer, History, 33–37 (*JSP*, H2:46–49).

25. Revelation, Aug. 30, 1831, [3], Newel K. Whitney Papers [D&C 63:65] (*JSP*, D2:55).

deception."[26] Booth's last interview may have occurred on September 6 at his home in Nelson, which was also located in Portage County, a few miles east from Hiram. On this day a conference of elders, which included Smith, Rigdon, and Cowdery, met in Nelson, possibly at the home of Charles Hulet, to silence Booth "from preaching."[27] There is no record of any further action being taken against Booth, but in his September 20, 1831, letter to Partridge, he said that he was "no longer a member of the Mormonite Church."[28]

In the face of severe criticism and apostasy, on Sunday, September 11, Smith dictated a revelation concerning the law of forgiveness, specifically Smith's. The revelation began by announcing that the Lord would be lenient: "There are those among you who have sinned but verily I say for this once for mine own glory & for the salvation of Souls I have forgiven you your sins." It assured the church that Smith was still their leader: "I will be mercyfull unto you for I have given unto you the Kingdom & the keys of the mysteries of the kingdom shall not be taken from my Servent Joseph while he liveth in-as-much as he obeyeth mine ordinances." Concerning Smith's critics, the revelation declared: "There are those who have sought occasion against him without a cause nevertheless he hath sinned but verily I say unto you I the Lord forgiveth sins unto those who confess their sins before me & ask forgiveness who have not sinned unto death. ... For he that forgiveth not his brother his tresspasses standeth condemned before the Lord for there remaineth in him the greater sin I the Lord will forgive whom I will forgive but of you it is required to forgive all men & ye had ought to say in your hearts let God Judge between me & thee."[29]

The revelation also singled out Ezra Booth and Isaac Morley, who had traveled to Missouri together, because "they kept not the Law neither the commandment they sought evil in their hearts & I the Lord withheld my spirit they condemned for evil that thing in which there was no evil."[30] It is not known in what way Booth and Morley had violated God's law, but Smith was likely the object of their condemnation and they were possibly among those alluded to in the revelation who had "sought occation against him without

26. Booth, Letter to Ira Eddy, Sep. 12, 1831, "Mormonism—No. I," *Ohio Star*, Oct. 13, 1831, [3].

27. Minutes, Sep. 6, 1831, Minute Book 2, 6 (*JSP*, D2:59–61). Other meetings were held at the home of Charles Hulet. Dibble, Reminiscences, [6].

28. Booth, Letter to Ira Eddy, Nov. 12, 1831, "Mormonism—No. VII," *Ohio Star*, Nov. 24, 1831, [1].

29. Revelation, Sep. 11, 1831, Revelation Book 1, 109 [D&C 64:3, 5–7, 9–11] (*JSP*, D2:63–64).

30. Revelation, 109 [D&C 64:15–16] (*JSP*, D2:64).

a cause." Both men were in the party with Smith that had just returned to Kirtland, and it may be that the revelation alludes to Booth's account of some unnamed men criticizing Smith for "extensive cowardice" for refusing to travel in the canoe and taking the stage to St. Louis.[31] The revelation turned to Partridge, who during Smith's visit to Missouri had disagreed with the Mormon prophet, eliciting a rebuke from Smith and invective from Rigdon. The revelation declared that Partridge was forgiven but that "Satan Seeketh to destroy his soul."[32] Indeed, Smith's problems with Partridge were far from over.

The revelation repeated the directive given in the August 30 revelation to sell Morley's farm.[33] Joseph and Emma Smith, who had been living on Morley's farm since April 1831, had already made plans to move to the home of John and Elsa Johnson in Hiram, which occurred on the following day. Concerning Frederick G. Williams's farm, where Smith's parents were living, the revelation directed that it not be sold and then made a significant statement in justification: "For I the Lord willeth to retain a strong hold in the Land of Kirtland for the space of five years in the which I will not overthrow the wicked that thereby I may save some."[34] To some of Smith's followers, this may have seemed like a delay in the gathering to Zion, but after the expulsion of the Mormons from Jackson County in the summer of 1833, the date September 11, 1836 (exactly five years from the date of this revelation), will become a prophecy for the redemption of Zion. In an August 16, 1834, letter to his exiled brethren in Missouri, Smith announced that September 11, 1836, was "the appointed time for the redemption of Zion."[35] Although it would ultimately fail, Smith did all he could to make it happen.

As Cowdery and Newel K. Whitney were about to embark on their fundraising campaign, the revelation provided some incentive to potential donors: "Verily it is a day of Sacrifice & a day for the tithing of my People for he that is tithed shall not be burned."[36] The "Laws of the Church of Christ" instructed members to consecrate their property to the church and receive back an inheritance, but money was needed to purchase the land to begin the

31. Booth, Letter to Ira Eddy, Nov. 12, 1831, "Mormonism—No. VII," *Ohio Star*, Nov. 24, 1831, [1].

32. Revelation, Sep. 11, 1831, Revelation Book 1, 109 [D&C 64:17] (*JSP*, D2:64).

33. Revelation, 110 [D&C 64:20] (*JSP*, D2:65); Revelation, Aug. 30, 1831, [2], Newel K. Whitney Papers [D&C 63:38–40] (*JSP*, D2:52).

34. Revelation, Sep. 11, 1831, Revelation Book 1, 110 [D&C 64:21] (*JSP*, D2:65).

35. Joseph Smith, Letter to Lyman Wight and Others, Aug. 16, 1834, JS Letterbook 1, 86 (*JSP*, D4:106).

36. Revelation, Sep. 11, 1831, Revelation Book 1, 110 [D&C 64:23] (*JSP*, D2:65).

process.[37] Moreover, Smith needed a way of getting funds from those who would not consecrate their property for years to come or not at all. Over a year later, Smith explained in a letter to W. W. Phelps that "it is conterary to the will and commandment of God that those who receive not the inherttenc [inheritance] by consecration agree[a]ble to his law which he has given that he may tithe his people to prepare them against the day of vengence and burning should have there names enrolled with the people of God."[38]

The revelation addressed the issue of the church's contracting debt with the world (that is, non-members), which had been forbidden in the February 1831 laws of the church.[39] According to Booth, when Smith ordered Partridge to borrow the money to purchase land in the town of Thompson for the Colesville branch to settle on, the prophet's command shook Partridge's faith.[40] This issue was no doubt revisited during this period of apostasy, for the revelation attempted to explain: "Behold it is said in my Laws or forbidden to get in debt to thine enemies but Behold it is not said at any time that the Lord should not take when he please & pay as seemeth him good." Some like Booth and Ryder regarded such an explanation as a distinction without a difference. Regardless, "the rebelious shall be cut off out of the Land of Zion & shall be sent away & shall not inherit the Land."[41]

Hiram, Ohio

On Monday, September 12, Smith attended a conference of elders in Kirtland to discipline three Ohio members: "George Miller, a Priest in the Church of Shalersville, John Woodard an Elder in the Church of Orange, and Benjamin Bragg a Priest in the Church of Warrensville."[42] Later that day, he moved his family to Hiram, located in Portage County about twenty-five miles southeast of Kirtland, to live with recent converts John and Elsa Johnson and some of their children.[43] Joseph, Emma, and the twins occupied the "back room" on the main floor.[44]

---

37. Revelation, Feb. 9, 1831, "The Laws of the Church of Christ," Revelations Collection [D&C 42:30–38] (*JSP*, D1: 251–52).

38. Joseph Smith, Letter to William W. Phelps, Nov. 27, 1832, JS Letterbook 1, 2 (*JSP*, D2:319).

39. Revelation, Feb. 9, 1831, "The Laws of the Church of Christ," [6], Revelations Collection [D&C 42]; see also Revelation Book 1, 67 (*JSP*, D1: 255).

40. Booth, Letter to Ira Eddy, Nov. 21, 1831, "Mormonism—No. VII," *Ohio Star*, Nov. 24, 1831, [1].

41. Revelation, Sep. 11, 1831, Revelation Book 1, 111 [D&C 64:27–28, 35–36] (*JSP*, D2:65–66).

42. Minutes, Sep. 12, 1831, Minute Book 2, 6 (*JSP*, D2:67–68).

43. JS History, vol. A-1, 154 (DHC 1:215).

44. Staker, *Hearken, O Ye People*, 310, 315n6.

Seventeen-year-old Lorenzo Snow, who lived near Hiram, went to hear Smith speak to a group of about 250 people under a small bowery in the Johnsons' front yard. When Snow arrived with other family members, the meeting had already started and "Joseph Smith was standing in the door of Father Johnson's house, looking into the bowery and addressing the people." As Snow recalled decades later, his impression was that Smith "was not, at that time, what would be called a fluent speaker." Rather than giving an exposition on the scriptures, "His remarks were confined principally to his own experiences, especially the visitation of the holy angel, giving a strong and powerful testimony in regard to these marvelous manifestations. He simply bore his testimony to what the Lord had manifested to him, to the dispensation of the Gospel which had been committed to him, and to the authority that he possessed." This story-telling style of preaching was personable and engaging—possibly spellbinding—but that should not be taken to mean Smith could not preach with conviction and passion. "At first he seemed a little diffident and spoke in rather a low voice," Snow recalled, "but as he proceeded he became very strong and powerful, and seemed to affect the whole audience with the feeling that he was honest and sincere. It certainly influenced me in this way and made impressions upon me that remain until the present day." As Snow listened, the rumors that a false prophet had moved into the neighborhood began to melt away. "I thought to myself," Snow said, "that a man bearing such a wonderful testimony as he did, and having such a countenance as he possessed, could hardly be a false prophet."[45]

In late September, a newspaper published in Hudson, Portage County, Ohio, reported that Booth and Symonds Ryder, another defector, "made a public renunciation of the Mormon faith" at a camp meeting held in nearby Shalersville.[46] Ryder had been converted following Smith's healing of Elsa Johnson's arm in March 1831 largely through the efforts of his friend Booth, but soon after became concerned when he read "the Law of the Church"

---

45. LeRoi C. Snow, "How Lorenzo Snow Found God," *Improvement Era* (Salt Lake City), Feb. 1937, 82–83. At this point, Snow explores the possibility that Smith was either delusional or a deliberate deceiver, stating: "When he testified that he had had a conversation with Jesus, the Son of God, and had talked with Him personally, as Moses talked with God upon Mount Sinai, and that he had also heard the voice of the Father, he was telling something that he either knew to be false or to be positively true." Some have taken this as evidence that as early as 1831 Smith claimed to have seen the Father and Son in his first vision of 1820, but it is unclear if Snow had shifted his argument to an example that clearly illustrated his point or was referring to what he remembered Smith saying on that occasion. If the latter, the preponderance of the evidence on the first vision would suggest Snow's memory had been tainted by what he later learned.

46. "Renunciation of Mormonism," *Observer and Telegraph* (Hudson, OH), Sep. 29, 1831, [3].

Smith had revealed in February 1831, particularly its demand that members consecrate their property to the church.[47] The oft-repeated story that Ryder apostatized because his name was misspelled in one of Smith's revelations is likely untrue. The story was first told at Ryder's funeral in 1870 by the Reverend Burke A. Hinsdale, Ryder's friend.[48] Ryder himself gave a different reason. While Smith was in Missouri, Ryder and other recent converts were able to read some of Smith's revelations and "become acquainted with the internal arrangement of their church, which revealed to them the horrid fact that a plot was laid to take their property from them and place it under the control of Joseph Smith the prophet."[49] Ryder published the text of the "Law of the Church" in Portage County's *Western Courier* on September 6 anonymously.[50] What made publication even more irresistible was the revelation's injunction to keep its contents secret. As Ryder explained, church leaders "were commanded not to communicate it to the world, nor even to their followers, until they become strong in the faith."[51]

Within days after being silenced, Booth began writing a series of nine letters to the Reverend Ira Eddy critical of Smith and the church. In October, these letters began appearing in the *Ohio Star*, a newspaper printed in Ravenna, Portage County, with the stated intent "to prevent the spread of a delusion."[52] Booth became the first Mormon apostate to provide the public with detailed insider information. He not only gave firsthand accounts of some major Mormon events, including the introduction of the high priesthood in June 1831 and the church's first conference in Missouri, but also the texts of some of Smith's previously unpublished revelations. Booth's letters were immediately reprinted by E. D. Howe in the *Painesville Telegraph*. Rigdon denounced Booth's letters as "an unfair and false representation of the

47. Revelation, Feb. 9, 1831, "The Laws of the Church of Christ," Revelations Collection [D&C 52:30–39] (*JSP*, D1:251–52).

48. Hinsdale, "Life and Character of Symonds Ryder," 252. See also discussion in Staker, *Hearken, O Ye People*, 294–96.

49. Symonds Rider, Letter to A. S. Hayden, Feb. 1, 1868, in Hayden, *Early History of the Disciples*, 221. Historian Mark L. Staker observes that the revelation states that the properties were to be "laid before the bishop of my church," and that "Joseph Smith was not, therefore, the designated recipient although, as one of the poor, he eventually received some assistance while living in Hiram." Staker, *Hearken, O Ye People*, 295. This objection is hardly significant since Partridge operated under Smith's direction.

50. "Secret Bye-Laws of the Mormonites," *Western Courier* (Ravenna, OH), Sep. 1, 1831, [1]; rept. "Secret Bye-Laws of the Mormonites," *Painesville (OH) Telegraph*, Sep. 13, 1831, [1].

51. "Secret Bye Laws of the Mormonites," *Western Courier*, Sep. 1, 1831, [1].

52. Booth, Letter to Ira Eddy, Sep. 12, 1831, "Mormonism—No. I," *Ohio Star*, Oct. 13, 1831, [3].

subjects on which they treat" and challenged Booth and Ryder to a public debate, which apparently never happened.[53]

Other church leaders like Rigdon, David Whitmer, and John Whitmer followed Smith and moved to Hiram. The Rigdons and their six children moved into an old cabin across the road from the Johnson home, which John Johnson had recently expanded. Newly married David and Julia Jolley Whitmer occupied another nearby cabin.[54] According to his history, Smith resumed working on his Bible revision project in the "forepart of October."[55] However, Folio 2 of New Testament Manuscript 2, which begins with Matthew 26:1, is dated September 26, 1831. John Whitmer continued serving as Smith's scribe until Rigdon assumed this responsibility probably in November when Whitmer left for Missouri.[56]

Conferences

On October 11 Smith held a conference at the Johnson farm and said he wanted the elders to stay and hold another meeting on the next day when he would give them instructions about the "ancient manner of conducting meetings as they were led by the Holy Ghost ... [because] this was not perfectly known by many of the Elders in this Church."[57] No record of the second meeting exists, but it was possibly the reappearance of spiritual excesses during his absence in Missouri that prompted Smith to give directions on the proper manner of conducting meetings.

The minutes also indicate that Cowdery proposed that six elders be assigned to "visit the several branches of this church setting them in order and also make known the situation of brs Joseph Smith Jr and Sidney Rigdon," and that David Whitmer and Reynolds Cahoon were given that assignment.[58] In his diary, Cahoon wrote that the main purpose was "to obtain money or Property for Brs Joseph & O[t]hers to finish the translation."[59]

On October 25 Smith attended a two-day general conference at Serenus Burnett's house in Orange, Cuyahoga County, Ohio, fifteen miles south of Kirtland (about halfway between Kirtland and Hiram), which was attended

53. "To the Public," *Ohio Star,* Dec. 15, 1831.

54. See Staker, *Hearken, O Ye People,* 310.

55. JS History, vol. A-1, 154 (DHC 1:215).

56. The handwriting changes from John Whitmer to Sidney Rigdon at Mark 10:1. Faulring et al., *Joseph Smith's New Translation of the Bible,* 67, 305, 334. John Whitmer and Cowdery left Kirtland for Missouri on November 20, 1831. Whitmer, History, 38; *JSP,* H2:49.

57. Minutes, Oct. 11, 1831, Minute Book 2, 8 (*JSP,* D2:75).

58. Minutes, 8–9 (*JSP,* D2:75).

59. Cahoon, Diary, Nov. 9, 1831.

by twelve high priests, seventeen elders, four priests, three teachers, four deacons, and "a large congregation."[60]

Several of the elders met Smith for the first time at this conference. William E. McLellin, a new convert from Tennessee, wrote in his journal that he "first saw brother Joseph the Seer, also brothers Oliver, John [Whitmer] & Sidney and a great many other Elders" at this conference, which provided "much spiritual edification & comfort."[61] Joel Hills Johnson, who had converted five months earlier in Amherst, Lorain County, Ohio, recalled that on this occasion "I first beheld the face of the Prophet and Seer Joseph Smith," and that "when I was introduced to him, he laid his hands upon my shoulders and says to me 'I suppose you think that I am a great green lub[b]erly fellow.'" Johnson, four years older than Smith, later remarked that Smith was, in fact, large, tall, and beardless. "I conversed very freely with him upon many subjects relative to his mission," Johnson recalled, adding that he "received much instruction and was highly edified and blessed of the Lord during the conference and returned home rejoicing."[62]

Rigdon was first to speak. "When God works all may know it," he declared, "for he makes his children one, for he by his Holy Spirit binds their hearts from Earth to Heaven." When the elders assemble, they should "assemble themselves in perfect faith and humble themselves before the Lord and their wills being swallowed up in the will of God"—that is, the will of God as communicated through Smith.[63]

Smith spoke about being "sealed in the Lamb's Book of life." He declared, "Could we all come together with one heart and one mind in perfect faith the vail might as well be rent to day as next week or any other time and if we will but cleanse ourselves and covenant before God, to serve him, it is our privilege to have an assurance that God will protect us at all times."[64] Smith's teachings increasingly focused on the necessity of moral perfectionism to achieve a state of purity or sanctification. This was not unusual, but Smith coupled this teaching with Millenarianism as well as the promise of seeing God in mortality.[65] A January 2, 1831, revelation dictated in New

---

60. Minutes, Oct. 25–26, 1831, Minute Book 2, 10–15 (*JSP*, D2:78–87); JS History, vol. A-1, 156 (DHC 1:219). This is the first extant record to list a deacon's presence at a meeting.

61. McLellin, Journal, Oct. 25–26, 1831 (Shipps and Welch, *Journals of William E. McLellin*, 44–45).

62. Johnson, Autobiographical Sketch and Journal, 16.

63. Minutes, Oct. 25–26, 1831, Minute Book 2, 11 (*JSP*, D2:81).

64. Minutes, 11.

65. See Harrell, *"This Is My Doctrine,"* 328–30.

York declared: "The day soon cometh that ye shall see me & know that I am for the ... vail of darkness shall soon be rent & he that is not purified shall not abide the day."[66]

The introduction of the high priesthood in June 1831 included the concept of entering into God's presence. As explained in Alma 13, those who were "ordained unto the High Priesthood of the holy order of God, [were] to teach his commandments unto the children of men, that they also might enter into his rest." Moreover, those who entered this "holy order ... were sanctified, and ... after being sanctified by the Holy Ghost, having their garments made white, being pure and spotless before God, could not look upon sin save it were with abhorrence; and there were many, exceeding great many, which were made pure, and entered into the rest of the Lord their God."[67] Smith will continue to hold this promise out to his followers: perfect obedience to the law of God as revealed through him as the way to achieve purification and sanctification in God's presence, both individually and as a people. This incentive motivated Smith's followers to participate in his mission to establish Zion in Missouri—where the Saints will dwell in peace with their God.

This theme was reemphasized by Rigdon, who declared: "I bear testimony that God will have a pure people who will give up all for Christ's sake and when this is done they will be sealed up unto eternal life." Smith followed, explaining that "the order of the High priesthood is that they have power given them to seal up the Saints unto eternal life," and that "it was the privilege of every Elder present to be ordained to the High priesthood." Smith and Rigdon had a profound effect on those in attendance, for many in the congregation "bore their testimonies and made commitments to consecrate their all to the Lord."[68]

Hyrum Smith said that "he thought best that the information of the coming forth of the book of Mormon be related by Joseph himself to the Elders present that all might know for themselves." Joseph, aware that critics were informing the public about his involvement in folk magic and money digging, responded that "it was not intended to tell the world all the particulars of the coming forth of the book of Mormon, & also said that it was not expedient for him to relate these things &c."[69]

---

66. Revelation, Jan. 2, 1831, Revelation Book 1, 50 [D&C 38:8] (*JSP*, D1:231).

67. Book of Mormon, 1830 ed., 259–60 [Alma 13:6, 11–12].

68. Minutes, Oct. 25–26, 1831, Minute Book 2, 11 (*JSP*, D2:81–82).

69. Minutes, 13 (*JSP*, D2:84).

As early as September 1829, more than a year before Cowdery and the other missionaries appeared in northern Ohio, Eber D. Howe reprinted an article from the *Palmyra Freeman* that was based on information from Martin Harris claiming that in the "fall of 1827," Smith had been "visited in a dream by the spirit of the Almighty, and informed that in a certain hill in that town, was deposited this Golden Bible," that he discovered with the plates "a huge pair of Spectacles," and that he translated the record "by placing the Spectacles in a hat, and looking into it."[70] Howe also reprinted articles from the *Palmyra Reflector*, published by Abner Cole, a justice of the peace who was familiar with Smith's early association with a company of money-diggers in the Palmyra area. He described in detail the money diggers' use of peep stones and folk magic to procure buried treasures from their guardian spirits and linked Smith's involvement in these activities with his discovery of gold plates and subsequent production of the Book of Mormon.[71] On March 22, 1831, Howe published a letter from unidentified persons in Palmyra confirming the veracity of Cole's reporting, stating among other things: "Smith and his father belonged to a gang of money-diggers, who had followed that business for many years, Jo pretending he could see the gold and silver by the aid of what they called a '*peep stone*.'"[72]

This situation may have prompted Hyrum's request, but Joseph knew that giving an account of the discovery of the gold plates in the presence of his father, two brothers, the three witnesses, and five of the eight witnesses would only tend to confirm what critics were saying. Still, in the coming years Smith will attempt to supply the public with a version of his story that was more acceptable to mainstream Christians, while at the same time accusing his critics of lying.

In closing, Smith told the congregation that "he intended to do his duty before the Lord and hoped that the brethren would be patient as they had a considerable distance," referring to the difficulty of managing affairs in Kirtland from Hiram. Regarding his work on his Bible revision, he said that "the promise of God was that the greatest blessings which God had to bestow should be given to those who contributed to the support of his family while

---

70. *Painesville Telegraph*, Sep. 22, 1829; *Palmyra (NY) Freeman*, Aug. 11, 1829, [2]; also reprinted in *Advertiser and Telegraph* (Rochester, NY), Aug. 31, 1829 (*EMD*, 2:221–22); and *Niagara (NY) Courier*, Aug. 27, 1829.

71. See *Palmyra (NY) Reflector*, June 1, 12, July 7, 1830, Jan. 6, Feb. 1, 14, 28, 1831 (*EMD*, 2:230–48). See also *Palmyra Reflector*, Feb. 14, 1831, and Feb. 28, 1831; reprinted in *Painesville Telegraph*, Feb. 22, 1831; and Mar. 8, 1831.

72. *Painesville Telegraph*, Feb. 22, 1831 (*EMD*, 3:8–10).

translating the fulness of the Scriptures … and except the church recieve the fulness of the Scriptures that they would yet fall."[73]

In the evening session, Orson Hyde, Simeon Carter, Emer Harris, and Hyrum Smith were appointed to aid David Whitmer and Reynolds Cahoon "to visit the Churches and obtain means for the support of br. Joseph Smith jr. & those appointed to assist him in writing & copying the fulness of the Scriptures," and if they failed to do so, "they would yet fall."[74] The February 1831 revelation concerning the Lord's law mentioned that the Bible revision was "for thy Salvation," and instructed that it not be spoken of until finished.[75] Concerning Smith's Bible revision, Ezra Booth wrote in October 1831 that "it was intended to have kept this work a profound secret, and strict commandments were given for that purpose; and even the salvation of the church was said to depend upon it."[76] According to a letter of recommendation Emer Harris received from Cowdery, these men were appointed "to go two by two to visit the churches, set them in order, explain the mysteries of the Kingdom unto them, and also obtain whatever they should feel free to give for the support of the families of Bro. Joseph and his scribes, while they are employed in translating, writing and copying the fulness of the Sacred Scriptures."[77]

Rigdon then said it was "the privilege of those Elders present to be ordained to the High Priesthood, telling them that if they then should doubt God would withdraw his Spirit from them."[78] Evidently some elders were having trouble accepting the existence of the high priesthood in a New Testament church. The minutes name fifteen men who were ordained to the high priesthood by Cowdery, including David Whitmer and William E. McLellin, both of whom subsequently questioned the propriety of their ordinations.[79] Nearly four decades later, McLellin recalled that Smith "asked if we were willing to take upon us the office? I arose and said that I was willing to do anything that was the will of God, but I did not understand the duties of the office, and

---

73. Minutes, Oct. 25–26, 1831, Minute Book 2, 13 (*JSP*, D2:84–85).

74. Minutes, 14 (*JSP*, D2:85).

75. Revelation, Feb. 9, 1831, [4], Revelations Collection [D&C 42:56–57] (*JSP*, D1:254).

76. Booth, Letter to Ira Eddy, Oct. 2, 1831, in "Mormonism—No. II," *Ohio Star*, Oct. 20, 1831, [3].

77. Letter of Recommendation for Emer Harris, in Historical Department, Journal History of the Church, Oct. 26, 1831.

78. Letter of Recommendation.

79. Whitmer, *An Address to All Believers in Christ*, 35, 49, 64–65; [William E. McLellin], "Our Tour West in 1847," *Ensign of Liberty*, Aug. 1849, 104; see also Larson and Passey, *William E. McLellin Papers*, 388, 397, 441.

asked an explanation. Br. Joseph said we were to take upon us the office, and it would explain its duties."[80] Contemporaneously, McLellin recorded that he had been "ordained to the High-Priesthood of the Holy order of God," and "though I felt unworthy, I was ordained and took upon me the high responsibility of that office."[81] In later years, McLellin argued that Jesus was the only high priest of the gospel dispensation and that the office is not mentioned in the New Testament portion of the Book of Mormon or the original version of the "Articles and Covenants of the Church of Christ."[82]

Cowdery also ordained one priest as an elder and thirteen others as priests. McLellin noted at the time that "a number of others present were ordained to the lesser Priest-Hood."[83] The term "lesser priesthood" was used to distinguish other priesthood holders from the "high priesthood," hence elders were included in the bottom tier until a September 1832 revelation clarified that the office of elder was an appendage of the high priesthood.[84]

On the following day, Rigdon rebuked some of the elders "who were ordained to the High priesthood last evening, saying that the Lord was not well pleased with some of them because of their indifference to be ordained to that office." He then explained "the power of that office." The record then lists five men who said they were willing to "receive the rebuke in meekness," including Orson Hyde and Frederick G. Williams.[85] Whitmer and McLellin were not included in the list.

The reasons are not clear, but Smith and Rigdon were receiving some resistance to their introduction of the high priesthood. It may have been for the reasons McLellin later outlined, or it may have been because he believed that the manifestation of satanic power at the June conference was a sign of God's displeasure, or both. Concerning the introduction of the high priesthood, John Corrill later remarked that "some doubting took place among the elders, and considerable conversation was held on the subject. The elders not fairly understanding the nature of the endowments, it took some time to reconcile all their feelings."[86]

---

80. William E. McLellin, Letter to D. H. Bays, May 24, 1870, in *Saints' Herald* (Independence, MO), Sep. 15, 1870, 553 (Larson and Passey, *William E. McLellin Papers*, 458).

81. McLellin, Journal, Oct. 25–26, 1831 (Shipps and Welch, *Journals of William E. McLellin*, 44–45).

82. See Larson and Passey, *William E. McLellin Papers*, 388, 397, 441.

83. McLellin, Journal, Oct. 25, 1831 (Shipps and Welch, *Journals of William E. McLellin*, 45).

84. Revelation, Sep. 22–23, 1832, [1], Newel K. Whitney Papers [D&C 84:29] (*JSP*, D2:296–97).

85. Minutes, Oct. 25–26, 1831, Minute Book 2, 15 (*JSP*, D2:86).

86. Corrill, *Brief History*, 18 (*JSP*, H2:145).

Cowdery recorded in the minutes that he and David Whitmer had received "directions" earlier that morning, no doubt from Smith, "respecting the choice of the twelve, [which] was that they would be ordained & sent forth from the Land of Zion."[87] This referred to a June 1829 revelation directing Cowdery and Whitmer, as Book of Mormon witnesses, to "search out the twelve" who were to "ordain priests and teachers."[88] Cowdery had issued his own revelation calling himself an apostle, who would ordain priests and teachers and build up the church. It is interesting that during this conference Cowdery "by appointment" did all the ordaining, not just priests and teachers, but also an elder and other high priests.

---

87. Minutes, Oct. 25–26, 1831, Minute Book 2, 15 (*JSP*, D2:87).
88. Revelation, June 1829-B, BC XV:31, 35, 42 [D&C 18:29, 32, 37] (*JSP*, D1:72–73).

7

Publishing the Revelations

*Whatsoever they shall speak when moved upon by the Holy Ghost
shall be Scripture.*
—Revelation, Nov. 1, 1831, Revelation Book 1, 113 [D&C 68:4]

On his return to Hiram from the Orange conference, Joseph Smith was accompanied by his father and William E. McLellin, who sprained his ankle
while walking, causing Joseph Sr. to give up his horse to McLellin. After arriving at Kirtland, McLellin asked the Mormon prophet to heal his ankle,
and recorded his response in his journal: "He immediately turned to me and
asked me if I believed in my heart that God through his instrumentality would
heal it. I answered that I believed he would. He laid his hands on it and it was
healed although It was swelled much and had pained me severely."[1]

Smith left Kirtland on October 28, 1831, again accompanied by McLellin, and traveled southward thirty-two miles to Nelson in Portage County,
five miles east of Hiram, possibly staying the night with Charles Hulet.[2]
Shortly after returning to the Johnson farm in Hiram on the following day,
Smith dictated a revelation at McLellin's request.[3] McLellin, who was the
scribe on this and other occasions, described Smith's general practice: "The
scribe seats himself at a desk or table, with pen, ink and paper. The subject
of enquiry being understood, the Prophet and Revelator enquires of God.
He spiritually sees, hears and feels, and then speaks as he is moved upon by
the Holy Ghost, the 'thus saith the Lord,' sentence after sentence, and waits
for his amanuenses to write and then read aloud each sentence. Thus they

---

1. McLellin, Journal, Oct. 26, 1831 (Shipps and Welch, *Journals of William E. McLellin*, 45).
2. Shipps and Welch, 45. Charles Hulet was an early convert living in Nelson (Cannon and
Cook, *Far West Record*, 12n1).
3. Revelation, Oct. 29, 1831, William E. McLellin, Notebook, 1877, [9]–10 [D&C 66] (*JSP*,
D2:87–92). See also Shipps and Welch, *Journals of William E. McLellin*, 45.

proceed until the revelator says Amen, at the close of what is then communicated." To well-educated McLellin, it was a sign of Smith's inspiration that he could "thus deliver off in broken sentences, some of the most sublime pieces of composition which I ever perused in any book."[4]

In later years, McLellin, who had come to question Smith's decision to stop using the seer stone, said the stone was not used for this revelation.[5] Nevertheless, McLellin recalled: "I went before the Lord in secret, and on my knees asked him to reveal the answer to five questions through his Prophet, and that too without his having any knowledge of my having made such request. I now testify in the fear of God, that every question which I had thus lodged in the ears of the Lord of Sabbaoth, were answered to my full and entire satisfaction. I desired it for a testimony of Joseph's inspiration. And I to this day consider it to me an evidence which I cannot refute."[6]

The revelation began by acknowledging McLellin's recent conversion: "Behold thus saith the Lord u[n]to you my servant William, Blessed are you inasmuch as you have turned away from your inequities and have received my truths." He was no doubt thrilled to hear deity speak directly to him, but what he most wanted to know came next: "Verily I say unto you my servant Wm. that you are clean but not all Repent therefore of those things which are not pleasing in my sight saith the Lord for the Lord will shew them unto you."[7] Thus McLellin received an answer to one of his questions: were his baptism and confirmation accepted by God?

Another question McLellin had pertained to God's will concerning him: What does God want me to do? "Behold Verily I say unto you," the Lord declared, "that it is my will that you should proclaim my Gospel from land to land and from City to City. Yea in those regions round about where it hath not been proclaimed. Tarry not many days in this place."[8] According to McLellin, "I had expected to remain here [in Hiram] and read and write for some weeks and probably months, but having received the will of

---

4. *Ensign of Liberty* (Kirtland, OH), Aug. 1849, 98–99. McLellin was a follower of David Whitmer and applied the same description of receiving revelation to him.

5. McLellin told Joseph Smith III in 1872: "In Oct. 1831 I wrote a revelation as [Joseph Smith] delivered it. And I know he used no [seer] stone to see then." McLellin to Joseph Smith III, July 1872 (Larson and Passey, *William E. McLellin Papers*, 484). In 1870 McLellin wrote Mark H. Forscutt: "The revelations given by or through J. Smith after he ceased to give them by the use of the Interpreter ... cannot be altogether depended upon." McLellin, Letter to Mark H. Forscutt, Oct. 1871, [4], CCLA, in Larson and Passey, 479.

6. "Things in Kirtland," *Ensign of Liberty*, Jan. 1848, 61.

7. Revelation, Oct. 29, 1831, McLellin, Notebook, 1877, [9] [D&C 66:1, 3] (*JSP*, D2:90).

8. Revelation, [9] [D&C 66:4–5] (*JSP*, D2:90–91).

the Lord I determined to obey it."[9] Following the revelation's command, McLellin and Samuel Smith, Joseph's younger brother, would leave Hiram on November 16.

Two more questions pertained to when he should consecrate his property to the church and move to Zion? The answers came in the instruction to "go not up unto the Land of Zion as yet But in as much as you can send. Send, otherwis[e] think not of thy property." The final possible question related to the first and was easily surmised: "Commit not adultery, [a] temptation with which thou hast been troubled."[10] Exactly how McLellin had been tempted with adultery is unclear, but his wife, Cynthia Ann, whom he married in 1829, had died recently, leaving McLellin to experience "many lonesome & sorrowful hours."[11] "This revelation [gave] great joy to my heart," McLellin recorded in his journal, "because some important questions were answered which had dwelt upon my mind with anxiety yet with uncertainty."[12]

On the next day, Sunday, October 30, McLellin addressed a congregation of "brethren & sisters" at the Johnson farm, which included Sidney Rigdon, Oliver Cowdery, and Joseph Smith.[13] It may have been at this meeting that Smith dictated a short revelation inspired by Jesus's prayer in Matthew 6:10 for the kingdom of God to come on earth as well as the prophecy in Daniel 2:33–34 that the kingdom of God would grow to fill the world: "The keys of the kingdom of God is committed unto man on the Earth & from thence shall the Gospel roll forth unto the ends of the Earth as the stone which is hewn from the Mountain without hands shall roll forth untill it hath filled the whole Earth yea a voice crying prepare ye the way of the Lord prepare ye the supper of the Lamb make ready for the Bridegroom. ... Wherefore may the kingdom of God go forth that the kingdom of heaven may come that thou O God may be glorified in heaven so on Earth that thine enemies may be subdued for thine is the honour power & glory forever & ever Amen."[14] Declaring that his church was the stone that would grow to fill the earth and destroy all worldly kingdoms only eighteen months after its founding was audacious, to say the least.

---

9. McLellin, Journal, Nov. 16, 1831 (Shipps and Welch, *Journals of William E. McLellin*, 47).

10. Revelation, Oct. 29, 1831, McLellin, Notebook, 1877, [9]–[10] [D&C 66:6, 10] (*JSP*, D2:91).

11. McLellin, Letter to "Beloved Relatives," Aug. 4, 1832, [3].

12. McLellin, Journal, Oct. 29, 1831 (Shipps and Welch, *Journals of William E. McLellin*, 46).

13. McLellin, Oct. 30, 1831 (Shipps and Welch, 46–47).

14. Revelation, Oct. 30, 1831, Revelation Book 1, 112 [D&C 65] (*JSP*, D2:92–94). See also Isa. 40:3; Dan. 2:33–34; Matt. 3:3, 16:19, 22:2; Rev. 19:9.

The phrase "keys of the kingdom" evokes Jesus's words to the apostle Peter in Matthew 16:19—"And I will give unto thee the keys of the kingdom of heaven: and whatsoever thou shalt bind on earth shall be bound in heaven: and whatsoever thou shalt loose on earth shall be loosed in heaven." Only five days earlier Smith had explained that "the order of the High priesthood is that they have power given them to seal up the Saints unto eternal life."[15] Zebedee Coltrin recorded in his missionary diary that on November 15, 1831, he and others visited the "Shalersville" branch and that "Br David [Whitmer] seeled them up unto Eternal life."[16]

Conference

Two days later, on November 1, a special two-day conference consisting of ten elders was held in an upstairs room of the Johnson home—the room in which Smith was working on his Bible revision. This "translating" room was prepared while Smith was attending the October conference in Orange. Being the largest room upstairs, it was probably originally the bedroom of John and Elsa Johnson, which was vacated after another room was created by partitioning off a large workspace on the west end of the second floor.[17]

At this conference, it was decided to print 10,000 copies of a Book of Commandments containing Smith's revelations, but not without controversy.[18] The minutes are silent, but reminiscent accounts by David Whitmer and McLellin claim the proposal to print Smith's revelations was met with some resistance. Whitmer said that he and "a few of the brethren" objected to publishing Smith's revelations because they believed "that it was not the will of the Lord that the revelations should be published."[19] One major reason was that some revelations invoked secrecy. A March 1831 revelation, for example, commanded: "Keep these things from going abroad unto the world that ye may accomplish this work in the eyes of the people & in the eyes of your enemies that they may not know your works untill ye have accomplished the thing which I have commanded you."[20] Whitmer said he objected

---

15. Minutes, Oct. 25–26, 1831, Minute Book 2, 11 (*JSP*, D2:81).

16. Zebedee Coltrin, Diary, Nov. 15, 1831.

17. Staker, *Hearken, O Ye People*, 314.

18. Minutes, Nov. 1–2, 1831, Minute Book 2, 15–16 (*JSP*, D2:94–98). This was later changed to 3,000 copies on April 30, 1832. Literary Firm, Minutes, Apr. 30, 1832, Minute Book 2, 25 (*JSP*, D2:239).

19. Whitmer, *Address to All Believers in Christ*, 54. Whitmer mistakenly gave the date of the conference as "the spring of 1832," although he gave the correct location as Hiram.

20. Revelation, ca. Mar. 7, 1831, Revelation Book 1, 76 [D&C 45:72] (*JSP*, D1:280). See also Revelation, May 1829, BC, IX:8 [D&C 10:35–37] (*JSP*, D1:40–41); Revelation, Mar. 1830, BC, XVI:22 [D&C 19:21] (*JSP*, D1:90).

to publishing the revelations and "withstood Brothers Joseph and Sydney to the face." According to Whitmer, Smith responded with a prophetic threat: "Any man who objects to having these revelations published, shall have his part taken out of the Tree of Life and out of the Holy City." Such a threat was designed to silence all opposition, but Whitmer continued to press his case by issuing his own prophecy, that "if they sent those revelations to Independence to be published in a book, the people would come upon them and tear down the printing press, and the church would be driven out of Jackson county." In response, Whitmer recalled, "Brothers Joseph and Sydney laughed at me."[21]

In a later interview, Whitmer asked Smith if he was going to publish all the revelations, and when Smith answered in the affirmative, Whitmer asked a pointed question: "Are you going to publish that revelation for Oliver and Hiram [Page] to go to Kingston and get out a copyright for the Book of Mormon?"[22] After a long pause, Smith answered, "No." Whitmer then asked, "Why, not, Brother Joseph?" Smith reluctantly responded, "BECAUSE … IT WAS NOT TRUE."[23] McLellin said "hours were spent" discussing whether to publish the revelations before "it was finally decided to have them printed."[24]

According to McLellin, after Rigdon, Cowdery, and he had drafted a preface to the Book of Commandments and presented it to the conference, the "Conference picked it all to pieces" and requested that Smith replace it through revelation.[25] The minutes record that the "Preface [was] received by inspiration" during a recess between the morning and afternoon sessions.[26] McLellin remembered that Smith, who was "sitting by a window," dictated the preface "by the Spirit," while Rigdon served as scribe. "Joseph would deliver a few sentences and Sydney would write them down," McLellin said, Rigdon "then read them aloud, and if correct, then Joseph would proceed and deliver more."[27]

---

21. Whitmer, *Address to All Believers in Christ*, 55.

22. Revelation, ca. Early 1830, Revelation Book 1, 30–31 (*JSP*, D1:108–12). The revelation directed four men—Oliver Cowdery, Joseph Knight, Sr., Hiram Page, and Josiah Stowell—to travel to Kingston, Upper Canada, to sell the Book of Mormon's copyright for a Canadian edition, which they failed to do.

23. John L. Traughber to [James T. Cobb?], ca. 1881, in Wyl, *Mormon Portraits*, 311 (*EMD*, 5:334). Traughber said, "I have this from both Dr. W. E. McLellin … and David Whitmer, both of whom have read the revelation. Dr. McLellin was secretary of the council in which David talked to Joe about it."

24. William E. McLellin, Letter to John L. Traughber, Dec. 14, 1878, in Larson and Passey, *William E. McLellin Papers*, 510.

25. "Letter from Elder W. H. Kelley," *Saints' Herald*, Mar. 1, 1882, 67.

26. Minutes, Nov. 1–2, 1831, Minute Book 2, 15 (*JSP*, D2:97).

27. "Letter from Elder W. H. Kelley," *Saints' Herald*, Mar. 1, 1882, 67.

Speaking in the voice of God, the dictated preface warned the church and the world of the dire consequences of rejecting the new revelations. The revelation began: "Hearken O ye People of my Church ... ye People from afar & ye that are upon the Islands of the sea listen ... for verily the voice of the Lord is unto all men & there is none to escape." The Mormon missionaries are to be "the voice of warning ... in these last days," and are to go out into the world, "for I the Lord have commanded them Behold this is mine authority & the authority of my servents & my preface unto the Book of my Commandments which I have given them to Publish unto you O Inhabitants of the Earth." In keeping with the early understanding of authority as derived from the revealed commands of God and angels, the revelation further stated: "Commandments were given [that they] might have power to lay the foundation of this Church & to bring it forth out of obscurity & out of darkness the only true & living Church upon the face of the whole Earth with which I the Lord am well pleased speaking unto the Church collectively & not individually."[28]

The revelation described the tribulations and destruction awaiting the wicked at the end of the world and warned: "They who will not hear the voice of the Lord neither his servants neith[er] give heed to the words of the Prophets & Apostles shall be cut off from among the People."[29] At the conference in Orange on October 25–26, Smith had explained that the high priesthood included the "power ... to seal up the Saints unto eternal life," in this revelation that power was extended to include "power ... to seal both on Earth & in Heaven the unbelieveing & rebelious ... up unto the day when the wrath of God shall be poured out upon the wicked without measure."[30]

Concerning the problem of the revelations sounding more like Smith than God, the revelation explained: "Behold I am God & have spoken it these commandments are of me & were given unto my Servents in their weakness after the manner of their Language that they might come to understanding." Nevertheless, "whether by mine own voice or by the voice of my Servents it is the same for Behold & Lo the Lord is God & the Spirit beareth record & the [record] is true & the truth abideth for ever & ever

---

28. Revelation, Nov. 1, 1831, Revelation Book 1, 125–27 [D&C 1:1–2, 4–6, 30] (*JSP*, D2:105–106).

29. Revelation, 126 [D&C 1:14] (*JSP*, D2:105–106).

30. Revelation, 125 [D&C 1:8–9] (*JSP*, D2:105). See Minutes, Oct. 25–26, 1831, Minute Book 2, 11 (*JSP*, D2:81).

Amen."[31] Despite the weakness in language, Smith's inspired utterances were to be regarded as the voice of God.

When the conference resumed, Smith said "inasmuch as the Lord had bestowed a great blessing upon us in giving commandments and revelations, asked the conference what testimony they were willing to attach to these commandments which should shortly be sent to the world." While some of the elders said "they were willing to testify to the world that they knew that they were of the Lord," others hesitated, owing to their concern about the language in the revelations. The minutes are silent about such hesitation, but Smith's history states that after the preface to the Book of Commandments was dictated, "some conversation was had concerning Revelations and language."[32]

In response, Smith dictated a revelation challenging the elders to have the wisest among them attempt to compose a revelation.[33] The revelation declared that some of the elders had not received a spiritual conviction concerning the revelations because of "fears" in their hearts. The source of this trepidation was their familiarity with Smith, his manner of speech, and the wording of his revelations. As the revelation stated, "Your eyes have been upon my Servent Joseph & his language you have known & his imperfections you have known & you have sought in your hearts knowlege that you might express beyond his language."[34] The preface had also declared that the commandments were given to God's "Servents in their weakness after the manner of their Language."[35] To overcome the hesitation to endorse the publication of Smith's revelations, the revelation challenged the elders to choose the "most wise" among them to write a revelation "like unto" what they considered the "least" of Smith's revelations, and if he failed, the revelation reasoned, they would be "Justified" in testifying to the world that Smith's revelations are "true" and that "there is no unrighteousness in it," meaning Smith's dictation of revelation. As a further apologetic, the revelation paraphrased a passage in James about spiritual gifts—"That which is

---

31. Revelation, 126–27 [D&C 1:24, 38] (*JSP*, D2:106–107).

32. JS History, vol. A-1, 161 (DHC 1:224).

33. Revelation, ca. Nov. 2, 1831, Revelation Book 1, 114–15 [D&C 67] (*JSP*, D2:108–10). Although the earliest copy of the revelation bears the date of November 2, 1831, Smith's history implies that this revelation was dictated at the November 1 meeting in response to the conversation about perceived weaknesses in the revelations. JS History, vol. A-1, 161 (DHC 1:224). The minutes for the November 1 meeting mention both the "Preface received by inspiration" and that a "Revelation [was] received relative to the same." Minutes, Nov. 1–2, 1831, Minute Book 2, 16 (*JSP*, D2:97).

34. Revelation, ca. Nov. 2, 1831, Revelation Book 1, 115 [D&C 67:3, 5] (*JSP*, D2:109).

35. Revelation, Nov. 1, 1831 [D&C 1:24] (*JSP*, D2:106).

righteous cometh down from above from the father of lights."[36] Otherwise, if they fail to testify, they stand condemned before God.

The revelation closed by encouraging the elders who had been ordained to the high priesthood to seek the ultimate charismatic experience—seeing the face of God. "It is your privilege & a promise I give unto you that have been ordained unto the ministry," the revelation declared, "that in as much as ye strip yourselves from Jealesies & fears & humble yourselves before me … you shall see me & know that I am." The revelation then described the manner in which God would be seen: "Not with the carnal neither natural [mind] but with the spiritual for no man hath seen God at any time in the flesh but by the Spirit of God … wherefore continue in patience untill ye are perfected."[37] A week earlier, Smith had declared at the conference in Orange that "could we all come together with one heart and one mind in perfect faith the vail might as well be rent to day as next week or any other time."[38] Smith knew that such a charismatic experience would be interpreted by followers as proof of his mission and ministry.

According to Smith's history, McLellin tried and failed to produce an imitation revelation. The wording of Smith's history reveals a major impediment for McLellin: "It was an awful responsibility to write in the name of the Lord." Smith no doubt knew that followers would find speaking in God's voice without the authority of the Holy Spirit an impassable barrier. Nevertheless, those who witnessed McLellin's failure "to imitate the language of Jesus Christ" were "renewed [in] their faith … [and] in the truth of the commandments and revelations" given through their prophet.[39]

On the following day, November 2, according to the minutes, "the Revelation of last evening [was] read" by Cowdery and "the brethren then arose in turn and bore witness to the truth of the Book of Commandments." After which, Smith "expressed his feelings & gratitude concerning the commandment & Preface received yesterday."[40]

About this time, a formal undated endorsement or testimony to the Book of Commandments was drafted and signed by five attendees of the conference: Sidney Rigdon, Orson Hyde, William E. McLellin, Luke Johnson, and

36. Revelation, ca. Nov. 2, 1831, Revelation Book 1, 115 [D&C 67:6–8] (*JSP*, D2:109). Cf. James 1:17.

37. Revelation, 115 [D&C 67:10–14] (*JSP*, D2:109). Compare Visions of Moses, June 1830 [Moses 1:11].

38. Minutes, Oct. 25–26, 1831, Minute Book 2, 11 (*JSP*, D2:81).

39. JS History, vol. A-1, 162 (DHC 1:226).

40. Minutes, Nov. 1–2, 1831, Minute Book 2, 16 (*JSP*, D2:98).

Lyman Johnson. Subsequently thirteen others signed it, although four of the attendees listed in the minutes did not: David Whitmer, Oliver Cowdery, John Whitmer, and Peter Whitmer Jr. Since they were all Book of Mormon witnesses, there was perhaps an intentional avoidance of repeating their names. However, David Whitmer may have remained opposed to publishing Smith's revelations. Smith's history implies that he dictated the testimony during the conference.[41] The testimony, which was likely intended to be published in the back of the Book of Commandments, declared: "We the undersigned feel willing to bear testimony to all the world of mankind ... that god hath born record to our souls through the Holy Ghost shed forth upon us that these commandments are given by inspiration of God & are profitable for all men & are verily true."[42]

Printing Smith's revelations was an important step in the institutionalization of charisma. Not only did it strengthen Smith's leadership position but it facilitated the codification and standardization of early Mormon group behavior since the published revelations became the "law" by which church councils could try members and the justification for disciplinary measures taken.

At some point during the first day of conference, Smith dictated a revelation for Orson Hyde, Luke Johnson, Lyman Johnson, and William E. McLellin, who approached Smith and requested to know the Lord's will concerning them.[43] These four high priests were called to "proclaim the everlasting Gospel by the spirit of the living God from people to people & from land to land in the congregations of the wicked." The revelation then made an astounding declaration: "Whatsoever they shall speak when moved upon by the Holy Ghost shall be Scripture shall be the will of the Lord shall be the mind of the Lord shall be the voice of the Lord & shall be the power of God unto Salvation."[44] A September 1830 revelation, which declared that Smith was the only one "appointed to Receive commandments & Revelations" for the church, gave Cowdery permission to issue commandments to the church when moved upon by the spirit but not to

41. JS History, vol. A-1, 162 (DHC 1:226).

42. Testimony, ca. Nov. 2, 1831, Revelation Book 1, 121 (*JSP*, D2:110–14; *JSP*, MRB:215). The Testimony was not included in the unfinished Book of Commandments, but a version of it appeared without signatures in D&C, 1835 ed., 256, which incorrectly implied that it had been signed by the twelve apostles.

43. Revelation, Nov. 1, 1831, Revelation Book 1, 113–14 [D&C 68] (*JSP*, D2:98–103). The copy of the revelation in Revelation Book 1 is dated November 1, 1831, but Joseph Smith's history arranges the revelation at the end of the two-day conference. JS History, vol. A-1, 157–63 (DHC 1:227–29).

44. Revelation, 113 [D&C 68:1, 4] (*JSP*, D2:99–101).

write them down.[45] This allowed charisma to flourish without competing with Smith's authority. According to McLellin, a few months later when he requested Smith to inquire of the Lord concerning a certain matter that troubled him, Smith suggested that McLellin seek his own answer. McLellin said that when he read the revelation to Smith, the prophet "shed tears of joy" and said: "Brother William, that is the mind and the will of God, and as much a revelation as I ever received in my life. You have written it by the true spirit of inspiration."[46]

Smith's revelation went on to discuss other matters dealing with "certain items as made known in addition to the Laws & commandments which have been given to the church," referring to the "Law" given in February 1831.[47] With Edward Partridge in Missouri, the revelation directed "other Bishops to be set apart unto the church to minister even according to the first." These bishops were to be high priests "appointed by a confrenc[e] of high priests."[48] Accordingly, Newel K. Whitney will be called as the second bishop on December 4.[49] The revelation also stipulated that bishops can only "be tried or condemned for any crime save it be before a confrence of high priests."[50]

The revelation addressed the responsibilities of parents to teach their children the gospel and to have them baptized at the age of eight, otherwise "the sin be upon the head of the parents for this shall be a Law unto the inhabitants of Zion."[51] This was an item Smith wished to add to the "Law" as revealed the previous February.[52] A June 1829 revelation had instructed that children were not to be baptized until they had reached the "years of accountability," but an exact age was not given by Smith until sometime between February 1 and March 7, 1831, as he revised Genesis 17:11, which explained "that children are not accountable before me till eight years old."[53]

---

45. Revelation, Sep. 1830 [D&C 28:2] (*JSP*, D1:185); see also Revelation, Feb. 1831 [D&C 43:2–4] (*JSP*, D1:258).

46. William E. McLellin, Letter to Orson Pratt, Apr. 29, 1854, CHL, in Larson and Passey, *William E. McLellin Papers*, 434.

47. Revelation, Feb. 9, 1831 [D&C 42:1–72] (*JSP*, D1:245–56); Revelation, Feb. 23, 1831 [D&C 42:73–93] (*JSP*, D1:264–67).

48. Revelation, Nov. 1, 1831, Revelation Book 1, 114 [D&C 68:14–15] (*JSP*, D2:102). This is the first significant reference to the office of high priest.

49. Revelation, Dec. 4, 1831, Newel K. Whitney Papers, BYU [D&C 72:1–8] (*JSP*, D2:146–50).

50. Revelation, Nov. 1, 1831, Revelation Book 1, 114 [D&C 68:22] (*JSP*, D2:102). This was changed in 1835 to read that any high priest can only be tried by the First Presidency.

51. Revelation, 114 [D&C 68:25] (*JSP*, D2:102).

52. Revelation, Feb. 9, 1831 [D&C 42:1–72] (*JSP*, D1:245–56); Revelation, Feb. 23, 1831 [D&C 42:73–93] (*JSP*, D1:264–67).

53. Revelation, June 1829-B, BC XV:46 [D&C 18:42] (*JSP*, D1:73); Old Testament Revision 1, 41 [I.V. Gen. 17:11] (Faulring et al., *Joseph Smith's New Translation of the Bible*, 64).

Finally, the revelation directed that Cowdery "cary these sayings unto the land of Zion," which included a reprimand of their conduct: "I the Lord am not well pleased with the inhabitants of Zion for there are idlers among them & their children also are growing up in wickedness."[54] According to Smith's history, Cowdery had been assigned by a conference to carry all the revelations to Missouri for publication there, while Smith was requested to "arrange and get them in readiness by the time he left, which was to be by the 15th of the month [of November], and possibly before."[55]

On the day after conference, November 3, Smith dictated a fairly long revelation that became known as the "appendix" because it was intended to conclude the Book of Commandments.[56] According to Smith's history, it came in response to the elders' questions about "the gathering" and "preaching the gospel to the inhabitants of the earth."[57] Exhibiting a strong millenarian theme, the revelation wove many Bible passages into a text. The revelation began: "Hearken oh ye People of my Church—saith the Lord your God & hear the word of the Lord concerning you," and then warned that the end is near when "the Lord shall suddenly come to his temple" and "shall come down with a curse to Judgement yea upon all the Nations that forget god. Wherefore prepare ye prepare ye oh ye my People Sanctify yourselves gether ye together oh ye People of my Church upon the Land of Zion all you that have not been commanded to tarry go ye out from Babylon."[58] This seems to direct all who were not specifically commanded to tarry to go to the land of Zion, contrary to previous instructions to await Smith's approval.[59]

The Mormon elders—like the ancient apostles—were sent "unto the nations which are afar off unto the ilands of the sea send forth unto foreign lands call upon all nations firstly upon the gentiles & then upon the Jews." These missionaries were to instruct their converts to "go ye forth unto the

---

54. Revelation, Nov. 1, 1831, Revelation Book 1, 114 [D&C 68:31, 32] (*JSP*, D2:103).

55. JS History, vol. A-1, 166 (DHC 1:229).

56. Revelation, Nov. 3, 1831, Revelation Book 1, 116–21 [D&C 133] (*JSP*, D2:114–21). An early copy of the revelation in the handwriting of Sidney Rigdon bears the endorsement "An appendix to Revelation." Revelation, Nov. 3, 1831, [6], in *JSP*, MRB:405. When the revelation was first published in the May 1833 issue of *The Evening and the Morning Star*, W. W. Phelps introduced it as "the close" or "the Appendix" to the Book of Commandments. "Revelations," *The Evening and the Morning Star* (Independence, MO), May 1833, [1]. The revelation received the heading "Appendix" as section C [100] in the 1835 edition of the Doctrine and Covenants, 247–250.

57. JS History, vol. A-1, 166 (DHC 1:229).

58. Revelation, Nov. 3, 1831, Revelation Book 1, 116 [D&C 133:1–2, 4] (*JSP*, D2:116). Cf. Mal. 3:1; Isa. 34:5.

59. See Revelation, Aug. 30, 1831 [D&C 63:41] (*JSP*, D2:52); Revelation, Aug. 1, 1831 [D&C 58:44] (*JSP*, D2:19); see also Revelation, Sep. 11, 1831 [D&C 64:21–22] (*JSP*, D2:65).

Land of Zion [in Missouri] that the borders of my People may be enlarged & that her stakes may be strengthened. ... Yea let the cry go forth among all people awake & arise & go forth to meet the Bride-groom Behold & Lo the Bride-groom Cometh ... Watch therefore for ye know neither the day nor the hour let them therefore which are among the gentiles—flee unto Zion & let they which be of Judah flee unto Jerusalem."[60] Smith was thus attempting to set up a Mormon Zionism that would prove as volatile as modern-day Jewish Zionism. Of course, this perpetual immigration would not only increase Smith's power and influence as a religious leader, but he would wield considerable political and economic power as well.

The revelation then alluded to Revelation 14:6–7, which has since become a favorite proof text for the Book of Mormon—"For behold the Lord God hath sent forth the Angel crying through the midst of Heaven saying prepare ye the way of the Lord & make his paths strait. ... I have sent forth mine Angel flying throug[h] the midst of heaven having the everlasting Gospel who hath appeared unto some & hath committed it unto man who shall appear unto many that dwell on the Earth & this gospel shall be preached unto every Nation & kindred & tongue & People."[61] The angel had already appeared to the three witnesses, after having appeared to Mary Musselman Whitmer, David and John's mother: Smith anticipated there would be others.[62]

The revelation alluded to another proof text in Genesis 49:26, which links Smith's followers to Jacob's blessing of his grandson Ephraim, son of Joseph. It declared that in the last days the ten lost tribes would return from the "North countries" and come "unto the Children of Ephraim my servents & the boundaries of the everlasting hills shall trembl at their presence."[63] A September 1831 revelation had proclaimed that "the rebelious are not of the blood of Ephraim," and an early copy of an October 1831 revelation said that it was "given to Wm. E. McLelin a true decendant from Joseph who was sold into Egypt down through the loins of Ephraim his son."[64]

The revelation next alluded to David Whitmer's objection that publishing the revelations would violate the injunction in some of them to keep

---

60. Revelation, Nov. 3, 1831, Revelation Book 1, 116 [D&C 133:8–10] (*JSP*, D2:117). Cf. Isa. 54:2; Matt. 25:6, 13.

61. Revelation, 117, 118 [D&C 133:17, 36–37] (*JSP*, D2:117).

62. On Mary Musselman Whitmer's visionary experience, see Edward Stevenson, "The Thirteenth Witness to the Plates of the Book of Mormon," *Juvenile Instructor*, Jan. 1, 1889, 23 (DHC 5:262–63).

63. Revelation, Nov. 3, 1831, Revelation Book 1, 117, 118 [D&C 133:30–33] (*JSP*, D2:117).

64. Revelation, Sep. 11, 1831 [D&C 64:35–36]; Revelation, Oct. 29, 1831 [D&C 66] (*JSP*, D2:92).

them from the world: "[When] these commandments were given they were commanded to be kept from the world in the day that they were given but now are to go forth unto all flesh & this according to the mind & the will of the Lord who reigneth over all flesh."[65]

Finally, the revelation warned those who reject Smith's revelations: "Behold & Lo there is none to deliver you for ye obeyed not my voice when I called unto you all out of the Heavens ye believed not my Servants & when they were sent unto you ye received them not wherefore they sealed up the testimony & bound up the Law & ye were delivered up unto darkness these shall go away into outer darkness where there is weeping & wailing & gnashing of theeth [teeth] Behold the Lord your God hath spoken it Amen."[66]

Five days later, on November 8, Smith attended a special conference at the Johnson residence to discuss the publication of the Book of Commandments. Of the ten men who attended the previous conference, three were not present at this meeting: Orson Hyde, David Whitmer, and Lyman Johnson. While Hyde may have left with Hyrum Smith on their preaching mission, Whitmer and Johnson were apparently still in Hiram. Johnson attended the conference on the following day, but Whitmer, who may have been protesting the publication of the revelations, did not show up until the meeting on November 12.[67]

The November 8 meeting began with Rigdon discussing "the errors or mistakes which are in commandments and revelations, made either by the translation in consequence of the slow way of the scribe at the time of receiving or by the scribes themselves." There was no mention of Smith's limited linguistic skills. Yet Smith was permitted to "correct those errors or mistakes which he may discover by the holy Spirit while reviewing the revelations & commandments & also the fulness of the scriptures." The conference also authorized Cowdery to correct "all the writings which go forth to the world through the Printing press," that is, "except the revelations and commandments."[68] However, an examination of the earliest collection of revelations titled "A Book of Commandments & Revelations of the Lord given to Joseph the Seer" shows that Cowdery did make changes and that

---

65. Revelation, Nov. 3, 1831, Revelation Book 1, 118 [D&C 133:60] (*JSP*, D2:120).

66. Revelation, 118, 120–21 [D&C 133:71–73] (*JSP*, D2:121). Cf. Isa. 8:16; Matt. 8:12; 22:13; 25:30.

67. Minutes, Nov. 8–9, 1831, Minute Book 2, 16–17 (*JSP*, D2:121–24); "History of Orson Hyde," 8.

68. Minutes, Nov. 8, 1831, Minute Book 2, 16 (*JSP*, D2:123).

they were "often … substantive in nature, clarifying and expanding the meaning of several items."[69]

According to Smith's history, Smith reviewed the revelations in preparation for Cowdery and John Whitmer taking them to Independence, Missouri, for printing.[70] McLellin remembered that following this meeting, Smith, Rigdon, and Cowdery spent hours reading and revising the revelations and that they were sent to Missouri with Cowdery and Whitmer "in a bound blank book."[71] The men may have worked for hours, but extant manuscripts show that only minor changes were made, mostly in Rigdon's handwriting, before Cowdery and Whitmer left for Missouri with the book of revelations on November 20. The revelations will undergo further corrections and emendations by Cowdery, Whitmer, and Phelps in Missouri before being printed in the unfinished Book of Commandments in 1833.[72]

Uniting Zion and Kirtland

On November 11, 1831, Smith held a special conference in Hiram with seven other elders dealing with the various duties of the elders.[73] The minutes state that Cowdery read the "Commandments concerning the duties of the Elders," but while the record does not specify which commandments were read, it probably refers to the revelation Smith dictated on this day concerning the hierarchal structuring of the priesthood that would significantly change how the elders viewed their authority.[74] Indeed, those who thought the office of elder was the highest office in the church and questioned the need for the high priesthood were likely stunned by this revelation.

It is noteworthy that this revelation is addressed "To the Church of Christ in the Land of Zion" and pertains to an "addition to the Church Laws respecting Church business." Carried by Cowdery and Whitmer to Missouri, the main objective of this revelation was, by introducing the office of president of the high priesthood (which Smith alone would occupy), to put Edward Partridge in his place and curb the independent manner in which he fulfilled his duty as bishop. To justify the new office, the offices of deacon,

---

69. *JSP*, MRB:6.

70. JS History, vol. A-1, 172 (DHC 1:235).

71. McLellin, Letter to John L. Traughber, Dec. 14, 1878, in Larson and Passey, *William E. McLellin Papers*, 510.

72. *JSP*, MRB:6–7.

73. Minutes, Nov. 11, 1831, Minute Book 2, 17 (*JSP*, D2:126–29).

74. Revelation, Nov. 11, 1831-B, Revelation Book 1, 122–23 [D&C 107:59–100] (*JSP*, D2:132–36). Significant additions were made before publication in the 1835 Doctrine and Covenants [D&C 107:1–58, 70, 76–78, 93–98] (*JSP*, D4:308–21).

teacher, priest, elder, and high priest were organized into quorums of various sizes with presidents appointed for each. "Wherefore it must needs be that one be appointed of the high Priest hood to preside over the Priest hood & he shall be called President of the high Priest hood of the Church or in other words the Presiding high Priest over the high Priesthood of the Church. ... And again the duty of the president of the office of the High Priesthood is to preside over the whole church & to be like unto Moses."[75]

This hierarchal ordering of the priesthood placed Smith over Partridge in all matters. As the revelation specifically explained, the duty of the president of the high priesthood was "the administring of ordinances & blessings upon the Church by the Laying on of the hands wherefore the office of a Bishop is not equal unto it for the office of a Bishop is in administering all temporal things. ... Wherefore now let every man learn his duty & to act in the office in which he is appointed in all diligence."[76]

Within days, Rigdon wrote a scathing letter to church leaders in Missouri complaining about Partridge, which Cowdery and Whitmer probably carried to Missouri along with this revelation. Among other things, Rigdon accused Partridge of "having insulted the Lord's prophet in particular & assumed authority over him in open violation of the Laws of God."[77] Rigdon presumably had in mind Partridge's confrontation with Smith the previous summer over the selection of land in Missouri, when according to Ezra Booth, Partridge told Smith, "I wish you not to tell us any more, that you know these by the spirit when you do not."[78] On January 24, 1832, a Missouri conference of the priesthood determined that although Rigdon's charges against Partridge were "detrimental to his character and standing as a Bishop in the church of Christ," it had "no legal right to proceed to a trial of the same in the absence of one of the parties." Instead, it was "recommend that the Elders stationed in this land converse with the said Bishop (Edward Partrage) on this subject and write the said Sidney a friendly humiliating letter advising that this difficulty be settled and thereby the wound in the Church be healed."[79]

---

75. Revelation, 122, 123 [D&C 107:59, 65–66, 91] (*JSP*, D2:133–35).

76. Revelation, 122, 123 [D&C 107:67–68, 99] (*JSP*, D2:134, 135).

77. Sidney Rigdon, Letter to John Corrill and Isaac Morley, Nov. 14, 1831, which is not extant but mentioned in Oliver Cowdery, Letter to Joseph Smith, Jan. 28, 1832, JS Collection (*JSP*, D2:174–75); and in Minutes, Mar. 10, 1832, Minute Book 2, 23 (Cannon and Cook, *Far West Record*, 40–41, 235).

78. Ezra Booth, Letter, Nelson, Portage Co., OH, to Ira Eddy, Nov. 21, 1831, "Mormonism—No. VII," *Ohio Star*, Nov. 24, 1831, [1].

79. Oliver Cowdery, Letter to Joseph Smith, Jan. 28, 1832, JS Collection (*JSP*, D2:174–75).

Rigdon's charges against Partridge were again discussed at another meeting in Independence, Missouri, on March 10, 1832, where Partridge said: "If Br. Joseph has not forgiven him he hopes he will, as he is & has always been sorry." The conference recommended that Rigdon should "ask himself whether he was not actuated by his own hasty feelings rather than the Spirit of Christ." They also decided, in light of Partridge's humility and confession, that Rigdon should "forever bury the matter ... and thereby the wound in the Church be healed & they walk together as brothers filling the important stations in the Kingdom of God in Honor to themselves & the advancement of our Redeemer's Cause."[80]

The restructuring of the priesthood also created another layer in the church's court system. The president of the high priesthood, with a council of twelve other high priests, formed the highest court of appeal in the church to decide "the most important business of the church & the most difficult cases of the church. ... For this is the highest court of the church of God & a final desision upon controvers[i]es." Should Smith transgress, he was to be tried "before the common court of the church who shall be assisted by twelve counsellors of the high Priesthood & their desicision upon his head shall be an end of controversy concerning him thus none shall be exempt from the justice of the Laws of God."[81]

Also on this day, Smith dictated a revelation appointing John Whitmer to accompany Cowdery to Missouri and to assist in printing the revelations. The revelation began, "For my Servent Olivers sake it is not wisdom in me that he should be intrusted with the commandments & moneys which he shall carry unto the Land of Zion except one go with him who will be true & faithfull wherefore I the Lord willeth that my Servent John (Whitmer) shall go with my servent Oliver." Whitmer was instructed to "continue in writing & makeing a history of all the important things which he shall observe & know concerning my Church & also that he receive council & assistance from my Servent Oliver & others." Whitmer had started writing a history on June 12, 1831, but keeping track of Smith and events in Kirtland from Missouri was impossible. Nevertheless, Whitmer was instructed to "travel many times from place to place & from Church to Church that he may the more easily obtain knowledge Preaching & expounding writing cop[y]ing & selecting & obtain[in]g all things

---

80. Minutes, Mar. 10, 1832, Minute Book 2, 22 (Cannon and Cook, *Far West Record*, 41–42).
81. Revelation, Nov. 11, 1831-B, Revelation Book 1, 123 [D&C 107:79–84] (*JSP*, D2:134–35).

which shall be for the good of the Church & for the rising generations."[82] If Smith anticipated Whitmer's preserving for posterity the fulfillment of prophecy and the phenomenal growth of his Missouri Zion, he would be disappointed, for instead, Whitmer recorded the disastrous demise of Smith's Zionic vision.

On the following day, November 12, Smith attended a conference where he said he wished to have Cowdery, Whitmer, and the "sacred writings ... dedicated to the Lord by the prayer of faith." He also requested to have his scribes—Oliver Cowdery, Martin Harris, John Whitmer, and Sidney Rigdon—financially compensated for their labor. It was voted that Smith "be appointed to dedicate & consecrate these brethren & the sacred writings & all they have entrusted to their care, to the Lord."[83]

Smith also sought financial compensation for those who helped him in "temporal things" in New York, specifically his father, Joseph Sr., and brother Hyrum, Peter Whitmer Sr., Christian Whitmer, Jacob Whitmer, Hiram Page, and David Whitmer, as well as for the "labors" of Samuel H. Smith, Peter Whitmer Jr., William Smith, and Don Carlos Smith. The conference voted that these individuals "be remmemberd to the Bishop in Zion as being worthy of inheritances among the people of the Lord according to the laws of said Church."[84] Since Partridge had been given the responsibility to "[divide] unto the saints their inheritance" in Zion, the conference was recommending that these brethren were to be given priority.[85]

The conference voted that Smith's revelations be "prized" by the church more than "the riches of the whole Earth." They also appointed Smith, Cowdery, John Whitmer, and Rigdon to be managers of the revelations.[86] A revelation Smith dictated on this day stated that in addition to these individuals, Martin Harris and William W. Phelps, the church's printer, were to be "stewards over the revelations & commandments" and to "manage" them "& the concerns thereof yea the profits thereof." These six men formed the Literary Firm and were permitted to use the profits from the publication of the revelations "for their necessities & their wants." Any surplus money was

---

82. Revelation, Nov. 11, 1831-A, Revelation Book 1, 122 [D&C 69:3–4, 7–8] (*JSP*, D2:131–32).

83. Minutes, Nov. 12, 1831, Minute Book 2, 18 (*JSP*, D2:137–38).

84. Minutes, 18 (*JSP*, D2:138).

85. Revelation, July 20, 1831 [D&C 57:7] (*JSP*, D2:11); see also Revelation, May 20, 1831, Revelation Book 1, 86 [D&C 51:3] (*JSP*, D1:316).

86. Minutes, Nov. 12, 1831, Minute Book 2, 18 (*JSP*, D2:138).

to be "given into my storehouse & the benefits thereof shall be consecrated unto the inhabtants of Zion."[87]

Cowdery and Whitmer left Ohio for Independence, Missouri, on November 20, 1831, carrying the book of Smith's revelations with them.[88]

---

87. Revelation, Nov. 12, 1831, Revelation Book 1, 124 [D&C 70:3, 5, 7–8] (*JSP*, D2:140). The Literary Firm will be modified in the formation of the United Firm on April 26, 1832.

88. Whitmer, History, 38 (*JSP*, H2:49).

8

The Vision

DECEMBER 1831–APRIL 1832

When I came to read the vision of the different glories of the eternal world, and of the sufferings of the wicked, I could not believe it at first. … After I had prayed over it and Joseph had explained it I could see that it was nothing but good sense accompanying the power of God.

—*Joseph Young, "Discourse,"* Deseret News, *Mar. 18, 1857, 11*

Before leaving Ohio with Oliver Cowdery in November 1831, John Whitmer had assisted Joseph Smith as a scribe for the revision of the New Testament up to Mark 9:1, where the handwriting changes to Sidney Rigdon's.[1] Work on the revision was interrupted when Smith dictated a revelation on December 1 calling the Lord's "Servents"—Smith and Rigdon—to proclaim the gospel "in the regions round about … for the space of a season." The revelation instructed them to challenge their enemies to debate in public and private, promising that "no weapon that is formed against you shall prosper and if any man lift his voice against you he shall be confounded in mine own due time."[2] The pressure to confound one's enemies was not conducive to a search for truth but often led to misrepresentation and personal attacks.

The need for this preaching tour was instigated by the activities of former Smith followers Ezra Booth and Symonds Ryder, who began publishing and preaching against Mormonism in Portage County the previous September. On November 24, after publishing six letters from Booth, the *Ohio Star* declared, "We have reason to believe that these letters are exerting an

---

1. New Testament Revision 2, 24 [second numbering] [I.V. Mark 9:1] (Faulring et al., *Joseph Smith's New Translation of the Bible*, 67, 334).

2. Revelation, Dec. 1, 1831, [1], Newel K. Whitney Papers [D&C 71:1–2, 6–10] (*JSP*, D2:145–46).

important influence in opening the eyes of many of the really deluded sub-jects of Mormonism."[3] According to Smith's history, the "scandalous letters" produced "excited feelings" that demanded a response.[4]

Encouraged by Smith's revelation, Rigdon invited Booth to attend a public lecture in Ravenna on Sunday, December 25, where he would "review" Booth's letters and expose them as "an unfair and false representation of the subjects on which they treat." In response to Ryder's public declarations that the Book of Mormon was an "imposition"—deception or imposture—on the public, Rigdon also challenged Ryder to a debate in Hiram.[5] Both men declined.[6]

Ryder, who had returned to being a leader of the Disciples of Christ, responded in a letter to the *Ohio Star*, observing that if Rigdon wished to discuss the matter with him in private nothing was stopping him since "our dwellings are but about sixty rods apart." As to a public debate, nothing would be gained since "to undertake to correct him of his errors before the public, would be a most arduous task for me. His irascible temper, loquacious extravagance, impaired state of mind, and want of due respect to his superi-ors, I fear would render him in such a place, unmanageable, and I therefore fail of accomplishing the desired object."[7] According to Smith's history, Rig-don still lectured in Ravenna, and Smith and he preached in Shalersville "and other places, setting forth the truth."[8]

Smith and Rigdon went first to Kirtland. On Sunday, December 4, they attended a meeting consisting of "several of the Elders and members assem-bled together to learn their duty and for edification," according to Smith's history, but also identified in a revelation dictated at the time as a conference of high priests.[9] The first revelation Smith dictated called merchant Newel K. Whitney as bishop in the east to replace Edward Partridge who was now bishop in Missouri.[10]

After Whitney's ordination, Smith dictated another revelation concern-ing the duty of the bishop. Whitney's main responsibility was to oversee and supply the material needs of the elders preaching the gospel and the poor from the bishop's storehouse, which he operated from his dry goods store

3. "Mormonism," *Ohio Star* (Ravenna, OH), Nov. 24, 1831, [3].

4. JS History, vol. A-1, 179 (DHC 1:241).

5. Sidney Rigdon, "To the Public," *Ohio Star*, Dec. 15, 1831, [3].

6. Sidney Rigdon, "To the Public," *Ohio Star*, Jan. 12, 1832, [3].

7. Symonds Ryder, Letter to Editor, *Ohio Star*, Dec. 29, 1831.

8. JS History, vol. A-1, 179 (DHC 1:241).

9. JS History, vol. A-1, 176 (DHC 1:239); D&C 72:1.

10. Revelation, Dec. 4, 1831-A, Newel K. Whitney Papers [D&C 72:1–8] (*JSP*, D2:146–50).

in Kirtland. The revelation also stated Whitney was to provide for the needs of the stewards over the revelations: "And again let my servents who are appointed as stewards over the litterary concerns of my church have claim for assistence in all things upon the Bishop or Bishops ... that the revelations may be published and go forth unto the ends of the earth that they also may obtain funds which shall benefit the church in all things."[11]

A third revelation concerned the need for a certificate for those going to Zion. A November 3, 1831, revelation had instructed "all you that have not been commanded to tarry" in the east to gather to Zion.[12] Now they were told to first get "a certificate from three Elders of the church or a certificate from the Bishop."[13]

Smith and Rigdon pursued their public relations mission, preaching in Kirtland, Shalersville, Ravenna, and other places, aided by other missionaries, until January 10, 1832, when Smith dictated a revelation commanding the two men to return to revising the Bible "untill it be finished."[14] The revelation also instructed the elders to continue preaching "in the reagions round about" until the next conference.[15] On January 2, a church conference appointed Orson Pratt and Reynolds Cahoon "to visit the doubting members." Cahoon recorded in his diary that they "visited some members in Painsvill some in Chardon some in Kirtland and Made report to the Church," and noted that they "found some gilty and cut them off from the church."[16] While Booth's letters had a marked effect in the Kirtland and Hiram areas, baptisms continued. Peter Whitmer Jr. went to Shalersville and baptized John and Nancy Follet.[17] Ambrose Palmer, who lived in Norton in Portage County, admitted he was affected by Booth's lectures against Mormonism until he heard Cahoon, David Whitmer, and Lyman E. Johnson preach, which "left an impression on the minds of many, that was not easily eradicated" and resulted in his and other baptisms in the area.[18]

---

11. Revelation, Dec. 4, 1831-B, [2], Newel K. Whitney Papers [D&C 72:20–21] (*JSP*, D2:153). This revelation was evidently given after Whitney's ordination since it mentions "the Bishop which has been ordained" (D&C 72:9).

12. Revelation, Nov. 3, 1831, Revelation Book 1, 116 [D&C 133:4] (*JSP*, D2:116).

13. Revelation, Dec. 4, 1831-C, [1], Newel K. Whitney Papers [D&C 72:25] (*JSP*, D2:154).

14. JS History, vol. A-1, 179 (DHC 1:241); Revelation, Jan. 10, 1832, [1], Newel K. Whitney Papers [D&C 73:4] (*JSP*, D2:156).

15. Revelation, Jan. 10, 1832, [1], Newel K. Whitney Papers [D&C 73:4] (*JSP*, D2:156).

16. Reynolds Cahoon, Diary, Jan. 2 and 17, 1831.

17. Peter Whitmer, Jr., Journal, Dec. 1831.

18. Ambrose Palmer, Letter to Oliver Cowdery, Jan. 28, 1833, *LDS Messenger and Advocate*, Jan. 1835, 62.

President of the High Priesthood

Smith and Rigdon had not returned to their work long before they had to attend a general conference in Amherst Township, Lorain County, Ohio, located about fifty miles west of Kirtland, where on January 25 Smith was sustained as president of the high priesthood and ordained by Rigdon.[19] William E. McLellin later wrote that there were "between 70 and 80 official characters there from different states."[20] There are no extant minutes of the conference, but, according to Smith's history, "considerable business was done to advance the kingdom."[21]

At this conference, Smith dictated two revelations about the office of elder. Orson Pratt remembered that at least one of these revelations was "written in the presence of the whole assembly."[22] In the first, McLellin was chastised "for the murmerings of his heart and he sinned."[23] This may have had something to do with an abrupt end to his previous mission. An October 29, 1831, revelation instructed McLellin to travel with the prophet's brother Samuel Smith to the "Eastern lands" and to "bear testimony in every place, unto every people."[24] However, Samuel Smith wrote, "Becaus of disobedience our way was hedged up before us Brother William was taken Sick and I returned about the 25 of december (1831)."[25] Whatever happened, the revelation reassigned McLellin: "Therefore verily I say unto my servant William I revoke the commission which I gave unto him to go unto the eastern countries and I give unto him a new commission and a new commandment." Apparently, at this time, no one questioned that such a quick reversal could be considered as inconsistent with God's omniscience. McLellin's new assignment was to go with Luke Johnson into "the south countries."[26]

The revelation also called five pairs of elders on missions, commanding them to go "from house to house and from village to village and from City to City." Following Jesus's instruction to his disciples in the Gospels, the

---

19. Smith's ordination by Rigdon is mentioned in William E. McLellin, Editorial, *Ensign of Liberty* (Kirtland, OH), Jan. 1848, 61; "History of Orson Pratt," 12b; "History of Orson Pratt. (Written by himself, March, 1858.)," *Deseret News*, June 2, 1858, 62.

20. McLellin, Letter to "Beloved Relatives," Aug. 4, 1832, [4].

21. JS History, vol. A-1, 180 (DHC 1:243). The minutes of an October 25–26, 1831, general conference note that "another General Conference" was to be held in Amherst on January 25, 1832. Minutes, Oct. 25–26, 1831, Minute Book 2, 15 (*JSP*, D2:87).

22. "History of Orson Pratt," 12.

23. Revelation, Jan. 25, 1832-A, [1], Newel K. Whitney Papers [D&C 75:7] (*JSP*, D2:159).

24. Revelation, Oct. 29, 1831, McLellin, Notebook, 1877, [9] [D&C 66:7] (*JSP*, D2:91).

25. Samuel Smith, Diary, ca. Dec. 25, 1831, [1].

26. Revelation, Jan. 25, 1832-A, [1], Newel K. Whitney Papers [D&C 75:6–9] (*JSP*, D2:159–60).

revelation repeated previous revelations in admonishing the missionaries: "whatsoever house ye enter and they receive you not ye shall depart speedily from that house and shake off the dust of your feet as a testimoney against them." The next sentence, however, is intriguing: "And you shall be filled with joy and gladness and know this that in the day of judgement you shall be judges of that house and condemn them and it shall be more tollarable for the heathen in the day of judgement than for that house."[27] The phrase "filled with joy and gladness" is not found in the Gospels and was undoubtedly intended to immunize the missionaries against rejection and imbue them with confidence that they would indeed have the final word in all disputes.

In a second revelation, dictated later the same day, seven more pairs of missionaries were called. Whereas the first group of missionaries had volunteered, this second group of elders desired to know God's will concerning them, perhaps hesitating because of concerns about supporting their families. The revelation seemed sensitive to these concerns, declaring that "it is the duty of the church ... to support the families of those who are called and must needs be sent unto the world to proclaim the gospel unto the world."[28] Recently appointed Bishop Newel K. Whitney was probably responsible for organizing the effort to take care of these families.

Universalist Heavens

After conference, Smith and Rigdon returned to Hiram and to their work on revising the Bible.[29] About February 1832, Luman A. Shurtliff, at the time a Campbellite, rode on a sleigh to nearby Ravenna, Portage County, to hear Rigdon and Smith speak. He recalled, disappointingly, "I did not get much information by this meeting & thought I had herd Sidney preach much better" before his conversion to Mormonism. He thought Smith did not look anything like a prophet, perhaps expecting an older man with grey hair and a beard. "He looked green and not verry intelligent," Shurtliff remembered. "I felt disapointed and returned holm rather cast down."[30]

The weather was unusually cold in January and February as Smith and Rigdon worked on the New Testament.[31] On February 16, 1832, Smith reached John 5:29, which speaks of a time when "all who are in their graves ... shall

---

27. Revelation, [2] [D&C 75:13–20] (*JSP*, D2:160). See Matt. 26:26–29; Mark 14:22–25; Luke 22:19–20; D&C 24:15; 60:15; Weber, "'Shake Off the Dust of Thy Feet.'"

28. Revelation, Jan. 25, 1832-B, [1] [D&C 75:23–36] (*JSP*, D2:161–63).

29. JS History, vol. A-1, 183 (DHC 1:145).

30. Shurtliff, Autobiography, 52.

31. Staker, *Hearken, O Ye People*, 320.

come forth; they that have done good, unto the resurrection of life; and they that have done evil, unto the resurrection of damnation." In the manuscript, Rigdon first wrote "damnation," but then canceled it and wrote "the unjust."[32]

This passage figured prominently in the debates between Universalists and orthodox believers in heaven and hell. It was difficult for Universalists to escape the implications of the "resurrection of damnation," and they usually resorted to a figurative interpretation or, like Smith, suggested a substitution for the word "damnation." In 1809, for example, Universalists in Boston responded to the orthodox use of John 5:29 against their beliefs: "We are inclined to believe the quotation should be rendered thus: 'They shall come forth to the resurrection of *condemnation*,' which places those characters precisely in the same situation, where *every one must be*, before he is a proper subject for pardon and forgiveness; because pardon is never granted until sentence of condemnation has been pronounced on the guilty."[33] They argued that the substitution was justified because "that *word*, in the original Greek, which is here translated, *damnation* ... is translated *condemnation*, in other parts of scripture; and in some other passages, *judgment*."[34]

Smith may have been inspired in his word choice by Acts 24:15, where Paul says to Felix: "There shall be a resurrection of the dead, both of the just and unjust." Removing "damnation" from the binary description of human destiny opened up new possibilities. According to Smith's history, he had already surmised "that if God rewarded every one according to the deeds done in the body, the term 'heaven,' ... must include more kingdoms than one."[35] A revelation dictated to Martin Harris, a believer in universal salvation, in March 1830 revealed that Smith was privately a Universalist despite the anti-Universalist rhetoric found in the Book of Mormon.[36]

Some Universalists of Smith's day believed that there was no hell after death; others advocated for a temporary hell that existed only between death and the resurrection. Opponents of Universalism like the Reverend Bradstreet of Cleveland, Ohio, quoted Revelation 14:10–11, which states that

---

32. New Testament Revision 2, 114 [I.V. John 5:29] (Faulring et al., eds., *Joseph Smith's New Translation of the Bible*, 454). It should be noted that the Book of Mormon, in reflecting the language of John 5:29, referred to the "resurrection of endless damnation" (Mosiah 16:11; cf. Hel. 12:26; 3 Ne. 26:5).

33. *An Address from the Berean Society of Universalists in Boston*, 25; emphasis in original.

34. *Address*, 24.

35. JS History, vol. A-1, 183 (DHC 1:245).

36. Revelation, Mar. 1830, BC XVI:7–12 [D&C 19:5–12] (*JSP*, D1:89–90). See Vogel, "Anti-Universalist Rhetoric in the Book of Mormon"; Ford, "The Book of Mormon, the Early Nineteenth-Century Debates over Universalism."

the wicked "shall be tormented with fire and brimstone ... and the smoke of their torment ascendeth up forever and ever: and they have no rest day nor night."[37] Whereas the Universalist who reviewed Bradstreet's work referred to Revelation 20:13–14 and argued that "it must be remembered that Mr. B[radstreet]'s hell in which ... all the wicked will be tormented eternally, was also cast into this same lake of fire. ... It must also be borne in mind that *before* this hell of Mr. B[radstreet]'s was cast into the lake of fire it delivered up all the dead that were in it—of course they were not cast into the lake with hell."[38] This was in keeping with Smith's March 1830 revelation wherein Jesus declared that those who do not repent "must suffer," although not eternally.[39]

Smith and Rigdon's new text of John 5:29, as they later wrote, "caused us to marvel for it was given unto us of the spirit and while we meditated upon these thing[s] the Lord touched the eyes of our understandings and they were opened and the glory of the lord shone round about and we beheld the glory of the son on the right of the Father."[40] What they then saw was a series of visions that took them from the depths of hell, through a multi-layered heaven, to the highest heaven where God dwells.

Although some of Smith's contemporaries speculated about multiple heavens, Smith's primary source of inspiration was the Bible.[41] The text of the vision Rigdon and he experienced alludes to Jesus's statement in John 14:2 that in his Father's house are "many mansions," and 1 Corinthians 15:40–42, where the Apostle Paul writes that the bodies of the resurrected differ from one another in glory just as the stars, moon, and sun differ in glory.[42] Smith may have also been inspired by Paul's statement in 2 Corinthians 12:2, where he had been "caught up to the third heaven." In naming these heavens, Smith borrowed the terms *celestial* and *terrestrial* from Paul, who was merely contrasting the nature of heavenly and earthly bodies, and added a third, *telestial*, which was possibly inspired by the Greek word *telos,* meaning "the end," which appears in 1 Corinthians 15:24: "Then cometh the *end*, when he [Christ] shall have delivered up the kingdom to God, even

37. Bradstreet, *A Sermon on Future Punishment*, 21; see also Hopkins, *An Inquiry Concerning the Future State of those who die in their Sins*, 20, 46–47.

38. Anon., Review, *Gospel Advocate*, Aug. 6, 1824, 236–37.

39. Revelation, Mar. 1830, BC XVI:7–12 [D&C 19:5–12] (*JSP*, D1:89–90).

40. "The Vision," Feb. 16, 1832, Revelation Book 2, 2 [D&C 76:19] (*JSP*, D2:186).

41. See Haws, "Joseph Smith, Emanuel Swedenborg, and Section 76"; Bowen, "Present in the World of Glory."

42. Compare John 14:2/D&C 76:111; and 1 Cor. 15:40–42/D&C 76:96–98.

the Father. ... For he must reign, till he hath put all enemies under his feet. The last enemy that shall be destroyed is death." Included in his description of the "telestial world," Smith explained: "These are they who are cast down to hell and suffer the wrath of Almighty God, until the fulness of times, when Christ shall have subdued all enemies under his feet, and shall have perfected his work; When he shall deliver up the kingdom, and present it unto the Father, spotless."[43] Later, Smith will add "and bodies telestial" to his revision of 1 Corinthians 15:40.[44]

The vision describes those who are resurrected unto the highest or celestial glory, who are permitted into the presence of God and Christ, as those who are baptized into Smith's church, keep all the commandments, and are "sealed by the holy spirit of promise." This group includes especially those who "are priests of the most high after the order of Melchesadeck which was after the order of Enoch which was after the order of the only begotten son."[45] Those who enter the "terrestrial world" are those "who died with out Law ... who are honorable men of the earth who were blinded by the craftiness of men." In other words, those Christians who do not respond to the Mormon message and may have had missionaries wash their feet against them.

The vision explains that the only people not saved in one of the three heavens are those who apostatize from his church and knowingly rebel against God. "There is no forgiveness in this world nor in the world to come" for apostates who have "denied the holy ghost after having received it and having denied the only begoten son of the fathe[r] crucifying him unto themselves and putting him to an open shame."[46] This passage alludes to Jesus's words in the synoptic gospels about "blasphemy against the Holy Ghost" being unpardonable and the statement in Hebrews 6 that it is impossible to "renew" apostates who "crucify to themselves the Son of God afresh, and put him to an open shame" (Matt. 12:31–32; Mark 3:29; Luke 12:10; Heb. 6:4–6).

In excluding apostates from an otherwise universal salvation, the vision resolved a major objection of the anti-Universalists, for the unpardonable sin of blasphemy against the Holy Ghost was a chief orthodox argument against universal restoration. The *Gospel Advocate* reported in 1823 that "BLASPHEMY

---

43. "The Vision," Feb. 16, 1832, Revelation Book 2, 5 [D&C 76:106–107] (*JSP*, D2:188). Cf. 1 Cor. 15:24–26.
44. See Faulring et al., eds., *Joseph Smith's New Translation of the Bible*, 509.
45. "The Vision," Feb. 16, 1832, Revelation Book 2, 5–6 [D&C 76:51–53, 57] (*JSP*, D2:188).
46. "The Vision," 4 [D&C 76:31–35] (*JSP*, D2:187).

AGAINST THE HOLY GHOST is frequently urged as an unanswerable objection to the salvation of those by whom it is committed. How often we hear it conceded by the most zealous abettors [that is, one who encourages another to commit a crime] for the doctrine of endless sufferings, that if they could discover any way by which the final salvation of those who have sinned against the Holy Spirit, could be possible, they should entertain some hopes of the ultimate bliss of the whole human family."[47] An 1821 article in the *Presbyterian Magazine* thus argued: "There is an unpardonable sin, for which prayer would be altogether useless; and that for this plain reason, it is declared to be *irremissible*. Our Lord has declared it so. It is the sin against the Holy Ghost. Now, it is clear, if this sin be unpardonable, the person guilty of it must for ever lie under the *ban* of vindicatory justice, and consequently his punishment must be eternal. ... We conclude, then, that all men cannot be exempted from eternal punishment upon the ground of a vicarious atonement, because all were not embraced in its design."[48]

According to Philo Dibble, about a dozen onlookers watched as Smith and Rigdon sat motionless staring into space as the vision unfolded. One would say, "What do I see?" And then he would describe what he saw, and the other would say, "I see the same." This process continued for several hours. At the end of the vision, Dibble reported that Smith "sat firmly and calmly," while Rigdon was "limp and pale." Smith remarked with a smile, "Sidney is not used to it as I am." Dibble said that he "saw the glory, and felt the power, but did not see the vision."[49]

Some may argue that Rigdon was in a hypnotic-like trance and assert that Smith was leading the former through a series of suggestions, or what might be called guided imagery or creative visualization.[50] Smith was made aware of Rigdon's capacity for visionary experience when the latter began receiving revelations shortly after meeting Smith in New York in December

---

47. *Gospel Advocate* (Buffalo, NY), Sep. 26, 1823, 293; see also Jan. 16, 1824, 7–8.

48. *Presbyterian Magazine* (Philadelphia, PA), Mar. 1821, 123–24; see also Cleaveland, *An Attempt to Nip in the Bud, the Unscriptural Doctrine of Universal Salvation*, 9; Hopkins, *An Inquiry Concerning the Future State of those who die in their Sins*, 26, 38–39, 72–73, 76; *Methodist Magazine*, June 1820, 213; "Evidences of Endless Punishment," *New York Missionary Magazine, and Repository of Religious Intelligence* (New York, NY), 1802, 415; *Utica (NY) Christian Magazine*, Aug. 1813, 61.

49. Philo Dibble, "Recollections of the Prophet Joseph Smith." *Juvenile Instructor* (Salt Lake City), May 15, 1892, 303–304.

50. S. M. Kosslyn et al., "Neural Foundations of Imagery"; Barrett, "Dissociaters, Fantasizers, and their Relation to Hypnotizability."

1830.[51] As ultimate interpreter of the vision, Smith could create the impression of a shared vision.

Those in the Campbellite movement who knew him before his conversion to Mormonism were not surprised by Rigdon's visionary experiences. As early as 1831, Alexander Campbell noted Rigdon's "peculiar mental and corporeal malady, to which he has been subject for some years. Fits of melancholy succeeded by fits of enthusiasm accompanied by some kind of nervous spasms and swoonings which he has, since his defection [to Mormonism], interpreted into the agency of the Holy Spirit, or the recovery of spiritual gifts."[52] Newel K. Whitney, who was acquainted with Rigdon years before they both joined the Mormons, recalled in 1844: "He was always either in the bottom of the cellar or up in the garret window."[53] Jedediah Grant confirmed that Rigdon's mood swings persisted throughout his life: "Elder R[igdon]. would not only soar as it were to the highest Heaven in raptures of delight, but when dark clouds overpowered his horizon he would also sink into the lowest state of despondency."[54] His brother Loammi Rigdon, a physician, traced his younger brother's mental state to a brain injury he received at the age of seven. Loammi confirmed that Sidney had "received such a contusion of the brain as ever afterward seriously to affect his character, and in some respects, his conduct. ... He still manifested great mental activity and power, but was to an equal degree inclined to run into wild and visionary views on almost every question."[55] Such a consistent portrayal of Rigdon has led one of his biographers to speculate that he suffered from some form of manic-depressive illness, the manic phase of which included religious "hallucinations."[56]

News of the vision spread quickly in Hiram and beyond, and it was immediately seen as a form of universalism. The Utica, New York, *Evangelical Magazine and Gospel Advocate* reported in March 1832 that the Mormons were attempting to "embrace and teach Universalism," to the dismay of the Universalists. The editors of the paper had received a letter from a resident of

---

51. Booth to Ira Eddy, Dec. 6, 1831, "Mormonism—Nos. VIII–IX," *Ohio Star*, Dec. 8, 1831, [1].

52. Alexander Campbell, "Sidney Rigdon," *Millennial Harbinger* (Bethany, WV), 1831, 100–101.

53. *Times and Seasons* (Nauvoo, IL), Sep. 15, 1844, 686.

54. Grant, *Collection of Facts*, 7.

55. As reported by Anthony H. Dunlevy in Patterson, *Who Wrote the Book of Mormon*, 14, which quotes the now-missing *Baptist Witness* (Pittsburgh, PA), Mar. 1, 1875. Dunlevy was evidently related to Dr. John C. Dunlevy, Loammi Rigdon's medical partner in Warren County, Ohio. See Van Wagoner, *Sidney Rigdon*, 13n13.

56. See Van Wagoner, *Sidney Rigdon*, 116–18.

Chagrin reporting that some Mormon elders have "gone to those on whom they had pronounced curses for their unbelief, and asked forgiveness" for "their want of charity for unbelievers."[57]

It is perhaps significant that Smith's hosts, John and Elsa Johnson, were apparently sympathetic to the Universalists before their conversions to Mormonism, while many of their neighbors were vehemently opposed.[58] While most of Smith's followers welcomed the new doctrine, many struggled. Brigham Young, for example, admitted that he was confused by "the Vision" because it was "directly contrary and opposed to my former education," but he decided to suspend judgment. "I did not reject it," he said; "but I could not understand it."[59] His brother Joseph likewise confessed, "I could not believe it at first. Why the Lord was going to save everybody," but after praying and hearing Smith's explanation, he eventually accepted it.[60] In early spring 1833 Lyman Johnson and Orson Pratt discovered that Ezra Landon, who presided over a branch of the church in Geneseo, New York, claimed that the "vision was of the Devil ... & other members joined him." After laboring with the Geneseo branch, Landon and the others accepted the vision and "promised obedience to all the commands of God."[61] However, in September Pratt and Johnson discovered that Landon was again speaking against the vision, and the following December a conference of elders excommunicated him.[62]

The United Firm

On February 29, 1832, Smith and Rigdon traveled thirty miles to Kirtland, where on the following day they held a meeting with Bishop Whitney, Reynolds Cahoon, Joseph Coe, and Hyrum Smith.[63] At the meeting, Smith dictated a revelation instructing Rigdon, Whitney, and him to organize a "permanent and everlasting establishment and firm" to manage the "Literary and Merchantile establishments" of the church "both in this place and in the

---

57. "Changes of Mormonism," *Evangelical Magazine and Gospel Advocate* (Utica, NY), Mar. 17, 1832, 67.

58. Staker, *Hearken, O Ye People*, 262, 277.

59. Brigham Young, Sermon, in "Special Conference of the Elders," *Deseret News, Extra* (Salt Lake City), Sep. 14, 1852, 24–25.

60. Joseph Young, "Discourse," *Deseret News*, Mar. 18, 1857, 11.

61. John Murdock, Journal, May 1–2, 1833.

62. Orson Pratt, Journal, Sep. 16, Dec. 29 and 31, 1833; see also Murdock, Journal, Dec. 29, 1833; "To Whom It May Concern," *The Evening and the Morning Star* (Independence, MO), Feb. 1834, 2:134.

63. Notation in Revelation Book 2, 11 (*JSP*, MRB:435); Hyrum Smith, Diary and Account Book, Mar. 1, 1832, [21].

land of Zion."[64] Despite the optimistic tone, what became known variously as the United Firm, "United Order," or the "Order of Enoch"—intended to generate an income for the church and its members—dissolved two years later when efforts to raise money to pay its debts were unsuccessful.[65]

The revelation stated that the firm was established for the temporal "salvation" of its members, who were to be equal share holders, and declared: "If ye are not equal in earthly things ye cannot be equal in obtaining heavenly thing[s]."[66] Of the three men, only Whitney had substantial assets that he was now being commanded to share equally. The revelation instructed the members to bind themselves with "a bond or an everlasting covenant which cannot be broken."[67] Violation of this agreement would result in excommunication, for, as the revelation stated, "He who breaketh it shall loose his office & standing in the church and shall be delivered over unto the buffitings of satan untill the day of redemption."[68]

The revelation also required Smith, Rigdon, and Whitney to travel to Missouri and "sit in councel" with the church in Zion, "otherwise satan seeketh to turn there hearts away from the truth that they become blinded & understand not the things which are prepared for them."[69] A formal complaint Rigdon drafted about this time indicates that the leadership in Kirtland was concerned about procedural irregularities in the Missouri church. After reviewing the minutes of a January general conference, it was discovered that appointments were being made by the conference independent of church leadership and hence "illegal." In making certain appointments, the Missouri conference "assum[ed] a power with which it has not been invested," "infring[ed] on the rights of the Bishops councellers," and "assum[ed] authority to which they had no right."[70] In exactly one month, Smith, Rigdon, and Whitney will embark on their mission to regulate the Missouri church and unite them financially with Kirtland.

---

64. Revelation, Mar. 1, 1832, [1], Newel K. Whitney Papers [D&C 78:3–4] (*JSP*, D2:198).

65. Cook, *Joseph Smith and the Law of Consecration*, 57–70; Parkin, "Joseph Smith and the United Firm."

66. Revelation, Mar. 1, 1832, [1], Newel K. Whitney Papers [D&C 78:6] (*JSP*, D2:198–99).

67. The words "a bond or" are missing from the copy of the revelation in the Newel K. Whitney papers at BYU, but they appear in the copy of this revelation that John Whitmer made in Revelation Book 1, and Joseph Smith inserted them in the copy in Revelation Book 2. See Revelation Book 1, 145; Revelation Book 2, 16.

68. Revelation, Mar. 1, 1832, [1], Newel K. Whitney Papers [D&C 78:11–12] (*JSP*, D2:199).

69. Revelation, [1] [D&C 78:9–10] (*JSP*, D2:199).

70. Rigdon et al., Charges against Missouri Conference Preferred to Joseph Smith, ca. Mar. 1832 (*JSP*, D2:222–29).

On March 8, four days after returning to Hiram, Smith ordained Rigdon and Jesse Gause as "councillers of the ministry of the presidency of th[e] high priesthood."[71] The November 1831 revelation that appointed Smith as president of the high priesthood made no mention of counselors.[72] Gause, a schoolteacher who was of Quaker stock but joined the Shaker community at North Union in 1829, had only recently been baptized. After serving briefly as Smith's scribe for the Bible revision, Gause was sent on a mission with Zebedee Coltrin; however, he abandoned the mission in August 1832 and disappeared from Mormon history, dying in Chester County, Pennsylvania, in 1836.[73] He was excommunicated in December 1832 and replaced as Smith's counselor by Frederick G. Williams in January 1833.[74]

In preparation for the impending trip of Kirtland's leaders to Missouri, Thomas Marsh, who apparently was acting as branch president, ordained Titus Billings an elder on March 10 and authorized him "to take the lead of [the] Kirtland Church" in his absence.[75] Two days later, a meeting was held in Kirtland, where those going to Missouri "convvenentted to Consecrate their properties to the Bishop at Zion after their arrival."[76]

On March 15 Smith dictated a revelation at Hiram for Jesse Gause, which gave instructions to him concerning his duties as counselor. The revelation stated that Gause was "called even to be a high Priest in my church and councellor unto my servant Joseph unto whom I have given the keys of the Kingdom which belongs always to the prisidency of the high Priesthood," promising that if he "acts faithfully unto the end thou shalt have a crown of Immortality and eternal life in the mansions which I have prepared in the house of my father."[77]

Apparently, Smith hoped to complete the revision of the New Testament before leaving for Missouri at the end of the month, but only reached Revelation 11, when a March 20 revelation instructed Rigdon and him to "omit

71. Notation, Mar. 8, 1832, in Revelation Book 2, 10–11 (*JSP*, D2:201–204).

72. Revelation, Nov. 11, 1831-B, Revelation Book 1, 122–23 [D&C 107:65, 78–79] (*JSP*, D2:133–36).

73. Jennings, "The Consequential Counselor." Gause's scribal work dates to between March 8 and 20, 1832, and his handwriting appears sporadically on pages 136–49 of the New Testament Revision 2, folio 4, which coincides with 2 Thessalonians 3–James 2. Faulring et al., *Joseph Smith's New Translation of the Bible*, 529–47; Jennings, 183.

74. See Smith, Journal, Dec. 3, 1832 (*JSP*, J1:10); Revelation, Jan. 5, 1833, [1], Revelations Collection [uncanonized] (D2:361).

75. Hyrum Smith, Diary and Account Book, 22 (Mar. 10, 1832).

76. Hyrum Smith, Diary and Account Book, 22–23 (Mar. 13, 1832).

77. Revelation, Mar. 15, 1832, Revelation Book 2, 17–18 [D&C 81:1–2, 6] (*JSP*, D2:208).

the translation for the present time" and travel to Missouri immediately.[78] With John 6, Smith began employing a short notation system that was keyed to the printed edition of the Bible he and Rigdon were using, which enabled them to move rapidly through the New Testament.[79] Following his appointment as Smith's counselor on March 8, Gause occasionally sat in for Rigdon as scribe when Smith dictated his revisions for 2 Thessalonians through the Epistle of James.[80] About March 20, Smith dictated answers to questions about the Revelation of John, chapters 4–11. During this process, Smith's followers learned that they were living at the end of the 6,000th year of the earth's 7,000-year existence, when God will send forth his angels to save or destroy life, to "seal up unto life, or to cast down to the regions of darkness," and that the 144,000 mentioned in Revelation 7 were "high Priests ordained unto the holy order of God to administer the everlasting Gospel."[81] While Archbishop Ussher famously dated Adam's creation to 4004 BCE as early as the seventeenth century, W. W. Phelps calculated in the August 1832 issue of *The Evening and the Morning Star* that the first man was created 4,159 years before Christ, which meant that there remained only "NINE years" until "the begining of the seven thousandth year, or sabbath of creation."[82]

Another intriguing document created at this time testifies to Smith's fascination with the "pure language" spoken by Adam and the patriarchs until the confusion of tongues at the Tower of Babel (Gen. 11:1–9). When the Book of Mormon's Jaredites were dispersed from Babel to the American continent, they requested God to keep their language pure, which was granted.[83] When Smith emended Genesis in December 1830, he added mention of a "book of remembrance" that was kept among the ancient patriarchs, written "in the Language of Adam ... which was pure & undefiled."[84] Smith and the early Mormons associated the pure language with the gift of tongues, a kind of ecstatic speech practiced by some Christian groups, including the early Mormons.[85]

---

78. Revelation, Mar. 20, 1832, Newel K. Whitney Papers [uncanonized] (*JSP*, D2:218).

79. Faulring et al., *Joseph Smith's New Translation of the Bible*, 58, 454, 575.

80. Faulring et al., 529–47; Jennings, "The Consequential Counselor," 183.

81. Answers to Questions about the Book of Revelation, ca. Mar. 4–20, 1832, Revelation Book 1, 142, 143 [D&C 77:7–8, 11] (*JSP*, D2:211, 212).

82. "Present Age of the World," *The Evening and the Morning Star*, Aug. 1832, [5]–[6] (see *JSP*, D2:212n94).

83. Book of Mormon, 1830 ed., 539–40 [Ether 1:33–37].

84. Old Testament Revision 1, 11 [Moses 6:4, 6] (Faulring et al., eds., *Joseph Smith's New Translation of the Bible*, 97).

85. See Vogel and Dunn, "'The Tongue of Angels.'"

The original holograph of Smith's revelation is not extant, but it was copied into the revelation book by John Whitmer with the notation that it had been previously "copied by Br [John] Johnson." Like the revelation about the early chapters of John's Revelation, it too was given in a question and answer format: "What is the name of God in pure language[?] Answer Awmen." Continuing in this manner, this document gave Adamic names for the Son of God, man, and angels as "Son Awmen," "sons Awmen," and "Ang[e]ls-men."[86] Smith may have been inspired by the promise in Revelation 3:12, which states, "Him that overcometh ... I will write upon him the name of my God ... and I will write upon him my new name." What name? Verse 14 may have suggested an answer to him: "These things saith the Amen, the faithful and true witness, the beginning of the creation of God." As used here, Amen, which means "truth," is one of the titles for Christ. Inspired by the same passage, Anglican priest Robert S. Hawker published a hymn in 1818 titled "Amen," which begins: "We bless thee, O thou great Amen." Another line reads "God's Christ is your Amen," and twice more calls Christ "the great Amen."[87] It seems probable that Smith's adoption of "Awmen" as a synonym for God was inspired by "the Amen"—pronounced Ah-man—of Revelation 3:14.

On March 20 Smith dictated a revelation that commanded Bishop Whitney to purchase the paper for printing the Book of Commandments in Missouri and for Smith and Rigdon to suspend work on the Bible revision and take the paper with them to Zion.[88] In a January 1832 letter, Cowdery had informed Smith that publication of the revelations could begin as soon as he obtained an adequate supply of paper and suggested that Martin Harris purchase the paper and bring it to Independence.[89] Smith's revelation excused Harris and directed Whitney to make the purchase. To the question, "Shall we finish the translation of the New testament before we go to Zion or wait till we return"? The answer was that there should "be no delays" and that Smith and Rigdon should "omit the translation for the present time" and deliver the paper to Cowdery as soon as possible.[90]

About this time, Smith dictated another revelation concerning the bishops and explained what happens to the property consecrated to the bishop

86. "A Sample of Pure Language," ca. Mar. 4–20, 1832, Revelation Book 1, 144 (*JSP*, D2:213–15).

87. Hawker, *The Abba, Amen, and Corpus Christi Hymns*, 7–8.

88. Revelation, Mar. 20, 1832, Newel K. Whitney Papers [uncanonized] (*JSP*, D2:216–18). See also Revelation Book 2, 19.

89. Cowdery, Letter to Joseph Smith, Jan. 28, 1832, [3], JS Collection (*JSP*, D2:179).

90. Revelation, Mar. 20, 1832 [uncanonized] (*JSP*, D2:216–18).

should he apostatize.[91] Cowdery's January 1832 letter had contained the minutes from a Missouri conference held on January 23–24, which included a resolution that "moneys or properties" consecrated to the church "be expended for the use and benefit of this church" and that if a bishop was removed from office, "such money or properties … shall be handed over to his successor."[92] The revelation clarified, "The property or that which they [bishops] receive of the church is not their own but belongeth to the church wherefore it is the property of the Lord and it is for the poor of the church to be administered according to the law."[93]

There was another reason why properties handed over to the bishop were not the bishop's personal property. One purpose of Smith's trip to Missouri was to inform members of the newly organized United Firm and to place Bishop Partridge under its covenant and bond, thus joining the churches in Kirtland and Zion economically. The revelation explained that "bishops are accountable before the Lord for their stewardships … in the which they are appointed by commandment jointly with you my servents," referring to Smith and Rigdon.[94] The commandment given on March 1, 1832, stipulated that the United Firm, which was to include Partridge, would manage the "Literary and Merchantile establishments" of the church.[95] Under this arrangement, the question of the disposition of properties should the bishop apostatize was no longer an issue.

Similar to the November 1831 revelation defining and limiting the bishop's office, this revelation emphasized that while Partridge presides over the church in Missouri, he nevertheless serves under the president of the high priesthood, an office Smith would hold as long as he does not transgress. As the revelation declared, "The office of the presidency of the high Priesthood I have given authority to preside with the assistence of his councellers over all the Concerns of the church wherefore stand ye fast claim your Priesthood in authority yet in meekness and I am able to make you abound and be fruitfull and you shall never fall for unto you I have given the keys of the kingdom and if you transgress not they shall never be taken from you."[96]

---

91. Revelation, ca. Mar. 8–24, 1832, Newel K. Whitney Papers [uncanonized] (*JSP*, D2:219–22). The only copy of this revelation is dated and endorsed by Newel K. Whitney: "Duty of Bishops &c To Joseph & Sidney march 1832."

92. Cowdery, Letter to Joseph Smith, Jan. 28, 1832, [2], JS Collection (*JSP*, D2:174).

93. Revelation, ca. Mar. 8–24, 1832, [1] [uncanonized] (*JSP*, D2:220–21).

94. Revelation, [1] [uncanonized] (*JSP*, D2:221).

95. Revelation, Mar. 1, 1832, [1], Newel K. Whitney Papers [D&C 78:3–4] (*JSP*, D2:198).

96. Revelation, ca. Mar. 8–24, 1832, [1] [uncanonized] (*JSP*, D2:221–22).

This reiterated the September 11, 1831, revelation that proclaimed, "I have given unto you the Kingdom & the keys of the mysteries of the kingdom shall not be taken from my Servent Joseph while he liveth in-as-much as he obeyeth mine ordinances."[97]

Tar and Feathers

Although a March 20, 1832, revelation had instructed Smith and Rigdon to leave for Missouri without delay, they would not begin their journey until April 1. Meanwhile, anger in Hiram was brewing and soon would erupt in violence. The apostasy of Ezra Booth and Symonds Ryder, the latter of whom occupied the next farm east of the Johnsons, apparently convinced John Johnson's son John Jr., and bothers Eli and Edward, to apostatize as well. Another son, Olmsted, who was visiting his parents, resisted conversion, whereupon Smith prophesied that "he would never return to see his father again." Olmsted subsequently took sick and died in Virginia in 1834.[98] The division in the Johnson family no doubt created tension in the home in which Joseph, Emma, and the twins resided.

A few hours before sunrise on March 25, Smith and Rigdon were dragged out of their beds by a mob, attacked, then tarred and feathered. According to Smith's account, he was asleep on a trundle bed with one of the sick twins and Emma was near him with the other baby when he awoke to Emma's screams. A mob of about a dozen men instantly carried him out the door, one of the men tearing out a clump of his hair in the process. In his struggle to get free, Smith kicked the man who was holding one of his feet in the face. The man tumbled to the ground. As they carried Smith about 330 yards from the house, the men passed Rigdon lying on the ground. Smith supposed he was dead and pleaded for his own life. The men ripped off his clothes and began to beat him. One man, according to Smith's account, "fell on me and scratched my body with his nails like a mad cat, and then muttered out:—'*God damn ye, that's the way the Holy Ghost falls on folks.*'" While smearing Smith's body with tar, one of the men tried to force the tar paddle into his mouth. When Smith turned his head away, the paddle broke. Another man tried to force a vial of acid into his mouth, breaking one of his front teeth.[99]

---

97. Revelation, Sep. 11, 1831, Revelation Book 1, 109 [D&C 64:4–5] (*JSP*, D2:63).

98. JS History, vol. A-1:205 (DHC 1:260). Staker, *Hearken, O Ye People*, 333.

99. JS History, vol. A-1, 205–208 (DHC 1:261–64). The account of Smith being attacked by a mob in Smith's history was composed under his direct supervision on February 9–10, 1843. On February 9, 1843, Smith "gave a relation of the Mob in Hyrum which was written for the History," and on the following day he "reviewed the History of the Mob in Hyrum and the first

When the mob left him, Smith staggered to the Johnson home. Emma mistook the tar for blood and fainted. Someone threw Smith a blanket, and he entered the house. Meanwhile, John Johnson grabbed a club and dispersed the mob surrounding Rigdon, hitting one of them and chasing others off his property. Regaining consciousness, Rigdon staggered through the darkness to his home. "My friends spent the night in scraping and removing the tar, and washing and cleansing my body," Smith recalled. In 1843 he reported that in the morning despite his battered condition, which included a possible broken rib, a missing front tooth, and a bald spot on his head, he went to Sunday meeting as usual and preached, with a slight whistle, to a congregation that included some of the mobbers.[100]

Ryder stated that the mob consisted of men from Hiram, Shalersville, and Garrettsville.[101] Other participants came from Nelson, Mantua, and possibly Freedom.[102] Reportedly the twenty-plus mobbers disguised themselves by blackening their faces.[103] Nevertheless, Smith identified Ryder as the leader, claiming that he heard him being addressed by name and giving orders. Smith also identified three other participants.[104] Luke Johnson, a son of John and Elsa Johnson who was not there, named several other participants, including Dr. Richard A. Dennison from nearby Norton.[105]

Johnson asserted that the mobbers had torn off Smith's clothes "for the purpose of emasculating him, and had Dr. Dennison there to perform the operation; but when the Dr. saw the Prophet stripped and stretched on the plank, his heart failed him, and he refused to operate."[106] Johnson is alone in reporting the planned castration. Castration is unusual for a tar and feathering, and some researchers have connected it with another account that seems

Journey to Missouri." Smith, Journal, Feb. 9–10, 1843 (*JSP*, J2:257–58). Smith said he was carried a total of sixty rods, or 990 feet, or 330 yards. On Smith's missing front tooth, see Staker, *Hearken, O Ye People*, 369–70n69.

100. JS History, vol. A-1, 208 (DHC 1:264). On Smith's possible broken rib, whistle, and bald spot, see Staker, *Hearken, O Ye People*, 350, 367n50, 369–70n69 and n70.

101. Ryder, Letter to Amos S. Hayden, Feb. 1, 1868, in Hayden, *Early History of the Disciples*, 221.

102. Staker, *Hearken, O Ye People*, 346.

103. Sidney Rigdon estimated in 1844 that there were "20 or 30 ruffians." Minutes, Apr. 6, 1844, Nauvoo, IL, General Church Minutes. On the use of black face, see Marinda Nancy Johnson Hyde, Autobiography, in Tullidge, *Women of Mormondom*, 404; "Triumphs of the Mormon Faith," *Geauga Gazette* (Painesville, OH), Apr. 17, 1832, [3].

104. JS History, vol. A-1, 208 (DHC 1:264). Smith also identified Pelatiah Allen and two other participants by their last names only—McClentic and Streeter.

105. Luke Johnson, "History of Luke Johnson," *LDS Millennial Star* (Liverpool, Eng.), Dec. 31, 1864, 834–36; Staker, *Hearken, O Ye People*, 351–53, 379.

106. Johnson, "History of Luke Johnson," *LDS Millennial Star*, Dec. 31, 1864, 835.

to offer an explanation.[107] Church of Christ minister Clark Braden, who in his 1884 debate with E. L. Kelley of the RLDS Church, stated without giving a source that Smith was attacked in March 1832 by a mob, which "was led by Eli Johnson, who blamed Smith with being too intimate with his sister Marinda, who afterwards married Orson Hyde."[108] Most scholars of Smith's polygamy have criticized Braden's statement for its inaccuracy and lack of documentation.[109]

The skepticism is justified. Braden, who probably did not know of the threatened castration, nevertheless made several incorrect assumptions. He evidently assumed Eli was Marinda's oldest brother from the statement in Smith's history that "Eli Johnson, Edward Johnson, and John Johnson, Jr., had apostatized."[110] Eli and Edward, however, were brothers of John Sr., not sons. Braden apparently believed that the "Eli" mentioned in Smith's account as being responsible for bringing the tar bucket was Eli Johnson.[111] He also incorrectly assumed that Smith had married sixteen-year-old Marinda as a plural wife in 1832, rather than in 1842.[112] Braden made this clear when he stated: "Brigham Young, in after years, twitted Hyde with this fact, and Hyde, on learning its truth, put away his wife, although they had several children." What Young taunted Hyde about was Smith's polyandrous marriage to Marinda in 1842. Braden probably based his statement on Ann Eliza Young's 1876 comment that Young "informed his apostle that [Marinda] was his wife only for time, but Joseph's for eternity."[113] Orson and Marinda divorced in 1870. Others besides Braden may have incorrectly assumed Smith had married Marinda while he lived with her father in 1832, which may explain why she stated in an 1877 history that "during the whole year that Joseph was an inmate of my father's house I never saw aught in his daily life or conversation to make me doubt his divine mission."[114]

The motive for the mobbing of Smith and Rigdon was religious, and the attempt to pour acid into Smith's mouth was probably to punish him for what was perceived as blasphemy and to stop him from preaching.

---

107. See Brodie, *No Man Knows My History*, 119.
108. Braden and Kelley, *Public Discussion*, 202.
109. Hales, *Joseph Smith's Polygamy*, 1:42–48; Compton, *In Sacred Loneliness*, 642; Richard S. Van Wagoner, *Mormon Polygamy*, 4, 224–25n4; Staker, *Hearken, O Ye People*, 346–53.
110. JS History, vol. A-1:205 (DHC 1:260).
111. JS History, vol. A-1:206 (DHC 1:263).
112. On Marinda Nancy Johnson Hyde's polyandrous marriage to Joseph Smith, see Compton, *In Sacred Loneliness*, 238–39; Hales, *Joseph Smith's Polygamy*, 1:272–74.
113. Ann Eliza Webb Young, *Wife No. 19*, 324–26.
114. Marinda Nancy Johnson Hyde, Autobiography, in Tullidge, *Women of Mormondom*, 404.

The inhabitants of Hiram specifically and Portage County generally were horrified by Smith's and Rigdon's revision of the Bible and vision of three heavens. Ryder's disaffection was precipitated by his discovery of the written revelation containing the law of consecration, which he interpreted as "the horrid fact that a plot was laid to take their property from them and place it under the control of Joseph Smith the prophet."[115] Olmstead and John Johnson Jr. were no doubt unhappy about the prospect of losing their inheritance. Samuel F. Whitney, brother of Bishop Whitney, claimed that some of Johnson's sons were in the mob and that "they were angry because their father was urged by Jo and Rigdon to let them have his property."[116] In 1844 Orson Hyde accused Rigdon of holding "an old grudge" against the Johnson family, in particular, his wife, Marinda, "because Father Johnson, after giving him and his family a living for a long time, building a stone house for them to live in &c., would not give him his farm and all his property; for he once demanded of Father Johnson a deed of all his property without offering one dollar as an equivalent."[117]

Mormonism was also causing unrest in the neighborhood because families were being divided. One of Johnson's sons and two brothers apostatized. Another son rejected Mormonism outright. Symonds Ryder had apostatized, but his wife remained a believer. Another participant in the mobbing, Benjamin Hinkley, Hiram township's schoolteacher and brick-maker, had joined the Mormons in 1831 with his wife and children but soon changed his mind.[118] Ryder said the mobbing "had the desired effect, which was to get rid of them. They soon left for Kirtland."[119]

Prior to the mobbing, according to the *Geauga Gazette*, Smith and Rigdon had responded to threats of physical harm by declaring that "it could not be done—that God would not suffer it; that those who should attempt it, would be miraculously smitten on the spot, and many such like things, which the event proves to be false."[120] Nevertheless, Rigdon remarked in 1844 that, before being tarred and feathered, he and Smith "had been locked up for weeks and had no time only to eat."[121] Luke Johnson testified in 1837

115. Ryder, Letter to Amos S. Hayden, Feb. 1, 1868, in Hayden, *Early History of the Disciples*, 221.

116. S. F. Whitney, Statement to Arthur B. Deming, Mar. 1885, *Naked Truths about Mormonism* (Oakland, CA), Jan 1888, 4.

117. *Speech of Orson Hyde*, 28.

118. Staker, *Hearken, O Ye People*, 348, 365–66n31.

119. Symonds Ryder, Letter to Amos S. Hayden, Feb. 1, 1868, in Hayden, *Early History of the Disciples*, 221.

120. "Triumphs of the Mormon Faith," *Geauga Gazette*, Apr. 17, 1832, [3].

121. Minutes, Apr. 6, 1844, Nauvoo, IL, General Church Minutes.

that after the attack, Smith's followers were "ordered to arm ourselves for defence, that we might be prepared to resist similar aggressions."[122]

On Monday, March 26, the day after the mobbing, Smith went to see Rigdon who was experiencing homicidal delusions from having his head knocked on the ice. "The next morning I went to see elder Rigdon," Smith recounted in his history, "and found him crazy, and his head highly inflamed, for they had dragged him by his heels, and those too, so high from the earth he could not raise his head from the rough frozen surface, which lacerated it exceedingly."[123] Rigdon recalled in 1844 that "they broke into my house [and] drag[ged] me out of my bed—out of the door my head beating on the floor. They drag[ge]d me over the wood pile[,] and on they went my head thumping on the frozen ground, after which they threw tar and feathers on me—and endeavored to throw aqua fortes [nitric acid] in my face but I turned my face and it missed me."[124]

Apparently the mobbing had exacerbated Rigdon's old brain injury. When he saw Smith, he asked his wife to bring him his razor because he wanted to kill Smith. After she left the room, he asked Smith to bring his razor to him. When Smith asked why, he said to kill his wife, probably for not bringing the razor. Rigdon "continued delirious some days," Smith said.[125]

Two days later, Rigdon was recovered enough to load up an uncovered wagon, leave Hiram with his sick family, and move back to Kirtland "on account of the mob," which Smith said continued to "menace Father Johnson's house for a long time." On March 31 mob action again forced Rigdon to move five miles south from Kirtland to Chardon.[126]

Meanwhile, Joseph and Emma's adopted son, eleven-month-old Joseph Murdock Smith, died on March 29.[127] The bereaved parents blamed the mob, which, according to Emma, "left the door open when they went out with [Joseph], the child relapsed and died."[128] When John Murdock learned of the death of little Joseph, he wrote in his journal that the mob was

---

122. "Much Interest and Anxiety," *Painesville Telegraph*, June 9, 1837, [2].

123. JS History, vol. A-1, 208 (DHC 1:265).

124. Minutes, Apr. 6, 1844, Nauvoo, IL, General Church Minutes.

125. JS History, vol. A-1, 208 (DHC 1:265).

126. See Sidney Rigdon, Notes, Feb. 13, 1843, Sidney Rigdon Collection, CHL, in Vogel, ed., *History of Joseph Smith*, 8:5; cf. JS History, vol. A-1, 209 (DHC 1:265).

127. Smith Family Genealogy, in JS History, vol. A-1, 9 (*EMD*, 1:576). Smith's official history is probably incorrect in dating Joseph Murdock Smith's death to Friday, March 30, 1831 (DHC 1:265).

128. Joseph Smith III, "Last Testimony of Sister Emma," *Saints' Herald*, Oct. 1, 1879, 1.

"unbelieving and hard."[129] With such matters weighing heavily on his mind, Smith departed Hiram on April 1, leaving a pregnant Emma in the care of John and Elsa Johnson.

---

129. Murdock, Journal, 7.

9

Uniting Kirtland and Zion

APRIL–SUMMER 1832

If ye are not equal in earthly things ye cannot be equal in obtaining heavenly thing[s].

—Revelation, Mar. 1, 1832, Newel K.
Whitney Papers [D&C 78:6]

On Sunday, April 1, 1832, Joseph Smith left Hiram with Newel K. Whitney, Peter Whitmer, and Jesse Gause in George Pitkin's wagon and traveled about twenty miles southeast to Warren, where he met Sidney Rigdon. Continuing their journey the next day, they arrived at Wellsville, a distance of fifty miles, and then another twenty-one miles to Steubenville, where they arrived the following day, April 3.[1]

Somewhere along this journey Smith began to worry about Emma, who was in the early stages of pregnancy. In a letter, he advised Emma to go to Kirtland, although there was a mob there, too, and stay with Bishop Whitney's family until he returned.[2] However, Emma was unable to stay with the Whitneys because Elizabeth's aunt was visiting and objected to Emma staying. Instead, Emma stayed briefly with Reynolds Cahoon, then with father and mother Smith, and finally with Dr. Frederick G. Williams, where Joseph found her "very disconsolate" on his return.[3]

---

1. See JS History, vol. A-1, 209 (DHC 1:265–66). The account in Smith's history is based on notes provided by Rigdon. Rigdon, Statement, 1842; Vogel, *History of Joseph Smith*, 8:5–6. Rigdon's statement probably dates to February 13, 1843, when Smith's journal records: "Elder Rigdon came in early in the morning and gave a brief history [of] the 2d visit of the Presidency to Jackson Co, Missouri." Smith, Journal, Feb. 13, 1843 (*JSP*, J2:263). About the same time, Newel K. Whitney gave an account of his trip to Missouri. Whitney, Statement, 1842, 1 (Vogel, *History of Joseph Smith*, 8:7–8).

2. See JS History, vol. A-1, 209 (DHC 1:266). Smith's letter to Emma, which is mentioned in Smith's history, is not extant.

3. JS History, 209. This information appeared when Smith's History was first published in *Times and Seasons*, Sep. 2, 1844, 624, but was deleted in the B. H. Roberts edition. Cf. DHC 1:266.

Meanwhile, on Wednesday, April 4, Smith and company boarded a steamboat and traveled twenty-six miles down the Ohio River to Wheeling, Virginia (now West Virginia), where they purchased a large quantity of paper for printing the Book of Commandments. From Wheeling, they traveled by steamer to Cincinnati, and joined a group of Mormons from Kirtland headed by Titus Billings on their way to Missouri. After traveling about a hundred miles southwest, both companies boarded a steamer at Louisville, Kentucky, and traveled 260 miles to St. Louis. Smith and company left the other group and traveled the remaining 240 miles by stage, arriving at Independence, Missouri, on April 24.[4]

Two days after his arrival, Smith was "acknowledged by the High priests in the land of Zion to be President of the High Priesthood, according to commandment and ordination in Ohio, at the Conference held in Amherst January 25. 1832." The minutes of this meeting also state that "the right hand of fellowship [was] given [Smith] by the Bishop Edward Partridge in the land of Zion in the name of the church."[5] Thus Partridge and the Missouri church acknowledged Smith's authority over them.

The council then settled the conflict between Rigdon and Partridge that began during Smith and Rigdon's first visit to Missouri in July 1831, when Partridge resisted Smith's oversight regarding the purchase of land.[6] In a November 14, 1831, letter, Rigdon accused Partridge of "having insulted the Lord's prophet in particular & assumed authority over him in open violation of the Laws of God."[7] On January 24, 1832, a Missouri conference reviewed Rigdon's charges against Partridge, which they considered "detrimental to his character and standing as a Bishop in the church of Christ," but dismissed them as outside their authority.[8] On March 10, another Missouri conference considered Rigdon's charges, and again dismissed them because they believed the matter had been settled before Rigdon had left Missouri

---

4. JS History, vol. A-1, 209–10 (DHC 1:266).

5. Minutes, Apr. 26–27, 1832, Minute Book 2, 24 (*JSP*, D2:231); Revelation, Nov. 11, 1831-B, Revelation Book 1, 122 [D&C 107:65] (*JSP*, D2:134).

6. In a letter to Partridge, dated September 20, 1831, Ezra Booth wrote: "When you intimated to Joseph that the land which he and Oliver had selected, was inferior in point of quality to other lands adjoining, had you seen the same spirit manifested in me, which you saw in him [Smith], would you not have concluded me to be under the influence of violent passions, bordering on madness, rather than the meek and gentle spirit which the Gospel inculcates?" Booth, Letter to Ira Eddy, Nov. 21, 1831, "Mormonism—No. VII," *Ohio Star* (Ravenna, OH), Nov. 24, 1831, [1].

7. Rigdon's letter is not extant, but was quoted in Minutes, Mar. 10, 1832, Minute Book 2, 22–23 (Cannon and Cook, *Far West Record*, 41).

8. Oliver Cowdery, Letter to Joseph Smith, Jan. 28, 1832, [2], JS Collection (*JSP*, D2:174).

and therefore, as the record states, "we cannot consider them justifiable."[9] According to Smith's history, "a difficulty or hardness which had existed between Bishop Partridge and Elder Rigdon was amicably settled, and when we came together in the afternoon all hearts seemed to rejoice."[10] The minutes state, "All differences settled & the hearts of all run together in love."[11]

On the same day, Smith dictated a revelation, which began by acknowledging Rigdon and Partridge's reconciliation—"Inasmuch as ye have forgiven one another your tresspasses even so I the Lord forgive you." The revelation then instructed nine men—Smith, Whitney, Rigdon, and Martin Harris from Ohio, and Partridge, Sidney Gilbert, John Whitmer, Cowdery, and W. W. Phelps from Missouri—to form a United Firm, "bound together by a bond & Covennant that cannot be broken," to oversee the church's business and publishing interests, both in Ohio and Missouri. The revelation reasoned, "Ye call upon my name for revelations & I give them unto you & inasmuch as ye keep not my sayings which I give unto you ye become transgressors. ... I give unto you this commandment that ye bind yourselves by this covenant & it shall be done according to the Laws of the Land."[12]

Every man in the United Firm would have "equal claims on the properties ... according to his wants & his needs," with the surplus going to "the Lords Storehouse to become the common property of the whole Churc[h]." The revelation expressed optimism about the future of the Firm, for it was to be "an everlasting firm" for the participants and their "Successor[s]." Membership was not voluntary. Should anyone "sin against th[e] covenant & hardeneth his heart against it shall be dealt with according to the laws of my Church & shall be delivered over to the buffitings of Satan untill the day of Redemption."[13]

The following day, Smith formally organized the United Firm under the names of "Gilbert, Whitney & Company in Zion, And Newel K. Whitney & company in Kirtland Geauga Co. Ohio." Phelps and Gilbert were assigned to "draft the bond" for the new Firm.[14] In a single move Smith had bound the two branches of the church and resolved his financial needs, thus

---

9. Minute Book 2, Mar. 10, 1832 (Cannon and Cook, *Far West Record*, 40–41).

10. JS History, vol. A-1, 210 (DHC 1:267).

11. Minutes, Apr. 26–27, 1832, Minute Book 2, 25 (*JSP*, D2:232).

12. Revelation, Apr. 26, 1832, Revelation Book 1, 128, 129 [D&C 82:1, 4, 11–12, 15] (*JSP*, D2:235–36).

13. Revelation, 128 [D&C 82:18, 20–21] (*JSP*, D2:236–37).

14. Minutes, Apr. 26–27, 1832, Minute Book 2, 25 (*JSP*, D2:233). The agreement is no longer extant.

enabling him to continue working on the Bible revision. His confirmation as president of the high priesthood had also helped to clearly define his authority over the church and place Partridge and the Missouri church more firmly under his control.

After visiting the Colesville Branch in Kaw Township, Smith attended a meeting of the Literary Firm on April 30, the first since its organization in November 1831. The group, consisting of Smith, Rigdon, John Whitmer, Cowdery, Phelps and Jesse Gause, "ordered ... that three thousand copies of the book of Commandments be printed [in] the first edition," a third of the 10,000 ordered on November 1, 1831.[15] They also ordered "the printing of an Alminack for Zion this season be left at the option of brs. William Oliver & John," which was not done, as well as "the Hymns selected by sister Emma ... corrected by br. William W. Phelps," which was completed in Kirtland in 1835.[16]

On the same day, Smith dictated a short revelation about the care of widows and orphans, specifically what should happen if they are living on consecrated land at the time of the death of their husbands or fathers. The question may have come up during Smith's visit to the Colesville Saints a couple of days earlier, where two widows and their children lived.[17] Or it may have been in anticipation of conflict with the Gentiles. Whatever the reason, the revelation declared concerning widows, "If they are not found transgressors they remain upon their inheritances."[18]

Either later the same day or on the following day, May 1, Smith attended the meeting of the United Firm, which resolved to borrow "fifteen thousand dollars for five years or longer at six per cent anually or semianually as the agreement can be made, & that N. K. Whitney & co. be appointed to negotiate the same."[19] The purpose of this loan was not stated, but it was probably to supply the Gilbert and Whitney stores in Missouri and Kirtland.[20]

---

15. Literary Firm, Minutes, Apr. 30, 1832, Minute Book 2, 25 (*JSP*, D2:239); see Minutes, Nov. 1–2, 1831, Minute Book 2, 15 (*JSP*, D2:97).

16. Minutes, Apr. 30, 1832, Minute Book 2, 26 (*JSP*, D2:240). Emma Smith had been commanded in an 1830 revelation to "make a selection of Sacred Hymns as it shall be given thee." Revelation, July 1830-C, Revelation Book 1, 35 [D&C 25:11] (*JSP*, 1:164).

17. See *JSP*, D2:241.

18. Revelation, May 31 [Apr. 30], 1832, [1], Newel K. Whitney Papers [D&C 83:3] (*JSP*, D2:240–43). In 1835 this was emended to acknowledge the church's limited power: "and if they are not found transgressors they *shall have fellowship in the church, and if they are not faithful, they shall not have fellowship in the church; yet they may* remain upon their inheritances *according to the laws of the land.*" D&C, 1835 ed., LXXXVIII:1; emphasis added. Cf. D&C 83:3.

19. United Firm, Minutes, ca. May 1, 1832, Minute Book 2, 26 (*JSP*, D2:244–46).

20. Staker, *Hearken, O Ye People*, 230–31.

Nothing is known about Smith's activities during the remainder of his stay in Missouri. On May 6 Smith, Rigdon, and Whitney left Independence by stagecoach.[21] After traveling about 490 miles, Whitney jumped from a runaway coach and broke his leg in several places. The closest town was Greenville, Indiana, about twelve miles before New Albany, and the three men went there to find lodging. After situating Smith and Whitney at Porter's tavern, Rigdon continued the remaining 380 miles to Kirtland, arriving on May 26.[22]

Smith and Whitney would remain at Porter's tavern for the next four weeks. The owner, Daniel D. Porter, had a brother named James who was a physician, and he was probably the Porter brother whom Smith said attended to Whitney.[23] During this stay, Smith believed he was poisoned, which caused him to vomit blood so violently that he dislocated his jaw. According to Smith's history, he went to Whitney and asked for a blessing and he was immediately healed.[24]

Meanwhile, on May 26, a conference was held at Independence, Missouri, "to take into consideration a certain transgression of our br. Oliver committed in the fall of 1830 in the Township of Mayfield Cuyahoga County State of Ohio."[25] Cowdery's "transgression" consisted in proposing marriage to a woman in Ohio when he was already engaged to be married to Elizabeth Ann Whitmer in New York.[26] The timing of Cowdery's censure is curious. The minutes explain that Cowdery's case was not reviewed by church authorities because "some of the Elders supposed that the affair had been adjusted last year when brother Oliver made his confession to the individuals injured & received their forgiveness."[27] So, why the sudden interest in Cowdery's case?

The formal review of Cowdery's case was perhaps instigated by Smith, who may have learned of Cowdery's indiscretion from Booth's letters. Booth had heard about the situation from Peter Whitmer Jr. and Frederick G.

---

21. JS History, vol. A-1, 214 (DHC 1:271). The account of the return trip is partly based on notes provided by Rigdon and Whitney. Rigdon Statement, 1842, 2; Whitney Statement, 1842, 1, in Vogel, *History of Joseph Smith*, 8:5–8; see also note 1 above.

22. On May 26, 1832, Reynolds Cahoon recorded: "Br Sidney arived hear [here] with much intiligence from Zion." Reynolds Cahoon, Diary, [36].

23. JS History, vol. A-1, 214–15 (DHC 1:271). On the Porters, see *History of the Ohio Falls Cities and Their Counties*, 2:295.

24. JS History, vol. A-1, 215 (DHC 1:271).

25. Minutes, May 26, 1832, Minute Book 2, 27 (Cannon and Cook, *Far West Record*, 49).

26. Booth, Letter to Ira Eddy, Nov. 29, 1831, "Mormonism—Nos. VIII–IX," *Ohio Star*, Dec. 8, 1831, [1].

27. Minutes, May 26, 1832, Minute Book 2, 27 (Cannon and Cook, *Far West Record*, 49).

Williams when Booth traveled to Missouri with Smith in the summer of 1831 and later complained that, despite the offense, Cowdery "is set on high, to prepare work for the press; and no commandment touches him, only to exalt him higher."[28] Smith may have wished to knock Cowdery's reputation down a peg. At the same time, it may have been part of the Missouri church's way of asserting its authority. Apparently following Smith's departure, leaders in Missouri had second thoughts about Smith's attempt to put them under Kirtland's control. On June 2 John Corrill, second counselor to Partridge, wrote a letter to church leaders in Kirtland accusing Smith of "seeking after monarchial power and authority," which was taken to Kirtland by Sidney Gilbert who arrived in late June, shortly before Smith and Whitney.[29] Whatever the reason, Cowdery "frankly confessed" his error "to the satisfaction of all present; it was resolved that these proceedings be recorded for the benefit & satisfaction of the Church of Christ."[30] Cowdery married Elizabeth Ann in December.

On June 2, 1832, Martin Harris arrived at Porter's tavern, possibly carrying a letter from Whitney's wife, Elizabeth, and the sad news that Hyrum Smith's three-year-old daughter had died at Kirtland. On June 6 Joseph wrote to Emma complaining that she had not yet written to him. "It would have been very consoling to me to have received a few lines from you," he wrote, "but as you did not take the trouble I will try to be contented with my lot knowing that God is my friend [and] in him I shall find comfort." Then in a gloomy and committed tone he declared: "I have given my life into his hands I am prepared to go at his Call I desire to be with Christ I Count not my life dear to me only to do his will." He also told her of his recent repentance. "I have visited a grove which is Just back of the town almost every day where I can be secluded from the eyes of any mortal and there give vent to all the feelings of my heart in meaditation and praiyr," he wrote. "I have Called to mind all the past moments of my life and am left to mo[u]rn and Shed tears of sorrow for my folly in Sufering the adversary of my Soul to have so much power over me as he has had in times past but God is merciful."[31] Smith may have wanted her forgiveness as well.

With the death of his and Emma's four infant children on his mind,

---

28. Booth, Letter to Ira Eddy, Nov. 21, 1831, "Mormonism—No. VII," *Ohio Star*, Nov. 24, 1831, [1].

29. The original letter is not extant, but was summarized in Orson Hyde and Hyrum Smith, Letter to Edward Partridge and Others, Jan. 14, 1833, JS Letterbook 1:21 (*JSP*, D2:373).

30. Minutes, May 26, 1832, Minute Book 2, 27 (Cannon and Cook, *Far West Record*, 49).

31. Joseph Smith, Letter to Emma Smith, June 6, 1832, [1] (*JSP*, D2:249–51).

Joseph wrote concerning the recent death of brother Hyrum's daughter: "I think we Can in Some degree simpathise with him but we all must be reconciled to our lots and Say the will of the Lord be done." Such thoughts no doubt increased his anxiety to return to his family. "I Should Like [to] See little Julia and once more take her on my knee," he wrote, "and converse with you on all the subjects which concerns us things I cannot [write or] is not prudent for me to write," adding, "I omit all the important things which could I See you I could make you acquainted with."[32] Despite his position of authority, Smith desired to maintain his privacy as a husband and father.

Smith told Emma that his "Situation is a very unpleasant one," that he and Whitney were anxious to leave, and that Whitney thinks he will be able to make the journey soon, which will enable them to arrive at Kirtland about June 20.[33] According to Whitney, Smith came to him one day and proposed that if he agreed, they would leave in the morning, that Porter "will take us in his waggon to the River there will be a ferry ready, & when we get across the river, a hack [horse] will be waiting which will take us to the Landing, where a boat will be in waiting & we will be going up the river before 10 oc[loc]k.—I told him I would go."[34]

The next day, Whitney and Harris found everything as Smith had said. Whitney recalled, "Before 10 oclock we were on a steam boat going up the River." After traveling about 369 miles northeast to Wellsville, Ohio, then on a stage about 95 miles north to Chardon, and finally in a wagon about ten miles northwest, they arrived at Kirtland about June 26.[35]

Keys of the Kingdom

After reuniting with Emma and little Julia at Kirtland, Smith returned with his family to the Johnson farm in Hiram. They had barely settled in when Hyrum came with an urgent plea for him to return to Kirtland with him to settle a difficulty in the church caused by first counselor Rigdon.

On the day before, July 5, Rigdon had preached at a meeting and, according to Reynolds Cahoon, "remarked that he had a revelation from the Lord & said that the kingdom was taken from the Church and left with him."[36] Lucy Smith reported that Rigdon had stated that "the keys of the

---

32. Smith, [2], [3] (*JSP*, D2:251–56).

33. Smith, [1] (*JSP*, D2:249).

34. Whitney, Statement, 1842, 2 (Vogel, *History of Joseph Smith*, 8:8). Cf. DHC 1:272.

35. Whitney. Smith and the others apparently left later than expected and therefore did not arrive about June 20 as anticipated. See discussion in *JSP*, D2:263n314.

36. Cahoon, Diary, July 5–6, 1832.

kingdom are rent from the church and there shall not be a prayer put up in this place to day. ... The keys of [the] kingdom are wrent [rent] from you and you never will have them again untill you build me a new house."[37] After his mobbing in Hiram, Rigdon had moved his family somewhere in Kirtland, but according to Cahoon, the day after his return from Missouri, Rigdon "moved to the flats," probably in temporary housing near the Whitney store, and was evidently unhappy about his situation.[38] In his July 31, 1832, letter to the Missouri church, Smith wrote that when Rigdon learned that they were questioning the recent reorganization of the priesthood, "his heart was grieved his spirits failed & for a moment he became frantick & the advisary taking the advantage, he spake unadvisedly with his lips."[39]

Charles C. Rich, who was present, remembered that Rigdon "came into the meeting and told the congregation they might as well go home as God had rejected them. He left the meeting but shortly returned and gave the meeting another speech, telling them it was useless to pray or do anything, that the Kingdom was sent from the people. This caused confusion in the congregation both before and after dismissal."[40] According to Lucy Smith, Rigdon's words "produced a great excitement in the minds of many of the sisters and some brethren—The brethren stared and turned pale—the sisters cryed." Whereupon Hyrum grabbed his hat and said, "I'll put a stop to this fuss pretty quick I am going for Joseph."[41]

Smith went immediately to Kirtland, where he preached the next day, Sunday, July 8. Rich remembered that "everybody turned out to meeting," and that Smith "denounce[ed] the doctrine of Rigdon as being false."[42] Rigdon was aware of a revelation received sometime in March 1832 that defined the role of bishops as well as "the presidency of the high Priesthood ... with the assistance of his councellers over all the Concerns of the church," and promised Smith "you shall never fall for unto you I have given the keys of the kingdom and if you transgress not they shall never be taken from you."[43] No doubt Smith quoted this revelation when he addressed the church and

37. Lucy Mack Smith, History, 1844–45, bk. 13, [5] (Anderson, *Lucy's Book*, 561–62). See also Lucy Mack Smith, *Biographical Sketches*, 195–97.

38. Cahoon, Diary, May 31, 1832.

39. Smith, Letter to William W. Phelps, July 31, 1832, 4, JS Collection (*JSP*, D2:265).

40. "History of Charles C. Rich," Charles C. Rich Papers, CHL, quoted in Cook, *The Revelations of the Prophet Joseph Smith*, 174.

41. Lucy Mack Smith, History, 1844–45, bk. 13, [5] (Anderson, *Lucy's Book*, 561).

42. "History of Charles C. Rich," quoted in Cook, *The Revelations of the Prophet Joseph Smith*, 174.

43. Revelation, ca. Mar. 8–24, 1832, Newel K. Whitney Papers [uncanonized] (*JSP*, D2:220–22).

"affirmed that the kingdom was ours & never Should be taked from the faithful."[44] According to Lucy Smith, Joseph preached a "comforting discourse" and "told the brethren to cast of[f] all their fears for they were under a great mistake that they were under no transgression," and declared: "I myself hold the Keys of this last dispensation and I forever will hold them in time and in eternity so set your hearts at rest for all is well."[45]

On the following day, Smith called a council of the priesthood and disciplined Rigdon by taking away his preaching license. In September 1844 Amasa Lyman reported that Smith "called Sidney into council and there told him he had lied in the name of the Lord; and says he, 'you had better give up your licence and divest yourself of all the authority you can, for you will go into the hands of satan, and he will handle you as one man handleth another, and the less authority you have the better for you.'"[46]

According to several accounts, Rigdon suffered a relapse of his mental agitation, which some interpreted as demonic in origin.[47] Rich reported that "the devil did handle him by pulling him out of bed and other rough methods."[48] Lucy Smith said that "he [had] the most astonishing encounters with the devil on the following night that ever a man had he said that he was dragged out of bed 3 times successively on the same night," adding that "his contrition of soul was apparently as great as a man could well live through."[49] In 1882 Philo Dibble gave a more miraculous account, reporting that "Sidney was lying on his bed alone" when "an unseen power lifted him from his bed, threw him across the room, and tossed him from one side of the room to the other."[50]

Smith compared Rigdon's repentance to the suffering of the apostle Peter, who, after denying he knew Jesus, "wept bitterly" (Matt. 26:75; Luke 22:62). Smith wrote in a July 31, 1832, letter to the Missouri church that Rigdon, "after receiving a severe chastisement resigned his commision and became a private member in the church, but has since repented like Peter of old and after a little suffering by the buffiting of Satan has been restored to his high standing in the church of God."[51] Three days previous to this letter,

---

44. Cahoon, Diary, July 8, 1832.
45. Lucy Mack Smith, History, 1844–45, bk. 13, [6] (Anderson, *Lucy's Book*, 563).
46. "Continuation of Elder Rigdon's Trial," *Times and Seasons*, Oct. 1, 1844, 660.
47. Van Wagoner, *Sidney Rigdon*, 115–18, 127.
48. "History of Charles C. Rich," quoted in Cook, *The Revelations of the Prophet Joseph Smith*, 174.
49. Lucy Mack Smith, History, 1844–45, bk. 13, [5] (Anderson, *Lucy's Book*, 563–64).
50. Dibble, "Philo Dibble's Narrative," 80.
51. Smith, Letter to William W. Phelps, July 31, 1832, 4, JS Collection (*JSP*, D2:265).

Hyrum Smith had recorded in his journal that "Brother Sidney was ordaind to the high preisthood the second time."[52]

Bible Revision Resumed

About July 20, 1832, Smith hired Frederick G. Williams to replace Rigdon as a scribe. Williams later reported that he was "constantly in Said Smiths employ" to the end of 1835.[53] Williams's handwriting begins with Revelation 12:1 and continues to the end of the New Testament manuscript, then picks up with Genesis 24:1.[54] According to Smith's history, he "recommenced the translation of the scriptures, and thus I spent most of the summer."[55] By the end of July Smith had finished reviewing the New Testament and returned to the Old Testament, writing to his brethren in Missouri on July 31, "We have finished the translation of the New testament great and marvilous glorious things are revealed, we are making rapid strides in the old book."[56]

In his revisions of the New Testament, Smith believed he was authorized by God to restore some of the "plain and precious things taken away from the book" by the Roman Church. In the Book of Mormon, the prophet Nephi saw that the American Gentiles would take the Bible to the Indians, but "because of the many plain and precious things which have been taken out of the Book, … an exceedingly great many do stumble, yea, insomuch that Satan hath great power over them." He also saw "other books" that would "establish the truth of the first."[57] He was therefore intent on resolving apparent contradictions, used to cast doubt on Bible authority, and remove sources of doctrinal disputes.

The declaration in John 1:18 that "no man hath seen God at any time" seemed to contradict Moses seeing God "face to face, as a man speaketh unto his friend" in Exodus 33:11. Smith changed it to read: "No man hath seen God at any time, *except he hath borne record of the son. for except it is through him no man can be saved.*"[58] Similarly, 1 John 4:12—"No man hath seen God at any time"—was changed to read: "No man hath seen God at any time, *except them who believe.*"

---

52. Hyrum Smith, Diary and Account Book, July 28, 1832.

53. Williams, Statement, no date, [1].

54. New Testament Revision 2, Folio 4, 152–54 [Rev. 12:1–22:9] (Faulring et al., *Joseph Smith's New Translation of the Bible*, 59, 575, 581); Old Testament Revision 2, 59–81 [Gen. 24:1–Neh. 10:30] (Faulring et al., 59, 666, 737, 745).

55. JS History, vol. A-1, 216 (DHC 1:273).

56. Smith, Letter to William W. Phelps, July 31, 1832, 5, JS Collection (*JSP*, D2:267).

57. Book of Mormon, 1830 ed., 30–32 [1 Ne. 13:20, 28–29, 32, 38–39, 40].

58. New Testament Revision 2, Folio 4, 105–106 [I.V. John 1:19] (Faulring et al., *Joseph Smith's New Translation of the Bible*, 443).

Matthew and Mark were emended to include two angels instead of one at Jesus's tomb on the morning of the resurrection, thus harmonizing them with Luke and John.⁵⁹ The conflict between the method of Judas Iscariot's suicide in Matthew 27:5 and Acts 1:18, of either hanging or jumping off a cliff, is resolved in Smith's blending of the two passages in Matthew, which explains that Judas "went, and hanged himself *on a tree. And straightway he fell down, and his bowels gushed out, and he died.*" The well-known contradiction in the story of Paul's vision on the road to Damascus, where in Acts 9:7 it is said that those who traveled with Paul "stood speechless, hearing a voice, but seeing no man," and in Acts 22:9 that those who were with him "saw indeed the light, and were afraid; but they heard not the voice," was corrected by replacing the passage in Acts 9:7 with a duplicate of Acts 22:9.

Jesus's prayer in the Sermon on the Mount includes the line in Matthew 6:13—"And lead us not into temptation, but deliver us from evil." Attempting to avoid the thought of God tempting his children, Smith changed it to read: "And *suffer us not to be led* into temptation but deliver us from evil."⁶⁰ Smith revised the simple dictum in Matthew 7:1, "Judge not, that ye be not judged," to read: "Judge not *unrighteously* that ye be not judged," an interesting change in light of Smith's establishment of the bishop's and church presidency's courts.⁶¹ Reflecting Book of Mormon teachings about the salvation of children, Smith added to Matthew 18:10–11: "Take heed that ye despise not one of these little ones ... for the son of man is come to save that which was lost *and to call sinners to repentance but those little ones have no need of repentance and I will save them.*"⁶² In other words, there was no original sin and no need to baptize children. He also inserted a passage in Matthew about Jesus's life between his birth and ministry: "And it came to pass that Jesus grew up with his brethren and waxed strong and waited upon the Lord for the time of his ministry to come and he served under his father and he spake not as other men neither could he be taught for he needed not that any man should teach him[.] and after many years the hour of his ministry drew nigh."⁶³

59. Compare Luke 24:4–6 and John 20:11–13 with Matt. 28:1–7 and Mark 16:5–6.

60. New Testament Revision 1, 13 [I.V. Matt. 6:14] (Faulring et al., *Joseph Smith's New Translation of the Bible*, 171). The passage, however, remained unchanged in the Book of Mormon (3 Ne. 13:12).

61. New Testament Revision 1, 15 [I.V. Matt. 7:2] (Faulring et al., 173).

62. New Testament Revision 1, 43 [I.V. Matt. 18:10–11] (Faulring et al., 202–203). Cf. Book of Mormon, 1830 ed., 161 [Mosiah 3:16].

63. New Testament Revision 1, 4 [I.V. Matt. 3:24–26] (Faulring et al., 162–63).

Smith also resolved other lesser-known difficulties. In John 5:31, Jesus declares: "If I bear witness of myself, my witness is not true," which seemed to conflict with John 8:14: "Though I bear record of myself, yet my record is true." In this case, Smith simply removed the word "not" in John 5:31.[64]

Orson Pratt reported in 1874 that he had been present "many times" when Smith was "translating the New Testament," and "wondered why he did not use the Urim and Thummim, as in translating the Book of Mormon." According to Pratt, on one occasion Smith "looked up and explained that the Lord gave him the Urim and Thummim when he was inexperienced in the Spirit of inspiration," but that he "had advanced so far that he understood the operations of that Spirit, and did not need the assistance of that instrument."[65] The fact that Smith called his revisions of the New Testament a "translation" seemed to imply that he was restoring the text to its original reading through the spirit, although evidence indicates he was reacting to the English text before him, not to the original Greek, which he could not read.

Trouble in Missouri

As Smith and Williams finished the revision of the New Testament and moved on to the Old, the Mormon leader received a letter from Phelps in Missouri, dated June 30, conveying criticisms and challenges to his leadership.[66] The harmony that had been achieved during his recent visit, when it appeared that "the hearts of all" ran "together in love," had dissipated in his absence.[67] On the morning of July 31 Smith dictated a letter to his new scribe addressed to Phelps but intended for all the leaders in Missouri.[68] Phelps's letter of complaint is not extant, but some of its content may be surmised from Smith's responses.

Smith's letter reveals that despite the apparent unity, concerns about the welfare of Zion lingered in his mind even as he left Missouri. He wrote that while Whitney was convalescing in Greenville, Indiana, he experienced "painful anxiety concerning" Zion and wondered "whether that fellowship and brotherly love continued … towards us which you professed when we left you." This led him to a nearby grove where he "communed with him

64. New Testament Revision 2, Folio 4, 114 [I.V. John 5:32] (Faulring et al., 454).

65. Orson Pratt, Discourse, June 27, 1874, *LDS Millennial Star* (Liverpool, Eng.), Aug. 11, 1874, 498–99.

66. William W. Phelps, Letter to Joseph Smith, June 30, 1832, which is not extant but mentioned in Smith, Letter to William W. Phelps, July 31, 1832, 1, JS Collection (*JSP*, D2:261).

67. Minutes, Apr. 26–27, 1832, Minute Book 2, 25 (*JSP*, D2:232).

68. Smith, Letter to William W. Phelps, July 31, 1832, JS Collection (*JSP*, D2:257–72).

who is altogeth[e]r lovely witnessed your case & viewed the conspiricy with much grief and learned the displeasure of heaven and veewed the frowns of the heavenly hosts upon zion & upon all the earth."[69]

Smith also mentioned that when he arrived in Ohio, he found a hand-delivered letter dated June 2, 1832, from John Corrill, a counselor to Partridge, which confirmed his fears about the continuation of the conflict between the Missouri church and leaders in Ohio.[70] According to a letter written in January 1833 by Hyrum Smith and Orson Hyde, Corrill's letter, which is also no longer extant, accused Smith "in rather an indirect way of seeking after Monarchal power and authority."[71] Apparently, the Missouri leaders questioned the propriety of Smith's appointment as president of the high priesthood, whereby Partridge and ostensibly the entire Missouri church were placed under his control. Despite his previous repentance, Partridge was among Smith's critics, evoking Smith's instruction to Phelps to "tell Bro Edward it is very dangerous for men who have received the light he has received to be a seeking after a sign."[72]

Smith understood that he was facing a "critical moment." The letter from Corrill, according to Smith, "gave us this inteligence, that the Devel had been to work with all his inventive immagination ... stirring up your hearts ... by raking up evry fault ... and not being content with bringing up those things which had been settled & forgiven & which they dare not bring to our faces but many with which we were charged with were absolutely false & could not come from any other sourse than the fath[e]r of all lies." Whatever the charges contained in Corrill's letter, Smith denied them. "I do not plead guilty of the charges made against me in that letter," Smith insisted. "I have not given occasion of offence to the brethren or sisters in zion, neither of Jealousy, or evel surmisings. I have ever been filled with the greatest anxiety for them, & have taken the greatest intrest for there welfare. I am a lover of the cause of Christ and of Virtue chastity and an upright steady course of conduct & a holy walk."[73]

Smith then criticized his accusers. "I dispise a hypocrite or a covenant breaker, I judge them not, God shall Judge them according to there works, ...

---

69. Smith, 3 (*JSP*, D2:264).

70. See JS History, vol. A-1, 215–16 (DHC 1:272), which states that Smith arrived in Kirtland "some time in June."

71. Orson Hyde and Hyrum Smith, Letter to Edward Partridge and Others, Jan. 14, 1833, JS Letterbook 1:21 (*JSP*, D2:373).

72. Smith, Letter to William W. Phelps, July 31, 1832, 4, JS Collection (*JSP*, D2:265).

73. Smith, 2–3, 3 (*JSP*, D2:263–64).

and now I conjure you and exhort mine accusers and the hypocrite in zion in the love of Christ yea in the name of Jesus of Nazreth to remember the covenant which they have made with God, and to me."[74] The hypocrites were those who had sustained him as president of the high priesthood but now sought to break their covenant.

Smith wrote with a great deal of concern and passion. "Excuse the warmth of feeling of your unworthy yet affectionate brother in the Lord," he announced at the outset. "What I write I write without sparing any (or the feeling of any) knowing that God will bear me up in what I write." As the prophet-leader, he threatened the Missouri church that "the buffitings of the advasary be upon all those among you who are eniquitous persons and rebelious. ... They do not have my right hand of fellowship."[75]

First Autobiography

About this time, Smith, with the help of Williams, began writing "A History of the Life of Joseph Smith Jr. an account of his marvilous experience and of all the mighty acts which he doeth in the name of Jesus Ch[r]ist ... and also an account of the rise of the church of Christ in the eve of time according as the Lord brought forth and established by his hand."[76] This history was aborted and never published during his lifetime. While it recounts Smith's life up to about April 1829, it is clear that the 1832 history was intended to be more than an autobiography. It begins with a preamble that delineates several miraculous events in Smith's life that were foundational to the Mormon restoration. When compared with later accounts, however, two things are absent from the terse descriptions of Smith's preamble: there is no mention of angelic ordination or Oliver Cowdery's participation. It was an account of Smith's experiences and acts, which he outlined and numbered as follows:

"Firstly, he receiving the testimony from on high," which alludes to a vision of Jesus he experienced in his mid-teens, as described later in this history.

"Secondly, the ministering of Angels." This refers to the appearance of an angel in association with the coming forth of the Book of Mormon, which Smith also described later in his history. As used here, the term "ministering of angels" is generic and echoes a similar statement in the preamble to the "Articles and Covenants of the Church of Christ," dictated by Smith two

---

74. Smith, 3–4 (*JSP*, D2:264).
75. Smith, 1–2 (*JSP*, D2:261–62).
76. Smith, "A History of the Life of Joseph Smith Jr.," 1832, JS Letterbook 1, 1–6 (*JSP*, D2:275–85; H1:3–16).

years earlier, which refers to the Book of Mormon as having been "confirmed to others by the ministering of angels, and declared unto the world by them."[77]

"Thirdly, the reception of the Holy Priesthood by the ministering of Angels to administer the letter of the Gospel, the Law and commandments as they were given unto him, and the ordinances." This should not be read as alluding to the later claim that John the Baptist had appeared and ordained Smith and Cowdery to the lesser or Aaronic priesthood, which included the authority to baptize. Leading Mormons John and David Whitmer and William E. McLellin testified that they had not heard about angelic ordination until it was published in 1834 and 1835, so there were no stories in circulation to which this statement could allude.[78] The Whitmers and McLellin would have understood this statement as a declaration that the authority to baptize had been derived from Smith's having received the "ministering of angels" in association with the coming forth of the Book of Mormon. Indeed, the "Articles and Covenants" had declared that "God visited him by an holy angel," who "gave unto him commandments which inspired him from on high."[79] The innovation here was to call the authority derived from the angel's command "holy priesthood," but this would evolve as well.

In the month following their 1829 baptisms, Smith dictated a revelation that reminded Cowdery, "Thou hast been baptized by the hand of my servant [Joseph Smith] according to that which I have *commanded* him: Wherefore he hath fulfilled the thing which I *commanded* him."[80] Prior to revealing the angel-ordination story in his 1834 history, Cowdery stated what was more widely known: "After writing the account given of the Savior's ministry to the remnant of the seed of Jacob, upon this continent, it was easily to be seen ... that amid the great strife and noise concerning religion, none had authority from God to administer the ordinances of the gospel ... and we only waited for the commandment to be given, 'Arise and be baptized.'"[81]

77. Articles and Covenants, ca. Apr. 1830, "The Mormon Creed," *Painesville (OH) Telegraph*, Apr. 19, 1831 [D&C 20:10] (*JSP*, D1:121).

78. On David and John Whitmer, see Gurley, Jr., "Questions asked of David Whitmer," 2 (*EMD*, 5:137); "Report of Elders Orson Pratt and Joseph F. Smith," *Deseret News* (Salt Lake City), Nov. 16, 1878 (*EMD*, 5:50). On William E. McLellin, see *True L[atter] D[ay] Saints' Herald* (Plano, IL), Sep. 15, 1870, 556 (*EMD*, 5:329n9); McLellin, Letter to Joseph Smith III, July 1872 (*EMD*, 5:329). See also Vogel, "Evolution of Early Mormon Priesthood Narratives," 58–60, 64.

79. Articles and Covenants, ca. Apr. 1830, "The Mormon Creed," *Painesville Telegraph*, Apr. 19, 1831 [D&C 20:6–7] (*JSP*, D1:121).

80. Revelation, June 1829-B, BC XV:6–7 [D&C 18:7] (*JSP*, D1:71); emphasis added.

81. Oliver Cowdery, Letter to W. W. Phelps, Sep. 7, 1834, *LDS Messenger and Advocate* (Kirtland, OH), Oct. 1834, 15 (*EMD*, 2:419–20).

The command came, according to Smith and Cowdery, on May 15, 1829.[82] In her 1845 history, Lucy Smith remembered what she had been told about this event: "One morning, they sat down to their work, as usual, and the first thing which presented itself through the Urim and Thummim [seer stone], was a commandment for Joseph and Oliver to repair to the water, and attend to the ordinance of Baptism. They did so ... they had now received authority to baptize."[83]

"Fourthly, a confirmation and reception of the High Priesthood after the Holy Order of the Son of the Living God [with] power and ordinance from on high to preach the Gospel in the administration and demonstration of the spirit, the Keys of the Kingdom of God conferred upon him and the continuation of the blessings of God to him &c." This refers to the introduction of the "high Priesthood" at the June 1831 conference. It is important to note that at this time there were only two priesthoods: the "holy priesthood"—which consisted of elders, priests, teachers, and deacons—and high priests holding the high priesthood. This view of the priesthood will undergo modification when Smith dictates an important revelation on priesthood in September 1832.

In the course of outlining his early history, Smith claimed that he had a vision of Jesus when he was fifteen, or in 1821. Less polished than the history he began in 1838, the 1832 account, written in his own hand, contains no reference to the appearance of God the Father:

> While in the attitude of calling upon the Lord ... a piller of light above the brightness of the sun at noon day come down from above and rested upon me and I was filled with the spirit of God and the Lord opened the heavens upon me and I saw the Lord and he spake unto me saying Joseph my Son thy Sins are forgiven thee. ... Behold I am the Lord of glory I was crucifyed for the world that all those who believe on my name may have Eternal life behold the world lieth in sin at this time and none doeth good no not one they have turned aside from the Gospel and keep not my commandments they draw near to me with their lips while their hearts are far from me and mine anger is kindling against the inhabitants of the earth to visit them acording to th[e]ir ungodliness and to bring to pass that which hath been spoken by the mouth of the prophets and Ap[o]stles behold and lo I come quickly as it [is] written of me in the cloud clothed in the glory

---

82. JS History, vol. A-1, 18 (DHC 1:41); and Oliver Cowdery, introduction to blessings, Sep. 1835, Patriarchal Blessing Book, 1:8–9 (*EMD*, 2:452).

83. Lucy Mack Smith, *Biographical Sketches*, 131 (*EMD*, 1:381).

of my Father[.] and my Soul was filled with love and for many days I could rejoice with great joy and the Lord was with me.[84]

Although different than later accounts that describe the appearance of two personages, this account was nevertheless consistent with Book of Mormon theology, where Jesus is both the Father and Son—which is recognized by theologians as modalism or Sabellianism, where the Father and Son are different modes of the same person.[85] King Benjamin, for example, told his people about 124 BCE that "the time cometh, and is not far distant, that with power, the Lord Omnipotent who reigneth, who was, and is from all eternity to all eternity, shall come down from Heaven, among the children of men, and shall dwell in a tabernacle of clay. ... And he shall be called Jesus Christ, the Son of God, the Father of Heaven and Earth, the creator of all things, from the beginning."[86] In the first part of the Book of Mormon, Nephi saw a vision of the "condescension of God" and was told that the "virgin" whom he saw was "the mother of God, after the manner of the flesh."[87] When Nephi saw the virgin "bearing a child in her arms," the angel declared: "Behold the Lamb of God, yea, even the Eternal Father."[88] About 148 BCE, the prophet

---

84. JS History, 1832, JS Letterbook 1, 3 (*JSP*, H1:12–13). In 2012 Steven C. Harper, formerly a BYU professor of church history and doctrine and since an editor of the Joseph Smith Papers, published a book on Smith's first vision in which he tried to explain the absence of the Father in the 1832 account: "We could interpret the 1832 account to mean that Joseph saw one being who then revealed another while referring to both beings as 'the Lord': 'the Lord [Father] opened the heavens upon me and I saw the Lord [Son].'" Harper, *Joseph Smith's First Vision*, 91. The problem is that the only identification of "the Lord" in the text is with Jesus, who opened the heavens to reveal himself. In the 1832 account there are not two personages in the light and the Father is not there to introduce the Son, but instead the Son introduces himself. Harper's interpretation is anachronistic for 1832 since, as discussed below, Smith's earliest theology described Jesus as both the Father and the Son.

85. Vogel, "The Earliest Mormon Concept of God." Writers wishing to harmonize the Book of Mormon's apparent modalism with Smith's later teaching on the Godhead cite other passages which seem to contradict the oneness demanded by modalism. Bruening and Paulsen, "The Development of the Mormon Understanding of God," 129. The problem is that these other passages refer to such things as the voice of the Father introducing the Son, the Son praying to the Father, the subjection of the Son to the will of the Father, and the Son ascending to the Father (3 Ne. 11:6–8, 32, 36; 15:1, 18–19; 18:27; 26:2, 5, 15), which have direct parallels in the New Testament, but such passages never discouraged modalists, who interpret them as different modes of God rather than as separate persons. Since all theological positions have to explain *oneness* in light of passages implying *separateness*, I argue priority should be given to the unique and explicit modalistic passages in the Book of Mormon. Boyd Kirkland has similarly argued that "the more specific Book of Mormon statements on the relationship between the Father and the Son should serve as the framework for understanding the theology of 3 Nephi rather than vice-versa." Boyd Kirkland, "Jehovah as the Father," *Sunstone*, Autumn 1984, 43n7.

86. Book of Mormon, 1830 ed., 160 [Mosiah 3:5, 8].

87. Book of Mormon, 1830 ed., 25 [1 Ne. 11:16, 18, 26].

88. Book of Mormon, 1830 ed., 25 [1 Ne. 11:21].

Abinadi, before being martyred, explained the oneness of the Father and the Son in words that modalists would have understood:

> And now Abinadi saith unto them, I would that ye should understand that God himself shall come down among the children of men, and shall redeem his people; and because he dwelleth in flesh, he shall be called the Son of God: and having subjected the flesh to the will of the Father, being the Father and the Son; the Father, because he was conceived by the power of God; and the Son, because of the flesh; thus becoming the Father and Son: and they are one God, yea, the very Eternal Father of Heaven and of Earth.[89]

The 1832 account was also consistent with changes Smith had made recently to his revision of the New Testament. For example, in Luke 10:22, Jesus declares that "no man knoweth who the Son is, but the Father; and who the Father is, but the Son, and he to whom the Son will reveal him." Smith changed this to read: "No man knoweth that the son is the Father, and that the Father is the son, but him to whom the Son will reveal it."[90] In Matthew 9 Smith added an exchange between the Pharisees and Jesus, wherein they ask Jesus why he would not accept them with their baptism, "seeing we keep the whole law" of Moses. Jesus answers: "Ye keep not the law if ye had kept the law ye would have received me for I am he who gave the law."[91]

While the appearance of Jesus to young Joseph Smith was not a unique claim among those who had been exposed to the revivalist fires of the Burnt-Over District, it would have nevertheless been surprising to his followers.[92] All they knew at this point, as stated in the preamble of the Articles, was that prior to the 1823 appearance of the angel, "it truly was manifested" to Smith "that he had received a remission of his sins."[93] Without further details, readers of the "Articles and Covenants" would have assumed Smith's "manifestation" was no different from what was required of them to be members: to witness "unto the church that they truly repent of all their sins,

---

89. Book of Mormon, 1830 ed., 186 [Mosiah 15:1–4].

90. New Testament Revision 2, Folio 3, 70 (Faulring et al., *Joseph Smith's New Translation of the Bible*, 393).

91. New Testament Revision 1, 22 [I.V. Matt. 9:18–19] (Faulring et al., 179–80). Cf. 3 Nephi 15:5.

92. It has been widely recognized that the 1832 account fits well into nineteenth-century revivalism. See Lambert and Cracroft, "Literary Form and Historical Understanding."

93. Articles and Covenants, ca. Apr. 1830, "The Mormon Creed," *Painesville (OH) Telegraph*, Apr. 19, 1831 [D&C 20:5] (*JSP*, D1:121).

and ... truly manifest by their works that they have received of the gift of Christ unto the remission of their sins."[94]

Despite having been called as an apostle in 1835, McLellin, who will be excommunicated in 1838 and was apparently unaware of the publication of Smith's first vision account in 1842, questioned how Smith and Cowdery could call themselves "apostles" in the 1830 Articles since they had not seen Jesus.[95] "For them to make such a profession was simply false in every sense of the word," McLellin argued in 1878. "They could not be apostles of Jesus unless they had seen him."[96] McLellin added that "the Apostles of Christ at Jerusalem, and all his Disciples in America saw, heard, and felt, hence they could bear a firm witness and testimony that they most positively knew what they declared. Did Smith & Cowdery thus know? They did not. They never in the early days of the church so professed or declared."[97] McLellin's statements show not only that knowledge of Smith's first vision was unknown even among leading Mormons but also that a claim to have seen Jesus before the church's organization would have enhanced Smith's authority claims.

Before discontinuing his history, Smith made a claim for Cowdery, who at this time was in Missouri, that appears nowhere else and seems incongruous with Cowdery's later seeing the angel with the plates as one of three special witnesses to the Book of Mormon. According to Smith, prior to meeting Cowdery in April 1829, "[the] Lord appeared unto a young man by the name of Oliver Cowd[e]ry and shewed unto him the plates in a vision."[98] Thus Smith and Cowdery were apostles at the time the church was founded.

Besides the absence of the Father, there are other differences, even contradictions, between the 1832 and 1838 accounts. In 1838 Smith said he prayed to "know which of all the sects was right, (for at this time it had never entered into my heart that all were wrong) and which I should join."[99] In 1832 he said he had already concluded prior to his vision that there was no true church on earth. In this account, Smith said: "By Searching the Scriptures I found that mankind did not come unto the Lord but that they had apostatised from the true and liveing faith and there was no society or denomination that built

---

94. Articles and Covenants, ca. Apr. 1830 [D&C 20:37] (*JSP*, D1:123). On the lack of awareness of Joseph Smith's claimed vision of deity among early Mormons, see James B. Allen, "Emergence of a Fundamental."

95. Articles and Covenants, ca. Apr. 1830 [D&C 20:2–3] (*JSP*, D1:120).

96. Quoted in Larson and Passey, eds., *The William E. McLellin Papers*, 404.

97. William E. McLellin, Notebook, 1877, 43, in Larson and Passey, eds., *The William E. McLellin Papers*, 424.

98. JS History, 1832, JS Letterbook 1, 6 (*JSP*, H1:16).

99. JS History, vol. A-1, 3 (DHC 1:6).

upon the Gospel of Jesus Christ as recorded in the new testament"[100] Given his conclusion that all the churches were apostate, where could he go for salvation? He declares: "Therefore I cried unto the Lord for mercy for there was none else to whom I could go and obtain mercy." The first words Jesus spoke in this account were "Joseph my Son thy Sins are forgiven thee … I was crucifyed for the world that all those who believe on my name may have Eternal life."[101] In other words, Smith was saved despite the apostate condition of the churches. That was his answer. In 1832 there was no revival, no confusion over which church to join, and no command by deity to join none of the churches. Instead, Smith was motivated by a need for salvation and forgiveness of sins, not a quest to find the true church.

The 1832 history includes an account of the three appearances on the night of September 21–22 (incorrectly dated to 1822, rather than 1823) of the angel who revealed the location of the gold plates of the Book of Mormon buried in a nearby hill in Manchester, New York. After three attempts to remove the plates, seventeen-year-old Smith was told that he was not yet ready. This history mentions Smith's marriage to Emma, his obtaining the plates on September 22, 1827, and his relocation to Harmony, Susquehanna County, Pennsylvania.[102]

In his own hand, Smith described copying some of the characters from the plates and Martin Harris taking them to the learned in the East. There is no mention of Professor Charles Anthon pronouncing the characters and the accompanying translation correct, as in the 1838 account. Instead, alluding to Isaiah 29:11, Harris says, "Read this I pray thee and the learned said I cannot." Smith presented himself as the "unlearned" of Isaiah 29:12, for whom "the Lord had prepared spectacles for to read the Book." The history ends by telling the story of Harris's losing the 116-page translation manuscript and being replaced by Cowdery as scribe.[103]

If this history had been completed, it would have likely been printed in the newly launched periodical *The Evening and the Morning Star* published by Phelps in Independence. The timing of its composition and emphasis on Smith's reception of authority through various charismatic experiences may be seen as an effort to bolster Smith's position as the church's founder in response to the recent challenges from the Missouri leaders.

---

100. JS History, 1832, JS Letterbook 1, 2 (*JSP*, H1:11–12).
101. JS Letterbook 1, 3 (*JSP*, H1:12–13).
102. JS Letterbook 1, 4–5 (*JSP*, H1:14).
103. JS Letterbook 1, 5 (*JSP*, H1:15).

10

Return to Kirtland

You cannot find in the New Testament part of the Bible or Book of
Mormon where one single high priest was ever in the Church of Christ.
—David Whitmer, An Address to All Believers in Christ
(Richmond, MO: David Whitmer, 1887), 62

On September 12, 1832, Joseph, a pregnant Emma, and their adopted
daughter, Julia, moved back to Newel K. Whitney's white store on the Kirtland flats.[1] Smith's presence in Kirtland was needed to better supervise the
economic and institutional growth of his church and to more quickly deal
with correspondence from Missouri.

One of the first things Smith did after he got settled in was to issue a
major revelation about priesthood, which he began dictating to his scribe
Frederick G. Williams on the evening of September 22. They were joined by
"six Elders," many of whom had just returned from missions in the eastern
states. Later, the group swelled to include "Eleven high Priests save one."[2]
At this time, there were twelve leading high priests in Kirtland—Smith,
Sidney Rigdon, Joseph Smith Sr., Hyrum Smith, Ezra Thayer, Zebedee Coltrin, Newel K. Whitney, John Murdock, Frederick G. Williams, Joseph Coe,
Samuel Smith, and Orson Hyde—but Samuel Smith and Orson Hyde were
still on a mission in the East.[3] Sentence-by-sentence, Smith concluded the
six-page revelation early the next morning.[4]

---

1. [Emma Smith], List, ca. 1845, in Lucy Smith, History, 1844–45, Miscellany; Staker, *Hearken, O Ye People*, 251, 377.

2. Revelation, Sep. 22–23, 1832, [1], [2], Newel K. Whitney Papers [D&C 84:1] (*JSP*,
D2:293, 297).

3. See *JSP*, D2:297n60; Orson Hyde and Hyrum Smith, Letter to Edward Partridge and
Others, Jan. 14, 1833, JS Letterbook 1, 20–25 (*JSP*, D2:372).

4. According to Evan Greene, the revelation was dictated on "the night of the 22nd and 23rd
of September, 1832." Lula Greene Richards, "Brief Life Sketch of Evan Melbourne Greene,"
typescript, 2, private possession, quoted in *JSP*, D2:289n17.

The revelation discussed the two orders of priesthood mentioned in the preamble of Smith's history, but with more precision. It referred to the "lesser Priesthood" and "greater Priesthood" and for the first time identified the lesser with Aaron, the brother of Moses and first high priest, through whose lineage the Israelite priesthood descended. The claim that the restored church would include the Levitical or Aaronic priesthood, which ministered under the Law of Moses, was the most controversial aspect of this revelation. Indeed, most Christians in Smith's day believed the Old Testament priesthood ended with the Law of Moses and was superseded by Christ's priesthood, as explained in Hebrews 7.

The revelation anticipated criticism and offered two defenses. First, it alluded to the promise in Exodus 40:15 that Aaron's sons would be given "an everlasting priesthood throughout their generations," when it declared "the Lord confirmed a priesthood also upon Aaron and his seed throughout all their generations of the Jews. which priesthood also continueth and abideth for ever with the Priesthood which is after the holiest order of God"—meaning the high priesthood. Second, the revelation echoed the Lord's promise in Malachi 3:3 to "purify the sons of Levi, and purge them as gold and silver, that they may offer unto the Lord an offering in righteousness." Thus the revelation predicted the fulfilling of this promise, stating that "the sons of Moses, and also the sons of Aaron shall offer an acceptable offering and sacrifice in the house of the Lord which house shalt be built unto the Lord in this generation, upon the consecrated spot as I have appointed"—meaning Independence, Missouri.[5]

The revelation's discussion of the high priesthood also contains rhetoric to justify its existence in the church. The letters Smith received from Missouri complaining about his recent appointment as president of the high priesthood have not survived, but they may have included skepticism about the high priesthood. If so, some of those objections would have been the same ones that were subsequently raised by David Whitmer, who in later years judged Smith's introduction of the high priesthood as a mistake. "You cannot find in the New Testament part of the Bible or Book of Mormon where one single high priest was ever in the Church of Christ," Whitmer observed in 1887. "The office of Elder is spoken of in many places, but not one word about a High Priest being in the church." The New Testament only

---

5. Revelation, Sep. 22–23, 1832, [1], [2], Newel K. Whitney Papers [D&C 84:18, 31] (*JSP*, D2:295, 297).

speaks of Christ as "the Apostle and High Priest of our profession" and "a Priest for ever after the order of Melchisedec," Whitmer argued. He concluded that "the office of High Priests was established in the church almost two years after its beginning by men who had drifted into error."[6] William E. McLellin similarly decided that "the Gospel dispensation, can have but One High Priest—Christ Jesus! ... The highest office in it for man on earth now or in the Apostolic age is the Apostleship. Christ set in his church 'First, Apostles.' [1 Cor. 12:28] &c.—and so on to the Deacons."[7]

The revelation built upon the discussion of the high priesthood in Alma 13, which expands and interpolates the description in Hebrews 7 of Christ being a priest after the order of Melchizedek, a contemporary of Abraham. Alma 13 turned Hebrews 7 on its head and made Melchizedek a priest after the order of the Son of God. According to Alma's first-century BCE discourse, Melchizedek was one in a long line of high priests who were ordained "after the order of the Son of the only begotten of the Father, which is without beginning of days or end of years."[8] Whitmer interpreted "this holy order of priesthood" as merely "a type of Christ's order," and that Christ "[did] away with all types and shadows under the old law, himself alone being our great and last High Priest."[9]

However, the September 1832 revelation explained that Aaron and his sons were given the "lesser Priesthood," whereas the line of high priests before Aaron held the "greater Priesthood." According to the revelation, Moses had received the "holy Priesthood ... under the [hand of his] father in law, Jethro," who had received it through a long line of successive ordinations, which included Melchizedek, back to Adam.[10] This was news to Bible readers, although Alma 13 had said of Melchizedek, "there were many before him, and also there were many afterwards, but none were greater."[11] In the history he wrote about this time, Smith referred to the first bestowal of authority as the "holy Priesthood," but the revelation linked this term with the "greater Priesthood," explaining that because Israel rebelled, the Lord "took Moses out of there midst and the holy Priesthood also, and the lesser

6. Whitmer, *An Address to All Believers in Christ*, 62–63. Heb. 3:1; 7:17.

7. William E. McLellin, Letter to Joseph Smith III, Jan. 10, 1861, in Larson and Passey, eds., *William E. McLellin Papers*, 441.

8. Book of Mormon, 1830 ed., 259 [Alma 13:9].

9. Whitmer, *Address*, 67.

10. Revelation, Sep. 22–23, 1832, [1], Newel K. Whitney Papers [D&C 84:6–16] (*JSP*, D2:293).

11. Book of Mormon, 1830 ed., 260 [Alma 13:19].

Priesthood continued" with Aaron and his sons.[12] This is significant because it created two distinct priesthoods with different origin stories, which justified separate restorations.

The September 1832 revelation also restructured the church offices, explaining that "the offices of Teacher and Deacon are necessary appendages belonging to the lesser Priesthood, which priesthood was confirmed upon Aaron and his sons." The revelation explained, rather anachronistically, that "the offices of Elder & Bishop [both of which predated the June 1831 endowment of the High Priesthood] are necessary appendages belon[g]ing unto the high Priesthood."[13] In other words, the high priesthood was not an addition to the authority upon which the church was organized in April 1830, but a fullness of what was already there.

This revelation laid the groundwork for Smith and Cowdery's subsequent claims to angelic ordination, explaining that although the lesser priesthood had "continue[d] with the house of Aaron among the children of Israel until John [the Baptist]. ... He was ... ordained by the Angel of God at the time he was eight days old unto this power to overthrow the kingdom of the Jews."[14] However, John was a special case that Smith had not yet applied to himself.

The 1832 revelation stated that without the greater or high priesthood "no man can see the face of God, even the Father, and live"—which is puzzling since previously Smith had penned an account of his First Vision of deity a decade earlier.[15] In an 1880 sermon, Apostle Orson Pratt attempted to explain this discrepancy by claiming that Smith "had been already ordained before this world was made," apparently alluding to Alma 13.[16] In his discourse on the high priesthood, Alma explained: "I would that ye should remember that the Lord God ordained Priests, after his holy order, which was after the order of his Son. ... And this is the manner after which they were ordained, being called and prepared from the foundation of the world, according to the foreknowledge of God."[17] Similarly, a revelation Smith dictated the following December explained that "the [high] priesthood hath continued through the lineage of your fathers—for ye are lawful heirs, according to the flesh, and have been hid from the world with

12. Revelation, Sep. 22–23, 1832, [1], Newel K. Whitney Papers [D&C 84:25] (*JSP*, D2:296).

13. Revelation, [2] [D&C 84:29–30] (*JSP*, D2:297).

14. Revelation, [1] [D&C 84:27–28] (*JSP*, D2:296).

15. Revelation, [1] [D&C 84:22] (*JSP*, D2:295).

16. Orson Pratt, "The Divine Authority of the Holy Priesthood," Oct. 10, 1880, *Journal of Discourses*, 22:29.

17. Book of Mormon, 1830 ed., 258 [Alma 13:1, 3].

Christ in God—therefore your life and the priesthood have remained, and must needs remain through you and your lineage."[18] At this point, Smith saw no need to claim his authority came through angelic ordination—God's will was enough.

This revelation promised that "whoso is faithful unto the attaining of these two Priesthoods of which I have spoken and the magnifying there calling are sanctified by the spir[i]t unto the renewing of there bodies that they become the sons of Moses and of Aaron and the seed of Abraham. ... Therefore all that my father hath shall be given unto him and this is according to the oath and the covenant which belongeth to the Priesthood." The revelation apparently addressed those questioning the addition of the high priesthood, warning: "Whoso breaketh this covenant after he hath received it, and altogether turneth therefrom shall not have forgiveness in this world nor in the world to come."[19] This is similar to what Smith wrote to W. W. Phelps the previous July, when he declared that he "dispise[d] a hypocrite or a covenant breaker," and exhorted followers in Missouri to "remember the covenant which they have made with God, and to me"—referring to sustaining him as president of the high priesthood the previous April.[20]

The revelation spoke disapprovingly of the Missouri church, recommending that they "be upbraded ... for there rebellion against you at the time I sent you." Speaking directly to the church in Missouri, the revelation declared, "Your minds in times past have been darkened because of unbelief and because you have treated lightly the things you have received which vanity and unbelief hath brought the whole church under condemnation and this condemnation resteth upon the children of Zion even all, and thay shall remain under this condemnation until they repent and remember the new covenant even the book of Mormon and the former commandments which I have given them, not only to say but to do according to that which I have writen."[21]

The Missouri church responded. In the January 1833 issue of *The Evening and the Morning Star*, editor Phelps devoted several pages to the Book of Mormon and wrote: "The inhabitants of Zion are brought under condemnation for neglecting the book of Mormon, from which they not only

---

18. Revelation, Dec. 6, 1832, Revelation Book 2, 32 [D&C 86:8–10] (*JSP*, D2:327).

19. Revelation, Sep. 22–23, 1832, [2], Newel K. Whitney Papers [D&C 84: 33–34, 38, 41] (*JSP*, D2:297).

20. Joseph Smith, Letter to William W. Phelps, July 31, 1832, 3–4, JS Collection (*JSP*, D2:264).

21. Revelation, Sep. 22–23, 1832, [2]–[3], Newel K. Whitney Papers [D&C 84:54–57, 76] (*JSP*, D2:298–99).

received the new covenant, but the fulness of the gospel."[22] David Pettegrew remembered: "Upon my arrival at Jackson County we were reproved by the Lord, through revelation for treating lightly the book of Mormon and the former revelations, and were to remain under condemnation if we did not repent. ... Soon after this, Bishop Partridge appointed a Solemn asembley in all the branches, which was to be held as a day of confession and repentance. he went from branch to branch exorting, until he had gone through them all, and in a few months, we were informed that we had repented, and the angel's were rejoicing over us."[23] On February 26, 1833, Partridge met with a special council of high priests at Independence, Missouri, and reported "the effect of the proceedings of the Solemn Assemblies as held throughout Zion." It was resolved that Cowdery, Phelps, and John Corrill "write an epistle to our brethren in Kirtland," which was written and accepted, after which they "all kneeled before the Lord & asked him to effect a perfect harmony between us & our brethren in Kirtland which was the desire of our hearts."[24]

Three years before the organization of the Quorum of Twelve Apostles, the revelation declared, "For you are mine Apostles, even Gods High priests ye are they whom my father hath given me, ye are my friends."[25] This was the first attempt to institutionalize apostleship. As previously discussed, Cowdery and David Whitmer had been assigned to search out the twelve in June 1829, which they apparently resisted. Instead, the apostleship remained a charismatic calling linked to the eldership in the 1830 Articles and Covenants.[26] Here there seems to be an attempt not only to link the apostleship to the twelve leading high priests in Kirtland but to place the entire church under their administration.

The revelation concluded by launching a missionary program. Like early Christians, Mormon missionaries were commanded to travel lightly and without "purse or scrip"—meaning money—and to rely on church members and the kindness of strangers for food and lodging.[27] Repeating previous instructions, they were commanded to wash their feet privately against those

---

22. "Some of Mormon's Teaching," *The Evening and the Morning Star* (Independence, MO), Jan. 1833, [4].

23. Pettegrew, Journal, 15.

24. Minutes, Feb. 26, 1833, Minute Book 2, 34 (Cannon and Cook, *Far West Record*, 60–61).

25. Revelation, Sep. 22–23, 1832, [3], Newel K. Whitney Papers [D&C 84:63] (*JSP*, D2:299).

26. Revelation, June 1829-B, BC XV:42 [D&C 18:37] (*JSP*, D1:73); Articles and Covenants, ca. Apr. 1830, BC XXIV:32 [D&C 20:38] (*JSP*, D1:123).

27. Revelation, Sep. 22–23, 1832, [3]–[4], Newel K. Whitney Papers [D&C 84:78, 86] (*JSP*, D2:300). Matt. 10:10.

who reject them, "whether in heat or in cold."[28] The Lord warned that the missionaries should move quickly because "plagues shall go forth and it shall not be taken from the earth untill I have completed my work which shall be cut short in righteousness"—probably a reference to the cholera epidemic that swept through Europe and was then afflicting the waterways of the United States.[29]

The revelation instructed Bishop Newel K. Whitney to go to New York City, Albany, and Boston, and "warn the people of those cities with the sound of the gospel with a loud voice of the desolation and utter abolishment which awaits them if they do reject these things, for if they do reject these things the hour of thei[r] Jodgment is nigh and there house shall be left unto them dessolate."[30] According to John Whitmer, it was understood that "the Lord gave a Commandment for Joseph the seer and N. K. Whitney the Bishop at Kirtl[a]nd to go and cry repntanc [repentance]" to those cities.[31] The Lord closed by warning that in "a little while" he would "exhert the powers of heaven … and ye shall see it and know that I am and that I will come and reign with my people."[32]

To the Eastern United States

In early October 1832 Smith left a very pregnant Emma in Kirtland and traveled with Bishop Whitney to Albany, New York City, and then Providence and Boston.[33] "My leg was not perfectly well," Whitney recalled in 1843, "but I proceeded with Joseph … to fulfill the Revelation."[34] While they were in New York City purchasing goods for the United Firm, Smith and Whitney lodged at the four-story Pearl Street House and Ohio Hotel, in lower Manhattan Island near the merchants of dry goods and their warehouses.

Whitney mentioned that they visited Bishop Benjamin T. Onderdonk of the Episcopal Church, and Smith may have used his church to fulfill his desire to preach.[35] "This day I have been walking through the most splended part of the city of New Y[ork]— the buildings are truly great and wonderful

---

28. Revelation, [4] [D&C 84:92] (*JSP*, D2:301). Mark 6:11; Luke 10:10–11; Revelation, Jan. 25, 1832-A, [2], Newel K. Whitney Papers [D&C 75:20] (*JSP*, D2:160).

29. Revelation, Sep. 22–23, 1832, [4], Newel K. Whitney Papers [D&C 84:97] (*JSP*, D2:301). See "The Cholera," *The Evening and the Morning Star*, Aug. 1832, [17]; Rosenberg, *The Cholera Years*.

30. Revelation, [5] [D&C 84:114–15] (*JSP*, D2:303–304).

31. Whitmer, History, 39 (*JSP*, H2:51).

32. Revelation, Sep. 22–23, 1832, [6], Newel K. Whitney Papers [D&C 84:119] (*JSP*, D2:304).

33. JS History, vol. A-1, 240 (DHC 1:295).

34. Whitney, Statement, ca. Feb. 13, 1843, [2] (Vogel, *History of Joseph Smith*, 8:8).

35. Whitney, [2].

to the astonishing of eve[r]y beholder," Smith wrote to Emma on October 13; "yet when I reflect upon this great city like Ninavah not desearning their right hand from their left yea more then two hundred thousand souls my bowels is filled with compasion towards them and I am determined to lift up my voice in this city."[36] The revelation that had brought them to the city had instructed Smith and Whitney to warn the people of impending destruction should they remain unrepentant.[37] Having lived entirely in small farming communities among those who shared his simple puritanical values, Smith found plenty to denounce in the crowded, affluent metropolis.

His letter to Emma reveals a hyper-religious moralizing and a struggle to deal with culture shock: "The inequity [iniquity] of the people is printed in every countinance. ... All is deformity their is something in every countinance that is disagreable with few exceptions," he wrote. "After beholding all that I had any desire to behold I returned to my room to meditate and calm my mind. ... It is [with] much pepleccity [perplexity] of mind [that] I prefer reading and praying and holding communeion with the holy spirit and writing to you then walking the streets and beholding the distraction of man." Smith condemned all that he saw as only a prophet could: "The anger of the Lord kindled because they Give him not the Glory therefore their iniquities shall be visited upon their heads and their works shall be burned up with unquenchable fire. ... Oh how long Oh Lord Shall this order of things exist and darkness cover the Earth and gross darkness cover the people." He had some conversations that "gave satisfaction," including a long discussion into the night with a young man from New Jersey who had nearly died from cholera. Smith wrote that he "took advantage" of the young man's state of mind and "opened a long discours with him," reporting that "he received my teaching appearanly [apparently] with much pleasure and became very strongly attacht [attached] to me."[38]

Smith wrote that when he escaped the unfamiliar world into the quiet of his room, "the thoughts of home of Emma and Julia rushes upon my mind like a flood" and that he "wish[es] for [a] moment to be with them [and] my breast is filled with all the feelings and tenderness of a parent and a Husband." Alluding to Emma's pregnancy, he wrote: "I feel as if I wanted to say something to you to comfort you in your beculier [peculiar] triel and presant

---

36. Joseph Smith, Letter to Emma Smith, Oct. 13, 1832, [1], [2] (*JSP*, D2:307, 312).

37. Revelation, Sep. 22–23, 1832, [5]–[6], Newel K. Whitney Papers [D&C 84:114] (*JSP*, D2:304).

38. Smith, Letter to Emma Smith, Oct. 13, 1832, [1], [3] (*JSP*, D2:307, 312–13).

affliction I hope God will give you strength that you may not faint." He knew there was more to her suffering than the late stages of pregnancy could explain: "I feel for you for I know your state and that others do not but you must cumfort yourself knowing that God is your friend in heaven and that you have one true and living friend on Earth your Husband."[39] No doubt Emma was worried about losing yet another child or even of dying, which had nearly happened when she lost her twins the previous year.

While Whitney spent his day in the warehouses "Selecting goods," Smith said, "I have nothing to do but to Sit in my room and pray for him that he may have strength to indure his labours for truly it is a tedious job to stand on the feet all day to select goods."[40] Smith and Whitney may have also attempted to negotiate a loan for the United Firm. Whitney had been given responsibility for securing a loan in a meeting about May 1, 1832. If they made such an attempt, they were apparently unsuccessful.[41]

After visiting Boston where "Joseph Prophecied u[n]to that citty," the two men returned to Kirtland, arriving on November 6, "immediately after the birth of my son, Joseph Smith 3d."[42] Both Emma and the infant survived.

Brigham Young

On November 8, 1832, Brigham Young, his brother Joseph, and Heber C. Kimball came to Kirtland to meet the leader of the church they had embraced in western New York. They first called on their friend John P. Greene, who had recently moved to Kirtland, and together they went to call on the prophet. They eventually found him in the woods chopping wood with some other brethren. "Here my joy was full at the privilege of shaking the hand of the Prophet of God, and received the sure testimony by the spirit of prophecy, that he was all that any man could believe him to be, as a true Prophet," Brigham later recalled.[43]

After a hearty welcome, Smith invited Young and the others to his home on the upper floor of the Whitney store, where they were eventually joined by other brethren, probably in what was called the "council room." Young said they were conversing "upon the things of the kingdom," when Smith called upon him to pray. "In my prayer," Young recalled, "I spoke in tongues.

---

39. Smith, [1]–[2] (*JSP*, D2:312–13).
40. Smith, [3] (*JSP*, D2:313).
41. Minutes, ca. May 1, 1832, Minute Book 2, 61 (*JSP*, D2:246); Staker, *Hearken, O Ye People*, 231.
42. Samuel Smith, Diary, Nov. 26, 1832; and JS History, vol. A-1, 240 (DHC 1:295).
43. Brigham Young, "History of Brigham Young," *Deseret News* (Salt Lake City), Feb. 10, 1858, [1].

As soon as we arose from our knees the brethren flocked around [Smith], and asked his opinion concerning the gift of tongues that was upon me." They expected that Smith would condemn the gift as he had done when he first arrived in Kirtland in the winter of 1831. Surprisingly, Smith said, "No, it is of God," explaining that "it was the pure Adamic language."[44]

At this time, Smith astonished those present by also speaking in tongues. Smith's official history states, "I received the gift myself."[45] According to an early draft of Young's history, Smith declared that "the same spirit and gift is upon me, and I wish to speak in an unknown tongue, which he did and he interpreted, declaring it was the pure language which he spoke, and exhorted the brethren to seek after that gift."[46]

Smith was apparently impressed with Young and made a statement about Young's leadership qualities, although later reports of it were colored by the knowledge that Young, as president of the Quorum of the Twelve Apostles, had succeeded Smith. In fact, Young had just begun to establish himself as Smith's legitimate successor when an insertion was made in Smith's official history recording what Smith reportedly said after meeting Young for the first time. The insertion, which was made by scribe Thomas Bullock in January 1845, represents Smith declaring, "Brother Joseph Young is a great man, but Brigham is a greater, and the time will come when he will preside over the whole Church."[47] Young repeated this prediction in his history, but added that it was made in his absence.[48] According to Levi W. Hancock, who was hired to renovate the upper floor of Whitney's store, after Young and the others had left, Smith said to him: "Brigham Young is a great man and one

---

44. Young, "History of Brigham Young," [1]. According to Heber C. Kimball, the branch in Columbia, Pennsylvania, was speaking in tongues since the fall of 1831 and was "the first Branch of the Church that received the gift of tongues," that missionaries from that branch were instrumental in converting him and Young, and that the Mendon, New York, branch became the second to experience tongues. Heber C. Kimball, "History of Brigham Young," *LDS Millennial Star* (Liverpool, Eng.), July 30, 1864, 488; and Aug. 20, 1864, 535. Young recounted his first reception of the gift: "A few weeks after my baptism [in April 1832] I was at bro. Kimball's house one morning, and while family prayer was being offered up, bro. Alpheus Gifford commenced speaking in tongues; soon the Spirit come on me, and I spoke in tongues, and we thought only of the day of Pentecost, when the apostles were clothed upon with cloven tongues of fire." Brigham Young, "History of Brigham Young," *Deseret News*, Feb. 10, 1858, [1].

45. JS History, vol. A-1, Addenda, 2, Note A (DHC 1:297), which was added by Thomas Bullock, possibly on Jan. 14, 1845. Vogel, *History of Joseph Smith*, 1:212n42.

46. Historian's Office, Brigham Young History Drafts, 4.

47. JS History, vol. A-1, Addenda, 2, Note A (DHC 1:297), which was added by Thomas Bullock, possibly on Jan. 14, 1845. Vogel, *History of Joseph Smith*, 1:213; see also 212n42.

48. Young, "History of Brigham Young," *Deseret News*, Feb. 10, 1858, [1].

day the whole kingdom will rest upon him."[49] What that meant in the context of 1832 or how it was interpreted by Hancock at the time is unclear.

Heber C. Kimball remembered that following Young's interview with Smith, "the gift of tongues became general in the Church in Kirtland."[50] A week later, Zebedee Coltrin recorded in his diary that he attended a prayer meeting and saw "Joseph Smith and heard him Speak with Tongues and Sing in Tongues also."[51] Between November 1832 and October 1833 Coltrin mentioned several meetings at which tongues was manifested.[52] At a church conference held on January 22, 1833, Smith "spake in an unknown Tongue he was followed by Br Zebede Coltrin and he by Bro William Smith after this the gift was poured out in a miraculous manner until all the Elders obtained the gift together with several of the members of the Church both male & female Great and glorious were the divine manifestation of the Holy Spirit, Praises were sang to God & the Lamb besides much speaking & praying all in tongues."[53] The Kirtland Revelation Book, in which Frederick G. Williams began copying and recording Smith's revelations in late February or early March 1832, includes the words of an unattributed song that was "sang by the gift of Tongues & Translated" on February 27, 1833, which was inspired by Smith's expansion of Genesis concerning Enoch's vision and prophecy about the latter-day Zion.[54] Gideon Carter reported in May 1833 that the Kirtland church was "sharing bountifully in the blessings of the Lord, and many have the gift of tongues and some the interpretation thereof."[55]

If Mormons were surprised by Smith's acceptance of Young's gift and his subsequent encouragement of the practice, it was even more perplexing to outsiders like Eber D. Howe, who remarked in 1834: "On the opening of the year 1833, the 'gift of tongues' again made its appearance at [Mormon] head-quarters, and from thence extended to all their branches in different

49. Levi W. Hancock, Statement, ca. 1845.

50. Kimball, "History of Brigham Young," *LDS Millennial Star*, Aug. 20, 1864, 535.

51. Coltrin, Diary, Nov. 14, 1832.

52. Coltrin, Diary, Nov. 14, 17, 18, 1832, Jan. 24, 1833, Mar. 10, 1833, and Oct. 17, 1833.

53. Minutes, Jan. 22, 1833, Minute Book 1, 7 (*JSP*, D2:381).

54. Revelation Book 2, 48–49 (*JSP*, MRB:509–11). See Moses 7. A drastically altered version of the song appears on a broadside titled: "Mysteries of God, As revealed to Enoch, on the Mount Mehujah, and sung in tongues by Elder D[avid] W. Patton [sic], of the 'Church of Latter Day Saints,' (who fell a Martyr to the cause of Christ, in the Missouri persecution,) and interpreted by Elder S[idney]. Rigdon." No place or date of publication, CHL. The broadside necessarily dates to after Patten's death on October 24, 1838, and before Rigdon's excommunication in September 1844. See Marquardt, *The Joseph Smith Revelations*, 96.

55. Gideon H. Carter, Letter to Missouri Brethren, May 1833, *The Evening and the Morning Star*, July 1833, 108.

parts. Whether the languages now introduced, differed materially from those practiced two or three years previous, (and pronounced to be of the Devil,) we have not been informed."[56]

Continuing Problems in Missouri

On November 27, 1832, Smith wrote to Phelps in Independence about the consecration of property and the importance of keeping records.[57] In contrast with his previous letter, when Smith chastised Phelps for his "cold and indifferent manner,"[58] he now praised Phelps, telling him that he had "the most implicit confidence in you as a man of God having obtained this confidence by a vision of heavn."[59] The letter exhibits the continuing difficulties between Smith and leaders in Missouri, which is probably reflected in the fact that a letter discussing items relevant to church administration is addressed to Phelps rather than Bishop Partridge.

Smith was writing because "I wish to communicate some things … which are lying with great weight upon my mind." The first thing is the question of "what shall becom[e] of all these who are assaying to come up unto Zion in order to keep the commandments of God and yet receive not there inheritance by consecration by order or deed from the bishop."[60] Phelps may have alerted Smith to this problem in a previous letter that is no longer extant. In the November 1832 issue of *The Evening and the Morning Star*, Phelps noted that some individuals had not received an inheritance because they had not obeyed the commandment to consecrate their properties.[61] There seems to have been a lack of confidence in the system.

Intending to motivate his followers to consecrate their property to the bishop, Smith directed John Whitmer, as the Lord's clerk, "to keep a hystory and a general church reccord of all things that transpire in Zion and of all those who consecrate properties and receive inheritances legally from the bishop and also there manner of life and the faith and works and also of all the apostates who apostatize after receiving ther inheritances." He then instructed that those refusing to enter into the law of consecration not be entered into church records. "It is conterary to the will and commandment

---

56. Howe, *Mormonism Unvailed*, 132.

57. Smith, Letter to William W. Phelps, Nov. 27, 1832, JS Letterbook 1, 1–4 (*JSP*, D2:315–21). The main portion of this letter was subsequently published in *The Evening and Morning Star*, Jan. 1833, [61]; and included as section 85 in the 1876 edition of the Doctrine and Covenants.

58. Smith, Letter to William W. Phelps, July 31, 1832, 1, JS Collection (*JSP*, D2:261).

59. Smith, Letter to William W. Phelps, Nov. 27, 1832, JS Letterbook 1, 1 (*JSP*, D2:318).

60. Smith, Letter to Phelps, 1 (*JSP*, D2:318).

61. "To the Saints," *The Evening and the Morning Star*, Nov. 1832, [46].

of God," he declared, "that those who receive not the inherttenc [inheritance] by consecration … should have there names enrolled with the people of God, neithe[r] is the[ir] geneology to be kept or to be had where it may be found on any of the reccords or hystory of the church there names shall not be found neithe[r] the names of ther fathers or the names of the children writen in the book of the Law of God saith the Lord of hosts."[62] This was equivalent to being left out of the Lamb's Book of Life, a threat repeated several times in the book of Revelation (Rev. 3:5; 13:8; 17:8; 20:12, 15; 21:27; 22:19).

Wishing to impress followers in Missouri with the seriousness of the subject, Smith stamped it with his prophetic authority: "Yea thus saith the still small voice which whispereth through and pierceth all things and often times it maketh my bones to quake while it maketh manifest." Then, writing in God's voice, he declared: "It shall come to pass that I the Lord God will send on[e] mighty and strong holding the scepter of power in his hand clothed with light for a covering whose mouth shall utter words Eternal words while his bowels shall be a fountain of truth to set in order the house of God and to arange by lot the inheritance of the saints whose names are found and the names of their fathers and of their children enroled in the Book of the Law of God."The one mighty and strong "holding the scepter of power" was Smith, who would be sent to replace Partridge, "who was called of God and appointed" but nevertheless "puteth forth his hand to steady the ark of God" and therefore "shall fall by the shaft of death like as a tree that is smitten by the vived shaft of lightning."[63] Here Smith used a powerful metaphor from the Old Testament story of God striking Uzzah dead for reaching out to steady the Ark of the Covenant when the oxen stumbled because Uzzah was not authorized (2 Sam. 6:1–7; see also Num. 4:15–20). Partridge may have attempted to steady the ark when he began issuing deed forms that required those entering into the law of consecration to sign over all property to the bishop, both real and personal, and rather than giving stewardships of private property, as the revelations directed, the bishop only leased land and loaned

---

62. Smith, Letter to William W. Phelps, Nov. 27, 1832, JS Letterbook 1, 1–2 (*JSP*, D2:318–19).

63. Smith, Letter to Phelps, 3 (*JSP*, D2:319–20). In January 1834 Oliver Cowdery reported: "Brother Joseph says, that the item in his letter that says, that the man that is called &c. and puts forth his hand to steady the ark of God, does not mean that any one had at the time, but it was given for a caution to those in high standing to beware, lest they should fall by the shaft of death as the Lord had said." Letter to John Whitmer, Jan. 1, 1834, in Cowdery, Letterbook, 15. However, it is important to note that by this time the Mormons had been ejected from Jackson County and the law of consecration was no longer enforced.

other kinds of property.[64] Smith will specifically address this situation in a subsequent letter to Partridge dated May 2, 1833.[65]

In the name of the Lord, Smith pronounced more condemnations on those who refused to enter into the law of consecration: "All they who are not found write [written] in the book of remmemberance shall find none inheritance in that day but they shall be cut assunder and their portion shall be appointed them among unbelievers where is wailing and gnashing of teeth. ... And they who are of the high Priesthood whose names are not found written in the book of the Law or that ar[e] found to have appostitized or to have been cut off out of the church as well as the lesser Priesthood or the members in that day shall not find an inheritance among th[e] saints of the most high." Smith then compared their fate with the children of the Israelite priests in Ezra 2:61–62, who because they could not find their names in the genealogical register were considered "polluted" and were "put from the priesthood."[66]

Smith closed by acknowledging his limitations as a letter-writer: "Oh Lord God deliver us in thy due time from the little narrow prison almost as it were totel darkness of paper pen and ink and a little narrow prison and imperfect language."[67]

Also on this day, November 27, Smith bought a blank book in which "to keep a minute acount of all things that come under my observation &c," writing in his own hand, "Oh may God grant that I may be directed in all my thoughts Oh bless thy Servant Amen."[68] Unfortunately, after December 6 the journal goes silent until October 4, 1833. On November 29, despite troubles in Missouri, Smith was able to record in his journal, "This Evening my mind is calm and serene for which I thank the Lord."[69]

Miscellaneous Activities

Smith's first journal gives a brief glimpse into the day-to-day activities of the Mormon leader during this period. On November 29 Smith and scribe Frederick G. Williams rode to Chardon to visit the prophet's sisters Sophronia Stoddard and Katharine Salisbury. In the evening, Williams "Prophcyed tha[t] next spring I should go to the city of PittsBurg to

---

64. Two deed forms from this period survive: one undated for Titus Billings (DHC 1:365–67n), and the other for Joseph Knight, Jr., dated October 12, 1832. Joseph Knight Jr. and Edward Partridge, Deed of Stewardship, Oct. 12, 1832, CHL, quoted in *JSP*, D3:73n99.

65. See Joseph Smith, Letter to Edward Partridge, May 2, 1833, [1], JS Collection (*JSP*, D3:76).

66. Smith, Letter to William W. Phelps, Nov. 27, 1832, JS Letterbook 1, 3 (*JSP*, D2:320).

67. Smith, 4.

68. Smith, Journal, Nov. 27, 1832 (*JSP*, J1:9).

69. Smith, Journal, Nov. 28, 1832 (*JSP*, J1:9).

establish a bishopwrick and within one year I should go to the city of New York." While this did not come to pass, Williams's prediction conveyed optimism about the future, of which Smith seemed less certain. "Lord spare the life of thy servent Amen," Smith wrote in the journal. The following day Smith and Williams returned to Kirtland, stopping on the way at a Mr. King's house and "bore testimony to him and Family."[70]

On December 1 Smith bore testimony to a Mr. Gilmore and "wrote and corrected revelations &c." in preparation for their publication in Missouri. The next day he went to Sunday meeting as usual. On December 3 he attended a conference of elders, after which he was visited by Solomon Humphrey from the East; in the evening he attended another meeting, during which his counselor Jesse Gause and William E. McLellin were excommunicated, Gause for denying the faith, McLellin for failing to fulfill his mission assignment. On December 4 he was unwell and rested at home most of the day, but in the evening he wrote: "[I] feel better in my mind then I have for a few days back Oh Lord deliver thy servent out of temtations and fill his heart with wisdom and understanding." On December 5 he began copying letters into the same book following his aborted history, worked on his Bible revision, and in the evening attended a council meeting. On December 6 he continued working on his Bible revision and "received a Revelation explaining the Parable [of] the wheat and the tears [tares] &c."[71]

In Matthew 13, Jesus declares: "The kingdom of heaven is likened unto a man which sowed good seed in his field: But while he slept, his enemy came and sowed tares among the wheat." At harvest time, the owner instructed his servants to first gather the tares and burn them, then gather the wheat into the barn. At the request of his disciples, Jesus explained that the field is the world, the good seed is the children of the kingdom, the tares are the devil's children, and the reapers are the angels who will be sent before the end of the world to gather out the wicked and burn them (Matt. 13:24–30, 36–43).

Although Smith was primarily working on the Old Testament with Williams, between late July 1832 and early February 1833 he was also reviewing the New Testament revision with Sidney Rigdon assisting occasionally.[72] During this time, Smith and Rigdon revised the text of Matthew 13:30, changing it from "I will say to the reapers, gather ye together first the tares" to "gather ye together first the wheat into my barn, and the tares are bound

---

70. Smith, Journal, Nov. 29–30, 1832 (*JSP*, J1:9–10).
71. Smith, Journal, Dec. 1–6, 1832 (*JSP*, J1:10).
72. See Faulring et al., eds., *Joseph Smith's New Translation of the Bible*, 59.

in bundles to be burned."[73] This modification made the parable more suitable for Smith's instruction that the saints "flee unto Zion" and the Jews to Jerusalem to escape the coming destruction of the wicked world.[74]

The December 6 revelation, which was originally dictated to Rigdon, reflects this change, with the Lord telling the angels to "first gather out the wheat," but also making an interesting statement about the priesthood: "Therefore thus saith the Lord unto you with whom the priesthood hath continued through the lineage of your fathers, for ye are lawful heirs according to the flesh and have been hid from the world with christ in God."[75] This claim to the priesthood is consistent with Alma 13, which speaks of foreordination to the high priesthood, and the September 22–23, 1832, revelation, which explained that anciently the high priesthood had been transmitted from individual to individual "through the linage of thare fathers" and that those who were "faithful unto the attaining" of the priesthood became, through "the renewing of the bodies ... the sons of Moses and of Aaron and the seed of Abraham."[76] Thus Mormon priesthood holders were biologically qualified to hold the Aaronic or Levitical priesthood as well as the high priesthood, which had been conveyed through patriarchal lineage from father to son from Adam to Moses, either through an untraceable lineage or the miraculous transformation of their bodies.

Prophecy on War

In December 1832 the nation was on the verge of civil war when South Carolina nullified the Federal Tariff Acts of 1828 and 1832 and threatened to secede from the Union and President Andrew Jackson prepared to take military action. These events were being followed closely by the newspapers, including the *Painesville Telegraph*, which declared in mid-December that "civil war" was at hand and "unless some signal interposition shall arrest the course of events ... our national existence is at an end."[77] On Christmas Day, when the volatile situation seemed certain to explode at any moment into a

---

73. New Testament Revision 1, 34 [I.V. Matt. 13:30] (Faulring et al, 192); New Testament Revision 2, 25 (first numbering) [I.V. Matt. 13:30] (Faulring et al., 267).

74. Revelation, Nov. 3, 1831, Revelation Book 1, 116 [D&C 133:12–14] (*JSP*, D2:116).

75. Revelation, Dec. 6, 1832, Revelation Book 2, 32 [D&C 86:6, 8–9] (*JSP*, D2:327). Cf. Col. 3:3. A notation that concludes the revelation reads: "given by Joseph the seer and writen by Sidney the scribe an[d] Councellor, & Transcribed by Frederick [G. Williams] assistent scribe and councellor."

76. Book of Mormon, 1830 ed., 258 [Alma 13:3]; Revelation, Sep. 22–23, 1832, [1], [2], Newel K. Whitney Papers [D&C 84:14–15, 31–34] (*JSP*, D2:295, 297).

77. "South Carolina Convention," *Painesville (OH) Telegraph*, Dec. 21, 1832, [2]; "Nullification," *Painesville Telegraph*, Dec. 21, 1832, [2]–[3]; News Item, *Painesville Telegraph*, Dec. 21, 1832, [3].

national Armageddon, Smith dictated his well-known "Prophecy on War." This prophecy declared:

> Verily thus saith the Lord, concerning the wars that will shortly come to pass begining at the rebellion of South Carolina which will eventually terminate in the death and missery of many souls, and the days will come that war will be poured out upon all Nations begining at this place for behold the southern states shall be divided against the Northern States, and the Southern States will call on other [Nations] even the Nation of Great Britian as it is called and they shall also call upon other Nations in order to defend themselves against other Nations and thus war shall be poured out upon all Nations.[78]

Thus the approaching civil war, according to Smith, would lead to world war. The revelation gave other details. While America was divided in war, "slaves shall rise up against there Masters who shall be Martialed and disaplined for war." Nat Turner's bloody slave rebellion in southeastern Virginia the previous August made this prediction all too real. The revelation further predicted that "the remnants who are left of the land"—the Indians—"will martial themselves also and shall become exceding angry and shall vex the Gentiles with a soar vexation." The combination of war, famine, plague, and other natural disasters will bring "a full end of all Nations." The coming war was the beginning of the end, the revelation warned, "wherefore stand ye in holy places and be not moved untill the day of the Lord come, for be hold it cometh quickly saith the Lord. Amen."[79]

With the nation gripped by the terror of war and the possible dissolution of the Union, Smith seized the opportunity to legitimize his mission to build a utopian theocracy in the west. On January 4 he wrote to Noah C. Saxton, editor of the *American Revivalist and Rochester Observer* published in Rochester, New York, declaring: "By the authority of Jesus Christ, that not many years shall pass away before the United States shall present such a scene of <u>bloodshed</u> as has not a parallel in the hystory of our nation pestalence hail famine and earthquake will sweep the wicked of this generation from off the face of this Land. ... The people of the Lord, those who have complied with the requsitions of the new covenant have already commenced gathering togethe[r] to Zion which is in the State of Missouri."[80] When Saxton

---

78. Revelation, Dec. 25, 1832, Revelation Book 2, 32–33 [D&C 87:1–3] (*JSP*, D2:330–31).

79. Revelation, 33 [D&C 87:4–8] (*JSP*, D2:330–31).

80. Joseph Smith, Letter to Noah C. Saxton, Jan. 4, 1833, JS Letterbook 1, 17–18 (*JSP*, D2:355); emphasis in original.

published a portion of Smith's letter the following month, Smith dashed off a letter to the editor warning that he had written his previous letter "by the commandment of God" and demanded that it be published in its entirety otherwise "the sin be upon your head."[81] Saxton ignored the warning. By March 1833 the immediate threat of civil war had subsided, and Smith's Prophecy on War remained unpublished during his lifetime.[82]

The Olive Leaf

On December 27–28, 1832, Smith attended a conference with nine other high priests in the "translating room" above Whitney's store. According to the minutes, Smith arose and said, "To receive revelation and the blessings of heaven it was necessary to have our minds on god and exercise faith and become of one heart and of one mind." He then instructed them to "prey seperately and vocally to the Lord for to reveel his will unto us concerning the upbuilding of Zion, & for the benifit of the sa[i]nts and for the duty and employment of the Elders." Afterward, each man stood, expressed his feelings, and pledged to keep the commandments. Then Smith began to dictate a long revelation that was not finished when the meeting was adjourned at 9:00 p.m. and had to be completed when the men reconvened the next morning. When Smith finished dictating, the conference ended "in harmony with the brethren and gratitude to our heavenly Father for the great manifestation of his holy spirit."[83]

In contrast to previous threats of blotting out the names of transgressors, this revelation assured "the first Elders of this Church of Christ" that "the Angels rejoice over you … and [you] are recorded in the book of the names of the sanctified even they of the celestial world."[84] The revelation is significant for its theological materialism and naturalism. Inspired by the natural theologians of the day who were trying to synthesize theology and science, the revelation equated the "light of Christ" with the physical light of the sun, moon, stars, and Earth: "The light which now shineth; which giveth you light, is through him which enlightneth your eyes; which is the same light that quickneth your understandings, which light, procedeth forth from

---

81. Joseph Smith, Letter to Noah C. Saxton, Feb. 12, 1833, JS Letterbook 1, 27–28 (*JSP*, D3:9–10).

82. When the Compromise of 1850 rekindled the conflict between the north and south, the prophecy was included in *The Pearl of Great Price*, a pamphlet published by Franklin D. Richards in 1851 in England, and in 1876 it was added to the Doctrine and Covenants as section 87.

83. Minutes, Dec. 27–28, 1832, Minute Book 1, 3–4 (*JSP*, D2:331–34).

84. Revelation, Dec. 27–28, 1832, Revelation Book 2, 34 [D&C 88:2] (*JSP*, D2:336). Verses 1–126 were dictated on December 27–28, 1832, and verses 127–41 on January 3, 1833.

the presence of God; to fill the emencity of space; the light which is in all things which giveth life to all things, which is the law by which all things are govorned, even the power of God, who sitteth upon his throne; who is in the bosom of eternity, who is in the midst of all things."[85] Thus solving the problem of how there could be light before the creation of the sun in the Genesis account of Creation.

The revelation also equated the celestial, terrestrial, and telestial worlds of the February 1832 revelation with the planets and stars and explained the Earth's ultimate destiny: "Earth abideth the law, of a celestial kingdom, for it filleth, the measur of its creation; and transg[r]esseth not the law wherefore it shall be sanctified, yea notwithstanding it shall die, it shall be quickened again, and shall abide the power, by which it was quickened, and the righteous shall inherit it."[86] The revelation also affirmed: "All kingdoms have a law given; and there are many kingdoms; for there is no space, in the which there is no kingdoms; and there is no kingdom, in which there is no space, either a greater or a lesser kingdom, and unto every kingdom, is given a law, and unto every law there are certain bounds also, and conditions, all beings who abide not, in those conditions, are not justified."[87] The revelation's inference that all the planets and stars were kingdoms and hence inhabited was consistent with the February 1832 revelation's declaration that through Christ "the worlds are made and were created and the inhabitants thereof are begotten sons and daughters unto God."[88]

The concept of a plurality of inhabited worlds was prevalent in Smith's day. Many justified their belief by referring to the passage in Isaiah 45:18, which declares that "God ... created [the earth] not in vain, he formed it to be inhabited." The Revered Amos Pettengill, for example, reasoned in 1826 that "Jehovah intimates that it would have been inconsistent for him to create the Earth, had he not designed it to be inhabited. ... As he shows us a number of other worlds, ... must we not infer from his perfections that he acted consistently in creating them, that he created them not in vain, but to be inhabited?"[89] Deist Thomas Paine asserted that "the immensity of space will appear to us

85. Revelation, 34–35 [D&C 88:11–13] (*JSP*, D2:337). On the influence of natural theology, especially the plurality of worlds concept, on Smith and other early Mormons, see Paul, "Joseph Smith and the Plurality of Worlds Idea"; Paul, *Science, Religion, and Mormon Cosmology*; Vogel and Metcalfe, "Joseph Smith's Scriptural Cosmology."

86. Revelation, Dec. 27–28, 1832, Revelation Book 2, 36 [D&C 88:21–22] (*JSP*, D2:338).

87. Revelation, 37 [D&C 88:36–39] (*JSP*, D2:338–39).

88. "The Vision," Feb. 16, 1832, Revelation Book 2, 3 [D&C 76:24] (*JSP*, D2:186).

89. Pettengill, *A View of the Heavens*, 64.

to be filled with systems of worlds; and that no part of space lies at waste, any more than any part of our globe of earth and water is left unoccupied."[90]

The revelation became poetic in its description of God's creation: "The Earth rolls upon her wings, and the sun giveth her light by day, and the moon, giveth her light by night, and the stars also giveth there light as they roll upon, there wings, in there glory in the midst, of the power, of God." The revelation asked: "Unto what shall I liken *these kingdoms*, that ye may understand"? The answer took the form of a parable in which a farmer visited his servants one at a time working in different areas of a field. "Therefore," the revelation stated, "unto this parable, will I liken all *those kingdoms; and the inhabitants thereof.*"[91] In 1833 Oliver Cowdery referred to this revelation for proof that "the vast creations of the Almighty ... [are] all inhabited by intelligent beings" and that "they all are [to be] visited with the light of his [Jesus's] countenance, according to the revelation of his own character."[92]

The revelation revisited the subject of sanctification as a prerequisite for seeing God: "Therefore sanctify yourselves that your minds become single to God, The days come, that you shall see him, for he will, unveil his face unto you, and it shall be in his own time, and in his own way, and according, to his own will."[93] A November 1831 revelation had promised the elders a vision of deity provided they humble and perfect themselves, and the September 1832 revelation added the requirement of the high priesthood.[94] When this December revelation was sent to Missouri the next month, Smith said the Lord had "promised us great things, yea even a visit from the heavens to honor us with his own presence."[95] Indeed, in the Book of Mormon Jesus had promised that believing Gentiles would assist in gathering and converting the Indians and in building the holy city of the New Jerusalem, and then "the powers of heaven shall be in the midst of this people; yea, even I will be in the midst of you."[96]

The revelation instructed these leading elders to "tarry" at Kirtland, to call a "solemn assembly," and to "organize yourselves, and prepare yourselves, and sanctify yourselvs yea purify your hearts, and clean your hands, and your

90. Paine, *The Age of Reason*, 41.
91. Revelation, Dec. 27–28, 1832, Revelation Book 2, 37–39 [D&C 88:42–61] (*JSP*, D2:338–40).
92. [Oliver Cowdery], "Signs in the Heavens," *The Evening and the Morning Star*, Dec. 1833, 116.
93. Revelation, Dec. 27–28, 1832, Revelation Book 2, 39–40 [D&C 88:68–69] (*JSP*, D2:341).
94. Revelation, ca. Nov. 2, 1831, Revelation Book 1, 115 [D&C 67:10] (*JSP*, D2:109–110); Revelation, Sep. 22–23, 1832, [1], Newel K. Whitney Papers [D&C 84:22] (*JSP*, D2:295).
95. Smith, Letter to William W. Phelps, Jan. 11, 1833, JS Letterbook 1, 19 (*JSP*, D2:367).
96. See Book of Mormon, 1830 ed., 497, 501 [3 Ne. 20:22; 21:23–25].

feet, before me, that I may make you clean." This will shortly become the "School of the Prophets," which was intended to prepare the elders for the ministry. "I give unto you a commandment, that you shall teach one another, the doctrines, of the kingdom ... that ye may be inst[r]ucted more perfectly, in theory, in principle, in doctrine ... that ye may be prepared, in all things when I shall send you again, to magnify the calling, whereunto I have called you, and the mission with which, I have commissioned you."[97]

Having recently returned from his mission of warning the major cities in the East of the coming destruction by famine, plague, and war, Smith now prepared to launch a major missionary program to do the same. "Behold I send you out, to testify, and to warn the people," the revelation declared to these missionaries; "therefore tarry ye, and labour diligently, that you may be perfected, in your ministry to go forth among the gentiles, for the last time, ... that there souls may escape the wrath of God, the dessolation, of abomination, which awaiteth the wicked, both in this world, and in the world to come."[98] The revelation then described in detail the tribulations and destructions preceding the Second Coming, drawing on many Bible passages.

After the missionaries have finished dividing the wheat from the tares and the Earth is "ready to be burned," then "the face of the Lord shall be unveiled," that is, in the heavens above the earth with his angels. Believing Mormons will then "be quickened and be caught up to meet him."[99] This passage ties in with the high priesthood and the power of translation. According to the February 1832 vision, those who would ultimately be saved in the highest heavenly kingdom were those "priests of the Most High, after the order of Melchizedek. ... These are they whom he shall bring with him, when he shall come in the clouds of heaven."[100] Speaking about the Melchizedek Priesthood in 1840, Smith noted that "the doctrine of translation is a power which belongs to this Priesthood."[101] After the ascension of the Saints, the dead in Christ will be resurrected from their graves, and "they also shall be caught up to meet him in the midst of the pillar of heaven" and become part of those "who shall descend with him first." Much like the Book of Revelation, Smith's revelation described seven angels blowing their trumpets in

---

97. Revelation, Dec. 27–28, 1832, Revelation Book 2, 40–41 [D&C 88:70, 74, 77–78, 80] (*JSP*, D2:341).

98. Revelation, 41 [D&C 88:81, 84–85] (*JSP*, D2:341–42).

99. Revelation, 43 [D&C 88:96] (*JSP*, D2:343). See 1 Thess. 4:17.

100. "The Vision," Feb. 16, 1832, Revelation Book 2, 5–6 [D&C 76:57, 63] (*JSP*, D2:188).

101. Joseph Smith, Discourse, Oct. 5, 1840, JS Collection (Ehat and Cook, *The Words of Joseph Smith*, 41).

succession, Satan being bound, and a thousand years of peace, after which Satan and his armies fight God's armies led by Michael the Archangel.[102]

In closing, the revelation repeated the command to organize a school, appoint a teacher, and learn "out of the best books." The deportment of those attending the school was to be serious at all times: there was to be no trivial speech or laughter and discussion was to be harmonious and respectful. It also instructed that a special building be provided for the school, that the elders should "establish, an house, even an house of prayer and house of fasting, an house of faith, an house of Learning, an house of glory, an house of order an house of God."[103] This would eventually become a temple, which at the time was variously referred to as the "school," the "house of the Lord," or the "chapel."

On January 3, 1833, Smith added an appendage to his previous revelation, giving further instructions about the school of the elders. Participants were to greet one another with uplifted hands and a holy salutation. The revelation incidentally mentioned that this house was not only for the school but also to be "prepared for the presidency."[104]

When Smith sent a copy of the revelation to officials in Missouri, he included a cover letter to Phelps, dated January 11, 1833, in which he referred to the revelation as "the Olieve leaf ... plucked from the tree of Paradise" and "the Lords message of peace to us." By olive leaf, Smith may have meant the revelation was being sent as a peace offering and a reminder that he was God's oracle. The message of peace was God's acceptance of Smith and the other Kirtland leaders despite the recent reception of letters of criticism and complaint from Missouri. Smith made this clear to Phelps: "For though our Brethren in Zion, indulge in feelings towards us, which are not according to the requirements of the new covenant yet we have the satisfaction of knowing that the Lord approves of us & has accepted us, & established his name in kirtland."[105] Indeed, the revelation began by declaring that the "Angels rejoice over you," assured them that their names were recorded in the "book ... of the sanctified," and announced that the Lord was sending them "another comfortor ... even the holy spirit of promise."[106]

---

102. Revelation, Dec. 27–28, 1832, Revelation Book 2, 43–44 [D&C 88:97–115] (*JSP*, D2:343–45).

103. Revelation, 45–46 [D&C 88:117–126] (*JSP*, D2:345–46).

104. Revelation, Jan. 3, 1833, Revelation Book 2, 47–48 [D&C 88:127–137] (*JSP*, D2:347–48). Verses 138–141 were added for the 1835 edition of the Doctrine and Covenants.

105. Smith, Letter to William W. Phelps, Jan. 11, 1833, JS Letterbook 1, 18 (*JSP*, D2:365–67).

106. Revelation, Dec. 27–28, 1832, Revelation Book 2, 34 [D&C 88:2–3] (*JSP*, D2:336–37).

In his letter, Smith expressed fear that Zion might be lost due to their "self Justification" to the point "past being redeemed" and issued a strong prophetic warning: "For if Zion, will not purify herself so as to be approved of in all things in [God's] sight he will seek another people for his work will go on untill Isreal is gathered & they who will not hear his voice must expect to feel his wrath. ... Let me say unto you, seek to purefy yourselves, & also all the inhabitants of Zion lest the Lords anger be kindled to fierceness, repent, repent, is the voice of God, to Zion." The possible loss of Zion was seriously being considered in Kirtland: "The Brethren in Kirtland pray for you unceasingly, for knowing the terrors of the Lord, they greatly fear for you."[107]

This revelation also marked a turning point in Smith's ongoing troubles with the Missouri leaders, for Smith was now willing to make a long-term investment in Kirtland. As Smith wrote to Phelps, "You will see that the Lord commanded us in Kirtland to build an house of God, & establish a school for the Prophets, this is the word of the Lord to us, & we must— yea the Lord helping us we will obey, as on conditions of our obedience, he has promised us great things, yea even a visit from the heavens to honor us with his own presence."[108] Smith's decision to develop both communities simultaneously would prove to be a greater task than anticipated.

On January 5 Smith dictated a revelation naming Williams as a counselor in the presidency of the high priesthood to replace Gause, who had apostatized.[109] "Verily verily I say unto you thou art calld to be a Councillor & scribe unto my servant Joseph," the revelation declared and then issued a difficult request: "I say unto you, my Servant Joseph is called to do a great work and hath need that he may do the work of translation for the salvation of souls. ... Let thy farm be consecratd f[o]r bringing forth of the revelations, and tho[u] shalt be blessed and lifted up at the last day even so Amen." At the time of this revelation, Smith's parents had occupied the 144-acre farm since May 1831.[110] Williams subsequently consecrated his farm when he joined the United Firm on March 15, 1833; his ordination to the presidency

---

107. Smith, Letter to William W. Phelps, Jan. 11, 1833, JS Letterbook 1, 19 (*JSP*, D2:367).

108. Smith, Letter to Phelps, 19.

109. Revelation, Jan. 5, 1834 [1833], Revelations Collection [uncanonized] (*JSP*, D2:356–61). The year "1834" is a later insertion. Because the revelation mentions Williams helping Smith "do the work of translation," evidently referring to the Bible revision which was completed in July 1833, the 1834 insertion is probably wrong (*JSP*, D2:356–57).

110. Revelation, May 15, 1831, Revelation Book 1, 85 [uncanonized] (*JSP*, D1:312–13); Lucy Mack Smith, History, 1844–45, bk. 12, [6] (Anderson, ed., *Lucy's Book*, 540); Williams, "Account on Farm," no date; Williams, Statement, no date.

followed three days later.[111] The Williams donation would form the south-west quarter of the planned city of Kirtland, which included a portion of the future temple block that was to contain two additional buildings, one for the presidency and another for a printing house.[112] The plan apparently was to fund the printing of the revelations in Missouri through the sale of lots from the Williams farm.[113] On January 9 the Firm agreed to pay Williams $300 per year for his service as "assistant scribe" to Smith.[114]

Rebellion in Zion

On Sunday, January 13, 1833, Smith attended a conference of twelve high priests and three elders to discuss "the subject of Rebelion in Zion." The meeting was presided over by Rigdon, who had convened the Ohio conference to fulfill the command in the September 1832 revelation to call the Missouri leaders to repentance "for there rebellion against you at the time I sent you."[115] The conference also discussed how best to respond to the two letters written by Phelps and Sidney Gilbert in December 1832 that contained criticisms and accusations against Smith and the Ohio leaders. To address these issues, the conference assigned Orson Hyde and Hyrum Smith to compose an "Epistle to the brethren in Zion." The following day the letter was read and "unanimously sanctioned" by the conference.[116]

The letter began with Hyde and Hyrum Smith explaining the authority by which they were calling them to repentance, noting that previous letters to them "upon this subject have failed to bring to us that satisfactory confession." They reminded the Missouri leaders that at the time Smith left Missouri, "all matters of hardness and misunderstanding were settled and buried (as they supposed) and you gave them the hand of fellowship but afterwards you brought up all these things again in a sensorious spirit," which was received in a letter from John Corrill, a counselor to Partridge, dated June 2, 1832. According to Hyde and Hyrum Smith, the letter, which is not extant, also accused "Bro Joseph in rather an indirect way of seeking after Monarchal

---

111. Minute Book 1, Mar. 15 and 18, 1833. Williams did not actually deed the farm to Joseph Smith until May 1834 (Geauga Co., OH, Deed Records, vol. 18, 477–78, May 5, 1834).

112. Plat of Kirtland, OH, ca. 1833 (*JSP*, D3:208–20).

113. Parkin, "Joseph Smith and the United Firm," 17, 21.

114. Notation, ca. Jan. 9, 1833, Minute Book 1, 5 (*JSP*, D2:361–63).

115. Revelation, Sep. 22–23, 1832, [3], Newel K. Whitney Papers [D&C 84:76] (*JSP*, 2:299).

116. Minute Book 1, Index, [1]; Minutes, Jan. 13–14, 1833, Minute Book 1, 5–6 (*JSP*, D2:369–71). The Joseph Smith Papers editors suggest the possibility that this was a president's court, which required twelve high priests. *JSP*, D2:369–70. See also Revelation, Nov. 11, 1831-B, Revelation Book 1, 123 [D&C 107:78–79] (*JSP*, D2:134).

power and authority." This referred to Smith's being sustained as president of the high priesthood in Missouri on April 26, 1832. "We are sensable that this is not the thing Bro J[oseph] is seeking after, but to magnify the high office and calling whereunto he has been called and appointed by the command of God and the united voice of this Church," they insisted. They advised them to remember the fate of those in the Book of Mormon and Bible who questioned the authority of the prophets.[117] They gave no examples, but may have had in mind Laman and Lemuel, who rebelled against their younger brother Nephi because he "thinks to rule over us," and the children of Israel, who accused Moses of seeking to make himself "a prince over us."[118]

Next, they turn to Gilbert's letter of December 10, 1832, which is also no longer extant. According to Hyde and Hyrum Smith, this letter contained "low, dark, & blind insinuations" and "an uneassness ... and a fearfulness that God will not provide for his saints in their last days and these fears lead him on to covitousness." Gilbert, who had been appointed as the church's financial agent in Missouri and manager of the church's store in Independence, had evidently expressed concern about the feasibility of the United Firm and questioned the motives of the Ohio leaders in establishing such a system. He was more conservative than the Ohio leaders wanted, and so they directed him to exercise faith, to accept more risk than he was accustomed, and promised that the Lord would bless him.[119] Gilbert's covetousness was alluded to when Smith responded to Gilbert's letter in April 1833, and advised him to "trust in god" and reprimanded him for "with holding credit" from the poor.[120]

Orson and Hyrum then turned to Phelps's December 15, 1832, letter, also not extant, which they said "betrays a lightness of spirit that ill becomes a man plased [placed] in the important and responsable station that he is placed in." Concerning Phelps's suggestion that Smith move to Missouri, they respond: "Br J[oseph]. will not settle in Zion until she repent and purify herself & abide by the new covenant, and remember the commandments which have been given her." They called the Missouri church to repentance and warned them of impending destruction should they continue in rebellion: "We have the best of feelings, and feelings of the greatest anxiety for

---

117. Orson Hyde and Hyrum Smith, Letter to Edward Partridge and Others, Jan. 14, 1833, JS Letterbook 1, 21 (*JSP*, D2:373–74).

118. See Book of Mormon, 1830 ed., 71 [2 Ne. 5:2–5]. Cf. Num. 16:12–13.

119. Hyde and Smith, Letter to Edward Partridge and Others, Jan. 14, 1833, JS Letterbook 1, 21 (*JSP*, D2:373–74).

120. Joseph Smith, Letter to "brethren in Zion," Apr. 21, 1833, JS Letterbook 1, 34 (*JSP*, D3:68).

the welfare of Zion we feel more like weeping over Zion than we do like rejoicing over her, for we know the judgments of God that hang over her and will fall upon her except she repent and purify herself before the Lord and put away from her evry foul spirit—we now say to Zion <u>this once</u> in the name of the Lord, Repent! Repent!" They assured the Missouri leaders that it is not their desire to rule over them: "Let not satan tempt you to think we want to make you bow to us to domaneur [domineer] over you for God knows this is not the case." They reiterated and clarified what Smith said in his January 11 letter to Phelps: "If the people of Zion did not repent the Lord would seek another place, and another people, Zion is the place where the Temple will be built, and the people gathered but all people upon that holy Land being under condemnation, the lord will cut off if they repent not and bring another race upon it that will serve him."[121]

Having delivered their message, Orson and Hyrum concluded, "We now feel that our garments are clean from you, and all men, when we have washed our feet & hands according to the commandment We have written plain at this time but we believe not harsh, Plainness is what the Lord requires and we should not feel ourselves clean unless we had done so."[122]

---

121. Hyde and Smith, Letter to Edward Partridge and Others, Jan. 14, 1833, JS Letterbook 1, 23 (*JSP*, D2:376–77); emphasis in original.

122. Hyde and Smith, 21–24 (*JSP*, D2:375–77).

School of the Prophets

JANUARY–MAY 1833

The most likely Method to stock the Church with a faithful Minis-
try, in the present Situation of Things, the publick Academies being
so much corrupted and abused generally, is, To encourage private
Schools, or Seminaries of Learning, which are under the Care of
skilful and experienced Christians.

—*Gilbert Tennent*, The Danger of an Unconverted
Ministry, Considered in a Sermon on Mark VI. 34
(2nd ed.; Boston: Rogers and Fowle, 1742), 11

In their January 14, 1833, letter to the Missouri church, Orson Hyde and
Hyrum Smith mentioned that "The School of the Prophets will commence
if the Lord will in 2 or 3 days"[1] The name was inspired by similar schools
established in eighteenth-century America to train Protestant clergy. Both
Harvard and Yale were called "schools of the prophets" because they produced
many of the professional clergy, but soon private "schools of the prophets"
were founded by New Light Congregationalists and New Side Presbyterians,
who suspected that the scholarly clergy were "unconverted." New Brunswick,
New Jersey, Presbyterian minister Gilbert Tennent, for example, suggested
that "Pious and experienced Youths, who have a good natural Capacity, and
great Desires after the Ministerial Work, from good Motives, might be sought
for, and found up and down in the Country, and put to Private Schools of the
Prophets."[2] These "schools of the prophets" operated until they were replaced
by more formal seminaries and academies in the early nineteenth century.[3]

---

1. Orson Hyde and Hyrum Smith, Letter to Edward Partridge and Others, Jan. 14, 1833, JS
Letterbook 1:24 (*JSP*, D2:377).

2. Gilbert Tennent, *The Danger of an Unconverted Ministry, Considered in a Sermon on Mark*
VI. 34 (2nd ed.; Boston: Rogers and Fowle, 1742), 11.

3. Darowski, "Schools of the Prophets"; Kling, "New Divinity Schools of the Prophets,
1750–1825."

The designation "school of the prophets" was based on references in the Old Testament to a "company of prophets" and the "sons of the prophets" (1 Sam. 19:18–24; 2 Kgs. 2; and 4:38–44). Early American theologian Jonathan Edwards explained that "because God intended a constant succession of prophets from Samuel's time, therefore in his time was begun a school of the prophets; that is, a school of young men, trained up under some great prophet, who was their master and teacher in the study of divine things, and the practice of holiness, to fit them for this office as God should call them to it."[4]

The organization of the school of the prophets in Kirtland occurred on the second day of a two-day conference. On the first day, January 22, 1833, Joseph Smith led the congregation in speaking in tongues. He was followed by Zebedee Coltrin and William Smith, who also spoke in tongues. Afterward, as the minutes record, "The gift was poured out in a miraculous manner until all the Elders obtained the gift together with several of the members of the Church both male & female Great and glorious were the divine manifestation of the Holy Spirit, Praises were sang to God & the Lamb besides much speaking & praying all in tongues."[5]

The next day Smith attended the first meeting of the school of prophets. According to Coltrin, "There were many powerful manifestation[s] of the holy spirit" and "much useful instruction was obtain by the gift and power of the holy spirit and also the gift of tongues and the interpretation thereof."[6] The minutes of the meeting record that "after much speaking praying and singing, all done in Tongues," each member of the school washed his own hands, face, and feet in a ritual of self-purification. Afterward, Smith "guirded himself with a towel and again washed the feet of all the Elders wiping them with the towel," beginning with his own father, who first blessed his son that "he should continue in his Priests office untill Christ come." After Smith completed the ordinance, he declared "through the power of the Holy Ghost that the Elders were all clean from the blood of this generation," while at the same time "that those among them who should sin wilfully after they were thus cleansed and sealed up unto eternal life should be given over unto the buffettings of Satan until the day of redemption." Moved by the spirit of the moment, Frederick G. Williams then washed Smith's feet "as a token of his fixed determination to be with him in suff[er]ing or in rejoicing, in life or in death and to be continually on his right hand."[7]

---

4. Edwards, *The Works of President Edwards*, 3:224.
5. Minutes, Jan. 22–23, 1833, Minute Book 1, 6–7 (*JSP*, D2:380–81).
6. Coltrin, Diary, Jan. 24, 1833.
7. Minutes, Jan. 22–23, 1833, Minute Book 1, 7–8 (*JSP*, D2:381–82).

The purpose of this ritualistic washing should be distinguished from the previous instruction to missionaries to wash their feet as a testimony against those who had rejected their message, which was to be performed on location, whereas in this instance the washing was intended to be performed by an officiator in the House of the Lord not only to cleanse but to seal up to eternal life, the function of the high priesthood. Following Jesus's example in the New Testament, other groups such as the Mennonites, Church of the Brethren, and Baptists practiced the ritual of foot washing as an expression of humility.[8]

According to Coltrin, "The meeting was dismissed by uplifted hand to the most high in token of the everlasting covenants in which covenant we received each other into fellowship in a determination to share in each others burdens whether in prosperity or adversity," which is what the January 3, 1833, revelation commanded.[9]

From January to April the school met occasionally, but little is known of their activities as a school other than, as Coltrin later informed, "Elder Orson Hyde was the teacher," who "saluted the brethren with uplifted hands, and they also answered with uplifted hands." In addition to training the elders for their missions, the meetings were also occasions for observing the sacrament, performing ordinations, receiving revelations, and experiencing various spiritual manifestations. According to Coltrin, "The Sacrament was also administered at times when Joseph appointed, after the ancient order; that is, warm bread to break easy was provided, and broken into pieces as large as my fist, and each person had a glass of wine and sat and ate the bread and drank the wine; and Joseph said that was the way that Jesus and his deciples partook of the bread and wine; and this was the order of the church anciently, and until the church went into darkness." Decades later Coltrin reminisced: "The brethren always went fasting; they went in the morning, remained until about four oclock in the afternoon, when each had a glass of wine and a piece of bread, after the ancient pattern."[10] Of course, fasting followed by the consumption of alcohol did not cause spiritual manifestations, but it may have aided in achieving a relaxed and receptive state of consciousness. Some studies have shown that alcohol consumption

---

8. See "Footwashing," in *The Mennonite Encyclopedia*, 2:347; Grow, "'Clean from the Blood of This Generation.'" See John 13:4–17.

9. Coltrin, Diary, Jan. 24, 1833; Revelation, Jan. 3, 1833, Revelation Book 2, 47 [D&C 88:132–133] (*JSP*, D2:347–48).

10. School of the Prophets Salt Lake City Minutes, Oct. 3, 10, 1883.

increases a person's susceptibility to suggestion, especially if one is already prone to mystical experiences.[11]

Coltrin remembered that on one occasion "the gift of tongues fell upon me and I spoke under its influence." When Smith heard Coltrin speaking from his "translation room," he came into the classroom and said, "God bless you, Brother Coltrin, that is the Spirit of God," and instructed Coltrin to continue. Coltrin said he not only continued, but "the gift of tongues and of prophecy rested on the greater part of the brethren present," which lasted well into the night.[12]

While Smith encouraged the men of the school of the prophets to speak in tongues, he continued to combat what he considered inappropriate, excessive expressions of religious enthusiasm. On February 6 Smith and his counselors wrote to a congregation of believers in Thompson, Ohio, about sixteen miles east of Kirtland. The letter introduced them to their new leader, Salmon Gee, explaining "that through him you may be kept from evil spirits and all strifes and discensions."[13] A few days after Smith and his counselors sent this letter, John Murdock, who had baptized many in Thompson, wrote a letter to Gee and his congregation that contrasted his own experience of the gift of tongues with the improper practice of some Thompson members, particularly Thomas King, who was attempting to block Gee's appointment. Murdock explained that he had been able "to speak the praises of God and the mysteries of the kingdom in other tonges according to promise and this without throwing me down or wallowing me on the ground or any thing unbecoming or immoral … so that I know that those odd actions and strange noises is not caused by the spirit of the Lord as is represented by brothe[r] King therefore in the name of the Lord Jesus Christ by the spirit of the Living God, according to the authority of the holy Priesthood commited to me I command Brother Thomas King (as though I were present) to cease from your diabolical acts of in thusiasm [enthusiasm] and also from acting as an

---

11. Rebecca Semmens-Wheeler, Zoltan Dienes, and Theodora Duka, "Alcohol Increases Hypnotic Susceptibility," *Consciousness and Cognition,* 22, no. 3 (Sep. 2013): 1082–1091; Kim Van Oorsouw, Herald Merckelbach, and Tom Smeets, "Alcohol Intoxication Impairs Memory and Increases Suggestibility for a Mock Crime: A Field Study," *Applied Cognitive Psychology* 29, no. 4 (July–Aug. 2015): 493–501. Other studies have shown alcohol has a negligible or even opposite effect. See David L. R. Maij, Michiel van Elk, and Uffe Schjoedt, "The Role of Alcohol in Expectancy-driven Mystical Experiences: A Pre-registered Field Study Using Placebo Brain Stimulation," *Religion, Brain & Behavior* 9, no. 2 (2019): 108–25.

12. Zebedee Coltrin, Address, Feb. 5, 1878, Minutes of the High Priests, Spanish Fork, UT, CHL.

13. Joseph Smith et al., Letter to "the Church of Christ in Thompson," Feb. 6, 1833, JS Letterbook 1, 25–26 (*JSP,* D3:6).

Elder ... [and] to submit and let brother Gee be upheld by the prayer of faith of every brother & sister and if there be this union of spirit & prayer of faith, evry false spirit shall be bound and cast out from among you."[14]

On February 27 the school of the prophets met in an adjoining room in the Whitney store where Smith dictated a revelation containing one of Mormonism's most distinguishing tenets: the prohibition of tobacco, alcohol, coffee, and tea—better known as "The Word of Wisdom." It came as a result of Emma's complaining about cleaning the floor after meetings. According to Brigham Young, who was not present but heard from others, tobacco juice was often "spit all over the floor" of the small room in which the school met, and "the smoke was so dense you could hardly see across the room."[15] Coltrin, who was present, recalled that Smith came out of his "translating room" and read the revelation to the members of the school. "There were twenty out of the twenty-one who used tobacco," Coltrin remembered, "and they all immediately threw their tobacco and pipes into the fire."[16] On another occasion, Coltrin explained that "those who gave up using tobacco [also] eased off on licorice root."[17] Licorice was thought to improve digestion or repress a cough, and it was common to chew on the root after it had been soaked in gin or whiskey. There was also an elixir or medicinal concoction for cough consisting of alcohol, opium, and licorice flavoring.[18]

The revelation containing Mormonism's new health code declared: "I have warned you & forewarned you by giving unto you this word of wisdom by Revelation, that inasmuch as any man drinketh wine or Strong drink among you behold it is not good, neither mete in the sight of your Father ... & again Strong drinks are not for the belly, but for the washing of your bodies, & Tobacco is not for man but is for bruises & all sick cattle to be used with judgement & skill."[19] For centuries tobacco had been used to treat a variety of ailments, including bruises, as well as a variety of maladies in cattle

---

14. John Murdock, Letter to Salmon Gee, Feb. 11, 1833, in JS Letterbook 1, 26–27.

15. Brigham Young, Discourse, Feb. 8, 1868, in George D. Watt, Discourse Shorthand Notes, Feb. 8, 1868, Pitman Shorthand Transcriptions, CHL, as quoted in *JSP*, D3:12n57; see also Brigham Young, "School of the Prophets," Feb. 8, 1868, *Journal of Discourses*, 12:158.

16. School of the Prophets Salt Lake City Minutes, Oct. 3, 1883; School of the Prophets Saint George Records, Dec. 23, 1883.

17. School of the Prophets Salt Lake City Minutes, Oct. 10, 1883.

18. Coxe, *The American Dispensatory*, 606; Paris, *Pharmacologia*, 2:221, 321.

19. Revelation, Feb. 27, 1833, "A Word of Wisdom," Gilbert, Notebook, [113] [D&C 89:4–8] (*JSP*, D3:20–21). Joel Hills Johnson remembered that the revelation was dictated in the evening. Johnson, Notebook, [1].

and other livestock. By 1833, however, tobacco use was falling into disfavor among a growing number of physicians as well as clergy.[20]

The Mormons were not the first to discourage the use of alcoholic beverages. At the time this revelation was dictated, there were already thousands of temperance societies throughout the United States advocating for a moderate, or temperate, use of alcohol, if not for complete abstinence.[21] When Kirtland's Temperance Society was formed in October 1830, it boasted more than 200 members. By February 1833—about four weeks before Smith dictated this revelation—the Kirtland distillery closed due to a lack of business.[22] Many of Smith's converts in the area came from Alexander Campbell's Disciples of Christ, which as early as 1830 strongly disapproved of the excessive use of alcohol.[23] The revelation, however, authorized the continued use of wine in the sacrament, although it advised that it "should be wine of your own make."[24]

The revelation also declared that "hot drinks are not for the body or belly."[25] Although some of Smith's contemporaries expressed concern about the consumption of tea and coffee, calls for moderation or prohibition were not as loud or persistent as those against alcohol and tobacco.[26] Apparently some of Smith's followers questioned what the revelation meant by "hot drinks" to excuse their continued use of tea and coffee, which prompted Joseph and Hyrum Smith, according to Joel Johnson, to rebuke them at a Sabbath meeting in Kirtland in July 1833 and to identify coffee and tea as the "hot drinks" prohibited by the revelation.[27] According to Coltrin, "There was no easing off on Tea and Coffee; these they had to give up straight off or their fellowship was jeopardized."[28] By May 1835, William W. Phelps wrote to

20. See Stewart, "A History of the Medicinal Use of Tobacco, 1492–1860"; Richardson, *The New-England Farrier, and Family Physician*, 37, 53, 254, 281, 307, 321; Clater, *Every Man His Own Cattle Doctor*, 193, 277, 342; "Tobacco," *Millennial Harbinger* (Bethany, WV), June 7, 1830, 281–83; "M'Allister's Dissertation on Tobacco," *Journal of Health* (Philadelphia), July 14, 1830, 329–31; Bush, "Word of Wisdom," 172–73.

21. See Blocker, *American Temperance Movements*; Peterson, "An Historical Analysis of the Word of Wisdom," 7–8; Bush, "The Word of Wisdom in Early Nineteenth-Century Perspective," 164–67; see also "Temperance," *Painesville (OH) Telegraph*, Nov. 22, 1832, [2].

22. Crary, *Pioneer and Personal Reminiscences*, 24–25, 68.

23. "Four Great Sources of Health," *Millennial Harbinger*, June 7, 1830, 279–80.

24. Revelation, Feb. 27, 1833, Gilbert, Notebook, [113] [D&C 89:6] (*JSP*, D3:21). On the use of wine in the sacrament, John Corrill wrote in 1839: "Bread and wine are used as emblems, but for wine they prefer the pure juice of the grape when they can get it." Corrill, *Brief History*, 47 (*JSP*, H2:195).

25. Revelation, Feb. 27, 1833, Gilbert, Notebook, [113] [D&C 89:9] (*JSP*, D3:21).

26. Bush, "Word of Wisdom," 170–72.

27. Johnson, Notebook, [1]. Hyrum Smith again identified tea and coffee as the prohibited "hot drinks" in 1842 in Nauvoo. "The Word of Wisdom," *Times and Seasons*, June 1, 1842, 800.

28. School of the Prophets Salt Lake City Minutes, Oct. 10, 1883.

his wife, Sally, that the members of the church in Kirtland uniformly "drink cold water; and don't even mention tea and Coffee."[29]

Still, opinions varied among Smith's followers about how strictly the revelation's instructions were to be followed, largely due to the revelation's opening statement that it was given as "a word of wisdom for the benefit of the Saints in these last days" and "not by commandment or Constraint."[30] However, most probably considered the word of God to be binding and discontinued the use of the banned substances, believing that only those weak in the faith would put their wisdom above God's. Coltrin, for example, reported that he was among the members of the school of the prophets who "laid aside their pipes and use of tobacco" and that he "never used it since."[31] Joel Johnson, another member of the school, said that although he "had used Tobbacco smoke and chew 15 years and always used strong drink Tea and Coffe[e]," he immediately "laid them all aside."[32] Not until February 1834 would disobedience to the Word of Wisdom be considered a transgression worthy of excommunication.[33]

Nevertheless, many members believed that it was permissible for tea or alcohol to be consumed for medicinal purposes. George A. Smith remembered that Emma Smith offered tea and coffee to refresh travelers in May 1833, and that in June 1834 Joseph Smith gave him whiskey when he was suffering from cholera.[34] This loophole, however, was closed on December 4, 1836, when a meeting of the church in Kirtland headed by Sidney Rigdon voted unanimously to "discountenance the use intirely of all liquors from the Church in Sickness & in health," with the only exception being "wine at the Sacraments."[35] Despite this decision, there is evidence that some leading members, including Oliver Cowdery and Brigham Young, continued the use of tea and alcohol in cases of sickness.[36]

In addition to the prohibition of alcohol, tobacco, coffee and tea, the revelation recommended the use of "all wholesome herbs ... & every fruit in

---

29. William W. Phelps, Letter to Sally Phelps, May 26–27, 1835, 1.

30. Revelation, Feb. 27, 1833, Gilbert, Notebook, [113] [D&C 89:9] (*JSP*, D3:20–21).

31. School of the Prophets Saint George Records, Dec. 23, 1883.

32. Johnson, Notebook, [1].

33. Minutes, Feb. 20, 1834, Minute Book 1, 39–40 (*JSP*, D3:451–52).

34. Smith, "History of George A. Smith by Himself," ca.1857–75, 10, 31.

35. Woodruff, Journal, Dec. 4, 1836 (Vogel, *Wilford Woodruff Journals*, 1:100).

36. When charged with breaking the Word of Wisdom in January 1838, Cowdery defended himself by saying he "had drank tea three times a day this winter on account of his ill health." Minutes, Jan. 26, 1838, Minute Book 2, 95; Cannon and Cook, *Far West Record*, 136. When Young and others left Nauvoo, Illinois, in the fall of 1839, church members prepared tea and "tonic bitters" for them because of their sickness. Historian's Office, Brigham Young History Drafts, 27.

the season thereof ... to be used with prudence & thanksgiving," while at the same time advising that the "flesh ... of beasts & of fowls ... be used sparingly ... only in times of winter or of famine."[37] Although some people advised against eating meat, the suggestion was contrary to prevailing wisdom.[38] Smith's followers seemed to understand it more in terms of conservation than as a dietary restriction for the promotion of health. John Corrill, for example, wrote in 1839: "Wasting of flesh, or taking of life of animals unnecessarily, or for sport, was forbidden."[39]

Finally, alluding to Isaiah 40:31, the revelation promised that "all saints who remember to keep & do these sayings walking in obedience to the commands shall receieve health in their navel & marrow to their bones ... & shall run & not be weary & walk & not faint."[40]

Presidency Reorganized

On March 8, 1833, Smith dictated a revelation about the presidency of the high priesthood, which began by declaring that his (Smith's) sins were forgiven "according to thy petition" and that "the keys of this kingdom shall never be taken from you whilst thou art in the world neither in the world to come."[41] The keys of the presidency included running the "School of the prophets which I have commanded to be organized that thereby they may be perfected in their ministry."[42] Rigdon, who had come under condemnation in July 1832 for claiming the keys had been taken from the church, was also "forgiven" of his sins, along with Frederick G. Williams. Both men—called as Smith's scribes and counselors, although Williams had yet to be ordained—were to be "accounted as equal with thee in holding the keys of this Last Kingdom."[43] Making Smith's counselors "equal" with him was probably motivated by the recent charge from Missouri officials that Smith wanted "monarchial power."[44]

The revelation summarized Smith's calling in the moment and immediate

---

37. Revelation, Feb. 27, 1833, Gilbert, Notebook, [113]–[114] [D&C 89:10, 12–13] (*JSP*, D3:21).

38. See Bush, "Word of Wisdom," 168–69.

39. Corrill, *Brief History*, 47 (*JSP*, H2:195). See also Revelation, May 7, 1831, Revelation Book 1, 81 [D&C 49:19, 21] (*JSP*, D1:302).

40. Revelation, Feb. 27, 1833, Gilbert, Notebook, [113]–[114] [D&C 89:18, 20] (*JSP*, D3:22–24).

41. Revelation, Mar. 8, 1833, [1], Newel K. Whitney Papers [D&C 90:1–3] (*JSP*, D3:27).

42. Revelation, [1] [D&C 90:7] (*JSP*, D3:28).

43. Revelation, [1] [D&C 90:6] (*JSP*, D3:28).

44. Orson Hyde and Hyrum Smith, Letter to Edward Partridge and Others, Jan. 14, 1833, JS Letterbook 1, 21 (*JSP*, D2:373).

future: "I say unto you I give unto you a commandment that you continue in this ministry and presidency and when you have finished the translation of the prophets you shall from thence forth preside over the affairs of the Church and the School and from time to time as shall be manifest by the comfo[r]ter receive revelations to unfold the mystres [mysteries] of the kingdom and set in order the churches."[45]

Concerning the present living accommodations of Smith's counselors, the revelation instructed: "Let there be a place provided as soon as it is possable for the family of thy councellor & scribe even Frederick and let mine Aged servant Joseph [Smith Sr.] continue with his family upon the place where he now lives and let it not be sold untill the mouth of the Lord shall name and let thy councellor even Sidney remain where he now resides untill the mouth of the Lord shall name."[46] In October 1831 a conference decided that "Br Frederick G Williams' family be provided with a comfortable dwelling by this Church," which after seventeen months still had not been done.[47] Determining if this promise was fulfilled is difficult, but the Williams family was displaced by Hyrum Smith's family on April 11, 1833. On this day, Hyrum recording in his journal: "Arived at kirtland the 10 of April rested a Part of a Day Moved into Brother F G Williams [house] and He moved out the 11th the 12th commenced Work on the farm."[48] Where the Williams family went is uncertain, but they finally settled on a seventeen-acre farm on the Kirtland flats northeast of the Whitney store, which was purchased from Newel K. Whitney on April 20, 1834.[49]

The revelation also instructed Smith to "write this commandment and say unto your brethren in Zion in Love greeting that I have called you also to preside over Zion in mine own due time therefore let them cease wear[y]ing me concerning this matter."[50] This refers to Smith's delay in moving to Missouri. Responding to W. W. Phelps's request that the Mormon leader move to Independence, Orson Hyde and Hyrum Smith wrote the previous January that "Brother Joseph will not settle in Zion until she repent and purify herself, and abide by the new covenant, and remember the commandments that

---

45. Revelation, Mar. 8, 1833, [2], Newel K. Whitney Papers [D&C 90:12–14] (*JSP*, D3:28).
46. Revelation, [2] [D&C 90:19–21] (*JSP*, D3:29–30).
47. Minutes, Oct. 10, 1831, Minute Book 2, 7 (Cannon and Cook, *Far West Record*, 16).
48. Hyrum Smith, Diary, Apr. 10–12, 1833.
49. Newel K. Whitney, Deed to Frederick G. Williams, Apr. 20, 1834, Geauga Co., OH, Deed Records, vol. 19, 203–204.
50. Revelation, Mar. 8, 1833, [3], Newel K. Whitney Papers [D&C 90:32–33] (*JSP*, D3:31).

have been given her, to do them as well as say them."[51] The Lord explained that although Zion has begun to repent, there were "many things" for which he was "not well pleased" and then concluded by chastising its leaders—the "strong ones" of Zion—promising to "chasten her untill she overcome and are clean before me for she shall not be moved out of her place."[52]

On March 15 Smith dictated a short revelation that added Williams as a "lively member" of the United Firm.[53] A note in the minute book indicates that Williams was "received into the United firm in full partnership agreeable to the specification of the bond."[54] Williams joined the other nine men in the firm who were "bound together by a bond & Covenant that cannot be broken" wherein they were "to have equal claims on the properties" belonging to the firm "according to his wants & his needs."[55] This fulfilled the command Williams had received the previous January to "let thy farm be consecratd f[o]r bringing forth of the revelations."[56]

Three days after joining the United Firm, Williams was finally ordained as Smith's second counselor in the presidency of the high priesthood more than two months after being called to replace Jesse Gause. On March 18, at a meeting of high priests in the school of the prophets, Rigdon requested that he and Williams be ordained, after which Joseph Smith ordained them as "equal with him in holding the Keys of the Kingdom and also to the Presidency of the high Priest hood."[57] Having first become equal in financial and temporal matters of the church, which required the consecration of his property, Williams was now made equal to Smith and Rigdon in ecclesiastical authority. This would not be the last time Smith would use church office as an inducement or reward for cooperation.

The minutes of this meeting also state that someone addressed those present, probably Smith, and promised that "the pure in heart that were present should see a heavenly vision, and after remaining for a short time in secret prayer the promise was verified to many present having the eyes

---

51. Orson Hyde and Hyrum Smith, Letter to Edward Partridge and Others, Jan. 14, 1833, JS Letterbook 1, 22 (*JSP*, D2:375).

52. Revelation, Mar. 8, 1833, [3], Newel K. Whitney Papers [D&C 90:35–37] (*JSP*, D3:31–32).

53. Revelation, Mar. 15, 1833, Revelation Book 2, 55 [D&C 92] (*JSP*, D3:35–37).

54. Notation, ca. Mar. 15, 1833, Minute Book 1, 11 (*JSP*, D3:38).

55. Revelation, Apr. 26, 1832, Revelation Book 1, 128–29 [D&C 82:11, 15, 18] (*JSP*, D2:236).

56. Revelation, Jan. 5, 1833, [1], Revelations Collection (*JSP*, D2:361).

57. Minutes, Mar. 18, 1833, Minute Book 1, 16–17 (*JSP*, D3:40–42); Revelation, Jan. 5, 1833, Revelations Collection (*JSP*, D2:361). Two days after he had been ordained to the presidency of the high priesthood, Williams received a license from Smith and Rigdon. License for Frederick G. Williams, Mar. 20, 1833, CHL (*JSP*, D3:43–46).

of their understandings opened so as to behold many things." Smith then distributed the sacrament, which as usual broke their fast and consisted of a plenitude of bread and wine.[58] According to the minutes, after partaking of the sacrament, "many of the brethren saw a heavenly vision of the saviour and concourses of angels and many othe[r] thing[s] of which each one has a record of what they saw &c."[59] No such records exist, but despite the use of the singular "a vision" in the minutes, it is clear that the manifestations were individualistic, subjective, and not objectively experienced by everyone present.[60]

Fifty years later, Zebedee Coltrin apparently described this event to the school of the prophets in Salt Lake City, giving more details about what preceded his visionary experience: "When we were all togather, Joseph having givan instructions, and while engaged in silent prayer, kneeling, with our hands uplifted each one praying in silence, no one whispered above his breath."[61] John Murdock remembered: "The Prophet told us if we would humble ourselves before God, and exercise strong faith, we should see the face of the Lord."[62] According to Coltrin, "A personage walked through the room from east to west, and Joseph asked if we saw him. I saw him and suppose the others did, and Joseph answered that is Jesus, the Son of God, our elder brother."[63] John Murdock said: "And about midday the visions of my mind were opened, and the eyes of my understanding were enlightened, and I saw the form of a man, most lovely, the visage of his face was round and fair as the sun. His hair a bright silver grey, Curled in most majestic form, His eyes a Keen penetrating blue, and the skin of his neck a most beautiful white and he was Covered from the neck to the feet with a loose garment, pure white: whiter than any garment I have ever before seen. His countenance was most penetrating, and yet most lovely; And while I was endeavoring to Comprehend the whole personage from head to feet it slip[p]ed from me, and the vision was closed up."[64] Coltrin's description of the personage was different: "Jesus was clothed in modern clothing, apparently of gray cloth."[65]

---

58. See Coltrin's statement in School of the Prophets Salt Lake City Minutes, Oct. 3 and 11, 1883.

59. Minutes, Mar. 18, 1833, Minute Book 1, 17 (*JSP*, D3:42–43).

60. For a discussion of the mechanisms that make group hallucination possible, see Zusne and Jones, *Anomalistic Psychology*, 135; Green and McCreery, *Apparitions*, 41–42; see also Vogel, "The Validity of the Witnesses' Testimonies," 105–108.

61. School of the Prophets Salt Lake City Minutes, Oct. 3, 1883.

62. Murdock, Autobiography, 26.

63. School of the Prophets Salt Lake City Minutes, Oct. 3, 1883.

64. Murdock, Autobiography, 26.

65. School of the Prophets Salt Lake City Minutes, Oct. 10, 1883.

In his 1883 reminiscence, Coltrin said Smith instructed the men to resume praying as before and that he soon saw "another personage surrounded as with a flame of fire" move through the room, and that Smith said it was "the Father of our Lord Jesus Christ." Coltrin is unique in reporting this second vision. When asked about the kind of clothing the Father was wearing, Coltrin said he could not tell because his glory was so great but that he was seated on a chair. After this vision closed, according to Coltrin, the prophet told the men to resume praying and that "in a very short time he drew our attention and said to us that Bro. Reynolds Cahoon was about to leave us—and told us to look at him." Coltrin said Cahoon "was on his knees, and his arms were extended," and it appeared to him as if Cahoon's "hands and wrists, head, face and neck down to his shoulders were as a piece of amber—clear and transparent, his blood having apparently left his veins." Coltrin reported that as soon as the men looked, Cahoon's appearance changed to normal, and that "Joseph said that in a few minutes more Bro. Cahoon would have left us."[66]

Coltrin also reported that following these visionary experiences, Smith said: "Brethren now you are prepared to be the Apostles of Jesus Christ, for you have seen both the Father and the Son, and know that They exist, and that They are two separate Personages."[67] In the September 1832 revelation, the Lord had already called them "mine apostles, even God's high priests," but if Coltrin's memory is correct, Smith's theology may have begun to distinguish the Father and Son as separate personages, if not separate persons.[68]

On March 23 Smith met with a council of high priests and elders at Whitney's store "for the purpose of appointing a committee to purchase land in Kirtland, upon which the Saints might build a stake of Zion."[69] Joseph Coe, Moses Dailey, and Ezra Thayer were assigned to investigate and if possible "make purchase of certain farms." Thayer was specifically asked to "obtain the price of Pete[r] French farm."[70] The three men left immediately to perform their assignment while the other men remained "in prayer and fasting." The council reconvened after three hours, and Joseph Coe and Moses Dailey reported that Elijah Smith agreed to sell his farm for $4,000,

---

66. School of the Prophets Salt Lake City Minutes, Oct. 3, 1883.

67. School of the Prophets.

68. The Lectures on Faith, which were given during the 1834–35 session of the school of the prophets, later explained: the Godhead consisted of "two personages"—the Father, "a personage of spirit," and the Son, "a personage of tabernacle." Lecture 5, par. 2, D&C, 1835 ed., 52–53.

69. JS History, vol. A-1, 282 (DHC 2:335).

70. Minutes, Mar. 23, 1833–A, Mar. 23, 1833–B, Minute Book 1, 15–16, 18–19 (*JSP*, D3:46–50).

and Thomas Morley agreed to sell his for $2,100.[71] Ezra Thayer reported that Peter French agreed to sell his 103-acre farm for $5,000. The following month, Coe made a down payment of $2,000 and agreed to pay the remaining $3,000 in two equal installments by April 1835.[72] Purchase of the French farm was significant since it was centrally located, bordering Whitney's land to the north and Frederick G. Williams's to the south. It also included a two-story brick building near the Whitney store that would later serve as the John Johnson Inn, as well as a brickyard, which Smith's history explained was "essential to the building up of the city."[73] Most importantly, the temple would be built on the southern edge of French property.

At the same meeting, Smith assigned more than a dozen elders to serve missions both to proselytize and to solicit funds from church members.[74] Coltrin explained that the newly-acquired properties "made it necessary to call the Elders out of school for the purpose of going again into the world and procuring means for Paying for the farms."[75] One of the missionaries, David W. Patten, explained in his journal that "the Elders of the Chirch that were there ware again sent out Buy the commandment of god to visit the Churches and advise them to come to Kirtland and settle there."[76] Smith and Williams were assigned "to visit the several churchs as shall be given by the spirit."[77]

With the elders leaving on missions, the school of the prophets was temporarily discontinued. A revelation Smith dictated the following June explained that "my servants sinned a verry grievous sin and contentions arose in the school of the prophets, which was verry grievous unto me saith your Lord. therefore I sent them forth to be chastened."[78] Existing records provide no additional information on the nature of this contention.

Tradition of Their Fathers

A clue to the possible cause of the "contention" in the school of the prophets may have been provided in a revelation Smith dictated on May 6, 1833. This revelation begins by drawing heavily on John 1, but it was unrelated

71. These farms were never acquired by the church. See *JSP*, D3:48n282 and n283.

72. Geauga Co., OH, Deed Records, vol. 17, 38–39, 360, Apr. 10, 1833. Thayer was a witness to the deed, which required that one of the payments was due on April 10, 1834, and the second on the same date in 1835.

73. JS History, vol. A-1, 283 (DHC 2:336).

74. Minutes, Mar. 23, 1833, Minute Book 1, 15–16 (*JSP*, D3:50–54).

75. Coltrin, Diary, Mar. 23, 1833.

76. Patten, Journal, Mar. 25, 1833.

77. Minutes, Mar. 23, 1833, Minute Book 1, 16 (*JSP*, D3:54).

78. Revelation, June 1, 1833, Revelation Book 2, 60 [D&C 95:10] (*JSP*, D3:107).

to Smith's work of revising the Bible, the New Testament portion of which had been completed three months earlier.[79] Rather, the revelation picked up themes in a December 1832 revelation related to the school of the prophets, which promised that if their "eye be single to my glory, your whole bodies shall be filled with light, and there shall be no darkness in you, and that body, which is filled with light comprehendeth all things; therefore ... you shall see him, for he will, unveil his face unto you, and it shall be in his own time, and in his own way, and according, to his own will."[80] The same revelation also reflected John 1 when it declared that "the light shineth in darkness, and the darkness compre[hen]deth it not, nevertheless, the day shall come, when you shall, comprehend even God, ... then shall ye know, that ye have seen me, that I am, and that I am the true light."[81]

The May 1833 revelation began by reiterating this same promise: "Evry soul who forsaketh their sins and cometh unto me and calleth on my name and obeyeth my voice and keepeth all my commandments shall see my face and know that I am."[82] The revelation then expanded on the previous revelation's the light-versus-darkness metaphor, explicating John 1 more fully and directly while also introducing new theological concepts such as the relationship between the Father and Son, the pre-mortal existence of the human spirit, free agency, and original sin. Possibly Smith felt a need to explain these principles because they were related to the "contentions [that] arose in the school of the prophets" mentioned in the subsequent June 1833 revelation, or he need to explain why only some experienced visions while others did not, or both.[83] Significantly, the revelation warned Smith's followers that the "wicked one cometh and taketh away light and truth through disobeidienc [disobedience] from the children of men and becaus[e] of the tradition of their fathers."[84] The source of "contentions" may have been certain inherited traditions or creeds relating to the nature of the Godhead and other theological issues.

In the May 1833 revelation, for example, Jesus declared: "I am the true light that lighteth evry man who cometh into the world; ... I am in the fathe[r] and the father in me and the fathe[r] and I are one." Explaining this

79. Revelation, May 6, 1833, [1]–[4], Newel K. Whitney Papers [D&C 93:1–37] (*JSP*, D3:85–89). Cf. John 1:1–34. Minutes, Feb. 2, 1833, Minute Book 1, 9 (Collier and Harwell, *Kirtland Council Minute Book*, 7).

80. Revelation, Dec. 27–28, 1833, Revelation Book 2, 39–40 [D&C 88:67–68] (*JSP*, D2:340–41). Cf. Matt. 6:22–23.

81. Revelation, 38 [D&C 88:49–50] (*JSP*, D2:339). Cf. John 1:5.

82. Revelation, May 6, 1833, [1], Newel K. Whitney Papers [D&C 93:1] (*JSP*, D3:85–86).

83. Revelation, June 1, 1833, Revelation Book 2, 60 [D&C 95:10] (*JSP*, D3:107).

84. Revelation, [4] [D&C 93:39] (*JSP*, D3:89–90).

oneness, Jesus said he was "the father because he gave me of his fulness and the son becaus I was in the world and made flesh my tabernacle and dwelt among the sons of men."[85] This statement was similar to a passage in the Book of Mormon, which declared that Jesus was both "the Father and the Son," and then explained that he was "the Father, because he was conceived by the power of God; and the Son, because of the flesh."[86] These passages point to Jesus's dual nature. Despite the logical and theological incoherence, the Fourth Ecumenical Council held in Chalcedon in 451 CE decided that Jesus was "perfect in divinity and humanity, truly God and truly human."[87] The two-nature doctrine of Jesus Christ, as one scholar of Smith's theology noted, "is nowhere expressly found in the New Testament," but nevertheless "persisted and was popular at the time of Joseph Smith."[88]

The Book of Mormon provides a clearly stated modalistic context for Christ's Sonship—it declares that "God himself shall come down among the children of men."[89] This meant that Jesus was literally the Father. The May 1833 revelation, however, implies something more nuanced when Jesus states that he is the "father because he gave me of his fulness," but qualifies this by stating that "John saw that [the Son] received not of the fulness at first ... but continued from grace to grace until he received a fulness and thus he was called the son of God because he received not of the fulness at the first."[90] This concept was apparently unique to Smith, but theologians of his day would have seen anything less than a fullness of the Father as denying the divinity of Jesus.[91] In John, Jesus is the Son because he is "full of grace and truth," and humans, not Jesus, are described as receiving Jesus's "fulness ... grace for grace" (John 1:16). Smith's revelation explained this discrepancy by implying that John was incomplete—despite his recent inspired translation of it—and promising that the "fulness of John's record is hereafter to be revealed."[92]

---

85. Revelation, May 6, 1833, [1], Newel K. Whitney Papers [D&C 93:1–4] (*JSP*, D3:86).

86. Book of Mormon, 1830 edition, 186 [Mosiah 15:2–3].

87. As quoted in McGrath, *Christian Theology*, 224.

88. Harrell, *"This Is My Doctrine,"* 160.

89. Book of Mormon, 1830 edition, 186 [Mosiah 15:1].

90. Revelation, May 6, 1833, [1], [2], Newel K. Whitney Papers [D&C 93:4, 12–14] (*JSP*, D3:86, 88).

91. As nineteenth-century American theologian Humphrey Moore expressed: "It is absurd to say that Christ possesses divine attributes only in a limited degree. Divine attributes are infinite, or in the greatest possible degree. What is less is not divine. If this be not true, it is impossible to draw a line of distinction between human and divine attributes." Moore, *Treatise on the Divine Nature*, 104.

92. Revelation, May 6, 1833, [2], Newel K. Whitney Papers [D&C 93:6] (*JSP*, D3:88).

Smith's revelation also expanded John's description of Jesus as an uncreated being, who was "in the beginning with God" (John 1:1–2), to include humans—"man was also in the begining with God."[93] While there is no clearly-stated doctrine of the pre-mortal existence of the human spirit in the Bible, as early as June 1830 Smith added a passage to his revision of Genesis that said "the Lord God created all things … spiritually before they were naturally upon the face of the Earth," including "all the children of men."[94] The revelation also seems to imply that man's spirit was made from God's glory, which like God is eternal and uncreated. Man was in the beginning with God because "inteligence or the Light of truth was not created or made neith[er] indeed can be. … The glory of God is inteligence or in other words light & truth."[95] Mormon scholar Charles R. Harrell has observed that this teaching "is similar to the ancient Gnostic doctrine of emanation" and compatible with the contemporary teachings of Unitarian-Universalist Hosea Ballou, who, according to religious historian E. Brooks Holifield, "blurred the distinction between the human and the divine by contending that human beings embodied a divine principle, having been created from the 'fulness' of God rather than from nothing."[96]

The revelation rejected the Calvinist doctrine of Original Sin, declaring that "evry spirit of man was innocent in the begining, and God having redeemed man from the fall man became again in their infant state innocent before God."[97] As early as December 1830, Smith's revision of Genesis had explained that "Christ hath atoned for original guilt wherein the sins of the Parents cannot be answered upon the heads of the Children for they are whole from the foundation of the world." While this absolved humankind of Adam's transgression, it did not free them from inheriting a sinful nature as a result of the Fall. As the Lord told Adam, "Inasmuch as thy Children are conseived in sin even so when they begin to grow up sin conseiveth in

---

93. Revelation, [3] [D&C 93:29] (*JSP*, D3:89).

94. Old Testament Revision 1, 5 [Moses 3:5] (Faulring et al., *Joseph Smith's New Translation of the Bible*, 88). See Harrell, *"This Is My Doctrine,"* 207–209.

95. Revelation, May 6, 1833, [3], [4], Newel K. Whitney Papers [D&C 93:29, 36] (*JSP*, D3:89).

96. Harrell, *"This Is My Doctrine,"* 208; Holifield, *Theology in America*, 229. Ballou, for example, wrote: "The truth undoubtedly is, that just as far as we can look into creation, providence and redemption, and see the harmony and beauty of them, and see that all were calculated for the good of created intelligences. … Were we not created *of his fulness?* … I know it has been said, that God created all things out of nothing, &c.; but such an idea never will be imbibed by me." Ballou, *A Treatise on Atonement*, 84.

97. Revelation, May 6, 1833, [4], Newel K. Whitney Papers [D&C 93:38] (*JSP*, D3:89).

their hearts."[98] By Smith's time, as Harrell has observed, New England theologians began to distinguish "between original *sin*, which is the depraved nature that all inherit, and original *guilt*, which is the culpability for Adam's sin," and that "the belief that an individual begins life with a clean slate, free of the guilt of Adam's sin, was becoming increasingly popular."[99]

The May 1833 revelation reiterated several points that had been revealed through Smith's revision of Genesis, of which most of the men of the school of the prophets were likely unaware. In Smith's revision of Genesis, Adam received a revelation in which God not only explained that Jesus atoned for "original guilt," but, similar to the May 1833 revelation, declared: "I made the world, & men before they were in the flesh."[100] The revelation mentioned the "agency of man," and the Genesis revision stated that Adam's children were "agents unto themselves."[101] Most interestingly, in Smith's revision of Genesis, God taught Adam the gospel of Christ and the plan of salvation, which consisted of faith, repentance, baptism, and the gift of the Holy Ghost, and then declared: "I give unto you a commandment to teach these things freely unto your Children."[102] Similarly, in the May 1833 revelation, the Lord reminded its recipients: "I have commanded you to bring up your Children in light and truth."[103]

The last half of the revelation chastised Smith, his counselors Rigdon and Williams, and Bishop Whitney for various things, but especially for failing to teach their families the commandments. Concerning Smith, the revelation stated: "Joseph you have not kept the commandments and must needs stand rebuked before the lord your family must needs repent and forsake some things and give more earnest heed unto your sayings or be removed out of their place."[104]

---

98. Old Testament Revision 1, 14 [Moses 6:54–55] (Faulring et al., *Joseph Smith's New Translation of the Bible*, 101).

99. Harrell, *"This Is My Doctrine,"* 264.

100. Old Testament Revision 2, 17 [Moses 6:51, 54], adds "in the flesh" above the line (Faulring et al., *Joseph Smith's New Translation of the Bible*, 612).

101. Revelation, May 6, 1833, [3], Newel K. Whitney Papers [D&C 93:31] (*JSP*, D3:89); Old Testament Revision 1, 14 [Moses 6:56] (Faulring et al., *Joseph Smith's New Translation of the Bible*, 101).

102. Old Testament Revision 1, 14 [Moses 6:58] (Faulring et al., *Joseph Smith's New Translation of the Bible*, 102). In November 1831 Smith dictated a revelation in which parents were instructed to teach their children the doctrines of faith, repentance, baptism, and the gift of the Holy Ghost, otherwise "the sin be upon the head of the parents." Revelation, Nov. 1, 1831-A, Revelation Book 1, 114 [D&C 68:25–28]; *JSP*, D2:102.

103. Revelation, May 6, 1833, [5], Newel K. Whitney Papers [D&C 93:47–48] (*JSP*, D3:90).

104. Revelation, [4] [D&C 93:40] (*JSP*, D3:90).

12

House of the Lord

APRIL–JULY 1833

*Joseph rose and reminded them that they were not making a house
for themselves or any other man but a house for God . . .*
—*Lucy Mack Smith, History, 1844–45, book 14, [1]–[2]*

In compliance with a December 1832 revelation instructing that a house
be built for the school of the prophets, Joseph Coe, acting on behalf of the
church, purchased the 103-acre tract of land from Peter French on April
2, 1833, on which the temple would eventually be built.[1] On May 4 a conference of high priests met and appointed Hyrum Smith, Jared Carter, and
Reynolds Cahoon to collect money by subscription to build the temple.[2]
The three men apparently did not act quickly enough, for on June 1 Joseph
Smith dictated a revelation chastising them for not taking steps toward the
construction of the Lord's House: "Ye have sinned against me a verry grievous sin in that ye have not considered the great commandment in all things
that I have given unto you concerning the building of mine house for the
preparation wherewith I deign to prepare mine Apostles to prune my vineyard for the last time."[3]

Blessings Promised

The same day that Joseph dictated the revelation, Hyrum Smith, Carter, and
Cahoon issued a circular for collecting funds by subscription to construct the
temple school. "Unless we fulfil this command," they warned, "we may all

---

1. Revelation, Dec. 27–28, 1833, Revelation Book 2, 46 [D&C 88:119] (*JSP*, D2:345);
Geauga Co., OH, Deed Records, vol. 17, 38–39, 359–360 (Apr. 10, 1833); Parkin, "Joseph Smith
and the United Firm," 19–22; Staker, *Hearken, O Ye People*, 414.
2. Minutes, May 4, 1833, Minute Book 1, 20 (*JSP*, D3:81–82).
3. Revelation, June 1, 1833, Revelation Book 2, 59 [D&C 95:3–4] (*JSP*, D3:106). See Revelation, Dec. 27–28, 1832, Revelation Book 2, 45–46 [D&C 88:119] (*JSP*, 2:345).

dispare of obtaining the great blessing that God has promised to the faithful of the Church of Christ." They encouraged church members to "make evry possable exertion to aid temporally as well as spiritually in this great work that the Lord is bringing about and is about to accomplish."[4]

The "great blessing" was the Lord's command to "build an house in the which house I design to endow those whom I have chosen with power from on high, for this is the promise of the Father unto you. Therefore, I commanded you to tarry even as mine Apostles at Jerusalem."[5] The building of the House of the Lord was thus tied to the promise made in the January 1831 revelation that those who obeyed the command to move to Ohio would be "endowed with power from on high."[6] The reference to Jesus's instruction for his apostles to tarry at Jerusalem until they were "endued with power from on high" alludes to the Day of Pentecost when the apostles were "filled with the Holy Ghost, and began to speak with other tongues" (Luke 24:49; Acts 2:1–4). Although the promise was designed to create an incentive to begin construction of the temple, some of Smith's followers may have wondered about the meaning of this statement since they had already been endowed with the high priesthood in June 1831 and were currently speaking in tongues and serving missions.

The revelation stipulated that the inner court of the House of the Lord was to be 55 feet by 65 feet and that it was not to be constructed "after the manner of the world" but "after the manner which I shall show unto three of you whom ye shall appoint and ordain unto this power."[7] At this time, Smith, Rigdon, and Williams were assigned by a conference of high priests "to obtain a draft or construction of the inner court of the house."[8] According to Truman O. Angell, a principal worker on the temple, Williams later said that the three men were shown "the plan or model of the House to be built" in a vision.[9] When the presidency sent plans for a similar structure to church leaders in Missouri in late June 1833, Williams wrote on the draft, "For your satisfaction we inform you that … the size form and dime[n]sions of the house were given us of the Lord."[10]

---

4. Hyrum Smith et al., Letter to "the Churches of Christ," June 1, 1833, in JS Letterbook 1, 36–38; see also JS History, vol. A-1, 297–300 (DHC 1:349–50).

5. Revelation, June 1, 1833, Revelation Book 2, 59–60 [D&C 95:8–9] (*JSP*, D3:106–107).

6. Revelation, Jan. 2, 1831, Revelation Book 1, 52 [D&C 38:32] (*JSP*, 1:232).

7. Revelation, June 1, 1833, Revelation Book 2, 60 [D&C 95:13–15] (*JSP*, D3:107).

8. Minutes, June 3, 1833, Minute Book 1, 12 [ca. 1 June 1833] (*JSP*, D3:104).

9. Angell, Autobiography, 14–15.

10. Plan of the House of the Lord, June 1–25, 1833 (*JSP*, D3:145).

The plans were unique in calling for identical halls on the first and second floors: one for worship, the other for the school of the prophets. The building was unlike other churches in its arrangement of four-tiered pulpits at both ends of each hall. The exterior of the temple incorporated a "mixture of Georgian, Federal, Greek Revival, and Gothic elements."[11] The box-shaped building was Federal in style and the bell tower and dominant roof pediment added Greek Revival elements, while the pointed tops of the windows were Gothic. With the addition of a vestibule at the entrance, which contained stairways and a vestry, the exterior dimensions of the Kirtland House of the Lord were about 79 feet by 59 feet.[12]

Construction Begins

On June 4, 1833, Smith attended a conference in the translating room in the Whitney store to consider "how the french farm should be disposed of," but "the councel could not agree who should take the charge of it."[13] The council decided to seek revelation on that matter, and Smith dictated a revelation that stipulated that Whitney take charge of the farm and directed that John Johnson, who had just sold his farm in Hiram and moved to Kirtland, be added to the United Firm and eventually to superintend the two-story brick tavern on the former French farm.[14] As a result, the farm was transferred to N. K. Whitney & Co. on June 17.[15]

On June 6 Smith attended a meeting of high priests who voted that the building committee (Hyrum Smith, Reynolds Cahoon, and Jared Carter) "proceed immediately to commence building the House or obtaining material, Stone Brick Lumber &c"[16] It was probably at this meeting, according to Lucy Smith's history, that "some thought that it would be better to build a frame others said that a frame was too costly kind of a house and the majority concluded upon the putting up a log house," after which "Joseph rose and reminded them that they were not making a house for themselves or any other man but a house for God— And shall we brethren build a house for Our

---

11. Robison, *First Mormon Temple*, 16.

12. See Plan of the House of the Lord in Kirtland, OH (four fragments), ca. June 1833 (*JSP*, D3:91–102); and Plan of the House of the Lord, June 1–25, 1833 (*JSP*, D3:131–346). Text and drawing are in the handwriting of Frederick G. Williams.

13. Minutes, June 4, 1833, Minute Book 1, 13 (*JSP*, D3:110).

14. Revelation, June 4, 1833, Revelation Book 2, 60–61 [D&C 96] (*JSP*, D3:111–12).

15. Geauga Co., OH, Deed Records, vol. 17, 360–61 (June 17, 1833). John Johnson was delayed in taking control of the Inn until the fall of 1833 because of an agreement Peter French had with Thomas Knight, who was using the main floor as a store. Staker, *Hearken, O Ye People*, 414–15.

16. Minutes, June 6, 1833, Minute Book 1, 21 (*JSP*, D3:112–15).

God of logs. No brethren I have a better plan than that I have the plan of the house of the Lord given by himself. … He then gave them the plan in full of the house of the Lord at Kirtland with which when the brethren heard they were highly delighted." Lucy said that the men left the meeting and followed their prophet up the hill to the Smiths' field of wheat. When Joseph pointed out the location of the future temple, Hyrum ran to the nearby house to get his scythe, explaining to his inquiring mother that he was determined to be "the first at the work" of building the House of the Lord. "In a few minutes," Lucy remembered, "the fence was removed [and] the young wheat cut."[17]

Lucy also thought Hyrum had begun digging on the same day, but Hyrum wrote in his journal on June 7: "This Day Commenced making Preparation for the Building the House of the Lord."[18] Joseph's history also incorrectly dated the beginning of construction to June 5 based on an insertion Willard Richards made in the 1840s: "June 5 Geo. A. Smith drawed the first load of stone for the Temple and Hyrum Smith & Reynolds Cahoon commenced digging the trench for the walls of the Lord's House and fin[i]shed the same with their own hands."[19] An excavation four to five feet deep and somewhat larger than 79 by 59 feet had to be dug first, which took about six weeks. The first cornerstone was laid on July 23, and construction of the foundation walls began.[20] George A. Smith remembered that the "first two loads of Rock taken to the Temple ground were hauled from Stanard's Quarry by Harvey Stanly & myself."[21]

By fall, a 28-inch-wide stone foundation had been completed and some girders were in place to support the floor. About this time, it was determined that the walls of the temple could not be made of brick as originally planned since the Mormons who took over French's old brickyard were unsuccessful in making quality bricks in the quantity needed, nor could they afford to purchase bricks elsewhere.[22] Consequently, construction was temporarily halted in late 1833. On October 10 Williams wrote to Missouri leaders that a council had decided to "discontinue the building of the temple for

---

17. Lucy Mack Smith, History, 1844–45, book 14, [1]–[2] (Anderson, ed., *Lucy's Book*, 581–82).

18. Hyrum Smith, Diary, June 7, 1833.

19. JS History, vol. A-1, 302 (DHC 1:353). It was copied into vol. A-2, 201, about May 28–29, 1845. Vogel, *History of Joseph Smith*, 1:263n65.

20. [William W. Phelps], "The House of God," *Messenger and Advocate*, July 1835, 147; Notes for Joseph Smith History, ca. 1843, [1], in *JSP*, MRB:659.

21. George A. Smith, "History of George A. Smith by Himself," 10.

22. Robison, *The First Mormon Temple*, 32–33. On April 2, 1833, a council of high priests appointed Frederick G. Williams to superintend the operation of the church's brickyard. Minutes, Apr. 2, 1833, Minute Book 1, 19 (*JSP*, D3:55–56).

the winter for want of materials and to prepare and get all things ready to recommence it early in the spring."[23]

Meanwhile, Artemus Millet, one of Brigham Young's Canadian converts and an experienced builder of large-scale projects, arrived in Kirtland to inspect the work. At Young's recommendation, Hyrum Smith had written to Millet to request his assistance. As Millet recalled, "Hyrum Smith wrote to me that it was the will of the Lord that I should go and work on the temple in Kirtland. When I went the work was suspended and I returned, sold out on credit and took my family in April 1834 to Kirtland."[24] During his visit, Millet resolved the construction problem by suggesting that the temple walls be constructed of rubble stone covered with stucco, a common practice in Canada.[25]

Prior to Millet's arrival, irreversible mistakes in construction had already occurred due to the lack of skill and experience of the workers. The walls of the foundation should have had a wider footing to spread out the weight, which would later result in the building settling about two inches and the walls cracking. The 9-by-12-inch girders supporting the first floor were rough-hewn and marred by defects such as knots; they were also oriented on the foundation walls sideways, making them weaker, and together with the inadequate number of supporting piers in the basement has resulted in the failure of one girder. According to one architectural study of the Kirtland Temple, "Given the weakness of the girders supporting the floor of the lower court, the floor must have creaked and groaned during the services," and it was with "extreme good fortune that the floor of the lower court did not collapse during the temple dedicatory services."[26] A change in number of windows resulted in the wall separating the inner court from the vestibule bisecting the first of six evenly-spaced windows. Other design flaws raise the question of how much of the inspired construction was left up to interpretation.

Charismatic Challenges from Vermont

In mid-April 1833 Smith received a letter from John S. Carter in Benson, Vermont, reporting difficulties the branch under his care was experiencing and asking about preparations for gathering to Zion. In early March 1833 Carter recorded in his journal that the Benson congregation was "under some trials" and stated that a "division in feeling has taken place."[27] Adding

---

23. Frederick G. Williams, Letter to "Dear Brethren," Oct. 10, 1833, JS Letterbook 1, 57–58.
24. Millet, Reminiscences, 3.
25. Robison, *The First Mormon Temple*, 32–34.
26. Robison, 30, 32.
27. John S. Carter, Journal, Mar. 3, 1833.

to the difficulties Carter was attempting to settle were the charismatic claims of Jane Sherwood. On March 10 Carter wrote: "Sister Sherwood appears to have visions of the Lord. Oh. God, let us not be deceived! She has seen greate things, but does not as yet tell all."[28] On April 5 he recorded that he "heard Sister Sherwood relate her vision of seeing an Angel" and that she claimed to have "visions of God concerning that which must come hereafter perporting indeed that the powr of God's Judgment has come, & astonishing things soon are to take place."[29]

Smith responded on April 13, mentioning in his postscript that he had also received two letters from Sherwood's husband, Henry G. "As it respects the vision you speak of," Smith began, "we do not consider ourselves bound to receive any revelation forom [from] any one man or woman without being legally constituted and ordained to that authority and given sufficien[t] proof of it, I will inform you that it is contrary to the economy of God for any member of the Church or any one to receive instruction for those in authority hig[h]er than themselves, therefore you will see the impropriety of giving heed to them, but if any have a vision heavenly or a visitation from an hevenaly [heavenly] messenger it must be for their own benefit and instruction, for the fundimental principals, government and doctrine of the church is invested in the keys of the kingdom."[30]

This statement shows how Smith kept control of the church and insulated himself from usurpers. As early as September 1830, a revelation had denounced Hiram Page's claim of receiving revelations through a seer stone, declaring that "no one shall be appointed to Receive commandments & Revelations in this Church excepting my Servant Joseph for he Receiveth them even as Moses." The same revelation instructed Oliver Cowdery, "Thou shalt not command him which is at thy head."[31] While this revelation pertained to Smith as leader of the church, his letter to Carter explicitly applied the principle to local leaders as well as every leader in the developing hierarchy. Drawing on the September 1832 revelation, Smith explained that "the office of Elders is an appendege to the high priesthood" and that the high priesthood "centers & concentrates in one" president. With apparent sensitivity to recent criticism of his appointment as president of the high priesthood and accusations

---

28. Carter, Mar. 10, 1833.
29. Carter, Apr. 5, 1833.
30. Joseph Smith and Frederick G. Williams, Letter to John S. Carter, Apr. 13, 1833, JS Letterbook 1, 29–30 (*JSP*, D3:59).
31. Revelation, Sep. 1830-B, Revelation Book 1, 40, 41 [D&C 28:2, 6] (*JSP*, D1:185).

of seeking authority over others, Smith explained to Carter that "the duty of a high priest is to administer spriitual and holy things and to hold Communeion with God but not to exorcise [exercise] monarchal government."[32]

In his letter, Carter also apparently sought advice about the gathering to Zion. On March 24 he had noted in his journal that some members of the branch in Benson had already "made their calculation to go up to Zion," though "their way appears hegged [hedged] up."[33] Smith responded that "with respect to preparing to go to Zion first it would be pleasing to the lord that the Church or Churches going to Zion should be organised, and appoint a suitable person who is well acquainted with the Conditions of the Church & and be sent to Kirtland to inform the Bishop and procure licence from him."[34]

No doubt weary of continual pressure to resolve all disputes, Smith's response explained another principle that was to be resolved with the eventual publication of his revelations: "We never enquire of at the hand of God for special revelation only in case of ther being no previous revelation to suit the case. ... It is a great thing to enquire at the hand of God or to come into his presence and we feel fearful to appro[a]ch him upon subject[s] that are of little or no consequen[ce] to satisfy the enqueries of individuals especially about things the knowledge of which men aught to obtain in all cencerity before God for themselves in humility by the prayer of faith."[35]

Carter mentioned in his journal receiving this letter in late April as well as another letter from Smith in early May containing additional "answers to important questions."[36] Apparently taking Smith's advice to seek personal revelation, Carter and many Benson branch members moved to Kirtland the following September.[37]

Reconciliation with Missouri Officials

On Sunday, April 21, 1833, Smith responded to a letter the Missouri leaders had sent in late February, which is no longer extant. It must have provided relief to Smith and the Kirtland leaders, because it "contained the conffescion of our brethren" in Missouri "all of which was to our entire satisfaction."[38] After holding solemn assemblies throughout the Missouri

---

32. Smith and Williams, Letter to Carter, Apr. 13, 1833, JS Letterbook 1, 30 (*JSP*, D3:61).
33. Carter, Journal, Mar. 24, 1833.
34. Smith and Williams, Letter to Carter, Apr. 13, 1833, JS Letterbook 1, 30 (*JSP*, D3:61–62).
35. Smith and Williams, 31 (*JSP*, D3:62–63).
36. Carter, Journal, Apr. 23–24 and May 7, 1833.
37. Carter, Journal, Aug. 21–22 and Sep. 5, 1833; see also Barnouw, "The Benson Exodus of 1833."
38. Joseph Smith, Letter to "brethren in Zion," Apr. 21, 1833, JS Letterbook 1, 33 (*JSP*, D3:66).

branches "to effect a perfect harmony between" them and their "brethren in Kirtland," the Missouri high priests appointed Oliver Cowdery, W. W. Phelps, and John Corrill to write an epistle to the Ohio leaders reporting the general repentance of the Missouri church and confessing that it was a mistake to challenge Smith's leadership.[39] Smith reported to the Missouri officials that their letter "was read by the Brethren in Kirtland with feelings of the deepest interest knowing as we did that the anger of the Lord was kindled against you and [no]thing but repentance of the greatest humility would turn it away and I will assure you that expressions of Joy beemed on evry countenance when they saw that our epistle and the revelation was received by our brethren in Zion & it had its desired effect."[40]

Smith also responded to Sidney Gilbert's December 10 and February 24 letters, both of which are no longer extant. Regarding the first letter, which was described by Orson Hyde and Hyrum Smith as containing "low, dark, & blind insinuations," Smith said that "upon mature reflection and inquiry at the hand of the Lord" the leadership in Ohio found it "unreconcilable" because it contained "hints ... not clearly explained" and that "it is necessary that there should be no disgise in them but that evry subject writen from brethren should be plain to the understanding of all." Regarding the second letter, Smith said that it "was not written in that contrition of heart which it should have been for it appeared to be writen in too much of a spirit of justification." Hyde and Hyrum Smith's previous letter to Bishop Partridge had mentioned Gilbert's hesitancy to extend credit to poor members and reprimanded him for his "fearfulness," covitousness," and lack in faith that God will "provide for his saints in their last days." Speaking of Gilbert in the present letter, Smith said: "It is his duty to assist all the poor brethren that are pure in heart and that he has done rong in with holding credit from them as they must have assistence for the Lord established him in Zion for that express purpose."[41]

Smith also revealed his plans for his inspired revision of the Bible, stating that "it is not the will of the Lord to print any of the new translation in the Star but when it is published it will all go to the world together in a volume by itself, and the new Testament and the book of Mormon will be printed together."[42] Editor Phelps had already published an extract from Smith's

39. Minutes, Feb. 26, 1833, Minute Book 2, 33 (Cannon and Cook, *Far West Record*, 60–61).

40. Smith, Letter to "brethren in Zion," Apr. 21, 1833, JS Letterbook 1, 33 (*JSP*, D3:66–67).

41. Smith, 33–34 (*JSP*, D3:67–68); see also Orson Hyde and Hyrum Smith, Letter to Edward Partridge and Others, Jan. 14, 1833, JS Letterbook 1, 21 (*JSP*, D2:374).

42. Smith, Letter to "brethren in Zion," 35 (*JSP*, D3:68).

translation of the Old Testament in *The Evening and the Morning Star*,[43] but the prospect of printing the entire Bible in the same volume as the Book of Mormon must have seemed overly ambitious, if not cost-prohibitive.

In a postscript Smith mentioned John Corrill's "confession [which] gave me great satisfaction and all thing[s] are now settled on my part."[44] Following Smith's visit to Missouri in the summer of 1832, during which he was sustained as president of the high priesthood, Corrill, a counselor to Partridge, sent a letter to Kirtland (not extant) that, according to Hyde and Hyrum Smith, accused Smith of "seeking after Monarchal power and authority."[45] In a July 1832 letter Smith responded that Corrill's letter contained "absolutely false" charges.[46] Orson and Hyrum's January 14, 1833, epistle rejected the charge that Smith sought power but rather was attempting to "magnify the high office and calling whereunto he has been called and appointed by the command of God."[47] Corrill may have acquiesced to Smith's taking control over all aspects of the Missouri church, but his commitment to republican liberty would eventually lead him to oppose Smith and to withdraw from the church in 1838.[48]

Smith wrote a follow-up letter to Bishop Partridge on May 2, 1833, concerning the law of consecration and stewardship.[49] In the previous letter, he could only advise the Missouri leaders "to make yourselves acquainted with the commandments of the Lord and the Laws of the State and govern yourselves accordingly."[50] Smith evidently had second thoughts about leaving the decision to the Missouri leadership. The system Partridge had set up whereby he retained ownership of all consecrated property and leased small portions to members as stewardships was a concept that was not being supported in Missouri courts. One precedent-setting case was reported in the July 1833 issue of *The Evening and the Morning Star* involving "one Bates from New-London, Ohio," who had won a lawsuit against Partridge for fifty

---

43. See "Extract from the Prophecy of Enoch," *The Evening and the Morning Star* (Independence, MO), Aug. 1832, [2]–[3] [Moses 7].

44. Smith, Letter to "brethren in Zion," Apr. 21, 1833, JS Letterbook 1, 36 (*JSP*, D3:70).

45. Hyde and Smith, Letter to Edward Partridge and Others, Jan. 14, 1833, JS Letterbook 1, 21 (*JSP*, D2:373).

46. Smith, Letter to William W. Phelps, July 31, 1832, 3, JS Collection (*JSP*, D2:263).

47. Hyde and Smith, Letter to Edward Partridge and Others, Jan. 14, 1833, JS Letterbook 1, 21 (*JSP*, D2:373–74).

48. Winn, "'Such Republicanism as This.'"

49. Smith, Letter to Edward Partridge, May 2, 1833, JS Collection (*JSP*, D3:71–77).

50. Smith, Letter to "brethren in Zion," Apr. 21, 1833, JS Letterbook 1, 35 (*JSP*, D3:68).

dollars.[51] Apparently writing about the same case on March 4, 1833, the Reverend Benton Pixley informed readers of the *Cincinnati Journal* that an unnamed plaintiff sued Partridge "to recover certain moneys sent to [the bishop] ... *to purchase an inheritance for himself and for the saints of God in Zion in these last days.*" Pixley also noted that "several others on this decision stand ready to make s[i]milar demands on the Bishop." Pixley advised anyone considering the consecration of their property to the "Bishop" to "be sure and keep back enough to purchase and possess a little home of their own, independent of the Bishop, for their own heirs and not for his, and that they receive also enough to purchase at least one year's provision."[52]

In his letter to Partridge, Smith counseled him to grant inheritances by deed, rather than lease, and that it should be considered an "everlasting inheritance" and a "private stewardship." Should the member apostatize or be excommunicated he or she would retain the property on which they were living but the portion that was consecrated for the poor would be retained by the bishop legally as a charitable donation. By following this policy, Smith assured Partridge, "no man can take any advantage of you in law."[53] The Mormon occupation of Jackson County was nearing an end, and there was little time to implement Smith's plan. However, according to one historian, the law of consecration was observed in other Mormon settlements in Missouri by members simply consecrating their surplus property to the church, not by the bishop deeding stewardships, as Smith instructed.[54]

Smith closed his letter by acknowledging the reconciliation that had taken place between the leaders of both Mormon centers: "And now b[r]other Edward, be assured that we all feel thankful, that the brethren in Zion are beginning to humble themselves, & trying to keep the commandments of the Lord, which is our prayer to God, you may all be able to do, and now, may the grace of God be with you all, amen."[55]

---

51. "The Elders Stationed in Zion to the Churches Abroad," *The Evening and the Morning Star,* July 1833, 110.

52. "Still Later from Mount Zion," *Cincinnati (OH) Journal,* Mar. 22, 1833, 46, italics in original; see also "Mormonism," *Painesville (OH) Telegraph,* Apr. 26, 1833, [3].

53. Smith, Letter to Edward Partridge, May 2, 1833, JS Collection (*JSP,* D3:76). A redaction made prior to the 1835 publication of Smith's May 20, 1831, revelation reflects the instruction he gave to Partridge in this letter. It reads, "If he shall transgress, and is not accounted worthy to belong in the church, he shall not have power to claim that portion which he has consecrated unto the bishop for the poor and the needy of my church: therefore, he shall not retain the gift, but shall only have claim on that portion that is deeded unto him." Revelation, May 20, 1831, in D&C XXIII:1, 1835 ed. [D&C 51:5] (cf. *JSP,* D1:316).

54. Cook, *Revelations,* 135n6.

55. Smith, Letter to Edward Partridge, May 2, 1833, JS Collection (*JSP,* D3:77).

Excommunication of Philastus Hurlbut

About June 1, 1833, Smith attended a conference of high priests in the translating room in the second story of Whitney's store and considered the case of Philastus Hurlbut, who was accused of "unchristian conduct with the female sex while on a mission to the east."[56] According to Orson Hyde, who was Hurlbut's missionary companion, "it was at my instance that a charge was preferred against him before the Council of the Church for an attempt at seduction and crime." Hurlbut was not present, but the council decided that "his commission be taken from him and that he be no longer a member of the Church of Christ."[57]

Since Hurlbut had been tried by the "Bishop's council of High Priests," he appealed to the "President's council of high priests," which met on June 21, 1833, to hear his case. With Smith presiding, the council decided that Hurlbut's excommunication had been "decided correctly," but that he should be forgiven and reinstated based on his "liberal confession."[58] According to George A. Smith, the prophet opposed the decision, stating that Hurlbut was "not honest" and "what he has promised he [will] not fulfill," because "what he has confessed is not the thoughts and intents of his heart [and] time will prove it."[59]

Two days later, on June 23, Hurlbut's case was again taken up because Salmon Gee, who had been appointed to preside over the church in Thompson, testified that Hurlbut while passing through Thompson on his way to Pennsylvania publicly declared that "he deceived Joseph Smith's God, or the spirit by which he is actuated &c &c."[60] As George A. Smith later explained, "Hurlbut stated to the Branch in Thompson, Ohio ... I have proved that Council has no wisdom, I told them I was sorry I confessed and they believed it to be an honest confession. I deceived the whole of them and made them restore me to the Church."[61] This resulted in Hurlbut's immediate excommunication.

---

56. Minutes, June 3, 1833 [ca. June 1, 1833], Minute Book 1, 12 (*JSP*, D3:102–104). The minutes are dated June 3, but in addition to Hurlbut's case, the minutes also mention the reception of the revelation giving the dimensions of the temple, which is dated June 1, 1833. See Revelation Book 1, 181; and Revelation Book 2, 59–60 [D&C 95] (*JSP*, D3:106–108).

57. Orson Hyde, Letter to George J. Adams, June 7, 1841, in Winchester, *Plain Facts*, 26.

58. Appeal and Minutes, June 21, 1833, Minute Book 1, 21–22 (*JSP*, D3:116–17).

59. George A. Smith, Discourse, Nov. 15, 1864, in George D. Watt, Discourse Shorthand Notes, Nov. 15, 1864, Pitman Shorthand Transcriptions, as quoted in *JSP*, D3:116–17; see also Staker, *Hearken, O Ye People*, 597; and George A. Smith, "Historical Discourse," Nov. 15, 1864, *Journal of Discourses*, 11:8.

60. Minutes, June 23, 1833, Minute Book 1, 22 (*JSP*, D3:119–20).

61. George A. Smith, Nov. 15, 1864, *Journal of Discourses*, 11:8; see also George A. Smith, Discourse, Nov. 15, 1864, in Pitman Shorthand Transcriptions, CHL, as quoted in Staker, *Hearken, O Ye People*, 597.

Smith later noted in his journal that once Hurlbut learned of his excommunication, he "saught the distruction of the sainst [saints] in this place and more particularly myself and family." From the beginning, Hurlbut had been no ordinary convert. Shortly after his baptism, Hurlbut had a long conversation with Smith about the Book of Mormon, during which he very pointedly said, as Smith recalled, "if he ever became convinced that the Book of Mormon was false, he would be the cause of my destruction &c."[62] True to his word, Hurlbut soon began giving anti-Mormon lectures in the area. By mid-August 1833, Smith wrote to church leaders in Missouri that he and his followers in Ohio were "suffering great persicution on account of one man by the name of Docter Hurlburt who has been expeled from the chirch for lude and adulterous conduct and to spite us he is lieing in a wonderful manner and the peapl [people] are running after him and giveing him mony to b[r]ake down mormanism which much endangers our lives at preasnt [present]."[63] Hurlbut would eventually be hired by a group of leading citizens opposed to the growth of Mormonism in Geauga County to collect damaging information against Smith in New York, Pennsylvania, and elsewhere, which he did between August and December 1833.

Bible Revision Finished

Shortly after completing the translation of the New Testament on July 31, 1832, Williams began writing in the Old Testament manuscript at Genesis 24:1, where Rigdon had stopped. Williams's handwriting continues uninterrupted to Nehemiah 10:30, where Smith took over briefly.[64] Then Williams resumes from Psalm 11 to the end of Malachi, where Williams wrote, "Finished on the 2d day of July 1833."[65] According to one scholar, Smith had made "changes to the wording of approximately three thousand verses in the King James Version and added hundreds of details not found in the Bible."[66]

While Smith and Williams worked their way through the Old Testament, they also revisited the New Testament, making additional emendations, which was finished on February 2, 1833, when Williams wrote in

---

62. Joseph Smith, Journal, Jan. 28, 1834 (*JSP*, J1:27).

63. Joseph Smith, Letter to William W. Phelps and Others, Aug. 18, 1833, [3], JS Collection (*JSP*, D3:267–68).

64. Frederick G. Williams' handwriting appears in Old Testament Revision 2, 59–81 [Gen. 24:1–Neh. 10:30], and Joseph Smith's on 81–83 [Neh. 11–Psalm 10]. See Faulring et al., *Joseph Smith's New Translation of the Bible*, 59, 666, 737, 745.

65. Old Testament Revision 2, 83–119 [Psalm 11–Malachi]. See Faulring et al., *Joseph Smith's New Translation of the Bible*, 59, 745, 851.

66. See *JSP*, D2:xxix, which cites Jackson, "Joseph Smith and the Bible," 29.

the Minute Book, "This day completed the translation and the reviewing of the New testament and sealed up no more to be brokin till it goes to Zion."[67]

On March 9 Smith dictated a brief revelation concerning what he was to do with the Apocrypha, which at that time was still in many Protestant Bibles. Much like the Old and New Testaments, according to the revelation, the Apocrypha too is "mostly translated correct," but "there are many things contained therein that are not true which are interpolations by the hands of men"—ironically, Smith was also interpolating and passing it off as a translation. Nevertheless, Smith was instructed that it was "not needful that the Apocrypha should be translated."[68]

As early as the seventeenth century, English theologian John Toland feared that "in the dark ages of popery, those we commonly call apocryphal books, were added to the Bible, so at the same time, and in as ignorant ages before, several others might be taken away, for not suiting all the opinions of the strongest party." Expressing a similar view to Smith's, Toland believed that the Apocrypha contained some truth but was "strangely adulterated, and full of interpolations."[69] By the 1820s, the Apocrypha was looked upon with such suspicion that the British and Foreign Bible Society as well as the American Bible Society removed it from the Bibles they distributed.[70]

Further Response to Missouri Leaders

On July 2 the presidency of the high priesthood wrote a second letter to Mormon leaders in Missouri in response to three letters they received: one from Phelps and Cowdery, and two others from David Whitmer and Sidney Gilbert. Rigdon again wrote on behalf of the presidency: "I Sidney [Rigdon] write this in great haste in answer to yours to Bro Joseph as I am going off immediately in company with Bro Frederick [G. Williams], to proclaim the gospel we think of starting to morrow having finished the translation of the bible a few hours since."[71]

Apparently Hurlbut's threats to destroy Mormonism had little effect at this time, for Rigdon wrote that "doors are opening continually for proclaiming [the gospel] the spirit of bitterness among the people is fast subsiding a

---

67. Minutes, Feb. 2, 1833, Minute Book 1, 9 (Collier and Harwell, *Kirtland Council Minute Book*, 7); see also Frederick G. Williams, Statement, n.d.

68. Revelation, Mar. 9, 1833, Revelation Book 2, 55 [D&C 91:1–3] (*JSP*, D3:32–35).

69. Toland, *Amyntor, or, A Defense of Milton's Life*, 49–50, 55.

70. See discussion in *JSP*, D3:33–34.

71. Sidney Rigdon, Joseph Smith, and Frederick G. Williams, Letter to "Brethren," July 2, 1833, JS Letterbook 1, 51–52 (*JSP*, D3:165–68). None of the letters sent from Missouri are extant.

spirit of enquiry is taking place," adding that he had preached "last Sunday at Chardon our county seat" to a "general turn out" of people and that he had received "a pressing invitation for more meetings." Rigdon also mentioned that "Bro Joseph is going to take a tower [tour] with Bro George James of Brownhelm as soon as he (George) comes to this place."[72] James, who was the leader of a branch in Brownhelm Township in Lorain County, Ohio, located approximately fifty miles southwest of Kirtland, never showed up. On April 4, 1834, he confessed to a council of high priests that he failed to "magnify his calling" and explained "that his pecuniary affairs called his attention at home which prevented his fulfilling the promise he made to Bro. Joseph in going out to proclaim the Gospel."[73]

One of the letters must have mentioned the gift of tongues among the Mormons in Missouri, which caused Rigdon to issue a warning: "As to the gift of tongues, all we can say is that in this place we have received it as the ancients did we wish you however to be careful lest in this you be deceived … Satan will no doubt trouble you about the Gift of tongues unless you are careful you cannot watch him too closly nor pray to[o] much may the Lord give you wisdom in all things."[74] The appearance of tongues among Missouri church members about this time was documented by John Whitmer, who wrote that "in June 1833 we received th[e] gift of tongues in Zion."[75] In a July 29, 1833, letter to Smith and Cowdery, Whitmer gave more details: "God is pouring out his Spirit upon his people so that most all on last thursday at the school [of the prophets] received the gift of tongues & spake & prophesied; The next day David [Whitmer] called his branch together and most of them received the gift of tongues many old things are coming to light that had it not been for this gift would have remained in the dark & brought the wrath of God, upon the inhabitants of Zion."[76] Rigdon's warning would prove prophetic since church leaders in Missouri will face challenges from charismatic tongue-speakers in less than a year.

The presidency instructed that the Book of Commandments be sent to Kirtland, the printing of which was nearing completion: "Consign the Box of the book of the Commandments to N K Whitney & Co Kirtland Geauga Co Ohio care of Killy and Walworth Cleaveland Cuyahoga County

72. Sidney Rigdon et al., Letter to "Brethren," 53 (*JSP*, D3:167).

73. Minutes, Apr. 4, 1834, Minute Book 1, 48 (*JSP*, D4:4).

74. Sidney Rigdon et al., Letter to "Brethren," July 2, 1833, JS Letterbook 1, 52 (*JSP*, D3:167).

75. John Whitmer, History, 39 (*JSP*, H2:51).

76. John Whitmer, Letter to Oliver Cowdery and Joseph Smith, July 29, 1833, JS Letterbook 2, 52 (*JSP*, D3:188–90).

Ohio." This refers to Thomas M. Kelley and Ashbel W. Walworth, who ran a shipping business in Cleveland.[77] It is unknown if Missouri church officials received this letter before mob violence destroyed the Mormon press in Independence on July 20, 1833, and the Saints were driven from the county shortly afterward.

---

77. See *JSP*, D3:167n10.

PART TWO

Failure of Charisma

13

Zion Lost

... and it came to pass that Zion was not for God received it up into his own bosom and from thence went forth the saying Zion is fled.
—Bible Revision 1, 19 [Moses 7:69]

By November 1832 the Mormon community in Jackson County, Missouri, had swelled to more than 800.[1] With indifference to the original setters, the Saints had rechristened Jackson County the Mormon holy land—the prophesied land of Zion and location of the future New Jerusalem temple. If that was not motivation enough for the gathering, Joseph Smith's revelations had declared that Zion was to be "a city of refuge, a place of safety for the saints of the Most High God," and that "it shall come to pass among the wicked, that every man that will not take his sword against his neighbor must needs flee unto Zion for safety."[2] In his January 4, 1833, letter to the editor of the *American Revivalist, and Rochester Observer,* Smith had warned his fellow Americans to "flee to Zion before the overflowing scourge overtake you."[3] His confidence prevented him from foreseeing the turn of events just over the horizon. Instead of a place of refuge, by the year's end,

---

1. John Whitmer recorded that around March 1832 there were 402 "disciples living in this land Zion," and that by December there were "538 individuals in this land b[e]longing to th[e] church." Whitmer, History, 38–39 (*JSP,* H2:50, 51). According to William E. McLellin, most of this increase occurred when a group of "near 100 of our brethren ... women & children" arrived in Jackson County from Portage County, Ohio, in June 1832. McLellin, Letter to "Beloved Relatives," Aug. 4, 1832, [7]. In the November 1832 issue of *The Evening and the Morning Star,* W. W. Phelps noted that "the number of the disciples which have come from the east, and which have been baptized in this region, is 465[.] Children and those not members, about 345[.] Total 810." "The Gathering," *The Evening and the Morning Star,* Nov. 1832, [45].
2. Revelation, ca. Mar. 7, 1831, Revelation Book 1, 75–76 [D&C 45:66, 68] (*JSP,* D1:280).
3. Joseph Smith, Letter to Noah C. Saxton, Jan. 4, 1833, JS Letterbook 1:18 (*JSP,* D2:355).

Zion would become a place of danger and a place from which approximately 1,200 Mormons had to flee.[4]

Jackson Countians were becoming increasingly alarmed by the steady influx of what they considered Smith's fanatical, deranged followers. In the spring of 1832, handbills were posted in various places warning the Mormons to leave the county; they were ignored.[5] According to John Whitmer, the anti-Mormons held a meeting in Independence in March 1832 to decide "how they might destroy the saints."[6] Bishop Edward Partridge reported that this meeting was broken up by Indian agent Marston Clark, but "still the hostile spirit of individuals was no less abated."[7] This was followed by several nights of harassment during which Mormon homes were struck by stones or pieces of brick, shattering some windows, and in a few instances shots were fired, after which "the persecution abated in some degree."[8]

One cause of non-Mormon concern was mentioned in Smith's July 31, 1832, letter, in which he chastised Missouri leaders for allowing "ignorant & unstable Sisters, & weak members … [to] prophe[s]y falsely which excites many to believe that you are putting up the Indians to slay the Gentiles which exposes the lives of the Saints evry where."[9] Such prophesying was inspired by the Book of Mormon, which predicted that the Indians would not only assist believing Gentiles in building a New Jerusalem but would destroy their Gentile oppressors.[10]

In April 1833 about 300 citizens met in Independence to plan the removal or destruction of their Mormon neighbors, but it broke up due to a drunken brawl.[11] Finally, in mid-July non-Mormons held meetings and drafted resolutions that would culminate in the expulsion of the Mormons. Meanwhile, unaware of the anger and danger that was brewing in Jackson County, church leaders in Kirtland envisioned a great and glorious future for Zion.

---

4. Parley P. Pratt and John Corrill estimated that there were 1,200 Mormons in Jackson County before they were expelled in November 1833. Pratt, *History of the Late Persecution*, 25; Corrill, *Brief History*, 20 (*JSP*, H2:149).

5. Parley P. Pratt et al., "'The Mormons' So Called," *The Evening and the Morning Star* (Independence, MO), Extra, Feb. 1834, [1].

6. Whitmer, History, 38 (*JSP*, H2:50).

7. [Edward Partridge], "A History, of the Persecution, of the Church of Jesus Christ, of Latter Day Saints in Missouri," *Times and Seasons* (Nauvoo, IL), Dec. 1839, 17 (*JSP*, H2:207–208).

8. Parley P. Pratt et al., "'The Mormons' So Called," *The Evening and the Morning Star*, Extra, Feb. 1834, [1].

9. Smith, Letter to William W. Phelps, July 31, 1832, 5, JS Collection (*JSP*, D2:266).

10. Book of Mormon, 1830 ed., 488, 497, 500, 501 [3 Ne. 16:15; 20:16–17; 21:12, 23]; Micah 5:8–9.

11. JS History, vol. A-1, 290 (DHC 1:342).

Plat of the City of Zion

During June 1833, Kirtland leaders worked on the plat of the city of Zion as well as a draft of the architectural design for the House of the Lord to be built in Independence, which were sent to Missouri leaders with a cover letter dated June 25, 1833.[12] Although the drawings and explanations were drafted by second counselor Frederick G. Williams, the letter that accompanied them indicates that the entire presidency was involved in their creation.

The master plan for the "City of Zion" plots a one-square-mile grid with forty-nine city blocks and sixteen 132-foot-wide straight streets that run east-west and north-south and intersect at right angles. While this grid pattern was not unusual for urban areas at the time, the provision for ten-acre city blocks divided into half-acre lots was larger than usual, resulting in fewer blocks than normally the case.[13] Forty-six blocks were reserved for residences, which were to house "15 to 20 thousand people," an unrealistic estimate since an average of sixteen individuals would have to occupy each dwelling to reach the lowest estimate. Nevertheless, the plan restricted one house per lot "to be built 25 feet back from the street leaving a small yard in front to be planted in a grove according to the taste of the builder the rest of the lot for gardens &c all the houses to be of brick and stone."[14]

The plat also provided three central blocks of fifteen acres each for storehouses and temples. In the instructions, the presidency explained that barns and stables were to be built at the city's northern and southern boundaries, not among the houses, and that farms and grazing areas were also to be located outside city limits. Optimistically, the presidency instructed that "where this square is laid off and supplied lay off another in the same way and so fill up the world in these last days and let every man live in the City for this is the City of Zion."[15] Smith's vision was expansive, if also unrealistic.

The plat made no provision for businesses, implying that all the needs of the community were to be supplied through the bishop's storehouses,

---

12. Plat and Explanation of the City of Zion, ca. early June–June 25, 1833 (*JSP*, D3:121–131); Plan of the House of the Lord for Zion, ca. June 1–25, 1833 (*JSP*, D3:131–46). The text and drawings are in the handwriting of Williams. For the cover letter, see Smith et al., Letter to Edward Partridge and Others, June 25, 1833, JS Collection (*JSP*, D3:147–58). The package was postmarked in Kirtland on June 26, 1833.

13. Jackson, "The Mormon Village," 224–27.

14. Plat and Explanation of the City of Zion, ca. early June–25 June 1833, [1] (*JSP*, D3:128).

15. Plat and Explanation, [1]. Historian Mario S. De Pillis has noted that Smith's one square mile plat "seemed perfectly logical, for under its secular name of 'section,' one square mile formed the basic unit of the official federal square survey of all of the public domain west of Pennsylvania." De Pillis, "Christ Comes to Jackson County," 29.

according to the law of consecration. There was also no provision for a court-house, a central feature of most American communities. Instead, the three larger blocks in the center contained a complex of twenty-four houses of the Lord. One of the three central blocks was designated for twelve temples for the presidency, a second block of twelve more temples for the lesser priesthood, and a third block for the bishop's storehouses.[16] From these multipurpose buildings, the various branches of the priesthood were to administer a theocratic government. The bishop's court, for example, was to be held in the three temples reserved for the use of the bishop.

The organization of this complex of temples reflected church administration as it was conceived in 1833, for while there were temples for the presidency of the high priesthood, bishops, high priests, and elders in one lot, and the presidency of the lesser priesthood, priests, teachers, and deacons in another lot, there were no temples for the twelve apostles or high council. While Smith and his counselors were particular in declaring that "the plot for the City and the size form and dime[n]sions of the house were given us of the Lord," in less than two years it would become outdated.[17]

In their letter the presidency instructed that the temple marked on the plat with an "x" was "to be built immediately in Zion for the presidency as well as all purposes of Religion and instruction."[18] The location of this temple was no doubt the same "spot of ground" that was dedicated by Sidney Rigdon in August 1831 and subsequently purchased by Partridge.[19] The first of the twenty-four temples to be constructed in Zion was to be "composed of stone and brick of the best kind" and measure "Eighty Seven feet Long and Sixty one feet wide and ten feet taken of[f] on the east end for the stairway leaves the inner court 78 by 61 feet," slightly larger than its Ohio counterpart.[20] Like the Kirtland temple, there were to be four tiers of ascending pulpits at each end of the building occupied by the presiding officers of the two branches of the priesthood, following the same organization of the twenty-four temples. Similarly, there were no seats for the twelve

---

16. Plat and Explanation, [2] (*JSP*, D3:129).

17. Plan of the House of the Lord for Zion, June 1–25, 1833, [2] (*JSP*, D3:145).

18. Smith et al., Letter to Edward Partridge and Others, June 25, 1833, [1], JS Collection (*JSP*, D3:151).

19. Whitmer, History, 32 (*JSP*, H2:45); see also Howard, "The Spot for the Temple," *Saints' Herald*, June 1987, 9–10; and Romig, *Early Independence, Missouri*, 15–18.

20. Plan of the House of the Lord for Zion, June 1–25, 1833, [1], [2] (*JSP*, D3:140–41, 142). By revelation, the inner court of the House of the Lord in Kirtland was to be fifty-five feet by sixty-five feet long. Revelation, June 1, 1833, Revelation Book 2, 60 [D&C 95:15] (*JSP*, D3:107).

apostles or high counselors. Instead, the benches that they later occupied in Kirtland, located on both sides of the east-facing pulpits, are designated in the plans for "visiting officers."[21]

The cover letter, which was dictated by Rigdon on behalf of the presidency to scribes Williams and Orson Hyde, began in a spirit of reconciliation and unity: "We desire with all our hearts, the prosperity of Zion and the peace of her inhabitents for we have as great an intrest in the welfare of Zion as you can have," and assured Missouri leaders near the end that "day and night we pray for the salvation of Zion."[22]

They advised that the Book of Commandments should be published unbound to expedite its circulation. Concerning the publication of Smith's Bible revision, plans had changed. Instead of being printed by Phelps in Missouri, the "New translation" will be printed by the presidency when "we can attend to it ourselves, and this we will do as soon as the Lord permit."[23] The following August, the presidency wrote to inform Missouri officials that "we have to print the new translation here at kirtland for which we will prepare as soon as possible."[24] On September 11, 1833, Smith and the members of the Kirtland branch of the United Firm met with Oliver Cowdery and decided to establish a press in Kirtland under the firm of F. G. Williams & Co. to publish the *Latter Day Saints' Messenger and Advocate* and to continue the *Evening and Morning Star* with Cowdery as editor.[25]

Due to the large influx of Mormons into Jackson County, the presidency proposed adding two more bishops, Isaac Morley and John Corrill.[26] Parley P. Pratt remembered that in the summer of 1833 "immigration had poured into the County of Jackson in great numbers; and the Church in that county now numbered upwards of one thousand souls."[27] In the July 1833 issue of *The Evening and the Morning Star*, Phelps estimated that there were "near seven hundred" baptized members in Zion, which along with children and other family members "probably amount to more than twelve hundred souls"

21. Plan of the House of the Lord for Zion, June 1–25, 1833, [1] (*JSP*, D3:142).

22. Smith et al., Letter to Edward Partridge and Others, June 25, 1833, [1], [3], JS Collection (*JSP*, D3:148, 156).

23. Smith et al., [1], [2] (*JSP*, D3:148, 154).

24. Rigdon et al., Letter to Edward Partridge and Others, Aug. 6, 1833, [3], JS Collection (*JSP*, D3:233); see also Revelation, Aug. 2, 1833, Revelation Book 2, 64–66 [D&C 94:10] (*JSP*, D3:206).

25. Minutes, Sep. 11, 1833, Minute Book 1, 24 (*JSP*, D3:297–301).

26. Smith et al., Letter to Edward Partridge and Others, June 25, 1833, [1], JS Collection (*JSP*, D3:150).

27. Pratt, *Autobiography*, 99.

in the Missouri Mormon community.[28] This was in contrast to the estimated 150 "disciples" in Kirtland mentioned in the presidency's letter. In the postscript the presidency said, concerning "the size of Bishopricks," that "when Zion is once properly regulated there will be a Bishop to each square," referring to the one-mile-square on the plat map of the city of Zion and the addition of other connecting squares that Smith envisioned would eventually fill up the world.[29]

After informing them of the addition of John Johnson to the United Firm, the presidency ordered that there be an exchange of a "power of Agency," or power of attorney, to facilitate economic and land transactions between the two branches of the Firm.[30]

They reminded Partridge "to be sure to get a form according to law for secureing a gift, we have found by examineing the Law that a gift cannot be retained without this."[31] The Kirtland leaders further advised Partridge that how much a man retained as a private stewardship and how much he consecrated to the church was a matter of conscience and should be voluntary: "For, to give the Bishop power to say how much every man shall have and he be obliged to comply with the Bishops judgment, is giveing to the Bishop more power than a King." On the other hand, "to let every man say how much he needs and the Bishop obliged to comply with his judgment, is to throw Zion into confusion and make a Slave of the Bishop." The process of consecration is to be done by "mutual consent of both parties," for "there must be a balance or equalibrium of power between the bishop and the people, and thus harmony and good will may be preserved among you." They therefore instructed that the bishop determine how much property was to be retained, but if the man consecrating the property disagreed, he "must show reasonably to the Bishop that he wants as much as he claims." However, "in case the two parties cannot come to a mutual agreement, the Bishop is to have nothing to do about receiveing their consecrations and the case must be laid before a council of twelve high Priests."[32]

---

28. "The Elders Stationed in Zion to the Churches Abroad," *The Evening and the Morning Star*, July 1833, 110.

29. Smith et al., Letter to Edward Partridge and Others, MO, June 25, 1833, [3], JS Collection (*JSP*, D3:155, 157).

30. Smith et al., [3] (*JSP*, D3:150–51, n436).

31. Smith et al., [3] (*JSP*, D3:151). This direction reiterates Smith's previous counsel to Partridge concerning the use of a legal deed whereby the church could retain consecrated land as a charitable donation. Smith, Letter to Edward Partridge, May 2, 1833, [1], JS Collection (*JSP*, D3:76).

32. Smith et al., Letter to Edward Partridge and Others, June 25, 1833, [2], JS Collection (*JSP*, D3:153).

The presidency also addressed what they considered false doctrine being taught by the Hulet brothers, Charles and Sylvester, who believed in the eventual salvation of the devil, his angels, and the sons of perdition who apostatize from Mormonism. "Say to the Brethren Hulits and to all others that the Lord never authorized them to say that the Devil nor his angels nor the Sons of perdition should ever be restored, for their state of destiny was not revealed to man, is not revealed, nor ever shall be revealed save to those who are made partakers thereof, consequently, those who teach this doctrine have not received it of the Spirit of the Lord." Agreeing with Cowdery's pronouncement that it was "the doctrine of devils," they "command[ed] that this doctrine be taught no more in Zion" and "sanction[ed] the decission of the Bishop and his council in relation to this doctrine being a bar of communion."[33] The Hulets may have reasoned that if "eternal punishment" of mankind was figurative and hell was only temporary, it may also be the case for Satan. Even Universalists debated among themselves whether or not there was a hell in which there was to be a temporary punishment, and some speculated that Satan may yet be restored.[34]

The presidency announced: "We have commenced building the House of the Lord in this place, and it goes on rapidly," which signaled that the gathering and construction of a temple in Jackson County were not as urgent as one might have supposed from Smith's utterances and warnings about the wars and plagues that were soon to overtake the wicked. Moreover, the five years that Kirtland was to be a stronghold was soon to end, and Smith was only beginning to construct an edifice that would barely be finished before that time expired.[35]

When the package of city and temple plans arrived at Independence on July 29, 1833, John Whitmer and Phelps quickly wrote a lengthy letter to inform Smith and other church leaders in Kirtland of the recent violent confrontation with a mob, destruction of the press, and threat of expulsion from the county. It is a "time of confusion among us," Whitmer began, "although the enemy has accomplished his design in demolishing the Printing establishment they cannot demolist [demolish] the design of our God, for his

---

33. Smith et al., [2]–[3] (*JSP*, D3:155).

34. See, for example, Patrides, "The Salvation of Satan." The concept of Satan's salvation traces back as early as the second century CE, when theologian Origen discussed *apocatastasis*, or "the idea that all things will be ultimately reconciled to God through Christ—including the damned in hell and even Satan and his demons." Moore, "Personal and Cosmic Eschatology," 878.

35. Revelation, Sep. 11, 1831, Revelation Book 1, 110 [D&C 64:21] (*JSP*, D2:65).

decrees will stand & his purposes must be accomplished notwithstanding the great rage of Satan, which we can behold in his followers."[36]

Confrontation and Appeasement

The spark that ignited a riot appeared in the July 1833 issue of the church's monthly paper *The Evening and the Morning Star* published by Phelps at Independence. The offending article was titled "Free People of Color," which invited free Black members of the church in other states to migrate to Missouri and join fellow Mormons in gathering in Zion. The purpose of the article was to inform Black Mormons that Missouri law required them to have a legal certificate of citizenship and to warn them to exercise "great care" and "prudence" and to "Shun every appearance of evil," which sounded to the Missourians like a clandestine operation to import free blacks into their county. Phelps also associated "abolishing slavery" with "the wonderful events of this age."[37] It made little difference to the Missourians that Phelps had prefaced his comments by stating that concerning "slaves we have nothing to say." Missouri church leaders may have been officially neutral on slavery, but that did not stop individual Mormons most of whom were from northern states from expressing their repulsion.[38]

Warren Jennings, a scholar of Missouri Mormonism, noted: "What prompted Phelps to print such an article is something of an enigma."[39] When Phelps's article appeared, there were two known Black converts, Black Pete in Ohio and Elijah Able in Maryland. As late as 1839, Parley P. Pratt admitted that "one half dozen negroes or mulattoes never have belonged to our Society, in any part of the world."[40] It may be that Phelps's article was an attempt to drive out the Missourians by threatening to bring free Blacks into the county. If so, it backfired. Missourians were strongly opposed to free Blacks in their

---

36. John Whitmer (with postscript by Phelps), Letter to Oliver Cowdery and Joseph Smith, July 29, 1833, JS Letterbook 2, 52 (*JSP*, D3:188).

37. "Free People of Color," *The Evening and the Morning Star*, July 1833, 109, 111.

38. I disagree with Thomas Spencer's assertions that the Mormons "were in no way abolitionists" and that it was a "baseless charge in order to incite as much anger as possible against the Mormons." Spencer, "'Persecution in the Most Odious Sense of the Word,'" 6–7. In an 1881 interview, David Whitmer, one of the church leaders in Missouri, admitted that "the church was composed principally of Eastern and Northern people who were opposed to slavery," and that "their only crime was that they were opposed to slavery." "Mormonism," *Kansas [MO] City Daily Journal*, June 5, 1881. Alexander Doniphan, a Clay County attorney who was hired by the Mormons in 1833, remembered that the Mormons were "northern people, who, on account of their declining to own slaves and their denunciation of the system of slavery, were termed 'free soilers.'" "Mormonism," *Kansas City Daily Journal*, June 12, 1881.

39. Jennings, "Factors in the Destruction of the Mormon Press in Missouri," 65.

40. Pratt, *Late Persecution of the Church*, 11.

state. At this time, there were 360 slaves and no free Blacks in Jackson County.[41] The announcement that abolitionist Mormons intended to encourage free Blacks to enter the county was like pouring gasoline on a fire.

Despite Phelps's issuing a retraction in a July 16 "Extra," non-Mormons demanded that the Mormons leave the county and issued a manifesto listing their grievances, among which was the recent article "inviting free Negroes and mulattoes from other states to become Mormons and remove and settle among us." They feared that "the introduction of such a caste [of free blacks] amongst us, would corrupt our blacks and instigate them to bloodshed."[42] The death of about sixty-one white people during Nat Turner's slave rebellion in Virginia in 1831 made this fear real. It also added a frightening dimension to Smith's December 25, 1832, prophecy that civil war would soon break out in the United States and that "Slaves shall rise up against their Masters who shall be Marshialed and disaplined for war."[43] It is unknown if the Missourians knew about the unpublished revelation, but they accused the Mormons of "tampering with our slaves, and endeavoring to sow dissentions and raise seditions amongst them."[44] The Mormons later denied the charge, arguing that it would be foolish to attempt such a thing as it would also endanger their lives.[45] Nevertheless, the Missourians contended that the introduction of free Blacks would be "the surest means of driving us from the County."[46] They also dismissed the retraction in the *Star*, which claimed that the article was designed to discourage the migration of free Blacks, as "weak" and disingenuous since it "contained an extract from our laws, and all necessary directions and *cautions* to be observed by colored brethren, to enable them upon their arrival here, to claim and exercise the rights of citizenship."[47]

---

41. Jennings, "Factors in the Destruction of the Mormon Press in Missouri," 68.

42. The original manifesto of the citizens of Jackson County is not extant, but it was transcribed in a letter to Missouri governor Daniel Dunklin and published in the December 1833 issue of *The Evening and the Morning Star*. See "To His Excellency, Daniel Dunklin," *The Evening and the Morning Star*, Dec. 1833, 114. Russell Hicks, an attorney and Jackson County clerk, later admitted that he drafted the manifesto. *Daily Missouri Republican*, Jan. 20, 1834.

43. Revelation, Dec. 25, 1832, Revelation Book 2, 33 [D&C 87:4] (*JSP*, D2:330).

44. "To His Excellency, Daniel Dunklin," *The Evening and the Morning Star*, Dec. 1833, 114.

45. See "The Outrage in Jackson County, Missouri," *The Evening and the Morning Star*, Jan. 1834, 122.

46. "To His Excellency, Daniel Dunklin," *The Evening and the Morning Star*, Dec. 1833, 114. Militia colonel Thomas Pitcher later denied slavery was an issue in the conflict, saying, "I don't think that Matter had anything to do with it. The Mormons ... did not interfere with the negroes and we did not care whether they owned slaves or not." "Mormon History," *Kansas City Journal*, June 19, 1881. His post-Civil War opinion, however, is contradicted by the manifesto.

47. Minutes, July 20, 1833, "Mormonism," *Western Monitor* (Fayette, MO), Aug. 2, 1833, as quoted in JS History, vol. A-1, 333 (DHC 1:397). Original not located.

According to the Missourians, the Mormons posed an existential threat to non-Mormons. "They declare openly that their God hath given them this county of land, and that sooner or later they must and will have the possession of our lands for an inheritance."[48] The Reverend Isaac McCoy, a noted Baptist missionary to the Indians living in Jackson County, later remarked that he heard Mormons declare "perhaps hundreds of times, that this county was theirs, the Almighty had given it to them, and that they would surely have entire possession of it in a few years."[49] Indeed, the plat of the city of Zion required total possession of the county. As the editors of the Joseph Smith Papers have noted, "Attempts to implement the plan of Zion would have necessitated major changes in existing roads and structures and undoubtedly caused significant political strife. The plat appears to disregard existing streets, structures, and, consequently, anyone already living or operating a farm or business at this location who might not accede to this plan."[50] David Whitmer remembered, "There were among us a few ignorant and simple-minded persons who were continually making boasts to the Jackson county people that they intended to possess the entire county."[51] To the Missourians, such talk meant that either they or the Mormons had to leave the county, and the citizens of Jackson County were determined that it was not going to be them. They therefore concluded: "We believe it a duty we owe ourselves to our wives and children, to the cause of public morals, to remove them from among us, as we are not prepared to give up our pleasant places, and goodly possessions to them."[52]

Jackson Countians believed that there was no negotiating with the Mormons. Their determination to possess the land was tied to Book of Mormon prophecy and fixed by Smith's revelations. Indeed, the Mormons' fanatical delusion was clearly manifest in their claims to "converse face to face with the most high God, to receive communications and revelations direct from heaven; to heal the sick by laying on hands, and in short, to perform all the wonder working miracles wrought by the inspired apostles and prophets of old." To the Missourians, the Mormons "openly blaspheme the most high God, and cast contempt on his holy religion, by pretending to receive revelations direct from heaven, by pretending to speak unknown tongues; by direct

---

48. "To His Excellency, Daniel Dunklin," *The Evening and the Morning Star*, Dec. 1833, 114.
49. Isaac McCoy, "The Disturbances in Jackson County," *Missouri Republican* (St. Louis), Dec. 20, 1833, [2]–[3].
50. *JSP*, D3:124.
51. "Mormonism," *Kansas City Daily Journal*, June 5, 1881, [1].
52. "To His Excellency, Daniel Dunklin," *The Evening and the Morning Star*, Dec. 1833, 114.

inspiration, and by diverse pretences derogatory of God and religion, and to the utter subversion of human reason."[53]

The Missourians believed time was running out because soon the influx of Mormons would give them superior voting power and it would not be long before they controlled the entire county. They therefore determined to "rid our society" of the Mormons, as they said, "peaceably if we can, forcibly if we must." The Missourians admitted that their remedy was extra-legal—"Believing as we do, that the arm of the civil law does not afford us a guarantee, or at least a sufficient one against the evils which are now inflicted upon us"—but that their "expedient" actions were justified by the "law of nature" and the "law of self preservation."[54] The manifesto, which was signed by about 300 people, concluded by calling a meeting at the county courthouse in Independence on July 20, 1833.

On the appointed day, about 500 citizens convened at the courthouse to rid their community of the Mormon menace. Seven prominent men were appointed to draft a set of resolutions, which was read after the meeting reconvened later the same day.[55] This declaration reiterated many of the complaints voiced in the manifesto and urged non-Mormons to "act not from the excitement of the moment, but under a deep and abiding conviction, that the occasion is one that calls for cool deliberation, as well as energetic action." It reasoned that they were justified in using an extra-legal process because their "peculiar situation" was unforeseeable and "therefore unprovided for by the laws" and that "delays incident to legislation, would put the mischief beyond remedy." Citizens must act now, it argued, or see their county taken over by the continual influx of Mormons, not to mention free Blacks, and themselves driven out. It was a matter of "self-preservation, good society, public morals, and the fair prospects" to the old settlers.

For the Missourians, the Mormons were "pretended Christians" who made superstitious pretensions to miracles, revelations, visions, and unknown tongues, but at the same time, they insisted that they were not involved in religious persecution. "Of their pretended revelations from heaven—their personal intercourse with God and his angels—the maladies they pretend to heal by the laying on of hands—and the contemptible gibberish with

---

53. "To His Excellency," 114.

54. "To His Excellency," 114.

55. Minutes, July 20, 1833, in "Mormonism," *Western Monitor*, Aug. 2, 1833; original not located. For a partial reprint, see *Missouri Intelligencer and Boon's Lick Advertiser* (Columbia), Aug. 10, 1833. Mulder and Mortensen, *Among the Mormons,* 77–80. For convenience, I have used JS History, vol. A-1, 330–35 (DHC 1:395–99).

which they habitually profane the Sabbath, and which they dignify with the appellation of unknown tongues, we have nothing to say, vengeance belongs to God alone." Rather, their concerns were economic and political. The Mormons were for the most part poor and uneducated, "little above the condition of our blacks." Most of all, they were abolitionists, who in time would command political power through the steady stream of migration. "It requires no gift of prophecy," they observed, "to tell that the day is not far distant when the civil government of the county will be in their hands. When the sheriff, the justices, and the county judges will be Mormons, or persons wishing to court their favor from motives of interest or ambition."[56] The Reverend McCoy later added: "It was easily perceived that as matters were progressing, at no distant day they would control all county business."[57] While the Missourians claimed their expulsion of the Mormons was motivated solely by economic and political concerns, the Mormons made no such distinction. Indeed, Smith's revelations did not distinguish between the spiritual and the temporal. One historian has noted that "Smith's revelations created the dynamics for both loyalty and hostility" for "they gave him political power."[58] There was nothing more repugnant to Missourian sensibilities than the thought of being governed by men who were loyal to a purported prophet living in a distant state. It violated the basic American principles of republicanism and local sovereignty.

Jackson County residents became increasingly concerned for their safety. "We are daily told, and not by the ignorant alone, but by all classes of them," they observed in their July 20 statement, "that we, (the Gentiles,) of this county are to be cut off, and our lands appropriated by them for inheritances. Whether this is to be accomplished by the hand of the destroying angel, the judgments of God, or the arm of power, they are not fully agreed among themselves." Nevertheless, they pointed to "recent remarks in the *Evening and Morning Star*" that "show plainly that many of this deluded and infatuated people have been taught to believe that our lands were to be won from us by the sword."[59]

The remarks in the *Star* referred to were probably the publication of Smith's August 1831 revelation in the February 1833 issue, which declared:

---

56. "To His Excellency, Daniel Dunklin," *The Evening and the Morning Star,* Dec. 1833, 114.
57. Isaac McCoy, "The Disturbances in Jackson County," *Missouri Republican* (St. Louis), Dec. 20, 1833, [2]–[3].
58. Harper, "'Dictated by Christ,'" 281.
59. "To His Excellency, Daniel Dunklin," *The Evening and the Morning Star,* Dec. 1833, 114.

"Wherefore the land of Zion shall not be obtained but *by purchase, or by blood*, otherwise there is none inheritance for you. And if by purchase behold you are blessed; and if by blood, as you are forbidden to shed blood, lo, your enemies are upon you, and ye shall be scourged from city to city, and from synagogue to synagogue, and but few shall stand to receive an inheritance."[60] While the purpose of the revelation was to convince believers that purchasing the land was the wisest course to take, some interpreted it as saying one way or another all the land was to be their inheritance, perhaps to encourage non-Mormon Gentiles to sell out and move. The Reverend McCoy reported in December 1833:

> Reports believed by many to be true, for the correctness of which I cannot vouch, says that they repeatedly declared that if the Almighty should not give it [Jackson County] to them by any other miracle, it would be done by their sword—by blood, &c. However erroneous these reports might have been, such sayings, appeared to the people very near akin to so many remarks which were common among them, and unfortunately for the Mormons, these reports were believed to be true, and the effect upon the public mind was accordingly.[61]

The following year, Missouri church leaders in exile in neighboring Clay County found it necessary to dispel a rumor that the Mormons planned to "regain our possessions, and even Jackson county, 'by the shedding of blood,'" by emphasizing the phrase in the revelation declaring that "you are forbidden to shed blood."[62] Few minds were changed though.

The Jackson County committee issued five demands that were unanimously adopted:

1. Mormon migration to Jackson County must stop immediately.
2. Mormons in the county must pledge to leave within a reasonable time.
3. The Mormon press must discontinue all printing operations.
4. Mormon leaders are to assist in accomplishing these resolutions.
5. Those who fail to comply should consult those among them who have "gifts of divination, and of unknown tongues," to inform them of the consequences that await them.[63]

---

60. "A Revelation Given, August 30, 1831," *The Evening and the Morning Star*, Feb. 1833, 70; emphasis added. See also Revelation, Aug. 30, 1831, [1], Newel K. Whitney Papers [D&C 63:30–31] (*JSP*, D2:51); *The Evening and the Morning Star*, Feb. 1833, 70.

61. Isaac McCoy, "The Disturbances in Jackson County," *Missouri Republican*, Dec. 20, 1833, [2]–[3].

62. "An Appeal," *The Evening and the Morning Star*, Aug. 1834, 184.

63. "'Regulating' the Mormonites," *Missouri Republican*, Aug. 9, 1833, [3].

A committee of twelve men was appointed to visit the Mormon leaders. After two hours, the committee returned and reported that they spoke with Phelps, editor of the *Star*, Edward Partridge, storekeeper Sidney Gilbert, and some others, and that "they declined giving any direct answer to the requisitions made of them, and wished an unreasonable time for consultation, not only with their brethren here, but in Ohio." This was deemed unacceptable. Immediately, a mob of 400–500 citizens descended on the Mormons and vandalized the press, throwing the uncut sheets of the unfinished Book of Commandments into the street, and then tore off the roof and knocked the walls down. Afterward, they began to vandalize Gilbert's store several blocks away, but stopped because the proprietor promised to vacate the premises by July 23. In a final symbolic act of public humiliation, they tarred and feathered Partridge and another Mormon, Charles Allen, in front of the courthouse.[64] The actions taken by Jackson Countians were hardly surprising or exceptional. Collective acts of violence directed at ethnic, racial, religious, and political minorities were frequent in Jacksonian America. A common notion at the time was that the majority held a sovereign right to expel people they considered nuisances from their communities.[65]

Three days later, on July 23, non-Mormons held another public meeting at Independence. After a committee of seventeen men was appointed, the meeting adjourned for two hours while the committee conferred with the Mormon leaders. When the committee returned, it announced that an "amicable agreement" had been put into writing. The agreement stipulated that Cowdery, Phelps, McLellin, Partridge, Lyman Wight, Simeon Carter, Peter and John Whitmer, and Harvey H. Whitlock, and one half of the Mormons leave Jackson County by January 1834, and the rest by April. John Corrill and Sidney Gilbert were permitted to remain as general agents to wind up church business.[66]

Mormon leaders would later complain that the agreement was made under duress. In their September 1833 petition to Missouri governor Daniel Dunklin, they said a weapon-bearing mob of about 500 captured several leading Mormon men and threatened their lives and the lives of all

64. See account of the mob's actions in "To His Excellency, Daniel Dunklin," *The Evening and the Morning Star*, Dec. 1833, 114. For a history of the press and its destruction, see Romig and Siebert, "First Impressions."

65. Grimsted, *American Mobbing*; Brown, *Strain of Violence*; Feldberg, *The Turbulent Era*.

66. Minutes, July 23, 1833, "Mormonism," *Western Monitor*, Aug. 2, 1833; original not located. For convenience, I have used JS History, vol. A-1, 335–37 (DHC 1:394–95). See also "To His Excellency, Daniel Dunklin," *The Evening and the Morning Star*, Dec. 1833, 115.

Mormons in the county if they did not agree to leave the county.[67] According to John Whitmer, "The whole county turned out and surrounded us
came to W W Phelps, and my hous and took us upon the publick square as
also Partridge Corrill, Morly, and gilbert and wer[e] determined to massacre us unless we agreed to leav th[e] county immediately."[68] Partridge later
wrote, "Seeing the determination of the mob, some few of the leading elders
offered their lives, provided that would satisfiy them, so as to let the rest of
the society live, where they then lived, in peace; they would not agree to this,
but said that every one should die for themselves, or leave the county. At that
time, the most, if not all, of our people, in Jackson, thought they would be
doing wrong, to resist the mob, even by defending themselves; consequently
they thought, that they must quietly submit, to whatever yoke was put upon
them, even to the laying down of their lives."[69] Finally, after agreeing to leave
the county, the Mormon leaders negotiated a delay of five to eight months.

"Waiting Patiently"

Corrill wrote: "This agreement having been made in duress, the Mormons
considered it illegal, and not binding, and supposed that the Governor, or authorities, would protect them, if applied to, and not suffer them to be driven
off in that manner."[70] According to Partridge, at the time the Mormon leaders made the agreement with representatives of the Missourians, they did
not intend to keep it but "hop[ed] that ... providence would kindly open
the way for them, to still live there in peace." Very few Mormons, Partridge
wrote, "believed that they would have to leave it [Jackson County], thinking
that the government would protect them, in their constitutional rights."[71]

Within days of the agreement, Cowdery left Independence to confer with
the presidency in Kirtland.[72] On July 29, 1833, the day the package containing plans for the city of Zion and one of its twenty-four temples arrived,
John Whitmer wrote to Cowdery and Smith and informed them of recent
events in Jackson County and included copies of the mob's manifesto and
the Mormon agreement to leave the county. Addressing Cowdery, Whitmer
said: "Nothing in particular has transpired since you left here save the gifts

67. "To His Excellency, Daniel Dunklin," *The Evening and the Morning Star,* Dec. 1833, 114.

68. Whitmer, History, 43 (*JSP*, H2:55).

69. [Edward Partridge], "A History, of the Persecution, of the Church of Jesus Christ, of
Latter Day Saints in Missouri," *Times and Seasons,* Dec. 1839, 18 (*JSP*, H2:211).

70. Corrill, *Brief History,* 19 (*JSP*, H2:147).

71. [Partridge], "History, of the Persecution," 19 (*JSP*, H2:211).

72. JS History, vol. A-1, 330 (DHC 1:395).

are breaking forth in a marvellous manner." The outpouring of the gift of tongues in the midst of severe persecution was a comfort and a sign that God had not forsaken them. "Marvellous to tell in the midst of all the rage of persecution," Whitmer wrote, "God is pouring out his Spirit upon his people so that most all on last thursday [July 25] at the school [of the elders] received the gift of tongues & spake & prophesied." On the following day, Whitmer reported, "David [Whitmer] called his branch together and most of them received the gift of tongues many old things are coming to light that had it not been for this gift would have remained in the dark & brought the wrath of God, upon the inhabitants of Zion." In a postscript Phelps reported that "David [Whitmer] says he can speak in all the tongues on earth."[73]

Persecution could not shake the Mormon community's faith. It was with some degree of satisfaction that Whitmer reported: "There are very few that have denied the faith in consequence of this transaction."[74] Of course, the Missourians did not care if any Mormons lost their faith; they just wanted them out of their county. If anything, persecution created more cohesion among believers. As one historian of communal groups has observed, "Through the experience of persecution and conflict, defenses are built up and strengthened, so that the group is made immune to (prepared for) future and more extreme attacks on it. ... In addition, persecution gives the ends of group existence more meaning and importance, because they hold enough threat for the outgroup to lead it to take steps against the organization. The group's increased self-esteem thus strengthens it in the face of disaster."[75] Nevertheless, Whitmer "greatly fear[ed] for some of they who call themselves disciples."[76]

Whitmer suggested that persecution was God's way of purifying the church: "My daily prayer is that the Lord will cleanse Zion of all the remaining wickedness that is on this Holy Land."[77] A September 1832 revelation had threatened "a scourge and a Judgment" that would be "poured out upon the children of Zion" if they continued to pollute the Lord's "holy land."[78] After mentioning recent cases of cholera in nearby Lexington, he suggested

---

73. Whitmer, Letter to Oliver Cowdery and Joseph Smith, July 29, 1833, JS Letterbook 2, 52–56 (*JSP*, D3:186–98).

74. Whitmer, 52 (*JSP*, D3:190).

75. Kanter, *Commitment and Community*, 102.

76. Whitmer, Letter to Oliver Cowdery and Joseph Smith, July 29, 1833, JS Letterbook 2, 52 (*JSP*, D3:190).

77. Whitmer, 52.

78. Revelation, Sep. 22–23, 1832, [2], Newel K. Whitney Papers [D&C 84:58–59] (*JSP*, D2:298).

it could be the means of cleansing the land of Zion. "Our daily cry to God is deliver thy people from the hand of our enemies send thy destroying angels, O God in the behalf of thy people [I pray] that Zion may be built up according to the plan of our Lord through his servants to us, received this mail." Near the end of his letter, he revisited the subject: "We need the prayers of all the disciples of our Redeemer for it is a time of great anxiety to behold the cleansing of this Church & also the land from wickedness & abominations." Missouri Mormons were confident that God would not reveal his will concerning Zion and its temple without providing a means of accomplishing it. Thus Whitmer closed his part of the letter: "We are waiting with inexpressible anxiety to hear the word of the Lord concerning Zion, ... which will be as balm to the wounded bosom, or as a smile of the Redeemer to a soul in distress, my heart is full and I say O my God will thou not deliver, yea wilt thou not come down that the mountains may flow down at thy presence &c." Phelps followed, declaring: "In our present situation I have nothing to write, I wait for the word of the Lord: For his will and not ours will be done."[79]

Cowdery would not arrive in Kirtland until August 9. Meanwhile, Smith continued dictating revelations and letters about establishing Zion while in complete darkness regarding the perilous situation in Missouri. On August 6, in response to two letters from Jackson County, dated early July, Smith and his counselors sent a letter to church leaders in Missouri that included copies of three recently-received revelations.

The first revelation, dictated on August 2, was described by the presidency as "the communication which we received from the Lord concerning the school [of the elders] in Zion."[80] This revelation directed that Parley P. Pratt continue to preside over the school and for church leaders to build "speedily" the House of the Lord in which the school can meet. Completion of the temple would bring great blessings, for "all the pure in heart that shall come into it shall see God." Concerning the predicted calamities preceding Jesus's second coming, the revelation declared: "Let Zion rejoice while all the wicked shall mourn. ... Nevertheless Zion shall escape if she observe to do all things whatsoever I have commanded her but if she observe not to do whatsoeve[r] I have commanded her I will visit her according to all

---

79. Whitmer, Letter to Oliver Cowdery and Joseph Smith, July 29, 1833, JS Letterbook 2, 52, 55 (*JSP*, D3:190, 196).

80. Rigdon et al., Letter to Edward Partridge and Others, Aug. 6, 1833, JS Collection (*JSP*, D3:230).

her works with sore afflictions with pestilence with plague with sword with vengence with devouring fire."[81]

At the time Smith dictated this revelation, he was unaware of what had already transpired in Zion. Nevertheless, the revelation concluded by declaring: "I, the Lord, have accepted of her offering; and if she sin no more none of these things shall come upon her; And I will bless her with blessings, and multiply a multiplicity of blessings upon her, and upon her generations forever and ever, saith the Lord your God. Amen."[82] The acceptance of the "offering" of the Missouri church probably refers to their confession and repentance for criticizing Smith and the other Ohio leaders, which they reported in an epistle in early 1833.[83] Smith responded on April 21, "With Joy we received your general epistle writen the 26 of Feby which contained the conffescion of our brethren concerned all of which was to our entire satisfaction."[84]

The declaration of forgiveness and promise of protection in the August 2 revelation coming after the mob's attack and the signing of the agreement to leave Jackson County by church leaders would make shifting responsibility for losing Zion to the sins of the Missouri church difficult. Nevertheless, Pratt, who was mentioned in the revelation, tried to do just that. "This revelation," he later wrote in his *Autobiography*, "was not complied with by the leaders and Church in Missouri as a whole (notwithstanding many were humble and faithful); therefore, the threatened judgment was poured out to the uttermost, as the history of the five following years will show."[85] He did not elaborate. Rather than question his prophet, Pratt blamed fellow believers.

On the same day, August 2, Smith dictated another revelation directing that the Mormons in Kirtland build three buildings of the same construction and size—one for worship, one for the presidency, and one for printing "as soon … as means can be obtained."[86] When this revelation was copied into the presidency's August 6 letter to Missouri leaders, they said it was "also binding on you" and that "you at Zion have to build two houses as well as the one of which we have sent the pattern."[87] This was unrealistic for

---

81. Revelation, Aug. 2, 1833-A, Revelation Book 2, 62–64 [D&C 97:3–4, 10, 16, 21, 25–26] (*JSP*, D3:200–202).

82. Revelation, 64 [D&C 97:27–28] (*JSP*, D3:203).

83. This epistle is no longer extant but was mentioned in Minutes, Feb. 26, 1833, Minute Book 2, 33 (Cannon and Cook, *Far West Record*, 60–61).

84. Joseph Smith, Letter to "brethren in Zion," Apr. 21, 1833, JS Letterbook 1, 33 (*JSP*, D3:66).

85. Pratt, *Autobiography*, 102.

86. Revelation, Aug. 2, 1833-A, Revelation Book 2, 64–66 [D&C 94] (*JSP*, D3:203–207).

87. Rigdon et al., Letter to Edward Partridge and Others, Aug. 6, 1833, [4], JS Collection (*JSP*, D3:236–37).

both places, even if an agreement had not been signed for the Mormons to leave Jackson County. The two revelations of August 2 were not only constrained by Smith's knowledge of events—or lack thereof—but they made more probable the likelihood that Smith and church leaders would attempt to resist removal.

A third revelation the presidency included in their August 6 letter was dictated earlier the same day and included instruction about how to deal with the growing opposition to the church and persecution of its members. It may have been prompted by a July 9, 1833, letter from Cowdery, no longer extant but mentioned in the presidency's letter, which possibly expressed concern about the rising tensions and threats of violence in Jackson County. This revelation advised church members to bear persecution patiently, to "renounce war and proclaim peace," and to be law-abiding citizens, "waiting patiently on the Lord." Martyrs for the faith will be eternally blessed: "I will try you and prove you herewith and whoso layeth down his life in my cause for my name sake shall find it again even life eternal therefore be not afraid of your enemies for I have decreed in my heart saith the Lord that I will prove you in all things whether you will abide in my covenant even unto death that ye may be found worthy." Nevertheless, the revelation explained that self-defense was permissible, but the Lord promised increasing blessings each time Mormons resisted striking back.[88] Although retribution, no matter how delayed, is still vigilantism, it was a widely-accepted remedy where government mechanisms failed to protect individuals or communities.[89] Finally, the revelation implied that persecution was connected to unfaithfulness: "Behold I the Lord am not well pleased with many who are in the church at Kirtland for they do not forsake their sins and their wicked ways the pride of their hearts and their covetiousness and all their detestable things. ... If ye observe to do whatsoever I command you I the Lord will turn all wrath and indignation from you and the gates of hell shall not prevail against you."[90]

Unaware of the destruction of the printing press in Missouri, the presidency in summarizing the content of the three revelations said regarding Smith's Bible revision: "You are to print an Edition of the scriptures there at the same time we do here so that two additions [editions] will be struck

---

88. Revelation, Aug. 6, 1833, Revelation Book 2, 67–69 [D&C 98:2, 12–14, 16, 23–31] (*JSP*, D3:224–27).

89. See Gilje, *Rioting in America*; Grimsted, *American Mobbing*.

90. Revelation, Aug. 6, 1833, Revelation Book 2, 68 [D&C 98:19–20] (*JSP*, D3:225–26).

at the same time."[91] The letter and revelations were mailed to Independence two days before Cowdery arrived in Kirtland.[92] Frederick G. Williams wrote, "Immediately after the arrival of bro Oliver we sat in council to know what should be done, the decission of the councel was that measurs should be immediately taken to seek redress by the Laws of our country."[93]

The day following his arrival, Cowdery wrote to Phelps and other church leaders in Missouri, advising them to "look out another place to locate on" and assuring them that "an other place of beginning will be no injury to Zion in the end." He also told them to "make out your bill of damages immediately" and "do not remove any faster to your new home than you bound yourselves to, but pray for the Lord to deliver, for this is his will that you should, & fear not for his arm will be revealed."[94] In other words, search out a new place of settlement but delay moving until the last possible moment while praying for God to intervene.

Cowdery said that the agreement was necessary and approved by the Lord, for "there was no other way to save the lives of all the church in Zion, or the most: and any who are dissatisfied with that move, are not right & have cause to repent." Nevertheless, "This great tribulation would not have come upon Zion had it not been for rebelion ... against the one to whom were intrusted the keys, & from thence it has spread down to the lowest & least member!" Cowdery was referring to the "rebellion" of the Missouri church leaders against Smith and the Kirtland leadership in 1832 and early 1833, particularly Smith's claim to be president of the high priesthood. Cowdery also blamed church members "who were void of understanding were continually telling that which was not true, & putting false coloring to the things of God! I mean those whose mouths are continually open, & whose tongues cannot be stayed from tatling!"—referring to Mormons who antagonized other inhabitants of Jackson County by boasting about plans to establish Zion and drive them out of the county. "The church will never have peace while such remain in her," Cowdery warned, "therefore, brethren purge them out. ... It was necessary that these things should come upon us: not only justice demands it, but there was no other way to cleanse the church."[95]

---

91. Rigdon et al., Letter to Edward Partridge and Others, Aug. 6, 1833, [4], JS Collection (*JSP*, D3:237).

92. Oliver Cowdery, Letter to William W. Phelps and Others, Aug. 10, 1833, [1] (*JSP*, D3:240). Cowdery reported having been "hindered three days ... in waiting for a conveyance."

93. Frederick G. Williams, Letter to "Dear Brethren," Oct. 10, 1833, JS Letterbook 1, 56.

94. Cowdery, Letter to William W. Phelps and Others, Aug. 10, 1833, [1] (*JSP*, D3:240–41).

95. Cowdery, [1] (*JSP*, D3:241).

Cowdery addressed the inability of the Missouri church to fulfill the three revelations the presidency had sent to them a few days earlier, instructing them to "Read them carefully & keep them from false brethren & tatlers." One of the revelations would have particularly concerned the Missourians since it authorized retaliation and vigilantism. He assured them that "all things concerning Zion will come to pass in the due time of the Lord," and implored: "Don't be discouraged but be patient."[96]

Smith added a postscript to Cowdery's letter expressing solidarity: "Brethren if I were with you I should take an active part in your sufferings & although nature shrinks yet my spirit would not let me forsake you unto death God helping me." In closing, he prayed: "Oh be of good cheer for our redemption draweth near Oh God save my Brethren in Zion Oh brethren give up all to God forsake all for Christ sake."[97]

Resistance

Eight days later, on August 18, Smith wrote a long emotion-evoking letter to the Missouri leaders. In his own hand, Smith began prayerfully: "O thou disposer of all Events, thou dispencer of all good! in the name of Jesus Christ I ask thee to inspire my heart ... guide my peen [pen] to note some kind word to these my Brotheren in Zion that like the rays of the sun upon the Earth [that] wormeth [warmeth] the face thereof so let this word I write worm [warm] the hearts of my Brotheren. ... Give unto thy servent Joseph a word that shall refresh the hearts and revi[v]e the spir[i]ts yea souls of those afflicted ones who have been called to leave their homes and go to a strange land not knowing what should befall them." Likening their situation to the trial of faith Abraham faced when God commanded him to sacrifice his only son, Smith further prayed: "O Lord what more dost thou require at their hands before thou wilt come and save them"?[98]

Smith assured his brethren that they were not alone in their suffering, that the Saints in Kirtland were also experiencing significant trials. "There is no saifty for us here," he informed them, "but evevery man has to wa[t]ch their houses every night to keep off the Mob[b]ers Satan has Come down in Great wrath upon all the Chirch of God and the[re] is no saifty."[99] According to George A. Smith, who arrived in Kirtland in May 1833, "In

---

96. Cowdery, [2] (*JSP*, D3:242, 243).

97. Cowdery, [2] (*JSP*, D3:243).

98. Smith, Letter to William W. Phelps and Others, Aug. 18, 1833, [1], JS Collection (*JSP*, D3:262).

99. Smith, [1] (*JSP*, D3:263).

consequence of the persecution which raged against the Prophet Joseph and the constant threats to do him violence it was found necessary to keep continual guard to prevent his being murdered by his enemies. ... I took a part of this service."[100] "We are no safer here in Kirtland then you are in Zion," Smith told Missouri leaders, "the cloud is gethering arou[nd] us with great fury and ... all hell and the com[bined] pow[e]rs of Earth are Marsheling their forces to overthrow us."[101]

Smith mentioned that the main source agitating the public mind against Mormonism in Ohio was former member Philastus Hurlbut, who had been excommunicated the previous June. "We are suffering great persicution on account of one man by the name of Docter Hurlburt," Smith reported. Hurlbut "is lieing in a wonderful manner and the peopl are running after him and giveing him mony to brake down mormanism which much endangers our lives at preasnt but god will put a stop to his carear soon and all will be well."[102] In fact, Hurlbut will collect affidavits from Smith's former neighbors and relatives in Palmyra and Manchester, New York, and Harmony, Pennsylvania, and they will be published in 1834 by E. D. Howe.[103]

Smith likened the church's position to that of the Israelites fleeing Egypt, "with the red Sea before them and the Egyptions ready to fall upon them to distroy them and no arm could deliver but the arm of God and this is the case with us we must wait on God to be gratious and call on him with out ceaseing to make bare his arm for our defence for naught but the arm of the almighty can Save us." However, he explained that "only in the arm of Jehovah none else can deliver and he will not deliver unless we prove ourselves faithful to him in the severeest trouble." Then, as their prophet, he declared: "I verily know that he will spedily deliver Zion for I have his immutible covenant that this shall be the case but god is pleased to keep it hid from mine eyes the means how exactly the thing will be done."[104] This "immutible covenant" refers to the revelation Smith dictated a few days earlier on August 6 and sent to Missouri, which stated that the Lord had heard their prayers and that he "giveth this promise unto you with an immutable covenant that they shall be fulfilled and all things wherewith you have been afflicted shall

---

100. George A. Smith, Memoirs and Autobiography, 12.

101. Smith, Letter to William W. Phelps and Others, Aug. 18, 1833, [2], JS Collection (*JSP*, D3:264).

102. Smith, [3] (*JSP*, D3:267–68).

103. Howe, *Mormonism Unvailed*, 231–69.

104. Smith, Letter to William W. Phelps and Others, Aug. 18, 1833, [1], [2], JS Collection (*JSP*, D3:264).

work together for your good and my names glory."[105] Smith interpreted this as the deliverance of Zion, although he could not say how it would be done.

Rather than place the blame on the Missouri church as Pratt and Cowdery had done, Smith said, "This affliction is sent upon us not for your sins but for the sins of the church. ... God has suffered it not for your sins but that he might preprare you for a grateer [greater] work that you might be prepared for the endowment from on high."[106] Before leaving New York in 1831, Smith had dictated a revelation that promised that followers would be "endowed with power from on high" in Ohio.[107] Some believed this was fulfilled with the introduction of the high priesthood in June 1831, but in June 1833 Smith dictated a revelation that promised the Saints an endowment of "power from on high" in the temple they were to build in Kirtland.[108] In 1839 church historian John Corrill described the high priesthood as "the endowment" of "a new order" of "bestowed authority," and then wrote that some of the elders questioned this and did not understand "the nature of the endowments," showing that he had come to understand that the promised endowment of power was not a single event.[109]

For the time being, there was to be no Mormon retaliation against Jackson County. "If our kingdom were of this world then we would fight," Smith said, "but our weapons are not carnal yet mighty and will bind satan ere long under our feet. ... In the mean time god will send Embasadors to the authorities of the government and sue for protection and redress that they may be left with out excuse that a ritious [righteous] Judgement might be upon them."[110] Soon after receiving this letter, Missouri Mormons petitioned the state to intervene.

Smith again assured the Missouri church leaders that despite the threats of their enemies to "distroy Zion ... we have had the word of the Lord that you shall [be] deliverd from you[r] dainger and shall again flurish in spite of hell [this] god has communicated to me by the gift of the holy ghost that this should be the case after much p[rayer] and suplication and also that an other printing office must be built the Lord knows how and also it is the

---

105. Revelation, Aug. 6, 1833, Revelation Book 2, 66 [D&C 98:3] (*JSP*, D3:224).

106. Smith, Letter to William W. Phelps and Others, Aug. 18, 1833, [1], [2], JS Collection (*JSP*, D3:264).

107. Revelation, Jan. 2, 1831, Revelation Book 1, 52 [D&C 38:32] (*JSP*, D1:232).

108. Revelation, June 1, 1833, Revelation Book 2, 59–60 [D&C 95:8] (*JSP*, D3:106).

109. Corrill, *Brief History*, 18 (*JSP*, H2:145).

110. Smith, Letter to William W. Phelps and Others, Aug. 18, 1833, [2], JS Collection (*JSP*, D3:266, 267).

will of the Lord that the Store shou[ld] be kept."[111] Smith wished to inspire followers not to lose faith in Zion. With his charismatic reputation in jeopardy, he chose to double down on revelation, promising that Zion would be delivered from its enemies. This, too, would ultimately prove to be incorrect.

In his August 10 letter, Cowdery had raised the possibility that Missouri members "may be under the necessity to sell some of our lands, but be wise, hold on to the sacred places."[112] Eight days later, Smith strictly forbade the sale of any Jackson County land to non-Mormons: "It is the will of the Lord that ... not one foot of land perchased should be given to the enimies of God or sold to them but if any is sold let it be sold to the chirch." He therefore advised that those who were bound by the agreement with the mob "to leave the land to make a show as if to do [it] untill the Lord delivr."[113] In their July 1834 appeal to "the people and constituted authorities of this nation, and to the ends of the earth," Missouri church leaders declared that to sell their land in Jackson County "would amount to a denial of our faith, as that land is the place where the Zion of God shall stand, according to our faith and belief in the revelations of God."[114]

In closing, Smith instructed Missouri church leaders to "be wise and not let the knowledge I give unto you be known abroad for your sak[e]s." Indeed, the Missourians would not be pleased to learn that the Mormons were planning to resist removal. As far as Smith was concerned, all options were still on the table. "I conclude by telling you that we w[a]it the Comand of God to do whatever he ple[a]se and if he shall say go up to Zion and defend thy Brotheren by the sword we fly and we count not our live[s] dear to us."[115]

Although Smith evoked secrecy in his August 18 letter, Mormons in the Kirtland area were openly discussing plans to resist the evacuation of their Missouri Zion. As early as August 16, E. D. Howe in nearby Painesville reported rumors that "some Davids or Golia[t]hs are to be dispatched immediately by the prophet to the relief of the brethren in the wilderness."[116] On August 30 he reported that the elders "in this vicinity, under the wing of the prophet and far removed from danger, appear determined to send on a reinforcement. The

---

111. Smith, [3] (*JSP*, D3:268).

112. Cowdery, Letter to William W. Phelps and Others, Aug. 10, 1833, [2] (*JSP*, D3:243).

113. Smith, Letter to William W. Phelps and Others, Aug. 18, 1833, [3], JS Collection (*JSP*, D3:268).

114. "An Appeal," *The Evening and the Morning Star*, Aug. 1834, 183.

115. Smith, Letter to William W. Phelps and Others, Aug. 18, 1833, [3], JS Collection (*JSP*, D3:268, 269).

116. Report, *Painesville (OH) Telegraph*, Aug. 16, 1833, [3].

Lord has been consulted, we are told, and the prophet has given orders to retain the Hon. Henry Clay as counsel, to prosecute the aggressors."[117]

Meanwhile, plans were moving ahead to found the city of Zion and construct a temple in Independence, despite the agreement to leave Jackson County. On August 13 Partridge wrote to Frederick G. Williams with some questions about the plat of the city and architectural plans for the temple.[118] However, his letter arrived in Kirtland in early September, after Williams had revised the plat and plans and sent them to Independence with Orson Hyde and John Gould, who arrived in Jackson County in late September.[119] On the revised plans for the temple, Cowdery explained: "Those patterns previously sent you, per mail, by our brethren, were incorrect in some respects; being drawn in grate haste. They have therefore drawn these, which are correct. The form of the city was also incorrect, being drawn in haste. We send you another."[120] Among other things, the revised plat omitted a third central block that was to contain the bishop's storehouses, and instead of the city covering one square mile, it was now 1.5 square miles. This increased the total number of lots from 976 to 2,600, which was more realistic for housing the projected 15,000–20,000 inhabitants.[121] About this time, Partridge drew up his own revision of the two remaining central blocks, which rearranged the twenty-four temples into three across and four down, instead of four across and three down.[122] While Partridge's belief that it was his prerogative to change the prophet's plan perhaps reveals something about his mindset, Kirtland's swift revisions to a plan written in "haste" did not inspire confidence.

In late September the Missouri leaders followed Smith's advice and drafted a petition to Governor Daniel Dunklin that reported the destruction of the press, tarring and feathering of Partridge, and various abuses Mormons in Jackson County were enduring. The petitioners explained that they were appealing to state officials for assistance because nearly all local civil and military authorities were anti-Mormons and were unresponsive to any "civil process" initiated by Mormons for damages against the mob. In desperation they declared: "We appeal to the Governor for aid; asking him by express proclamation, or other wise, to raise a sufficient number of

---

117. Editorial, *Painesville Telegraph*, Aug. 30, 1833, [3].

118. Partridge's letter is not extant but was mentioned in Smith's letter to Vienna Jaques. Smith, Letter to Vienna Jaques, Sep. 4, 1833, [3], JS Collection (*JSP*, D3:296).

119. "History of Orson Hyde," 12.

120. Revised Plan of the House of the Lord, ca. Aug. 10–ca. Sep. 4, 1833 (*JSP*, D3:279).

121. See discussion in *JSP*, D3:246.

122. See Edward Partridge, Proposal for Zion's City Center, ca. late Sep. 1833 (*JSP*, D3:308–13).

troops, who, with us, may be empowered to defend our rights, that we may sue for damages in the loss of property ... that the law of the land may not be defied, nor nulified, but peace restored to our country."[123] The petition was signed by most of the Mormons in Jackson County and taken to Jefferson City by Hyde and Phelps, where they presented it to Dunklin on October 7.[124] On October 19 Dunklin, a staunch conservative who held a strict constructionist interpretation of both federal and state constitutions, responded that he could do nothing to help them and that they must appeal to local authorities for redress as an "experiment" to see "whether the laws can be peaceably executed or not." However, if local authorities proved unresponsive, he said it was his duty "to take such steps as will enforce a 'faithful execution'" of the law.[125]

The authors of the appeal had informed Dunklin that mobbers had threatened that "if any of the mormons attempted to seek redress by law or other wise, for character, person or property, they should *die!*"[126] True to their word, John Corrill later reported, "as soon as the people found out that we had petitioned the Governor for protection, and that we were about to appeal to the law for redress, they became very angry, and again commenced hostilities."[127]

On Sunday, October 20, the Missouri leaders made a public announcement that they would not leave the county but instead "we as a people should defend our lands and houses."[128] According to the Reverend McCoy, "While the other citizens little apprehended it, the Mormons procured powder and lead and distributed it among them and also guns."[129] Corrill said, "The Mormons then began to prepare for self-defence, but were badly armed."[130] An Ohio newspaper later reported that the Mormons "had erected a temporary bulwark, and supplied themselves with fire locks for

---

123. "To His Excellency, Daniel Dunklin," *The Evening and the Morning Star*, Dec. 1833, 115.

124. See Corrill, *Brief History*, 19 (*JSP*, H2:147); JS History, vol. A-1, 346 (DHC 1:410–15). About the same time, church leaders in Missouri sent a similar petition to President Andrew Jackson. This has not been located but was mentioned in their second petition to Jackson. See Partridge et al., Petition to President Andrew Jackson, Apr. 10, 1834.

125. Dunklin's response is found in Dunklin, Letter to Edward Partridge and Others, Oct. 19, 1833, in Phelps, Collection of Missouri Documents; it was also published in "To His Excellency, Daniel Dunklin," *The Evening and the Morning Star*, Dec. 1833, 115.

126. "To His Excellency, Daniel Dunklin," *The Evening and the Morning Star*, Dec. 1833, 115.

127. Corrill, *Brief History*, 19–20 (*JSP*, H2:147).

128. Unidentified author, Letter to "Dear brethren," Oct. 30, 1833, in "The Outrage in Jackson County, Missouri," *The Evening and the Morning Star*, Dec. 1833, 119 (*JSP*, D3:335).

129. Isaac McCoy, "The Disturbances in Jackson County," *Missouri Republican* (St. Louis), Dec. 20, 1833, [2]–[3].

130. Corrill, *Brief History*, 20 (*JSP*, H2:147).

the purpose of *nullifying*, in accordance with the legal advisement of their prophet, the treaty they had entered into."[131] The *Painesville Telegraph* similarly reported: "It is said that, since the previous affair, the Prophet had sent orders to the brethren there, to 'stand by their arms,' instead of leaving the place as they had agreed. They had accordingly erected some kind of baricade and supplied themselves with arms."[132] According to William E. McLellin, Smith and other leaders in Kirtland had sent Orson Hyde and John Gould to Missouri not only with revised plans for the city of Zion but also with instructions for "the members of the church to stand in their own defence, raise weapons and defend themselves. Fight when opposed and oppressed. This the members were quick to do."[133] According to Partridge, the Mormons armed themselves "hoping that, when it should be understood, would dampen the hostile spirit of those who were, at that time, continually threatening them. But it had a contra effect."[134]

McCoy reported that the more peace-loving part of the community tried to mediate between the Mormons and the mob, but neither side would listen. He related a story about one of his neighbors pleading with a Mormon to stand down, but he was answered that the Mormons "had resolved to fight while one of them remained alive." According to McCoy, "My neighbor then appealed to his professions of religion, and reminded him that the Bible forbade such a course as he said they had resolved upon," but the Mormon replied that "the Israelites had been authorized by the Bible to drive out the Canaanites, and he pleaded a similar privilege for his society."[135]

After "the leaders of the mob" heard rumors that they "would be called upon to bind themselves to keep the peace" when court opened on Monday, October 28, they became enraged. On Saturday, October 26, more than fifty of the mob met at Independence and "voted ... to move the 'mormons'" out of the county.[136] One speaker declared that "he would expell them [Mormons] if he had to wade up to his neck in blood."[137] In their November 1839 petition to Congress, Smith, Rigdon, and Elias Higbee insinuated that the

---

131. "More Nullification," *Ashtabula (OH) Republican*, Dec. 7, 1833, [2]; italics in original.

132. "More Trouble in the Mormon Camp," *Painesville Telegraph*, Nov. 29, 1833, [3].

133. Larson and Passey, eds., *The William E. McLellin Papers*, 417; see also 326, 390, 426, 485, 511.

134. [Edward Partridge], "A History, of the Persecution," *Times and Seasons*, Dec. 1839, 19 (*JSP*, H2:213).

135. Isaac McCoy, "The Disturbances in Jackson County," *Missouri Republican*, Dec. 20, 1833, [2]–[3].

136. Unidentified author, Letter to "Dear brethren," Oct. 30, 1833, in "The Outrage in Jackson County, Missouri," *The Evening and the Morning Star*, Dec. 1833, 119 (*JSP*, D3:335).

137. Greene, *Facts Relative to the Expulsion*, 17.

sudden outburst of violence against the Mormons was unprovoked, claiming that prior to this anti-Mormon meeting the Saints "had faithfully observed the treaty" between Mormons and non-Mormons.[138] This was not true. Not long after the agreement, the anti-Mormons became suspicious when, as McCoy reported, they noticed that the Mormons "appeared to be preparing fields with a view of remaining." Suspicion turned to certainty when the Mormons petitioned the governor and "instituted a law suit for damages which had been done [to] their property."[139] Then the public announcement on October 20 removed all doubt, and the situation quickly escalated to open confrontation.

When court opened on Monday, October 28, there was "no mob, but great threats."[140] On the same day, the law firm of Doniphan, Atchison, Rees, and Wood, located at Liberty, Clay County, contacted church leaders in Missouri and offered to be their legal counsel for $1,000, explaining that their high price was due to the probable loss of business in defending the Mormons. They requested to be informed immediately of the church's decision since the mob would probably hire them instead. However, they explained: "We prefer to bring your suits, as we have been threatened by the mob we wish to show them we disregard their empty bravadoes."[141] Two days later, Phelps accepted their proposal and promised to pay them the full amount within six months.[142] However, the attempt to put the leaders of the mob under bonds to keep the peace proved futile; local justices of the peace were either sympathetic to the mob or feared retaliation. When the Mormons caught Richard McCarty stoning the Gilbert & Whitney store on the night of November 1 and took him to Esq. Samuel Weston, the justice refused to prosecute him. A second attempt to obtain a peace warrant from

---

138. Smith et al., Memorial to the United States Senate and House of Representatives, ca. Oct. 30, 1839–Jan. 27, 1840, 4 (*JSP*, D7:147).

139. Isaac McCoy, "The Disturbances in Jackson County," *Missouri Republican*, Dec. 20, 1833, [2]–[3]. McCoy's account of the Mormons working their fields was verified by Mormon David Pettegrew, who wrote that he was at work in his field when a neighbor remarked: "Mr Pettegrew, you are at work, as though you intended to remain here." Pettegrew responded, "I thought I had 'right to stay upon my own land.'" The neighbor shouted, "We are determined to drive you away from this Country, and we will stop you from emigrating here." Pettegrew, "A History of David Pettegrew," 17.

140. Unidentified author, Letter to "Dear brethren," Oct. 30, 1833, "The Outrage in Jackson County, Missouri," *The Evening and the Morning Star*, Dec. 1833, 119 (*JSP*, D3:336).

141. William T. Wood et al., Letter to William W. Phelps and Others, Oct. 28, 1833, in Phelps, Collection of Missouri Documents.

142. William W. Phelps et al., Letter to William T. Wood and Others, Oct. 30, 1833, in Phelps, Collection of Missouri Documents.

circuit judge William Silvers also failed. According to Partridge, Silvers said that "if he did he feared that his life would be in danger."[143]

During the escalation of the conflict, McCoy later reported, Jackson Countians "strongly suspected" that the Mormons were "secretly tampering with the neighboring Indians, to induce them to aid in the event of open hostility," although he could not prove it.[144] The rumors were probably unfounded but may have been based on recent communications from Ohio. On October 10 Frederick G. Williams wrote a letter to his brethren in Missouri and reported that through the gift of tongues Elizabeth Whitney, wife of Newel Whitney, had predicted that certain persons would go among the Indians and "great things would be done by them ... that if we will not fight for ourselves, the Indians will fight for us." Though it may be true, Williams advised, "it is not needful that it should be spoken, for it is of no service to the saints and has a tendency to stir up the people to anger—no prophecy spoken in tongues should be made public."[145] Otherwise, the Missourians may have feared the Mormons may try to fulfill predictions in the Book of Mormon that "if the Gentiles do not repent," the Indians will "go forth among them ... as a lion among the beasts of the forest, and as a young lion among the flocks of sheep, who, if he goeth through both treadeth down and teareth in pieces, and none can deliver."[146]

Expulsion

A concerted campaign to harass and terrorize the Mormons in Jackson County was launched in late October. Groups of marauding mobbers began stoning houses, breaking windows, whipping the men, and committing various other depredations. In their 1839 petition to Congress, Smith, Rigdon, and Higbee implied that some Mormon women were sexually assaulted, stating that "their women [were] grossly insulted; and their daughters brutally

---

143. [Edward Partridge], "A History of the Persecution, of the Church of Jesus Christ, of Latter Day Saints in Missouri," *Times and Seasons*, Jan. 1840, 20, 33 (*JSP*, H2:214, 215). McCarty was in the process of countersuing for assault and false imprisonment when the Mormons were expelled from the county. See [Partridge], 34, in *JSP*, H2:217–18; "Civil War in Jackson County!" *Missouri Republican*, Nov. 12, 1833, [3].

144. Isaac McCoy, "The Disturbances in Jackson County," *Missouri Republican*, Dec. 20, 1833, [2]–[3]; Jennings, "Isaac McCoy and the Mormons," 62–82.

145. Frederick G. Williams, Letter to "Dear Brethren," Oct. 10, 1833, JS Letterbook 1, 59 (DHC 1:419).

146. Book of Mormon, 1830 ed., 497 [3 Ne. 20:16]; cf. Micah 5:8–9. See also Book of Mormon, 1830 ed., 488, 500, 501 [3 Ne. 16:15; 21:12, 23].

abused before their mother's eyes."[147] In his 1844 letter to the Pennsylvania legislature, Rigdon used the term "rape" when listing the crimes committed against the Mormons in Missouri.[148]

Late in the evening of October 31, a gang of about fifty mobbers attacked a settlement of Mormons about ten miles west of Independence near the Big Blue River, destroying twelve houses, including David Whitmer's, and beating two men nearly to death.[149] The next night the mob moved about five miles farther west and attacked another settlement of Mormons from Colesville, New York, on the prairie, during which Parley P. Pratt was injured and two Missourians were taken prisoners but released the next morning.[150] On the same night, another mob attacked the Mormons at Independence, injuring some and damaging property, including the Gilbert & Whitney store. The men looting the store fled when they saw about thirty Mormon men led by Lyman Wight approach.[151] On the night of November 2 the mob again attacked the Big Blue settlement, tearing off the roofs of two houses and shooting at the owner of one, grazing his scalp. They also shot at a group of Mormons without wounding anyone; one mobber was hit in the leg when the Mormons returned fire, causing the mob to flee.[152]

On November 3 Joshua Lewis, Hiram Page, Parley P. Pratt, and apparently Thomas Marsh were sent to Lexington to ask circuit judge John F. Ryland for a peace warrant against the leaders of the mob. According to Pratt, Ryland refused, fearing the mob, and advised "us to fight and kill the mob whenever they came upon us."[153] However, in a letter to Smith's

---

147. Smith et al., Memorial to the United States Senate and House of Representatives, ca. Oct. 30, 1839–Jan. 27, 1840, 5 (*JSP*, D7:147).

148. Sidney Rigdon, "To the Honorable, the Senate and House of Representatives of Pennsylvania," *Times and Seasons*, Feb. 1, 1844, 418–23.

149. William W. Phelps, Letter to "Dear brethren," Nov. 6, 1833, "The Outrage in Jackson County, Missouri," *The Evening and the Morning Star*, Dec. 1833, 119; [Edward Partridge], "A History, of the Persecution," *Times and Seasons*, Dec. 1839, 19 (*JSP*, H2:213); Orson Hyde in "Civil War in Jackson County!" *Missouri Republican*, Nov. 12, 1833, [3]; Orrin Porter Rockwell, Affidavit, Feb. 3, 1840, National Archives, Washington, DC, in Johnson, *Mormon Redress Petitions*, 526.

150. Pratt, *History of the Late Persecution*, 13; Pratt, *Late Persecution*, 32–33.

151. [Partridge], "History, of the Persecution," 20 (*JSP*, H2:214–15); "The Outrage in Jackson County, Missouri," *The Evening and the Morning Star*, Dec. 1833, 120; and "From Missouri," *The Evening and the Morning Star*, Jan. 1834, 124.

152. [Partridge], "History, of the Persecution," 33 (*JSP*, H2:215–16); "Civil War in Jackson County!" *Missouri Republican*, Nov. 12, 1833, [3]; "The Outrage in Jackson County, Missouri," *The Evening and the Morning Star*, Dec. 1833, 119; "From Missouri," *The Evening and the Morning Star*, Jan. 1834, 125.

153. Pratt, *History of the Late Persecution*, 16.

attorneys, Doniphan and Atchison, dated November 24, 1833, Ryland asked: "I wish to know whether Joshua Lewis and Hiram Page handed the writ to the sheriff of Jackson [county], that I made and issued on their affidavit against some of the ringleaders of the mob in Jackson county, dated sixth of this month."[154] Since Pratt and Marsh had left Lexington the day before, they may have been unaware that Lewis and Page had succeeded. Regardless, it was too late.

On Monday, November 4, there was a skirmish near Big Blue between a mob of about fifty and a company of about thirty Mormons headed by David Whitmer. Several were wounded on both sides. Two Missourians were killed; one Mormon was wounded and died the next day.[155] According to Lieutenant Governor Lilburn W. Boggs, a resident of Independence at the time, news of the battle reached the village about 8:00 p.m. by an express messenger, who had left the scene of the battle but nevertheless gave an exaggerated, incorrect account.[156] In their petition to Congress, Smith, Rigdon, and Higbee wrote: "When the news of this battle was spread abroad, the public mind became much inflamed against our people; the militia collected in arms from all quarters, and in great numbers; and being excited to fury by false accounts which had been circulated against us."[157] The false rumors were apparently that the Mormons were the aggressors, having ambushed a small company of the mob that was merely attempting to negotiate peace with the Mormons, and that the Mormons had killed up to twenty in the battle.[158] The fog of war had descended on Jackson County; non-Mormons became fearful that Smith's followers had launched a full-scale revolt.

During the early morning hours of November 5, several Mormon leaders, who had been secured in the jail for their own safety, were "visited by

---

154. John F. Ryland, Letter to Amos Rees, Nov. 24, 1833, in Phelps, Collection of Missouri Documents.

155. On the Battle of Big Blue, see JS History, vol. A-1, 369–70 (DHC 1:429–31); Whitmer, History, 44 (*JSP*, H2:56); "The Outrage in Jackson County, Missouri," *The Evening and the Morning Star*, Dec. 1833, 119; [Edward Partridge], "A History, of the Persecution," *Times and Seasons*, Jan. 1840, 33–34 (*JSP*, H2:215–17); "From Missouri," *The Evening and the Morning Star*, Jan. 1834, 125; Corrill, *Brief History*, 20 (*JSP*, H2:148).

156. Lilburn W. Boggs, Letter to the editor, Nov. 26, 1833, *Missouri Republican*, Dec. 6, 1833, [3].

157. Smith et al., Memorial to the United States Senate and House of Representatives, ca. Oct. 30, 1839–Jan. 27, 1840, 5 (*JSP*, D7:148).

158. Pixley to *New York Observer*, Nov. 7, 1833, rept. in *Christian Watchman* (Boston), Dec. 13, 1833 (Mulder and Mortensen, *Among the Mormons*, 80–83); "The Outrage in Jackson County, Missouri," *The Evening and the Morning Star*, Dec. 1833, 118; [Edward Partridge], "A History, of the Persecution," *Times and Seasons*, Jan. 1840, 34; Lilburn W. Boggs, Nov. 26, 1833, Letter to the editor, *Missouri Republican*, Dec. 6, 1833, [3].

some influencial men," including Boggs, "who told them that the mob had now become desperate, and that the whole county had become enraged, and nothing would stop them from massacreing the whole society."[159] The Mormon leaders, "on seeing the rage of the people," decided to leave Jackson County immediately "rather than to have so many lives lost as probably would be."[160] They fled northward into Clay County, where on November 17 John Corrill wrote: "We saw plainly that the whole county were enraged, and preparing for a general massacre the next day. We then thought it wisdom to stop the shedding of more blood; and by agreeing to leave immediately we saved many lives; in this we feel justified."[161]

At about 10:00 a.m. Col. Thomas Pitcher called out the militia to "suppress the insurrection," as Boggs later described it. "I approved of the course adopted by Col. Pitcher, as the only means of saving bloodshed, and of restoring order."[162] The Mormons insisted that it was a "pretended militia."[163] Hyde wrote on November 8, 1833: "They called it, 'calling out the militia!' probably for the purpose of lessening the magnitude of their crime in the eyes of community."[164] Boggs objected to Hyde's accusation, stating that none of the depredations against the Mormons were committed by the militia, only after the militia was disbanded.[165] Even before the militia had mustered, another messenger arrived with the news that a group of about 150 armed Mormons led by Lyman Wight was marching toward Independence.

When Wight and company arrived at the western border of the village, they learned that the prisoners had been released and that an agreement had been reached to vacate the county immediately. After setting up camp near the proposed temple site, they were approached by Pitcher and the militia. Pitcher demanded that they surrender their arms as well as three men who participated in the Battle at the Blue, which they reluctantly obeyed and

---

159. [Edward Partridge], "A History, of the Persecution," *Times and Seasons*, Jan. 1840, 34 (*JSP*, H2:218).

160. "From Missouri," *The Evening and the Morning Star*, Jan. 1834, 125.

161. [John Corrill], Letter to "Dear brethren," Nov. 17, 1833, "The Outrage in Jackson County, Missouri," *The Evening and the Morning Star*, Dec. 1833, 120.

162. Lilburn W. Boggs, Letter to the editor, Nov. 26, 1833, *Missouri Republican*, Dec. 6, 1833, [3].

163. [Edward Partridge], "A History, of the Persecution," *Times and Seasons*, Jan. 1840, 35 (*JSP*, H2:220).

164. "The Outrage in Jackson County, Missouri," *The Evening and the Morning Star*, Dec. 1833, 118; [Edward Partridge], "A History, of the Persecution," *Times and Seasons*, Jan. 1840, 35 (*JSP*, H2:219).

165. Lilburn W. Boggs, Letter to the editor, Nov. 26, 1833, *Missouri Republican*, Dec. 6, 1833, [3].

then disbanded.[166] "Immediately after the surrender," according to Boggs, "the Militia returned to town and were dismissed, with the exception of a small guard intended to guard the Mormons."[167]

The disarming of Wight's men was followed by the unleashing of the mob upon the Mormon community. Small companies spread throughout the county terrorizing various Mormon settlements, destroying property and driving Mormons out of their homes by force and pursuing them through the wilderness despite the cold and harsh weather conditions. Many wandered several days without food, either individually or in hastily-formed groups. According to Smith, Rigdon, and Higbee, "The houses of the Mormons, in the county of Jackson which they had abandoned, numbering about two hundred, were burned down, or otherwise demolished by the mob."[168] Around 1,200 Mormons were displaced, fleeing into all neighboring counties, with the majority moving north into Clay County.[169] On November 7, as Pratt reported, "the shore [of the Missouri river] began to be lined on both sides of the ferry, with men, women and children, goods, waggons, boxes, chests, and provisions. … Hundreds of people were seen in every direction. Some in tents and some in the open air, around their fires, while the rain descended in torrents."[170] Partridge remembered that "Everetts ferry [that was] on the road leading from Independence to Clay Co. was thronged for near two weeks in crossing the Saints."[171]

On November 6 Hyde and John Gould left Independence for Kirtland, where on the 25th they informed Smith of the hostilities.[172] Phelps wrote to

---

166. [Partridge], "A History, of the Persecution," *Times and Seasons*, Jan. 1840, 35 (*JSP*, H2:219–20); Lilburn W. Boggs, Letter to the editor, Nov. 26, 1833, *Missouri Republican*, Dec. 6, 1833, [3]. According to Pratt, the men who were arrested for their participation in the Battle of the Blue were "imprisoned; but were dismissed in a day or two without trial." Pratt, *History of the Late Persecution,* 20. Pitcher was later charged with "misdemeanor in office" for his actions against the Mormons in Jackson County, but although he was admonished for confiscating the Mormons' weapons by a court of inquiry held at Liberty, Missouri, beginning in December 1833, he was ultimately acquitted. Boggs, Letter; "Mormon History," *Kansas City (MO) Daily Journal,* June 19, 1881, 12; John Whitmer, Daybook, Dec. 19–21, 1833; see also *JSP*, H2:63n193, 73n220.

167. Lilburn W. Boggs, Nov. 26, 1833, Letter to the editor, *Missouri Republican,* Dec. 6, 1833, [3].

168. Smith et al., Memorial to the United States Senate and House of Representatives, ca. Oct. 30, 1839–Jan. 27, 1840, 5–6 (*JSP*, D7:148–49); see also Pratt, *History of the Late Persecution,* 23.

169. Partridge wrote: "Other companies fled towards the Missouri river; and in a short time the most of the church, were under way for Clay county; some few went east, and others south." [Partridge], "A History, of the Persecution," 36 (*JSP*, H2:222).

170. Pratt, *History of the Late Persecution,* 22.

171. Partridge, History, Manuscript, ca. 1839, [14].

172. "The Outrage in Jackson County, Missouri," *The Evening and the Morning Star,* Dec. 1833, 118; Smith, Journal, Nov. 25, 1833 (*JSP*, J1:20).

the Kirtland leaders on November 6 and 7, recounting events in Missouri, including the Battle at the Blue and the mob's subsequent retaliation on various Mormon settlements.[173]

By mid-November the evacuation of the Mormons from Jackson County was nearly complete with most of the refugees eventually crossing the Missouri River into Clay County, where they received more humane treatment. On November 14 Phelps wrote from Clay County to church leaders in Ohio: "The situation of many is critical having nothing to buy food with, and having raised none the passed season. Great destruction is said to be making with the property left. ... The Savior said, Blessed are ye when ye are hated of all men for my name's sake—and I think we have come to that. Now is the hour that tries our souls ... and we mean to be saved, even if we die—for life with the present prospect before us, is not very desirable!"[174] On November 17 Corrill also wrote to church leaders in Ohio: "We are literally in a scattered, miserable condition, not knowing what we shall be called to pass through next. The brethren, generally bare it patiently and feel cheerful, trusting in God, and but few deny the faith."[175]

At the time of the expulsion, Partridge had purchased about 2,100 acres of land in Jackson County for the church, and several Mormons had also purchased lots in Independence on their own.[176] The total loss was estimated in 1840 at $120,000, which in today's dollars would be more than $4,000,000.[177]

Crisis of Faith

Smith could have said he was commanded by God to establish Zion without specifying a location, but a revelation he dictated on July 20, 1831, declared that "the place which is now called Independence is the centre place, & the spot for the Temple is lying westward upon a lot which is not far from the court-house."[178] Tying Zion to a geographic spot by revelation was a

---

173. William W. Phelps, Letter to "Dear brethren," Nov. 6–7, 1833, "The Outrage in Jackson County, Missouri," *The Evening and the Morning Star*, Dec. 1833, 119 (*JSP*, 3:336–41).

174. [William W. Phelps], Letter to Church Leaders, Nov. 14, 1833, "The Outrage in Jackson County, Missouri," *The Evening and the Morning Star*, Dec. 1833, 119 (*JSP*, D3:343).

175. [John Corrill], Letter to "Dear brethren," Nov. 17, 1833, "The Outrage in Jackson County, Missouri," *The Evening and the Morning Star*, Dec. 1833, 120.

176. See *JSP*, D3:374n294.

177. Smith et al., Memorial, to the United States Senate and House of Representatives, ca. Oct. 30, 1839–Jan. 27, 1840, 6 (*JSP*, D7:149).

178. Revelation, July 20, 1831, Revelation Book 1, 93 [D&C 57:1–3] (*JSP*, D2:7–8). This revelation was not included in the 1833 Book of Commandments but was first published as section XXVII in the 1835 Doctrine and Covenants.

miscalculation from which he would never fully recover. His next misstep was to choose a location already occupied by settlers who opposed the Mormon takeover of their community. He underestimated the resolve of the non-Mormon inhabitants of Jackson County to protect their community, continuing to make plans for the city of Zion even after learning about the destruction of the press and agreement by church leaders to leave.

While the loss of their holy land caused some Mormons to question their faith, most saw it as a test of their devotion. Parley P. Pratt's November 12, 1833, prophecy that "we shall be enabled to return to our houses by the first of next Jany & enjoy the fruit of our labor & none to molest or make afraid" underscores how incomprehensible the loss of Zion was to believers.[179] Pratt felt anxious to rescue fellow believers who were questioning how the Lord could permit their enemies to eject them from the holy land while at the same time command them to build a city and a central temple. His prophecy reflects his confidence that government officials would correct the injustice that was being inflicted on the Mormons. He was so sure of this that he was willing to stake his prophetic reputation on it: "If it does not come to pass we may call him a false prophet." We can only wonder what Pratt felt when 1833 passed without returning to Zion.

The loss of Zion was a blow to the Mormon psyche and a challenge to Smith's authority. He had not seen this coming. He and Rigdon had laughed two years earlier when David Whitmer predicted that publishing the revelations would result in destruction and expulsion.[180] Maintaining his prophetic status in the midst of this crisis would be difficult. A similar crisis occurred when the ancient Israelites lost their homeland to the Assyrians and Babylonians: their prophets explained the loss as the result of sin and prophesied about a future period of restoration. Smith will adopt a similar strategy.

---

179. [Edward Partridge], Letter to Joseph Smith, ca. Nov. 14–19, 1833, [1], JS Collection (*JSP*, D3:347).

180. Whitmer, *Address to All Believers in Christ*, 55.

14

Tribulation and Blessings

OCTOBER 1833–JANUARY 1834

After much tribulation cometh the blessing.
—*Joseph Smith to Edward Partridge and Others,*
Dec. 10, 1833, JS Letterbook 1, 71

While his Missouri followers were facing severe persecution and defying demands to vacate Jackson County, Smith was on a proselytizing tour through New York and Upper Canada, having left Kirtland with Rigdon and New York convert Freeman Nickerson on October 5, 1833.[1] Nickerson had traveled to Kirtland and persuaded Smith to accompany him to Upper Canada to speak to members of his family, including his son Moses.[2] On October 10 Frederick G. Williams described Smith's intentions when he wrote that he had "gone down the Lake to Niagara from thence expect to go into Canada as far as Long point U[pper] C[anada] and to preach in all the most noted places on the way."[3]

On Sunday, October 6, Smith, Rigdon, and Nickerson arrived at Springfield, Pennsylvania, where there was a branch of the church. Rigdon was invited to speak to the congregation, which may have been assembled at the home of Andrews and Elizabeth Tyler.[4] Their son, Daniel, who later recalled meeting Smith at his father's house, said, "He was a meek, humble, sociable and very affable man, as a citizen, and one of the most intelligent of men, and a great Prophet."[5] Prior to Smith's arrival, Elizabeth had experienced a vision of Michael the Archangel "sitting upon a white cloud, clothed in white from head

---

1. Smith, Journal, Oct. 5, 1833 (*JSP*, J1:12).
2. Gates, *Lydia Knight's History*, 16–23 (*JSP*, J1:12n25).
3. Frederick G. Williams, Letter to "Dear Brethren," Oct. 10, 1833, JS Letterbook 1, 57.
4. Smith, Journal, Oct. 6, 1833 (*JSP*, J1:12 and n. 28).
5. Daniel Tyler, "Recollections of the Prophet Joseph Smith," *Juvenile Instructor* (Salt Lake City), Feb. 1, 1892, 93.

to foot. He had on a peculiar cap, different from any she had ever seen, with a white robe, underclothing, and moccasins." Daniel remembered that "the Prophet informed her that she had had a true vision, and it was of the Lord," for "he had seen the same angel several times."[6] Following another meeting the same evening during which Smith and others bore testimony, Smith recorded in his journal: "Oh God Seal our te[s]timony to their hearts Amen."[7]

The next day, October 7, Smith "continued at springfield."[8] It may have been on this day that Smith spoke at a meeting held in the Tyler home. According to Daniel, "During his short stay he preached at my father's residence, an humble log cabin. ... His discourse was, I think, entirely on the first principles of the gospel, and he quoted many passages of scripture. ... It seemed as though the gates of heaven were opened and a living stream flowed directly to the holy man of God. It also filled the house where we were sitting."[9]

Perrysburg

Smith, Rigdon, and Nickerson left Springfield on October 8 and, after traveling four days, arrived at Freeman's home in Perrysburg, New York. On this day, Smith recorded: "I feel very well in my mind the Lord is with us but have much anxiety about my family."[10] Shortly after arriving, Smith dictated a revelation in which he and Rigdon were assured, "Your families are well they are in mine hands and I will do with them as seemeth me good."[11] They were commanded to "lift up your voices unto this people [and] speak the thoughts that I shall put into your hearts and you shall not be confounded before men."[12] The Lord instructed them to declare the gospel "in my name in solemnity of heart in the spirit of meekness," and promised that "the holy Ghost shall be shed forth in bearing record unto all things whatsoever ye shall say."[13]

The revelation also stated that Rigdon "should be spokesman unto this people yea verily I will ordain you unto this calling even to be a spokesman unto my servant Joseph and I will give unto him power to be mighty in testimony and I will give unto thee power to be mighty in expounding all scriptures that thou mayest be a spokesman unto him and he shall be a

---

6. Tyler, 93.

7. Smith, Journal, Oct. 6, 1833 (*JSP*, J1:12).

8. Smith, Journal, Oct. 7, 1833 (*JSP*, J1:12).

9. Daniel Tyler, "Recollections of the Prophet Joseph Smith," *Juvenile Instructor*, Feb. 1, 1892, 93, 94.

10. Smith, Journal, Oct. 8–12, 1833 (*JSP*, J1:12–14).

11. Revelation, Oct. 12, 1833, [1], Newel K. Whitney Papers [D&C 100:1] (*JSP*, D3:324).

12. Revelation, [1] [D&C 100:5] (*JSP*, D3:324).

13. Revelation, [1] [D&C 100:7–8] (*JSP*, D3:324).

revelator unto thee that thou mayest know the certanty of all things pertaining to the things of my kingdom on the earth."[14] Rigdon later mentioned that he had been "consecrated a spokesman" to Smith.[15] This effectively placed Rigdon in Cowdery's calling as Smith's spokesman, another indication that Cowdery's influence was waning.[16] Alexander Campbell described Rigdon as "the great orator of the Mahoning [Reformed Baptist] Association."[17] Smith was impressed by Rigdon's speaking talents, recording in his journal shortly after their return from Canada that Rigdon was "a man of great power of words and can gain the friendship of his hearrers very quick."[18]

The revelation closed by assuring believers that "Zion shall be redeemed altho she is chasened for a little season. ... Therefore let your hearts be comforted for all things shall work together for good to them that walk uprightly and to the sactifycation [sanctification] of the church for I will raise up unto myself a pure people that will serve me in righteousness and all that call on the name of the Lord and keep his commandments shall be saved."[19]

The day after this revelation was dictated, Smith made an entry in his journal that reflected his and Rigdon's ministerial roles: "Brother Sidney preached & I bear record to the people."[20] John P. Greene, who attended the meeting, stated that Rigdon "preac[h]ed in the demmonstrtion [demonstration] of the Spirrit."[21] Smith recorded that he and Rigdon spoke to "a large congregation" and that "the Lord gave his Spirit in a remarkable manner."[22]

Canada

On October 14 Smith, Rigdon, and Nickerson continued their journey toward Canada, accompanied by Freeman's wife, Huldah, and their son Levi. On October 18 they arrived at Mount Pleasant, Upper Canada (now Ontario), where they were "kindly received" by Eleazer F. Nickerson, Freeman and Huldah's other son. After preaching in the morning and again in the evening to "a very large" congregation at Eleazer's home on October 20 Smith recorded "what may be the result we cannot tell but the p[r]ospect is

---

14. Revelation, Oct. 12, 1833, [1]–[2] [D&C 100:9–11] (*JSP*, D3:324–25).

15. Quorum of the Twelve Apostles, Minutes, Aug. 7, 1844.

16. On Cowdery's role as Smith's spokesman, see 2 Ne. 3:18; see also D&C 23:1–2.

17. Alexander Campbell, "Anecdotes, Incidents, and Facts," *Millennial Harbinger* (Bethany, WV), Sep. 1848, 523.

18. Smith, Journal, Nov. 19, 1833 (*JSP*, J1:18).

19. Revelation, Oct. 12, 1833, [2], Newel K. Whitney Papers [D&C 100:13, 15–17] (*JSP*, D3:325).

20. Smith, Journal, Oct. 13, 1833 (*JSP*, J1:14).

21. Greene, Diary, Oct. 13, 1833.

22. Smith, Journal, Oct. 13, 1833 (*JSP*, J1:14).

flattering." On the following day, Smith and Rigdon spoke with a Methodist minister, who was unprepared to deal with the two Americans. "He could not stand against our words," Smith recorded.[23]

On October 22 Smith and Rigdon traveled to Colborne Village, where they held a meeting in the evening. A second meeting was held the next evening despite a heavy snow storm, during which they were challenged by a Wesleyan Methodist who "was very tumultious but destitute of reason or knawledge he would not give us oppertunity to reply." Nevertheless, "we find that conviction is resting on the minds of some [and] we hope that great good may yet be done in canada which O Lord grant for thy names sake."[24]

On October 24 Smith and Rigdon left Colborne and traveled south to Waterford in the adjoining county of Norfolk and spoke to a small congregation, then returned to Mount Pleasant. In the evening they preached to a large congregation, after which Eleazer declared his "full beleif in the truth of the work" and he and his wife, Eliza, expressed their desire to be baptized on the following Sunday. Reflecting on his and Rigdon's preaching in the area, Smith wrote: "Great excitement prevailes in every place where we have been the result we leave in the hand of God."[25]

On Sunday, October 27, Smith and Rigdon preached to a large congregation at Mount Pleasant, after which twelve people were baptized, including Freeman's two sons, Moses and Eleazer.[26] Moses later recalled that after listening to Smith and Rigdon for "some days," he "became much interested; and, finally convinced of its truthfulness."[27] Shortly after returning to Kirtland, Smith wrote to Moses and reflected on his stay in Mount Pleasant: "You remember the testimony which I bore in the name of the Lord Jesus, concerning the great work which he has brought forth in the last days. You know my manner of communication, how that in weakness and simpleness I declared to you what the Lord had brought forth by the ministering of his holy angels to me, for this generation."[28]

On the following day Smith held a meeting at 10:00 a.m., after which "two came forward and were baptized" and then "confirmed ... at the watter's

---

23. Smith, Journal, Oct. 18–21, 1833 (*JSP*, J1:14–15).

24. Smith, Journal, Oct. 22–23, 1833 (*JSP*, J1:15).

25. Smith, Journal, Oct. 24–25, 1833 (*JSP*, J1:15).

26. Smith, Journal, Oct. 27, 1833 (*JSP*, J1:15, 19–20).

27. "Autobiography of Moses C. Nickerson," *True Latter Day Saints' Herald* (Plano, IL), July 15, 1870, 425.

28. Joseph Smith, Letter to Moses Nickerson, Nov. 19, 1833, JS Letterbook 1, 64–65 (*JSP*, D3:359).

edge." During a meeting the same evening, twelve people who had been baptized the previous day were confirmed, after which Eleazer was ordained an elder and became the leader of the new branch. Smith later recorded that "the spirit was given in great power to some and the rest had great peace" and prayed "may God carry on his work in this place till all shall know him. Amen." He also mentioned that "one of the sisters got the gift of toungues," possibly Lydia Goldthwaite Bailey, the future wife of Newel Knight, "which made the saints rejoice." Smith prayed, "may God increase the gifts among them for his sons sake."[29]

As Lydia recalled, the meetings were held in the "Nikerson store-house." Afterward the family was "all seated around the wide, old-fashioned fireplace in the parlor listening to the Prophet's words and full of rejoicing," when Moses said he wished to hear someone speak in tongues. According to Lydia, Smith said: "If one of you will rise up and open your mouth it shall be filled, and you shall speak in tongues." For some reason, everyone looked to Lydia. As told by her biographer in 1883, Lydia was "enveloped as with a flame, and, unable longer to retain her seat, she arose and her mouth was filled with the praises of God and His glory. The spirit of tongues was upon her, and she was clothed in shining light, so bright that all present saw it with great distinctness above the light of the fire and the candles."[30] No doubt Moses was pleased with the result of his request. On December 29, 1833, he wrote to Rigdon: "Your labors while in Canada have been the beginning of a good work: there are 34 members attached to the church at Mount Pleasant, all of whom appear to live up to their profession, five of whom have spoken in tongues, and three sing in tongues."[31]

On Tuesday morning, October 29, Smith and Rigdon left Mount Pleasant for Kirtland, accompanied by Freeman and his wife and son.[32] Before leaving, Lydia remembered that "while the team was being hitched up, Joseph paced back and forth in the sitting room in deep study." Finally, he spoke to those gathered to see him off, explaining that he had been "pondering on Sister Lydia's lonely condition, and wondering why it is that she has passed through so much sorrow and affliction and is thus separated from all her relatives." The twenty-one-year-old Lydia was estranged from her

29. Smith, Journal, Oct. 28, 1833 (*JSP*, J1:16).

30. Gates, *Lydia Knight's History*, 20–22.

31. Moses Nickerson, Letter to [Sidney Rigdon], Dec. 29, 1833, in *The Evening and the Morning Star*, Feb. 1834, 134.

32. Smith, Journal, Oct. 29, 1833 (*JSP*, J1:16).

husband, Calvin Bailey, an abusive drunkard who had abandoned his wife and child. Turning to Lydia, Smith said: "Sister Lydia, great are your blessings. The Lord, your Savior, loves you, and will overrule all your past sorrows and afflictions for good unto you. Let your heart be comforted. You are of the blood of Israel descended through the loins of Ephraim. You shall yet be a savior to your father's house. Therefore be comforted, and let your heart rejoice, for the Lord has a great work for you to do. Be faithful and endure unto the end and all will be well."[33] Thereafter, Smith stepped up into the wagon and rode off toward Lake Erie.

After crossing the lake at Nickerson's expense, the group arrived at Buffalo on October 31.[34] The next day, Smith and Rigdon continued their journey southwest toward Kirtland, while the Nickersons traveled south to their home in Perrysburg.[35]

Return to Kirtland

Smith and Rigdon arrived in Kirtland on November 4 at 10:00 a.m., "after a fateagueing journey."[36] Their trip to Canada was hailed as a great success by Cowdery, who in his November 12 letter to Samuel Bent of Pontiac, Michigan, mentioned that "bro. Joseph S. & Sidney R. have returned from Canada, where they raised up a church of fourteen members. The Lord was with them truly, and their testimony had great effect on the minds of hundreds."[37]

Smith was relieved when he "found his family all well," which was "according to the promise of the Lord" given in an October 12, 1833, revelation, "for which blessings I feel to thank his holy name; Amen."[38] On November 19 Smith wrote to Moses Nickerson and stated: "We found our families, and the church in this place, well, generally: nothing of consequence transpire[d] while we were abscent, except the death of one of our brethren, a young man of great worth as a private citizen among us, the loss of whom we justly mourn."[39]

---

33. Gates, *Lydia Knight's History,* 22–23.

34. Smith, Journal, Oct. 29, 1833 (*JSP,* J1:16). Gates, *Lydia Knight's History,* 22, mentions Freeman Nickerson funding Smith and Rigdon's return to Kirtland.

35. Smith, Journal, Oct. 31, 1833 (*JSP,* J1:16); Joseph Smith, Letter to Moses Nickerson, Nov. 19, 1833, JS Letterbook 1, 62 (*JSP,* D3:356).

36. Smith, Journal, Nov. 4, 1833 (*JSP,* J1:16); Joseph Smith, Letter to Moses Nickerson, Nov. 19, 1833, JS Letterbook 1, 62 (*JSP,* D3:356).

37. Oliver Cowdery, Letter to Samuel Bent, Nov. 12, 1833, Cowdery, Letterbook, 10.

38. Smith, Journal, Nov. 4, 1833 (*JSP,* J1:16); Revelation, Oct. 12, 1833, [1], Newel K. Whitney Papers [D&C 100:1] (*JSP,* D3:324).

39. Joseph Smith, Letter to Moses Nickerson, Nov. 19, 1833, JS Letterbook 1, 63 (*JSP,* D3:357). The man who died was probably twenty-three-year-old David Johnson, who died on October 31, 1833, after a long illness. Obituary for David Johnson, *The Evening and the Morning Star,* Dec. 1833, 117.

For eight consecutive days following his return to Kirtland, November 5–12, while the Saints in Missouri were fleeing Zion, Smith recorded that "nothing of note transpired."[40] On the ninth day, November 13, Smith was awakened at 4:00 a.m. to see the annual Leonid meteor shower, which he interpreted as a "fullfillment of the word of God as recorded in the holy scriptures and a sure sign that the coming of Christ is clost at hand." Adding his prayer, Smith journalized: "Oh how marvellous are thy works Oh Lord and I thank thee for thy me[r]cy unto me thy servent Oh Lord save me in thy kingdom for Christ sake Amen."[41]

The meteor shower was also observed by Smith's followers in Missouri on their way to Liberty, Clay County, Missouri. Writing to Smith shortly afterward, Edward Partridge said: "The heavens were literally filled with meteors or shooting stars as they are called. ... It is said that they struck the ground in Independence & in other places round about. ... During this sight our people rejoiced but the worlds people were much frightened."[42] Partridge's daughter Eliza later wrote, "Some of our enemies thought the day of judgment had come and were very much frightened but the Saints rejoiced and considered it as one of the signs of the Latter days."[43] How the Partridges learned this is not explained, but Jackson County resident Josiah Gregg confirmed the report, stating that the meteor shower caused many of its inhabitants "to wonder whether, after all, the Mormons might not be in the right; and whether this was not a sign sent from heaven as a remonstrance for the injustice they had been guilty of towards that chosen sect."[44]

Smith still had not learned of the expulsion of his people when he wrote to Moses Nickerson on November 19. "We have received letters from our breth[r]en in Missouri of late," he wrote, "but we cannot tell from their contents the probable extent that those persons who are desirous to expel them from that country, will carry their unlawful and unrighteous purposes. ... How far they will be suffered to execute their threats we know not, but we trust in the Lord, and leave the event with him to govern in his own wise providence."[45]

In his letter, Smith expressed concern about the welfare of his new converts

---

40. Smith, Journal, Nov. 5–12, 1833 (*JSP*, J1:16).

41. Smith, Journal, Nov. 13, 1833 (*JSP*, J1:16–18). Cf. Rev. 6:13.

42. [Partridge], Letter to Joseph Smith, ca. Nov. 14–19, 1833, [1], JS Collection (*JSP*, D3:347–48).

43. Eliza Maria Partridge Lyman, Journal, 9–10.

44. Gregg, *Commerce of the Prairies*, 1:317–18.

45. Joseph Smith, Letter to Moses Nickerson, Nov. 19, 1833, JS Letterbook 1, 63–64 (*JSP*, D3:357–58).

in Canada. "You are aware, no doubt, dear brother, that anxieties inexpresible croud themselves continually upon my mind for the saints, when I consider the many temptations with which we are subject from the cunning and flattery of the great adversary of our souls. And I can truely say, that with much fervency I have called upon the Lord in behalf of our brethren in Canada." He reminded them of the nearness of the Second Coming, encouraging them to keep the commandments and to remember the testimony he bore while he was with them. "I pray that the Lord may enable you to treasure these things up in your mind," he wrote, "for I know that his Spirit will bear testimony to all who seek diligently after knowledge from him. I hope you will search the scriptures, to see whether these things are not also consistant with those things that the ancient prophets and apostles have written."[46]

Blessings

In his journal entry for November 19, Smith revealed something about himself and his attitude toward his fellow man: "This day my hart is somewhat sorrowfull but feel to trust in the Lord. ... I have learned in my travels," he said, "that man is trecheous [treacherous] and selfish but few excepted."[47] Despite his affable demeanor, Smith admitted to a strong suspicion and cynicism toward others. This would make him distrustful, skeptical of motives, wary, and constantly on the lookout for deception, malice, and betrayal. He then assessed the characters of his two counselors, expressing disappointment.

Rigdon is a "great and good man," but several faults prevent Smith from placing confidence in him: "selfishness and independence of mind"—things that made Rigdon less malleable. "Brother Sidney is a man whom I love but is not capab[le] of that pure and stedfast love for those who are his benefactors as should possess the breast of a Presedent of the chu[r]ch of Christ," Smith wrote. Concerning Frederick G. Williams, Smith had less worry. Williams is "not a man of many words but is ever wining because of his constant mind. ... He is perfectly honest and upright, and seeks with all his heart to magnify his presidency in the church of ch[r]ist, but fails in many instances, in consequence of a want of confidence in himself." Nevertheless, Williams—unlike Rigdon—"is one of those men in whom I place the greatest confidence and trust for I have found him ever full of love and Brotherly kindness. ... He shall ever have place in my heart and is ever intitled to my

46. Smith, 64–65 (*JSP*, D3:359).
47. Smith, Journal, Nov. 19, 1833 (*JSP*, J1:18).

confidence."[48] Assessing the personality and character of his followers was a useful ability for a leader who wanted to utilize their talents and direct them toward building the organization.

At this point in his journal, Smith pronounced blessings on his two counselors: "Blessed be brother Frederick, for he shall never want a friend; and his generation after him shall flourish. The Lord hath appointed him an inheritance upon the land of Zion." Smith had more to say about Rigdon: "And again, blessed be brother Sidney, also, notwithstanding he shall be high and lifted up, yet he shall bow down under the yoke like unto an ass that coucheth beneath his burthen; that learneth his master's will by the stroke of the rod: thus saith the Lord. Yet the Lord will have mercy on him, and he shall bring forth much fruit." Perhaps referring to Rigdon's bouts with depression, Smith promised: "The Lord shall make his heart merry as with sweet wine because of him who putteth forth his hand and lifteth him up from out of deep mire, and pointeth him out the way, and guideth his feet when he stumbles; and humbleth him in his pride."[49]

About mid-November, Smith moved from the Whitney white store, where he and his family had lived since September 1832, about a quarter-mile south into a house situated on the hill above the Kirtland Flats near the lot where the House of the Lord was being constructed.[50] On November 22 Smith's younger brother Don Carlos moved in with him and began learning the printing trade with Cowdery, who had recently purchased a press and type in New York.[51] Soon, two other apprentice printers, Phineas Young and Wilbur Denton, also moved in with Smith as boarders.[52]

News from Missouri
On November 25 Orson Hyde and John Gould arrived in Kirtland from Jackson County and "brough[t] the melencholly intelegen [intelligence] of the riot in Zion" and the expulsion of the Mormons from Jackson County.[53] About the same time, Smith received a letter from W. W. Phelps, dated November 6–7, 1833, a portion of which Cowdery printed the following month in the first Kirtland issue of *The Evening and the Morning Star*, containing

48. Smith (*JSP*, J1:18–19).
49. Smith (*JSP*, J1:19).
50. [Emma Smith], List, ca. 1845, in Lucy Mack Smith, History, 1844–45, Miscellany.
51. Smith, Journal, Nov. 22, 1833 (*JSP*, J1:21).
52. Smith, Journal, Dec. 9 and 11, 1833 (*JSP*, J1:21).
53. Smith, Journal, Nov. 25, 1833 (*JSP*, J1:20).

information about the final days of the conflict as well as the ongoing exodus of the Mormons from Jackson to Clay County.[54]

On December 5 Smith wrote a letter to Edward Partridge at Liberty, Clay County, noting the reception of Phelps's letter containing "the painful intelegence of the rage of the enemy and your present unsettled situation."[55] He repeated information he had received from various sources, though he was uncertain about some of its accuracy. Indeed, some of it was incorrect. He instructed them to "collect every particular concerning the Mob from the begining and send us a correct statement of fact as they transpired from time to time that we may be enabled to give the public correct information on the subject," that is, through Cowdery's publication of *The Evening and the Morning Star*.[56] Because of the lack of reliable, complete information, he wrote, "it is difficult for us to advise and can only say that the destenies of all people are in the hands of a Just God." Nevertheless, instead of blaming Missouri Mormons in the midst of their crisis, Smith contextualized persecution as a sign of the true followers of Christ. "One thing is sure," he wrote, "they who will live Godly in Christ Jesus shall suffer persecution," quoting 2 Timothy 3:12, and reminded them that "it is to be expected they will pass through great tribulation according to John the Revelator [Rev. 7:14]." Indeed, as Smith informed them, persecution of the church was universal: "The inhabitants of this county threaten our distruction and we know not how soon they may be permitted to follow the examples of the Missourians."[57]

Repeating his previous instruction, he said: "I would inform you that it is not the will of the Lord for you to sell your Lands in Zion."[58] He also instructed them "not to murmur at the dealings of God with his creature you are not as yet brought into as trying circumstances as were the ancient Prophets & apostles."[59] He advised: "It is your privelege to use every lawful means in your power to seek redress for your grievances of your enemies and prosecute them to the extent of the Law." However, he had to deliver the disappointing news that "it will be impossible for us to render you any assistance in a temporal point of view as our means are already exhausted and

54. "The Outrage in Jackson County, Missouri," *The Evening and the Morning Star*, Dec. 1833, 119 (*JSP*, 3:336–41).

55. Joseph Smith, Letter to Edward Partridge, Dec. 5, 1833, JS Letterbook 1, 65 (*JSP*, D3:369).

56. Smith, 67 (*JSP*, D3:371). See also "The Outrage in Jackson County, Missouri," *The Evening and the Morning Star*, Dec. 1833–June 1834, 118–23, 129, 137–39, 159–60, 167–68.

57. Smith, Letter to Partridge, JS Letterbook 1, 67–69 (*JSP*, D3:371–72).

58. Smith, 67 (*JSP*, D3:371). For his previous instruction, see Smith, Letter to William W. Phelps and Others, Aug. 18, 1833, [3], JS Collection (*JSP*, D3:268).

59. Smith, Letter to Partridge, Dec. 5, 1833, JS Letterbook 1, 68 (*JSP*, D3:372).

are deeply in debt and know no means whereby we shall be able to extricate ourselves." This was due to the recent purchase of land and acquisition of a new printing press and type.

Uncertain of the situation in Missouri, Smith further advised followers that if Jackson County was completely vacated by the Mormons, it would not be wise to "recommence hostilities with them," but if some of his followers were armed and still on their land, they "should maintain the ground as Long as there is a man Left. as the spot of ground upon which you were located is the place appointed of the Lord for your inheritance and it was right in the sight of God that you contend for it to the last, you will recollect that the Lord has said that Zion should not be moved out of her place therefore the land should not be sold but held by the brethren until the Lord in his wisdom opens a way for your return."[60]

On December 10 a package of several letters from Partridge, Phelps, and John Corrill arrived in Kirtland, having been mailed on November 19. Later the same day, Smith dictated a consoling letter to his Missouri followers: "When we learn your sufferings, it awakens every sympathy of our hearts; it weighs us down; we cannot refrain from tears, yet we are not able to realize, only in part, your sufferings."[61] After mentioning the receipt of their letters in the morning's mail, which Smith said "gave us the melancholy inteligence of your flight from the land of your inheritance having been driven before the face of your enemies in that place," Smith struggled to make sense of the loss of Zion. His followers no doubt wanted to know how God could allow it to happen.

Smith acknowledged his own puzzlement. "I cannot learn from any communication by the spirit to me that Zion has forfeited her claim to a celestial crown notwithstanding the Lord has caused her to be thus afflicted," he wrote. Nevertheless, he suggested "it may be some individuals ... have walked in disobedience and forsaken the new covenants; all such will be made manifest by their works in due time." Smith perhaps hoped his Missouri followers would find someone to blame besides him, but would God allow the wicked to destroy Zion, the printing press, the nearly-finished Book of Commandments, because of the sins of the few? Later in the letter, Smith suggested that such was the case: "I am sensable that ... those who are innocent are compelled to suffer for the iniquities of the guilty," and this was

---

60. Smith, 69–70 (*JSP*, D3:374).
61. Joseph Smith, Letter to Partridge and Others, Dec. 10, 1833, JS Letterbook 1, 70 (*JSP*, D3:376).

because sinners were allowed to remain in the church whereby "all is brought into bondage together."[62]

Smith then referenced several revelations that seemed to explain their unexpected situation, although in hindsight the events should not have surprised them. "I have always expected that Zion would suffer sore affliction from what I could learn from the commandments which have been given," Smith explained.[63] This alluded to an August 2, 1833, revelation that promised Zion would escape latter-day calamities "if she observe to do all things whatsoever I have commanded her but if she observe not to do whatsoeve[r] I have commanded her I will visit her according to all her works with sore afflictions with pestilence with plague with sword with vengence with devouring fire."[64] However, this same revelation declared that the Lord had forgiven Zion and promised "if she sin no more none of these things shall come upon her; And I will bless her with blessings, and multiply a multiplicity of blessings upon her, and upon her generations forever and ever, saith the Lord your God. Amen."[65] The timing of this divine declaration, coming after the Missouri leaders had agreed to leave Jackson County, is problematic for Smith's use of it.

Smith continued, "I would remind you of a certain clause in one [revelation] which says that after much <u>tribulation</u> cometh the <u>blessing</u>."[66] The revelation containing this clause was given in August 1831 and declared: "Ye cannot behold with your natural eyes ... the glory which shall follow after much tribulation for after much tribulation cometh the blessings Wherefore the day cometh that ye shall be crowned with much glory."[67] The revelation promised "blessings" in the "kingdom of heaven" for individuals who would endure tribulations, even unto death, to establish Zion.

Because of these and other passages in his revelations, including "one received of late," Smith assured his Missouri followers: "I know that Zion, in the own due time of the Lord will be redeemed."[68] This alluded to a revelation Smith dictated the previous October assuring believers that "Zion shall

---

62. Smith, 71 (*JSP*, D3:377).

63. Smith, 71 (*JSP*, D3:376).

64. Revelation, Aug. 2, 1833-A, Revelation Book 2, 64 [D&C 97:26] (*JSP*, D3:202).

65. Revelation, 64 [D&C 97:27–28] (*JSP*, D3:203).

66. Joseph Smith, Letter to Partridge and Others, Dec. 10, 1833, JS Letterbook 1, 71 (*JSP*, D3:376).

67. Revelation, Aug. 1, 1831, Revelation Book 1, 94 [D&C 58:3–4] (*JSP*, D2:14).

68. Joseph Smith, Letter to Partridge and Others, Dec. 10, 1833, JS Letterbook 1, 71 (*JSP*, D3:376–77).

be redeemed altho she is chasened for a little season."[69] This was dictated after Smith had learned of the recent escalation of conflict in Missouri and was meant as encouragement that their sufferings would be short. At that time, Smith did not anticipate the loss of Zion and believed that persecution would cease when the Mormons achieved numerical superiority.

At this point, Smith dared not give a timetable for Zion's redemption: "How many will be the days of her purification, tribulation and affliction, the Lord has kept hid from my eyes; and when I enquire concerning this subject the voice of the Lord is, Be still, and know that I am God!" In fact, Smith had little to offer his followers by way of explanation or resolution: "Now there are two things of which I am ignorant and the Lord will not show me—perhaps for a wise purpose in himself. ... And they are these, Why God hath suffered so great calamity to come upon Zion; or what the great moving cause of this great affliction is. ... And again by what means he will return her back to her inheritance with songs of everlasting Joy upon her head."[70]

Smith repeated his previous instruction for Missouri Mormons not to sell their Jackson County lands,[71] only this time in the strongest possible terms: "It is better that you should die in the ey[e]s of God, then that you should give up the Land of Zion, the inheritances which you have purchased with your monies; for evry man that giveth not up his inheritances, though he should die yet when the Lord shall come, he shall stand upon it, and with Job in his flesh he shall see God." Smith was willing to pay a high price to maintain his charismatic integrity. He then advised his Missouri followers to appeal to the judge, then to the governor, then to the president, "seeking evry lawful means to obtain redress of your enemies &c &c and pray to God day and night to return you in peace and in safety to the Lands of your inheritance."[72] Smith hinted that he was preparing to fight back when he advised Phelps to find a place for a press "in Liberty" or "some other place," and to "collect all the information, and give us a true history of the begining and rise of Zion, and her calamities &c."[73]

---

69. Revelation, Oct. 12, 1833, [2], Newel K. Whitney Papers [D&C 100:13] (*JSP*, D3:325). Cf. Ps. 46:10.

70. Joseph Smith, Letter to Partridge and Others, Dec. 10, 1833, JS Letterbook 1, 71 (*JSP*, D3:377).

71. See Joseph Smith, Letter to Partridge, Dec. 5, 1833, JS Letterbook 1, 70 (*JSP*, D3:374); Revelation, Dec. 16–17, 1833, Revelation Book 2, 83 [D&C 101:99] (*JSP*, D3:397).

72. Joseph Smith, Letter to Partridge and Others, Dec. 10, 1833, JS Letterbook 1, 73 (*JSP*, D3:379). Cf. Job 19:26.

73. Smith, 74 (*JSP*, D3:380).

Finally, unable to let go of his vision for Zion, Smith prayed: "O My God! ... I ask thee in the name of Jesus Christ, to return thy people unto their homes, & there inheritances, to enjoy the fruit of their Labors; that all the waste places may be built up; that all the enemies of thy people, who will not repent and turn unto thee be distroyed from off the face of that Land; and let an house be built and established unto thy name, and let ... the borders of Zion be enlarged forever, ... and let all the saints ... flee unto Zion, ... and let her be organized according to thy law." Then, in closing, Smith prayed for his followers: "Give thy holy spirit unto my brethren ... [and] deliver them from all evil; and when they turn there faces towards Zion and bow down before thee and pray may their sins never com[e] up before thy face ... and may they depart from all their eniquities."[74]

Revelation

On December 16 Smith began dictating a long revelation to Cowdery, which occupied the entire evening and continued until the early morning hours of the next day.[75] Ira Ames, who had recently moved to Kirtland from New York, remembered that he and Martin Harris went to Smith's home one morning in December 1833 and "found Joseph and Oliver Cowdery at breakfast," and that Cowdery greeted them and said, "we have just received news from heaven," referring to the manuscript copy of the revelation on the table.[76]

In his December 10, 1833, letter to church leaders in Missouri, Smith struggled to explain the loss of Zion, but this new revelation clearly stated that the Mormons were expelled from Jackson County because of their transgressions. "Verily I say unto you concerning your brethren who have been afflicted and persecuted and cast out from the Land of their inheriten[ces]," the revelation began. "I the Lord have suffered the affliction to come upon them wherewith they have been afflicted in consequence of their transgressions." Later, the revelation reiterated this accusation, stating that "many but not all ... were found transgressors therefore they must needs be chastened." Smith's Missouri followers were afflicted because "there were jar[r]ings and contentions envyings and strifes and lustful and covetous desires among them Therefore by these things they poluted their inheritances." Such vague language applied to a large population made it difficult to deny.

---

74. Smith, 75 (*JSP*, D3:381).

75. Revelation, Dec. 16–17, 1833, Revelation Book 2, 73–83 [D&C 101] (*JSP*, D3:386–97); see also Revelation Book 1, 183–89, which dates the revelation to Dec. 16–17, 1833 (*JSP*, MRB:343–55).

76. Ames, Autobiography and Journal, [10].

They were also "slow to hearken unto the voice of the Lord their God" and "they esteemed lightly my council."[77]

Smith's followers accepted this explanation. The day before Smith dictated this revelation, Phelps, in Missouri, wrote a letter to Smith in which he referred to the loss of Zion as a "necessary chastisement" and exclaimed: "I know it was right that we should be driven out of the land of Zion, that the rebellious might be sent away."[78] Following the riot in Independence, John Whitmer wrote to Smith and revealed: "My daily prayer is that the Lord will cleanse Zion of all the remaining wickedness that is on this <u>Holy Land</u>."[79] Cowdery had written to church leaders in Missouri on August 10, 1833, and declared: "This great tribulation would not have come upon Zion had it not been for rebelion ... against the one to whom were intrusted the keys, & from thence it has spread down to the lowest & least member!" Cowdery was probably referring to Partridge and other leaders who had been hesitant to accept Smith as president of the high priesthood. "It was necessary that things should come upon us," Cowdery declared. "There was no other way to cleanse the church."[80] The Missouri leaders accepted blame for the loss of Zion despite an August 2, 1833, revelation declaring their forgiveness.[81]

The revelation explained that because of transgression Smith's Missouri followers were being "chastened and tried even as Abraham who was commanded to offer up his only son for all those who will not endure chastening but deny me cannot be sanctified."[82] Thus the loss of Zion was an Abrahamic test of faith. Abraham followed God's command even when sacrificing his "only son" would have prevented the fulfillment of God's promise to make him the father of many nations (Gen. 12:2–3; 22:1–14). Similarly, the loss of Zion conflicted with God's command to purchase Jackson County land "for an everlasting inheritance."[83] Prior to this revelation, Smith had told the Missouri leaders that "the affliction of my Brotheren reminds me of Abraham offering up Isaac his only son but my Brotheen [brethren] have been

77. Revelation, Dec. 16–17, 1833, Revelation Book 2, 73, 76 [D&C 101:1–2, 6–8, 41] (*JSP*, D3:389, 392).

78. William W. Phelps, Letter to "Dear Brethren," Dec. 15, 1833, "Later from Missouri," *The Evening and the Morning Star*, Jan. 1834, 128 (*JSP*, D3:383).

79. John Whitmer, Letter to Oliver Cowdery and Joseph Smith, July 29, 1833, JS Letterbook 2:52–56 (*JSP*, D3:190).

80. Oliver Cowdery, Letter to William W. Phelps and Others, Aug. 10, 1833, [1] (*JSP*, D3:241).

81. Revelation, Aug. 2, 1833-A, Revelation Book 2, 64 [D&C 97:27–28] (*JSP*, D3:203).

82. Revelation, Dec. 16–17, 1833, Revelation Book 2, 73 [D&C 101:4] (*JSP*, D3:389).

83. Revelation, July 20, 1831, Revelation Book 1, 93 [D&C 57:5] (*JSP*, D2:11).

called to give up even more than this their wives and their children yea and their own life also."[84]

The revelation also provided hope that the Lord would be merciful to the Missouri Mormons. "Therefore let your hearts be comforted concerning Zion. ... Zion shall not be moved out of her place notwithstanding her children are scattered they that remain and are pure in heart shall return and come to their inheritances they and their children with songs of everlasting joy to build up the waste places of Zion and all these things that the prophets might be fulfilled."[85] Smith's words were woven from Isaiah 51, which predicted the restoration of the Jews to the holy land and the rebuilding of Jerusalem as their capital, a time when the Lord will "comfort Zion" and "all her waste places," a time when "the redeemed of the Lord shall return, and come with singing unto Zion; and everlasting joy upon their head ... and sorrow and mourning shall flee away" (Isa. 51:3, 11). Like the Jews, the Mormons too had lost their Zion and Smith found himself in a similar situation as the ancient prophets. However, an American Zion was a distinctive feature of the Book of Mormon and Smith's revelations, neither of which had anticipated a loss and restoration, and so Smith had to fashion his rhetoric from the Old Testament.

Through a parable about a nobleman and his "vineyard," which contained twelve olive trees, the revelation explained how Mormons were to reclaim their lands. However, the opening part of the parable alludes to the cause of the expulsion. After planting the trees, the servants build a hedge around them, set watchmen, and begin to build a tower as the nobleman commanded them.

> While they were yet Laying the foundation thereof they began to say among themselves and what need hath my Lord of this tower and consulted for a Long time saying among themselves what need hath my Lord of this tower seeing this is a time of peace might not this money be given to the exchangers for there is no need of these things and while they were at varience one with another they become very slothful and they harkened not unto the commandment of their Lord and the enemy came by night and broke down the hedge and the servants of the nobleman arose and were affrighted and fled and the enemy distroyed their works and broke down the Olive trees.[86]

---

84. Smith, Letter to William W. Phelps and Others, Aug. 18, 1833, [1], JS Collection (*JSP*, D3:262).

85. Revelation, Dec. 16–17, 1833, Revelation Book 2, 73 [D&C 101:16–19] (*JSP*, D3:389). Cf. Isa. 51:3.

86. Revelation, 76–77 [D&C 101:47–51] (*JSP*, D3:393).

Smith's allegory of a watchman was inspired by various passages in the Bible (Ezek. 33:2–9; Isa. 21:6; Jer. 51:12), which he adapted to criticize his followers who questioned the command to build, not one, but three temples in Missouri. The parable continued by calling for the use of force to redeem Zion:

> And the Lord of the vineyard said unto one of his servants, go and gather togethe[r] the residue of my servants and take all the strength of mine house which are my wariors my young men and they that are of middle age also among all my servants who are the strength of mine house ... and go ye straitway unto the Land of my vineyard and redeem my vineyard for it is mine I have bought it with money therefore get ye straitway unto my Land break down the walls of mine enemies th[r]ow down their tower and scatte[r] their watchmen and inasmuch as they gather to gether against you avenge me of mine enemies that by and by I may come with the residue of mine house and possess the Land.[87]

The servant to whom the Lord of the vineyard spoke was of course Joseph Smith, as indicated in a subsequent revelation.[88] The servant asked the lord: "When shall these things be"? The Lord answered that it would be done according to his will, and ordered his servant: "Go ye strait way and do all things whatsoever I have commanded you." The parable ends with the declaration: "And his servant went straitway and done all things whatsoever his Lord commanded him and afte[r] many days all things were fulfilled."[89]

Smith was prepared to lose some of his followers in the struggle for the land of Zion. The revelation promised a glorious afterlife to the martyrs of the faith. "All they that suffer persecution for my name and endure in faith though they are called to lay down their lives for my sake yet shall they partake of all this glory wherefore fear not even unto death."[90] Similarly, an August 1833 revelation had declared, "And whoso layeth down his life in my cause for my name sake shall find it again even life eternal therefore be not afraid of your enemies."[91]

Despite being expelled from the Mormon holy land, the revelation commanded Smith's followers to purchase as much land as possible, both in Jackson County and the surrounding region, with money raised from

---

87. Revelation, 77–78 [D&C 101:55–57] (*JSP*, D3:393–94).

88. Revelation, Feb. 24, 1834, in Hyde and Pratt, Notebook of Revelations, [12] [D&C 103:21] (*JSP*, D3:461).

89. Revelation, Dec. 16–17, 1833, Revelation Book 2, 79 [D&C 101:60] (*JSP*, D3:394).

90. Revelation, 76 [D&C 101:35] (*JSP*, D3:392).

91. Revelation, Aug. 6, 1833, Revelation Book 2, 67 [D&C 98:13–14] (*JSP*, D3:225).

branches of the church outside of Missouri. To facilitate the purchase of these lands, the revelation instructed that "all the churches [in the east] gather to gether all their monies ... and let honorable men be appointed even wise men and send them to purchace the lands [in Missouri] ... and in this way they may establish Zion."[92] Meanwhile, Missouri Mormons were to "importune for redress, and redemption by the hand of those who are placed as rulers and are in authority over you," and to work up the chain of command, from judge to the governor to the president of the United States, much as Smith had advised in his December 10 letter.[93]

Smith had previously strictly prohibited the sale of Jackson County property. In this revelation, the Lord specifically commanded Sidney Gilbert not to sell the church's storehouse, stating that to do so would be "a very soar and grievous sin against me." The revelation then reiterated Smith's previous instruction: "It is my will that my people should claim and hold claim upon that which I have appointed unto them though they should not be permited to dwell thereon." Meanwhile, the Lord declared, "a commandment I give unto all the churches that they shall continue to gather to gether into the places which I have appointed," observing a previous commandment to do so in an orderly fashion.[94]

This revelation was printed in Kirtland as a broadsheet and posted publicly.[95] According to Eber D. Howe, editor of the *Painesville Telegraph*, the printed broadsheet had also been "privately circulated" among church members.[96] Howe also indicated that the printed revelation was "taken up by all their priests and carried to all their congregations, some of which were actually sold for one dollar per copy."[97] The revelation was sent to the Missouri leaders in a January 22, 1834, letter. At the same time, Smith and his counselors informed them that they had already petitioned Missouri governor Dunklin on their behalf and that they were also planning to send the same to US president Jackson.[98] Missouri leaders had reason to be concerned

---

92. Revelation, Dec. 16–17, 1833, Revelation Book 2, 80 [D&C 101:70–74] (*JSP*, D3:395).

93. Revelation, 81–82 [D&C 101:76, 86–89] (*JSP*, D3:395–97); Joseph Smith, Letter to Edward Partridge and Others, Dec. 10, 1833, JS Letterbook 1, 73 (*JSP*, D3:379).

94. Revelation, Dec. 16–17, Revelation Book 2, 80, 83 [D&C 101:67, 96–97, 99] (*JSP*, D3:394, 397).

95. *Verily, I say unto you, concerning your brethren who have been afflicted* (Kirtland, OH: ca. Jan. 1834); copy at CHL.

96. "A Scrap of Mormonism," *Painesville (OH) Telegraph*, Jan. 24, 1834, [1].

97. Howe, *Mormonism Unvailed*, 155.

98. Joseph Smith et al., Letter to "brethren in Christ Jesus scattered abroad," Jan. 22, 1834, JS Letterbook 1, 79–80 (*JSP*, D3:409–11).

about their safety following the public disclosure of the Kirtland leadership's plan to retake Zion by force. In a March 1834 letter to Partridge, Phelps, and other Missouri leaders, Smith indicated that the decision to publish the revelation was based on the fact that it had already gone "into the hands of the world by stealth, through the means of <u>false</u> brethren." Because the Kirtland leadership worried that the revelation would "reach the ears of the President and Governor, with a false coloring, being misrepresented," they decided to publish it themselves "in its own proper light."[99] If Dunklin read the revelation, he no doubt concluded he was dealing with dangerous religious fanatics and that it would be unwise to encourage or associate himself with them in what could escalate into a full-fledged conflict between the two parties.

More Blessings

Smith and the elders met in Kirtland on December 18, 1833, to dedicate the new printing press, which was confirmed by Rigdon and Hyrum Smith. They then printed a compositor's "take" of the first issue of the *Evening and the Morning Star* to be published in Kirtland with Cowdery as the new editor.[100]

Later that day, as Smith dictated an account of the dedication for his journal with Cowdery as scribe, the former suddenly began pronouncing blessings for Cowdery and several Smith family members. Concerning Cowdery, Smith said: "Blessed of the Lord is bro Oliver nevertheless there are two evils in him that he must needs forsake or he cannot altogeth[er] escape the buffettings of the advers[ar]y[.] if he shall forsak these evils he shall be forgiven and shall be made like unto the bow which the Lord hath set in the heavens he shall be a sign and an ensign unto the nations."[101] These two evils are never identified. Based on statements Brigham Young and others made in Utah, D. Michael Quinn has suggested: "In 1833 newly married Cowdery had either committed adultery or entered into an unauthorized plural marriage which Smith defined as adulterous."[102] This does not seem likely given the fact that Cowdery would later accuse Smith of the same thing, which would have opened him up to Smith's countercharge, and sexual impropriety was never mentioned in the list of nine offenses when

---

99. Joseph Smith, Letter to Edward Partridge, William W. Phelps, and other members of the United Firm, Mar. 30, 1834, Cowdery, Letterbook, 33–34 (*JSP*, D3:493).

100. Smith, Journal, Dec. 18, 1833 (*JSP*, J1:21).

101. Smith, Journal, Dec. 18, 1833 (*JSP*, J1:21–23). Cf. Isa. 5:26; 11:12. When copying his blessing into the Patriarchal Blessing Book in October 1835, Cowdery expanded it but deleted this part. Patriarchal Blessing Book 1, 12 (*JSP*, D5:512).

102. Quinn, *The Mormon Hierarchy*, 17.

Cowdery was excommunicated in April 1838. Other historians, including myself, reject the accusations of Young and other Utah Mormons against Cowdery as suspiciously convenient and unpersuasive.[103]

Rather, the phrase "two evils in him" seems to imply character flaws. An April 1830 revelation warned Cowdery to "beware of pride, lest thou shouldst enter into temptation."[104] Based on the April 1838 charges against Cowdery, Mormon writers Hyrum M. Smith and Janne M. Sjodahl suggested that "*pride* and covetousness were the sins that beset him."[105] Among other things, Cowdery was charged with selling his Jackson County lands contrary revelation, seeking "filthy lucre" through the practice of law, refusing to submit to church authorities in his temporal affairs, and writing an insulting letter to the Missouri leaders.[106]

Despite Cowdery's character flaws, Smith saw other traits worthy of his blessing: "Behold he is blessed of the Lord for his constancy and steadfastness in the work of the Lord wherefore he shall be blessed in his generation and they shall never be cut off and he shall be helped out of many troubles and if he keep the commandments and harken unto the council of the Lord his rest shall be glorious."[107]

At the same time, Smith pronounced blessings on his parents. "Blessed is my mother for her soul is ever fill[ed] with benevolence and philanthropy … and shall be comforted in the midst of her house and she shall have eternal life." Concerning his father, he said: "Blessed is my father for the hand of the Lord shall be over him for he shall see the affliction of his children pass away and when his head is fully ripe he shall behold himself as an olive tree whose branches are bowed down with much fruit he shall also possess a mansion on high."[108]

Smith then pronounced blessings on his brothers. Hyrum was blessed "for the integrity of his heart," and promised that "he shall be a shaft in the hand of his God to execute Judgment upon his enemies." Samuel was blessed because the Lord will call him by name and "he shall be made a teache[r] in the hous of the Lord." William's blessing is noteworthy, being described as "the fi[e]rce Lion who divideth not the spoil because of his strength and in

103. Compton, *In Sacred Loneliness*, 645; Hales, *Joseph Smith's Polygamy*, 1:134–36; Hales, "'Guilty of Such Folly?'"; Lawrence Foster, *Religion and Sexuality*, 300n35.

104. Revelation, Apr. 1830-A, Revelation Book 1, 29 [D&C 23:1] (*JSP*, D1:131).

105. Smith and Sjodahl, *Doctrine and Covenants Commentary*, 119–20.

106. Minutes, Apr. 12, 1838, Minute Book 2, 118–19 (*JSP*, D6:85–97).

107. Smith, Journal, Dec. 18, 1833 (*JSP*, J1:23).

108. Smith.

the pride of his heart he will neglect the more weighty matters until his soul is bowed down in sorrow and then he shall return and call on th[e] name of his God and shall find forgivness and shall wax valient … notwithstanding his rebelious heart."[109]

Finally, Smith asked God to bless "the residue [his sisters?] of my fathers house" that they may "ever come up in remembrance before thee that thou mayest save them from the hand of the oppressor and establish their feet upon the rock of ages that they may have place in thy house and be saved in thy kingdom."[110]

Case against Hurlbut

By mid-December 1833, Philastus Hurlbut was giving lectures in the Kirtland area against Smith and the Book of Mormon.[111] His lectures included readings from affidavits he had collected the previous four months in Ohio, New York, Pennsylvania, and Massachusetts. "Hurlbut returned to Ohio and lectured on the Origin of Mormonism and the Book of Mormon," Howe remembered. "I heard him Lecture in Painesville."[112] Howe was so impressed with Hurlbut's findings that he would include them in his book *Mormonism Unvailed* published in the fall of 1834.

During the previous August and September, Hurlbut had visited the relatives and friends of the late Solomon Spalding (Spaulding) in Conneaut, Ohio, and Springfield, Pennsylvania, who testified that the Book of Mormon's narrative, including its plots and characters, even down to the names, were virtually identical to a manuscript novel Spalding had shared with them twenty years earlier. Spalding, a graduate of Dartmouth College and former minister, had moved to New Salem (now Conneaut) in 1809 and soon began writing a romance about the ancient builders of the earthen mounds found in the region. Failing in business and health, he moved to Amity (now Pittsburgh), Pennsylvania, where he spent his last years writing and reading portions of his manuscript to friends and neighbors until his death in 1816.[113]

In an attempt to track down the incriminating manuscript, Hurlbut visited Spalding's widow, Matilda Spalding Davidson, in Massachusetts. While she had "no distinct knowledge" of the manuscript's contents, she told him her husband's papers were stored at a cousin's house in Otsego County, New

---

109. Smith (*JSP*, J1:23–24).
110. Smith (*JSP*, J1:24).
111. Winchester, *The Origin of the Spaulding Story*, 9–11.
112. Howe, Affidavit, Apr. 8, 1885.
113. Whittier and Stathis, "The Enigma of Solomon Spalding."

York.[114] The untitled manuscript Hurlbut found was obviously not the source of the Book of Mormon but instead described the accidental discovery by fourth-century Roman sailors of an already settled New World.[115] Hurlbut's witnesses and others subsequently insisted that Spalding had written another manuscript titled "Manuscript Found," which was written in a biblical style and based on the popular theory that the American Indians were descended from the lost ten tribes of Israel.[116]

The Spalding theory became the dominant theory of the Book of Mormon's origin during the nineteenth century because it provided an explanation for the assumption that a twenty-three-year-old farmer with a limited education could not have produced a book of any quality. As early as 1831, the supposition that Smith was too ignorant to have authored the Book of Mormon prompted some to speculate that Rigdon was the real author.[117] Howe admitted that he had no "positive proof" to connect Rigdon with Mormon origins, but he nevertheless speculated that while Rigdon was living in Pittsburgh in 1823 or 1824, he may have removed Spalding's manuscript from the printing office of Patterson & Lambdin, where Spalding's manuscript presumably laid for nearly a decade.[118]

The Spalding theory thrived because it was commonly believed that Smith dictated to his scribes from behind a curtain, where they imagined he was reading from a manuscript prepared by Rigdon, which combined Spalding's historical narrative with Rigdon's theology. This view of translation was derived from Howe's publication of a February 1834 letter from Charles Anthon, a professor of classics at Columbia University who had been visited by Martin Harris in 1828 seeking his opinion about a sample of characters said to have been copied from the gold plates of the Book of Mormon. During his interview with the "simple-hearted farmer," Anthon learned that Smith claimed to translate with a "large pair of spectacles" from "behind a curtain, in the garret of a farm house."[119] In fact, however, Smith quickly discarded the plates and spectacles, came out from behind the curtain, and dictated in

---

114. Howe, *Mormonism Unvailed*, 287–88; Dickinson, *New Light on Mormonism*, 22.

115. This manuscript is now in the library of Oberlin College, Oberlin, Ohio, a transcription of which is available in Jackson, ed., *Manuscript Found*.

116. Vogel, *Indian Origins and the Book of Mormon*, 35–52.

117. Bennett, Diary, Aug. 7–8, 1831; [James Gordon Bennett], "Mormonism—Religious Fanaticism—Church and State Party," Part I, *Morning Courier and Enquirer*, Sep. 24, 1831 (*EMD*, 3:282, 289).

118. Howe, *Mormonism Unvailed*, 100, 289–90.

119. Charles Anthon to E. D. Howe, Feb. 17, 1834, Howe, *Mormonism Unvailed*, 270 (*EMD*, 4:379).

the open with his face buried in his hat and his money-digging seer stone in the crown, claiming the characters and translation appeared in the spiritual light emanating from the stone. According to eye-witnesses—Emma Smith, Martin Harris, David Whitmer, and others—the stone-in-hat method was used for the entire Book of Mormon as well as much of the manuscript that Martin Harris lost in 1828.[120]

There is no reason to doubt the sincerity of either Hurlbut or his witnesses, who were trying to recover twenty-year-old memories about a manuscript dealing with a similar theme as the recently read Book of Mormon. They were sincere, but their memories had played a trick on them. Perhaps they were victims of what psychologists today call false memory syndrome, wherein vague memories are augmented through suggestion.[121] As an untrained interviewer, Hurlbut may have asked leading questions and unintentionally influenced the outcome of his investigation. The Spalding theory has fallen into disrepute among most serious students of the subject in favor of Smith as the sole author, at least for those seeking a naturalistic explanation.[122]

In November and December 1833 Hurlbut had also collected affidavits from the residents of Palmyra and Manchester, New York, regarding Smith's character and early career as a treasure seer. He also solicited and received a letter from Smith's father-in-law, Isaac Hale, living in Harmony, Pennsylvania, post-marked December 22, 1833. Hurlbut's trip to the Palmyra area was probably inspired by the affidavit appearing in the *Painesville Telegraph* in 1831 regarding Smith's treasure-seeking activities and signed by ten Palmyra residents.[123] From Willard Chase, a near-neighbor of the Smiths, Hurlbut learned that Smith had obtained a seer stone while digging a well on the Chase property in 1822. According to Chase, who claimed he was the real owner of the stone, "Joseph put it into his hat, and then his face into the top of his hat," and in the darkness he claimed that "he could see in it." Chase said, "After obtaining the stone, he began to publish abroad what wonders he could discover by looking in it."[124] Other neighbors supplied stories recounting specific instances of Smith using the stone to locate

---

120. Lancaster, "The Translation of the Book of Mormon"; Vogel, *Joseph Smith*, 120, 382.

121. Loftus, "Memory Malleability"; Loftus and Pickrell, "The Formation of False Memories"; Zaragoza and Mitchell, "Repeated Exposure to Suggestion and the Creation of False Memories."

122. Bush, "The Spalding Theory Then and Now"; Roper, "The Mythical 'Manuscript Found'"; see my comments in Vogel, ed., *Mormonism Unvailed*, 408–12.

123. Unidentified Palmyra Resident [Abner Cole?] to Editor, Mar. 12, 1831, *Painesville Telegraph*, Mar. 22, 1831, 2 (*EMD*, 3:8–10).

124. Howe, *Mormonism Unvailed*, 240–41 (*EMD*, 3:65–66).

buried treasures, which no amount of ceremonial magic incantations and digging could uncover. According to these accounts, Smith explained away such failures by appealing to folk-magic lore about guardian spirits who protected the treasures from discovery by moving them through the earth by magic enchantment to another location.[125]

Chase also gave Hurlbut an account of the discovery of the gold plates, which he had obtained from Joseph Sr. in 1827, that fit comfortably with treasure-seeking lore about guardian spirits and seemed to be an extension of Smith's previous activities as a treasure seer. According to his account, Joseph Jr. had learned of the plates from an apparition of "a spirit," who instructed him to go to the place of burial dressed in black and riding a black horse. Upon arriving at the spot, he located the large stone that was the lid of the stone box containing the plates. After removing the plates and setting them on the ground, he replaced the stone lid but was surprised to discover the plates had disappeared. Again removing the lid, he found that the plates had magically returned to the box but was "hindered" when he tried to remove them. He then noticed there was something else in the box that looked "like a toad, which assumed the appearance of a man, and struck him on the side of his head." Smith made two more attempts to gain possession of the plates, each time being struck by the spirit, the last knocking him "three or four rods, and hurt him prodigiously." When Smith inquired why he could not have the plates, the spirit said he had not followed orders precisely in setting the plates down and not leaving immediately. The spirit then instructed Smith to return in one year and to bring his brother Alvin with him. However, Alvin died in the interim, which prevented Smith from getting the plates until he could find someone to replace him. Three years later, Smith took his new wife, Emma, to the location and, as he claimed, obtained the plates.[126] Excluding the transforming toad, Chase's account can be corroborated by friendly sources such as Lucy Smith, Joseph Knight Sr., and Martin Harris.[127]

Hurlbut's affidavits were explosive, and Smith and leading Mormons did little more than to dismiss them as lies. On January 13, 1834, Cowdery wrote to his brother in New York that "Hurlbut is now in this country pedling slanders."[128] On January 22 Orson Hyde writing to Missouri church leaders

---

125. The most comprehensive examination of the Smith family's early involvement in treasure searching and the folk-magic context of Joseph Smith's discovery of the gold plates is Quinn, *Early Mormonism and the Magic World View*.

126. Howe, *Mormonism Unvailed*, 238–39 (*EMD*, 3:66–72).

127. See Quinn, *Early Mormonism and the Magic World View*, 136–77.

128. Oliver Cowdery, Letter to Lyman Cowdery, Jan. 13, 1834, Cowdery, Letterbook, 22.

on behalf of the Kirtland presidency mentioned that "Doctor P[hilastus] Hurlbut ... has been to the State of New York and gathered up all the rediculous stories that could be invented and some affidavits respecting the character of Bro Joseph and the Smith family and he exhibeted them to numerous congregations in Chagrin Kirtland Mentor and Painesville and fired the minds of the people with much indignation against Bro Joseph and the Church."[129]

Hurlbut's anger toward the Mormon leader grew to the point of issuing death threats against Smith. George A. Smith, who became one of the prophet's bodyguards during this time, remembered that "in delivering lectures he [Hurlbut] had said he would wash his hands in Joseph Smith's blood."[130] Hyde's letter on behalf of the presidency mentioned that "Hurlbut also made many harsh threats &c that he would take the life of Bro Joseph if he could not distroy Mormonism without."[131]

Smith took legal action against Hurlbut on December 21, 1833, when he filed a complaint against him with Kirtland justice of the peace John C. Dowen, which stated that he had reason to fear that Hurlbut "would Beat wound or Kill him or injure his property." Dowen issued an arrest warrant for Hurlbut, who was brought before Painesville justice William Holbrook on January 4. Holbrook ordered Hurlbut to remain in custody until the preliminary examination, which was set to begin on January 13.[132]

Meanwhile, persecution against the Mormons in the Kirtland area escalated. One non-Mormon resident of nearby Mentor noted on January 6 that a group had "threatend mob[b]ing" the Mormons and observed that "Smith has four or five armed men to gard him every night."[133] Cowdery wrote that on the night of the 8th their enemies "came out ... about 12 o'clock at night, a little west & fired cannon, we suppose to alarm us, but no one was frightened, but all prepared to defend ourselves if they made a

129. Smith et al., Letter to "brethren in Christ Jesus scattered abroad," Jan. 22, 1834, JS Letterbook 1, 81 (*JSP*, D3:411).

130. George A. Smith, "Historical Discourse," Nov. 15, 1864, *Journal of Discourses*, 11:8.

131. Smith et al., Letter to "brethren in Christ Jesus scattered abroad," Jan. 22, 1834, JS Letterbook 1, 81 (*JSP*, D3:411–12).

132. Ohio v. D. P. Hurlbut, Mar. 31, 1834, Geauga Co., OH, Court of Common Pleas, Final Record, vol. P, 431–32. Dowen later claimed that when Hurlbut said he would "kill" Joseph Smith, "he meant he would kill Mormonism." Dowen, Statement, Jan. 2, 1885, 3.

133. B. F. Norris, Letter to Mark Norris, Jan. 6, 1834, Mark Norris Papers, Burton Historical Collection, Detroit Public Library, MI, as cited in Grua, "Joseph Smith and the 1834 D. P. Hurlbut Case," 38.

sally upon our houses."[134] Concerning this persecution, Heber C. Kimball remembered: "Our enemies were raging and threatening destruction upon us, and we had to guard ourselves night after night, and for weeks were not permitted to take off our clothes, and were obliged to lay with our fire locks in our arms."[135] Smith had earlier expressed his fear that events in Jackson County might be repeated in Ohio.[136]

On January 13–15 Smith attended the preliminary hearing of *Ohio v. Doctor Philastus Hurlbut* at Painesville. Heber C. Kimball later recalled: "I carried him [Smith] from Kirtland to Painesville, with four or five others, in my wagon every morning for five days, and brought them back in the evening. We were often waylaid, but managed to elude our enemies by rapid driving and taking different roads."[137]

Sixteen witnesses, including Smith (who was represented by Benjamin Bissell), testified of Hurlbut's alleged threat against the Mormon prophet.[138] Hurlbut's attorney, James A. Briggs, who mistakenly reversed the circumstances of the legal action, later recalled that the proceedings "attracted a great deal of curiosity" and that court was held in "the old Methodist Church in Painesville," which "was filled to overflowing."[139] According to Briggs, "During the examination I said to Bissel, 'Let us get a statement from Smith of how he found the golden plates of the Mormon Bible.' Bissel at first objected to my question, but then withdrew the objection, and then Prophet Smith told us the whole story of digging for and the finding of the plates in Palmyra, N.Y. Smith testified that in digging he touched the plates. He was kicked by an unseen power out of the hole in the earth."[140] On another occasion, Briggs said: "During the examination of Smith, he gave the history of the finding of the golden plates of the Mormon Bible, how he was kicked by the Devil when he uncovered the plates and stooped down to get them. It was an interesting story; and, although it had nothing to do with the case

134. Oliver Cowdery, Letter to W. W. Phelps and John Whitmer, Jan. 21, 1834, Cowdery, Letterbook, 22.

135. "Elder Kimball's Journal," *Times and Seasons*, Jan. 15, 1845, 771.

136. Joseph Smith, Letter to Edward Partridge, Dec. 5, 1833, JS Letterbook 1, 67–69 (*JSP*, D3:371–72).

137. "Elder Kimball's Journal," *Times and Seasons*, Jan. 15, 1845, 771.

138. Ohio v. D. P. Hurlbut, Mar. 31, 1834, Geauga Co., OH, Court of Common Pleas, Final Record, vol. P, 431–32.

139. James A. Briggs, Letter to John Codman, Mar. 1875, *International Review* (New York, NY), Sep. 1881, 222.

140. James A. Briggs, Statement to Arthur Deming, Mar. 22, 1886, *Naked Truths about Mormonism* (Oakland, CA), Jan. 1888, 4 (*EMD*, 1:206).

under investigation, the Court, his own attorney, and the people all desired to hear the narration, and it came out under oath."[141]

The court ruled in Smith's favor and affirmed that he indeed "had reason to fear" Hurlbut. Justice Holbrook ordered Hurlbut to "enter into a recognizance to keep the peace generally and especallly towards" Smith and to appear before the court of common pleas at the start of its next term on March 31, 1834.[142] Writing on behalf of the presidency on January 22, Orson Hyde said: "Bro Joseph took him with a peace warrant and after 3 days trial and investigating the merits of our religion in the town of Painesville by able attorney[s] on both sides he was bound over to the County Court. thus his influence was pritty much distroyed, and since the trial the spirit of hostility seames to be broken down in a good degree but how long it will continue so we cannot say."[143] Cowdery reported that one "very grave judge" boasted that Hurlbut was only bound over to appear at the County Court in Chardon, so that "the lawyers might have a fair opportunity of *rediculing*, and *scandalizing*, Jo. Smith, as he was pleased to call him."[144]

Despite his success against Hurlbut, Smith and his followers in the Kirtland area continued to experience persecution. On January 31, Oliver A. Crary, the township clerk, filed the names of twenty-two heads of households (including Smith, Joseph Smith Sr., Rigdon, Hyrum Smith, Samuel Smith, John Smith, Zebedee Coltrin, and John Murdock) who had been formally warned out of town by the overseers of the poor for Kirtland Township.[145] The order was issued to Constable William G. Crary on October 21, 1833, but not returned for more than three months.

Described as "the earliest known anti-Mormon actions taken by local government officials against [Joseph Smith] and his followers in Ohio," these warnings out were typically perfunctory actions taken by the overseers to avoid the financial responsibility of caring for the poor, but they may have also been used by Kirtland officials to prevent legal residence and thus deny the Mormons of their right to vote.[146] Howe later explained that

---

141. James A. Briggs, Letter to John Codman, Mar. 1875, *International Review*, Sep. 1881, 222.

142. Ohio v. D. P. Hurlbut, Mar. 31, 1834, Geauga Co., OH, Court of Common Pleas, Final Record, vol. P, 431–32.

143. Joseph Smith et al., Letter to "brethren in Christ Jesus scattered abroad," Jan. 22, 1834, JS Letterbook 1, 81 (*JSP*, D3:411–12).

144. Oliver Cowdery, Editorial, *The Evening and the Morning Star*, Apr. 1834, 150.

145. Roswell D. Cottrell and John Parks, Warrant, Kirtland Township, Geauga Co., OH, to William G. Crary, Oct. 21, 1833, Kirtland Township Trustees Minutes, 114–15. Filed Jan. 31, 1834 (*JSP*, D3:325–31).

146. *JSP*, D3:326. Benton, *Warning Out in New England*.

tensions between Mormons and other residents of Kirtland were exacerbated by "boasts that in a short time they [the Mormons] would control all the county offices and elect a member of Congress from their own ranks." Consequently, Howe continued, "many of our citizens thought it advisable to take all the legal means within their reach to counteract the progress of so dangerous an enemy in their midst, and many law suits ensued."[147] These warnings out may have been a part of the strategy described by Howe.

On the same day that clerk Crary copied the warrant authorizing the warnings out into the township minutes, the *Painesville Telegraph* published a statement of intent by a committee of ten men, including Crary, which had been "appointed by a public meeting held in Kirtland … for the purpose of ascertaining the origin of the Book of Mormon" and "to avert the evils which threaten the Public by the location in this vicinity, of Joseph Smith Jun. otherwise known as the Mormon Prophet—and who is now, under pretence of Divine Authority, collecting about him an impoverished population, alienated in feeling from other portions of the community, thereby threatening us with an insupportable weight of pauperism."[148] The committee also announced that Hurlbut's research and findings would soon be published.

---

147. Howe, *Autobiography and Recollections of a Pioneer Printer*, 44–45.
148. "To the Public," *Painesville Telegraph,* Jan. 31, 1834, [3].

15

Redeeming Zion

JANUARY–MAY 1834

Behold I say unto you, the redemption of Zion must needs come by
power.
— *Revelation, Feb. 24, 1834, Orson Hyde and Orson Pratt,*
Notebook of Revelations, [11], CHL [D&C 103:15]

Bishop Partridge presided over a conference in Clay County, Missouri, on January 1, 1834. The conference decided to send Parley P. Pratt and Lyman Wight to confer with the presidency in Ohio about the situation in Missouri.[1] Pratt later said that he and Wight were sent "to counsel with President Smith and the Church at Kirtland, and take some measures for the relief or restoration of the people thus plundered and driven from their homes."[2] A plan to restore the Mormons to their homes would necessarily involve force. On December 15 Phelps wrote to Smith and explained that "Governor [Dunklin] is willing to restore us, but as the constitution gives him no power to guard us, when back, we are not willing to go. The mob sware, if we come *we shall die!*"[3] The obvious solution was for the Saints to provide their own protection, and the need for a larger force may have led Pratt and Wight to meet with the Kirtland leadership. They were unaware that Smith had already dictated a revelation commanding him to gather "the strength of mine house which are my wariors my young men and they that are of middle age" and go "straitway" to Missouri and redeem Zion by armed force if necessary.[4] Wight may have been chosen to accompany Pratt because of his leading role

---

1. JS History, vol. A-1, 413 (DHC 2:1); Pratt, *Autobiography*, 114; John Whitmer, Day Book, Jan. 1, 1834.
2. Pratt, *Autobiography*, 114.
3. William W. Phelps, Letter to "Dear Brethren," Dec. 15, 1833, "Later from Missouri," *The Evening and the Morning Star* (Kirtland, OH), Jan. 1834, 128 (*JSP*, D3:384); italics in original.
4. Revelation, Dec. 16–17, 1833, Revelation Book 2, 77–78 [D&C 101:55–57] (*JSP*, D3:393–94).

during the previous conflict. According to Wight's journal, he and Pratt left Missouri on January 12 and arrived in Kirtland on February 22.[5]

Advice

On January 22 Smith, Rigdon, and Williams wrote to the scattered Saints and their leaders in their Clay County asylum in response to Phelps's December 15, 1833, letter asking "what is best to do ... *till Zion is redeemed!*"[6] Regarding the inability of the governor to provide a standing army to protect the Mormons after being returned to their homes, the presidency instructed them to petition Dunklin "and pray him to notify the [US] President of your situation and also petition the President yourselves according to the direction of the Lord."[7] The December 16–17, 1833, revelation had commanded Missouri church leaders to "importune at the feet of the President," which was not done until the following April.[8] "We exhort you to prosecute and try every lawful means to bring the mob to Justice as fast as circumstances will permit," Smith, Rigdon, and Williams wrote. "With regard to your tarrig [tarrying] in Clay county we cannot say you must be governed by circumstances. perhaps you will have to hire out or take farms to cultivate to obtain your bread until the Lord deliver."[9] Clearly, the redemption of Zion was going to take longer than Parley P. Pratt had prophesied.

The letter mentioned that a petition signed by sixty Mormon men had been sent to Dunklin about a week earlier, along with a printed copy of the December revelation, and that the same would soon be done for the president. "We Shall do all that is in our power to assist you in every way we can," they promised. "We know your case is a trying one but be patient and not murmr against the Lord and you shall see that all these things shall turn to your greatest good." Yet the overall message of the letter was disappointing. "We shall not be able to send you any more money at present unless the Lord put it into our hands unexpectedly," they wrote, but assured, "our calls for money

---

5. Wight, Journal, 401–402 (Jan. 12, 1834).

6. William W. Phelps, Letter to "Dear Brethren," Dec. 15, 1833, "Later from Missouri," *The Evening and the Morning Star*, Jan. 1834, 128 (*JSP*, D3:385); italics in original.

7. Joseph Smith, Sidney Rigdon, and Frederick G. Williams, Letter to "brethren in Christ Jesus scattered abroad," Jan. 22, 1834, JS Letterbook 1, 79 (*JSP*, D3:409).

8. Revelation, Dec. 16–17, 1833, Revelation Book 2, 82 [D&C 101:88] (*JSP*, D3:396); Partridge et al., Petition to Andrew Jackson, Apr. 10, 1834, in Phelps, Collection of Missouri Documents; Sidney Gilbert et al., Letter to Andrew Jackson, Apr. 10, 1834, in Phelps, Collection of Missouri Documents; William W. Phelps et al., Letter to Daniel Dunklin, Apr. 10, 1834, in Phelps, Collection of Missouri Documents.

9. Joseph Smith et al., Letter to "brethren in Christ Jesus scattered abroad," Jan. 22, 1834, JS Letterbook 1, 80 (*JSP*, D3:410).

are many and pressing."[10] The December revelation had instructed that all the branches of the church were to "gather to gether all their monies" and purchase "all the Land which can be purchaced in Jackson County and the counties round about."[11] Nothing was certain at this point, but "there is a prospect of the eastern churches doing something pretty handsome toward the deliverance of Zion in the course of a year if Zion is not delivered otherwise."[12]

Referring to the December revelation, the presidency reminded the Missouri leaders that it said "this affliction came upon you because of your sin [thereby] polluting your inheritances &c" (D&C 101:1–2, 6), and then added, "yet there is an exception of some namely the heads of Zion for the Lord said your brethren in Zion begin to repent, and the Angels rejoice over them &c."[13] The second part is a reference to a March 1833 revelation that dealt with the reconciliation of Missouri and Ohio leaders and had nothing to do with exempting leaders from the subsequent revelation's accusation of sins. Indeed, the Missouri leaders had only *begun* to repent but still had "many things to repent of" and that "the Lord will contend with Zion and plead with her strong ones." The March revelation therefore did not exclude the leadership in its pronouncement that "your brethren" in Missouri "have been afflicted in consequence of their transgressions."[14] Neither were they exempt from the December revelation's accusation that Zion had been afflicted because of sin. In their letter, the presidency sidestepped the implications of Smith's August 1833 revelation that declared the church in Zion was forgiven and promised protection, which had been dictated before Smith learned that his followers had already signed an agreement to leave Jackson County.[15] Now, in their January 1834 letter, the presidency declared: "Therefore this affliction came upon the Church to chastin those in transgression, and prepare the hearts of those [leaders] who had repented for an end[o]wment from the Lord."[16] This endowment was to take place in the temple in Kirtland.[17]

The presidency also mentioned that the persecution in the Kirtland area had somewhat abated, partly due to Philastus Hurlbut being placed under

10. Smith et al., Letter, 80–81 (*JSP*, D3:410–11).

11. Revelation, Dec. 16–17, 1833, Revelation Book 2, 80 [D&C 101:71–72] (*JSP*, D3:395).

12. Joseph Smith et al., Letter, Jan. 22, 1834, JS Letterbook 1, 80 (*JSP*, D3:410–11).

13. Smith et al. (*JSP*, D3:411).

14. Revelation, Mar. 8, 1833, [3], Newel K. Whitney Papers [D&C 90:34–36] (*JSP*, D3:31–32).

15. Revelation, Aug. 2, 1833-A, Revelation Book 2, 64 [D&C 97:27–28] (*JSP*, D3:203).

16. Joseph Smith et al., Letter to "brethren in Christ Jesus scattered abroad," Jan. 22, 1834, JS Letterbook 1, 80 (*JSP*, D3:411).

17. Revelation, June 1, 1833, Revelation Book 2, 59 [D&C 95:8] (*JSP*, 3:106).

bonds to keep the peace.[18] Six days later, Smith, Cowdery, and Williams prayed that Hurlbut would not succeed in his lawsuit against them and that "God would soften the hearts" of five prominent non-Mormon men that "they might obey the gospel, or, if they would not repent, that the Lord would send faithful saints, to purchase their farms, that this stake may be strengthened, and its borders enlarged, O lord, grant it for Christ's sake: Amen."[19] Together these men owned more than forty acres in the northern and eastern sections of Kirtland, as well as a sawmill and a gristmill.[20] Rather than easing tensions, the desire to convert or expel non-Mormons contributed to the persecution and opposition they were experiencing.

Trial of Martin Harris

On February 12, 1834, Smith met with the high priests and elders at his home, a two-story frame house located a little north of the cemetery and temple lot into which he had recently moved his family from the Whitney store. This meeting was called to consider certain statements made by Book of Mormon witness Martin Harris derogatory to Smith's character. Smith arose and spoke of "the dignity of the office which has been conferred upon me by the ministering of the Angel of God, by his own voice and by the voice of this Church"—that is, the office of president of the high priesthood derived charismatically from the appearance of the angel who called him to translate the Book of Mormon, various revelations, and the common consent of the membership.[21] This was perhaps to remind the council of his authority and how it was obtained, despite any character flaws they might discover in him.

Smith also reminded them of Jesus's warning not to judge too harshly: "He said, that no man was capable of judging a matter in council without his own heart was pure; and that we frequently, are so filled with prejudice, or have a beam in our own eye, that we are not capable of passing right descissions, &c." He then stressed how important it was to pay attention, not to whisper, or leave the room. "Our acts are recorded, and at a future day they will be laid before us, and if we should fail to judge right and injure our fellow beings, they may there prehaps condemn us ... beyond any

---

18. Smith et al., Letter to "brethren in Christ Jesus scattered abroad," Jan. 22, 1834, JS Letterbook 1, 81 (*JSP*, D3:411–12).

19. Joseph Smith, Journal, Jan. 28, 1834 (*JSP*, J1:27–28).

20. Portions of this land were subsequently sold to Joseph Smith on October 23, 1835, and November 2, 1836. See Geauga Co., OH, Deed Records, vol. 21, 227, Oct. 23, 1835; vol. 22, 567–68, Nov. 2, 1836, cited in *JSP*, J1:27–28n79.

21. Minutes, Feb. 12, 1834, Minute Book 1, 27 (*JSP*, D3:429).

thing which I am able to express." Finally, he reminded them of the eternal consequences of their decision: "Ask yourselves, brethrn, how much you have exercised yourselves in prayer since you heard of this Council; and if you are now prepared to sit in judgment upon the soul of your brother."[22] While ostensibly speaking on Harris's behalf, Smith was also pleading his own case.

The record then states: "Bro Joseph then went on to give us a relation of his situation at the time he obtained the record, the persecution he met with &C. He also told us of his transgressing at the time he was translateing the Book of Mormon." His transgression was in letting Harris take the translation manuscript back to Palmyra after asking the Lord three times before being told he could, which resulted in Harris's losing it. In conclusion, Smith "prophecied that he should stand and shine like the sun in the firmament when his enemies and the gainsayers of his testimony should be put down and Cut off and their names blotted out from among men."[23]

The council then considered the charges preferred against Harris by Rigdon. The charges, based on the report of Alpheus C. Russell, were that Harris had asserted that "Joseph drank too much liquor when he was translating the Book of Mormon and that he wrestled with many men and threw them &c. ... [and] that he [Harris] exalted himself above bro. Joseph, in that he said bro. Joseph knew not the contents of the book of Mormon until it was translated but that he himself knew all about it before it was translated." In his defense, "Bro. Martin said he did not tell Esqr Russell that bro. Joseph drank too much liquor while translateing the book of Mormon, but this thing took place before the book of Mormon was translated. He confessed that his mind was darkend and that he had said many things inadvertently calculateid to wound the feelings of his bretheren and promised to do better." Harris was forgiven and the council "gave him much good advice."[24]

No doubt this advice included a request for him not to speak of such matters publicly. Among other things, Hurlbut's witnesses accused Smith of drinking excessively, and with Harris confirming those accusations, it was difficult to dismiss Hurlbut's affidavits as lies.

High Council Organized

On February 17, Smith held a meeting at his house and organized the standing "Presidents Church Council," later known as the "high Council of the

---

22. Minutes, 27–28 (*JSP*, D3:429–30). Cf. Matt. 7:3–5.
23. Minutes, 28 (*JSP*, D3:430).
24. Minutes, 28–29 (*JSP*, D3:430–31).

Church of Christ," which consisted of twelve high priests "for the purpose of settling important difficulties which might arise in the church, which could not be settled by the Church, or the bishop's council to the satisfaction of the parties."[25] The members of the council were Smith's father and brother Samuel, Uncle John Smith, John Johnson and his son Luke, brothers John and Jared Carter, Oliver Cowdery, Martin Harris, Joseph Coe, Orson Hyde, and Sylvester Smith. The presidents of the high priesthood—Smith, Rigdon, and Williams—were also presidents of the Kirtland high council. By the draw of lots, Cowdery became the first speaker and would later refer to himself as the "first High Counsellor."[26]

Smith said the council was organized according to "the order of Councils in ancient days ... as shown to him by vision." He claimed the Apostle Peter was the president of the council, having been appointed by Jesus, and that he had "two men" as counselors.[27] The Kirtland council was to serve as "an ensample to the high priests in their Councils abroad." However, if the parties were not satisfied with the decision of these lower courts, they could appeal to the bishop's court, and if still unsatisfied to the "presidents Council," or Kirtland high council, "which is an end of all strife."[28] In practice, however, the council's authority was not limited to appeals but extended to deciding cases in the Kirtland stake as well as making administrative decisions and regulating church affairs.

The organizational meeting concluded with a vote proposing that "Bro Joseph" review the minutes and "make all necessary corrections by the spirit of inspiration."[29] Accordingly, on the following day, Smith "laboured ... with all the strength and wisdom that [God] had given him in making the corrections necessary." On February 19 Smith presented the corrected minutes to a council of sixty-two members of the priesthood, who, after hearing the revised minutes read three times and suggesting at least one additional correction, unanimously voted to accept them "for a form, and constitution of

25. See Minutes, Feb. 17, 1834, Minute Book 1, 29–31 (*JSP*, D3:435–39); and Revised Minutes, Feb. 18–19, 1834, Minute Book 1, 31–35 [D&C 102] (*JSP*, D3:439–44).

26. Minutes, Feb. 17, 1834, Minute Book 1, 31 (*JSP*, D3:433); JS History, 1834–36, 17 (*JSP*, H1:32).

27. Minutes, Feb. 17, 1834, Minute Book 1, 29–30 (*JSP*, D3:437).

28. Minutes, 30 (*JSP*, D3:438). This explanation of the appeals process was replaced in the revised minutes with a general statement that the council was organized "for the purpose of settling important difficulties which might arise in the church, which could not be settled by the Church, or the bishop's council to the satisfaction of the parties." Revised Minutes, Feb. 18–19, 1834, Minute Book 1, 32 [D&C 102:2] (*JSP*, D3:440).

29. Minutes, Feb. 17, 1834, Minute Book 1, 31 (*JSP*, D3:438).

the high Council of the Church of Christ hereafter." Among other things, Smith blessed his two counselors with "wisdom to magnify their office, and power over all the power of the adversary," and then blessed the twelve members of the high council with "wisdom and power to counsel in righteousness upon all subjects that might be laid before them."[30]

Smith received a blessing from his father, who said: "Joseph, I lay my hands upon thy head, and pronounc[e] the blessings of thy progenitors upon thee, that thou mayest hold the keys of the mysteries of the Kingdom of heaven until the coming of the Lord, Amen." Joseph Sr. also blessed his son Samuel, and John Johnson blessed his son Luke.[31]

Smith then charged his counselors "to do their duty in righteousness and in the fear of God," then "charged the twelve Counsellors in a similar manner, all in the name of Jesus Christ." After which the congregation "all raised [their] hands to heaven in token of the everlasting Covenant, and the Lord blessed us with his spirit." Smith declared that "the Council was organized according to the ancient order, and also according to the mind of the Lord."[32]

The first case was heard the same day, when Ezra Thayer charged Curtis Hodges with "loud speaking, and a want of clearness in articulation." The council rebuked Hodges, after which he confessed and was forgiven.[33] The next day, the council considered the case of members in Pennsylvania refusing to partake of the sacrament because the elder administering it did not observe the Word of Wisdom. They decided that transgressing the Word of Wisdom was grounds for losing one's office in the church.[34] The high council will play a key role in maintaining stability in the Mormon community.

Change of Plans

When Smith dictated the December revelation, he did not know that Dunklin had suggested that the state could provide a military escort for the Mormons returning to Jackson County, but that he was not authorized to provide a standing army to protect them once they had returned. Smith's original plan was for the Mormons to arm themselves and repossess their Jackson County lands, which could be bloody. With help from the governor and the state

---

30. Minutes, Feb. 19, 1834, Minute Book 1, 36 (*JSP*, D3:445).

31. Minutes, 37 (*JSP*, D3:446).

32. Minutes, 37.

33. Minutes, 38–39 (*JSP*, D3:447–48).

34. Minutes, Feb. 20, 1834, Minute Book 1, 39–40 (*JSP*, D3:451–52). The council's decision was published in "To the Churches of Latter Day Saints," *LDS Messenger and Advocate*, Nov. 1836, 412.

militia, the Jackson Countians would be less likely to resist. Once reestablished on their lands, the Mormons could provide their own protection.[35]

On January 7, 1834, Cowdery wrote to Samuel Bent in Pontiac, Michigan, and mentioned the recent reception of correspondence from Missouri that informed them that "there was a prospect that the Governor of Missouri was about to reinstate the brethren upon their land."[36] On January 13, Cowdery wrote to his brother Lyman: "I have been informed that the governor of that state has offered to reinstate my friends again upon their own lands and also has issued his proclamation to call out three hundred men from the adjoining counties that a court might be held."[37] One source of Cowdery's information was probably the reception of Phelps's December 15 letter, which explained that Missouri Mormons were unwilling to take up the governor's offer to restore them to their lands because they feared what the mob would do once the government troops withdrew.[38]

Two days after arriving in Kirtland from Missouri, Pratt and Wight appeared before the Kirtland high council on Feb. 24, 1834, as "representatives from Zion, to represent ... the state of the Church in that place."[39] They asked the council, "When, how and by what means Zion was to be redeemed from our enemies"? The council reported that the exiled Mormons were comfortably situated in Clay County, "but the idea of being driven away from the land of Zion pained their very souls and they desired of God, by earnest prayer, to return with songs of everlasting joy as said Isaiah, the Prophet." They also reported that "none of their lands were sold into the hands of our enemies except a piece owned by bro. Wm. E. Mc.Lellin of thirty acres which he sold into the hands of the enemy, and seven acres more which he would have sold to the enemy if a brother had not come forward & purchased it and paid him his money."[40]

Smith arose before the council and the large congregation that had gathered at his house and declared that "he was going to Zion to assist in

---

35. See Crawley and Anderson, "The Political and Social Realities of Zion's Camp."

36. Oliver Cowdery, Letter to Samuel Bent, Jan. 7, 1834, Cowdery, Letterbook, 18.

37. Oliver Cowdery, Letter to Lyman Cowdery, Jan. 13, 1834, Cowdery Letterbook, 20.

38. William W. Phelps, Letter to "Dear Brethren," Dec. 15, 1833, "Later from Missouri," *The Evening and the Morning Star* (Independence, MO), Jan. 1834, 128 (*JSP*, D3:382–86).

39. Minutes, Feb. 24, 1834, Minute Book 1, 41 (*JSP*, D3:454). According to Lyman Wight, he and Pratt left Missouri on January 12, 1834, and arrived in Kirtland on February 22. Wight, Journal, 401–402 (Jan. 12, 1834).

40. Minutes, Feb. 24, 1834, Minute Book 1, 41–42 (*JSP*, D3:456). According to land records, McLellin sold nearly seven acres of Jackson County land to church member James Newberry on December 14, 1833. However, there is no extant record of McLellin making another sale in late 1833 or early 1834. *JSP*, 3:456n200.

redeeming it." After requesting the council to sanction his going to Zion, which was given "without a dissenting voice," Smith called for volunteers. About thirty to forty men came forward. It was decided that they would go by land, and Smith was nominated and accepted as the "Commander in Chief of the Armies of Israel and the leader of those who volunteered to go and assist in the redemption of Zion"[41]

According to McLellin, "Wight being fully imbued with the war spirit he soon got an order issued by the Presidency to the entire church to gather up their munitions of war, and come up to Kirtland the first of May."[42] As leader of the armed defense of the Mormons in Jackson County, Wight was an eager militant. However, McLellin was unaware that Smith had already decided to respond with force before the arrival of Wight and Pratt. What changed with their arrival was a sense of urgency. It was time to make the allegory in the December revelation reality. As historians Peter Crawley and Richard L. Anderson observed, "Joseph Smith had little choice but to respond with a pledge of help from the Church in Kirtland. His failure to do so at this critical juncture would certainly have been interpreted as an abandonment of the Missouri Saints. All at the council meeting must have been convinced that the time for the redemption of the nobleman's vineyard spoken of in the parable was at hand."[43]

On the same day, Smith dictated a revelation about the persecution and redemption of Zion. In the voice of God, Smith declared: "I will give unto you a revelation & commandment, that you may know how to act in the discharge of your duties concerning the salvation & redemption of your brethren who have been scattered from the land of Zion." The revelation explained that Zion was to be "chastened for a little season, with a sore & grievous chastisement; because they did not hearken all together unto the precepts & commandments which I gave unto them."[44] The qualifying phrase "all together" placed blame on the Missouri church as a whole for its lack of unity and conformity not just to the commandments but to unspecified precepts. The December revelation had stated that Smith's followers were expelled from Jackson County because "there were jar[r]ings and contentions envyings and strifes and lustful and covetous desires" among them.[45]

---

41. Minutes, Feb. 24, 1834, Minute Book 1, 42 (*JSP*, D3:456–57).

42. Larson and Passey, *William E. McLellin Papers*, 418.

43. Crawley and Anderson, "The Political and Social Realities of Zion's Camp," 411.

44. Revelation, Feb. 24, 1834, in Hyde and Pratt, Notebook of Revelations, [7]–[8] [D&C 103:1, 4] (*JSP*, D3:459–60).

45. Revelation, Dec. 16–17, 1833, Revelation Book 2, 73 [D&C 101:6–7] (*JSP*, D3:389).

The need to maintain group purity and harmony thus made the organization of the high council all the more vital.

The revelation predicted the return of the exiled Mormons to Jackson County: "I have decreed that your brethren who have been scattered shall return to the lands of their inheritances & build up the waste places of Zion; for after much tribulation, as I have said unto you in a former commandment, commeth the blessing."[46] This passage combined two previous revelations with Smith's reasoning as articulated in his December 10, 1833, letter to the Missouri leaders. "I would remind you of a certain clause in one [revelation] which says that after much <u>tribulation</u> cometh the <u>blessing</u>," Smith wrote.[47] Smith's use of the August 1831 revelation was questionable since the revelation attempted to explain the persecution, not the complete removal, of the Mormons in Jackson County. In the same letter, Smith prayed: "O My God! ... I ask thee in the name of Jesus Christ, to return thy people unto their homes, & there inheritances, to enjoy the fruit of their Labors; that all the waste places may be built up."[48] This also found its way into Smith's December 16–17 revelation, which predicted that the children of Zion "shall return and come to their inheritances they and their children with songs of everlasting joy to build up the waste places of Zion and all these things that the prophets might be fulfilled."[49]

The revelation instructed Smith to organize armed companies and march to Jackson County for the relief of Missouri followers. "Behold I say unto you, that the redemtion of Zion must needs come by power; therefore, I will raise up unto my people a man who shall lead them like as Moses led the children of Israel; for ... ye must needs be led out of bondage by power, & with a stretched out arm. ... Therefore, let my servant Joseph, say unto the strength of my house, my young men, & the middle aged, Gather ye together unto the land of Zion."[50] This revelation declared that Smith was the servant in the allegory of the vineyard in the December revelation, who was commanded to gather "the strength of mine house which are my wariors my young men and they that are of middle age" and go "straitway" to Missouri

46. Revelation, Feb. 24, 1834, in Hyde and Pratt, Notebook of Revelations, [9]–[10] [D&C 103:11–12] (*JSP*, D3:460).

47. Joseph Smith, Letter to Edward Partridge and Others, Dec. 10, 1833, JS Letterbook 1, 71 (*JSP*, D3:376); Revelation, Aug. 1, 1831, Revelation Book 1, 94 [D&C 58:3–4] (*JSP*, D2:14).

48. Smith, Letter to Partridge and Others, JS Letterbook 1, 75 (*JSP*, D3:381).

49. Revelation, Dec. 16–17, 1833, Revelation Book 2, 73 [D&C 101:18–19] (*JSP*, D3:389). Cf. Isa. 51:3.

50. Revelation, Feb. 24, 1834, in Hyde and Pratt, Notebook of Revelations, [11]–[13] [D&C 103:15–17, 22] (*JSP*, D3:460–61).

and redeem Zion: "Break down the walls of mine enemies th[r]ow down their tower and scatte[r] their watchmen and inasmuch as they gather to gether against you avenge me of mine enemies that by and by I may come with the residue of mine house and possess the Land."[51] As "Commander in Chief of the Armies of Israel," Smith was prepared to lose some followers. Drawing on Jesus's words in the Gospels, the revelation declared: "Let no man be afraid to lay down his life for my sake; for whoso layeth down his life for my sake shall find it again; & whoso is not willing to lay down his life for my sake is not my dissiple."[52]

The plan was to restore the Mormons to their lands and buy out the non-Mormons, at least the chief instigators: "Let all the churches send up wise men with their moneys & purchase lands, even as I have commanded them." Rigdon, Pratt, and Wight were assigned to gather recruits, as many as 500 but no fewer than 100. The revelation also instructed eight men to travel east in pairs to solicit funds and recruit volunteers.[53]

Recruiting and Fundraising

The February 24 revelation assigned Pratt to travel with Smith.[54] Two days later, the two men left Kirtland on a three-week mission through New York and western Pennsylvania to "obtain volenteers for Zion." They arrived at Westfield, New York, on March 1 and stayed with Brother Job Lewis for four days. On Sunday, March 2, Pratt and Smith preached to a small congregation that "seems strong in the faith." Later that evening, Smith wrote: "O may God keep them in the faith, and save them and lead them to Zion." The next day, he recorded: "O may God bless us with the gift of utterance to accomplish the journey and the errand on which we are sent, and return safe to the land of Kirtland, and find my family all well. O Lord bless my little children with health and long life, to do good in their generation for Christ's sake, Amen."[55]

On March 4 Smith and Pratt, joined by John Gould, left Westfield and went thirty-three miles to Villanova and stayed the night with Reuben Mc-Bride.[56] According to McBride, "Joseph Smith and Parley P. Pratt Came to my House and held a meeting in that neighbourhood[.] at the close of

---

51. Revelation, Dec. 16–17, 1833, Revelation Book 2, 77–78 [D&C 101:55–57] (*JSP*, D3:393–94).

52. Revelation, Feb. 24, 1834, in Hyde and Pratt, Notebook of Revelations, [14], [D&C 103:27] (*JSP*, D3:461). Cf. Mark 8:35.

53. Revelation, [13], [15]–[18] [D&C 103:22–24, 29–34] (*JSP*, D3:461–63).

54. Revelation, [17] [D&C 103:37] (*JSP*, D3:462).

55. Smith, Journal, Feb. 26, Mar. 2–3, 1834 (*JSP*, J1:28–29).

56. Smith, Journal, Mar. 4, 1834 (*JSP*, J1:31).

the meeting Joseph Called for volenteers to go up to Redeem Zion [and] I volunteered to go."[57]

In the morning, Smith and Pratt left Villanova and traveled about fourteen miles to the home of Freeman Nickerson in Perrysburg, where they held a meeting, during which Smith "Related unto them what had hapened to our Brethren in Zion" and "opened to them the prophesyes and revelations concerning the order of the gathering to Zion and the means of her Redemtion." Pratt wrote in Smith's journal: "Brother Joseph Prophesyed to them and the spirit of the Lord came mightily upon them and with all redyness the yo[u]ng and mid[d]le aged volenteered for Zion." They also held two other meetings in the evening at different locations. On March 6 Smith and Pratt held another meeting at Nickerson's home, but a few unbelievers disrupted the meeting.[58]

After instructing Gould and a Brother Matthews to begin gathering recruits in the area into companies and prepare to depart from Kirtland for Zion on May 1, Smith and Pratt, accompanied by Nickerson, continued their journey on March 7. Later that night, they could not find lodging due to the circuit court being in session, forcing them to continue traveling in the dark and rain to Ellicottville, where they stayed. In the morning, they traveled about twenty miles and arrived at Farmersville, located in the eastern border of Cattaraugus County, to the house of Marcellus McCown. Later that evening, they visited the home of an Esquire Walker and "found them very friendly and somewhat believing, and tarried all night."[59]

On Sunday, March 9, Smith, Pratt, and Nickerson preached in the schoolhouse at Farmersville. As a result of many inquiries, they appointed another meeting in nearby Freedom for Monday. The next day, the three men traveled about ten miles north to Freedom, where they preached to two large congregations who responded favorably.[60] On the same day, Smith wrote to Partridge and the others in Missouri, as he later explained, "to comfort your hearts if possible, and keep you from fainting."[61] No longer extant, Smith's letter likely contained an update on his recruiting efforts. They

57. Reuben McBride, Reminiscence, 1.
58. Smith, Journal, Mar. 5–6, 1834 (*JSP*, J1:31–32).
59. Smith, Journal, Mar. 7–8, 1834 (*JSP*, J1:32).
60. Smith, Journal, Mar. 9–10, 1834 (*JSP*, J1:32).
61. Joseph Smith, Letter to Edward Partridge and Others, ca. Mar. 10, 1834, which is not extant but mentioned in Joseph Smith, Letter to Edward Partridge and other members of the United Firm, Mar. 30, 1834, Cowdery, Letterbook, 30 (*JSP*, D3:490).

stayed overnight with Cowdery's older brother, Warren A., a physician and druggist, who would join Smith's church within a few months.[62]

On March 11 Smith, Pratt, and Nickerson preached and baptized twenty-one-year-old Heman T. Hyde.[63] Pratt later recalled that Heman's Presbyterian mother, Polly, told him that "she would much rather have followed him to an earthly grave than to have seen him baptized. Soon afterward, however, herself, her husband, and the rest of the family, with some thirty or forty others, were all baptized and organized into a branch of the Church—called the Freedom branch."[64] According to Polly's grandson, after hearing Smith tell the story of the coming forth of the gold plates, Polly said: "Mr. Smith, if what you say is not true, hell is too good a place for you." Smith replied: "I know it, Mrs. Hyde, but the testimony I have borne to you is true and you may know it." That night she prayed about it, and the next day she was baptized.[65] It was probably on this occasion that eight-year-old Samuel Miles first met Smith in company with his newly-baptized father. Late in life, he remembered Smith's "kind manner and gentle words" as "he took me by the hand." Miles later reported that based on this first encounter with Smith as well as subsequent observations of "his noble deportment when before the people; his easy, jovial appearance when engaged in the sports ... combined to give me a very favorable opinion of this noble man."[66]

Later the same day, Smith, Pratt, and Nickerson rode nine miles and stayed the night at Steward's tavern. On the following day, they rode thirty-six miles to Edmund Bosley's home in Livonia, New York, where Pratt preached on March 13.[67]

On March 14 the three men traveled about ten miles northwest to Avon and stayed with Alvah Beaman, an old acquaintance of the Smith family who as a rodsman had participated in treasure digs in Manchester and was present when Smith brought the gold plates home in September 1827.[68] Pratt later remarked: "Among those whose hospitality we shared in that vicinity

---

62. Smith, Journal, Mar. 10, 1834 (*JSP*, J1:32–34). Warren Cowdery's baptism date is unknown, but it was prior to his September 1 letter to Oliver Cowdery. See *The Evening and the Morning Star*, Sep. 1834, 189.

63. Smith, Journal, Mar. 11, 1834 (*JSP*, J1:34).

64. Pratt, *Autobiography*, 117.

65. William Hyde, Autobiographical Sketch, [7]–[8].

66. Samuel Miles, "Recollections," *Juvenile Instructor* (Salt Lake City), Mar. 15, 1892, 173.

67. Smith, Journal, Mar. 11–13, 1834, 62 (*JSP*, J1:34).

68. Smith, Journal, Mar. 14, 1834, 62 (*JSP*, J1:34). On Alvah Beaman, see Quinn, *Early Mormonism and the Magic World View*, 39, 59, 256, 388nn78–79; Vogel, *Joseph Smith*, 96, 100–101, 600–601n73, 602n103.

[of Geneseo] was old Father Beaman and his amiable and interesting family. He was a good singer, and so were his three daughters; we were much edified and comforted in their society, and were deeply interested in hearing the old gentleman and Brother Joseph converse on their early acquaintance and history."[69] Beaman's daughter Mary recalled: "This was the first time I ever beheld a prophet of the Lord, and I can truly say at the first sight that I had a testimony within my bosom that he was a man chosen of God to bring forth a great work in the last days. His society I prized, his conversation was meat and drink to me. The principles that he brought forth bind the testimony that he bore of the truth of the Book of Mormon made a lasting impression upon my mind."[70]

On March 15 Rigdon and Wight arrived at the Beaman residence in Avon "to the Joy of our Souls," as Smith would subsequently record in his journal.[71] Mary Beaman Noble recalled the arrival of others, and that "Sidney Rigdon and Joseph and Brigham Young, Luke and Lyman Johnson, and twelve or fourteen of the traveling elders had a council to my father's. I, in company with my sisters, had the pleasure of cooking, and serving the table, and waiting on them, which I considered a privilege and blessing."[72] One of the missionaries from Ohio was John Murdock, who recorded in his journal that the conference attempted to reclaim Ezra Landon, who had been excommunicated on December 31, 1833, for rejecting the vision of three heavens. According to Murdock, the conference tried to show Landon "his rong," but their effort was "all in vane."[73]

Joseph Young remembered that when he arrived, Smith greeted him, calling out "there's Brother Joseph Young." After shaking hands, Young said: "Br Joseph I want to talk with you." Smith suggested that they go into the barn. After climbing into the loft and situating themselves on the hay, Smith said: "Br Joseph Young, Br — will go down to hell until the day of redemption."

---

69. Pratt, *Autobiography*, 117–18.

70. Noble and Noble, Reminiscences, [5]–[6].

71. Smith, Journal, Mar. 15, 1834, 62 (*JSP*, J1:34). Smith's journal locates Beaman in Livonia, which contradicts the March 17, 1834, minutes of a conference held at Avon, Livingston County, New York, "at the house of Alvah Beeman." Minutes, Mar. 17, 1834, Minute Book 1, 42 (*JSP*, D3:487). Livingston County records indicate that Alvah Beaman sold his property in Livonia on January 20, 1831, and bought land in Avon on January 22 and March 26, 1831. Doxey, "The Early Latter-day Saints in Livingston County, New York," 87n35.

72. Noble and Noble, Reminiscences, [5]–[6].

73. Murdock, Journal, Mar. 15, 1834. Murdock seems to locate the conference at "Br Bosley's," presumably Edmund Bosley in Livonia, while Orson Pratt locates it in Geneseo. Pratt, Journal, Mar. 15, 1834.

Young said: "Br Joseph, you astonish me." "Well," Smith responded, "it is true, for he has always put himself in my way, and wishes to supplant me and take this work out of my hands; but the Lord wont suffer him to do it." According to Young, the conversation then shifted to "his then present mission; which was to gather up the strength of the Lords house, to go up [to Missouri and] redeem Zion, or replace the Saints in Jackson County. He hinted to me a wish that I should go in that company. He did not however urge me."[74]

The suppressed name is probably Oliver Cowdery, of whom Smith said the previous December had "two evils in him that he must needs forsake, or he cannot altogether escape the buffetings of the adversary."[75] It was Cowdery who from the beginning wanted to replace Smith as translator but failed, who argued with Smith about the status of John the Beloved, who before the organization of the church issued his own revelation calling himself "an Apostle of Jesus Christ" with authority from God to ordain priests and teachers and thus "build up his church," who joined the Whitmers in demanding that Smith alter the Articles and Covenants.[76] Young's account is cryptic and it is uncertain why Cowdery's name came up. It may be that during his search for a printing press the previous October, Cowdery had stopped to visit the Youngs and others in the Mendon branch.[77] Brigham Young and Heber C. Kimball had moved to Kirtland the previous fall, but brothers Joseph and Phineas Young were still living in the area, and their conversations with Cowdery may have caused them concern. Cowdery may have continued this behavior after his return to Kirtland, causing Smith to reprimand him about the "two evils in him," which in Smith's mind may have been pride and coveting power. Joseph Young may have suppressed Cowdery's name because he was a relative by marriage. Phineas Young's wife, Lucy Pearce Cowdery, was Cowdery's half-sister and was still living.

On Sunday, March 16, Smith, Pratt, Wight, and the Beamans traveled

---

74. Joseph Young Sr., Letter to Lewis Harvey, Nov. 16, 1880, 3. Young said he met Smith "in the town of Lima, Livingston County." The villages of Avon and Lima are eight miles apart, but the townships are neighboring and Young may have been mistaken about where the Beamans lived.

75. Smith, Journal, Dec. 18, 1833 (*JSP*, J1:21–22).

76. On Cowdery's attempt to translate, see Revelation, Apr. 1829-D, in BC VIII [D&C 9] (*JSP*, D1:48–50). For Cowdery's revelation, see Cowdery, "A Commandment from God unto Oliver how he should build up his church & the manner thereof," ca. June 1829 (*EMD*, 2:409–12; *JSP*, MRB:21–23). On Cowdery's disagreements with Smith about John the Beloved and the Articles and Covenants, see JS History, vol. A-1, 15, 51 (*EMD*, 1:74, 128; *JSP*, H1:284, 426).

77. The possibility that Cowdery may have visited the Youngs in the Mendon area seems suggested by his mention in an October 30, 1833, letter that he had arranged for Phineas Young to come to Kirtland and work with him in the print shop. Oliver Cowdery, Letter to Ambrose Palmer, Oct. 30, 1833, in Cowdery, Letterbook, 5.

about ten miles southwest to Geneseo, where Rigdon preached to "a very large congregation."[78] Pratt later wrote that in Geneseo, he and Smith "met with the other Elders who had started from Kirtland on the same mission, and with others who were local, and held a general Conference," at which both men "addressed the crowds in great plainness of speech with mighty power."[79] Mary Beaman Noble remembered that the meeting was held in a barn in what was called the "Orton neighborhood." She recalled that Rigdon preached and that "Brother Joseph bore testimony of the truth of the Book of Mormon, and of the work that had come forth in these last days. Never did I hear preaching sound so glorious to me as that did. I realized it was the truth of heaven, for I had testimony of it myself."[80]

A resident of Henrietta, New York, who was also in attendance, later published a scathing account of Smith's discourse as well as a conversation he had with the Mormon leader following the meeting in the *Evangelical Magazine and Gospel Advocate*. The reporter included a harsh description of Smith: "In his person, he is about six feet in height, neither attenuated nor corpulent. His eyes are rather dull than expressive, hair of a light brown, and his countenance unmarked by any peculiar expression indicative of intense thought or extraordinary intellect. ... His manner is ungainly, his diction coarse, and his delivery slow and labored. There is nothing in his appearance or language to excite much attention, save his presumptuous impiety." Regarding Smith's discourse, the reporter said:

> A multitude was assembled to hear what this impudent ignoramus would say; most of whom were surprised that he said so little and made so ordinary an appearance. He did not attempt to preach, but made some few statements with regard to himself and his clumsy compilation of pretended oracles. He said many would disbelieve that a recent revelation had been made to him, (!!!) and in view of himself and the "Book of Mormon," would raise the cry of false prophet! delusion!! &c., but that a revelation from heaven was given to him, and by him had been faithfully transcribed, for the benefit of all who should receive his testimony!

After the meeting ended, the openly disbelieving reporter tried to press Smith for proof of his mission, but the Mormon leader kept walking, mounted his horse, and rode off. "Here this Baal of the Mormonites, irritated and vexed

---

78. Smith, Journal, Mar. 16, 1834, 62 (*JSP*, J1:34).
79. Pratt, *Autobiography*, 117–18.
80. Noble and Noble, Reminiscences, [6].

by the manner in which the conversation had been carried on, murmured out something which became inaudible in the distance, as he urged on his horse and was soon out of the reach of my voice."[81]

On March 17 Smith presided over a conference of six other high priests and six elders at the Beaman residence in Avon. After opening the conference with prayer, Smith "introduced the object of our meeting, which was to obtain young men and middle aged to go and assist in the redemption of Zion according to the commandment, and for the church to gather up their riches and send them to purchase lands according to the commandments of the Lord." In addition to raising funds for the relief of Zion, Smith pushed to raise at least $2,000 to "deliver Kirtland from Debt." Church leaders in Kirtland had incurred significant debt as a result of the purchase of the French farm, Newel K. Whitney's purchase of goods in New York on behalf of the United Firm, and Cowdery's recent purchase of a printing press. Smith proposed that Edmund Bosley and Isaac McWithy "go with him to bro. Perry's and see if, by their united efforts, they could not raise Two Thousand Dollars for the relief of Kirtland."[82] "Bro. Perry" may have been Asahel Perry, who served as branch president in Middlebury, New York. However, this plan may have been scrapped since the minutes of the meeting state that it was voted that Roger Orton and fathers Bosley, Nickerson, and McWithey "should exert themselves to obtain the said Two Thousand Dollars for the present relief of Kirtland. They all agreed to do all they could to obtain it; and they firmly believed that they could obtain the amount by the first of April." It was also voted that Orson Hyde remain and preach in the area until the money is raised, at which time he was to "bring it immediately to Kirtland."[83]

Smith's journal indicates that he stayed in Livonia with Edmund Bosley on March 18 and in the morning "Started for home." Smith, Rigdon, and Wight traveled west about forty-five miles to Bennington Township, New York, where they spent the night at Isaac McWithy's tavern.[84] On March 20

---

81. M.L.F., "Interview with the Mormon Prophet," *Evangelical Magazine and Gospel Advocate* (Utica, NY), Apr. 5, 1834, 107.

82. Minutes, Mar. 17, 1834, Minute Book 1, 42–43 (*JSP*, D3:487). On the church's debts at this time, see *JSP*, D3:485, 486n312.

83. Minutes, 43 (*JSP*, D3:487).

84. Smith, Journal, Mar. 18–19, 1834 (*JSP*, J1:35). Smith's journal does not name his traveling companions, but the March 17, 1834, minutes directed him to travel with Rigdon and Wight. Minutes, Mar. 17, 1834, Minute Book 1, 43 (*JSP*, D3:487–88). Isaac McWithy is listed in the 1830 US Census, Bennington, Genesee Co., NY, 136; and Genesee Co., NY, Deed Records, Apr. 7, 1832, vol. 29, 337, microfilm, U.S. and Canada Record Collection, FHL. McWithy's tavern is mentioned in JS History, vol. A-1, 448 (DHC 2:45).

Smith, Rigdon, and Wight traveled southeast about twenty miles to Joseph Holbrook's at Wethersfield, Genesee (now Wyoming) County, New York, arriving about noon. After a short rest, they continued on their journey and tried three times to find free lodging but finally had to pay a man named Reuben Wilson in China, about seventeen miles southwest from Wethersfield.[85]

On March 22 the three men reached Perrysburg, New York, and stayed at Vinson Knight's home. On the following day, Sunday, they moved to Father Freeman Nickerson's house, also in Perrysburg, where they held a meeting. After two days, Smith, Rigdon, and Wight, accompanied by Father Nickerson, traveled southwest about thirty-five miles to Father Job Lewis's home in Westfield, New York.[86] In the morning, Smith and his companions resumed their journey, traveling about sixty miles to Elk Creek, Pennsylvania. The next day, they traveled about thirteen miles northwest to Springfield, where they found Rigdon, who at some point had left the group. Smith and the others continued west about thirty-five miles, stopping about sixteen miles east of Painesville, Ohio.[87]

Return to Kirtland

On March 28 Smith, Rigdon, and Wight traveled about twenty-seven miles and arrived at Kirtland, where Smith wrote in his journal: "Came home found my Family all well and the Lord be praised for this blessing." The next day, Smith remained home and recorded: "Had much Joy with my Family." Smith spent Sunday, March 30, with his family and only left them to attend church to hear Rigdon "preach the word of life &c."[88]

Later that day, Smith dictated a letter to Partridge, Phelps, and other United Firm members, mentioning that several letters from Missouri awaited him when he returned to Kirtland, some of which criticized him and other Kirtland leaders. These letters are no longer extant, but according to Smith, they contained "sharp, piercing, & cutting reproofs," apparently for errors in the printed broadside of the December 1833 revelation and the slow response of Kirtland leaders to the needs of the Missouri church.[89]

In response, Smith wanted Missouri Mormons to know that "God, in his wisdom, and in the order of his Providence, is preparing all things before his

---

85. Smith, Journal, Mar. 20, 1834 (*JSP*, J1:35). See Matt. 10:9–15; D&C 24:18; 84:77–78, 86–94.
86. Smith, Journal, Mar. 22–25, 1834 (*JSP*, J1:36).
87. Smith, Journal, Mar. 26–27, 1834 (*JSP*, J1:36).
88. Smith, Journal, Mar. 28–30, 1834 (*JSP*, J1:36–37).
89. Joseph Smith, Letter to Edward Partridge and other members of the United Firm, Mar. 30, 1834, Cowdery, Letterbook, 30–38 (*JSP*, D3:490–98).

face for the redemption of Zion." He assured them that the Kirtland leaders "are crying day & night to God for the deliverance and prosperity of Zion; and many are preparing with all zeal to do all that lies in their power to accomplish the great work, and it will be seen in due time, that the saints in this region are not slack towards you."[90]

Addressing their criticisms, Smith responded defensively: "O, how wounding & how poignant must it be to receive chastisements & reproofs for things that we are not guilty of from a source we least expect them, arising from a distrustful, a fearful, & jealous spirit."[91] Apparently, Phelps had mentioned "glaring errors in the Revelation," referring to the broadside of the December revelation. The errors were minor misspellings and grammatical mistakes, which Smith again defended: "We would say, by way of excuse, that we did not think so much of the orthography, or the manner, as we did of the subject matter; as the word of God means what it says & it is the word of God, as much as Christ was God, although he was born in a stable & was rejected by the manner of his birth, notwithstanding he was God. What a mistake!" Smith argued that if the eternal God could condescend to become mortal flesh through an ordinary and lowly birth, the word of God is still his word although it might be clothed in imperfect and unremarkable language. In other words, if Jesus was rejected because of his low-status birth, Phelps should be careful not to criticize the word of God because he chose to speak through an unlearned farm boy. Smith then compared Phelps to the "laughing philosophers," who amused themselves by finding fault with humanity for its weakness and folly.[92]

Smith blamed the "mistakes in punctuation, or spelling" on Cowdery's haste in printing the revelation amidst persecutions in the Kirtland area: "When he and I, and all the church in Kirtland had to lie every night for a long time upon our arms to keep off mobs … to save our lives and the press." Despite these hardships, the revelation was printed "that the word of God might be printed & sent forth by confidential brethren to the different churches; for the churches are just like you—they will not receive anything but by revelation!"[93] This last comment reveals an aspect of the dynamic between Smith and his followers: because they distinguished between Smith's

---

90. Smith, 30 (*JSP*, D3:490).
91. Smith, 31 (*JSP*, D3:491).
92. Smith, 31–32 (*JSP*, D3:491–92).
93. Smith, 32–33 (*JSP*, D3:492).

speaking as a man and his inspired pronouncements, it put pressure on him to produce revelations and pseudepigraphic translations.

In a postscript, Cowdery shifted the blame to his apprentices: "Every article is generally inspected before it goes out. There are many errors in spelling which cannot be avoided yet, well the boys are young and it is not as it was with us four or five proofreaders, and with the incessant labor which is necessary for us to perform it could not be expected that everything would be perfect." Besides, Cowdery wrote, "I will just remind you that your reproofs, though designed for the best, are calculated to make a different impression when written than when given orally."[94] Whatever the explanations, it seems Smith bristled at criticism of any kind, even minor, inconsequential notes from a proofreader. Smith finished by warning that "men should not attempt to steady the ark of God!"—meaning Phelps should not attempt to correct those above him in authority.[95]

Smith approved of the Missouri leaders hiring Robert W. Wells, an attorney in Jefferson City, to sue for damages in Jackson County, although he had no means of paying Wells: "We have neither gold nor silver, we have run into debt for the press, and also to obtain money to pay the New York debt for Zion, and have received but a very few dollars for the Star and printing as yet, no means of speculation to gain or make money, yet we think that the money can be had, and that there will be no difficulty on this subject." He suggested that one possible means of obtaining money was to sell their Jackson County lands to other Mormons when they arrive from the east in a few months, and when their cases are settled to use that money to purchase new property in Zion.[96]

At this time, Smith was undecided as to whether he would go to Zion with the company: "Once more I design coming unto [you]; but when, it has not been revealed: whether it will be with Parley & Lyman I cannot now say; but once more I design to come <u>mob</u> or no <u>mob</u>, <u>enemy</u> or no <u>enemy</u>!" In closing his reply, he advised restraint and the avoidance of violence: "There needs be no difficulty in relation to the revelations for they show plainly from the face of them, that no blood is to be shed except in self-defense; and that the law of God as well as man gives us a privilege. ... Be united, brethren, in all your moves, and stand by each other even unto death you may prevail."[97]

---

94. Smith, 37–38 (*JSP*, D3:497–98).
95. Smith, 34 (*JSP*, D3:494).
96. Smith, 34–35 (*JSP*, D3:494–95).
97. Smith, 35 (*JSP*, D3:495).

Another letter waiting for Smith from Phelps, dated February 27, 1834, reported on the court of inquiry held at Independence regarding Col. Pritchard's activities in Jackson County leading to the expulsion of the Mormons. "I have just returned from Independence, the seat of war in the west," Phelps wrote. He reported that he and about a dozen Mormons were escorted by the militia to Independence on February 23, and that in the morning they were visited by District Attorney Amos Rees and Attorney General Robert W. Wells, who informed them that "all hopes of *criminal prosecution*, was at an end." The reason, Wells explained, was that although he had been sent by Dunklin to investigate, he was unable to penetrate the mob's death oath to protect one another. When a mob gathered, the judge ordered that the Mormon witnesses be returned to their homes. As Phelps wrote, "We were marched out of town to the tune of Yankee doodle in quick time, and soon returned to our camp ground without the loss of any lives. ... Thus ends all hope of 'redress.'"[98]

Phelps also noted, "The mob has quit whipping, and now beat with clubs." He named four Mormons who attempted to return to their homes in Jackson County and were beaten with clubs. To prevent other Mormons from returning to their property, the mob resorted to burning some houses and hay stacks.[99] Two months later, Phelps reported that the mob had burned "nearly all" of the Mormon-owned buildings in Jackson County.[100] John Corrill corroborated this statement the following month, stating that "for fear that we would return and enjoy our dwellings again, they set fire to, and burned them down."[101] Despite these discouraging reports, Smith continued making plans for the redemption of Zion. Meanwhile, he had other pressing matters to deal with in Kirtland.

Philastus Hurlbut Trial

On March 31, 1834, Smith traveled about ten miles Chardon to testify for the prosecution in *State of Ohio v. D. P. Hurlbut*.[102] At a preliminary hearing in Painesville on January 13–15, Justice Holbrook had ordered Hurlbut to keep the peace and to appear before the court of common pleas at the

---

98. William W. Phelps, Letter to "Dear Brethren," Feb. 27, 1834, "The Outrage in Jackson County, Missouri," *The Evening and the Morning Star*, Mar. 1834, 139 (*JSP*, D3:469–71).

99. Phelps, 139 (*JSP*, D3:471–72).

100. "The Outrage in Jackson County, Missouri," *The Evening and the Morning Star*, May 1834, 160.

101. "The Outrage in Jackson County, Missouri," 168.

102. Smith, Journal, Mar. 31, 1834 (*JSP*, J1:37).

start of its next term, March 31.[103] However, Hurlbut's case was delayed for several days as the court worked through several cases on its docket.

Smith remained at Chardon, apparently staying at a Brother Rider's house, where he spent the next day preparing subpoenas for witnesses. He also prophesied in his journal that Hurlbut would not prevail in the case against him and pronounced a curse upon him: "The Lord shall destroy him who has lifted his heel against me even that wicked man Docter P Hurlbert[.] he will deliver him to the fowls of heaven and his bones shall be cast to the blast of the wind for he lifted his arm against the Almity therefore the Lord shall destroy him."[104] On April 2–3 Smith "attended court at Chardon" in the Hurlbut case before Judge Matthew Birchard adjourned court for the weekend.[105]

When Smith returned to Chardon on Tuesday, April 8, he found that the courthouse, a large log cabin, "was filled almost to suffocation, with an eager and curious crowd of spectators, to hear the Mormon trial," as the *Chardon Spectator and Geauga Gazette* would later report.[106] During the trial, the court heard from seventeen prosecution witnesses and seven defense witnesses.[107] According to the *Spectator*, "One witness, who testified to the threats of Hurlbut, on cross-examination being asked the reason why she had not communicated these threats to Smith, answered that she did not believe Hurlbut, or any other human being, had the power to hurt the prophet;—but Joe himself appears to have placed little reliance upon his divine invulnerability;—for he testified that he became afraid of bodily injury from the defendant."[108]

Samuel F. Whitney, a non-Mormon brother of Bishop Newel K. Whitney, remembered that Smith "was on the witness stand ... three or four hours" and "testified he had no arms, and that his house was not guarded." Whitney, a defense witness, said he was asked if he thought Smith was "a man of truth and veracity," and he answered no, "for Jo knew he had sworn

103. See Transcript of Proceedings, Chardon, Geauga Co., OH, ca. Apr. 9, 1834, State of Ohio v. D. P. Hurlbut, Geauga Co., OH, Court of Common Pleas, Final Record, vol. P, 431–32; see also Grua, "Joseph Smith and the 1834 D. P. Hurlbut Case."

104. Smith, Journal, Apr. 1, 1834 (*JSP*, J1:37). Probably Ezekiel Rider who is listed in the Geauga County tax records for 1833 (*JSP*, J1:37n119). Ironically, it would be Smith who would meet an early, tragic end, while Hurlbut lived out his years as a United Brethren minister and other occupations before dying in Sandusky County, Ohio, in 1883, at age seventy-four.

105. Smith, Journal, Apr. 2–4, 1834 (*JSP*, J1:37).

106. "Mormon Trial," *Chardon Spectator and Geauga Gazette* (Chardon, OH), Apr. 12, 1834, 3.

107. Witness List, Chardon, Geauga Co., OH, ca. Apr. 2, 1834, State of Ohio v. D. P. Hurlbut, Geauga Co., OH, Court of Common Pleas, Witness Docket 1831–35, 110; see Grua, "Joseph Smith and the 1834 D. P. Hurlbut Case," 45.

108. "Mormon Trial," *Chardon Spectator and Geauga Gazette*, Apr. 12, 1834, 3.

to things [during trial] which he was well aware I knew were not true." Whitney gave an example: "Jo had told me a short time previous, while I was painting my brother's store (he at that time was living in the dwelling part of it), that he had a sword and pistol, and that his house was guarded by six men every night."[109] George A. Smith later confirmed that shortly after he arrived in Kirtland in May 1833, he served as one of Smith's bodyguards and that the Mormon prophet "found necessary to keep continual guard to prevent his being murdered by his enemies."[110]

On the following day, April, 9, Judge Birchard ruled that Smith "had ground to fear" physical harm from Hurlbut, ordered Hurlbut to post a $200 bond to keep the peace for six months and pay court costs of $112.59.[111] Afterward, Smith had Cowdery write in his journal that the verdict was "in answer to our prayer for which I thank my heavenly father."[112]

Although he had prevailed in his case against Hurlbut, Smith was unhappy with Whitney's testimony. The day after the trial, Smith confronted Whitney in his brother's store and called him a liar. Whitney said, "I asked him if he was a prophet of the Lord. He replied he was. I said, 'Blessed are they who trust in the Lord, and nothing shall offend them;' he being very angry all the time. I inquired if he had the gift of healing; he said he had. I told him if he would perform one miracle I would become a convert to his faith. ... I see you have a lying tongue and a short memory, and if you will cure that I will embrace the faith." According to Whitney, "The conversation began in the morning and lasted two hours," during which "Jo shook his fist in my face, raved around violently, and threatened to whip me."[113]

Cowdery's report of the trial in the April issue of *The Evening and the Morning Star* became an occasion to destroy Hurlbut's influence in the community. He challenged the committee supporting Hurlbut's research into Smith's character to be consistent and "expose *his* [Hurlbut's] character, and hold him up to the view of community, in the true light which his crimes

---

109. Samuel F. Whitney, "Statement of Rev. S. F. Whitney on Mormonism," *Naked Truths about Mormonism* (Oakland, CA), Jan. 1888, 3.

110. George A. Smith, Memoirs and Autobiography, 12.

111. Smith, Journal, Apr. 9, 1834 (*JSP*, J1:38); Docket Entry, Ruling, Chardon, Geauga Co., OH, Apr. 9, 1834, State of OH v. D. P. Hurlbut, Geauga Co., OH, Court of Common Pleas, Final Record, vol. M, 193; Docket Entry, Costs, Chardon, Geauga Co., OH, ca. Apr. 9, 1834, State of OH v. D. P. Hurlbut, Geauga County Court of Common Pleas, Execution Docket, vol. F, 82.

112. Smith, Journal, Apr. 9, 1834 (*JSP*, J1:38).

113. Samuel F. Whitney, "Statement of Rev. S. F. Whitney on Mormonism," *Naked Truths about Mormonism*, Jan. 1888, 3. Whitney evidently alluded to Psalm 119:165: "Great peace have they which love thy law: and nothing shall offend them."

merit."[114] Of course, for unbelievers, at least, Hurlbut's character had nothing to do with the merits of his research and the affidavits he collected.

United Firm Dissolved

On April 7, 1834, during the break in the Hurlbut trial, Smith, Newel K. Whitney, Cowdery, Frederick G. Williams, and Heber C. Kimball met in the translating room on the upper floor of the Whitney store to pray for a way to pay the United Firm's debts, as well as for Smith to prevail in his case against Hurlbut and "that he [Hurlbut] be put to shame."[115] Destruction of the press and loss of the Gilbert & Whitney Store in Missouri hurt the Firm financially, and it went into further debt when Cowdery purchased a new press and Whitney purchased goods in New York in October 1833.

On the same day, Smith, Williams, and Cowdery wrote to Orson Hyde, who had been left in Livingston County, New York, to collect a donation of $2,000 for the relief of the Kirtland debt and to finance the Missouri expedition. In a letter to the Kirtland leaders, dated March 31, which is no longer extant, Hyde reported that he was unable to obtain the money. After acknowledging the receipt of Hyde's letter, they wrote that they were "much grieved" by the news of his failure "to succeed according to our expectations." Nevertheless, Smith still hoped that Hyde would accomplish his mission, telling Hyde that he, Whitney, Williams, and Cowdery "retired to the Translating room ... and unbosomed our feelings before God ... that you in the meraculus providence of God will succeed in obtaining help." Smith then proceeded to pressure Hyde: "The fact is that unless we can obtain help I myself cannot go to Zion and if I do not go it will be impossible to get my brethren in Kirtland any of them to go and if we do not go it is in vain for our eastern brethren to think of going up to better themselves by obtaining so goodly a land which now can be obtained for one dollar and a quarter p[e]r acre and stand against that wicked Mob for unless they do the will of God, God will not help them and if God does not help them all is vain."[116]

Smith's desperation is apparent when he drew upon his prophetic charisma: "I proph[es]y I speak the truth I Lie not God shall take away their tallant and give it to those who have no tallant and shall prevent them from ever obtaining a place of reffuge or an inheritance upon the Land of Zion. ... I therefor beseech you to conjure [adjure] them in the name of the Lord

---

114. [Oliver Cowdery], editorial, *The Evening and the Morning Star*, Apr. 1834, 150.
115. Smith, Journal, Apr. 7, 1834 (*JSP*, J1:38).
116. Joseph Smith et al., Letter to Orson Hyde, Apr. 7, 1834, JS Letterbook 1:82 (*JSP*, D4:7–8).

by the Love of God to lend us a helping hand and if all this will not soften their hearts to administer to our necessity for Zion sake turn your back up on them and return speedily to Kirtland and the blood of Zion be upon their heads. ... What man shall ... be found turning a deaf ear to the voice of his servant God shall speak in due time and all will be declared amen."[117]

Despite Smith's threats, the church only received a total of $167 in donations "from the East for the benefit of Zion."[118] Smith went anyway. In fact, only two days after he threatened that he would not go to Missouri if he failed to receive significant donations, he was making plans to do just that. A notation in Smith's journal under April 9, 1834, reads: "Remember to carry the bond between A S Gilbert & N K Whitney and have them exchangd when I go to Zion."[119] This is the earliest indication that Smith had decided to go to Missouri with the Camp of Israel, probably due to the completion of his case against Hurlbut.

A payment of $1,500 was due on the French farm on April 10, 1834, but there is good reason to believe that Whitney was unable to make the payment.[120] By April 1834, N. K. Whitney & Co. was in financial trouble, owing more than $4,400 to New York firms.[121] The firm owed an additional $630.15 for Cowdery's purchase of a press.[122] In total, N. K. Whitney & Co. had $8,000 in debts.[123] On the same day, April 10, Smith met with the members of the United Firm of Ohio, and "it was agreed that the firm should be desolv[e]d and each one have their stewardship set off to them."[124] It is unclear what their "stewardship" entailed, but it possibly has reference to a division or redistribution of the company's assets.

Preparations to Go to Zion

Also, on April 10, Cowdery responded to Phelps's letter of March 26, assuring him that the brethren, both in Kirtland and abroad, are "now in the might

---

117. Smith et al., 83 (*JSP*, D4:8–9).

118. Account with the Church of Christ, ca. Aug. 11–29, 1834, [1], JS Collection (*JSP*, D4:138).

119. Smith, Journal, Apr. 9, 1834 (*JSP*, J1:38).

120. According to a biographical sketch of John Tanner, when he arrived at Kirtland in January 1835, he loaned Smith $2,000 to prevent foreclosure of the French farm, suggesting that the April 1834 payment had not been made. Tanner, "Sketch of an Elder's Life," in *Scraps of Biography*, 12.

121. "New York Account Book Sept. 1834," Newel K. Whitney Papers; Circular, *New-York Spectator* (New York, NY), Aug. 30, 1832, [3]; Madsen, "Tabulating the Impact of Litigation on the Kirtland Economy," 234.

122. F. G. Williams & Co. Account Book, 1833–35, 1.

123. Newel K. Whitney, Order to Joseph Smith, Apr. 18, 1834, JS Collection (*JSP*, D4:10–13).

124. Smith, Journal, Apr. 10, 1834 (*JSP*, J1:38).

of labor & toil for Zion." Redeeming Zion was imperative, Cowdery said, since "it is of but <u>little</u> consequence to proclaim the everlasting gospel to men and warn them to flee to Zion for refuge when there is no Zion. ... So Zion must be redeemed, and then the saints can have a place to flee to for safety."[125]

On Sunday, April 13, Smith was sick and unable to attend church.[126] Lyman Wight recorded in his journal that he preached to a "large congregation" in Kirtland about the expulsion and suffering of the Saints in Missouri and "the necessity of those of like faith sympathizing with their brothers and sisters," following which "about seventy volunteered to fly to their relief even if death should be the consequence thereof" and "many donated largely of their substance to supply the wants of the needy." Wight also recorded that he "spent the night with Bro. Joseph, and had much conversation with him concerning our peculiar circumstances."[127]

Over the next few days, Smith purchased hay, oats, and a horse on credit to Frederick G. Williams and Co., and then plowed and planted the oats on the Williams farm, where his parents lived.[128]

On April 17 Smith attended a meeting during which Rigdon discussed the "deliverance of Zion and the building of the Lords house in Kirtland." After the lecture, Smith spoke and "requested the brethren and sisters to contr[i]bute all the money they could for the deliverence of Zion," and then collected $29.68.[129]

Trip to Medina County

On April 18 Smith, Rigdon, Cowdery, and Zebedee Coltrin left Kirtland for New Portage, Ohio, to attend a conference. They dined at the home of W. W. Williams in Newburgh, about twenty-six miles west of Kirtland and about five miles south of Cleveland. Continuing their journey after dark, they were harassed by three men but "escaping their hands through the providence of the Lord," they managed to reach a tavern where they spent the night.[130]

In the morning, they continued their journey, traveling south about twenty-seven miles to Copley, Medina County (now Summit County), Ohio, where they stopped at the home of Joseph Bosworth, a former Campbellite

---

125. Oliver Cowdery, Letter to W. W. Phelps, Apr. 10, 1834, Cowdery, Letterbook, 39.

126. Smith, Journal, Apr. 13, 1834 (*JSP*, J1:40).

127. Wight, Journal, 443 (Sep. 13, 1834).

128. Smith, Journal, Apr. 14–16, 1834 (*JSP*, J1:40); F. G. Williams & Co., Account Book, 1833–35, 6.

129. Smith, Journal, Apr. 17, 1834 (*JSP*, J1:40); see also Account with the Church of Christ, ca. Aug. 11–29, 1834, [1], JS Collection (*JSP*, D4:139).

130. Smith, Journal, Apr. 18, 1834 (*JSP*, J1:40–41).

and visionary.[131] After dinner, they went another five miles south to Jonathan Taylor's in Norton. Shortly after arriving, Smith, Rigdon, Cowdery, and Coltrin went into the wilderness and prayed for those going to the land of Zion, especially for God "to give brother Joseph strength, and wisdom, and understanding sufficient to lead the people of the Lord" to a successful outcome. They then gave one another priesthood blessings, conferring on Smith "all the blessings necessary to qualify him to stand before the Lord in his high calling; and he return again in peace and triumph, to enjoy the society of my breth[r]en." They blessed Cowdery in preparing the revelations for publication in the Doctrine and Covenants. They also blessed Rigdon to lead the church in Smith's absence and to help Cowdery publish the *Star* and Doctrine and Covenants. They then blessed Coltrin with a long life that he may "see Zion built up and Kirtland established forever."[132]

On the morning of the following day, Sunday, April 20, Coltrin "noticed that Joseph seemed to have a far off look in his eyes, or was looking at a distance." Then he stepped between Cowdery and Coltrin, took each man by the arm, and said, "Let's take a walk." He led them to a patch of "beautiful grass, and grapevines and swamp birch interlaced." After each man had prayed as Smith instructed, Smith declared, "Now brethren, we will see some visions." According to Coltrin, "Joseph lay down on the ground on his back and stretched out his arms, and we laid [our heads] on them." In a few moments, as Coltrin later recounted, "The heavens gradually opened, and we saw a golden throne, on a circular foundation, and on the throne sat a man and a woman, having white hair and clothed in white garments. Their heads were white as snow, and their faces shone with immortal youth. They were the two most beautiful and perfect specimens of mankind I ever saw." Smith said, "They are our first parents, Adam and Eve." Concerning the two beings, Coltrin remembered: "Adam was a large broad shouldered man, and Eve, as a woman, was as large in proportion."[133] As with Rigdon two years earlier, Smith was the interpreter of a shared vision.

Later, the same day, Smith attended a meeting where Rigdon "entertained a large congregation of saints, with an interesting discourse upon the 'Dispensation of the fulness of times.'"[134]

On April 21 Smith presided over a conference of elders held at the home

131. On Joseph Bosworth, see *JSP*, D3:431–35.
132. Smith, Journal, Apr. 19, 1834 (*JSP*, J1:41–42).
133. Zebedee Coltrin, in School of the Prophets Salt Lake City Minutes, Oct. 11, 1883.
134. Smith, Journal, Apr. 20, 1834 (*JSP*, J1:42).

of a Brother Carpenter in Norton Township, during which Smith got a few volunteers for the Camp of Israel and $36.37 for the relief of Zion.[135] According to Smith's journal, it was "a glorious time."[136] Smith spoke first, presenting a defense of his charismatic authority and the need for new revelations. He began by reading Joel 2:28, which predicts that in the last days "your sons and your daughters shall prophesy." He then explained that because of what God had revealed to him, "we are differently situated from any other people that ever existed upon this earth." He referred to prophecies about God saving a "remnant" in Zion, and then said: "Now, if God should give no more revelations, where will we find Zion and this remnant? He said that the time was near when desolation was to cover the Earth, and then God would have a place of deliverance in his remnant, and in Zion, &c."[137] This justified the reception of revelations beyond the Book of Mormon.

He next reviewed his reception of authority through "translating the Book of Mormon, the revelation of the priesthood of Aaron, the organization of the Church in the year 1830, the revelation of the high priesthood, and the gift of the Holy Spirit poured out upon the church, &c."[138] Unfortunately, the minutes of this meeting are too brief to determine what was meant by the "revelation of the Priesthood of Aaron," and Cowdery's announcement of his and Smith's ordination by an angel prior to their baptisms in May 1829 was still five months away. However, it parallels "revelation of the High Priesthood," which was connected to the June 1831 conference in Kirtland. Regardless, there is no reason to believe that Smith's description went beyond a revealed command from God for him and Cowdery to baptize one another.[139]

To those who may have been questioning Smith's revelations that located Zion in Independence, Smith argued: "Take away the book of Mormon, and the revelations, and where is our religion? We have none; for without a Zion and a place of deliverance, we must fall, ... for God will gather out his saints from the gentiles and then comes desolation or destruction and none can escape except the pure in heart who are gathered, &c."[140] Smith used fear of

135. Minutes, Apr. 21, 1834, Minute Book 1, 43–47 (*JSP*, D4:14–19). Possibly Richard Carpenter who was living in Norton Township in 1830 (*JSP*, D4:14n57). See also Account with the Church of Christ, ca. Aug. 11–29, 1834, [1], JS Collection (*JSP*, D4:139).

136. Smith, Journal, Apr. 21, 1834 (*JSP*, J1:42).

137. Minutes, Apr. 21, 1834, Minute Book 1, 43–44 (*JSP*, D4:15). See 3 Ne. 21:22–26; Ether 13:5–6.

138. Minutes, 44 (*JSP*, D4:15).

139. Vogel, "Evolution of Early Mormon Priesthood Narratives," 66.

140. Minutes, Apr. 21, 1834, Minute Book 1, 44 (*JSP*, D4:15–16).

the coming destruction to motivate followers to build Zion in the wilderness, both of which rested on Smith's revelations.

Rigdon spoke next. The Second Coming "is now just before us," he declared; "for if they are not gathered, they must wail because of his coming," because they will be destroyed with the wicked and not reign with Jesus a thousand years. He reasoned that "it was in vain for men in this generation to think of laying up and providing inheritances for their children except they laid it up in the place where deliverance was appointed by the voice of God."[141] Ironically, two days later, Rigdon will be given his home and tannery in Kirtland as a stewardship, "for a blessing upon him, and his seed after him."[142] He "urged the importance of an obedience" to the "revelation ... requiring the saints to go up for the deliverance of those who had been driven from their inheritances, ... & those who could not go, should help those who are going to means for their expenses."[143]

Rigdon then discussed the necessity of building the temple in Kirtland, in which the elders were to receive the endowment of power before being sent out as missionaries, as promised in a June 1833 revelation. He likened it, as did also the revelation, to the ancient apostles receiving the Holy Ghost on the Day of Pentecost in fulfillment of Jesus's instruction to "tarry ye in the city of Jerusalem, until ye be endued with power from on high" (Acts 2:1–4; Luke 24:49).[144] Building two capitals of Mormonism simultaneously not only seemed inconsistent with the urgent need to redeem Zion as a refuge from the coming holocaust, but it also shows that Smith and Rigdon were not afraid to ask a lot from church members.

Cowdery and others also spoke on the deliverance of Zion and the need for donations. Smith prophesied "that if Zion was not deliverd the time was near when all of this church, whereever they might be found, would be persecuted and destroyed."[145] At the close of the meeting, Smith "laid hands upon certain children & blessed them in the name of the Lord."[146]

---

141. Minutes, 45 (*JSP*, D4:16).

142. Revelation, Apr. 23, 1834, Hyde and Pratt, Notebook of Revelations, [24] [D&C 104:22] (*JSP*, D4:24).

143. Minutes, Apr. 21, 1834, Minute Book 1, 45–46 (*JSP*, D4:17); Revelation, Feb. 24, 1834, in Hyde and Pratt, Notebook of Revelations, [7]–[18] [D&C 103] (*JSP*, D3:457–63).

144. Minutes, Apr. 21, 1834, Minute Book 1, 46 (*JSP*, D4:17–18); Revelation, June 1, 1833, Revelation Book 2, 59–60 [D&C 95:8] (*JSP*, D3:106–107).

145. Minutes, Apr. 21, 1834, Minute Book 1, 46 (*JSP*, D4:17).

146. Minutes, 47 (*JSP*, D4:19).

The next day, April 22, Smith returned to Kirtland to prepare for his departure to Missouri.[147]

Financial Matters

Having dissolved the United Firm on April 10, 1834, Smith moved to dissolve his debts with the other members. Williams said that "about the time" Smith received a long revelation about the reorganization of the United Firm on April 23, he also received another revelation instructing members of the firm "to balan[ce] all accounts & give up all notes & demands that they had against each other & all be equal which was done."[148] This required Williams to forgive all debts owed him by the other members of the firm, including Smith's for the use of Williams's farm, loans of money, livestock, farming tools, wagons, and other things. This included $27.00 "for Joseph Smith Jr expenses to the east"; $6.00 "for J. Smith Jr. expenses at Court at Chardon"; and purchases of wheat, oats, and a horse as recently as April 14.[149] At one point, Williams said, Smith "gave me his note to the amount several Hundred Dollars."[150] In two undated statements, Williams said: "I frequently assisted him by letting him have money & other things among which was the use of my Farm in Kirtland for two years for which I never took any note or Security," adding in an earlier version that he "re[ceive]d no compensation though he [Smith] frequently promised me."[151]

On the day of Smith's revelation, Bishop Whitney prepared a document listing the balance of accounts owed him by other members of the firm, including Smith, who owed the largest amount, $1,151.31. At the top, Whitney wrote: "Joseph said it was the will of the Lord the accounts ... should be balanced ... in full without any value rec[eive]d"—meaning the debts were to be forgiven. He added with emphasis: "Joseph said it must be don[e]."[152] In total, the other members of the firm no longer owed Whitney $3,635.35.

Also on April 23, Smith met with Rigdon, Williams, Whitney, John Johnson, and Cowdery to pray for God to help Zebedee Coltrin, who had gone to borrow money from Jacob Myers Sr., who lived in Worthington, Ohio, approximately 150 miles southwest of Kirtland.[153] Myers had recently sold a

---

147. Smith, Journal, Apr. 22, 1834 (*JSP*, J1:42).
148. Williams, Statement, n.d.
149. F. G. Williams & Co. Account Book, 6.
150. Williams, Statement, n.d.
151. Williams, Statement, n.d.; Williams, "Statement of facts relative to J Smith & myself," n.d.
152. Newel K. Whitney, Balances Due, Apr. 23, 1834, Newel K. Whitney Papers (*JSP*, D4:31–33).
153. Smith, Journal, Apr. 23, 1834 (*JSP*, J1:42).

mill and land for $10,250.[154] It is not known if Coltrin succeeded, but it was possibly related to Whitney's April 18 authorization for Smith to obtain a loan of between $1,000 and $8,000 in the name of N. K. Whitney & Co.[155]

On the same day, Smith dictated another revelation concerning the distribution and reorganization of the United Firm. Despite the earlier decision on April 10 to dissolve the firm, this revelation directed that it be reorganized as a separate entity from the Missouri branch, explaining that while the "United Firm" was "everlasting," "immutable," and "unchangeable," the covenant had been broken through "transgression" and "covetousness & feigned words, therefore you are dissolved as a United Firm with your brethren" in Missouri. The revelation declared that God will not be "mocked," and that the guilty will be cursed, punished, and delivered "over unto the buffetings of Satan."[156] The identities of the guilty and the nature of their transgression were not disclosed.

The revelation instructed them to "organize yourselves and appoint every man his stewardship"—meaning that each member was to do business in his own name. The properties held by the firm were divided and given as stewardships to Rigdon, Martin Harris, John Johnson, Smith, Cowdery, Williams, and Whitney. Specifically, Rigdon was given his house and lot and was responsible for management of the tannery, while Cowdery was given land next to the printing shop, the management of which he was to share with Williams. Whitney was given "the houses & lot where he now resides, & the lot & building on which the store stands, & the lot also which is on the corner south of the store, & also the lot on which the Ashery is situated." Smith was given the temple lot as well as the farm where his parents were then living, land that had been purchased from Peter French and consecrated by Frederick G. Williams in March 1833. Nevertheless, the men were reminded that they were only stewards of what belonged to God, and therefore God through Smith could still tell them what to do with their stewardships.[157]

The revelation also called for the establishment of two treasuries: one for

154. Jacob Myers, Deed to Joseph Kanagy, Mar. 27, 1834, Richland Co., OH, Deed Books, 1814–1913, vol. 11, 464, microfilm 386,085, U.S. and Canada Record Collection, FHL (*JSP*, D4:12).

155. Newel K. Whitney, Order to Joseph Smith, Apr. 18, 1834, JS Collection (*JSP*, D4:13).

156. Revelation, Apr. 23, 1834, Hyde and Pratt, Notebook of Revelations, [19]–[21], [32] [D&C 104:1–10, 53] (*JSP*, D4:22–23, 28).

157. Revelation, Apr. 23, 1834, Hyde and Pratt, Notebook of Revelations, [21]–[30], [31]–[34] [D&C 104:11–46, 49–51, 55–59] (*JSP*, D4:23–29). On May 3, 1834, Ezra Thayer deeded the tannery (located east of the Whitney store) to Sidney Rigdon. Staker, *Hearken, O Ye People*, 405; *JSP*, D4:24n113.

the Literary Firm's publication of "sacred things," and the other for profits gained from their individual stewardships. Any faithful member of the firm can request money from the latter treasury, if needed, by the common consent of the other members. Meanwhile, God will soften the hearts of the debtors, especially in New York. The revelation instructed the members of the firm that if there was "a chance to loan [borrow] money... even until you shall loan [borrow] enough to deliver yourselves from bondage, it is your privilege. ... I give unto you the privilege this once."[158] However, there is no evidence that the United Firm in either Missouri or Ohio was ever organized on the plan outlined in this revelation.[159]

On April 25 Wilford Woodruff, who had been baptized in 1833 in Richland, New York, arrived in Kirtland in the evening to participate in the approaching expedition of Zion's Camp to Missouri. Woodruff later remembered the first time he met the Mormon prophet: "I saw him out in the field with his brother Hyrum: he had on a very old hat and was engaged shooting at a mark." After introductions, Smith invited Woodruff to stay at his home, which he gladly accepted. While the men were leaving the field, Smith remarked that "this was the first hour he had spent in recreation for a long time." Shortly after arriving home, Smith brought out a wolf skin and asked Woodruff to help him tan it because he wanted to use it on his wagon seat during the long trip to Missouri. "I pulled off my coat," Woodruff said, and "went to work and helped him, and felt honoured in so doing."[160] Woodruff wrote that he "boarded at [Smith's] house most of the time for a week," and later said: "I watched him pretty closely, to see what I could learn."[161] Woodruff must have been favorably impressed because he would not only serve dutifully as a member of Zion's Camp, but he would soon become one of the twelve apostles and later the LDS Church's fourth president.

About this time, Kirtland began to be crowded with volunteers preparing to march to Missouri with Smith, including brothers Joseph and Brigham Young. However, Joseph Young was still fearful about participating in the expedition, having expressed hesitation about going to Missouri while Smith was visiting Livingston County, New York, during a recruiting trip in March 1834. Smith tried to ease Young's anxiety by declaring: "Br Joseph, if you will

158. Revelation, Apr. 23, 1834, Hyde and Pratt, Notebook of Revelations, [35]–[43] [D&C 104:60–82, 84–86] (*JSP*, D4:20–30).

159. See *JSP*, D4:28n131; 29n135.

160. Wilford Woodruff, "Early Events of the Church," Jan. 10, 1858, *Journal of Discourses*, 7:101.

161. Woodruff, 101.

go with Br Brigham and me up to Missouri, and will keep my counsel, both you and Brigham; I promise you in the name of the Lord, that I will lead you there and back again, and there shall not a hair of your heads fall."[162] The three men shook hands to seal the covenant.

Woodruff also remembered that on the evening of April 26 "several of the brethren came in and talked with brother Joseph, and asked what they should do, for they had not means to bear their expenses from there to Missouri." Smith responded, "I am going to have some money soon." The next morning, according to Woodruff, Smith received a letter containing $150 from a "sister Voce, of Boston."[163] The account record for the Zion's Camp lists under April 1834 "cash receivd from the East for the benefit of Zion," $50; and "cash received from Boston for the benefit of Zion," $100. According to this record, Smith had collected at least $332.65 at the time of his departure from Kirtland.[164]

On Sunday, April 27, according to Woodruff, a priesthood meeting was held in the log schoolhouse, during which Rigdon, Hyde, Orson Pratt, Smith and others preached. "It appeared to me," Woodruff wrote, that "there was more light made manifest at that meeting respecting the gospel and Kingdom of God than I had ever receieved from the whole Sectarian world."[165] In later years, Woodruff recalled that Smith invited the men to bear their testimonies of the restored gospel. Afterward, Smith arose and said: "Brethren, I am very much edified and interested in listening to your testimony. But I want to tell you that you know no more concerning the result of this work and what lies before you as the Elders of Israel, and before this people, than a parcel of little children." This startled Woodruff and the others. As Woodruff remembered, Smith told them that "this work would fill the whole earth, and that all nations would have to hear the proclamation of the Gospel." Smith's expansive vision implied that there was much work to be accomplished before the Second Coming and that the end of the world was not as near as they and he had assumed. Smith further said: "This work will fill the Rocky Mountains with tens of thousands of Latter-day Saints, and there will be

---

162. Joseph Young Sr., Letter to Lewis Harvey, Nov. 16, 1880, 4; Historian's Office, Brigham Young History Drafts, 7–8.

163. Woodruff, "Early Events of the Church," Jan. 10, 1858, *Journal of Discourses*, 7:101. This may have been fifty-four-year-old Mary Vose or her twenty-six-year-old niece Ruth Vose, both wealthy converts. See *JSP*, D4:138n182. In his 1882 history of Zion's Camp, Woodruff gave $250 as the amount. Woodruff, "History and Travels of Zion's Camp," 3.

164. Account with the Church of Christ, ca. Aug. 11–29, 1834, JS Collection (*JSP*, D4:138–39).

165. Woodruff, Journal, Apr. 27, 1834 (Vogel, *Wilford Woodruff Journals*, 1:24).

joined with them the Lamanites who dwell in those mountains, who will receive the Gospel of Christ at the mouth of Elders of Israel, and they will be united with the Church and the kingdom of God, and bring forth much good." At this time, Woodruff thought nothing of the statement, but later believed it was fulfilled in the Mormon settlement of Utah.[166]

Nevertheless, it is doubtful that Smith envisioned the headquarters of his church being established in the Rocky Mountains, along with the main body of his followers. In fact, he was optimistic about the success of Zion's Camp. On April 28 he dictated a revelation about reserving $3,000 in lands in Zion for "inheritances in due time" for members of the Kirtland branch of the United Firm.[167] However, when the revelations were published in the Doctrine and Covenants the following year, this revelation was not included.

On May 1 about twenty Mormon men, including Woodruff and Brigham and Joseph Young, left Kirtland with four baggage wagons, traveling to New Portage, Ohio, to await the arrival of the main body of Zion's Camp.[168]

Two days later Smith presided over a conference of elders to discuss a change in the church's name, from "Church of Christ" to "The Church of the Latter-Day Saints." According to the minutes, "a motion was made by Sidney Rigdon, and seconded by Newel K. Whitney, that this church be known hereafter by the name of THE CHURCH OF THE LATTER DAY SAINTS," which was unanimously approved.[169] The minutes give no reason for the change. Some have suggested that it was merely to distinguish the church from Alexander Campbell's organization, also called the Church of Christ.[170] However, this does not explain why the Mormons felt a need to distinguish themselves after five years of converting and interacting with the Campbellites. It is also difficult to explain why a strongly Christian primitivist organization would relinquish the name of Christ, especially considering how the Book of Mormon mocked churches that took other names (e.g., 3 Ne. 27:5–8). Historian Michael Marquardt has suggested that the change may have been an attempt to frustrate the church's creditors in New York from taking legal action against them.[171] This would also explain the dissolution of the United

---

166. Wilford Woodruff, Discourse, ca. June 12–13, 1892, *Millennial Star* (Liverpool, Eng.), Sep. 19, 1892, 605.

167. Revelation, Apr. 28, 1834, Hyde and Pratt, Notebook of Revelations, [44] (*JSP*, D4:33–35).

168. Woodruff, Journal, May 1, 1834 (Vogel, *Wilford Woodruff Journal*, 1:24).

169. Minutes, May 3, 1843, "Communicated," *The Evening and the Morning Star*, May 1834, 160 (*JSP*, D4:42–44).

170. *JSP*, D4:43.

171. H. Michael Marquardt, "An Appraisal of Manchester as Location for the Organization of the Church," *Sunstone*, Feb. 1992, 54. LDS historian Michael MacKay argues that Smith would

Firm and reorganization of the Kirtland branch, as well as the use of code names for the firm and its members and assets in the revelations when they were published the next year in the Doctrine and Covenants.[172] This was only a delay tactic at best, but Smith was desperate. Whitney had told him on April 18 that $4,000 was needed immediately and another $4,000 by September, and there is no indication that this was accomplished.[173]

On Sunday, May 4, Smith preached to the Saints in the shade of the new schoolhouse. According to E. D. Howe, "The Prophet had a general meeting of his troops and all the brethren in the neighborhood," during which Smith and Rigdon "harangued them to deeds of valor, to perseverance, and to a renewal of their faith in his commandments—dwelling largely, of course, on ancient persecutions of the Christians—their own persecution, and the beauties of martyrdom, as sure passports to glory—assuring them that they should all return, safe and sound, if they followed his instructions."[174] George A. Smith remembered that Smith "promised the brethren that if they would all live as they should, before the Lord, keeping his commandments, & not, like the children of Israel murmur against the Lord & his servants, they should all safely return & not one of them should fall upon the mission they were about to undertake, for if they were united & exercised faith, God would deliver them out of the hands of their enemies, but should they like the children of Israel forget God & his promises & treat lightly his commandments, He would visit them in his wrath & vex them in his sore displeasure."[175]

Before leaving Kirtland with Zion's Camp on May 5, Smith made several land transactions. On this day, Williams deeded his 1.5-acre farm to Smith for $177.70.[176] This was the farm that Smith's parents had been using for two

---

not have made the name change public if he were trying to elude creditors, but a public announcement would be necessary to argue in court that a new organization had been formed and would not be responsible for the debts of the former. Indeed, the publication of the minutes in the May 1834 issue of *The Evening and the Morning Star* is singular. MacKay, *Sacred Space*, 88–89.

172. Concerning the use of code names in the 1835 Doctrine and Covenants, LDS historian Max Parkin wrote that "the Prophet was concerned about protecting members of the firm ... from unnecessary scrutiny by a sometimes unfriendly public and peering creditors." Parkin, "Joseph Smith and the United Firm," 58. Orson Pratt explained in 1852 that "fictitious names, which Joseph substituted for the real names in certain revelations" so that "their creditors in Cainhannoch (New York) should not take advantage of this Church firm." Orson Pratt, Letter to Brigham Young, Nov. 20, 1852, [2]–[3]. See D&C, 1835 ed., XCVIII:13 [D&C 104:81].

173. Newel K. Whitney, Order, to Joseph Smith, Apr. 18, 1834, JS Collection (*JSP*, D4:12–13 and 12n46).

174. Howe, *Mormonism Unvailed*, 156.

175. George A. Smith, Memoir and Autobiography, 11b.

176. Frederick G. Williams, Deed for property in Kirtland Township, Geauga Co., OH, to Joseph Smith, May 5, 1834, Geauga County Deed Records, vol. 18, 477–78.

years. On the same day, Smith also purchased the remaining 103 acres of Williams's property for $2,200.[177] This action fulfilled a January 5, 1833, revelation commanding Williams to consecrate his farm, which he did when he joined the United Firm in March 1833.[178] It also fulfilled his April 23, 1834, obligation to forgive all debts owed him by other members of the United Firm.[179] In addition, Smith received a deed from John and Alice Johnson for land valued at $222.30.[180] Although the wording of the deeds indicates that Smith paid for the property in full at the time of signing, it seems doubtful that any money changed hands.

Smith rushed to settle his business affairs before leaving for Missouri since he did not know how long he would be gone.[181] The plan was for Zion's Camp and the Missouri militia to escort the Mormons back to their lands in Jackson County and for Smith and his company to provide protection after the militia withdrew.

177. Williams, Deed for property in Kirtland Township, Geauga Co., OH, to Joseph Smith, May 5, 1834, Geauga County Deed Records, vol. 18, 480–81.

178. Revelation, Jan. 5, 1834 [1833] [uncanonized], Revelations Collection (*JSP*, D2:356–61).

179. Williams, Statement, n.d.; and Williams, "Statement of facts relative to J Smith & myself," n.d. According to Oliver Cowdery, Williams later regretted losing his farm to Smith. Cowdery, Letter to Warren Cowdery and Lyman Cowdery, June 2, 1838, [3].

180. John and Alice (Elsa) Johnson, Deed for property in Kirtland Township, Geauga Co., OH, to Joseph Smith, May 5, 1834, Geauga County Deed Records, vol. 18, 478–79 (*JSP*, D4:46–48). This deed was subsequently deemed invalid because at this time the land was owned by Newel K. Whitney, who deeded it to the Johnsons in 1836. On January 4, 1837, the Johnsons again deeded the land to Joseph Smith. See *JSP*, D4:45–46.

181. On April 30 Smith also paid debts to various persons amounting to $50. Smith, Journal, Apr. 30, 1834 (*JSP*, J1:43). The source of the money is unknown.

16

Army of Israel

MAY–JULY 1834

I say unto you, my friends, … find favor in the eyes of the people,
until the armies of Israel become very great.
—*Revelation, June 22, 1834, Revelation*
Book 1,[200] [D&C 105:26]

On May 5, 1834, Smith marched out of Kirtland at the head of the approximately hundred-man Army of Israel, more generally known as Zion's Camp.[1] On the first day, they traveled about twenty-seven miles south to Streetsboro, Ohio, and stayed in a Mr. Ford's barn.[2] The next day the camp traveled about twenty-three miles southwest to New Portage, where they joined the advance contingent of more than twenty men who had left Kirtland on May 1. Although this group would be joined by others along the way and number a little more than 200 men, about twelve women, and ten children, it was fewer than the 500 recommended by the February 1834 revelation.[3]

On May 7–8 Smith organized the camp into companies of twelve headed by a captain and appointed Frederick G. Williams as paymaster. It was decided that everyone in the camp should put their money into a general fund along with the donations collected prior to the march that could then be distributed as needed under Smith's direction. "Some of the brethren had

---

1. Heber C. Kimball, "Elder Kimball's Journal," *Times and Seasons* (Nauvoo, IL), Jan. 15, 1845, 771; JS History, vol. A-1, 477 (DHC 2:63). The account of Zion's Camp in Smith's history (vol. A-1, 477–528) was compiled by Willard Richards in June–August 1843 and chiefly relied on Kimball's account published in *Times and Seasons*, Jan. 15–Apr. 15, 1845, 771–869. It was later revised by George A. Smith, a participant in the events described, in August 1845. See Vogel, ed., *History of Joseph Smith*, 1:lxxxv–lxxxviii, lxxxviii n. 19.

2. Kimball, "Elder Kimball's Journal," *Times and Seasons*, Jan. 15, 1845, 771; JS History, vol. A-1, 477–78, and Addenda, 16, Note 20 (DHC 2:63).

3. On the members of Zion's Camp, see Backman, comp., *A Profile of Latter-day Saints of Kirtland, Ohio, and Members of Zion's Camp*, 93–95; Revelation, Feb. 24, 1834, in Hyde and Pratt, Notebook of Revelations, [15]–[16] [D&C 103:32–34] (*JSP*, D3:462).

considerable, and some had little or none," Heber C. Kimball remembered, "yet all became equal."[4] The company's funds and expenditures were carefully noted in a record kept by Williams, which documents that on May 8, 1834, there was a total of $1,659.59 of consecrated funds collected.[5]

Marching Through Ohio

Having completed the organization of the camp on the morning of May 8, Smith armed himself with Wilford Woodruff's sword and led the camp as it marched through Ohio, traveling about twelve miles southwest to Chippewa Township.[6] Woodruff wrote, "Our march was similar to the ancient Israelites. Our horses, waggons and tents were in readiness and we were led by Joseph. Our Company now consisted of twenty baggage waggons and rising of one hundred & fifty men. The men were armed with dirks pistols Swords & rifles For self defence."[7] The food was simple and scarce, and every night the camp prayed and then retired at the sounding of a trumpet. At 4:00 a.m., they were awakened by the trumpet to pray and prepare for another day of travel.[8]

On May 9 the camp traveled about seventeen miles southwest to Wooster, Ohio, and on the following day another thirty-three miles west, passing through Mansfield and stopping at Richfield, Ohio, where they were joined by Lyman E. Johnson, Willard Snow, and others from Vermont. On Sunday, May 11, Sylvester Smith preached to the camp, after which they partook of the sacrament. Later, they were joined by eight more men.[9] Woodruff recorded, "We made it a practice of pitching our tents on Saturday night and not remove them untill Monday morning[.] we had preaching on the Lords day[.] Brother Joseph often addressed us in the name of the Lord while on our journey and often while addressing the camp he was clothed upon with much of the spirit of God[.] his precepts were very instructive and interesting."[10]

---

4. Kimball, Autobiography, ca. 1842–58, 8; Kimball, "Elder Kimball's Journal," *Times and Seasons*, Jan. 15, 1845, 771; JS History, vol. A-1, 478–79 (DHC 2:65).

5. Williams's record is no longer extant, but Orson Hyde later used it to create two records presented at the trial of Sylvester Smith (Aug. 28–29, 1834). See Account with the Church of Christ, ca. Aug. 11–29, 1834, JS Collection (*JSP*, D4:135–55); and Account with the Camp of Israel, ca. Aug. 11–29, 1834, JS Collection (*JSP*, D4:156–63).

6. JS History, vol. A-1, 478 (DHC 2:64); Woodruff, "The History and Travels of Zion's Camp," 7. Woodruff recorded: "According to Brother Joseph's request I delivered him my sword for his own use." Woodruff, Journal, May 8, 1834 (Vogel, *Wilford Woodruff Journals*, 1:24).

7. Woodruff, Journal, May 8, 1834 (Vogel, *Wilford Woodruff Journals*, 1:24–25).

8. Kimball, "Elder Kimball's Journal," *Times and Seasons*, Jan. 15, 1845, 771; JS History, vol. A-1, 478 (DHC 2:64–65).

9. Heber C. Kimball, "Elder Kimball's Journal," *Times and Seasons*, Jan. 15, 1845, 771–72; JS History, vol. A-1, 478–79 (DHC 2:65).

10. Woodruff, Journal, May–June 1834 (Vogel, *Wilford Woodruff Journals*, 1:24–25).

On Monday, May 12, Smith led the company about thirty-five miles and camped on the Sandusky Plains near some Indian settlements. On the following day the camp passed through some woods, where the road was muddy. "In many instances," Kimball wrote, "we had to fasten ropes to the wagons to haul them out of the sloughs and mud holes."[11] While encamped at Bellefontaine, Ohio, on May 14, Sylvester Smith complained about the lack of food, although his captain, Brigham Young, was doing his best to get supplies for his men.[12]

On May 15 Smith led Zion's Camp about thirty-five miles south and, after fording Mad River, set up camp a little west of Springfield, Ohio. During the night, Smith found Moses Martin asleep while on guard duty. Taking Martin's sword, Smith left him sleeping.[13]

The next day, while the company was passing through the woods on its way toward Dayton, Smith, who was riding in a wagon with his brother Hyrum, Ezra Thayer, and cousin George A. Smith, said he felt "depressed in spirit and lonesome" and that he believed "that there had been a great deal of bloodshed in that place." He further remarked that "whenever a man of God is in a place where many have been killed, he will feel lonesome and unpleasant, and his spirits will sink."[14] According to this account, which was apparently inserted into Smith's official history in 1845 by George A. Smith, the camp soon left the woods and discovered a farm on which there was a large mound of earth. This sixty-foot mound appeared to be of human construction and reportedly was filled with "human bones" from some great battle. The general opinion in Smith's day was that such mounds were used anciently for the mass burial of a white-skinned race that was destroyed in a great war with the ancestors of the Indians.[15] The account mentions that the mound was "covered with apple trees," which was a common method of guessing the ages of the mounds at more than a thousand years.[16]

At dinner some of the men expressed fear about "milk sickness," which they had seen exhibited in people and cattle along the way. Milk sickness causes trembling, vomiting, and severe intestinal pain in people who consume milk or meat from a cow that has fed on the white snakeroot plant, a

---

11. Heber C. Kimball, "Elder Kimball's Journal," *Times and Seasons*, Jan. 15, 1845, 772.

12. Kimball, 772; JS History, vol. A-1, Addenda, 6–7, Note 1 (DHC 2:65–66), which was added by Thomas Bullock about Aug. 21–31, 1845. Vogel, *History of Joseph Smith*, 1:lxxxviii.

13. JS History, vol. A-1, Addenda, 7, Note 1 (DHC 2:66).

14. JS History.

15. Vogel, *Indian Origins and the Book of Mormon*, 53–69.

16. Vogel, 29.

member of the daisy family that grows in the Ohio River Valley. Symptoms appear several hours after ingestion, and death within two to ten days.[17] The cause of milk sickness was not understood until later in the nineteenth century, but Smith promised that if they followed his command, they would not be harmed. This account, no doubt remembered by George A. Smith in 1845, concludes by having the prophet declare that "although we passed through neighborhoods where many of the people and cattle were infected with the sickness, yet my words were fulfilled."[18]

When the camp passed through Dayton, locals asked what such a large group was up to but were answered evasively. After the camp settled in for the night, a court-martial was held and Moses Martin was tried for falling asleep while on guard duty the night before. Martin defended himself, saying that "he was overcome with fatigue, and so overpowered that he could not keep awake." Smith decided to acquit him with a warning and took the occasion to lecture the camp.[19]

On May 17, after traveling forty miles, Zion's Camp crossed the Ohio state line into Wayne County, Indiana, and set up camp in Richland. At this point in the journey, Kimball noted: "Our feet were very sore and blistered, and our stockings were wet with blood, the weather being very warm."[20]

Sylvester Smith Rebels

On the evening of May 17, according to Kimball's account, a dispute arose between Sylvester Smith and others in the camp, and Joseph Smith (no relation) was called upon to arbitrate the matter. He warned them that misfortune would befall them all if they did not repent, and that it would begin to happen before they left their present campsite.[21]

This may have been the incident involving Sylvester's refusing to share bread with Parley P. Pratt, which was brought up by Smith and others at Sylvester's trial the following August. Smith testified that on hearing a complaint about Sylvester, he went with Pratt and John S. Carter to Sylvester's

---

17. See Milk sickness, wikipedia.org; Knight, *A Guide to Poisonous House and Garden Plants*, 117–18.

18. JS History, vol. A-1, Addenda, 7, Note 1 (DHC 2:66–67); Vogel, *History of Joseph Smith*, 1:lxxxviii.

19. JS History.

20. Kimball, "Elder Kimball's Journal," *Times and Seasons*, Jan. 15, 1845, 772; JS History, vol. A-1, Addenda, 4, Note 2 (DHC 2:68).

21. Kimball, "Elder Kimball's Journal," *Times and Seasons*, Jan. 15, 1845, 772; JS History, vol. A-1, Addenda, 4, Note G (DHC 2:65–66), which was added by Thomas Bullock between May–July 1845. Vogel, *History of Joseph Smith*, 1:lxxxviii; 2:78n211.

tent and confronted Sylvester, who justified his actions. Details are lacking, but Sylvester's possession of extra bread may have been due to rationing in his company, of which Pratt was not a member. However, Smith said he "rebuked brother Sylvester ... because if this was so, brethren might frequently retire to rest, without food, and as long as he (brother Sylvester) had bread he was bound. to impart to those who had none, and that under these circumstances, brother Sylvester, had conducted contrary to the principles of Christ, and that his (Sylvester's) mind was darkned in consequence of this covetous spirit."[22] At this trial, Brigham Young said that when Sylvester resisted Smith's reprimand concerning the bread, Smith "reproved him sharply." Luke Johnson testified that he did not witness the transaction but heard Smith reprove Sylvester and "thought at the time the reproofs were rather severe, but had learned since, they were not any more severe than were just."[23]

Levi Hancock, who was the cook for Sylvester's company, remembered decades later that "Sylvester lost the spirit of peace and became dissatisfied with John Carter and called him an old jackass and many other names which soon brought dissatisfaction in our tent." On hearing this, Smith rebuked Sylvester for "sowing the seeds of discord." Sylvester responded that he did not care "if Joseph was a Prophet he was not afraid and would contradict him in the face of all present." Smith said, "If I have not told you the truth then God never spoke by me," and walked away. "We all said that is enough. We believed Joseph," Hancock wrote; thereafter "Sylvester became more calm and acted like a saint; [and] for sometime we had peace."[24]

In the morning, on May 18, according to Kimball, "we found almost every horse in the camp so badly foundered that we could scarce lead them a few rods to the water." The members of the camp interpreted this as "the effects of discord" and a fulfillment of Smith's warning. When Smith learned of the situation with the horses, he declared that "all those who would humble themselves before the Lord, should know that the hand of God was in this misfortune, and their horses should be restored to health immediately, and by twelve o'clock the same day the horses were as nimble as ever, with the exception of one of Sylvester Smith's which soon afterwards died."[25]

As this was Sunday, the camp did not travel but held the usual church

---

22. Minutes, Aug. 28–29, 1834, Minute Book 1, 62–63 (*JSP*, D4:126).

23. Minutes, 62, 69 (*JSP*, D4:126, 131).

24. Levi Hancock, Autobiographical Sketch, 138.

25. Kimball, "Elder Kimball's Journal," *Times and Seasons*, Jan. 15, 1845, 772; JS History, vol. A-1, Addenda, 4, Note G (DHC 2:68–69).

services. After the meeting, Smith sat on the ground in his tent and wrote a letter to Emma in response to "the few lines [she] wrote and sent by the ha[n]d of Brother Lyman [which] gave me satisfaction and comfort." Smith appreciated Emma's support, but he must have felt some guilt for leaving his family. "I am sensible of the dut[i]es of a Husband and Father," he began, "and that I am well and I pray God to let his blessings to rest upon you and the Children and all that are a round you untill I return to your society." He asked her to continue writing as it was "a consolation to me ... in my lonely moments which is not easily discribed," and he promised to write her "every Su[n]day if I can and let you know how I am." Smith added, "In this way I can have the privelege to communicate some of my feelings that I should not dare to reveal as you know that my situation is a very critacal one." Despite the dire predictions the previous day, Smith assured Emma that "all the Kirtland Brothen [brethren] are well and cannot fail." Closing his brief letter, he wrote: "O may the blessings of God rest upon you is the prayer of your Husband until death."[26]

Indiana and Illinois

On Monday, May 19, Smith and Zion's Camp traveled thirty-one miles through Indiana, mostly on the National Road, which ran from Maryland through Indiana and into Illinois, but also on some muddy by-roads. John M. Chidester remembered, "Zion's Camp, in passing through the state of Indiana, had to cross very bad swamps, consequently we had to attach ropes to the wagons to help them through, and the Prophet was the first man at the rope in his bare feet. This was characteristic of him in all times of difficulty."[27] After traveling all day, the camp stopped in Franklin Township, Indiana.[28]

The next day Smith led the camp through about twenty-five miles of muddy roads to Greenfield, Indiana. While resting there, three men came into the camp inquiring about their intent and who the leader was, but got no clear answer.[29] On this day, the *Huron Reflector* in Norwalk, Ohio, stated that "in obedience to a revelation communicated to their great Prophet, Joseph

---

26. Joseph Smith, Letter to Emma Smith, May 18, 1834, [1] (*JSP*, D4:50). "Brother Lyman" was likely either Lyman Johnson or Amasa Lyman. *JSP*, D4:50n234.

27. John M. Chidester, "Recollections of the Prophet Joseph Smith," *Juvenile Instructor*, Mar. 1, 1892, 151.

28. JS History, vol. A-1, 480 (DHC 2:69), which is an interlinear insertion probably added under George A. Smith's direction in August 1845. Vogel, *History of Joseph Smith*, 2:79n230.

29. Kimball, "Extracts from H. C. Kimball's Journal," *Times and Seasons*, Feb. 1, 1845, 787–88; JS History, vol. A-1, 480, and Addenda, 7–8, Note 3 (DHC 2:69–70); Vogel, *History of Joseph Smith*, 2:79n235, n240.

Smith, three hundred young men are to 'go well armed and equipped to defend the *promised land* in Missouri,'" and that the Mormons were marching through the country "with the Book of Mormon in one hand and a musket in the other."[30] Such a large group of armed men passing through their communities naturally raised an alarm. As the camp approached Indianapolis, they were warned that they would meet with resistance should they attempt to pass through the city. On the following day, Smith ordered the camp to pass through Indianapolis in small groups so as not to attract attention.[31]

Over the next three days Smith led the camp about seventy-five miles, passing Belleville and Greencastle, Indiana, crossing the Wabash River in ferry boats, then continuing another ten miles into Edgar County, Illinois, and setting up camp. On Sunday, May 25, there was no meeting in the camp, but the day was spent "washing and baking" and otherwise preparing for the next day's travel. During the day a man came into the camp and swore the group would never make it over the Mississippi River alive, which caused many to surmise that he was a spy from Jackson County.[32]

On Monday, May 26, Smith led Zion's Camp through Paris, Illinois, and across a sixteen-mile prairie. Near Embarras River, Smith lectured his men not to kill wild animals unnecessarily. He then astonished them by shooting a squirrel and walking away, leaving it on the ground. Orson Hyde picked it up and said it would be cooked and not wasted. Late that night, Smith fired his gun to sound a false alarm to show the camp how the moon's light filtered through trees made it appear there were campfires on the prairie before them. It also provided an opportunity to test the readiness of the camp.[33]

On the following day Smith led the camp over the Kaskaskia River, transporting their baggage on two skiffs and swimming across with their wagons and horses. The next day, the camp reached Decatur, Illinois, where another horse died. While encamped at Decatur on May 29, Smith led the men through a sham battle to alleviate growing tension and unrest caused by a lack of provisions. During the exercise, Kimball cut his hand severely on a sword. The camp then crossed the prairie and stopped to dine near

---

30. "Mormonism," *Huron Reflector* (Norwalk, OH), May 20, 1834, [2]; italics in original.

31. JS History, vol. A-1, 480, and Addenda, 8, Note 4 (DHC 2:70); Vogel, *History of Joseph Smith*, 2:80n245.

32. JS History, vol. A-1, 480, and Addenda, 8, Notes 4 and 5 (DHC 2:70–71); Vogel, *History of Joseph Smith*, 2:81nn272 and 284; Kimball, "Elder Kimball's Journal," *Times and Seasons*, Jan. 15, 1845, 772.

33. JS History, vol. A-1, 480, and Addenda, 8–9, Note 5 (DHC 2:70–72); Vogel, *History of Joseph Smith*, 2:81n284.

Springfield, Illinois, at which time Smith wrote a letter to the Missouri church leaders wanting to know the situation there and requesting them to send someone to meet them.[34]

On May 30 Smith led the camp through Springfield, which caused considerable curiosity among the locals, and after traveling about three miles farther, they camped on Spring Creek, where they learned that Hyrum Smith and his company from Michigan were about fifty miles north of them.[35] On the following day Smith led the camp to within one mile of Jacksonville, Illinois, where they camped and prepared for the sabbath.[36] On Sunday, June 1, Smith and others preached all day to a crowd from Jacksonville. The Mormon preachers must have stuck closely to biblical proof texts since the non-Mormons who attended thought they were listening to representatives of different denominations such as the Methodists, Universalists, and Campbellites.[37]

Zelph and a Prophecy

On June 2 the camp passed through Jacksonville and continued to the banks of the Illinois River. Despite threats from enemies, they ferried over the river and set up camp on the western bank.[38] On the following day Smith and some of his men visited a nearby Indian burial mound and unearthed the skeletal remains of a man, which they brought back to the camp. In the afternoon, Smith stood on a wagon and delivered a prophecy. Levi Hancock said he did not go to the mound with the others but "saw some bones that were brought back with a broken arrow," which were "laid down by our camp." Addressing Sylvester Smith, the prophet said: "This is what I told you and now I want to tell you that you may know what I meant."[39] According to Kimball, "The Lord had told him [Smith] that there would a scourge come upon the camp, in consequence of the fractious and unruly spirits that appeared among them and they should die like sheep with the rot; still if they would repent and humble themselves before the Lord, the

---

34. Kimball, "Elder Kimball's Journal," *Times and Seasons*, Jan. 15, 1845, 772; JS History, vol. A-1, 481, and Addenda, 9, Note 6 (DHC 2:74–75); Vogel, *History of Joseph Smith*, 2:84n327. Smith's letter is not extant.

35. JS History, vol. A-1, Addenda, 10, Note 7 (DHC 2:76–77); Vogel, *History of Joseph Smith*, 2:86n375.

36. JS History (DHC 2:77–78); Vogel, *History of Joseph Smith*, 2:86n375.

37. Kimball, "Elder Kimball's Journal," *Times and Seasons*, Jan. 15, 1845, 772–73; JS History, vol. A-1, Addenda, 11–12, Note 7 (DHC 2:77–78); Vogel, *History of Joseph Smith*, 2:88n411.

38. Kimball, "Extracts from H. C. Kimball's Journal," *Times and Seasons*, Feb. 1, 1845, 788.

39. Hancock, Autobiography, 140.

scourge in a great measure might be turned away; but, as the Lord lives, this camp will suffer for giving way to their unruly temper."[40] Woodruff inserted a note in Smith's manuscript history: "Thare was not a dry Eye in Camp, all ware bathed in tears."[41] Apparently, Smith used the grave mounds and the skeleton as a reminder to his men of what happened to the Nephite armies when they became rebellious.

Kimball also reported that as the camp was about to continue, "we felt anxious to know who the person was who had been killed by that arrow." Apparently enwrapped in vision, Smith said that "he had been an officer who fell in battle, in the last destruction among the Lamanites, and his name was Zelph. This caused us to rejoice much, to think that God was so mindful of us as to show these things to his servant."[42] Woodruff similarly reported that it was revealed to Smith that the skeleton belonged to a man named Zelph, who was "a white Lamanite" and "a warrior under the great prophet Onandagus that was known from the hill Camorah or east sea to the Rocky mountains." Onandagus was apparently derived from the Onondaga ("Hill Place") Indian Nation, one of the tribes belonging to the five-nation confederacy of the Iroquois who occupied western New York. According to Woodruff, Smith also discovered that Zelph had been "killed in battle with an arrow," the stone head of which "was found among his ribs." Observing that one of his thigh bones had been broken and healed, Smith explained that "this was done by a stone flung from a sling in battle years before his death." Unlike other Lamanites, Zelph was "a man of God," who had "the curs[e]" of dark skin "taken from him or at least in part." Woodruff wrote that he put the broken thigh bone in his wagon and brought it with him to Missouri.[43]

When the camp arrived near Atlas, Illinois, they purchased twenty-five gallons of honey and twelve Missouri-cured hams that were slightly damaged or rotting on the outside. Someone subsequently threw six of the hams down at Smith's tent door, angrily declaring, "We don't eat dirty, stinking

---

40. Kimball, "Extracts from H. C. Kimball's Journal," *Times and Seasons*, Feb. 1, 1845, 788.

41. Woodruff inserted this note in red ink in the left margin of JS History, vol. A-2, 320, possibly in December 1859. Vogel, *History of Joseph Smith*, 2:92n477.

42. Kimball, "Extracts from H. C. Kimball's Journal," *Times and Seasons*, Feb. 1, 1845, 788.

43. Woodruff, Journal, May–June 1834 (Vogel, *Wilford Woodruff Journals*, 1:24–25). For an analysis of the Zelph episode, see Godfrey, "The Zelph Story." Archaeologists have since located this approximately thirty-foot high mound along the Illinois River about one mile south of Valley City, Illinois. This mound, which has been designated the Naples-Russell Mound Number 8, sits high above the river on top of a 300-foot bluff. It has been classified as a Hopewell burial mound of the Middle Woodland period of the North American pre-Columbian era, which dates from roughly 50 BCE to CE 250. Farnsworth, "Lamanitish Arrows and Eagles with Lead Eyes."

meet." Smith ordered Zebedee Coltrin to fry up some of the damaged ham, and he and his company feasted on it.[44] That night, a great uneasiness pervaded the camp. As Kimball recalled, "Guns were fired in almost all directions through the night. Brother Joseph did not sleep much, if any, but was through the camp, pretty much during the night."[45]

In the morning, on June 4, Smith and the company traveled about five miles to the banks of the Mississippi River, where it took two days to cross into Missouri by repeatedly using a ferry. The members of the camp were extremely apprehensive after hearing rumors that 400 Missourians were waiting for them on the Missouri side.[46] While encamped "on the banks of the Mississippi" River, near Atlas, Illinois, and awaiting the arrival of a boat, Smith dictated a letter to Emma which downplayed the difficulties the expedition was encountering. He told her the camp was experiencing a "tolerable degree of union," and gave her the impression that all members had sufficient food. In fact, the camp was experiencing disharmony over the quality and quantity of food, and the day before Smith had chastised its members for rebellion.[47]

Smith, nevertheless, complained about the physical strain of traveling. "I have been able to endur[e] the fatigue of the journey far beyond my most sanguine expectations," he reported, "except have been troubled some with lameness, have had my feet blistered, but are now well, and have also had a little touch of my side complaint."[48] The long days of walking no doubt pained his lower left leg from which pieces of bone had been removed during a childhood leg operation, and his "side complaint" may refer to an injury he received when he was attacked by the mob in Hiram, Ohio, in 1832, and may have been aggravated while pulling wagons out of the mud.

Smith confessed that "our numbers and means are altogether too small for the accomplishment of such a great enterprise. ... Now is the time for the Church abroad to come to Zion. It is our prayer day and night that God will open the heart of the Churches to pour in men and means to assist us, for the redemption and upbuilding of Zion." Such help never materialized. Smith reported that the enemy has been kept at bay because they are presently "terrified" due to their spies miscalculating their numbers. "The Lord

---

44. JS History, vol. A-1, Addenda, 5, Note I, and 12, Note 8 (DHC 2:80–81); Vogel, *History of Joseph Smith*, 2:93nn481 and 487.

45. Kimball, "Extracts from H. C. Kimball's Journal," *Times and Seasons*, Feb. 1, 1845, 788.

46. Kimball, 788.

47. Joseph Smith, Letter to Emma Smith, June 4, 1834, JS Letterbook 2, 56–57 (*JSP*, D4:54–57).

48. Smith, 57 (*JSP*, D4:54).

shows us to good advantage in the eyes of their spies," he wrote, "for in counting us the[y] make of our 170 men from five to seven hundred. ... The general report is that four or five hundred Mormons are traveling through the country well armed, and disciplined; and that five hundred more has gone a south west [course] and expect to meet us, and also another company are on a rout North of us, all these things serve to help us, and we believe the hand of the Lord is in it."[49] While Smith attributed this to God, the camp's numbers may have been exaggerated intentionally to arouse opposition against the Mormons.

Smith also reflected on the two burial mounds encountered while passing through Illinois, especially the discovery of Zelph. According to Smith, the camp was "wandering over the plains of the Nephites, recounting occasionaly the history of the Book of Mormon, roving over the mounds of that once beloved people of the Lord, picking up their skulls & their bones, as a proof of its divine authenticity."[50] Smith connected his revelation about Zelph and the burial mounds with the history recounted in the Book of Mormon, which like the folklore about the ancient Mound Builders described a great war in which a white race was destroyed by the ancestors of the Indians.[51]

If it were not for missing their families and loved ones, Smith said, "our whole journey would be as a dream, and this would be the happiest period of all our lives."[52] Smith enjoyed the camaraderie and the opportunity to lead; it must have been bonding for many of its participants, who began reuniting annually in 1864 to commemorate their experience.[53]

Missouri

On June 5 the camp finished crossing the river and then set up "in a little oak grove" on the western bank near the town of Louisiana, Missouri, where the Mormon leader and Sylvester Smith had another altercation. This time it was about the prophet's dog, Old Major, a large English mastiff, which according to George A. Smith was "greatly attached to Joseph and was generally by his side, keeping close watch of every thing that approached the camp."[54] According to Kimball, "There was some feelings of hostility manifested again by Sylvester Smith, in consequence of a dog growling at him

---

49. Smith, 57 (*JSP*, D4:56).
50. Smith, 57–58 (*JSP*, D4:57).
51. Vogel, *Indian Origins and the Book of Mormon*, 53–69.
52. Joseph Smith, Letter to Emma Smith, June 4, 1834, JS Letterbook 2, 58 (*JSP*, D4:57).
53. "Festival of the Camp of Zion," *Deseret News* (Salt Lake City), Oct. 17, 1864, 5.
54. George A. Smith, Memoirs and Autobiography, 29; Baugh, "Joseph Smith's Dog, Old Major."

while he was marching his company up to the camp, he being the last that came over the river."[55]

The next morning, according to Brigham Young, there was "considerable complaint and murmuring concerning the dog." Smith reprimanded the complainers for being so easily insulted and uncompromising: "I will descend to the spirit that is in the camp, to show you the spirit you are of for I want to drive it from the camp," and then declared: "The first man that kills that dog, ... I will whip him!" Sylvester interrupted, "If that dog bites me I will kill him." "If you do," Joseph said firmly, "I will whip you." Sylvester defiantly remarked, "If you do, I shall defend myself the best way that I can!"

Young remembered that Joseph then asked the men "if they were not ashamed of such a spirit?" "I am," he said, and reproved them "for condescending to that spirit,—that they ought to be above it, that it was the spirit of a dog, and men ought never to place themselves on a level with beasts. but be possessed of a more noble disposition. He then said he had decended to that spirit in order to show the spirit which was among them."[56] George A. Smith remembered that Joseph also told Sylvester that "he was possessed of a wicked spirit and said in the name of the Lord that if he did not get rid of that spirit the day would come when a dog should bite him, and gnaw his flesh and he would not be able to resist it." Unimpressed, Sylvester accused Joseph of "prophesying lies in the name of the Lord."[57]

David Elliott said he was not present when Smith made the remarks about the dog but heard about the episode afterward and that "during the forenoon he learned that there were many of the bretheren dissatisfied with brother Joseph's remarks, concerning the dog in the morning." He confessed that he harbored some "disagreeable feelings" until he "heard brother Joseph give a further explanation, which perfectly satisfied his mind." Orson Hyde said he was present when Joseph reproved Sylvester, but did not think his reproofs were unjust. Furthermore, "he did not consider this reproof had any tendency to lessen the esteem of the brethren for brother Smith, but if they had, in consequence of a confession in general terms, from brother Smith, about that time, he thought that sufficient to heal every hard feeling then existing against him, or that might exist."[58]

On the morning of June 7, a small company with two wagons joined Zion's

---

55. Kimball, "Extracts from H. C. Kimball's Journal," *Times and Seasons* Feb. 1, 1845, 788.
56. Minutes, Aug. 28–29, 1834, Minute Book 1, 67 (*JSP*, D4:129–30).
57. George A. Smith, Memoir and Autobiography, 29.
58. Minutes, Aug. 28–29, 1834, Minute Book 1, 62, 67–68 (*JSP*, D4:125, 130).

Camp from nearby Bowling Green, Missouri. Later the same day, Smith led the company about twenty miles northwest and set up camp east of Paris, Missouri, near the Salt River, where there was a branch of the church known as the Allred settlement. On the following day, Sunday, the camp held church services. Later that day, they were joined by the Michigan contingent lead by Hyrum Smith and Lyman Wight, which added nine men, three women, and three boys to the expedition.[59] The camp now consisted of approximately 205 men, twelve women, and ten children.[60] The camp was even more conspicuous as it traveled the remaining 140 miles with twenty-five baggage wagons, each pulled by with two or three horses.[61]

Woodruff recorded that the meeting of the two groups was "joyful," and Lyman O. Littlefield, a thirteen-year-old boy who traveled with his father, Waldo, in Hyrum Smith's party, remembered that the prophet "received our little company with manifestations of friendship and joy."[62] Decades later, Littlefield recalled seeing the Mormon leader: "I first beheld him a tall, well-proportioned man, busily mingling with the members of Zion's Camp, shaking hands with them, meeting them with friendly greetings and carefully seeing to their comforts."[63]

The company remained on Salt River three more days, during which Smith reorganized the camp into groups of ten with a captain over each. Lyman Wight was designated as the general of the army of Israel; Smith was "acknowledged as Commander in-Chief."[64] Smith also chose twenty men as his lifeguards with Hyrum Smith as captain and George A. Smith as armor-bearer. "I took care and kept his arms loaded and in order," George recalled. "They consisted of a brace of fine silver mounted brass barrelled horse pistols, which had been taken from a British Officer in the war of 1812, a Rifle, also a Sword. ... I generally accompanied him wherever he went, carrying these arms with me, whenever he discharged either of them I reloaded it, and acted as a personal guard."[65] During their encampment at Salt River, Wight marched the men onto the prairie, where he inspected their firelocks

---

59. Kimball, "Extracts from H. C. Kimball's Journal," *Times and Seasons*, Feb. 1, 1845, 789; Manscill, "Journal of the Branch of the Church of Christ in Pontiac, ... 1834," 171, 174.

60. Bradley, *Zion's Camp 1834*, 28; Radke, "We Also Marched," 149.

61. Kimball, "Extracts from H. C. Kimball's Journal," *Times and Seasons*, Feb. 1, 1845, 789.

62. Woodruff, Journal, May–June 1834 (Vogel, *Wilford Woodruff Journals*, 1:25); Lyman O. Littlefield, "The Prophet Joseph Smith in Zion's Camp," *Juvenile Instructor*, Jan. 1, 1892, 57.

63. Littlefield, "The Prophet Joseph Smith in Zion's Camp," 56–57.

64. George A. Smith, Memoir and Autobiography, 30; see also Kimball, "Extracts from H. C. Kimball's Journal," *Times and Seasons*, Feb. 1, 1845, 789.

65. George A. Smith, Memoir and Autobiography, 30–31.

and ordered them discharged as a test. From this point, their guns were kept loaded. After drilling the army of Israel for several hours, Wight marched them back to camp.[66]

Before leaving Salt River on June 12, Smith dispatched Hyde and Parley P. Pratt to Jefferson City to ask Missouri governor Dunklin to provide a guard to reinstate the Mormons on their lands in Jackson County.[67] The Mormons in Clay County were under the impression that Dunklin would provide such a military escort and conveyed that information to Smith. As early as November 1833, Missouri attorney general Robert Wells had indicated that the governor would be open to sending "an adequate force" to accompany the exiled Mormons back to Jackson County.[68] In December 1833 William W. Phelps informed Smith that Dunklin was willing to restore the Saints to their lands but could not station troops in Jackson County to protect them.[69] In February 1834 Dunklin offered a militia escort to the Mormons wishing to participate as witnesses in the grand jury hearing in Independence concerning Colonel Thomas Pitcher's taking Mormon arms the previous November. At the same time, Dunklin suggested that if some of the Mormons wished to repossess their homes, this same escort should "see that they are permitted to take possession peaceably, and protect them in such possession during the trial."[70] However, without continued protection, none of the Mormons dared to accept the offer.

During the next three days, Smith led Zion's Camp about fifty miles to the Chariton River. On the way, Kimball's horses got loose through negligence of the guards, Frederick G. Williams and Roger Orton, and Kimball had to pursue them for ten miles. Williams and Orton, according to Kimball, "received a very severe chastisement from Brother Joseph," especially Orton, who specifically had charge of Kimball's team.[71]

On Sunday, June 15, while camped on the Chariton River, Pratt and Hyde returned from Jefferson City with word that Dunklin would not reinstate the Saints on their lands in Jackson County. According to Pratt, a

---

66. Kimball, "Extracts from H. C. Kimball's Journal," *Times and Seasons*, Feb. 1, 1845, 789.

67. JS History, vol. A-1, Addenda, 13, Note 11 (DHC 2:88–89; Vogel, *History of Joseph Smith*, 2:103n115). See also Pratt, *Autobiography*, 123.

68. Robert W. Wells, Letter to Alexander Doniphan and David R. Atchison, Nov. 21, 1833, Phelps, Collection of Missouri Documents.

69. William W. Phelps, Letter to "Dear Brethren," Dec. 15, 1833, "Later from Missouri," *The Evening and the Morning Star*, Jan. 1834, 128 (*JSP*, D3:384).

70. Daniel Dunklin, Letter to David R. Atchison, Feb. 5, 1834, "Mormon Difficulties," *Missouri Intelligencer and Boon's Lick Advertiser* (Columbia), Mar. 8, 1834, [1].

71. Kimball, "Extracts from H. C. Kimball's Journal," *Times and Seasons*, Feb. 1, 1845, 789.

council was held with the leaders of the camp at which he and Hyde explained that Dunklin "readily acknowledged the justice of the demand," but told them that he "dare" not call out the militia "for fear of deluging the whole country in civil war and bloodshed."[72]

Dunklin expressed his views on the crisis in a June 6, 1834, letter to Colonel John Thornton, where he admitted that "a more clear, and indisputable right does not exist, than that the Mormon people, who were expelled from their homes in Jackson county, to return and live on their lands." He stated his belief that opposition to the Mormons was religion-based, and defended the Saints' constitutional right "to believe and WORSHIP JO SMITH as a MAN, an ANGEL, or even as the only TRUE AND LIVING GOD, and to call their habitation ZION, the HOLY LAND, or even heaven itself." He also defended their constitutional "right to bear arms, IN DEFENCE OF THEMSELVES." However, he strongly objected to the approach of Smith's army of Israel: "If citizens march there in arms from other counties, without order from the commander-in-chief, or some one authorized by him, it would produce a very different state of things. Indeed, the Mormons have no right to march to Jackson county in arms, unless by the order or permission of the commander-in-chief.—Men must not 'levy war' in taking possession of their rights, any more than others should in opposing them in taking possession." Nevertheless, Dunklin, not understanding the Mormon attachment to their Zion, suggested that the best resolution would be for "the Mormons to sell out their lands in Jackson county, and to settle somewhere else, where they could live in peace."[73]

Dunklin's refusal to provide military support was a fatal blow to Smith's plan of redeeming Zion. "Should they cross the river" into Jackson County, warned one resident of Lexington, Missouri, "there will be a battle, and probably much blood shed." Jackson County had received reinforcements from neighboring counties and non-Mormons far out-numbered the Mormons. "If they had crossed the river," a resident of Lafayette County declared, "I very much question if one would have been left to tell the tale."[74]

Pratt remembered that after he and Hyde delivered their report, Smith "called on the God of our fathers to witness the justice of our cause and the

---

72. Pratt, *Autobiography*, 123–24.

73. Daniel Dunklin, Letter to John Thornton, June 6, 1834, *The Evening and the Morning Star*, July 1834, 175–76; emphasis in original.

74. "The Mormon Controversy," *Daily National Intelligencer* (Washington, DC), July 23, 1834, [3].

sincerity of our vows, which we engaged to fulfill, whether in this life or in the life to come. For, as God lives, truth, justice and innocence shall triumph, and iniquity shall not reign."[75] Charles C. Rich recorded in his journal that the council decided that despite Dunklin's refusal to help "that we should go on armed and equiped."[76]

Bishop Partridge

Later that day (June 15), the camp crossed the Chariton River and set up camp on the west bank. Bishop Edward Partridge soon visited the camp from Liberty with "much information ... concerning the hostile feelings and prejudices that existed against us in Missouri in all quarters."[77] Traveler John K. Townsend, who spent more than a month in Independence, made an entry in his journal on March 20, 1834, stating that "the villages here are now in a constant state of feverish alarm. Reports have been circulated that the Mormons are preparing to attack the town, and put the inhabitants to the sword, and they have therefore stationed sentries along the river for several miles, to prevent the landing of the enemy. The troops parade and study military tactics every day, and seem determined to repel, with spirit, the threatened invasion."[78]

In their April 10, 1834, petition to US president Jackson, Missouri Mormon leaders said that the mob consisted of "from three to five hundred, most of them equipped with fire-arms."[79] In a May 1 letter to Kirtland officials, Phelps reported that on April 26 a false rumor circulated in Jackson County that the Mormons were "crossing the Missouri, to take possession of their lands," which so alarmed the inhabitants that a company was formed, composed of "nearly all the county ... 'prepared for war,'" and on the following day marched as far north as "old McGee's above Blue [River]" without discovering any Mormon troops. Nevertheless, "the scene closed by burning our houses, or many of them."[80] John Corrill wrote: "Several nights in succession were they in burning our houses, and I am informed, that they have

---

75. Pratt, *Autobiography*, 123–24.

76. Rich, Diary, June 14, 1834.

77. Kimball, "Extracts from H. C. Kimball's Journal," *Times and Seasons*, Feb. 1, 1845, 789.

78. Townsend, *Narrative of a Journey*, 25.

79. Edward Partridge et al., Petition to Andrew Jackson, Apr. 10, 1834, William W. Phelps, Collection of Missouri Documents.

80. William W. Phelps, Letter to church leaders, May 1, 1834, "The Outrage in Jackson County, Missouri," *The Evening and the Morning Star*, May 1834, 160 (*JSP*, D4:40–41). On April 25, 1834, John Whitmer noted in his daybook: "Mob gathered above blue 150 or 200." Whitmer, Daybook, Apr. 25, 1834.

burned them all, except a very few which are occupied by other families."[81] In their May 7 letter to Dunklin, Sidney Gilbert and Phelps reported that "the mob of Jackson county have burned our dwellings—as near as we can ascertain, between one hundred and one hundred and fifty were consumed by fire in about one week."[82]

The inhabitants of Jackson County were further alarmed by an April 29 letter from the postmaster at Chagrin, Ohio, to the postmaster at Independence, which warned that Smith and his followers were recruiting volunteers to march to Jackson County to engage in a "holy war" to *restore Zion ... by force of arms,*" and reported that the Mormons "have emmissaries among the neighboring Indians, trying to provoke their ignorant people to join them" in their invasion.[83]

In Clay County, John Whitmer noted in his daybook under May 1 that "the mob from Jackson are trying to get help from this Co. to drive us from here."[84] Partridge later remembered that around this time Jackson County residents "frequently sent over word to Clay co. that they were coming over to drive" church members "from that place."[85] Under June 1, 1834, Whitmer wrote in his history that "the Jackson County mob, have sent a Mr. Samuel Campbell to harangue the people of Clay County on the subject of Mobocracy," and that "Campbell succeeded in embittering the minds of some, and the Idea that Joseph should v[e]nture to bring an armed force into this uper country to afford relief to the poor and afflicted saints, enraged the enemy."[86]

Meanwhile, Mormons in Clay County were preparing for the arrival of Zion's Camp and the possible outbreak of war. According to Whitmer, "The Saints here are preparing with all possible speed to arm themselves and otherwise prepare to go to Jacckson Co. when the Camp arrives, for we have had some hints from Joseph th[e] seer that this will be our privilege: so we were in hopes that the long wished for day will soon arrive. and Zion be redeemed to the Joy and satisfaction of the poor suffering saints."[87] The "hints from Joseph th[e] seer" probably refers to the February 24, 1834, revelation,

---

81. "The Outrage in Jackson County, Missouri," *The Evening and the Morning Star*, June 1834, 168.

82. Sidney Gilbert and William W. Phelps, Letter to Daniel Dunklin, May 7, 1834, in Phelps, Collection of Missouri Documents.

83. "Another Mormon War Threatened!," *Missouri Intelligencer and Boon's Lick Advertiser* (Columbia), June 7, 1834, [3]; italics in original.

84. Whitmer, Daybook, May 1, 1834.

85. "A History, of the Persecution," *Times and Seasons*, Feb. 1840, 49 (*JSP*, H2:224).

86. Whitmer, History, 66 (*JSP*, H2:75).

87. Whitmer, 66–67 (*JSP*, H2:75).

which declared that the Saints "must needs be led out of bondage by power" and that they would see "the redemption of Zion."[88]

No doubt Partridge informed Smith that despite repeated efforts Missouri Mormons had been unsuccessful in regaining possession of their arms from Colonel Pitcher, who had illegally confiscated them the previous November and refused to return them. On June 4 Dunklin issued a second order to Pitcher to return the arms (fifty-two guns and one pistol) to the Mormons, which was never obeyed.[89] In his 1839 history Corrill wrote that at the time the Mormons surrendered their weapons "Pitcher and others faithfully agreed" to return the weapons as soon as the Mormons left Jackson County, "but this they afterwards refused to do, although required to do so, by a written order from the Governor, and the Mormons have never received the guns nor an equivalent for them to this day."[90]

Judge Ryland's Mediation

As the possibility of war loomed over western Missouri, Ray County judge John F. Ryland wrote to Sidney Gilbert at Liberty on June 10 to arrange a meeting between the Mormon leaders and representatives of the citizens of Jackson County to be held on Monday, June 16, at Liberty, "to settle or allay the disturbances between the 'Mormons' and the people of Jackson County." He wrote, "I call upon you, in the name of humanity, therefore to leave no efforts untried to collect your Brethren at Liberty as requested—Should my efforts to make peace fail of success, there can at least be no wrong or Sin in the attempt, and I shall enjoy the consolation of having done my duty as a man as well as a christian."[91] Corrill and Gilbert responded on June 14, saying that while they respected his good intention, they were nevertheless "entertaining some fears, that your honor, in his zeal for peace, might unwarily recommend a sale of our lands in Jackson County we have thought it expedient to give seasonable notice that no such proposition could possibly be acceded to by our society."[92]

On June 16 the Missouri Mormon leaders met with Ryland and representatives of Jackson County at the courthouse in Liberty. Ryland told

---

88. Revelation, Feb. 24, 1834, Hyde and Pratt, Notebook of Revelations, [11] [D&C 103:17–18] (*JSP*, D3:461).

89. Daniel Dunklin, Letter to Thomas Pitcher, June 4, 1834, in Phelps, Collection of Missouri Documents.

90. Corrill, *Brief History*, 20 (*JSP*, H2:148).

91. John F. Ryland, Letter to Sidney Gilbert, June 10, 1834, in Phelps, Collection of Missouri Documents.

92. John Corrill and Sidney Gilbert, Letter to John F. Ryland, June 10, 1834, in Phelps, Collection of Missouri Documents.

the two groups "in an impressive and forcible manner" of "the destructive and inevitable consequences which would result from an obstinate refusal to bring this disagreeable and truely deplorable state of things to an amicable end."[93] The Jackson County committee proposed that either the citizens of their county purchase all Mormon lands within thirty days or the Mormons buy out the Jackson citizens, which they knew the Mormons could not do in thirty days, especially since it required the purchase of all the "lands and improvements on public lands" currently held by Jackson County citizens.[94]

Later the same day, the Mormon committee submitted their answer, signed by Phelps, William E. McLellin, Gilbert, Corrill, and Isaac Morley, stating "we are not authorized to say to you that our brethren will submit to your proposals." Anticipating the arrival of Smith and Zion's Camp, they announced that they would call a meeting to consider the Jackson committee's propositions and determine what action to take, either on Saturday, June 21, or Monday, June 23.[95]

Division

While negotiations were underway in Liberty, the camp left the Chariton River and traveled about twenty-three miles to Grand River. After ferrying over the river, they encamped on the west bank. In attempting to demonstrate his faith, Martin Harris played with a black snake with his bare feet and got bit. According to George A. Smith, the prophet reproved Harris for trifling with God's promises, saying that "it was presumption for any man to provoke a serpent to bite him, but if a man of God was accidentally bitten by a poisonous serpent, he might have faith, or his brethren have faith for him, so that the Lord would hear his prayer and he be healed, but when a man designedly provoked a serpent to bite him, the principle was the same as when a man drinks deadly poison knowing it to be such, in that case no man had any claim on the promises of God to be healed."[96] Smith's remarks alluded to Mark 16:18 (repeated in Mormon 9:24), where Jesus promised protection to his faithful followers, which is generally considered by New Testament scholars to be part of a second-century addition to the Gospel. Almost a century before snake-handling took hold among Appalachian Pentecostals

---

93. "The Mormons," *Missouri Intelligencer and Boon's Lick Advertiser* (Columbia), June 28, 1834, [3].

94. "Proposition of the Jackson Committee to the Mormons and Their Answer," June 16, 1834, 1–4, Phelps, Collection of Missouri Documents.

95. "Proposition," 4.

96. George A. Smith, Memoir and Autobiography, 34.

and other charismatic Christians, Smith similarly interpreted the spurious passage literally, but sensibly.[97]

On June 17, after traveling about twenty-five miles and crossing Wakenda Creek in Carroll County, there was a disagreement about the safest place to camp, having learned that a party of men was waiting on the Missouri River to the south to attack them at night. Smith followed Hyrum's advice—which he declared "in the name of the Lord"—to begin crossing a twenty-five-mile prairie. Lyman Wight disagreed, and about twenty men followed him into the woods, where they set up camp and began preparing supper. Sylvester Smith, who was Wight's adjutant, convinced some to turn back to the woods, saying: "Are you following your general, or some other man?" Smith and most of the camp went eight miles onto the prairie and camped.[98]

Later that evening, when Wight's group caught up with Smith and the main body of the camp, Smith reproved Wight and Sylvester. According to George A. Smith, Wight "promised that he would stand by the Prophet for ever and never forsake him again let the consequence be what it would; but Sylvester Smith manifested refractory feelings."[99] Luke S. Johnson testified at Sylvester's trial on August 29 that later the same evening (June 17) "Wight & Sylvester, were called upon to give an account of themselves, why they had sought to divide the camp? They both acknowledged that they had been out of the way by so doing and were reproved for their conduct."[100] Smith punctuated his reproof by throwing a trumpet in Sylvester's direction, which at Sylvester's trial became an issue. Sylvester believed the Mormon leader threw the trumpet at him in anger, whereas others like Johnson and Hyrum Smith thought Joseph had merely tossed it on the ground near Sylvester.[101]

---

97. On the last chapter in the Gospel of Mark being a second-century addition, see, e.g., Ehrman, *Misquoting Jesus*, 65–68. On the history of snake handling in the United States, see Hood and Williamson, *Them That Believe*.

98. JS History, vol. A-1, 14–15, Note 15 (DHC 2:100–101); Vogel, *History of Joseph Smith*, 1:lxxxviii; 2:114n93; George A. Smith, Memoir and Autobiography, 34; Luke S. Johnson and Hyrum Smith testimonies in Minutes, Aug. 28–29, 1834, Minute Book 1, 63–65 (*JSP*, D4:126, 128); John M. Chidester, "Recollections of the Prophet Joseph Smith," *Juvenile Instructor*, Mar. 1, 1892, 151.

99. George A. Smith, Memoir and Autobiography, 35. George A. Smith, writing in the 1850s, remembered that Joseph reprimanded Lyman Wight and Sylvester Smith the morning of June 18, whereas Luke S. Johnson testified at Sylvester's trial on August 29, 1834, that it occurred on the evening of June 17 (see below).

100. Luke S. Johnson testimony in Minutes, Aug. 28–29, 1834, Minute Book 1, 65 (*JSP*, D4:128).

101. Luke S. Johnson and Hyrum Smith testimonies in Minutes, Aug. 28–29, 1834, Minute Book 1, 64–66 (*JSP*, D4:127–29).

On June 18 Smith awoke in poor health and left the affairs of the camp in Wight's command. The camp traveled seventeen miles, Smith riding in Heber C. Kimball's wagon, before stopping for breakfast at 10:00 a.m. Continuing about five miles, the camp stopped within a mile of Richmond, Missouri, where it was learned that their enemies were preparing an attack. Upon arriving at the campsite, Smith jumped from the wagon and went into the brush to pray for the camp's safety. He reportedly received an assurance that they would be safe until morning.[102]

Providential Storm

In the morning, Smith hurried the camp to march nine miles before breakfast. About noon, the camp moved on but made little progress due to the wagons breaking down. They decided to set up camp between two branches of Fishing River a few miles east of Liberty. "Just as we halted and were making preparations for the night," Kimball recalled, "five men rode into the camp, and told us we should see hell before morning, and such horrible oaths as came from their lips, I never heard before. They told us that sixty men were coming from Richmond, Ray county, who had sworn to destroy us, also, seventy more were coming from Clay county, to assist in our destruction."[103] While such threats were concerning to some, Joseph Holbrook remembered that Smith calmly said, "Stand still and see the salvation of God."[104]

According to Kimball, it was not more than twenty minutes after these men left the camp that a furious storm of wind, rain, hail, and lightening hit the region, which lasted through the night and prevented an attack. "It seemed as though the Almighty had issued forth his mandate of vengeance," Kimball wrote.[105] John Whitmer wrote that "God interposed and sent a storm of Thunder lightning and rain at an astonishing rate. Which stoped our enemies in consequence of the flood of water which swelled the River and made it impassable."[106] Woodruff, who also believed the storm was providential, reported that the rain was so torrential that "our beds were soon afloat & our tents blown down over our heads," which caused many of the camp to flee into a nearby Baptist church. "As the Prophet Joseph Came in shaking the water from his hat & clothing. He says Boys there is some

---

102. JS History, vol. A-1, Addenda, 15, Note 15 (DHC 2:101–102); Vogel, *History of Joseph Smith*, 1:lxxxviii; 2:114n93; George A. Smith, Memoir and Autobiography, 35.

103. Kimball, "Extracts from H. C. Kimball's Journal," *Times and Seasons*, Feb. 1, 1845, 790.

104. Joseph Holbrook, Autobiography and Journal, 37.

105. Kimball, "Extracts from H. C. Kimball's Journal," *Times and Seasons*, Feb. 1, 1845, 790.

106. Whitmer, History, 67 (*JSP*, H2:76).

meaning to this, God is in this storm, we sung praises to God & lay all night on benches under Cover while our Enemies were in the falling storm."[107] In his journal, Woodruff recorded that the storm caused the mob to reconsider their plans to attack the camp, "for while they were comeing against us the Lord rained upon them rain and great hail So that it was expedient for them to seek Shelter from the storm and after the storm they dispersed and would not go against the camp."[108] Nathan Baldwin, a twenty-two-year-old participant, recalled that "all were conscious that God was engaged in the conflict, and thankful that they were under his special care and kind protection."[109]

Fishing River Encampment

The next day, June 20, Smith instructed the camp to discharge their firearms to check for possible moisture, which was done without a single misfire.[110] Because the storm had made Fishing River impassable, the camp could not continue their westward movement toward Liberty but instead proceeded northward between the branches of the river. As the camp moved through the country, they could see evidence of the storm's destructive force. After traveling about four miles, they set up camp on land owned by church member John Cooper, situated on the Fishing River about twelve miles east of Liberty.[111]

The approach of the Mormon company put Jackson County into a state of panic. Corrill wrote on June 14 that some men were warning the inhabitants that "the 'Mormons' are coming upon them, mob like, to kill their women and children." He reported that these men "raised an alarm a few days ago in which the whole county of Jackson was in an uproar; men riding in different directions and proclaiming, 'the Mormons are coming,—they are now crossing the river—they are coming to kill, destroy,' &c." Panic and fear were such that "some women and children left their houses, and fled to the woods, and elsewhere, while the men, 2 or 300, gathered together, to oppose the 'Mormons,' as they supposed, in their return." Among other things, the Jackson men set guards along the river, especially at the places where the ferries operated, to prevent a Mormon invasion. "I have been

---

107. Wilford Woodruff, Note added in JS History, vol. A-2, 331–32; Vogel, *History of Joseph Smith*, 2:117n133.

108. Woodruff, Journal, May–June 1834 (Vogel, *Wilford Woodruff Journals*, 1:25).

109. Baldwin, Account of Zion's Camp, 1882, 12.

110. JS History, vol. A-1, Addenda, 16, Note 16 (DHC 2:105); Vogel, *History of Joseph Smith*, 1:lxxxviii; 2:118n151.

111. "Amasa Lyman's History," *LDS Millennial Star*, Aug. 11, 1865, 502.

credibly informed," Corrill wrote, "that they have since continued to guard the river at the different crossing places, from one end of Jackson county to the other."[112]

On June 21, at the request of Judge Ryland, a delegation of six men from Clay and Ray counties, headed by Clay County sheriff Cornelius Gilliam, visited the Fishing River encampment "to meet the Mormons under arms, and obtain from the leaders thereof the correctness of the various reports in circulation—the true intent and meaning of their present movements, and their views generally regarding the difficulties existing between them and the citizens of Jackson county."[113] Smith took a small company into a grove and formed a circle with Gilliam in the center, who explained his purpose for visiting the camp.

Smith spoke next, giving "an open and frank avowel" of the camp's "views and intentions in emigrating to this country with their arms."[114] According to Kimball, "Brother Joseph arose and began to speak and the power of God rested upon him. He gave a relation of the sufferings of our people in Jackson county, and also of all our persecutions and what we had suffered by our enemies for our religion; and that we had come one thousand miles to assist our brethren, to bring them clothing, and to reinstate them upon their own lands; that we had no intentions to molest or injure any people, but only to administer to the wants of our afflicted brethren." [115] After Smith had delivered a lengthy speech, Kimball noted that the delegation had been "melted ... into compassion," and Reuben McBride remembered that the delegation was "very much afected" by Smith's words "and Some Shed tears."[116]

The delegation left determined to quell the excitement. Gilliam was given a written statement that declared: "It is our intention to go back upon our lands in Jackson county, by order of the Executive of the State, if possible. We have brought our arms with us for the purpose of self defense, as it is well known to almost every man of the State that we have every reason to put ourselves in an attitude of defense, considering the abuse we have suffered in Jackson county." This statement included a counter-proposal to the one that had been offered days earlier by the Jackson County committee.

---

112. John Corrill, Letter to the Editor, June 14, 1834, *The Evening and the Morning Star*, June 1834, 168.

113. *Missouri Enquirer*, July 2, 1834; rept. *The Evening and the Morning Star*, July 1834, 176.

114. Sidney Gilbert et al., Letter to Daniel Dunklin, June 26, 1834, in Phelps, Collection of Missouri Documents.

115. Kimball, "Extracts from H. C. Kimball's Journal," *Times and Seasons*, Feb. 15, 1845, 804.

116. Kimball, 804; McBride, Reminiscence, 6.

Reluctant to give up their holy land, Smith and the Missouri Mormon leaders suggested that the Mormons purchase only the property of those citizens who wished to leave if the Mormons returned to Jackson County and that the Mormons be compensated for the damages they had incurred.[117] This proposal had little chance of succeeding since the Mormons had no leverage in the situation and the people of Jackson County had little reason to compromise or cooperate.

The two parties remained intractable. On June 23 Samuel C. Owens, chair of the Jackson County committee, dismissed the Mormon declaration, claiming that it "was gotten up for the sole purpose of allaying public excitement against" the camp "and without much regard to their real object in coming here." He quoted Smith's August 1831 revelation that "the land of Zion shall not be obtained but by purchase or by blood, otherwise there is none inheritance for you," and accused Smith of duplicity.[118] "Thus it would seem, that either the Revelation is false, or the statement made by Joseph Smith and others to the people of Clay county is false."[119]

While each blamed the other, public sentiment turned against the Mormons. John Whitmer wrote: "The mob of Jackson Co proposed to sell to us, or buy our possessions in a manner that they knew that we could not comply with if we were ever so willing, which served to blind the mind of those who had heretofore said nothing, but now advised us to comply because they thought we had better have someth[i]ng than nothing for our possessions."[120] Nevertheless, armed conflict was averted. Without military assistance from Governor Dunklin and considering the public's general hostility, Mormon leaders had no choice but to return to Ohio without redeeming Zion.

Prophecy and Revelation

On the following day, Sunday, June 22, the camp was on edge, fearing an attack.[121] Orson Hyde preached, after which Smith held a council "to determine what steps" to take.[122] According to Kimball, "Bro. Joseph called the

---

117. *Missouri Enquirer*, July 2, 1834; rept. *The Evening and the Morning Star*, July 1834, 176. See also Joseph Smith et al., Declaration, June 21, 1834, JS Collection (*JSP*, D4:65–69).

118. Revelation, Aug. 30, 1831, [1], Newel K. Whitney Papers [D&C 63:29] (*JSP*, D2:51). However, the revelation continued, "& if by purchase or by blood you are blessed & if by blood as ye are forbidden to shed blood lo your enemies are upon you" (cf. D&C 63:30–31). The more relevant revelation was dictated in December 1833, which declared the army of Israel would knock down the towers of the gentiles and scatter their watchmen (D&C 101:55–58).

119. "Proposition of the Mormons," *Painesville (OH) Telegraph*, Aug. 8, 1834.

120. Whitmer, History, 66–67 (*JSP*, H2:75).

121. Rich, Diary, June 22, 1834.

122. William F. Cahoon, Autobiographical Sketch, 43.

camp together, and told us that in consequence of the disobedience of some who had not been willing to listen to his words, but had been rebellious, God had decreed that sickness should come upon us, and we should die like sheep with the rot; and said he, 'I am sorry, but I cannot help it.'" Smith's words, Kimball recalled, "pierced me like a dart."[123] Prior to Smith's declaration, cholera had already made an appearance. Kimball reported that Joseph Hancock had been "taken with the cholera during the storm" that occurred on June 19, and apparently Ezra Thayer and Thomas Hayes were also sick.[124] Cholera continued to spread through the camp for the next two weeks afflicting about sixty-eight members, thirteen of whom died.[125]

During the council, Smith dictated a revelation that "show[ed] the mind of God concerning the redemption of Zion."[126] The revelation—known as the Fishing River Revelation—explained why Zion's Camp failed to accomplish its mission and why Zion was not to be redeemed at that time. "Behold, I say unto you," the Lord declares, "were it not for the transgressions of my people, speaking concerning the church, and not individuals, they might have been redeemed, even now."[127] It must have been difficult for those who had sacrificed so much to march to Missouri to hear this. Smith's revelation allowed him to avoid responsibility, while blaming the church as a whole encouraged them to blame each other.

Nevertheless, the revelation hinted at who was most to blame: "Behold, they have not learned to be obedient to the things which I require at their hands, but are full of all manner of evil, and do not impart of their substance as becometh saints, to the poor and afflicted among them, and are not united according to the union required by the law of the celestial kingdom."[128] From the beginning, Smith had been frustrated by the lack of funds and manpower. The 500 volunteers his February 1834 revelation called for did not materialize and his treasury was paltry.[129] But then why was Zion's Camp not aborted? Many must have been questioning their leadership. This was a serious failure of Smith's leadership and charismatic powers.

The revelation defended church leaders and placed the blame squarely on

---

123. Kimball, "Extracts from H. C. Kimball's Journal," *Times and Seasons*, Feb. 15, 1845, 804.

124. Kimball, 804; Hancock, Autobiography, 147–48; George A. Smith, Memoir and Autobiography, 38.

125. Divett, "His Chastening Rod," 12.

126. Holbrook, Autobiography and Journal, 38.

127. Revelation, June 22, 1834, Revelation Book 1, 199 [D&C 105:2] (*JSP*, D4:73).

128. Revelation, 199 [D&C 105:3–4] (*JSP*, D4:73).

129. Revelation, Feb. 24, 1834, in Hyde and Pratt, Notebook of Revelations, [15]–[16] [D&C 103:31–34] (*JSP*, D3:462).

the membership. "I speak not concerning those who are appointed to lead my people, who are the first elders of my church, for they are not all under this condemnation," the Lord explained. "But I speak concerning the churches abroad." The revelation singled out those who did not donate the $2,000 that Smith had asked for when he was recruiting in the east the previous February and March, those who said "we will not go up to Zion, and will keep our moneys." Because of this lack of support, the Lord declared, "My people must needs be chastened until they learn obedience, if it must needs be by the things which they suffer. ... Therefore, in consequence of the transgressions of my people, it is expedient in me that mine elders should wait for a little season for the redemption of Zion."[130]

The elders are to wait to be more "prepared" and learn "more perfectly concerning their duty," and "this cannot be brought to pass until mine elders are endowed with power from on high; for, behold, I have prepared a greater endowment and blessing to be boured [poured] out upon them, inasmuch as they are faithful."[131] The revelation thus delayed the redemption of Zion until after the temple in Kirtland was completed and the elders were endowed with power. Sociologist Joseph Zygmunt, who has studied the effects of prophetic failure on various millenarian and charismatic groups, observes that "if the causes of prophetic failures are identified as internal to the movement itself, being construed, for instance, as reflecting the incomplete spiritual readiness of believers to inherit the new earth, a cycle of collective self-purification, spiritual regeneration, and moral unbuilding may ensue. ... The movement may, in fact, become more or less permanently reorganized around such goals of spiritual edification and perfection, seeing their pursuit as being in the service of prophetic fulfillment. Millennial hopes remain intact but they come to be drawn upon to sustain motivation for more enduring patterns of preparatory action."[132] Little wonder that the dedication of the completed Kirtland temple in March and April 1836 was accompanied by spiritual renewal, purification, and solemn covenants to support the leadership.

The revelation therefore called for a temporary truce: "For behold, I do not require at their hands to fight the battles of Zion; for as I have said in a former commandment, even so I will fulfil: I will fight your battles."[133] Many

---

130. Revelation, June 22, 1834, Revelation Book 1, 199 [D&C 105:6–9] (*JSP*, D4:73–74).

131. Revelation, 199 [D&C 105:10–12] (*JSP*, D4:74).

132. Zygmunt, "When Prophecies Fail," 98.

133. Revelation, June 22, 1834, Revelation Book 1, 199 [D&C 105:14] (*JSP*, D4:74). See also Revelation, Aug. 6, 1833, Revelation Book 2, 71 [D&C 98:37] (*JSP*, D3:227).

must have wondered why they had armed themselves, traveled such a great distance, called themselves the "army of Israel," appointed a commander-in-chief and a general, and practiced military maneuvers. What the army of Israel could not accomplish, the Lord promised to fulfill by sending the cholera epidemic to destroy the Saints' enemies in Jackson County: "Behold the destroyer I have already sent forth to destroy and lay waste mine enemies, and not many years hence they shall not be left to pollute mine heritage, and to blaspheme my name. upon the lands which I have consecrated for the gathering together of my Saints."[134] This too failed to materialize.

The revelation instructed the Mormons to "carefully gather together as much in one region as can be consistently with the feelings of the people." They are to keep suing for "Justice" and "redress" and grow "until the army of Israel becomes very great" and Smith has "time to gather up the strength of my house." The revelation reiterated a previous command to continue "purchasing of all the lands in Jackson county that can be purchased, and in the adjourning counties round about."[135]

After the purchase of lands in Jackson County, Zion's Camp will again assemble for war: "After these lands are purchased I will hold the armies of Israel guiltless in taking possession of their own lands, and of throwing down the towers of mine enemies that may be upon them, and scattering their watchmen and avenging me of mine enemies, unto the third and forth generation of them that hate me. But firstly let my army become very great, and let it be sanctified before me, that it may become fair as the sun, and clear as the moon, and that her banners may be terrible unto all nations."[136] The revelation then reiterated Smith's aspiration for world dominance, stating "that the kingdoms of this world may be constrained to acknowledge that the kingdom of Zion, is, in very deed, the kingdom of our God and his Christ; therefore, let us become subject unto her laws."[137]

Zion's Camp was not a complete waste of time. "I have heard their prayers, and will accept their offering," the Lord declared. "And it is expedient in me that they should be brought thus far for a trial of their faith."

---

134. Revelation, June 22, 1834, Revelation Book 1, 199 [D&C 105:15] (*JSP*, D4:74).

135. Revelation, [200]–[201] [D&C 105:24–28] (*JSP*, D4:75–76). See also Revelation, Dec. 16–17, 1833, Revelation Book 2, 80 [D&C 101:70–71] (*JSP*, D3:395); Revelation, Feb. 24, 1834, in Hyde and Pratt, Notebook of Revelations, [13] [D&C 103:23] (*JSP*, D3:461).

136. Revelation, June 22, 1834, Revelation Book 1, [201] [D&C 105:30–31] (*JSP*, D4:76–77). See also Revelation, Dec. 16–17, 1833, Revelation Book 2, 76–79 [D&C 101:44–60] (*JSP*, D3:393–94).

137. Revelation, June 22, 1834, Revelation Book 1, [201] [D&C 105:32] (*JSP*, D4:77).

Those who passed this test would soon be blessed: "Verily I say unto you it is expedient in me, that the first elders of my church should receive their endowment from on high in mine house which I have commanded to be built unto my name in the land of Kirtland." The revelation then instructed that Smith choose by the spirit those who are to receive the future endowment of power, "and they shall be sanctified, and in as much as they, follow the counsels which they receive they shall have power after many days to accomplish all things pertaining to Zion."[138]

Concerning this revelation, John Whitmer wrote: "Thus our fond hopes of being redeemed at this time were blasted at least for a season."[139] According to William Cahoon, "Many in the camp murmured because we were not permited at this time to restore our Brethren & Sisters to their Homes and defend them there at all hazards."[140] George A. Smith remembered that "several of the brethren apostatized because they were not to have the privilege of fighting."[141] Nathan Tanner also recalled that some declared "they had rether die than to return with out a fite" and then "gave vent to their Rath on a patch of Pawpaw brush" some distance from the camp, mowing it "down like grass."[142]

The next day, June 23, a council of high priests assembled to fulfill the instruction to choose those who are to receive power from on high upon completion of the temple. Those selected were: Partridge, Phelps, Isaac Morley, Corrill, John Whitmer, David Whitmer, Sidney Gilbert, Peter Whitmer Jr., Simeon Carter, Newel Knight, Thomas B. Marsh, Wight, Parley P. Pratt, Christian Whitmer, and Solomon Hancock.[143] However, Christian Whitmer and Sidney Gilbert died before their appointments could be fulfilled.

Cholera

On the morning of June 24, Smith and the camp marched for Liberty, but they were met by a group of men headed by General David R. Atchison, a Clay County attorney representing the Mormons, who urged that they not enter the town because "the feelings of the people of that place was much enraged against" the camp. Smith therefore led the camp to Sidney Gilbert's

138. Revelation, [200]–[201] [D&C 105:19, 33, 35–37] (*JSP*, D4:75, 77).
139. Whitmer, History, 67–68 (*JSP*, H2:77).
140. William F. Cahoon, Autobiographical Sketch, 43.
141. George A. Smith, Memoir and Autobiography, 38.
142. Nathan Tanner, Address, [13].
143. Minutes, June 23, 1834, Minute Book 2, 41–42 (*JSP*, D4:80–84).

home at Rush Creek, about two miles southeast of Liberty, and set up camp in a nearby field owned by church member George Burket.[144]

During the "night the cholera came upon us, as we had been warned by the servant of God," Kimball recalled. "About 12 o'clock at night we began to hear the cries of those who were seized with the cholera, and they fell before the destroyer."[145] George A. Smith later remarked that "many of the brethren were violently attacked with cholera, their moans were truly terrific, some falling to the ground while they were on guard."[146]

Smith and his brother Hyrum tried to administer to the sick, but were themselves seized by the disease. Kimball described Smith's unsuccessful attempt to heal: "Brother Joseph, seeing the sufferings of his brethren, stepped forward to rebuke the destroyer, but was immediately seized with the disease himself; and I assisted him a short distance from the place when it was with difficulty he could walk."[147] Hyrum, who was also suddenly inflicted by severe abdominal cramps, said "it seized us like the talons of a hawk."[148]

In the morning of June 25, according to Woodruff, Smith "remarked that it was the duty of the Camp to brake up and disperse and take up their abode around among the brethren lest the Scourge should be more severe."[149] Despite being sick, Smith wrote to the church's attorneys in Liberty, which he sent by express, announcing that Zion's Camp "shall be immediately dispersed" as a "pacific measure" to ease tensions between the Mormons and Jackson County residents, although he and his people intend to pursue the matter lawfully.[150]

Later the same evening, thirty-eight-year-old John S. Carter was the first to die from cholera. Thirty minutes later Seth Hitchcock also died, followed by three others the same evening. In all, at least thirteen would succumb to the disease. Their corpses were hastily buried without coffins. Cholera also raged among the residents of Clay County, claiming the lives of Sidney

144. "Extracts from H. C. Kimball's Journal," *Times and Seasons*, Mar. 15, 1845, 838; see also Kimball, Autobiography, ca, 1842–58, 15–16; George A. Smith, Memoir and Autobiography, 38–39; Woodruff, Journal, May–June 1834 (Vogel, *Wilford Woodruff Journals*, 1:25).

145. "Extracts from H. C. Kimball's Journal," *Times and Seasons* Mar. 15, 1845, 838. On the experience of cholera in Zion's Camp, see Divett, "His Chastening Rod," 10–12.

146. George A. Smith, Memoir and Autobiography, 39.

147. "Extracts from H. C. Kimball's Journal," *Times and Seasons*, Mar. 15, 1845, 838.

148. George A. Smith, Memoir and Autobiography, 39.

149. Woodruff, Journal, May–June 1834 (Vogel, *Wilford Woodruff Journals*, 1:25).

150. Joseph Smith, Letter to John Thornton, Alexander Doniphan, and David R. Atchison, June 25, 1834, in JS History, vol. A-1, 505 (*JSP*, D4:86).

Gilbert on June 29 and six-year-old Phebe Murdock, daughter of John and Julia Murdock, on July 6.[151]

During the first night of deaths, the terrified members of the camp began praying for their lives. "I felt to weep and pray to the Lord, that he would spare my life that I might behold my dear family again," Kimball wrote. "I felt to covenant with my brethren, and I felt in my heart never to commit another sin while I lived."[152] The camp's struggle with cholera was interpreted by members as a fulfillment of Smith's June 3 prophecy, which he repeated on June 22. However, only two days earlier, Smith had promised that God would send the "destroyer" to attack their enemies. How could the people of Jackson County not think God was on their side when the opposite happened? Interpreting cholera as God's vengeance may have been the only thing on which the Mormons and Jackson Countians agreed.

Little is known of Smith's activities during the last week of June. George A. Smith mentioned that he went to David Whitmer's residence in western Clay County on June 28, where he found Joseph and Hyrum and that the former gave him a concoction of whiskey and flour to alleviate the symptoms of cholera.[153] Smith's history states that he spent "the last days of June … with my old Jackson county friends, in the western part of Clay county."[154]

When cousin Jesse N. Smith died on July 1, George A. Smith remarked to the prophet that he wished it had been him instead. Joseph replied: "You do not know the mind of the Lord on these things." He further remarked that "if his work had been done, you would have had to tumble me into the ground with a coffin."[155] About this time, according to his history, Smith crossed the Missouri River into Jackson County with a few others to be able to say that his feet had touched the "goodly land" of Zion.[156]

On July 2 Smith visited Wight and others near Liberty. Many camp members came there, and Smith told them that they could avoid a second wave of cholera by humbling themselves and covenanting to obey God's commandments, which they did.[157] Woodruff recalled that the "Prophet seemed more bowed down with sorrow at the Loss of his brethren than I

151. "Afflicting," *The Evening and the Morning Star*, July 1834, 176; "Deaths," *The Evening and the Morning Star*, Aug. 1834, 182; Murdock, Journal, June 26, July 6, 1834; JS History, vol. A-1, 509 (DHC 2:119–20). See also Parkin, "Zion's Camp Cholera Victims Monument Dedication."

152. "Extracts from H. C. Kimball's Journal," *Times and Seasons*, Mar. 15, 1845, 839.

153. George A. Smith, Memoir and Autobiography, 42.

154. JS History, vol. A-1, 506 (DHC 2:120).

155. George A. Smith, Autobiography, 43.

156. JS History, vol. A-1, 506 (DHC 2:120).

157. JS History, 506.

Ever saw him in my life. at the same time he was clothed upon with the spirit of God & with humility and when all the Brethren Covenanted with uplifted hands to heaven that they would humble themselves before the Lord and keep his commandments and obey the council of the Prophet the power of God rested upon them and we were all bathed in tears and there was not another case of cholera among the saints from that hour."[158]

Missouri High Council Organized

On July 3 Smith called a meeting at Wight's residence, located about four miles south of Liberty, where he organized a high council of twelve men and the first Missouri stake with David Whitmer as president and Phelps and John Whitmer as counselors or assistant presidents.[159] Woodruff recorded that Smith "Chastised David Whitmore & others for unfaithfulnes. said their hearts were not set upon the building up the Kingdom of God as they should be. after He was chastised He was set apart under the hand of Joseph to Preside over the Land of Zion."[160] George A. Smith remembered that "Brother Joseph said that it was his wish to appoint brother David Whitmer president, 'but I am afraid to do so, for I fear that his wife, his boy, and his, corn will engross more of his attention than the welfare of Zion, that he will neglect his duty and lay the foundation of his own downfall and that of others."[161] While Smith appointed Whitmer at this time, he delayed ordaining him until July 7. Smith also formally disbanded Zion's Camp and instructed the men, who were given a written discharge, to return home. The remaining camp funds were divided among its members—Smith got $1.16.[162]

Four days later, on July 7, Smith met with the newly-organized high council at Wight's residence and gave them instructions about their callings.[163] After the congregation sustained those who had been appointed on July 3, Smith, according to the minutes, "ordained the three Presidents. David Whitmer as President and William W. Phelps & John Whitmer assistants and their twelve Counsellors."[164]

---

158. Woodruff inserted this note in red ink in the left margin of JS History, vol. A-2, 340, possibly in December 1859. Vogel, *History of Joseph Smith*, 2:133n147.

159. Minutes, July 3, 1834, Minute Book 2, 43 (*JSP*, D4:88–90). On the location of Lyman Wight's residence in Clay County, see Berrett, *Sacred Places*, 4:173.

160. Woodruff, Journal, July 3, 1834 (Vogel, *Wilford Woodruff Journals*, 1:26).

161. George A. Smith, Memoir and Autobiography, 50.

162. Account with the Camp of Israel, ca. Aug. 11–29, 1834, JS Collection (*JSP*, D4:159).

163. Minutes, ca. July 7, 1834, Minute Book 2, 43–45 (*JSP*, D4:90–96). There is some question as to whether the meeting occurred on Monday, July 7, or Tuesday, July 8. See *JSP*, D4:90–91.

164. Minutes, 44 (*JSP*, D4:93).

In his history, John Whitmer wrote that Smith not only ordained his brother, David, as "President of Zion" but "at the same time he ordained David Whitmer Prophit Seeer Revelator & translator."[165] This was interpreted to mean that David Whitmer, as president of the high council in Missouri, held the second-highest office in the church, after Smith, and hence was Smith's putative successor should he be removed through death or transgression. Smith seemed to confirm this at a March 1838 meeting in Far West, Missouri, when he gave attendees "a history of the ordination of David Whitmer, which took place in July 1834, to be a leader, or a prophet to this Church, which (ordination) was on conditions that he (J. Smith jr) did not live to God himself."[166] According to William E. McLellin, Smith said that "the time has come when I must appoint my successor in office," and "DAVID WHITMER IS THE MAN."[167] In 1887 David Whitmer said Smith "had so much confidence in me that in July, 1834, he ordained me his successor as 'Prophet Seer and Revelator' to the Church. ... I did not know what he was going to do until he laid his hands upon me and ordained me. ... There are men now living who were present in that council of elders when he did it."[168] In 1847 Martin Harris, Leonard Rich, and Calvin Beebe signed a statement testifying that they had attended the meeting and heard Smith state "that the time had come when he must appoint his Successor in office. Some have supposed that it would be Oliver Cowdery; but, said he, Oliver has lost that privilege in consequence of transgression. The Lord has made it known to me that David Whitmer is the man."[169] Smith's passing over Cowdery because of "transgression" probably relates to the "two evils" Smith had mentioned in his blessing on Cowdery the previous December.[170]

The minutes record that Smith gave instructions on the council's "high calling" and read the revised minutes of the organization of the high council in Kirtland the previous February. Most importantly, "he also informed them if he should now be taken away that he had accomplished the great work which the Lord had laid before him, and that which he had desired

---

165. Whitmer, History 94–95 (*JSP*, H2:105).

166. Zion high council and bishopric, Minutes, Mar. 15, 1838, Minute Book 2, 108 (*JSP*, D6:42).

167. William E. McLellin, Letter to Davis H. Bays, May 24, 1870, in *True Latter Day Saints' Herald* (Plano, IL), Sep. 15, 1870, 555; emphasis in original.

168. Whitmer, *An Address to All Believers in Christ*, 55. Whitmer incorrectly remembered that the ordination took place at the Fishing River encampment.

169. *Ensign of Liberty* (Kirtland, OH), Dec. 1847, 43.

170. Smith, Journal, Dec. 18, 1833 (*JSP*, J1:21–22).

of the Lord, and that he now had done his duty in organizing the High Council, through which Council the will of the Lord might be known on all important occasions in the building up of Zion, and establishing truth in the earth."[171] Harris, Rich, and Beebe also remembered that immediately following his ordination of Whitmer as a "Prophet, Seer, Revelator, and Translator before God," Smith "seemed to rejoice that that work was done, and said, now brethren, if any thing should befal me, the work of God will roll on with more power than it has hitherto done. Then, brethren, you will have a man who can lead you as well as I can."[172] After returning to Ohio, he similarly stated: "I supposed I had established this church on a permanent foundation when I went to the Missourie and indeed I did so, for if I had been taken away it would have been enough."[173]

After the organization of the high council, Edward Partridge "desired to have the prayers of all the Church that he might be able to act in his station in righteousness."[174] Previously, Partridge had been acknowledged as "head of the Church of Zion,"[175] and the bishop's court was the highest authority in the Missouri church, but with the appointment of David Whitmer as president and the establishment of the high council as an appellate court, Partridge's authority as bishop was greatly diminished.

Despite Phelps's appointment as a counselor to David Whitmer in the presidency of the high council of Zion, Smith made a motion that Phelps be released to assist Cowdery in "the printing establishment" in Kirtland. After discussion, David Whitmer "decided that it is the duty of Br. W. W. Phelps to go to Kirtland to assist in the printi[n]g business and that his family remain in this region of country and that he have an honorable discharge in his station in this place for a season."[176] It was also decided that newly-ordained President Whitmer should also go to Kirtland—as one of the three witnesses to the Book of Mormon—as well as John Whitmer and William E. McLellin.[177] The absence of the presidency in Missouri left the church there without leadership, which led to confusion and strife. Smith later defended this decision, explaining in an August 1834 letter that it was important that

---

171. Minutes, ca. July 7, 1834, Minute Book 2, 43–44 (*JSP*, D4:93).

172. *Ensign of Liberty*, Dec. 1847, 43–44.

173. Smith, Journal, Nov. 12, 1835 (*JSP*, J1:97).

174. Minutes, ca. July 7, 1834, Minute Book 2, 44 (*JSP*, D4:94).

175. Minutes, Sep. 11, 1833, Minute Book 2, 36 (Cannon and Cook, *Far West Record*, 65).

176. Minutes, ca. July 7, 1834, Minute Book 2, 44–45 (*JSP*, D4:94–95).

177. Minutes, 45 (*JSP*, D4:95).

the "first Elders" of the church obtain an endowment of power in Kirtland, which did not occur until March and April 1836.[178]

Smith's Departure

On July 9, after speaking to a congregation gathered at the home of Thomas B. Marsh in eastern Clay County for about an hour and sealing them up to eternal life, Smith left to return to Kirtland, accompanied by Hyrum Smith, Frederick G. Williams, William E. McLellin, and others.[179] However, before leaving, Smith borrowed money from the Missouri leaders and had a total of $218.16 for the return trip to Ohio, which he apparently distributed to his company along the way.[180] George A. Smith remembered that the small group, consisting of about eighteen persons, two wagons, and a buggy, traveled about eighteen miles to their former Fishing River campsite the first day, after some of them had waded across the river.[181]

On July 12 Smith's company passed through Chariton, Missouri, where they found the town "nearly abandoned, in consequence of the cholera, the inhabitants having fled in every direction."[182] After crossing the Illinois River on June 18, George A. Smith, Williams, and four others separated from the company to dine at the home of a Mr. Eldred. As they were attempting to catch up with the company, they found Joseph waiting for them in Carrollton, Illinois, "feeling quite uneasy, [and] fearing we had tarried on account of a spirit of disunion."[183] Nine days later, after passing through Greenfield, Charlottesville, and Middleton, the company reached Little Lewisville, Indiana, where Joseph Smith, brothers Hyrum and William, and Williams boarded a stagecoach back to Kirtland, leaving behind George A. Smith and "the other boys who were left with his wagons [and] eight dollars a piece" for their expenses.[184]

---

178. Joseph Smith, Letter to Lyman Wight and Others, Aug. 16, 1834, JS Letterbook 1, 85 (*JSP*, D4:104).

179. JS History, vol. A-1, 525 (DHC 2:135); George A. Smith, History, 50; McLellin, Journal, July 9, 1834 (Shipps and Welch, eds., *The Journals of William E. McLellin*, 131).

180. Account with the Camp of Israel, ca. Aug. 11–29, 1834, JS Collection (*JSP*, D4:160); George A. Smith, Memoir and Autobiography, 50–51, 57–58.

181. George A. Smith, Memoir and Autobiography, 51.

182. George A. Smith, 52.

183. George A. Smith, History, 54–55.

184. George A. Smith, Memoir and Autobiography, 57–58.

17

Fallout

Gen. Joe Smith, with his army of fanatics returned to his old head-
quarters in this county … This expedition may be considered as one
of the veriest "wild goose chases" to be found upon record.
—*"The Mormon War,"* Painesville (OH) Telegraph, *Aug. 8, 1834*

Joseph Smith returned to Kirtland about August 1, 1834, "after a tedious journey from the midst of enemies, mobs, cholera, and excessively hot weather."[1] He also returned to massive fallout for his failure to redeem Zion. According to one historian, the failure of Zion's Camp "seriously demoralized many of Smith's followers, thus contributing to a major apostasy crisis a few years later."[2]

William McLellin later expressed what may have been the sentiment of many of Smith's followers: "Now in all the past history of nations or individuals I have never seen so much folly and weakness displayed as in this warrior raid to upper Mo. [Missouri], by Smith and followers. Thousands of dollars paid out—worse than wasted; and most valuable time … wasted, as well as may lives lost, and much human suffering endured; and not one particle of good accomplished, but … myriads of evil to all concerned in following a prophet who did not nor could not see what was before him."[3] Joseph Young, who with his brother Brigham had reluctantly participated in the expedition, later wrote: "This was a stumbling block as it turned out; … even the Saints themselves, many of them, looked upon it with disfavor; and their remarks on the subject showed that they could not, or did not

---

1. JS History, vol. A-1, 528 (DHC 2:139). George A. Smith's Autobiography dates his arrival to August 4 and Joseph Smith's "a few days before." George A. Smith, Memoir and Autobiography, 58.

2. Winn, *Exiles in a Land of Liberty*, 101.

3. McLellin, Notebook, ca. 1880, 37, in Larson and Passey, eds., *The William E. McLellin Papers*, 418.

371

understand, that the Lord had a hand in these things; but they had not eyes to see his providence. Some few of the saints accused Joseph the Prophet in these matters and their murmurings brought chastisement upon them and left them in the dark and hence they strayed away and lost their faith."[4]

During the remainder of 1834 and into 1835, Smith was forced to deal with criticism, dissention, and challenges to his authority. To keep the church from splintering, Smith expanded the church's hierarchy, thus inviting more followers to deepen their commitment to the organization. He also redefined authority in ways that made challenges to his leadership less threatening and less likely. This is consistent with what historians and sociologists have learned from the study of various millenarian and charismatic groups. In his study of prophetic leaders, social scientist Anthony B. van Fossen has observed that "to survive the failure of an important specific prophecy, a movement must become more hierarchal—demoting the unreliable and consigning nonbelievers to insignificance but, most importantly, elevating the prophet and his original and most trusted apostles and disciples."[5] Sociologist Joseph Zygmunt similarly observed: "The general problem confronting the group is to prevent non-confirmation from being interpreted as disconfirmation. This requires the social and ideological reinforcement of beliefs, a restructuring of expectations in a direction that makes them more easily 'confirmable' or 'renewable' by the group itself," a process that can be aided by "the gradual institutionalization of the movement."[6]

Sylvester Smith Trial

Not long after returning to Kirtland, Sylvester Smith began airing his grievances publicly. In an August 16 letter to Missouri leaders, Smith wrote that Satan "had taken the advantage of our brothe[r] Sylvest[er] Smith and others who gave a false colloring to allmost every transaction from the time that we left Kirtland untill we returned, and thereby Stirred up a great difficulty in the Church against me accordingly." He also wrote, "I was met in the face and eyes as soon as I had got home ... and the cry was Tyrant,! Pope!! King!!! Usurper!!!! Abuser of men!!!!! Angel!!!!! False proph[e]t!!!!! Prophecying Lies in the name of the Lord!!!!!!! and taking Consecrated monies!!!!!!!! and every other lie to fill up and complete the cattelogue."[7] At the time Smith

---

4. Joseph Young Sr., Letter to Lewis Harvey, Nov. 16, 1880, 6.

5. Van Fossen, "How Do Movements Survive Failures of Prophecy?" 175.

6. Zygmunt, "When Prophecies Fail," 96.

7. Joseph Smith, Letter to Lyman Wight and Others, Aug. 16, 1834, JS Letterbook 1, 84 (*JSP*, D4:103–104).

wrote this, he was confident that he was about to be exonerated by Sylvester's public confession, but the matter was far from over.

On August 9 Sylvester accused the Mormon leader of misusing "monies and other properties" of the camp, "proph[e]sying lies in the name of the Lord," and "abusing" his "character." By August 11, knowledge of these accusations had spread in every direction, forcing Smith to confront Sylvester publicly. Church leaders called for a meeting of the priesthood at the new schoolhouse, a two-story building with an attic near to where the temple was being constructed, "for the purpose of investigating a matter of difficulty growing out of certain reports or statements made by brother Sylvester Smith; one of the High counsellors of this Church, accusing brother Joseph Smith Junr. with criminal conduct during his journey to and from Missouri this Spring & Summer."[8]

Joseph Smith began, speaking at "considerable length" about "the circumstances of their journey to and from Missouri," and "very minutely laid open the causes out of which those jealousies of brother Sylvesters and others had grown. He made a satisfactory statement concerning his rebukes and chastisements upon Sylvester & others, and also concerning the distribution of monies and other properties, calling on brethren present who accompanied him to attest to the same."[9]

Sylvester followed Smith, making "some observations relative to the subject of their difficulties, and begun to make a partial confession for his previous conduct, asking forgiveness for accusing brother Joseph publicly on the Saturday previous."[10] Regardless of the merits of his accusations, Sylvester no doubt realized that the institution could not bear its leader being publicly criticized by a member of the high council.

After Sidney Rigdon spoke against Sylvester and others, it was decided to address the issue through a formal council, which was formed with Bishop Newel Whitney presiding. John Smith and others suggested that Sylvester make a public confession and publish it in *The Evening and the Morning Star*, and Samuel Smith said that he should also "send by letter, to those who are in the same transgression with himself, and inform them of this decision." Orson Hyde said that "the confession ought to be as liberal

---

8. Minutes, Aug. 11, 1834, Minute Book 1, 52 (*JSP*, D4:99–100). Sylvester Smith later told Oliver Cowdery that reports "censuring the conduct" of Joseph Smith were circulating in the churches "abroad." Sylvester Smith, Letter to Oliver Cowdery, Oct. 28, 1834, in *LDS Messenger and Advocate* (Kirtland, OH), Oct. 1834, 11.

9. Minutes, Aug. 11, 1834, Minute Book 1, 52 (*JSP*, D4:99).

10. Minutes, 52 (*JSP*, D4:100).

as the accusation." John P. Greene said that Sylvester should "do this for the salvation of the Churches abroad."[11]

Oliver Cowdery "proposed that this council send a certificate or resolution, informing the churches abroad, that the conduct of brother Joseph, has been investigated, and that he has acted in a proper manner and in every respect has conducted himself to the satisfaction of the church in Kirtland, and also let brother Sylvester make a proper confession." It was then decided that a committee of three should write such a statement and that it should be published in the *Star*. At this time, Sylvester said "he was willing to publish a confession in the Star."[12]

Redemption of Zion Reset

On August 16 Smith dictated a letter to the Missouri officials that mentioned his having been troubled by Sylvester Smith's false accusations. "In consequence of having to combat all these" accusations, he wrote, "I have not been able to regulate my mind so as to write to give you council and the information that you needed." At this time, the Mormon leader believed the matter had been settled, but this statement reveals how personally upsetting such allegations were to him. "I have succeeded in putting all gainsayers and enemies to flight unto the present time and not withstanding the advisary Laid a plan which was more subtle than all others, I now swim in good <u>clean</u> pure water with my head out! as you will see by the next star."[13] In this expectation, Smith would soon become frustrated as Sylvester would have second thoughts.

Shifting to the concerns of the Missouri church, Smith said he would give "such council as the spirit of the Lord may dictate." As Governor Dunklin did not have the authority to commission a standing force in Jackson County to protect the Mormons, Smith instructed William Phelps to write a petition to the governor requesting him to call on President Andrew Jackson for authorization to establish such a force.[14] However, since Dunklin had even refused to escort the Mormons to Jackson County and allow Zion's Camp to provide protection, there was little chance that he would follow Smith's suggestions. Nevertheless, a petition circulated throughout the rest

---

11. Minutes, 53 (*JSP*, D4:100).

12. Minutes, 52–54 (*JSP*, D4:100–101).

13. Joseph Smith, Letter to Lyman Wight and Others, Aug. 16, 1834, JS Letterbook 1, 84–85 (*JSP*, D4:104).

14. Smith, 85–86 (*JSP*, D4:104–105).

of 1834 and 1835, garnering several hundred signatures before being sent to Dunklin on December 31, 1835.[15]

Smith then authorized Lyman Wight, who had been the general of the army of Israel, to use force if attacked, that if their enemies "endeaver to take life or tear down homes ... to gather up the little army and be set over Immediately into Jackson County and trust in God and do the best he can in maintaining the ground." No doubt, this would be a suicide mission. On the other hand, Smith advised, if "peace prevails use every effort to prevail on the churches to gather to those regions and situate themselves to be in readiness to move into Jackson Co. in two years from the Eleventh of September next which is the appointed time for the redemption of Zion."[16] Smith derived September 11, 1836, for the redemption of Zion from a September 11, 1831, revelation that said that God would "retain a strong hold in the Land of Kirtland for the space of five years," after which he would "not hold any guilty that shall go with open hearts up to the Land of Zion."[17] However, retaining Kirtland as a stronghold had nothing to do with the timing of Zion's establishment. "Following the 1833 forced removal to Clay County," historians Ronald E. Romig and Michael S. Riggs observe, "the exegesis of the earlier 1831 revelation morphed into a retrospective spiritual rationalization to rally support for a second effort to reclaim Jackson County by September 11, 1836."[18] Smith's interpretation was not only an exegetical leap, but its use in buying such a limited amount of time would prove unwise, resulting in yet another unfulfilled prediction. "Now my beloved brethren," Smith wrote, "you will learn by this we have a great work to do, and but little time to do it in and if we dont exert ourselves to the utmost in gathering up the strength of the Lords house that this thing may be accomplished behold their remaineth a scorge for the Church."[19]

Sylvester had yet to publish his confession, so things were still up in the air when Smith concluded his letter: "The church seems to be in a languid cold disconsolate state. ... When the head is sick the whole body is faint, for when the church lifts up the head the Angel will bring us good

---

15. William W. Phelps et al., Letter to Daniel Dunklin, Dec. 30, 1835; and Daniel Dunklin, Letter to William W. Phelps and Others, Jan. 22, 1836, in Phelps, Collection of Missouri Documents.

16. Joseph Smith, Letter to Lyman Wight and Others, Aug. 16, 1834, JS Letterbook 1, 86 (*JSP*, D4:106).

17. Revelation, Sep. 11, 1831, Revelation Book 1, 110 [D&C 64:21–22] (*JSP*, D2:65).

18. Romig and Riggs, "Reassessing Joseph Smith's 'Appointed Time for the Redemption of Zion,'" 29.

19. Joseph Smith, Letter to Lyman Wight and Others, Aug. 16, 1834, JS Letterbook 1, 86 (*JSP*, D4:106).

tidings even so Amen."[20] Smith must have felt uncertain about his future and looked to the church for help.

The high council in Clay County, Missouri, read Smith's letter on September 10. As Smith had directed, Phelps drafted a petition to Dunklin requesting him "to petition the President of the United States for a guard of troops to be stationed in Jackson Co. sufficient to protect this unfortunate people in their rights."[21] This petition apparently circulated among the Saints and by December 30, 1835, had been forwarded to Dunklin from Kirtland with "several hundred" signatures attached. In his history, John Whitmer wrote that while the petition was circulating, "the saints were humbling themselves before the Lord," but "some were making preperation to leave the land ... doubting the truth of the book of Mormon" and "denying the faith."[22] The failure of Zion's Camp and the desperation of the petition were difficult for some of Smith's followers to accept. For them, the promise of being guided by an omniscient and all-powerful God had collapsed.

Sylvester Smith Again

On August 23 the high council censored Sylvester and adopted resolutions written by Oliver Cowdery, Thomas Burdick, and Orson Hyde concerning Joseph Smith's conduct toward Sylvester during the expedition to Missouri. These resolutions, which were ordered to be printed in the *Star* and circulated in the churches abroad, stated that Sylvester's accusations were "calculated to create an unfavorable influence, as regards the moral character and honesty of our brother [Joseph Smith]." After a thorough investigation, the high council assured the membership that their president was "worthy of [their] esteem and fellowship, and that those reports, could have originated in the minds of none, except, such as either from a misunderstanding or a natural jealousy, are easily led to conceive of evils where none exist." Such accusations were "calculated to create an evil prejudice in the minds of [the] community, to prevent, if possible the increase of light, the better to effect their own purposes and keep men in error."[23]

The resolutions were followed by the testimony of Lyman E. Johnson and Heber C. Kimball, who "having accompanied brother J. Smith Junr. to and from Missouri, certify that the above is a correct statement concerning

---

20. Smith, 87 (*JSP*, D4:107–108).
21. William W. Phelps et al., Letter to Daniel Dunklin, Dec. 30, 1835, in Phelps, Collection of Missouri Documents; Whitmer, History, 69 (*JSP*, H2:78).
22. Whitmer, History, 70 (*JSP*, H2:78–79).
23. Resolutions, ca. Aug. 23, 1834, Minute Book 1, 55–56 (*JSP*, 5:111–12).

his character and conduct."[24] Both would soon be chosen as a member of the Quorum of Twelve Apostles.

No doubt the use of such strong language in condemning Smith's accusers was responsible for Sylvester's lack of cooperation. After the resolutions were read, accepted, and ordered printed, "Brother Sylvester objected against abiding by the decision of the former council, and proceeded to justify himself in his former conduct." Upon hearing Sylvester's protest, the council decided that "in consequence of the stand our brother Sylvester Smith has taken against the former decision of this council, that we judge him guilty of a misdemeanor unbecoming a man in his high station, and except a humble confession be made, to this council, he stands rebuked and disqualified to act further in his office in the church, until he make proper satisfaction, or till a trial before the bishop assisted by twelve high priests can be had."[25]

Joseph Smith and his counselors were present when Sylvester was again tried before Bishop Whitney and the high council on August 28. Rigdon made the complaint against Sylvester, stating that he "has refused to submit to the decision of a council of the high priests and elders of this church held in this place on the eleventh of this month"—which was to publish a confession and apology to Joseph Smith. Next Sylvester "continues to charge said Joseph, contrary to the decision of the before mentioned council with improper conduct in his proceedings as president of the church of the Latter-Day Saints during his journey the past season, to the state of Missouri. As these things are exceedingly grievous to many of the Saints in Kirtland, and very prejudicial to the cause of truth in general, I therefore require that you summon the high council of this church, to investigate this case that a final [decision] may be had upon the same."[26]

The trial lasted two days; the council heard testimony from eleven witnesses about Joseph Smith chastising Sylvester regarding Sylvester's insulting John S. Carter, his refusing to share his bread with Parley P. Pratt, his threatening to kill Smith's dog, and whether or not Smith threw a trumpet at Sylvester. The testimony was universally in favor of Joseph Smith. Cowdery probably possessed the records that Sylvester could have used in his defense—the history of the camp written by Frederick G. Williams, which Williams had mailed to Cowdery—but nothing was said about them.[27]

24. Resolutions, 58 (*JSP*, 5:114).

25. Minutes, Aug. 23, 1834, Minute Book 1, 55 (*JSP*, 5:109).

26. Minutes, 58 (*JSP*, D4:122).

27. In an appended note to Joseph Smith's June 4, 1834, letter to Emma, Williams mentioned his writing "all the particulars of our journey" in weekly letters to Oliver Cowdery and in a

Regarding Sylvester's accusation that Smith had mishandled camp funds, Orson Hyde put together two accounts based on Williams's records as treasurer of the expedition: one showing the contributions and general expenses of the camp, another showing Joseph Smith's contributions and personal expenses while on the expedition.[28] The original records are not extant, but Williams told the council that "the account exhibited was correctly taken from his accounts."[29] The accounts that Hyde provided satisfied the council that Sylvester's accusations were without foundation, but they do raise some questions. The account for the church's expenditures for the expedition shows that it spent $391.91 more than its receipts of $1,659.59 of consecrated funds, which Hyde reconciled by adding $391.91 from an old account.[30] Yet, according to Hyde's accounting, when the camp disbanded in Clay County, the remaining funds, amounting to $233.70, were "distributed among the companies ... it being the balance left of the consrecrated moneys."[31]

There was apparently no discussion concerning Sylvester's accusing Smith of "proph[e]sying lies in the name of the Lord." Sylvester no doubt shared the disappointment of many that Zion had not been redeemed by power as Smith's December 1833 and February 1834 revelations had predicted.[32] Smith loyalists in the council accepted the new revelation and blamed the failure of Zion's Camp on Sylvester and others who had complained.[33]

The council decided against Sylvester and he was given an ultimatum: "That if brother Sylvester Smith will acknowledge the following items of complaint before this council & publish the same in print, that he can remain yet a member of this church, otherwise he is expelled from the same." Sylvester was to acknowledge that he "willfully and maliciously lied" when he accused Smith of "prophesying lies in the name of the Lord," that he "maliciously told falsehoods" when he said Joseph had abused and insulted him, and that he "wickedly and maliciously insulted" the council's "just and

"journal." Joseph Smith, Letter to Emma Smith, June 4, 1834, JS Letterbook 2, 58 (*JSP*, D4:58). This history is not extant. George A. Smith reported that it had been lost. George A. Smith, Memoir and Autobiography, 43.

28. See Account with the Camp of Israel, ca. Aug. 11–29, 1834, JS Collection (*JSP*, D4:135–51); Account with the Church of Christ, ca. Aug. 11–29, 1834, JS Collection (*JSP*, D4:156–63).

29. Minutes, Aug. 28–29, 1834, Minute Book 1, 70 (*JSP*, D4:132).

30. See discussion in *JSP*, D4:137.

31. Account with the Camp of Israel, ca. Aug. 11–29, 1834, JS Collection (*JSP*, D4:149).

32. Revelation, Dec. 16–17, 1833, Revelation Book 2, 77–78 [D&C 101:55–57] (*JSP*, D3:393–94); Revelation, Feb. 24, 1834, in Hyde and Pratt, Notebook of Revelations, [11]–[13] [D&C 103:15–17, 22] (*JSP*, D3:460–61).

33. Revelation, June 22, 1834, Revelation Book 1, 199 [D&C 105:2] (*JSP*, D4:73).

righteous decisions." Sylvester complied and signed the complaint as "just and true."[34] Later, someone, likely Sylvester himself, crossed out his name and wrote under it, "The above was signed for fear of punishment."[35] It makes little sense that someone in high office such as Sylvester Smith would intentionally lie about transactions witnessed by many others of his faith, apparently without any motive to do so.

This confession was never published, but Sylvester managed to make another, less self-incriminating confession on October 28, 1834, that was published by Cowdery the same month in the *Latter Day Saints' Messenger and Advocate*. In this confession, Sylvester exonerated Smith, acknowledging that the prophet "had conducted [himself] worthily, and adorned his profession as a man of God, while journeying to and from Missouri," and that "I am now perfectly satisfied that the errors of which I accused him, before the council, did not exist, and were never committed by him; and my contrition has been and still continues to be deep, because I admitted thoughts into my heart which were not right concerning him, and because that I have been the means of giving rise to reports which have gone abroad, censuring the conduct, of bro. J.S. jr. which reports are without foundation."[36]

Sylvester managed to retain his membership, though a council headed by Joseph Smith removed him from the high council on September 24 and replaced him with Hyrum Smith. Sylvester's last act as a high counselor was to give "his own assent with thankfulness" to the decision of the council.[37] According to William McLellin, the affair "entirely killed Sylvester in the eyes of the world." McLellin subsequently criticized the actions taken against Sylvester, believing he had been a scapegoat to cover Joseph Smith's sins and save the church from embarrassment. According to McLellin, Sylvester at first refused to sign the "lie bill" until an "older brother took him out and persuaded him to sign it and thus save the church and Joseph." Sylvester returned to the proceedings and told the council: "If you will take all the responsibility before God for the act of signing: I will take the responsibility before the world." The council agreed.[38] Later, in 1834, E. D. Howe wrote that following

34. Minutes, Aug. 28–29, 1834, Minute Book 1, 71–72 (*JSP*, D4:132–33).

35. Minutes, 72 (*JSP*, D4:120, 133n164; *JSP*, J1:173, Jan. 25, 1836).

36. Sylvester Smith, Letter to Oliver Cowdery, Oct. 28, 1834, *LDS Messenger and Advocate*, Oct. 1834, 10–11.

37. Minutes, Sep. 24, 1834, Minute Book 1, 74–76 (*JSP*, D4:173–76).

38. McLellin, Letter to Joseph Smith III, July 1872, 3, in Larson and Passey, eds., *The William E. McLellin Papers*, 486.

Smith's return, "There was a constant uproar among the brethren, for three or four weeks, which only terminated in a sham trial of the Prophet."[39]

New Portage

On September 5 Smith left Kirtland with Cowdery to attend a conference to be held on the 8th in New Portage, where there was a branch of about 100 Saints headed by Ambrose Palmer.[40] Two days later, Smith and Cowdery attended a church service and heard Jared Carter and Rigdon preach "cheering truths ably and eloquently."[41] That same evening, Cowdery wrote to Phelps in Liberty, Missouri, and gave an account of his first meeting Joseph Smith on April 5, 1829, and his service as Smith's scribe, writing the text of the Book of Mormon under Smith's inspired utterance. Cowdery revealed that he and Smith were ordained by an angel prior to baptizing one another in the Susquehanna River. Four years after the church had been organized this detail changed how the membership viewed both the source and nature of Smith's and Cowdery's authority.[42]

Motivation for making such a disclosure, as Cowdery explained, was that it "might … prove especially beneficial to yourself, by confirming you in the faith of the gospel." According to Cowdery, "After writing the account given of the Savior's ministry to the remnant of the seed of Jacob, upon this continent," in 3 Nephi, "it was as easily to be seen, that amid the great strife and noise concerning religion, none had authority from God to administer the ordinances of the gospel. For, the question might be asked, have men authority to administer in the name of Christ, who deny revelations? … We only waited for the commandment to be given, 'Arise and be baptized.'"[43]

In the context of May 1829, the divinely revealed commandment was the authority. In 3 Nephi, Nephi received "power" from the resurrected Jesus to baptize by oral command. Jesus called Nephi to him and said: "I give unto you power that ye shall baptize this people when I am again ascended into heaven. And again the Lord called others, and said unto them likewise; and he gave unto them power to baptize" (3 Ne. 11:21–22). This commission

---

39. Eber D. Howe, *Mormonism Unvailed*, 163.

40. Oliver Cowdery, Letter to William W. Phelps, Sep. 7, 1834, *LDS Messenger and Advocate*, Oct. 1834, 14; Ambrose Palmer, Letter to Oliver Cowdery, Jan. 28, 1835, in *LDS Messenger and Advocate*, Jan. 1835, 62.

41. Cowdery, Letter to William W. Phelps, Sep. 7, 1834, *LDS Messenger and Advocate*, Oct. 1834, 16.

42. The following discussion of Smith and Cowdery's introduction of angelic ordination in 1834 and 1835 is based on Vogel, "Evolution of Early Mormon Priesthood Narratives."

43. Cowdery, Letter, Sep. 7, 1834, *LDS Messenger and Advocate*, Oct. 1834, 13–15.

authorized them to baptize using the following words: "Having authority given me of Jesus Christ, I baptize you in the name of the Father, and of the Son, and of the Holy Ghost. Amen" (3 Ne. 11:25). While Protestants generally believed their authority to baptize was derived from the command in the Bible, Smith's followers believed they were baptizing, preaching, and gathering to Zion by direct command of God as revealed through their prophet.

The command came, according to Smith and Cowdery, on May 15, 1829.[44] In her 1845 history, Smith's mother, Lucy, remembered what she had been told about this event: "One morning, they sat down to their work, as usual, and the first thing which presented itself through the Urim and Thummim [i.e., seer stone], was a commandment for Joseph and Oliver to repair to the water, and attend to the ordinance of Baptism. They did so. ... They had now received authority to baptize."[45]

This concept of authority changed when Cowdery revealed that the chain of ordinations could be traced back to his and Smith's ordination by an angel. According to Cowdery, who used especially elevated language: "After we had called upon [God] in a fervent manner ... on a sudden, as from the midst of eternity, the voice of the Redeemer spake peace to us, while the veil was parted and the angel of God came down clothed with glory, and delivered the anxiously looked for message, and the keys of the gospel of repentance!—What joy! what wonder! what amazement!" Using language familiar to Bible readers, Cowdery said that the angel's "voice, though mild, pierced to the center, and his words, 'I am thy fellow servant,' dispelled every fear"—reminding readers of the angel's words to John the Revelator (Rev. 19:10).[46] "We listened—we gazed—we admired! 'Twas the voice of the angel from glory—'twas a message from the Most High!" Cowdery wrote. "We were rapt in the vision of the Almighty! Where was room for doubt? No where: uncertainty had fled, doubt had sunk, no more to rise, while fiction and deception had fled forever!" By extension, how could Phelps or anyone doubt, especially since there were two witnesses to the same vision. "We received under his hand the holy priesthood, as he said, 'upon you my fellow servants, in the name of Messiah I confer this priesthood and this authority,

---

44. JS History, vol. A-1, 18 (*EMD*, 1:75); and Oliver Cowdery, introduction to blessings, Sep. 1835, Patriarchal Blessing Book, 1:8–9 (*EMD*, 2:452).

45. Lucy Mack Smith, *Biographical Sketches*, 131 (*EMD*, 1:381).

46. The angel's words to John the Revelator were, "I am thy fellowservant, and of thy brethren the prophets" (Rev. 19:10). The quality of the voice being "mild" yet piercing has parallels as well: Hel. 5:30; 3 Ne. 11:3; D&C 85:6.

which shall remain upon earth, that the sons of Levi may yet offer an offering unto the Lord in righteousness!'"[47]

Cowdery's use of the term "priesthood" was anachronistic since "priesthood" was not used to describe authority before the June 1831 introduction of the high priesthood; the term did not even appear in the founding 1830 "Articles and Covenants."[48] The reference to the "sons of Levi" was also problematic since the notion of a greater and lesser priesthood, with the lesser being associated with the Levitical priesthood, did not figure into Mormon discourse until September 1832 when Smith dictated his revelation on priesthood.[49] Cowdery took the words in Malachi 3:3—that "the Lord ... shall suddenly come to his temple ... and he shall purify the sons of Levi ... that they may offer unto the Lord an offering in righteousness," which had been used in the 1832 revelation to justify the continuance of the Old Testament priesthood—and placed them in the angel's mouth.[50]

This disclosure was news to Phelps and others in Missouri and elsewhere. David Whitmer, who at the time was president of the Missouri church, repeatedly said he never heard about the angelic bestowal of authority until years later. Though he had first met Smith and Cowdery within weeks of their alleged angelic ordinations and conveyed them from Harmony, Pennsylvania, to his father's house in Fayette, New York, where they completed the translation of the Book of Mormon, he stated in 1885: "I never heard that an angel had ordained Joseph and Oliver to the Aaronic priesthood until the year 1834 5 or 6."[51] McLellin recalled in 1877: "I never heard of John the Baptist ordaining Joseph and Oliver."[52] In an 1872 letter to Smith's son, Joseph III, McLellin wrote: "But as to the story of John, the Baptist ordaining Joseph and Oliver on the day they were baptized: I never heard of it in the church for years, altho I carefully noticed things that were said. And today I do not believe the story."[53]

---

47. Oliver Cowdery, Letter to W. W. Phelps, Sep. 7, 1834, *LDS Messenger and Advocate*, Oct. 1834, 15–16 (*EMD*, 2:420–21).

48. Vogel, "Evolution of Early Mormon Priesthood Narratives," 67; "Articles and Covenants," ca. Apr. 1830, in BC XXIV [D&C 20] (cf. *JSP*, D1:116–26).

49. Revelation, Sep. 22–23, 1832, Newel K. Whitney Papers [D&C 84] (*JSP*, D2:289–304); Vogel, "Evolution of Early Mormon Priesthood Narratives," 64–68.

50. Revelation, Sep. 22–23, 1832, [2] [D&C 84:31] (*JSP*, D2:297).

51. Gurley, "Questions asked of David Whitmer at his home in Richmond Ray County Mo. Jan 14–1885," 2, back (*EMD*, 5:137).

52. William E. McLellin, Letter to J. L. Traughber, Aug. 25, 1877, [1], in Larson and Passey, eds., *The William E. McLellin Papers*, 508.

53. McLellin, Letter to Joseph Smith III, July 1872, 4, in Larson and Passey, eds., *The William E. McLellin Papers*, 491.

Not only did Whitmer and McLellin never hear the story of angelic ordination, they believed such ordination was unnecessary. McLellin argued in 1872: "An angel never ordained a man to any office since the world began. Then say you how did Joseph and Oliver get authority to start? I answer, that a revelation from the Lord gives a man both power and authority to do whatever it commands. The Lord commanded Joseph to baptize, confirm, and ordain Oliver, then Oliver to do the same for him. This was legal and valid."[54] After his 1886 interview with David Whitmer, Edward Stevenson reported: "David said the prophet of God received the command from God, and that was sufficient authority. He did not seem to understand the necessity of the connecting link of Ordinations."[55] This concept of authority was consistent with contemporary church records, where the claim of angelic ordination is not only missing but divine command as the source of authority is emphasized. In the month following their 1829 baptisms, Smith dictated a revelation that reminded Cowdery, "Thou hast been baptized by the hand of my servant [Joseph Smith] according to that which I have *commanded* him: Wherefore he hath fulfilled the thing which I *commanded* him."[56] Significantly, the claim of angelic ordination is absent from the "Articles and Covenants"—which begins by stating the authority upon which the church was organized, including a summary of the miraculous events preceding that organization, yet is completely silent about angelic ordinations.

Cowdery's willingness to alter history for Smith began as early as July 1830, when he testified at the first of Smith's trials in South Bainbridge and Colesville, New York. Smith was arrested on the old 1826 charge of being a stone gazer, and he pled the statute of limitations since more than three years had elapsed.[57] The prosecution apparently countered that three years had not elapsed since Smith had continued to use the same stone in producing the Book of Mormon. Cowdery testified that Smith translated the Book of Mormon with "two transparent stones, resembling glass, set in silver bows," contrary to other eyewitnesses who uniformly described Smith using a seer stone placed in the crown of a hat, into which he put his face, and in the darkness the translation would appear in luminous writing on the

54. William E. McLellin, Letter to Mark H. Forscutt, Oct. 1, 1871, in *True L[atter] D[ay] Saints' Herald* (Plano, IL), Aug. 1, 1872, 472 (Larson and Passey, eds., *The William E. McLellin Papers*, 477).

55. Stevenson, Letter to Franklin D. Richards, Feb. 12, 1886, 2.

56. Revelation, June 1829-B, BC XV:6–7 [D&C 18:7] (*JSP*, D1:71); emphasis added.

57. Colesville justice Joel K. Noble remembered that "Jo. plead in bar statue of limitations." Noble, Letter to Jonathan B. Turner, Mar. 8, 1842, 2 (*EMD*, 4:108).

stone, which he read to a scribe—who most of the time was Cowdery.[58] In his letter to Phelps, Cowdery repeated this inaccurate claim: "Day after day I continued, uninterrupted, to write from [Smith's] mouth, as he translated, with the *Urim* and *Thummim*, or, as the Nephites would have said, 'Interpreters,' the history, or record, called 'The book of Mormon.'"[59] By calling the spectacles *Urim and Thummim* and associating it with the Old Testament's description of two stones connected with Aaron's breastplate, Smith and Cowdery shrouded the instrument in mystery and obscured its link to seer stones. The story of Smith translating with the spectacles became the official version Smith and Cowdery repeatedly told, and the stone-in-hat story disappeared.

McLellin noted that "Oliver wrote his letters [to Phelps] after … he had assisted for two days and evenings in the high council in Kirtland in August 23rd and 24th, 1834, to screen J. Smith from deserved punishment."[60] Cowdery, with Thomas Burdick and Orson Hyde, had drafted the resolution against Sylvester Smith.[61] Cowdery's history was written a full month before Sylvester made his confession, although both appeared in the October 1834 issue of the *Messenger and Advocate*. Despite whatever misgivings Joseph Smith harbored about Cowdery, the two began working together closely following Smith's return to Kirtland. Indeed, Smith was with Cowdery when he wrote his account of his and Smith's ordination by an angel in May 1829, and when it was published the following month, he promised further installments of early Mormon history with Smith's assistance.[62]

The introduction of this angelic ordination story not only enhanced Smith's leadership and bound other priesthood holders to him—making secession of the Missouri church and schism less likely—it raised Cowdery to prominence as a co-receiver of special authority. That both Cowdery and Smith were

---

58. Cowdery's testimony is reported in [Abram W. Benton], "Mormonites," *Evangelical Magazine and Gospel Advocate* (Utica, NY), Apr. 9, 1831, 120 (*EMD*, 4:97). Emma, who told Joseph III in 1879 that "Oliver Cowdery and your father wrote in the room where I was at work," specifically stated that the spectacles were not used after Harris lost the 116 pages in June 1828. Joseph Smith, III, "Last Testimony of Sister Emma," *Saints' Herald*, Oct. 1, 1879, 290 (*EMD*, 1:542); Emma Smith Bidamon, Letter to Emma Pilgrim, Mar. 27, 1870 (*EMD*, 1:532). For an examination of eyewitness testimony about Smith's method of translation, see Lancaster, "The Translation of the Book of Mormon."

59. Cowdery to Phelps, 14 (*EMD*, 2:419).

60. William E. McLellin, Letter to Mark H. Forscutt, Oct. 1, 1871, [1], CCLA (Larson and Passey, eds., *The William E. McLellin Papers*, 475).

61. Minutes, Aug. 23, 1834, Minute Book 1, 54–55 (*JSP*, 5:109).

62. Oliver Cowdery, Letter to William W. Phelps, Sep. 7, 1834, *LDS Messenger and Advocate*, Oct. 1834, 13.

ordained by the angel, rather than Cowdery simply witnessing Smith's ordination, says something significant about the new dynamic of their relationship. In less than three months, Cowdery's new status will be officially recognized when he is ordained as assistant or copresident by Rigdon.

Meanwhile, on September 8 Smith and Cowdery attended a conference of elders at New Portage, apparently to resolve some conflicts among its members. Smith and Cowdery "united in anointing with oil and laying hands upon a sick sister, who said she was healed." The minutes do not record the illness, but seem equivocal about the result, as the sister "requested us to pray that her faith fail not, saying, if she did not doubt, she should not be afflicted any more."[63]

Smith then spoke on "false spirits and other items," after which branch president Ambrose Palmer spoke and wished to be counseled by Smith about a few policies. First, he described the trial of a Brother Carpenter at which another brother spoke in tongues and declared that Carpenter should not be shown any lenience. Smith explained that the gift of tongues "was not given for the government of the Church ... that it was contrary to the rules and regulations of the Church, because, in all our decisions we must judge from actual testimony." Smith "advised that we speak in our own language in all such matters, and then the adversary cannot lead our minds astray."[64]

The second issue involved the handling of people who speak out of order in conference. Palmer had presided at a conference during which several spoke out of order and Joseph B. Bosworth, branch clerk and high priest, refused to submit to order. It was decided by unanimous vote that Bosworth "acted out of place in opposing brother Palmer in a former council, when requested to take his seat, that the business might proceed according to order," and that a letter signed by the clerk of this conference, Cowdery, be sent to Bosworth informing him of the decision.[65]

Return to Kirtland

Shortly after returning to Kirtland, Smith attended a high council meeting on September 24, during which Sylvester Smith was removed as a member. Four days later, Sylvester wrote an apology for accusing the prophet of wrongdoing during the march of the army of Israel. At the same meeting, a committee, consisting of Smith, Cowdery, Rigdon, and Williams, was

---

63. Minutes, Sep. 8, 1834, Minute Book 1, 49 (*JSP*, D4:165).
64. Minutes, 49–50 (*JSP*, D4:165).
65. Minutes, 50–52 (*JSP*, D4:165–68).

appointed to arrange the revelations and other items of doctrine for publication. The council also decided that high priests would be ordained only by the council at Kirtland.[66]

On the same day, Smith wrote a letter to Cowdery in which he railed about Alexander Campbell's *Millennial Harbinger* and its misrepresentations of "Joe Smith! false prophet!" The letter, which appeared in the September 1834 issue of *The Evening and the Morning Star*, amounts to little more than a personal attack. Smith accused Campbell and his followers—those "who profess to be 'Reformers, and Restorers of ancient principles'"—of having "corrupt hearts," which condition has been exposed to the world through their attack on him, "by crying delusion, deception, and false prophets, accusing the innocent, and condemning the guiltless, and exalting themselves to the stations of gods, to lead blind-fold, men to perdition!"[67]

Smith characterized the *Harbinger* as saying, "*Joe* Smith! *Joe* Smith! imposture! imposture!" This may refer to Campbell's recent article about the languid and apostate condition of Christianity, wherein he states in passing: "Every few years gives us an Anna Lee, a Jemima Wilkinson, a Joanna Southcoat, a Joe Smith, a religious Robinson Crusoe."[68] Campbell's dismissing him with other prophets probably angered Smith. Since publishing a critique of the Book of Mormon in 1831, Campbell had said little about Mormonism, which seems to have frustrated Smith.[69] "Mr. Campbell was very lavish of his expositions of the falsity and incorrectness of the book of Mormon, some time since," Smith wrote, "but of late, since the publication of the Evening and the Morning Star, has said little or nothing, except some of his back-handed *cants*."[70] During the previous months, Cowdery repeatedly attacked Campbell and the *Harbinger* in *The Evening and the Morning Star* without a response from Campbell.[71] Smith continued to taunt Campbell for his failure to respond: "Perhaps, he is of opinion that he so completely overthrew the foundation on which it was based, that all that is now wanting

---

66. Minutes, Sep. 24, 1834, Minute Book 1, 74–76 (*JSP*, D4:173–76).

67. Joseph Smith, Letter to Oliver Cowdery, Sep. 24, 1834, *The Evening and the Morning Star*, Sep. 1834, 192 (*JSP*, D4:169).

68. "Christendom in Its Dotage," *Millennial Harbinger* (Bethany, WV), Aug. 1834, 374.

69. See Campbell, *Delusions*.

70. Joseph Smith, Letter, in *The Evening and the Morning Star* (Kirtland, OH), Sep. 1834, 192 (*JSP*, D4:170).

71. See "Communications," Jan. 1834, 123; "Millennium. No. II," 127; "Millennium. No. III," Feb. 1834, 131; "Faith of the Church of Christ in These Last Days. No. II," Apr. 1834, 145–46; Editorial Comments, Apr. 1834, 150; "Faith of the Church of Christ in These Last Days. No. IV," June 1834, 163.

to effect an utter downfall of those who have embraced its principles is, to continue to *bark* and *howl*, and cry, *Joe* Smith! false prophet! and ridicule every man who may be disposed to examine the evidences which God has given to the world of its truth!"[72]

Through Cowdery's paper, Smith wished to inform Campbell that "while he is breathing out scurrility he is effectually showing the honest, the motives and principles by which he is governed, and often causes men to investigate and embrace the book of Mormon, who might otherwise never have perused it."[73] Smith's hyperbole seems intended to provoke Campbell into an exchange. In December 1835, Smith will challenge Campbell to a public debate, which was also ignored.[74] From his success in recruiting Campbell's followers during the first years of his movement in northern Ohio, Smith perhaps hoped to instigate a more general disaffection from Campbellism, resulting in another large influx of converts that could strengthen the army of Israel.

According to Smith's history, he spent the first part of October working on the temple, despite limited funds and means.[75] On October 8 he wrote McLellin a letter of introduction and sent him to the branch in Florence, about seventy miles southwest of Kirtland. McLellin recorded the main portion of Smith's letter in his journal and noted that Smith had sent him to the churches in that place and vicinity to "fill a promise that he had made for to go himself."[76] In mid-October, McLellin visited the branches of the church in Brownhelm, Amherst, and Florence, Ohio, and found them in discord, dissension, and "low in spirits."[77]

Michigan

Meanwhile, on October 16 Smith left Kirtland with Cowdery, Hyrum Smith, David Whitmer, Williams, and Roger Orton to visit the Saints in Pontiac, Michigan, where five months earlier Hyrum and Lyman Wight left with a contingent of the army of Israel. At 9:00 p.m. they boarded the steamer *Monroe* at Fairport, Ohio, and made a short stop at Cleveland before

---

72. Smith, Letter, in *The Evening and the Morning Star*, Sep. 1834, 192 (*JSP*, D4:170).

73. Smith, 192.

74. Joseph Smith, Letter to "the Elders of the Church of the Latter Day Saints," ca. Nov. 30–Dec. 1, 1835, *LDS Messenger and Advocate*, Dec. 1835, 228 (*JSP*, D5:96).

75. JS History, vol. B-1, 557 (DHC 2:167).

76. Joseph Smith, Letter to Moses Daley, ca. Oct. 8, 1834, partly quoted in McLellin, Journal, Oct. 26, 1834 (*JSP*, D4:178).

77. See Shipps and Welch, *The Journals of William E. McLellin*, 140–44.

continuing across the lake and up the Detroit River, landing at Detroit at 4:00 a.m. on October 18.[78] They then took a stage to Pontiac.[79]

Decades later, Edward Stevenson, who was fourteen at the time, remembered that Smith's arrival caused "a great stir" in the settlement and that a large congregation gathered in an old log schoolhouse on Sunday, October 19, to hear the Mormon prophet and Book of Mormon witnesses speak. Smith did not disappoint, for, according to Stevenson, Smith, who he described as "a plain but noble looking man," stood behind a table and "began relating his vision and before he got through he was in the midst of the Congregation with uplifted hand. ... His countanance seemed to me to assume a heavenly witeness and his voice was so peirseing and forcible for my part it so inpressed me as to become indellibly imprinted on my mind." Smith's presentation proved effective, for, as Stevenson recalled, "there was not one person present who did at the time being, or who was not convicted of the truth of his vision, of An Angle [angel] to him."[80] Stevenson also remembered that "The 3 witnesses bore their testimonies as to seeing the Angle, and hearing his voice," although Martin Harris is not known to have been present, and that "there were meny who were babtized."[81]

Smith's visit to Pontiac was brief, for he and Cowdery had returned to Kirtland by November 5, when Williams noted in his account book that Cowdery had incurred a debt of $14.23½ for "expenses to & from Mishigan," and that Smith owed $13.16.[82]

Financial and Legal Troubles

Former Mormon Dennis Lake sued Smith in November 1834, demanding

---

78. The trip to Pontiac was chronicled by Cowdery, Letter, Oct. 20, 1834, *LDS Messenger and Advocate*, Oct. 1834, 2–7.

79. JS History, vol. B-1, 557 (DHC 2:168), says they arrived on Monday, October 20, but Cowdery's account implies that it was on the morning of Saturday, October 18. Cowdery, Letter, Oct. 20, 1834, *LDS Messenger and Advocate*, Oct. 1834, 6.

80. Stevenson, Autobiography, 19–20. In later accounts, Stevenson changed Joseph Smith's telling about the appearance of the angel to the appearance of the Father and Son. See *EMD*, 1:35–40. Later in the same history, following his account of 1838 events, Stevenson added a statement concerning Smith's 1834 visit to Michigan: "We were highly honoured by entertaining a Prophet of God who had stood in the presance of God The Father and JESUS Christ his only Begotten (in that way) upon this Earth, and while we herd him tell in his plain simple way about this vision and also of the visit of Maroni The Angle [angel] to him." Stevenson, Autobiography, 65. While it is not impossible for Smith to have added the Father to his first vision account by 1834, it is more likely that Stevenson's memory had been influenced by information obtained during the intervening years or conflated Smith's October 1834 and August 1835 visits to Pontiac. Stevenson also remembered that he brought Smith "some very early apples and he dined with us," which fits the August 1835 visit.

81. Edward Stevenson, Autobiography, 20.

82. F. G. Williams & Co. Account Book, 12 (Nov. 5, 1834).

payment for his labor and expenses while on the expedition to Missouri with Zion's Camp. The suit was filed with Kirtland justice of the peace John C. Dowen, who issued a summons for Smith to appear before him on November 28. After the parties gave "the proofs & allegations," Dowen adjourned the court until December 4, at which time he ruled in Lake's favor and ordered Smith to pay $63.67 plus court costs of $8.04. Smith, concerned that the case could set a precedent, filed an appeal to the Geauga County Court of Common Pleas on December 10 and entered into a $150 recognizance promising to pay whatever the court decided.[83] The case would be resolved in June 1835 in Smith's favor.

On November 25 Smith dictated a revelation calling Cowdery's recently-baptized older brother, Warren, as a high priest over the branch at Freedom, New York. This was apparently in response to two letters Oliver had received from Warren: one in September mentioning that the Freedom branch needed "a preacher" who could "do us good, by strengthening and building us up in the most holy faith," and another in October in which Warren told Oliver that he "had thoughts of requesting you to enquire what is the will of the Lord concerning me," stating that he sometimes thought he could be "useful in the vineyard of the Lord."[84] Accordingly, Smith dictated a revelation for Oliver's brother, beginning with a warning that "the coming of the Lord draweth nigh, and it overtaketh the world as a thief in the night," then declaring in the voice of God: "There was joy in heaven when my servant Warren bowed to my scepter and separated himself from the crafts of men. Therefore, blessed is my servant Warren, for I will have mercy on him, and notwithstanding the vanity of his heart, I will lift him up."[85]

On the evening of November 28, Smith presided over a meeting of the high council, which met to decide if three representatives of the branch in Lewis Township, New York, should remain in Kirtland for the winter or continue to Missouri, where they were to purchase lands as directed in a December 1833 revelation.[86] The high council advised the three represen-

---

83. Docket Entry, Kirtland Township, Geauga Co., OH, D. Lake v. Joseph Smith, Justice of the Peace Court, copied in Transcript of Proceedings, ca. June 19, 1834, Geauga County Court of Common Pleas, Final Record, vol. Q, 506–507.

84. Warren Cowdery, Letter to Oliver Cowdery, Sep. 1, 1834, *The Evening and the Morning Star*, Sep. 1834, 189; Warren Cowdery, Letter to Oliver Cowdery, Oct. 28, 1834, *LDS Messenger and Advocate*, Nov. 1834, 22.

85. Revelation, Nov. 25, 1834, Revelation Book 2, 116 [D&C 106] (*JSP*, D4:180–82).

86. Revelation, Dec. 16–17, 1833, Revelation Book 2, 80 [D&C 101:72–73] (*JSP*, D3:395); see also D&C 103:23; 105:27–29. The revelation instructed that branches of the church "gather together all their monies" and send "wise men" to Missouri to purchase lands.

tatives to remain at Kirtland for the winter and to loan the church $430, which would be repaid with interest by April 15, 1835.[87] John H. Tippets later wrote that he, his sister Caroline, and cousin Joseph H. Tippets stayed in Kirtland "thro[u]gh the winter spring and sumer" and "obtained a greate deal of good in struction."[88] According to Eleanor Wise Tippets, John's wife, her non-Mormon father-in-law "upbraided his son for lending" the money to Smith, but she said that Smith later "returned to John H Tippets, every dollar due."[89] The promissory notes were signed by Joseph Smith, Oliver Cowdery, and Frederick G. Williams, which might indicate that the loan was for the Cowdery-Williams printing establishment and its most pressing need to print and bind the revelations.

On November 29 Smith and Cowdery united in prayer giving thanks "for the relief which the Lord had lately sent us" and entering into a covenant that if God will prosper them in business enough to pay their debts, they will pay a tenth to aid the poor.[90] The next day, Smith recorded that he received prophetic assurance "that in a short time the Lord would arrange his providences in a merciful manner and send us assistance to deliver us from debt and bondage."[91] Nevertheless, Smith and his church were in financial difficulty even as they made strenuous efforts to construct the temple and publish his revelations.

---

87. Minutes, Nov. 28, 1834, Minute Book 1, 77–80 (*JSP*, D4:182–88).
88. John H. Tippets, Autobiography, 20–22.
89. Tippets, 25.
90. Smith, Journal, Nov. 29, 1834 (*JSP*, J1:46–47; *JSP*, D4:188–91).
91. Smith, Journal, Nov. 30, 1834 (*JSP*, J1:47).

18

Hierarchy

DECEMBER 1834–JULY 1835

I am aware, that I am standing in a far more responsible station in
this church now, than I have ever heretofore …
—Oliver Cowdery to Elizabeth Cowdery,
May 4, 1834, Oliver Cowdery, Letterbook, 42

As Smith resolved his public dispute with Sylvester Smith, and Sylvester published an apology in the October 1834 issue of the *Latter Day Saints' Messenger and Advocate*, Eber D. Howe was writing a preface to his exposé *Mormonism Unvailed: or, A Faithful Account of That Singular Imposition and Delusion, from Its Rise to the Present Time,* which was released for sale in late November.[1] Howe's work received a favorable review in Alexander Campbell's *Millennial Harbinger* in January 1835, which praised Howe for his "detection of this fraud."[2]

On December 4 a judgment was rendered against Joseph Smith in favor of Dennis Lake, who sued Smith for labor and expenses while on the expedition to Missouri with Zion's Camp.[3] Though Smith prevailed on appeal the following June, the unfavorable judgment was no doubt a source of embarrassment, adding to the pressures surrounding the debacle of Zion's Camp and his failure to redeem Zion.

---

1. The sale of Howe's book was announced in "Mormonism Unvailed," *Painesville* (OH) *Telegraph,* Nov. 28, 1834, [3].

2. "Mormonism Unvailed," *Millennial Harbinger* (Bethany, WV), Jan. 1835, 44–45.

3. Transcript of Proceedings, ca. June 19, 1835, County Court of Common Pleas, Court Record, vol. Q, 506–507.

Cowdery's Rise to Power[4]

The next day, December 5, Smith and his counselors—Rigdon and Williams—met with Cowdery in the evening. This meeting was held by the "direction of the Holy Spirit" to discuss "the welfare of the Church."[5] Smith ordained Cowdery to be "a President of the high and holy priesthood, to assist in presiding over the Chu[r]ch, and bearing the keys of this kingdom." While ordaining Cowdery, Smith said: "Let him hear thy voice, and recieve the ministring of the holy angels—deliver him from temptation, and the power of darkness—deliver him from evil, and from those who may seek his destruction, … endow him with power from on high, that he may write, preach, and proclaim the gospel to his fellowmen in demonstration of the Spirit and of power … may his faith never fail."[6]

Cowdery thus became the first assistant-president of the church, surpassing Rigdon and Williams in authority. As Cowdery explained in an unpublished history that he began writing about this time, "The office of Assistant President is to assist in presiding over the whole chu[r]ch, and to officiate in the absence of the President, according to his rank and appointment, viz: President Cowdery, first; President Rigdon Second, and President Williams Third, as they were severally called. The office of this Priesthood is also to act as Spokesman—taking Aaron for an ensample."[7]

Only five months previous, according to William McLellin, Smith had ordained David Whitmer in Missouri as his successor, explaining that Cowdery had lost the privilege due to transgression.[8] Now, on this day, Cowdery is elevated in authority over the entire church, second only to Smith. The move was so unexpected that Cowdery felt compelled to explain the action in the new history he was keeping for Smith: "The reader may further understand, that the reason why High Counsellor Cowdery was not previously ordained to the Presidency, was, in consequence of his necessary attendance in Zion [Missouri], to assist Wm. W. Phelps in conducting the printing business; but that this promise was made by the angel while in

---

4. The following discussion of Cowdery's rise to power recapitulates Vogel, "Evolution of Early Mormon Priesthood Narratives," 68–69. On the development of Smith's teachings about authority, priesthood, and organization of the Mormon hierarchy, see Prince, *Power from on High*; Vogel, "Evolution of Early Mormon Priesthood Narratives"; Quinn, *The Mormon Hierarchy*; Smith, "Early Mormon Priesthood Revelations"; and MacKay, *Prophetic Authority*.

5. Smith, Journal, Dec. 5, 1834 (*JSP*, J1:47–48).

6. JS History, 1834–36, 19 (*JSP*, H1:36–37; D4:198–99).

7. JS History, 1834–36, 17 (*JSP*, H1:32; D4:196).

8. *Ensign of Liberty* (Kirtland, OH), Dec. 1847, 43. See discussion in chapter 16.

company with President Smith, at the time they received the office of the lesser priesthood."[9]

Cowdery's claim, first made public in October 1834, that he and Smith were ordained by an angel in May 1829 prior to their baptisms is anachronistic, but in drawing on this new claim to justify his rise in the developing hierarchy, Cowdery added further anachronistic elements, claiming that the angel had told them about the offices of president and assistant president of the high priesthood. The high priesthood was not introduced until June 1831, and it was not until November 1831 that a president of the high priesthood was appointed by revelation in response to the challenge of Edward Partridge. Even then, counselors for the president were not provided until March 1832.

Cowdery's excuse for the delay of his ordination is curious since there had been more than ample opportunity to perform such an ordination before December 1834. Following organization of the church on April 6, 1830, Smith and Cowdery were together until Cowdery left Fayette, New York, on his mission to Missouri in October. Cowdery and Smith were reunited when the latter visited Missouri in mid-July and early August 1831, during which time Cowdery was not ordained to the newly-revealed high priesthood. He was present in Hiram, Ohio, on November 11, 1831, when Smith dictated the revelation appointing him as President of the High Priesthood, which did not mention Cowdery's co-presidency. Smith and Cowdery were again reunited in late April 1832 when Smith made a second visit to Missouri with counselors Rigdon and Jesse Gause and was sustained as president of the high priesthood, and then left without ordaining Cowdery. When Cowdery returned to Kirtland in August 1833 following destruction of the press in Missouri, there were additional opportunities to ordain him, but none were as obvious as when Cowdery assisted Smith on April 19, 1834, and "confirmed upon" Rigdon authority as first counselor "to preside over the Church in the abscence [sic] of brother Joseph."[10] When Smith left Kirtland for Missouri the following month at the head of Zion's Camp, it was Rigdon, not Cowdery, who presided over the church for the next three months.[11]

At the December 5 meeting, Smith dictated a short revelation rebuking leaders and members for the informal manner in which they addressed one another. The revelation instructed members of the priesthood to be addressed

---

9. JS History, 1834–36, 17 (*JSP*, H1:34; D4:196).

10. Smith, Journal, Apr. 19, 1834 (*JSP*, J1:41).

11. Vogel, "Evolution of Early Mormon Priesthood Narratives," 68–69.

with "the respect due the office, calling, and priesthood."[12] Thus, instead of "Brother Joseph," it was "President Smith." Cowdery explained that prior to this revelation, the use of titles was shunned for fear that it would lead to pride, spiritual abuse, and "vain ambition," which many members had experienced in their former religious affiliations. Such informality, however, fostered disrespect and distrust of those in authority. In contrast to sectarian leaders, "the true principle of honor in the church of the saints, [is] that the more a man is exalted, the more humble he will be, if actuated by the Spirit of the Lord," for "the greatest is least and servant of all; as said our Savior."[13] This instruction was probably a reaction to the disrespect Smith felt from some members of Zion's Camp; it also suited the upcoming expansion of the hierarchy.

Patriarch

On December 6 another meeting was held attended by Presidents Smith, Cowdery, Rigdon, and possibly Williams; high councilors Joseph Smith Sr., Hyrum Smith, and Samuel Smith; Reynolds Cahoon, counselor to Bishop Whitney; high priest William Smith; and elder Don Carlos Smith. At this meeting, "a lengthy discussion was held upon the subject of introducing a more refined order into the Church," including "the propriety of ordaining others to the office of Presidency of the high priesthood." According to the minutes, Smith ordained Hyrum to the presidency, and Rigdon ordained Joseph Sr. to the same.[14] In another record that he began writing the following year, Cowdery said that Joseph Sr. was also ordained as church patriarch at this time.[15]

Three days later, on December 9, the Smith family gathered for a feast at Joseph Smith's home. Afterward, Joseph Sr. gave a patriarchal, or father's, blessing to each of his children and their spouses, including Joseph and Emma. Joseph Sr.'s blessing on his namesake is revealing of his childhood as well as his place in the family dynamic:

Thou hast sought to know his ways, and from thy childhood thou hast meditated much upon the great things of his law. Thou hast suffered much in

---

12. JS History, 1834–36, 17 (*JSP*, H1:34–35; D4:197).

13. JS History, 18 (*JSP*, H1:35–36; D4:198). See Matt. 20:26–27; D&C 50:26.

14. Minutes, Dec. 5–6, 1834, in JS History, 1834–36, 20 (*JSP*, H1:37–38; D4:200).

15. While some historians have dated Joseph Sr.'s ordination to December 18, 1833, when he blessed his family and church leaders, Cowdery wrote that Joseph Sr. was ordained to the authority of "president and patriarch, under the hands of his son Joseph, myself, Sidney Rigdon, and Frederick G. Williams, presidents of the church" on December 6, 1834. Patriarchal Blessing Book, 1:9. See also introduction to Blessing from Joseph Smith Sr., Dec. 9, 1834, in *JSP*, D4:200.

thy youth, and the poverty and afflictions of thy father's family have been a grief to thy soul. Thou hast desired to see them delivered from bondage, for thou hast lov'd them with a perfect love. Thou hast stood by thy father, and like Shem, would have covered his nakedness, rather than see him exposed to shame: when the daughters of the Gentiles laughed, thy heart has been moved with a just anger to avenge thy kindred. Thou hast been an obedient son: the commands of thy father and the reproofs of thy mother, thou hast respected and obeyed—for all these things the Lord my God will bless thee.[16]

Like one of his main Book of Mormon characters, Nephi, Joseph Jr. had stood by his father's dream-visions, which declared the apostate condition of the religious world, whereas his mother, Lucy, and three older siblings had joined the Presbyterian Church during the Palmyra revival of 1824–25.[17]

School of the Elders

During the first weeks of December, a School of the Elders was established in Kirtland. According to Smith's history, the school met in the schoolroom on the lower story of the printing office, was "well attended," and its participants "gave the most studious attention to the all important object, of qualifying themselves, as messengers of Jesus Christ, to be ready to do his will."[18] About the same time, many of the elders in Kirtland began attending a grammar school taught by McLellin and Thomas Burdick. The students studied geography, grammar, and writing, among other things.[19]

During the winter, Smith and Rigdon delivered lectures on theology in the School of the Elders that became the seven "Lectures on Faith," later published in the 1835 Doctrine and Covenants.[20] Jedediah M. Grant remembered that "Elders Smith, Rigdon, and others, acted as teachers" in the school, and Harrison Burgess said the theological lectures were given during evening sessions and were devoted to "instruction in the principles of our Faith and religion."[21] Five of the lectures are followed by catechisms in a question-and-answer format: "Q. What is faith? A. It is the assurance

---

16. Joseph Smith Sr., Blessing to Joseph Smith and Emma Smith, Dec. 9, 1834, Patriarchal Blessing Book, 1:3–5 (*JSP*, D4:200–208).

17. Vogel, *Joseph Smith*, 62 63, 131–35.

18. JS History, vol. B-1, 557–58, 562 (DHC 2:175–76, 180).

19. William W. Phelps, Letter to Sally Phelps, Dec. 18, 1835, in "Some Early Letters of William W. Phelps," *Utah Genealogical and Historical Magazine* (Salt Lake City), Jan. 1940, 30; McLellin, Journal, Dec. 22, 1834, in Shipps and Welch, eds., *The Journals of William E. McLellin*, 152; McLellin, Notice, Feb. 27, 1835, *LDS Messenger and Advocate* (Kirtland, OH), Feb. 1835, 80.

20. The Lectures remained in various editions of the Doctrine and Covenants until 1921.

21. Grant, *A Collection of Facts,* 8; Harrison Burgess, Autobiography, 4.

of things hoped for, the evidence of things not seen: Heb. 11:1," and the like. Catechisms were used in various denominations as a simple means of instructing children and new converts on the major principles of the faith. The Mormon Lectures presented lessons on various theological topics such as faith, God as the object of faith, God's attributes, the true nature of the Godhead, what faith requires of believers, and the effects of faith.

The fifth lecture on the nature of the Godhead may be the most controversial. This is largely due to its capturing what Smith believed about the relationship between the Father and Son midway through his career, before he announced in 1842 that "the Father, and the Son are persons of Tabernacle; and the Holy Ghost [is] a spirit."[22] In contrast, the fifth lecture described the Godhead as consisting of "two personages"—"the Father being a personage of spirit, … the Son, who was in the bosom of the Father, a personage of tabernacle, … possessing the same mind with the Father, which mind is the Holy spirit, that bears record of the Father and the Son, and these three are one."[23] While still sounding like the Book of Mormon's modalistic theology, the lecture made a subtle shift by never declaring that Jesus was both the Father and the Son.[24] Instead, the Father remains a personage of spirit outside the body of Jesus and enters only via the Holy Spirit which *emanates* from God and is "shed forth upon all who believe on his name and keep his commandments."[25]

It appears that this view—that the Son was filled by an emanation from the Father—was an attempt to avoid the charge of patripassianism, that is, the belief that the Father suffers death on the cross. The concept of emanation was not unique to Smith or Rigdon. In 1829 British theologian Edward Burton noted that Sabellius, a third-century modalist, "thought to avoid this difficulty [of patripassianism], by making the divinity of the Son an actual emanation from the Father." Burton explained, "Sabellius adopted in part

---

22. Joseph Smith, Editorial, *Times and Seasons* (Nauvoo, IL), Sep. 15, 1842, 926. This was formulated in April 1843 as: "The Father has a body of flesh & bone as tangible as mans the Son also, but the Holy Ghost is a personage of spirit" (D&C 130:22).

23. Lectures on Faith, D&C, 1835 ed., 52–53.

24. The Book of Mormon repeatedly declares Jesus is both the Father and the Son (1 Ne. 11:16, 26; Mosiah 3:5, 8; 15:1–5, 7; Alma 11:28–29, 38–39; 3 Ne. 1:14; Ether 3:14). For a discussion of the Book of Mormon's modalism, see Vogel, "The Earliest Mormon Concept of God"; Harrell, *"This Is My Doctrine,"* 109–11.

25. D&C, 1835 ed., 54. This is consistent with the account in the Book of Mormon where the Father talks with Nephi III the day before his birth and declares "on the morrow come I into the world … to do the will, both of the Father and of the Son—of the Father because of me, and of the Son because of my flesh" (3 Ne. 1:13–14).

the system of emanations, and supposed the Son and the Holy Ghost to be unsubstantial emanations from the Father, like light from the sun. ... There was therefore some resemblance between the doctrine held by Sabellius and that of the Gnostics: for both of them believed the divinity, which was in Jesus, to be an emanation from God." Burton also spoke of "that tenet of Sabellianism, by which the divinity of the Son was supposed to have no previous personal existence. It was merely an emanation, sent forth upon that express occasion by God."[26] Thus, as of 1835, the Son, in Smith's theology, remained only a vessel for the Father's spirit emanation, if not his spirit personage. As the lecture states, "The Son ... possess[es] all the fulness of the Father, or, the same fulness with the Fathe[r]; being begotten of him. ... The Father and Son possess the same mind, ... the Son being filled with the fulness of the Mind of the Father, or, in other words, the Spirit of the Father."[27]

Because the fifth lecture described the Father and Son as personages but not the Holy Spirit, some have concluded that this represents a shift to binitarianism.[28] Binitarianism, the belief that the Godhead consists of two personages and that the Holy Spirit is "a divine emanation of God," was popular among primitivistic Christians such as David Millard, a leader in the "Christian Connexion" movement, and apparently Alexander Campbell, as well.[29] However, while the lecture described the Son as a "personage" of flesh, it fails to define the Son as a *person* distinct from the Father and therefore may only be a variation of modalism—albeit, one that allows for the simultaneous appearance of the Father and Son. The binitarian-like formulation of the Godhead in the fifth lecture may be due, in part, to former Campbellite Rigdon's participation in preparing the lectures.[30]

About the same time the lectures were being delivered, Smith's recitals of his first vision began to reflect the same view of the Godhead. In his 1832 history, Smith described only one personage appearing to him: "I

---

26. See Burton, ed. *An Inquiry into the Heresies*, 590, 591, 594.

27. D&C, 1835 ed., 53, 54.

28. Van Hale, "Defining the Mormon Doctrine of Deity," *Sunstone*, Jan. 1985, 26; Boyd Kirkland, "Jehovah as the Father: The Development of the Mormon Jehovah Doctrine," *Sunstone*, Autumn 1984, 37.

29. Vogel, "The Earliest Mormon Concept of God," 25–27.

30. For evidence of Rigdon's possible influence on the "Lectures on Faith," see Gentry, "What of the Lectures on Faith?," 13–19; Reynolds, "The Case for Sidney Rigdon as Author of the Lectures on Faith"; and discussion in *JSP*, D4:458–59. In the 1837 edition of his book, binitarian primitivist David Millard declared: "Instead of the holy Ghost being a distinct person, it is represented in scripture as the Spirit of a person; or a divine emanation from God, which he diffuses or pours out." Millard, *The True Messiah*, 86; see also 80, 217.

saw the Lord and he spake unto me saying ... behold I am the Lord of glory I was crucifyed for the world."[31] This version was congruent with the Book of Mormon's theology. However, when Smith related his experience in November 1835, he not only said that "a personage appeared in the midst of [a] pillar of flame," but that "another personage soon appeared like unto the first."[32] Several decades later, Edward Stevenson recalled hearing Smith, during a visit to Pontiac, Michigan, probably in August 1835, describe "the visit of the Father and the Son, and the conversation he had with them."[33]

Response to Howe

Following the release of Eber D. Howe's *Mormonism Unvailed* in November 1834, Smith and Cowdery decided to respond indirectly through the history Cowdery was writing, which appeared in the *Latter Day Saints' Messenger and Advocate* in the form of letters to William Phelps in Missouri. What would become an eight-part history of Smith and the church's founding began in the October issue with the announcement of a May 1829 ordination by an angel, followed in the November issue with a history of the church, from the patriarchs to "the ministry of the apostles of that church; ... till it lost its visibility on earth; was driven into darkness, or till God took the holy priesthood unto himself, where it has been held in reserve to the present century."[34] In his third letter, which appeared in the December issue, Cowdery wrote that one aim of the history he was about to give was "to convince the public of the incorrectness of those scurrilous reports [i.e., Howe's new book] which have *inundated* our land."[35]

In the same issue, Smith responded specifically to his "accusers," admitting that in his youth he "fell into many vices and follies," due to "a light and too often vain mind." He said he engaged in "foolish and trifling conversation," although not in any "gross and outrageous violations of the peace

---

31. JS History, 1832, 3 (*JSP*, H1:13).

32. Smith, Journal, Nov. 9–11, 1835 (*JSP*, J1:88).

33. Stevenson, *Reminiscences of Joseph, the Prophet*, 4. In his autobiography, Stevenson wrote about Smith's October 1834 visit and his account of the angel and then later added that he and his family "were highly honoured by entertaining a Prophet of God who had stood in the presence of God The Father and JESUS Christ his only Begotten." Stevenson, Autobiography, 19–20, 65. It seems probable that Stevenson had conflated Smith's October 1834 and August 1835 visits to Pontiac, Michigan, especially since Stevenson also remembered that he brought Smith "some very early apples and he dined with us," which fits the August 1835 visit.

34. Oliver Cowdery, Letter to W. W. Phelps, *LDS Messenger and Advocate*, Nov. 1834, 28.

35. Oliver Cowdery, Letter to W. W. Phelps, *LDS Messenger and Advocate*, Dec. 1834, 42 (*EMD*, 2:423).

and good order of the community."[36] Mormon historian Richard Anderson interpreted this disclaimer as an allusion to treasure-seeking even though Smith avoided explicit details about treasure quests.[37]

In his third letter, Cowdery described the "great awakening" in Palmyra, New York, where "large additions were made to the Methodist, Presbyterian, and Baptist churches." This religious excitement was touched off under the preaching of Methodist minister George Lane, who had a profound effect on a young Joseph Smith. Soon a harmonious revival transitioned to a competition for converts and sectarian strife, and Smith's mother and three older siblings joined the Presbyterian Church. While Cowdery dates these events to Smith's "15th year," or 1820, the revival actually occurred during the winter of 1824–25.[38] In his fourth letter, Cowdery said that Smith was actually seventeen and the year was 1823. He then described the glorious appearance of an angel to Smith on the night of September 21–22. From this angel, Smith learned about the gold plates hidden in a nearby hill, which he said "gave a history of the aborigines of this country, and said they were literal descendants of Abraham."[39] Cowdery's fifth, sixth, and seventh letters explicated various scriptures dealing primarily with the restoration of Israel in the last days, which he said were "rehearsed by the angel," who he said was Moroni, the last recorder in the Book of Mormon, on the night he appeared to Smith.[40] The obvious aim of rehearsing these long Bible passages was to inspire the Mormons in Missouri, who believed they had been called by God to fulfill ancient prophecy about the establishment of Zion.

In his final letter, published in October 1835, Cowdery elaborated on Smith's first attempt to take the gold plates from their place of deposit in the hill. On the morning following his vision of the angel, Smith climbed the hill near his home, located the plates, and uncovered them by removing a large stone. Cowdery explained that when Smith touched the plates, he received a "shock ... by an invisible power, which deprived him, in a measure of his natural strength," and that Smith had "heard of the power of enchantment, and a thousand like stories, which held the hidden treasures of the

36. Joseph Smith, Letter to Oliver Cowdery, *LDS Messenger and Advocate*, Dec. 1834, 40 (*EMD*, 1.42).

37. Anderson, "The Mature Joseph Smith," 495.

38. Oliver Cowdery, Letter to W. W. Phelps, *LDS Messenger and Advocate*, Dec. 1834, 42 (*EMD*, 2:423–24); Vogel, *Joseph Smith*, 58–59

39. Oliver Cowdery, Letter to W. W. Phelps, *LDS Messenger and Advocate*, Feb. 1835, 78–80 (*EMD*, 2:427–30).

40. Oliver Cowdery, Letters to W. W. Phelps, *LDS Messenger and Advocate*, Mar. 1835, 95–96; Apr. 1835, 108–12; and July 1835, 155–59 (*EMD*, 2:427–50).

earth, and [Smith] supposed that physical exertion and personal strength was only necessary to enable him to yet obtain the object of his wish." Smith made two more attempts to remove the plates, but each time he failed, finally exclaiming: "Why can I not obtain this book?" The angel appeared and explained that it was because he had not kept the commandments.[41]

Smith thus concealed his involvement in treasure searching—it was only something he had heard about. In fact, before 1823, Smith had been an active treasure seer in the Palmyra-Manchester area, occasionally drawing on folklore about enchanted treasures to explain his failures. In a statement published in Howe's book, former Smith family neighbor Willard Chase recounted how Joseph obtained a seer stone while digging a well for the Chase family in 1822. Another neighbor, William Stafford, said on one occasion while digging for treasure on Smith property, Joseph claimed to have seen a spirit in his stone, who caused a treasure to slip away through the ground before the diggers could reach it.[42]

Chase's account of Smith's attempt to remove the plates from the hill varies from the Smith-Cowdery version and contains elements more akin to treasure-searching lore. According to a conversation he had with Joseph's father in 1827, Chase said Joseph Jr. was "hindered" from removing the plates, and that he "saw in the box something like a toad, which soon assumed the appearance of a man, and struck him on the side of his head." Making a third attempt to get the plates, Smith was again struck by the "spirit," who "knocked him three or four rods, and hurt him prodigiously."[43] Smith, through Cowdery, responded to Howe's publication of such affidavits indirectly when he quotes the angel telling him in 1823: "This is the sign: When these things begin to be known, that is, when it is known that the Lord has shown you these things, the workers of iniquity will seek your overthrow: they will circulate falsehoods to destroy your reputation, and also will seek to take your life."[44]

Cowdery no doubt referred to Howe's publication of the affidavits Philastus Hurlbut had gathered, including the general affidavits signed by sixty-two residents of Palmyra and Manchester, when he wrote that Smith's

---

41. Oliver Cowdery, Letter to W. W. Phelps, *LDS Messenger and Advocate*, Oct. 1835, 197–98 (*EMD*, 2:458–59).

42. Howe, *Mormonism Unvailed*, 238–41 (*EMD*, 2:60–61, 65–66). On Joseph Smith's treasure-seeking career, see Quinn, *Early Mormonism and the Magic World View*.

43. Howe, *Mormonism Unvailed*, 242 (*EMD*, 2:67).

44. Oliver Cowdery, Letter to W. W. Phelps, *LDS Messenger and Advocate*, Oct. 1835, 199 (*EMD*, 2:461).

"character has been so shamefully traduced" by those who accuse him of being "a lazy, idle, vicious, profligate fellow."[45] The Palmyra affidavit declared that both Josephs Sr. and Jr. were "considered entirely destitute of *moral character, and addicted to vicious habits,*" while the Manchester affidavit said the Smith family "were not only a lazy, indolent set of men, but also intemperate; and their word was not to be depended upon."[46] Cowdery countered these accusations by claiming he had "the testimony of many persons with whom I have been intimately acquainted, and know to be individuals of the strictest veracity, and unquestionable integrity," which "strictly and virtually agree in saying, that he was an honest, upright, virtuous, and faithfully industrious young man."[47] Most of the leading citizens of Palmyra and Manchester who signed Hurlbut's affidavits probably had only a passing acquaintance with the Smiths; they nevertheless held a common cultural assumption that treasure digging was idleness and drinking alcohol, especially to the point of intoxication, was a vicious habit and moral failing. Despite Cowdery's defense, Smith had confessed that in his youth he "fell into many vices and follies," and in his unpublished 1832 history he had similarly admitted that he "fell into transgression and sinned in many things which brought a wound upon my soul."[48]

Cowdery discussed Smith's treasure-seeking employment with Josiah Stowell in November 1825. Stowell, who lived in South Bainbridge, was attempting to locate a lost Spanish mine about thirty miles down the Susquehanna River in Harmony, Pennsylvania, near the home of Isaac Hale, Smith's future father-in-law. If we are to believe Cowdery, who obtained his information from Smith, Stowell traveled 130 miles to the Smiths' Manchester home only to hire Joseph Jr. as "a common laborer." Cowdery attempted to dismiss the actual reason Stowell hired Smith by stating that if Smith had "not been accused of digging down all, or nearly so, the mountains of Susquehannah, or causing others to do it by some art of nicromancy, I should leave this, for the present, unnoticed."[49] When Joseph Jr. was sued by Stowell's relatives in March 1826 for being a "glass-looker," he confessed to Judge Albert Neely that "he had a certain stone, which he had occasionally looked at to determine

---

45. Cowdery, 200 (*EMD*, 2:462).

46. Howe, *Mormonism Unvailed*, 261–62 (*EMD*, 2:18–21, 48–55).

47. Oliver Cowdery, Letter to W. W. Phelps, *LDS Messenger and Advocate*, Oct. 1835, 200 (*EMD*, 2:462).

48. JS History, 1832, 4 (*JSP*, H1:13).

49. Oliver Cowdery, Letter to W. W. Phelps, *LDS Messenger and Advocate*, Oct. 1835, 200–201 (*EMD*, 2:463–64).

where hidden treasures in the bowels of the earth were, that he professed to tell in this manner where gold mines were a distance under ground, and had looked for Mr. Stowel several times and [had] informed him where he could find those treasures, and Mr. Stowel had been engaged in digging for them ... that he has occasionally been in the habit of looking through this stone to find lost property for 3 years."[50]

Cowdery also apparently hinted at Smith's 1826 legal trouble, claiming that "some very officious person complained of him as a disorderly person, and brought him before the authorities of the country; but there being no cause of action he was honorably acquainted."[51] The person who initiated the lawsuit was Peter G. Bridgeman, Stowell's nephew, who charged Smith with being a "disorderly person and an Impostor." While "Impostor" was not a criminal offense, New York law at the time included under "disorderly persons" the following description: "All jugglers [deceivers], and all persons *pretending* to have skill in physiognomy, palmistry, or like crafty science, or *pretending* to tell fortunes, or to discover where lost goods may be found ... shall be deemed and adjudged disorderly persons."[52] Smith's defense apparently was that he was a true seer, and thus the law did not pertain to him. However, since the law made no such distinction and assumed all persons engaged in such activity were fraudulent, Justice Neely instructed the constable to notify two other justices in anticipation of a formal trial.[53] The reason Smith was not prosecuted is unclear, but South Bainbridge resident Abram W. Benton, who was familiar with the case, reported in 1831 that Smith was "condemned" by Neely's court but that, "considering his youth, (he then being a minor) and thinking he might reform his conduct, he was designedly allowed to escape."[54] Whatever the case, Cowdery, presumably under Smith's influence, was engaging in hyperbole when he claimed that Smith had been "honorably acquitted" in South Bainbridge.

---

50. Docket Entry, Bainbridge, Chenango Co., NY, Mar. 20, 1826, People v. Joseph Smith, Chenango Co., NY, Justice of the Peace Court. The now-missing court record was published in "A Document Discovered," *Utah Christian Advocate* (Salt Lake City), Jan. 1886, [1] (*EMD*, 4:249–50).

51. Oliver Cowdery, Letter to W. W. Phelps, *LDS Messenger and Advocate*, Oct. 1835, 201 (*EMD*, 2:465).

52. *Laws of the State of New-York, Revised* (1813), 1:114, sec. 1; emphasis added. See also *A New Conductor Generalis*, 108. Noah Webster's *Compendious Dictionary of the English Language* (1806) defines a "juggler" as "one who juggles, a cheat, a deceiver," and "juggling" as "the act of playing tricks, deceit" (168).

53. Philip DeZeng, Bill of Costs, 1826 (*EMD*, 4:263).

54. [Abram W. Benton], "Mormonites," *Evangelical Magazine and Gospel Advocate* (Utica, NY), Apr. 9, 1831, 120 (*EMD*, 4:96).

Despite Cowdery's announcement that he intended to publish "a full history of the rise of the church of the Latter Day Saints, and the most interesting parts of its progress, to the present time," his serial history ended at this point.[55]

Apostles

In mid-December 1834, the anticipated redemption of Zion received encouragement when church leaders in Ohio read the text of Governor Dunklin's message to the Missouri legislature, in which he blasted Jackson County for expelling the Mormons. "As yet none have been punished for those outrages, and it is believed that under our present laws, conviction for any violence committed upon a Mormon, cannot be had in Jackson county," Dunklin told the legislature. "It is for you to determine what amendments the laws may require so as to guard against such acts of violence for the future."[56] In the December issue of the *Messenger and Advocate*, Cowdery editorialized: "One thing, and only one, is wanting to put matters in a train for the restoration of this afflicted people to their own land [is] for the Legislature to 'amend,' or make provision in the law to guard against the outrage of mobs, hereafter—when this is done, violence, in that land ceases forever!" At this time, Cowdery was confident that such would be the case.[57] However, no new legislation was enacted.[58]

Through January 1835, Smith was engaged in the School of the Elders and in preparing the lectures on theology for publication in the forthcoming Doctrine and Covenants, the copyright for which Smith obtained on January 14, 1835.[59] On January 18 Smith presided at a meeting of the high council to consider the case of some brethren from Bolton, New York, who had come to Kirtland seeking advice about whether they should move to Missouri. One member of the group, John Tanner, had recently sold his saw and flour mills and about 2,200 acres of land. According to the minutes, Rigdon and then Smith spoke on the importance of "preparing a place in which the Elders might be endowed, and of printing and sending out the word of the Lord." Smith decided that Tanner should assist him in "build[ing]

---

55. Oliver Cowdery, Letter to William W. Phelps, Sep. 7, 1834, *LDS Messenger and Advocate*, Oct. 1834, 13.

56. Oliver Cowdery, Editorial, *LDS Messenger and Advocate*, Dec. 1834, 41.

57. Cowdery, 41.

58. Jennings, "Zion Is Fled," 238.

59. JS History, vol. B-1, 563 (DHC 2:180). Copyright for Doctrine and Covenants, Jan. 14, 1835, Copyright Records, OH, 1831–48 (Department of State), unnumbered volume.

up the cause by tarrying in Kirtland."[60] According to his son, Nathan, John Tanner loaned Smith $2,000, which was used to pay the mortgage on the temple block and prevent a foreclosure.[61]

On Sunday, February 8, after church service, Smith invited Brigham and Joseph Young to his home. According to Brigham, while he and his brother were singing, Smith had a vision showing the new order of the priesthood as well as the post-mortal condition of those who had died in Zion's Camp.[62] Joseph Young remembered that Smith wept and said: "Brethren, I have seen those men who died of the cholera in our camp; and the Lord knows, if I get a mansion as bright as theirs, I ask no more." He then said to Brigham, "I wish you to notify all the brethren living in the branches, within a reasonable distance from this place, to meet at a general conference on Saturday next. I shall then and there appoint twelve Special Witnesses, to open the door of the Gospel to foreign nations, and you ... will be one of them." After speaking at length about the duties of the twelve apostles, he told Joseph Young, "Brother Joseph, the Lord has made you President of the Seventies."[63] The office of seventy is not mentioned in the Book of Mormon, but both Moses and Jesus appointed seventy men to ecclesiastical duties (Ex. 24:1, 9–11; Luke 10:1–24).

On Saturday, February 14, Smith presided at a meeting in the schoolhouse "of those who journeyed to Zion for the purpose of laying the foundation of its redemption last season with as many more of the Brethren & Sisters as felt disposed to attend."[64] If some were disappointed by the failure of Zion's Camp to redeem Zion, perhaps they might view it as useful in an unexpected way. Smith began by eulogizing those who had died by reading John 15: "Greater love hath no man than this, that a man lay down his life for his friends" (v. 13). Other verses in the same chapter also seemed appropriate for the occasion: "If they have persecuted me, they will also persecute you" (v. 20); and "Ye have not chosen me, but I have chosen you, and ordained you, that ye should go and bring forth fruit" (v. 16). After prayer, Smith instructed that all the men who had participated in Zion's Camp, more than fifty, should sit together.

Smith explained that the meeting had been called by God's command

---

60. Minutes, Jan. 18, 1835, Minute Book 1, 82–83 (*JSP*, D4:215–18).

61. [John Tanner], "Sketch of an Elder's Life," 12; Nathan Tanner, "History of John Tanner," 2.

62. Brigham Young, "Home Manufactures," May 7, 1861, *Journal of Discourses*, 9:89.

63. Young, *History of the Organization of the Seventies*, 1–2.

64. Minutes, Feb. 14–15, 1835, Minute Book 1, 147 (*JSP*, D4:224–25).

and according to a vision that he had. After he related some of the circumstances, trials, and sufferings during the march of Zion's Camp, he said, "God had not designed all this for nothing." God remembered their sacrifice and willingness to lay down their lives, he said; it was therefore "the Will of God, that they should be ordained to the ministry and go forth to prune the vineyard for the last time, or the coming of the Lord, which was nigh, even fifty six years, should wind up the scene."[65] This was a significant delay for those who believed the Second Coming was imminent and building Zion was urgent. Smith concluded by promising that soon they would be "endowed with power from on high."

After an hour of adjournment, Smith instructed the three Book of Mormon witnesses—Oliver Cowdery, David Whitmer, and Martin Harris—to choose the Twelve Apostles, which the minutes state was according to a June 1829 revelation.[66] (In fact, the revelation had only mentioned Cowdery and Whitmer.) After prayer, the witnesses chose the following men:

1. Lyman E. Johnson	7. William E. McLellin
2. Brigham Young	8. John F. Boynton
3. Heber C. Kimball	9. Orson Pratt
4. Orson Hyde	10. William Smith
5. David W. Patten	11. Thomas B. Marsh
6. Luke S. Johnson	12. Parley P. Pratt

Eight of these designated apostles had marched with Zion's Camp, while Patten, McLellin, and Marsh were already living in Missouri and Boynton was on a mission in Maine at the time. During the next two days, nine of the twelve would be ordained; Parley P. Pratt, Orson Pratt, and Marsh were out of town and were ordained soon after.[67] At this point, the apostles were considered special witnesses with proselytizing responsibilities, but in the following days and months, Smith would explain their position in his evolving hierarchy.

Although the Three Witnesses were to choose the Twelve, Smith appointed Brigham Young and urged them to include his, Smith's, younger

---

65. Minutes, 147 (*JSP*, D4:225). Smith similarly said in 1843 that he was once praying "very earnestly to know the time of the coming of the Son of Man," when he heard a voice declaring: "Joseph, my son, if thou livest until thou art eighty-five years old, thou shalt see the face of the Son of Man" (D&C 130:14–15). Both statements point to the year 1891. See Erickson, "Joseph Smith's 1891 Millennial Prophecy."

66. Revelation, June 1829-B, BC XV [D&C 18] (*JSP*, D1:71–73).

67. Parley P. Pratt was ordained on February 21, 1835, and Orson Pratt and Thomas Marsh on April 26, 1835.

brother William.[68] In an 1885 interview, David Whitmer said that he and Cowdery "were appointed" to select the apostles but that Smith "insisted that his brother William Smith should be put in as it was the only way by which he could be saved."[69] In a letter to Brigham Young, Cowdery later revealed that he and Whitmer had originally selected his brother Phineas Young as one of the Twelve, but "owing to Brother Joseph's urgent request at the time, Brother David and myself yielded to his wish, and consented for William to be selected, contrary to our feelings and judgment, and to our deep mortification ever since."[70]

The ordinations were performed by the Three Witnesses, with Cowdery probably acting as the voice for most. Lyman E. Johnson, for instance, was ordained and blessed "in the name of Jesus Christ, that he should bear the tidings of salvation to nations, tongues and people, until the utmost corners of the earth shall hear the tidings. ... And that he should live until the gathering was accomplished, according to the Holy Prophets ... and that he shall see the Saviour come and stand on the Earth with power and great glory." If the Second Coming was delayed, it was not far off. Many of the ordination blessings on the Twelve emphasized their calling as missionaries with special powers to convince and convert. Brigham Young, for instance, was blessed "that he might go forth and gather the Elect preparatory to the great day of the coming of the Lord ... that he may come to Zion with many sheaves ... that he may do wonders in the name of Jesus, that he may cast out Devils, heal the sick, raise the dead, open the eyes of the blind ... and that heathen nations shall even call him God himself, if he did not rebuke them."[71]

According to the minutes, Lyman E. Johnson, Brigham Young, and Heber C. Kimball were ordained on the first day and six others on the day following. Orson Hyde was blessed that "He shall be equal in holding the keys of the kingdom. He shall stand on the earth and bring souls till Christ comes. ... He shall be like unto one of the three Nephites."[72] This hints at the hierarchal status of the Twelve—that they were to be considered equal with Smith and his counselors. Being like one of the three Nephite disciples meant that Hyde would never taste death but remain on Earth until Jesus returned.

---

68. On Smith choosing Brigham Young, see Young, *History of the Organization of the Seventies*, 1.
69. Gurley, "Questions asked of David Whitmer," 4.
70. Oliver Cowdery, Letter to Brigham Young, Feb. 27, 1848.
71. Minutes, Feb. 14–15, 1835, Minute Book 1, 149–50 (*JSP*, D4:228–29).
72. Minutes, 151 (*JSP*, D4:230).

David W. Patten was blessed that he might have "power to smite his enemies before him with utter destruction," and that he might "continue till the Lord comes." (Patten became the first Mormon martyr during a conflict with Missourians in 1838.) Luke S. Johnson was blessed that "the angels shall bear him up till he shall finish his ministry." (Johnson apostatized in 1838.) William McLellin was blessed that "the Tempter shall not overcome him, nor his enemies prevail against him." (McLellin also left the church in 1838.) John F. Boynton was told that he should "see the face of thy Redeemer in the flesh." (Boynton apostatized as well.) William Smith was blessed that he "shall be preserved and remain on the earth until, Christ shall come to take vengeance on the wicked."[73] (Smith drifted from one Mormon schismatic group to another following his older brother's death in 1844.)

According to Heber Kimball, after the ordination blessings were given by Cowdery, Whitmer, and Harris, "the first presidency laid their hands on us, and confirmed these blessings and ordination."[74]

It was probably at this two-day meeting that Cowdery gave a general charge to the Twelve.[75] After reading the June 1829 revelation, he said: "Our minds have been on a constant stretch to find who these Twelve were. When the time should come, we could not tell, but we sought the Lord by fasting and prayer, to have our lives prolonged to see this day, to see you." Explaining the source of their apostolic authority, Cowdery continued: "You have been ordained to the Holy Priesthood, You have received it from those who had their power and authority from an angel." This was the angel who delivered the plates to Smith and appeared to the Three Witnesses, who testified that an angel had shown them the plates and that "the voice of the Lord commanded us that we should bear record of it."[76] This heavenly command was the authority that they were now passing on to the Twelve in obedience to the command in the June 1829 revelation. He then told them that their ordinations would not be complete until they "receive a testimony from Heaven for yourselves, so that you can bear testimony to the truth of the Book of Mormon. And that you have seen the face of God. ... Never cease

---

73. Minutes, 152–54 (*JSP*, D4:229–33)

74. Kimball, Autobiography, ca. 1852–58, 22.

75. Cowdery's general charge to the Twelve was recorded under February 21, but his reference to "the other three" apostles who were "not present," evidently referring to Parley P. Pratt, Orson Pratt, and Thomas B. Marsh, implies that it was given sometime during the February 14–15 meetings. See *JSP*, D4:237–38.

76. Testimony of Three Witnesses, Book of Mormon, 1830 ed., [589]; Vogel, "Evolution of Early Mormon Priesthood Narratives," 69–70.

striving until you have seen God, face to face. … If the Saviour in former days laid his hands on his deciples. Why not in the latter Days."[77]

Cowdery also reminded them that they were "not to go to other nations till you receive your endowments. Tarry at Kirtland until you are endowed with power from on high." This meant that the temple would have to be completed first, which was more than a year away. Cowdery took each man by the hand, asking, "Do you with full purpose of heart take part in this ministry, to proclaim the gospel with all diligence with these your brethren, according to the tenor and intent of the charge you have received"? Each answered in the affirmative.[78] Parley P. Pratt called this the "Oath and Covenant of the Apostleship."[79]

When Hyde subsequently began keeping the "Record of the Transactions of the Twelve," he included a brief account of this ordination-blessing meeting, wherein he said that the Three Witnesses were present and that "part of the revelation given in Fayette N.Y. June 1829 relative to the choosing of twelve apostles, was taken into consideration, and it was ascertained that the time had come when they should be chosen."[80] One reason for the five-plus year delay in choosing the Twelve was that this revelation left Cowdery and Whitmer out of the proposed hierarchy and relegated them to missionary work. Cowdery especially resisted this arrangement by issuing his own revelation about the same time, which called him "an Apostle of Jesus Christ by the will of God" and explained "how he should build up [Christ's] church and the manner thereof."[81] Cowdery's revelation not only failed to mention twelve apostles but it gave him authority to build up the church by ordaining priests and teachers, which Smith's revelation had given to the Twelve. According to early convert Ezra Booth, Smith rejected Cowdery's revelation as having been inspired by Satan.[82] A compromise seems to have been worked out when, in the months following the April 1830 organization of the church, the "Articles and Covenants" (D&C 20) was drafted, which failed to mention a Quorum of Twelve Apostles but instead equated the

---

77. Minutes, Feb. 21, 1835, Minute Book 1, 158–60 (*JSP*, D4:242–44).

78. Minutes, 162, 164 (*JSP*, D4:245, 247).

79. Pratt, *Autobiography*, 127.

80. Minutes, Feb. 14, 1835, in Record of the Twelve Apostles, 1 (*JSP*, D4:233); Revelation, June 1829-B, BC XV [D&C 18] (*JSP*, D1:71–73).

81. Oliver Cowdery, "A commandment from God unto Oliver," ca. June 1829, JS Collection (*EMD*, 2:409–12; *JSP*, MRB:21–23). The exact date is not given, but it was "Written in the year of our Lord & Savior 1829." Since the document, at several points, depends on Doctrine and Covenants 18, it was probably composed sometime during or shortly following June 1829.

82. Howe, *Mormonism Unvailed*, 214 (*EMD*, 2:409).

apostleship with the charismatic office of elder.[83] Now that Cowdery was safely within the hierarchy, he was less inclined to resist Smith's desire to establish the apostleship as an office in the church.

Parley P. Pratt, who was in New Portage at this time, would not be ordained until February 21; and after returning to Kirtland from their missions, Thomas B. Marsh and Orson Pratt were ordained on April 26, 1835, completing the quorum.[84]

On February 27 Smith met with nine of the new apostles, as well as counselors Rigdon and Williams and Bishop Whitney, at his home in the evening. He instructed them on the importance of keeping records, although his own journal-keeping had lapsed and would not resume until September 1835. "I have for myself learned a fact by experience which on reflection gives me deep sorrow," he began. "It is a truth that if I now had in my possession every decision which has been given had upon important items of doctrine and duties since the rise of this church, they would be of incalculable worth to the saints." He instructed the Twelve to "let the oldest of your number preside, and let one or more be appointed to keep a record of your proceedings and on the decision of every important item, be it what it may, let such decision be noted down, and they will ever after remain upon record as law, covenants and doctrine." He even prophesied that if they neglected to do so, the time would come that they would "fall by the hands of unrighteous men." He imagined that such a record would create alibis for them when enemies tried to falsely accuse them before the law. Nevertheless, he promised that if they kept a careful record, "it will be one of the most important and interesting records ever seen."[85] McLellin and Hyde were appointed clerks for the Twelve.

After discussing the purpose of the Twelve, Smith said they were "called to [be] a travelling high council to preside over all the churches of the saints among the gentiles when there is no presidency established. They are to travel and preach among the Gentiles until the Lord shall command them to go to the Jews. They are to hold the keys of this ministry—to unlock the door of the kingdom of heaven unto all nations and preach the Gospel unto every creation. This is the virtue pow[e]r and authority of their Apostleship—Amen."[86]

---

83. Articles and Covenants, ca. Apr. 1830, BC XXIV:32 [D&C 20:38] (*JSP*, D1:123).
84. Minutes, Feb. 21, 1835, Minute Book 1, 154–57 (*JSP*, D4:239–42).
85. Minutes, Feb. 14, 1835, in Record of the Twelve Apostles, 1–2 (*JSP*, D4:249).
86. Record of the Twelve Apostles, 3 (*JSP*, D4:252).

Smith explained the source of their authority, which differed from Cowdery's explanation, but, significantly, still did not appeal to angelic ordination: "In the first place God manifested himself to me and gave me authority to establish his church, and you have received your authority from God through me; and now it is your duty to go and unlock the kingdom of heaven to foreign nations, for no man can do that thing but yourselves."[87]

Seventies

On February 28 Smith organized the Quorum of Seventy, an office inspired by Luke 10:1: "After these things the Lord appointed other seventy also, and sent them two and two before his face into every city and place, whither he himself would come." At this two-day meeting, forty-nine men—forty-four of whom had participated in Zion's Camp—were blessed. Of those blessed, forty-three were also ordained as members of the Seventy. Seven men— Sylvester Smith, Joseph Young, Zebedee Coltrin, Hazen Aldrich, Levi Hancock, Leonard Rich, and Lyman Sherman—were appointed presidents over the Seventy.[88]

The Seventy were to act as Smith's missionary force to gather converts to raise an even-larger army to redeem Zion by September 11, 1836. Soon after their ordinations, many of the Seventy left Kirtland in pairs in all directions, serving brief proselytizing missions in various states. On December 28, 1835, a meeting was held at which the Seventy reported that 175 individuals had been baptized thus far through their efforts.[89] On this day, Smith said, "My heart was made glad while listning to the relations of those that had been labouring, in the vinyard of the Lord with such marvelous success."[90]

The ordination blessings of the Seventy, performed by various members of the presidency, promised special powers, predicted future events, and gave a glimpse into early Mormon beliefs. Roger Orton's blessing, for instance, said, "If there be no other way to escape [your enemies], you shall walk upon waters. ... You shall have power to heal the sick, open the eyes of the blind, loose the tongue of the dumb and cause the lame to leap as an heart." Jaazeniah B. Smith was promised that "if you shall command the wicked to be smitten they shall be smitten, and you shall turn rivers out of their course if needful." Harvey Stanley was told, "You shall see the face of your Redeemer

---

87. Record of the Twelve Apostles, 4 (*JSP*, D4:252).
88. Minutes, Feb. 28–Mar. 1, 1835, Minute Book 1, 164–71 (*JSP*, D4:255–86).
89. Minutes, Dec. 27, 1835, *LDS Messenger and* Advocate, Jan. 1836, 253.
90. Smith, Journal, Dec. 28, 1835 (*JSP*, J1:139).

and he shall lay his hand upon you." Lyman Sherman was assured, "You shall lead a flock to Zion from the abodes of poverty." And Lyman Smith, who died about two years later, was promised: "You shall be the son of the waters and preach in ships & on ships, and whole crews shall be converted and follow you to Zion."[91]

On the following day, Sunday, March 1, Smith presided over another ordination-blessing meeting of the Seventy. Previous to administering the sacrament, Smith spoke: "How long do you suppose a man may partake of this ordinance unworthily and the Lord not withdraw his spirit from him? How long will he thus trifle with sacred things and the Lord not give him over to the buffitings of Satan until the day of Redemption? The church should know if they are unworthy, from time to time, to partake, The servants of the Lord will be forbidden to administer it. Therefore our heart ought to humble themselves, and we to repent of our sins, and put away evil from among us."[92]

Before the afternoon break, thirty-four men were ordained and blessed, apparently by the presidency, including Joseph Young and Sylvester Smith. Not all the blessings were for the Seventies; some were for those who participated in Zion's Camp, sometimes referred to as "Zion blessings."[93] These blessings were in partial fulfillment of a promise made in the revelation disbanding Zion's Camp the previous June, which stated that those who had participated would be rewarded with "a great endowment and blessing."[94]

During the afternoon, Smith, with others, may have attended the funeral of Seth Johnson, who had contracted cholera during the march of Zion's Camp but never fully recovered and lingered in a weakened condition until February 19, 1835, when he died at age thirty.[95] Following the break, eight more ordination-blessings were given, bringing the major shift to an institutionally-based authority to a close. By expanding church administration, Smith hoped it would serve both as a reward for loyalty and a deterrent to apostasy.

At one of the meetings of the Seventy, according to Joseph Young, Smith declared: "Brethren, some of you are angry with me, because you did not fight in Missouri; but let me tell you, God did not want you to fight. He

---

91. Minutes, Feb. 28–Mar. 1, 1835, Minute Book 1, 165–67 (*JSP*, D4:259–61).
92. Minutes, Mar. 1, 1835, Minute Book 1, 172 (*JSP*, D4:265–66).
93. Park, "Zion Blessings in the Early Church."
94. Revelation, June 22, 1834, Revelation Book 1, 199 [D&C 105:12] (*JSP*, D4:74).
95. Obituary, *LDS Messenger and Advocate*, Feb. 1835, 74.

could not organize His kingdom with twelve men to open the Gospel door to the nations of the earth, and with seventy men under their direction to follow in their tracks, unless He took them from a body of men who had offered their lives, and who had made as great a sacrifice as did Abraham. Now the Lord has got His Twelve and His Seventy, and there will be other quorums of Seventies called, who will make the sacrifice, and those who have not made their sacrifices and their offerings now, will make them hereafter."[96] Even the spectacular failure of Zion's Camp could be construed as fulfilling God's purposes.

More Blessings and Meetings

Temple construction was funded by donations of labor, money, and other resources. The outer fifty-foot stone walls of the temple had been completed by December 1834, but the edifice stood without a roof until July 1835. Stuccoing of the outside and plastering of the inside did not begin until November.[97] On March 7–8 Smith attended meetings where 121 men who helped build the temple were blessed by Sidney Rigdon: forty-five on March 7 and seventy-six on March 8. On the first day, Smith made "remarks to the Church, upon the propriety and necessity of purifying itself."[98] Those involved in the building of the temple pledged to continue until it was finished.

On March 12, in response to "pressing requests" from church branches in the eastern United States to hold conferences that year, Smith met with the Twelve Apostles and, contrary to Cowdery's instruction that they remain in Kirtland until they received their endowment of power, proposed that they go on their "first mission through the Eastern States, to the Atlantic Ocean." It was therefore decided that the Twelve should leave for their mission on May 4, and that they should hold meetings in various towns in New York, Canada, Vermont, Massachusetts, New Hampshire, Maine, and Upper Canada, and then return in October.[99]

On March 26 Smith went to Huntsburg, about seventeen miles southeast from Kirtland, with William McLellin, Lyman Johnson, David Patten, Parley Pratt, John Boynton, and others to attend a two-day public debate

---

96. Young, *History of the Organization of the Seventies*, 14.

97. Kimball, Autobiography, ca. 1842–58, 48–51; "The House of the Lord," *LDS Messenger and Advocate*, July 1835, 147; JS History, vol. B-1, 595, 606, 619, 660, 684; Robison, *The First Mormon Temple*, 45–58.

98. Minutes, Mar. 7–8, 1835, Minute Book 1, 192 (*JSP*, D4:281).

99. Minutes, Mar. 12, 1835, Record of the Twelve Apostles, 4 (*JSP*, D4:289); Orson Hyde and William E. McLellin, Letter to the Editor, Mar. 8, 1835, *LDS Messenger and Advocate*, Mar. 1835, 90.

between McLellin and J. M. Tracy, a Campbellite preacher. McLellin said that when he was challenged to the debate, he received a note from Tracy in which he "pledged himself to prove that 'the book of Mormon was not a divine revelation.'" Recalling the debate in a letter to Cowdery the following month, McLellin reported: "The debate continued two days, about eight hours each, the parties speaking alternately thirty minutes. When the interview closed a majority of the congregation arose, by an anxious urgency on the part of Mr. T[racy]. to testify thereby that they did not believe in the divinity of the book of Mormon. But when I asked them if they had been convinced that it was false by Mr. Tracy's arguments, (if I might call them such,) there was not one to answer 'Yes.'" As a result, McLellin converted two people, who were immediately baptized.[100]

On the day after the debate, Sunday, Smith preached for about three hours at Huntsburg. McLellin recorded that another meeting was held on Monday and that he baptized four more people before he, Smith, and the others returned to Kirtland.[101]

Legal Troubles

On March 31 Rigdon applied to Geauga County for a license to marry, but Judge Matthew Birchard refused to grant it, contending that Rigdon was not a "regularly ordained minister of the gospel within the meaning of the Statute."[102] Birchard's judgment may have been the result of the church's not being incorporated in Ohio at that time. On January 21, 1838, Vilate Kimball wrote to her husband, Heber, in England: "This church has never ben organized agreable to the Laws of the State of Ohio, until last week. consequently every Elder that has married a couple, is liable to five hundred dollars fine."[103] Rigdon will be indicted the following June and tried on October 20 for having performed the marriage of Orson Hyde and Marinda Johnson on September 4, 1834, but discharged when it was discovered that a license he received in 1826 as a Campbellite minister was still technically valid.[104]

---

100. William E. McLellin, Letter to Oliver Cowdery, Apr. 16, 1835, *LDS Messenger and Advocate*, Apr. 1835, 102.

101. William E. McLellin, Journal, Mar. 23, 1835 (Shipps and Welch, eds., *The Journals of William E. McLellin*, 153).

102. State of OH v. Sidney Rigdon, Mar. 7, 1835, Geauga Co., OH, Court of Common Pleas, Final Record, vol. M, 380–81.

103. Vilate Kimball, Letter to Heber C Kimball, Jan. 19, 21, and 24, 1838; see also *JSP*, J1:110n163.

104. Bradshaw, "Joseph Smith's Performance of Marriages in Ohio," 23–24. The *Chardon Spectator and Geauga Gazette* reported: "Rigdon produced a license of the Court, which had been granted to him several years ago, as a minister of the gospel of that sect usually called

Smith had his own legal troubles about this time. On April 21 Justice of the Peace Lewis Miller of Painesville issued a warrant for his arrest for assaulting his brother-in-law Calvin Stoddard, husband of his oldest sister Sophronia, in Kirtland earlier the same day. The altercation occurred during an argument over whether "there was water in a certain lot," which resulted in Smith striking Stoddard "with a flat hand," knocking him to the ground. The complaint was not filed by Stoddard, but by Grandison Newell, a merchant and antagonist of the Mormons living in nearby Mentor who apparently claimed to have witnessed the fight. Constable Samuel Brown arrested Smith the same day. At the preliminary hearing, attorneys Benjamin Bissell and Ira Paine defended Smith, while Henry Payne and Hiram Willson represented the state. After issuing subpoenas for five witnesses, Miller adjourned until the following day, releasing Smith on bail.[105]

On April 22 Miller heard testimony from Smith's parents and brothers Hyrum and William, but apparently not from Stoddard. The justice found that there was enough evidence to send the case to the Geauga County Court of Common Pleas and ordered Smith to enter into a recognizance for $200 to appear at the court's June session.[106]

Meetings of the New Hierarchy

On Sunday, April 26, according to previous appointment, Smith held a meeting in the unfinished temple with the newly-organized Apostles and Seventies, together with "a numerous concourse of people." The purpose of the meeting, according to Apostle Orson Hyde, who kept the minutes, was "to receive our charge and instructions from President Joseph Smith Jun relative to our mission and duties."[107]

During the meeting, Orson Pratt arrived from his mission. Although he incorrectly remembered the date as April 5, Heber Kimball said: "We were all assembled together with the exception of Brother Orson Pratt who had not yet been with us.—At this time while we were praying, and wishing

Campbellites, but who call themselves disciples, to continue so long as he remained a minister in regular standing in that denomination. The prosecution then undertook to prove by proof that he had abandoned that church, and joined the Mormons, and held principles inconsistent with his former faith. It appeared that the society of disciples kept written minutes of their proceedings, and no church record of his dismissal being offered, the Court rejected the testimony, and a *nolle prosequi* was entered." *Chardon Spectator and Geauga Gazette* (Chardon, OH), Oct. 30, 1835, 3.

105. Docket Entry, Painesville Township, Geauga Co., OH, Apr. 21–22, 1835, State of OH v. Joseph Smith for Assault and Battery, Lewis Miller, Docket Book (fragment), 332; *Painesville* (OH) *Telegraph*, June 26, 1835, [3].

106. Miller, 332.

107. Minutes, Apr. 26, 1835, Record of the Twelve Apostles, 5 (*JSP*, D4:295).

for his arrival, while opening the meeting he entered the house, we rejoiced at his presence, and thanked the Lord for it."[108] Pratt wrote in his journal that he "arrived in Kirtland on the 26th, about ten o'clock in the forenoon; walked into the meeting and learned that they had been prophesying that I would arrive there, so as to attend that meeting, although not one of them knew where I was."[109] At this time both Pratt and Thomas Marsh were ordained apostles and blessed by Cowdery, the record stating: "makeing our number complete."[110]

Two days later, on April 28, the apostles met in the schoolroom to finalize preparations for their mission to the eastern states, and it was decided to leave Kirtland from Johnson's Tavern on May 4.[111]

On May 2 Smith presided over a "grand council" of the priesthood, consisting of the presidency of the high priesthood, the Twelve Apostles, most of the Seventy with their presidents, Bishops Whitney and Partridge and their counselors, the Kirtland high council, and other elders.[112] The Twelve were seated by age: Thomas Marsh, who was appointed to preside over the quorum, David Patten, Brigham Young, Heber Kimball, Orson Hyde, William McLellin, Parley Pratt, Luke Johnson, William Smith, Orson Pratt, John Boynton, and Lyman Johnson.

Smith gave instructions concerning the authority and duties of the new officers, stating that "the Twelve will have no right to go into Zion or any of its stakes and there undertake to regulate the affairs thereof where there is a standing High Council. But it is their duty to go abroad and regulate all matters relative to the different branches of the Church. When the Twelve are together, or a quorum of them in any Church, they will have authority to act independently and make decisions, and those decisions ...are valid." Smith further instructed that "the Seventy are not to attend the conferences of the Twelve unless they are called upon or requested to by the Twelve."[113]

Smith then spoke about the anticipated return to Zion and moved that the church officers "never give up the struggle for Zion, even until Death, or until Zion is Redeemed." The voting was "unanimous" in favor of Smith's

---

108. "Extracts from H. C. Kimball's Journal," *Times and Seasons*, Apr. 15, 1845, 869. Kimball incorrectly remembered the date as April 5, 1835.

109. Orson Pratt, Journal, Apr. 26, 1835.

110. Minutes, Apr. 26, 1835, Record of the Twelve Apostles, 5 (*JSP*, D4:295).

111. Minutes, 5.

112. See Orson Pratt, Journal, May 2, 1835.

113. Minutes, May 2, 1835, Minute Book 1, 187–88 (*JSP*, D5:302).

proposition and made "with apparent deep feeling."[114] The editors of the Joseph Smith Papers observe that these comments "suggest that these groups' assignments were necessary components in Zion's redemption. ... This was certainly one aspect of the Twelve's mission to church branches in the eastern United States. Likewise, preaching by the Seventy was characterized in January 1836 as helping 'gather up the elect of God out of every nation,' thereby allowing Zion to 'be builded, a holy city.'"[115]

As planned, the Twelve left Kirtland on their missions early in the morning on May 4, and the Seventy would soon spread out in all directions. Smith had responded to the failure of Zion's Camp by blessing and rewarding those who had participated. By giving them a greater stake in the organization, Smith hoped to ensure their continued loyalty. Perhaps they would learn through their own increased responsibility the difficulties of leadership. At the same time, by expanding the authority base under him, Smith also increased his own power.

Revising the Revelations

About the time Cowdery began writing his history of Smith and the church in letters to Phelps in Missouri, which included an account of his and Smith's ordination by an angel in May 1829, he also announced that he had discovered many errors in the *Evening and Morning Star* that he was about to reprint in Kirtland, especially in its printing of the revelations. Cowdery explained "that in the first 14 numbers, in the Revelations, are many errors, typographical, and others, occasioned by transcribing manuscript[s]; but as we shall have access to originals, we shall endeavor to make proper corrections."[116] When the first issue of the *Star* was reprinted in January 1835, which included an edited and expanded version of the "Articles and Covenants of the Church of Christ" that would appear in the Doctrine and Covenants later the same year, Cowdery said that he and the others were "not a little surprised to find the previous print [of the revelations] so different from the original." This untrue assertion shows Cowdery's willingness to alter history and the revelations under the guise of correcting mistakes. Continuing, Cowdery asserted: "We have given them a careful comparison, assisted by individuals whose known integrity and ability is uncensurable.

---

114. Minutes, 191, CHL (*JSP*, D5:305).

115. *JSP*, D4:300, quoting Sylvester Smith, Editorial, *LDS Messenger and Advocate*, Jan. 1836, 254.

116. "Prospectus for Re-printing the First and Second Volumes of The Evening and the Morning Star," *The Evening and the Morning Star* (Kirtland, OH), Sept. 1834, 192.

Thus saying we cast no reflections upon those who were entrusted with the responsibility of publishing them in Missouri, as our own labors were included in that important service to the church, and it was our unceasing endeavor to have them correspond with the copy furnished us. We believe they are now correct. If not in every word, at least in principle."[117]

Among the many emendations in Cowdery's reprint of the Articles are references to traveling bishops, high councilors, high priests, all of which did not exist when the document was created about April 1830.[118] While the Articles were updated in early 1835, by the time they appeared as Section II in the Doctrine and Covenants about September 1835, the offices of apostle and seventy were conspicuously missing.

Smith also added phrases in a March 1829 revelation that seemed to allude to his and Cowdery's ordinations two months later, inserting the words "hereafter you shall be ordained and go forth and deliver my words unto the children of men" and "you must wait yet a little while, for ye are not yet ordained."[119] To a September 1830 revelation warning Smith not to purchase wine for the sacrament from his enemies, Smith added a long section naming various ancient figures from the Bible and Book of Mormon who would one day drink the fruit of the vine with Jesus. In mentioning John the Baptist, Smith's expansion added: "which John I have sent unto you, my servants, Joseph Smith, jr. and Oliver Cowdery, to ordain you unto this first priesthood which you have received, that you might be called and ordained even as Aaron."[120] This addition not only named the angel who had ordained Smith and Cowdery, but it made it appear that their ordinations had been mentioned as early as September 1830.

Smith's expansion also revealed an angelic origin for the apostleship: "Peter, and James, and John, whom I have sent unto you, by whom I have ordained you and confirmed you to be apostles and especial witnesses of my name, and bear the keys of your ministry: and of the same things which I revealed unto them; unto whom I have committed the keys of my kingdom, and a dispensation of the gospel for the last times."[121] Rather than being

---

117. Notice, *Evening and Morning Star*, June 1832 [Jan. 1835], 16.

118. Compare BC XXIV with D&C, 1835 ed., II. For an examination of the changes, see Marquardt, *The Joseph Smith Revelations*, 66–68.

119. Revelation, Mar. 1829 [ca. Aug. 1835], D&C, 1835 ed., XXXII:2–3 [D&C 5:6, 17] (cf. *JSP*, D1:16–19). See Marquardt, *The Joseph Smith Revelations*, 26–29.

120. Revelation, Sep. 4, 1830 [ca. Aug. 1835], D&C, 1835 ed., L:2 [D&C 27:8] (*JSP*, D4:411). See Marquardt, *The Joseph Smith Revelations*, 72–73.

121. Revelation, Sep. 4, 1830 [ca. Aug. 1835], D&C, 1835 ed., L:3 [D&C 27:12–13] (*JSP*, D4:411). See Marquardt, *The Joseph Smith Revelations*, 73.

apostles through charismatic experiences such as seeing Jesus or angels, Smith and Cowdery were ordained by those with undisputed authority to be apostles.

Although Smith had made it appear that he had been talking about the visitation of the ancient apostles since September 1830, it was nevertheless news to those who had been his followers from the early days. When asked by Orson Pratt in 1878, "Can you tell the date of the bestowal of the Apostleship upon Joseph, by Peter, James and John?" David Whitmer said: "I do not know, Joseph never told me."[122] Significantly, Pratt, who first met Smith at the Whitmer home in Fayette in October 1830, did not know the answer. On February 12, 1886, Edward Stevenson wrote to Apostle Franklin D. Richards: "I enquired of David and ... John [Whitmer] ... who say that they do not have any knowledge of, neither do the Records show concerning Peter, James, and John's coming to the Prophet Joseph."[123] William McLellin, one of the original Twelve Apostles, recalled in 1877: "I heard not[hing] of James, Peter, and John" ordaining Smith and Cowdery.[124] McLellin said that although he had heard Smith tell the story of the church's founding "probably more than twenty times, I never heard of ... Peter, James and John."[125] In a notebook, McLellin wrote: "In 1831 I heard Joseph tell his experience ... many times about angels visits, ... but I never heard one word of ... Peter, James, and John's visit and ordination. Till It was told some year or two afterward in Ohio."[126]

The visitation of the ancient apostles was not mentioned in the Articles and Covenants—the foundational document of the church—where instead authority was said to have been derived from divine and angelic commands. Apparently, it had not occurred to Cowdery to mention Peter, James, and John restoring the apostolic keys when he spoke to the newly-organized Quorum of Twelve Apostles in February 1835. Instead, he told them that they had been "ordained to this holy priesthood" by "those who have the power and authority from an angel"—referring to the commission the Three Witnesses received from the angel who showed them the plates in late June

---

122. "Report of Elders Orson Pratt and Joseph F. Smith," *Deseret News* (Salt Lake City), Nov. 16, 1878 (*EMD*, 5:50).

123. Stevenson, Letter to Franklin D. Richards, Feb. 12, 1886, 1–2.

124. McLellin, Letter to John L. Traughber, Aug. 25, 1877 (Larson and Passey, eds., *The William E. McLellin Papers*, 508).

125. William E. McLellin, Letter to Davis H. Bays, May 24, 1870, in *True L[atter] D[ay] Saints' Herald* (Plano, IL), Sep. 15, 1870, 556 (Larson and Passey, eds., *The William E. McLellin Papers*, 462).

126. McLellin, Notebook, 1877, 10 (Larson and Passey, eds., *The William E. McLellin Papers*, 68).

1829.[127] Thus, the September 1830 revelation was emended to include references to a visitation of John the Baptist and Apostles Peter, James, and John sometime after Cowdery spoke to the Twelve in February but before Smith left Kirtland in August 1835.

Another revelation Smith emended was originally dictated in April 1829 as a translation of a record written on parchment by John the Beloved and "hidden up" somewhere in the Middle East. This pseudepigraphic revelation claimed that Jesus granted John's wish to have "power over death," resolving a dispute between Cowdery and Smith, as well as many of their contemporaries, over the meaning of Jesus's words to Peter in John 21:22 concerning John: "If I will that he tarry till I come, what is that to thee?" Was this to be understood literally or as hyperbole? According to this revelation, John was to remain alive to "bring souls" unto Christ until the Second Coming. In 1835 Smith added wording where Jesus declares: "I will make thee [Peter] to minister for him [John] and for thy brother James; and unto you three I will give this power and the keys of this ministry until I come."[128] Thus the expanded revelation provided pseudepigraphic evidence that Peter, James, and John had been given special keys that they passed on to Smith and Cowdery at some undisclosed time.

Smith also revised and expanded a revelation originally dictated in November 1831 about the offices of bishop and president of the high priesthood, then combined it with instructions on priesthood—which he gave to the newly-appointed apostles in late winter or early spring 1835—and a vision he had about the Seventies before publishing it as section III in the 1835 edition of the Doctrine and Covenants.[129] The November 1831 revelation had stipulated that "a Bishop must be chosen from the high Priesthood," but the expansion added an exemption: "unless he is a literal descendant of Aaron." In such case, he would have "a legal right to the presidency of this

---

127. Minutes, Feb. 14–15, 1835, Minute Book 1, 152–54 (*JSP*, D4:229–33).

128. Revelation, Apr. 1829-C [ca. Aug. 1835], D&C, 1835 ed., XXXIII [D&C 7] (cf. *JSP*, D1:48). See Marquardt, *The Joseph Smith Revelations*, 33–35.

129. Cf. Revelation, Nov. 11, 1831-B, Revelation Book 1, 122–23 [cf. D&C 107:59–100] (*JSP*, D2:132–36); and Instruction on Priesthood, Mar. 1–May 4, 1835, D&C, 1835 ed., 82–89, sec. III [D&C 107] (*JSP*, D4:312–21). While section III was published in the 1835 Doctrine and Covenants without date or explanation, the editors of the Joseph Smith Papers have suggested that Smith's 1835 instructions on priesthood date to after March 1, 1835, when the Quorum of Seventy was fully organized, and before the Twelve left Kirtland on May 4, 1835, on their mission to the east and Canada. *JSP*, D4:309–10. Section III is a compilation of several items on priesthood organized in three main sections: Instructions given by Joseph Smith in 1835 regarding the Twelve, Seventy, high councils, and patriarchs (D&C 107:1–57); a revised version of the November 1831 revelation (vv. 58–92, 99); and an 1835 vision about the Seventy (vv. 93–98).

priesthood, to the keys of this ministry, to act in the office of bishop independently, without counsellors."[130] A non-descendant of Aaron therefore needs a higher priesthood to perform the duties of a bishop. This explanation was perhaps designed to respond to those who, like Alexander Campbell, criticized the Book of Mormon for having the Lehites (who were of the wrong tribe)—and, by extension, the Mormons themselves—offer sacrifice and officiate in temples.[131]

Shortly after organizing the Quorum of Twelve Apostles, Smith held several meetings with nine of its members to give them instructions concerning their duties and powers in association with other offices in the hierarchy. According to Heber Kimball, "One evening when we were assembled to receive instruction, the revelation ... on Priesthood was given to Brother Joseph as he was instructing us, and we praised the Lord."[132] The first part of Smith's 1835 instructions defined the authority of the five quorums of church government—the presidency, the Twelve, the Seventy, the bishopric, and the high councils in Kirtland and Missouri—as being "equal in authority and power," which, as historian Lyndon W. Cook observed, "tempered the earlier supremacy of the presidency of the high priesthood."[133] This sharing of authority must have pleased Cowdery and the Whitmers, who resisted the establishment of a hierarchy as well as anyone who had complained that Smith was seeking monarchial authority. "In viewing the subject," John Corrill wrote, "I saw that there were several different bodies that had equal power; I thought, therefore, they would serve as a check upon each other, and I concluded there was no danger where the full power and authority was reserved to the people."[134]

Probably the most important feature of the instructions pertained to the patriarchal priesthood, which was associated with the high priesthood. The Twelve were responsible for ordaining "evangelical ministers"—meaning

---

130. Instruction on Priesthood, D&C, 1835 ed., III:32, 34 [D&C 107:69, 76] (*JSP*, D4:318, 319). The same instruction about descendants of Aaron was also added to another November 1831 revelation. Compare Revelation, Nov. 1, 1831-A, Revelation Book 1, 113–14 [D&C 68] (*JSP*, D2:99–103); and Revelation, ca. June 1835, D&C, 1835 ed., 73–74, sec. XXII [D&C 68:15–21] (*JSP*, D4:357–58). This expansion was made before the revelation appeared in Cowdery's Kirtland reprint of *The Evening and the Morning Star*, Oct. 1832 [June 1835], 73.

131. Campbell, *Delusions*, 11.

132. Autobiography, ca. 1842–58, 54.

133. Instruction on Priesthood, Mar. 1–May 4, 1835, D&C, 1835 ed., III:11–15 [D&C 107:21–37] (*JSP*, D4:314–15); Cook, *The Revelations of the Prophet Joseph Smith*, 216.

134. Corrill, *Brief History*, 25 (*JSP*, H2:157–58).

patriarchs—"in all large branches of the church."[135] The instructions explained that the patriarchal priesthood was "instituted in the days of Adam, and came down by lineage" from father to son until Noah, and that three years previous to his death, the first patriarch gathered the "residue of his posterity ... into the valley of Adam-ondi-ahman," including seven generations of those whom he had ordained to the high priesthood, and "bestowed upon them his last blessing." On this occasion, according to the revelation, "the Lord appeared unto them, and they rose up and blessed Adam, and called him Michael, the prince, the Archangel"—thus identifying Adam with God's Archangel, who in Jude 1:9 contended with the devil for Moses' body, and in Revelation 12:7 fought against the dragon and his angels; and the great prince, who in Daniel 12:1 delivered all those whose names are written in God's book. Then, Adam, "being full of the Holy Ghost, predicted whatsoever should befall his posterity unto the latest generation." The revelation concludes the 1835 instructions by declaring: "These things were all written in the book of Enoch, and are to be testified of in due time."[136]

This promise of a pseudepigraphic Book of Enoch may have resulted from Smith's sense that his followers needed ancient justification for some of his recent innovations. Smith and Cowdery were no doubt aware, even at this time, that Josephus had mentioned that "in consequence of the prophecy of Adam, that the world should be destroyed once by water and again by fire, Enoch wrote a history or an account of the same, and put [it] into two pillars one of brick and the other of stone."[137] The Book of Enoch, however, would not be forthcoming; instead, the case would be made in Smith's translation of the Book of Abraham in the coming months.

Printing the Revelations

On February 14, 1835, Smith and his counselors—Cowdery, Rigdon, and Williams—filed a copyright for the Doctrine and Covenants.[138] Three days later, this committee met to approve the publication of the Doctrine and Covenants and compose a preface intended to contain "the leading items of

---

135. Instruction on Priesthood, D&C, 1835 ed., III:17 [D&C 107:39] (*JSP*, D4:316). On May 4, 1835, Bishop Partridge was blessed by Joseph Smith, Sr., "the evangelist." See Marquardt, *Early Patriarchal Blessings*, 30.

136. D&C, 1835 ed., III:18–29 [D&C 107:41–57] (*JSP*, D4:316–17).

137. "Egyptian Mummies—Ancient Records," *LDS Messenger and Advocate*, Dec. 1835, 236; Flavius Josephus, Antiquities of the Jews, Book 1, chap. 2, sect. 3, in Whiston, *Josephus Complete Works*, 27.

138. Copyright for Doctrine and Covenants, Feb. 14, 1835.

the religion which we have professed to believe."[139] The preface announced that in addition to Smith's revelations, the Doctrine and Covenants would also contain seven theological lectures on faith given at the School of the Elders. According to Cowdery, the publication would give church members "a perfect understanding of the doctrine believed by this society."[140]

The preface addressed the anti-creedal sentiments of members like David Whitmer, who had objected to publishing Smith's revelations in 1831: "There may be an aversion in the minds of some against receiving any thing purporting to be articles of religious faith, in consequence of there being so many now extant; but if men believe a system, and profess that it was given by inspiration, certainly, the more intelligibly they can present it, the better. It does not make a principle untrue to *print* it, neither does it make it true not to print it."[141]

Phelps and John Whitmer arrived at Kirtland from Missouri on May 16.[142] Whitmer recorded that when they arrived, they found that "the house of the Lord was reared and the stonework thereof completed the rafters were Just put up and the first story of the steeple raised."[143] Phelps and his son Waterman boarded with Joseph and Emma.[144] On May 18 Whitmer recorded that he attended a meeting, and "contrary to my feelings or expectations I was appointed to Edit the Messenger and Advocate."[145] This freed Cowdery to work on printing the revelations with Phelps. On May 26 Phelps wrote to his wife, Sally, in Liberty, Missouri, and included sample prints of "the Six first forms of the Doctrines and Covenants," indicating that typesetting had reached page 98.[146]

On May 26 a meeting was held in Kirtland to divide up Jackson County land among the faithful Saints in anticipation of the redemption of Zion. According to John Whitmer, a list of sixty-three names in the order they were to receive inheritances in Zion was generated, "according to the dictation of the Spirit of the Lord through Joseph the Revelator."[147] On the next day, Phelps broke open his letter to his wife written the previous day to add among other things: "The order of receiving inheritances in Zion when it is

139. Joseph Smith et al., "Preface," Feb. 17, 1835, D&C, 1835 ed., [iii] (*JSP*, D4:236).
140. Oliver Cowdery, Editorial, *LDS Messenger and Advocate*, May 1835, 122.
141. Joseph Smith et al., "Preface," Feb. 17, 1835, D&C, 1835 ed., [iii] (*JSP*, D4:236).
142. John Whitmer, Day Book, May 16, 1835; Phelps, Diary, May 16, 1835.
143. John Whitmer, History, 71 (*JSP*, H2:79).
144. JS History, vol. B-1, 592; Bowen, "The Versatile W. W. Phelps," 62.
145. John Whitmer, Day Book, May 18, 1835.
146. William W. Phelps, Letter to Sally Phelps, May 26–27, 1835, [1].
147. Whitmer, History, 71–72 (*JSP*, H2:79–81).

redeemed was commenced to day in council—Elder Martin [Harris] for his great good in assisting to bring for[th] the Book of Mormon, &c is No 1 President Smith No 2—mine is No 16."[148]

On Sunday, May 31, Smith spoke for three and a half hours on a text Phelps gave him: "This is my beloved Son; hear ye him!" Phelps wrote to his wife that Smith "preached one of the greatest sermons I ever heard ... and unfolded more mysteries than I can write at this time."[149] The text was probably Mark 9:7 or Luke 9:35—"This is my beloved Son: hear him"—which Smith's contemporaries often quoted as "hear ye him," either by blending or shortening Matthew 17:5: "This is my beloved Son, in whom I am well pleased; hear ye him."[150] Smith's exposition possibly included an account of his first vision, which may have begun to distinguish between the Father and Son as two personages in conformity with the recently-published fifth lecture in the Lectures on Faith.[151] In three months, during a visit to his followers in Pontiac, Michigan, Smith described being "in the presance of God The Father and JESUS Christ."[152] While rehearsing his vision the following November, he said, "A personage appeared in the midst of this pillar of flame," and then "another personage soon appeared like unto the first."[153]

On June 1 Bishop Partridge and Counselor Isaac Morley received a recommendation signed by Smith and other church presidents authorizing them to collect "moneys or other properties in their hands for the good of the poor and afflicted, or for any other purpose."[154] They had been assigned by a council on May 29 to "visit the churches in the east and obtain donations for the poor saints, and also to counsel the br[ethren]."[155] The "poor and afflicted" were those who had been driven from their lands in Jackson County. The June 1835 issue of the *Messenger and Advocate* announced that Partridge, accompanied by Morley, was "on his way to the east" and admonished church members to "donate liberally for the benefit of those who have

---

148. Phelps, Letter to Sally Phelps, May 26–27, 1835, [3].

149. William W. Phelps, Letter to Sally Phelps, June 2, 1835, included in Joseph Smith et al., Letter to John Burk and Others, June 1–2, 1835, JS Collection (*JSP*, D4:336).

150. See, e.g., Henry, *An Exposition of the Old and New Testament*, 3:140; Anon., *Reflections on the Character of Our Saviour*, 13; *Christian Spectator* (New Haven, CT), May 1, 1823, 233.

151. The fifth and sixth lectures were published in *LDS Messenger and Advocate*, May 1835, 122–26.

152. Edward Stevenson, Autobiography, 65.

153. Smith, Journal, Nov. 9, 1835 (*JSP*, J1:87).

154. Smith et al., Recommendation for Edward Partridge and Isaac Morley, June 1, 1835, JS Collection (*JSP*, D4:322–325).

155. Edward Partridge, Diary, May 29, 1835.

been so inhumanly dispossessed of their homes."[156] Partridge and Morley left on their mission on June 2 and traveled through Ohio, Pennsylvania, New York, and other parts of New England, returning around November 1.[157] The editors of the Joseph Smith Papers observe that "this focus on obtaining funds for Missouri church members was part of a larger ongoing effort to restore the Saints to Jackson County by 11 September 1836."[158]

Also on June 1, Smith, Cowdery, Phelps, and John Whitmer wrote to John Burk, president of the elders in Liberty, Clay County, explaining that the elders did not have authority to conduct disciplinary councils. Rather, the letter stated, "the high council has been organized expressly to administer over in all her spiritual affairs; And the bishop and his council are set over her temporal matters: so thus the elders' acts are null and void." This situation was no doubt caused by the lack of leadership in Missouri. The presidency of the high council—David Whitmer, Phelps, and John Whitmer—ten of the twelve high counselors, as well as Partridge and his counselors, had left Missouri to attend the dedication of the Kirtland temple and to receive the promised endowment of power from on high, which was still eight months away. Phelps, who wrote the letter on behalf of the others, admonished the Missouri church to "prepare with one heart and one mind to redeem Zion, that goodly land of promise, where the willing and the obedient shall be blessed."[159]

On June 15 Smith wrote a letter to his "brethren in the Lord" in Liberty, Missouri, informing them of his plans to publish the New Translation of the Bible and requesting donations and loans "to accomplish the work as a great means towards the salvation of Men."[160] This apparently failed since Smith's Bible revision remained unpublished during his lifetime. Indeed, it made little sense to request donations from people for whom other donations were simultaneously being collected.

Zion's Camp Lawsuit

Former Mormon Dennis Lake won a lawsuit against Smith the previous November for losses he sustained while taking part in Zion's Camp. Kirtland Justice John C. Dowen ruled that Smith must pay $63.67 plus $8.04 in

---

156. "Bishop Partridge," *LDS Messenger and Advocate*, June 1835, 139.

157. Edward Partridge, Report, Oct. 31, 1835; Edward Partridge and Isaac Morley, Letter to the Editor, Nov. 10, 1835, *LDS Messenger and Advocate*, Nov. 1835, 220–21.

158. *JSP*, D4:323.

159. Joseph Smith et al., Letter to John Burk, June 1, 1835, [1], JS Collection (*JSP*, D4:330).

160. Joseph Smith, Letter to "brethren in the Lord," June 15, 1835, [1], JS Collection (*JSP*, D4:347).

costs. On December 10 Smith filed an appeal to the Geauga County Court of Common Pleas, which would not convene for another five months.[161]

On May 7, 1835, Lake filed a declaration, claiming that Smith owed him $200 for his labor and financial contributions to the camp. According to Brigham Young, who had been called as a witness, Lake charged Smith "$30 a month for going up in Zion's camp to Missouri" and claimed Smith "had promised him a lot of land."[162] Within a few days, Smith's attorney, Benjamin Bissell, entered a plea disputing the claim that Smith had made the implied contract with Lake.[163] On June 19, before the jury could render a verdict, Judge Matthew Birchard ruled that Lake had failed to prove that a contract between him and Smith existed and therefore dismissed the case, ordering Lake to pay the court's costs totaling $36.50.[164]

Trial for Assault

Smith appeared in the courthouse in Chardon on June 16 after a grand jury indicted him the previous April for "assault and Battery" for striking his brother-in-law Calvin Stoddard. Reuben Hitchcock was the prosecuting attorney, but it is unknown who represented Smith. Smith pleaded "guilty, unless the Court on hearing the evidence adduced shall be of opinion that he is not guilty."[165] According to the *Painesville Telegraph*, "by consent of the parties, the case was submitted to the Court without Jury."[166]

On June 20 Judge Matthew Birchard heard testimony from Stoddard, William Smith, Lucy Mack Smith, and a man named Burgess (possibly Mormon William Burgess or one of his sons, Harrison or Horace). According to the *Telegraph*, which subsequently published what appears to be a transcript of the trial, Stoddard testified that "Smith had irritated him in a controversy about water—he had affirmed that there was water in a certain lot, which Smith denied." On the day in question, as Smith turned and

---

161. Docket Entry, Kirtland Township, Geauga Co., OH, D. Lake v. Joseph Smith, Justice of the Peace Court, copied in Transcript of Proceedings, ca. June 19, 1834, Geauga County Court of Common Pleas, Final Record, vol. Q, 506–507.

162. "History of Brigham Young," *Deseret News*, Feb. 10, 1858, 385.

163. Transcript of Proceedings, ca. June 19, 1835, Geauga County Court of Common Pleas, Final Record, vol. Q, 507–508.

164. Transcript of Proceedings, ca. June 19, 1835, Geauga County Court of Common Pleas, Final Record, vol. Q, 506–507; Docket Entry, Costs, Chardon, Geauga Co., OH, ca. June 19, 1835, D. Lake v. Joseph Smith, Geauga County Court of Common Pleas, Execution Docket, vol. F, 312.

165. Indictment, Chardon, Geauga Co., OH, June 16, 1835, State of OH v. Joseph Smith for Assault and Battery, copied in Transcript of Proceedings, Geauga County Court of Common Pleas, Final Record, vol. Q, 497–98.

166. Trial Report, *Painesville Telegraph*, June 26, 1835, [3].

walked away towards his house, Stoddard followed him yelling, "I don't fear you, or no other man." Stoddard said, "Smith then came up and struck him on the forehead with his flat hand—the blow knocked him down, when Smith repeated the blow four or five times." The blows were "very hard," Stoddard said, so hard that they made him temporarily "blind." Stoddard told Birchard that the matter had been resolved prior to trial. "Smith afterwards came to him and asked his forgiveness," Stoddard reported, and that he "was satisfied" and therefore "had forgiven him," just as he "would forgive any man who would injure him and ask his forgiveness."[167]

William Smith testified that he "Saw Stoddard come along cursing and swearing," and that when "Joseph went out—Stoddard said he would whip him, and drew his cane upon Joseph—Joseph struck him once or twice." William said that he "cautioned Joseph to stop, that he had done enough." On cross-examination, Stoddard said he "Had a cane," but "did not attempt to strike him, or threaten."

Lucy Smith said she was "upstairs" and "heard Stoddard talking loud," and that he "called Joseph 'a d—d false prophet, and a d—d one thing [and] another.'" She said she "saw Joseph slap him," but "did not hear Stoddard say he would flog him" and "did not see Stoddard attempt to strike him."

Burgess testified that "Stoddard struck at Smith first, and raised his cane in a threatening attitude when down."

The judge decided that Smith was "not guilty as he Stands charged" and "ordered that he be discharged from said Indictment."[168] The *Telegraph* indicated that Birchard made his decision because "the injured party was satisfied" and because "the assault might perhaps be justified on the principle of self-defence."[169]

On June 22 Smith wrote to the editor of the *Painesville Telegraph*, requesting that since the paper had published a notice "of my being bound over to the Court of Common Pleas, to keep the peace, for an assault upon the person of my brother-in-law," that it should also report "my honorable acquital before said court, last week, there being no evidence to prove the same."[170]

---

167. The substance of the testimony given at the trial comes from Trial Report, *Painesville Telegraph*, June 26, 1835, [3].

168. Transcript of Proceedings, June 16, 1835, Geauga County Court of Common Pleas, Final Record, vol. Q, 497–98.

169. Trial Report, *Painesville Telegraph*, June 26, 1835, [3].

170. Joseph Smith, Letter to the Editor of the *Painesville Telegraph*, June 22, 1835, *Painesville Telegraph*, June 26, 1835, [3] (*JSP*, D4:347–49).

Four days later, the paper not only obliged Smith by publishing his letter to them but also a response, followed by a transcript of the trial. According to the *Telegraph*, at the time of the preliminary hearing in Painesville "Stoddard ... could not be obtained as a witness, as he had, it appeared, been suddenly induced to leave the State. He returned a few days since when his presence at court was secured, much against his will." He nevertheless provided testimony that the intra-family dispute had been resolved in the interim. The *Telegraph* also questioned why Burgess, a Mormon who provided crucial testimony in support of Smith, was not brought forward at the preliminary hearing "although present in the place at the time—a circumstance that induced many to suppose his evidence was manufactured for the occasion."[171]

Evangelical Order

On Sunday, June 21, according to his official history, Smith preached on the Evangelical Order.[172] While the details of the sermon are unknown, Smith likely outlined the contents of his recent instructions on priesthood about the six generations of the high and patriarchal priesthood among Adam's posterity and the responsibility of the Twelve to ordain patriarchs.[173] Why Smith associated the term "evangelist" with the office of patriarch is puzzling since in the New Testament it simply refers to a preacher of the gospel (Eph. 4:11). Historian and Smith biographer Richard L. Bushman observed that the former term quickly vanished in favor of the latter and suggested that Smith initially used the term "evangelist," although "patriarch" more appropriately "conveyed the duties of the office," because the word "evangelist" appeared "in the New Testament, the model for Church organization."[174]

On June 18 a meeting was held at which $950 was subscribed by the Mormons in the Kirtland area to build the temple, and on June 25 another $6,232.50 was raised.[175] At the latter meeting, Smith, Phelps, and John Whitmer pledged $500 each, and Cowdery pledged $750, which Smith's history claims was "paid within one hour; and the people were astonished."[176]

---

171. Editorial, *Painesville Telegraph*, June 26, 1835, [3].

172. JS History, vol. B-1, 595 (DHC 2:234), composed by Willard Richards in September 1843. Vogel, *History of Joseph Smith*, lxxxix. The source for this is unknown.

173. Instruction on Priesthood, Mar. 1–May 4, 1835, D&C, 1835 ed., III:17–29 [D&C 107:39–57] (*JSP*, D4:316–17).

174. Bushman, *Joseph Smith*, 261.

175. [William W. Phelps], "The House of God," *Messenger and Advocate*, July 1835, 148.

176. JS History, vol. B-1, 595 (DHC 2:234). The source or authority for this statement is unknown.

Indeed, the source of these funds is a historical mystery as well. Phelps noted in the July 1835 issue of the *Messenger and Advocate* that the Saints had already spent about $10,000 and estimated that "the whole cost, when finished, will probably be from twenty to thirty thousand" dollars.[177]

---

177. [William W. Phelps], "The House of God," *Messenger and Advocate*, July 1835, 147.

19

Mummies and Papyrus

*Valuable Discovery of hiden reccords that have been obtained from
the ancient bur[y]ing place of the Egiyptians.*
—Joseph Smith, "Valuable Discovery," ca. early July 1835,
Joseph Smith Egyptian Papers, CHL

About the last of June or first of July 1835, an Irish immigrant named Michael Chandler arrived in Kirtland with four Egyptian mummies, two rolls of papyri, and an assortment of fragments.[1] Chandler claimed he had inherited eleven mummies and several Egyptian papyri from his recently deceased uncle, Antonio Lebolo, the legendary Italian antiquarian.[2] After exhibiting and selling some of his Egyptian artifacts in several major cities, including Baltimore, Pittsburgh, New Orleans, and Cleveland, Chandler heard that Joseph Smith had translated the Book of Mormon from "Reformed Egyptian," so, eager to sell what remained of his relics, he traveled to Kirtland.

On July 3 Smith and other church leaders paid a fee to view Chandler's mummies and papyri.[3] According to Oliver Cowdery, "The morning Mr. Chandler first presented his papyrus to Brother Smith, he was shown by the latter, a number of characters like those upon the writings of Mr. C[handler].

---

1. Oliver Cowdery said Chandler arrived "the last of June, or first of July" (Oliver Cowdery, Letter to William Frye, Dec. 22, 1835, "Egyptian Mummies—Ancient Records," *LDS Messenger and Advocate* [Kirtland, OH], Dec. 1835, 235; hereafter "Egyptian Mummies"). Phelps said the mummies were brought to Kirtland "last of June." William W. Phelps, Letter to Sally Phelps, July 19, 1835. John Whitmer said it was "About the first of July 1835." Whitmer, History, 76 (*JSP*, H2:86). Cowdery's letter to Frye was copied into Cowdery, Letterbook, 68–74. For a more detailed treatment of Joseph Smith's purchase and initial translation of the Egyptian papyri, see Vogel, *Book of Abraham Apologetics*.

2. "Egyptian Mummies," 234. Chandler's claim that Lebolo was his uncle has never been verified. See Donl Peterson, *The Story of the Book of Abraham*, 88.

3. On July 3, 1835, Frederick G. Williams recorded in his account book: "to see the mummies 68½." F. G. Williams & Co. Account Book, July 3, 1835.

which were previously copied from the plates containing the history of the Nephites, or Book of Mormon."[4] Indeed, Smith's "Reformed Egyptian" characters—as found on the so-called "Anthon Transcript"—share some points of similarity with hieratic and demotic Egyptian. Remarkable as this might at first appear, equal results can be produced by comparing Smith's characters with the Latin alphabet and Arabic numerals.[5]

Cowdery also said that Chandler solicited Smith's "opinion concerning his antiquities, or a translation of some of the characters," that Smith "gave him the interpretation of some few for his satisfaction."[6] On July 6 Chandler supplied Smith with a certificate attesting to Smith's ability as a translator: "This is to make known to all who may be desirous, concerning the knowledge of Mr. Joseph Smith, jr. in deciphering the ancient Egyptian hieroglyphic characters, in my possession, which I have, in many eminent cities, shown to the most learned: And, from the information that I could even learn, or meet with, I find that of Mr. Joseph Smith, jr. to correspond in the most minute matters."[7]

No doubt Smith made good use of Chandler's statement, for it implied that the learned could partially verify Smith's gift to translate ancient languages. However, there is reason to question the motive behind Chandler's statement. As LDS scholar Terryl Givens observes, "Given Chandler's desire to unload his inherited mummies and papyri on a prospective buyer, his ignorance of ancient languages, and the unlikelihood that strangers in New York and Philadelphia would refer him to the presumed charlatan Joseph Smith, we do well to see in Chandler more flattery than sincerity."[8] Moreover, the details of Jean-François Champollion's decipherment of the Rosetta Stone were not

---

4. "Egyptian Mummies," 235.

5. In 1942 Mormon researcher Ariel L. Crowley found that 97 of the 225 characters on the well-known Whitmer document were similar to demotic Egyptian. Ariel L. Crowley, "The Anthon Transcript ... II. The Identification of the Characters as Egyptian," *The Improvement Era*, Feb. 1942, 79–80, 124–25; reprinted in Crowley, *About the Book of Mormon*, 23–26. Concerning this effort, Mormon scholar Stanley Kimball observed: "Honorable as such attempts are and fascinating though they may be, the net result is generally a striking comparison of the similar characters and an ignoring of the dissimilar characters. By this very method it may be 'proved' that we speak Russian in this country." Stanley B. Kimball, "Charles Anthon and the Egyptian Language," *The Improvement Era*, Oct. 1960, 765. My own comparison to the English alphabet accounted for 104 of the characters, while numbers or digits accounted for another thirty-nine.

6. "Egyptian Mummies," 235.

7. "Egyptian Mummies" (*JSP*, D4:364–65).

8. Givens, *The Pearl of Greatest Price*, 120. The editors of the Joseph Smith Papers state, "It is possible that Chandler supplied the certificate to JS in an attempt to curry his favor so that he would purchase the mummies and papyri. ... He may have believed the certificate would help motivate JS or investors to make the purchase." *JSP*, D4:362–63.

yet widely known in the United States, so it is unlikely that the learned could decipher any Egyptian characters.[9] LDS scholars Robin Scott Jensen and Brian Hauglid agree that "neither Chandler nor any other American at that time would likely have been able to make such an attestation authoritatively."[10]

Nevertheless, an opportunity presented itself to Smith: the prospect of possessing actual ancient documents that he could display in public, something that was not possible with the Book of Mormon or Book of Enoch. Smith also learned from Chandler that any translation he would eventually offer to the public could not be verified or exposed by the learned.

Smith expressed his interest in purchasing the papyri, but Chandler insisted on selling the mummies and records together for $2,400, a substantial sum for that day.[11] Smith quickly made arrangements for the purchase by Joseph Coe, a wealthy member of the Kirtland high council. In an 1844 letter to Smith, Coe explained the circumstances of the purchase: "Previous to closing the contract with Chandler I made arrangements with S[imeon]. Andrews to take one third part and your Self & Co. one third leaving one third to be borne by myself. Andrews soon paid his $800 I took $800 out of Geauga Bank which paid a large portion of my share, but yours together with the interest remained unto the Spring of 1836 if I mistake not." According to Coe, he was at first hesitant, but having been assured by Smith "that the burthen would be but temporary; that the profits arising from the work when translated would be more than adequate to the defraying all the expence."[12]

Abraham and Joseph

Smith soon discovered that he had purchased one male and three female mummies. Mary Ann Sterns Winters, who as a child saw the mummies in the Kirtland temple, said: "They frightened me very much—they had such an unearthly look to me. They were dark in color, and hard as metal, and the cloth they were wrapped in was petrified like the bodies."[13] Smith also found two badly damaged scrolls: one on the breast of the male mummy, another on one of the females. While Smith apparently assumed he had in his possession unique Egyptian documents, the writing associated with the male mummy was actually an ordinary Egyptian funerary text dating to the Ptolemaic period, about 250 to 150 years BCE, known as the Book

---

9. See Parkinson et al., *Cracking Codes*, 41.

10. *JSP*, R4:xx.

11. Today, $2,400 is roughly the equivalent of $80,000.

12. Joseph Coe, Letter to Joseph Smith, Jan. 1, 1844, JS Collection.

13. Winters, "An Autobiographical Sketch," 4.

of Breathings or Breathing Permit, which allowed the owner, a priest by the name of Hôr (or Horos), to regain the ability to breathe in the afterlife.[14] The record found on the breast of one of the female mummies was the Book of the Dead belonging to Ta-sherit-Min (or Semminis), dating from about 300 to 100 BCE.[15]

Soon Smith announced that one of the scrolls contained the writings of Abraham and another scroll the record of the ancient patriarch Joseph—the two Old Testament characters, besides Moses, who had dealings with the Egyptians. Smith's official history dates this discovery to between July 5 and 9, 1835. An entry composed by scribe Willard Richards in September 1843, no doubt under Smith's direction and probably with the help of fellow scribe and participant W. W. Phelps, states: "I, with W. W. Phelps and O[liver]. Cowdery, as scribes, commenced the translation of some of the characters or hieroglyphics, and much to our joy found that one of the rolls contained the writings of Abraham; another the writings of Joseph of Egypt, &c. a more full account of which will appear in its place, as I proceed to examine or unfold them."[16]

On July 19 Phelps wrote to his wife, Sally, in Missouri: "As no one could translate these writings they were presented to President [Joseph] Smith. He soon knew what they were and said that the rolls of papyrus contained the sacred record kept by Joseph in Pharaoh's court in Egypt and the teachings of Father Abraham." Phelps added that when Smith read Sally's recently-received letter, he remarked that "it was as easy to shed tears while reading that letter as it was when reading the History of Joseph in Egypt."[17] In an appended note, Smith assured Sally that her separation from her husband was only "for a short season" and prophesied that "as the Lord God liveth the redemtion of Zion is nigh at hand, and we shall live to see it."[18]

---

14. *JSP*, R4:8; Ritner, *The Joseph Smith Egyptian Papyri*, 86.

15. *JSP*, R4:12; Ritner, *The Joseph Smith Egyptian Papyri*, 151.

16. JS History, vol. B-1, 596 (DHC 2:236). This entry in Smith's history was composed by Richards on September 15, 1843. Vogel, *History of Joseph Smith*, 2:240n22. The history was read to Smith and approved by him regularly. On November 8, 1843, for instance, Smith recorded in his journal: "from 9 to 11½ A.M.— Interv[ie]w with Phelp[s] an[d] Richa[r]ds clerks—read & hea[r]d read the history." Smith, Journal, Nov. 8, 1843 (*JSP*, J3:127). The previous day Richards and Phelps had reached page 729 in volume B-1, which recounts the events of April 1836. Richards, Journal, Nov. 7–8, 1843.

17. William W. Phelps, Letter to Sally Phelps, July 19–20, 1835. A partial transcription with some variant readings is also available in Leah Y. Phelps, "Letters of Faith from Kirtland," *Improvement Era*, Aug. 1942, 529.

18. Joseph Smith, Letter to Sally Phelps, July 20, 1835. Leah Y. Phelps, "Letters of Faith from Kirtland," *Improvement Era*, Aug. 1942, 529 (*JSP*, D4:370–71).

About this time, Smith may have dictated a rough draft of Abraham 1:1–3 to Phelps, Cowdery, or to both at the same time, which Phelps later copied into a blank translation book, the only extant copy.[19] These three verses explicitly identified the writer of one of the scrolls as Abraham:

> In the land of the Chaldeans, at the residince of my fathers, I, Abraham, saw, that it was needful for me to obtain another place of residence, and seeing there was greater happiness and peace and rest, for me, I sought for the blessings of the fathers, and the right whereunto I should be ordained to administer the same: Having been a follower of righteousness; desiring to be one who possessed great Knowledge; a greater follower of righteousness; a possessor of greater Knowledge; a father of many nations; a prince of peace; one who keeps the commandments of God; a rightful heir; a high priest, holding the right belonging to the fathers, from the begining of time; even from the begining, or before the foundation of the earth, down to the present time; even the right of the first born, or the first man, who is Adam, or first father, through the fathers, unto me.[20]

Smith's translation begins with Abraham in Chaldea, near the site of the legendary tower of Babel, before he leaves in search of the Promised Land in Canaan, only to flee farther south into Egypt to avoid a famine (Gen. 11:31–12:10). It also picks up the theme in Smith's recent instruction on priesthood, which traced the high and patriarchal priesthood from Adam to Noah and promised to provide details in a forthcoming Book of Enoch.[21] Where the Old Testament was silent, Smith's Abraham was explicit. For those who may have questioned Smith's revelations, especially after they had proved wrong about the redemption of Zion, Smith returned to translating ancient records to foster confidence in his followers that his recent hierarchical innovations, particularly the high and patriarchal priesthood, had ancient authority. It was no longer authority derived from revealed commandments, but authority restored through angelic ordination and handed down in an unbroken succession of legitimate ordinations.

---

19. Book of Abraham Manuscript-C, 1 (*JSP*, R4:219). The five sheets comprising this document were subsequently removed from the book, and the document itself is the only manuscript—out of the three translation manuscripts produced in Kirtland—to contain a rough version of the first three verses of the Book of Abraham. The rest of this document, the longest of the three Kirtland documents, is in the handwriting of Warren Parrish, who did not become a scribe until late October 1835. *JSP*, R4:217.

20. Book of Abraham Manuscript-C, 1 (*JSP*, R4:219).

21. Instruction on Priesthood, ca. Mar. 1–May 4, 1835, D&C, 1835 ed., III:17–29 [D&C 107:39–57] (*JSP*, D4:316–17).

Identity of the Mummies

A second passage in Smith's official history, which, following the entry for July 17, 1835, reads: "The remainder of this month, I was continually engaged in translating an alphabet to the Book of Abraham, and arrangeing a grammar of the Egyptian language as practiced by the ancients."[22] This refers to three small nearly identical booklets containing the "Egyptian alphabet" in Smith, Cowdery, and Phelps's handwriting, as well as a bound "Grammar and Alphabet of the Egyptian Language," the greater portion of which is in Phelps's handwriting. The Alphabets function more as dictionaries, recording a sign in the left margin, then in the next column a name, and finally an explanation or definition. The same characters in the Alphabets were later copied into the bound Grammar and their definitions were expanded into five "degrees" of meaning. Three of the degrees are preceded by brief lectures on Egyptian grammar, which primarily explain the degree system and the multiple layers of meaning compressed into a single Egyptian character.

How the Alphabets relate to the Book of Abraham is not stated, but the first of its five parts deals with the Ta-sherit-Min papyrus—which Smith identified with Old Testament Joseph—and fragments from the Book of the Dead for a man named Amenhotep, which are not extant but survive as copies by Smith's scribes in two similar booklets. One of these notebooks is titled "Valuable Discovery of hid[d]en reccords that have been obtained from the ancient bur[y]ing place of the Egyptians," which appears on the cover in the handwriting of Frederick G. Williams above the signature of Joseph Smith.[23] In addition to containing copies of hieratic Egyptian texts, both booklets include an English "translation" of a few characters in the handwriting of Cowdery and Phelps, apparently written simultaneously as Smith dictated.[24] On the first page of Phelps's notebook appear the following two sentences under the heading "A Translation of the next page" with "in part" added in pencil: "Katumin, Princess, daughter of On-i-tas King of Egypt, who began to reign in the year of the world, 2962. Katumin was born in the 30th year of the reign of her father, and died when she was 28 years old, which was the year 3020."[25]

---

22. JS History, vol. B-1, 597 (DHC 2:238). Like the first statement previously quoted, this entry was also composed by Willard Richards on September 16, 1843, no doubt with the help of Smith and/or Phelps. Vogel, *History of Joseph Smith*, 2:244n13.

23. Historical Introduction, *JSP*, R4:27.

24. The simultaneous transcription is determined by comparing the different ways Phelps and Cowdery made the same corrections in the middle of their texts. Vogel, *Book of Abraham Apologetics*, 48 (*JSP*, R4:31, 35).

25. Notebook of Copied Egyptian Characters, 1 (*JSP*, R4:35).

On the opposite page are four lines of hieratic characters, which according to Robert K. Ritner, an Egyptologist at the University of Chicago's Oriental Institute, were taken from Chapter 46 of the now-missing Amenhotep Book of the Dead.[26] Underneath these characters, Phelps wrote: "Over this stood the figure of a woman," which Ritner explains was actually "the *male* owner, Amenhotep."[27] Cowdery evidently referred to the Amenhotep fragments, as well as to the circular hypocephalus (now Facsimile 2 of the Book of Abraham), when he wrote in December 1835 that in addition to the two rolls, "two or three other small pieces of papyrus, with astronomical calculations, epitaphs, &c. were found with others of the Mummies."[28] Cowdery's version of the same words in the "Valuable Discovery" notebook identified the specific characters that were "in part" translated in Phelps's notebook.

If one uses Bishop James Ussher's 4004 BCE as the date of Creation, as Smith and his contemporaries did, then 2,962 years after Creation is 1042 BCE and 3,020 years is 984 BCE. According to Smith's/Rigdon's "Lectures on Faith" delivered in Kirtland during the winter of 1834–35, Abraham died in the 2,183rd year of the world, or 1821 BCE, which is 809 years before the birth of Katumin (b. 1012 BCE).[29] According to Adam Clarke's widely-circulated Bible commentary, Joseph son of Jacob/Israel died in 1635 BCE, or 623 years before the birth of Katumin.[30]

Apparently, Smith's first translations pertained to the identities of the mummies. According to two independent reports, when Smith's mother later exhibited the mummies in Nauvoo, Illinois, she identified them as King Onitas and his family. Shortly after viewing the mummies and papyri in Nauvoo in 1843, Charlotte Haven told her mother that Lucy Smith introduced her and her companions to "King Onitus and his royal household,—one [mummy] she did not know."[31] In December 1843 LaFayette Knight wrote that he visited Smith in Nauvoo and examined the four mummies "one of which his Mother told me was King Onitus, on whose breast was found the writing of Abr[a]ham."[32]

---

26. Ritner, *The Joseph Smith Egyptian Papyri*, 211. Since Cowdery described only two rolls of papyrus, Smith only possessed a fragment of the Amenhotep papyrus, which Chandler probably sold to someone prior to his arrival at Kirtland. "Egyptian Mummies," 236.

27. Ritner, *The Joseph Smith Egyptian Papyri*, 210.

28. "Egyptian Mummies," 234.

29. D&C, 1835 ed., 24.

30. Clarke, *The Holy Bible*, Ex. 1:6.

31. Charlotte Haven, Letter to her mother, Feb. 19, 1843, "A Girl's Letters from Nauvoo," *Overland Monthly* (San Francisco, CA), Dec. 1890, 623.

32. LaFayette Knight, Letter to James H. and Sharon Fellows, Dec. 21, 1843.

While the Katumin passage in the Valuable Discovery notebooks is about a specific princess and king, the Kah-tou-man of the Alphabets is a generic term applied to a royal female lineage extending back to the reputed discovery of Egypt by the daughter of Noah's son Ham before the Flood waters had fully receded. The first part of the Alphabets, which apparently blends characters from the Katumin epitaph and record of Joseph, is about various aspects of the royal Kah-tou-man family line, and, as developed in the five degrees of the bound Grammar, the purpose of the passage is apparently to explain how two records of Hebrew patriarchs came into the possession of an Egyptian mummy. In the fifth degree, the term "Kah tou mun" is defined as "a lineage with whom a record of the fathers was intrusted by tradition of Ham, and according to the tradition of their elders, by whom also the tradition of the art of embalming was kept."[33] While Smith tried to account for the Egyptian royal family's possession of the records of two Hebrew prophets, he did not explain why, after being handed down for several generations, they should be buried with mummies.

The Pure Language

The first thirteen of fifty-nine characters of part 2 of the Alphabets are also not about Abraham or the Hôr papyrus. In fact, they are not even Egyptian characters.[34] Rather, they were taken from a document that predated the arrival of the Egyptian papyri and purported to contain characters and words from the "pure language" spoken by Adam and his posterity before the confusion of tongues at the tower of Babel (Gen. 11:1–9). On May 26, 1835, more than a month before Smith acquired the Egyptian papyri, Phelps, who was living with Smith and working as his scribe, wrote to his wife in Missouri and included "A specimen of some of the 'pure language.'"[35] Like the Egyptian Alphabets, this text is arranged in columns, although with different names and definitions but identical characters in the first column:

---

33. Grammar and Alphabet of the Egyptian Language, 4 (*JSP*, R4:123); hereafter GAEL.

34. In 1968 University of Chicago Egyptologist Klaus Baer observed that the first thirteen characters "differ in general appearance" from the other characters in the Alphabets and do not appear to be hieratic Egyptian. Baer, "The Breathing Permit of Hôr," 128–29.

35. William W. Phelps, Letter to Sally Phelps, May 26–27, 1835. Phelps arrived at Kirtland on May 16, 1835, and may have come across this material while working on printing the Doctrine and Covenants. Phelps recorded on May 25 that he "Worked in the office" until Saturday, May 30. On June 16 he recorded: "Commenced cop[ying]. rev[elations]. at 3 [p.m.] [at] Josephs." This perhaps refers to the revelations Phelps copied into his journal. On June 17 Phelps recorded: "Compared revelations." William W. Phelps, Diary and Notebook, May 25–30, and June 16–17, 1835.

ah	ahman–	God.
anz	sonahman=	Son of God
aintz	saunsahman	sons of God ordain[ed]
aine	anglo–	angels
oh	oleah	the Earth

The names and definitions of all but the last character were given by Smith as early as March 1832, while he and his family were living in Hiram, Ohio, with John Johnson and his family. This related document is headed "A Sample of pure Language given by Joseph the Seer as copied by Br Johnson," and conveys the same information in a question and answer format, only without characters:

Question What is the name of God in pure Language
Answer Awman.

Q [what is] The meaning of the pure word A[w]man
A It is the being which made all things in all its parts.
Q What is the name of the Son of God.
A The Son Awman.
Q What is the Son Awman.
A It is the greatest of all the parts of Awman which is the Godhead the first born.
Q What is man.
A This signifies Sons Awman. the human family the children of men the greatest parts of Awman Sons the Son Awman
Q What are Angels called in pure language.
A Awman Angls-man
Q What are the meaning of these words.
A Awman's Ministerring servants Sanctified who are sent forth from heaven to minister for or to Sons Awman the greatest part of Awman Son. Sons Awman Son Awman Awman[36]

Before obtaining the papyri, Smith was preoccupied with the concept of a pure Adamic language. The Book of Mormon includes the story of a people called the Jaredites whose language was not confounded at the tower of Babel. God allowed the Jaredites to preserve their language pure and uncorrupted and sent them to the American continent (Ether 1:33–37; Gen. 11:1–9). As early as November 1830, Smith had emended Genesis to include

---

36. "A Sample of Pure Language," ca. Mar. 4–20, 1832, Revelation Book 1, 144 (*JSP*, MRB:265; *JSP*, D2:213–15).

mention of a "book of remembrance" that was kept among the ancient patriarchs, written "in the language of Adam ... which was pure and undefiled."[37] As early as August 1831, Smith declared that Independence, Missouri, was the location of the prophesied city of Zion, which in the original language was "Zomar."[38] In his instruction to the Twelve Apostles, probably dictated in March or April 1835, Smith said that Adam called together seven generations of patriarchal high priests and "the residue of his posterity, who were righteous, into the valley of Adam-ondi-ahman, and there bestowed upon them his last blessing."[39]

Both Zomar and Adam-ondi-Ahman appear in one of Smith's definitions in the bound Grammar. A character defined as "mans first residence fruitful garden A val[le]y a place of happiness" in the Alphabets is developed in the fifth degree in the bound Grammar as "The place appointed of God for the residence of Adam; Adam ondi= Ahman a fruit garden ... great valley or plain given by promise, fitted with fruit trees and precious flowers, made for the healing of Man; ... place of happiness—purity, holiness, and rest: even Zomar—Zion."[40]

Book of Enoch Aborted

Why would Smith include his sample of the pure language in an Egyptian alphabet and grammar? The answer may be found in the widespread belief that ancient Egyptian hieroglyphics were visual representations of the language Adam spoke. Seventeenth-century German Jesuit Athanasius Kircher, as Umberto Eco explains, "firmly believed that ancient Egyptian was the perfect, Adamic language, and, according to the 'hermetic' tradition, he identified the Egyptian Hermes Trismegistus with Moses and said that hieroglyphs were Symbols, that is, expressions that referred to an occult, unknown, and ambivalent content."[41] Eco also notes that Kircher believed "the symbols were initiatory because they were wrapped in an impenetrable and

---

37. Old Testament Revision 1, 11 [Moses 6:4, 6], in Faulring et al., eds., *Joseph Smith's New Translation of the Bible*, 97. On date, see Faulring et al., 57.

38. Ezra Booth, Letter to Ira Eddy, Nov. 14, 1831, "Mormonism—No. VI," *Ohio Star* (Ravenna, OH), Nov. 17, 1831. In Howe's reprint of Booth's letter, the name appeared as "Zomas." Howe, *Mormonism Unvailed*, 199.

39. Instruction on Priesthood, ca. Mar. 1–May 4, 1835, D&C, 1835 ed., III:28 [D&C 107:53–55] (*JSP*, D4:317). In 1838 Smith located Adam-ondi-Ahman eighty miles north of Zomar, explaining that "it is the place where Adam shall come to visit his people, or the Ancient of days shall sit as spoken of by Daniel the Prophet." Smith, Journal, May 19, 1838 [D&C 116] (*JSP*, J1:271); Dan. 7:13–14.

40. GAEL, 23 (*JSP*, R4:161).

41. Eco, *Serendipities*, 60.

indecipherable enigma, to protect them from the idle curiosity of the vulgar multitudes."[42] Nevertheless, Kircher produced a three-volume dictionary of the Egyptian language titled *Oedipus Aegyptiacus,* filled with invented translations in which a few characters sometimes yield many words. If, as Smith believed, Egypt had been settled by the daughter of Ham, then the Egyptian language would not have been affected by the subsequent confusion of tongues at the tower of Babel and Egyptian hieroglyphics would be closer to the pure Adamic language than even Hebrew.

Another reason is that any so-called "Book of Enoch" would have been written originally in the pure language. If Phelps's pure-language specimen of characters, names, and definitions were part of Smith's preliminary effort to produce a pseudepigraphic Book of Enoch, perhaps the characters and translation were intended to bolster confidence in Smith's followers that any eventual translation would have come from an actual record that—like the Book of Mormon's gold plates—would never be exhibited to the public. If so, Smith may have prepared his specimen of pure language characters for the same reasons he produced a facsimile of Book of Mormon characters (the "Anthon Transcript") seven years earlier.

If Smith was, in fact, preparing to produce a pseudepigraphic Book of Enoch to support his introduction of the patriarchal priesthood, it was interrupted by the arrival of the Egyptian papyri—which Smith used to accomplish the same thing: to lend ancient support for his recent introduction of the patriarchal priesthood. This is evident in part 2 of the Alphabets and bound Grammar as well as in the first lines of the Book of Abraham.

Less than two weeks before the arrival of Michael Chandler, Smith preached on the "Evangelical Order," meaning patriarchal priesthood.[43] When Chandler arrived with his papyri, Smith was able to translate real ancient records that the learned had declared were undecipherable. Smith only had to persuade colleagues—especially Phelps—that he was actually translating. After identifying the mummies and authors of the two rolls of papyrus, Smith began recording his ideas in the Egyptian Alphabets. It would only be natural for him to transfer his thoughts about Adam, Enoch, and patriarchal priesthood to the Egyptian project. In doing so, the narrative necessarily shifted to patriarchs who had dealings with Egypt—most obviously Abraham and Joseph—and who lived after the corruption of language at the

---

42. Eco, 60.
43. JS History, vol. B-1, 595 (DHC 2:234).

tower of Babel. Smith therefore explained that Abraham had access to the records of previous patriarchs—presumably Adam's Book of Remembrance and the Book of Enoch. Thus Abraham is made to declare: "The records of the fathers, even the patraarch's, concerning the right of priesthood, the Lord my God preserved in mine own hands, therefore a Knowledge of the beginning of creation, and also of the planets and of the Stars, as it was made Known unto the fathers, have I Kept even unto this day."[44]

In discussing the record of Old Testament Joseph in December 1835, Cowdery made an explicit connection to the Book of Enoch and revealed the possible source of Smith's inspiration. Cowdery said that upon the papyrus scroll of Joseph son of Jacob/Israel was found a drawing of "Enoch's Pillar, as mentioned by Josephus, ... our present version of the bible does not mention this fact, ... but Josephus says that the descendants of Seth were virtuous, and possessed a great knowledge of the heavenly bodies, and, that, in consequence of the prophecy of Adam, that the world should be destroyed once by water and again by fire, Enoch wrote a history or an account of the same, and put [it] into two pillars one of brick and the other of stone; and that the same were in being [or existence] at his (Josephus') day."[45]

No doubt Smith was familiar with Josephus, a first-century CE Roman-Jewish historian who also mentioned a prophecy of Adam, a record of Enoch, and knowledge of "heavenly bodies, and their order" being handed down by the descendants of Seth. [46] Smith's familiarity with Josephus is evident in part 1 of the bound Grammar, where it is said that Abraham "was fore warned of God to go down into Ah=meh=strah, or Egypt, and preach the gospel unto the Ah meh strah ans"—which seems to reflect Josephus' reference to Egypt as "Mestree, and the Egyptians Mestreans."[47]

Phelps's copy of the pure language was not simply a summary of Smith's 1832 answers to questions, it added new material about "the Earth" and divided humankind into "sons of God," or those ordained, and the "children of men." Similarly, part 2 of the Alphabets builds on the version of the pure language in Phelps's letter to Sally Phelps by multiplying and refining the categories. The first nine characters discuss: God, the firstborn son, two grades of angels (spirits and resurrected beings), four grades of ministers

---

44. Book of Abraham Manuscript-B, Nov. 1835, 5–6 [Abr. 1:31] (*JSP*, R4:213–14).

45. "Egyptian Mummies," 236.

46. Flavius Josephus, Antiquities of the Jews, Book 1, chap. 2, sect. 3, in Whiston, *Josephus Complete Works*, 27.

47. GAEL, 6 (*JSP*, R4:127). Antiquities of the Jews, Book 1, chap. 6, sect. 2, in Whiston, *Josephus Complete Works*, 31.

(high priests, lesser priests, priests ordained but not of God, and unordained ministers), and, finally, "all mankind."

Similar to Smith's 1835 instruction on priesthood (D&C 107), characters 10–14 list five generations of patriarchal high priests, tracing the line of authority from Adam to "Baeth-ku," the "fifth high priest from Adam," who was Mahalaleel, Enoch's grandfather. Character 15 represents humankind's first residence on Earth, followed by five degrees of improvement, which leads to the earth in its "purified" state, then to all the "heavenly bodies," and finally to the "Celestial kingdom, God's residence."[48] This is where the work of defining characters in part 2 of the Alphabets ends. Later, Cowdery inserts the names to numbers 24–41 in Smith's Alphabet. Shortly after October 1835, Smith and new scribe Warren Parrish add the last name—Kolob, number 42—to two of the Alphabets, leaving characters 43–59 blank.

The Hôr Papyrus

Following the pure-language characters, part 2 of the Alphabets begins copying characters from the Hôr Papyrus, which Smith identified with Abraham. These characters were taken from one of the four vertical columns that flank the vignette at the beginning (or right-hand side) of the scroll that became Facsimile 1 in the published the Book of Abraham, bringing the total number of characters to fifty-nine. The characters in the three remaining columns were copied without names or definitions into parts 3–5 of the Alphabets, with two exceptions. The two characters in part 3 were named but not defined. One is "Iota nitah veh ah que," later defined in the grammar volume as "see, saw seeing, or having seen" as "increased five times from the fourth." The other named character relates to Smith's early translation of the first three verses of the Book of Abraham. The character is a man holding a staff, although Smith and his scribes did not recognize it as such. To them, it was lines and dots, each part of which had meaning. In the Alphabets, it is named "Kiah broam = Kiah brah oam = zub zool oan." This character appears at the beginning of the Grammar, where "Kiah brah oam," an obvious variant of the name Abraham, is defined as "Coming down from the beginning—right by birth—and also by blessing, and by promise—promises made; a father of many nations; a prince of peace; one who keeps the commandment of God; a patriarch; a rightful heir; a high priest."[49]

---

48. Egyptian Alphabet-A, 2; Egyptian Alphabet-B, 2; Egyptian Alphabet-C, 2 (*JSP*, R4:58, 76–77, 89).

49. GAEL, 3 (*JSP*, R4:221). Cf. Gen. 12:2; 17:4–5.

The last two characters in the Alphabets are not copied from the columns flanking the vignette, but are taken from the beginning of the horizontal lines of the text that immediately follow, which have since flaked off and are no longer visible.[50] These two characters are translated in the Alphabets as "The land of the Chaldeans" and "The father of the faithful," which are the same phrases keyed to the same characters in the left margin of Phelps's transcription of the first three verses of the Book of Abraham.[51] In Smith's Alphabet, the translation of the characters was canceled by Cowdery, who then inserted a translation of the second character in all five degrees of its meaning:

> In the first degree Ah-broam—signifies The father of the faithful, the first right, the elders second degree—same sound—A follower of righ-tiousness—Third degree—same sound—One who possesses great Knowledge—Fourth degree—same sound—A follower of righteousness, a possessor of greater knowledge. Fifth degree—Ah-bra-oam. The father of many nations, a prince of peace, one who keeps the commandments of God, a patriarch, a rightful heir, a high priest.[52]

The fact that the three characters dealing with Abraham in the Alphabets also appear in the lecture on grammar at the beginning of the bound Grammar suggests a chronology of composition. Another important observation is that the same three characters appear in the margin of Phelps's transcription of the first three verses of Abraham, implying a possible sequence of events. Still, another observation is that besides these three characters, there are no subsequent characters from the Hôr papyrus in the Grammar, which suggests that the translation was interrupted by work on the Grammar. This is a problem for some LDS scholars who have attempted to distance Smith from the Alphabets and Grammar volume by arguing that Smith's translation of the entire Book of Abraham preceded the Alphabets and Grammar and that those works were produced by Smith's scribes, not Smith, who were attempting to reverse engineer Smith's translation.[53]

In the Alphabets, the definitions end with character 23, which discusses the Celestial Kingdom or residence of God. The bound Grammar continues

---

50. See Ritner, *The Joseph Smith Egyptian Papyri*, 84, 99; Baer, "The Breathing Permit of Hôr," 129; Brian Hauglid, *A Textual History of the Book of Abraham*, 58; Egyptian Alphabets-A, 4, -B, 4, and -C, 4 (*JSP*, R4:68–69, 83, 93).

51. See Egyptian Alphabet-C, 4 (*JSP*, R4:93); Book of Abraham Manuscript-C, 1 (*JSP*, R4:219).

52. Egyptian Alphabet-A, [5] (*JSP*, R4:70–71).

53. For an examination of attempts to distance Joseph Smith from the Alphabets and bound Grammar, see Vogel, *Book of Abraham Apologetics*, 7–9, 37–40, 85–93, 96–101.

this theme, defining the next two characters (24 and 25) as "an other Kingdom. govrned by different laws. a second king. or governed by another, or second person not having been exalted"; and "Another Kingdom governed by different laws, composed of subjects who receive their place at a future period, and governed by those who are under the directions of another; a kingdom whose subject[s] differ one from another in glory; ... [they] behold not the face of God."[54]

These definitions correspond to the Terrestrial and Telestial Kingdoms of Smith's and Rigdon's 1832 vision of three heavens.[55] The definitions are followed by three kingdoms of the devil, two names of which are derived from the Greek word Hades (the underworld): "Dah tu Hah dees" and "Hahdees."[56] While Hades does not appear in the King James Version of the Bible, it appears in the Greek manuscripts of the Old and New Testaments and is translated variously as "Hell," "grave," or "pit." Smith's contemporaries used the term as a synonym for "Hell." The Grammar then returns to the Celestial Kingdom, which is "above all other glories, as the [sun] excels in light the Moon in light, this glory excels being filled: with the same glory equaility."[57]

This is followed by four Masonic-like characters. Character 32 looks like a man with his arms raised above his head, which reminded Smith of the Masonic "sign of distress," wherein initiates pledge upon seeing the sign given by a brother Mason to "fly to his relief at the risk of my life."[58] In the Alphabets, Smith names it "Ho-hah-oop" but does not define it. Later, in the bound Grammar, the character is defined as one who has been "appointed to intercede for another; [or] invocation."[59] Characters 33 and 34 are V and U shapes, apparently abstractions of the raised arms. They are not found on the papyrus but are similarly defined in the Grammar as "a sign among the Egyptians that is used for influence or power: [or] a sign made use of for one to escape his enemies."[60]

The appearance of Masonic-like signs/gestures at the time of the patriarchs is a theme Smith discussed as early as April 1829, when he dictated the account in the Book of Mormon of Alma's commanding his son Helaman to suppress the records of the Jaredites so that people may not know "the

---

54. GAEL, 23, 27 (*JSP*, R4:161, 169).
55. "The Vision," Feb. 16, 1832, Revelation Book 2, 1–10 [D&C 76] (*JSP*, D2:179–92).
56. GAEL, 29, 31, 33 (*JSP*, R4:173, 177, 181).
57. GAEL, 23 (*JSP*, R4:161).
58. Morgan, *Illustrations of Masonry*, 74; see also illustration on page 76.
59. GAEL, 31 (*JSP*, R4:177).
60. GAEL, 27 (*JSP*, R4:169).

mysteries and the works of darkness, and their secret works, ... retain all their oaths, and their covenants, and their agreements in their secret abominations; yea, and all their signs and their wonders ye shall retain from this people."[61] The next month, Smith dictated the account in the Book of Ether of a conspiracy to murder the Jaredite king Omer, which states that "Akish did administer unto them the oaths which was given by them of old, who also sought power, which had been handed down even from Cain, who was a murderer from the beginning."[62] In October 1830, as part of his revision of the King James Bible, Smith expanded Genesis to include an account of Cain making a secret oath with Satan and exclaiming: "Truly I am Mahon the master of this great secret"—thereafter "Cain was called Master Mahon," an allusion to "Master Mason," the third degree of Freemasonry.[63]

At this point Smith took a break from his Egyptian project, stopping with character 35, where the method of copying the characters into the bound Grammar changed and the subject becomes an elaborate ordering of the cosmos, which Smith's journal records as beginning on the first of October.[64]

Trip to Michigan

Prior to leaving for Michigan, Smith attended a series of meetings. On August 4 he met with the presidencies of the Kirtland and Missouri high councils to consider letters from Warren A. Cowdery in Freedom, New York, and William E. McLellin, who was in the east conducting conferences with the Twelve. In a letter dated July 29, 1835, Cowdery mentioned that Jared Carter came to his branch soliciting donations for the temple and that it was the first time he and his branch realized the importance of doing so, although the Twelve held a conference there the previous May on their way east. Cowdery's statement displeased church leaders because it seemed to indicate that the Twelve "failed in [the] out set, to fill their great and important mission, as they know that God has commanded us to build a house in which to receive an endowment, previous to the red[e]mption of Zion, and that Zion could not be redeemed until this takes place."[65]

The presidencies were also concerned by McLellin's letter to his wife.

---

61. Book of Mormon, 1830 ed., 328 [Alma 37:21, 27].

62. Book of Mormon, 1830 ed., 553 [Ether 8:15].

63. Old Testament Revision 1, 9 [Moses 5:30–31] (Faulring et al., eds., *Joseph Smith's New Translation of the Bible*, 94).

64. Smith, Journal, Oct. 1, 1835 (*JSP*, J1:67); Vogel, *Book of Abraham Apologetics*, 103, 114–15, 121. This will be discussed in the next chapter.

65. Council of Presidencies and Others (Including Joseph Smith), Letter to Quorum of the Twelve, Aug. 4, 1835, JS Letterbook 1, 91 (*JSP*, D4:375).

McLellin, who had taught school before going on a mission with the Twelve, evidently was not pleased with the way Sidney Rigdon was running the school, having received a report from Orson Hyde, who had briefly returned to Kirtland. This was taken by the council as an insult to the church and one of its presidents. They therefore reprimanded both McLellin and Hyde, writing: "We hereby inform Elders Mc.Lellin and Hyde that we withdraw our fellowship from them until they return and make satisfaction face to face."[66]

Both matters would be settled once the Twelve returned to Kirtland in late September. Meanwhile, the council sent a scathing letter to the Twelve: "We further inform the twelve, that as far as we can learn from the churches through which you have traveled, that you have set yourselves up as an indepandant counsel subject to no authority of the church—a kind of out laws. This impression is wrong, and will if presisted in, bring down the wrath and indignation upon your heads."[67] What the Twelve did to deserve such a reprimand is unclear, but they had been given "authority to act independently and make decisions."[68] The minutes of the council were sent to the Twelve, who were in Maine at this time.

On August 8 Smith presided with Oliver Cowdery and Rigdon at a meeting at which the "sons of Zion," referring to those who had participated in Zion's Camp, were blessed.[69] Two days later the high council met to hear Smith's complaint against Reynolds Cahoon who "had failed to do his duty in correcting his children, and instructing them in the way of truth & righteousness. ... Elder Cahoon confessed the correctness of the decision, and promised to make public acknowledgement before the church."[70] Contemporary records lack detail, but Smith apparently mentioned this event in a March 10, 1843, journal entry: "When in Kirtland I saw Elder [Reynolds] Cahoon's boy steal a cucumber, put it in his pocket. I told Cahoon of it. At the same time his boy came up and denied it saying he had an apple [and] let it fall and picked it up. There said Cahoon I did not believe he stole it. His boys drove their cows among mine while the women were milking to endanger their safety. I rebuked him and threatened him and made him confess in public next day."[71]

---

66. Council, Letter, 91 (*JSP*, D4:376).

67. Council, Letter, 91–92 (*JSP*, D4:376).

68. See Minutes, May 2, 1835, Record of the Twelve Apostles, 6 (*JSP*, D4:307).

69. Minutes, Aug. 8, 1835, Minute Book 1, 95 (*JSP*, D4:378–80). See Park, "Zion's Blessings in the Early Church," 27–37.

70. Minutes, Aug. 10, 1835, Minute Book 1, 96 (*JSP*, D4:380–82).

71. Smith, Journal, Mar. 10, 1843 (*JSP*, J2:302–303).

In mid-August 1835 Smith left Kirtland with Frederick Williams on a trip to Michigan. Little is known about their departure besides the passing notice in the August 18 minutes that Smith and Williams were "absent."[72] It was probably during this visit to the church in Pontiac, as Edward Stevenson recalled decades later, that Smith described "the visit of the Father and the Son, and the conversation he had with them."[73] Stevenson apparently conflated this visit with another visit Smith made to Pontiac in October 1834. In his autobiography, Stevenson only mentioned the first visit, during which Smith spoke to the congregation and gave an account of his vision of the angel. Afterward, Smith dined with the Stevenson family, and, as Stevenson recalled, they "were highly honoured by entertaining a Prophet of God who had stood in the presence of God The Father and JESUS Christ his only Begotten." Stevenson, who was fourteen at the time, also remembered that he brought Smith "some very early apples and he dined with us," which better fits the mid-August 1835 visit.[74]

On August 17, while Smith was still in Michigan, Cowdery and Rigdon presided over a general assembly of the priesthood and "a very large portion of the church" that approved the Doctrine and Covenants as scripture.[75] Many of the church's leadership were also absent—the Twelve, Bishop Partridge and his counselor Isaac Morley, eight members of the Kirtland high council, and ten members of the Missouri high council, including President David Whitmer.[76]

After several Zion blessings were given in which some were promised to return to Zion and receive an inheritance, an unbound copy of the Doctrine and Covenants was passed around as a representative of each quorum testified to its inspiration. Phelps said the book "was well arranged and calculated to govern the church in righteousness, if followed would bring the members to see eye to eye." John Whitmer testified that he knew "it to be true. and from.

---

72. Minutes, Aug. 17, 1835, Minute Book 1, 98 (*JSP*, D4:398).

73. Stevenson, *Reminiscences of Joseph*, 4.

74. Stevenson, Autobiography, 19–20, 65. The harvest period for Jonathan apples is normally in mid to late September, while the harvest season for Red Delicious apples is normally from late September to early October.

75. Minutes, Aug. 17, 1835, Minute Book 1, 98–106 (*JSP*, D4:382–96); also published in "General Assembly," *LDS Messenger and Advocate*, Aug. 1835, 161–64; and "General Assembly," D&C, 1835 ed., 255–57.

76. The reason for Whitmer's absence may have been his continued objection to publishing Smith's revelations. He had been present but did not sign the Testimony attesting to the truth of Smith's revelations in early November 1831 and did not attend the following week to discuss plans to publish them. Minutes, Nov. 1–2, 1831, Minute Book 2, 15–16 (*JSP*, D2:94–98); Minutes, Nov. 8, 1831, Minute Book 2, 16–17 (*JSP*, D2:121–24).

God." John Smith added that "we have at length receivd the long wished for document to govern the church in righteousness and bring the Elders to see eye to eye."[77] An article in the May 1835 issue of the *Messenger and Advocate* said the Doctrine and Covenants would give church members "a perfect understanding of the doctrine believed by this society."[78] It was voted that "they would receive the Book as the rule of their faith & practice, and put themselves under the guidance of the same."[79] The publication of Smith's revelations was another important step in stabilizing charismatic authority.

At the meeting, Phelps read "a chapter of Rules for Marriage among the saints" and Cowdery read "an instrument containing certain principles or items upon laws in general. & church government," both of which were accepted and ordered to be printed in the book.[80] The authorship of the two documents is not stated in the minutes, but historians have generally attributed both to Cowdery.[81] The statement on marriage may have been written so that priesthood members could claim the right to solemnize marriages. Several months earlier the Geauga County Court of Common Pleas denied Rigdon a license to perform marriages partly because he was not a "regularly ordained minister of the gospel, within the meaning of the [1824] Statute [on marriage]."[82] While that statute permitted "religious societies" to perform marriages "agreeably to the rules and regulations of their respective churches," Rigdon could point to no such provision among the Mormons.[83] The statement required that all marriages be performed legally and publicly with a properly-worded covenant, and that they be recorded by a clerk.

The statement on marriage also took occasion to deny rumors that the church endorsed fornication and polygamy. Among other things, it stated: "Inasmuch as this church of Christ has been reproached with the crime of fornication, and polygamy: we declare that we believe, that one man should have one wife."[84] Later claims by Utah Mormons, particularly Brigham

---

77. Minutes, Aug. 17, 1835, Minute Book 1, 103–104 (*JSP*, D4:393–94).

78. Editorial, *LDS Messenger and Advocate*, May 1835, 122.

79. Minutes, Aug. 17, 1835, Minute Book 1, 104 (*JSP*, D4:394).

80. Minutes, 106 (*JSP*, D4:396); Statement on Marriage, ca. Aug. 1835, D&C, 1835 ed., 251–52, sec. CI (*JSP*, D4:476–78); Declaration on Government and Law, ca. Aug. 1835, D&C, 1835 ed., 252–54, sec. CII [D&C 134] (*JSP*, D4:482–84).

81. *JSP*, D4:384, 476.

82. State of OH v. Sidney Rigdon, Mar. 7, 1835, Geauga Co., OH, Court of Common Pleas, Final Record, vol. M, 380–81.

83. An Act Regulating Marriages [Jan. 6, 1824], *Statutes of Ohio*, 2:1407, sec. 2.

84. Statement on Marriage, ca. Aug. 1835, in D&C, 1835 ed., 251 (*JSP*, D4:477–78). The Article on Marriage was removed from the Doctrine and Covenants in 1876.

Young, that Cowdery had included the proclamation disavowing plural marriage over Smith's objections are not credible.[85] After public acknowledgment in 1852 that some Mormons were practicing plural marriage, the 1835 statement denying the practice was difficult to explain. According to Young, Smith had rejected Cowdery's proposal, stating he would "have nothing to do with it."[86] In 1869 Joseph F. Smith recorded in his diary that Young explained that "Cowdry wrote it, and incisted on its being incerted in the Book D.&C. contrary to the thrice expressed wish and refusal of the Prophet Jos. Smith."[87] In 1835, Young was in the east with the Twelve and in 1869 gave no authority or source for his assertions. Moreover, Smith seemingly approved of the statement, referring to it when he subsequently performed marriages. On December 3, 1835, he recorded in his journal that he joined his scribe Warren Parrish and Martha H. Raymond in wedlock "according to the articles, and covenants of the Church of the latter day Saints."[88]

In asserting that Smith opposed the statement on marriage, Young implied that Smith was at this time privately espousing the need for a restoration of polygamy as practiced by the patriarchs, which is also suspect. Rather, it makes more sense to interpret the denial as a response to accusations dating back to as early as 1831 that the Mormons believed in communal wives. These accusations may have stemmed from the Morley Family's possible sympathy for similar Owenite communities, which practiced a form of free love. The *Evangelical Magazine and Gospel Advocate*, for instance, reported on February 5, 1831, that the Mormons "have all things in common, and dispense with the marriage covenant."[89] Recalling his 1832 visit to the Kirtland area, Henry Carroll said: "It was claimed all things were common, even to free love, among the Mormons at Kirtland."[90] Cowdery's use of the phrase "fornication, and polygamy" seems to refer to such accusations.[91]

The general assembly also voted unanimously to accept the declaration regarding governments and laws in general. Among other things, the declaration stated: "We believe that all men are bound to sustain and uphold the

---

85. Hales, *Joseph Smith's Polygamy*, 1:156–58.

86. Brigham Young, Discourse, Sep. 8, 1867, in George D. Watt, Discourse Shorthand Notes, Sep. 8, 1867, Pitman Shorthand Transcriptions, CHL, cited in *JSP*, D4:467.

87. Joseph F. Smith, Diary, Oct. 9, 1869; Joseph F. Smith, "Plural Marriage," July 7, 1878, *Journal of Discourses*, 20:29.

88. *JSP*, J1:70; see also under Jan. 14 and 20, 1836, where Joseph Smith performed marriages "according to the rules and regulations of the Church of the Latter Day Saints" (*JSP*, J1:104, 116).

89. "Infatuation," *Evangelical Magazine and Gospel Advocate* (Utica, NY), June 18, 1831, 198.

90. Henry Carroll, Statement to Arthur B. Deming, *Naked Truth about Mormonism* (Oakland, CA), Apr. 1888, 3.

91. See Hales, *Joseph Smith's Polygamy*, 1:165–68.

respective Governments in which they reside, while protected in their inherent and inalienable rights by the laws of such Governments, and that sedition and rebellion are unbecoming every citizen thus protected, and should be punished accordingly; and that all Governments have a right to enact such laws as in their own judgments are best calculated to secure the public interest, at the same time, however, holding sacred the freedom of conscience." This declaration should be read as a subtle criticism of Missouri for having forced the Mormons out of Jackson County in 1833. "We believe that Rulers, States and Governments have a right, and are bound to enact laws for the protection of all citizens in the free exercise of their religious belief; but we do not believe that they have a right, in justice, to deprive citizens of this privilege, or proscribe them in their opinions, so long as a regard and reverence is shown to the laws, and such religious opinions do not justify sedition nor conspiracy."[92]

It also may be read as a justification for Zion's Camp and the planned second attempt at Zion's redemption: "We believe that men should appeal to the civil law for redress of all wrongs and grievances, where personal abuse is inflicted, or the right of property or character infringed, where such laws exist as will protect the same; but we believe that all men are justified in defending themselves, their friends and property, and the Government, from the unlawful assaults and encroachments of all persons, in times of exigencies, where immediate appeal cannot be made to the laws, and relief afforded."[93]

Finally, the declaration contained a statement intended to alleviate the fears of the slaveholders in Jackson County: "We do not believe it right to interfere with bond-servants, neither preach the gospel to, nor baptize them, contrary to the will and wish of their masters, nor to meddle with, or influence them in the least to cause them to be dissatisfied with their situations in this life, thereby jeopardizing the lives of men: interference we believe to be unlawful and unjust, and dangerous to the peace of every Government allowing human beings to be held in servitude."[94] As Smith was planning to return to Jackson County in the spring, the leadership was preparing the way by adopting a noninterference position on the slavery question. The previous February, the church founded a Democratic-leaning paper called the *Northern Times*, edited by Cowdery, which opposed abolition.[95]

---

92. Declaration on Government and Law, ca. Aug. 1835, in D&C, 1835, ed., 252–53 [D&C 134:5, 7] (*JSP*, D4:483).

93. D&C, 1835, ed., 253 [D&C 134:11] (*JSP*, D4:484).

94. D&C, 1835, ed., 253–54 [D&C 134:12] (*JSP*, D4:484).

95. See Crawley, *Descriptive Bibliography*, 1:51–53; "Abolition," *Northern Times* (Kirtland, OH), Oct. 9, 1835, [2].

Patriarchal Blessings

Although Smith and Williams returned to Kirtland on August 23,[96] Smith would not resume the Abraham project until October. On September 11 Phelps wrote to his wife in Missouri: "Nothing has been doing in the translation of the Egyptian Record for along time, and probably will not for some time to come."[97]

On August 27 Joseph Smith Sr. held a patriarchal blessing meeting in which many were blessed, including Martin Harris.[98] Lorenzo Snow, who attended one of the senior Smith's patriarchal blessing meetings in the Kirtland temple in 1836, later recalled how he was impressed by the content of the blessings. "After listening to several patriarchal blessings pronounced upon the heads of different individuals with whose history I was acquainted, and of whom I knew the Patriarch was entirely ignorant," Snow said, "I was struck with astonishment to hear the peculiarities of those persons positively and plainly referred to in their blessings. I was convinced that an influence, superior to human prescience, dictated his words."[99] Upon examination, the blessings tend mostly to contain occasional generalized statements to which recipients attach meanings. The blessings provide a glimpse into early LDS culture, give fatherly advice, and make promises about receiving power and witnessing mass conversions, the redemption of Zion, and the Second Coming.

On September 2 Smith, Cowdery, and others went to New Portage, Ohio, to attend a conference on the 4th and preach on the following day. Little else is known other than they returned to Kirtland on the 8th.[100]

On Sunday, September 13, Smith presided at a meeting in the unfinished temple. According to Truman O. Angell, who worked on the temple as a carpenter, the "meeting assembled in the Temple on a loose floor which had been arranged for carpenters benches," and "the house was partly filled, the people being seated on work benches and other things."[101] Smith displayed the new still-blank Patriarchal Blessing Book, which had been purchased "by a contribution of the Saints in Kirtland, in the latter part of the year 1834," and then

---

96. JS History, vol. B-1, 606 (DHC 2:253).

97. W. W. Phelps, Letter to Sally Phelps, Sep. 11, 1835, [2]; Van Orden, "Writing to Zion," 563.

98. Patriarchal Blessing Book, 1:16–20, 28, 138–39.

99. LeRoi C. Snow, "How Lorenzo Snow Found God," *Improvement Era*, Feb. 1937, 83–84.

100. JS History, vol. B-1, 612 (DHC 2:273); Notice, *LDS Messenger and Advocate*, July 1835, 153. On September 2, 1835, Frederick G. Williams noted in his account book: "for O. Cowdery's & others expenses to New Portage 3.00." F. G. Williams & Co. Account Book, Sep. 2, 1835.

101. Truman O. Angell, Autobiography, 8–9.

handed it to a group of men to be examined.[102] A Brother Aldrich apparently complained that the large leather-bound book was too expensive. He may have also insinuated that church leaders asked for more money than they needed and kept the rest for themselves. Joseph and Hyrum Smith reprimanded Aldrich, accusing him of being "under the influence of an evil spirit."[103]

On Monday, September 14, Smith presided at a meeting of the high council where it was decided that "the laborer is worthy of his hire" and therefore that Joseph Smith Sr. was to be paid $10 per week as a patriarch plus expenses.[104] Frederick Williams was appointed a scribe and recorder of blessings and also compensated at $10 per week plus expenses; and Oliver Cowdery was to be appointed Church Recorder, charging ten cents per folio or per one hundred words.[105] In accordance with a July 1830 revelation, the council instructed Emma Smith to prepare a new selection of hymns to be printed by Phelps.[106]

Meanwhile, Henry Green was voicing his disapproval of how Joseph and Hyrum Smith treated Aldrich the previous day. At a meeting of the high council on Wednesday, September 16, Joseph Smith issued a complaint against Green and a high council court was convened. Sylvester Smith testified that Green said that "brother Aldrich was justified in what he said, and that Presidents Joseph & Hyrum Smith were wrong in abusing the old man," and that "if any man should do so by him, he should call him a scoundrel, and that he should say that any man who would talk as Joseph did must have the Devil in him." Lorin Babbitt said he heard Green say that although the Smith brothers accused Aldrich of "having an evil Spirit, yet if the truth was known the Devil was in them. ... For if any man should ask my opinion and then abuse me in this way, I should call him a scoundrel or a knave." The council found that Smith was justified in rebuking Aldrich and that Green was wrong to criticize him. The "Presidency of the High council," which included Smith, decided that "brother Green be & is now excluded from this church, and shall be a member no more until he come in by the ordinance

102. See George A. Smith and Wilford Woodruff, "A History of this Record," Patriarchal Blessing Book, vol. 1, front flyleaf; also Jonathan M. Holmes, Statement, Feb. 7, 1843, JS Collection.

103. See Minutes, Sep. 16, 1835, Minute Book 1, 108–113 (*JSP*, D4:415–20). The Joseph Smith Papers editors are probably correct in arguing that the "Brother Aldrich," described as an "old man," was sixty-seven-year-old Andrew Hazen Aldrich, father of Hazen Aldrich, who was present in Kirtland in August 1835. *JSP*, D4:389n171, 415–20.

104. Minutes, Sep. 14, 1835, Minute Book 1, 107 (*JSP*, D4:414). See Luke 10:7; D&C 31:5; 84:79; 106:3.

105. Cowdery, "Account Book of Writing," 1.

106. Minutes, Sep. 14, 1835, Minute Book 1, 108 (*JSP*, D4:414–15). See D&C 25:11.

of baptism." This was agreed to by the entire council except Joseph Coe, who suggested that Green be allowed to confess and retain his membership and, if not, there should be a rehearing since Green was late to the meeting. As the council was about to adjourn, Coe demanded an explanation from Smith, who responded: "When a heinous crime is committed & indignity offered to the high council then it is the privilege of the Presidency of the High council to stamp it with indignation under foot & cut off the offender as in the case just decided." Coe withdrew his objection.[107]

The minutes of Green's trial show how both office and hierarchy insulated Smith from criticism. Samuel H. Smith said that "President [Joseph] Smith was in the lines of his duty when he reproved bro. Aldridge for his evil, and consequently brother Green must have been wrong in opposing him." Levi Jackman said that "brother Green could not be justified in opposing the servant of the Lord, while in the actual discharge of his duty." Frederick Williams said that Green had acted "foolishly … in questioning the integrity of the heads of the church."[108]

On September 22 Smith dictated blessings for David Whitmer, John Whitmer, John Corrill, and Phelps, which Oliver Cowdery recorded and then copied into the Patriarchal Blessing Book.[109] In copying them, Cowdery wrote that they were "given … by vision, to Joseph Smith, jr. the Seer, September 22, 1835, and recorded Oct. 2, 1835."[110] On September 22 Cowdery made the first entry in Smith's new journal: "This day Joseph Smith, jr. labored with Oliver Cowdery, in obtaining and writing blessings. We were thronged a part of the time with company, so that our labor, in this thing, was hindered; but we obtained many precious things, and our souls were blessed. O Lord, may thy Holy Spirit be with thy servants forever. Amen." Following Cowdery's entry, Smith echoed: "This day Joseph Smith, Jr. was at home writing blessings for my most beloved Brotheren," then added: "I, have been hindered by a multitude of visitors but the Lord has blessed our Souls this day."[111]

Among the visitors Smith and Cowdery received were Ezra Thayer and Noah Packard, the latter of whom loaned the building committee $1,000. Smith jubilantly wrote in his journal: "Oh! may God bless him a hundred

---

107. See Minutes, Sep. 16, 1835, Minute Book 1, 108–13 (*JSP*, D4:416–20).
108. Minutes, 110–11 (*JSP*, D4:417–18).
109. Patriarchal Blessing Book, 1:13–15.
110. Patriarchal Blessing Book, 1:14.
111. Smith, Journal, Sep. 22, 1835 (*JSP*, J1:61–62).

fold! even of the things of [the] Earth, for this ritious [righteous] act. My heart is full of desire to day, to be blessed of the God, of Abraham; with prosperity, untill I will be able to pay all my depts; for it is the delight of my soul to be honest; Oh Lord that thou knowes[t] right well! help me and I will give to the poor."[112]

The blessings Smith pronounced on these men reflected their roles in the approaching redemption of Zion. Among other things, Smith said in blessing David Whitmer that "the Lord hath appointed [him] to be the captain of his host," and that under Smith's leadership, he would "build up the waste places of Zion." Smith predicted that Whitmer would become "a mighty shaft ... in the quiver of the Almighty in bringing about the redemption of Zion, and in avenging the wrongs of the innocent," and promised that "he shall yet stand upon the land of Zion, from whence he has been driven, and shall find inheritance there; and shall be a ruler in Zion until he is old and well stricken in years."[113]

In blessing John Whitmer, Smith referred to his calling as Church Historian, saying that "he shall make a choice record of Israel unto the memory of his name" and promised that "he shall be made mighty in the hands of his God in bringing to pass the redemption of Zion."[114] Of Corrill, Smith declared that "there are none that surpass him in understanding pertaining to architecture: unto this end hath the Lord raised him up, ... for he shall build the house of the Lord in Zion."[115] Of Phelps, Smith said: "He shall be a wise lawyer in Israel. ... Behold, he shall have understanding in all sciences and languages, and with his brother Oliver [Cowdery] shall write and arrange many books for the good of the church, that the young may grow up in wisdom: these shall remain for a memorial unto their names." Smith also promised Phelps that "his days shall be prolonged upon the land of Zion," where he would live until he was "old and bowed down with many years."[116]

In the evening, Cowdery blessed Smith. When he copied it into the blessing book, Cowdery wrote an introduction explaining that after recording the blessings of the four Missouri leaders "at the mouth of the Seer," he

---

112. Smith (*JSP*, J1:62).

113. Joseph Smith, Blessing to David Whitmer, Sep. 22, 1835; copied Oct. 2, 1835, Patriarchal Blessing Book, 1:13–14 (*JSP*, D4:429–30).

114. Joseph Smith, Blessing to John Whitmer, Sep. 22, 1835; copied Oct. 2, 1835, Patriarchal Blessing Book, 1:14 (*JSP*, D4:432–33).

115. Joseph Smith, Blessing to John Corrill, Sep. 22, 1835; copied Oct. 3, 1835, Patriarchal Blessing Book, 1:14 (*JSP*, D4:433–34).

116. Joseph Smith, Blessing to William W. Phelps, Sep. 22, 1835; copied Oct. 3, 1835, Patriarchal Blessing Book, 1:14–15 (*JSP*, D4:435–36).

"greatly desired to know the mind of the Spirit concerning my brother, with whom I had labored so many years." He accordingly "besought the Lord in prayer and fasting, who opened the heavens upon me, and thus, while in the heavenly vision, I wrote the following blessing, which is a part of that which was shown and declared should come upon my brother: therefore, let no one doubt their correctness and truth; for they will verily be fulfilled."[117]

Cowdery's blessing emphasized Smith's role as a translator of ancient records, including the sealed portion of the gold plates and other Nephite records. "The records of past ages and generations, and the histories of ancient days shall he bring forth: even the record of the Nephites shall he again obtain, with all those hid up by Mormon, and others who were righteous, and many others, till he is overwhelmed with knowledge." Cowdery's promise that the "Urim and Thummim" should remain "in his hands" probably refers to Smith's possession of the brown stone used in translating the Book of Mormon as well as a white stone, both of which date to the early days of Smith's activities as a treasure seer. Alluding to Smith's recent instruction on priesthood that mentioned the evangelical priesthood being handed down among the patriarchs after Adam, Cowdery declared that Smith would continue to possess "the keys of the evangelical priesthood, also, for an everlasting priesthood forever, even the patriarchal; for, behold, he is the first patriarch in the last days. He shall sit in the great assembly and general council of patriarchs, and execute the will and commandment of God under the direction of the Ancient of Days." In closing, Cowdery promised Smith that "he shall remain to a good old age, even till his head is like the pure wool. ... Thus closes the vision, and thus it shall be."[118]

---

117. Oliver Cowdery, Blessing, to Joseph Smith, Sep. 22, 1835; copied Oct. 3, 1835, Patriarchal Blessing Book, 1:15 (*JSP*, D4:437–41).

118. Patriarchal Blessing Book, 1:15–16 (*JSP*, D4:437–41).

20

Abraham's Cosmology

For it was a maxim among the rabbins, that "whatsoever was in the earth, the same was also found in heaven."
—*Adam Clarke,* The Holy Bible, Containing the Old and New Testaments ..., *Gal. 4:26*

On September 24, 1835, Smith met with the high council in his home to discuss "the redeemtion of Zion." During the meeting, Smith said, "It was the voice of the spirit of the Lord" instructing him to petition Missouri governor Daniel Dunklin to restore the Saints to their lands in the "spring," adding that "we go next season to live or dy [die] ... in Jackson County."[1] John Whitmer recorded in his history that the leadership of the church's "war department" was organized "by revelation" at this meeting, and that David Whitmer was "appointed ... Capt of the Lords hosts," with Frederick Williams and Rigdon as his assistants, and that Smith was named as "the seer to stand at the head," with Hyrum Smith and Cowdery as assistants.[2] Smith underscored the seriousness of this meeting when he wrote: "We truly had a good time and Covena[n]ted to struggle for this thing u[n]till death shall disolve this union and if one falls that the rest be not discouraged but pe[r]sue this object untill it is acomplished which may God grant u[n]to us in the name of Christ our Lord." Articles of Enrollment were drawn up listing the names of volunteers willing to go with the army of Israel to Missouri in the spring to redeem Zion. Smith prayed, "I ask God in the name of Jesus that we may obtain Eight hundred men or one thousand well armed and that they may acomplish this great work even so Amen."[3]

---

1. Smith, Journal, Sep. 24, 1835 (*JSP*, J1:64).
2. Whitmer, History, 81, (*JSP*, H2:90).
3. Smith, Journal, Sep. 24, 1835 (*JSP*, J1:64).

Return of the Twelve

On September 26 the Twelve returned to Kirtland in the morning from their six-month mission to the east and Canada.[4] In the evening, the presidency, consisting of Smith, Rigdon, David Whitmer, Phelps, John Whitmer, Hyrum Smith, and Cowdery, met to consider criticisms of the Twelve. First, Warren A. Cowdery's August 4 letter from Freedom, New York, complaining that the Twelve had not properly instructed them about donating money to build the temple was judged to be false. Second, regarding the letter William McLellin wrote to his wife complaining about Rigdon's school, which was based on information he had received from Orson Hyde, McLellin and Hyde were found to be at fault—they confessed and were forgiven.[5]

On Sunday, September 27, Smith attended a meeting at which apostles Thomas Marsh, David Patten, Brigham Young, and Heber Kimball preached. Afterward, Smith wrote in his journal: "The Lord poured out his Spirit, and my soul was edified."[6] On the following day Smith and Cowdery attended a meeting of the high council, which met to try Gladden Bishop on a charge preferred by the Twelve "for advancing heretical doctrines which were derogatory to the character of the church."[7] While conducting a conference in Bradford, Massachusetts, the previous month, the Twelve discovered that Bishop "had erred in Spirit and in Doctrine and was considerably inclined to enthusiasm and much lifted up." At this time, the council suspended Bishop "until he become more instructed and also get his spirits and feelings amalgamated with his brethren."[8] He appealed to the high council in Kirtland, which sustained the decision of the Twelve. After Bishop confessed and asked for forgiveness, he was restored to full fellowship and ordained an elder.[9]

In later years, Brigham Young interpreted the Bishop trial in a way to support the view that the Twelve were superior to the high council, adding an addendum to Smith's history in which Smith declared a later understanding of the Twelve's authority: "An attempt was made in the foregoing council to criminate the Twelve before the High Council for cutting off Gladdon Bishop, at their Bradford Conference; but the attempt totally failed. I decided that the High Council had nothing to do with the Twelve, or the decisions of the

---

4. Smith, Journal, Sep. 26, 1835 (*JSP*, J1:64).

5. Minutes, Sep. 26, 1835, Minute Book 1, 119 (*JSP*, D4:442).

6. Smith, Journal, Sep. 27, 1835 (*JSP*, J1:66).

7. Minutes, Sep. 28–29, 1835, Minute Book 1, 120 (*JSP*, D4:449).

8. Record of the Twelve Apostles, Aug. 7, 1835.

9. Minutes, Sep. 28, 1835, Minute Book 1, 120–22 (*JSP*, D4:450–51).

Twelve; but if the Twelve erred they were accountable only to the General Council of the authorities of the whole church, according to the Revelation."[10]

The revelation Young referred to was Smith's 1835 instructions on priesthood (D&C 107), which only mentioned equality among the presiding quorums that included the high council in Kirtland.[11] The minutes indicate that there was "much altercation … whether [Bishop's] case could be legally brought before this court or not, which was decided in the affirmative."[12] At a January 16, 1836, meeting of the Twelve, it was discussed how their feelings were "hurt on account of some remarks made by President H[yrum]. Smith on the trial of Gladden Bishop," because he insinuated that their previous trial of Bishop had been "discountenanced." At the same meeting, it was mentioned that it was the Twelve "who had by their request thrown [Bishop's] case before the high council in Kirtland for investigation."[13] In doing so, they may have followed the precedence of allowing those tried by councils of high priests "abroad" to "appeal to the high Council at the seat of the general government of the Church, and have a re-hearing."[14] Bishop himself remembered that the discussion "condemn[ed], the unhallowed, tyranical course of the twelve, which very much mortified their pride."[15] Although the high council sustained the decision of the Twelve regarding Bishop—deciding that it had been made "in righteousness"—tensions between the Twelve and other church leaders in Kirtland continued.

The next day, Smith and Cowdery attended two trials. One involved Phineas H. Young for borrowing copies of the Book of Mormon and selling them. Later the same day, Cowdery complained that Lorenzo Young had called at Smith's house and declared that poor people should not have children. Both Youngs confessed and were forgiven.[16] Concerning the activities of this day, Smith wrote: "In all these I acted on the part of the defence for the accused to plead for mercy. The Lord blessed my soul, and the council was greatly blessed, also. Much good will no doubt, result from our labors during the two days in which we were occupied on the business of the Church."[17]

---

10. JS History, vol. B-1, Addenda, 2, Note E (DHC 2:285), which was added by Willard Richards between May 12–June 7, 1845. This addition was based on Brigham Young Memoranda for Book B-1, ca. May 10–July 1845. Vogel, *History of Joseph Smith*, 2:475n31; 7:540–41.

11. See discussion in Quinn, *The Mormon Hierarchy*, 156–60.

12. Minutes, Sep. 28, 1835, Minute Book 1, 120 (*JSP*, D4:449).

13. Smith, Journal, Jan. 16, 1836 (*JSP*, J1:157).

14. Revised Minutes, Feb. 18–19, 1834, Minute Book 1, 34–35 [D&C 102:24, 27] (*JSP*, D3:443).

15. Saunders, *A Transcription of "Zion's Messenger,"* 32.

16. Minutes, Sep. 28–29, 1835, Minute Book 1, 124–25 (*JSP*, D4:452–55).

17. Smith, Journal, Sep. 29, 1835 (*JSP*, J1:66–67).

Cowdery Begins Recording Blessings

In mid-late September 1835, Cowdery began copying blessings Joseph Smith Sr. had given to his children and their spouses in December 1834 on the first eight pages of the new Patriarchal Blessing Book.[18] From late September to October 2, Cowdery copied Joseph Jr.'s December 18, 1833, blessings of his parents, brothers Hyrum, Samuel, William, and Don Carlos, and Cowdery on pages 9–12.[19] Then, on October 2, Cowdery copied the mid-November 1833 blessings of Frederick Williams and Rigdon on page 13, which Cowdery mistakenly dated to December 18, 1833.

Comparison between Cowdery's 1835 copies and the 1833 versions in Smith's journal shows that the blessings were altered and expanded, presumably under Smith's direction.[20] As the editors of the Joseph Smith Papers observe, "Most sections of the 1835 texts are expansions of and alterations to the earlier blessing texts, while other passages correspond word for word." Specifically, they further observe, "over eighty percent of the text of JS's blessing for his father and mother is not found in the earlier journal version. Nearly ninety percent of the text of JS's blessing to Don Carlos Smith is new or different from the earlier journal version, and an even greater portion of the blessing to Oliver Cowdery is new or altered. In the 1835 patriarchal blessing book, the texts of JS's blessings to Sidney Rigdon and Frederick

---

18. Patriarchal Blessing Book, 1:1–8 (Marquardt, *Early Patriarchal Blessings,* 11–19). Cowdery began recording Joseph Sr.'s December 9, 1834, blessings of his children and their spouses into the Patriarchal Blessing Book sometime between September 15 and 28, 1835. The first recording date is September 28, 1835, which appears at the end of the blessing for Samuel H. Smith on page 10. Cowdery apparently began copying the blessing after September 15, 1835, because that is the date on which Joseph Sr. blessed his youngest son, Don Carlos, and his new wife Agnes, which Cowdery copied on pages 7–8.

19. Hyrum's blessing is dated September, Samuel and William's September 28, Don Carlos' October 1, and Cowdery's October 2, 1835.

20. The Joseph Smith Papers editors acknowledge Cowdery expanded the blessings Smith gave to Cowdery, Williams, Rigdon, and Smith family members in November and December 1833 when he transcribed them into the new Patriarchal Blessing Book in September 1835. However, they are reluctant to involve Smith in the expansions and place the blessings into an appendix because "JS's role in the expansions is not clear." *JSP,* D4:487. They argue that Smith's journal only states that he worked with Cowdery on September 22, when the blessings of the Missouri brethren were composed. D4:486. "In summary, there is no direct evidence that JS was involved in expanding and editing the 1833 blessings in September or October of 1835, and there are reasons to think he was not—but there remains a possibility that he, with Cowdery, authored the alterations to those blessings around the same time he bestowed blessings on John and David Whitmer, John Corrill, and William W. Phelps on 22 September 1835." D5:509. However, Smith's journal is far from comprehensive and is also silent about the expansions Smith had previously made to his earlier revelations. That said, it is possible that Cowdery sometimes acted independently with Smith's approval.

G. Williams contain, respectively, sixty-six and seventy-nine percent new or different words from the journal versions."[21]

Nevertheless, as he had done with the expansions to Smith's earlier revelations, Cowdery tried to conceal the fact that the blessings had been altered. At the time Cowdery recorded the blessings, he noted that they "were given by vision and the spirit of prophecy, on the 18th of December, 1833, and written by my own hand at the time; and I know them to be correct and according to the mind of the Lord." He then claimed that the blessings, as recorded in the book, contained "the words which fell from [Joseph Smith's] lips while the visions of the Almighty were open to his view."[22]

As a bridge between the blessings of father Smith and his prophet son, Cowdery explained that Joseph Sr. got his authority to give blessings from Joseph Jr., who was "the first elder, and first patriarch of the church." He then outlined various angelic visitations Smith had received, beginning with the angel who had revealed the gold plates, followed by the angel who ordained him and Smith prior to their baptisms: "He was ordained by the angel John, unto the lesser or Aaronic priesthood, in company with myself, in the town of Harmony, Susquehannah County, Pennsylvania, on Fryday, the 15th day of May, 1829, after which we repaired to the water, even to the Susquehannah River, and were baptized, he first ministering unto me and after—I to him."[23] Cowdery had not named the angel in his letter to Phelps the previous September, but here he reflects information from Smith's expansion of his September 1830 revelation, which mentioned that John the Baptist ordained Smith and Cowdery "unto this first priesthood which you have received, that you might be called and ordained even as Aaron."[24]

Cowdery further explained that prior to this first reception of authority, "our souls were drawn out in mighty prayer—to know how we might obtain the blessings of baptism and of the Holy Spirit, according to the order of God." He then drew on language Smith had recently used in his translation of the first three verses of the Book of Abraham:[25]

---

21. *JSP*, D5:508.

22. Patriarchal Blessing Book, 1:9 (Marquardt, *Early Patriarchal Blessings*, 3).

23. Patriarchal Blessing Book, 1:8 (Marquardt, 3).

24. Revelation, Sep. 4, 1830 [ca. Aug. 1835], D&C, 1835 ed., L:2 [D&C 27:8] (*JSP*, D4:411).

25. Book of Abraham Manuscript-C, 1 [Abr. 1:2] (*JSP*, R4:219); Patriarchal Blessing Book, 1:8–9 (Marquardt, *Early Patriarchal Blessings*, 3).

Book of Abraham Manuscript Phelps (ca. July 1835)	Patriarchal Blessing Book Cowdery (late September 1835)
"I *sought* for the blessings of the *fathers*, and the *right* whereunto I should be ordained to *administer the same*: Having been a *follower of righteousness*; *desiring* to be one who *possessed great Knowledge*; a greater follower of righteousness; a *possessor of greater knowledge*; …"	"and we diligently *saught* for the *right* of the *fathers* and the authority of the holy priesthood, and the *power to ad-min[ister] in the same*: for we *desired* to be *followers of righteousness* and the *possessors of greater knowledge*, even the knowledge of the mysteries of the kingdom of God."

By late September 1835, Phelps had entered the opening verses of the Book of Abraham into the translation book, which Cowdery may have had access to, if not in manuscript form. After this, Cowdery made a direct reference to the papyrus Smith had identified as the record of ancient Joseph: "Therefore, we repaired to the woods, even as our father Joseph said we should, that is to the bush, and called upon the name of the Lord, and he answered us out of the heavens, and while we were in the heavenly vision the angel came down and bestowed upon us this priesthood; and then, as I have said, we repaired to the water and were baptized."[26]

The first blessing Cowdery copied was Smith's December 18, 1833, blessing of his father, but the material added to Joseph Sr.'s blessing did not exist until 1835. Using language from Smith's 1835 instructions on priesthood (D&C 107), the 1833/1835 blessing emphasized Smith Sr.'s calling as a patriarch, an office he did not occupy until a year after the original 1833 blessing: "Blessed of the Lord is my father, for he shall stand in the midst of his posterity and shall be comforted by their blessings when he is old and bowed down with years, and shall be called a prince over them, and shall be numbered among those who hold the right of patriarchal priesthood, even the keys of that ministry: for he shall assemble together his posterity like unto Adam; and the assembly which he called shall be an ensample for my father."[27] The blessing then quoted directly from Smith's expansion about Adam blessing his posterity and Jesus Christ appearing to them in

---

26. Patriarchal Blessing Book, 1:8–9 (Marquardt, *Early Patriarchal Blessings*, 3).
27. Patriarchal Blessing Book, 1:9 (*JSP*, 4:488; Marquardt, *Early Patriarchal Blessings*, 4).

"the valley of Adam-ondi-ahman."[28] Smith Jr. continued: "So shall it be with my father: he shall be called a prince over his posterity, holding the keys of the patriarchal priesthood over the kingdom of God on earth, even the Church of the Latter Day Saints; and he shall sit in the general assembly of patriarchs, even in council with the Ancient of Days when he shall sit and all the patriarchs with him—and shall enjoy his right and authority under the direction of the Ancient of Days."[29]

On October 2, 1835, Cowdery copied a blessing into the Patriarchal Blessing Book that Smith gave to him in 1833, which was now expanded to reflect Cowdery's new status as the officer in the church next to Smith in authority, explaining that Cowdery "shall sit in the council of the patriarchs, with his brother Joseph and with him have part in the keys of that ministry when the Ancient of Days shall come. ... For he shall have part with me in the keys of the kingdom of the last days, and we shall judge this generation by our testimony: and the keys shall never be taken from us, but shall rest with us for an everlasting briesthood [priesthood], forever and ever. ... He shall be equal in the councils of Israel." The expanded 1835 blessing then referred to a second angelic ordination Smith and Cowdery had received, which also fulfilled the prophecy of ancient Joseph:

> These blessings shall come upon him [Cowdery] according to the blessings of the prophecy of Joseph, in ancient days, which he said should come upon the Seer of the last days and the Scribe that should sit with him, and that should be ordained with him, by the hand of the angel in the bush, unto the lesser priesthood, and after receive the holy priesthood under the hands of those who had been held in reserve for a long season; even those who received it under the hand of the Messiah, while he should dwell in the flesh, upon the earth, and should receive the blessings with him, even the Seer of the God of Abraham, Isaac and Jacob, saith he, even Joseph of old.[30]

Cowdery did not name the ancient apostles, but Smith's 1835 expansion of the 1830 revelation not only mentioned the appearance of John the Baptist but also "Peter, and James, and John, whom I have sent unto you,

---

28. Patriarchal Blessing Book, 1:9 (*JSP*, 4:488; Marquardt, *Early Patriarchal Blessings*, 4). Compare Instruction on Priesthood, ca. Mar. 1–May 4, 1835, D&C, 1835 ed., III:28–29 [D&C 107:53–55] (*JSP*, D4:317).

29. Patriarchal Blessing Book, 1: 9 (*JSP*, 4:488; Marquardt, *Early Patriarchal Blessings*, 4). See Dan. 7:9–10; and Revelation, Sep. 4, 1830 [ca. Aug. 1835], D&C, 1835 ed., L:2 [D&C 27:11] (*JSP*, D4:411).

30. Patriarchal Blessing Book, 1:12 (*JSP*, D5:513–14; Marquardt, *Early Patriarchal Blessings*, 8–9).

by whom I have ordained you and confirmed you to be apostles."[31] This expanded revelation retroactively provided Smith and Cowdery with authority to organize the Quorum of Twelve Apostles, which they had done the previous February 1835, while the expansion to the 1831 revelation gave the new apostles authority to "ordain evangelical ministers," or patriarchs.[32]

The new 1835 emendation of Cowdery's blessing also omitted a phrase that was critical of him, one that admonished him to forsake the "two evils in him" and warned that if he failed to do so he would be unable to "escape the buffettings of the advers[ar]y."[33] He also turned a conditional phrase into a positive declaration. The phrase promised blessings *if* Cowdery kept the commandments and obeyed council, but as he copied it into the book it became: "He shall be helped out of all his troubles *because* he shall keep the commandments of the Lord and hearken unto all his council."[34] Similar to an 1829 revelation that promised him with ability to translate ancient Nephite records, Cowdery's expanded blessing promised that "he shall be blessed with the blessings of the lasting hills ... even the records that have been hid from the first ages, from generation to generation he shall be an instrument in the hands of his God, with his brother Joseph, of translating and bringing forth to the house of Israel."[35]

Cowdery's late September 1835 introduction to Joseph Sr.'s blessings and the expanded portion of the blessing Cowdery had received from Joseph Jr. in 1833 strongly suggest that Smith and Cowdery might use the Egyptian papyri as pseudepigraphic evidence not only to support their recent introduction of angelic ordinations but also the 1831 introduction of the high priesthood, the 1834 introduction of the patriarchal priesthood, and the 1835 organization of the Quorum of Twelve Apostles.

Celestial Hierarchy[36]

While copying blessings, Cowdery took a break on the first of October to work with Smith and Phelps on the Egyptian alphabet. Later that day, Cowdery wrote in Smith's journal, apparently from dictation: "This after

---

31. Revelation, Sep. 4, 1830 [ca. Aug. 1835], D&C, 1835 ed., L:3 [D&C 27:12] (*JSP*, D4:411).

32. Instruction on Priesthood, Mar. 1–May 4, 1835, D&C, 1835 ed., III:17 [D&C 107:53–55] (*JSP*, D4:316).

33. Smith, Journal, Dec. 9, 1833 (*JSP*, J1:22–23).

34. Compare Smith, Dec. 9, 1833 (*JSP*, J1:23); and Patriarchal Blessing Book, 1:12 (*JSP*, D5:512).

35. Patriarchal Blessing Book, 1:12 (*JSP*, D5:512; Marquardt, *Early Patriarchal Blessings*, 8).

36. My treatment of Joseph Smith's translation of Abrahamic cosmology from the Hôr papyrus recapitulates some of my discussion in *Book of Abraham Apologetics*.

noon labored on the Egyptian alphabet, in company with brsr. O. Cowdery and W. W. Phelps: The system of astronomy was unfolded."[37] After a break of about two months, Smith resumed work on his "Grammar and Alphabet of the Egyptian Language," where the last seven characters (36–42) describe a hierarchy of stars and planets organized much in the same manner in which Smith had recently organized the priesthood authorities in his church.

Like Cowdery, Smith was no doubt aware of passages in Josephus that mentioned that the descendants of Seth were "the inventors of that peculiar sort of wisdom which is concerned with the heavenly bodies, and their order."[38] And also that Abraham had "communicated" to the Egyptians "arithmetic, and delivered to them the science of astronomy, before Abram came into Egypt, they were unacquainted with those parts of learning; for that science came from the Chaldeans into Egypt, and from thence to the Greeks also."[39] It is no surprise therefore that Smith would include a discussion of astronomy in his account of Abraham in Egypt. Smith's Abraham received knowledge from God through the Urim and Thummim, which, expectedly, comported with contemporary understandings of cosmology, not ancient conceptions based on belief in a flat earth.

The first character of the seven is "Jah-ni-hah," which is defined in the first degree as "one delegated with redeeming power; a swift messenger; one that goes before another; one having redeeming power, a second person in authority"—possibly referring to the Son, or Christ.[40] The fifth degree adds, "one ... sent from the Celestial Kingdom."[41]

The next character's name is "Jah-oh-eh"—the earth—and its definition in each of the degrees leads to the unfolding of Egyptian astronomy, with the fifth degree blossoming into a long and elaborate explanation of the whole subject. In the first degree, Jah-oh-eh is "The earth including its affinity with the other planets, with their govering powers: which are fifteen: the earth; the sun, and the moon, first in their affinity; including one power."[42] Here the text described the solar system as it was then understood, which, as one 1829 book on astronomy described it, consisted of "the Sun, eleven

37. Smith, Journal, Oct. 1, 1835 (*JSP*, J1:67).

38. Flavius Josephus, Antiquities of the Jews, Book 1, chap. 2, sec. 3, in Whiston, *Josephus Complete Works*, 27.

39. Antiquities of the Jews, Book 1, chap. 8, sec. 2, in Whiston, *Josephus Complete Works*, 33.

40. GAEL, 33 (*JSP*, R4:181).

41. GAEL, 24 (*JSP*, R4:163).

42. GAEL, 27, 29–30, 31, 33–34 (*JSP*, R4:169, 173–75, 177, 181–83).

primary Planets, and eighteen Moons."[43] This same source then names the eleven primary planets: "Mercury, Venus, the Earth, Mars, Vesta, Juno, Pallas, Ceres, Jupiter, Saturn, and Uranus."[44] German-born British astronomer William Herschel discovered the planet Uranus in 1781, but Neptune and Pluto were not observed until 1846 and 1930. Vesta, Juno, Pallas, and Ceres were counted as planets from 1808 until 1845, but are now considered large asteroids in the asteroid belt between Mars and Jupiter. Thus Smith's text referred to the eleven primary planets, the sun and moon, and two yet-to-be-discovered planets. Smith elaborated on this system in the fifth degree:

> Jah-oh-eh The earth under the governing powers of oliblish, Enish go on dosh, and Kai-e van rash, which are the grand governing key or in other words, the governing power, which governs the fifteen fixed stars (twelve besides themselves) that governs the earth, sun, & moon, (which have their power in one,) with the other twelve moving planets of this system. Oliblish=Enish go on dosh, and Kaie ven rash, are the three grand central powers that govern all the other creations, which have been sought out by the most aged of all the fathers, since the begining of the creation, by means of the urim and Thummim.[45]

The pattern of fifteen "fixed stars," consisting of three "grand central stars" and twelve "fixed stars," as well as fifteen "moving planets" reflects Smith's recent organization of his church hierarchy. In February 1834, Smith organized the "standing" high council in Kirtland, which included three presidents and twelve high priests. In July 1834, Smith organized another high council to preside over the church in Missouri, again with three presidents and twelve high priests. In February 1835, the Quorum of Twelve Apostles was organized. Described as the "Traveling Presiding High Council," they operated under the direction of the three presiding presidents.[46]

In October 1835, as Smith dictated his Egyptian cosmology, the Kirtland temple was under construction and the plans for the first floor included a system of pulpits at the east and west ends of the hall, one for the Melchizedek Priesthood leaders and the other for the Aaronic Priesthood leaders. At the center of the west end of the hall were four ascending levels of three pulpits each, where the presidencies of the various quorums sat during meetings. Smith and his two counselors sat at the top. On the right were the

---

43. Banks, *Astronomy*, 19.
44. Banks, 19.
45. GAEL, 24 (*JSP*, R4:163).
46. D&C 102:3; 107:33.

twelve apostles, and on the left the twelve Kirtland high counselors. Thus Smith's text projected his priesthood organization into the heavens.

Administrative Duties

On October 2, while Cowdery was copying blessings into the Patriarchal Blessing Book, Smith "wrote a letter to be published in the Messenger and Advocate."[47] He wrote this letter, and two others to follow, to the "elders traveling through the world," whose mission it was "to warn the inhabitants of the earth to flee the wrath to come." In the letter, Smith explained why the Mormons settled in Jackson County, that "the very spot" had been designated by revelation as the "central spot" for the gathering of the believers and the "upbuilding of an holy city, which should be called Zion—Zion because it is to be a place of righteousness." He responded to "designing and wicked men" who claimed Mormons wanted to get Jackson County land "unlawfully" by force, declaring that such was never their intent. Rather, their plan was "to purchase, *with money*, lands, and live upon them—not infringing upon the civil rights of any individual, or community of people." Nevertheless, he acknowledged that misunderstanding occurred when "many [Mormons] ... having a zeal not according to knowledge, not understanding the pure principles of the doctrine of the church, have no doubt, in the heat of enthusiasm, taught and said many things which are derogatory to the genuine character and principles of the church; and for these things we are heartily sorry, and would apologize if apology would do any good."[48]

No apology would have been acceptable to Jackson Countians, because they had no intention of allowing the Mormons to take over their county. Smith had chastised church leaders in Missouri in a July 31, 1832, letter for allowing "ignorant & unstable Sisters, & weak members ... [to] prophe[s]y falsly which excites many to believe that you are putting up the Indians to slay the Gentiles which exposes the lives of the Saints evry where."[49] Missourians would have questioned the genuineness of such an apology since a denial that the Mormons were in league with the Indians was not the same as denying their potential to do so in the future, as the Book of Mormon prophesied.[50]

---

47. Smith, Journal, Oct. 2, 1835 (*JSP*, J1:67).

48. Joseph Smith, Letter to "the Elders of the Church of Latter Day Saints," Oct. 2, 1835, *LDS Messenger and Advocate* (Kirtland, OH), Sep. 1835, 179–80 (*JSP*, D5:7–10). The publication of the *Messenger* was evidently about a month behind schedule. Cf. D&C 52:2, 42; 57:1–3.

49. Joseph Smith, Letter to William W. Phelps, July 31, 1832, 5, JS Collection (*JSP*, D2:266).

50. Book of Mormon, 1830 ed., 488, 497, 500, 501 [3 Ne. 16:15; 20:16–17; 21:12, 23]; Micah 5:8–9.

Still, the Mormons had every intention of buying out or driving out the non-Mormon settlers and turning the county into their theocratic Zion, as the plat of the city of Zion clearly shows.[51] No force or league with the Indians was necessary since, as Jackson Countians understood, the Mormons would inevitably possess the entire county by their sheer numbers, which the non-Mormons were unwilling to allow.

In the remainder of the letter, Smith instructed the elders to teach the "first principles of the gospel, which are repentance, and baptism for the remission of sins, and the gift of the Holy Ghost by the laying on of the hands," and quoted many Bible passages in support.[52] This instruction was perhaps intended to curb discussion of prophecy and plans dealing with Zion.

On October 3 Smith participated in a case brought before the high council against John Gould, who was visiting Kirtland from Freedom, New York. Gould allegedly "ma[de] expressions ... calculated to do injury to the great cause which we have espoused and manifesting a very strong dissatisfaction against the teachings of the Presidency of the church."[53] According to Smith's journal, Gould was charged "for giving credence to false and slanderous report instigated to Injure bro Sidney Rigdon."[54] It is unknown why Gould was so upset, but he ultimately confessed and was forgiven. In the afternoon, Smith entertained most of the Twelve at his home, exhibiting and explaining to them some of the ancient Egyptian records, while Cowdery continued copying blessings.[55]

On October 5 Smith attended a meeting of the Twelve and told them it was God's will that they should move their families to Missouri the following spring. He also instructed them to attend the school of the prophets in the fall and observe the ordinance of the washing of feet, which had been performed when the school had been organized in 1833 (D&C 88:136–39). Afterward, Smith wrote in his journal: "May God spare the lives of the twelve with one accord to a good old age for christ the redeemers sake amen."[56]

On October 6 Smith visited his sick father and stayed until early evening, returning the next day to administer herbal medicine and pray: "May God

51. The editors of the Joseph Smith Papers note, "Attempts to implement the plan of Zion would have necessitated major changes in existing roads and structures and undoubtedly caused significant political strife." *JSP*, D3:124.

52. Joseph Smith, Letter to "the Elders of the Church of Latter Day Saints," Oct. 2, 1835, *LDS Messenger and Advocate*, Sep. 1835, 180–82 (*JSP*, D5:10–15).

53. Minutes, Oct. 3, 1835, Minute Book 1, 126 (*JSP*, D5:15–18).

54. Smith, Journal, Oct. 3, 1835 (*JSP*, J1:67).

55. Smith (*JSP*, J1:68); Patriarchal Blessing Book, 1:14–16.

56. Smith, Journal, Oct. 5, 1835 (*JSP*, J1:68).

grant to restore him immediately to health for Christ the redeemers sake Amen."[57] The same day, Smith pronounced a blessing on Newel Whitney, which was recorded in his journal by Frederick Williams and in the Patriarchal Blessing Book by Cowdery.[58] Cowdery prefaced his transcription: "The following blessing was given by president Joseph Smith, Jr. through the Urim and Thummim, according to the spirit of prophecy and revelation."[59] In association with his recent translation of the Egyptian papyri, Smith apparently resumed using a seer stone.

Translation Recommenced

On October 7 Frederick Williams made an entry in Smith's journal that the Mormon prophet had "recommenced translating the ancient records."[60] By "recommenced," Williams probably meant since October 1, when Egyptian astronomy began to be unfolded. Continuing, Smith defined the 38th character—the moon—as the "lesser light" that passes between the earth and sun "forming an eclipse." However, his definitions of the 39th character—Flos isis, or the sun—are surprising because the sun, while described as "the King of the day," is also considered a "central moving planet, from which, those other gove[rn]ing moving planets receive their light."[61]

In referring to the sun as both *central* and *moving* as well as a *planet*, Smith was reflecting the belief in his day, especially among natural theologians, that the solar system was part of a larger system that moved around other systems, which in turn moved around the throne of God. Commenting on the phrase "heaven of heavens" in Deuteronomy 10:14, Bible commentator Adam Clarke said that "the words were probably intended to point out the immensity of God's creation, in which we may readily conceive one system of heavenly bodies, and others beyond them, and others still in endless progression through the whole vortex of space, every *star* in the vast abyss of nature being *a sun*, with its peculiar and numerous attendant worlds! Thus there may be systems of systems in endless gradation up to the throne of God."[62] In his book *Philosophy of a Future State*, first published in

---

57. Smith (*JSP*, J1:69).

58. Smith, Journal, Oct. 7, 1835 (*JSP*, J1:69–70; *JSP*, D5:18–21); Patriarchal Blessing Book, 1:33–34 (Marquardt, *Early Patriarchal Blessings*, 54–55).

59. Patriarchal Blessing Book, 1:33 (Marquardt, *Early Patriarchal Blessings*, 54).

60. Smith, Journal, Oct. 7, 1835 (*JSP*, J1:71). Frederick Williams's handwriting appears in Joseph Smith's journal for October 3–7, 1835.

61. GAEL, 34 (*JSP*, R4:183).

62. Clarke, *The Holy Bible*, Deut. 10:14.

Philadelphia in 1825, natural theologian Thomas Dick commented on the phrase "throne of God":

> It is now considered by astronomers, as highly probable, if not certain, from late observations, from the nature of gravitation, and other circumstances, that all the systems of the universe revolve round one common centre,— and that this centre may bear as great a proportion, in point of magnitude, to the universal assemblage of systems, as the sun does to his surrounding planets. And, since our sun is five hundred times larger than the earth, and all the other planets and their satellites taken together; on the same scale, such a central body would be five hundred times larger than all the systems and worlds in the universe. Here, then, may be a vast universe of itself; an example of material creation, exceeding all the rest in magnitude and splendour, and in which are blended the glories of every other system. If this is in reality the case, it may, with the most emphatic propriety, be termed, *The Throne of God.* ... This grand central body may be considered as the *Capital* of the universe.[63]

Smith's definition of Flos-isis moved beyond the sun to include in the fourth degree "the high[es]t degree of light," which illuminates "the face of Millions of planets."[64] This is elaborated in the fifth degree to describe a grand center of light:

> Flos isis— The highest degree of light, because its component parts are light. The gover[n]ing principle of light Because God has said Let this be the centre for light, and let there be bounds that it may not pass. He hath set a cloud round about in the heavens, and the light of the grand govering or 15 fixed stars centre there; and from there its is drawn, by the heavenly bodies according to their portions; according to the decrees that God hath set, as the bounds of the ocean, that it should not pass over as a flood, so God has set the bounds of light lest it pass over and consume the planets.[65]

Smith believed the sun was in an orbit around this grand light center, which is why he described it as both a central and moving planet. Indeed, he included the name of the sun—Flos-isis—among the fifteen moving planets. In referring to the sun as a planet, Smith reflected the belief among contemporaries that all the planets were inhabited worlds, including the sun.

---

63. Dick, *Philosophy of a Future State*, 224–25. Dick's book was discussed by Oliver Cowdery in *LDS Messenger and Advocate*, Nov. 1836, 423.

64. GAEL, 28 (*JSP*, R4:171).

65. GAEL, 25 (*JSP*, R4:165).

Astronomer William Herschel was one of the earliest from the scientific community to receive popular notice for his ideas about the inhabitants of the sun and moon. As one scholar summarized his views, Herschel "thought it [was] possible that there was a region below the Sun's fiery surface where men might live, and he regarded the existence of life on the Moon as 'an absolute certainty.'"[66] The Reverend J. L. Blake's *First Book in Astronomy, Adapted to the Use of Common Schools*, which went through many editions, included a discussion about the sun in 1831.

> [The sun] was formerly supposed to consist of liquid fire. ... By modern astronomers this theory has been found untrue. They have supposed, with more plausibility, that it is a solid body, surrounded by a luminous atmosphere. ... The similarity of the sun to the other globes of the system, in solidity, atmosphere, surface diversified with mountains and vallies, and rotation on its axis, lead us to conjecture that it is inhabited, like the rest of the planets, by beings whose organs are adapted to their peculiar circumstances. Dr. Elliot, an English astronomer, allows his imagination, in speaking of it, to depict the most delightful rural scenery, with purling brooks, meandering streams, and rolling oceans, and with all the vicissitudes of foul and fair weather. And as the light of the sun is eternal, so he imagined, were its seasons. Hence, the Doctor infers, that this luminary offers one of the most blissful habitations which the mind of man is capable of conceiving.[67]

A revelation Smith dictated in 1832 became poetic in its description of God's creation when it declared: "The earth rolls upon her wings, and the sun giveth her light by day, and the moon, giveth her light by night, and the stars also giveth there light as they roll upon, there wings, in there glory in the midst, of the power, of God." The revelation then asked: "Unto what shall I liken *these kingdoms*, that ye may understand"? The answer was given in the form of a parable in which a farmer visits his servants one at a time working in different areas of a field and concludes, "unto this parable, will I liken all *those kingdoms* [i.e., the earth, sun, moon, and stars]; and *the inhabitants thereof.* "[68] The parable implies that the earth, sun, moon, and stars are inhabited, which is precisely how early Mormons understood it. Hyrum Smith alluded to this revelation when he declared in a public discourse in

---

66. Moore, *New Guide to the Moon*, 128. See also Kawaler and Veverka, "The Habitable Sun"; and Schaffer, "'The Great Laboratories of the Universe.'"

67. Blake, *First Book in Astronomy, Adapted to the Use of Common Schools*, 16, 17–18.

68. Revelation, Dec. 27–28, 1832, Revelation Book 2, 37–38 [D&C 88:45–46, 51–57, 60–61] (*JSP*, D2:339–40); emphasis added.

Nauvoo in 1843 that *"every* Star that we see is a world and is inhabited the same as this world is peopled. The Sun & Moon is inhabited & the Stars … are inhabited the same as this Earth. … They are under the same order as this Earth."[69]

Returning to the bound Grammar, characters 40 and 41—Kli-flos-isis and Veh-Kli-flos-isis—are measurements of time dealing with the twelve fixed stars. Three of the degrees for Veh-Kli-flos-isis as well as all five degrees of the last character, Kolob—numbers 41 and 42—are written in the handwriting of Warren Parrish, whom Smith hired as a scribe on October 29, 1835.[70] Smith saved the best for last, for in the fifth degree we are told "Kolob. signifies the first creation nearer to the celestial [kingdom], or the residence of Lord, first in government, the last pertaining to the measurement of time, the measurement according to celestial time which signifies, one day to a cubit which day is equal to a thousand years according to the measurement of this Eearth or Jah=oh=eh."[71]

The length of Kolob's revolution recalls Thomas Dick's speculations about the enormity of the throne of God and the vastness of the system in orbit around it. However, the slowness of Kolob's revolution conflicts with definitions Smith previously dictated in early October 1835 where Kolob is one of twelve fixed stars under the rule of the three grand ruling stars and is described as "swifter than the rest of the twelve fixed stars; going before, being first in motion."[72]

In the first degree we are told "Kolob … signifies the first great grand governing fixed Star which is the fartherest that ever has been discovered by the fathers which was discovered by Methuselar and also by Abraham."[73] And in the second degree that "Kolob … signfies the wonder of Abraham the eldest of all the stars, the greatest body of the heavenly bodies that ever was discovered by man."[74] Perhaps Smith was familiar with Josephus' statement that the descendants of Adam's son Seth were "the inventors of that peculiar sort of wisdom which is concerned with the heavenly bodies, and their order."[75] And, also, that Abraham had "communicated" to the Egyptians "the science

69. Laub, Reminiscences and Journal, Apr. 27, 1843.

70. Smith, Journal, Oct. 29, 1835 (*JSP*, J1:76).

71. GAEL, 26 (*JSP*, R4:167).

72. GAEL, 25 (*JSP*, R4:165).

73. GAEL, 34 (*JSP*, R4:183).

74. GAEL, 32 (*JSP*, R4:179).

75. Antiquities of the Jews, Book 1, chap. 2, sec. 3, in Whiston, *Josephus Complete Works*, 27.

of astronomy."[76] Later, in Nauvoo in 1842, when Smith dictated chapter 3 of the Book of Abraham, he drew on this material in the Grammar (Abr. 3:1–4).

Domestic and Family Concerns

On October 8 Smith again visited his ill father, attending to his needs for several days. On Sunday, October 11, Smith prayed that his father would be restored to health, so that "I might be blessed with his company and advice, esteeming it one of the greatest earthly blessings to be blessed with the society of parents, whose mature years and experience renders them capable of administering the most wholesome advice." He wrote that he received the word of the Lord: "My servant, thy father shall live." Later that same evening, Smith and David Whitmer laid hands on Joseph Sr. and "rebuked the disease," after which the elder Smith arose, got dressed, and joined in the singing.[77] Two days later, on October 13, Smith visited his father, who had fully recovered, and then on the 15th helped Joseph Sr. pick apples in his orchard.[78]

On October 16 Smith was called into the printing office to settle a difficulty. In the evening, Smith went to the nearby Chagrin River and baptized nineteen-year-old Ebenezer Robinson, who had been working in the printing shop since May.[79] Shortly after Robinson had moved in with the Smiths as a boarder, Smith said to him, "When you are baptized I want to baptize you." Robinson made no reply, but about two months later he requested Smith to baptize him. Smith responded that he would attend to it later in the afternoon. "We then went to the printing office together, he to his council room which adjoined the room where I worked, and I to my work in the printing office. I worked until well on to the evening, feeling very anxious all the time, for it seemed that I could not live overnight without being baptized; after enduring it as long as I could, went to the door of [his] room, and gently opened it, (a thing I had never presumed to do before). As soon as Mr. Smith saw me he said, 'Yes, yes, brethren, Brother Robinson wishes to be baptized, we will adjourn and attend to that.'" After baptism, Robinson said, "I shouted aloud, 'Glory to God.' My heart was full to overflowing, and I felt that I had born again in very deed, both of water and of the spirit." In

---

76. Antiquities of the Jews, Book 1, chap. 8, sec. 2, in Whiston, 33.

77. Smith, Journal, Oct. 8–11, 1835 (*JSP*, J1:71).

78. Smith, Journal, Oct. 8, 13, 15, 1835 (*JSP*, J1:72).

79. Smith, Journal, Oct. 16, 1835 (*JSP*, J1:72); Ebenezer Robinson, "Items of Personal History of the Editor," *Return*, May 1889, 74.

coming out of the river, Robinson said Smith remarked to the brethren, "I am not afraid of Brother Robinson ever denying the faith."[80]

It may have been due to financial troubles when Smith wrote in his journal that he "called my family together and arranged my domestic concerns, and dismissed my boarders."[81] At least three men who worked in the print shop—Robinson, Samuel Brannan, and Phelps—apparently boarded with Smith at this time. Phineas Young, Wilbur Denton, and Don Carlos Smith, who had moved in with Smith in 1833, may have still been there.[82]

On Sunday, October 18, Smith attended a meeting in the unfinished temple, confirmed Robinson and several others who had been baptized, and blessed some children.[83] According to John Whitmer, "The Spirit of the Lord decended upon J. Smith Jr—the seer and he prophec[i]ed: saying the L[or]d has showd to me this day by the Spirit of Revelation that the distress, and sickness that has heretofore prevaled among the children of Zion will be mitigated from this time forth."[84] There is no record that the Mormon community was experiencing an unusual rate of illness at this time. It may be that Smith was promising that the upcoming redemption of Zion would not include a repeat of the cholera epidemic that had spread among the members of Zion's Camp in June 1834.

On October 23 Smith met with the presidents of the Missouri and Ohio churches and others to pray for God to relieve them of their debts and to "deliver Zion in the appointed time and that without the shedding of blood" and that God "will give us the blessings of the earth sufficient to carry us to Zion, and that we may purchase inheritances in that land."[85]

On Sunday, October 25, Smith attended church and heard Rigdon preach in the morning and Lyman E. Johnson in the afternoon. After the meeting, Smith witnessed Seymour Brunson marry William Perry and Eliza

---

80. Ebenezer Robinson, "Items of Personal History of the Editor," *Return*, Apr. 1889, 58; and May 1889, 74. I have changed Robinson's habit of speaking of himself in the plural to the singular. Following Joseph Smith's death, Robinson was affiliated a short time with Sidney Rigdon's organization, then baptized into the Reorganized Church of Jesus Christ of Latter Day Saints in 1863, and later joined David Whitmer's Church of Christ in 1888. He edited *The Return*, 1889-91, which was a Whitmerite periodical.

81. Smith, Journal, Oct. 17, 1835 (*JSP*, J1:72).

82. Ebenezer Robinson, "Items of Personal History of the Editor," *Return*, July 1889, 104; W. W. Phelps, Letter to Sally Phelps, Sep. 16, 1835; Smith, Journal, Nov. 22, 1833; and Dec. 9 and 11, 1833 (*JSP*, J1:21).

83. Smith, Journal, Oct. 18, 1835 (*JSP*, J1:72–73); Ebenezer Robinson, "Items of Personal History of the Editor," *Return*, May 1889, 74–76.

84. Whitmer, History, 81–82 (*JSP*, D5:21–23; H2:90).

85. Smith, Journal, Oct. 23, 1835 (*JSP*, J1:73, 111; *JSP*, D5:23–25).

Brown and blessed them "with long life and prosperity in the name of Jesus Christ."[86] Later that day, Smith attended a prayer meeting and exhorted the members for about one hour. Afterward, he recorded: "The Lord poured out his Spirit, and some glorious things were spoken in the gift of tongues, and interpreted, concerning the redemption of Zion."[87]

On October 26 Smith accompanied his brothers Hyrum, Samuel, and Don Carlos to the County Court in Chardon to answer charges against Samuel for not fulfilling his military duties. Samuel was fined $20 plus court costs because he was unable to show that he was exempt as a minister.[88] Joseph blamed their attorney, Benjamin Bissell, for not telling them to bring the proper documents. Evidently they brought a certificate signed by Frederick Williams stating that Samuel was an elder but did not bring proof of Williams's official status as clerk of the conference.[89] The judgment forced Samuel to sell one of his cows to pay the court.[90] Joseph was angry at Bissell and accused him of intentionally aiding the "ungodly" in their effort to exercise "unlawful power over us, and trample us under their unhallowed feet," and also cursed the court "in the name of Jesus Christ that the money that they have thus unjustly taken shall be a testimony against them and canker & eat their flesh as fire."[91]

On the morning of October 27, Smith was called to Samuel's home because his pregnant wife, Mary, was in a dangerous condition. Don Carlos was sent nine miles to Chardon after Frederick Williams, a Botanic or Thomsonian physician. Joseph went out into a field to pray and received inspiration that Mary would "be delivered of a living child, and be spared" from death.[92] In the evening, he preached in the schoolhouse to a large congregation.[93]

On October 29 Smith hired Warren Parrish to write for him at $15.00 per month and gave him a $16.00 advance out of the temple committee's store. Parrish wanted to find housing, so Smith agreed to pay him $19.00

---

86. Smith, Journal, Oct. 25, 1835 (*JSP*, J1:73). Brunson had obtained a license to perform marriages in Jackson County and may have been the only licensed Mormon. See Bradshaw, "Joseph Smith's Performance of Marriages in Ohio," 40.

87. Smith, Journal, Oct. 25, 1835 (*JSP*, J1:73).

88. State of OH v. Samuel Smith, Oct. 20, 1835, Geauga Co., OH, Court of Common Pleas, Final Record, vol. S, 97. This was an appeal from the decision of a court of inquiry held September 25, 1833, which had fined Samuel $1.75.

89. Smith, Journal, Oct. 26, 1835 (*JSP*, J1:75).

90. Samuel paid taxes on two cows in 1834–35. Cook, *Revelations*, 34.

91. Smith, Journal, Oct. 26, 1835 (*JSP*, J1:75).

92. Smith, Journal, Oct. 27, 1835 (*JSP*, J1:75–76; *JSP*, D5:25–26).

93. Smith, Journal, Oct. 26, 1835 (*JSP*, J1:76).

per month. Parrish began immediately to write for Smith, during which they noticed Bishop Partridge arriving from the east through the window.[94] Later that day, they were interrupted when Smith was called to testify at the high council concerning a complaint brought by his brother William against David Elliott of Willoughby for whipping his fifteen-year-old daughter, leaving marks on her arms and body. Based on his previous investigation of the parties in Willoughby, Joseph defended Elliott. Afterward, he wrote: "I was satisfied that the girl was in the fault, and that the neighbors were trying to create a difficulty."[95]

Instead of returning to their writing room, Smith decided that he and Parrish should go to Frederick Williams's house to get his "large journal." On the way, Smith "made some observations" to his scribe "concerning the plan of the city [of Kirtland], which is to be built up hereafter on this ground consecrated for a stake of Zion." While at Williams's house, Partridge and Phelps came in to examine the mummies that were being kept there.[96]

After Smith and Parrish returned to their "writing room" in Smith's home, Parrish began recording in the journal, concluding Cowdery's second letter to Phelps from the *Messenger and Advocate*, which Williams had begun.[97] Meanwhile, Whitney and his wife, Elizabeth, called on Smith with his non-Mormon parents, Samuel and Susanna, who had just arrived from Marlborough, Vermont. Edward Partridge and some others also called. At the request of Whitney's parents, Smith related the story of the coming forth of the Book of Mormon.[98]

In the afternoon, Smith attended a council where there was much debate. On returning home, Apostle John Boynton observed that long debates were not good, and Smith agreed, stating that "to[o] much, altercation was indulged in, on both sides and their debates protracted to an unprofitable length." Later, while Smith was at supper with Whitney and Partridge, Whitney said to Partridge that it occurred to him that in less than a year they could be seated around a similar table in the land of Zion—alluding to Smith's prediction that it would occur before September 11, 1836. Emma

94. Smith, Journal, Oct. 29, 1835 (*JSP*, J1:76); JS History, 1834–36, Oct. 29, 1835 (*JSP*, H1:105).
95. Minutes, Oct. 29, 1835, Minute Book 1, 127–29 (*JSP*, D5:27–29).
96. Smith, Journal, Oct. 29, 1835 (*JSP*, J1:76).
97. Smith, Journal, Oct. 29, 1835 (*JSP*, J1:76–77); JS History, 1834–36, Oct. 29, 1835 (*JSP*, H1:105). Cowdery had made two entries in the journal, December 5 and 6, 1834, and then skipped 24 pages, where he had Williams begin copying his eight historical letters to Phelps, which had appeared in the *Messenger and Advocate*. Williams had nearly completed the second letter on page 57, where Parrish's handwriting begins. *JSP*, H1:39.
98. Smith, Journal, Oct. 29, 1835 (*JSP*, J1:77).

expressed her wish that she could serve everyone at her table again "in the land of promise" and everyone concurred. Smith remarked in his journal: "my heart responded, amen; God grant it, I ask in the name of Jesus Christ."[99]

In the evening, accompanied by Emma and others, Smith attended the meeting of the high council and was asked to preside at the hearing of the continuation of the Elliott case. Lucy Smith was asked to testify, and she "began to relate circumstances that had been brought before the Church and settled," referring to the charges against Elliott settled earlier in the day. The council was now considering charges against Elliott's wife, Mary, for "abusing said E[lliott']s daughter ... and also abusing the rest of her children." Joseph said Lucy's testimony was irrelevant. William got angry and accused him of saying their mother was a liar. Joseph ordered William to sit down. William said he would only sit if Joseph "knocked him down." Parrish added in Smith's history that Joseph "became wounded and agitated in his feelings on account of the wilful and wicked stubbornness of his brother Wm." Joseph was about to leave when Joseph Sr. requested his son to stay. He complied, and the house was brought to order. The council decided that the charges were not fully sustained but that Elliott "ought to have trained his child in a way that she would not have required the rod at the age of fifteen years." Brother and Sister Elliott confessed, promised to do better, and were restored to fellowship.[100]

In the evening of the following day, Smith received an angry letter from William, who complained of being censured for his conduct at the council. Smith replied by letter that he was not responsible for what others did, that he thought they had departed on good terms, and that they should meet and talk.[101] The next day, October 31, William visited Joseph and Hyrum to discuss the situation, but he refused to be subjugated by the authority of the presidency and rushed out the door. A few hours later, William sent Smith his license and, according to Smith's journal, began to "spread the levanin [leaven] of iniquity among my brethren and especially prejudiced the mind of br. Samuel as I soon learned that he was in the streets exclaiming against me, which no doubt our enemys rejoiced at, and where the matter will end I know not." In the evening, after baptizing Newel Whitney's parents and

---

99. Smith.

100. Smith (*JSP*, J1:77–79); Minutes, Oct. 29, 1835, Minute Book 1, 127–29 (*JSP*, D5:28–29); JS History, 1834–36, Oct. 29, 1835 (*JSP*, H1:107).

101. Smith, Journal, Oct. 30, 1835 (*JSP*, J1:79–80). Neither letter that Joseph and William exchanged on this occasion is extant.

sister, Smith received a witness that William "would return to the church and repair the wrong he had done."[102]

On Sunday, November 1, Smith dictated a revelation for Reynolds Cahoon, a counselor in the Kirtland bishopric, that called him to repentance for "his iniquities his covetous and dishonest principles in himself and family" and for failing to "set his house in order." The previous August, Smith had brought charges against Cahoon before the high council for having "failed to do his duty in correcting his children, and instructing them in the way of truth & righteousness." After Smith read the revelation, Cahoon confessed and promised to do better.[103] On the same day, Smith attended church and heard John Corrill preach. During the afternoon meeting, Phelps spoke and Smith blessed some children.[104]

School of the Elders

On November 2, after spending the morning engaged in planning for the opening of the elder's school, Smith traveled with Rigdon, Cowdery, Williams, Parrish, and others to Willoughby Medical College to hear Dr. Daniel Peixotto lecture on physics. Peixotto, the first Jewish doctor to teach medicine in Ohio, had recently moved from New York City. Cowdery and Parrish approached Peixotto and invited him to teach Hebrew classes in Kirtland during the winter. Peixotto agreed and advised them to purchase appropriate books beforehand.[105]

After returning to Kirtland, a question arose about whether Williams or Cowdery should go to New York to make arrangements with a book bindery. Smith dictated a revelation that said Williams should not go unless he wanted to preach to his relatives.[106] It is unknown if Williams accompanied him, but soon after the revelation Cowdery left Kirtland for New York City, later explaining: "I went to purchase a bookbinding establishment and stock, and also a quantity of Hebrew books for the school."[107]

About this time, Artemus Millet and Lorenzo Young began plastering the

---

102. Smith, Journal, Oct. 31, 1835 (*JSP*, J1:80–81).

103. Smith, Journal, Nov. 1, 1835 (*JSP*, J1:81; *JSP*, D5:29–30); Minutes, Aug. 10, 1835, Minute Book 1, 96 (*JSP*, D4:380–82).

104. Smith, Journal, Nov. 1, 1835 (*JSP*, J1:81).

105. Smith, Journal, Nov. 2, 1835 (*JSP*, J1:82). See *JSP*, J1:82; *JSP*, H1:110; Grey, "'The Word of the Lord in the Original,'" 249–75.

106. Smith, Journal, Nov. 2, 1835 (*JSP*, J1:82; *JSP*, D5:30–32).

107. Oliver Cowdery, Letter to W. A Cowdery, Nov. 22, 1835, Cowdery Letterbook, 63. In his letter to John M. Henderson, dated November 2, 1835, Cowdery mentioned that he expected to "leave for New York in a day or two." Cowdery, Letterbook, 62.

outside of the temple.[108] In a letter to his wife in early November, Partridge wrote: "I expect that the house will not be finished till towards spring, though they push it as fast as they can. the lower windows are mostly in, and the lower room principally lathed. they are preparing to commence plastering soon."[109]

On November 3 Smith dictated a revelation that called the Twelve to repentance for their "covetous desires" and making themselves unequal, and warned that "they must all humble themselves before me, before they will be accounted worthy to receive an endowment, to go forth in my name unto all nations." The revelation named especially William Smith, David Patten, Orson Hyde, and William McLellin for unspecified sins. McLellin and Hyde had recently been chastised for criticizing Rigdon, and William Smith had gotten into a heated argument with Joseph Smith only a few days before. Nevertheless, all were called to "repent speedily and prepare their hearts for the solem assembly," which was to be held in the House of the Lord.[110] Hyde and McLellin visited Smith two days later and read the November 3 revelation. They were offended at first, but eventually admitted it was true. Brigham Young also came, read it, and accepted the reproof. Nevertheless, issues in the Twelve continued.[111]

Later the same day, Smith assisted in organizing the school of the prophets and "made some remarks upon the object of this school, and the great necessity of our rightly improving our time and reining up our minds to a sense of the great object that lies before us, viz: that glorious endowment that God has in store for the faithful." After dedicating the school, Smith attended a blessing meeting at Samuel Smith's home, where Joseph Sr. blessed Samuel's in-laws, Joshua and Susannah Bailey, and infant child, Susannah, then preached in the schoolhouse.[112] Smith began attending school regularly in the morning and lecturing on grammar in the evening on November 4.[113] George A. Smith remembered that he attended "the School of the Prophets, which school was held in the room under the Printing office, taught by Joseph Smith Jr. & Sidney Rigdon. I studied English Grammar about six weeks." Later, he said, "the school was removed to the attic story of the Temple."[114]

While many of Smith's followers recounted being immediately impressed

---

108. Smith, Journal, Nov. 2, 1835 (*JSP*, J1:96).
109. Edward Partridge, Letter to Lydia Partridge, Nov. 2–10, 1835, [2], JS Collection.
110. Smith, Journal, Nov. 3, 1835 (*JSP*, J1:83; *JSP*, D5:32–36).
111. Smith, Nov. 5, 1835 (*JSP*, J1:84).
112. Smith, Nov. 3, 1835 (*JSP*, J1:84).
113. Smith, Nov. 4, 1835 (*JSP*, J1:84).
114. George A. Smith, Memoir and Autobiography, 81.

by Smith's appearance and demeanor, this was not a universal experience. On November 6, for example, Smith met a man visiting Kirtland from the east, who expressed surprise that the Mormon prophet "was nothing but a normal man." Smith responded by quoting James 5:17–18, that "Elias was a man subject to like passions as we are"—yet God heard his prayers and performed great miracles. "Such is the darkness and ignorance of this generation," Smith wrote, "that they look upon it as incredible that a man should have any intercourse with his Maker."[115]

On November 7 Bishop Partridge and counselor Isaac Morley, who had recently returned to Kirtland from their fund-raising mission in the east, went to Smith to ask if they should return to Missouri or remain in Kirtland. Smith dictated a revelation that commanded them to remain in Ohio for a season and attend school while waiting for the solemn assembly.[116]

On Sunday, November 8, Smith went to church and heard Zerubbabel Snow preach in the morning and Joseph Young in the afternoon. Isaac Hill, who had previously been excommunicated for lying and trying to seduce a woman, confessed and asked to be forgiven. John Smith and Rigdon expressed reservations about Hill's confession, but Joseph spoke in his defense and convinced the two leaders that they were wrong. Hill was restored to fellowship. At home, Smith counseled John Smith and Rigdon, who both repented. At the same time, Smith received a revelation saying that John Whitmer and Phelps were "under condemnation before the Lord, for their iniquities." He also reprimanded John Corrill "for not partaking of the sacrament," and Emma Smith "for leaving the meeting before sacrament." Corrill repented. Emma "made no reply, but manifested contrition by weeping."[117]

Prophet Meets Prophet

On the morning of November 9, Smith was visited by an oddly-dressed man who introduced himself as "Joshua, the Jewish Minister." Although he fancied himself as a prophet, Joshua was, in fact, Robert Matthews, a religious eccentric who had recently been tried in New York for murder, for which he was acquitted but then imprisoned for four months for contempt of court and

---

115. Smith, Journal, Nov. 6, 1835 (*JSP*, J1:85).

116. Smith, Nov. 7, 1835 (*JSP*, J1:85; *JSP*, D5:36–37).

117. Smith, Nov. 8, 1835 (*JSP*, J1:85–86; *JSP*, D5:38–39). Phelps later scrape-erased "iniquities" in Smith's journal and wrote the word "errors," and also inserted "for which they made satisfaction the same day." This was likely done while Phelps worked on Smith's history with Willard Richards between 1842 and 1843 in Nauvoo.

for whipping his daughter.[118] After his release, Matthews discovered that he had lost the few followers he had and soon was on his way to Geauga County, apparently to meet Smith. What he intended is not clear, but if he thought to attach himself to Smith's organization or possibly to poach some of his converts, nothing materialized. During the course of their conversation, Smith related his early history, the first vision, the coming forth of the Book of Mormon, and the establishment of the Church of Christ, which Parrish recorded in his journal. In his recitation of the first vision, Smith said:

> A pillar of fire appeared above my head; it presently rested down upon me and filled me with joy unspeakable; a personage appeared in the midst of this pillar of flame, which was spread all around, and yet nothing consumed; another personage soon appeared like unto the first; he said unto me, "thy sins are forgiven thee"; he testified unto me that Jesus Christ is the Son of God; and I saw many angels in this vision. I was about fourteen years old when I received this first communication.[119]

As written by Parrish, the two personages were not identified, although the phrase "like unto the first" alludes to Hebrews 1:3, which describes Jesus as being in "the express image of his [Father's] person."[120] The fifth Lecture on Faith recently published in the Doctrine and Covenants signaled a move away from the strict modalism of the Book of Mormon and opened the possibility that the Father and Son could appear simultaneously, one as a personage of spirit and the other as a personage of tabernacle animated by the Holy Spirit or mind of the Father. This lecture thrice emphasized that the Son was made in "the express image and likeness of the personage of the Father."[121] According to Edward Stevenson, Smith had described his vision of the Father and Son during his visit to Pontiac, Michigan, the previous August.[122]

The two men went to a meeting, then dined together, after which Joshua started to explain world history in light of the prophecy in Daniel 2. The golden head, he said, was Nebuchadnezzar, king of Babylon, which is just about what everyone thought, but surprisingly he believed the "feet of the

---

118. Smith, Nov. 9, 1835 (*JSP*, J1:86–87; *JSP*, D5:39–47).

119. Smith, Journal, Nov. 9, 1835 (*JSP*, J1:88).

120. In March 1842, Joseph Smith said that in 1820 he saw "two glorious personages who exactly resembled each other in features, and likeness." Joseph Smith, "Church History," in *Times and Seasons*, Mar. 1, 1842, 707 (*JSP*, D9:181).

121. D&C, 1835 ed., 53–54. On the Book of Mormon's modalism, see Vogel, "The Earliest Mormon Concept of God"; Harrell, "*This Is My Doctrine,*" 109–11.

122. Edward Stevenson, Autobiography, 19–20, 65.

image are the government of these United States."[123] Matthews earlier taught that "President [Andrew] Jackson and his government were the toes of this image" and that "this was the last of the republican governments" and "declared this government at an end."[124] Matthews also said: "The silence spoken of by John the Revelator, which is to be in heaven for the space of half an hour, is between 1830 and 1851, during which time the judgments of God will be poured out; after that time there will be peace."[125] After a brief interruption, Matthews delivered a lecture on God's creation of light at Smith's request.[126]

Matthews stayed with Smith overnight, and in the morning the men continued conversing. When Smith inquired concerning his views on the resurrection, Matthews said the ancient apostle Matthias was resurrected in him, which was more like reincarnation than resurrection. Smith responded by telling him his doctrines were of the devil.[127] On the morning of their third day together, Smith told Matthews that he must leave. Smith wrote in his journal that in asking Matthews to depart, "I for once, cast out the devil in bodily shape, and I believe a murderer."[128]

Smith must have been intrigued by Matthews, having spent so much time with him. In some ways, Matthews may have reminded Smith of Luman Walters, one of his occult mentors in the 1820s in New York who also dressed differently and was similarly eccentric.[129] Soon after, the *Painesville Telegraph* reported: "The notorious impostor Matthias has performed a pilgrimage to the temple of the equally notorious Joe Smith, where he held forth his doctrines last week. It appears that the new pretender met with less encouragement than he anticipated from the Latter-Day-ites, and after a two days conference the *Prophets* parted, each declaring he had miraculously discerned a devil in the other!"[130]

Raising Expectations

On November 12 Smith met with nine of the Twelve and spoke to them about the ordinance of the washing of feet and the forthcoming solemn assembly and endowment. Regarding foot washing, Smith said: "This we have

---

123. Smith, Journal, Nov. 9, 1835 (*JSP*, J1:92).
124. Stone, *Matthews and His Impostures*, 167.
125. Smith, Journal, Nov. 9, 1835 (*JSP*, J1:93).
126. Smith (*JSP*, J1:95).
127. Smith, Nov. 10, 1835 (*JSP*, J1:95).
128. Smith, Nov. 11, 1835 (*JSP*, J1:95).
129. Quinn, *Early Mormonism and the Magic World View*, 117–20.
130. "Prophet Catch Prophet," *Painesville (OH) Telegraph*, Nov. 20, 1835, 3; italics in original.

not done as yet but it is necessary now as much as it was in the days of the Saviour, and we must have a place prepared, that we may attend to this ordinance, aside from the world."[131] Smith had introduced the foot-washing ordinance in the school of the prophets in 1833 but now connected it to the temple. Whereas other contemporary religious denominations viewed foot washing as an act of humility, Smith saw it as a purification ritual, which absolved recipients from the sins of the world.[132] Smith further explained: "The house of the Lord must be prepared, and the solem assembly called and organized in it according to the order of the house of God and in it we must attend to the ordinance of washing of feet ... that we may be one in feeling and sentiment and that our faith may be strong, so that satan cannot over throw us, nor have any power over us."[133]

Smith began to prepare the apostles' minds and raise expectations: "The endowment you are so anxious about you cannot comprehend now, nor could Gabriel explain it to the understanding of your dark minds, but strive to be prepared in your hearts, be faithful in all things that when we meet in the solem assembly ... we must be clean evry whit, let us be faithful and silent brethren, and if God gives you a manifestation, keep it to yourselves." Smith wanted to inspire charismatic experience without competition or challenges, and promised that "all who are prepared and are sufficiently pure to abide the presence of the Saviour will see him in the solem assembly."[134] A November 1831 revelation had similarly promised the elders a vision of deity, "not with the carnal neither natural mind, but with the spiritual."[135]

On November 13 Smith was visited by George Messinger Jr. of Bainbridge, New York, who came to Kirtland to inquire about the Hezekiah Peck family, Mormon converts from Chenango County then living in Clay County, Missouri. Messinger was a "Universalist Minister," who soon entered into a long debate with Smith, which was continued at Rigdon's house and lasted well into the evening. Smith and Rigdon "bore testimony to him of what we had seen and heard," evidently relating to Messinger their 1832 vision of three heavens. He "attempted to raise some objections but, the

---

131. Smith, Journal, Nov. 12, 1835 (*JSP*, J1:97).

132. "Footwashing," in *The Mennonite Encyclopedia*, 2:347; Grow, "'Clean from the Blood of This Generation,'" 131–34. Cf. John 13:4–17.

133. Smith, Journal, Nov. 12, 1835 (*JSP*, J1:98); see also Whitmer, History, 83 (*JSP*, H2:91).

134. Smith, Journal, Nov. 12, 1835 (*JSP*, J1:98–99).

135. Revelation, ca. Nov. 2, 1831, Revelation Book 1, 115 [D&C 67:10] (*JSP*, D2:110).

force of truth bore him down, and he was silent, although unbelieving."[136] Debate may have revolved around the existence of a temporary hell, which ultra-Universalists rejected.[137]

On November 14 Smith dictated a revelation calling Warren Parrish as his scribe, although Smith had hired him on October 29: "He shall see much of my ancient records, and shall know of hid[d]en things, and shall be endowed with a knowledge of hidden languages; and if he desire and shall seek it at my hand, he shall be privileged with writing much of my word, as a scribe unto me for the benefit of my people."[138] This alluded to his work on the Book of Abraham. About this time, Parrish made the last entries in Smith's "Grammar and Alphabet of the Egyptian Language," adding material to "Veh Kli flos-isis"—the "fo[u]rth fixed governing star"—at the ends of the fifth, fourth, and third degrees, and to "Kolob"—the "first creation nearer to the Celestial, or the residence of God"—at the end of all five degrees. Parrish also produced a short Book of Abraham Manuscript, covering Abraham 1:4–2:3, which he copied into the translation book following Phelps's transcription of the first three verses before adding fifteen more verses from Smith's dictation.[139]

On this day, Smith was visited by Erastus Holmes from Newbury, Ohio, who had recently been excommunicated from the Methodist church for receiving the Mormon Elders into his house. "I gave him a brief relation of my experience while in my juvenile years," Smith wrote, "say from six years old up to the time I received the first visitation of angels, which was when I was about fourteen years old; also the revelations that I received afterwards concerning the Book of Mormon, and a short account of the rise and progress of the church up to this date."[140] Smith may have begun with his leg operation at age seven, and he apparently included his first vision, although Parrish's reference to "first visitation of angels" is cryptic. Smith had told Robert Matthews earlier in the week, that in addition to the Father and Son he also saw angels. At the same time, Smith may have used the term angel with a special meaning. Within weeks, he will dictate the text of Abraham 1:15, which equates Jehovah with "the angel of his [God's] presence."[141]

---

136. Smith, Journal, Nov. 13, 1835 (*JSP*, J1:99). On Messinger as a preacher for the First Universalist Society of Smithville Flats, Chenango County, New York, see *JSP*, J1:99n137.

137. Miller, *The Larger Hope*, 111–26.

138. Smith, Journal, Nov. 13, 1835 (*JSP*, J1:99–100; *JSP*, D5:51–53).

139. See *JSP*, R4:89, 165–67, 171, 175, 179, 183, 203–15, 217–37.

140. Smith, Journal, Nov. 14, 1835 (*JSP*, J1:100).

141. See my discussion in the next chapter.

On Sunday, November 15, Smith attended a church meeting in the schoolhouse with Holmes and heard Rigdon preach on authority. After this meeting, Smith dined with Holmes, then attended another meeting where Isaac Hill's case was discussed and resolved after much controversy. Hill confessed and agreed to have it published in the *Messenger and Advocate*.[142]

On November 16 Smith "dictated a letter to the Advocate," which continued his previous letter "with a hope that it may be a benefit, and a means of assistance in their labors, while they are combating the prejudices of a crooked and perverse generation." He complained that his religion has been "misrepresented by almost all those whose crafts are in danger by the same" and that persecution has been the result of "false rumor and misrepresentations concerning my sentiments."[143] The main subject of the letter was the gathering of Israel in the last days: "Men and angels are to be co-workers in bringing to pass this great work; and a Zion is to be prepared, even a New Jerusalem, for the elect that are to be gathered from the four quarters of the earth, and to be established an Holy City, for the tabernacle of the Lord shall be with them."[144]

Smith argued that the Bible speaks of two Jerusalems, a new and an old: "Now many will be disposed to say, that this New Jerusalem spoken of, is the Jerusalem that was built by the Jews on the eastern continent: but you will see from Revelations, 21:2, there was a New Jerusalem coming down from God out of heaven, adorned as a bride for her husband. That after this the Revelator was caught away in the Spirit to a great and high mountain, and saw the great and holy city descending out of heaven from God. Now there are two cities spoken of here."[145] Smith's reasoning echoes Ether 13:3–5, which speaks of the New Jerusalem as being both built on the American continent and coming out of heaven. How John's vision of a New Jerusalem descending out of heaven proves there are two Jerusalems in different locations, as Smith maintained, is unclear.[146] John said in the previous verse that he saw "a new heaven and a new earth," but no one argued from this that there were two heavens and two earths. Smith's analysis differed from the mainstream interpretation that the New Jerusalem of Revelation 21:2

---

142. Smith, Journal, Nov. 15, 1835 (*JSP*, J1:100–101).

143. Smith, Nov. 16, 1835 (*JSP*, J1:101; *JSP*, D5:53–60); Joseph Smith, Letter to "the Elders of the Church of the Latter Day Saints," Nov. 16, 1835, *LDS Messenger and Advocate*, Nov. 1835, 209 (*JSP*, D5:54).

144. Smith, Letter (*JSP*, D5:55).

145. Smith, 210 (*JSP*, D5:57).

146. See discussion in Harrell, *"This Is My Doctrine,"* 418–21.

predicts that Jerusalem will be rebuilt. Adam Clarke linked the descent of the New Jerusalem with the belief among the Rabbis that in heaven there is a spiritual Jerusalem and that the earthly Jerusalem is merely a temporal counterpart to the ideal in heaven.[147]

Smith revived the old Puritan dream of America as the location of the New Jerusalem.[148] As Smith explained, "Now we learn from the Book of Mormon the very identical continent and spot of land upon which the New Jerusalem is to stand."[149] While the Book of Mormon locates the New Jerusalem on the "land northward" in the lands once occupied by the Jaredites, Smith's subsequent revelations located the holy city in Jackson County (Ether 13; D&C 57:1–2).

In closing, Smith instructed the elders not to proselytize children without the consent of their parents, wives without the consent of their husbands, or slaves and servants without the consent of their masters.[150] If Smith had any hope of redeeming Zion, he needed to ease tensions with the inhabitants of Jackson County by assuring them that Mormons respected slave owners.

On this day, Smith also dictated a letter and revelation in response to a letter from Harvey Whitlock. In his letter to Smith, Whitlock confessed his sins and asked the prophet to inquire of the Lord on his behalf with the prayer: "O breathe into the ears of thy servant the prophet, words suitably adapted to my case and situation."[151] In reading Whitlock's confession, Smith wrote that "the very flood gates of my heart were broken up; I could not refrain from weeping." The revelation that Smith dictated for Whitlock said: "Therefore let him prepare himself speedily and come unto you; even to Kirtland and inasmuch as he shall hearken unto all your council from henceforth he shall be restored unto his former state, and shall be saved unto the uttermost, even as the Lord your God liveth Amen."[152]

Later the same day, Alvah Beaman visited Smith asking for guidance. Smith told him it was the will of the Lord that he should move to Missouri in the spring. Still uncertain about what to do, Beaman requested a council to meet on his behalf. Accordingly, David Whitmer and others met in the

147. Clarke, *The Holy Bible*, Gal. 4:24–27; Rev. 21:2.

148. Vogel, *Religious Seekers*, 181–213.

149. Joseph Smith, Letter to "the Elders of the Church of the Latter Day Saints," Nov. 16, 1835, *LDS Messenger and Advocate*, Nov. 1835, 210 (*JSP*, D5:57).

150. Smith, 210–11 (*JSP*, D5:57–60).

151. Whitlock's letter was copied into Smith, Journal, Nov. 16, 1835 (*JSP*, J1:101–103).

152. Joseph Smith, Letter to Harvey Whitlock, Nov. 16, 1835, Smith, Journal, Nov. 16, 1835 (*JSP*, J1:101–105; *JSP*, D5:60–62).

evening and also advised Beaman that it was his duty to move to Missouri next spring. The same evening, Smith said it was "the word of the Lord" that Erastus Holmes should wait until he returned home to Newbury, Ohio, to be baptized, and that he should make the fifteen-mile trip by land instead of water because three men were lying in wait to take his life.[153] On the following day, November 17, Smith "exhibited the Alphabet of the ancient record" to Holmes and others; Smith then accompanied them to Frederick Williams's home to see the mummies. Afterward, Holmes started for Newbury and Smith returned home, dictated letters, and preached in the evening at the schoolhouse.[154]

On November 18 Smith, accompanied by his mother, wife, and Parrish, went to the home of Preserved Harris's in Mentor, Ohio, at about 11:00 a.m. and preached about the resurrection at the funeral of Nathan Harris, father of Martin and Preserved Harris. In the evening, Smith, at Bishop Whitney's invitation, attended a debate at the home of Joseph Smith Sr. When they arrived, some young elders were in the midst of a three-hour debate on the question: "Was it, or was it not, the design of Christ to establish His Gospel by miracles?" Smith recorded that the leader of the meeting decided in the negative, which he noted was a "righteous decision." Nevertheless, Smith found fault with the proceedings. "I discovered in this debate," he observed, "much warmth [excitement, animation] displayed; too much zeal for mastery; too much of that enthusiasm that characterizes a lawyer at the bar, who is determined to defend his cause, right or wrong. I therefore availed myself of this favorable opportunity to drop a few words upon this subject by way of advice, that they might improve their minds and cultivate their powers of intellect in a proper manner, that they might not incur the displeasure of heaven; that they should handle sacred things very sacredly and with due deference to the opinions of others, and with an eye single to the glory of God."[155] Smith was more interested in a search for the truth, not polemics and winning debates.

---

153. Smith, Journal, Nov. 16, 1835 (*JSP*, J1:105; *JSP*, D5:63–64).
154. Smith, Nov. 17, 1835 (*JSP*, J1:105).
155. Smith, Nov. 18, 1835 (*JSP*, J1:106).

21

Translating Abraham's Record

A Translation of some ancient Records, that have fallen into our hands, from the Catacombs of Egypt, purporting to be the writings of Abraham, while he was in Egypt, called the Book of Abraham, written by his own hand, upon papyrus.
　　　—*Joseph Smith,* Times and Seasons, *Mar. 1, 1842, 704*

On November 12, 1835, Smith noted in his journal that Artemus Millet and Lorenzo Young had started to plaster the outside of the Kirtland temple on November 2, but that a snowstorm on the 11th forced them to discontinue.[1] In a November 10 letter to his wife, Lydia, in Missouri, Edward Partridge reported that "about 1/3 of the outside of the house [is] plastered," and that "10 days or 2 weeks good weather more they will finish it on the outside."[2] Young later recounted: "I made a suitable tool and, before the mortar was dry, I marked off the walls into blocks in imitation of regular stone work."[3] Historian Mark L. Staker notes: "They also added ground, cobalt-glazed ceramics to the plaster to give it a bluish tinge, reminiscent of polished granite."[4] Smith also commented in his journal that Jacob Bump had started plastering the inside on the 9th, and Partridge mentioned that it was the lower room.[5]

On November 19 Smith visited the temple with scribes Williams and Parrish and inspected the plastering, observing that "the masons ... had commenced puting on the finishing coat of plastureing." Later that day,

---

1. Smith, Journal, Nov. 12, 1835 (*JSP*, J1:96).

2. Edward Partridge, Letter to Lydia Partridge, Nov. 2–10, 1835, [2].

3. Lorenzo Young, "Lorenzo Dow Young's Narrative," 43.

4. Staker, *Hearken, O Ye People*, 426; see also 437, where Staker debunks the "cherished story" that the Saints "smashed their best china to mix with the wall stucco."

5. Smith, Journal, Nov. 12, 1835 (*JSP*, J1:96); Partridge, Letter to Lydia Partridge, Nov. 2–10, 1835, [2].

Parrish wrote apparently at Smith's dictation: "I returned home and spent the day in translating the Egyptian records." On the following day, Parrish recorded: "We spent the day in translating, and made rapid progress."[6] Smith most likely dictated the text of Abraham 1:4–2:6 during these two days of translation, which Williams and Parrish recorded simultaneously.[7] Recalling his time as Smith's scribe, Parrish said: "I have set by his [Joseph Smith's] side and penned down the translation of the Egyptian Hieroglyphicks as he claimed to receive it by direct inspiration of heaven."[8]

Parrish did not mention the method Smith used to translate, but there is some indication that he briefly returned to using a seer stone, which had come to be called Urim and Thummim in Mormon sources. In August 1835 the *Cleveland Whig* reported that they were "credibly informed" by Phelps that Smith had examined the Egyptian papyri "through his spectacles."[9] Six and a half years later, as Smith was preparing to translate more of the Hôr papyrus in February 1842, Wilford Woodruff wrote in his journal: "The Lord is Blessing Joseph with Power ... to translate through the urim & Thummim Ancient records & Hyeroglyphics as old as Abraham or Adam."[10] In July 1842 Parley P. Pratt announced in the *Millennial Star* that the Book of Abraham "is now in course of translation by the means of the Urim and Thummim."[11] When Cowdery blessed Smith in September 1835, he promised that the "Urim and Thummim" should remain "in his hands."[12] Yet there is no direct statement that Smith dictated the Book of Abraham using the same method as he had with the Book of Mormon—that is, by placing a seer stone in the crown of his hat and inserting his face into its brim, thus creating darkness in which the spiritual light of the stone could shine.[13]

As Williams and Parrish wrote, they also copied groups of characters from the Hôr papyrus in the left margins of their manuscripts, except where the

---

6. Smith, Journal, Nov. 19–20, 1835 (*JSP*, J1:107). My treatment of Smith's translation of the Book of Abraham recapitulates some of my discussion in Vogel, *Book of Abraham Apologetics*.

7. For the two Book of Abraham manuscripts produced by Williams and Parrish, see *JSP*, R4:192–215. For a discussion of the textual evidence that the two men wrote simultaneously from Smith's dictation, see Vogel, *Book of Abraham Apologetics*, 17–20.

8. Warren Parrish, Letter to the editor, Feb. 5, 1838, *Painesville (OH) Republican*, Feb. 15, 1838.

9. "Another Humbug," *Cleveland (OH) Whig*, Aug. 5, 1835, 2.

10. Woodruff, Journal, Feb. 19, 1842 (Vogel, *The Wilford Woodruff Journals*, 1:494).

11. Editorial, *LDS Millennial Star* (Liverpool, Eng.), July 1842, 47.

12. Oliver Cowdery, Blessing to Joseph Smith, Sep. 22, 1835, Patriarchal Blessing Book, 1:16 (*JSP*, D4:439).

13. On Smith's method of translating the Book of Mormon, see Lancaster, "The Translation of the Book of Mormon." For an extended, somewhat apologetic discussion, see MacKay and Frederick, *Joseph Smith's Seer Stones*.

dictated text corresponded with holes left in the damaged papyrus. These gaps were later filled with invented characters mixed with characters from part 1 of the Egyptian Alphabets. The nineteen groups of characters appear at the beginnings of paragraphs or groupings of text, which are sometimes awkwardly divided mid-sentence, showing a clear relationship between the characters and text. After Williams and Parrish wrote to Abraham 2:2, they apparently both drew the next group of characters in the margins of their manuscripts, but only Williams wrote the translation next to it, stopping at Abraham 2:6.

Sacrifice of Abraham

Phelps had been the scribe for the opening verses of the Book of Abraham, which announced Abraham's desire to leave Chaldea, the land of his fathers, for a better place, and to claim his right to be ordained to the high and patriarchal priesthood.[14] Abraham 1:4–20 tells the story of the attempted sacrifice of Abraham by the priest of Pharaoh in the Chaldean city of Ur. The story was inspired by the first vignette on the Hôr papyrus, which corresponds to Facsimile No. 1 in the Book of Abraham, as published in the March 1, 1842, issue of the *Times and Seasons*. In fact, Facsimile 1 is mentioned twice in the text, once for the likeness of the bedstead or altar upon which Abraham was placed for sacrifice and once for the representation of the gods who appear under the altar (Abr. 1:12, 14). Most Egyptologists recognize Facsimile 1 as depicting the reanimation of the Egyptian god Osiris, which inclines them to restore the vignette in ways that do not correspond to Smith's narrative. To Smith, this partly-intact vignette looked like human sacrifice, and no doubt the attempted sacrifice of Isaac by Abraham came to mind—where "Abraham stretched forth his hand, and took the knife to slay his son," but God called out to him to stop (Gen. 22:10). At some point after the vignette was mounted on thick paper, someone drew a knife in the priest's right hand. Later, in Nauvoo, Reuben Hedlock, in consultation with Smith, made a printing plate with the knife in the left hand.[15]

Despite the isolated story of Abraham's attempted sacrifice of Isaac, Egyptologists have challenged the Book of Abraham's assertion that human

---

14. Book of Abraham Manuscript-C, ca. July–Nov. 1835, 1 (*JSP*, R4:219).

15. On February 23, 1842, Willard Richards recorded in Smith's journal: "Gave R. Hadlock [Hedlock] instructions concerning the cut for the altar & Gods in the Records of Abraham. As designed for the Times and Seasons." Smith, Journal, Feb. 23, 1842 (*JSP*, J2:36). On March 1, 1842, Richards recorded: "During the fore-noon at his office. & printing office correcting the first plate or cut. of the Records of father Abraham, prepared by Reuben Hadlock for the Times & Seasons." Smith, Journal, Mar. 1, 1842 (*JSP*, J2:39).

sacrifice was a general practice of the Egyptians at the time of Abraham—especially, that the human sacrifices that were being performed "after the manner of the Egyptians" (Abr. 1:9, 11) occurred "in the land of the Chaldeans" (Abr. 1:1), specifically, in "the land of Ur, of the Chaldees" (Abr. 2:1), by "the priest of Elkenah [who] was also the priest of Pharaoh" (Abr. 1:7). As University of Chicago Egyptologist Robert Ritner noted, "Wherever one locates Ur of Chaldees, human sacrifice dictated there by 'priests of Pharaoh' is unbelievable to credible scholars of the Ancient Near East."[16]

The Book of Abraham states that Abraham's life was sought because he preached against idolatry, stating that his "fathers having turned from their righteousness ... unto the worshipping of the gods of the heathens, utterly refused to hearken to my voice. ... Therefore they turned their hearts to the sacrifice of the heathen in offering up their children unto their dumb idols, and hearkened not unto my voice, but endeavored to take away my life by the hand of the priest of Elkenah" (Abr. 1:5, 7). While this element is absent from the account of Abraham's life in Genesis, the idolatry of Abraham's father, Terah, has long been assumed based on Joshua 24:2, which states that "Terah, the father of Abraham, ... served other gods."[17] Not only Terah's idolatry but non-canonical writings that mention Abraham's preaching against his father's idolatry were well-known to Smith's contemporaries. For example, *A New Complete English Dictionary*, published in London in 1760, under "A'Bram," reads:

> He [Abraham] spent the first years of his life in his father's house, where they adored idols. Many are of opinion, that he himself was at first engaged in this way of worship; but that God giving him better understanding he renounced it; and for this reason, as some believe, suffered a severe persecution from the Chaldeans, who threw him into a fiery furnace; from which God miraculously rescued him. ... Jewish writers tell us, that Terah, Abraham's father, made and sold images, or representations of sun, moon, and stars to worship; and that Abraham being well skilled in the Astronomy of those times, learned from thence, that the heavenly bodies could neither make nor move themselves by their own power; but that there was one only

---

16. Robert K. Ritner, "'Translation and Historicity of the Book of Abraham'—A Response," oi.uchicago.edu. Accessed Apr. 25, 2021. See also the comments of Christopher Woods, Associate Professor of Sumerology in the Oriental Institute at the University of Chicago, in "The Practice of Egyptian Religion at 'Ur of the Chaldees'?," in Ritner, *The Joseph Smith Egyptian Papyri*, 73–74.

17. Andrew H. Hedges admits that knowledge of "Abraham's father's idolatry," based on Joshua 24:2 and nonbiblical traditions, was readily available to Smith's contemporaries. Hedges, "A Wanderer in a Strange Land," 185–86.

God, who created, preserved, and governed all things, and that therefore they ought to worship him alone.[18]

The published minutes of an anti-Masonic convention held in Massachusetts in 1829 include the following statement about Abraham and his father:

Those who did not emigrate with their venerable ancestor, Shem, fell under the tyranny and idolatry of Nimrod; for the Bible informs us, that Nahor, Terah, and perhaps Serug, bowed to idols. Indeed, ancient story informs us, Terah was a manufacturer of idols. This gave offence to Abraham; and in the absence of Terah, one day, Abraham broke up his father's idols. This so enraged Terah, that he accused Abraham before Nimrod, to have him punished for condemning his gods.[19]

According to Smith's narrative, Abraham was rescued at the last minute by "the angel of his [God's] presence," who "stood by me, and immediately unloosed my bands. And his voice was unto me: Abraham, Abraham, behold, my names is Jehovah, and I have heard thee, and have come down to deliver thee" (Abr. 1:15–16). This echoes Isaiah 63:9, which states, concerning Israel's flight from Egypt, "the angel of his presence saved them; and in his love, and in his pity, he redeemed them." This, together with other passages that equate angel with Jehovah (e.g., Gen. 16:7, 13; Ex. 33:2, 14), led some of Smith's contemporaries to associate "the angel of his presence" with Jehovah himself. Yet others took this a step farther and asserted that Jesus was the Jehovah-angel. Matthew Henry's Bible commentary explained that "the angel of [God's] presence" is "to be understood of Jesus Christ, the eternal Word, that angel of whom God spake to Moses, Exod. xxiii.20, *whose voice Israel was to obey.*"[20]

Patriarchs and Race

The Book of Abraham states that in retribution for the attempted sacrifice of Abraham, the Lord not only destroyed the altar and gods but also "smote the priest that he died," following which there was "great mourning in Chaldea, and also in the court of Pharaoh; which Pharaoh signifies king by royal blood" (Abr. 1:20). This leads into a six-verse parenthetical statement that

---

18. Marchant et al., *A New Complete English Dictionary*, under "A'Bram." See also Stackhouse, *An History of the Holy Bible*, 1:192.

19. Sanborn, *Minutes of an Address*, 11.

20. Henry, *A New Family Bible*, under Isa. 63:9. However, the Jehovah-angel-Jesus connection was a point of contention among Smith's contemporaries. See, for example, Belsham, *A Calm Inquiry*, 196–201.

begins by announcing that the Pharaoh was "a descendant from the loins of Ham, ... and thus the blood of the Canaanites was preserved in the land" (Abr. 1:21–22). The remainder of the excurses and accompanying three groups of characters, which were added later in a different hand in the margin, correspond to a gap in the papyrus. These verses discuss the history of Egypt's founding by Egyptus, daughter of Ham and his wife Zeptah, who, after the waters of the Flood receded, "settled her sons in it; and thus, from Ham, sprang that race which preserved the curse in the land" (Abr. 1:21–27).[21] Both the text and the invented characters were adapted and expanded from part one in the Egyptian Alphabets and the Grammar and Alphabet of the Egyptian Language pertaining to Katumin and her mother. It is unclear how Smith came up with the name Egyptus, but it appears in Josephus as a man's name from a later time.[22]

What Smith meant by preserving the curse in the land may be best explained in a letter Phelps wrote to Cowdery on February 6, 1835:

> Is or is it not apparent from reason and analogy as drawn from a careful reading of the Scriptures, that God causes the saints, or people that fall away from his church to be cursed in time, with a *black skin*? Was or was not Cain, being marked, obliged to inherit the curse, [upon] he and his children, forever? And if so, as Ham, like other sons of God, might break the rule of God, by marrying out of the church, did or did he not, have a Canaanite wife, whereby some of the *black seed* was preserved through the flood, and his son, Canaan, after he laughed at his grand father's nakedness, heired [inherited] three curses: one from Cain for killing Abel; one from Ham for marrying a black wife, and one from Noah for ridiculing what God had respect for?[23]

Significantly, Phelps's letter was written five months before Smith procured the Egyptian papyri, which indicates that the Book of Abraham reflected what was already being discussed among Smith's followers about race and curses. In fact, both Phelps and Smith were expressing a version of what many of Smith's contemporaries believed was the origin of the Black race. Those who wanted to justify African slavery, however, did not refer to

---

21. In the dictated manuscripts, Ham's wife is named Zeptah, who is not mentioned in Genesis. Later, prior to publication in 1842, Smith changed Zeptah to Egyptus, making it appear that Ham's wife and daughter had the same name. Metcalfe, "The Curious Textual History of 'Egyptus' the Wife of Ham."

22. Flavius Josephus, Against Apion, Bk. 1, sec. 15, in Whiston, *Josephus Complete Works*, 612.

23. William W. Phelps, Letter to Oliver Cowdery, Feb. 6, 1835, *LDS Messenger and Advocate* (Kirtland, OH), Mar. 1835, 82.

Ham's wife but rather to Ham's son, Canaan. According to the biblical account, Ham had seen the drunken and naked Noah passed out in his tent; and when Noah found out he was displeased and cursed Ham's son, Canaan, saying: "Cursed be Canaan; a servant of servants shall he be unto his brethren" (Gen. 9:25). No doubt the pro-slavery persecutors of the Mormons in Missouri shared the views reported in John Blake's 1834 book *The Family Encyclopedia of Useful Knowledge and General Literature*: "In consequence of this irreverent act on the part of Ham, some have fancifully conjectured, that not only Ham and Canaan, but all their posterity, became slaves, and the color of their skin was suddenly rendered black; and accordingly they maintain, that all the blacks have descended from Ham and Canaan."[24]

As early as 1831, Smith's revelations had explained that the mark God had put upon Cain for murdering his brother Abel was black skin. In his revision of the Bible, Smith dictated to his scribe that Enoch beheld in vision that humankind "were a mixture of all the seed of Adam save it was the seed of Cain, for the seed of Cain were black, and had not place among them."[25] In August 1832 Phelps published Smith's "Prophecy of Enoch," which included the preceding statement, in *The Evening and the Morning Star*, perhaps in the hope of currying favor in the eyes of the suspicious, slave-holding Missourians.

While some of Smith's contemporaries associated Cain's curse with black skin, it remained to be explained how the curse was preserved through the Flood. One editor of a London newspaper noted that "doctors of divinity have differed as to what kind of mark was set upon Cain, some have asserted that his colour was changed to black, whence the negro race have sprung, but a difficulty is again started here, as Noah and his family according to the bible history must have pro-created the present race."[26] In America anti-slavery Quaker Elihu Coleman highlighted the problem in his 1733 pamphlet, reporting the incongruent belief among his contemporaries that "there was a mark set upon Cain, and they do believe that these negroes are the posterity of Cain, ... and that Canaan was to be a servant of servants to his brethren, whom they take to be of the same linage: But if we do but

---

24. Blake, *The Family Encyclopedia of Useful Knowledge*, 434.

25. Old Testament Manuscript 1, 16 [Moses 7:22] (Faulring et al., *Joseph Smith's New Translation of the Bible*, 105). This passage would have been dictated between December 1830 and March 7, 1831. Faulring et al., 57. Moses 7 was published in the August 1832 issue of *The Evening and the Morning Star* (18).

26. "Continuation of Reply to the Rev. Thomas Hartwell Horne's Pamphlet, Entitled Deism Refuted, &c. From Page 415," *The Republican* (London), Apr. 14, 1820, 445.

observe, and read in the genealogy of Cain, we may find that they were all drowned in the old world, and that Canaan was of the line of Seth."[27]

Smith initially solved the problem by having Canaan's curse include black skin. As early as 1831, while working on his revision of the Bible, Smith reinforced the pro-slavery interpretation of the passage in Genesis: "And [Noah] said, Blessed be the Lord God of Shem; and Canaan shall be his servant, *and a veil of darkness shall cover him, that he shall be known among all men.*"[28] Earlier in his revision, Smith added a passage where Enoch saw a vision of "the world for the space of many generations" in which he seemed to allude to Africa: "For behold, the Lord shall curse the land with much heat, and the barrenness thereof shall go forth forever; and there was a blackness came upon all the children of Canaan, that they were despised among all people."[29]

Smith therefore initially described a separate cursing of Canaan rather than a transmission of the curse through Ham's interracial marriage. In the intervening years between Smith's working on his Bible revision and dictating the text of the Book of Abraham, his ideas about the origin of the Black race apparently evolved and were possibly influenced by Phelps.[30]

While Ham and Zeptah had other children, their daughter Egyptus would have had no claim to the patriarchal priesthood. Still, the Book of Abraham makes a point of saying that although her son Pharaoh was a "righteous man" who imitated the patriarchal government of his fathers, he was nevertheless "cursed … pertaining to the Priesthood" (Abr. 1:26). Pharaoh was therefore an illegitimate ruler not only because he was of the wrong race but because he had the wrong lineage. Nevertheless, the Book of Abraham states that "the Pharaohs would fain claim it from Noah, through Ham, therefore my father was led away by their idolatry" (Abr. 1:27), which may have been influenced by Isaiah 19:11, where the princes of the Egyptian city Zoan declare to Pharaoh, "I am the son of the wise, the son of ancient kings."[31]

---

27. Coleman, *Testimony against that Anti-Christian Practice of Making Slaves,* 16.

28. Old Testament Manuscript 1, 25 [Gen. 9:26; I.V. Gen. 11:30] (Faulring et al., *Joseph Smith's New Translation of the Bible,* 118); emphasis added.

29. Old Testament Manuscript 1, 16 [Moses 7:20] (Faulring et al., 118).

30. A useful discussion of Smith's evolving ideas on race may be found in Bingham, "Curses and Marks."

31. A chronology accompanying the publication of some eighteenth- and nineteenth-century Bibles lists the founding of Egypt by one of Noah's grandsons and then states: "Egypt is called the land of Ham, and the Egyptian Pharaohs boasted themselves to be the sons of ancient Kings." See *The Holy Bible, Containing The Old Testament and the New* (London: Charles Bill, 1706); *The Holy Bible, According to the Authorized Version* (Oxford, Eng.: Clarendon Press, 1818), unpaginated index at end of both volumes.

The right of kingship among the patriarchs is not mentioned in Genesis, but it is a key theme in Josephus, who described the right to govern being handed down through the patriarchs, that Enos "delivered the government to Cainan his son," and that several generations later Methuselah "delivered the government" to his son Lamech. When Lamech had "governed seven hundred and seventy-seven years, [he] appointed Noah his son to be ruler of the people ... and retained the government nine hundred and fifty years."[32]

While later Mormons interpreted Abraham as banning Blacks from all priesthood offices, the context of Abraham 1:26 is patriarchal priesthood. There is no indication that Smith envisioned an elaborate priesthood organization existing before Moses. To this point, his revelations spoke only of a line of patriarchal ordinations, to which Shem was preferred over Ham. How this applied to Smith's church was never explicitly stated during Smith's lifetime, and historians have debated whether or not Brigham Young correctly interpreted Smith's teachings on this matter.[33] Nevertheless, Smith's revelations strengthened the dubious theological notions of white Europeans concerning the origin of a black race and biblical justification for slavery.

While Smith was always sympathetic to slave owners, Mormons who migrated to Missouri from the north brought their anti-slavery attitudes with them. Smith understood that in order to retake Jackson County and establish his Zionic community, he needed to defuse the highly charged, volatile issue of slavery. The racial aspects of the Book of Abraham are best understood in this context. Without explicitly addressing slavery, the Book of Abraham supported the white supremacist ideology of slave owners by denouncing Ham's interracial marriage as "that which is forbidden" (Abr. 1:23) and asserting that because of him, the "curse" of black skin was "preserved" through the Flood (Abr. 1:24). By delegitimizing Pharaoh's patriarchal government because he was "cursed ... pertaining to the Priesthood" (Abr. 1:26), Smith signaled that Blacks would never be rulers in the patriarchal government that he was proposing for his Missouri Zion.

Abraham and the Famine

In Genesis, a famine is not mentioned until after Abraham leaves Ur and is traveling in Canaan, which forces him to go into Egypt (Gen. 12:10). In

---

32. Antiquities of the Jews, Book 1, chap. 3, sect. 4, in Whiston, *Josephus Complete Works*, 28.

33. See Mauss, "The Fading of the Pharaohs' Curse." Restricting Blacks from holding the priesthood (as well as receiving the temple endowment) became LDS Church policy under Brigham Young until 1978.

Abraham, the famine appears while Abraham is still in Ur as God's retribution for attempting to sacrifice Abraham (Abr. 1:29–30). Smith used the famine to explain the death of Abraham's brother Haran, whereas Genesis gives no cause (Abr. 2:1; Gen. 11:28). The famine in Ur also causes Terah to repent, but later, when the famine "abated" in Haran, he returns to his former practice (Abr. 1:30; 2:5). When the Book of Abraham mentions the famine in Canaan, it becomes a "continuation" of the famine (Abr. 2:21). Rather than create two famines in Abraham's day, it was necessary to maintain one long famine that briefly abates to avoid conflict with Genesis 26:1, which mentions in connection with another famine in the days of Isaac: "there was a famine in the land, beside the first famine that was in the days of Abraham."

After writing about the marriage of Abraham and his brother, Nehor, to Sarai and Milcah, in Abraham 2:2, which parallels Genesis 11:29, there was apparently a break in Smith's dictation, when Parrish stopped writing and Williams continued for four more verses that deal with Abraham's call.

Abraham's Call

In Genesis, Abraham does not receive his call and command to move to Canaan until after he leaves Ur and is located in Haran. In Smith's day, there was debate about whether Abraham received one or two calls: one in Ur, located in Chaldea, another in Haran, in northern Mesopotamia. The debate centered on Stephen's words to the Jewish Sanhedrin in Acts 7, which locates God's appearance to Abraham and the command for him to depart as occurring in Ur, rather than in Haran: "And he [Stephen] said, Men, brethren, and fathers, hearken; The God of glory appeared unto our father Abraham, when he was in Mesopotamia, before he dwelt in Charran [Haran], And said unto him, Get thee out of thy country, and from thy kindred, and come into the land which I shall shew thee" (Acts 7:2–3).

According to Adam Clarke, "There is great dissension between commentators concerning the call of Abram; some supposing he had *two* distinct calls, others that he had but *one*." Clarke conjectured that when Terah, Abraham, Lot, and their new wives left Ur, "this was, no doubt, in consequence of some Divine admonition."[34] Under Acts 7:2, Clarke wrote: "It seems most probable that Abraham had *two* calls, one in *Ur*, and the other in *Haran*."[35] In Abraham 2, Smith attempted to resolve this conflict by creating two calls. In creating the first call in Ur, Smith borrowed wording from Genesis 12:1,

---

34. Clarke, *The Holy Bible*, Gen. 12:1.
35. Clarke, Acts 7:2.

which was the call Abraham later received in Haran, rather than from Acts 7:3: "Now the Lord had said unto me: Abraham, get thee out of thy country, and from thy kindred, and from thy father's house, unto a land that I will show thee" (Abr. 2:3; cf. Gen. 12:1).

Concerning Abraham's departure from Ur, Genesis 11:31 states that Terah "took" Abraham and Lot, and their wives, to Haran. Since Abraham 1:16–18 and 2:3 had Jehovah command Abraham to leave Ur, Smith changed it to read: "I left the land of Ur" and "I took Lot" and the others to Haran, "and also my father followed after me" (Abr. 2:4). When the famine "abated," Terah "turned again unto his idolatry," and therefore remained in Haran when Abraham received a second call and left with the others (Abr. 2:5). At this point, Williams stopped writing from Smith's dictation.[36]

Translation Pauses

Cowdery returned from New York City on the evening of November 20, bringing with him several Hebrew books for the school, and presented Smith with a Hebrew Bible, lexicon, and grammar, a Greek lexicon, and Noah Webster's Dictionary.[37] Among the Hebrew books Cowdery brought were an 1833 edition of the *Biblia Hebraica*, the 1835 edition of Moses Stuart's *A Grammar of the Hebrew Language*, and the 1832 edition of Josiah Gibbs's *A Manual Hebrew and English Lexicon*, all described by historian Matthew J. Grey as "some of the highest quality resources available at that time."[38] On the following day Smith studied the Hebrew alphabet at home and then, in the evening, attended Hebrew class, where it was decided to release Dr. Peixotto, who could only teach the rudiments of Hebrew, and search for a new instructor in New York City, where Cowdery said he had become "quite intimately acquainted with a learned Jew, with whom I held several conversations."[39]

On Sunday, November 22, Smith attended church in the nearly-finished temple and heard Simeon Carter preach on Matthew 7, and in the afternoon

---

36. Williams had discontinued writing from dictation with Abraham 2:5. Later, when he resumed writing in his document by copying from another document, presumably Parrish's text in the translation book, he accidentally repeated the same text at the end of his manuscript and then continued with Abraham 2:6, which ends abruptly, implying that his document is incomplete. See *JSP*, R4:201.

37. Smith, Journal, Nov. 20, 1835 (*JSP*, J1:107); Oliver Cowdery, Letter to Warren A. Cowdery, Nov. 22, 1835, Cowdery Letterbook, 63.

38. Grey, "'The Word of the Lord in the Original.'"

39. Oliver Cowdery, Letter to Warren A. Cowdery, Nov. 22, 1835, Cowdery Letterbook, 63.

attended another meeting in the schoolhouse.[40] In the evening, Smith attended a council of high priests and elders in the case of Andrew Jackson Squires, who confessed that he had temporarily joined the Methodists and requested to be reinstated. During this meeting, Smith "spoke at considerable length on the impropriety of turning away from the truth and going after a people so destitute of the spirit of righteousness as the Methodists."[41] According to Smith's journal, the case caused "considerable altercation" among members of the council, and Squires was only restored after a "keen rebuke" and "severe chastisement."[42]

On November 23 Smith was visited by some of the brethren who wanted to see the Egyptian papyri, and later he studied Hebrew.[43] In the evening, Hyrum invited him to attend the wedding of Newel Knight and Lydia Goldthwaite, but when Hyrum told him of his intention to get Seymour Brunson to perform the ceremony, as Brunson had obtained a license while in southern Ohio, Joseph said he would perform the ceremony himself. As Lydia Knight later explained: "Hyrum looked at his brother in astonishment at this announcement. ... The law of Ohio did not recognize the 'Mormon' Elders as ministers, and it was a punishable offense for a lay man to officiate in that capacity. In fact, several Elders had been arrested and fined for the performance of this act." Hyrum replied, "Very well, you know best. We will be very glad to have you do so."[44]

While Smith was performing the marriage ceremony the next evening, he remarked that "marriage was an institution of h[e]aven institude [instituted] in the garden of Eden, that it was necessary that it should be Solemnized by the authority of the everlasting priesthood." The words which he was later reported to have spoken to marry them were original: "You covenant to be each others companions through life, and discharge the duties of husband & wife in every respect to which they assented, I then pronounced them husband & Wife in the name of God and also the blessings that the Lord confered upon adam & Eve in the garden of Eden; that is to multiply and replenish the earth, with the addition of long life and prosperity."[45]

---

40. Smith, Journal, Nov. 22, 1835 (*JSP*, J1:109).

41. Minutes, Nov. 22, 1835, Minute Book 1, 131 (*JSP*, D5:69).

42. Smith, Journal, Nov. 22, 1835 (*JSP*, J1:109).

43. Smith, Journal, Nov. 23, 1835 (*JSP*, J1:109).

44. Gates, *Lydia Knight's History*, 30. Lydia misdated her marriage to November 23 instead of November 24, 1835. The conversation between Joseph and Hyrum occurred the day before, which she mistakenly dated to November 22. Hartley, "Newel and Lydia Bailey Knight's Kirtland Love Story and Historic Wedding."

45. Smith, Journal, Nov. 24, 1835 (*JSP*, J1:110).

Newel Knight later said: "We received much Instruction from the Prophet concerning matrimony, & what the ancient order of God was, & what it must be again concerning marriage."[46] According to Lydia, Smith addressed the spectators: "Our elders have been wronged and prosecuted for marrying without a license. The Lord God of Israel has given me authority to unite the people in the holy bonds of matrimony and from this time forth I shall use that privilege to marry whomsoever I see fit."[47]

This is the first known marriage performed by Smith. Over the next two months, he performed ten more marriages, and a total of nineteen by June 1837.[48] Rigdon had been indicted the previous June and tried in October for performing the marriage of Orson Hyde and Marinda Johnson on September 4, 1834, but acquitted because it was determined his minister's license as a Campbellite was still valid.[49] Smith perhaps proceeded based on his belief that the publication of the statement on marriage in the Doctrine and Covenants the previous August fulfilled the 1824 Ohio statute on marriage, which permitted marriages to be performed by "the several religious societies agreeably to the rules and regulations of their respective churches."[50]

Although Smith emphasized priesthood authority in his journal entry, the statement on marriage allowed that weddings could be performed by either priesthood holders or "other authority."[51] According to John C. Dowen, a justice of the peace in Kirtland from 1833 to 1839, because "Mormons were not permitted to marry couples" in Geauga County, "they often had me perform the legal marriage ceremony, and afterward Joe Smith would, as he claimed, marry them according to the gospel."[52] Still, the Knight-Goldthwaite and other marriages were filed with the county under Smith's name.

Another potential problem with the Knight-Goldthwaite marriage was that Lydia had not officially divorced her first husband, Calvin Bailey, who had abandoned her and her child three years earlier. Lydia, who apparently needed some persuading, recalled in her history that Newel explained that "according to the law she was a free woman, having been deserted for three years with nothing provided for her support."[53] However, as M. Scott

---

46. Newel Knight, Autobiography and Journal, ca. 1846, [60].

47. Gates, *Lydia Knight's History*, 31.

48. Geauga County Marriage Records, Book C, 141–42, 144, 165, 188–89, 233–34; Bradshaw, "Joseph Smith's Performance of Marriages in Ohio," 24.

49. Bradshaw, 23.

50. An Act Regulating Marriages [Jan. 6, 1824], *Statutes of Ohio*, 2:1407, sec. 2.

51. Statement on Marriage, ca. Aug. 1835, in D&C, 1835 ed., 251 (*JSP*, D4:477).

52. Dowen, Statement, Jan 2. 1885, 5.

53. Gates, *Lydia Knight's History*, 28.

Bradshaw points out, "Newel seems to have been unaware that earlier in 1835 the state legislature adopted a new bigamy statute … [that] lengthened to five years the time required to constitute abandonment—a requirement which Lydia would not have met." Nevertheless, Lydia subsequently learned that Bailey was probably dead at the time anyway.[54]

Translation Resumes

Meanwhile, Parrish had copied the text of Abraham thus far dictated into the translation book, following the first three verses Phelps had transcribed a few months earlier, skipped a line, copied the four verses dictated to Williams in his absence, and then continued recording Smith's dictation of Abraham 2:6–18.[55] On November 24 Parrish recorded in Smith's journal: "In the after-noon, we translated some of the Egyptian records," and on the following day that they "spent the day in Translating."[56] These are the last two entries in Smith's Kirtland journal which mention translation.

Abraham 2:6 introduces Abraham's second calling, but, instead of repeating Genesis 12:1, Smith created three new verses, which describe God appearing to Abraham and commanding him: "Arise, and take Lot with thee; for I have purposed to take thee away out of Haran, and to make of thee a minister to bear my name in a strange land which I will give unto thy seed after thee for an everlasting possession, when they hearken to my voice" (Abr. 2:6). Then Smith continued with the remainder of Abraham's call in Genesis 12:2–3, expanding them in much the same way as he had done in his Bible revision in 1830–33.

Abraham 2:9–11	Genesis 12:2–3
9 And I will make of thee a great nation, and I will bless thee *above measure*, and make thy name great *among all nations*, and thou shalt be a blessing *unto thy seed after thee, that in their hands they shall bear this ministry and Priesthood unto all nations*;	2 And I will make of thee a great nation, and I will bless thee, and make thy name great; and thou shalt be a blessing:

---

54. Bradshaw, "Joseph Smith's Performance of Marriages in Ohio," 32–33.

55. Book of Abraham Manuscript-C, ca. July–Nov. 1835, 7–10 (*JSP*, R4:231–37). For a discussion of the textual evidence that Parrish wrote Abraham 2:7–18 from Smith's dictation, see Vogel, *Book of Abraham Apologetics*, 25–26.

56. Smith, Journal, Nov. 24–25, 1835 (*JSP*, J1:109–110).

10 *And I will bless them through thy name; for as many as receive this Gospel shall be called after thy name, and shall be accounted thy seed, and shall rise up and bless thee, as their father;*

11 And I will bless them that bless thee, and curse them that curse thee; and in thee *(that is, in thy Priesthood) and in thy seed (that is, thy Priesthood), for I give unto thee a promise that this right shall continue in thee, and in thy seed after thee (that is to say, the literal seed, or the seed of the body)* shall all the families of the earth be blessed, *even with the blessings of the Gospel, which are the blessings of salvation, even of life eternal.*

3 And I will bless them that bless thee, and curse him that curseth thee: and in thee shall all families of the earth be blessed.

Smith made other changes to the Genesis account. Genesis 12:5, for instance, states that when Abraham left Haran for Canaan, he took, among other things, "the souls that they had gotten in Haran." Abraham 2:15 changed this to read: "the souls we had won in Haran"—which made it sound more like those whom Abraham had converted. Commenting on Genesis 12:5, Adam Clarke stated: "This may apply either to the persons who were employed in the service of Abram, or to the persons he had been the instrument of converting to the knowledge of the true God; and in this latter sense the Chaldee paraphrasts understood the passage, translating it, *The souls of those whom they proselyted in Haran.*"[57] Smith also changed Abraham's age when he left Haran, from seventy-five to sixty-two (Gen. 12:4; Abr. 2:14), following his earlier practice of changing the ages of the patriarchs in his Bible revision without any apparent reason.[58]

Smith's dictation in Kirtland ended with an embellishment of Genesis 12:6, which describes Abraham's journey from Haran to Canaan via Sichem to the plain of Moreh. In Abraham 2:16–18, Smith added "by way of Jershon,"

---

57. Clarke, *The Holy Bible*, Gen. 12:5.

58. Old Testament Manuscript 1, 11–12, 19, in Faulring et al., *Joseph Smith's New Translation of the Bible*, 97–98, 110. This portion of the manuscript was composed before March 7, 1831 (Faulring et al., 57), and emended in Cowdery's handwriting probably in 1835.

where Abraham stopped to offer sacrifice to God and pray that "the famine might be turned away from my father's house, that they might not perish."

On November 26 Parrish made the last entry in Smith's Kirtland journal to mention the Egyptian materials until 1842: "We spent the day in transcribing Egyptian characters from the papyrus."[59] It has been suggested that the "transcribing" of Egyptian characters refers to the addition of characters in the margins of the three Kirtland translation manuscripts.[60] However, Parrish's shorter document ends with a group of characters without English text next to it, which implies that the characters in that document were written as the dictation proceeded. When Parrish copied this text into the translation book, the last two groups of characters were misaligned and had to be scrape-erased and moved up a few lines, which suggests that in that instance the characters were copied before the English text. The "transcribing [of] Egyptian characters from the papyrus" could have been for the new text Parrish had added to the translation book or one or more of the single sheets of hieratic text among the Kirtland Egyptian Papers.[61]

On the same day, Smith complained that he was "severely afflicted with a cold." The next day, both Smith and Parrish were sick, and they blessed one another. On November 28 Smith said that he was "considerably recovered from my cold, & I think I shall be able in a few days to translate again, with the blessing of God."[62] However, there is no evidence for any additional translation of the papyri during the remainder of Smith's residence in Kirtland, although he called the west room in the third story of the temple his "translating room."[63]

Smith was frequently visited by those who wanted to view the mummies and papyri, requests he always obliged. In February 1836 Joseph Coe, who had helped to purchase the Egyptian artifacts, proposed to put the mummies and papyri on display at John Johnson's Inn in Kirtland, apparently with the view of charging money to help recoup some of his losses.[64] "I complied with his request," Smith wrote in his journal, "and only observed that they must be managed with prudence and care especially the manuscripts."[65]

---

59. Smith, Journal, Nov. 26, 1835 (*JSP*, J1:110–11).

60. Hauglid, *Textual History of the Book of Abraham*, 216n21.

61. For these loose sheets with hieratic texts, see Copies of Egyptian Characters, ca. summer 1835-A and -B; and Copy of Hypocephalus, ca. July 1835–Mar. 1842 (*JSP*, R4:44–47, 50–51).

62. Smith, Journal, Nov. 26–28, 1835 (*JSP*, J1:110–12).

63. Smith, Journal, Dec. 31, 1835 (*JSP*, J1:140).

64. Joseph Coe, Letter to Joseph Smith, Jan. 1, 1844, JS Collection; see also Todd, *Saga of the Book of Abraham*, 196–200.

65. Smith, Journal, Feb. 17, 1836 (*JSP*, J1:186).

By November 25, the mummies and records were back in the temple, somewhere in the "upper rooms," according to Wilford Woodruff, probably on display in Smith's "translating room," where meetings were often held.[66]

Troubles with Anti-Mormons

On Sunday, November 29, Smith went to church and heard Isaac Morley preach in the morning; in the afternoon he heard Bishop Partridge. "Their words were words of wisdom," he wrote in his journal, "like apples of gold in pictures of silver, spoken in the simple accents of a child, yet sublime as the voice of an angel."[67] Partridge wrote in his journal that "Prest. Smith bore testimony that br. Morley & Myself had preached by the spirit & to his satisfaction."[68]

On November 30 Smith "spent the day in writing a letter to the Messenger & Advocate on the Subject of the Gathering," which he finished on the following day.[69] In this last of a three-part open letter published in the *Messenger and Advocate,* Smith likened his mission of gathering converts to his Missouri Zion to Jesus's parable of the wheat and tares in Matthew 13, where the wheat is harvested and gathered into a barn before the field and tares are burned.[70] Smith also likened the Book of Mormon to Jesus's parable of the mustard seed "coming out of the ground," and, although "accounted the least of all seeds," he wrote, we can "behold it branching forth; yea, even towering, with lofty branches, and God-like majesty, until it becomes the greatest of all herbs: ... and God is sending down his powers, gifts and angels, to lodge in the branches thereof."[71]

Smith's narrative switches to attacking his enemies. The Church of the Latter Day Saints, he declared, is "like an impenetrable, immovable rock in the midst of the mighty deep, exposed to storms and tempests of satan, but has, thus far, remained steadfast and is still braving the mountain of waves of opposition." As examples of Satan's "pitchfork of lies," Smith named E. D. Howe's *Mormonism Unveiled,* which was published the previous year, and Alexander Campbell's periodical the *Millennial Harbinger,* which reviewed

---

66. Woodruff, Journal, Nov. 25, 1836 (Vogel, *The Wilford Woodruff Journals*, 1:98).

67. Smith, Journal, Nov. 29, 1835 (*JSP*, J1:112).

68. Partridge, Diary, Nov. 29, 1835.

69. Smith, Journal, Nov. 30, 1835 (*JSP*, J1:113).

70. Joseph Smith, Letter to "the Elders of the Church of the Latter Day Saints," Nov. 30–Dec. 1, 1835, *LDS Messenger and Advocate*, Dec. 1835, 225–27 (*JSP*, D5:91–94). Smith quoted and discussed the parable of the sower (Matt. 13:3–12), the parable of the wheat and tares (Matt. 13:24–30), and the parable of the mustard seed (Matt. 13:31–32).

71. Smith, 227 (*JSP*, D5:94–95).

the Book of Mormon in 1831. "And we hope that this adversary of truth will continue to stir up the sink of iniquity, that the people may the more readily discern between the righteous and the wicked."[72]

Smith criticized Campbell for neglecting the gift of the Holy Ghost and gifts of the spirit, which Campbell believed were only necessary to establish the primitive church, and challenged him to "a public investigation of these matters." Campbell was well-known for public debates, but it is unclear if Smith intended to debate Campbell himself or have Rigdon or one of his elders do it.[73]

Smith also named "the right honorable Doct[or] P[hilastus]. Hurlburt, who is the legitimate author" of *Mormonism Unveiled*. Doctor was Hurlbut's first given name, but to Smith, he was "not so much a doctor of physic, as of falsehood." Hurlbut supplied many of the affidavits of Smith's former neighbors in Manchester and Palmyra, New York, and Harmony, Pennsylvania, but Howe wrote the bulk of the book.[74] Nevertheless, Smith attempted to discredit Howe's book by associating Hurlbut with it, mentioning that Hurlbut had recently been "bound over to court for threatening life."[75]

Next, Smith turned to the "ringleaders" of the anti-Mormons in nearby Mentor, where there was a large congregation of Campbellites. Smith singled out Orris Clapp, a leading Mentor Campbellite and associate of Hurlbut, "who has of late immortalized his name by swearing that he would not believe a Mormon under oath, and by his polite attention to Hurlburt's wife, which cost him (as we have been informed) a round sum."[76] Rigdon later accused Clapp of immorality and used it to discredit Campbellism.[77] Clapp's son Matthew, according to Smith, testified that "the Book of Mormon had been proved false an hundred times, by Howe's book; and also that he would not believe a Mormon under oath." Smith suggested that "the far-famed Mentor mob: all sons and legitimate heirs of the same spirit of Alexander Campbell, and 'Mormonism Unveiled,'" be judged "by their fruits."[78]

From this letter and an earlier one published in the September 1834 issue

---

72. Smith, 227 (*JSP*, D5:95).

73. Smith, 228 (*JSP*, D5:96).

74. Vogel, ed., *Mormonism Unvailed*, xxiii–xxiv.

75. Joseph Smith, Letter to "the Elders of the Church of the Latter Day Saints," Nov. 30–Dec. 1, 1835, *LDS Messenger and Advocate*, Dec. 1835, 228 (*JSP*, D5:96–97).

76. Smith, 228 (*JSP*, D5:97).

77. Sidney Rigdon, Letter to Oliver Cowdery, *Messenger and Advocate*, Apr. 1836, 298–99; "Persecution," *Messenger and Advocate*, Jan. 1837, 436–39.

78. Joseph Smith, Letter to "the Elders of the Church of the Latter Day Saints," Nov. 30–Dec. 1, 1835, *LDS Messenger and Advocate*, Dec. 1835, 228 (*JSP*, D5:97–98).

of *The Evening and the Morning Star,* Smith was trying to provoke Campbell into an exchange that might result in another mass conversion of his Disciples.[79] If successful, it could provide the needed numbers for Smith's Army of Israel and ensure the redemption of Zion.

On December 2 Smith, accompanied by Emma and their two children, Parrish, and others, traveled by sleigh to Painesville. On the way, Smith was mocked by two men on Mentor Street. As he passed them in their sled, they yelled, "Do you get any revelation lately"? This was followed by foul words Smith could not hear clearly. "This is a fair sample of the character of Mentor Street inhabitants, who are ready to abuse and scandalize, men who never laid a straw in their way," Smith later wrote in his journal.[80] The previous April, Parley P. Pratt had been egged while preaching on the steps of the large Campbellite church in Mentor.[81] Smith further reflected, "I was led to marvel at the longsuffering and condescension of our heavenly Father, in permitting these ungodly wretches to possess this goodly land, … and we rejoice that the time is at hand, when the wicked who will not repent, will be swept from the earth with the besom of destruction, and the earth becomes an inheritance for the poor and the meek."[82]

In Painesville, Smith and company visited Harriet Howe, the believing sister of E. D. Howe. After a while, Smith left his family and went into town with Parrish to conduct business and visit Horace Kingsbury, a Mormon who owned a variety and jewelry store. According to an early history, Smith and Parrish also visited "at the bank, and at various other places."[83] Smith may have been attempting to get credit from the bank, using Kingsbury as a cosigner, although the visit to the jewelry store may have been connected to Parrish's wedding on the evening of the following day. The ceremony was performed by Smith, who gave a brief address on matrimony and then married Parrish and Martha H. Raymond. Smith said he "pronounced them husband and wife in the name of God according to the articles, and covenants of the Church of the Latter Day Saints."[84]

---

79. See Joseph Smith, Letter to Oliver Cowdery, Sep. 24, 1834, *The Evening and the Morning Star* (Kirtland, OH), Sep. 1834, 192 (*JSP,* D4:169–71).

80. Smith, Journal, Dec. 2, 1835 (*JSP,* J1:113–14).

81. Pratt, *A Short Account of a Shameful Outrage.* Pratt subsequently sued Grandison Newell, ringleader of the mob, and received a judgment in his favor for $47. *Chardon Spectator and Geauga Gazette,* Oct. 30, 1835.

82. Smith, Journal, Dec. 2, 1835 (*JSP,* J1:113–14).

83. JS History, 1834–36, 139 (*JSP,* H1:137).

84. Smith, Journal, Dec. 3, 1835 (*JSP,* J1:113–14).

Financial Relief

On December 4 Smith and Vinson Knight went to Painesville and withdrew $350 from "Painsvill Bank," or Bank of Geauga, on three months' credit, which they obtained under the names of Frederick G. Williams & Co., Newel K. Whitney, John Johnson, and Vinson Knight. After returning to Kirtland, Smith settled with Knight and Hyrum Smith, paying Knight $245. "I feel heartily thankful to my heavenly Father, and ask him in the name of Jesus Christ, to enable us to extricate ourselves from all embarrassments whatever, that we may not be brought into disrepute, in any respect, that our enemies may not have any power over us." Smith said he "also paid, or have it in my power to pay J[ob] Lewis."[85] Smith had borrowed $100 from Lewis in March 1834, probably when he was in Westfield, New York, but Lewis never got paid, which led to his angry confrontation with Smith and subsequent excommunication.[86]

Smith spent part of the day at home studying Hebrew. In the evening, he was visited by non-Mormon John Hollister, a closed communion Baptist from Portage County, Ohio, who remained overnight at the Smith home. In the morning, he confessed to Smith that he thought he knew a lot about religion, but after their conversation, he came to think otherwise. After breakfast, Smith studied Hebrew with Frederick Williams and Cowdery. Later, Smith complained that he was experiencing "some indisposition of health," so he rested for a while. Afterward, he received his mail, for which he was required to pay the postage.[87] As this was becoming a "common occurrence," Smith wrote a letter of complaint to the editor of the *Messenger and Advocate,* informing the public that he would no longer pay postage on incoming mail.[88]

After Smith preached at the schoolhouse on the evening of December 8, some of the brethren in attendance proposed hauling wood for him, suggesting that his "remarks included an expression of material and financial need." Entries in Smith's journal for the next two days support this. On the following day, Smith was visited by an Elder Packard, who forgave a $12.00 debt.

---

85. Smith, Dec. 3–4, 1835 (*JSP*, J1:115). JS History, 1834–36, 140 (*JSP*, H1:138), revises this to $250.

86. On Lewis's excommunication for accosting Smith in the street and demanding payment, see Minutes, May 23, 1836, Minute Book 1, 175 (Collier and Harwell, *Kirtland Council Minute Book,* 175).

87. Smith, Journal, Dec. 4–5, 1835 (*JSP*, J1:115–16).

88. Joseph Smith, Letter to the Editor, Dec. 5, 1835, *LDS Messenger and Advocate,* Dec. 1835, 240 (*JSP*, D5:103–104).

James Aldrich paid another $12.00 debt for Smith. An additional twenty other men paid Smith a total of $40.50, to which Parrish added $5.00. John Tanner and Shadrach Roundy donated food. "My heart swells with gratitude inexpressible," Smith wrote in his journal, "when I realize the great condescension of my heavenly Father, in opening the hearts of these, my beloved brethren to administer so liberally, to my wants and I ask God in the name of Jesus Christ, to multiply, blessings, without number upon their heads." On December 10, as previously proposed, the brethren chopped and hauled wood for Smith. A grateful Smith wrote a blessing for them in his journal: "I invoke the rich benediction of heaven to rest upon them, and their families ... and the way be prepared for them, that they may journey to the land of Zion and be established, on their inheritances, to enjoy undisturbe[d], peace and happiness for ever, ... which blessings I ask in the name of Jesus of Nazareth. Amen."[89]

Later the same day, Smith assisted about 200 men for an hour in putting out a fire in the lumber kiln, located on the flats near the sawmill and Whitney store. Three days later, the "board kiln, took fire again."[90] The kiln was used for drying and seasoning wood used in constructing the temple; its loss delayed the temple's completion.[91]

On December 12 Smith reprimanded a young lady for daring to question the authenticity of the Egyptian papyri. In the evening, he attended a debate at William Smith's and argued in favor of the question: "Was it necessary for God to reveal himself to man, in order for their happiness"? His participation was cut short when he was called away to bless an ailing Angeline Works, taking John Corrill with him. The next day, he returned with Parrish and married Ebenezer Robinson and Angeline Works, who was still recovering her health.[92]

Troubles with the Twelve

On December 15 Smith was at home and received many visitors, some wanting to see the papyri. In the afternoon, he was visited by Orson Hyde, who handed him a letter of complaint, claiming, among other things, that, contrary to revelation, the temple committee—Hyrum Smith, Reynolds Cahoon, and

---

89. Smith, Journal, Dec. 8–10, 1835 (*JSP*, J1:117–19); and JS History, 1834–36, 143 (*JSP*, H1:141).

90. Smith, Journal, Dec. 10–13, 1835 (*JSP*, J1:120–22).

91. JS History, 1834–36, 145 (*JSP*, H1:143).

92. Smith, Journal, Dec. 12–13, 1835 (*JSP*, J1:121).

Jared Carter—was being too generous to William Smith.[93] Smith claimed to have lost the letter and Hyde gave him a copy two days later, which he read to Smith himself. Hyde complained that while the Twelve were in the east holding conferences, "we strained every nerve to obtain a little something for our familys and regularly divided the monies equally for aught I know, not knowing that William had such a fountain at hom[e] from whence he drew his support." This fountain was the mercantile firm of Cahoon, Carter & Co., which appears to have been open for business by October 1835.[94] "I ascertained that Elder W[illia]m Smith could go to the store and get whatever he pleased," Hyde wrote, "and no one to say why do ye so, until his account has amounted to seven Hundred Dollars or there abouts."[95]

No doubt Smith was worried about division among the Twelve and what that might mean for the upcoming endowment in the temple, so he must have been relieved when the issue with Hyde and the temple committee was "settled amicably."[96] This was done by extending credit equally to all members of the Twelve.[97]

On December 16 McLellin, Brigham Young, and Jared Carter visited Smith, who exhibited the papyri and "explained many things concerning the dealings of God with the ancients, and the formation of the planetary system."[98] Smith used the word "formation" in his journal not to refer to creation but to the form or structure of the system, that is, the hierarchical organization of the planets, which Smith had detailed in his translation of characters from the Hôr papyrus in early October.[99] When Warren Parrish rewrote this portion of Smith's journal for Smith's contemporary history, he clarified that "formation" meant "especially the system of astronomy as taught by Abraham, which is contained upon these manuscripts."[100]

In the evening, Smith attended the continuation of the debate at William Smith's home exploring the question: "Was it necessary for God to

---

93. Smith, Dec. 15, 1835 (*JSP*, J1:123). On the uncanonized revelation to the Twelve referred to by Hyde, which stated that the Twelve should be treated equally, see Smith, Journal, Nov. 3, 1835 (*JSP*, J1:83; *JSP*, D5:32–36).

94. Advertisement, *Northern Times* (Kirtland, OH), Oct. 9, 1835, [4].

95. Orson Hyde, Letter to Joseph Smith, Dec. 15, 1835, Smith, Journal, Dec. 17, 1835 (*JSP*, D5:104–109; *JSP*, J1:124–28).

96. Smith, Journal, Dec. 17, 1835 (*JSP*, J1:128).

97. JS History, vol. B-1, Addenda, Note G (Vogel, *History of Joseph Smith*, 2:332; DHC 2:337–38).

98. Smith, Dec. 16, 1835 (*JSP*, J1:123–24).

99. Smith, Oct. 1, 1835 (*JSP*, J1:67).

100. JS History, 1834–36, Dec. 16, 1835 (*JSP*, H1:147).

reveal himself to mankind in order for their happiness"?[101] A decision was given in favor of the affirmative side, which was Joseph Smith's side. Nevertheless, Smith apparently suggested that the debate club be discontinued. A month earlier he had expressed his disapproval about the group, saying there was "too much of that enthusiasm that characterizes a lawyer at the bar, who is determined to defend his cause, right or wrong."[102] Becoming enraged, hot-tempered William Smith physically attacked his older brother and Jared Carter. Suddenly, the dysfunction of the Smith family was public and William's jealous resentment of Joseph's control over the family erupted into full view. "I am grieved beyond expression," Joseph wrote in his journal, "and can only pray God to forgive him inasmuch as he repents of his wickedness, and humbles himself before the Lord."[103]

More details of the altercation were recounted by Joseph in his letter to William two days later. Joseph said that he had not gone to William's house intending to break up the club. Nevertheless, he felt it was his duty as one of the presidents to speak out "when folly and that which militates against truth and righteousness, rears its head."[104] Smith apparently expressed his worry that exposure to skepticism would damage the faith of some, particularly when the subject of miracles had been explored on November 18. Almon Babbitt, a member of the Quorum of Seventy who had participated in the debate, responded that "a man must be a very weak man if he could not argue ag[a]inst the truth without being swerved." Babbitt said he could read Thomas Paine's *Age of Reason*, a well-known work critical of religion, the Bible, and miracles, "or any other work without being swerved" in his faith. At this, according to Babbitt, Joseph "got mad because he got overpowered in argument," and that "there would have been no disturbance if he had not got mad."[105]

At some point, as Smith recounted in his letter, William McLellin attempted to speak, but William Smith rudely interrupted him. Joseph said, "Do not have any feelings." In other words, "Do not react so emotionally." Hyrum asked to speak, and William said he could so long as he did not abuse school members in his house. Joseph tried to reason with William, but

---

101. See Smith, Journal, Dec. 12, 1835 (*JSP*, J1:120–21).
102. Smith, Nov. 18, 1835 (*JSP*, J1:106).
103. Smith, Dec. 16, 1835 (*JSP*, J1:124).
104. Joseph Smith, Letter to William Smith, ca. Dec. 18, 1835, Smith, Journal, Dec. 18–19, 1835 (*JSP*, J1:131; *JSP*, D5:117).
105. Minutes, Dec. 28, 1835, Minute Book 1, 132 (*JSP*, D5:125).

he "manifested an inconsiderate and stubborn spirit." Then, in frustration, Joseph said to William, "You [are] as ugly [hateful] as the devil."

Joseph Sr., attempting to maintain control over the increasingly embarrassing situation, "commanded silence." William replied that he "would say what [he] pleased in [his] own house." Father Smith responded, "Say what you please, but let the rest hold their tongues."

Joseph Jr. responded, "I will speak, for I built the house, and it is as much mine as yours" (in his letter to William, Smith admitted, "I should have said that I helped finish the house"). This infuriated William, who lunged at Joseph, probably to eject him from the house. Joseph tried to pull off his coat to better defend himself, but William was too quick, and in the scuffle Joseph aggravated a side injury he had received from the Hiram mob in 1832. Other men pulled the two brothers apart, and Joseph left. In his letter, Joseph said that in addition to "a lame side," he had received "marks, of violence … upon my body" and that he "returned home, not able to sit down, or rise up, without help."[106]

Smith biographer Richard L. Bushman has pointed out that fighting for honor was common in Smith's day, but this does not change what the encounter reveals about Smith's character and Smith family dynamics.[107] The dysfunction between Joseph and William became evident when, contrary to the judgment of Cowdery and David Whitmer, Joseph insisted that William be included in the Quorum of the Twelve Apostles as a means of saving his younger brother. As a member of the Twelve, William was under Joseph's control, and disagreeing with his older brother carried great social and institutional ramifications, which exacerbated the already strained Smith family dynamics. From William's point of view, there was no winning with Joseph. Cloaked in the mantle of the prophet, Joseph seemed always to get his way. In a previous dispute, Joseph had used his high office to prevail in a matter that was important to William: the beating of a young girl by her parents. Even with Hyrum and Parrish as arbiters, William stood no chance, especially when his anger was characterized as a character flaw and the issue was framed as an inability to follow authority. At this arbitration, William complained that Joseph was "always determined to carry [his] points whether they were right or wrong, and therefore he would not stand an equal chance

---

106. Smith, Journal, Dec. 18, 1835 (*JSP*, J1:132–33). In Smith's 1834–36 history, he states that he returned home "with marks of violence upon my body, with a lame side, I left your habitation bruised and wounded." JS History, 1834–36, 159 (*JSP*, H1:156).

107. Bushman, "The Character of Joseph Smith," 27.

with [him]." If William's gravitation towards reason and debate is any indication of his personality, Joseph's authoritarianism and arbitrariness certainly would have been frustrating. Now, Joseph was telling him what to do in his own home, and it did not matter what arguments William could devise because disagreeing with Joseph meant he was "justifying himself" and "treating the authority of the Presidency with contempt."[108] William was expected to be silent and conform to the decisions of the president—his brother—or church councils, which were under Joseph's control.

The next evening, December 17, Mother and Father Smith visited Joseph to discuss his difficulty with William. They agreed to move out of William's house and instead live with Joseph and Emma.[109]

On December 18 Hyrum delivered a letter to Joseph from William, which he read aloud to him. In the letter, William asked for forgiveness and, after being called to account for his actions by the Twelve the day before, offered to resign from the apostleship to avoid "falling from so high a station." A contrite William begged to keep his membership: "Do not cast me off for what I have done but strive to save me in the church as a member[.] I do repent of what I have done to you and ask your forgiveness—I concider the transgression the other evening of no small magnitude,—but it is done and I cannot help it now—I know brother Joseph you are always willing to forgive. But I sometimes think when I reflect upon the many injuries I have done you I feel as though confession was not hardly sufficient—but have mercy on me this once and I will try to do so no more."[110]

Hyrum sided with Joseph and believed William was wrong. Concerning Hyrum, Joseph wrote in his journal: "I could pray in my heart that all my brethren were like unto my beloved brother Hyrum, who possesses the mildness of a lamb and the integrity of a Job, and in short the meekness and humility of Christ, and I love him with that love that is stronger than death; for I never had occasion to rebuke him, nor he me which he declared when he left me to day."[111]

On the same day, Joseph began writing a letter to his younger brother, which he completed the next day. Among other things, Joseph explained that he had acted "in the spirit of my calling and in view of the authority of

---

108. Smith, Journal, Oct. 31, 1835 (*JSP*, J1:80).

109. Smith, Dec. 17, 1835 (*JSP*, J1:128–29).

110. William Smith, Letter to Joseph Smith, Dec. 18, 1835, Smith, Journal, Dec. 18, 1835 (*JSP*, J1:130; D5:114–15).

111. Smith, Journal, Dec. 18, 1835 (*JSP*, J1:129).

the priesthood that has been confered upon me," and that it was his "duty to reprove whatever I esteemed to be wrong[,] fondly hoping in my heart that all parties, would consider it right, and therefore humble themselves, that satan might not take the advantage of us, and hinder the progress of our School," referring to the school of the elders.[112]

Despite William's insubordination, Joseph refused to accept his resignation. "You desire to remain in the church, but forsake your apostleship," he wrote, "this is a stratigem of the evil one, when he has gained one advantage, he lays a plan for another, but by maintaining your apostleship in rising up, and making one tremendeous effort, you may overcome your passions, and please God."[113] He then reminded William how indebted the family was to him, both spiritually and temporally, stating, "I brought salvation to my fathers house, as an instrument in the hand of God, when they were in a miserable situation." Near the end of his letter, Joseph gave William some advice: "And if at any time you should concider me to be an imposter, for heavens sake leave me in the hands of God, and not think to take vengance on me your self. Tyranny usurpation, and to take mens rights ever has been and ever shall be banished from my heart."[114]

On December 19, the day Joseph finished his letter and sent it to William, he wrote in his own hand in his journal, "I have had many solemn feelings this day Concerning my Brothe[r] William and have prayed in my heart to fervently that the Lord will not cast him off but he may return to the God of Jacob and magnify his apostleship and calling may this be his happy lot for the Lord of Glorys Sake Amen."[115]

Smith spent Christmas Day at home with his family. In the evening, he was visited by Jonathan Crosby, who later recalled: "He showed me the records of the mummies and explained them to me. He could read them."[116] Also on this day, Cowdery concluded his long letter to William Frye of Lebanon, Illinois, about the Egyptian papyri. In a postscript not included in his publication of the letter in the December 1835 issue of the *Messenger and Advocate*, Cowdery stated: "There are a great number of Elders in Kirtland now, many of whom are attending an English school. We are expecting a Hebrew school to commence in a few weeks if we get a room prepared. The

---

112. Joseph Smith, Letter to William Smith, ca. Dec. 18, 1835, Smith, Journal, Dec. 18–19, 1835 (*JSP*, J1:131; *JSP*, D5:117).

113. Smith (*JSP*, J1:134; *JSP*, D5:120).

114. Smith (*JSP*, J1:134; *JSP*, D5:121).

115. Smith, Journal, Dec. 19, 1835 (*JSP*, J1:135).

116. Crosby, Autobiography, 14.

most of those Elders who are now in the school are studying and reviewing grammar, History, writing, &c. The House of the Lord is being finished as fast as can be expected considering the smallness of the means in the hands of the church."[117] In his history, John Corrill wrote, "In the fall, and early part of the winter of '35, the elders gathered in to Kirtland, to the number, I should think, of three or four hundred, who remained there through the winter. Schools were instituted for the use of the elders and others. Some studied grammar and other branches."[118]

On December 26 Smith resumed his study of Hebrew with Parrish and Williams.[119] In Smith's contemporary history, Parrish recorded that Smith "commenced regularly, & systematically, to study the venerable Hebrew language; we had paid some little attention to it before."[120] Their study of Hebrew was interrupted by Lyman Sherman, one of the presidents of the Seventy, who asked Smith for "the word of the Lord" concerning his duty. Smith then dictated a revelation in which the Lord forgave Sherman's sins and commanded him to "wait patiently until the solemn assembly" and then he will be called on a mission.[121]

On Sunday, December 27, the Seventy held a meeting and reported on their missionary activities during "the past season … in various States … generally with good success." According to the minutes, 175 individuals were baptized in 1835 because of the efforts of the Seventy.[122] This influx of converts was a component of Smith's effort to raise an army to redeem Zion. On the next day, Smith attended another meeting of the Seventy during which an account of their travels and missionary labors was given: "The meeting was interesting indeed, and my heart was made glad while listening to the relations of those that had been labouring, in the vinyard of the Lord with such marvelous success."[123]

On December 28 Smith attended a high council meeting to testify against Almon W. Babbitt for "misrepresenting" and "traducing" his character, asking the council to investigate so that "my character and influence

---

117. Oliver Cowdery, Letter to William Frye, Dec. 22, 1835, Cowdery, Letterbook, 75; "Egyptian Mummies–Ancient Records," *LDS Messenger and Advocate*, Dec. 1835, 233–37.

118. Corrill, *A Brief History*, 22 (*JSP*, H2:153).

119. Smith, Journal, Dec. 26, 1835 (*JSP*, J1:137).

120. JS History, 1834–36, 163 (*JSP*, H1:160).

121. Revelation, Dec. 26, 1835, Smith, Journal, Dec. 26, 1835 [D&C 108] (*JSP*, J1:137–38; *JSP*, D5:122–23).

122. Minutes, Dec. 27, 1835, *LDS Messenger and Advocate*, Jan. 1836, 253–54.

123. Smith, Journal, Dec. 28, 1835 (*JSP*, J1:139). It is possible that there was only one meeting and that one of the accounts is misdated.

may be preserved as far as it can in righteousness." Babbitt blamed Smith for the disruption at the debating club, claiming that Smith "got mad because he was overpowered in argument." Evidently Babbitt was standing "by the door of the house" and said these things to those nearby and "appeared dissatisfied with J. Smith's bad spirit," but Lyman Wight thought it was Babbitt who "showed a bad spirit against J. Smith." Babbitt later told others that "we would not have had any difficulty if J. Smith had not have got mad." According to Brigham Young, "Babbitt said Smith would not have wanted the school broke up, if they had not got defeated." Referring to the altercation between Joseph and William, Babbitt joked that "if they could not overpower by argument, they would by knocking down."

Rigdon delivered the decision that Babbitt "had let the adversary get the possession of his heart, in consequence of which he has spoken things falsely to the injury of J. Smith Junr. and by injuring him he has insulted the feelings of the Church of Christ. And that he shall confess publically to the satisfaction of his brethren." Babbitt confessed that what he said was "in anger" and that he did not intend to "rise up in rebelling against the government of the Church," but that "he thought he would give B[rother] J. Smith as good as he sent." He further said that he "confesses that he had injured J.S. character and is sorry for it, but … cannot confess all that President Rigdon has said in his speech."[124] According to Smith's journal, the council adjourned without a full confession from Babbitt after "parleying [discussing] with him a long time, and granting him every indulgence."[125]

On December 29 Smith attended a blessing meeting at Oliver Olney's with Emma, his parents, and Parrish. About fifteen people received patriarchal blessings from Joseph Sr., including Lyman Wight.[126]

In the evening, Smith preached in the schoolhouse for three hours to a large congregation, during which he made some indirect but pointed remarks to some Presbyterians who were present.[127] It may have been at this meeting that Smith expressed sorrow over the rebellion of his brother William and others. Daniel Tyler said that he went to a meeting in the schoolhouse on the flats where Smith presided. Even before the meeting began, Tyler said he "gazed upon the man of God" and "perceived sadness in his countenance and tears trickling down his cheeks." After the hymn was sung, Smith arose and

---

124. Minutes, Dec. 28, 1835, Minute Book 1, 131–34 (*JSP*, D5:123–27).
125. Smith, Journal, Dec. 28, 1835 (*JSP*, J1:138).
126. Smith, Dec. 29, 1835 (*JSP*, J1:139).
127. Smith.

delivered the opening prayer. "Instead, however, of facing the audience, he turned his back and bowed upon his knees, facing the wall," Tyler said. "This, I suppose, was done to hide his sorrow and tears." The seventy-five-year-old Tyler said that although he had heard many prayers in his day, "never until then had I heard a man address his Maker as though He was present listening as a kind father would listen to the sorrows of a dutiful child. ... There was no ostentation, no raising of the voice as by enthusiasm, but a plain conversational tone, as a man would address a present friend."[128]

Tyler said that when Smith addressed the congregation, "he spoke of his many troubles, and said he often wondered why it was that he should have so much trouble in the house of his friends, and he wept as though his heart would break." Among the things Smith said during his long sermon, Tyler remembered one extraordinary statement. "The Lord once told me," Smith declared, "that if at any time I got into deep trouble and could see no way out of it, if I would prophesy in His name, he would fulfill my words," and then added: "I prophesy in the name of the Lord that those who have thought I was in transgression shall have a testimony *this night* that I am clear and stand approved before the Lord."[129] In other words, go home and pray about him and receive a spiritual witness that he is still God's chosen prophet. Smith's altercation with his brother was not only embarrassing but seemed to many to be incongruent with his high and holy calling as a prophet. Finding himself in "deep trouble," Smith drew on his prophetic gift and threw the matter into the arena of subjective experience.

On New Year's Day, Smith reflected on his problems and the challenges of the coming year: "Notwithstanding, the gratitude that fills my heart on retrospecting the past year, and the multiplied blessings that have crowned our heads, my heart is pained within me because of the difficulty that exists in my fathers family." Smith's comments reveal that the Smith family's troubles extended beyond William's rebellion to other family members, most notably his brother-in-law, Calvin Stoddard, with whom he had a physical altercation the previous April. Reflecting on his relationship with his younger brother and brother-in-law, Smith wrote: "the powers of darkness, seeme[d to] lower over their minds and not only theirs but cast a gloomy shade over the minds of my brothers and sisters, which prevents

---

128. Daniel Tyler, "Recollections of the Prophet Joseph Smith," *Juvenile Instructor*, Feb. 15, 1892, 127. Tyler said, "The next Sabbath his brother William and several others made humble confessions before the public." This occurred on Sunday, January 3, 1836.

129. Tyler, 128.

them from seeing things as they really are." Seeing things "as they are" meant seeing them as Smith saw them and agreeing with his views. Smith worried that this "division in the family" threatened "to overthrow us and the Church" and "to prevent the saints from being endowed, by causing a division among the 12 also among the 70, and bickerings and jealousies, among the Elders and official members of the church, and so the leaven of iniquity foments and spreads among the members of the church." There was a lot at stake, and Smith was "determined that nothing on my part shall be lacking to adjust and amicably dispose of and settle all family difficulties, on this day."[130]

Later the same day, with help of his father and other family members, Smith reconciled with William. When William, Hyrum, and Uncle John Smith came to Smith's house, Smith invited them into a private room with Joseph Sr. and Martin Harris. Father Smith opened with prayer and then expressed himself on the matter "in a verry feeling and pathetic manner even with all the sympathy of a father whose feeling[s] were wounded deeply on the account of the difficulty that was existing in the family." Smith's journal notes that as the patriarch spoke, "the spirit of God rested down upon us in mighty power, and our hearts were melted." William then "made an humble confession" and asked Joseph's forgiveness for "the abuse he had offered," and Joseph asked his younger brother to forgive him "wherein [he] had been out of the way." The two men agreed to support one another and keep any future disagreements between themselves. They then called Emma, Mother Smith, and Parrish into the room and repeated the covenant to them. The Smiths were relieved and overcome with emotion. "Tears flowed from our eyes," Smith recorded in his journal. "It was truly a jubilee and time of rejoicing." Joseph then closed the meeting with prayer.[131]

An addendum to Smith's history, probably inserted by George A. Smith, states that after the reconciliation the group "all unitedly administered by laying on of hands to my cousin George A. Smith, who was immediately healed of a severe rheumatic affection [infection] all over the body, which caused excruciating pain."[132] In his autobiography, George said that he had been "attacked with inflamatory rheumatism, which swelled my legs, right arm and shoulder," leaving him without the use of the affected arm and in

---

130. Smith, Journal, Jan. 1, 1836 (*JSP*, J1:140–41).
131. Smith (*JSP*, J1:141).
132. JS History, vol. B-1, Addenda, 3, Note I (DHC 2:354), which was added by Wilmer Benson, probably on June 18, 1845. Vogel, *History of Joseph Smith*, 2:346, n32.

the "most excruciating pain." Shortly before being healed, George confided to Joseph that he was becoming discouraged because of his condition. Joseph's response provides a glimpse into his tenacity and determination. George recalled, "He told me I should never get discouraged, whatever difficulties might surround me, if I was sunk in the lowest pit of Nova Scotia and all the Rocky Mountains pile on top of me, I ought not to be discouraged but hang on, exercise faith and keep up good courage and I should come out on the top of the heap." After the blessing, George said, "my pain instantly left me and I gradually recovered my strength and the use of my limbs."[133]

Orson Johnson, a member of the high council, had already preferred charges against William Smith on December 29 for "Unchristianlike conduct in speaking disrespectfully of President Joseph Smith ... and the revelations & commandments given through him" and "for attempting to inflict personal violence on President J. Smith."[134] Despite the brothers' reconciliation, the council considered Johnson's complaint on January 2. William "humbly confessed" and was forgiven. He also promised to make the same confession before the church on the Sabbath. Babbitt also admitted wrongdoing and was forgiven.[135] Joseph's relief was evident in this day's journal entry: "Our hearts were made glad on the occasion, and there was joy in heaven, and my soul doth magnify the Lord, for his goodness and mercy endureth forever."[136]

On Sunday, January 3, Smith, Rigdon, and Hyrum gave Lorenzo Barnes, a Seventy, his Zion blessing, promising: "Thou shalt remane untill the coming of the Son of man in the clowds of heaven y[e]a thou shalt view the winding up seen of all things & stand with the hundred forty & four thousand on Mount Zion."[137] Smith also attended church and heard Rigdon preach "on the subject of revelation." In the afternoon, he attended a meeting where "William Smith made his confession to the Church to their satisfaction, and was cordially received into fellowship again." The same evening, Smith heard William preach "a fine discourse." In his journal, Smith expressed relief for the restoration of unity in his family and the church: "This

---

133. George A. Smith, Memoir and Autobiography, 81–82.

134. Orson Johnson, Charges against William Smith, Dec. 29, 1835, Minute Book 1, 135 (*JSP*, D5:128).

135. Minutes, Jan. 2, 1836, Minute Book 1, 135–36 (*JSP*, D5:128–31).

136. Smith, Journal, Jan. 2, 1836 (*JSP*, J1:142).

137. Joseph Smith et al., Blessing to Lorenzo Barnes, Jan. 3, 1836, Lorenzo Barnes, Reminiscences and Diaries, vol. 2, [51]–[52] (*JSP*, D5:131–35).

day has been a day of rejoicing to me, the cloud that has been hanging over us has burst with blessings on our heads, and Satan has been foiled in his attempts to destroy me and the Church, by causing jealousies to arise in the hearts of some of the brethren, and I thank my heavenly father for, the union and harmony which now prevails in the Church."[138]

---

138. Smith, Journal, Jan. 3, 1836 (*JSP*, J1:142–43).

$\mathscr{P}entecost$

JANUARY–MARCH 1836

Our duty, in our present circumstances ... is to seek such a revival of
religion as commenced in the Day of Pentecost ...
> —*John Brown,* On the Means and Manifestations
> of a Genuine Revival of Religion *(Edinburgh, Scot.:*
> *William Oliphant and Son, 1840), 38*

On January 4, 1836, Smith met with others in his "translating room," which was the westernmost of the five rooms on the third story of the temple, and organized a school to study Hebrew.[1] Dr. Daniel Peixotto sent notice the day previous that he would not be able to start teaching the Hebrew class until the next Wednesday; class members voted to release him as the teacher. Instead, William McLellin and Orson Hyde were assigned to visit Hudson Seminary, about thirty miles south of Kirtland, to secure a replacement. Smith, who had been studying Hebrew on his own and with others, became the instructor until a teacher could be obtained.[2]

On the following day, the Hebrew school met and divided into classes. During the first day of instruction, Smith got into an "unpleasant" dispute with Orson Pratt over the pronunciation of a Hebrew word, causing Smith to write in his journal that Pratt has a "stubborn spirit, which I was much grieved at."[3]

On January 6 Smith attended Hebrew school and labored to resolve his conflict with Pratt, who confessed that he should not have made an issue over a small matter and asked forgiveness. McLellin returned from Hudson with news that he had hired Joshua Seixas, "highly celebrated as

---

1. See Robison, *The First Mormon Temple,* 55, figs. 4–7.
2. Smith, Journal, Jan. 4, 1836 (*JSP,* J1:143).
3. Smith, Journal, Jan. 5, 1836 (*JSP,* J1:145); JS History, 1834–36, 170 (*JSP,* H1:167).

a hebrew schollar," for a seven-week term for $320 for forty students.[4] Seixas, a Sephardic Jew from New York City, had taught Hebrew at various institutions in the East since the 1820s and in 1833 published his own textbook, *A Manual Hebrew Grammar*. With his family, he had moved to Ohio in the fall of 1835 to teach at Oberlin Collegiate Institute and Western Reserve College in Hudson. The Hebrew class continued to meet in the temple until Seixas arrived on January 26.

On January 7 Smith attended a feast at Bishop Newel Whitney's to which the poor were invited. This was said to be "after the order of the Son of God … according to the instructions of the Savior" in Luke 14:13–14: "When thou makest a feast, call the poor, the maimed, the lame, the blind: And thou shalt be blessed." Among other things, they sang the Songs of Zion and spoke about the approaching gathering to Mount Zion.[5] Elizabeth, Whitney's wife, remembered that the feast lasted for three days, with "Prophet Joseph and his two Counselors being present each day, talking, blessing, and comforting the poor."[6] According to Smith's journal, he was not present on the second day but instead attended the Hebrew School. On the last day of the feast, January 9, Smith received a note from Whitney informing him that the "voice of the spirit" had promised that Brother Joseph would make an appearance. Smith dismissed the school and went to the feast with his wife and parents.[7]

Priesthood Meetings

On January 13 Smith presided over a "Grand Council" of church leaders from Kirtland and Clay County (Missouri), which met in the attic story of the printing office to call and ordain several men to fill vacancies in the Kirtland bishopric and high council, which had been created when Cowdery, Joseph Smith Sr., and Hyrum Smith were called as assistant presidents and Luke Johnson and Orson Hyde were called as apostles. Five members of the Missouri high council had been replaced the previous week.[8] A committee consisting of Joseph Smith, Rigdon, Hyrum Smith, Phelps, and David Whitmer was assigned to draft the rules and regulations to govern

---

4. Smith, Journal, Jan. 6, 1836 (*JSP*, J1:145). On Seixas, see Goldman, "Joshua/James Seixas (1802–74)"; LeRoi C. Snow, "Who Was Professor Seixas?," *Improvement Era*, Feb. 1936, 67–71.

5. Smith, Journal, Jan. 7, 1836 (*JSP*, J1:146).

6. [Elizabeth Ann Smith Whitney], "A Leaf from an Autobiography," *Woman's Exponent*, Nov. 1, 1878, 83. Orson F. Whitney attributed this statement to "Mother Whitney." "The Aaronic Priesthood," *Contributor*, Jan. 1885, 129–30.

7. Smith, Journal, Jan. 9, 1836 (*JSP*, J1:146–47; *JSP*, D5:135–38).

8. Minutes, Jan. 6, 1836, Minute Book 2, 67.

the House of the Lord, which they wrote up and printed the following day.[9] After Rigdon spoke about the upcoming endowment, the meeting closed.[10]

Reflecting on this day, Smith wrote optimistically: "This has been one of the best days that I ever spent, there has been an entire unison of feeling expressed in all our proceedings this day, and the Spirit of the God of Israel has rested upon us in mighty power, and it has been good for us to be here, in this heavenly place in Christ Jesus, and altho much fatiegued with the labours of the day, yet my spiritual reward has been verry great indeed."[11]

Two days later Smith met with priesthood leaders in the temple's third-story "council room." Smith "organized the authorities of the church agreeably to their respective offices." The rules and regulations of the temple were read three times. Rules that prohibited whispering during meetings or interrupting speakers were discussed, debated, and eventually adopted.[12] When the vote was taken by quorums, the high councils of Kirtland and Zion voted before the Twelve, which caused some consternation among the members of the Twelve. Nevertheless, Cowdery, who had just returned from attending the Democratic Party convention in Columbus, recorded that "several Quorams of the authorities of the Church met today, and transacted important business preparatory to the endowment. The Spirit of the Lord was in our midst."[13]

On January 16 Smith attended a special council meeting to resolve resentment that members of the Twelve harbored towards others in the hierarchy. Representing the Twelve as their president, Thomas Marsh outlined three complaints. First, the presidency of the Kirtland high council had suspended two apostles, Hyde and McLellin, and chastised the rest based on a letter from Warren Cowdery of Freedom, New York, that charged the Twelve with not having explained the importance of donating to the building of the temple. Second, the Twelve were unhappy that on the previous day they voted after the high councils of Kirtland and Zion, whereas they previously had been placed next to the First Presidency. Third, the Twelve were upset by Hyrum Smith's remarks at the September 28, 1835, trial of Gladden Bishop, whom the Twelve had previously tried while they were in the east, and felt

9. Smith, Journal, Jan. 14, 1836 (*JSP*, J1:151–53; D5:143–45).

10. Minutes, Jan. 13, 1836, Minute Book 1, 200–203 (*JSP*, D5:138–43); Smith, Journal, Jan. 13, 1836 (*JSP*, J1:148–51).

11. Smith, Journal, Jan. 13, 1836 (*JSP*, J1:151).

12. Minutes, Jan. 15, 1836, Minute Book 1, 203–205 (*JSP*, D5:146–48); Smith, Journal, Jan. 15, 1836 (*JSP*, J1:153–56).

13. Cowdery, Diary, Jan. 15, 1836.

Hyrum had questioned their authority. They also complained that the high council presidency had disregarded their charge against Warren Cowdery for unchristian conduct, for which they were criticized by Oliver Cowdery (Warren's younger brother), who "on a certain occasion had made use of language to one of the twelve that was unchristian and unbecoming any man, and that they would not submit to such treatment."[14]

Smith responded that he had not lost confidence in the Twelve; that the letter may have been too harsh, but so was McLellin's response; and the sitting order in the last meeting was only temporary, that "the Twelve are not subject to any other than the first Presidency." To increase unity, Smith proposed that they all enter into a covenant: "I will now covenant with you before God, that I will not listen to nor credit any derogatory report against any of you, nor condemn you upon any testimony beneath the heavens, … until I can see you face to face, and know of a surety; and I do place unlimited confidence in your word, for I believe you to be men of truth; and I ask the same of you; when I tell you anything, that you place equal confidence in my word, for I will not tell you, I know anything, which I do not know."[15]

Presidents Rigdon and Williams voiced their support for Smith. Rigdon said he should have charged Warren Cowdery and put him to trial. Cowdery, in fact, would be tried on March 5, 1836, and on the 7th he wrote a confession and had it published in the *Messenger and Advocate*.[16] Marsh called for a vote, and the Twelve voted that they were "perfectly satisfied" and all felt a "perfect unison," and they manifested their willingness to covenant with Smith by raising their hands.[17]

Washings and Anointings

In the evening, Oliver Cowdery and John Corrill met with Smith at his home. According to Cowdery's diary, "after pure water was prepared, [we] called upon the Lord and proceeded to wash each other's bodies, and bathe the same with whiskey, perfumed with cinnamon. This we did that we might be clean before the Lord for the Sabbath, confessing our sins and covenanting to be faithful to God." It is unknown why Smith chose this occasion to

---

14. Smith, Journal, Jan. 16, 1836 (*JSP*, J1:156–58; *JSP*, D5:148–54).

15. Smith (*JSP*, J1:158–59; D5:151–53).

16. "Notice," *LDS Messenger and Advocate* (Kirtland, OH), Feb. 1836, 263. Warren Cowdery's trial was not recorded in the Minute Book, but Oliver Cowdery mentioned it in his diary. Cowdery, Diary, Mar. 5, 1836.

17. Smith, Journal, Jan. 16, 1836 (*JSP*, J1:159–60; D5:153–54).

introduce this ritual, but he was apparently attempting to follow the example of the ancient Aaronic priests and Levites who officiated in the tabernacle in the wilderness and later in the temple in Jerusalem. "While performing this washing unto the Lord with solemnity," Cowdery wrote, "our minds were filled with many reflections upon the propriety of the same, and how the priests anciently used to wash always before ministering before the Lord."[18] The Old Testament mentions only washing with water followed by an anointing with perfumed olive oil (Ex. 30:19–31). Smith's ritual had more to do with the cleansing practices of his day. A February 1833 revelation called the "word of wisdom" had discouraged drinking "strong drinks," or distilled spirits, but allowed its use in cleaning bodies.[19] Washing with cinnamon-infused whiskey symbolized the importance of being pure before entering the Lord's presence. "As we had nearly finished this purification," Cowdery noted, "bro. Martin Harris came in and was also washed."[20]

On Sunday, January 17, Smith presided over a meeting in the school-house, arranging the quorums in order of authority: the First Presidency, the Twelve, the Seventy, and the high councils of Kirtland and Zion. The meeting became highly emotional when Rigdon turned the time over to each member of the presidency and Twelve to speak. According to Smith's journal, "The Lord poured out his Spirit upon us, and the brethren began to confess their faults one to the other and the congregation were soon overwhelmed in tears and some of our hearts were too big for utterance, the gift of toungs, came upon us also like the rushing of a mighty wind, and my soul was filled with the glory of God."[21] Cowdery recorded: "The Holy Spirit rested upon us. O may we be prepared for the endowment,—being sanctified and cleansed from all sin."[22]

Seixas would not arrive in Kirtland for another week, yet Smith recorded in his journal on January 19 that those attending the school of the elders were reading Hebrew. "It seems as if the Lord opens our minds in a marvelous manner to understand his word in the original language," he wrote, "and my prayer is that God will speedily endue us with a knowledge of all languages and tongues, that his servants may go forth for the last time to bind

---

18. Cowdery, Diary, Jan. 16, 1836.

19. Revelation, Feb. 27, 1833, "A Word of Wisdom," Gilbert, Notebook, [113] [D&C 89:7] (*JSP*, D3:20–21).

20. Cowdery, Diary, Jan. 16, 1836.

21. Smith, Journal, Jan. 17, 1836 (*JSP*, J1:160–61).

22. Cowdery, Diary, Jan. 17, 1836.

up the law, and seal up the testimony."[23] Cowdery spent the day recording blessings and thinking about the promised endowment, writing in his diary that he felt a strong desire to dedicate himself to the Lord and prayed: "O my God, my soul desires to see thee as thy favored ones in days of old."[24]

On January 21 John W. Olived, a minister from Connecticut, came to Smith's door and asked Joseph Sr. "if the pro[p]het lives here"? Senior Smith replied that he did not understand. Olived repeated his question several times and finally asked "if Mr. Smith lives here"? Joseph Sr. replied: "O yes Sir I understand you now." When Joseph Jr. came into the room, he answered several questions, including: "Wherein we differ from other christian denomination[s]"? Smith responded, "We believe the bible, and they do not." When the minister remarked that he believed the Bible, Smith told him to be baptized by immersion "for the remission of sins" followed by the "laying on of hands for the reseption of the Holy Ghost." Olived reportedly "manifested much surprise." Smith then excused himself to attend school.[25]

In the afternoon, Smith met with the presidency in the attic story of the printing office and washed their bodies in "pure water" and also perfumed their bodies and heads "in the name of the Lord."[26] Cowdery described the washing and anointings: "At about three o'clock P.M. I assembled in our office garret, having all things prepared for the occasion, with presidents Joseph Smith, jr. F. G. Williams, Sidney Rigdon Hyrum Smith, David Whitmer, John Whitmer and elder John Corrill, and washed our bodies with pure water before the Lord, preparatory to the annointing with the holy oil. After we were washed, our bodies were perfumed with a sweet smelling oderous wash," probably with the same cinnamon-infused whiskey used five days earlier.[27]

In the evening, Smith again met with the presidency in his office on the third floor of the temple. The high councils of Kirtland and Zion and both bishoprics were present in the adjacent rooms. Smith began by consecrating the oil and then anointing and blessing his father, after which each member of the presidency did the same—"all blessing him to be our patraark [patriarch]." Joseph Sr. then anointed and blessed each of them in order of their age, blessing and sealing upon Joseph Jr. "the blessings of Moses, to lead Israel in the latter days." Afterward each of the presidents blessed Smith,

23. Smith, Journal, Jan. 19, 1836 (*JSP*, J1:164).
24. Cowdery, Diary, Jan. 19, 1836.
25. Smith, Journal, Jan. 21, 1836 (*JSP*, J1:166).
26. Smith (*JSP*, J1:166–67).
27. Cowdery, Diary, Jan. 21, 1836.

prophesying great things concerning him.[28] Cowdery wrote that the presidents "were annointed with the same kind of oil and in the man[ner] that were Moses and Aaron, and those who stood before the Lord in ancient days, and those in the other rooms with annointing oil prepared for them."[29]

Concerning this introduction of washings and anointings, Phelps wrote to his wife: "We are preparing to make ourselves clean, by first cleansing our hearts, forsaking our sins, forgiving every body, all we ever had against them; ano[in]ting washing the body; putting on clean decent clothes, by annointing our heads, and by keeping all the commandments."[30]

In the presence of these leaders, Smith had a vision of the celestial kingdom and saw among other inhabitants his oldest brother, Alvin, and wondered how he could have been there since he had never been baptized. The voice of the Lord then declared that "all who have died with[out] a knowledge of this gospel, who would have received it, if they had been permited to tarry, shall be heirs of the celestial kingdom of God." Not only those like Alvin, who died before the restoration, but "all that shall die henseforth, without a knowledge of it, who would have received it, with all their hearts, shall be heirs of that kingdom, for I the Lord will judge all men according to their works according to the desires of their hearts."[31] Smith mentioned that he "also beheld the Terrestial kingdom," but subsequently had it crossed out, perhaps worried that it might create a problem with his 1832 vision of three heavens—when he stated that the heirs of the terrestrial kingdom had "died without Law; ... who are the sprits of men kept in prison whom the son visited and preached the gospel unto them ... who received not the testimony of Jesus in the flesh but afterwards received it ... who are honorable men of the earth who were blinded by the craftiness of men."[32] Instead, Smith continued to describe the celestial kingdom: "I also beheld that all children who die before they arive to the years of accountability, are saved in the celestial kingdom of heaven."[33]

Smith said that he saw the Twelve in a foreign land standing in a circle and Jesus looking upon them and weeping. He saw McLellin healing the

28. Smith, Journal, Jan. 21, 1836 (*JSP*, J1:166–67, 170).

29. Cowdery, Diary, Jan. 21, 1836.

30. William W. Phelps, Letter to Sally Phelps, Jan. 1836, [4].

31. Smith, Journal, Jan. 21, 1836 (*JSP*, J1:167–68; D5:158–59); D&C 137. The text of this vision also mentions "I saw father Adam, and Abraham and Michael," which seemingly contradicts earlier statements that Adam and Michael were the same person (D&C 27:11); see also Cowdery, Letterbook, 15 (Jan. 1, 1834).

32. "The Vision," Feb. 16, 1832, Revelation Book 2, 7 [D&C 76:75] (*JSP*, D2:189).

33. Smith, Journal, Jan. 21, 1836 (*JSP*, J1:168; D5:160). See also Moses 6:54.

lame and Brigham Young preaching "in a strange land, in the far southwest, in a desert place, upon a rock in the midst of about a dozen men of colour who, appeared hostile." He saw an angel with "a drawn sword" protecting him. Finally, he saw the Twelve in the celestial kingdom and the redemption of Zion.[34] (Unfortunately, the redemption of Zion, for which the endowment in the temple was preparatory, would never materialize and half of the Twelve would soon apostatize.)

Warren Parrish, who was the scribe for these entries in Smith's journal, wrote that after his own anointing, he "saw in a vision the armies of heaven protecting the Saints in their return to Zion— & many things that [Smith] saw."[35] The difference in visionary experiences highlights their subjective, individualistic nature; such visionary experiences did not prevent Parrish, for example, from denouncing both the Book of Mormon and Smith's revelations in 1838. At this time, he did not try to explain away his own visionary experiences but alleged concerning Smith and Rigdon, "having a knowledge of their private characters and sentiments, I believe them to be confirmed Infidels, who have not the fear of God before their eyes, notwithstanding their high pretensions to holiness, and frequent correspondence with the Angels of Heaven, and the revelations of Jesus Christ by the power of the Holy Ghost."[36]

Father Smith then anointed and blessed the bishops of Kirtland and Zion and their counselors, who were confirmed by the presidents. The high councils of Kirtland and Missouri were invited into the room, and Hyrum Smith anointed John Smith, president of Kirtland high council, and David Whitmer anointed Simeon Carter, president of Missouri high council. Carter and Smith then anointed the other high counselors.[37]

According to Smith's journal, these anointings were followed by visionary experiences, during which "some of them saw the face of the Saviour, and others were ministered unto by holy angels, and the spirit of prophecy and revelation was poured out in mighty power, and loud hosanahs, and glory to God in the highest, saluted the heavens for we all communed with the h[e]avenly host's."[38] Cowdery recorded: "The glorious scene is too great to be described in this book, therefore, I only say, that the heavens were opened

---

34. Smith (*JSP*, J1:168; D5:159–60).

35. Smith (*JSP*, J1:170).

36. Warren Parrish, Letter to the Editor, Feb. 5, 1838, *Painesville (OH) Republican*, Feb. 15, 1838, [3].

37. Smith, Journal, Jan. 21, 1836 (*JSP*, J1:170).

38. Smith.

to many, and great and marvelous things were shown."[39] Edward Partridge wrote that "a number saw visions & others were blessed with the outpouring of the Holy Ghost and we shouted hosanna to the most high."[40] Such experiences were not unlike what other charismatic religious groups experienced in their meetings and revivals.[41] The meeting finally ended after 1:00 a.m.

On January 22 Smith attended the Hebrew school but "spent the time in rehearsing to each other the glorious scenes that transpired on the preceding evening, while attending to the ordinance of holy anointing."[42] In the evening, the holy anointing was repeated with the addition of the Twelve and presidents of the Seventy.[43] Smith ordained, blessed, and anointed Thomas Marsh, who then anointed and blessed the other members of the Twelve in order of their age, followed by Smith pronouncing blessings upon their heads. According to Smith's journal: "The heavens were opened and angels ministered unto us."[44] Years later, Apostle Heber C. Kimball said that "when the Twelve in a circle were anointed, [the ancient apostle] John stood in their midst."[45] How they knew this—whether it was visionary, felt, or declared to them by Smith—is not explained.

The Twelve anointed and blessed the presidents of the Seventy and gave them authority to bless the other seventies. Sylvester Smith jumped to his feet and declared that "the heavens were opened" and that he saw "the horsemen of Israel and the chariots thereof." After Don Carlos Smith was anointed and blessed as president of the high priests by the presidents of Kirtland and Missouri, Rigdon closed the meeting "by invoking the benediction of heaven upon the Lords anointed." The group of gathered priesthood officials then "shouted a loud hosannah" and for the next half hour were enwrapped in a spontaneous expression of various kinds of ecstatic experience, including speaking in tongues, visions, and the loss of physical power.[46] Partridge wrote that the hosanna shout was performed according to Smith's instruction, and that "the shout & speaking in unknown tongues lasted 10 or 15 minutes," during which also "a number saw visions as they declared unto us."[47]

---

39. Cowdery, Diary, Jan. 21, 1836.

40. Partridge, Diary, Jan. 21, 1836.

41. See Taves, *Fits, Trances, and Visions*.

42. Smith, Journal, Jan. 22, 1836 (*JSP*, J1:171).

43. Joseph Smith's journal does not mention the Kirtland and Missouri bishoprics, but they are included in Cowdery, Diary, Jan. 22, 1836.

44. Smith, Journal, Jan. 22, 1836 (*JSP*, J1:171).

45. School of the Prophets Provo Records, May 18, 1868.

46. Smith, Journal, Jan. 22, 1836 (*JSP*, J1:171–72).

47. Partridge, Diary, Jan. 22, 1836.

When the meeting ended at about 2:00 a.m., Smith said he went home and that "the spirit & visions of God attended me through the night," possibly reflecting Smith's belief that dreams with religious content were visions.[48]

On the following day, January 23, Smith attended school as usual, but everyone wanted to talk about the events of the previous night. Alva Beaman, who had recently been appointed as president of the elders quorum and was not present the previous night, expressed skepticism and then, after being chastised, repented and promised "he would try to resist Satan in [the] future."[49] Cowdery recorded that he went to the office but did not get much work done and instead "Conversed considerable time with president Rigdon on the subject of his vision concerning the return of the Ten Tribes." Later the same evening, Cowdery was visited by Apostle Marsh, who "talked much upon the subject of visions: he greatly desired to see the Lord." With visionary experiences already occurring among some of the leaders, many were looking to the approaching endowment with great excitement and expectation. "Brother Marsh is a good man," Cowdery wrote, "and I pray that his faith may be strengthed to behold the heavens open."[50]

The next day Smith met the several quorums in the room under the printing office and instructed the high council of Kirtland to confess their sins. In the evening, he met with the presidency in the room over the printing office to discuss the "endowment & the preparation necessary for the solemn Assembly which is to be called when the House of the Lord is finished."[51] Cowdery recorded that the presidency "conversed upon the time of, and preparation and sanctification for the endowment."[52]

Performance of the holy anointing continued on January 28, when Smith and his counselors met with the quorums of high priests and elders in the evening in his third-story office in the temple. After the presidency anointed and blessed the presidents of these quorums, Smith left them to perform the ordinance on the other members and went into the adjoining room where the Twelve and Seventy were assembled. Smith instructed the presidents of the Twelve and Seventy "to call upon God with uplifted hands to seal the blessings which had been promised to them by the holy anoint[in]g," which they had previously received. While Smith was speaking, Sylvester Smith, as he later

---

48. Smith, Journal, Jan. 22, 1836 (*JSP*, J1:172). This concept was expressed in Lehi's declaration in 1 Nephi 8:2: "Behold, I have dreamed a dream; or, in other words, I have seen a vision."

49. Smith, Journal, Jan. 22, 1836 (*JSP*, J1:172).

50. Cowdery, Diary, Jan. 23, 1836.

51. Smith, Journal, Jan. 24, 1836 (*JSP*, J1:172–73).

52. Cowdery, Diary, Jan. 24, 1836.

reported, saw "a pillar of fire rest down & abide upon the heads of the quorem as we stood in the midst of the Twelve." After the Twelve and Seventy finished their sealing prayers, Rigdon with uplifted hands led them in a hosanna shout.[53]

Roger Orton, one of the seven presidents of the Seventy, said he saw "a mighty Angel riding upon a horse of fire with a flaming sword in his hand followed by five others—encircle the house & protect the saints even the Lords anointed from the power of Satan & a host of evil spirits which were striving to disturb the saints." William Smith said he "saw the h[e]avens op[e]ned & the Lords host protecting the Lords anointed," that is, all the anointed leaders, not just Smith. Zebedee Coltrin, also one of the seven presidents of Seventy, said he "saw the saviour extended before him as upon the cross" and then "crowned with a glory upon his head above the brightness of the sun."[54] Smith's journal records that he also had "a glorious vision" without describing it. Another of the Seventy, Harrison Burgess, apparently recalling this occasion, said he remembered that "Joseph Exclaimed aloud, 'I behold the Saviour, the Son of God.'"[55]

Following this meeting, Smith returned home elated, writing in his journal: "I retired to my home filled with the Spirit, and my soul cried Hosanna to God and the Lamb through the silent watches of the night, and while my eyes were closed in sleep, the visions of the Lord were sweet unto me; and his glory was round about me, praise the Lord."[56]

Hebrew Lessons

On January 26 Joshua Seixas began teaching Hebrew to Smith and other Mormons in Kirtland, using his own textbook, which was designed for a six-week curriculum.[57] The plan was for Seixas to teach from 10:00 a.m. to 11:00 a.m. and from 2:00 p.m. to 3:00 p.m. "His introduction pleased me much," Smith wrote. "I think he will be a help to the class in learning the Hebrew."[58] Interest in Kirtland was such that Seixas was held over several weeks to teach additional classes. For eight of the next nine weeks, he taught Hebrew every day but Sundays on the third floor of the temple to 80–120 students.[59]

---

53. Smith, Journal, Jan. 28, 1836 (*JSP*, J1:174).
54. Smith (*JSP*, J1:174–75).
55. Burgess, Autobiography, 4.
56. Smith, Journal, Jan. 28, 1836 (*JSP*, J1:175).
57. See Seixas, *A Manual Hebrew Grammar*, iv. On Smith as a student of Hebrew, see Grey, "'The Word of the Lord in the Original.'"
58. Smith, Journal, Jan. 26, 1836 (*JSP*, J1:173).
59. On the Hebrew school, see Ogden, "The Kirtland Hebrew School (1835–36)"; and Grey, "'The Word of the Lord in the Original.'"

On January 30, after the Hebrew school, Smith showed Seixas and others the papyri. "Mr. Seixas, our Hebrew teacher, examined them with deep interest, and pronounced them to be original beyond all doubt," Smith observed. "He is a man of excellent understanding, and has a knowledge of many languages, which were spoken by the ancients, and he is an honorable man so far as I can judge yet."[60] Of course, Seixas could not read Egyptian, although Smith implied that his knowledge of ancient languages was perhaps pertinent in this situation.

Following two weeks of intensive grammar lessons, Seixas had his classes begin translating portions of the Hebrew Bible in the third week, which included passages dealing with the account of creation in Genesis 1, from which Smith would later draw for his continued translation of the Book of Abraham in Nauvoo, Illinois, in 1842, and his famous 1844 King Follett funeral discourse.[61]

On February 15 Smith recorded: "On this day we commenced translating the Hebrew-language, under the instruction of professor Seixas, and he acknowledg's that we are the most forward of any class he ever taught, the same length of time."[62] Smith proved to be a good student, for he and nine others were selected by Seixas to receive additional instruction.[63] After attending Hebrew school on February 17, Smith recorded: "My soul delights in reading the word of the Lord in the original, and I am determined to persue the study of the languages until I shall become master of them, if I am permitted to live long enough."[64]

On March 7 Smith met with the Hebrew class in Seixas's room in the evening and translated Genesis 17. This marked the end of Seixas's six-week course in Hebrew. After the class was dismissed, the school committee remained to discuss the possibility of retaining Seixas for another quarter, but no agreement was reached. The next day Smith met with the Hebrew class and translated most of Genesis 22. On his own, he translated Exodus 3:1–10, which together with Psalms 1–2, were to be "our next lesson."[65] Seixas

---

60. Smith, Journal, Jan. 30, 1836 (*JSP*, J1:178).

61. On the influence of Hebrew on Smith's dictation of Abraham 3–5 in 1842, see Zucker, "Joseph Smith as a Student of Hebrew"; Grey, "'The Word of the Lord in the Original'"; and Grey, "Approaching Egyptian Papyri through Biblical Language." On Smith's April 7, 1844, King Follett funeral sermon, see Ehat and Cook, *The Words of Joseph Smith*, 340–62.

62. Smith, Journal, Feb. 15, 1836 (*JSP*, J1:186).

63. Smith, Journal, Feb. 19, 1836 (*JSP*, J1:187). The nine others were Cowdery, Phelps, Rigdon, Partridge, McLellin, Hyde, Orson Pratt, Sylvester Smith, and Parrish.

64. Smith, Journal, Feb. 17, 1836 (*JSP*, J1:186).

65. Smith, Journal, Mar. 8, 1836 (*JSP*, J1:195). In the Edward Partridge papers, there is a sixteen-page booklet of his translations from the Hebrew Bible of Genesis 13 and 22, Exodus

kept teaching until March 11, then left the following day. He returned with his family on March 14, after a two-week vacation, to give additional instruction until March 29, for a total of eight weeks and two days.[66]

In addition to attending classes taught by Seixas, Smith also studied Hebrew on his own. As the editors of the Joseph Smith Papers have observed, "Between 23 November 1835 and 29 March 1836, J[oseph] S[mith]'s journal mentions his studying Hebrew—whether in class, with colleagues, or by himself—no fewer than seventy times."[67]

On March 30 Seixas gave Smith a certificate verifying the completion of his course in Hebrew: "Mr Joseph Smith Junr has attended a full course of Hebrew lessons under my tuition; & has been indefatigable in acquiring the principles of the Sacred Language of the Old Testament Scriptures in their original tongue. He has so far accomplished a knowledge of it, that he is able to translate to my entire Satisfaction."[68] In his journal Smith stopped short of prophesying of his teacher's conversion. "I believe the Lord is striving with him, by his holy spirit, and that he will eventually embrace the new and everlasting covenant ... but I forebear lest I get to prophesying upon his head."[69] Despite the united prayer of Smith and others, Seixas remained Jewish.[70]

Organizing the Quorums

While attending Hebrew classes, Smith continued to conduct church business. On January 30 he attended a "conference of the Presidency of the Church" and determined "that no one be ordained to an office in the Church in Kirtland without the voice of the several quorums when assembled for church business." This was a change from the 1835 version of the Articles and Covenants, which stipulated that a vote of the church or branch be taken.[71] Smith and his counselors also instructed Alvah Beaman, president of the elders quorum, to make a list of elders in his quorum, including any not belonging to a quorum.[72] The list that Beaman presented to the presidency four days later was used to select members for a second quorum of seventies.[73]

15, and Psalms 1. Partridge, Scriptural Passages, ca. 1836. Partridge was in Smith's Hebrew class. Smith, Journal, Feb. 19, 1836 (*JSP*, J1:187).

66. Smith, Journal, Mar. 7–11, 1836 (*JSP*, J1:195–96).

67. Historical Introduction, *JSP*, D5:216.

68. Seixas, Certificate to Joseph Smith, Mar. 30, 1836 (*JSP*, D5:214–16).

69. Smith, Journal, Feb. 19, 1836 (*JSP*, J1:187).

70. Cowdery, Diary, Feb. 15, 1836.

71. Articles and Covenants, ca. Apr. 1830 [ca. Aug. 1835], D&C, 1835 ed., II:16 [D&C 20:65–66] (*JSP*, D1:123). This will be clarified on February 12, 1836. Minute Book 1, 137 (*JSP*, D5:172).

72. Minutes, Jan. 30, 1836, Minute Book 1, 137 (*JSP*, D5:164).

73. *JSP*, D5:164–65n320.

In the evening, Smith held a meeting in the third story of the temple, organized the quorums, and instructed the presidents of the Seventy on the holy anointing. "Having set all the quorems in order," he wrote, "I returned to my house being weary with continual anxiety & labour in putting all the Authorities in [order] & in striving to purify them for the solemn assembly according to the commandment of the Lord."[74] Nevertheless, Smith spent two more days organizing and instructing the quorums.[75]

Sealings

On February 6 Smith met with the anointed quorums in the third story of the temple in the evening to "seal all of their blessings" and "bring [them] to the order which God had shown to me."[76] The quorums were divided into three groups: high priests and elders in the west room, the Seventy and Twelve in the second room, and the bishoprics in the third room. Smith gave them strict instructions about how to conduct a sealing meeting, with the apparent goal of promoting spiritual manifestations.

They were to begin with "solemn prayer before god without any talking or confusion," which is to be concluded "with a sealing prayer by Pres. Rigdon." Following this, "all the quorums are to shout with one accord a solemn hosannah to God & the Lamb with an Amen—amen & amen—& then all take seats & lift up their hearts in silent prayer to God & if any obtain a prophecy or vision to rise & speak that all may be edefied & rejoice together." Smith's technique differed little from the revivalists', which moved, encouraged, and even pressured congregations to experience various religious phenomena, such as fits, trances, fainting, or tongues. Such phenomenon spread through camp meetings by what nineteenth-century skeptics called "religious enthusiasm," or an emotional/psychological self-enforcing loop of expectation, anticipation, and suggestion.[77] Boston Congregationalist minister Charles Chauncy, a critic of the emotionalism often displayed at revivals during the 1740s, described the effect of Methodist George Whitefield's hell-fire and damnation style of preaching the "*sensible Perceptions* [of the 'Multitudes'] arose to such a Height, as that they *cried out, fell down, swooned away*, and to all Appearance, were like persons in *Fits*." More than a century before the social "contagion" theory of Gustave Le Bon, Chauncy explained

---

74. Smith, Journal, Jan. 30, 1836 (*JSP*, J1:178).

75. Smith, Journal, Jan. 31, and Feb. 1, 1836 (*JSP*, J1:178–79).

76. Smith, Journal, Feb. 6, 1836 (*JSP*, J1:180–81). See also Cowdery, Diary, Feb. 6, 1836.

77. For an extended discussion of revival phenomena and various psychological explanations, see Taves, *Fits, Trances, and Visions*.

the phenomenon as a result of suggestibility, where the speaker influences "*one* or *two* weak *Women*," who shriek in despair for their souls, and their "Shrieks catch from one to another, till a great Part of the Congregation is affected." According to Chauncy, this heightened state of mind led to a variety of spiritual manifestations: "Visions now became common, and trances also, the subjects of which were in their own conceit transported from earth to heaven, where they saw and heard most glorious things; conversed with Christ and holy angels."[78]

However, this was not easily achieved, for Smith reported: "I had considerable trouble to get all the quorums united in this order—I went from room to room repeatedly & charged each separately—assuring them that it was according to the mind of God." The elders had not followed Smith's directions, and when Don Carlos Smith (president of the high priests meeting in the same room) tried to remind them of their instructions, some of the elders said "they had a teacher of their own," referring to President Alvah Beaman. Smith said, "This caused the spirit of the Lord to withdraw ... & this quorem lost th[e]ir blessing in a great measurs."[79] On hearing about this in the third room with the Bishops, Smith sent Presidents Hyrum Smith and Oliver Cowdery to help the elders. The elders quorum record states that "there seemed to be a cloud of darkness in the room. Press. O[liver]. Cowdery & H[yrum]. Smith came and gave some instructions ... and the cloud was broaken and some shouted, Hosanna and others spake in tongues." When Smith returned, he "reprimanded us for our evil deeds which was the cause of our darkness. He prophesied saying this night the key is turned to the nations; and the angel John is about commencing his mission to prophesy before kings, and rulers, nations tongues and people."[80]

The other quorums were more compliant. Consequently, the Seventy "enjoyed a great flow of the holy spirit [and] many arose & spok[e] testifying that they were filled with the holy spirit which was like fire in their bones so that they could not hold their peace but were constrained to cry hosannah to God & the Lamb & glory in the highest." William Smith saw in vision the Twelve and the seven presidents of Seventy in England and prophesied that

---

78. Charles Chauncy, "A Letter from a Gentleman in Boston to Mr. George Wishart ... of Edinburgh," in Bushman, ed., *The Great Awakening*, 118–19. Charles-Marie Gustave Le Bon (1841–1931) is known for his 1895 work *The Crowd: A Study of the Popular Mind*, considered one of the seminal works on crowd psychology.

79. Smith, Journal, Feb. 6, 1836 (*JSP*, J1:181).

80. Kirtland Elders Quorum, "Record," Feb. 6, 1836. Cook and Backman, *Kirtland Elders' Quorum Record*, 6.

"a great work would be done by them in the old countries & God was already beginning to work in the hearts of the p[e]ople." Zebedee Coltrin, one of the seven presidents, saw "the Lords Host," and others spoke in tongues and prophesied. Despite the trouble with the elders, Smith said: "This was a time of rejoicing long to be remembered! praise the Lord."[81]

Cowdery recorded that "their anointing blessings were sealed by uplifted bands and praises to God," that "many saw visions, many prophesied, and many spoke in tongues," and that the meeting "closed a little before 12 o'clock."[82]

Regulating Ordinations

On Sunday, February 7, Smith attended church in the room below the printing office with the quorums seated in order and heard the confession and exhortation of the bishopric of Zion. In the afternoon, the bishopric of Kirtland and Rigdon preached. In the evening, Smith met with the Presidency and Seventy in the loft above the printing office to choose more seventies and bless Alvin Winegar, one of the "Zion brethren."[83] These Seventy will be formerly called and ordained during the coming week.[84]

On February 12 Smith met with the quorums in the school room on the third floor of the temple in the evening to discuss restricting ordinations to protect the church. In his preliminary remarks, Smith observed that "many are desiring to be ordained to the ministry, who are not called and consequently the Lord is displeased." Next, he said, "many already have been ordained who ought [not] to hold official stations in the church because they dishonour themselves and the church and bring persecution swiftly upon us, in consequence of their zeal without k[n]owledge—I requested the quorum's to take some measures to regulate the same."[85] Two resolutions passed requiring the unanimous vote of the general authorities in Kirtland and a general conference in the branches before a man could be ordained.[86] This clarified what had been discussed on January 30, which had only mentioned ordinations in Kirtland.

The Twelve met in the temple the next day to amend the second part of the resolution to say that the general conference is to be appointed by them in

---

81. Smith, Journal, Feb. 6, 1836 (*JSP*, J1:181–82).

82. Cowdery, Diary, Feb. 6, 1836.

83. Smith, Journal, Feb. 7, 1836 (*JSP*, J1:182); Smith et al., Blessing to Alvin Winegar, Feb. 7, 1836 (*JSP*, D5:165–68); Cowdery, Diary, Feb. 7, 1836.

84. Kirtland Elders Quorum, "Record," Feb. 8 and 11, 1836 (Cook and Backman, *Kirtland Elders' Quorum Record*, 7, 8); Stephen Post, Journal, Feb. 13, 1836; Record of the Seventies, vol. A, 6–8.

85. Smith, Journal, Feb. 12, 1836 (*JSP*, J1:184–85).

86. Minutes, Feb. 12, 1836, Minute Book 1, 137–38 (*JSP*, D5:170–73); Smith, Journal, Feb. 12, 1836 (*JSP*, J1:184–85).

accordance with Smith's instructions on priesthood given the previous spring and published as Doctrine and Covenants 3, rather than by local leaders.[87] The Twelve's amendment was rejected by the high council of Kirtland on February 17, by the high council of Zion on the following evening, and by the presidency on February 22, at which time the original resolutions of February 12 were "unanimously ... adopted without amendments."[88] The new policy requiring the approval of the general authorities in Kirtland before ordaining a man was apparently practiced only briefly and soon abandoned as impractical.[89]

On February 24 Smith attended a meeting of the quorums to consider the impropriety of ordaining a large number of men seeking official positions in the church. Consequently, only seven of the twenty-six men applying for ordination were approved. In addition to recording licenses and conference minutes, Hyde, Cowdery, and Sylvester Smith were appointed to draft regulations for ordaining men. The Twelve and seven presidents of the Seventy were assigned to organize missionaries to proselytize in the region around Kirtland.[90]

On March 3 Smith met with several quorums in the evening to discuss the resolutions on ordinations and licenses that had been initially proposed on February 12 and 24. The goal was to centralize priesthood licensing and regulate ordinations to assure conferences and branches that the traveling elders were legitimate officers. Consequently, the first of six resolutions ordered that all licenses be issued from the church's Kirtland headquarters and recorded in a book. Other resolutions dealt with appointing a chair and clerk, re-issuing licenses to current holders, and publishing newly issued licenses in the church newspaper. The resolutions were accepted unanimously by all the quorums.[91]

Smith was sustained as the standing chair and Frederick Williams as clerk to issue licenses, while Rigdon and Cowdery were sustained as president and clerk pro tempore. A vote was taken among the Twelve to see if they would withdraw their amendment to the February 12 resolutions and all but three—John F. Boynton, Lyman E. Johnson, and Orson Pratt—were willing.[92]

87. Instruction on Priesthood, Mar. 1–May 4, 1835, D&C, 1835 ed., III:11–13, 16–17, 30 [D&C 107:23–24, 33, 35, 38–39, 58] (*JSP*, D4:314–15).

88. Minutes, Feb. 17, 18, and 22, 1836, Minute Book 1, 139 (*JSP*, D5:179–80).

89. See Minutes, June 10, 1836, and Oct. 2, 1837, Minute Book 1, 210, 247 (Collier and Harwell, *Kirtland Council Minute Book*, 175–76, 193–94).

90. Smith, Journal, Feb. 24, 1836 (*JSP*, J1:189).

91. Minutes, Mar. 3, 1836, Minute Book 1, 140–43 (*JSP*, D5:180–85); and Smith, Journal, Mar. 3, 1836 (*JSP*, J1:193). See also minutes in *LDS Messenger and Advocate*, Feb. 1836, 266–68.

92. Smith, Journal, Mar. 3, 1836 (*JSP*, J1:194). As chairman, Joseph Smith signed nearly 300 new licenses by June 1836. See Kirtland Elders' Certificates, 1–157.

On Sunday, March 13, Smith met with the presidency and some of the Twelve and "counseled with them upon the subject of removing to Zion this Spring." Moving the church's headquarters to Missouri was a necessary, long-overdue step in the redemption of Zion. "We conversed freely upon the importance of her redemption," he wrote, "the necessity of the Presidency removing to that place, that their influence might be more effectually used in gathering the saints to that country; and we finally came to the resolution to emigrate on or before the 15th of May next if kind Providence smiles upon us, and opens the way before us."[93] This meant that almost immediately after the dedication of the Kirtland Temple, not only would an army of missionaries fan out in every direction, but the church's leadership would move to Missouri, leaving Kirtland's Mormon population greatly reduced and diminishing due to immigration to Zion.

Six days later Smith met with the several quorums in the temple and "gave some instructions relative to the sealing power, in a short but powerful address" and "made some remarks respecting the coming meeting, and gave out some appointments." Rigdon "sealed the blessings of the Lord on those who had been anointed, by prayer and with a shout of Hosanna to God and, the Lamb."[94] Later the same day, Apostles Boynton, Johnson, and Pratt met with Smith and the presidency to discuss their insistence on amending the February 12 resolution concerning ordinations in branches outside Kirtland to include oversight by the Twelve; they eventually withdrew their objections.[95]

On March 26 Smith spent the day in his office with the presidency and others preparing for the dedication of the temple and meeting of the solemn assembly which was to occur on the following day.[96] Cowdery wrote that he, Rigdon, Warren A. Cowdery, and Parrish met with Smith in his temple office and "assisted in writing a prayer for the dedication of the house."[97] The prayer was likely set in type on the press of the *Messenger and Advocate* that night and printed as a broadside for Smith to read at the dedication.

Dedication[98]

The day for dedicating the House of the Lord had finally arrived nearly three

---

93. Smith, Journal, Mar. 13, 1836 (*JSP*, J1:197).

94. Kirtland Elders Quorum, "Record," Mar. 19, 1836 (Cook and Backman, *Kirtland Elders' Quorum Record*, 12).

95. Minutes, Mar. 19, 1836, Minute Book 1, 144 (*JSP*, D5:185).

96. Smith, Journal, Mar. 26, 1836 (*JSP*, J1:199).

97. Cowdery, Diary, Mar. 26, 1836.

98. The minutes of the dedication of the Kirtland Temple were recorded in Smith's journal under March 27, 1836 (*JSP*, J1:200–211), and published in "Kirtland, Ohio, March 27th, 1836,"

years after the ground had been broken. Anticipation about the promised endowment of power must have been high on March 27, when 500–600 Saints gathered before the massive olive-green doors were even opened. Meanwhile, Smith and other officials were inside the temple dedicating and consecrating the pulpits. With the general authorities seated in the pulpits according to their order of authority, the presidents assisted in seating between 900 and 1,000 people in the pews. When "every seat and aisle were crowded," the doors were ordered closed.[99] According to George A. Smith, "The congregation was so large that we could not all get in; and when the house was full, then, of course, the doors were closed, and no more admitted. This caused Elder Frazier Eaton, who had paid seven hundred dollars towards building the house, to apostatize, because he did not get there early enough to [attend] the meeting."[100] A simultaneous meeting was held in the nearby schoolhouse, which also crowded to capacity and caused some to congregate outside during the eight-hour dedication.

The atmosphere in the temple must have been electric as the congregation sat in anticipation of what was about to transpire. The room in which they sat featured a high vaulted or elliptical ceiling and was well-lighted with two large arched windows at the east and west ends and five and a half smaller gothic-styled windows on each side. It was well-ornamented with moldings, pillars, and an elaborate four-tiered system of pulpits at the east and west ends. Each of the three ascending tiers consisted of three connected semi-circled pulpits, where the presidents of the various quorums were seated. John Corrill, who was in charge of finishing the temple, described the pulpits and the order of seating:

> These pulpits were alike in each end of the house, and one was for the use of the Malchisedec [Melchizedek], or high priesthood, and the other for the Aaronic, or lesser priesthood. The first, or higher apartment, was occupied by the first presidency over all the church; the second apartment, by the President of the high priests, and his two counsellors; the third by three of the High Priests; and the fourth by the President of the Elders, and his two counsellors. The highest apartment of the other pulpit was occupied by the Bishop of the church and his two counsellors; the next by the President of the priests and his two counsellors; the third by the President of the

LDS *Messenger and Advocate*, Mar. 1836, 274–81 (*JSP*, D5:188–209; hereafter Minutes), which Oliver Cowdery said were written by him. Cowdery, Diary, Mar. 31, 1836.

99. Minutes, Mar. 27, 1836, 274 (*JSP*, D5:191).

100. George A. Smith, "Historical Discourse," *Journal of Discourses*, Nov. 15, 1864, 11:9.

teachers and his two counsellors; and the fourth by the President of the deacons and his two counsellors.[101]

These two systems of pulpits were flanked on either side by four rows of short benches, originally intended in 1833 for "visiting officers,"[102] but now were occupied at the west end by the high council of Kirtland and Quorum of the Twelve, and the east end by the high council of Zion (Missouri) and the seven presidents of the Seventy. With these newly-organized quorums displayed in their assigned pulpits, the transition from an egalitarian leadership of elders to a hierarchy of leaders and disciplinary councils was complete and provided the stability necessary for the continued expression of the charismatic gifts, which was about to take place.

At 9:00 a.m., Rigdon began the meeting by reading Psalm 96, which entreats listeners to "sing unto the Lord a new song," for "strength and beauty are in his sanctuary," and to "bring an offering, and come into his courts" (vv. 1, 6, 8); and Psalm 24, which declares that the "earth is the Lord's, and the fulness thereof" (v. 1), a passage previously used to encourage donations and consecration of property to the church (D&C 104:17). This psalm also mandates that only those with "clean hands, and a pure heart" should "receive the blessing from the Lord" and "stand in his holy place," where "the King of glory shall come in" (vv. 3–7). A significant contribution of $960 was collected on this occasion.[103]

The choir, seated in special pews in the four corners of the room, led by M. C. Davis, sang Hymn 19—"Ere Long the Veil Will Rend in Twain"— about the return of Jesus.[104] After Rigdon prayed, another hymn was sung about one day praying in the appointed city of Zion.

Rigdon then spoke for two and a half hours, preaching from the text of Matthew 8:18–20, but more particularly from verse 20: "The foxes have holes, and the birds of the air have nests; but the Son of man hath not where to lay his head." He drew tears from listeners when he said it was because of their sacrifice in building the temple, despite threats from their enemies that the walls would never be raised, that the Lord no longer needed to say, "The Son of Man hath not where to lay His head." Rigdon observed that Jesus declared this, although the Jews had synagogues and a temple. This was because they

---

101. Corrill, *Brief History*, 21–22 (*JSP*, H2:151, 153).
102. Plan of the House of the Lord, ca. June 1–25, 1833, [1] (*JSP*, D3:142). See Petersen, "The Kirtland Temple," 405–409.
103. Smith, Journal, Mar. 27, 1836 (*JSP*, J1:201).
104. Minutes, Mar. 27, 1836, 274 (*JSP*, D5:191).

"were not led by revelation." Indeed, "*This* ... was the grand difficulty among them," that is, "Their unbelief in present revelation." This situation prevailed, Rigdon declared, until Smith began his career. The sectarians worship "according to outward forms" and "the precepts and commandments of men," which is why "the Son of Man hath not where to lay His head." Despite the many spacious churches built by sectarians, there is "not one except this, on the face of the whole earth, that was built by divine revelation."[105]

According to Cowdery, Rigdon's "whole soul appeared to be fired with his subject. ... The comparison drawn between the different religious sects of ancient and modern times, was perfectly natural, and simple yet it was done in that confident, masterly manner, accompanied with those incontrovertible proofs of his position, that was directly calculated to cheer and gladden the hearts of the Saints."[106] Smith's journal noted that Rigdon's prayer and sermon were "very forcible and sublime, and well adapted to the occasion."[107]

Rigdon then called on the several quorums and the congregation to sustain Smith as a "Prophet and Seer," which was unanimously manifested. Afterward, another hymn about the return of Jesus was sung, followed by a fifteen-minute intermission.

Dedicatory Prayer

The afternoon session opened by singing "Adam-ondi-Ahman," a hymn about the return of the earth to its paradisiacal state and worshiping "Jesus face to face." Afterward, Smith gave a short sermon, then called on the quorums and congregation to sustain each of the quorums. Another hymn about Zion followed that included the lines: "Come, let us seek our God today!" and "Peace to this sacred house!" Finally, Smith stood to dedicate the temple. However, some were surprised when he read a long, eloquently-written prayer, which had been composed the previous night and printed as a broadside.[108] According to George A. Smith, Smith's reading of the prayer "was a great trial of faith to many. 'How can it be that the prophet should read a prayer?' What an awful trial it was, for the Prophet to read a prayer!"[109] Much of the prayer was a combination of quotes from and allusions to

---

105. Minutes, 275–76 (*JSP*, D5:194–96).

106. Minutes, 276 (*JSP*, D5:195).

107. Smith, Journal, Mar. 27, 1836 (*JSP*, J1:203).

108. Smith (*JSP*, J1:204–10); Minutes, Mar. 27, 1836, 277–80 [D&C 109] (*JSP*, D5:199–206); and Broadside, "Prayer, at the Dedication of the Lord's House in Kirtland, Ohio, March 27, 1836."

109. George A. Smith, "Historical Discourse," Nov. 15, 1864, *Journal of Discourses*, 11:9.

various passages of scripture from the Bible as well as revelations Smith had previously dictated.[110]

Smith's prayer began by thanking God, "who keepest covenant[s] and showest mercy unto thy servants," and then declared that the saints have obeyed his commandment to build a house to his name and asked God to accept it, that "the Son of Man might have a place to manifest himself to his people." He then quoted a December 1832 revelation commanding that a "solemn assembly" be called, and asked for "a fulfillment of the promises" made in an August 1833 revelation "that thy glory may rest down upon thy people, and upon this thy house which we now dedicate to thee, that it may be sanctified and consecrated to be holy, and that thy holy presence may be continually in this house; and that all people who shall enter upon the threshhold of the Lord's house may feel thy power and be constrained to acknowledge that thou hast sanctified it, and that it is thy house, a place of thy holiness."[111]

Smith prayed that the temple would fulfill its purpose as a house of learning and training for missionaries: "And we ask thee, holy Father, that thy servants may go forth from this house, armed with thy power, and that thy name may be upon them and thy glory be round about them, and thine angels have charge over them; and from this place they may bear exceeding great and glorious tidings, in truth, unto the ends of the earth."[112] Later, he prayed: "Let the anointing of thy ministers be sealed upon them with power from on high: let it be fulfilled upon them as upon those on the day of Pentecost: let the gift of tongues be poured out upon thy people, even cloven tongues as of fire, and the interpretation thereof. And let thy house be filled, as with a rushing mighty wind, with thy glory."[113]

Smith hoped to replicate the experience of the ancient apostles, who were instructed by Jesus to "tarry ye in the city of Jerusalem, until ye be endued with power from on high," before beginning their missions to take the gospel to the world (Luke 24:49). This was fulfilled on the Day of Pentecost, which was celebrated by the Jews fifty days after Passover. According to Acts 2:1–6, when the apostles met to observe this holiday, there was a sound like a "rushing mighty wind" that filled the house, and "cloven tongues" like a

---

110. Cook, *Revelations*, 218, 330n3.

111. Minutes, Mar. 27, 1836, 277–78 [D&C 109:1–13] (*JSP*, D5:199–200); Revelation, Dec. 27–28, 1832, Revelation Book 2, 45–46 [D&C 88:118–20] (*JSP*, D2:345); Revelation, Aug. 2, 1833-A, Revelation Book 2, 63 [D&C 97:15–17] (*JSP*, D3:202).

112. Minutes, Mar. 27, 1836, 278 [D&C 109:22–23] (*JSP*, D5:202). See Revelation, Jan. 2, 1831, Revelation Book 1, 51-52 [D&C 38:32–33] (*JSP*, D1:232).

113. Minutes, 278–79 [D&C 109:22–23, 35–37] (*JSP*, D5:202–203).

flame of fire appeared above each of their heads as they spoke in tongues to a gathered multitude of mixed nationalities, yet miraculously "every man heard them speak in his own language." This did not happen in Kirtland, but the Saints were looking for any charismatic experience as a sign of God's acceptance of the temple and their reception of special power.

The building of the temple was a magnificent accomplishment, but it could not fully compensate for the failure to redeem Zion. Smith therefore prayed for God to "remember those who have been driven by the inhabitants of Jackson county, Missouri, from the lands of their inheritance, and break off, O Lord, this yoke of affliction, that has been put upon them. … O Lord, how long wilt thou suffer this people to bear this affliction, and the cries of their innocent ones to ascend up in thine ears, and their blood to come up in testimony before thee, and not make a display of thy power in their behalf? … Make bear thine arm O Lord, and redeem that which thou didst appoint a Zion unto thy people!"[114] Smith hoped that the missionary program he was about to launch would gather recruits for the army of Israel that would help to redeem Zion with power and thus repair his reputation as a prophet.

Finally, Smith prayed: "O hear, O hear, O hear us, O Lord, and answer these petitions, and accept the dedication of this house, unto thee, the work of our hands, which we have built unto thy name; and also this church to put upon it thy name … and let these thine anointed ones be clothed with salvation, and thy saints shout aloud for joy. AMEN AND AMEN."[115]

After Smith's dedicatory prayer, the choir sang Hymn 90—"The Spirit of God Like a Fire Is Burning"—which was composed by Phelps and includes the inspiring lines: "The visions and blessings of old are returning | The angels are coming to visit the earth"; "We'll wash and be washed, and with oil be anointed, | Withal not omitting the washing of feet; | For he that receiveth his penny appointed | Must surely be clean at the harvest of wheat."[116] Afterward, Smith asked each quorum if they accepted the dedicatory prayer and considered the house dedicated; all quorums unanimously said yes.[117]

Testimony

After the sacrament of bread and wine was administered, Smith "bore record of his mission."[118] His journal gives more detail, stating that he "bore

---

114. Minutes, 279 [D&C 109:47, 49, 51] (*JSP*, D5:203–204).
115. Minutes, 280 (*JSP*, D5:206).
116. *A Collection of Sacred Hymns*, 120–21.
117. Minutes, Mar. 27, 1836, 281 (*JSP*, D5:208).
118. Minutes, 281 (*JSP*, D5:208).

testimony of the administering of angels."[119] Stephen Post recorded that Smith "testified of the Angel of the Lord appearing unto him to call him to the work of the Lord, & also of being ordained under the hands of the Angel of the covenant."[120] Smith was followed by others bearing testimony. Don Carlos Smith "bore record of the truth of the work of the Lord in which we are engaged," and Cowdery "testified of the truth of the book of Mormon, and of the work of the Lord in these last days."[121]

Frederick Williams "bore record that a Holy Angel of God, came and set between him and J. Smith sen. while the house was being dedicated."[122] To be closer to the congregation, Smith had given up his seat in the middle of the top pulpit to his father. According to Smith's journal, the "angel entered the window" while Rigdon was "making his first prayer … and remained there during his prayer."[123] Post, a seventy, recorded Williams more specifically saying the angel entered the window behind the pulpit.[124] Edward Partridge recorded that "Williams saw an angel" but interlinearly inserted "or rather the Savior," possibly conflating it with what another person saw.[125] Years later, Truman Angell recalled that Smith identified this angel as the apostle Peter.[126] Joseph Sr. was unaware of the angel's presence, which must have been something Williams experienced alone. When Phelps wrote to his wife about the meeting, he simply said: "An Angel came in on the first seat during the prayer," leading her and others in Missouri to assume everyone had seen it.[127]

The angel was not mentioned in the minutes published in the *Messenger and Advocate*, but Smith's journal added that David Whitmer "saw angels in the house."[128] However, George A. Smith remembered that Whitmer said he saw three angels during the priesthood meeting, which was held later in the evening.[129]

Hyrum Smith, on behalf of the building committee, commended those who had sacrificed to build the temple. In closing, Rigdon made a few

---

119. Smith, Journal, Mar. 27, 1836 (*JSP*, J1:210).
120. Post, Journal, Mar. 27, 1836.
121. Minutes, Mar. 27, 1836, 281 (*JSP*, D5:208).
122. Minutes, 281.
123. Smith, Journal, Mar. 27, 1836 (*JSP*, J1:210–11).
124. Post, Journal, Mar. 27, 1836.
125. Partridge, Journal, Mar. 27, 1836.
126. Angell, Autobiography, 16.
127. Phelps, Letter to Sally Phelps, Apr. 1836, [1].
128. Smith, Journal, Mar. 27, 1836 (*JSP*, J1:211).
129. George A. Smith, "Historical Discourse," Nov. 15, 1864, *Journal of Discourses*, 11:10.

remarks, gave a short prayer, and led the congregation in the hosanna shout.[130] Smith's journal records: "We then sealed the proceedings of the day by a shouting hosanah to God and the Lamb 3 times sealing it each time with Amen, Amen, and Amen."[131]

Apparently, this inspired Brigham Young to deliver a spontaneous display of speaking and singing in tongues, followed by fellow apostle David Patten, who interpreted and then gave a short exhortation in tongues himself. The congregation, which had maintained a "quiet demeanor during the whole exercise," was dismissed with Smith's blessing a little after 4:00 p.m.[132]

Eliza R. Snow remembered only that "angels appeared to some, while a sense of divine presence was realized by all present, and each heart was filled with 'joy inexpressible and full of glory.'"[133] William McLellin, however, later expressed disappointment in the proceedings: "When that noble structure the Temple in Kirtland was dedicated, after only being partly finished, it was done without any power being sent forth, or manifested in any degree to the large congregation assembled in it. I was present and know what I saw."[134]

Priesthood Meeting

In the evening, Smith met with more than 400 members of the priesthood quorums and instructed them concerning the ordinance of the washing of feet to be conducted on Wednesday.[135] Benjamin Brown, an elder visiting from New York, recorded that Smith opened the meeting by declaring "the day of Penticost was continued"; and Post wrote that Smith expounded on "the order of dedicating a house to God" and gave further instructions "relative to our preaching & to our endowment."[136]

Several attendees described an unusual and spontaneous outpouring of the gifts of prophecy and tongues. In his contemporary account, Brown, drawing on language from Acts 2, reported that "many prophesied in the name of the Lord then began to speak in tongues and it filled as it were the whole house, perhaps there were forty speaking at once Cloven tongues of

130. Minutes, Mar. 27, 1836, 281 (*JSP*, D5:209).

131. Smith, Journal, Mar. 27, 1836 (*JSP*, J1:211).

132. Minutes, Mar. 27, 1836, 281 (*JSP*, D5:209).

133. Tullidge, *Women of Mormondom*, 95. Cf. 1 Pet. 1:8.

134. William E. McLellin, Letter to Joseph Smith III, July 1872, [4] (Larson and Passey, eds., *The William E. McLellin Papers*, 493).

135. JS History, vol. B-1, Addenda, Note J, 4 (DHC 2:428); Smith, Journal, Mar. 27, 1836 (*JSP*, J1:211).

136. Benjamin Brown, Letter to Sarah M. Brown, Mar. 1836 [ca. Apr. 1836]; Post, Journal, Mar. 27 and 28, 1836.

fire was seen to sit on many of them [and] an hand was seen laid upon one [brother] when he spake in tongues to the lamanites."[137] Decades later, he wrote that "the Spirit of the Lord, as on the day of Pentecost, was profusely poured out. Hundreds of the Elders spoke in tongues, but many of them being young in the Church, and never having witnessed the manifestation of this gift before, felt a little alarmed. This caused the Prophet Joseph Smith to pray the Lord to withhold the Spirit. Joseph then instructed them on the nature of the gift of tongues, and the operation of the Spirit generally. We had a most glorious and never-to-be-forgotten time. Angels were seen by numbers present, and the first endowments were received."[138]

According to an addendum in his history, Smith gave instructions on the spirit of prophecy and "called on the Congregation to speak, and not to fear to prophesy good concerning the saints, for if you prophecy ... the downfall of the enemies of Zion, and the rising of the Kingdom of God, it shall come to pass.—do not quench the spirit for the first one that opens his mouth shall receive the spirit of prophecy." George A. Smith arose and began to prophesy, "when a noise was heard like the sound of a rushing mighty wind which filled the temple, and all the congregation simultaneously arose being moved upon by an invisible power many began to speak in Tongues and prophesy others saw glorious visions." According to this addition, which was probably inserted by George A. Smith in 1845, Joseph Smith "beheld the Temple was filled with angels," which he "declared to the congregation."[139] This account, like Brown's, highlights Smith's guiding followers into charismatic experiences.

In his earlier account, Brown gave more details, stating that "many Visions [were] seen, one saw a pillar or cloud rest down upon the house bright as when the sun shines on a cloud like as gold, two others saw three personages hovering in the room with bright keys in their hands. ... Father Stephens saw on sunday evening two rows of Angels through the House, at another time the glory of God came down on the Elders from the head down half way."[140] Brown was reporting the subjective experiences of some of those who attended. He did not mention his participation in the phenomena, nor did he claim to have seen anything himself. Even his report that "the west end of the

---

137. Brown, Letter.

138. Brown, *Testimonies for the Truth*, 10–11.

139. JS History, vol. B-1, Addenda, Note J, 3–4 (DHC 2:428), which was added by Wilmer Benson probably on June 18, 1845. See Vogel, *History of Joseph Smith*, 2:413n121.

140. Brown, Letter to Sarah M. Brown, Mar. 1836 [ca. Apr. 1836].

House was illuminated by a light from heaven seen on the outside by many" is too vague to assess properly. It is unclear if the same light that was seen by those outside the temple was seen by anyone inside. Of course, the pulpits at the west end of the temple where Smith sat would have been well lit for the meeting, and perhaps some on the outside reported what they thought was an unusual intensification of the light, perhaps caused by the movement of the veils. The lower court was fitted with a series of heavy canvas curtains or veils "painted white" rolled up on long polls and suspended from the ceiling, which could be lowered to the floor by a system of ropes and pulleys hidden in the pillars thereby dividing the lower court into four compartments. Another series of shorter curtains suspended above the Melchizedek and Aaronic pulpits could also be lowered to divide each of the four tiers of pulpits into small compartments.[141] Those outside the temple may have observed the effects of artificial light on the whitened veils when they were lowered or possibly an increase in light when they were raised.

The last entry in Cowdery's diary reports his attendance at this meeting and includes an account of visions he experienced: "The Spirit was poured out—I saw the glory of God, like a great cloud, come down and rest upon the house, and fill the same like a mighty rushing wind. I also saw cloven tongues, like as of fire rest upon many ... while they spake with other tongues and prophesied."[142]

Solemn Assembly of the Priesthood

On March 28 the Twelve met and had a "general confession" for being "light-minded and vain, and in many things have done wrong ... [and] grieved or wounded the feelings of the Presidency." This likely resulted from the Twelve's opposition to one of the February 12 resolutions regarding ordinations outside Kirtland and their attempt to amend it. They also asked Smith for a "written revelation" to guide them on their missions, but it is unclear if one was given.[143]

On the following day, March 29, after attending the last day of Hebrew school with Seixas, Smith and other members of the presidency met in "the most holy place" in the temple—created by lowering the veils to enclose the Melchizedek pulpits—to seek revelation regarding moving the authorities

---

141. For a description of the veils, see Corrill, *Brief History*, 22 (*JSP*, H2:153); and West, *A Few Interesting Facts*, 5; see also Robison, *The First Mormon Temple*, 85–93.

142. Cowdery, Diary, Mar. 27, 1836.

143. Quorum of the Twelve Apostles, Letter to Joseph Smith, Mar. 28, 1836, Minute Book 1, 198 (*JSP*, D5:210–11).

of the church to Zion and other matters. After uniting in prayer, Smith was inspired that they should call the presidents of the Missouri church and two bishoprics and meet three times, and that they should "fast through the day and also the night, and that during this, if we would humble ourselves, we should receive further communications" from God.[144]

When the other officers arrived and took their seats in the veiled pulpits, the meeting continued. Smith instructed them to remain in the holy place to attend to the washing of one another's feet and partake of the sacrament of bread and wine "that we might be made holy" before God and become "qualified to officiate in our calling upon the morrow in washing the feet of the Elders." Smith concluded this day's entry: "The Holy Spirit rested down upon us and we continued in the Lords house all night prophesying and giving glory to God."[145]

Partridge recorded that the washing of feet lasted "till about dusk," after which those present "partook of bread and wine a feast." He also reported that some of those present "prophesied and spake in tongues & shouted hosannas."[146] Phelps said it was "a solemn scene" and wrote that "they partook of the sacrament, as the Passover, having fasted all day they feasted on bread and wine; were filled with the spirit of their endowment, and prophesied many terrible things: The meeting continued till day light in the morning."[147]

At 8:00 a.m., on March 30, the doors were opened, allowing members of the various quorums of the Kirtland stake—about 300 men—to enter the lower court of the temple to attend the solemn assembly of the priesthood.[148] According to George A. Smith, some women were upset that the solemn assembly was exclusively for men, and when they heard about the washings, they suspected "some mischief was going on, and some of them were right huffy about it."[149]

Joseph Smith addressed the congregation and said "we had passed through many trials and afflictions since the organization of this church and that this is a year of Jubilee to us and a time of rejoicing, and that it was expedient for us to prepare bread and wine sufficient to make our hearts glad,

---

144. Smith, Journal, Mar. 29, 1836 (*JSP*, J1:211–12).

145. Smith (*JSP*, J1:212–13).

146. Partridge, Diary, Mar. 29, 1836.

147. Phelps, Letter to Sally Phelps, Apr. 1836, [2].

148. Minutes, Mar. 30, 1836, Smith, Journal, Mar. 30, 1836 (*JSP*, J1:213–16; D5:216–21).

149. George A. Smith, "Gathering and Sanctification of the People of God," *Journal of Discourses*, Mar. 18, 1855, 2:215.

as we should not probably leave this house until morning."[150] Seven days before celebrating the sixth year of the church's existence, Smith identified this year as a year of Jubilee. The Israelite Jubilee was observed every fifty years, or at the end of seven seven-year or sabbatical cycles, and mandated that all slaves be freed, all debts forgiven, and all fields lay fallow (Lev. 16; 25:8–10). Leviticus 25:13 probably attracted Smith's attention: "In this year of jubile ye shall return every man unto his possession." For Smith, the Year of Jubilee represented a time of rejoicing, redemption, and restoration, a year when all things would be made right, when Zion would be redeemed and his prophetic reputation rehabilitated.

Following Smith's remarks, tubs of water and towels were brought in and the Presidency washed the feet of the Twelve, while at the same time "pronouncing many prophecy's and blessings upon them in the name of the Lord Jesus." According to Smith's journal, the Twelve began to prophesy and utter "cursings upon the enemies of Christ who inhabit Jackson county Missouri."[151] Smith's journal mentions no other washings, but Post, who referred to this washing of feet as "the last ordinance of the endowment" that was administered to "those who are clean from [the] blood of the generation in which they live," wrote that "the washing commenced by the Presidents who first washed the 12 & the 7 Presidents of the Seventies" and that "the 12 & 7 then commenced washing until the whole were washed."[152] This apparently took until nearly 7:00 p.m., when the ordinance was sealed with a hosanna shout.[153]

Smith announced that "the time that we were required to tarry in Kirtland to be endued would be fulfilled in a few days, and then the Elders would go forth."[154] Phelps explained that the Jubilee and Passover that began with the solemn assembly ended with the church's anniversary celebration on April 6.[155] Smith advised the elders "not to contend" with sectarians because it will only bring down persecution upon them, which he "pronounced as a prophesy, sealed with a Hosanna & amen."[156] John Corrill explained that Smith told the elders, who were now "endowed with power to go forth and build up the Kingdom," to act cautiously "and avoid contention, and not

---

150. Smith, Journal, Mar. 30, 1836 (*JSP*, J1:213; D5:218).
151. Smith (*JSP*, J1:213–14; D5:219).
152. Post, Journal, Mar. 30, 1836.
153. Smith, Journal, Mar. 30, 1836 (*JSP*, J1:214; D5:219).
154. Smith (*JSP*, J1:214; D5:219).
155. Phelps, Letter to Sally Phelps, Apr. 1836, [3].
156. Smith, Journal, Mar. 30, 1836 (*JSP*, J1:214–15; D5:219–20).

meddle with other orders of Christians, nor proclaim against their doctrines, but to preach the gospel in its simplicity, and let others alone."[157]

Concerning the Seventies, Smith instructed that they were "not called to serve tables or preside over churches to settle difficulties, but to preach the gospel and build them up." He further declared: "The seventies are at liberty to go to Zion if they please or go wheresoever they will and preach the gospel and let the redemtion of Zion be our object, and strive to affect it by sending up all the strength of the Lords house whereever we find them."[158] This was an allusion to previous revelations about finding recruits for the army of Israel.[159] Smith then proposed that all enter into a solemn covenant "that if any more of our brethren are slain or driven from their lands in Missouri by the mob that we will give ourselves no rest until we are avenged of our enimies to the uttermost." According to Smith's journal, "this covenant was sealed unaminously by a hosanna and Amen."[160]

At this point, the bread and wine were brought in and Smith observed that "we had fasted all the day; and lest we faint; as the Saviour did so shall we do on this occasion, we shall bless the bread and give it to the 12 and they to the multitude, after which we shall bless the wine and do likewise."[161] Phelps wrote that "the sacrament was administered, as the feast of the Passover for the first time in more than 1800 years."[162] John Corrill noted: "The sacrament was then administered, in which they partook of the bread and wine freely, and a report went abroad that some of them got drunk: ... A similar report, the reader will recollect, went out concerning the disciples, at Jerusalem, on the day of penticost. This was followed by a marvellous spirit of prophecy. Every man's mouth was full of prophecying."[163] McLellin remembered that money was collected and "a wagon sent nine miles to Painesville, and a barrel of wine procured," and that "the Twelve were required to take large servers, and set glasses of wine and lumps of bread, and go through the house and serve the brethren. I did my part of the serving. ... All the latter part of the night I took care of Samuel H. Smith, perfectly unable to help

---

157. Corrill, *Brief History*, 26 (*JSP*, H2:158).

158. Smith, Journal, Mar. 30, 1836 (*JSP*, J1:215; D5:220).

159. See Revelation Dec. 16–17, 1833, Revelation Book, 78–79 [D&C 101:55–58] (*JSP*, D3:393–94); Revelation, Feb. 24, 1834, Hyde and Pratt, Notebook and Revelations, [12]–[13] [D&C 103:22] (*JSP*, D3:461); Revelation, June 22, 1834, Revelation Book 1, 200 [D&C 105:16] (*JSP*, D4:75).

160. Smith, Journal, Mar. 30, 1836 (*JSP*, J1:215; D5:220).

161. Smith (*JSP*, J1:214; D5:219). Matt. 15:32–38; 3 Ne. 18:1–11; 20:1–9.

162. Phelps, Letter to Sally Phelps, Apr. 1836, [2].

163. Corrill, *Brief History*, 23 (*JSP*, H2:154). Acts 2:13, 15.

himself. And I had others removed from the house, because they were unfit to be in decent company."[164]

Finally, Smith announced to those present that he had "now completed their organization of the church and we had passed through all the necessary ceremonies," and that "they now were at liberty after obtaining their lisences to go forth and build up the kingdom of God."[165] By the end of May, Smith will issue more than 300 licenses, which fulfilled his March 3 resolution to centralize licensing.[166]

At 9:00 p.m., Smith and the other presidents left the meeting in charge of the Twelve and went home. According to Smith's journal, "the brethren continued exhorting, prophesying and speaking in tongues until 5 o clock in the morning." As Smith had previously promised that "all who are prepared and are sufficiently pure to abide the presence of the Savior will see him in the solemn assembly," he was careful to note in his journal that in his absence "the Saviour made his appearance to some, while angels minestered unto others, and it was a penticost and enduement indeed, long to be remembered for the sound shall go forth from this place into all the world, and the occurrences of this day shall be handed down upon the pages of sacred history to all generations, as the day of Pentecost, so shall this day be numbered and celebrated as a year of Jubilee and time of rejoicing to the saints of the most high God."[167]

McLellin had a different opinion about the proceedings, writing decades later that "the attempted endowment in the Temple in Kirtland in 1836" was "an entire failure."[168] As he remembered: "No display of power from God was given. All the power given was the power of man. It was manifested in ordinations, in washing and anointing, and blessings by the authority of men. The Heads or Leaders claimed that by laying on their hands in their ordinations and ordinances 'The whole power of the church rested on each one of those of the assembly, and that was their endowment.'" He went on to say that "some of them partook of the wine so freely so as to become badly intoxicated! But

164. William E. McLellin, Letter to John L. Traughber, Jan. 5, 1879 (Larson and Passey, eds., *The William E. McLellin Papers*, 516).

165. Smith, Journal, Mar. 30, 1836 (*JSP*, J1:215; D5:220–21).

166. Smith, Journal, Mar. 3, 1836 (*JSP*, J1:191–94; D5:182–84); Kirtland Elders' Certificates, 1–157.

167. Smith, Journal, Mar. 30, 1836 (*JSP*, J1:215–16; D5:221). For Smith's promise that some would see Jesus at the solemn assembly, see Smith, Journal, Nov. 12, 1835 (*JSP*, J1:99; D5:51).

168. McLellin, Notebook, ca. 1880, 4 (Larson and Passey, eds., *The William E. McLellin Papers*, 383). McLellin misdated these events to April 6, 1836.

when I look back upon those times and scenes I feel a kind of shudder, to think that intelligent good men could be so infatuated and blindly led."[169]

McLellin may have been jesting when he said, "It was more an endowment of <u>wine</u> than power from God."[170] Of course, the wine did not cause hallucinations, but by breaking down their inhibitions, it may have made them more susceptible to speaking in tongues, prophesying, possibly even visions. Indeed, the dedicated temple—the House of the Lord—was itself a suggestive space for spiritual experience. Even the whitened veils, which were apparently lowered after Smith left, provided a favorable background for visionary experiences.[171]

McLellin was so troubled about what he had witnessed in the temple that "in a day or two, I, individually, went to Joseph and told him plainly that I was disppointed." Smith asked, "What do you want?" McLellin responded, "I wanted knowledge and power from God; that as an Apostle I might go forth to the nations of the earth, and preach to them in their own <u>lip</u> the pure gospel of the Lord." McLellin remembered that Smith then laid his hands on his head and prophesied: "Go South on a mission. Go to the tops of the highest hills, and to the bottom of the lowest valleys, or ravines, and call fervently on God, and before you return, you shall receive all that you desire." McLellin said that he followed Smith's instructions, but that while he was praying in a deep ravine in the woods in Kentucky about the last of June 1836, he heard "a still, small voice" say, "Get up and go home," which he obeyed.[172] McLellin returned to Kirtland with mixed feelings about Smith.

---

169. McLellin, 15 (Larson and Passey, eds., 396).

170. McLellin, Letter to John L. Traughber, Dec. 14, 1878, 7 (Larson and Passey, eds., *The William E. McLellin Papers*, 512).

171. Stephen Post wrote that "the house was divided into parts by curtains & they prophesied spake and sang in tongues in each room." Post, Journal, Mar. 30, 1836. Edward Partridge recorded that at one point "the priests teachers & deacons [were] in one corner the vails having been let down, and the other officers occupied the rest of the lower room." Partridge, Diary, Mar. 30, 1836.

172. McLellin, Letter to John L. Traughber, Dec. 14, 1878, 7–8 (Larson and Passey, eds., *The William E. McLellin Papers*, 512).

23

Keys, Money, Land

MARCH–SEPTEMBER 1836

Behold, I will send my messenger, and he shall prepare the way before me: and the Lord, whom ye seek, shall suddenly come to his temple, even the messenger of the covenant, whom ye delight in: behold, he shall come...

—*Malachi 3:1*

On March 31, 1836, Smith and other church authorities repeated the dedication meeting of the previous Sunday for those who could not attend the first, during which "the Spirit of God rested upon the congregation, and great solemnity prevailed."[1] Phelps wrote that the second dedication "was a sublime scene, surpassing the first in sublimity and solemnity as well as in order. The singing was grand. The Addresses were the best that could be and majesty exceeded any thing I have witnessed in the last days."[2] The second dedication lasted until 9:00 p.m., five hours longer than the first.

Raising Money

On April 2 Smith, Frederick Williams, Rigdon, Cowdery, Phelps, David Whitmer, and John Whitmer, members of F. G. Williams & Co., met in the upper story of the printing office to discuss discharging the debts of the printing establishment and raising funds for the purchase of land in Zion. Rigdon and Williams were appointed to settle the debts of the United Firm. At this time, there was a partial division of stock, and Phelps and John Whitmer, who were preparing to return to Missouri, were released from their responsibilities in the printing office.[3] F. G. Williams &

---

1. Smith, Journal, Mar. 30, 1836 (*JSP*, J1:216).
2. Phelps, Letter to Sally Phelps, Apr. 1836, [2].
3. F. G. Williams & Co., Minutes, Apr. 2, 1836, Minute Book 1, 199 (*JSP*, D5:222–24); and Smith, Journal, Apr. 2, 1836 (*JSP*, J1:217).

Co. will eventually be dissolved on June 7, when Cowdery "purchased the entire establishment."[4]

When discussing the "redemption of Zion," Smith was quite animated, for Warren Cowdery, Smith's new scribe, wrote in Smith's journal that "the positive manner in which he expressed himself on this, his favorite theme, was directly calculated to produce conviction in the minds of those who heard him, that his whole soul was engaged in it."[5] Smith and Oliver Cowdery were appointed to "raise all the money they can in Righteousness, for a season, to send by, or to certain wise men, appointed to purchase land in Zion, in obedience to a revelation or command of the Lord for the mutual benefit of the said company or firm aforesaid."[6] A December 1833 revelation had instructed Smith to appoint "wise men and send them to purchase" as much Jackson County land as possible.[7] According to John Whitmer's history, on March 11, 1836, Edward Partridge, Isaac Morley, John Corrill, and Phelps were appointed as "wise men" who would soon return to Missouri "with some money [to] purchase land for the saints—to seek a place for them &c."[8] In a letter sent the following month to his wife, Phelps wrote that he "could not get ready to start for Missouri" when he planned because he "had to wait to raise Money to purchase land."[9]

Immediately after the meeting, Smith and Cowdery began raising money for the redemption of Zion, traveling throughout the region. According to Smith's journal, "their success was such in one half day, as to give them pleasing anticipation, and assure them that they were doing the will of God and that his work prospered in their hands."[10] Despite this positive assessment, Smith and Cowdery met with some resistance. Charges were subsequently preferred against Preserved Harris and Isaac McWithy for "a want of benevolence to the poor, and charity to the church." At the hearing, Smith said he and Cowdery approached McWithy "for money to send up to Zion, but could get none," and that they also failed to get money from Father Lyon because of McWithy's influence.[11]

---

4. "Notice," *LDS Messenger and Advocate* (Kirtland, OH), June 1836, 329.

5. Smith, Journal, Apr. 2, 1836 (*JSP*, J1:217).

6. F. G. Williams & Co., Minutes, Apr. 2, 1836, Minute Book 1, 199 (*JSP*, D5:223–24).

7. See Revelation, Dec. 16–17, 1833, Revelation Book 2, 80 [D&C 101:73] (*JSP*, D3:395). See also D&C 103:23; 105:28.

8. Whitmer, History, 83 (*JSP*, H2:92).

9. Phelps, Letter to Sally Phelps, Apr. 1836, [3].

10. Smith, Journal, Apr. 2, 1836 (*JSP*, J1:216).

11. Minutes, June 16, 1836, Minute Book 1, 217–18 (*JSP*, D5:253).

Special Keys

On April 3 Smith attended Easter Sunday service in the temple with about a thousand people. In the afternoon, he attended another meeting where he, the other presidents, and the Twelve officiated over the sacrament.[12] According to Stephen Post, the administration of the sacrament and blessing of children took place simultaneously in the four sections of the temple's lower court, the veils having been lowered, and "the presidency took the pulpit during the confirmation & blessing of the children."[13] While Smith and Cowdery were behind the veils that formed the Holy of Holies in the highest tier of the Melchizedek Priesthood pulpits, as they would later report, they bowed "in solemn, but silent prayer to the Most High." After prayer they arose and, according to Smith's account, they saw a vision of Christ, who accepted the temple, followed by Moses, Elias, and Elijah, who delivered priesthood keys.[14]

Their written account begins by stating that the vision occurred in "the eyes of their understandings," and they "saw the Lord standing upon the breastwork of the pulpit." Among other things, Jesus declared: "I have accepted this house and my name shall be here; and I will manifest myself to my people, in mercy, in this House, Yea I will appear unto my servants and speak unto them with mine own voice, if my people keep my commandments and do not pollute this Holy House."

After this vision closed, another opened and "Moses appeared before them and committed unto them the Keys of the gathering of Israel from the four parts of the Eearth and the leading of the ten tribes from the Land of the North." This reception of keys gave co-presidents Smith and Cowdery authorization to launch their missionary program and to recommence gathering the elect out of every country to their Missouri Zion.

After this, Elias appeared and "committed the dispensation of the gospel of Abraham, saying, that in them and their seed all generations after them should be blessed." This referred to the continuation of the patriarchal priesthood through Smith and Cowdery, which priesthood was mentioned in Smith's recent translation of the Book of Abraham, and prior to that in

---

12. Smith, Journal, Apr. 3, 1836 (*JSP*, J1:219).

13. Post, Journal, Apr. 3, 1836.

14. Smith, Journal, Apr. 3, 1836 (*JSP*, J1:219–22; D5:226–29). The April 3, 1836, visions of Smith and Cowdery were recorded by Warren Cowdery in the third person but were converted into the first person by Willard Richards in October 1843 for Smith's official history. JS History, vol. B-1, 727–28; Vogel, *History of Joseph Smith*, 1:xc; 2:420. The later version was added to the Doctrine and Covenants in 1876 [D&C 110].

his spring 1835 instructions to the Twelve.[15] Abraham had sought for his "appointment unto the Priesthood according to the appointment of God unto the fathers concerning the seed" (Abr. 1:4). The Lord told Abraham:

> I will make of thee a great nation, and I will bless thee above measure, and make thy name great among all nations, and thou shalt be a blessing unto thy seed after thee, that in their hands they shall bear this ministry and priesthood unto all nations, and I will bless them through thy name; for as many as receive this Gospel shall be called after thy name, and shall be accounted thy seed ... and in thee (that is, in thy priesthood) and in thy seed (that is, thy priesthood), for I give unto thee a promise that this right shall continue in thee, and in thy seed after thee (that is to say, the literal seed, or the seed of the body), shall all the families of the earth be blessed, even with the blessings of the Gospel, which are the blessings of salvation, even of life eternal. (Abr. 2:9–11)

Prior to this, Smith's instructions to the Twelve included a discussion of the patriarchal priesthood: "The order of this priesthood was confirmed to be handed down from father to son, and rightly belongs to the literal descendants of the chosen seed, to whom the promises were made."[16] This expansion traced this priesthood from Adam to Noah, which implied that President-Patriarch Joseph Smith Sr., who had been ordained as such in December 1834, represented a continuation of the seed of the patriarchs.[17] When Cowdery expanded Smith's 1833 blessing of Joseph Sr. in September 1835, he wrote that he was to "be called a prince over his posterity, holding the keys of the patriarchal priesthood over the kingdom of God on earth, even the Church of the Latter Day Saints." He was also to "sit in the general assembly of patriarchs, even in council with the Ancient of Days when he shall sit and all the patriarchs with him and shall enjoy his right and authority under the direction of the Ancient of Days."[18]

Similarly, on October 2, 1835, Cowdery copied a blessing into the Patriarchal Blessing Book that Smith gave him in 1833 that Cowdery also expanded to reflect his new status as co-president with Smith, explaining that Cowdery "shall sit in the council of the patriarchs, with his brother Joseph and with him have part in the keys of that ministry when the Ancient

---

15. Instruction on Priesthood, Mar. 1–May 4, 1835, D&C, 1835 ed., III:18–29 [D&C 107:40–57] (*JSP*, D4:316–17).

16. Instruction on Priesthood, D&C, 1835 ed., III:18 [D&C 107:40] (*JSP*, D4:316).

17. Quinn, *The Mormon Hierarchy*, 32–35.

18. Patriarchal Blessing Book, 1:9 (*JSP*, D4:488; Marquardt, *Early Patriarchal Blessings*, 4).

of Days shall come. ... For he shall have part with me in the keys of the kingdom of the last days, ... and the keys shall never be taken from us, but shall
rest with us for an everlasting briesthood [priesthood], forever and ever."[19]

While Elias bestowed keys pertaining to the patriarchal priesthood,
which was tied to the right to rule among the ancient patriarchs as well as
in Smith's planned City of Zion, Smith's circa August 1835 expansion to
a September 1830 revelation implied that there were keys yet to be given,
describing Elias as holding "the keys of bringing to pass the restoration of all
things, or restorer of all things spoken by the mouth of all the holy prophets
since the world began, concerning the last days," which alluded to Acts 3:21.[20]

Finally, after this vision, Smith and Cowdery saw "Elijah, the Prophet,
who was taken to Heaven without tasting death, also stood before them,
and said, behold the time has fully come which was spoken of by the mouth
of Malachi, testifying, that he should be sent before the great and dreadful
day of the Lord come, to turn the hearts of the Fathers to the children, and
the children to the fathers, lest the whole earth be smitten with a curse.
Therefore, the Keys of this dispensation are committed into your hands, and
by this ye may know that the great and the dreadful day of the Lord is near,
even at the doors."

Smith's 1835 expansion of his September 1830 revelation also implied
a possible future reception of keys from Elijah, who held "the keys of the
power of turning the hearts of the fathers to the children, and the hearts of
the children to the fathers, that the whole earth may not be smitten with
a curse," which alluded to Malachi 4:5–6.[21] Seven years later, in Nauvoo,
Smith asserted that Elijah's keys pertained to the power to "seal" for eternity
marriages and parent-child relationships for both the living and the dead.[22]
Smith's vision of Elijah in 1836 represents a bestowal of keys for the last dispensation to fulfill ancient prophecy. This was Phelps's understanding when
he told his wife: "There was a manifestation of the Lord to Br Joseph and
Oliver, by which they learned that the great & terrible day of the Lord as
mentioned by Malichi, was near, even at the doors."[23]

The appearance of both Elias and Elijah to Smith and Cowdery is problematic since Elias is the Greek form of the Hebrew name Elijah. The same

---

19. Patriarchal Blessing Book, 1:12 (*JSP*, D5:513–14; Marquardt, 8).
20. Revelation, Sep. 4, 1830 [ca. Aug. 1835], D&C, 1835 ed., L:2 [D&C 27:6] (*JSP*, D4:411).
21. Revelation [D&C 27:9].
22. See Smith, Journal, Aug. 27, 1843 (*JSP*, J3:86–87); and Ehat and Cook, *The Words of Joseph Smith*, 43–44, 240–41, 244, 329–31.
23. Phelps, Letter to Sally Phelps, Apr. 1836, [3].

problem exists in Smith's expansion of his September 1830 revelation, where Elias and Elijah are mentioned as separate individuals.[24] Smith similarly confused Isaiah and Esaias, also Hebrew and Greek forms of the same name, claiming Esaias was a contemporary of Abraham (D&C 76:100; 84:13). In his study of early Mormon doctrine, LDS author Charles R. Harrell recognized that Smith's distinction between Elias and Elijah was erroneous and that "in the KJV, no such distinction exists, nor would it make sense because Elias and Elijah are one and the same" and "obscures the simple New Testament idea that Elijah came in the person of John the Baptist who was filled with the spirit of Elijah."[25]

Smith and Cowdery now held keys—power—not shared by other priesthood officers, and as joint presidents of the church, they were beyond the reach of any usurper. This, together with their claim the previous year to having been ordained by John the Baptist and apostles Peter, James, and John, made it extremely difficult to break away from the main body of the church. Brigham Young understood this when he subsequently defended Smith against other apostles and church leaders attempting to replace Smith, saying that "they might rail and abuse slander him so much as they pleased they could not destroy the appointment of the Prophet of God, they were only destroying their own authority.—cut the thread that bound them to the Prophet and to God and sink themselves to hell."[26]

The account of the temple visions in Smith's journal remained unpublished until 1852 when it appeared in the *Deseret News* as part of Smith's history and again in 1876 as Doctrine and Covenants 110.[27] Nevertheless, the content of the visions was apparently known at the time.[28] Mary Ann Stearns Winters, Parley P. Pratt's step-daughter, recalled that shortly after the

---

24. Revelation, Sep. 1830 [ca. Aug. 1835], D&C, 1835 ed., L:2 [D&C 27:6, 9] (*JSP*, D4:411).

25. Harrell, *"This Is My Doctrine,"* 66. See Luke 1:17. Mormon intellectual Samuel Brown has attempted to extricate Joseph Smith from his Elias/Elijah blunder, unsuccessfully in my view. Brown, "The Prophet Elias Puzzle."

26. Historian's Office, Brigham Young History Drafts, 14.

27. "Life of Joseph Smith," *Deseret News*, Nov. 6, 1852; Cook, *The Revelations of Joseph Smith*, 220.

28. To explain the introduction of angelic ordinations in 1834 and 1835 that were said to have occurred five years earlier, Ronald O. Barney suggests that Smith had an "idiosyncratic disposition to conceal his personal experiences with heaven" because he considered them sacred, which does not explain why Cowdery failed to mention them or why they were absent from foundational texts such as the "Articles and Covenants of the Church of Christ" (D&C 20). Barney believes Smith's handling of the 1836 Kirtland Temple manifestations supports his thesis, arguing that "there is no evidence that he publicized the fantastic and marvelous encounter except perhaps to a handful of the faithful." Barney, "Joseph Smith and the Conspicuous Scarcity of Early Mormon Documentation," 387–88. In my opinion, this argument from silence is contradicted by the evidence.

Kirtland manifestations her mother took her into the temple and "showed me the place on the pulpit where the Savior had stood when He appeared to the Prophet, and where afterwards Moses and Elias came and delivered the keys for the gathering of the Saints (Israel), and the redemption of the dead."[29] A week after the visions, on April 10, non-Mormon Lucius Pomeroy Parsons, who lived in Kirtland Mills, wrote to his sister about recent events, including the "solemn assembly" in the temple, where, Parsons reported, the Mormons say "they have had wonderful manifestations there of late behind the curtains ... they report that the Savior appeared personly [personally] with angels and endowed the Elders with power to work Miracles."[30]

Missionaries

Smith's journal entries end here, probably as a result of sending scribe Warren Parrish on a mission to Tennessee, and do not resume until March 13, 1838, after Smith had arrived at Far West, Missouri.[31] Phelps wrote that the elders began leaving Kirtland on missions on April 1, 1836.[32] Smith and Frederick Williams issued forty-one licenses on March 30, forty-seven on March 31, and twenty-six on April 1, with nearly 300 new licenses being issued by June 1836.[33] During the following week most of the ordained men left Kirtland to proselytize and raise money to purchase land for the redemption of Zion.

The church met in the temple on April 6 to observe its sixth anniversary. Phelps wrote that the day "was set apart as [a] day of prayer, to end The feast of the passover. and in honor of the Jubilee of the church: it being Six years to this day."[34] Heber Kimball remembered that "the meeting continued on through the night, the spirit of prophecy was poured out upon the Assembly. ... Also Angels administered to many, for they were seen by many." He also recalled that "a marvellous spirit of prophecy" continued for several days, and that the men visited "from house to house, administering bread and wine, and pronouncing blessings upon each other."[35]

---

29. Winters, "An Autobiographical Sketch," 3. This account is influenced by what she later learned about the meaning of the visions.

30. Parsons, Letter to "Dear Sister" [Pamelia Parsons], Apr. 10, 1836, 2. This account is influenced by what she later learned about the meaning of the visions.

31. On Parrish's arrival in Tennessee before May 28, 1836, see *LDS Messenger and Advocate*, June 1836, 331.

32. Phelps, Letter to Sally Phelps, Apr. 1836, [2].

33. Kirtland Elders' Certificates, 1–157.

34. Phelps, Letter to Sally Phelps, Apr. 1836, [3].

35. Kimball, "History of Heber Chase Kimball," 43.

Bishop Partridge and his counselors, Isaac Morley and John Corrill, and President Phelps left Kirtland on the morning of April 9 to return to Missouri. Smith and other leaders followed them as far as Chardon, where rain forced them to stay overnight. In the morning Smith blessed them and sent them on their way.[36]

Neutrality on Slavery

About this time, Smith wrote an anti-abolitionist letter to Cowdery to be published in the *Messenger and Advocate*, which appeared in the April 1836 issue along with two other articles on the same topic.[37] In being anti-abolitionist, Smith was not necessarily pro-slavery. As Phelps subsequently wrote, "We have taken no part for or against slavery, but are opposed to the abolitionists, and consider that men have a right to hold slaves or not according to law."[38] Such a nuanced position allowed the church to remain essentially neutral about slavery, which they believed was a necessary position to take if their relationship with Jackson Countians were ever to improve.

Apparently Smith was motivated to comment on slavery by the recent lecture in Kirtland by abolitionist John Alvord, a student from nearby Oberlin College, who, according to a report, was "well received" and was able to form an antislavery society with about eighty-six members.[39] In his letter, Smith explicitly said: "I do not believe that the people of the North have any more right to say that the South *shall not* hold slaves, than the South have to say the North shall."[40] Smith also quoted the favorite pro-slavery proof text in Genesis 9:25–26 concerning Noah's cursing his grandson Canaan with multi-generational servitude, and then declared: "I can say, the curse is not yet taken off from the sons of Canaan."[41] Smith clearly stated his church's policy regarding slavery: "We have no right to interfere with slaves, contrary to the mind and will of their masters. In fact, it would be much better, and

---

36. JS History, vol. B-1, 728 (DHC 2:436). Possibly based on information provided by Phelps about Nov. 7, 1843. Vogel, *History of Joseph Smith*, 2:421n93. See also Partridge, Journal, Apr. 9–10, 1836.

37. Joseph Smith, Letter to Oliver Cowdery, ca. Apr. 9, 1836, *LDS Messenger and Advocate*, Apr. 1836, 289–91 (*JSP*, D5:231–43). See also Warren Parrish, "For the Messenger and Advocate" and "The Abolitionists," *LDS Messenger and Advocate*, Apr. 1836, 295–96, 299–301.

38. "Public Notice," *Messenger and Advocate*, Aug. 1836, 360.

39. "Anti-Slavery Intelligence," *Philanthropist* (Cincinnati), Apr. 22, 1836, [2].

40. Smith, Letter to Oliver Cowdery, ca. Apr. 9, 1836, *LDS Messenger and Advocate*, Apr. 1836, 289 (*JSP*, D5:238).

41. Smith, 290 (*JSP*, D5:240).

more prudent, not to preach at all to slaves, until after their masters are converted, and then teach the master to use them with kindness."[42]

When the citizens of Clay County demanded that the Mormons leave the county in June 1836, in part, because they believed the Mormons were dangerous to societies "where slavery is tolerated and practiced,"[43] Smith and his counselors sent a letter, dated July 25, 1836, to alleviate tensions by denying the accusation and sending a copy of Smith's anti-abolitionist article.[44] Regardless, the Mormons were soon pushed out of Clay County and would eventually form their own county.

Smith Family Arrivals

On May 14 Cowdery preferred a charge before the high council against Wilkins J. Salisbury, Smith's brother-in-law, and Charles Kelly of the Quorum of Seventy for "unchristian like conduct." Two days later, the high council met to consider, among other things, Cowdery's charges against Salisbury and Kelly. Smith testified that Salisbury had brought "unnecessary persecution on him," that he neglected his family and left them without food and wood just before the solemn assembly. John Johnson testified to Salisbury's drunkenness, and McLellin claimed that "he had been intimate with every woman he could since he belonged to the church." Hyrum Smith testified to his neglecting his family, and believed that when Salisbury left town without explanation, "he never intended to return." Salisbury confessed to tale-bearing and drinking, but denied the "charge of unchastity to his wife, suggested by J. Smith Junr. as stated by Wm. E. McLellin." The high council disfellowshipped him "until there be a thorough reformation."[45]

Later the same day, Smith's cousin Elias Smith arrived at Kirtland after traveling 500 miles from St. Lawrence County, New York, with news that his father, Silas, and family were on their way and that grandmother Mary Duty Smith, wife of the deceased Asael Smith, had landed at Fairport Harbor, Ohio. The next day, Joseph and Hyrum traveled eleven miles to Fairport and brought their ninety-three-year-old grandmother to Kirtland. According to an addendum in Smith's history, probably added by Smith's cousin George

---

42. Smith, 291 (*JSP*, D5:242). See D&C 134:12, which was included in the 1835 Doctrine and Covenants as CII:12.

43. "Public Meeting," *Far West* (Liberty, MO), June 30, 1836; reprinted in "Public Meeting," *LDS Messenger and Advocate*, Aug. 1836, 354.

44. Sidney Rigdon, Joseph Smith, Oliver Cowdery, Frederick G. Williams, and Hyrum Smith, Letter to John Thornton and Others, July 25, 1836, *LDS Messenger and Advocate*, Aug. 1836, 355–359 (*JSP*, D5:258–68).

45. Minutes, May 16, 1836, Minute Book 1, 205–207 (*JSP*, D5:243–47).

A. Smith in 1845, "My Grand Father Asael Smith long ago predicted that there would be a prophet raised up in his family, and my Grand Mother was fully satisfied that it was fulfilled in me. My Grand Father Asahel, Died in East Stockholm St Lawrence Co New York, after having received the Book of Mormon, and read it nearly through, and he declared that I was the very prophet, that he had long known would come in his family."[46] In his own history begun in 1857, George A. wrote less dramatically that during a visit of Joseph Sr. and Don Carlos to St. Lawrence County, New York, in August 1830, "the old Gentleman said, that he always knew that God was going to raise up some branch of his family to be a great benefit of to mankind," and that subsequently he "fully believed the book of Mormon" after reading it "nearly through" before his death on October 31, 1830.[47] George A.'s father, John, similarly wrote: "Father received with gladness, that which Joseph [Sr.] communicated; and remarked, that he had always expected that something would appear to make known the true Gospel."[48]

On May 18 Smith's uncle, Silas Smith, and family arrived at Kirtland from the east. Almost two weeks after her arrival, Mary Duty Smith died, unbaptized, on May 27. After Rigdon preached the funeral sermon, she was buried in the cemetery between the temple and Smith's home.[49]

Money Problems

Mounting debts associated with land transactions, the Camp of Israel expedition, publication of the Doctrine and Covenants, and construction of the House of the Lord forced Smith to borrow money, plunging him further into debt. John Corrill later wrote that the temple cost "nearly $40,000" to construct and that the building committee "found themselves 13 or $14,000 in debt." In all, Corrill estimated that "the church found itself something like fifteen or twenty thousand dollars in debt, as near as I can recollect."[50]

The mercantile partnership of Rigdon, Smith & Cowdery was formed, and on June 15 the firm purchased wholesale goods from Buffalo merchant Jonathan F. Scribner on credit for $796.65.[51] This was followed by a series of

46. JS History, vol. B-1, Addenda, 5, Note R (DHC 2:442–43), which was inserted by Wilmer Benson possibly on July 15, 1845. Vogel, *History of Joseph Smith*, 2:428–29n30.

47. George A. Smith, History, 2, 4 (back), Note 2.

48. Extract from John Smith's Journal, quoted in Lucy Mack Smith, *Biographical Sketches*, 155.

49. JS History, vol. B-1, Addenda, 5–6, Note R, (DHC 2:443), which was added by Wilmer Benson possibly on July 15, 1845. Vogel, *History of Joseph Smith*, 2:428–29n30.

50. Corrill, *Brief History*, 21, 26 (*JSP*, H2:151, 159).

51. See Transcript Proceedings, Oct. 20, 1840, Scribner v. Rigdon et al., Geauga Co., OH,

similar purchases from several other Buffalo merchants.[52] "Notwithstanding they were deeply in debt," wrote Corrill, "they had so managed as to keep up their credit, so they concluded to try mercantile business. Accordingly, they ran in debt in New York, and elsewhere, some thirty thousand dollars, for goods, and, shortly after, some fifty or sixty thousand more, as I was informed."[53] Records are incomplete, but the editors of the Joseph Smith Papers note: "Debts incurred during this period that were subsequently litigated included at least $34,000 for which Joseph Smith was defendant and at least $13,000 for which members of the temple committee were defendants."[54]

On June 16 the high council met in the temple to consider Smith's charges against two wealthy Mormons, Preserved Harris and Isaac McWithy, for "a want of benevolence to the poor, and charity to the church." The charges were sustained against Harris, who was disfellowshipped, but McWithy defended himself. Smith testified against McWithy, stating that "he in company with Prest. O[liver]. Cowdery called upon the accused for money to send up to Zion but could get none." Afterward, according to Smith, he approached McWithy again and "asked him if he would sell his farm." Although he was offered $3,000 and an additional $400 or $500 to help him migrate to Zion, McWithy eventually declined and influenced Father Lyon not to give as well.[55]

Frederick Williams, who had already sacrificed his farm and given Smith much of his own money, said the case before the high council was an important one because God has commanded the church to care for the poor and to build up Zion "and we have not means to do it unless the rich assist. & because the rich have not assisted, the heads of the church have to suffer and are now suffering under severe embarrassments and are much in debt."[56] Rigdon said "many things concerning the law of God upon the subject of property, showing clearly that it is the duty of the saints to offer their all to the will of

---

Court of Common Pleas, Final Record, vol. X, 530–32; Reuben Hitchcock on behalf of Hitchcock & Wilder, Statement of Account, [between July 9 and Nov. 6, 1838], JS Collection (*JSP*, D6:289).

52. These purchases were as follows: Jonathan Scribner, June 16; John Newbould and Martin Birge, June 17; George Walbridge, Gurdon Coit, and Mead & Betts, June 18; Daniel Ketchum, June 20; and Gardner & Patterson, June 27. Promissory notes for all except John Newbould are found in Joseph Smith Office Papers. On John Newbould, see Invoice, June 17, 1836; and Transcript of Proceedings, Oct. 24, 1837, Newbould v. Rigdon, Smith & Cowdery, Geauga Co., OH, Court of Common Pleas, Final Record, vol. U, 351.

53. Corrill, *Brief History*, 26–27 (*JSP*, H2:159–60).

54. *JSP*, H2:160n120. See Madsen, "Tabulating the Impact of Litigation on the Kirtland Economy."

55. Minutes, June 16, 1836, Minute Book 1, 217–18 (*JSP*, D5:253).

56. Minutes, 214 (*JSP*, D5:250).

God for the building up of the Kingdom & for the sustenance of the poor …
& he that is not willing to make this sacrifice cannot be considered a saint
of the most High God & [he is] unworthy of the fellowship of the Saints."[57]

McWithy's reputation for stinginess was such that someone prophesied
against him during the March 27, 1836, dedication of the temple.[58] In later
years, Brigham Young recalled McWithy as "a man who had plenty of money,
and refused to loan it, or use it for the advancement of the cause of truth.
He would not put his money out to usury." During the trial, according to
Young, McWithy told the council, as "tears rolled down his checks," that "he
had always been a Christian, and had done so much for the Churches, and
for the Priests, and been so liberal since he had been in this Church, which
was between three and four years," and estimated that he had "given away in
my life time two hundred and fifty dollars." Young said he spoke up and said
that if he remained at home working instead of traveling as a missionary for
four months out of each of the years McWithy was in the church "and give
no more than two hundred and fifty dollars, I should be ashamed of myself."[59]

After several men testified against McWithy for his lack of charity, he
eventually asked for forgiveness. Because the minutes end abruptly, it is uncertain what happened to McWithy, but he "seems to have distanced himself
from the church after this trial."[60]

On June 22 Joseph Smith Sr. and John Smith left Kirtland on a mission
to the eastern states to give patriarchal blessings. Smith accompanied his
father and uncle as far as Painesville, then returned home.[61] After traveling
more than 2,000 miles and visiting various branches and relatives in New
York, Vermont, New Hampshire, and Pennsylvania, the two family patriarchs returned on October 2, 1836.[62]

Fanny Alger

About late spring 1836, Emma discovered Joseph was having an affair with

---

57. Minutes (*JSP*, D5:251).

58. Leonard Rich mentioned that McWithy feared the "fulfilment of a prophecy delivered against him at the dedication." Minutes, June 16, 1836, Minute Book 1, 216 (*JSP*, D5:252).

59. Brigham Young, "Use and Abuse of Blessings," June 5, 1853, in *Journal of Discourses,*
1:255–56.

60. *JSP*, D5:248.

61. JS History, vol. B-1, Addenda, 4, Note M (DHC 2:446–47), which was added by Wilmer
Benson possibly on July 15, 1845, under George A. Smith's direction. Smith, Memoirs and Autobiography, 83; Vogel, *History of Joseph Smith*, 2:432n89.

62. JS History, vol. Book B-1, Addenda, 4, Note N (DHC 2:467), which was added by
Wilmer Benson possibly on July 15, 1845, under George A. Smith's direction. Smith, History, 54;
Smith, Memoirs and Autobiography, 87; Vogel, *History of Joseph Smith*, 2:451–52, n32.

their nineteen-year-old live-in maid Fanny Alger.[63] According to McLellin, he heard a rumor and subsequently confirmed it with Emma when he visited her in Nauvoo in 1847 that "one night she missed Joseph and Fanny Alger. She went to the barn and saw him and Fanny in the barn together alone. She looked through a crack and saw the transaction!!!"[64] A reporter for the *Salt Lake Tribune* wrote in 1875 that McLellin said that Emma told him that she saw "with her own eyes" her husband with "the hired girl ... in a barn on the hay mow ... through a crack in the door!"[65]

Prior to Emma's discovery, Eliza R. Snow, an unmarried thirty-two-year-old school teacher, moved in with the Smiths and may have shared a room with Fanny.[66] During the school term, Snow became "well acquainted" with Fanny and remembered that "Emma made such a fuss about" the young lady.[67] Snow may not have understood what occurred between Joseph and Fanny as she later expressed surprise when Smith in Nauvoo taught her polygamy and she became one of his wives. Snow had assumed that polygamy was for the next life, but events in Nauvoo would cause her to reconsider what had happened in Kirtland between Smith and Alger.[68] Later, in Utah, Eliza would tell historian Andrew Jenson that Alger was "one of the first wives Joseph married," although she seems not to have had any reason to believe in 1836 that there had been a formal marriage.[69]

Snow's reference to "fuss" alluded to Emma's angered removal of Fanny from the Smith house in the middle of the night. After she was evicted from the Smith home, Alger went to stay with Chauncey and Eliza Jane Webb "until she could be sent to her relatives."[70] Eliza Jane said that "Fanny Alger had lived in Joseph's family several years, and when she left there she came and lived with me a few weeks."[71] Chauncey implied that Fanny was pregnant when she came to live with them: "Emma was furious, and drove

---

63. On the probable timing of Emma's discovery of Smith's affair with Alger, see Hales, *Joseph Smith's Polygamy*, 1:103, which dates the discovery to May–June 1836; Bradley, "Mormon Polygamy before Nauvoo? The Relationship of Joseph Smith and Fanny Alger"; and Hales, "Fanny Alger and Joseph Smith's Pre-Nauvoo Reputation," 147–50. Alger is apparently pronounced with a hard "g."

64. McLellin, Letter to Joseph Smith III, July 1872, 3 (Larson and Passey, *The William E. McLellin Papers*, 489).

65. J. H. Beadle, "Jackson County," *Salt Lake Tribune*, Oct. 6, 1875, 4.

66. Snow, "Sketch of My Life," 7.

67. Eliza R. Snow, Interview, ca. 1887, Andrew Jenson Notes, Andrew Jenson Papers, Joseph Smith polygamy folder, Document 10, CHL, in Hales, *Joseph Smith's Polygamy*, 1:113–14.

68. Snow, "Sketch of My Life," 13.

69. Snow, Interview, ca. 1887, in Hales, *Joseph Smith's Polygamy*, 1:113.

70. Young, *Wife No. 19*, 67.

71. Eliza Jane Webb, Letter to Mary Bond, Apr. 24, 1876.

the girl, who was unable to conceal the consequences of her celestial relation with the prophet, out of her house."[72] While Fanny's pregnancy is doubtful, Chauncey's account implies that Smith and Alger had a sexual relationship that lasted several months before being discovered by Emma.[73]

According to the Webbs' daughter, Ann Eliza, Emma had been "extremely fond" of Fanny and the betrayal so enraged her that "Joseph was obliged to send, at midnight, for Oliver Cowdery, his scribe, to come and endeavor to settle matters between them."[74] If true, Smith could not have chosen a worse ally since Cowdery was the probable author of the statement on marriage recently published in the Doctrine and Covenants, which disavowed the practice of polygamy, and he would later describe Smith's relationship with Alger as "a dirty, nasty, filthy affair."[75]

Rumors began to circulate that Smith had committed adultery, adding to dissension in the church. "By degrees it became whispered about," Ann Eliza Webb reported, "that Joseph's love for his adopted daughter was by no means a paternal affection, and his wife discovering the fact, at once took measures to place the girl beyond his reach."[76] Fanny Brewer, a member of the church in Boston, reported that when she arrived in Kirtland in the spring of 1837, she found the town abuzz with two rumors about the Mormon prophet: that Smith had hired two men to murder arch-enemy Grandison Newell, and that "an unlawful intercourse between himself and a young orphan girl residing in his family, and under his protection!!!"[77] Fanny was not an orphan, but the description served to amplify Alger's victimization.

Benjamin F. Johnson, age seventeen, remembered Fanny as "a vary nice & Comly young woman about my own age. towards whoom not only my-Self but every one Seemed <u>partial</u> for the ameability of her character" and that even before her eviction from the Smith home, "it was whispered … that Joseph <u>Loved</u> her." Before Smith's sudden departure from Kirtland the following winter, Johnson recalled that "there was Some trouble with Oliver Cowdery. and whisper Said it was Relating to a girl then living in his Family." Johnson subsequently learned from Warren Parrish "that He himself &

---

72. Chauncey Webb, Statement, in Wyl, *Mormon Portraits*, 57.

73. One candidate for a possible child of Joseph Smith and Fanny Alger, Orrison Smith, has been eliminated through genetic testing. Hales, *Joseph Smith's Polygamy*, 1:298.

74. Young, *Wife No. 19*, 66.

75. Oliver Cowdery, Letter to Warren Cowdery, Jan. 21, 1838, in Cowdery Letterbook, 81. In the manuscript letter, the word "affair" is written over "scrape."

76. Young, *Wife No. 19*, 66.

77. Fanny Brewer, Letter, Boston, Sep. 13, 1842, in Bennett, *The History of the Saints*, 85–86.

Oliver Cowdery did know that Joseph had Fanny Alger as a wife for They were Spied upon & found together." Reflecting on these events more than a half-century later, Johnson said: "And I Can now See that as at Nauvoo—So at Kirtland That the Suspician or Knowledge of the Prophets Plural Relation was one of the Causes of Apostacy & disruption at Kirtland altho at the time there was little Said publickly [by church officials] upon the Subject."[78] Rumors of Smith's impropriety must have remained hushed among the Mormons since it was never picked up by their enemies or trumpeted in the press. It also helped that Alger's family left Kirtland in September.[79] On their way to Missouri, the Algers stopped in Dublin, Indiana, where Fanny quickly married non-Mormon Solomon Custer on November 16.[80]

How Smith's relationship with Alger began is less well known. The sources on this question are contradictory and incomplete. One late source dates the beginning of the relationship to about March 1833, with the full knowledge of fifteen-year-old Fanny's parents, and names Levi Hancock as the officiator, but it is too anachronistic and problematic to be accepted without corroboration. This account was added to Hancock's autobiography by his son Mosiah fourteen years after his father's death in 1882 and frames Smith's relationship with Alger as if it existed in an established underground polygamous culture much as it existed in Utah at the time Mosiah was writing.[81] After reviewing the available sources, researcher Brian Hales concluded that "Joseph Smith's relationship with Fanny Alger began in late 1835 or early 1836 and was not discovered until after the April 1836 dedication of the Kirtland Temple."[82]

If Smith's subsequent proposals to other women are any indication, the Mormon prophet likely overcome Fanny's resistance by telling her it was commanded by God. This assumes he framed the proposal as a form of marriage. Some of his first polygamist marriages in Nauvoo reported that he approached them with the story that God had commanded him to marry them, but that he resisted doing so until an angel with a drawn sword threatened to kill him if he did not fully obey the command.[83] For example, Mary Elizabeth Rollins Lightner reported that Smith approached her in 1842, shortly after her mar-

78. Johnson, Letter to George F. Gibbs, Apr.–Oct. 1903, 26–27.

79. On the month that the Alger family left Kirtland, see "Died," Obituary of Samuel Alger, *Deseret News* (Salt Lake City), Oct. 14, 1874, 7. The authority of this date is unstated.

80. On Alger's marriage to Custer, see Van Wagoner, *Mormon Polygamy*, 9.

81. Mosiah Lyman Hancock, "Autobiography of Levi Ward Hancock," ca. 1896, 61–64.

82. Hales, *Joseph Smith's Polygamy*, 1:107.

83. See Hales, *Joseph Smith's Polygamy*, 1:186–98.

riage to Adam Lightner, and told her that "[he] was commanded [by God] to take me for a wife" and that an "angel came to him three times, the last time with a drawn sword and threatened his life" if he did not obey.[84]

For Smith, the justification for marriage with plural partners was present from the beginning. The Book of Mormon condemned polygamy as practiced by David and Solomon, without mentioning the patriarchs. Through Nephi's brother, Jacob, the Lord declared that the two Israelite kings had "many wives and concubines, which thing was abominable before me." At this time, the Lord also commanded the Nephites: "For there shall not any man among you have save it be one wife; and concubines he shall have none." However, the door was left open to follow the example of the patriarchs: "For if I will, saith the Lord of Hosts, raise up seed unto me, I will command my people; otherwise they shall hearken unto these things" (Jacob 2:23–30). This passage was not anti-polygamy but rather permitted it so long as the union was authorized through divine command. In the context of June 1829, this would mean that Smith could take another wife if authorized by revelation, either through his seer stone or a burning in the bosom.

Later, in Utah, many of the early Mormons who were then openly living polygamy claimed that Smith began teaching that plural marriage was a correct principle in the early 1830s.[85] According to Joseph B. Noble, "the Prophet Joseph told him that the doctrine of celestial marriage was revealed to him while he was engaged on the work of translation of the scriptures [meaning his revision of the Bible in 1831–33], but when the communication was first made the Lord stated that the time for the practice of that principle had not arrived."[86] If true, Smith may have been discussing the principle as early as February or March 1831 while working on Genesis, where he encountered the account of patriarch Abraham taking another wife (Gen. 16:1–6).[87] According to Benjamin Johnson, as early as 1835 he learned from his brother-in-law Lyman R. Sherman that Smith was teaching "that the ancient order of plural marriage was again to be practiced by the Church." Sherman also told Johnson that Jared Carter had requested Smith to give him another wife, which the prophet "would not permit."[88]

Perhaps such talk inspired some of Smith's followers to begin practicing

84. Lightner, "Statement," Feb. 8, 1902; Lightner, Reminiscences, ca. 1905, 18.

85. Hales, *Joseph Smith's Polygamy*, 1:85–91.

86. Joseph B. Noble, Sermon, Quarterly Conference Minutes, Centerville, Davis County, UT, June 11, 1883, quoted in Andrew Jenson, "Plural Marriage," *Historical Record*, July 1887, 232–33.

87. On dating, see Faulring et al., *Joseph Smith's New Translation of the Bible*, 57.

88. Johnson, Letter to George F. Gibbs, 26.

polygamy, independent of church sanction. The August 1835 statement on marriage published in the 1835 Doctrine and Covenants implied that polygamy had been an issue among Smith's followers when it stated that since the church had been "reproached with the crime of fornication, and polygamy," it was therefore necessary that "we declare that we believe, that one man should have one wife."[89]

The statement did not give any specifics of this reproach, but Oliver Cowdery, the likely author of the statement, probably had in mind the 1834 case of Joseph Wood. On February 3, 1834, a council of elders and high priests met to consider the complaint of Jabez G. Fosdick, a church leader in the Pontiac, Michigan, area, against Joseph Wood, a high priest and visiting missionary. In this letter, signed by Joseph Smith, as Moderator, Fosdick was informed of the decision of the council to excommunicate Wood for "indulging in an idle, partial, overbearing and lustful spirit and not magnifying his holy calling." Wood seems to have offered a rationale for his behavior that required a response from Smith—"We were very sorry to learn that Bro. J. Wood had gone so far astray and offered such violence to the pure principles of the Gospel of Christ. ... Every principle incubated among you which is contrary [t]o virtue, to industry, to wisdom, to good order, to propriety, and in fine, to the pure principles of godliness ... is entirely foreign from the feelings of our breasts, and is that upon which we look down with feelings of the utmost disapprobation. ... We cannot look upon any principle contrary to the above with any degree of allowance."[90] While Smith charged Wood with being unvirtuous and lustful, without Fosdick's letter of complaint, which is apparently not extant, it remains unexplained why Smith felt the need to disavow such behavior and proclaim that it is "entirely foreign from the feelings of our breasts."

On March 7, 1834, while Smith and Rigdon were away from Kirtland, Cowdery responded to a follow-up letter from Fosdick and other church leaders in Michigan inquiring about Joseph Wood's excommunication for adultery. This letter is also not extant, but Cowdery's response implies that Wood, who had been a missionary in the Pontiac area, had defended his actions by alleging that Smith and other church leaders in Kirtland were secretly condoning adultery or some form of polygamy, which Cowdery denied: "I am sensible, that many reproaches are and will be heaped upon

---

89. Statement on Marriage, ca. Aug. 1835, in D&C, 1835 ed., CI (*JSP*, D4:477–78).

90. Joseph Smith and Orson Hyde, Letter to [J. G.] Fosdick, Feb. 3, 1834, Cowdery Letterbook, 23–24 (*JSP*, D3:422–25). In the manuscript letter, "lustful" is underlined three times.

us falsely by apostates; but we are endeavoring to have a conscious void of offence in the sight of heaven; and if we maintain this, we are certain, that when the trying hour arrives, we shall shine in the Kingdom of our God, while liars and adulterers meet their just reward." Written two years before he would learn of Smith's relationship with Alger, Cowdery advised the Pontiac leaders not to give credence to Wood's accusations, for "a man who will leave a virtuous companion and follow adulterous practices, you will not expect but little truth!" Cowdery, who equated polygamy with adultery, expressed an attitude that would soon bring him into conflict with Smith: "That sacred marriage covenant is, in my opinion of too precious a nature to be trifled with, without justice overtaking the breaker of it sooner or later. With regard to our honesty and righteousness, as individuals of whom Mr. Wood spake, I can say, by our fruits we are to be known, and so far from doing anything in the dark, brethren, come and prove us critically as you please, & then of course you will be satisfied."[91]

Concern that church members were secretly practicing polygamy led the seventies, who met in the temple on April 29, 1837, to resolve to disfellowship any of its members "who is guilty of polygamy or any offence of the kind."[92] In November 1837 one of the frequently-asked questions for which Smith was preparing answers was: "Do the Mormons believe in having more wives than one?"[93] His answer, which did not appear in the *Elders' Journal* until July 1838, after he had relocated to Missouri, was: "No, not at the same time. But they believe that if their companion dies, they have a right to marry again."[94] Smith was probably distinguishing what the church taught publicly from what was taught privately by its leader. Regardless, it is a testament to the persistence of the rumors. If Smith regarded his relationship with Alger as a legitimate marriage, what kind of marriage was it? Who officiated? By what authority?

The sources that name an officiator are mixed, but in the context of late 1835 or early 1836, it seems probable that Smith would have linked polygamous marriage to the high and patriarchal priesthoods. Hancock family lore naming Levi Hancock as the officiator who married Smith and Alger seems

---

91. Oliver Cowdery, Letter to J. G. Fosdick, Samuel Bent, and Elijah Fordham, Mar. 7, 1834, Cowdery Letterbook, 28–29. Wood subsequently repented and was rebaptized, but in November 1840 was again disfellowshipped. *Times and Seasons*, Mar. 1, 1841, 335. Later, he openly practiced polygamy after joining William Smith's faction in 1851. Shepard and Marquardt, *Lost Apostles*, 340–43.

92. Minutes, Apr. 29, 1837, *LDS Messenger and Advocate*, May 1837, 511.

93. Joseph Smith, Editorial, *Elders' Journal* (Kirtland, OH), Nov. 1837, 28–29.

94. Joseph Smith, Editorial, *Elders' Journal* (Far West, MO), July 1838, 43.

unlikely given that Levi was an elder in 1833 and then ordained a seventy in February 1835.[95] According to Eliza Jane Webb, "Fanny Alger's mother says Fanny was sealed to Joseph by Oliver Cowdery in Kirtland in 1835–or 6."[96] Given Cowdery's involvement with the 1835 statement on marriage and subsequent accusations, Cowdery is not a likely officiator. More probable is that Smith acted as his own officiator, Fanny responded affirmatively, and Smith then pronounced them husband and wife by the authority of the patriarchal priesthood invested in him by God.[97] This may clarify Emma's comment to McLellin in 1847 that "she knew her husband the Prophet practiced both adultery and polygamy."[98] If she knew there had been an officiator, Emma likely would have defined Joseph's relationship with Alger as polygamous, not adulterous, which is clearly how she viewed it.

Far West, Missouri

Edward Partridge, Isaac Morley, John Corrill, and Phelps returned to Liberty, Missouri, on May 6, 1836, and soon after Partridge and Phelps began searching for a permanent place for the Mormon community. "After my arrival at home," Partridge wrote in his journal, "I spent a few days in attending to my own affairs: then, in company with br. W. W. Phelps, I took a tour in looking at the country north."[99] On June 2 Phelps wrote to Oliver Cowdery and mentioned that since his return to Missouri he had been "constantly engaged in viewing the country."[100] He and Partridge eventually located a desirable "mill seat on Shoal creek," about thirty-five miles northeast of Liberty for the future site of Far West in what would eventually become Caldwell County.[101]

Meanwhile, rumors of "Another Mormon Invasion" in the spring circulated in northwestern Missouri, and Clay County citizens grew anxious for the Mormons to leave. Report was received in Clay County from "persons of undoubted veracity" in Kirtland, which claimed that "the Mormons in that place and its vicinity, to the number of 1500 or 2000, are arming and coming

---

95. See *JSP*, D5:572; Cook, *Revelations of the Prophet Joseph Smith*, 76.

96. Webb, Letter to Mary Bond, Apr. 24, 1876.

97. Interestingly, Smith's scribe and church historian Willard Richards married one of his plural wives in Nauvoo in 1845 without a ceremony but by "mutually acknowledg[ing] each other husband and wife." See Smith, *Nauvoo Polygamy*, 649n315.

98. McLellin, Notebook, ca. 1880, 14 (Larson and Passey, eds., *The William E. McLellin Papers*, 395).

99. Partridge, Diary, May 6, 1836.

100. William W. Phelps, Letter to Oliver Cowdery, June 2, 1836, *LDS Messenger and Advocate*, July 1836, 340–41.

101. Partridge, Diary, May 6–June 29, 1836.

on to the upper Missouri ... [in] another attempt to take Zion," and that "no doubt can remain but that the peace of this section is again to be disturbed by a military array of ragamuffins, headed by the modern Mohamed."[102] Clay County resident Anderson Wilson explained the reason for concern over the growing Mormon presence. The Mormons "have been flocking in here faster than ever and making great talk what they would do," he wrote. "A letter from Ohio Shows plainly that they intend to Emigrate here til they outnumber us. Then they would rule the Contry at pleasure." Continuing, he said: "They have got a revelation from Smith that they Shal have the Missouri By money or Blood. ... We are to Submit to a mormon government or trample under foot the laws of our Contry." Wilson explained that he and others had taken up arms against the Mormons and were resolved to "fight by each others Side & die like Ishmael in the presence of our brethren."[103]

On a second scouting tour in the region north of Ray County, Partridge and Phelps were accompanied by Morley and Corrill, the latter of whom purchased seven eighty-acre lots in what would become Rockford (later Mirabile) Township on June 22, 1836, on behalf of himself, Cowdery, and Smith. Among the applications Corrill submitted at Lexington, Missouri, two were for Smith: one for 400 acres for $500, and another for a little more than seventy-eight acres for $98.20, totaling 478 acres for $598.20, paid in cash.[104]

On June 29 non-Mormons held a public meeting at Liberty and demanded that Mormons leave. A "Committee of nine" was organized to draft resolutions and negotiate the departure of the Mormons from Clay County. According to their resolutions, they were worried about civil war breaking out between the Mormons and hostile Clay Countians. Primarily, they believed the Mormon leaders, despite agreeing to make Clay County a temporary asylum for their people, were "determined to violate that promise and make Clay County their 'permanent home,'" citing the rapid emigration of Mormons and their purchases of large sections of land.[105] At this time,

---

102. "Another Mormon Invasion," *Missouri Republican* (St. Louis), May 17, 1836, [2].

103. Anderson Wilson and Emelia Faucett Wilson, Letter to Samuel and Ann [Nancy] Wilson, July 4, 1836, in Stokes, "Wilson Letters, 1835–1849," 504–509.

104. Register's Office, Certificate to Joseph Smith, Lexington, Lafayette Co., MO, June 22, 1836, Land Entry Case File 7873, Record Group 49; and Register's Office, Certificate to Joseph Smith, Lexington, Lafayette Co., MO, June 22, 1836, Land Entry Case File 7874, Record Group 49, Records of the Bureau of Land Management, National Archives and Records Administration, Washington DC. For a discussion of these purchases and a transcription of the second application, see *JSP*, D5:253–58.

105. "Public Meeting," *Messenger and Advocate*, Aug. 1836, 353–55; reprinted from "Public Meeting," *Far West* (Liberty, MO), June 30, 1836.

Mormons owned nearly 1,000 acres of land in Clay County.[106] On July 1 the Mormons held a public meeting and, while denying many of the accusations of the non-Mormon committee, agreed to move into another part of the state of Missouri, stating: "Notwithstanding the necessary loss of property and expense we incur in moving, we comply with the requisitions of their resolutions in leaving the county of Clay … and that we will also exert ourselves to stop the tide of emigration of our people to this county."[107]

Phelps wrote a letter to Missouri governor Dunklin on July 7 to inform him of their determination to settle on land north of Ray County.[108] A week later, Elisha Cameron and Cornelius Gilliam began serving as guides for Partridge, Phelps, and John Whitmer during a nine-day expedition to northwest Missouri.[109] On July 25 a general assembly authorized Phelps, Whitmer, Partridge, Morley, and Corrill "to search out land for the Church to settle upon &c."[110]

Meanwhile, Phelps's July 1 letter reporting on recent negotiations with the Clay County committee had reached Kirtland, and on July 25 the First Presidency responded: "We are sorry that this disturbance has broken out— [but] we do not consider it our fault," and advised them to "give no occasion, and if the people will let you dispose of your property, settle your affairs, and go in peace, go."[111] On the same day, the First Presidency wrote to John Thornton (chair) and others of the Clay County committee, responding to their June 29 resolutions and demands. They denied the charge, for example, that Mormons believe they will possess northern Missouri "at all hazards and in defiance of all consequences," which they blamed on "the whims and vain notions of some few uninformed" Mormons, and suggested that "where the idea could have originated is unknown to us. … There is nothing in all our religious faith to warrant it." In fact, they knew precisely where such ideas came from.

They denied that the Mormons wanted to make Clay County their "permanent home," but insisted that they were only there until they could regain "the quiet possession of their homes in Jackson county"—which, in light of

---

106. Parkin, "A History of the Latter-day Saints in Clay County," 207, 318–19.

107. "Public Meeting," *Messenger and Advocate*, Aug. 1836, 359–60.

108. William W. Phelps et al., Letter to Daniel Dunklin, July 7, 1836, in Phelps, Collection of Missouri Documents.

109. Parkin, "History of the Latter-day Saints in Clay County," 268.

110. Minutes, July 25, 1836, Minute Book 2, 69 (Cannon and Cook, *Far West Record*, 104–105).

111. Sidney Rigdon et al. (including Joseph Smith), Letter to William W. Phelps and Others, July 25, 1836, *LDS Messenger and Advocate*, Aug. 1836, 359 (*JSP*, D5:269-70).

the nearly 1,000 acres of Clay County lands purchased by the Mormons, was unconvincing. They also denied the charge that the Mormons continued to communicate with the Indians, declaring "from the pulpit, that the Indians are a part of God's chosen people, and are destined, by heaven, to inherit this land, in common with themselves," and argued that Mormons are just as worried about the Indians as anyone. "Another charge brought against our friends," the Mormon leaders wrote, "is that of being dangerous in societies 'where slavery is tolerated and practiced,'" and recommended that they read Smith's anti-abolitionist article in the April issue of the *Latter Day Saints' Messenger and Advocate*, which they sent with their letter.[112] Finally, they agreed that the Mormons will leave Clay County, but could not say where they will settle next.[113]

In August, the Mormons began leaving Clay County and settling at their new location near the future site of Far West in the area south of Shoal Creek. On August 8 Phelps and Whitmer purchased the town plot and four adjacent eighty-acre tracts in their own names with church funds, for which they will later be disciplined.[114] Partridge subsequently wrote, "In a few months nearly or quite all the best land of the territory, now known as Caldwell county, was purchased by the saints, several hundred buildings erected, and great preparations made for a crop the coming season."[115]

Trip to Salem

On July 25 Smith left Kirtland in the afternoon for the East on a secret mission with Rigdon, Hyrum Smith, and Cowdery. At 7:00 p.m., they boarded the steamer *Charles Townsend* at Fairport and arrived at Buffalo about 10:00 p.m. the following day. They lodged in Farmer's Hotel, where they met Orson Hyde on his way to Canada and Moses C. Nickerson returning from Canada. The next day they took a canal boat, arrived at Utica, New York, at about 8:00 a.m. on July 29, and immediately boarded a railroad car for Schenectady. After six hours, they arrived and quickly boarded a baggage train for Albany, where they arrived the same evening. On July 30 Smith and the others boarded the steamer *John Mason*, which took them to the steamer *Erie*, which stopped at Catskill, West Point, and finally New York

---

112. Joseph Smith, Letter to Oliver Cowdery, ca. Apr. 9, 1836, *LDS Messenger and Advocate*, Apr. 1836, 289–91 (*JSP*, D5:231–43).

113. Sidney Rigdon et al. (including Joseph Smith), Letter to John Thornton and Others, July 25, 1836, *LDS Messenger and Advocate*, Aug. 1836, 355–59 (*JSP*, D5:258–68).

114. Minutes, Apr. 7, 1837, Minute Book 2, 68–69 (Cannon and Cook, *Far West Record*, 110).

115. [Partridge, Edward], "A History, of the Persecution, of the Church of Jesus Christ, of Latter Day Saints in Missouri," *Times and Seasons*, Mar. 1840, 65 (*JSP*, H2:230).

City. During his stay, Smith visited part of New York City which had been burned in the 1835 fire.[116]

Smith and the others apparently left New York City on August 4, traveling aboard a steamer to Newport, Rhode Island, where they took steam cars to Boston. From there, they traveled by stage to Salem, Massachusetts, a busy seaport located on Massachusetts Bay about fifteen miles north of Boston that Cowdery described as a quiet and "pleasantly situated town with fifteen thousand inhabitants." Shortly after arriving, they rented a house on Union Street and for three weeks spent part of their time visiting historic sites and, according to Smith's history, "teaching the people from house to house, and preaching publicly, as opportunity presented."[117]

On August 6 Smith dictated a revelation that revealed the main reason for his sudden departure from Kirtland and extended stay in Salem: "I have much treasure in this city for you, for the benefit of Zion. ... I will give this city into your hands; ... and its wealth pertaining to gold and silver shall be yours. Concern not yourselves about your debts, for I will give you power to pay them. ... And inquire diligently concerning the more ancient inhabitants and founders of this city; For there are more treasures than one for you in this city."[118]

Ebenezer Robinson, who worked in the printing office in Kirtland with Don Carlos Smith, later wrote that the Prophet's younger brother told him that Joseph had learned about possible treasure from "a brother Burgess" who had come to Kirtland and "stated that a large amount of money had been secreted in the cellar of a certain house in Salem, Massachusetts, which had belonged to a widow, and he thought he was the only person now living, who had knowledge of it, or the location of the house." Robinson also said that Burgess met Joseph and the others in Salem but because "time had wrought such a change that he could not, for a certainty point out the house, and soon left."[119] The "brother Burgess" was evidently Jonathan Burgess, from whom Smith and the others borrowed $100 on August 17.[120]

---

116. Oliver Cowdery, Letter, Aug. 3 [4], 1836, *Messenger and Advocate*, Sep. 1836, 373–75.

117. Oliver Cowdery, Letter, Aug. 24, 1836, *Messenger and Advocate*, Oct. 1836, 386–93; News Item, *Essex Register* (Salem, MA), Aug. 25, 1836, [2]; Proper, "Joseph Smith and Salem," 97n27; JS History, vol. B-1, 749 (DHC 2:464).

118. Revelation, Aug. 6, 1836, Phelps, Diary and Notebook, 35–[37] [D&C 111:2, 4, 5, 9–10] (*JSP*, D5:277–78).

119. Ebenezer Robinson, "Items of Personal History of the Editor," *Return* (Davis City, IA), July 1889, 105–106.

120. See Joseph Smith et al., Promissory Note to Jonathan Burgess, Aug. 17, 1836, JS Collection (*JSP*, D5:280). Little is known about Jonathan Burgess, but he is listed as attending a church council in 1837 in Kirtland and being approved for ordination as a priest. Minutes, Nov. 2, 1837, Minute Book 1, 258 (Collier and Harwell, *Kirtland Council Minute Book*, 202).

On August 19 Smith wrote to Emma and explained the reason for his re-maining in Salem and not returning with Hyrum: "With regard to the graat [great] object of our mishion. you will be anxtiou [anxious] to know, we have found the house since Brother Burjece left us, very luckily and providentialy, as we had one spell been most discouraged, but the house is ocupied and it will require much care and patience to rent or b[u]y it, we think we shall be able to effect it if not now within the course of a few months, we think we shall be at home about the middle of septtember."[121]

It is not known how Smith located the house, but it does not appear that he used his treasure seeing stone, although James Colin Brewster, who had been a young stone gazer himself in Kirtland, implied such was the case. Re-sponding to John Taylor's 1842 description of treasure hunting as a "ridiculous and pernicious" practice, Brewster asked: "Who was the author of this prac-tice among the Mormons [in Kirtland]?" He then answered his own question: "If he has a good memory, he will remember the house that was rented in the city of Boston [Salem], with the expectation of finding a large sum of money buried in or near the cellar."[122] However, it is doubtful that Smith would use the terms *luck* and *providence* to describe his use of the stone.

On the same day that Smith dictated his revelation, Rigdon and Cowdery toured the East India Marine Society Museum and signed the registry; three days later, Smith did the same.[123] Cowdery mentioned visiting other places such as the Boston naval yard, Bunker Hill, the ruins of the Charlestown Ursuline Convent burned by an anti-Catholic mob in 1834, and locations related to the famous late-seventeenth-century witch trials.[124] During his stay in Salem, Smith was visited by Brigham and Joseph Young and Lyman E. Johnson, who were on missions in the East.[125]

On August 20 Rigdon preached in the afternoon at the Lyceum in Salem. According to one newspaper, "Notices were sent round on Saturday" announcing that "Mr. Rigdon of Ohio would preach at the Lyceum that

---

121. Joseph Smith, Letter to Emma Smith, Aug. 19, 1836 (*JSP*, D5:280–83).

122. See "Notice," *Times and Seasons*, Dec. 1, 1842, 32; Brewster, *Very Important!* 4; see also Vogel, "James Colin Brewster."

123. Oliver Cowdery and Sidney Rigdon, Aug. 6, 1836, and Joseph Smith, Aug. 9, 1836, Guest Book, vol. J, East India Marine Society Records. See photograph in *JSP*, D5:276; see also Proper, "Joseph Smith and Salem," 94.

124. Oliver Cowdery, Letter, Aug. 24, 1836, *Messenger and Advocate*, Oct. 1836, 386–93.

125. JS History, vol. B-1, Addenda, 4, Note O, which was inserted by Wilmer Benson pos-sibly on July 15, 1845, under Brigham Young's direction. Vogel, *History of Joseph Smith*, 2:451n24. In a later history, Brigham mentioned that he "met with the Prophet in Salem." Historian's Office, Brigham Young History Drafts, 12.

afternoon, on the subject of the Christian religion." The same paper reported that "the preacher was a man of very respectable appearance, apparently about forty years of age, and very fluent in his language." Rigdon surprised his audience by not talking about the Book of Mormon, but instead delivered a sermon based on Galatians 1:8: "Though we, or an angel from heaven, should preach any other gospel than that which we have preached to you, let him be accursed." He declared that "he rejected the other prevalent systems of faith" and "he considered them all destitute of truth" because "none can be true Christians, except those who have received the Holy Ghost, and who have power to see visions, dream dreams, look into futurity, utter prophecies, handle poisonous reptiles or drink any deadly thing, without receiving any injury, of healing the sick by laying their hands upon them, and the gift of speaking with other tongues, as on the day of Pentecost." The reporter noted that Rigdon abruptly ended his discourse and left "without giving any evidence that he himself possessed any of the above powers."[126] If Smith was present, he apparently remained silent.

Rigdon again spoke at the Lyceum on August 24 and complained about the newspaper coverage of his previous preaching. This time Rigdon was challenged from the audience by the Reverend Joshua Himes, pastor of the First Christian Church in Boston. According to the *Boston Daily Times,* "Himes answered this Rigdon on the spot, exposed his deceptions, unraveled his absurdities, and so effectually stopped his mouth that not even his accustomed imprudence could bear him out of the scrape."[127] Later the same year, Himes gave an account of his exchange with Rigdon and reported that Rigdon "was confounded, though he attempted to extricate himself by his sophistry, in which he abounds, yet it only made a bad matter worse. ... His object was to deceive and lead astray the innocent disciples of Christ. He, however, did not make many disciples on this occasion."[128] The newspaper also reported that "Joe Smith, the original founder of the sect and the high priest and prophet of his tribe of impostors, was also present, and was obliged to undergo the 'searching operation' of divers questions which were propounded to him by those who knew more of his history than he was aware," and then added: "He did not pass through the ordeal unscathed. He

126. "Mormonism," *Essex Register* (Salem, MA), Aug. 22, 1836, [3].
127. "Mormonism—Again," *Boston Daily Times*, Aug. 26, 1836, [2].
128. Joshua Himes, "Joe Smith-ism, Alias Mormonism," *Christian Palladium* (Union Mills, NY), Dec. 15, 1836, 243–44.

seemed to be borne down with ... guilt and shame. It may take him a day or two to get that load off his stomach."[129]

According to Robinson, the Mormons ultimately "found a house which they felt was the right one, and hired it. Needless to say, they failed to find either that treasure, or the gold and silver spoken of in the revelation."[130] Apparently, Smith and the others left Salem the same day. According to the *Essex Register,* "It is said they retain possession of the tenement leased by them in Union Street, and intend to return to this city next spring."[131]

Smith and the others returned to Kirtland empty-handed shortly before the purchase of land on September 13 and 14, 1836.[132] How Smith explained his failure to find "treasure ... for the benefit of Zion" in Salem is unknown.[133] He may also have arrived before the September 11 deadline for the redemption of Zion; the record is equally silent about that failure as well.

---

129. "Mormonism—Again," *Boston Daily Times,* Aug. 26, 1836, [2].
130. Ebenezer Robinson, "Items of Personal History of the Editor," *Return,* July 1889, 105–106.
131. News Item, *Essex Register,* Aug. 25, 1836, [2].
132. See next chapter.
133. Revelation, Aug. 6, 1836, Phelps, Diary and Notebook, 35 [D&C 111:2] (*JSP,* D5:277).

24

Heaven's Bank

SEPTEMBER 1836–MAY 1837

I have listened to him with feelings of no ordinary kind, when he declared that the audible voice of God, instructed him to establish a Banking-Anti Banking institution, which like Aaron's rod should swallow up all other Banks.
—*Warren Parrish, Feb. 5, 1838, Letter to the Editor,*
Painesville (OH) Republican, *Feb. 15, 1838, [3]*

Shortly after returning from Salem, Smith purchased two large tracts of land in Kirtland on September 13 and 14, 1836: one as a member of Rigdon, Smith & Cowdery for $1,800 for thirty-nine acres of land, the other for a thirteen-acre lot adjoining the first in his own name for $200.[1] In all, Smith purchased, either on his own or in partnership, about 440 acres in the Kirtland area during the fall of 1836.[2] The editors of the Joseph Smith Papers note: "These acquisitions seem to have been motivated by a desire to make land available for church members newly arriving in Kirtland and, perhaps, to provide real estate backing for the establishment of a bank in Kirtland."[3] Backing the bank with landholdings would prove to be a mistake when the real-estate bubble burst the following year.

Smith planned to buy store goods on credit in New York and then convert the goods into property acquisitions for speculative purposes that involved dividing large tracts of land into smaller lots and selling them at higher

---

1. Hiram and Permelia Dayton, Deed for property in Geauga Co., OH, to Rigdon, Smith & Cowdery, Sep. 13, 1836, Geauga Co., OH, Deed Record, vol. 22, 305; William and Elizabeth Draper, Deed for property in Geauga Co., OH, to Joseph Smith, Sep. 14, 1836, Geauga Co., OH, Deed Record, vol. 22, 428–29.

2. See *JSP*, D5:xxvii. According to the editors of the Joseph Smith Papers, "This figure represents the acres of land documented in extant Geauga County deed records. There may have been additional land purchased by Smith and his associates." *JSP*, D5:xxviin58.

3. *JSP*, D5:xxvii.

prices to arriving Mormons. In October 1836, Smith traded about $17,000 in store goods as down payments on more than 1,025 acres of property near the temple. With these property transfers, Smith ran out of inventory and had to close the store he operated across the road from his house. A second store run by Rigdon, Smith, and Cowdery in Chester Township, located immediately south of Kirtland Township, lasted another year, although it too was used to convert merchandise into land.[4]

On October 5 Smith, in partnership with brothers William and Don Carlos and newly arrived convert William Miller, bought a large tract of land consisting of 239 acres in southwestern Kirtland Township from Peter French on credit for $11,777.50.[5] Historian Mark L. Staker observes, "During the first ten days in October, leaders purchased over $36,595.70 in property on credit. At that point, the identifiable debt for store goods and land associated with Joseph Smith, who was presumably acting for the Church, amounted to more than $50,000."[6]

Safety Society Bank

The earliest indication that Smith was planning to establish his own bank is an invoice for the purchase of goods by Cowdery and Hyrum Smith in New York City, dated October 11, 1836, payable in six months at the "Kirtland Safety Society Bank"—suggesting that there were plans for a bank prior to their leaving Kirtland, probably in late September.[7] While the two men were in New York City, they purchased four "booksafes," evidently for use in the bank, from merchant Jesse Delano on October 15.[8] Cowdery also arranged to have three, possibly four, metal plates—each containing multiple denominations—made for printing the Kirtland Safety Society Bank's bills, which Cowdery ordered from the firm Underwood, Spencer, Bald & Hufty in New York City, which he picked up at their office in Philadelphia in December.[9]

---

4. Staker, *Hearken, O Ye People*, 453–54.

5. Peter and Sarah French, Deed for property in Kirtland Township, Geauga Co., OH, to William Miller, William Smith, Don Carlos Smith, and Joseph Smith, Oct. 5, 1836, Geauga Co., OH, Deed Record, vol. 23, 94–95. On the same day the same parties entered into a mortgage agreement: William Miller, William Smith, Don Carlos Smith, and Joseph Smith, Mortgage for property in Kirtland Township, Geauga Co., OH, to Peter French, Oct. 5, 1836, Geauga Co., OH, Deed Record, vol. 22, 383–84 (*JSP*, D5:293–99).

6. Staker, *Hearken, O Ye People*, 454.

7. Winthrop Eaton, Invoice, New York City, New York Co., NY, to Smith & Cowdery, Kirtland Township, Geauga Co., OH, Oct. 11, 1836, JS Office Papers.

8. Jesse Delano, Bill, Oct. 15, 1836, JS Office Papers (*JSP*, D5:300–301).

9. JS History, vol. B-1, 750 (DHC 2:468). See also *JSP*, D5:302 and n. 79; 331 and n. 190.

The firm later sued Cowdery and others when they defaulted on a promissory note for $1,450.[10]

Rigdon was first to invest in the Safety Society, purchasing 2,000 shares on October 18 for an initial payment of $630; later, he purchased an additional 1,000 shares, which brought his number of shares to the maximum that any one person could hold.[11] On October 22 Smith purchased 3,000 shares of stock and made an initial payment of $1,342.69.[12] By November 2, the day of the first stockholder meeting, sixty subscribers had purchased nearly half of the bank's 80,000 stocks and paid nearly $7,000 in initial payments.[13]

At the 2 November organizational meeting Orson Hyde presented the constitution of the Kirtland Safety Society Bank, which was received with unanimous approval. During the meeting, thirty-two directors were elected; from this group, six were chosen to form a committee to run the bank. The directors also elected Rigdon as president and Joseph Smith as cashier.

Smith may have conceived the bank as a means of stimulating Kirtland's economy to sustain and support the gathering of the Mormons. If successful, the bank could also provide funds for the purchase of lands in Jackson County. However, the bank was misconceived and doomed to failure. Article 1, for example, stipulated that the "capital stock of said Bank shall not be less than four millions of dollars; to be divided into shares of fifty dollars each."[14] This would require 80,000 stockholders. The editors of the Joseph Smith Papers note: "The amount of the Kirtland Safety Society's capital stock was an ambitious and unlikely, if not impossible, objective."[15] By January 1837 the society had collected nearly $12,000 in specie or banknotes from more than 100 investors, each of whom had paid at least 26.25 cents per share as the first installment on their stock subscriptions.[16] When the charter was considered by the Ohio legislature in February 1837, the amount of its capital stock was reduced from $4 million to $300,000, which was still too high.[17]

Another problem was that the Kirtland society was underfunded because its administrators were too lenient, allowing several to make only partial

10. Transcript of Proceedings, Apr. 16, 1839, Underwood et al. v. Rigdon et al., Geauga Co., OH, Court of Common Pleas, Final Record, vol. X, 34–36; *JSP*, D5:331n189.

11. Kirtland Safety Society Stock Ledger, 1836–37, 1–2.

12. Ledger, 13–14.

13. See *JSP*, D5:302.

14. Constitution of the Kirtland Safety Society, Nov. 2, 1836, *LDS Messenger and Advocate* (Kirtland, OH), Extra, Dec. 1836, [1] (*JSP*, D5:304).

15. *JSP*, D5:304n90.

16. See Kirtland Safety Society Stock Ledger, 13–14.

17. "In Senate," *Ohio State Journal and Columbus Gazette*, Feb. 14, 1837, [2].

initial payments while others paid nothing. On this matter, the editors of the Joseph Smith Papers also note: "The combination of relatively low share prices, an unusually high capital stock, and a very low initial installment payment for stock, some of which was never paid, meant that the society was low on funds from the outset."[18]

As required by law, Orson Hyde was assigned to go to Columbus to petition the legislature for an act of incorporation, which was unlikely due to the Democratic majority's dislike for private banks and paper money. The answer, however, would not come until February 1837.[19] Meanwhile, the society set up its office close to the temple, likely on the lot to the south.[20]

Pride

Even before Smith left on his trip to Salem in late July 1836, the Mormons in Kirtland began dreaming of getting rich. In early July, Ebenezer Robinson, after returning from a five-week mission, observed: "We discovered a great change had taken place in the church, especially with many of its leading official members. A spirit of speculation was poured out, and instead of that meek and lowly spirit which we felt had heretofore prevailed, a spirit of worldly ambition, and grasping after the things of the world, took its place. Some farms adjacent to Kirtland were purchased by some of the heads of the church, mostly on credit, and laid out into city lots, until a large city was laid out on paper, and the price of the lots put up to an unreasonable amount, ranging from $100 to $200 each, according to location."[21] Expectations for growth were such that in the summer of 1836 more than seventy citizens of Kirtland petitioned for an expansion of the original 1833 city plat, increasing the city's limits from one to two square miles, which was formalized in spring 1837.[22]

In mid-November 1836, one visitor to Kirtland remarked that he "was astonished to see that a city had sprung up since I was there last March." Describing the area around the temple on the bluff to the southern border of Kirtland Township, the reporter said: "I should think there were between 100 and 200 houses (perhaps more) new building, most of them are small and plain, but some of them are elegant. ... Most of the farms between the centre of Kirtland and the centre of Chester, they own; they also own a large store in

---

18. *JSP*, D5:290.

19. JS History, vol. B-1, 750 (DHC 2:468).

20. Staker, *Hearken, O Ye People*, 413.

21. Ebenezer Robinson, "Items of Personal History of the Editor," *Return* (Davis City, IA), July 1889, 105–106.

22. Staker, *Hearken, O Ye People*, 450, 458n43.

Chester, and do business under the firm of Rigdon, Smith, & Co. They trade on a large scale, and make market for everything that can be raised about here. ... Their village will undoubtedly be incorporated as a city next winter."[23]

The fleeting illusion of prosperity gave rise to vanity and pride. Cyrus Smalling, a member of the high council, said: "All the heads of the church, got lifted up in pride, and they imagined that God was about to make them rich, and they were to suck the milk of the Gentiles ... and then they would make the whole church rich."[24] John Corrill explained in 1839 that church leaders and others "did not fully understand the mercantile business, and, withal, they suffered pride to arise in their hearts, and became desirous of fine houses, and fine clothes, and indulged too much in these things, sup-posing for a few months that they were very rich. ... They also bought many farms at extravagant prices, and made part payments, which they afterwards lost, by not being able to meet the remaining payments."[25] John Whitmer wrote in his history that Smith and other leaders "established a bank for the purpose of Speculation and the whole church partook of the same Spirit, they were lifted up in pride, and lusted after the forbiden things of God."[26]

Even Smith got caught up in land speculation and created unrealistic expectations by overselling the bank. According to Warren Parrish, who had worked as a cashier for the short-lived bank, Smith "declared that the audible voice of God, instructed him to establish a Banking-Anti Bank-ing institution, which like Aaron's rod should swallow up all other Banks."[27] With such declarations, the bank's success seemed like a sure thing.

Setbacks

On December 22 Smith attended a conference of church officers in the temple to discuss problems created by the increase of Mormons, especially impover-ished members, moving to Kirtland. Historian Milton Backman estimated the number of Mormons in Kirtland and vicinity in 1835 was approximately 1,100, and that by 1838 the number had nearly doubled to 2,000.[28] It was de-cided that the poor should be taken care of by the churches where they reside

---

23. Anonymous, Munson, OH, Nov. 14, 1836, *Aurora* (Lisbon, OH), Jan. 19, 1837.

24. Cyrus Smalling, Letter from Kirtland, OH, Mar. 10, 1841, in Lee, *The Mormons*, 13. Cf. Isa. 60:16.

25. Corrill, *Brief History*, 26–27 (*JSP*, H2:159–60).

26. Whitmer, History, 86 (*JSP*, H2:95–96).

27. Warren Parrish, Letter to the Editor, Feb. 5, 1838, *Painesville (OH) Republican*, Feb. 15, 1838, [3].

28. Backman, *Heavens Resound*, 139–40.

and that all immigration to Kirtland be suspended until "wise men" can be sent in advance to prepare places for those moving to Kirtland.[29]

In the published minutes, Smith gave the impression that land was scarce in Kirtland: "Our houses are all full, and our lands mostly occupied, except those houses and lands that do not belong to the church, which cannot be obtained without great sacrifice."[30] Of course, this was untrue since, in the months preceding this conference, Smith and other church members had bought hundreds of acres in Kirtland. This new policy seems designed to set up a real estate operation and ensure land was purchased from Smith and other Mormon speculators by the "wise men" and not from non-Mormon competitors. With the extent of their landholdings unknown, speculators could charge higher prices.

On January 2, 1837, a meeting of the Kirtland Safety Society was held with Rigdon as chair and Warren Parrish as secretary to annul the previous articles—adopted the previous November—and adopt new articles under the name "Kirtland Safety Society Anti-Banking Company."[31] By the time of this meeting, there were 137 stockholders, including seventeen women.[32] Warren Cowdery described the new society as a "bank, or monied institution" that may have been "considered a kind of joint stock association."[33] The new articles avoided the use of banking terminology, replacing, for instance, "bank" with "company"; "stockholders" with "managers" or "members"; and "directors" with "managers." Instead of "President" and "Cashier," Rigdon became "Secretary" and Smith "Treasurer."

This change in the Safety Society made it necessary to alter the bills which had been previously printed and were waiting to be circulated. Using hand stamps, the word "BANK" was now preceded by "ANTI" and followed by "ING CO." in smaller typeface; the titles president and cashier following the signatures of Rigdon and Smith were canceled and replaced with "Tres" (Treasurer) and "Sec" (Secretary), which occurred only on the earliest bills and was almost immediately abandoned.[34] While local newspapers criticized

---

29. Minutes, Dec. 22, 1836, "Minutes of a Conference," *LDS Messenger and Advocate*, Jan. 1837, 443 (*JSP*, D5:322–23).

30. Minutes, 443 (*JSP*, D5:323).

31. Articles of Agreement, Jan. 2, 1837, "Articles of Agreement," *LDS Messenger and Advocate*, Jan. 1837, 441–43 (*JSP*, D5:324–31).

32. *JSP*, D5:324n162.

33. Warren A. Cowdery, Editorial, *Messenger and Advocate*, July 1837, 535; see also Walker, "Kirtland Safety Society and the Fraud of Grandison Newell," 44–47.

34. *JSP*, D5:332; Staker, *Hearken, O Ye People*, 479.

this stamping as an attempt to deceive, its discontinuance opened the company up to legal action.[35]

The published minutes included a postscript by Smith asking church members to invest in the institution. In quoting Isaiah 60:9–17, he added, possibly in jest, a parenthetical interpretation: "Surely the isles shall wait for me, and the ships of Tarshish first, and to bring thy sons from far, their silver and their gold (not their bank notes) with them."[36] Regardless, as the editors of the Joseph Smith Papers observe, "It demonstrates the Kirtland Safety Society's need for specie and not simply payment in banknotes."[37] The *Cleveland Weekly Advertiser* reported on February 2, 1837, that the society had $16,000 in "specie and bankable funds."[38] Warren Parrish, who was the society's clerk and later replaced Smith as treasurer, claimed in 1838: "I have been astonished to hear [Smith] declare that we had 60,000 Dollars in specie in our vaults and $600,000 at our command, when we had not exceeded $6,000 and could not command any more."[39]

The Safety Society was significantly underfunded due to the low price of stock and leniency of its officers and needed more capital before it could legally issue paper currency.[40] Consequently, Smith, Newel Whitney, and Rigdon obtained a loan for $3,000 from the Bank of Geauga in Painesville on January 2, signing a promissory note ensuring payment of the loan "forty five days after the date."[41] However, more than three months after the due date, the Bank of Geauga found it necessary to sue Smith, Whitney, and Rigdon.[42] On January 10 a second loan was obtained for $1,200 from the Commercial Bank of Lake Erie in Cleveland, due in four months.[43] This bank sued Smith and others in April 1838 for non-payment of another loan.[44]

---

35. "A New Revelation—Mormon Money," *Cleveland Weekly Gazette*, Jan. 18, 1837, [3].

36. Articles of Agreement, Jan. 2, 1837, "Articles of Agreement," *LDS Messenger and Advocate*, Jan. 1837, 443 (*JSP*, D5:329).

37. *JSP*, D5:329n187.

38. "Kirtland Safety Society," *Cleveland Weekly Advertiser*, Feb. 2, 1837, [3].

39. Warren Parrish, Letter to the Editor, Feb. 5, 1838, *Painesville Republican*, Feb. 15, 1838, [3]. The editors of the Joseph Smith Papers question Parrish's claim because he subsequently became a critic of Smith. *JSP*, D5:329n187; see also Staker, *Hearken, O Ye People*, 480.

40. *JSP*, D5:289–90.

41. Bank of Geauga Discount Book, Jan. 2, 1837.

42. Transcript of Proceedings, June 5, 1837, Bank of Geauga v. JS et al., Geauga Co., OH, Court of Common Pleas, Final Record, vol. U, 67–69.

43. Joseph Smith and Others, Promissory Note to Commercial Bank of Lake Erie, Jan. 10, 1837, JS Collection.

44. Transcript of Proceedings, Apr. 3, 1838, Commercial Bank of Lake Erie v. Cahoon, Smith, and Young, Geauga Co., OH, Court of Common Pleas, Final Record, vol. V, 5–6.

Bank Opens

The Safety Society appears to have opened for business on January 4, the earliest date found on extant bank notes as well as the date in the charges filed against Smith and Rigdon for illegally issuing banknotes for an unchartered bank.[45] Almost immediately, the bank was assailed by the newspapers, and some church members began questioning Smith's leadership.

On January 6 Wilford Woodruff, who had recently been ordained to fill a vacancy in the first quorum of seventy, wrote: "I visited the office of the Kirtland Safety Society & saw the first money that was issued by the Treasurer or Society," which "was given to Brother [Jacob] Bump (in exchange for other notes) who was the first to Circulate it." Woodruff also recorded that others were in the office, such as Frederick Williams, David Whitmer, S. Smith (possibly Sylvester Smith), and Warren Parrish, when the Prophet declared that he had received a revelation concerning the society earlier that morning, that he not only heard "the voice of the Spirit upon the Subject but even an audable voice." However, Smith "did not tell us at that time what the LORD said upon the subject but remarked that if we would give heed to the Commandments the Lord had given this morning all would be well."[46] This is similar to Parrish's 1838 statement that Smith "declared that the audible voice of God, instructed him to establish a Banking-Anti Banking institution, which like Aaron's rod should swallow up all other Banks (the Bank of Monroe excepted,) and grow and flourish and spread from the rivers to the ends of the earth, and survive when all others should be laid in ruins."[47] The mention of the Bank of Monroe probably indicates that Parrish was reporting a statement Smith made after he initiated business dealings with that institution in late January 1837.

The reason Smith felt the need to use his prophetic reputation to promote the Safety Society may have something to do with growing discontent over the church's involvement in land speculation and banking. There were enough grumblings among church members that Brigham Young addressed the subject four days later while attending a meeting of the seventies in the temple. Woodruff later wrote in his journal that Young "gave us an interesting exhortation & warned us not to murmer against Moses (or) Joseph or

---

45. Coin and Currency Collection, CHL (*JSP*, D5:331–40). Transcript of the Proceedings, Oct. 24, 1837, Rounds Qui Tam v. Joseph Smith; and Rounds Qui Tam v. Sidney Rigdon, Geauga Co., OH, Court of Common Pleas, Final Record, vol. U, 359–64. Staker, *Hearken, O Ye People*, 479, notes that Monday, January 9, 1837, was the official opening to the public.

46. Wilford Woodruff, Journal, Jan. 6, 1837 (Vogel, *The Wilford Woodruff Journals*, 1:104–105).

47. Warren Parrish, Letter to the Editor, Feb. 5, 1838, *Painesville Republican*, Feb. 15, 1838, [3].

the heads of the Church." On Sunday, January 15, Woodruff recorded that he attended a meeting in the temple and that "President Rigdon preached in the Spirit & exhorted the Church to union that they might be prepared to meet every trial & difficulty that awates [awaits] them."[48] Young later said, probably with some exaggeration, that "the people almost universally … believed honestly truly with all their hearts that Joseph didn't understand anything about temporal matters … [and] that they knew more than the prophet." Young asserted that if Smith would have received more support from the church, "wealth would have been poured into [the] laps of this people."[49] George A. Smith remembered that a member of the high council came to his father, John Smith, "with a complaint … that Joseph didn't know how to do business … and it was very wrong for him to do it." On another occasion, wealthy Joseph Coe told George that "Joseph was to have nothing to do with temporal things and began to express fears Joseph was about to lose the light of the Lord because his heart was set on temporal things."[50]

When David Whitmer spoke to the seventies on January 17, Woodruff recorded that "he warned us to humble ourselves before God lest his hand rest upon us in anger for our pride & many sins that we were runing into in our days of prosperity as the ancient Nephites did & it does now appear evident that a scourge awates this stake of Zion even Kirtland if their is not great repentance immediately … esspecially the heads of the Church."[51] On January 18 President Alvah Beaman spoke to the elders' quorum "and reproved them for murmuring ag[a]inst the pres. of the Church by relating a vision"; Hyrum Smith also reproved them for their "murmuring."[52]

On January 14 the society contracted with David Cartter, a young attorney in Akron, Ohio, about forty-five miles south of Kirtland, to represent the society as an agent with authority to make loans and exchange notes for a commission of 1.5 percent.[53] This agreement, signed by Rigdon, Smith, Frederick Williams, Reynolds Cahoon, David Whitmer, and Oliver Cowdery, uses the banking-specific terminology of the November 2, 1836,

48. Woodruff, Journal, Jan. 10 and 15, 1837 (Vogel, *The Wilford Woodruff Journals*, 1:105).

49. Brigham Young, Sermon, Sep. 11, 1853, 32, CHL, quoted in Staker, *Hearken, O Ye People*, 485.

50. George A. Smith, Sermons, Sep. 4, 1866, 33, and Nov. 13, 1864, 7, George D. Watt Papers, CHL, transcribed from Pitman shorthand by LaJean Purcell Carruth, 2009, quoted in Staker, *Hearken, O Ye People*, 485.

51. Woodruff, Journal, Jan. 17, 1837 (Vogel, *The Wilford Woodruff Journals*, 1:106).

52. Kirtland Elders Quorum, "Record," Jan. 18, 1837 (Cook and Backman, *Kirtland Elders' Quorum Record*, 23).

53. Rigdon et al. (Including Joseph Smith), Agreement with David Cartter, Jan. 14, 1837, JS Collection (*JSP*, D5:341–43).

constitution despite the reorganization on January 2, 1837, which shows that "the Kirtland Safety Society officers considered the institution a bank, despite its not yet being granted a charter by the Ohio legislature."[54] The society provided Cartter with $30,000 in notes. No doubt the bills Cartter was given were not the ones altered to read "antiBANKing," since Cartter's contract had been made with the "Managers of the Kirtland-safety-society-Bank." Nothing more is known about Cartter or if any of the banknotes were distributed in Akron, but the society's contract with him was unethical if not fraudulent.

On January 12 the Safety Society received some bad publicity when the *Cleveland Daily Gazette* warned the public about the circulation of the new bills. "During the past two days an emission of bills from the society of Mormons, has been showered upon us," the *Gazette* began. "As far as we can learn there is no property bound for their redemption, no coin on hand to redeem them with, and no responsible individuals whose honor or whose honesty is pledged for their payment. ... Aside from the violation of the statute rendering them void, and of course the notes given for them, we look upon the whole as a most reprehensible fraud on the public, and cannot conceal our surprise that they should circulate at all." After noting the alteration of the bills to read "antiBANKing," the *Gazette* noted: "We do not object to private or company banking, as a system, provided it is done *upon a system made safe*, but we consider this whole affair a deception, that there is still in force a section of the statute affixing a penalty of $1,000 to the issuing or passing unauthorized Bank paper like the present."[55]

On January 17 the *Gazette* again tried to warn customers not to take the Safety Society's banknotes, that it was a private stock company, not a chartered bank, and therefore could not guarantee redemption of its paper money. "The articles of association do not make a legal lien upon the property of the signers, for the redemption of the money," the *Gazette* noted. "And if they did, every thing relating to the concern is utterly [nugatory] in a court of law, on both sides." The Mormon notes "will doubtless redeem at first, but as far as we can learn, it is a stupendous fraud on the community." The *Gazette* lamented that "the LABORER WHO HOLDS A DOLLAR or two of the KIRTLAND SAFETY SOCIETY antiBANKing co's bills" will soon find that they are "void at law" and have no "credit ... with the community."[56]

---

54. *JSP*, D5:342n229.
55. A New Revelation—Mormon Money," *Cleveland Daily Gazette*, Jan. 12, 1837, [2].
56. *Cleveland Daily Gazette*, Jan. 17, 1837.

On January 19 an article appeared under the title "Rags! Mere Rags!!" in the *Ohio Star* at Ravenna warning readers of the "emission of Mormon money, purporting to be bank paper."[57] On the same day, the *Painesville Republican* reported that the Bank of Geauga refused to accept Kirtland's notes, forcing Painesville merchants or anyone doing business with the bank to reject them as well. However, based on the Safety Society's claim that "they have a large amount of specie on hand and have the means of obtaining much more, if necessary," the *Republican* suggested that the circulation of more paper currency "would be beneficial to community, and sensibly relieve the pressure in the market so much complained of."[58]

On January 20 the editors of the *Gazette* repeated their warning and expressed surprise at "the readiness with which these anti-banking *bank* bills are thrown into circulation without any *evidence* or *knowledge* of the solvency of the issues" and considered it "a most reprehensible fraud on the public."[59] On January 24 the *Gazette* criticized the *Herald* for its support of the illegal bills printed by the Kirtland society: "We do not suppose the Herald intended to advocate a breach of the law, though it looks mightily like it. This paper, in conjunction with the Advertiser, is now *pledged* in support of the Mormon money, and rest their argument upon the *present* redemption of the bills." Nevertheless, the *Gazette* warned the other papers that "at some future period *not* very remote," they will take occasion "to recall the subject to their minds, by announcing the fact that those bills are not redeemed and cannot be recovered."[60]

Such warnings went unheeded by many Mormons, who believed, like Willard Richards, a new convert and recent arrival in the Mormon capital, that the "Kirtland bills are as safe as Gold."[61] Encouraged by favorable comments in several area newspapers, they easily wrote off the warnings and criticisms of other papers as anti-Mormon propaganda. Brigham Young, Hyrum Smith, and others began immediately to purchase farms in and around Kirtland using the society's bills as down payments.[62]

One unforeseen threat to the Safety Society was led by Grandison Newell, a prominent resident of Mentor and enemy of the Mormons who organized a run on the bank in an attempt to force the bank to close by

57. "Rags! Mere Rags!!" *Ohio Star* (Ravenna), Jan. 19, 1837.
58. "Anti-Banking Company," *Painesville Republican*, Jan. 19, 1837.
59. "Mormon Currency," *Cleveland Daily Gazette*, Jan. 20, 1837, [2]; italics in original.
60. "Law *versus* Mobocracy," *Cleveland Daily Gazette*, Jan. 24, 1837.
61. Richards, Letter to Hepzibah Richards, Jan. 20, 1837.
62. Joseph Young, Letter, to Lewis Harvey, Nov. 16, 1880, 7–8.

draining its required reserve of specie. James Thompson, one of Newell's employees, claimed that shortly after the Kirtland bank began issuing bills, Newell began to "drive about the country and buy up all the Mormon money possible, and the next morning go to the bank and obtain the specie."[63] In a July 1837 editorial in the *Messenger and Advocate*, Warren Cowdery reported that "hundreds who were enemies, either came or sent their agents and demanded specie till the officers thought best to refuse payment."[64] The Safety Society's brief day book only covers the first half of January 1837 and contains entries for "redeemed" and "exchanged" currency from various named individuals and the occasional "stranger."[65] Historian Mark Staker suggests Newell's first redemption may have occurred as early as January 10 since Smith, as treasurer, withdrew $704 on that day.[66]

About this time, reports began to circulate that Rigdon refused to redeem banknotes for specie. According to one resident of Kirtland, the Mormons "continued to redeem with specie for ten days, and then shut up shop."[67] The *Cleveland Daily Gazette* reported on January 24 that the Mormon bank got "tired of redeeming their bills ... yesterday."[68] Two days later the *Gazette* reported that "*day-before-yesterday*," the Kirtland Safety Society "refused to cash its phantom money, as we were credibly informed."[69] Rigdon's action may have temporarily saved the society, but it angered the non-Mormon populace. On January 24 Woodruff recorded: "We had been threatened by a mob from Panesville to visit us that night & demolish our Bank & take our property but they did not appear."[70] George A. Smith said he was one of the men assigned guard duty, and "during the entire winter" it was his duty to "see if old Newel and his mob could come over and interfere with us."[71]

On January 27 the *Painesville Telegraph* claimed that the Mormons were attempting to redeem banknotes in land instead of specie.[72] On Saturday, January 28, the doors of the Kirtland Bank closed temporarily. Several days

---

63. James Thompson, Statement, *Naked Truths about Mormonism* (Oakland, CA), Jan. 1888, 3.

64. Warren A. Cowdery, Editorial, *Messenger and Advocate*, July 1837, 536.

65. Kirtland Safety Society, Daybook, ca. Jan. 4–16, 1837.

66. Staker, *Hearken, O Ye People*, 484.

67. C., Letter to Editor, Feb. 16, 1837, in "About Matters in Kirtland," *Ohio Observer* (Hudson, OH), Mar. 2, 1837.

68. "A Piece of News for the Herald.—Mormon Safety Society Notes," *Cleveland Daily Gazette*, Jan. 24, 1837, [2].

69. "Mormon Money Once More," *Cleveland Weekly Gazette*, Feb. 1, 1837. This report first appeared in the *Cleveland Daily Gazette* on Jan. 26, 1837.

70. Woodruff, Journal, Jan. 24, 1837 (Vogel, *The Wilford Woodruff Journals*, 1:106).

71. George A. Smith, Sermon, Sep. 26, 1863, 7–8, quoted in Staker, *Hearken, O Ye People*, 478.

72. *Painesville Telegraph*, Jan. 27, 1837, [3].

later, the *Painesville Telegraph* reported: "We understand that the Mormon bank, *alias* the KIRTLAND SAFETY SOCIETY ANTI-BANK-ING CO. suspended specie payments on Saturday last, agreeably to a *Revelation* of the Mormon Prophet we suppose."[73] The mob rumor may have contributed to the temporary closing, but there may have been other reasons as well.

On Sunday, January 29, Smith and Cowdery preached in the temple, according to Woodruff, and "JOSEPH blessed us in the name of the Lord & Said if we would be faithful we should rise above our imbarrements & be delivered from the hands of our enemies."[74] Despite strenuous efforts, nothing appeared to stop the collapse of Kirtland's artificial economy.

Bank of Monroe

On January 31 a meeting was held in the temple during which Smith and Rigdon spoke "on the temporal business of the Church & Petitioned for a Charter to the Assembly of the State for the Kirtland Safety Society & the presidency of the Church bought the Monroe Charter & we all lent a hand in esstablishing it that it might be benificial to us in forwarding the building of the temporal Kingdom."[75] The charter would not be presented to the Ohio senate until February 10, but the Mormon leadership had little hope of success. The Kirtland bank charter was being handled by Samuel Medary, a Whig from Geauga County, while the Mormons were predominantly Democrats, and although the Democrats were in the majority in the legislature, they opposed chartering any banks.[76]

Given doubts about the charter, an alternate plan was devised in late January 1837 whereby the officers of the Kirtland society made business arrangements with officers of the Bank of Monroe in Monroe, Michigan, apparently intending to become a branch of the bank with authority to act under its charter.[77] Bank of Monroe officials were probably eager to make a deal with the Mormons because an infusion of specie from the Kirtland Safety Society would allow them to print more bills and sponsor land speculation in Michigan.

In early February, Smith, Rigdon, Hyrum Smith, and Oliver Cowdery visited Monroe, probably traveling by boat across Lake Erie, to attend the

73. "How have the Mighty Fallen!!" *Western Reserve Chronicle* (Warren, OH), Feb. 7, 1837, [3]; reprinted from the *Painesville Telegraph*.
74. Woodruff, Journal, Jan. 29, 1837 (Vogel, *The Wilford Woodruff Journals*, 1:107).
75. Woodruff, Journal, Jan. 31, 1837 (Vogel, *The Wilford Woodruff Journals*, 1:107).
76. See Adams, "Chartering the Kirtland Bank."
77. The earliest record of this business arrangement is dated January 25, 1837. B. J. Hathaway, Receipt, Jan. 25, 1837, JS Office Papers.

bank's stockholders meeting on February 10, at which time Cowdery was appointed vice president and director of the Bank of Monroe.[78] Before leaving Kirtland, the firm of Oliver Cowdery & Co. was dissolved and transferred to Smith and Rigdon. Cowdery was also released as editor of the *Messenger and Advocate*, which was taken over by his brother Warren.[79]

On February 11 officials of the Kirtland Safety Society transferred $3,000 in Cleveland banknotes and $95 in gold coins to the Bank of Monroe. In return, Bank of Monroe officials transferred $20,026 in banknotes to officials of the Kirtland bank. The Safety Society received additional infusions of Monroe banknotes on February 14 and 18, the latter of which was made by Cowdery, who remained in Michigan, amounting to $5,600.[80] Soon the Safety Society began exchanging Kirtland bills with notes from the Bank of Monroe, which helped to improve confidence in the bank. One man from Russell, a town in Geauga County about ten miles south of the temple, who came to Kirtland to do business with Rigdon, refused "Mormon money" but accepted a lesser amount in Monroe bills.[81]

Unrest

On their return from Michigan in mid-February, Smith, Rigdon, and Hyrum Smith were met on the road approaching Kirtland by Brigham Young and William Smith, who warned them that "a plot was laid to waylay Joseph for the purpose of taking his life." This plot was led by one of Smith's followers, Solomon W. Denton, who was especially angered by Grandison Newell's run on the bank and the failure of the Kirtland bank charter.[82] By going "round by another road," they "arrived in Kirtland in safety."[83]

Smith soon learned that the same day on which he had met with officials of the Bank of Monroe, the Ohio senate had rejected the Safety Society's request for a charter.[84] Smith also learned that in his absence Samuel Rounds, a resident of Painesville, had initiated a lawsuit against him, Rigdon, and four other officers of the society. Rounds, acting on behalf of Grandison

---

78. "Bank of Monroe," *Monroe (MI) Times*, Feb. 16, 1837, 2; Staker, *Hearken, O Ye People*, 492–500.

79. "Notice," *LDS Messenger and Advocate*, Feb. 1837, 458–59.

80. Kirtland Safety Society, Account with Bank of Monroe, Feb. 11–Apr. 4, 1837; Staker, *Hearken, O Ye People*, 495.

81. G. S. Pelton, Statement, *Naked Truths about Mormonism*, Apr. 1888, 3.

82. Details about Denton's plot were discussed during a trial the following June. See "The State of Ohio vs. Joseph Smith, Jr.," *Painesville Telegraph*, June 9, 1837, [1].

83. Historian's Office, Brigham Young History Drafts, slip of paper attached to page 15.

84. Staker, *Hearken, O Ye People*, 491–92.

Newell, based his suit on an Ohio law granting private individuals the right to sue officials of unlicensed banks. While the legal actions against the four junior officers were concluded in their favor later that summer, a jury decided against Smith and Rigdon when their cases were brought to trial in October 1837.[85]

On Sunday, February 19, Smith spoke in the temple and denounced the dissenters. Woodruff recorded that Smith "for several hours addressed the Saints in the power of God." He noted that "Joseph had been absent from Kirtland on business for the Church," adding wryly, "though not half as long as Moses was in the mount," yet many Mormons "were stir'd up in their hearts & some were against him as the Israelites were against Moses." On this occasion, Woodruff wrote, Smith "arose in the power of God in their midst, as Moses did anciently, they were put to silence for the complainers saw that he stood in the power of a Prophet. O how weak is man."[86] On the following Sunday, February 26, Woodruff again recorded that Smith "addressed the Congregation of the saints in the power and spirit of God."[87]

On Sunday, March 12, Willard Richards "was set apart to accompany Elder Brigham Young on a special business mission to the east."[88] Young said that the "special mission [was] appointed us by the Prophet Joseph."[89] Over the next month and a half, Young and Richards visited Buffalo, Rochester, Albany, New York City, Boston, and Providence, as well as Martin Harris in Palmyra, New York, to raise funds for the struggling Safety Society.

When the Bank of Monroe temporarily closed its doors from March 16 to mid-May, it sent a shock wave through the Mormon community. The *Painesville Telegraph* announced the closure on March 31: "After having for its presiding officer about three weeks the wonderful and noted Oliver Cowdery," the "Monroe Mormon Bank closed its doors against all demands for specie."[90] According to one observer, the Bank of Monroe was forced to close due to "a constant pressure, for several months, on the Institution, urged on by false reports, and cunning *shavers*"—meaning those who take

---

85. Transcript of Proceedings, Rounds qui tam v. Joseph Smith, ca. Oct. 25, 1837, Geauga Co., OH, Court of Common Pleas, Final Record, vol. U, 362; Madsen, "Tabulating the Impact of Litigation on the Kirtland Economy," 241–45.

86. Woodruff, Journal, Feb. 19, 1837 (Vogel, *The Wilford Woodruff Journals*, 1:107–108).

87. Woodruff, Journal, Feb. 26, 1837 (Vogel, *The Wilford Woodruff Journals*, 1:108).

88. "History of Willard Richards," *Millennial Star* (Liverpool, Eng.), Feb. 1865, 120.

89. Brigham Young, "History of Brigham Young," *Deseret News Weekly* (Salt Lake City), Feb. 10, 1858, 386.

90. "For the Telegraph," *Painesville Telegraph*, Mar. 31, 1837, [3].

advantage of the desperate situation and leverage for reduced prices.[91] The Panic of 1837 had started in New York in February and was forcing banks throughout the United States to close in March, some temporarily, others permanently. After sixty days, the Bank of Monroe reopened and would operate until 1842.

Passage of the Free Banking Act on March 15, which required that bank officials be legal residents of the state, rendered Cowdery's position in the Bank of Monroe illegal. Cowdery returned to Kirtland about this time and subsequently was elected as a justice of the peace before May 25, 1837.[92]

Meanwhile, the Safety Society began defaulting on its loans. On March 24 Sheriff Abel Kimball arrested Smith, Newel Whitney, and Rigdon and brought them before the Geauga County Court of Common Pleas in Chardon for an unpaid loan of $3,000 from the Bank of Geauga in Painesville. The following day, Vinson Knight and Ira Bond signed a special bail for $8,000, which freed the three Mormon leaders until the next term of the court in June. [93] Upon release, Smith and Rigdon were rearrested in the case of *Kelley v. Rigdon, Smith & Cowdery* for an outstanding debt to Buffalo merchant Hezekiah Kelley for $2,014.74. At this time, Cowdery was still in Michigan and could not be found by the sheriff. Smith and Rigdon were released on $6,000 bail and ordered to appear at the forthcoming trial in June.[94]

Anniversary

For several days preceding the church's seventh anniversary, the various priesthood quorums held washing and anointing meetings in the temple. On the morning of the April 6 anniversary, the quorums held a solemn assembly in which the ordinance of the washing of the feet was observed for two to three hours.[95]

Meanwhile, the First Presidency and presidents of the seventies met in the west room of the attic story to seal the anointing of those who had been washed and anointed the previous evening. Six of the seven presidents of the

---

91. "The Bank of Monroe," *Monroe Times*, Mar. 16, 1837, 2.

92. Staker, *Hearken, O Ye People*, 501. Based on purchases at the Whitney store, Staker thinks Cowdery had returned to Kirtland before March 9, 1837. However, it is not clear if the purchases were made by Oliver or his wife.

93. Transcript of Proceedings, Bank of Geauga v. Joseph Smith, Newel Knight, and Sidney Rigdon, ca. June 6, 1837, Geauga County Court of Common Pleas, Final Record, vol. U, 67–69.

94. Transcript of Proceedings, Kelley v. Rigdon, Smith & Cowdery, ca. June 6, 1837, Geauga County Court of Common Pleas, Final Record, vol. U, 97–98.

95. "Anniversary of the Church of Latter Day Saints," *LDS Messenger and Advocate*, Apr. 1837, 486.

Seventy were high priests before their ordinations, and some assumed it was necessary to ordain Joseph Young, an elder, to the high priesthood as well. Smith declared this wrong—those who were high priests were moved to the high priests' quorum and six others were chosen from among the seventies to replace them.[96] This reorganization became necessary when Smith decided in another dispute that high priests held higher authority than seventies, which was not clear before. Zebedee Coltrin, one of the presidents of Seventy reassigned to the high priests' quorum, reported in 1879 that the debate over who had higher authority began when Benjamin Winchester, a seventy, told Jared Carter that he had no right to rebuke him because he "held a higher Priesthood than he did, and Jared contended that he didn't because [he] was a High Priest."[97] Joseph Young wrote in 1878 that this debate was carried on "with so much warmth that it amounted to jealousy."[98] When Smith decided that high priests held a higher office, it created a problem among the presidents of Seventy who were formerly high priests. Did they lose power when they became seventies, and did they have authority over Joseph Young who had previously been an elder? They wanted to retain authority by having Young ordained a high priest and by making it a requirement for future presidents of Seventy, but Smith decided the reverse because the other action would require rethinking the presidencies of all the quorums.

After returning to the lower hall, Smith addressed the quorums, explaining the order and duties of the priesthood. Among other things, he said: "The presidents, or presidency are over the church, and revelations of the mind and will of God to the church are to come through the presidency. This is the order of heaven and the power and privilege of this priesthood. It is also the privilege of any officer in this church, to obtain revelations so far as relates to his particular calling or duty in the church." Smith explained further, "The Seventies are to be taken from the quorum of elders and are not to be high priests. They are subject to the direction and dictation of the twelve, who have the keys of the ministry." He also noted that a bishop needed to be a high priest because he was not a descendant of Aaron.[99]

Smith then made a remark that was vague and puzzling to many of his

---

96. *Messenger and Advocate*, 486–87. Record of Seventies, Book A, 9, 18, records that the decision was made by Joseph Smith. See also Woodruff, Journal, Apr. 6, 1837 (Vogel, *The Wilford Woodruff Journals*, 1:112); Joseph Young, *History of the Organization of the Seventies*, 5. See D&C 107:93.

97. Coltrin's account was recorded in L. John Nuttall, Diary, May 31, 1879.

98. Young, *History of the Organization of the Seventies*, 4–5.

99. "Anniversary of the Church of Latter Day Saints," *LDS Messenger and Advocate*, Apr. 1837, 487 (*JSP*, D5:355).

followers. Even those taking notes could only write: "He here remarked something concerning the will of God, and said, that what God commanded, the one half of the church would condemn."[100] This may have been an allusion to the resistance he was experiencing with the Safety Society.[101] The remark, whatever it meant, recalled Jesus's comment that one of his disciples would betray him (Matt. 26:21–22). Lucy Smith remembered that about this time, Joseph gave a sermon in which he declared that "there is an evil in this very congregation ... making one third of you who are here this day so much my enemies that you will have a desire to take my life." Understandably, as Lucy reported, "the following week was much given to surmises and speculations as to who would be the traitors."[102]

Smith "rebuked and admonished his brethren frequently ... because he loved them; not because he wished to incur their displeasure or mar their happiness." He said that "such a course of conduct was not calculated to gain the good will of all," but it was his duty and responsibility as leader and prophet. "So you see, brethren the higher the authority the greater the difficulty of the station."[103]

The minutes did not capture Smith's intense emotion and passion as he spoke to his people. Woodruff wrote that Smith "addressed the Congregation for the term of three hours Clothed with the power, spirit, & image of GOD," during which "He unbosom'd his mind & feelings in the house of his friends" and "presented many things of vast importance to the minds of the Elders of Israel." Woodruff also gives insight into the effect that Smith's words had on followers: "I say such evidences presented in such a forcible manner ought to drive into oblivion every particle of unbelief & dubiety from the mind of the hearers, for such language sentiment principle & spirit cannot flow from darkness. Joseph Smith jr. is a prophet of God r[a]ised up for the deliverance of Israel as true as my heart now burns within me

---

100. *Messenger and Advocate*, 487.

101. While working on the official history in January 1844, Willard Richards edited this passage to read: "What [God] commands, <u>one half</u> the church will condemn. through ignorance and prejudice." In June 1845 a review committee composed of John Taylor, Brigham Young, Heber C. Kimball, and George A. Smith changed it to read: "If the church knew all the commandments, one half they would condemn through ignorance and prejudice." JS History, vol. B-1, 756; Vogel, *History of Joseph Smith*, 2:461, and n44; 7:573. This change shifted the meaning from one-half of the church to one-half of the commandments, while at the same time expanding it to apply to plural marriage.

102. Anderson, *Lucy's Book*, 595, 596.

103. "Anniversary of the Church of Latter Day Saints," *LDS Messenger and Advocate*, Apr. 1837, 487 (*JSP*, D5:356).

while I am penning thes[e] lines which is as true as truth itself." Concerning "that fountain of light, principle & virtue that came forth out of the heart & mouth of the prophet JOSEPH" on this occasion, Woodruff prayed: "O that they might be written upon our hearts as with an iron pen to remain forever that we might practice them in our lives."[104]

According to the minutes, Smith remarked that Kirtland must be built up and "more houses must be built." He "observed that large contracts had been entered into for land on all sides where our enemies had signed away their right. We are indebted to them to be sure, but our brethren abroad have only to come with their money, take these contracts, relieve their brethren of the pecuniary embarrassments under which they now labor, and procure for themselves a peaceable place of rest among us."[105] Woodruff recorded that "Joseph presented us in some degree the plot of the city of Kirtland (which is the strong hold of the daughter of Zion) as it was given him by vision." In this vision, Smith saw "the city extended to the east, west, North, & South[.] Steam boats will come puffing into the city[.] our Goods will be conveyed upon rail roads from Kirtland to many places & probably to Zion. houses of worship would be reared unto the most high[.] beautiful streets was to be made for the Saints to walk in[.] Kings of the earth would come to behold the glory thereof."[106] Smith concluded "by uttering a prophesy saying this place must be built up, and would be built up, and that every brother that would take hold and help secure and discharge those contracts that had been made, should be rich."[107]

Hyrum Smith chastised members who took money from immigrants for various reasons when it should be used to purchase land from the church and alleviate its debts. Rigdon addressed the church's debts and suggested using the missionary program to sell real estate. Like Smith, he concluded with a prediction that would come back to haunt him: "He then uttered a prediction, that if all would exert themselves as they might, three months should not pass away before we can shout victory over the adversary."[108] In that time, the Kirtland Bank would fold and the city's economy would collapse.

In the evening, another meeting was held in the temple that lasted "nearly

---

104. Woodruff, Journal, Apr. 6, 1837 (Vogel, *The Wilford Woodruff Journals*, 1:112–13).

105. "Anniversary of the Church of Latter Day Saints," *LDS Messenger and Advocate*, Apr. 1837, 488 (*JSP*, D5:356).

106. Woodruff, Journal, Apr. 6, 1837 (Vogel, *The Wilford Woodruff Journals*, 1:113).

107. "Anniversary of the Church of Latter Day Saints," *LDS Messenger and Advocate*, Apr. 1837, 488 (*JSP*, D5:357).

108. *Messenger and Advocate*, 488–89.

all night."[109] Smith's history barely mentioned this meeting, but Woodruff gave more details: "Joseph requested the congregation to speak their feelings freely & pray according to the spirit." Following this instruction, "the saints began to open their mouths & they were filled with language unto edification one a prayer another exortation some a doctrin & a psalm others a toungue, some an interpretation[.] Prophecy was also poured out upon us & all things was done decently & in order & the night was spent gloriously by the saints[.] much of the gifts of the gospel rested upon us. ... Thus was this day & night spent gloriously & those scenes will long be remembered. ... The meeting continued until break of day when we all dispersed to our homes with great Joy & consolation."[110] Smith's presence and ability to conduct such spirit-filled meetings was proof that God was with him despite rumors about Fanny Alger and the looming failure of his bank.

Divestiture

Despite the plea to church members to support the bank during the April 6 conference, Smith began preparing for the seizure of his property to pay outstanding debts.[111] Accordingly, on the next day he began transferring land to William Marks, who appears to have functioned as his agent.[112] On April 10 Smith transferred six properties, including the temple, to Marks.[113] Concerning the transfer of the temple, the editors of the Joseph Smith Papers note: "Had the land or building been seized for debts, it would have been a severe blow to the church, both financially and spiritually."[114]

On Sunday, April 9, Smith presided over a meeting in the temple for which Woodruff's journal provided the only record. Rigdon addressed the congregation and "laid before them their situation as to temporal things, as the gentiles are striving to besiege the Saints in Kirtland & would be glad to starve the saints to death," and that "the Presidency had used every means

---

109. JS History, vol. B-1, 758 (DHC 2:480).

110. Woodruff, Journal, Apr. 6, 1837 (Vogel, *The Wilford Woodruff Journals*, 1:113–14).

111. Promissory notes made out by the firms of Rigdon, Smith & Cowdery and Cahoon, Carter & Co. were due in April 1837, and subsequent litigation indicates that the firms defaulted on some of these notes. See *JSP*, D5:358–59 and n299.

112. Joseph Smith and Emma Smith, Deed for property in Kirtland Township, Geauga Co., OH, to William Marks, Apr. 7, 1837, Geauga Co., OH, Deed Record, vol. 23, 537–38.

113. For Smith's transfer of land to Marks, including the temple, see Joseph Smith and Emma Smith, Deed for property in Kirtland Township, Geauga Co., OH, to William Marks, Apr. 10, 1837, Geauga Co., OH, Deed Record, vol. 23, 536–37 (*JSP*, D5:357–62). For additional land transfers between Smith and Marks on the same day, see Geauga Co., OH, Deed Records, vol. 23, 535–36, 538–39; and vol. 24, 189, 353, 25:301–302.

114. *JSP*, D5:359.

for the deliverance of the Church but as many of the Church had refused Kirtlan[d] Currency which was their temporal salvation in Consequence of this they put strength in the hands of their enemies & those that had done this thing must suffer by it."[115]

Next, Smith "arose & like the lion of the tribe of JUDAH he poured out his Soul in the midst of the Congregation of the Saints." Woodruff, who was more impressed with Smith's style of preaching than Rigdon's, wrote: "Who can find languague to write his words & teachings as with an iron pen in a rock that they may stand for future generation[s] to look upon[?] A fountain of knowledge rolled from his mouth to the people which was the word of God." Smith's speech on such occasions reflected the language of his dictated revelations: simple, powerful, and full of scriptural allusions, echoes, and Bible-like imagery. Woodruff was taken by Smith's charisma: "There is not a greater man than Joseph standing in this generation. The gentiles … know not his principle, his spirit, his wisdom, virtue, phylanthropy, nor his calling. His mind like Enochs swells wide as eternity[.] Nothing short of a God can comprehend his Soul."[116]

According to Woodruff, Smith shifted blame for the failing bank and the faltering Kirtland economy: "Yea in the name of God he proclaimed that Severe Judgment awaited those characters that professed to be his friends & friends to humanity & the Kirtland Safety Society But had turned tr[a]itors & opposed the Currency & its friends which has given power into the hands of the enemy & oppressed the poor Saints[.] Such have become Covenant Breakers for which they will feel the wrath of God as true as Joseph is a prophet."[117]

Hiding Out

On April 13 Grandison Newell filed a complaint with Painesville justice of the peace Edward Flint, alleging that Smith had conspired with others to have him killed. An arrest warrant was issued, but there is no record of an arrest or bail.[118] The *Painesville Republican* reported on June 15 that "several weeks ago, a report was put in circulation in this neighborhood, that through the instigation of Mr. Smith jr., two men had made an attempt to take the life of one Grandison Newell, who resides in that neighborhood, and who is well known to be a violent enemy to them and opposed to them in religious

---

115. Woodruff, Journal, Apr. 9, 1837 (Vogel, *The Wilford Woodruff Journals*, 1:115).

116. Woodruff.

117. Woodruff.

118. Transcript of Proceedings, June 5, 1837, State of Ohio on Complaint of Newell v. Joseph Smith, Geauga Co., OH, Court of Common Pleas, Final Record, vol. T, 52–53.

and political matters. … At length, a warrant was issued by Justice Flint of this place, on the application of Newell, to apprehend Smith—but he was not to be found." At the same time, the *Republican* reported that a gang or committee had formed in Painesville and "repaired to Kirtland and made a formal demand of the leading members of the Mormon Society, that Smith should be delivered up, but being assured that he was actually absent, and that on his return he should be forthcoming, this self-constituted committee returned to their homes."[119]

Smith and Rigdon had fled Kirtland so suddenly that Smith did not even tell Emma or say goodbye to his children.[120] Nor was he able to officiate at the weddings of Woodruff to Phebe Carter and Jonathan Holmes to Marietta Carter on April 13 as he had planned. Woodruff noted in his journal that Frederick Williams performed his marriage to Phebe, adding: "President J. Smith Jr was expecting to Solemnize the ceremony, but his life was so beset & sought for by wicked and ungodly men for the testimony of JESUS, that he was under the necessity of fleeing from his house & home for a few days."[121]

Smith's whereabouts for the next few weeks, from April 13 until May 19, is largely unknown. According to Woodruff, he had fled to "some lonely place to seek a shelter to escape the blood thirsty gentiles hands."[122] Smith and Rigdon eventually made their way to the home of Benjamin Brown in Westfield, New York, some 107 miles east of Kirtland on the shores of Lake Erie. Lorenzo Brown, who was fourteen at the time, recalled in 1856: "In the spring 1837 we were visited by Presidents Joseph Smith and Sidney Rigdon who on account of persecutions heaped upon them after staying three days and nights in the woods concealed had finally left Kirtland for a season and were directed to our house[.] They stayed with us for a few days. I became acquainted with them but more particularly with the Prophet Joseph who was peculiarly adapted to the acquaintance of great and small."[123]

Next, the two Mormon leaders stopped in Fredonia, also on the shores of Lake Erie in Chautauqua County, New York, about thirteen miles east of Westfield. On June 7 the *Fredonia Censor* mentioned that "Sidney Rigdon, who held forth to a gaping multitude in this village a short time since, it appears was then making his escape from justice, having been much more free

---

119. "The Humbug Ended," *Painesville Republican*, June 15, 1837, [2].
120. Emma Smith, Letter to Joseph Smith, Apr. 25, 1837, JS Letterbook 2, 35.
121. Woodruff, Journal, Apr. 13, 1837 (Vogel, *The Wilford Woodruff Journals*, 1:116).
122. Woodruff.
123. Lorenzo Brown, Diary and Autobiography, [2].

in shelling out the bills of the pretended Mormon Bank at Kirtland, than he was in giving any thing in exchange for them."[124]

They may have spent part of their time on Martin Harris's farm in Palmyra, New York, where Newel Whitney in Kirtland addressed a letter to them on April 20 discussing various legal and financial matters. It is unknown if Smith and Rigdon received Whitney's letter, but it included an instruction: "Br Marten If Sidney & Joseph have left your place please forward this to them immediately."[125]

The pressing issue in Whitney's letter was a large sum of money owed to Timothy Martindale, a Kirtland farmer with extensive land holdings. In October 1836 Smith, Whitney, Reynolds Cahoon, and John Johnson became indebted to Martindale in the amount of $5,000, probably for land in Kirtland which may have served as financial security for the Safety Society. Payment was due on January 1, 1837, but Martindale was forced to begin legal proceedings against Smith, Whitney, Cahoon, and Johnson, who were arrested on February 22. With the help of fellow Mormons, the four men were released on $10,000 bail.[126]

Whitney informed Smith that in his absence he and the other defendants had visited Martindale on April 19 who insisted that "he will not settle otherwise than we pay him $2500 pay cost of Court & he keep the farm, or he will leave it to men to say how much we shall give him."[127] Of course, the court would probably render a judgment for the full $5,000, plus interest, which had reached $7,500 by April, and court costs.[128] Whitney reported that "Hyrum thinks best to pay the 2d payment if possible say 6500 $ certainly as soon as the 10th day of May as the farm is worth considirable to raise grain on this season &c. if any thing is done it must be done soon & if you can get the money (say 6500 $) deposit it in Bank and send a check or something that we can sell to Geauga Bank."[129] Smith and Rigdon may have traveled to Palmyra to try to obtain money from Martin Harris to pay

124. "Mormon Fugitive," *Fredonia (NY) Censor*, June 7, 1837.

125. Newel K. Whitney, Letter to Joseph Smith and Sidney Rigdon, Apr. 20, 1837, JS Letterbook 2, 61 (*JSP*, D5:370).

126. Transcript of Proceedings, June 5, 1837, Martindale v. Joseph Smith et al., Geauga Co., OH, Court of Common Pleas, Final Record, vol. U, 106–108.

127. Whitney, Letter to Joseph Smith and Sidney Rigdon, Apr. 20, 1837, JS Letterbook 2, 61 (*JSP*, D5:370).

128. Transcript of Proceedings, June 5, 1837, Martindale v. Joseph Smith et al., Geauga Co., OH, Court of Common Pleas, Final Record, vol. U, 106–108.

129. Whitney, Letter to Joseph Smith and Sidney Rigdon, Apr. 20, 1837, JS Letterbook 2, 61–62 (*JSP*, D5:370).

Martindale. Martindale's terms were apparently accepted, and the case of *Martindale v. Smith* was settled out of court sometime before June 5, 1837.[130]

On April 25, Emma Smith wrote to her husband in response to a letter she had received from him. Emma's letter was probably delivered to Joseph by hand. "Your letter was welcomed both by friends and foes," she wrote, "we were glad enough to hear that you was well, and our enemies think they have almost found you, by seeing where the letters were mailed."[131] The possibility that Smith's enemies saw the postmark on his letter to Emma in the Kirtland post office may explain Smith's arrest in Painesville the same day.

In discussing her finances and access to supplies, Emma mentioned that his store in Chester was inaccessible because "there is so many a watching that place that there is no prospect of my getting any thing of consequence there." She then wrote about the effect of his sudden departure on her and his three children: "I cannot tell you my feelings when I found I could not see you before you left, yet I expect you can realize them, the children feel very anxious about you because they dont know where you have gone." She also expressed her continuing faith in God: "I verily feel that if I had no more confidence in God than some I could name, I should be in a sad case indeed but I still believe that if we humble ourselves, and are as faithful as we can be we shall be delivered from every snare that may be laid for our feet, and our lives and property will be saved and we redeemed from all unreasonable encumbrances." She closed: "My time is out, I pray that God will keep you in purity and safety till we all meet again."[132] Emma's reference to "purity" makes one wonder if she was worried her husband may repeat his previous infidelity.

Emma repeated this worry in her May 3, 1837, letter to Joseph, who was still in hiding: "I hope that we shall be so humble and pure before God that he will set us at liberty to be our own masters in a few things at least." This second letter informed Smith that his creditors were coming after his property and other assets. Apparently even scribe Warren Parrish was seeking payment: "I spoke to Parish about the money, and he appeared rather indifferent and stiff. ... Brother Parish has been very anxious for some time to get the little mare, and I do not know but it would be your will to have him have her." Concerning her husband's financial matters, she could only

---

130. Record of Judgment, June 5, 1837, Martindale v. Joseph Smith et al., Geauga Co., OH, Court of Common Pleas, Final Record, vol. N, 189.

131. Emma Smith, Letter to Joseph Smith, Apr. 25, 1837, JS Letterbook 2, 35 (*JSP*, D5:371).

132. Emma Smith (*JSP*, D5:371–72).

express feelings of helplessness: "It is impossible for me to do any thing, as long as every body has so much better right to all that is called yours than I have." On a personal note, Emma requested Joseph to return as soon as possible: "My anxiety for your company at home, or else it is realy so that your matters and things would be much bettered by your presence just as soon as consistant, it is impossible for me to write what I wish you to know. ... I could hardly pacify Julia and Joseph when they found ou[t] you was not coming home soon."[133]

In addition to Parrish's indifference, there were signs that other members were displeased with Smith's leadership. The Kirtland high council, for instance, met on May 11 to consider charges against Alexander Badlam for accusing Cyrus Smalling of "joining a company to put down President Joseph Smith Jr."[134] Smalling had appealed the case from the quorum of seventies, where he had been found guilty.

Home Again

Smith returned to Kirtland by May 19, when he made a transaction at his store in Chester, which he found in financial ruin.[135] The store ledger shows a significant decrease in activity in April.[136] The store was effectively closed on May 22, when Smith charged $379.24 worth of household goods to his account, then removed them from the store.[137] He also took possession of twenty-seven promissory notes, the majority of which were settled in late May.[138]

While Smith's enemies were rejoicing over his stunning failure, his followers were experiencing humiliation and looking for answers from the man whom they considered to be God's mouthpiece.

---

133. Emma Smith, Letter to Joseph Smith, May 3, 1837, JS Letterbook 2, 35–36 (*JSP*, D5:372–76).

134. Minutes, May 11, 1837, Minute Book 1, 219 (Collier and Harwell, *Kirtland Council Minute Book*, 181). These minutes end abruptly with pages 220–25 missing.

135. "Bill of Goods Taken from the Chester Store," May 19–24, 1837, JS Office Papers; see also *JSP*, D5:367.

136. Rigdon, Smith & Co., Store Ledger, Sep. 1836–May 1837, in JS Letterbook 2, [1]–79.

137. "Bill of Goods Taken from the Chester Store," May 19–24, 1837, JS Office Papers.

138. Rigdon, Smith & Co., Notes Receivable to Joseph Smith, May 22, 1837, JS Collection (*JSP*, D5:382–85).

25

Dissenters and Lawsuits

MAY–AUGUST 1837

*Then shall the seers be ashamed, and the diviners confounded: yea,
they shall all cover their lips; for [there is] no answer of God.*
—*Micah 3:7*

One sign of a lack of confidence in the Safety Society came on May 22, 1837, when Woodruff, William F. Cahoon, and Sabra Granger each withdrew their original investments.[1] Others soon followed.

On May 23 Parley P. Pratt wrote a threatening letter to Smith about the faltering society and possible loss of his home. Pratt had purchased three lots from Smith for $2,000, and when he could not meet his financial obligation, Rigdon, as secretary of the Safety Society, demanded that Pratt forfeit his property as well as the house he had built. Pratt, who had just returned to Kirtland from a mission in Canada, likely expected leniency since he had been sent by the church on missions instead of working to pay for his property and house. However, Rigdon informed Pratt that Smith had already withdrawn money in anticipation of Pratt's paying his debt to the bank and that Smith "had Left it to the mercy of the Bank and could not help what ever course they might take to collect it." Pratt was angered by Smith's attitude, especially since he had received "the most sacred promise" from the prophet "that I should not Be ingured [injured]" by the transaction.[2]

The situation so annoyed Pratt that he threatened to bring charges against Smith "for Extortion, covetousness, and takeing advantage of your Brother By an undue religious influence ... such as saying it was the will of God that Lands Should Bear such a price and many other Prophesyings Preachings

---

1. See Kirtland Safety Society, Stock Ledger, 45, 55, 219 (*JSP*, D5:395).
2. Parley P. Pratt, Letter to Joseph Smith, May 23, 1837, "Parley P. Pratt's Letter," *Naked Truths about Mormonism* (Oakland, CA), Apr. 1888, 4 (*JSP*, D5:390–91).

and Statements of a like nature." Despite his continued belief in the Book of Mormon and Smith's revelations, Pratt declared: "I have at Length Become fully convinced that the whole scene of Speculation in which we have Been Engaged is of the Devel; I allude to the covetous Extortionary Speculating Spirit which has reigned in this place for the Last season; which Has given rise to Lying deceiveing and takeing the advantage of ones Nabour [neighbor] and In Short to Every Eavle [evil] work."[3] While Pratt never sued Smith, he did withdraw from the Safety Society by selling his shares of stock to Lorenzo Young on June 10, 1837.[4]

Parrish and the Dissenters

On Sunday, May 28, Smith attended a worship service in the temple, during which a dramatic confrontation erupted between Smith and Warren Parrish, who was the leader of the dissenters. Woodruff, who recorded the event, observed that "the same spirits of murmering, complaining, & of mutiny," which had come to his notice the previous February, "hath not slept" but "have been brewing in the family Circle in the secret Chamber & in the streets untill many & some in high places had risen up against Joseph the servent whom God had raised up to lead Israel. and they were striving to overthrow his influence & cast him down. ... But notwithstanding this thick cloud of darkness standing over Kirtland Joseph being unmoved in the cause entered the Congregation of the Saints arose in the stand & spake to the people in the name of the Lord in his own defence." Despite his failures, Smith spoke passionately against the dissenters, Woodruff testifying that "the Lord was with him by his power & spirit to the Convinceing of the honest that he would stand & his enemies fall."[5]

Woodruff also reported that Smith was followed by Rigdon and others who "spake in the spirit of God maintaining Joseph in his integrity." Near the end of the meeting, according to Woodruff, Parrish "arose ... in the blackness of his face & corruption of his heart stretched out his puny arm and proclaimed against Joseph." Parrish probably criticized Smith for his handling of the bank and perhaps even his relationship with Alger. Smith apparently said little or nothing, for Woodruff reported that "Joseph acted wisely while all saw the spirit of his foe."[6]

---

3. Pratt, 4 (*JSP*, D5:389–91).
4. Kirtland Safety Society, Stock Ledger, 227 (*JSP*, D5:395).
5. Wilford Woodruff, Journal, May 28, 1837 (Vogel, *The Wilford Woodruff Journals*, 1:121).
6. Woodruff. In this entry, Woodruff wrote "Warren [Parrish]" in shorthand.

On the following day, May 29, the high council met in the temple to deal with a complaint against Frederick Williams, David Whitmer, Parley Pratt, Lyman Johnson, and Parrish. The complaint, signed by Abel Lamb, Nathan Haskins, Harlow Redfield, Artemus Millet, and Isaac Rogers, charged that "their course for some time past has been injurious to the Church of God in which they are high officers."[7] The meeting was contentious, with the dissenters raising procedural objections. Parrish objected that the complaint as read was "not in accordance with the copy of which they received." Williams and Whitmer objected that only a bishop's court could try members of the church presidency (D&C 107:82–84). It was decided that Williams and Whitmer could not be tried by the present council and they were dismissed. Pratt objected to being judged by Smith and Rigdon since they had "previously expressed their opinion against him." Rigdon, Cowdery, and Williams recused themselves, and "the council and assembly then dispersed in confusion."[8]

On the same day, Apostles Lyman Johnson and Orson Pratt preferred charges against Smith before the bishop's council "for lying & misrepresentation—also for extortion—and for—speaking disrespectfully against his brethren behind their backs."[9] At the same time, Parrish preferred charges against Rigdon "for expressing an unbelief in the revelations of God, both old and new. also an unbelief in the agency of man and his accountability to God, or that there is such a principle existing as Sin—and also, for lying & declaring that God required it at his hands."[10]

Parrish, who wrote both complaints, went into more detail in a letter published in 1838 after his disaffection from the church: "For the year past their lives have been one continued scene of lying, deception, and fraud, and that too, in the name of God. But this I can account for in my own mind, having a knowledge of their private characters and sentiments, I believe them to be confirmed Infidels, who have not the fear of God before their eyes, notwithstanding their high pretensions to holiness, and frequent correspondence with the Angels of Heaven, and the revelations of Jesus Christ by the power of the Holy Ghost. ... What more favorable idea, can

---

7. Abel Lamb, Nathan Haskins, Harlow Redfield, Artemus Millet, and Isaac Rogers, Letter to "the Presidency of the Church of the Latter Day Saints," ca. May 28, 1837, Minute Book 1, 226–27 (*JSP*, D5:393).

8. Minutes, May 29, 1837, Minute Book 1, 226–30; see also Woodruff, Journal, May 29, 1837 (Vogel, *The Wilford Woodruff Journals*, 1:121).

9. Lyman Johnson and Orson Pratt, Charges against Joseph Smith Preferred to Bishop Newel K. Whitney and his council, May 29, 1837, Newel K. Whitney Papers (*JSP*, D5:397).

10. Warren Parrish, Complaint against Sidney Rigdon to the Bishop's Council, May 29, 1837, Newel K. Whitney Papers.

one entertain who has heard them say that man has no more agency than a wheelbarrow, and consequently is not accountable, and in the final end of all things no such principle will exist as sin."[11] Parrish's belief that Smith and Rigdon were infidels reflected his inability to accept the complexity of their faith. Like many of his contemporaries, Parrish assumed that only an infidel—a non-believer—would consciously deceive in God's name.

Newell Trial

On May 30 Smith went to Painesville "in company with the Presidency & many other official members of the church" to be tried for "endangering the life of [Grandison] Newel."[12] Smith appeared with Painesville attorney William Perkins and "some forty or fifty witnesses" before Justice of the Peace Edward Flint. After a preliminary hearing, a continuance was granted at the request of the prosecutor.[13] On Saturday, June 3, Smith returned to Painesville with attorneys William Perkins and Benjamin Bissell.[14] Newell was represented by James H. Paine, a prominent lawyer and descendant of Painesville's founding family. The *Painesville Republican* reported that "the trial was had in the methodist chapel, before a large collection of people who had assembled in expectation of hearing a disclosure of the murderous projects of the modern prophet."[15]

According to the *Painesville Telegraph*, which published a transcript of the trial in its June 9, 1837, issue, the prosecution's first witness was Orson Hyde. The Mormon apostle testified that "some time in January or February last," while he, Smith, and others were conversing in the "Mormon Bank" about the difficulties the Safety Society was experiencing, largely due to an apparent organized run on the bank's specie reserves to force its closure, Smith said that "it was possible a suit might be commenced against them; but, said he, I know of no one who would do such a thing, except it is Mr. Newell. Smith seemed much excited and declared that Newell should be put out of the way, or where the crows could not find him: he said destroying

11. Warren Parrish, Letter to the Editor, Feb. 5, 1838, *Painesville (OH) Republican*, Feb. 15, 1838, [3].

12. Woodruff, Journal, May 30, 1837 (Vogel, *The Wilford Woodruff Journals*, 1:121).

13. Transcript of Proceedings, June 5, 1837, State of Ohio on Complaint of Newell v. Joseph Smith, Geauga Co., OH, Court of Common Pleas, Final Record, vol. T, 52–53; "The Humbug Ended," *Painesville Republican*, June 15, 1837, [2].

14. Transcript of Proceedings, June 5, 1837, State of Ohio on Complaint of Newell v. Joseph Smith, Geauga Co., OH, Court of Common Pleas, Final Record, vol. T, 52–53. Perkins charged Smith $15.00 for representing him in this case. See Perkins on behalf of Perkins & Osborn, Statement of Account for Joseph Smith and others, ca. Oct. 29, 1838 (*JSP*, D6:255).

15. "The Humbug Ended," *Painesville Republican*, June 15, 1837, [2].

Newell would be justifiable in the sight of God, that it was the will of God, &c." However, Hyde said that he was "alarmed" by what Smith had said and that he subsequently spoke to him about it and that Smith assured him "he had no intention to hurt Newell, but that ... he felt injured, and had spoken rashly and inadvertently in the heat of passion."[16]

The prosecution's key witness Solomon Wilbur Denton, an excommunicated Mormon who once lived with Smith and worked in the printing office with Oliver Cowdery, testified that in mid-1835 Smith tried to hire him and a Mr. Davis to murder Newell.[17] According to Denton, after he had followed Smith's instruction to borrow a pair of pistols from Cowdery, he had another conversation with Smith in his garden at which time Smith "said this was a great work, and we must be very wise; then spake of Newell; said he had injured the society, and that it was better for one man to suffer than to have the whole community disturbed; that it was the will of Heaven that Newell should be put out of the way, and that he would take the responsibility, for the deed was justifiable in the sight of God, and would be rewarded: but when we had killed him, he wanted his body secreted if possible. ... Smith told him ... Heaven would reward the doers of a deed so just, &c." However, Denton said he and Davis discussed the matter, and "after some hurried expressions from each on the atrocity of the crime, they separated." Denton was prohibited from giving hearsay testimony on Davis, who was evidently unavailable. Denton said he was recently approached by Smith, who "told me he expected to be prosecuted, and that he had heard I would swear against him: he then urged upon me the necessity of favoring him and the [Mormon] society."[18]

In an attempt to substantiate Hyde's testimony, Newel Whitney, Luke Johnson, and Parrish were called to testify, all of whom said they did not remember Smith threatening Newell's life in the bank, as Hyde reported. Whitney said, "he has heard others say and has said himself, that if Newell should attack them at the head of a mob, he should be the first to suffer." Johnson testified that he "has heard Smith and others say, if Newell or any other man should head a mob against him, they ought to be put out of the way, and it would be our duty to do so."

---

16. "The Humbug Ended."

17. On Denton boarding with Smith, see Smith, Journal, Dec. 11, 1833 (*JSP*, J1:21); and his working with Cowdery in the printing office, see Oliver Cowdery, Letter to W. W. Phelps, Dec. 11, 1833, in Cowdery Letterbook, 13.

18. "The Humbug Ended," *Painesville Republican*, June 15, 1837, [2].

The defense called Rigdon, who testified that "about two years since he had heard Davis and Denton had conspired against the life of Mr. Newell; that on receiving this information, he went to Smith and stated the case to him, requesting him to see to it. ... Smith said he had known nothing of the conspiracy until then." Rigdon added that he was at the bank when Smith supposedly threatened Newell, "but never heard Smith make any threats, though we often discussed the question, how far we should suffer, before we offered violence in self-defence."

Hyrum Smith stated that when he and his brother Joseph returned from Michigan in February, they were informed that "Denton had said he would take defendant's life, and that he (Denton) would swear the defendant had threatened to destroy Mr. Newell." Hyrum further testified that when he and Joseph arrived in Kirtland, they "went to the Bank: there met Denton; spoke to him on the subject.—Denton declared it was an absolute falsehood: a lie as black as the depths of hell."

The *Painesville Telegraph* reported that "the arguments of the Counsel on both sides, were remarkably clear, able and eloquent; and the whole affair terminated by the Court's requiring Mr. Joseph Smith, Jr. $500 bonds for his appearance at Court. Rigdon, Hyde and Denton each $50 for their appearance as witnesses in the case."[19] The reporter for the *Painesville Republican* wrote that he "was much surprised to find that no testimony appeared, on which, any reliance could be placed, that went in the least degree to criminate the respondent, but rather to raise him in the estimation of men of candor. But the Justice of the Peace who had been selected to try the question, decided otherwise, and Mr. Smith was held to bail in the sum of $500, to appear at the Court of Common Pleas, at the next term, which commenced the Monday following."[20]

On Sunday, June 4, between court appearances, Smith set apart Heber Kimball to preside over a mission to England, the first foreign mission of the church.[21] According to Kimball, he was sitting in the lowest tier of the

---

19. "Much Interest and Anxiety," *Painesville (OH) Telegraph*, June 9, 1837.

20. "The Humbug Ended," *Painesville Republican*, June 15, 1837, [2].

21. Kimball seems uncertain about the date he was set apart, dating it to June 4, 1837, in his journal and "about the first day of June" in a reminiscent account. Heber C. Kimball, Journal, June 4, 1837, 7, in Kimball, *On the Potter's Wheel*, 4–5; Heber C. Kimball, "Synopsis of the History of Heber Chase Kimball," *Deseret News* (Salt Lake City), Apr. 14, 1858, 33; see also "Mission to England, or the First Foreign Mission of the Latter-Day Saints," *Millennial Star* (Liverpool, Eng.), Apr. 1841, 289. However, the record of his setting apart dates it to June 2, 1837, which might be the source of Kimball's confusion. Joseph Smith et al., Recommendation for Heber C. Kimball, ca. June 2–13, 1837 (*JSP*, D5:400). Yet Kimball was certain that it was on a Sunday.

Melchizedek pulpits in the temple when Smith came to him and whispered: "Brother Heber, the Spirit of the Lord has whispered to me, 'Let my servant Heber go to England and proclaim my gospel and open the door of salvation to that nation.'" Kimball was stunned, but "the moment I understood the will of my heavenly Father, I felt a determination to go at all hazards, believing that he would support me by his almighty power."[22]

Later the same day, Kimball met Smith and other members of the presidency at Rigdon's house, but as he was about to be set apart, Orson Hyde came into the room and said: "Brethren I acknowledge that I have sinned before my God and you, and I beg of you to forgive me." The presidency happily forgave Hyde, and the apostle proposed that he be allowed to accompany Kimball to England. Accordingly, the presidency set apart Kimball and Hyde as well as Joseph Fielding, an Englishman who had immigrated to Canada in 1832. In their blessing, they promised "that God would make me [Kimball] mighty in that nation in winning souls unto him, and angels should accompany me and bear me up, that my feet should never slip, that I should be mightily blessed and prove a source of salvation to thousands, not only in England but in America."[23]

The British mission was suggested by some Canadian converts, who expressed a desire to return to their homeland to preach the Mormon gospel. Consequently, Joseph Fielding, Isaac Russell, John Goodson, and John Snider from Canada were chosen to accompany Kimball and Hyde to England.[24]

On the same evening, Smith married Robert B. Thompson and Mercy R. Fielding.[25] Smith performed the ceremony at the home of John Gaylord before a small gathering of people that included several of the Twelve with their wives, Patriarch Joseph Smith Sr. and wife, Lucy, and Mercy's brother and sister, Joseph and Mary Fielding. Mercy later said: "After the marriage ceremony was over we listened with joy and profit to the words of instruction and counsel which fell from the inspired lips of Joseph Smith, each word carrying to our hearts deeper and stronger convictions that we were listening to a mighty Prophet of God. And yet there was not the slightest appearance of ostentation or conscious power on his part; he was as free and

---

22. Heber C. Kimball, "Synopsis of the History of Heber Chase Kimball," *Deseret News*, Apr. 14, 1858, 33.

23. Kimball, 33.

24. Pratt, *Autobiography*, 183.

25. Geauga Co., OH, Marriage Record, vol. C, 233.

sociable as though we had all been his own brothers and sisters, or members of one family. He was as unassuming as a child."[26]

The next day, Monday, June 5, Smith was again in court in Chardon for conspiring to have Grandison Newell killed. This time he appeared before Judge Van R. Humphrey of the Geauga County Court of Common Pleas, who ultimately dismissed the charges, stating: "The Court having heard the evidence adduced, are of the opinion that the complainant had no cause to fear as set forth in his said complaint—it is therefore adjudged by the court, that the said Joseph Smith Junior be discharged, and go thereof without day."[27] As in the previous trial, Smith was represented by William Perkins, who charged him $35.00.[28] The *Painesville Republican* reported that the trial "resulted in the entire *acquital* of Joseph Smith jr., of the charges alledged against him. This is said to be the *thirteenth* prosecution which has been instituted against Joseph Smith jr. for crime, since he became a Mormon, and notwithstanding *the prejudice against him,* he has never, in a single instance been convicted, on a final trial. This fact shows on the one hand, that a spirit of persecution has existed, and on the other hand it certainly furnishes some evidence that he has for some reason, been falsely accused, and that, he is indeed and in truth better than some of his accusers."[29]

While Humphrey regarded Denton's "evidence as worthless," Newell thought otherwise and wrote to the *Telegraph* to complain: "The president judge in sustaining his views of the testimony insinuated that my hatred, not my fear, induced the prosecution." Newell argued that Denton's testimony was credible and corroborated by Rigdon. However, Rigdon had only corroborated a rumor that Denton and Davis had conspired to murder Newell, not that Smith was involved. Newell also argued that Hyde's testimony was further corroboration for Denton's testimony: "Hyde's evidence would be a confirmation of Denton's. Denton's testimony was, that Smith in the spring of 1835, advised him to kill me. Now if Smith gave similar advice last February, does not that fact strengthen the statements of Denton"? Hyde only

---

26. Mercy R. Thompson, "Recollections of the Prophet Joseph Smith," *Juvenile Instructor,* July 1, 1892, 398.

27. Transcript of Proceedings, Chardon, Geauga Co., OH, ca. June 10, 1837, State of OH v. Joseph Smith, Geauga Co., OH, Court of Common Pleas, Final Record, vol. T, 53.

28. See Perkins, Statement of Account for Joseph Smith and Others, ca. Oct. 29, 1838, JS Collection (*JSP,* D6:255).

29. "The Humbug Ended," *Painesville Republican,* June 15, 1837, [2].

testified that Smith spoke in the heat of passion and provided no direct corroboration of an 1835 plot.[30]

The *Republican* criticized Newell on July 6 for using the justice system to attack Smith: "In preferring his complaint against Smith—why did he [Newell] depart from the common practice, and drag Mr. Smith and his witnesses through his own town a distance of nine miles from home, to Painesville, when there are two Justices of the Peace in Mentor, where he resides? Was it done to harass Mr. Smith and subject him to a greater bill of expense in defending himself?"[31] In a sarcasm-filled editorial published in Missouri the following year, Smith commented: "A poor persecuting booby by the name of Grandison Newel and who in fact was scarcely a grade above the beast that perish, went and swore out a state's warrant against the editor of this paper, saying that he was afraid of his life. In so doing, he swore a palpable lie and everybody knew it, and so did the court and decided accordingly."[32]

Lawsuits

The Kirtland economy was greatly affected by the national financial and bank panic of 1837, and the defaulting mercantile firms found themselves entangled in legal actions, Joseph Smith among the rest.[33] Between June and December 1837, Smith would be involved as a defendant or co-defendant in thirteen lawsuits for collection of debts, as well as fourteen others that would be filed following his departure to Missouri in January.[34] As summarized by legal historian Gordon Madsen, Smith was sued by two banks, five New York City merchants, two Buffalo merchants, one Painesville merchant, two Kirtland landowners, the engraver who made the plates for printing Safety Society banknotes, and Joseph Coe, who supplied one-third of the money to purchase the Egyptian papyri and mummies, among other smaller claimants.[35]

On the same day that Smith's trial in the Newell case ended, June 5, all parties appeared before the Court of Common Pleas in Chardon in the case of *Martindale v. Smith* and declared that the case had been settled out of court by mutual agreement.[36] The settlement likely involved ownership of the land in question reverting to Martindale, which, according to Whitney's

---

30. Grandison Newell, Letter to the Editor, *Painesville Telegraph*, June 30, 1837, [3].
31. "The Mormon Persecutor," *Painesville Republican*, July 6, 1837.
32. "Argument to Argument," *Elders' Journal* (Far West, MO), Aug. 1838, 58.
33. For a partial list of litigation involving Joseph Smith, see *JSP*, D5:387n120.
34. Madsen, "Tabulating the Impact of Litigation on the Kirtland Economy," 234.
35. Madsen, 236.
36. Transcript of Proceedings, June 5, 1837, Martindale v. Joseph Smith et al., Geauga Co., OH, Court of Common Pleas, Final Records, vol. U, 106–108; and vol. N, 189.

April 20, 1837, letter, Martindale had demanded.[37] Painesville attorney William Perkins charged Smith $5.00 to represent him.[38]

On the same day, the Court of Common Pleas convened for the case of *Patterson and Patterson v. Cahoon, Carter & Co.* and *Rigdon, Smith & Cowdery*, but the defendants did not appear and a judgment was rendered in favor of the plaintiffs for $610.37 plus court costs.[39] Smith also failed to appear in the case of *Holmes v. Dayton, Slitor, and Smith* for an unpaid note for $208.30.[40] Smith likely failed to appear in these cases because he was occupied by the others previously mentioned.

On the next day, June 6, Smith appeared in the case of *Kelley v. Rigdon, Smith & Cowdery*. Hezekiah Kelley, a merchant in Buffalo, New York, was represented by attorneys William Perkins and Salmon Osborn, who commenced two separate legal actions: one against Cahoon, Carter & Co., as the originator of the promissory note for $2,014.74; the other against Rigdon, Smith & Cowdery, as the endorser of the note. On June 18 of the previous year, Cahoon, Carter & Co. had purchased goods from New York City merchant Daniel Ketchum, which Rigdon, Smith & Cowdery evidently paid for, because on the same day they received a promissory note from the other Kirtland firm for the amount owed. Rigdon, Smith & Cowdery subsequently transferred the note to Buffalo merchant John Ayer, who, in turn, signed it over to Kelley.[41] Although Kelley succeeded in getting a judgment in his favor, he was unsuccessful in collecting the debt.

Also on June 6, Smith appeared in the case of *Bank of Geauga v. Joseph Smith, Newel K. Whitney, and Sidney Rigdon* and declared that the $3,000 debt had been settled by mutual agreement. The court ordered Smith and the other defendants to pay the court fees, then dismissed the case.[42]

---

37. Whitney, Letter to Smith and Rigdon, Apr. 20, 1837, JS Letterbook 2, 61–62 (*JSP*, D5:368–69, 370).

38. Perkins, Statement of Account for Joseph Smith and Others, ca. Oct. 29, 1838, JS Collection (*JSP*, D6:258).

39. Transcript of Proceedings, ca. June 5, 1837, Patterson and Patterson v. Cahoon, Carter & Co. and Rigdon, Smith & Cowdery, Geauga Co., OH, Court of Common Pleas, Final Record, vol. U, 126–28.

40. Transcript of Proceedings, ca. June 5, 1837, Holmes v. Dayton, Slitor, and Smith, Geauga Co., OH, Court of Common Pleas, Final Record, vol. U, 86–87.

41. D[aniel] Ketchum, Invoice, Buffalo, Erie Co., NY, to Cahoon, Carter & Co., June 18, 1836, Joseph Smith Office Papers; and Transcript of Proceedings, ca. June 6, 1837, Kelley v. Rigdon, Smith & Cowdery, Geauga Co., OH, Court of Common Pleas, Final Record, vol. U, 97–98.

42. Transcript of Proceedings, ca. June 6, 1837, Bank of Geauga v. Joseph Smith, Newel K. Whitney, and Sidney Rigdon, Geauga Co., OH, Court of Common Pleas, Final Record, vol. U, 67–69. The mutual agreement may have had something to do with a promissory note signed by Smith and others with the bank the previous day. Bank of Geauga Discount Book, June 5, 1837.

In an editorial in the June 1837 issue of the *Messenger and Advocate,* Warren Cowdery reflected on the prevailing economic downturn. "A great amount of merchandise was purchased on credit, and sold in this town during the summer, fall, and winter past. ... Men who were not thought worth fifty or an hundred dollars became purchasers to the amount of thousands. Notes, (some cash,) deeds, and mortgages passed and repassed, till all, or nearly all, vainly supposed they had become wealthy, or at least had acquired a competence. With the consciousness of having suddenly and without much effort enhanced the amount of his worldly fortune, every one thought he must clothe himself and family according to his circumstances & present prospects, he therefore made large bills with the merchants, and promised to pay in a few short months, or when the bank should open and begin to discount." Some hoped to purchase Safety Society bills at a discount, then use them at face value to pay debts. However, the bank failed and Kirtland's economy collapsed, leaving little ability to pay off debts. Cowdery lamented, "The day of speculation, we mean local speculation in real estate, appears to have gone by for the present, and the hour of adversity the time of trial—has come; payments are due, money scarce, credit impaired, and confidence gone!" The only consolation Cowdery could offer was that Kirtland was not alone: "We speak not of these, as calamities peculiar to our little town. We mention them because they are common to our whole country, and because causes of a similar nature have combined to produce nearly the same effect throughout our whole country."[43]

Resignation, Apostasy, Illness

On or about June 8 Smith and Rigdon sold their shares in the Safety Society and resigned as president and treasurer, and Frederick Williams and Warren Parrish were elected to replace them.[44] Williams and Parrish decided to continue making loans, although stockholders had withdrawn their funds in May and June. Several newspapers warned the public that the society "is about making a new emission of their worthless trash, 'using old paper and signed by [Dr]. Williams and one Parish, by the redemption of a few dollars

43. Warren A. Cowdery, Editorial, *LDS Messenger and Advocate,* June 1837, 520–22.

44. Sidney Rigdon, Receipt on behalf of Kirtland Safety Society to Samuel Phelps, June 8, 1837, JS Office Papers; Smith sold his shares of stock to Oliver Granger and Jared Carter. Kirtland Safety Society, Stock Ledger, 1–2, 273. A July 1837 editorial by Warren A. Cowdery implies that Smith and Rigdon resigned about the time Smith transferred his stock. Warren A. Cowdery, Editorial, *Messenger and Advocate,* July 1837, 535–41; and Smith's history implies that it happened before July 7, 1837. JS History, vol. B-1, 764; DHC 2:497. On Frederick G. Williams and Warren Parrish replacing Rigdon and Smith, see "Argument to Argument," *Elders' Journal,* Aug. 1838, 58.

of which they expect to get the old emission as well as the new, again into circulation.'"[45] Even Smith felt compelled to caution the public "to beware of speculators, renegades and gamblers, who are duping the unsuspecting and the unwary, by palming upon them, those bills, which are of no worth, here. I discountenance and disapprove of any and all such practices. I know them to be detrimental to the best interests of society, as well as to the principles of religion."[46]

Smith's resignation from the bank was followed by a firestorm of anger and apostasy. Some wondered if he should also resign as president of the church. It was a crushing defeat from which Smith struggled to overcome, both spiritually and financially.

Brigham Young later described a confrontation he and other Smith loyalists had with dissenters in the temple, the latter of whom had called a meeting "to asurtain how the Prophet Joseph could be deposed, and David Whitmer appointed President of the church." Despite Oliver Cowdery's position as co-president, he had not yet come out in opposition to Smith. Nevertheless, dissenters likely favored Whitmer over Cowdery because of the former's leadership qualities, for unlike Cowdery, who had served as a scribe, clerk, printer, and editor of the church's periodicals, Whitmer presided over the Missouri church and was publicly named as Smith's successor. Young said that he "rose up and in a plain and forcible manner told them that Joseph was a Prophet & I knew it; and that they might rail and abuse slander him so much as they pleased they could not destroy the appointment of the Prophet of God, they were only destroying their own authority.—cut the thread that bound them to the Prophet and to God and sink themselves to hell." Young recalled that many of the dissenters became "enraged at my decided opposition to their measures, and Jacob Bump (an old Pugilist [boxer]) was so exasperated he could not be still" and threatened to hit Young. "This meeting was broken up without the apostates being able to unite on any measures to overthrow the Prophet," Young said. "This was a crisis when earth & hell seemed leagued to overthrow the Prophet & church of God. The knees of the strongest men in the church faltered. During this siege of darkness I stood close by Joseph and with all the wisdom and power

---

45. "Look Out," *Daily Herald and Gazette* (Cleveland, OH), July 8, 1837, [3], quoting the *Painesville Telegraph* of the previous day; "Mormon Money," *Ohio Repository* (Canton, OH), July 20, 1837.

46. "Caution," *LDS Messenger and Advocate*, Aug. 1837, 560.

God bestowed upon me, put forth my utmost energies to sustain the servant of God and unite the quorums of the church."[47]

Parley Pratt sold his shares of stock in the Safety Society to Lorenzo Young on June 10.[48] Prior to leaving Kirtland for Missouri, Pratt publicly criticized Smith. Mary Fielding, who married Hyrum Smith the following December, attended this meeting and shortly after gave an account of it in a letter to her sister, Mercy Thompson. Apparently dating the meeting to Sunday, June 11, Mary said that the people were surprised to find Pratt had taken upon himself the responsibility of conducting morning services in the place of Smith, who, as Rigdon reported, was suffering a life-threatening illness. "We sat and heard him deliver a very plausable discourse," she wrote. "He [Pratt] labored through out to show that nearly all the Church had departed from God and that Brother J.S had committed great sins and he [Smith] told the People and that he had confessed his sins to God and he [God] had forgiven him. this he [Pratt] said was not sufficient, it was his [Smith's] duty to confess also." Mary wrote that Pratt "entely cleard him self of all blaim before he closed he advirted to the 2 Letters he had written to J.S and declared he would not retract anything he had said in them, except one charge prefered against Sidney Rigdon th[at] he recalled but all the rest was true." Pratt also denied "many reports that were in circulation about him amongst which was one that he had broaken a mattrimonial covenent … and solemnly call[e]d heaven & earth, and Angels to witness that he had conducted all his matrimonal affairs as a Man of God and a Man of honour. he affirmed that such reports had only been raised through envy and malice &c." According to Mary, Rigdon "with feelings of great disgust quickly dismist the large congregation of Saints."[49]

When the congregation met for the afternoon session, "the seen of confusion that presented itself I shuld never forget," Mary wrote. "Elders Pratts, Parish & many others disafected ones were present." Rigdon, who

---

47. Historian's Office, Brigham Young History Drafts, 14–15. It is unclear when the confrontation Young described occurred. The story was first composed in an 1837 context, but the draft of the account has "fall of 1836" written diagonally over the paragraph, which seems unlikely. The editors of the Joseph Smith Papers believe the event could have happened "as early as February 1837" (*JSP*, D5:363n1).

48. Kirtland Safety Society, Stock Ledger, 227.

49. Mary Fielding [Smith], Letter to Mercy Fielding Thompson, ca. June 1837, 1–2. Mary Fielding dated the meeting to "the Sunday after you left," which had to be after the marriage of Robert B. Thompson and Mercy R. Fielding at Kirtland on June 4, 1837. Geauga Co., OH, Marriage Record, vol. C, 233; DHC 4:411. The next Sunday was June 11, which also coincides with Smith's sickness. DHC 2:492–93.

was "bowed down with the sad condition of the Church," nevertheless stood and began to speak in "all his deepest afflictions … and in the most affecting language pourd forth his complaints." Among other things, he said he was "now sacrificeing his feelings & his Character and all that was dear to him, to the four winds of Heaven, claiming a share in the reproach heaped upon Bro J.S." Rigdon announced that "he could bear no more and he would bear no more. … He then left the Stand and went out of the house many others followed." Mary said she stayed a short time and "heard Oliver Cowdrey make a few remarks endeavoring to reconsile things a little," but "when Orson Pratt began I and a great many more left the Hous." She later learned that "Elder Parish last adressd the people after which the meeting broak up for the first time since the House of the Lord was built without commemorating the Lords Supper," which was very upsetting to the community of believers.[50]

Mary Fielding noted that "our beloved Brother Joseph Smith appeared, so far gone that Brother Rigdon told us that he should not wonder naturally speaking if he did not live till night," which explains why Rigdon was so disgusted by Pratt's harsh comments. Pratt was possibly positioning himself as a successor to Smith, when, according to Mary, he professed his innocence and "endeavored to show that he himself was a Prophet and all his conduct had been consistant with his profession except as he said the common foibles of his nature." Elsewhere, Mary explicitly mentioned that Smith subsequently declared that "he shall yet stand in his place and accomplish the work God has given him to do. however much many seek his removal," and added, "I was struck last Sunday to see elder Parish place himself right in Brother Josephs Stand."[51] Soon after the meeting broke up, Pratt left for Missouri, possibly never to see Smith again.

On June 13 Heber Kimball, Orson Hyde, Willard Richards, who had been set apart the previous day, and Joseph Fielding left for England but first visited Smith, who was unable to raise his head from his pillow.[52] Their departure was an extraordinary act of faith. They did not know if their prophet would live or die or if the church would survive its darkest trial of apostasy and schism. According to Kimball, fellow apostle John Boynton told him he was a "fool as to go at the call of the fallen prophet, Joseph Smith."[53] They were also leaving their families in dire condition economically. "Sisters

---

50. Mary Fielding, Letter to Mercy Fielding Thompson, ca. June 1837, 2–3.

51. Mary Fielding, 2, 4.

52. JS History, vol. B-1, 763 (DHC 2:492–93); Willard Richards, Journal, June 12–13, 1837.

53. Kimball, "History of Heber Chase Kimball," 55.

Kimball & Hyde seem to bear there loss with considerable fortitude and resignation," Mary Fielding wrote. "I pray the Lord to provide for them such things as are needful." Vilate Kimball, in particular, "is left in debt with nothing but Kirtland money to pay her way." Mary expressed doubt that the Safety Society's bills would ever be accepted by any merchant and wrote that Smith had said that "as many of the Bank directors are become unfaithful ... he does not know that it will rise again." He further said that the Kirtland Bank could never succeed "while some pull one way and some another," because "it requires the united efforts of all and when this will be the case the Lord only knows."[54]

Concern for Smith's survival was such that Jared Carter and others "met together in the House of the Lord where they fasted and pray[e]d for him nearly all night." According to Mary Fielding, "Bro. Carter saw in a vision a grave open to receive him. J.S. but saw the Earth fall in of its own accord and fill up the grave with no person in." No doubt this was interpreted as a sign that Smith would recover. And, indeed, Smith "began rapidly to recover and in 3 or 4 days after was ab[le] to be out in air," and "those who loved him of course rejoiced abundantly."[55]

On June 14, according to Smith's history, Dr. Levi Richards administered "herbs and mild food ... and in a few days I was able to resume my usual labors."[56] In her letter to her sister, Mary Fielding wrote: "Sister [Vilate] Kimble & I visited Brother Joseph yesterday and took supper with him he seemed quite comfortable is able to walk about and converse." She asked Smith when he was going to visit the Saints in Canada again, but he responded that it was impossible to give a particular time given the state of affairs in Kirtland and that they "must not expect too much from him he feels himself to be but a poor Creature and can do nothing but what God enables him to do." Mary reported that during their visit, Smith "told us something of his feelings during his sickness." He then described his illness in terms of a struggle between a good and evil spirit, the latter of whom was trying "with all his power to get his [Smith's] Spirit," and said he needed the prayers of others to overcome the evil spirit. "When he [was] too weak to pray himself," she wrote, "he had to call uppon his wife or some Friend to pray that the good

---

54. Mary Fielding, Letter to Mercy Fielding Thompson, ca. June 1837, 6.

55. Mary Fielding, 4.

56. JS History, vol. B-1, 763 (DHC 2:493). Composed by Willard Richards on January 24, 1844, possibly with Joseph Smith's help. Vogel, *History of Joseph Smith*, 2:473n103.

spirit might conquer." He also said that "he was blessest at time[s] with such glorious visions as made him quite forget that his body was afflicted."[57]

A passage in Smith's history, composed by Willard Richards in January 1844, likely with Smith's assistance, reflects on this period of sickness and apostasy: "This is one of the many instances that I have suddenly been brought from a state of health, to the borders of the grave, and as suddenly restored, for which my heart swells with gratitude, to my heavenly Father, and I feel renewedly to dedicate myself and all my powers to his service. While I was thus afflicted the enemy of all Righteousness was suggesting, Apostates reporting and the doubtful believing that my afflictions were sent upon me because I was in transgression, and had taught the church things contrary to godliness; but of this the Lord judge betwixt me and them, while I pray my Father to forgive them this wrong."[58]

On his way to Missouri, Pratt met Thomas Marsh, David Patten, and William Smith near Columbus, Ohio, on their way to Kirtland. They persuaded him to return to Kirtland. After arriving at the Mormon capital on July 8, Marsh told Mary Fielding that he believed "the difficultys between the Presidency & the twelve will very shortly be settled."[59] Once he arrived in Kirtland, Pratt reconciled with Smith. According to Pratt's autobiography, "I went to brother Joseph Smith in tears, and, with a broken heart and contrite spirit, confessed wherein I had erred in spirit, murmured, or done or said amiss. He frankly forgave me, prayed for me and blessed me. Thus, by experience, I learned more fully to discern and to contrast the two spirits, and to resist the one and cleave to the other."[60] Both Parley and Orson Pratt would make public confessions before leaving Kirtland to preach in the eastern United States.

Far West Temple

About this time, Smith received a letter from Phelps in Far West, Missouri, dated July 7, 1837, informing him and other leaders in Kirtland of the general situation in the new county of Caldwell as well as in Far West, center of the Mormon gathering. Phelps reported that a groundbreaking meeting was held for the construction of a temple at Far West on July 3, which 1,500 Saints attended. On this "great and glorious day ... the Spirit of the Lord

---

57. Fielding, Letter to Mercy Fielding Thompson, ca. June 1837, 3–4.

58. JS History, vol. B-1, 762–63 (DHC 2:493). Composed by Willard Richards on January 24, 1844, possibly with Joseph Smith's help. Vogel, *History of Joseph Smith*, 2:473n103.

59. Fielding, Letter to Mercy Thompson, July 8, 1837.

60. Pratt, *Autobiography*, 183–84.

was with us," Phelps wrote. They not only broke ground but nearly completed "a cellar for this great edifice, 110 long by 80 broad." Another meeting on July 4 resulted in several baptisms; in fact, Phelps reported, baptisms were occurring nearly every Sabbath. Far West is growing rapidly as Mormons arrive daily from other areas of Missouri and elsewhere, driving land sales up to $10.00 per acre. "We have about one hundred buildings, 8 of which are stores," he reported. "If the brethren abroad are wise, and will come on with means, and help enter the land and populate the Co. and build the Lord's House, we shall soon have one of the most precious spots on the Globe. God grant that it may be so."[61]

Phelps also noted that the "*mob*" in Daviess County to the north had ordered all Mormons in their county to leave and go into Caldwell County by August 1. Caldwell County had been organized on December 29, 1836, exclusively for the Mormons as a means of resolving conflict by segregating them from the non-Mormon populace. The understanding was that the Mormons were "not to settle in any other county except by permission of two-thirds of the residents of the township in which they desired to locate."[62] In late 1836 Alexander Doniphan, who introduced a bill in the Missouri legislature to create Caldwell County, later said that the compromise worked until the Mormons "commenced forming a settlement in Davis county, which, under their agreement, they had no right to do."[63] On August 7, 1838, a Carroll County committee reported: "And whereas it was distinctly understood, and expressly agreed upon by said Mormons and the other citizens of the upper part of the State of Missouri, that they (the said Mormons) might select a tract of country uninhabited, and locate themselves in peace, but they should not intrude upon the citizens of any of the adjoining counties, agreeably to which contract, the Mormons first settled that tract of country now known as Caldwell county, which met with the approbation of the counties adjoining. And whereas said Mormons have broken the covenant so by them made, and are now settling in Carroll county, contrary to the express wishes of the citizens thereof."[64]

Phelps did not mention his and John Whitmer's difficulty with the high

61. William W. Phelps, Letter to Joseph Smith, [July] 7, 1837, *LDS Messenger and Advocate*, July 1837, 529 (*JSP*, D5:401–404). Published as May 7, 1837, but corrected to July 7, 1837, in the "Erratum," which is consistent with the letter's content. *Messenger and Advocate*, Aug. 1837, 560.

62. Stevens, *Centennial History of Missouri*, 108.

63. "Mormonism," *Kansas City Daily Journal*, June 12, 1881, 1.

64. "The Mormons in Carroll County," *Missouri Republican* (St. Louis), Aug. 18, 1838, [2], daily edition.

council and bishopric over the purchase of land in their names using church funds as well as their laying out Far West and initiating the construction of a temple independently from other church authorities. In President David Whitmer's absence, who was still in Kirtland, Phelps and John Whitmer met in Far West on November 15, 1836, as members of the Missouri presidency, and appointed Jacob Whitmer, Elisha H. Groves, and George M. Hinkle "for a building committee to assist the Presidency to build the house of the Lord in said City."[65] This meeting became a major source of conflict, primarily because, as John Murdock wrote, "the two Presidents did all the business indepen[den]t of [the] Bishopric or High Council and the Church was dissatisfied."[66]

The following year Apostle Thomas B. Marsh wrote that after he and Elisha Groves returned from Kentucky and Tennessee in the summer of 1836, where they had collected $1,450 for the relief of "<u>Poor bleeding Zion</u>"— those who had been expelled from Jackson County—they delivered the money to Phelps and Whitmer, who instead "purchased land for their own emolument." This, Marsh wrote, brought them into conflict with other Missouri leaders "not only because they purchased land with Church funds, in their own name, for their own aggrandisement, but because they selected the place of the City Far West and appointed the spot for the House of the Lord to be built on, drew the plan of said house, and appointed and ordained a committee to build the same, without asking or seeking council, at the hand of either Bishop, High Council, or first presidency; when it was well understood that these authorities wer[e] appointed for the purpose of counciling on all important matters pertaining to the saints of God."[67]

On April 3 the high council issued questions to Phelps and Whitmer, including: "By what authority was this place pointed out for a city and house of the Lord, and by whom"? "Are the two Presidents entitled to the profits arising from the sale of lands on which the City is to be built in this place"? "Have the two Presidents authority to lay out a City, and build a house of God, independently of the Counsel of the high Council and Bishop and his Council"?[68]

On April 5–7 the high council convened to consider these and other questions. Phelps and Whitmer objected to the presence of Apostles Marsh and David Patten and Bishop Partridge and his counselors, but

65. Minutes, Nov. 15, 1836, Minute Book 2, 68 (Cannon and Cook, *Far West Record*, 102).
66. John Murdock, Journal, 17.
67. Thomas B. Marsh, Letter to Wilford Woodruff, ca. June 18, 1838, 2 (*JSP*, D6:157–58); published in *Elders' Journal*, July 1838, 37.
68. Minutes, Apr. 3, 1837, Minute Book 2, 72 (Cannon and Cook, *Far West Record*, 107–108).

their objection was unanimously rejected. "Prest. Phelps then said he would disolve the Council, upon which T. B. Marsh declared that if the council should be disolved he would prefer a charge against the two Presidents, before the Bishop & 12 High Priests"—meaning they would try Phelps and Whitmer for their membership in the church. Phelps and Whitmer then acquiesced.[69] As John Murdock wrote, "Phelps was for having the Bishopric and two Apostles to withdraw," but "I being the oldest of the council told him no, or I with the High Council would leave also. And at the snap of a whip the whole church will leave you. So he yielded the point."[70]

After discussing the matter with Phelps and Whitmer for three days, the council decided that the questions "were not generally satisfactorily answered," and they therefore "strongly rebuke[d] the late improper proceedings of the Presidents." Patten spoke with "apparent indignation" against them, stating that their actions had been "iniquitous & fradulent in the extreme, in unrighteously appropriating Church funds to their own emolument." On April 7 the high council ordered Phelps and Whitmer to transfer the town plot and adjacent four eighty-acre tracts "into the hands of the Bishop of Zion, & that the avails arising from the sale of said lands should be appropriated to the benefit & upbuilding of 'Poor Bleeding Zion'"—which was the purpose of raising the money.[71] Marsh recorded: "After l[a]boring diligently three days in succsssion, it was unanimously agreed upon, that the town Plat, with four eighties adjacent to the plat, should be at the disposal of the Bishop and his council the High Council, the two presidents, and the two apostles. During this labor the two presidents acknowledged they were wrong, and they, to all appearance, willingly suffered themselves to be corrected by the Council."[72]

Despite this power struggle, the high council resolved to follow Phelps and Whitmer's one-mile-square plat of the city of Far West and to proceed with their plan to build a temple. They even appointed presidents David Whitmer, John Whitmer, and Phelps to "superintend the building of the Lord's House, in this city, and receive revelations, visions, &c. concerning

---

69. Minutes, Apr. 5, 1837, Minute Book 2, 73 (Cannon and Cook, 109).

70. John Murdock, Journal, 17.

71. Minutes, Apr. 5–7, 1837, Minute Book 2, 73 (Cannon and Cook, *Far West Record*, 109–110). For the purpose of raising funds for Zion, see Minutes, July 25, 1836, Minute Book 2, 69 (Cannon and Cook, 104–105).

72. Thomas B. Marsh, Letter to Wilford Woodruff, ca. June 18, 1838, 3 (*JSP*, D6:158–59); *Elders' Journal*, July 1838, 37.

said house."[73] About this time, the high council assigned John Whitmer, Phelps, Partridge, Isaac Morley, and John Corrill to sell town plots, with Whitmer being the receiver of the money.[74]

Phelps and Whitmer again courted trouble when, in transferring the town plat of 640 acres and four 80-acre tracts to Partridge on May 17, they conditioned the transaction upon a mortgage and two bonds, requiring Partridge to pay them $1,450 for the land and to take responsibility for their pledges of $1,000 each for building the House of the Lord, which they had otherwise planned to pay using proceeds from the sale of land. [75] How they got Partridge to agree to these terms is a mystery because it undid what had been decided by the high council the previous month, but it may have had something to do with Partridge's purchase of four tracts of land from Phelps and Whitmer on the same day.[76] Marsh wrote about the unusual circumstances of the transfer, stating that "by some means they managed to bind the bishop in a mortgage of three thousand four hundred and fifty dollars." Also, Phelps and Whitmer still demanded the bishop pay the $2,000 they had pledged for building the temple, although "the affair of building the house has falen through." Once Partridge deposited the money in the building fund, Phelps and Whitmer planned to withdraw it, along with the "many people [who] have withdrawn ther subscription to it. ... A small part of which has been already paid to Wm. W. Phelps."[77]

While Marsh subsequently complained about the self-aggrandizing actions of Phelps and Whitmer, it is interesting to observe that on June 11 the high council granted Patten's request to have the church pay his debts so he can better preach the gospel. The council also agreed to give Patten and Marsh "a lot in the town of Far West, free of charge, and that the Bishop, if he approve, give a title."[78]

---

73. Minutes, Apr. 7, 1837, Minute Book 2, 68 (Cannon and Cook, *Far West Record*, 103–104). On April 13, 1837, John Whitmer and Phelps submitted a plat for Far West to Elias Higbee, a justice of the peace in Caldwell County. "Description of Far West Plat," 1837. This one-square-mile plat of Far West was divided into 121 blocks of land.

74. Minutes, undated [ca. Apr.–May 1837], Minute Book 2, 70–72 (Cannon and Cook, *Far West Record*, 106–107).

75. Partridge, Bonds to William W. Phelps and John Whitmer, May 17, 1837.

76. Edward Partridge and Lydia Partridge, Mortgage to William W. Phelps and John Whitmer, May 17, 1837. See *JSP*, D6:158n760.

77. Thomas B. Marsh, Letter to Wilford Woodruff, ca. June 18, 1838, 3 (*JSP*, D6:159–60); *Elders' Journal*, July 1838, 37–38.

78. Minutes, June 11, 1837, Minute Book 2, 76 (Cannon and Cook, *Far West Record*, 114–15).

Mortgaging God's House

On July 11, 1837, William Marks, Smith's land agent, mortgaged the land on which the temple was built to the New York mercantile firm of Mead, Stafford & Co. to satisfy a debt incurred in October 1836 when the Kirtland mercantile firms of Rigdon, Smith & Cowdery and Cahoon, Carter & Co. purchased goods to sell in their stores.[79] Smith had transferred the title of this land to Marks the previous April to prevent it from being lost to creditors, but they managed to work out a deal where the church retained use of the property while paying off the mortgage.[80] This deal required three annual payments, beginning on July 8, 1838, amounting to $4,393.77, not including interest.[81] If they failed to pay the promissory notes, then Mead, Stafford & Co. could take possession of the temple after July 8, 1840.[82] An addendum to the mortgage exempted "the mummies and ancient writings now in said temple ... because they are not owned by me or any of the other makers of the foregoing instrument."[83]

On Sunday, July 23, Smith dictated a revelation to Marsh, president of the Twelve Apostles, and the Twelve generally. Vilate Kimball, who made one of the earliest copies of the revelation, said she took it from "Elder Marshs book as he wrote it from Josephs mouth."[84] Marsh had designated July 24 as the day the Twelve would meet in Kirtland to prepare for their mission to England.[85] When Marsh reached Kirtland, he learned that Smith had already sent Kimball and Hyde to England and was troubled by several members of the quorum who were critical of Smith's leadership. On the day before the appointed day, Marsh wanted to know what he should do. The July 23 revelation assured Marsh that he was chosen to lead the Twelve: "Verily I say unto you my servant Thomas, thou art the man whom I have

---

79. Smith et al., Mortgage to Mead, Stafford & Co., July 11, 1837 (*JSP*, D5:404–410); also copied on July 14, 1837, into Geauga Co., OH, Deed Record, vol. 24, 211–14.

80. Joseph Smith and Emma Smith, Deed for property in Kirtland Township, Geauga Co., OH, to William Marks, Apr. 10, 1837, Geauga Co., OH, Deed Record, vol. 23, 536–37 (*JSP*, D5:357–62).

81. Reuben Hitchcock, Statement of Account on behalf of Hitchcock & Wilder, [Painesville, Geauga Co., OH?], ca. July 9 and Nov. 6, 1838, JS Collection (*JSP*, D6:285–90).

82. The first note, due July 8, 1838, appears not to have been paid, but the New York firm did not sue. According to a May 1841 letter from Joseph Smith to Oliver Granger, the church's agent in Kirtland, the mortgage for the House of the Lord seems to have been resolved by that time. Smith, Letter to Oliver Granger, May 4, 1841 (*JSP*, D8:135–38).

83. Smith et al., Mortgage to Mead, Stafford & Co., July 11, 1837 (*JSP*, D5:409).

84. Vilate Kimball, Letter to Heber C. Kimball, Sep. 6, 1837.

85. Thomas B. Marsh and David W. Patten, Letter to Parley P. Pratt, May 10, 1837, in JS Letterbook 2, 62–63.

chosen to hold the keys of my kingdom (as pertaining to the twelve) abroad among all nations, that thou mayest be my servant to unlock the door of the kingdom in all places where my servant Joseph, and my servant Sidney [Rigdon], and my servant Hyrum [Smith], cannot come, for on them have I laid the burden of all the Churches for a little season: wherefore whithersoever they shall send you, go ye, and I will be with you and in whatsoever place ye shall proclaim my name an effectual door shall be opened unto you that they may receive my word."[86] Smith wanted Marsh to understand that he was the chief apostle, but that he acted under the direction of the First Presidency. Marsh was not going to England, but he would soon play a role in establishing the presidency in Missouri.

Frederick Williams and Oliver Cowdery were probably not named in the revelation because of their sympathies with the dissenters. The Lord addressed the Twelve generally and instructed Marsh to "Admonish them sharply ... for all their sins ... and if they harden not their hearts and stiffen not their necks against me they shall be converted and I will heal them. ... Exalt not yourselves; rebel not against my servant Joseph for Verily I say unto you I am with him and my hand shall be over him; and the keys which I have given him, and also to youward shall not be taken from him untill I come."[87]

The Lord warned of the destruction that was about to come upon the inhabitants of the earth: "And as a whirlwind it shall come upon all the face of the earth saith the Lord." And then he seemed to allude to the dissenters and their takeover of the temple: "And upon my house shall it begin and from my house shall it go forth saith the Lord. First among those among you saith the Lord; who have professed to know my name and have not known me and have blasphemed against me in the midst of my house saith the Lord."[88]

Canada

Earlier in June, Smith could not tell Mary Fielding when he would be able to visit the Saints in Canada, but on July 27 he left Kirtland for Canada with Rigdon and Marsh, accompanied by Brigham Young and newly-baptized Albert P. Rockwood on their way to the East. At Painesville, they were "detained all day by malicious and vexatious law suits."[89] Painesville attorney William Perkins charged Smith $10.00 for "defending [him] successfuly in three suits

---

86. Revelation, July 23, 1837, Smith, Journal, July 23, 1837 [D&C 112:16–18] (*JSP*, J1:307–308; D5:416).

87. Revelation [D&C 112:12–13, 15] (*JSP*, J1:307; D5:415–16).

88. Revelation [D&C 112:23–26] (*JSP*, J1:308; D5:416–17).

89. JS History, vol. B-1, 767 (DHC 2:502; Vogel, *History of Joseph Smith*, 2:480).

before Flint, Kingsbury & Miller."[90] Edward Flint and Lewis Miller were justices of the peace in Painesville, and Kingsbury is probably Horace Kingsbury of Painesville, a Mormon who subsequently vouched for Smith's business integrity but named in a canceled paragraph in Smith's history as one of "our enemies [who] entered various complaints, and instituted several malicious suits against me and elder Rigdon."[91] Kingsbury—like Parley P. Pratt, who threatened to sue Smith—may have likewise subsequently repented.

According to Young, Smith was arrested and tried six times in Painesville. On the third time, Smith was held over for trial, and "Br. Anson Call who had lately joined the church stepped forward and proffered to become his bail. The Sheriff who was personally acquainted with br. Call took him to one side and advised him strongly against being Bail for the Prophet, asserting the Prophet would be sure to abscond and he would loose his farm; but br. Call willingly became his bail." Finally, as Smith got into his wagon to return to Kirtland, "an officer also jumped in and catching the lines with one hand put his other hand on Joseph's shoulder and said 'Mr. Smith you are my prisoner.' Joseph enquired what was the cause of action, the officer informed him that a Gentleman a few months previous had left a stove with him, for the price of which he was sued. brother Joseph replied 'I never wished to purchase the stove, but the gentleman insisted on me putting it up in my house, saying it would bring him custom.' Joseph left his watch and other property in security and we returned home to Kirtland."[92] Perkins subsequently charged Smith $1.00 for "time & trouble with Holbrook about watch."[93]

While working on this portion of Smith's history in January 1844, Willard Richards added two notes in pencil under July 27 and 29, 1837, in his journal: "Joseph went to canada—persecution at Paynsvill—Bishop Whitney can tell ... Court arrived on Mr. Rigdon &c for making spurious money."[94] In a letter to her husband, Heber, the following September, Vilate Kimball wrote that Smith's arrest in Painesville "was concerning Kirtland money,

---

90. See Perkins, Statement of Account for Joseph Smith and Others, ca. Oct. 29, 1838, JS Collection (*JSP*, D6:255). Perkins also credited Joseph Smith for "Cash to Perkins $1.00 do to [Salmon] Osborn $1" (*JSP*, D6:257).

91. JS History, vol. B-1, 767, 770, Note 6 (DHC 2:502). Horace Kingsbury, Statement, Oct. 26, 1838, JS Letterbook 2, 40 (DHC 3:174).

92. Historian's Office, Brigham Young History Drafts, 12; published in *Deseret News*, Feb. 10, 1858, 386. See also Call, Reminiscences, 1–2.

93. See Perkins, Statement of Account for Joseph Smith and Others, ca. Oct. 29, 1838 (*JSP*, D6:256; see under July 28, 1837). The identity of Holbrook is unknown.

94. Willard Richards, Journal, July 27 and 29, 1837. For the date Richards was working on vol. B-1, 767, see Vogel, *History of Joseph Smith*, 1:xci.

they continued in this way until they put four or five warents onto him, he then gave it up for that day and came home, the brethren all with him except Br Patten[.] he went on." According to Vilate, Smith and company started for Canada the following night, July 28, at about 11:00, and reached "the first port below Fairport where they got a boat and went off unmolested."[95]

After riding in a wagon all night, Smith and company arrived at Ashtabula, Ohio, early the next morning, July 29. Young remembered: "We tarried in Ashtabula through the day, wandering over the bluffs, and through the woods and on the beach of the Lake; bathing ourselves in her beautiful waters, until evening when a steamboat arrived from the West. We went on board and took passage, ... & we all lay down on the deck of the vessel for the night: We arrived in Buffalo early the next morning."[96] They then "took cars for the Falls," where, on July 30, Young and Rockwood parted for their mission field and Smith and the others proceeded to Toronto.[97]

During Smith's five-week absence from Kirtland, conflict between church leaders and dissenters escalated. At a meeting in the temple on Sunday, August 13, there was a fight between the dissenters, headed by Warren Parrish, and Smith loyalists, including members of the Smith family. According to Lucy Mack Smith, Joseph Sr., who was conducting the meeting, called upon Cowdery, as justice of the peace, to stop the dissenters, "but Oliver paid no attention."[98] The next day, Parrish filed a complaint against Joseph Sr. and eighteen others for assault. They were subsequently arrested and tried before Cowdery on August 25. Eliza Snow, who appeared as a witness, said she "found the court scene as amusing as the Temple scene was appalling. The idea of such a man as Father Smith—so patriarchal in appearance—so circumspect in deportment and dignified in his manners, being guilty of riot, was at once ludicrous and farcical to all sane-minded persons."[99] After the two-day trial, Cowdery found that "the charge against them was not sustained, and they were therefore discharged."[100]

Meanwhile, on August 21, Smith attended a conference at Scarborough, Upper Canada, during which he and others ordained twenty-eight-year-old

---

95. Vilate Kimball, Letter to Heber C. Kimball, ca. Sep. 11, 1837, [1].

96. Historian's Office, Brigham Young History Drafts, 13; *Deseret News*, Feb. 10, 1858, 386.

97. Brigham Young, Diary, July 27, 1837.

98. Lucy Mack Smith, History, 1844–45, bk. 14, [8] (Anderson, ed., *Lucy's Book*, 598).

99. Eliza R. Snow, *Biography and Family Record of Lorenzo Snow* (Salt Lake City: Deseret News Co., 1884), 21.

100. State of Ohio v. Joseph Smith Sr. et al., Transcript of Proceedings, Aug. 14, 25–26, 1837, Cowdery, Docket Book, 225–26.

John Taylor a high priest.[101] In the spring of 1836, Sampson Avard, a Thomsonian physician and recent convert from New York, had come to Toronto with falsified papers giving him authority over the churches in the area, replacing Taylor as the presiding elder. When Smith discovered this situation, he reprimanded Avard and reinstated Taylor. Taylor later explained that shortly after arriving in Canada, Smith summoned him, which surprised Taylor, and when he inquired why he had not sent for Avard, who was the presiding elder, Smith "was astonished and stated that he never was sent, and that I had no business to give up my presidency to him. I told him of the letter that he had from the High Priests Quorum. Br. Joseph said there must be some mistake about it, and imposition practised on me; and he seemed very much annoyed."

Taylor said that he borrowed a wagon and visited the churches in the Toronto area with Smith, Rigdon, and Marsh, traveling along the coast of Lake Ontario as far north as Whitby, where they held a conference in a large barn that was well attended. "The spirit of God was present," Taylor recalled, "the hearts of the Saints were made to rejoice and many who were out of the church believed." Another conference was held in Scarborough, at which Smith reproved Avard "very severely for coming to that place with fictitious papers," Taylor recalled. "He also reproved me for yielding up my office with so flimsy a pretext; but palliated it on account of my youth and inexperience. He then gave me a strict charge on no account whatever to give up any office or calling unless I receive orders from a proper legitimate source that could be relied upon, or otherwise I should be held responsible for any evil that accrued from it." Avard was ordered to return home and Taylor was reinstated as presiding authority. According to Taylor, Avard had obtained his papers from "an apostate party at Kirtland," and may have been a victim as well. Of his travels with Smith and company, Taylor said it was "as great a treat to me as I had ever enjoyed, as I had a daily opportunity of … participating in the rich stores of intelligence that flowed continually from the Prophet Joseph."[102]

Mary Isabella Hales Horne, a seventeen-year-old newlywed who hosted Smith's party at her home in Scarborough, later reported that a three-day conference was held in a barn that her husband had recently built. "On shaking hands with Joseph Smith," she recalled, "I received the Holy Spirit in such great abundance that I felt it thrill my whole system, from the crown

---

101. Sidney Rigdon and Joseph Smith, License for John Taylor, Aug. 21, 1837, transcribed in "History of John Taylor," 14. Taylor would later become LDS Church president.

102. Taylor, 13–14.

of my head to the soles of my feet. I thought I had never beheld so lovely a countenance. Nobility and goodness were in every feature."[103] Mary said that she and her husband traveled with Taylor, Smith, Rigdon, and Marsh on their tour of the several branches of the church and that Smith "gave the saints instructions on the organization and order of the Priesthood, respect for proper authority, corrected some of the mistranslations of the Bible, and took pleasure in answering questions pertaining to the gospel and the organization of the Church."[104]

While Smith was in Canada, Pamelia Rust Clark, wife of Kirtland miller Quartus Clark, was fatally injured in a carriage accident on Sunday, August 20. Pamelia's death was interpreted as a fulfillment of Smith's curse on Quartus for not selling his land to the Mormons.[105] In a letter to her sister Mercy, Mary Fielding Smith reported that "Clarke ... and his wife with some of their Children and other Friends were returning from the Presbyterian Meeting House in a very nice Carriage, about one minute after they passed the House of the Lord their Horses took fright and started off the side of the hill overthrew the Carriage and hurt Mr. C. and one Child considerably But Mrs. C so seriously as to prove fatal." Mary interpreted the tragedy as an act of God's just providence, noting that "on the day preceeding the accident She was heard to speak very unfavourably of our Church but is now gone to prove whether it is the Church of Christ or not." She also noted that "it is not quite a year since Bro J[oseph]. told Mr. C that the curse of God would be upon him for his conduct towards him and the Church." The prophet was frustrated with Clark because, as Mary reminded Mercy, "our people wished to purchas[e] his place, but he would not sell it on any reasonable terms and therefore kept it, and has been a trouble in the place but has prospered in business so much as to say he never prospered better and told a person some time ago that he was ready for another of Joseph Smiths Curses. I feel inclined to think he will never be heard to utter such words again. May the Lord forgive and save him and all others who raise their hand against the Lords anointed," Mary concluded, "for I see more clearly than ever that this is no trifling sin in the sight of God."[106]

Open-ended, subjectively-validated curses such as these tend to be easily

---

103. "Mary Hales Autobiography," in Hales, *Windows*, 30–31; see also *Woman's Exponent* (Salt Lake City), June 1, 1882, 1.

104. "The Prophet Joseph Smith: The Testimony of Sister M. Isabella Horne," *Relief Society Magazine* (Salt Lake City), Mar. 1951, 158.

105. *Painesville Telegraph*, Aug. 25, 1837.

106. Fielding, Letter to Mercy Fielding Thompson, ca. Sep. 1837, 3–4.

fulfilled. Interpreting events as providential acts of God, which Mormons and their contemporaries inherited from their Puritan forbearers, is a two-edged sword. No doubt Smith's enemies were at the same time interpreting his failures and misfortunes providentially as well.[107] Historian Keith Thomas has commented on the pitfalls of appeals to the doctrine of providence: "There was no way in which the theory once accepted could be faulted. If the wicked man encountered adversity this was clearly a punishment from God; if a godly man was smitten then he was being tested and tried. The pious Christian for whom events went well could thank God for his good fortune without in any way being worried by the equal prosperity of his reprobate neighbour, since he knew that the absence of worldly afflictions could sometimes be a dreadful sign of God's lost love. Indeed some suffering was almost essential as proof that God retained an interest in the person concerned."[108] Despite Mary's faith in Smith's charisma, Smith would soon return to Kirtland to defend himself against the accusations of those less impressed with his ability to foresee events.

---

107. While Calvin had cautioned against attempts to discern God's disposition by analyzing historical events, arguing that providences are "mysterious" and "hidden" from human understanding, late sixteenth- and early seventeenth-century Anglicans and Puritans in England developed a distinct view of providence and began viewing history as a form of revelation by which the "counsels of God" could be discerned. See VanderMolen, "Providence as Mystery, Providence as Revelation"; Viner, *The Role of Providence in the Social Order*, 18, 23–26, 27–113.

108. Thomas, *Religion and the Decline of Magic*, 82.

26

Persecution and Flight

No weapon formed against him shall prosper, and though the wicked
mar him for a little season, ... he shall roar in his strength, and the
Lord shall put to flight his persecutors.
—*Joseph Smith Sr., Blessing to Joseph Smith, Dec. 9, 1834,*
Patriarchal Blessing Book 1, 4, CHL

Smith and Rigdon returned to Kirtland from Canada "about the last of August" 1837.[1] They did not arrive in Sampson Avard's wagon about 10:00 p.m. as planned, but early the next morning on foot—wet, muddy, and exhausted from fleeing their enemies in Painesville. The following Sunday, Smith recounted their harrowing experience to a large congregation of Saints in the temple, while Rigdon convalesced at home, having sustained an injury from a fall during their flight. Both Vilate Kimball and Mary Fielding wrote detailed reports of Smith's account soon afterward.

In a letter to her husband Heber in England, Vilate reported that there was a plot to shoot Smith and "when the time came that he was expected home constables was employed to watch all the ports fare and neer." But when Smith, Rigdon, Marsh, and Avard left the boat at Ashtabula, they "took Doctor Avards hors and carriage (as he was in company with them) dressed themselves in disguise and got away unknown." At some point, the four men split, with Avard and Marsh accompanying Sisters Walton and Snider to Kirtland, and Smith and Rigdon riding in the wagon in disguise. However, they were recognized by a man who gave the alarm, and "within four miles of home they were arrested and taken back to Painsville for another mock trial on Kirtland money." As it happened, Smith and Rigdon were transported to Esquire Horace Kingsbury, a wayward Mormon whose

---

1. JS History, vol. B-1, 770 (DHC 2:508).

"heart was softend towards them and he showed them his back door and told them to make their escape if they could."[2]

The two men ran into the darkness, "but soon found themselves surrounded by their enemies on every side with lighted torches." According to Mary, "The first step they took was to find the woods as quick as possible where they thought they should be safe," but between them and the woods was a swamp through which they were forced to pass. At one point, Vilate wrote, their pursuers were so close that they found it necessary to lie down in the swamp behind a log and "almost hold their breath that they mite not be discovered." Mary remarked that "Brother J[oseph]. was obliged to entreat Brother Rigdon, after his exertion in running, while lying by a log to breath more softly if he meant to escape." The two men continued "climbing over fences or traveling through brush or corn fields until about 12 o'clock." Sometime during their flight, "they took each other by the hand and covenanted to live and die together." They wandered about five or six miles before they reached the road leading to Kirtland, and after walking "along muddy slippery roads till near 3 in the morning they arrived safe at home almost fainting with fatigue."[3]

Mary reported that although Rigdon's injury prevented him from attending church, Smith "appeared in the house of the Lord throughout the Sabbath in excellent spirits and spoke in a very powerful manner and blessed the congregation in the name of the Lord and I do assure you the saints felt the blessing and left the house rejoicing abundantly returning their blessing upon him."[4] Vilate reported that Smith had joked that it was the only time in their lives that he and Rigdon "thanked God for the darkness ... for it was all that saved them from their enemys."[5]

Negotiations and Reorganization

In the August issue of the *Messenger and Advocate*, Smith published a "Caution," warning that the Kirtland Bank notes were worthless.[6] The same issue also announced the publication of a new paper at Kirtland called the *Elders' Journal* to commence in October with Smith as editor.[7]

---

2. Vilate Kimball, Letter to Heber C. Kimball, ca. Sep. 11, 1837, [2].

3. Kimball, [2]; Mary Fielding [Smith], Letter to Mercy Fielding, ca. Sep. 1837, [2]–[3].

4. Fielding, [3].

5. Kimball, Letter to Heber C. Kimball, ca. Sep. 11, 1837, [2].

6. Joseph Smith, Notice, ca. late Aug. 1837, "Caution," *LDS Messenger and Advocate* (Kirtland, OH), Aug. 1837, 560.

7. [Warren Cowdery], "Prospectus," *LDS Messenger and Advocate*, Aug. 1837, 545–47.

With the assistance of Painesville attorney William Perkins, Smith managed to relieve some of his financial pressure, at least, temporarily. On the first of September the mercantile firms of Rigdon, Smith & Cowdery and Cahoon, Carter & Co. renegotiated their debts of more than $10,000 to several New York mercantile firms, which delayed payment for at least six months and up to three years.[8]

On Sunday, September 3, Smith presided over a conference that would later be referred to as a "re-organization of the Church,"[9] but, in fact, was a purging of Smith's critics. Reflecting on this meeting, Brigham Young later stated that the purpose was not only to "reorganize the church," but also "to disfellowship those of the Twelve and others seeking to bring disunion and destruction upon the church. The apostates and disaffected, not being united, were compelled to endure the chagrin of witnessing the accomplishment of the will of God and his Prophet."[10]

At this meeting, several men in the hierarchy were released from their positions and replaced, including eight members of the twelve-member high council and one of the seven presidents of the Quorum of Seventy. The conference also decided to disfellowship three members of the Quorum of the Twelve for rebellion and dissent. The object of the meeting was not only to reassert Smith's authority but to secure a vote of confidence and loyalty from the membership.

According to the minutes, Rigdon presented Smith to the membership "to know if he should still act as their Pres. as the presiding officer of the church."[11] A copy of the minutes prepared the next day emphasized Smith's office "as Prest. of the whole Church." The response was unanimous in favor.[12] Smith then presented Rigdon and Frederick Williams as "councillors to Pres. Smith and together with him to constitute the three first presidents of the church"— which was also sustained unanimously. While the action merely repeated what was already the case, Smith wanted to reinforce the fact and prepare the way for his move to Missouri. The significance of the sustaining vote was well understood by those attending the meeting, as indicated by a January 18,

---

8. See, for example, Joseph Smith et al., Promissory Note to Holbrook & Ferme, Sep. 1, 1837 (Ohio Historical Society, Columbus, OH); Joseph Smith et al., Promissory Note to Holbrook & Ferme, Sep. 1, 1837 (BYU). For a full listing of promissory notes, see josephsmithpapers.com, Calendar of Documents, under Sep. 1, 1837.

9. See Minutes, Nov. 7, 1837, Minute Book 2, 82 (*JSP*, D5:469).

10. "History of Brigham Young," *Deseret News*, Feb. 17, 1858, 393.

11. Minutes, Sep. 3, 1837, Minute Book 1, 234 (*JSP*, D5:422).

12. Joseph Smith, Letter to John Corrill and the Church in Missouri, Sep. 4, 1837, Smith, Journal, Mar.–Sept. 1838, 20 (*JSP*, J1:242; D5:428).

1838, letter Hepzibah Richards wrote to her brother Willard in England: "The presidents, Joseph [Smith] and Sidney [Rigdon] and Hiram [Hyrum Smith] returned from Missouri a few weeks since. They are elected to the first presidency, or to preside over all the churches instead of this place only."[13]

Next, Smith presented Cowdery, Hyrum Smith, Joseph Smith Sr., and John Smith as "assistant councillors"—this too was sustained unanimously.[14] According to Vilate Kimball, "Father John Smith was poot [put] in the place of David Whitmer (as he is going to Zion)."[15] Apparently, Whitmer, as president of the Missouri church, had been acting as an assistant president to Smith while in Kirtland.

In presenting his counselors, Smith introduced a subtle distinction. As the editors of the Joseph Smith Papers observe, "Previously, the church presidency consisted of JS as president and five assistant presidents. After December 1834, Cowdery ranked first among the assistants. Their separation here into counselors and assistant counselors with Cowdery among the latter clearly constituted a demotion for Cowdery, if not for Joseph Smith Sr. and Hyrum Smith, who were already ranked behind Rigdon and Williams."[16] The reshuffling of Cowdery was likely the result of a growing rift between Smith and Cowdery over the Fanny Alger affair and bank scandal. The next day, when Smith sent a copy of the minutes to the church in Missouri, he further commented that Cowdery "has been in transgression" and if he did not humble himself the church "will soon be under the necessity of raising their hands against him."[17] Describing the period just before Cowdery's departure to Missouri in September 1837, Desdemona W. Fullmer recalled that "Olover Cowdery with othrs would say to me are you such a fool as still to goo to hear Joseph the fallen prophet."[18] Cowdery was positioned to succeed Smith should Smith be removed through transgression, and Cowdery had information that could put that process into motion. Smith moved first to delegitimize him.

Smith then proposed Newel Whitney and his counselors as the bishopric for the Kirtland stake and received unanimous approval. However, when he presented the Twelve, all but Luke S. Johnson, Lyman E. Johnson, and John F. Boynton were sustained. The three men were instead disfellowshipped and

13. Hepzibah Richards, Letter to Willard Richards, Jan. 18–19, 1838, [2].
14. Minutes, Sep. 3, 1837, Minute Book 1, 234–35 (*JSP*, D5:422–23).
15. Vilate Kimball, Letter to Heber C. Kimball, ca. Sep. 11, 1837, [2].
16. *JSP*, J1:242n63.
17. Smith, Letter, Sep. 4, 1837, Smith, Journal, Mar.–Sept. 1838, 22 (*JSP*, J1:244; D5:430).
18. Fullmer, Autobiography, [1]–[2].

given the opportunity to confess and repent. Boynton, who was the only one present, attempted to confess, but because he justified his behavior "by reason of the failure of the bank, his ackowledgments appeared not to be satisfactory, by Elder Brigham Young in a plain and energetick manner."[19]

Boynton "again arose and still attributed his difficulties & conduct to the failure of the bank, stating that the bank he understood was instituted by the will & revelations of God, & he had been told that it never would fail let men do what they pleased." Smith countered Boynton, stating that "if this had been published, it was without authority, at least from him, he stated that he allways said that unless the institution was conducted upon righteous principles it would not stand."[20] True, Smith sometimes conditioned the bank's success on obedience, but for some, its failure seemed more to do with Smith's mismanagement as well as economic forces beyond his control than any lack of virtue on the part of the administrators and investors. Indeed, the founding of the bank was itself ill-conceived, and therefore troubling to some that God would command its establishment. The failure to obtain a charter was a defeat and challenged Smith's charismatic power and tested the hierarchal ecclesiastic structure he had erected two years earlier. Boynton's confession was rejected and he was disfellowshipped. However, seven days later he and the Johnson brothers made acceptable confessions and regained their membership as well as their place in the Quorum of Twelve.[21]

During the afternoon session, Smith presented the members of the high council. Objections were raised against five members: John Johnson, Joseph Coe, Joseph C. Kingsbury, Martin Harris, and John P. Greene. All were excommunicated except Greene, who was not present.[22] Vilate Kimball reported that "Harris ... was so angary he left the house."[23]

Smith next presented five new presidents of the Seventies to replace those who had been moved into the high priests quorum. They were sustained except for John Gould, who was replaced by Levi Hancock. A vote was taken to move the old presidents to the high priests quorum.[24] An additional statement in the copy of the minutes in Smith's journal reveals that the vote was perfunctory: "If any of the members of the quorum of the seventies should

---

19. Minutes, Sep. 3, 1837, Minute Book 1, 235 (*JSP*, D5:423).

20. Minutes, 236 (*JSP*, D5:424).

21. Minutes, Sep. 10, 1837, Minute Book 1, 240 (Collier and Harwell, *Kirtland Council Minute Book*, 188–89).

22. Minutes, Sep. 3, 1837, Minute Book 1, 236–37 (*JSP*, D5:424–25).

23. Vilate Kimball, Letter to Heber C. Kimball, ca. Sep. 11, 1837, [2].

24. Minutes, Sep. 3, 1837, Minute Book 1, 237–38 (*JSP*, D5:425).

be dissattisfied & would not submit to the Present order, and receive these last Presidents that they Should have power to demand their Lisence & they should no longer be concidered members of the church."[25] In other words, they had no say in the matter.

Missouri Leadership Given Notice

On the following day, September 4, Smith wrote a letter to John Corrill and the church in Zion (Missouri), in which he included the minutes of the conference of the previous day. Importantly, Smith's letter was addressed to Corrill, who was serving as "agent to the Church and Keeper of the Lord's store House,"[26] instead of Phelps and John Whitmer, members of the Missouri presidency. Phelps and Whitmer had been disciplined for buying land in their own names with church funds and had fallen out of favor with the Missouri church, although they retained their offices. On the same day, Smith dictated a brief revelation "making known the transgression of John Whitmer and W. W. Phelps." The revelation declared that Whitmer and Phelps "have done those things which are not pleasing in my sight," and warned that "if they repent not they shall be removed out of their places."[27]

Smith's letter began: "Joseph Smith Jr. Prest of the Church of Christ of Latter Day Saints in all the world To John Corroll [Corrill] & the whole Church in Zion."[28] By adding "in all the world," Smith "emphasized his authority over the church in Missouri and its presidency."[29] Smith explained why he was including a transcription of the minutes of the September 3 reorganization meeting: "You have undoubtedly been informed by letter & otherwise of our difficulties in Kirtland which are now about being settled and that you may have a knowledge of the same I subscribe to you the following minuits ... that you may know how to proceed to set in order & regulate the affairs of the Church in zion whenever they become disorganized."[30]

Smith was urging the Missouri church to similarly reorganize and closed his letter by warning them about David Whitmer and Oliver Cowdery, who were soon to leave Kirtland for Missouri. "Oliver Cowdery has been in

---

25. Smith, Letter, Sep. 4, 1837, Smith, Journal, Mar.-Sept. 1838, 22 (*JSP*, J1:243; *JSP*, D5:429–30).

26. See Minutes, May 22, 1837, Minute Book 2, 75 (Cannon and Cook, *Far West Record*, 113).

27. Revelation, Sep. 4, 1837, Smith, Journal, Mar.–Sep. 1838, 23 [uncanonized] (*JSP*, J1:245; D5:433).

28. Smith, Letter, Sep. 4, 1837, Smith, Journal, Mar.–Sept. 1838, 18 (*JSP*, J1:241; D5:427).

29. *JSP*, J1:241n60.

30. Smith, Letter, Sep. 4, 1837, Smith, Journal, Mar.–Sep. 1838, 19–20 (*JSP*, J1:241; D5:428).

transgression," he wrote, "but as he is now chosen as one of the Presidents or councilors I trust that he will yet humble himself & magnify his calling but if he should not, the church will soon be under the necessaty of raising their hands against him Therefore pray for him." Smith also said that "David Whitmer Leonard Rich & others have been in transgression but we hope that they may be humble & ere long make sattisfaction to the Church otherwise they cannot retain their standing."[31]

Smith had good reason to worry about the return to Missouri of these leaders. Cowdery had been demoted but still held high office and was armed with knowledge of Smith's infidelity. Whitmer also posed a threat to Smith's leadership, having been appointed as Smith's successor in 1834. In February 1837, dissenters named him to replace Smith as president of the church.[32] Another influential dissenter Smith named was Leonard Rich, one of the former presidents of the Seventies who had been moved to the high priests quorum.[33] Smith warned the Missouri leaders to "beware of all disaffected Characters for they come not to build up but to destroy & scatter abroad, Though we or an Angel from Heaven preach any other Gospel or introduce [any other] order of things than those things which ye have received and are authorized to received from the first Presidency let him be accursed."[34]

The letter referred the Missouri church to Hyrum Smith and Thomas Marsh for "further particulars." The two men hand-delivered the letter when they arrived at Far West in October 1837, a few weeks before Joseph Smith's arrival.[35] Hyrum also carried with him a power of attorney, dated September 5, 1837, which authorized him to make land transactions on behalf of Joseph and Emma Smith, as well as one for Oliver and Elizabeth Ann Cowdery drafted the same day.[36]

---

31. Smith, Letter, Sep. 4, 1837, Smith, Journal, Mar.–Sep. 1838, 22 (*JSP*, J1:244; D5:430).

32. Historian's Office, Brigham Young History Drafts, 14; Woodruff, Journal, Feb. 19, 1837 (Vogel, *The Wilford Woodruff Journals*, 1:107–108). In late May 1837 Abel Lamb made a formal complaint against David Whitmer for associating with the dissenters. Abel Lamb and Others, Letter to Joseph Smith and Others, ca. May 28, 1837, Minute Book 1, 226–27 (*JSP*, D5:393).

33. Rich was among the dissenters who signed Warren Parrish's February 5, 1838, letter to the editor of the *Painesville Republican*, see Feb. 15, 1838, [3].

34. Smith, Letter, Sep. 4, 1837, Smith, Journal, Mar.–Sep. 1838, 22 (*JSP*, J1:244; D5:431). Cf. Galatians 1:8.

35. Thomas B. Marsh, Letter to Wilford Woodruff, ca. June 18, 1837; *Elders' Journal* (Far West, MO), July 1838, 36; see also Marsh, History and Autobiography, [2].

36. Joseph Smith and Emma Smith, Power of Attorney to Hyrum Smith, Sep. 5, 1837, JS Collection (*JSP*, D5:433–37); Oliver Cowdery and Elizabeth Ann Cowdery, Power of Attorney to Hyrum Smith, Sep. 5, 1837.

Reconciliation

On Sunday, September 10, a meeting in the temple voted to accept the rules and regulations of the temple previously passed by the quorums on January 18, 1836. The high council minutes of the September 3 conference were read and the three apostles—Luke Johnson, Lyman Johnson, and John F. Boynton—who had been rejected at the previous meeting confessed and by the vote of the church were received into fellowship and retained their callings. John P. Greene, who was not present at the previous meeting but had been objected to along with others in the high council, was called on to address those objections. He confessed that he had been wrong and was received into fellowship and allowed to retain his office.

The purging and reorganizing of the hierarchy the previous Sunday evidently created much anger towards Smith and Rigdon. According to the minutes, Rigdon responded by "reproving some for the conjectures they had respecting Pres. Smith and himself, conniving together to remove certain individuals from office &c., or at least to use their influence so to do. This he informed them was a mistake, for he assured them that not one word had passed between them on the subject, neither had he a premeditated thought upon the subject. Pres Smith then corrected some mistakes of certain individuals which had been circulated by them concerning what he had said on the last Sabbath."[37]

Nevertheless, the move to reorganize and discipline the dissenters had brought about reconciliation among the church's leadership. Smith had already reconciled with Parley and Orson Pratt and Orson Hyde, who were serving a missions in the East and England. During the week before the September 10 meeting, Boynton and Lyman Johnson also reconciled with Smith. According to Vilate Kimball, she had been visited by Thomas Marsh, who said he and Smith "had met in counsel the evening before with Elders Boynton and Jonson that they had all become reconciled to each other, he said John [Boynton] and Limon Jonson were humble, ... and said they would come forward next Sunday and make their confession to the church." Luke Johnson had not yet returned to Kirtland from Missouri, but Marsh told Vilate that "he thought there would be no difficulty with him when he come[s] to find the rest all united." This was soon verified.

On September 11, 1837, Vilate described the events of the previous day:

---

37. Minutes, Sep. 10, 1837, Minute Book 1, 241 (Collier and Harwell, *Kirtland Council Minute Book,* 188–89).

"My Dear Heber, could you have ben in the house of the Lord here yesterday, surely your heart would have leapt for joy, as did mine. Br Luke got home last thursday, and let me tell you he was the first one to come forward yesterday and make a humble confession to the church; he was received into their full fellowship by a unanimus vote. he was succeeded by Br Limon and John, who also gave ample satisfaction, and was joyfully received by the unanimus vote of the church." Vilate reported that even "Elder Parrish (who had ben the most rebelous) is again restored to the fellowship of the Church, I never saw him so humble as he is now."[38] Finding themselves without status and community, some quickly acquiesced. These events may have been satisfying for Smith, but victory would prove to be temporary.

On September 12 Smith brought a complaint against Painesville constable Abram Ritch before Oliver Cowdery, a justice of the peace in Kirtland Township, accusing Ritch of "unlawful oppression by color of office." Painesville attorney William Perkins charged Smith $6.00 for "fees State vs Ritch on [his] complaint before Cowdery," dated September 15, 1837.[39] This charge may have had something to do with his recent arrests while passing through Painesville. Some of the arrests were legitimate, but apparently Smith thought at least one conducted by Ritch was an abuse of his authority. In response, Cowdery issued a warrant for the arrest of Ritch, who was brought before him two days later. Ten men were subpoenaed to testify, including associate judge of the Geauga County Court of Common Pleas Daniel Kerr and Painesville postmaster Benjamin Adams, neither of whom appeared. Among those who did testify at the preliminary hearing were Painesville merchants George Pease and Horace Kingsbury, the latter of whom was apparently a justice of the peace and lapsed Mormon, and hotel operator Orrin Blossom. Due to lack of evidence, Cowdery released Ritch.[40] Cowdery's judgment in the Ritch case may have further strained his relationship with Smith. A day or two afterward, Cowdery left Kirtland with his family for Missouri.[41]

On Sunday, September 17, a conference was held in the temple at which Bishop Newel Whitney nominated William Marks as the church's financial

---

38. Vilate Kimball, Letter to Heber C. Kimball, ca. Sep. 11, 1837, [2].

39. See William Perkins, Statement of Account for Joseph Smith and Others, ca. Oct. 29, 1838, JS Collection (*JSP*, D6:256).

40. Docket Entry, ca. Sep. 12–14, 1837, State of OH v. Ritch, Kirtland Township, Geauga Co., OH, Justice of the Peace Court, Cowdery, Docket Book, 224.

41. The last entry in Cowdery's docket Book is dated September 15, 1837. Cowdery, Docket Book, June 14–Sep. 15, 1837.

and land agent in Kirtland, apparently in anticipation of a mass migration of the church to Missouri. At the same time, George W. Robinson, Sidney Rigdon's son-in-law, was appointed to replace Cowdery as general church recorder, and the bishopric was assigned to write a memorial to the general church membership.[42]

In the evening, the elders met in the temple. Smith spoke about the importance of gathering the Saints and the duty of the quorums to accomplish it. According to the minutes, it was ascertained that "the places appointed for the gathering of the saints were at this time crowded to overflowing & that it was necessary that there be more Stakes of Zion appointed in order that the poor might have a place to gather to." Accordingly, the conference assigned Smith and Rigdon to organize more stakes, then divided the 109 elders who were present into eight companies to be sent in all directions.[43] Nine days after this meeting, Marcellus Cowdery, Oliver's nephew, informed George A. Smith: "Brother Joseph & Sidney expect to start soon to appoint 11 or 12 new Stakes of Zion" in Missouri. He also reported: "Brother Joseph & Sidney say that the Elders must be out all winter this year, no compulsion you know, but this is the word to the Elders, and great promises to those who go and are faithful."[44] According to Mary Fielding, "Some important things were shown to Bro. Jos[e]ph in vision … relative to the enlargment of our Borders." This had become necessary because of overcrowding both in Kirtland and Far West. She also reported that Rigdon said the Saints "will gather" and that "Earth and hell combined cannot hinder them for gather they will hence the necessaty of planting new stakes."[45]

On September 18 Whitney and his counselors issued a memorial to the Saints abroad. The memorial described the "great affliction" and "heavy burden" of the church at Kirtland in building the temple because "subscriptions failed" and credit was needed, which exposed them to "financial ruin in order that the work of the gathering might not fail." The memorial announced that because of the great numbers of poor, who rely on donations, Smith and Rigdon have been assigned to appoint other stakes of Zion where the poor can get help. Ten months before Smith dictated a revelation making tithing church policy, the bishopric quoted the command in Malachi 3:10 to "bring

---

42. Minutes, Sep. 17, 1837, Minute Book 1, 242 (*JSP*, D5:443; *Elders' Journal*, Nov. 1837, 17).

43. Minutes, 243–45 (*JSP*, D5:445–46).

44. John Smith and Marcellus Cowdery, Letter to George A. Smith, Sep. 26, 1837, [1].

45. Mary Fielding, Letter to Mercy Fielding Thompson and Robert Thompson, Oct. 7, 1837, [2].

ye all the tithes into the storehouse" and explained that the Saints are obligated under the law of God to pay a tithe.[46]

On Sunday, September 24, before Smith and Rigdon's departure, the temple was packed with 1,500 or more people to wish them godspeed. "We had a very affecting time the last Sabbath," Mary Fielding wrote. "Brother Rigdon received directions from the Lord in the morning as to the discourse he should deliver that day before he left us and truly it was marvelous, it was great it was glorious far beyond my power to describe. The tears flowed plentifully from Brother Jos[e]ph['s] eyes during the service." She also reported that Rigdon's address was about "the enlargement and future glory and purity of Zion when she arises and puts on her beautiful garments which must be before long," and that "after showing us what we have to do and what our privileges are and what our future blessedness would be he spoke out with a loud voice from the fullness of his heart, and let all the people say amen and amen. When it seemed as though all the congregation in one simultaneous voice responded with a loud amen it was the opinion of most that they had never heard the like before."[47]

Two days later, on September 26, Smith and Rigdon renegotiated their debts with the New York City firm of Bailey, Keeler & Remsen, which delayed payment for a year.[48] The next day, before their departure to Missouri, Smith and Rigdon drafted a power of attorney for Oliver Granger to become their agent to settle business affairs in Kirtland on their behalf, particularly their nearly $1,800 debt to Jonathan F. Scribner, who owned a hardware store in Buffalo, New York.[49] The wording of the power of attorney implies that Scribner had been paid with worthless Kirtland Safety Society money. Granger was apparently unsuccessful in satisfying the debt since on October 26, 1837, Scribner had a writ of summons issued against Smith, Rigdon, and

---

46. Newel K. Whitney et al., "To the Saints scattered abroad," Sep. 18, 1837, *Messenger and Advocate*, Sep. 1837, 561–64; also printed as a handbill. Crawley, *Descriptive Bibliography*, 1:68–69. On tithing, see D&C 119.

47. Fielding, Letter to Mercy Thompson, Oct. 7, 1837, [2]. Mary's letter is dated October 7, 1837, and "last Sabbath" would have been October 1, but Smith and Rigdon had left Kirtland on September 27, so she must have meant Sunday, September 24.

48. Joseph Smith et al., Promissory Notes to Bailey, Keeler & Remsen, Sep. 26, 1837. The three promissory notes are signed by Smith, Reuben Hedlock, Rigdon, John Gould, and Vinson Knight. The amounts are for $609.18 due Sep. 26, 1838; $609.18 due Mar. 26, 1839; and $609.18 due Sep. 26, 1839.

49. Sidney Rigdon and Joseph Smith, Power of Attorney to Oliver Granger, Kirtland Township, Sep. 27, 1837, JS Collection (*JSP*, D5:457–60); Jonathan F. Scribner, Invoice to Rigdon, Smith & Cowdery, June 16, 1836, JS Office Papers.

Cowdery. However, the case of *Scribner v. Rigdon, Smith & Cowdery* ended in October 1840 when Scribner or his representative failed to appear in court.[50]

Reorganization in Missouri

On September 27, a little more than a year after the appointed time of Zion's redemption and without an army, Smith and Rigdon left Kirtland for Missouri, accompanied by William Smith and Vinson Knight. Their purpose, as Smith would later write, was "visiting the Far West, and also to discover situations suitable for the location of the Saints who are gathering for a refuge and safety, in the day of the wrath of God which is soon to burst upon the head of this generation, according to the testimony of the prophets; who speak expressly concerning the last days."[51] Smith and company traveled southwest along the National Road through central Ohio and Indiana, holding a meeting in Norton, Ohio, and three in Dublin, Indiana, where the Alger family lived. (Fanny had recently married non-Mormon Solomon Custer on November 16, 1836.)[52] On October 12 they arrived at Terre Haute, where they held two meetings and Smith spoke.[53] The party continued west through Huntsville and Carrollton, Missouri, reaching Far West sometime before November 6.

Smith apparently stayed with George W. Harris, who in 1830 had married Lucinda Morgan, widow of famed anti-Masonic martyr William Morgan. Shortly after Smith's arrival, Cowdery paid him a visit at the Harris home, situated along Shoal Creek near Far West, and confronted him over the Alger affair in front of Thomas Marsh and George Harris, both of whom subsequently gave an account of it at Cowdery's trial before the Far West high council in April 1838.

According to Harris, Cowdery "seemed to insinuate that Joseph Smith jr was guilty of adultery," but when Smith asked Cowdery if he had "ever acknowledged to him that he was guilty of such a thing," Cowdery answered, "No." Marsh also testified that he was present and heard the conversation between Cowdery and Smith "last fall" at Harris's house, "when J. Smith asked him [Cowdery] if he [Smith] had ever confessed to him that he was

---

50. Transcript of Proceedings, Oct. 20, 1840, Scribner v. Rigdon, Smith & Cowdery, Geauga Co., OH, Court of Common Pleas, Final Record, vol. X, 530–32.

51. [Joseph Smith], Editorial, *Elders' Journal*, Nov. 1837, 27.

52. [Smith], 27.

53. Sidney Rigdon, Letter to Don Carlos Smith, Oct. 13, 1837, *Elders' Journal*, Oct. 1837, 7. Smith's speaking at Terre Haute is mentioned in Phebe Woodruff, Letter to Wilford Woodruff, Mar. 1, 1838.

guilty of adultery, when after considerable winking &c. he said <u>No</u>. Joseph then asked him if he ever told him that he confessed to any body, when he answered <u>No</u>."[54]

Further corroboration came from David Patten, who testified that he went to Cowdery to verify his accusation "respecting J. Smith's committing adultery with a certain girl, when he turned on his heel and insinuated as though he [Smith] was guilty; he then went on and gave a history of some circumstances respecting the adultery scrape stating that no doubt it was true. Also said that Joseph told him, he had confessed to Emma." Thomas Marsh testified that he was present when Patten "asked Oliver Cowdery if he Joseph Smith jr had confessed to his wife that he was guilty of adultery with a certain girl, when Oliver Cowdery cocked up his eye very knowingly and hesitated to answer the question yet conveyed the idea that it was true."[55]

Smith's denying that he confessed to committing adultery is not the same as denying that he had committed adultery. In pressing Cowdery to admit that he had not confessed, Smith seems to have alluded to the loyalty covenant that he had church leaders enter into on January 16, 1836: "I will now covenant with you before God, that I will not listen to nor credit any derogatory report against any of you, nor condemn you upon any testimony beneath the heavens, ... until I can see you face to face, and know of a surety; and I do place unlimited confidence in your word, for I believe you to be men of truth; and I ask the same of you; when I tell you anything, that you place equal confidence in my word, for I will not tell you, I know anything, which I do not know."[56] Because Smith could argue that his union with Alger was according to divine command and that they were thus married in the eyes of God, he could deny that he had committed adultery.

Prior to his departure from Missouri, Smith attempted to reconcile with Cowdery. According to Cowdery, "just before leaving, he [Smith] wanted to drop every past thing, in which had been a difficulty or difference—he called witnesses to the fact, gave me his hand in their presence, and I might have supposed of an honest man, calculated to say nothing of former matters." However, after returning to Kirtland, Smith began claiming that Cowdery had confessed he lied about him committing adultery. When

---

54. Minutes, Apr. 12, 1838, Minute Book 2, 123 (*JSP*, D6:90–91). Harris and Marsh had previously made affidavits, dated Feb. 15, 1838, concerning Cowdery's denial that Smith had confessed. Thomas B. Marsh, Letter to Joseph Smith, Feb. 15, 1838, in "Minutes of the Proceedings of the Committee of the Whole Church in Zion," *Elders' Journal*, July 1838, 44–46.

55. Minutes, Apr. 12, 1838, Minute Book 2, 123–24 (*JSP*, D6:91).

56. Smith, Journal, Jan. 16, 1836 (*JSP*, J1:159; D5:152–53).

Cowdery learned about this from his brothers in Kirtland, he wrote to Smith on January 21, 1838: "I learn from Kirtland, by the last letters, that you have publickly said, that when you were here I confessed to you that I had willfully lied about you—this compells me to ask you to correct that statement, and give me an explanation—until which you and myself are two."[57] By the time this letter reached Kirtland, Smith was on his way to Missouri. However, it would probably not have changed things since Smith had already begun his campaign to expel Cowdery and other Missouri officials from the church.

Meanwhile, on November 6, Smith attended a meeting of church leaders, who decided to alter the plat of Far West and to make each block containing four acres to be divided into four lots, thus decreasing lot sizes to better accommodate the anticipated influx of Mormons. They also decided to postpone building the temple "until the Lord shall reveal it to be His will to have it commenced."[58]

Later the same day, church leaders met again to continue the discussion of the town plan and the purchase of land. This may have been the occasion Edward Stevenson later described when Smith declared: "Since I have been here I perseive the spirit of selfishness, coveteousness, exists in the hearts of the saints which is not becomeing those who receive the spirit of the gosple, here are those who begin to spread out buying up all the land they are able to do, to the exclusion of the pooer ones, who are not so much blessed with this worlds goods. ... Now I want to tell you, that zion cannot be built up in eny such way. ... I tell you in the name of the God of Israel, if thare is not repentance with this people and a turning from such ungodlyness, covetousness and self will you will be broken up and scattered from this choice land to the four wines [winds] of Heaven."[59]

Discussion likely included the fact that John Whitmer and Phelps had purchased land in their own names without consulting church leaders and had kept the money from the sale of lots for their own benefit instead of turning it over to the bishop, for which they had been investigated and disciplined in April 1837 without the matter being fully resolved.[60] According to the November 7 minutes, "All difficulties were satisfactorily settled except a matter between J. Smith jr. Oliver Cowdery and T. B. Marsh." The council

---

57. Quoted in Oliver Cowdery, Letter to Warren Cowdery, Jan. 21, 1838, in Cowdery, Letterbook, [80]–[81] (*JSP*, D5:505).

58. Minutes, Nov. 6, 1837, Minute Book 2, 80–82 (*JSP*, D5:464–68).

59. Edward Stevenson, Autobiography, 40–41.

60. Minutes, Apr. 3–7, 1837, Minute Book 2, 73 (Cannon and Cook, *Far West Record*, 109).

did not attempt to settle their case at this time, but "referred [the matter] to themselves with the agreement that their settlement of the affair should be sufficient for the Council." The lack of the high council's involvement was perhaps because of Smith's Cowdery's, and Marsh's high ranking.[61]

In describing this meeting in a subsequent editorial, Smith included an item not mentioned in the minutes: "It was voted, that the work of the gathering to that place be continued, and that there is a plenty of provisions in the upper counties for the support of that place, and also the emigration of the Saints; also voted that other Stakes be appointed in the regions round about, therefore a committee was appointed to locate the same; consisting of Oliver Cowdery, David Whitmer, John Corrill, and Lyman Wight; who started on their mission before we left."[62]

The next day, November 7, Smith attended a conference that dealt with various matters of business, including the reorganization of church leadership similar to what had occurred in Kirtland on September 3, 1837.[63] Rigdon began the meeting by reading the minutes of the recent reorganization of the church in Kirtland so that Missouri Mormons might know who had been sustained and who had not.

Next, Smith presented Frederick Williams and Rigdon as his counselors, but Lyman Wight, recently elected as a colonel in the newly organized Caldwell County militia, objected to Williams because of a letter he had sent to Far West, which is no longer extant. Marsh and high councilman James Emmett also objected, but Edward Partridge seconded the nomination, stating that he did not see anything "criminal" in the letter. However, others objected to Williams and he was not sustained. Instead, Hyrum Smith, who had come to Missouri on business, was chosen to replace Williams.[64]

When David Whitmer was presented as president of the church at Far

---

61. Minutes, Nov. 6, 1837, Minute Book 2, 81–82 (*JSP*, D5:467–68).

62. *Elders' Journal*, Nov. 1837, 28 (*JSP*, D5:481). The members of the committee had changed by December 7 with David Patten and Frederick Williams replacing David Whitmer and John Corrill. Minutes, Dec. 7, 1837, Minutes 2, 92 (Cannon and Cook, *Far West Record*, 132).

63. Minutes, Nov. 7, 1837, Minute Book 2, 82–85 (*JSP*, D5:468–72; *Elders' Journal*, Nov. 1837, 29–30).

64. Williams's reputation had suffered from his involvement with the dissenters. In late May 1837, Abel Lamb and others characterized the recent conduct of Williams and other rebellious church leaders in Kirtland as "injurious to the church of God." Abel Lamb et al., Letter to "the Presidency of the Church of the Latter Day Saints," ca. May 28, 1837, Minute Book 1, 226–27 (*JSP*, D5:393). On December 17, 1837, a general assembly at Kirtland discussed Williams's standing in the church, but nothing was done to "reinstate Frederick G. Williams in the First Presidency." George W. Robinson, Letter to Thomas B. Marsh, Jan. 10, 1838; see also Williams, *The Life of Dr. Frederick G. Williams*, 528–31.

West, Marsh, who had previously written that the "church has had much sorrow ... on account of the unfaithfulness" of Whitmer and others,[65] objected, but after some discussion and Smith's support, he was sustained. Marsh also objected to John Whitmer and Phelps as counselors in the Missouri presidency, reading a complaint against them concerning their use of church funds to purchase lands in their own names, but after their confessions, both were sustained. Likewise, after some objections were overcome, the Missouri high council was also sustained, followed by the members of the Quorum of Twelve, including John Boynton, and Luke and Lyman Johnson, who had been rejected at the September 3 meeting but later confessed, as also Bishop Partridge and his counselors, Isaac Morley as patriarch, and John Corrill as "keeper of the Lord's Storehouse."

Apparently, Cowdery, who was clerk of the meeting, and the other assistant presidents were not presented to the conference for sustaining, possibly because Smith wanted to avoid a public confrontation with Cowdery. Another reason, as the editors of the Joseph Smith Papers observe, was that Cowdery, who had been appointed as a co-president next to Smith in authority on December 5, 1834, was being "silently displaced."[66] Writing to his brother Warren the following January, Cowdery, referred to the recent publication of the minutes of the November 7 reorganization meeting and observed: "You will see by the conference minutes from this place that we had a fudge when S[mith]. & R[igdon]. were here. If I am correctly informed a good many are dissatisfied with that way of proceeding."[67] The term *fudge* was slang for "an expression of contempt, applied to absurd or lying talk."[68] By referring to this meeting as "a fudge," Cowdery meant that the meeting was "a mere pretence, excuse, colour, or deception; a fiction without truth or reality."[69] Of this meeting, John Whitmer later wrote: "The situation of the Chirch both here and in Kirtland is in an unpleasant situation in consequence of the reorganization of its authorities, which was not satisfactory to all concerned. And has term[i]nated in the expulsion of some members."[70]

On November 10 the priesthood held a meeting, during which Rigdon

65. Marsh, Letter to Wilford Woodruff, ca. June 18, 1837; *Elders' Journal*, July 1838, 38.

66. *JSP*, J1:228.

67. Oliver Cowdery, Letter to Warren A. Cowdery, Jan. 21, 1838, Cowdery, Letterbook, 82; Minutes, Nov. 7, 1837, *Elders' Journal*, Nov. 1837, 29–30.

68. Rees, *Todd's Johnson's Dictionary of the English Language*, 91. See also discussion of the word "fudge" in *The Spectator*, Dec. 7, 1833, 1235.

69. Barclay, *A Complete and Universal English Dictionary*, under "fudge."

70. Whitmer, History, 85 (*JSP*, H2:94–95).

read the bishopric's September 18 memorial and prospectus of the *Elders' Journal*. The conference accepted Smith's modified plan for Far West. Whereas the original plan by Phelps and John Whitmer of April 1837 was one mile square with eight lots per block, Smith's plan was two miles square with a public square of ten acres in the center. The four main streets were to be eight rods wide and all other streets six rods, arranged to form four-acre blocks containing four buildings each. Partridge was appointed to "appraise the land adjacent to the present town plat."[71]

Shortly after November 12, Smith, Rigdon, accompanied by Hyrum and William Smith, left Far West for Kirtland.[72] However, the company only made it as far as the landing on the Missouri River near Richmond, Ray County, when they were forced to wait thirteen days for the river to rise enough to allow a steamer to pass. Meanwhile, Smith and the others lodged at the Hess home. John W. Hess, about thirteen at the time, remembered: "At that time Joseph was studying Greek and Latin, and when he got tired studying he would go and play with the children in their games about the house, to give himself exercise. Then he would go back to his studies as before. ... He used to take me up on his knee and caress me as he would a little child."[73] About November 25, Smith continued his journey.

"Vexatious Lawsuits"

When Smith arrived at Kirtland on or about Sunday, December 10, he found that Warren Parrish, Martin Harris, John Boynton, Luke Johnson, Joseph Coe, and other dissenters were trying to overthrow him and the church, denouncing its members as "heretics" for calling themselves "The Church of the Latter Day Saints," and were attempting to establish their own "Church of Christ."[74]

In a letter to her husband, Vilate Kimball wrote that during Smith's absence "there was a division took place in the church" in Kirtland and that "quite a large party desented from the church; being dissatisfied with the late reorganization of the church, and with the heads of the church alltogether,

---

71. Minutes, Nov. 10, 1837, Minute Book 2, 86 (*JSP*, D5:472–76; *Elders' Journal*, Nov. 1837, 30–31).

72. Smith was apparently still at Far West on November 12, 1837, when Benjamin Benson wrote an account of his 1795 vision at Smith's request from the previous day. Benjamin Benson, Letter to Joseph Smith, Nov. 12, 1837, JS Letterbook 2, 51 (*JSP*, D5:476–78.)

73. John W. Hess, "Recollections of the Prophet Joseph Smith," *Juvenile Instructor*, May 15, 1892, 302. Hess mistakenly dated Smith's visit to "autumn of 1838."

74. Thomas B. Marsh, Letter to Wilford Woodruff, ca. June 18, 1838; *Elders' Journal*, July 1838, 37, which states that Smith arrived at Kirtland "on, or about the 10th of December." Vilate Kimball wrote that Smith returned on December 10, 1837. Vilate Kimball, Letter to Heber C. Kimball, Jan. 19, 21, and 24, 1838, [1].

and all who uphold them; calling them Hereticks &c. ... They hold meetings every week; the tenor of their worship is to expose the iniquities of this church." Vilate did not deny the accusations of the dissenters but said, "I have every reason to believe that Joseph has humbled himself before the Lord, and repented of his past folly." Concerning the dissenters, she reported: "There is some of them, that I love, and have a great feeling, and pity for them; I know they have ben tryed to the very quick; and what greaves me the most of all is, that many things which they tell, I have no doubt but what are too true. Still I do not think they are justifyable in the course they have taken."[75]

Vilate also noted that "as soon as Presidents Smith and Rigdon got home from the west they were called upon to pay a fine of one thousand dollars each, for puting out Kirtland money. they were striped of every thing; even to food and rament."[76] This situation stemmed from separate judgments against Smith and Rigdon, which were obtained by Samuel D. Rounds, who acted on Grandison Newell's behalf, on October 24, 1837, while they were en route to Missouri.[77] The charges, filed on February 9, 1837, were based on an 1816 Ohio statute that granted private citizens the right to sue the officers of unauthorized banks (despite an 1824 statute that prohibited such lawsuits, a contradiction that was not resolved until 1840).[78] Smith and Rigdon were tried in absentia in the county court at Chardon on October 24 and fined $1,000 each plus court costs, which, according to the statute, was to be divided equally between the plaintiff and the state.

Efforts to collect the debt from Smith and Rigdon began in early November 1837, while they were still absent from Kirtland. Sheriff Abel Kimball made three attempts but obtained little personal property from Smith. He was more successful in confiscating items from Rigdon's home, which he sold at auction.[79] On March 1, 1838, after Rigdon and Smith had fled Kirtland permanently, Newell assigned or sold the judgments to William Marks and Oliver Granger, agents for Smith, for $1,600, which was paid in the

75. Vilate Kimball, Letter to Heber C. Kimball, Jan. 19, 21, and 24, 1838, [1], [3].

76. Kimball, [1].

77. Transcript of the Proceedings, Oct. 24, 1837, Rounds Qui Tam v. Joseph Smith; and Transcript of the Proceedings, Oct. 24, 1837, Rounds Qui Tam v. Sidney Rigdon, Final Record, vol. U, 359–64, Geauga Co., OH, Court of Common Pleas. Painesville attorney William Perkins charged Joseph Smith $25.00 for "trial Rounds Qui Tam against you" and $10.00 for "drawing bill of Exceptions for writ of Error." See William Perkins on behalf of Perkins & Osborn, Statement of Account for Joseph Smith and others, ca. Oct. 29, 1837 (*JSP*, D6:256).

78. See discussion in Walker, "The Kirtland Safety Society and the Fraud of Grandison Newell," 61–66.

79. See Abel Kimball, "Sheriff's Sale," *Painesville Telegraph*, Feb. 22, 1838, 3.

transfer of property.[80] From the proceeds of his auctions, the sheriff handed over to Newell an additional $604.50.[81] In all, Newell collected from his lawsuits against Smith and Rigdon $2,156.82, apparently retaining the 50 percent he owed to the state.[82]

On December 22 Brigham Young left Kirtland early in the morning fearing for his life, "in consequence of the mob, who threatened to take my life because [I] would proclaim publicly and privately that I knew by the power of the Holy Ghost that President Joseph Smith was a Prophet of the most high God, and that he had not transgressed and fallen as apostates declared."[83] During the last week of the year, John Smith, president of the Kirtland high council, called the council together to deal with the dissidents. On the first day of the new year, he wrote a letter to his son George and told him that during the previous week the council had excommunicated twenty-eight dissenters, including Cyrus Smalling, Joseph Coe, Martin Harris, Luke Johnson, John Boynton, and Warren Parrish. He estimated that since the previous spring the church councils had "cut off Between 40 & 50 from the ch[urc]h"—which he called a "mighty pruning."[84]

On January 1, 1838, Jacob Bump, likely one of the dissenters who had been excommunicated, made an oath before justice of the peace Warren A. Cowdery against Smith for the remaining $150 on an unpaid debt. Cowdery, who was also associated with the dissenters, issued a warrant for Smith's arrest, and recently excommunicated Constable Luke Johnson took

---

80. Grandison Newell, Assignment of the Rounds Judgment to Oliver Granger and William Marks, Mar. 1, 1838, Newel K. Whitney Papers. John and Nancy Isham, Deed to Grandison Newell, Mar. 1, 1838, Geauga Co., OH, Deeds, vol. 25, 423–24; and Winslow and Olive Farr, Deed to Grandison Newell, June 22, 1838, Geauga Co., OH, Deeds, vol. 26, 157–58. The first land transfer was for $1,300 and the second for $300.

81. Docket Entry, Costs, Chardon, Geauga Co., OH, ca. Oct. 25, 1837, Rounds qui tam v. Joseph Smith, Geauga Co., OH, Court of Common Pleas, Execution Docket, vol. G, 105.

82. Newell, using his son-in-law Henry Holcomb as a proxy, subsequently sued Smith's estate on behalf of the state, falsely claiming the 1837 judgment had not been satisfied, which enabled him to obtain brief ownership of the Kirtland Temple in 1862 before it was sold to William Perkins, Newell's attorney, who immediately sold it to Russell Huntley. Walker, "The Kirtland Safety Society," 98–140.

83. Historian's Office, Brigham Young History Drafts, 13. See also JS History, vol. B-1, 780 (DHC 2:529), which was probably added under Brigham Young's direction. See Vogel, History of Joseph Smith, 2:507n232. Hepzibah Richards wrote to her brother Willard in January 1838 that Young "left this place the 21 or 22 of December in company with Brother L[evi Richards], Mr. [Daniel S.] Miles and his eldest son." Hepzibah Richards, Letter to Willard Richards, Jan. 18–19, 1838, [1].

84. John Smith and Clarissa Smith, Letter to George A. Smith, Jan. 1, 1838, [1]. Historians have estimated that "between November 1837 and June 1838, possibly two or three hundred Kirtland Saints withdrew from the Church, representing from 10 to 15 percent of the membership there." Backman, The Heavens Resound, 328.

Smith into custody. At the trial, which was held on or soon after January 1, Cowdery rendered a judgment in favor of Bump and subsequently ordered Johnson to seize Smith's property to satisfy the debt.[85]

On January 2 Bump again gave an oath before Warren Cowdery against Joseph and Samuel Smith for collection of another unpaid debt of $43, which was originally owed to Ebenezer Jennings on October 3, 1837, who sold the note to Bump. Cowdery issued another warrant for Johnson to arrest the Smiths, but only Joseph was found and taken into custody. Joseph did not contest the judgment, and Cowdery issued an execution permitting the confiscation of personal property to satisfy the judgment, which, contrary to state statute, was served by Bump, who obtained property valued at $37.76, with an additional $7.28 received in May.[86]

On January 3 Warren Cowdery issued a summons for Smith and three others to appear before him on January 8 concerning an unpaid debt of $23 plus interest, which they as owners of a steam mill owed to Matthew Allen. On the appointed day, none of the defendants appeared, possibly because of the threat of mob violence, and Cowdery issued an order of execution to collect the judgment.[87] On January 24 Johnson stated that he collected only $9.25 of the debt, which led Allen to bring an action against Oliver Granger, who had become the surety for the payment of the debt.[88]

Reflecting on this period in her history, Lucy Smith recalled that some of the dissenters began suing her son Joseph, "and with this pretense they siezed upon every piece of property which they could have least pretext to lay hold upon." During the seizure of property to pay Smith's debts, Smith temporarily lost possession of the mummies and at least some of the Egyptian documents. Lucy remembered that the dissenters were "determined to get possession of some Mum[m]ies and the records which attended them and … accordingly they levied an execution upon them claiming that they belonged to Joseph and he was owing them a debt of 50 dollars."[89] In mid-January Hepzibah Richards wrote that "the mummies and records have been attached. Mummies sold, records missing."[90] She was evidently

85. Docket Entry, ca. Jan. 1, 1838, Bump v. Joseph Smith, in Cowdery, Docket Book, 280.

86. Docket Entry, ca. Jan. 2, 1838, Bump v. Samuel Smith and Joseph Smith, in Cowdery, Docket Book, 282.

87. Docket Entry, ca. Jan. 8, 1838, Allen v. Joseph Smith et al., in Cowdery, Docket Book, 293.

88. See Matthew Allen, Declaration, ca. May 4, 1838, Allen v. O. Granger, in Transcript of Proceedings, Geauga Co., OH, Court of Common Pleas, Final Record, vol. V, 148.

89. Lucy Mack Smith, History, 1844–45, bk. 14, [11] (Anderson, ed., *Lucy's Book*, 613–14).

90. Hepzibah Richards, Letter to Willard Richards, Jan. 18–19, 1838, [2].

unaware that Smith had regained possession of his Egyptian artifacts with the help of a sympathetic constable.

According to Lucy Smith, "By various strategems we kept them [the mummies and records] out of the hands of the rabble who were joined with the appostates in devising every invention to get these things into their possession."[91] The stratagem Lucy spoke about may have had something to do with a January 4, 1838, agreement Joseph made with Nicholas Markell for the return of the mummies and records. Markell agreed to "relinquish ... the box and records which James Markell has Levied in my favor as the property of J. Smith Jr. and my claim on the same."[92] Apparently, the mummies and Egyptian documents were seized by Constable Markell and given to his brother Nicholas to satisfy a debt; the latter Markell then conveyed the items to Smith. James and Nicholas were members of one of the founding families of Kirtland, as was also their brother, John P., who signed as a witness to the transaction. According to Markell family lore, someone related to Joseph Coe had obtained possession of the Egyptian artifacts in December 1837, but because Coe owed Justice Markell some money, the records were seized and handed to Smith.[93]

In the same document, Smith agreed to "conv[e]y the two undivided thirds of records and box Exclusive of the mummies." This seems to recognize that Smith was only a one-third owner of the Egyptian relics, and therefore they could not be auctioned to pay his or Coe's debts. The owner of the remaining third was Simeon Andrews.[94] Smith apparently became a two-thirds owner when Markell transferred the Egyptian artifacts to him, which Smith transferred to an unidentified party, who was probably named in the damaged and missing line of text at the top of the document. However, the file notation on the back of the document reads, possibly in John P. Markell's handwriting: "Articcle of Agremen[t] Between Joseph Smith Jun and Joseph Smith Sen." This seems confirmed by William Huntington's 1855 reminiscence that Joseph Sr. hid in his home during the winter of 1838 before leaving for Missouri, and also that "in my house the mummies and Egyptian records were hid to keep from sworn destruction by apostates."[95]

About this time, Sheriff Abel Kimball seized the contents in the printing

91. Lucy Mack Smith, History, 1844–45, bk. 14, [11] (Anderson, ed., *Lucy's Book*, 614).
92. Joseph Smith, Agreement, Jan. 4, 1838 (*JSP*, D5:489–92).
93. See *JSP*, D5:491n227.
94. Joseph Coe, Letter to Joseph Smith, Jan. 1, 1844, JS Collection.
95. Huntington, "A History of William Huntington," Jan. 1855, 13.

office and auctioned them on January 15.[96] The press was bought by Nathan Milliken, a critic of Smith and the church, who was suspected to have made the purchase on behalf of the dissenters and apostates.[97] Another auction was held at Johnson's Inn in Kirtland on March 5 for goods from Rigdon's home; the proceeds were handed to Grandison Newell.[98]

Kirtland Abandoned

The Kirtland Safety Society had failed for reasons beyond Smith's control, and God's, his critics surmised. He had lost at least $6,000, more money than any investor, and had taken out $4,200 in loans from local banks to save the society.[99] The collapse of the Kirtland economy brought a crush of creditors upon Smith demanding payment. E. D. Howe later remarked: "Many of our citizens thought it advisable to take all the legal means within their reach to counteract the progress of so dangerous an enemy in their midst, and many law suits ensued."[100] Between June 1837 and January 1838, Smith was involved in at least twenty-two lawsuits.[101] Lucy Smith later observed, "The persecution finally became so violent that Joseph regarded it as unsafe to remain any longer in Kirtland and began to make arrangements to move to Missouri."[102]

On January 7, as he was preparing to abandon Kirtland, Smith dashed off a brief letter to Partridge, written partly in the voice of God: "And again thus saith the Lord, let my people be aware of dissensions among them lest the enemy have power over them, Awake my shepherds and warn my people! for behold the wolf cometh to destroy them! receive him not."[103] This was a signal to Missouri leaders to begin making a purge of dissenters similar to what had been done in Kirtland. Smith's letter was read at a general assembly in Far West on February 5, the same day that church members voted to reject the Missouri presidency.[104]

On January 12—shortly before fleeing Kirtland—Smith dictated three short revelations in the presence of Rigdon, Bishop Vinson Knight, and clerk George Robinson. Significantly, the first made it more difficult to try

---

96. "Sheriff Sale," *Painesville Telegraph*, Jan. 5, 1838, [3].

97. See *JSP*, D6:132n623.

98. "Sheriff Sale," *Painesville Telegraph*, Feb. 22, 1838, [3].

99. See *JSP*, D5:xxxii and n87.

100. Howe, *Autobiography and Recollections*, 45.

101. See *JSP*, D5:xxxi.

102. Lucy Mack Smith, History, 1845, 241 (Anderson, ed., *Lucy's Book*, 615).

103. Joseph Smith, Letter and Revelation to Edward Partridge, Jan. 7, 1838, in Edward Partridge Jr., Genealogical Record, 52 (*JSP*, D5:492–94).

104. Minutes, Feb. 5, 1838, Minute Book 2, 96–99 (Cannon and Cook, *Far West Record*, 137–39).

or sustain charges against the First Presidency. The revelation was given in response to "A question asked of the Lord concerning the trying of the first Presidency of the Church of Latter Day Saints for transgression." No doubt Smith worried about what would happen once he was permanently in David Whitmer's and Oliver Cowdery's sphere of influence. A November 1831 revelation had instructed that the president of the high priesthood should be tried by the "common council of the church"—the bishop and his counselors—"assisted by twelve counselors of the High Priesthood," which remained unchanged when it was expanded and revised in the spring of 1835.[105] However, the new revelation stipulated that charges against the First Presidency should be sustained by three unimpeachable witnesses and ratified by a majority of the general membership in a majority of the stakes in Zion, rather than solely by a bishop's court. The revelation declared: "Except a majority is had by the voice of the Church of Zion, and the majority of her stakes, the charges will be considered not sustained." The revelation stated that this change was necessary to thwart "wicked and aspiring men."[106] Such a drastic change made it more difficult to try Smith on the Alger case and for the church in Zion to replace him with Whitmer or Cowdery.

A second revelation placed all stakes of Zion, including Far West, under the control of the First Presidency. In fact, "No stake shall be appointed except by the first presidency and this Presidency be acknowleged by the voice of the same, otherwise it shall not be counted as a stake of Zion."[107] This made it virtually impossible to remove Smith by a vote of the majority of the stakes of Zion, since by definition a stake of Zion must support the First Presidency, which determined what could be considered a stake.

Finally, a third revelation commanded the Presidency to "take their families as soon as it is practicable ... and move on to the west as fast as the way is made plain," and declared that "your labours are finished in this place, for a season, Therefore arise and get yourselves on to a land which I shall show unto you even a land flowing with milk and honey." The revelation commanded a general exodus of the church to Missouri as well: "Let all your faithfull friends arise with their families also and get out of this place and gather themselves together unto Zion and be at peace among yourselves O ye inhabitants of Zion or there shall be no saf[e]ty for you."[108]

---

105. Instruction on Priesthood, Mar. 1–May 4, 1835, D&C, 1835 ed., III:37 [D&C 107:82] (*JSP*, D4:320).

106. Revelation, Jan. 12, 1838-A, [2], Revelations Collection [uncanonized] (*JSP*, D5:494–98).

107. Revelation, Jan. 12, 1838-B, Revelations Collection [uncanonized] (*JSP*, 5:498–99).

108. Revelation, Jan. 12, 1838-C, Revelations Collection [uncanonized] (*JSP*, D5:500–502).

Although Smith had determined in November 1837 to move his family to Far West "as soon as our circumstances will admit," his departure was nevertheless sudden and unexpected.[109] According to Lucy Smith, "One evening before finishing his preparations for the contemplated journey, he sat in council at our houce. After giving them directions as to what he desired them to do, while he was absent from them, and as he was about leaving the room he said 'Well, brethren I do not recollect any thing more; but one thing, brethren, is certain; I shall see you again, let what will happen; for I have a promise of life five years, and they cannot kill me until that time has expired.' That night he was warned by the spirit, to make his escape with his family, as speedily as possible; he therefore arose from his bed, and took his family with barely beds and clothing sufficient for them, and left Kirtland in the dead hour of the night."[110]

Former apostle Luke Johnson later claimed that he, as one of Kirtland's sheriffs, prevented Sheriff Abel Kimball from arresting Smith by arresting the prophet himself: "I learned that Sherif Kimball was about to arrest Joseph Smith, on a charge of illegal banking, and knowing that it would cost him an expensive lawsuit and perhaps end in imprisonment, I went to the French Farm where he then resided, and arrested him on an execution for his person in the absence of Property to pay a judgement of 50$, which I had in my possession at the time, which prevented Kimball from arresting him. Joseph settled the execution and thanked me for my interference, and started that evening for Mo. this was the last time I ever saw the Prophet."[111]

In a letter Smith sent from Far West to the presidency in Kirtland, dated March 29, 1838, he lamented that because of "wicked vexatious Lawsuits for seven years past," his business had suffered so much that "I was not able to leave it, in as good a situation as I had antisipated, but if there are any wrongs, They shall all be noticed so far as the Lord gives me ability & power to do so."[112] Later, in May 1839, Smith assigned Oliver Granger to settle his debts in Kirtland.[113] In reviewing the suits for collection of debts against Smith between

---

109. *Elders' Journal*, Nov. 1837, 28 (*JSP*, D5:482). John Smith wrote on January 1, 1838, that Joseph Smith, Rigdon, and Hyrum Smith "mean to go to the west as soon as they can Settle their affairs here." John Smith and Clarissa Smith, Letter to George A. Smith, Jan. 1, 1838, [2].

110. Lucy Mack Smith, History, 1845, 241–42 (Anderson, ed., *Lucy's Book*, 615–16).

111. Historian's Office, "History of Luke Johnson," 6.

112. Joseph Smith, Letter to First Presidency, Mar. 29, 1838, in Smith, Journal, Mar.–Sep. 1838, 23 (*JSP*, J1:245).

113. Joseph Smith et al., Certificate to Oliver Granger, May 13, 1839, in Smith, Letterbook 2, 45–46 (*JSP*, D6:456–59); Joseph Smith, Letter to Oliver Granger, ca. July 22–28, 1840, in Smith, Letterbook 2, 159–61 (*JSP*, D7:360–66). See also Marks, "List of Demands on J Smith & S. Rigdon," Feb. 1–Apr. 19, 1838, JS Collection.

June 1837 and October 1842, legal historian Gordon Madsen estimated that Smith owed $34,460.94 as well as another $13,290.50 through his connection to the temple committee and a $4,500.00 mortgage on the temple, for a total debt of $52,251.44. Madsen determined that $45,649.12, or 87 percent, of this had been discontinued, settled, or satisfied, leaving an outstanding debt of $6,602.32. Much of the debt was paid after the Saints had abandoned Kirtland, mostly from the transfer and tithing of Kirtland property.[114]

Reflecting on Smith's difficulties in Kirtland, John Corrill, who had been appointed church historian in April 1838, wrote shortly after his own disaffection in 1839: "During their mercantile and banking operations they not only indulged in pride, but also suffered jealousies to arise among them, and several persons dissented from the church, and accused the leaders of the church with bad management, selfishness, seeking for riches, honor, and dominion, tyranising over the people, and striving constantly after power and property." On the other hand, he continued, "the leaders of the church accused the dissenters with dishonesty, want of faith, and righteousness, wicked in their intentions, guilty of crimes, such as stealing, lying, encouraging the making of counterfeit money, &c." This division in the church was exploited by Smith's enemies, who "rejoiced at this" and "assisted the dissenters what they could, until Smith and Rigden finally were obliged to leave Kirtland."[115]

According to Smith's history, Smith and Rigdon left Kirtland on horseback at about 10:00 p.m. on January 12.[116] However, in a letter Smith sent from Far West to the presidency in Kirtland, dated March 29, 1838, he said he arrived at Far West "after ... a journey of two months & one day," and his journal records that he arrived about eight miles from Far West on March 13 and entered the city the following day, which would date his departure to Saturday, January 13.[117] This date seems confirmed by Vilate Kimball, who, in a letter written shortly after Smith's departure, reported that "Presidents Smith and Rigdon fled last Saturday night, as for their lives; they went on horsback and their families followed after in Waggons, taking not much of any thing with them."[118] Smith and Rigdon traveled about sixty miles to New Portage in Norton Township, Ohio, where they waited for the arrival of

---

114. Madsen, "Tabulating the Impact of Litigation on the Kirtland Economy," 237, 240.

115. Corrill, *Brief History*, 27 (*JSP*, H2:160–61).

116. JS History, vol. B-1, 780 (DHC 3:1).

117. Smith, Journal, Mar.–Sep. 1838, 16; Joseph Smith, Letter to Presidency in Kirtland [William Marks, John Smith, and Reynolds Cahoon], OH, Mar. 29, 1838, in Smith, Journal, 23 (*JSP*, J1:237, 245).

118. Vilate Kimball, Letter to Heber C. Kimball, Jan. 19, 21, and 24, 1838, [1].

their families.[119] Meanwhile, Smith and Rigdon wrote to Phelps at Far West for assistance. This letter is not extant, but it was mentioned in the Far West high council minutes for February 24.[120] On the same day, Oliver Cowdery mentioned Smith's letter when writing to his brothers in Kirtland: "They call loudly for help from this place for money & waggons to help them forward." Writing before the council meeting, Cowdery said "what will be the result I am not able to say, but presume messengers will be sent to meet them."[121]

On January 15 the printing office was sold at auction to Nathaniel Milliken, one of the dissenters, to pay a church debt owed to Grandison Newell. Later the same night, the structure burned to the ground.[122] The dissenters suspected the fire had been set by the Mormons, while the Mormons claimed that the dissenters destroyed their own building so they could blame them. In his March 29, 1838, letter, Smith blamed the burning on the "Parrishites" and called them "Aristocrats or Anarchys."[123] However, the Mormons had the most to fear by the dissenters taking control of the press. As Vilate Kimball explained, the anti-Mormons and apostates "were calculating to print a paper here amediately [immediately] and publish the iniquities of this church. Sylvester Smith said he had a Journal of seven years that he wished to publish to the world. thus they made their calculations but they were niped in the bud: for about one oclock the same night, the printing office was discovered all in flames."[124] Less than two weeks after the destruction of the press, Parrish observed that "had it not been sacrificed upon the altar of reckless fanaticism, it would no doubt at this time have been speaking the truth."[125] Decades later, Benjamin F. Johnson said his brother-in-law, Lyman Sherman, set fire to the building.[126]

---

119. JS History, vol. B-1, 780 (DHC 3:2).

120. Minutes, Feb. 24, 1838, Minute Book 2, 100 (Cannon and Cook, *Far West Record*, 124).

121. Oliver Cowdery, Letter to Warren Cowdery and Lyman Cowdery, Feb. 24, 1838, in Cowdery, Letterbook, 87–88.

122. Hepzibah Richards, Letter to Willard Richards, Jan. 18–19, 1838, [1]; Vilate Kimball, Letter to Heber C. Kimball, Jan. 19, 21, and 24, 1838, [2].

123. Joseph Smith, Letter to Presidency in Kirtland, Mar. 29, 1838, in Joseph Smith, Journal, Mar.–Sep. 1838, 24 (*JSP*, J1:246).

124. Vilate Kimball, Letter to Heber C. Kimball, Jan. 19, 21, and 24, 1838, [2].

125. Warren Parrish, Letter to the Editor, Feb. 5, 1838, *Painesville (OH) Republican*, Feb. 15, 1838, [3].

126. Benjamin F. Johnson, "A Life Review," 24. Sherman and others were arraigned before Warren Cowdery on January 17–19, 1838, on the charge of arson but were acquitted for lack of evidence. Cowdery, Docket Book, 342. LDS historian Milton V. Backman Jr. has maintained that the Kirtland dissenters burned the print shop. Backman, "Flight from Kirtland," 149–50; Backman, *The Heavens Resound*, 349–50. Yet he never explained why the dissenters would burn their own property and thwart their publishing plans.

Vilate Kimball called the burning of the press a "singular providence," which "razed the indignation of this decenting party to a very high pich." In a letter to her husband Heber in England, she wrote a few days after the event: "Our Vilage was a scene of confusion; men runing to and fro, conculting [calculating] what mesures to take. ... There was a meting held in the Lords house the same evening."[127] Both Kimball and Hepzibah Richards reported that the purpose of the meeting was to organize night patrols. According to Richards, "Tuesday eve a meeting was held and a patrol consisting of 21 men, 3 for each night in the week, [was] chosen to guard the city to prevent further destruction by fire. A part of these men are members of the church—a part dissenters. We feel that we are in jeopardy every hour; though we possess a good degree of confidence that we shall be preserved and guided to a place of safety."[128]

John Smith wrote to his son George A. concerning "the state of affairs and of the church in Kirtland, for it is ... troublous times among us as a Church." He alluded to the bank's failure as the main cause of problems. "The Scarcity of money causes Disappointments which perplexes the people." He wrote that the dissenters were "striving to Distroy" the church "with a great Deal more Zeal than they ever had to build [it] up," and that their "greatest enmity is against their best friends and they cause law Suits by Scores by joining the enemy ... and we are at this [time] in rather Straitened [strained] circumstances."[129]

On January 18 Don Carlos Smith added a brief missive to John Smith's letter in which he described the dissenters' claims: "Those that have descented Still profess to have a belief in the book of Mormon, bible, and doctrine, and Covenants but they pretend the church has gone astray and left the foundation and they count them (the church) as heretics, the prophet also has transgressed, (according [to] their idea of things) and finally after summing the whole matter up he was a liar from the beginning, and yet (Say they) the book of Mormon is true, the revelations that come throw [through] him, are from god, &c. and many other things."[130]

On January 18–19 Hepzibah Richards wrote to her brother Willard in Bedford, England, describing recent events in the Kirtland area: "You had an

---

127. Vilate Kimball, Letter to Heber C. Kimball, Jan. 19, 21, and 24, 1838, [2].
128. Hepzibah Richards, Letter to Willard Richards, Jan. 18–19, 1838, [1].
129. John and Clarissa Smith, Letter to George A. Smith, Jan. 15 and 17, 1838, 1.
130. Don Carlos Smith, Letter, Jan. 18, 1838, 1–2, included in John Smith and Clarissa Smith, Letter to George A. Smith, Jan. 15 and 17, 1838.

opportunity to learn something of the spirit which was beginning to prevail here last spring. That spirit has continued to increase; or if at anytime it has appeared to be quelled it now appears that it was only preparing to operate with greater virulence, until it is generally believed that this place [Kirtland] will soon be trodden down by the enemies of that gospel which you preach. For some days past the aspect of things has been rapidly changing, and to the view of all appears to be gathering blackness."[131]

On January 21 Vilate Kimball reported that on the previous day Constable Luke Johnson had arrested Joseph Smith Sr., who was subject to a $500 fine for performing a marriage without a proper license. According to Kimball, "Brother Hiram told him if he did not let his Father go, he would have him up for the same crime." Apparently, former apostle Johnson had performed marriages as well. Hence, Kimball continued, "Luke was very glad to let him go; so he shoved the window and Father Smith made his escape." Vilate also reported: "Father Smith is now on his way to Far West in company with Carloss; they were obliged to flee and leave their families to follow after (if) they can."[132] In a January 22 letter Hepzibah Richards wrote that "the voice to this people, or to the honest in heart, is, 'Get ye out of this place'—and multitudes are preparing to flee. Some are going almost without any preparation."[133] On March 8 Lewis Robbins wrote to Wilford Woodruff in Maine informing him of troubles in Kirtland and that "Joseph & Sidney had gone to the far west with their family & the faithful are to follow them for Kirtland will be scorged. often have I herd Joseph Prophecy of these things for a year past."[134]

Meanwhile, on January 16, Smith and Rigdon left New Portage in covered wagons with their families for Far West.[135] In the ensuing days, the company took a familiar route, passing through Dayton and Eaton, Ohio, and arriving at Dublin, Indiana, where they would stay nine days. The lengthy stay may have caused Emma some uneasiness since it was the residence of the Alger family. Fanny, whom Emma had expelled from her home in the middle of the night, was now twenty and a married woman but not yet a mother.[136]

131. Hepzibah Richards, Letter to Willard Richards, Jan. 18–19, 1838, [1].

132. Vilate Kimball, Letter to Heber C. Kimball, Jan. 19, 21, and 24, 1838, [2].

133. Hepzibah Richards, Letter to Willard Richards, Jan. 22, 1838, in Historical Department, Journal History of the Church, Jan. 22, 1838.

134. Woodruff, Journal, Mar. 8, 1838 (Vogel, *The Wilford Woodruff Journals*, 1:175).

135. JS History, vol. B-1, 780 (DHC 3:2). A note among Joseph Smith's history papers dates Smith and Rigdon's departure to January 17, 1838. "Incidents of Joseph Smith's Journal," [3].

136. Fanny and Solomon Custer were the parents of six, possibly nine, children and lived in Dublin, Indiana, their entire married lives. *Richmond (IN) Telegram*, Apr. 2, 1885; Samuel Alger/

According to an addendum in Smith's history, probably supplied by Brigham Young in 1853 or 1854, when Smith and company "arrived in Dublin ... we found Bros Brigham Young Levi Richards and Daniel S. Miles, with others." Being short of funds, Smith proposed chopping wood for money, but Young advised Smith to rest and put his trust in the Lord. Within days, a "brother Tomlinson sold his farm ... and readily delivered to me [Smith] three hundred dollars which supplied our wants."[137]

About January 30 Smith and Rigdon left Dublin with Young, Richards, Miles, and about sixty others traveling different routes to Terre Haute, Indiana, arriving about February 10.[138] After resting briefly, they separated again and continued their journey, reaching Paris, Illinois, about February 11. Another note in Smith's history, which Young probably also supplied, states that "when we came to Paris Illinois, the news had reached there ahead of us that I [Smith] was on the way there, and the Excitement was so great that it was difficult for us to stay all night, and in the morning tho' the weather was Extreemly cold and strong I persued my journey leaving the most of the company because the families could not stand it to travil."[139] However, in a letter from Far West the following month, Smith remarked: "We left Pres. Rigdon 30 miles this side of Parris Illinois in consequence of the sickness of Br. G. W. Robinsons wife."[140]

About February 24 Brigham Young and his company rejoined Smith's company about four miles west of Jacksonville, Illinois, where there was a branch of the church. "After stopping a few days and resting," according to Young, "we proceeded to Quincy."[141] About March 2 Smith's group crossed the Mississippi River at Quincy, Illinois, and entered Missouri without Rigdon's group.[142] According to Young, "When we came to Quincy they said we

Clarissa Hancock Alger Family Group Sheet, FHL; Wayne Co., Indiana, census records 1850, 1860, 1880 (Dublin City); Compton, *In Sacred Loneliness*, 39–41, 641, 647; *Mormon Polygamy*, 227n14.

137. JS History, vol. B-1, Addenda, 10, Note 1; and vol. B-2, Addenda, 800, Note 1 (DHC 3:2); Vogel, *History of Joseph Smith*, 3:4, and n19. This story is also told in Historian's Office, Brigham Young History Drafts, 15–16; and "Incidents of Joseph Smith's Journal," [1].

138. JS History, vol. B-1, 780 (DHC 3:3); "Incidents of Joseph Smith's Journal," [3]. I have estimated the dates by dividing the distance between Dublin and Far West (521 miles) by the time it took to reach Far West (forty-two days), an average of 12.4 miles per day.

139. "Incidents of Joseph Smith's Journal," [4].

140. Joseph Smith, Letter to Presidency in Kirtland, Mar. 29, 1838, in Smith, Journal, Mar.–Sep. 1838, 26 (*JSP*, J1:247). See also John Wickliff Rigdon, "Life Story of Sidney Rigdon," 62, which mentions stopping because a wagon wheel came off.

141. Historian's Office, Brigham Young History Drafts, 16.

142. "Incidents of Joseph Smith's Journal," [4]; JS History, vol. B-1, 780 (DHC 3:3); Rigdon, "Life Story of Sidney Rigdon," 62. In his March 22, 1839, letter to land owner Isaac Galland, Smith said: "I have been in this State one year, the 12th, day of this month." Joseph Smith, Letter

could not pass the river the ice was so rotten and the water above it—but the Lord gave us strength and we crossed believing the Lord would deliver us which he did."[143] In his history, Young said Smith's horse, Charlie, was last to cross the river and broke the ice with every step but finally reached the shore.[144]

The company made their way about eighty-nine miles to Huntsville, Missouri, where they were met by John P. Barnard, a blacksmith, who had traveled about a hundred miles with his carriage to bring Smith and his family to his home near Far West.[145] "One day while crossing a large Prairie 6 or 8 miles from any house, we crossed a small stream," Young recalled. "The ground was frozen deep on each side and we sprung one of the axletrees of bro. Barnard's carriage. Bro. Barnard said we could not travel with it any farther. bro. Joseph looked at it, and said 'I can spring that iron axletree back so we can go on our journey'; bro. Barnard replied 'I am a blacksmith and used to work in all kinds of iron, and that axletree is bent so far round, to undertake to straighten it would only break it.' bro. Joseph answered 'I'll try it' he got a pry and we sprung it back to its place, and it did not trouble us any more till we arrived at Far West."[146]

On March 13 Smith and company arrived at Barnard's home at the Lyon Settlement on the Shoal and Log Creeks, about eight miles east of Far West. Smith was greeted by Thomas Marsh, John Corrill, Elias Higbee, and others, who escorted him into the village the next day.[147]

---

to Isaac Galland, Mar. 22, 1839, *Times and Seasons*, Feb. 1840, 53 (*JSP*, 6:382). This is doubtful since he could not travel the 200 miles by wagon to Far West in two days.

143. "Incidents of Joseph Smith's Journal," [2].
144. Historian's Office, Brigham Young History Drafts, 16.
145. Young, 17; Smith, Journal, Mar. 13, 1838 (*JSP*, J1:237).
146. Historian's Office, Brigham Young History Drafts, 17.
147. Smith, Journal, Mar. 13 and 29, 1838 (*JSP*, J1:237, 245); Berrett, *Sacred Places*, 4:335n23.

Survival of Charisma

27

Far West

MARCH–APRIL 1838

The City Far West should be built up spedily, by the gathering of my Saints …
           —*Revelation, Apr. 26, 1838, Joseph Smith, Journal,
           Mar.–Sep. 1838, 34 [D&C 115:17–18]*

While Smith and Rigdon were making their way towards Far West, the dutiful Thomas Marsh continued to purge the Missouri church of dissenters and apostates, similar to what had been done in Kirtland. On January 20, 1838, Marsh held a "social meeting" at his house attended by two apostles and several high counselors to discuss the rebellious behavior of the Missouri presidency—David and John Whitmer and Phelps—and Cowdery, a member of the church's presidency. A committee of three visited them to "enquire into their feelings and determinations."[1]

The four leaders were questioned about their sale of Jackson County lands contrary to a revelation forbidding it.[2] They "declared they had not broken revelation or Law of God in so doing and … declared they would not be controlled by an ecclesiastical power or revelation whatever in their temporal concerns." When asked about the word of wisdom, the Whitmers said they drank tea and coffee, but "they did not consider them to come under the head of hot drinks," and Cowdery said "he had drank tea three times a day this winter on account of his ill health."[3]

On January 30 a group of dissenters, including Frederick Williams, David

---

1. Minutes, Jan. 20, 1838, Minute Book 2, 94–95 (Cannon and Cook, *Far West Record*, 135).

2. In August 1833 Smith had ordered: "It is the will of the Lord … that not one foot of land perchased should be given to the enemies." Smith, Letter to W. W. Phelps and Others, Aug. 18, 1833, JS Collection (*JSP*, D3:268); see also Joseph Smith, Letter to Edward Partridge and Others, Dec. 10, 1833, in JS Letterbook 1, 73 (*JSP*, D3:379).

3. Minutes, Jan. 26, 1838, Minute Book 2, 95 (Cannon and Cook, *Far West Record*, 136).

Whitmer, Phelps, John Whitmer, Jacob Whitmer, and Lyman Johnson, met at Cowdery's home to discuss "the manner in which some of the Authorities … are still endeavoring to unite ecclesiastical with civil authority and force men under a pretense of incurring the displeasure of heaven to use their earthly substance contrary to their own interest and privilege; and also how said authorities are endeavoring to make it a rule of faith for said church to uphold a certain man or men right or wrong." Cowdery, David Whitmer, and Williams were appointed to draft resolutions, and Phelps, John Whitmer, and Johnson were assigned to find a place to settle where they "may live in peace."[4]

On February 4 Cowdery wrote his brothers Warren and Lyman in Kirtland, conveying news about disciplinary actions being taken against him and the Missouri presidency. "The radical principles taught when Messrs. Smith & Rigdon were here have given loose to the enthusiastick, and their seems to be a disposition prevalent to carry forward those damning doctrines to the subversion of the liberties of the whole church." Explaining the grounds for such discipline, Cowdery wrote: "Messrs. W. W. Phelps, J. Whitmer and myself had a partial claim to a few lots in Independence, Mo., sold some time since on some of the Jackson suits costs. We quit claimed our interest in and to the same for a small sum (and glad to get that) which has caused considerable stir." County records verify that Cowdery, Phelps, and John Whitmer sold their interest in four Jackson County lots on January 11, 1838.[5] "Not long since," Cowdery continued, "Messrs. D. & J. Whitmer, W. W. Phelps and myself were waited upon by (as they said) a committee of the High council who said the church was dissatisfied with our conduct &c. in selling those lots and not keeping the word of wisdom, and also, in not teaching the church to fulfil the consecration law. I told them that if I had property; while I live and was sane, I would not be dictated, influenced or controlled by any man or set of men by no tribunal of ecclesiastical pretences whatever." He lashed out at his former colleagues: "My soul is sick of such scrambling for power and self aggrandizement by a pack of fellows more ignorant than Balaam's ass. After I came to this country to enjoy peace, if I cannot, I shall go where I can. … Our hearts are encouraged, for we believe in God's holy word—we believe in enjoying equal rights and equal privileges

---

4. Minutes, Jan. 30, 1838, as transcribed in Oliver Cowdery, Letter to Warren A. Cowdery and Lyman Cowdery, Feb. 4, 1838, Cowdery, Letterbook, 85.

5. Jackson Co., MO, Deed Records, Jan. 11, 1833, vol. F, 54–56.

and we believe it to be our duty to separate ourselves from all who are disposed to fulminate pretended revelation and uphold corruption by lying."[6]

Trial of the Missouri Presidency

The next day, February 5, a general assembly convened at Far West to try the Missouri presidency. The meeting was presided over by Apostle Marsh, who read the September 4, 1837, revelation given at Kirtland that reprimanded John Whitmer and Phelps for selling land in Far West for their own profit and warned them to repent and humble themselves lest they be "removed out of their places."[7] Marsh also read a passage from the July 1834 "Appeal" to the citizens of Jackson County that was signed by twelve leaders in the Missouri church, including Whitmer and Phelps, which stated: "And to sell our lands would amount to a denial of our faith, as that is the place where the Zion of God shall stand, according to our faith and belief in the revelations of God."[8]

George M. Hinkle, one of the three members of the high council who interviewed the presidency, read the charges, discussed their responses, and spoke in an "energetic manner" against them. Bishop Partridge thought the trial was hasty and should be held by a bishop's court, but nevertheless read Smith's January 7 letter warning about the wolf among the sheep and instructing them to not receive the dissenters.[9] Lyman Wight said that in selling their lands in Jackson County, Phelps and Whitmer had "set an example which all Saints were liable to follow" and that "it was a hellish principle, and that they had flatly denied the faith in so doing."[10]

Others objected that the trial was illegal and that the matter should be handled by a bishop's court. In his letter to his brothers of the previous day, Cowdery reported that the Missouri presidency refused to attend the trial, stating that they will not "answer to a tribunal which is no tribunal," insisting: "If we have transgressed the law of God, try us by the law and according to the law."[11] They evidently were unaware that the procedure for trying the presidency had changed, or perhaps interpreted it as referring only to the First Presidency. John Murdock responded that the proceedings were

---

6. Oliver Cowdery, Letter to Warren Cowdery and Lyman Cowdery, Feb. 4, 1838, in Cowdery, Letterbook, 83–84.

7. Revelation, Sep. 4, 1837, Smith, Journal, Mar.–Sep. 1838, 23 (*JSP*, J1:245; D5:433).

8. "An Appeal," *The Evening and the Morning Star* (Kirtland, OH), Aug. 1834, 183.

9. Revelation, Jan. 7, 1838, Revelations Collection [uncanonized] (*JSP*, D5:492–94).

10. Minutes, Feb. 5–9, 1838, Minute Book 2, 98 (Cannon and Cook, *Far West Record*, 138).

11. Oliver Cowdery, Letter to Warren Cowdery and Lyman Cowdery, Feb. 4, 1838, in Cowdery, Letterbook, 84.

"perfectly legal, according to the instructions of President Joseph Smith jr." Marsh likewise said "the meeting was according to the direction of Brother Joseph, he therefore considered it legal." Moses Martin spoke "with great energy … in favor of the legality of the meeting and against the conduct of the Presidency of Zion, alleging that the present corruptions of the church here, were owing to the wickedness and mismanagement of her leaders."[12]

Marsh called for a vote and it was nearly "unanimous" in the negative except eight or ten, who "wished them to continue in office a little longer, or until Joseph Smith, Jun., arrived."[13] As per instructions in the January 12 revelation about the trial of the church presidency, which stipulated that each of the stakes be consulted in the decision, the trial was repeated with unanimous negative results at Carter's Settlement on the 6th; Durphy's Settlement on the 7th; Curtis Dwelling-house on the 8th; and Haun's Mill on the 9th.

On February 10 the high council and bishopric decided that "Oliver Cowdery, William W. Phelps, and John Whitmer, stand no longer as Chairman and Clerks to sign and record licenses." It was also decided that "Thomas B. Marsh and David W. Patten, be Presidents, pro tempore; of the Church of Latter-day Saints in Missouri, until Presidents Joseph Smith, Junior, and Sidney Rigdon, arrive in the land of Zion."[14] Historian Lyndon W. Cook wrote that Marsh's "motives appear to not have been pure," that he was "jealous to win greater recognition and influence," and that he "indulged in excessive behavior."[15] Nevertheless, he was acting as Smith's surrogate.

Five days later Marsh, not knowing that Smith was on his way to Missouri, sent a letter to the prophet which, among other things, informed him of the actions taken against the Missouri presidency. Following a transcription of the minutes of the trial, Marsh observed: "You will see by the above that quite a change has taken place among us of late, and we hope it is for the better; and we rejoice that we have a prospect of having things in a good degree straightened by the time you arrive here." Justifying these actions, he explained: "We saw plainly from the movement of things that the church was about to go to pieces, in consequence of the wickedness of those men. … Had we not taken the above measures, we think that nothing could have prevented a rebellion against the whole High council and bishop, so

---

12. Minutes, Feb. 5–9 1838, Minute Book 2, 97, 99 (Cannon and Cook, *Far West Record*, 137, 139).

13. Minutes, 99 (Cannon and Cook, 139).

14. Minutes, Feb. 10, 1838, Minute Book 2, 99 (Cannon and Cook, *Far West Record*, 141).

15. Cook, "'I Have Sinned Against Heaven,'" 394.

great was the disaffection against the presidents, that the people began to be jealous, that the whole authorities were inclined to uphold these men in wickedness, and in a little time the church, undoubtedly, would have gone, every man to his own way, like sheep without a shepherd."[16]

On February 24 the high council and bishopric met in the new school house at Far West to discuss, among other matters, Smith's request, via a letter from New Portage, Ohio, to Phelps, to help him move to Far West. The council decided to provide two wagons and $300.[17]

On the same day, Cowdery again wrote to his brothers in Kirtland and predicted that the arrival of Smith and Rigdon will result in disaster, just as their radical ideas had brought destruction to Kirtland: "I know not what will follow their arrival here, but I fear that a blast like that which has fallen on the devoted town of Kirtland will come after time is sufficient to test the impropriety of those plans advocated by some of this church." Cowdery further said of himself and the other former presidents: "We shall eventually go from this place, I have no doubt." He wrote about recent attempts to identify all those who "refuse to confess those disorganizing doctrines lately introduced into the church to be correct," or those who are "not friendly to Joseph," and regarded such actions as foolish and ungodly acts committed by "desperate & hot headed power seeking, ignorant men," which would only "drive the intelligent and independent to Declare their belief to an astonished world." He said that he had written very little about the cause of "divisions" in Kirtland, but promised that "in due time you will hear me speak." Cowdery may be alluding to polygamy or spiritual wifery, which had been mentioned in his 1835 statement on marriage, when he wrote: "I want to say, however, that if those who have taken a stand against those wicked doctrines heretofore taught, they may be instrumental in preserving the church of Christ on earth."[18]

On March 10, in anticipation of the trial of John Whitmer and Phelps, a letter of protest was sent to Marsh, acting president of the Missouri church with David Patten, which declared: "Sir: It is contrary to the principles of the revelations of Jesus Christ, and his gospel, and the laws of the land, to try a person for an offence, by an illegal tribunal, or by men prejudiced against

---

16. Thomas B. Marsh, Letter to Joseph Smith, Feb. 15, 1838, with Minutes, Feb. 5–9 and 10, 1838, in "Minutes of the Proceedings of the Committee of the Whole Church in Zion," *Elders' Journal* (Far West, MO), July 1838, 44–46 (*JSP*, D6:18–26).

17. Minutes, Feb. 24, 1838, Minute Book 2, 100 (Cannon and Cook, *Far West Record*, 142).

18. Oliver Cowdery, Letter to Warren Cowdery and Lyman Cowdery, Feb. 24, 1838, Cowdery, Letterbook, 88–89.

him or by authority that has given an opinion, or decision beforehand or in his absence"—signed "David Whitmer, W. W. Phelps, John Whitmer: Presidents of the Church of Christ in Mo."[19] Cowdery's transcription of the letter identifies the signers as "Presidents of the High C[ouncil] Church of Christ in Missouri." The letter was also attested to by "Oliver Cowdery, Clerk of the High Council of the Church of Christ in Mo.," a position from which he had been released, and it was addressed: "To T. B. Marsh, one of the travelling Councellors," which ignored Marsh's status as president pro tempore. Later the same day, Cowdery wrote to his brothers in Kirtland: "Whether this little document will cause those hotheaded men to consider their ways, I know not. I suppose however they will plead Smith's instructions & justify themselves in trying Presidents of the church before a rabble and call it legal!"[20] The council interpreted this as evidence of their wickedness and contempt for their authority, "by endeavoring to palm themselves upon the Church as her Presidents, after the Church had by a united voice, removed them from their presidential office."[21]

On the same day, various charges were brought against Phelps and Whitmer, but the main one was that in transferring lands that they had purchased in their own names with church funds into the hands of Bishop Partridge, they somehow "bound the Bishop in a heavy Mortgage, to pay them the above $2,000, in two years from the date thereof, a part of which they had already received, and claim the remainder." The $2,000 was their donation to the building of the Far West Temple, which they only pledged but never actually gave, intending to pay with the sale of town plots. When the project was suspended, they withdrew and claimed the bishop owed them the money. The council decided to disfellowship Whitmer and Phelps, who were "given over to the buffetings of Satan, until they learn to blaspheme no more against the Authorities of God, nor fleece the flock of Christ."[22]

Arrival

On March 14, "after a long & tedious journey of two months & one day," Joseph Smith arrived with his family at Far West, accompanied by Brigham

---

19. Minutes, Mar. 10, 1838, Minute Book 2, 105 (Cannon and Cook, *Far West Record*, 146–47).

20. Oliver Cowdery, Letter to Warren Cowdery and Lyman Cowdery, Mar. [10], 1838, Cowdery, Letterbook, 91.

21. Minutes, Mar. 10, 1838, Minute Book 2, 106[a] (Cannon and Cook, *Far West Record*, 147).

22. Minutes, 107 (Cannon and Cook, 148–49); see also Thomas B. Marsh, Letter to Wilford Woodruff, 1838, *Elders' Journal*, July 1838, 37–38.

Young, Levi Richards, and Daniel S. Miles.[23] They were escorted the last eight miles by Marsh, Corrill, Elias Higbee, and others, who had come to the Lyon Settlement the previous day to greet Smith.[24] According to Smith's journal, "As we ware about entering the town Many of the brethren came out to meet us who also withe open armes welcomed us to their bosoms."[25]

When Smith arrived, Far West was buzzing with activity and scattered construction projects. As later described by Partridge, "The town of Far West was laid out one mile square, and the most of the lots sold; and in one year from the time of the first settlement in Caldwell, there were from one hundred to one hundred and fifty dwelling houses erected in that place, six dry good stores in operation, one grocery and several mechanic shops."[26] When Warren Foote visited the town in September 1838, he wrote that "Far West is situated on a high rolling prairie between Shoal creek on the north, and Goose creek on the south, which empties into Shoal creek a short distance east of Far West. The houses are very scattering, and small, being chiefly built of hewed logs."[27]

According to Smith's journal, "We were immediately received under the hospitable roof of George W. Harris who treated us with all kindness possible. here we refreshed ourselves withe much satisfaction."[28] Smith had stayed with Harris and his wife, Lucinda, on his previous visit to Far West, but apparently at some point during Smith's residence in Missouri, according to a list of Smith's plural wives compiled in 1887 by Assistant Church Historian Andrew Jenson, Lucinda became "one of the first women sealed to the Prophet Joseph."[29] The term "sealed" avoided the difficult subject of Smith's polyandrous marriages to women who were already married to other men.[30] According to Sarah Pratt, while she was still married to Orson

---

23. Joseph Smith, Letter to the Presidency in Kirtland, OH, Mar. 29, 1838, Smith, Journal, Mar.–Sep. 1838, 16, 23 (*JSP*, J1:237, 245).

24. Smith, Journal, Mar. 14 and 29, 1838 (*JSP*, J1:237, 245); Berrett, *Sacred Places*, 4:335n23.

25. Smith, Journal, Mar. 14, 1838 (*JSP*, J1:237).

26. Edward Partridge, "A History of the Persecution, of the Church of Jesus Christ, of Latter Day Saints in Missouri," *Times and Seasons*, Mar. 1840, 66 (*JSP*, H2:232).

27. Warren Foote, Journal, Sep. 6, 1838.

28. Smith, Journal, Mar. 14, 1838 (*JSP*, J1:237).

29. Andrew Jenson, "Plural Marriage," *Historical Record: A Monthly Periodical Devoted Exclusively to Historical, Biographical, Chronological and Statistical Matters*, May [July] 1887, 233.

30. By 1843 Smith married at least fourteen women who were already married to other men. See Compton, "A Trajectory of Plurality"; Compton, *In Sacred Loneliness*, 1–23. Brian C. Hales argues—anachronistically, in my opinion—that these were eternity-only marriages that did not include sexual relations. Hales, *Joseph Smith's Polygamy*, 1:443–74. One of Smith's polyandrous wives, Sylvia Sessions Lyon, confessed on her deathbed that her oldest daughter, Josephine, was Smith's daughter. Fisher, Affidavit, Feb. 24, 1915. Recent genetic tests of Josephine's descendants

Pratt in 1841 in Nauvoo, Smith proposed to polygamously marry her, and when she later confided her "grief" to an older neighbor, who happened to be Lucinda Harris, Lucinda laughed and responded, "How foolish you are! I don't see anything so horrible in it. Why, I AM HIS MISTRESS SINCE FOUR YEARS!"[31] This four-year reference seemingly points to the two months when the Smiths lived with the Harrises in Far West as the beginning of the relationship.[32] Jenson found corroboration for Pratt's account from Harriet Cook Young, a plural wife of Brigham Young since 1843, who said she was "positive that she [Lucinda] was married to Joseph in Missouri."[33]

On the day after he arrived at Far West, March 15, Smith met with the high council and bishopric. According to the minutes, "President Joseph Smith jr took the charge of the Council." After resolving some policy issues, he gave participants "a history of the ordination of David Whitmer, which took place in July 1834, to be a leader, or a prophet to this Church, which (ordination) was on conditions that he (J. Smith jr) did not live to God himself."[34] Thus Smith reminded the Missouri leaders that he was in charge of the church and that David Whitmer had no claim on his office until removed by the procedures outlined in the January 12 revelation. Although the Missouri presidency had been dissolved and John Whitmer and Phelps excommunicated, David Whitmer still had some claim to authority that Smith felt a need to address.

Smith was less concerned with Cowdery. Although he was still considered a president of the church, he had been quietly demoted from his co-president status at the September 3 and November 7, 1837, reorganizational meetings

---

have demonstrated that she was, in fact, the biological offspring of Windsor Lyon, Sylvia's legal husband. Perego, "Was Joseph Smith the biological father of Josephine Lyon?" I suspect that Sylvia's mistaken belief about Josephine's paternity shows that she had concurrent sexual relationships with both Smith and Windsor.

31. Wyl, *Mormon Portraits*, 60.

32. Brian C. Hales questions the accuracy of Pratt's account of Harris's statement, arguing that four years "pinpoints the beginning of the alleged affair as the first half of 1837." Hales, *Joseph Smith's Polygamy*, 1:63. Hales has proposed 1842 as a more likely date for Smith's marriage to Lucinda, but more recently has expressed doubt about the marriage altogether. Hales, "Fanny Alger and Joseph Smith's Pre-Nauvoo Reputation," 130; Hales, *Joseph Smith's Polygamy*, 2:284–86. However, with two independent sources for the Missouri date and none for 1842, I see no reason to question it.

33. Lucinda Morgan Harris biographical information, in Andrew Jenson Collection, CHL, quoted in Hales, *Joseph Smith's Polygamy*, 1:61. Hales acknowledges that Cook was "a member of the polygamy inner circle in both Nauvoo and Utah," but questions the reliability of the source based on the silence of Eliza R. Snow, a plural wife of Joseph Smith and, after Smith's death, of Brigham Young.

34. Minutes, Mar. 15, 1838, Minute Book 2, 108 (*JSP*, D6:42). On Smith ordaining Whitmer as his successor, see Minutes, ca. July 7, 1834, Minute Book 2, 44 (*JSP*, D4:93).

in Kirtland. Unlike David Whitmer, Cowdery had few leadership qualities and preferred editing and clerking to church administration. Whitmer later told an interviewer that Cowdery, who was his brother-in-law, "was, in many respects, a peculiar man." Whitmer, on the other hand, was described by the same interviewer as having a "military bearing."[35] Whitmer's leadership qualities were such that Smith ordained him as his successor and appointed him as the president of the Missouri church. These same qualities served Whitmer well during his post-Mormon years, having subsequently become the leader of William McLellin's Church of Christ in 1847 and his own church with the same name in 1875, and was even elected as mayor of Richmond, Missouri, in 1867. Nevertheless, the Missouri leaders were about to deal with both Cowdery and Whitmer.

Two or three days after his arrival, Smith said his brother Samuel and family also arrived.[36] While walking with Samuel and others, Smith created what he called his "Political Motto," which was later committed to paper and signed by Joseph Smith, Thomas Marsh, David Patten, Brigham Young, Samuel Smith George Hinkle, and John Corrill. It begins with several patriotic platitudes:

> The Constitution of our country formed by the Fathers of liberty.
> Peace and good order in society. Love to God and good will to man.
> All good and wholesome Law's; And virtue and truth above all things
> And Aristarchy live forever!!!

By "Aristarchy," Smith meant a government that is administered by good and respectable men. The rest of the motto reads as a complaint against the inhabitants of Kirtland and Jackson County for persecuting the Mormons.

> But Wo to tyrants, Mobs, Aristocracy, Anarchy and Toryism: And all those who invent or seek out unrighteous and vexatious lawsuits under the pretext or color of law or office, either religious or political. Exalt the standard of Democracy! Down with that of Priestcraft, and let all the people say Amen! that the blood of our Fathers may not cry from the ground against us. Sacred is the Memory of that Blood which baught for us our liberty.[37]

Smith railed at his enemies for denying him and his people their religious liberty and betraying the democratic principles fought for in the Revolution.

---

35. P. Wilhelm Poulson, Letter to the Editor, Aug. 13, 1878, *Deseret Evening News*, Aug. 16, 1878 (*EMD*, 5:37).

36. Smith, Journal, Mar.–Sep. 1838, 16 (*JSP*, J1:237).

37. Smith, Journal, ca. Mar. 16–17, 1838 (*JSP*, J1:237–38; D6:44–45).

Using similar political language in his March 29, 1838, letter, Smith blamed the burning of the printing office on Parrish and the Kirtland dissenters, calling them "aristocrats or anarchists."[38] By "Toryism," Smith meant the apostates, who, similar to British sympathizers during the Revolution, aided non-Mormons in their persecutions. The "Wo" was a warning that signaled his growing impatience with persecutions.

In mid-March, Smith dictated inspired answers to five questions about Isaiah 11, which pertained to Zion being redeemed. The puzzling passage begins: "And there shall come forth a rod out of the stem of Jesse, and a Branch shall grow out of his roots: And the spirit of the LORD shall rest upon him, ... and he shall smite the earth with the rod of his mouth, and with the breath of his lips shall he slay the wicked. And righteousness shall be the girdle of his loins, and faithfulness the girdle of his reins" (vv. 1–5). The questions were possibly asked of Smith with the hope for a forceful redemption of Zion, but his answers tended to discourage such hopes.

> "Who is the stem of Jessee. ... It is Christ."
>
> "What is the rod. ... A servant in the hands of Christ who is partly a decendant of Jessee as well as of Ephraim or of the house of Joseph, on whome thare is Laid much power."
>
> "What is the Root of Jessee. ... It is a decendant of Jessee as well as of Joseph unto whom rightly belongs the Priesthood and the kees of the Kingdom for an ensign and for the geathering of my people in the Last day."[39]

Christian commentators have traditionally interpreted the stem (root) of Jesse as the Davidic dynasty and the branch as Jesus, whereas Smith interpreted the stem as Jesus and the rod as a latter-day servant, which he most likely understood as himself.[40] However, Smith was confused by the Hebrew poetic repetition in verse 1; hence, the stem and root refer to the same thing, and the branch and rod that grow out of the stem (trunk) also represent the same thing. Historian of early Mormon doctrine Charles R. Harrell has suggested that Isaiah 11 was "invoked by Joseph Smith to quell Church skeptics who questioned his divine calling."[41] Scott Esplin, a professor of religion at Brigham Young University, explained that Smith's

---

38. Joseph Smith, Letter to the Presidency in Kirtland, OH, Mar. 29, 1838, Smith, Journal, Mar.–Sep. 1838, 24 (*JSP*, J1:246).

39. "Quest. on Scripture," ca. Mar. 16–29, 1838, Smith, Journal, Mar.–Sep. 1838, 17 (*JSP*, J1:238–39; D&C 113).

40. E.g., Henry, *An Exposition of all the Books of the Old and New Testaments*, Isa. 11:1.

41. Harrell, *"This Is My Doctrine,"* 54.

interpretation "reveals that Joseph was not a fallen prophet, as his adversaries in Kirtland proclaimed."[42]

Elias Higbee, a member of the high council, asked two questions about Isaiah chapter 52, perhaps to provoke a plan for redeeming Zion in Jackson County by force.

What is ment by the command in Isiah 52d. Chap 1st. verse which saith Put on thy strength O Zion and what people had I[sa]iah referance to[?]

He had reference to those whome God should call in the last day's who should hold the power of Priesthood to bring again zion and the redemption of Israel. And to put on her strength is to put on the authority of the priesthood which she (zion) has a right to by lineage: Also to return to that power which she had lost

What are we to understand by zions loosing herself from the bands of her neck 2d. verse.

We are to understand that the scattered remnants are exorted to return to the Lord from whence they have fal[l]en which if they do the promise of the Lord is that he will speak to them or give them revelation See 6th. 7th. and 8th. verses The bands of her neck are the curses of God upon her or the remnants of Israel in their scattered condition among the Gentiles.[43]

Following the failure of Zion's Camp, Smith had predicted that the redemption of Zion would occur before September 11, 1836, and, although he made strenuous efforts to gather money to buy out non-Mormons in Jackson County, that date passed without fulfillment. The bank was established, in part, to raise funds for the redemption of Zion; that too failed. Naturally, Smith was reluctant to commit to another plan of redeeming Zion, which might jeopardize the building up of Caldwell County. Smith's answers skirted the issue of retaking Zion by force, and instead speak of Zion as the church or community of believers, power as the priesthood, and returning as repentance.

On March 29 Smith dictated a letter to his brethren in Kirtland in which he reported his arrival at Far West and included a copy of his motto. "I have nothing to do but to attend to my spiritual concerns or the spiritual affairs of the Church," he wrote despite the political substance of his motto.[44] According to John Corrill, "When Smith and Rigden first moved to Far West they

---

42. Esplin, "The Fall of Kirtland," 19.

43. "Questions by Elias Higby," Mar. ca. 16–29, 1838, Smith, Journal, Mar.–Sep. 1838, 18 (*JSP*, J1:238–39; D&C 113).

44. Smith, Letter to the Presidency in Kirtland, OH, Mar. 29, 1838, Smith, Journal, Mar.–Sep. 1838, 24 (*JSP*, J1:246; D6:58–59).

said that they did not intend to meddle with temporal concerns, but attend to their spiritual calling, and they relied upon the donations of the church for their support."[45] This plan became increasingly difficult to follow.

Smith also announced that "the difficulties of the Church had been ajusted before arrival here by a Judicious High Council," and that Phelps and John Whitmer had been excommunicated but that "D[avid] Whitmer remains as yit" to be dealt with. "The saints at this time are in union & peace & love prevails throughout, in a word Heaven smiles upon the saints in Caldwell," he wrote. He complained that his enemies in Kirtland were sending letters to Missouri containing falsehoods, "but have prevailed nothing." Nevertheless, he felt safe in Caldwell County. "We have no uneaseness about the power of our enemies in this place to do us harm."[46] It would not be long until trouble found him.

Near the end of the letter, Smith mentioned the arrival of George Robinson the day before and Rigdon's being detained at Huntsville, Missouri, due to the sickness of his wife. Five days later, Rigdon and his family arrived at Far West.[47]

On April 6 Smith presided over a conference, which was "assembled … to hold the anniversary of the church of Jesus Christ of Latter Day Saints."[48] The next day, Smith presided over a quarterly conference of the general authorities, "the first quarterly conference of the Church of Latter Day Saints Zion." After Smith "addressed the congregation at considerable length, on some important items," followed by Rigdon, who "continued the subject for a length of time," Apostle David Patten spoke about the Twelve, saying among other things that he was "doubtful of William Smith … respecting his faith in the work." He also said he could not recommend Apostles William McLellin, Luke and Lyman Johnson, and John Boynton. Seymour Brunson, a high priest, submitted nine charges against Cowdery, which will be considered at Cowdery's trial the following week.[49]

The conference continued on Sunday, April 8. Smith again presided and spoke about the Kirtland Bank and the word of wisdom, "giving the reason

---

45. Corrill, *Brief History*, 29 (*JSP*, H2:164).

46. Smith, Letter to the Presidency in Kirtland, OH, Mar. 29, 1838, Smith, Journal, Mar.–Sep. 1838, 24–25 (*JSP*, J1:246; D6:58–59).

47. Smith, 25 (*JSP*, J1:247; D6:61); JS History, vol. B-1, 786 (DHC 3:12, 13).

48. Minutes, Apr. 6, 1838, *Elders' Journal*, July 1838, 46–47 (*JSP*, D6:67–70). See also abbreviated minutes in Smith, Journal, Mar.–Sep. 1838, 29 (*JSP*, J1:250).

49. Minutes, Apr. 7–8, 1838, *Elders' Journal*, July 1838, 47 (*JSP*, D6:70–74); Minutes, Apr. 12, 1838, Minute Book 2, 118–19, (*JSP*, D6:85–87).

of its coming forth, saying it should be observed." On the second day of conference, a resolution passed stipulating that a member of the First Presidency should sign all licenses for the church's priesthood officers; prior to Smith's arrival, this had been conducted by David Whitmer, licensing chairman, and Phelps, licensing clerk, and then briefly by Marsh and Patten.[50]

On April 9 Smith and Rigdon sent a stern letter to John Whitmer, who had been called as church historian in 1831, requesting that he turn over his "notes" on the history of the church, promising to give him credit despite his "incompetency as a historian. ... Indeed, sir, we never supposed you capable of writing a history." They announced their intention to start writing a history "this week" that would appear in the *Elders' Journal*, which was revived in July, or possibly published as a pamphlet or book.[51] Whitmer never sent his history to Smith and Rigdon, who started writing what would become the official history of Joseph Smith and the church on April 27, 1838.[52] On the same day, the high council summoned Cowdery, Lyman Johnson, and David Whitmer to appear for trial on April 12 and 13. All three declined to participate.[53]

On April 11 Smith dictated a short revelation for Patten to prepare for a mission "next spring" with other members of the Twelve Apostles.[54] The revelation did not foresee that Patten would be fatally wounded in a conflict with non-Mormons on October 25, 1838, and therefore would not accompany the Twelve to the British Isles in April 1839.

Trial of Oliver Cowdery

On April 12 the bishop and high council met in Partridge's office to consider the charges against Cowdery listed by Seymour Brunson on April 7.[55] The trial was conducted by a "common council of the church," consisting of the bishop and twelve high priests, which was according to official instructions for trying "a president of the high priesthood," but not a member of the First

---

50. Minutes, Apr. 7–8, 1838, *Elders' Journal*, July 1838, 47 (*JSP*, D6:73–74). See also Joseph Smith et al., Resolution, ca. Apr. 8, 1838, License Record Book (*JSP*, D6:75–76).

51. Joseph Smith and Sidney Rigdon, Letter to John Whitmer, Apr. 9, 1838, Smith, Journal, Mar.–Sep. 1838, 28 (*JSP*, J1:249; *JSP*, D6:77–79). On Cowdery's transfer of the press from Kirtland to Far West and sale of it to John Whitmer, who then sold it to the high council in March or April 1838, see Crawley, *A Descriptive Bibliography*, 1:20.

52. In 1844 John Whitmer offered to sell his history, which he titled the "Book of John Whitmer," to the church, but the offer was declined. John Whitmer, Letter to William W. Phelps, Jan. 8, 1844, JS Office Papers; Willard Richards, Letter to John Whitmer, Feb. 23, 1844.

53. Minutes, Apr. 12, 1838, Minute Book 2, 118, 128, 132 (*JSP*, D6:87, 97, 103).

54. Revelation, Apr. 11, 1838, Smith, Journal, Mar.–Sep. 1838, 32 [D&C 114] (*JSP*, J1:257; *JSP*, D6:81–82).

55. Minutes, Apr. 12, 1838, Minute Book 2, 118–26 (*JSP*, D6:83–94).

Presidency.[56] Cowdery had been quietly removed as co-president the previous September without trial, and his trial by a bishop's court indicated his change of status—or rather, his change of status made it easier to try him.

The Missouri leaders were becoming increasingly dismayed with Cowdery, who had demonstrated his contempt for them when he added his signature as a testator to a letter the former presidents wrote to Marsh protesting the trial of Phelps and John Whitmer.[57] Cowdery did not attend his trial but sent a letter to Marsh that responded to some of the charges, asserted his independence in his temporal affairs, and resigned his membership in the church. Historians Donald Q. Cannon and Lyndon W. Cook described it as "an eloquent statement of constitutional law, property rights, and Cowdery's English heritage."[58]

The nine charges against Cowdery were read, as well as Cowdery's letter. Each charge was presented and debated, with some being withdrawn eventually.

First, Cowdery was charged with "stirring up the enemy to persecute the brethren by urging on vexatious Lawsuits and thus distressing the inocent," which was sustained.[59] This had nothing to do with Cowdery's persecuting the innocent, but with his pursuit of a career as a lawyer. Cowdery was not yet a lawyer but was aiding attorneys in advising and preparing paperwork to collect on small debts, including from Smith. The previous month, Cowdery wrote to his brothers in Kirtland: "We have some four or five suits to attend to at the next turn of the Circuit Court ... but we shall have to employ some one to advocate the suits in open Court."[60] Mormons were commanded by revelation to resolve problems before church councils and "not before the world," and they considered doing otherwise a transgression and a violation of fellowship.[61] In 1837 the seventies, for example, voted to "withdraw fellowship from all who are in the habit of promoting litigation among their brethren and still persist in so dooing."[62] Nevertheless, although sustained, the testimony on this charge was mostly speculation and not particularly strong.

56. See Revelation, ca. Mar. 1–May 4, 1835, D&C, 1835 ed., III:33, 37 [D&C 107:74, 82–84] (*JSP*, D4:318–19, 320); Revelation, Jan. 12, 1838-A, [1]–[3], Revelations Collection [uncanonized] (*JSP*, D5:496–98).

57. David Whitmer et al., Letter to Thomas B. Marsh, Mar. 10, 1838, Minutes, Mar. 10, 1838, Minute Book 2, 105 (Cannon and Cook, *Far West Record*, 147).

58. Cannon and Cook, *Far West Record*, 170n7.

59. Minutes, Apr. 12, 1838, Minute Book 2, 122–23 (*JSP*, D6:89–90).

60. Oliver Cowdery, Letter to Warren Cowdery and Lyman Cowdery, Mar. [10], 1838, Cowdery, Letterbook, 9.

61. Revelation, Feb. 23, 1831, "The rules and regulations of the Law," [7], Revelations Collection [D&C 42:89] (*JSP*, D1:267).

62. Record of Seventies, vol. A, 31–32 (July 30, 1837); and 37 (Dec. 5, 1837).

The second charge against Cowdery was "for seeking to destroy the character of President Joseph Smith jr, by falsly insinuating that he was guilty of adultery &c.," which was also sustained.[63] George W. Harris, with whom Smith had lodged during a visit to Far West in October and November 1837, testified concerning a conversation between Cowdery and Smith "last fall" in which Cowdery "seemed to insinuate that Joseph Smith jr was guilty of adultery," but that when Smith asked Cowdery if he had "ever acknowledged to him that he was guilty of such a thing," Cowdery answered, "No." Harris's testimony was corroborated by Marsh, who said he witnessed the confrontation. Marsh and David Patten testified that Cowdery repeated the accusation to them on a separate occasion.[64]

Smith then testified that "Cowdery had been his bosom friend, therefore he intrusted him with many things. He then gave a history respecting the girl business." Unfortunately, clerk Ebenezer Robinson did not record the details of Smith's story, which implied that Cowdery had learned about Alger from both Joseph and Emma. Smith would not have confessed to Cowdery that he had committed adultery because he believed divinely-sanctioned polygamy was not adultery. Emma and Cowdery thought otherwise. Cowdery stated his opinion of Smith and Alger's relationship in his January 21, 1838, letter to his brothers, in which he reported that when Smith visited Far West the previous fall, "A dirty, nasty, filthy scrape of his and Fanny Alger's was talked over in which I strictly declared that I had never deviated from the truth on the matters, and as I supposed was admitted by himself."[65]

The third charge was "for treating the Church with contempt by not attending meetings," which was also sustained given the fact that he was not present for his trial.[66]

The fourth and fifth charges were "for virtually denying the faith by declaring that he would not be governed by any ecclesiastical authority nor Revelation whatever in his temporal affairs," and "for selling his lands in Jackson County contrary to the Revelations."[67] In August 1833 Smith had said, "it is the will of the Lord ... that not one foot of land perchased should

---

63. Minutes, Apr. 12, 1838, Minute Book 2, 118 (*JSP*, D6:86).

64. Minutes, 123–24 (*JSP*, D6:90–91).

65. Oliver Cowdery, Letter to Warren Cowdery, Jan. 21, 1838, Cowdery, Letterbook, [80]–[81] (*JSP*, D5:505). At some point, the word "scrape" was canceled by writing "affair" over it. Noah Webster's 1828 *American Dictionary of the English Language* defines "scrape" as a "low word" meaning "Difficulty; perplexity; distress." The 1838 minutes use the term "adultery scrape." Minutes, Apr. 12, 1838, Minute Book 2, 124 (*JSP*, D6:91).

66. Minutes, Apr. 12, 1838, Minute Book 2, 126 (*JSP*, D6:93).

67. Minutes, 126.

be given to the enemies."[68] Missouri leaders were especially angered when Cowdery, Phelps, and John Whitmer sold their interest in four Jackson County lots on January 11, 1838.[69]

Cowdery considered these charges to be not only overstated but an abuse of ecclesiastical authority. He had previously told the committee: "If I had property: while I live and was sane, I would not be dictated, influenced or controlled by any man or set of men by no tribunal of ecclesiastical pretences whatever."[70] Cowdery's letter to Marsh, which had been read to the council, responded that the charges were a violation of his "Constitutional privileges and inherent rights," and criticized church authorities for attempting to "set up a kind of <u>petty</u> government, controlled and dictated by ecclesiastical influence, in the midst of this National and State Government ... [which] is, in my opinion, a direct attempt to make the secular power subservient to Church dictation—to the correctness of which I cannot in conscience subscribe—I believe that principle never did fail to produce Anarchy & confusion."[71] To Cowdery, Smith was the true anarchist, not the dissenters.

If Cowdery misunderstood Smith's intentions about establishing Zion on the western boundary of the United States, Rigdon apparently had a much better idea, having become privy to Smith's thinking when he attended "secret meetings" shortly after traveling to New York in December 1830 to meet Smith. Recalling this period in 1844, Rigdon denied that the meetings had anything to do "with designs against the government, and with laying plans to get money, &c." Nevertheless, he admitted that "we talked such big things that men could not bear them. ... God had great things to say for the salvation of the world, which, if they had been told to the public, would have brought persecution upon us unto death; so we were obliged to retire to our secret chambers, and commune ourselves with God."[72] While downplaying the perceived threat to civil government, Rigdon at the same time rejected the Jeffersonian doctrine of separation of church and state: "I discover one thing, mankind have labored under one universal mistake about this, viz: Salvation was distinct from government; i.e.; that I can build a church with-

---

68. Joseph Smith, Letter to W. W. Phelps and Others, Aug. 18, 1833, [3], JS Collection (*JSP*, D3:268); see also Joseph Smith, Letter to E. Partridge and Others, Dec. 10, 1833, JS Letterbook 1, 73 (*JSP*, D3:379).

69. Jackson Co., MO, Deed Records, vol. F, 54–56 (Jan. 11, 1833); and *JSP*, J1:253n94.

70. Oliver Cowdery, Letter to Warren Cowdery and Lyman Cowdery, Feb. 4, 1838, Cowdery, Letterbook, 83–84.

71. Minutes, Apr. 12, 1838, Minute Book 2, 126 (*JSP*, D6:93).

72. "Conference Minutes," *Times and Seasons*, May 1, 1844, 523 (*EMD*, 5:314).

out government, and that thing have power to save me. When God sets up a system of salvation, he sets up a system of a government; when I speak of government I mean what I say; I mean a government that shall rule over temporal and spiritual affairs."[73] Rigdon's willingness to entertain such ideas may explain his rapid rise to power over Cowdery.

Given the failure of the bank as well as Smith's unfulfilled prophecy to redeem Zion by September 11, 1836, prosecuting Cowdery on these charges would have been awkward and probably accounts for the apparent lack of discussion and the eventual dismissal of the two charges. Ironically, three months later, on July 3, 1838, Bishop Newel Whitney will sell the central church lots at Independence.[74]

The sixth charge was "for writing and sending an insulting letter to President T[homas] B. Marsh while on the High Council, attending to the duties of his office, as President of the Council and by insulting the whole Council with the contents of said letter."[75] This referred to Cowdery's attestation of the March 10, 1838, letter of Phelps and John and David Whitmer complaining that the council was "an illegal tribunal" and the outcome was predetermined.[76] This charge against Cowdery was also withdrawn.

The seventh charge was "for leaving his calling, in which God had appointed him, by Revelation, for the sake of filthy lucre, and turning to the practice of Law."[77] No doubt Cowdery had seen the writing on the wall and begun making preparations to support his family. At this time, Cowdery was only working with established lawyers trying to collect delinquent debts from the Mormons. On March 10 Cowdery wrote his brothers: "I am pressing my study as fast as health & circumstances will permit; and hope I may feel competent to apply for a license this summer."[78] This charge was sustained by the council.

The eighth charge was "For disgracing the Church by being connected in the 'Bogus' business [counterfeiting], as common report says," which was "sustained satisfactorily by circumstantial evidence."[79] Saying "common report" means they had no evidence, circumstantial or otherwise. This charge

---

73. "Conference Minutes," *Times and Seasons*, May 1, 1844, 524 (*EMD*, 5:315).

74. Jackson Co., MO, Deed Records, vol. F, 52 (July 3, 1838).

75. Minutes, 126.

76. Minutes, Mar. 10, 1838, Minute Book 2, 105 (Cannon and Cook, *Far West Record*, 146–47).

77. Minutes, Apr. 12, 1838, Minute Book 2, 126 (*JSP*, D6:93). See 1 Tim. 3:3, 8; Tit. 1:7, 11; and 1 Pet. 5:2.

78. Oliver Cowdery, Letter to Warren Cowdery and Lyman Cowdery, Mar. [10], 1838, Cowdery, Letterbook, 92.

79. Minutes, Apr. 12, 1838, Minute Book 2, 126 (*JSP*, D6:93).

is ironic given the fact that Smith and Rigdon had been convicted of issuing unauthorized banknotes.[80] They had also fraudulently represented their institution as a bank—which it was not—when they contracted David Cartter, a young attorney in Akron, Ohio, in mid-January 1837 to sell banknotes.[81]

Nevertheless, on this matter, Smith testified that a "Mr Sapham ... came to him and told him that a warrant was about to be issued against Oliver Cowdery for being engaged in making a purchase of Bogus money & dies to make the counterfeit money with. after which himself and President Rigdon went to see him, (Oliver) and talked with him about it, when he denied it after which they told him if he was guilty he had better leave the country; but if he was inocent to stand a trial & he should come out clear; but that night or the next he left the country."[82] Possibly in copying the minutes into the record book, Hosea Stout misread Ebenezer Robinson's "L" for an "S," which led the editors of the Joseph Smith Papers to suggest Smith's informant was Jonathan Lapham, a lawyer and justice of the peace in Cuyahoga County, Ohio, who was an active anti-Mormon.[83] Besides the absence of corroborating records of Cowdery's imminent arrest, it remains unexplained why the informant had gone to Smith, instead of Cowdery himself. Cowdery's leaving town did not imply guilt, as the church court surmised, only that he did not want to get arrested, which, ironically, Smith himself had done on several occasions. Moreover, Smith violated his pledge not to give rumor credit without checking with the person first, which is what he insinuated Cowdery did when he accused him of adultery. While Smith had insisted that he had not confessed such to Cowdery, Cowdery had not confessed to Smith either, leaving Smith to surmise Cowdery's guilt when he left town.

Smith had good reason for wanting Cowdery to leave Kirtland, fearing what he might say about Alger. Cowdery left Kirtland before September 17, 1837, when Rigdon said at a meeting that there was a need for a new recorder "to fill the place of O. Cowdery who had lately removed to the West."[84] This was after Cowdery had received John Whitmer's August 29, 1837, letter discussing his sending the press to Far West in exchange for land. "I have in reserve a lot for you, and W. W. P[helps] has another," Whitmer wrote. "I

---

80. Docket Entry, Costs, Chardon, Geauga Co., OH, ca. Oct. 25, 1837, Rounds qui tam v. Joseph Smith, Geauga Co., OH, Court of Common Pleas, Execution Docket, vol. G, 105.

81. Sidney Rigdon and Others (Including Joseph Smith), Agreement with David Cartter, Jan. 14, 1837, JS Collection (*JSP*, D5:341–43).

82. Minutes, Apr. 12, 1838, Minute Book 2, 125–26 (*JSP*, D6:93).

83. *JSP*, D6:93n462.

84. Minutes, Sep. 17, 1837, Minute Book 1, 242 (*JSP*, D5:443).

have ploughed yours, and will have it finced next Spring. we also have some timbered land for you, which we will let you have for the Press & type, when you come here we will make all things right. ... I hope that you will be in a situation to move to this place this fall—David will no doubt come this fall, we need him here very much."[85] Cowdery was already planning to move to Far West and did not leave suddenly as Smith claimed.

Having no firsthand evidence, Rigdon, in writing a letter warning Cowdery and others to leave Far West in June 1838, asserted that "during the full Career of Oliver Cowdery and David Whitmiers Bogus money business ... several gentlemen were preparing to commence a prosecution against Cowdry[.] He finding it out took with him Lyman E Johnson and fled to Far West with their families."[86] Writing to Phineas Young in Nauvoo in 1846, Cowdery denied having committed "crimes of theft, forgery, &c. Those which all my former associates knew to be false."[87]

Finally, the ninth charge was "for dishonestly Retaining notes after they had been paid and finally for leaving or forsaking the cause of God, and betaking [returning] himself to the beggarly elements of the world and neglecting his high and Holy Calling contrary to his profession," which was sustained.[88] Rigdon stated that in January 1837 he and Smith bought out Cowdery's interest in the print shop and gave him their notes. Later, in the spring, they permitted Cowdery to take one of the presses and some type in exchange for the return of their notes, and that Cowdery had taken the press and the type, "but the notes he did not give up."[89] The June 1838 letter warning Cowdery and other dissenters to leave Caldwell County stated that he "brought notes with him [to Missouri] upon which he had received pay and had promised to destroy them[.] Since here he made an attempt to Sell them to Mr Arthur of Clay County."[90] On this matter, the editors of the Joseph Smith Papers state: "There is no evidence, however, that Cowdery attempted to collect on the notes or sell them to a third party."[91]

---

85. John Whitmer, Letter to Oliver Cowdery and David Whitmer, Aug. 29, 1837. Cowdery arrived at Far West on October 20, 1837. John Whitmer, Day Book, Oct. 20, 1837.

86. Sidney Rigdon, Letter to Oliver Cowdery and Others, ca. June 17, 1838, in Transcript of Proceedings, Nov. 12–29, 1838, State of MO v. Joseph Smith et al. for Treason, [18] (*Document*, 105); hereafter Transcript.

87. Cowdery, Letter to Phineas Young, Mar. 23, 1846.

88. Minutes, Apr. 12, 1838, Minute Book 2, 119, 126 (*JSP*, D6:87, 93).

89. Minutes, 125 (*JSP*, D6:92).

90. Rigdon, Letter to Oliver Cowdery and Others, ca. June 17, 1838, in Transcript, [18] (*Document*, 105).

91. *JSP*, J1:254n97.

The trial record states that Cowdery's case "was not considered a difficult case," and consequently Cowdery was "considered no longer a member of the Church of Jesus Christ of Latter Day Saints."[92] In an 1843 letter to Brigham Young, Cowdery blamed his difficulty with the church on "ambitious and wicked men, envying the harmony existing between myself and the first elders of the Church, and hoping to get into some other men's birthright, by falsehoods, the most foul and wicked, caused all this difficulty from beginning to end. They succeeded in getting myself out of the Church; but since they themselves have gone to perdition."[93]

Trial of Lyman E. Johnson and David Whitmer

On April 13 Smith participated in a meeting of the Missouri church presidency and high council at which Alanson Ripley preferred charges against Lyman Johnson and David Whitmer.[94] Like Cowdery, neither Johnson nor Whitmer attended the trial but instead sent letters of protest and resignation.

Among the charges against Johnson were: "urging on vexatious lawsuits" against church leaders; declaring the high council proceedings were "illegal"; "seeking to injure the character of Joseph Smith jr by reporting that he had a demand against him of one thousand dollars, when it was without foundation in truth"; and "lying violent hands on our Brother Phineas Young."

Smith testified that "Lyman E. Johnson told him he had a thousand dollar note against him (J. Smith) which was not the case, but the note which he pretended to have was one given to Joseph Smith jr while acting as cashier in the Kirtland Bank."[95] Apparently, Johnson claimed he had an unpaid note from Smith for $1,000, while Smith denied the existence of such a note and claimed he had one against Johnson. According to Stephen Burnett, who wrote to Johnson on April 15, 1838, from Kirtland and related a conversation he had with Smith the previous September after Lyman had left Kirtland and moved to Far West, Smith claimed that "you had [a] bagg of money & could pay all of your debts if you would, I asked him if you did not loose [$6,000] by the bank & he said no not a cent." Smith also claimed that Johnson had borrowed "two thousand out of the bank which you never paid but exchanged a large amount with a broker in St Louis at 5 per cent for specie when you and Luke went west last fall and you bought land, hired

---

92. Minutes, Apr. 12, 1838, Minute Book 2, 126 (*JSP*, D6:93).
93. Oliver Cowdery, Letter to Brigham Young and Others, Dec. 25, 1843.
94. Minutes, Apr. 13, 1838, Minute Book 2, 126–33 (*JSP*, D6:94–104).
95. Minutes, 129–30 (*JSP*, D6:99).

a house built &c." According to Smith, Johnson had been loaned $2,000 in Safety Society bills, a "large amount" of which he exchanged for specie at 5 percent of the face value with a speculator in St. Louis, which could not have amounted to more than $400. If such a loan had been made to Johnson while Smith was cashier, it would necessarily date to before July 1837, not the fall. Concerning Smith's claim, the editors of the Joseph Smith Papers remark that there is no record of a large loan to Johnson among the records of the Safety Society, although they are incomplete.[96] Still, it is possible that Johnson was indebted to a bank that was no longer operating, and that Smith was personally indebted to Johnson. Burnett wrote that he believed Smith's claim was "a lie among the rest," but Johnson's reaction is unknown.[97]

The council decided that "Lyman E Johnson be no longer considered a member of the Church of Christ of Latter Day Saints, nor a member of the Quorum of the twelve Apostles of the Lamb and also be given over to the buffetings of Satan untill he learns to blaspheme no more against the authorities of God."[98]

On the same day, Ripley also preferred charges against Whitmer, who had been removed from the Missouri presidency in February. The charges were: "For not observing the word of wisdom, for unchristian-like conduct in neglecting to attend to meetings, in uniting with, and possessing the same spirit with the Dissenters, in writing letters to the Dissenters in Kirtland unfavorable to the cause and to Br Joseph Smith jr. ... For neglecting the duties of his calling. ... For seperating himself from the cause and the Church while he has a name among us. ... For signing himself President of the Church of Christ in an insulting letter to the High Council."[99]

The major reason for taking action against Whitmer was his contempt for the authorities who were responsible for his removal from office, continuing to refer to himself as president of the church in Missouri; the other charges were brought up to strengthen the case against him. Whitmer's breaking the word of wisdom was well known, even before he was stripped of his presidency in February, at which time he was allowed to retain the office of high priest. While Cowdery and Johnson corresponded with dissenters in Ohio, there is no evidence that Whitmer did the same.

Like Cowdery and Johnson, Whitmer also sent a letter, dated April 13,

96. *JSP*, D6:99n489.

97. Stephen Burnett, Letter to Lyman Johnson, Apr. 15, 1838, in JS Letterbook 2, 65.

98. Minutes, Apr. 13, 1838, Minute Book 2, 131 (*JSP*, D6:101).

99. Minutes, 131–32 (*JSP*, D6:101–102).

1838, in which he stated his reasons for not attending the council and why he resigned his membership. He declared the proceedings violated the revelations for trying presidents of the high priesthood, thus rejecting the previous trial which had removed him from office. The council considered Whitmer's letter contemptuous and excommunicated him without discussion. "Considering the stature of David Whitmer in the Church," observed Cannon and Cook, "the failure of the council to investigate the charges and hold a court is remarkable."[100] Smith was now without a rival.

Building Far West

Interestingly, on April 14, Smith presided over the high council to decide an appealed case of Nathan West, who declared publicly that he did not agree with the council's November 7, 1837, decision to withdraw support from shops selling liquor, tea, coffee, and tobacco, and said the word of wisdom did not "concern our Spiritual Salvation." Truman Wait, who had brought the charges against West, testified that West said "he did not consider the word of Wisdom given by Commandment or Constraint," which the revelation itself had declared, and Darwin Chase said he heard West say that "he would not believe the decision of the High Council if it did not coincide with the Book of Covenants." West now said he had changed his mind and supported the council's decision. Smith said that although West had "erred in spirit, therefore, feel to admonish him, but do not find any thing in him worthy of death or bonds."[101]

Brigham Young, who had been appointed pro tempore to the presidency of Zion on April 6, was having difficulty keeping up his church duties in Far West and tending to his sick wife and five children in Mill Creek, a settlement located about three miles from the Mormon capital. On April 17 Smith dictated a short revelation instructing Young to attend to his family until he is called on a mission.[102]

On April 21 Smith attended a meeting of the high council, during which a charge against Lyman Wight was submitted by John Anderson, which was put off until May 24, 1838. It was also resolved that the publication of the *Elders' Journal* continue in Far West under Marsh's editorship. Cowdery, who had purchased the printing press and type from the church in Kirtland, gave

---

100. Cannon and Cook, *Far West Record*, 178n14.

101. Minutes, Apr. 14, 1838, Minute Book 2, 133–35 (*JSP*, D6:104–107).

102. Revelation, Apr. 17, 1838, Smith, Journal, Mar.–Sep. 1838, 32 [uncanonized] (*JSP*, J1:257–58; D6:107–108).

it to John Whitmer in exchange for "timbered land" in Missouri.[103] Whitmer then sold the press and type to Marsh on April 17, 1838.[104] The high council ordered that the press and type be purchased by Bishop Partridge, and that "he be authorized to pay for the same out of the avails of the City lots or donations." The council also authorized Partridge to use church funds to build a schoolhouse and at least one storehouse in which to keep the consecrations to the poor, and "to assist, in making houses on, and fencing the lots in this City which are appropriated to the use of Joseph Smith jr. and Sidney Rigdon, with the avails arising from the town plot."[105]

Later the same day, Smith married Sylvia Sessions and Windsor Lyon. Four years later, twenty-three-year-old Sylvia—the mother of two children—would be polyandrously sealed to Smith in Nauvoo. She believed, incorrectly, that Smith was the biological father of her daughter Josephine, born on February 8, 1844.[106] On the day of her marriage to Windsor, Sylvia's mother, Patty Sessions, wrote in her journal: "Sylvia was married to Windsor P. Lyon, Smith performed the ceremony. David W. Patten was here when Sylvia was married and preached, while here, at Peregrine's. The next day the Prophet was there and a good time it was."[107] A week after performing this marriage, Smith defended Windsor's father, a widower named Aaron, before the high council for attempting to marry Sarah Jackson. Aaron claimed he had received a revelation that her missing husband was dead, which turned out to be false. Smith's scribe, George Robinson, recorded that Aaron Lyon was nearly excommunicated but was saved through the "profound eloquence" of Smith and George Harris.[108]

On April 26 Smith dictated a revelation concerning the building up of

103. John Whitmer, Letter to Oliver Cowdery and David Whitmer, Aug. 29, 1837.

104. Whitmer, Daybook, Apr. 17, 1838, [133].

105. Minutes, Apr. 21, 1838, Minute Book 2, 135–36 (*JSP*, D6:109–111).

106. See note 29 above.

107. [Emmeline Wells], "Patty Sessions," *Women's Exponent* (Salt Lake City), Nov. 1, 1884, 86.

108. Smith, Journal, Apr. 28, 1838 (*JSP*, J1:261–63; D6:124–28); Minutes, Apr. 28, 1838, Minute Book 2, 137–40, 157–59 (*JSP*, D6:119-24). Michael S. Riggs and John E. Thompson believe that "the incident between Aaron Lyon and Sarah Jackson was the likely trigger that stimulated Joseph Smith's receptiveness to consider 'taking another man's wife.'" Riggs and Thompson, "Joseph Smith, Jr., and 'The Notorious Case of Aaron Lyon,'" 118. Brian Hales counters that this interpretation is "purely conjectural" and that none of "the participants believed themselves to be involved polyandrously, nor is there any evidence to suggest they would have accepted a polyandrous relationship." Hales, *Joseph Smith's Polygamy*, 303n2. Riggs and Thompson further suggest that "Smith having been paired with Lucinda's husband George W. Harris to defend Aaron Lyon before the High Council, was a skillfully (and successfully) engineered effort to achieve damage control in the face of a potential public relations debacle" (110). But they do not explain how defending Lyon prevented the disclosure of his polyandrous marriage to Lucinda Harris.

Far West and the construction of a temple. "Let the City Far West, be a holy and consecrated land unto me, and it shall be called most holy for the ground upon which thou standest is holy."[109] Construction of a temple had been begun the previous summer when a cellar measuring 110 feet by 80 feet was dug, but in November Smith instructed that the building of the temple be "postponed until the Lord shall reveal it to be His will to have it commenced."[110] In this revelation, the Lord declared: "Therefore I command you to build an house unto me for the gathering together of my Saints that they may worship me, and let there be a begining of this work; and a foundation and a preparatory work, this following Summer; and let the begining be made on the 4th day of July next; and from that time forth let my people labour diligently to build an house, unto my name, and in one year from this day, let them recommence laying the foundation of my house; thus let them from that time forth laibour diligently untill it shall be finished, from the Corner Stone thereof unto the top thereof, untill there shall not any thing remain that is not finished." Still deeply in debt and the Kirtland Temple heavily mortgaged, Smith and Rigdon were instructed not to incur more debt, meaning the membership was expected to gather quickly to Caldwell County and to sacrifice much.[111]

This revelation signaled a change in Smith's plans for Caldwell County. Previously, the approach had been for temporary settlement while waiting for a return to Jackson County, but now Far West was to become a permanent stake of Zion, from which Mormon settlement was to branch out. The revelation anticipated that "the City Far West should be built up spedily, by the gathering of my Saints, and also that other places should be appointed for stakes in the regions round about as they shall be manifested unto my Servant Joseph from time to time."[112] Smith apparently had no plans to keep the Mormon settlement within the confines of Caldwell County, which conflicted with the understanding and expectations of non-Mormons in neighboring counties.[113]

The revelation is also noteworthy because it renamed the church as "the Church of Jesus Christ of Latter-day Saints," thus combining the

---

109. Revelation, Apr. 26, 1838, Smith, Journal, Mar.–Sep. 1838, 33 [D&C 115:7] (*JSP*, J1:258; D6:115).

110. Minutes, Nov. 6, 1837, Minute Book 2, 80–82 (*JSP*, D5:464–68).

111. Revelation, Apr. 26, 1838, Smith, Journal, Mar.–Sep. 1838, 33–34 [D&C 115:10–17] (*JSP*, J1:260; D6:115–16).

112. Revelation, 34 [D&C 115:17–18] (*JSP*, J1:260; D6:116).

113. LeSueur, "Missouri's Failed Compromise."

two previous names and responding to the criticism of the apostates, who accused the church of forsaking the name of Christ.[114] Marsh wrote to Wilford Woodruff in June 1838 and reported that the dissenters in Kirtland had established their own Church of Christ, calling Smith and other church leaders heretics for changing the name to "Church of the Latter Day Saints." Marsh argued that the dissenters "did not understand, that ... taking upon them the name of Latter day Saints, did not do away" with the name "Church of Christ." Still, in a postscript, Marsh announced that "Since Br. Joseph came to this place, we have been favored with a lengthy revelation in which many important items are shown forth," including that "the Church shall hereafter be called, 'the Church of Jesus Christ, of Latter Day Saints.'"[115]

---

114. Revelation, Apr. 26, 1838, in Smith, Journal, Mar.–Sep. 1838, 33 [D&C 115:3] (*JSP*, J1:258; D6:114).

115. Marsh, Letter to Wilford Woodruff, ca. June 18, 1838, 2, 4 (*JSP*, D6:156, 161); *Elders' Journal*, July 1838, 37–38.

Rooting Out Dissenters

APRIL–JUNE 1838

We have a company of Danites in these times, to put to rights phys-
ically that which is not righ[t], and to clense the Church of verry
great evils which hath hitherto existed among us ...
    —*George W. Robinson, in Joseph Smith, Journal, July 27, 1838*

In Missouri, Smith again found himself in conflict with the dissenters and
the non-Mormon community. Losing patience, he decided to fight back by
expelling dissenters and declaring war on persecutors. This would prove to
be a disastrous mistake and lead to his six-month incarceration with several
other church leaders. Meanwhile, he tried to cast himself as a victim of a
Satan-inspired scheme to destroy him and prevent his establishing the kingdom of God on earth.

Writing History

On April 27 Smith, with assistance from Rigdon and scribe George Robinson, began "writing a history of this Church from the earliest perion
[period] of its existence up to this date."[1] Working nearly every day until
May 4, they covered Smith's life to May 1829, when he and Cowdery baptized one another in the Susquehanna River in Harmony, Pennsylvania. This
Smith-Rigdon history draft is no longer extant, but its content may be deduced from where scribe James Mulholland's 1839 history draft begins. Both
drafts were then used to create what is known as Smith's official history of
the church.[2] Work on the history was derailed when other responsibilities
crowded Smith's schedule, and he was unable to return to the project until
June 1839, after relocating to Commerce (later Nauvoo), Illinois.[3] Smith

---

1. Smith, Journal, Apr. 27, 1838 (*JSP*, J1:260).
2. *JSP*, H1:xxii–xxiii, xxv.
3. Smith, Journal, June 11, 1839 (*JSP*, J1:340).

published his history serially in the *Times and Seasons*, beginning in March 1842, but he probably began dictating his history intending to publish it in the revived *Elders' Journal*, the first Missouri issue of which appeared in July 1838 under Smith's editorship but was discontinued after two issues.

Smith's goal was not simply to relate factual history, but to create sympathy for himself and his church and discredit his critics. Apologetic concerns are clear from the first lines: "Owing to the many reports which have been put in circulation by evil disposed and designing persons ... I have been induced to write this history so as to disabuse the public mind, and put all enquirers after truth into possession of the facts."[4] However, Smith was not opposed to putting his own false reports into circulation, as his handling of his former money-digging activities only a few pages into this history demonstrates. After describing what he reports as an 1820 encounter with deity and an 1823 vision of an angel in relation to the gold plates of the Book of Mormon, Smith denies accounts of his money digging and misrepresents his role in Josiah Stowell's 1825 mining operation in Pennsylvania, making it appear that he was nothing more than a hired hand. "After I went to live with him," he wrote, Stowell "took me among the rest of his hands to dig for the silver mine."[5] From reliable sources, we know that Smith was in fact a treasure seer who claimed to see treasures in the ground with a magical stone, which always seemed to elude the seekers by magically slipping away through the ground to another remote location.[6]

Smith's account of his first vision had a different purpose since it was not widely known and not part of any false stories circulating about him. A careful analysis of the 1838 account of the first vision narrative looks deeper than the surface story and pays attention to how Smith shaped his narrative to create meaning in his present circumstances. The first thing to notice is that Smith's account of his vision of deity occupies only about 100 words, whereas his description of the revival that precedes the vision and the persecution that follows occupies more than 2,000 words. This, together with the fact that both events are historically questionable, should alert us to their rhetorical importance.

According to Smith's 1838 narrative, when he was fourteen years old his community of Palmyra, New York, experienced a religious revival and

---

4. JS History, vol. A-1, 1 (*JSP*, H1:204).

5. JS History, 8 (*JSP*, H1:234).

6. Quinn, *Early Mormonism and the Magic World View*, 30–135; Vogel, *Joseph Smith*, 35–46, 72–75, 79–86.

his mother and three older siblings joined the Presbyterian Church, but he remained undecided about which church was true and which to join. The revival he described actually took place in 1824–25, not in 1820, as he claimed.[7] Neither the revival nor the puzzlement over which church to join appears in his 1832 history. In fact, in that earlier account Smith had already concluded prior to his vision that there was no true church on earth. "By Searching the Scriptures," he wrote in 1832, "I found that mankind did not come unto the Lord but that they had apostatised from the true and liveing faith and there was no society or denomination that built upon the Gospel of Jesus Christ as recorded in the new testament."[8] In 1832 it was the absence of a true church that drove Smith to pray concerning his salvation, but six years later, in 1838, Smith prayed to know "which of all the sects was right, (for at this time it had never entered into my heart that all were wrong)."[9]

In her own history, which she began in 1844, Lucy Smith made it clear that she did not join the Presbyterian Church until after her oldest son, Alvin, had died, which occurred on November 19, 1823. As she recalled, "Shortly after the death of Alvin, a man commenced labouring in the neighbourhood, to effect a union of the different churches, in order that all might be agreed, and thus worship God with one heart and with one mind. This seemed about right to me, and I felt much inclined to join in with them; in fact, most of the family appeared quite disposed to unite with their numbers; but Joseph, from the first, utterly refused even to attend their meetings. ... To gratify me, my husband attended some two or three meetings, but peremptorily refused going any more, either for my gratification, or any other person's."[10] With this division of the family, the issue of which church is true became urgent to the young Joseph.

Moving the revival to precede his 1820 vision reveals that, by 1838, Smith considered the revival to be significant in his development as a prophet as well as something about his rhetorical strategy. By doing so, he transformed a personal manifestation that his sins were forgiven into a reason for his not joining any of the churches. Both his conversion to Jesus in 1820 and the 1824–25 revival were important catalysts in his quest to find religious answers that would ultimately reunite his family. He drew on these experiences to create a narrative that would inspire his followers.

---

7. Walters, "New Light on Mormon Origins from the Palmyra Revival."

8. JS History, 1832, in JS Letterbook 1, 3 (*JSP*, H1:11–12).

9. JS History, vol. A-1, 3 (*JSP*, H1:214).

10. Lucy Mack Smith, *Biographical Sketches*, 90.

In describing the revival, Smith was not simply stating that he was confused about which church to join; he was also criticizing professors of the various denominations as hypocrites. Hence he declared: "Yet when the converts began to file off, some to one party and some to another, it was seen that the seemingly good feelings of both the priests and the converts were more pretended than real; for a scene of great confusion and bad feeling ensued; priest contending against priest, and convert against convert; so that all their good feelings one for another, if they ever had any, were entirely lost in a strife of words and a contest about opinions."[11] It was unnecessary to malign the sincerity of the entire religious world when all he needed was to provide a motivation for his prayer: not knowing which church to join. Since his attack was gratuitous, it was probably fueled by the anger he felt as the leader of a church that in 1838 was being persecuted and criticized by so-called Christians.

Smith's account of his vision, though brief, also contained a message for followers struggling against the powers of darkness in Missouri. According to Smith, when he attempted to pray, he was attacked by "some power" that prevented him from speaking. "Thick darkness gathered around me, and it seemed to me for a time as if I were doomed to sudden destruction," he said. "But, exerting all my powers to call upon God to deliver me out of the power of this enemy which had seized upon me, and at the very moment when I was ready to sink into despair and abandon myself to destruction … I saw a pillar of light exactly over my head, above the brightness of the sun, which descended gradually until it fell upon me. It no sooner appeared than I found myself delivered from the enemy which held me bound."[12] Likewise, Smith's followers could take courage that no matter how hopeless their situation seemed, God would ultimately deliver them from their enemies and Jesus would descend out of heaven and dwell with them a thousand years in their Missouri Zion.

In his 1838 account, Jesus does not appear alone, as in Smith's 1832 account, but with the Father, who says, "This is My Beloved Son. Hear Him!" Young Joseph does not wait to hear what Jesus might say but instead anxiously asks *his* question: "No sooner therefore did I get possession of myself so as to be able to speak, than I asked the personages who stood above me in the light, which of all the sects was right … and which I should join." In fact,

---

11. JS History, vol. A-1, 2 (*JSP*, H1:208).
12. JS History, 3 (*JSP*, H1:212, 214).

the question of which church is true and the answer that "I must join none of them" were anachronisms in the context of 1820 and signals invention.

What better way to discredit non-Mormon critics than to have Jesus declare that "all their creeds were an abomination in His sight," implying that Mormonism was now the only true creed. The "professors" of other creeds "were all corrupt" because "they draw near to me with their lips, but their hearts are far from me; they teach for doctrines the commandments of men: having a form of godliness, but they deny the power thereof"—a quote from Isaiah 29:13 and 2 Timothy 3:5. The former had been referenced in the 1832 account, the latter had not. Nevertheless, the phrase "having a form of godliness, but denying the power thereof" of 2 Timothy 3:5 worked its way into Mormon rhetoric before it showed up in Smith's 1838 first vision narrative and was especially suited for the situation in Missouri.[13] In 1833 the citizens of Jackson County had listed among the reasons for ejecting the Mormons from their community their belief in "wonder working miracles" and their claim "to receive communications and revelations direct from heaven."[14] Many of Smith's followers were with him because they were predisposed to favoring charismatic experience over lifeless religious forms, and they had felt out of place in the mainstream denominations of the day. Smith's account of his first vision tapped into their deepest sympathies.

Many historians have been puzzled by Smith's 1838 description of the persecution that arose against him immediately after his vision. According to Smith, "I soon found, however, that my telling the story had excited a great deal of prejudice against me among professors of religion, and was the cause of great persecution, which continued to increase; and though I was an obscure boy, only between fourteen and fifteen years of age, and my circumstances in life such as to make a boy of no consequence in the world, yet men of high standing would take notice sufficient to excite the public mind against me, and create a bitter persecution; and this was common among all the sects all united to persecute me."[15] This account seems exaggerated, especially since the claim of a vision of deity was hardly unique among Smith's contemporaries.[16] Yet Smith's intended audience could easily identify with this description, for it was certainly true in their present situation.

---

13. *The Evening and the Morning Star* (Independence, MO), Sep. 1832, 31; Apr. 1833, 85; *LDS Messenger and Advocate* (Kirtland, OH), Oct. 1835, 195; May 1836, 308, 309; July 1836, 346.

14. *The Evening and the Morning Star*, Dec. 1833, 114.

15. JS History, vol. A-1, 4 (*JSP*, H1:216).

16. Lambert and Cracroft, "Literary Form and Historical Understanding: Joseph Smith's First Vision," 33.

It is doubtful that the fourteen-year-old Joseph Smith was the object of intense persecution or that he would "attract the attention of the great ones of the most popular sects of the day, and in a manner to create in them a spirit of the most bitter persecution and reviling." However, this described his present circumstances. "While they were persecuting me, reviling me, and speaking all manner of evil against me falsely," Smith continued, "I was led to say in my heart, Why persecute me for telling the truth? I have actually seen a vision, and who am I that I can withstand God, or why does the world think to make me deny what I have actually seen? For I had seen a vision; I knew it, and I knew that God knew it, and I could not deny it, neither dared I do it, at least I knew that by so doing I would offend God, and come under condemnation."[17] Through this narrative, Smith hoped to create resolve in his followers and bind them closer to him by contextualizing their suffering as a continuation of Satan's attempt to destroy him, which was evident from the beginning of his career.

By May 2, 1838, Smith reached the part of his narrative which gave an account of the appearance of an angel on the night of September 21–22, 1823, who among other things revealed to him the location of an ancient record engraved in a golden book hidden in a nearby hill. The account, however, concealed the folk-magic elements of earlier versions.

The earliest accounts of the angel identify the heavenly messenger as a "spirit" who visited Smith three times in a "dream." About June 1829, Martin Harris, for instance, told people in Rochester that Smith had been "visited by the spirit of the Almighty in a dream, and informed that in a certain hill … was deposited a Golden Bible," and that "after a third visit from the same spirit in a dream, he proceeded to the spot."[18] Palmyra newspaperman Abner Cole reported in 1831 that Joseph Sr. described the "*spirit*" as a "little old man with a long beard."[19] Reporting on the activities of the first Mormon missionaries in Ohio under the direction of Oliver Cowdery, the *Painesville Telegraph* for November 30, 1830, said: "The new gospel they say was found in Ontario Co., N.Y. and was discovered by an angel of light, appearing in a dream to a man by the name of Smith." Locating treasures through dreams was not uncommon in Smith's day, and thrice repeated

---

17. JS History, vol. A-1, 4 (*JSP*, H1:216–18).

18. "Golden Bible," *Rochester (NY) Gem*, Sep. 5, 1829, 70 (*EMD*, 2:272).

19. *Palmyra (NY) Reflector*, Feb. 14, 1831, 101 (*EMD*, 2:245).

dreams were especially significant.[20] Former neighbor and fellow treasure seeker Willard Chase reported in 1833 that Joseph Smith Sr. informed him that the personage who appeared to his son "was the spirit of the prophet who wrote this book."[21]

In his 1838 account, Smith said the personage appeared in his room hovering above the floor, and that "he called me by name, and said unto me that he was a messenger sent from the presence of God to me, and that his name was Nephi."[22] Later, church historians in Utah changed the angel's name from Nephi, the first writer in the Book of Mormon, to Moroni, the last writer, to make it consistent with other sources.[23] Smith's 1835 expansion of his September 1830 revelation, for instance, declared: "The hour cometh that I will drink of the fruit of the vine with you on the earth, and with Moroni, whom I have sent unto you to reveal the Book of Mormon ... to whom I have committed the keys of the record of the stick of Ephraim."[24] Cowdery also named the angel Moroni in his history published in the *Messenger and Advocate* in April 1835 in Kirtland, Ohio.[25]

While it has generally been assumed that the name Nephi in the 1838 history was a scribal error, it is possible Smith was experimenting with the narrative and that the substitution occurred as part of his effort to downplay the folk-magic elements and to avoid the charge of necromancy. Changing the name to Nephi, who lived a thousand years before Moroni, allowed readers to assume a resurrected being had appeared to Smith instead of a spirit. Former apostle William McLellin, excommunicated in 1838, later said: "I have no doubt an angel ministered to Joseph, but it was not Moroni." Moroni, McLellin explained, "was a disimbodied spirit, and hence could not appear unto man to give him any manifestation. Therefore the statement of his appearing unto Joseph to reveal the place of the deposit of the plates is false. Angels can minister to man, but disimbodied spirits cannot, except they garb themselves in forms."[26] Nephi, on the other hand, would have been

---

20. See Quinn, *Early Mormonism and the Magic World View*, 138–40; Walker, "The Persisting Idea of American Treasure Hunting," 440.

21. Howe, *Mormonism Unvailed*, 242.

22. JS History, vol. A-1, 5 (*JSP*, H1:222).

23. Vogel, *History of Joseph Smith*, 1:12n21.

24. Revelation, Sep. 4, 1830 [ca. Aug. 1835], D&C, 1835 ed., L:2 [D&C 27:5] (*JSP*, D4:410–11).

25. Oliver Cowdery, Letter to W. W. Phelps, April 1835, "Letter VI," *LDS Messenger and Advocate*, Apr. 1835, 112.

26. McLellin, Notebook, ca. 1880, 11–12 (Larson and Passey, *The William E. McLellin Papers*, 391–92; see also 387).

among those saints who arose at Jesus's resurrection, as mentioned in Matthew (27:52–53) and the Book of Mormon (3 Ne. 23:11). This perhaps also explains why the 1838 history mentions the appearance of John the Baptist in May 1829 but not the subsequent visitation of Peter, James, and John. At the same time, Smith also avoided using the term "angel" but referred to Nephi as "messenger" and "heavenly messenger" instead—thus heading off objections by traditional Christians who understood angels to be special creations of God rather than dead or even resurrected mortals.

Within days of using the name Nephi, Smith reverted to Moroni when on May 8 he wrote answers to frequently asked questions that appeared in the July issue of *Elders' Journal*, stating that "Moroni ... being dead, and raised again therefrom, appeared unto me."[27] What occasioned Moroni's resurrection is not stated, but the importance of his having a body when he appeared to Smith in 1823 is clear. It may be that Smith intended to correct his previous use of Nephi but failed to do so before it was copied by James Mulholland in 1839 into the first volume of Smith's official history. Although Smith was editor of the *Times and Seasons* in 1842 when his history began to be printed, the Nephi designation slipped through in the April 15 issue, possibly because Smith was having difficulty keeping up with his many responsibilities and was leaning on John Taylor and Wilford Woodruff. The error was then perpetuated in subsequent printings of Smith's history, most notably in the *Pearl of Great Price* published by Apostle Franklin D. Richards in England in 1851.[28]

Smith said in 1838 that the angel told him that "God had a work for me to do, and that my name should be had for good and evil, among all nations, kindreds, and tongues; or that it should be both good and evil spoken of among all people"—another attempt to contextualize the controversy and persecution he attracted everywhere he went. The angel also told Smith about the location of the gold plates, which he said contained "an account of the former inhabitants of this continent, and the source from whence they sprang," as well as "the fullness of the everlasting gospel ... as delivered by the Savior to the ancient inhabitants."[29] The allusion to Jesus visiting

---

27. Joseph Smith, Answers to Questions, *Elders' Journal*, July 1838, 43. The entry for May 8, 1838, in Joseph Smith's journal reads: "Also in the after part of the day [I spent] in answering the questions proposed in the Elders' Journal." Smith, Journal, May 8, 1838 (*JSP*, J1:267). At what point after his death—presumably in the fifth century BCE—Moroni was resurrected is not stated, but the importance of his having a body when he first appeared to Smith is clear.

28. *The Pearl of Great Price* (Liverpool: F. D. Richards, 1851), 41.

29. JS History, vol. A-1, 5 (*JSP*, H1:222).

ancient America is anachronistic since that aspect of the narrative was a later development.[30]

Another anachronism occurs when Smith states that he was told that deposited with the plates were "two stones in silver bows, and these stones fastened to a breastplate constituted what is called the Urim and Thummim," and that the "use of these stones was what constituted seers in ancient or former times, and that God had prepared them for the purpose of translating the book."[31] The term "Urim and Thummim" (meaning in Hebrew "light and perfection") alludes to divining stones that were part of Aaron's breastplate in the Old Testament. While there was no attempt to claim the instrument buried with the plates was the same one used by Jewish high priests before the captivity, linking Smith's translation spectacles to the "Urim and Thummim" drew attention away from the folk-magic connection to seer stones. This apologetic defense was previously used by W. W. Phelps in Missouri in July 1832 and by Orson Hyde and Samuel H. Smith in Boston in August.[32] In fact, the idea that a large pair of spectacles was buried with the plates was not Smith's idea but was suggested by fellow seer Samuel Lawrence in 1825.[33] Nevertheless, Smith gave the impression that the Book of Mormon had been translated through the spectacles found with the plates, rather than what the earliest reliable sources say actually happened, that he dictated the text from peering into his treasure-seeing stone placed in a white top hat held to his face.[34]

Yet another anachronism in Smith's 1838 account is his claim that the angel quoted various Bible passages, including the prophecy in Malachi 4 about the Lord sending the prophet Elijah "before the great and dreadful day of the Lord," which Smith altered to read: "Behold I will reveal unto you the Priesthood by the hand of Elijah the prophet before the coming of the great and dreadful day of the Lord." Smith thus linked Malachi's prophecy to the 1836 appearance of Elijah in the Kirtland Temple.[35] Cowdery's 1834–35 history, published in the *Messenger and Advocate*, quoted at some length the angel's words and prophecies about the gathering of Israel in the last days but said nothing about Elijah's priesthood.

---

30. Metcalfe, "The Priority of Mosiah," 417–18.

31. JS History, vol. A-1, 5 (*JSP*, H1:222).

32. "Hosea Chapter III," *The Evening and the Morning Star*, July 1832, 14; "Questions proposed to the Mormonite Preachers and their answers," *Boston Investigator*, Aug. 10, 1832, 2.

33. Howe, *Mormonism Unvailed*, 243.

34. On Joseph Smith's method of translation, see Lancaster, "The Translation of the Book of Mormon."

35. JS History, vol. A-1, 5 (*EMD*, 1:65; *JSP*, H1:224).

According to Smith's 1838 account, the day after the heavenly messenger's appearance, September 22, 1823, he visited the hill to find the plates. However, his narrative again concealed various folk-magic elements of the original story. Historian Alan Taylor, who referred to Smith's revisions as "de-emphasis," suggested that Smith "recognized that a reputation for treasure-seeking was a handicap in communicating his message to an audience increasingly committed to rationality and a more abstract understanding of religion."[36] Similarly, historian Jan Shipps observed that "the prophet and those who participated with him in the compilation of the official *History of the Church* were anxious not to emphasize the prophet's early connection with the divining art," and that in "playing down this part of the prophet's background," they were attempting to avoid "charges that might endanger his reputation."[37] However, Smith did not merely glide over his early career as a treasure seer; he also removed the treasure-seeking and folk-magic elements from his account of the Book of Mormon's coming forth. In 1838, he was doing more than just maintaining his reputation; he was reinventing himself to become a more suitable, respectable religious leader. If Smith wanted to solidify and broaden his authority and influence, his story needed to sound more universal and mainstream Christian.

In his 1838 history, Smith said he was able to locate the plates because while he was conversing with the messenger, "the vision was opened to my mind that I could see the place where the plates were deposited, and that so clearly and distinctly that I knew the place again when I visited it."[38] Originally, Smith had said he located the plates with his seer stone. In an 1859 interview, Martin Harris said: "Joseph had a stone which was dug from the well ... [and] by means of this stone he first discovered these plates."[39] Willard Chase said that during the fall of 1827, Smith confessed to him that "if it had not been for that stone, (which he acknowledged belonged to me,) he would not have obtained the book."[40]

After locating the plates under a large rock, Smith said in his 1838 account: "I made an attempt to take them [the plates] out, but was forbidden by the messenger."[41] This obscures his original claim that when he attempted

---

36. Taylor, "Rediscovering the Context of Joseph Smith's Treasure Seeking," 26.
37. Shipps, "The Prophet Puzzle," 37.
38. JS History, vol. A-1, 6 (*JSP*, H1:226; DHC 1:13).
39. "Mormonism—No. II," *Tiffany's Monthly*, Aug. 1859, 163 (*EMD*, 2:302).
40. Willard Chase, Statement, ca. Dec. 11, 1833, in Howe, *Mormonism Unvailed*, 246 (*EMD*, 2:71–72).
41. JS History, vol. A-1, 6 (*JSP*, H1:232).

to remove the plates, he was thrown back by a supernatural force. According to Lucy, "He immediately reached forth his hand to take them, but instead of getting them, as he anticipated, he was hurled back upon the ground with great violence."[42] Chase's account of what Joseph Smith, Sr. told him is similar: Joseph Jr. "saw in the box something like a toad, which soon assumed the appearance of a man, and struck him on the side of his head.—Not being discouraged at trifles, he again stooped down and strove to take the book, when the spirit struck him again, and knocked him three or four rods, and hurt him prodigiously."[43] Cowdery's 1835 account also claimed Smith experienced three successive "shocks," each more powerful than the previous. Cowdery wrote that Smith initially interpreted these "shocks" within a treasure-seeking context, stating that he "had heard of the power of enchantment, and a thousand like stories, which held the hidden treasures of the earth, and supposed that physical exertion and personal strength was only necessary to enable him to yet obtain the object of his wish," and therefore persisted in his attempt to get the plates.[44]

Finally, in his 1838 history, Smith says that he was told by the messenger that "the time for bringing them [the plates] forth had not yet arrived, neither would until four years from that time, but he told me that I should come to that place precisely in one year from that time, and that he would there meet with me, and that I should continue to do so until the time should come for obtaining the plates."[45] However, he had earlier claimed that the messenger told him he would get the plates if he returned the next year with older brother Alvin but that Alvin's death prevented him from obtaining the plates in 1824. "After recovering from his fright," Chase said, "[Smith] enquired why he could not obtain the plates; to which the spirit made reply, because you have not obeyed your orders. He then enquired when he *could* have them, and was answered thus: come one year from this day, and bring with you your oldest brother, and you shall have them."[46] Joseph Knight, Sr., a fellow treasure seeker and early convert, gave a similar account, stating that Smith "exclaimed, 'why can't I stir this book?' and he was answered, 'you have not done right. You should have took the book and a gone right away. You

---

42. Lucy Smith, *Biographical Sketches*, 86.

43. Willard Chase, Statement, ca. Dec. 11, 1833, in Howe, *Mormonism Unvailed*, 242 (*EMD*, 2:67).

44. Oliver Cowdery, Letter to W. W. Phelps, Oct. 1835, in "Letter VIII," *Messenger and Advocate*, Oct. 1835, 197–98 (*EMD*, 2:458–59).

45. JS History, vol. A-1, 7 (*JSP*, H1:234).

46. Chase, Statement, ca. Dec. 11, 1833, in Howe, *Mormonism Unvailed*, 242 (EMD, 2:67).

can't have it now.' Joseph says, 'when can I have it?' the answer was 'the 22nd day of September next if you bring the right person with you.' Joseph says, 'who is the right person?' The answer was, 'your oldest brother.'"[47]

As soon as word got out that he had obtained possession of the plates and spectacles on September 22, 1827, Smith said, "the most strenious exertions were used to get them from me. Every stratagem that could be invented was resorted to for that purpose. The persecution became more bitter and severe than before, and multitudes were on the alert continualy to get them from me if possible but by the wisdom of God they remained safe in my hands untill I had accomplished by them what was required at my hand, when according to arrangement the messenger called for them, I delivered them up to him and he has them in his charge untill this day, being the Second day of May, One thousand Eight hundred and thirty eight."[48]

Smith's 1838 journal mentions only two more days of working on his history,[49] which apparently included the account of his relocation to Harmony, Pennsylvania, to live among Emma's relatives and his beginning to dictate his translation of the Book of Mormon, first to Martin Harris and then to Oliver Cowdery. Prior to beginning as scribe, Harris took a sample of characters and translation to Charles Anthon, a renowned linguist at New York City's Columbia University. According to Smith's account, Anthon pronounced the Book of Mormon characters "true characters," and that they were "Egyptian, Chaldeak, Assyriac, and Arabic." He also declared that Smith's translation was "correct, more so than any he had before seen translated from the Egyptian," which was something Anthon was unqualified to do. Anthon would later deny that he had said any such thing, and instead asserted that he immediately knew it was a hoax. Smith's version of the story reflects a need to emphasize his prophetic and seeric gifts, which was also evident in his recent handling of the Egyptian papyri.

This need was even greater with dissenters in Kirtland undermining the strength of the testimonies of the three and eight witnesses to the Book of Mormon and debating among themselves whether to continue believing in the book. In a letter written to recently-excommunicated Lyman Johnson, dated April 15, 1838, Stephen Burnett reported that Warren Parrish, Luke Johnson, and John Boynton were arguing that the Book of Mormon should be rejected, while Martin Harris, Cyrus Smalling, and Joseph Coe

47. Joseph Knight, Reminiscences, 1 (*EMD*, 4:13).
48. JS History, vol. A-1, 8 (*JSP*, H1:238).
49. Smith, Journal, May 3–4, 1838 (*JSP*, J1:264).

continued to believe in the book despite their rejection of Smith. Burnett said that Harris declared at a public meeting that "he never saw the plates with his natural eyes, neither Oliver [Cowdery] nor David [Whitmer] & also that the eight witnesses never saw them [with their natural eyes] & hesitated to sign that instrument for that reason, but were persuaded to do it." Upon hearing Harris's statement, Burnett said "the last pedestal gave way" and concluded: "If the witnesses whose names are attached to the Book of Mormon never saw the plates [with their natural eyes] as Martin [Harris] admits, [then] there can be nothing brought to prove that any such thing ever existed."[50] Three weeks later at another public meeting, according to Burnett, Harris said "he was sorry for any man who rejected the Book of Mormon for he knew it was true, he said he had hefted the plates repeatedly in a box [and at other times] with only a tablecloth or a handkerchief over them, but he never saw them only as he saw a city through a mountain." He also expressed regret about revealing the true nature of the experience of the eight witnesses, stating that "he never should have told that the testimony of the eight [witnesses] was false, if it had not been picked out of [h]im but should have let it passed as it was."[51] In March 1838, Parrish reported that "Harris ... told me and others a few days since that he never saw the plates with his natural eyes, but in a vision. He also said that Joseph, nor any other man, ever saw them in any other way."[52]

The Missouri draft of Smith's 1838 history may have included an account of Harris's loss of the entire translation manuscript written under his tenure as Smith's scribe and his subsequent replacement by Cowdery in April 1829, as well as an account of Smith and Cowdery's reception of authority from John the Baptist. As mentioned, Mulholland's 1839 draft picks up with Smith and Cowdery baptizing one another in the Susquehanna River on May 15, 1829.[53]

Answering Questions

According to Heber Kimball, Smith purchased a house in Far West, "which had been formerly occupied as a public house."[54] About the first of May,

---

50. Stephen Burnett, Letter to Lyman E. Johnson, Apr. 15, 1838, Smith Letterbook 2, 64 (*EMD*, 2:291). I have added "with their natural eyes" in brackets for clarity, which is implied from the context of Harris's statement.

51. Burnett, 64 (*EMD*, 2:291).

52. *Waldo (ME) Patriot*, May 4, 1838.

53. See *JSP*, H1:294.

54. Kimball, "History of Heber Chase Kimball," ca. 1842–58, 105–106.

Smith moved his family into a tavern, previously operated by Samuel Musick, located on the central block of the town.[55] Smith remained in the large structure until about June 23, when he began making preparations to purchase a home from George M. Hinkle, who was moving to De Witt, Missouri.[56]

On Sunday, May 6, Smith preached on various subjects, advising against hasty judgment and emphasizing the importance of hearing both sides. He then mentioned men who should come among them "grouling about their money" expecting that those who have less than they "aught to make up their loss." Smith's comments apparently alluded to the bank failure and those seeking to recover financial losses. He further warned the Saints to beware of them "for here and there they through [throw] out foul insinuations" to injure the church and "destroy the character of its Presidency," possibly a reference to Cowdery's accusations about Fanny Alger. He then talked about the mysteries, "giving them a history of the Plannets &c. and of Abrahams writings upon the Plannettary System &c."[57] This clearly refers to Smith's bound "Grammar and Alphabet of the Egyptian Language," which ends with a detailed description of the planetary system. In the afternoon, Smith spoke again, expounding on the word of wisdom.[58]

Two days later, on May 8, Smith answered questions frequently asked of him during his trip from Kirtland to Missouri in fall 1837 with Rigdon; Smith's answers were published in the July issue of the *Elders' Journal*:[59] they show how he treated such queries, an approach underlying the history he was then preparing. They also show why he "attract[ed] the attention of the great ones of the most popular sects of the day," why his message "create[d] a bitter persecution" that "was common among all the sects," and why it seemed to him that "all [were] united to persecute me."[60] The negative attention he attracted was not because he claimed to have seen God. Rather, it was because of his provocative message, expressed in deliberately blunt terms, that God had rejected every form of organized Christianity. This attitude is reflected in Smith's answers to the first three questions.

---

55. Samuel Musick, Receipt to Joseph Smith, July 14, 1838, JS Collection (*JSP*, D6:204–206).

56. On July 6, 1838, the high council assigned Edward Partridge to purchase Hinkle's house for Smith. Minutes, July 6, 1838, Minute Book 2, 150 (Cannon and Cook, *Far West Record*, 197).

57. Smith, Journal, May 6, 1838 (*JSP*, J1:266; D6:133–34).

58. Smith (*JSP*, J1:266).

59. Smith, Journal, May 8, 1838 (*JSP*, J1:267); Smith, Answers to Questions, *Elders' Journal*, July 1838, 42–44.

60. JS History, vol. A-1, 4 (*JSP*, H1:216–18).

Do you believe the b[i]ble? If we do, we are the only people under heaven that does. For there are none of the religious sects of the day that do.

Wherein do you differ from other sects? Because we believe the bible, and all other sects profess to believe their interpretations of the bible, and their creeds.

Will every body be damned but Mormons? Yes, and a great portion of them, unless they repent and work righteousness.[61]

Only days earlier, while working on his history, Smith claimed that Jesus had told him in his 1820 vision that all creeds "were an abomination in his sight" and that all who professed them were "corrupt."[62] While Smith was not alone in rejecting denominational creeds, he did not oppose creeds per se. Indeed, he had created his own creed, which he called covenants, the Law, revelations, and Lectures on Faith, the violation of which could result in excommunication. However, his creed differed from other creeds because his was God-inspired, while the others had been formulated by church councils and the interpretation and learning of men. Nevertheless, Smith's answers reveal that he, like other Christian primitivists, believed that their literalistic, fundamentalist readings of the Bible were value-free and non-interpretive.

To the question "Do you believe Joseph Smith, Jr., to be a prophet?" Smith answered: "Yes, and every other man who has the testimony of Jesus," and then quoted Revelation 19:10: "For the testimony of Jesus, is the spirit of prophecy." Smith's generous, disarming definition nevertheless did not fully convey the meaning of "prophet" his followers accepted.

To other questions, Smith simply denied that Mormons believed in "having all things common," or "having more wives than one," or having the power to "raise the dead," or that he had eloped with his wife, Emma. He did, however, acknowledge that he was "a money digger," but that "it was never a very profitable job to him, as he only got fourteen dollars a month for it."

To the question "Are the Mormons abolitionists?" Smith answered: "No, unless delivering the people from priestcraft and the priests from the power of Satan, should be considered such. But we do not believe in setting the Negroes free." The first part of the answer was perhaps a bit sarcastic, but the last part was an attempt to ease tensions and reverse the assumption that Mormons were anti-slavery northerners, which had resulted in the 1833 destruction of the Mormon press and their subsequent expulsion from Jackson County. Smith's answer to the next question, which asked if the Mormons

---

61. Smith, Answers to Questions, *Elders' Journal*, July 1838, 42. I have removed the numbers as well as the "Question" and "Answer" designations throughout.

62. JS History, vol. A-1, 3 (*JSP*, H1:214).

"stir up the Indians to war and to commit depredations," had a similar objective. "No," he said emphatically, "and those who reported the story, knew it was false when they put it into circulation." However, it was Smith who knew otherwise, for, as early as 1832, he had found it necessary to reprimand followers in Jackson County for speaking about Book of Mormon prophecies of Indian uprisings.[63] There is no evidence that Mormons actively tried to incite Indians to violence, at least before converting the tribes to Mormonism, which is what the Book of Mormon predicted; so, to the non-Mormon community, attempts to proselytize the Indians would be the same as stirring them up to warfare. Other questions mock Smith's critics.

> Do the Mormons baptize in the name of Jo Smith? No, but if they did, it would be as valid as the baptism administered by the sectarian priests.
> Does not Jo Smith profess to be Jesus Christ? No, but he professes to be his brother.

Two questions reflected non-Mormon concern with Smith's claim to continuing revelation and his expansion of the sacred canon of scripture.

> Is there anything in the Bible which licenses you to believe in revelation nowadays? Is there anything that does not authorize us to believe so? If there is, we have, as yet, not been able to find it.
> Is not the canon of the scriptures full? If it is, there is a great defect in the book, or else it would have said so.

Finally, to a question about "the fundamental principles" of Mormonism, Smith's answer would have been shared by other Christians: "The fundamental principles of our religion is the testimony of the apostles and prophets concerning Jesus Christ, 'that he died, was buried, and rose again the third day, and ascended up into heaven;' and all other things are only appendages to these, which pertain to our religion." In giving such answers Smith was proclaiming that Mormons were the only true Christians.

Financial Support

On May 9 Smith preached at the funeral of Thomas Marsh's ten-year-old son, James, and on the following day, he listened to Rigdon deliver a political address to a large gathering at the schoolhouse. According to Smith, Rigdon, responding to the May 5 speech of General Wilson, the Whig

---

63. Smith, Letter to William W. Phelps, July 31, 1832, JS Collection (*JSP*, D2:266). See 3 Ne. 20:15–20; 21:12–14.

candidate for Congress from Randolph County, reviewed the differences between Federalists (Whigs) and Democrats.[64] Mormons in Ohio were generally supporters of the Democratic Party and President Jackson, largely because anti-Mormons were Whigs.[65] This had not changed in Missouri. As Smith writes in his journal, "the Politics of this Church (with but few exceptions onley,) are that of the Democracy."[66]

On May 11 Smith attended a bishop's court in the case of Apostle William McLellin, who said that "he had no confidence in the heads of the Church, believing they had transgressed, and had got out of the way." This had led to his own downfall, confessing that he had discontinued praying, keeping the commandments, and "indulged himself in his lustful desires." When he heard that "the first presidency had made a general settlement and acknowledged their sins, he began to pray again, and to keep the commandments of God." Smith questioned him and elicited an admission that "he had seen nothing out of the way himself but ... judged from hearsay." In his journal, Smith remarked: "O!! foolish Man! what excuse is that thou renderest, for thy sins, that because thou hast heard of some mans transgression, that thou shouldest leave thy God, and forsake thy prayers, and turn to those things that thou knowest to be contrary to the will of God, we say unto thee, and to all such, beware! beware! for God will bring the[e] into Judgement for thy sins."[67] As with Cowdery, Smith got McLellin to admit that he had no firsthand information about the sins of the First Presidency. There are no minutes for McLellin's trial in the record of the high council, and Smith's journal copy gives no result, but presumably McLellin, who supported the dissenters, was excommunicated.[68]

On May 12 Smith and Rigdon petitioned the high council for financial assistance. The council decided to request Partridge to set aside two 80-acre lots for Smith and Rigdon next to the corporation (town square) belonging to the church. They also appointed a committee to consult with Smith and Rigdon and "to agree upon some particular price or wages for their services in the printing office & their saleries for the coming year." However, the council stipulated that the stipend was not for preaching or receiving revelations, "but for services rendered in the Printing establishment, in translating the Ancient

---

64. Smith, Journal, May 5 and 10, 1838 (*JSP*, J1:267–68).

65. See Hill, *Quest for Refuge*, 64–66; Parkin, "Mormon Political Involvement in Ohio."

66. Smith, Journal, May 10, 1838 (*JSP*, J1:268).

67. Smith, Journal, May 11, 1838 (*JSP*, J1:268).

68. See Historian's Office, "History of William E. McLellin," published in *Deseret News*, May 12, 1858, 49; and Porter, "The Odyssey of William Earl McLellin."

Records, &c."—showing that Smith and other church leaders viewed his work as a translator as different from dictating revelations.[69] The record left the amount of the stipend blank, but Ebenezer Robinson, who was the clerk of the meeting, remembered that it was $1,100 each per year. However, according to Robinson, the stipend was never paid because "the members of the church, almost to a man, lifted their voices against it. The expression of disapprobation was so strong and emphatic, that at the next meeting of the High Council the resolution voting them a salary, was recinded."[70]

This also implies that continued work on the translation was contemplated, although at this time the Egyptian artifacts had not yet arrived from Kirtland. Under May 24, 1838, William Swartzell, a fifty-six-year-old convert from Ohio, wrote that he saw Smith's "box of mummys" at Richmond landing.[71] Under 26 July, Swartzell wrote: "Doing nothing today, except looking at the hands employed in getting out logs for brother Joseph Smith's house, in which he intends translating the hieroglyphics of the Egyptian mummies."[72] However, Smith did not return to translating until 1842.

On May 14, two days after the high council had agreed to give Smith and Rigdon 80 acres each near the Far West town square, Smith plowed the garden of his new land, while Rigdon prepared material for the press.[73]

Daviess County

On May 18 Smith left Far West for the "north country" with Rigdon, Marsh, Patten, Partridge, Elias Higbee, Simeon Carter, and surveyor Alanson Ripley, "for the purpose of Laying off stakes of Zion" and "making Locations & laying claims [to land] for the gathering of the saints."[74] Laying claim to federal lands, according to the Preemption Act of 1830, required a survey and registration at the local branch of the General Land Office. However, while this land could be occupied, it would not become available for purchase from the federal government until November 1838.[75]

Smith and Rigdon had been assigned this task in September 1837 because it was determined that "the gathering of the saints [in Caldwell County] were at this time crowded to overflowing & that it was necessary

---

69. Smith, Journal, May 12, 1838 (*JSP*, J1:269).
70. Ebenezer Robinson, "Items of Personal History of the Editor," *Return* (Davis City, IA), Sep. 1889, 136–37.
71. Swartzell, *Mormonism Exposed*, 9.
72. Swartzell, 25.
73. Smith, Journal, May 14, 1838 (*JSP*, J1:270).
74. Smith, Journal, May 18, 1838 (*JSP*, J1:270).
75. See *JSP*, J1:273n149.

that there be more Stakes of Zion appointed in order that the poor might have a place to gather to."[76] When organized in December 1836, Caldwell County was "one-third timber and two-thirds prairie" and had a population of about 2,000. By the following November, the population had jumped to more than 7,000.[77] By summer 1838, several more thousand Mormons had moved to Caldwell County, especially to Far West. "In one year from the time of the first settlement in Caldwell," Partridge wrote in 1840, "there were from one hundred to one hundred and fifty dwelling houses erected in that place, six dry good stores in operation, one grocery and several mechanic shops. There were in the county, nearly or quite three hundred farms opened and several thousand acres under cultivation also, four saw and five grist mills doing good business."[78]

Mormon expansion was very much against the wishes of the people of Daviess County, who, along with the citizens of the other surrounding counties, understood that Caldwell had been created to keep the Mormons confined therein. Troubled by Mormon settlements in southern and western Daviess County, officials had warned the Mormons to leave the county by August 1, 1837.[79] The Mormons not only refused to leave, but Smith also intended to relocate more of his followers on large tracts of land in Daviess County.

Smith and company traveled about twenty-five miles and camped near the branch of Honey Creek and Grand River about five miles below Gallatin, the county seat. While encamped, Smith sent his dog after a wolf, but the wolf was too fast.[80]

On the morning of May 19, the company crossed Grand River at the mouth of the Honey Creek and traveled north along the river about eighteen miles to Lyman Wight's home, located in Grand River Township at the foot of a hill, which Smith named "Tower Hill" due to the remains of an "old Nephitish Alter" or "Tower."[81] Here, they set up their base camp in what

---

76. Minutes, Sep. 17, 1837, Minute Book 1, 243 (*JSP*, D5:445).

77. Brown, Cannon, and Jackson, *Historical Atlas of Mormonism*, 42.

78. "A History of the Persecution, of Latter Day Saints in Missouri," *Times and Seasons*, Mar. 1840, 66 (*JSP*, H2:232); see also *History of Caldwell and Livingston Counties, Missouri*, 118, 121; Berrett, *Sacred Places*, 4:288.

79. William W. Phelps, Letter to editor, [July] 7, 1837, *LDS Messenger and Advocate*, July 1837, 529; "A History of the Persecution, of Latter Day Saints in Missouri," *Times and Seasons*, Mar. 1840, 65 (*JSP*, H2:231).

80. Smith, Journal, May 18, 1838 (*JSP*, J1:271).

81. Wight had joined Cowdery in exploring Daviess County in November–December 1837 and had purchased land and a cabin from Adam Black about February 1838. Berrett, *Sacred Places*, 4:377; [Joseph Smith], editorial, *Elders' Journal*, Nov. 1837, 28.

they called "Robinson's Grove."[82] In the afternoon, Smith, Rigdon, and Robinson separated from the camp and continued about a half-mile up the river to Wight's ferry landing, where they selected a location for a city in an area known as "Spring Hill." The next month Smith would endow "Spring Hill" with special significance when he called the location Adam-ondi-Ahman because "it is the place where Adam shall come to visit his people, or the Ancient of Days shall sit, as spoken of by Daniel the Prophet."[83]

On Monday, May 21, Smith, Rigdon, and Robinson spent the day surveying and laying claim to land in Salem, Washington, and Grand River Townships then returned to Robinson's Grove. In the evening, the company held a council to discuss whether they should go farther north or try to secure all the free land around the future site of Adam-ondi-Ahman, especially along Grand River, as well as the land south between Adam-ondi-Ahman and Far West. It was decided to do the latter because Smith "felt impressed" to do so.[84]

The following day, Rigdon and some of the men left the camp, traveling east along the river, and found "some of the best locations in the country." After Rigdon's ground returned to the camp, Smith and Robinson left in the same direction but were unsuccessful. Later, Smith and some others left the camp in a westward direction to hunt game but only found "some ancient antiquities ... which conscisted of some stone mounds," which Smith thought "were made to seclude some valuable treasures deposited by the aborigionees of this land"—an assumption he carried over from his money-digging days.[85]

On May 23 Smith and the entire company went east from the camp, located lands to survey, and secured a claim on Grove Creek and near Adam-ondi-Ahman. In the evening, Smith and Rigdon went to Wight's cabin, while the other men returned to their tents in Robinson's Grove.[86] Recalling this period of surveying in Daviess County, Wight wrote: "About June [1838] Joseph Smith, together with many others of the principal men of the church, came to my house, and taking a view of the large bottom in the bend of the river, and the beautiful prairies on the bluffs, came to the conclusion that it would be a handsome situation for a town. We therefore commenced

82. Smith, Journal, May 19, 1838 (*JSP*, J1:271).
83. Smith [D&C 116] (*JSP*, J1:271); Dan. 7:13–14.
84. Smith, Journal, May 21, 1838 (*JSP*, J1:271–73).
85. Smith, Journal, May 22, 1838 (*JSP*, J1:273).
86. Smith, Journal, May 23, 1838 (*JSP*, J1:273).

surveying and laying off town lots, and locating government lands for many miles north of this place." He then reflected on the subsequent rapid growth of Adam-ondi-Ahman: "This beautiful country with its flattering prospects drew in floods of emigrants. ... There were upwards of two hundred houses built in this town, and also about forty families living in their wagons."[87]

On May 24 the company returned to the Grove Creek area to finish the survey there, and Smith returned to Far West, where he remained for a few days before returning to Daviess County.[88] In Smith's absence, the company continued to survey land near Grand River and in the area opposite Adam-ondi-Ahman.[89]

Smith had arrived at Far West just before his mummies and Egyptian artifacts arrived. Under May 24, 1838, William Swartzell, on his way to Far West with a company of Mormons from Ohio, wrote that he stayed the night at the river landing at Richmond, where he said "the Mormons land their goods for transportation across the country," and that he "saw here Joseph Smith's box of mummies."[90] Two days later, Swartzell and company arrived at Far West, where he was introduced to Smith. Because of his talent as a cook, Swartzell was "instantly installed into the important office of steward of Joseph Smith, Jr." He was also "chosen [as] an assistant surveyor, at a salary of one dollar per day, to help to lay off the Stake (or city) of Grand River."[91]

The mummies and other boxes containing the Egyptian papyri and Smith's papers probably arrived with Swartzell's company. According to a late reminiscence of Anson Call, who apparently arrived at Far West about this same time, "Joseph was much pleased with the arrival of the books, and said to us, 'Sit down and we will read to you from the Translation of the Book of Abraham.'" Judging by the two hours it took to read, the men read both the text of the Book of Abraham and the Grammar and Alphabet of the Egyptian Language.[92]

On May 28 Smith left Far West with Hyrum Smith and a company of about twenty to survey the lands north of Adam-ondi-Ahman.[93] Four

---

87. Lyman Wight, Journal, 155–56 (1839).
88. Smith, Journal, May 24, 1838 (*JSP*, J1:273).
89. Smith, Journal, May 25–26, 1838 (*JSP*, J1:274).
90. Swartzell, *Mormonism Exposed*, 25.
91. Swartzell, 9.
92. Call, "Copied from the Journal of Anson Call," Feb. 1879. Call's memory was faulty since he named Cowdery and Marsh as the readers, but Cowdery's participation at this time is doubtful since he had resigned from the church and was excommunicated the previous month. Call also dated the reading to his second visit to Far West in July, rather than his first visit about May.
93. Smith, Journal, May 28, 1838 (*JSP*, J1:274).

days later Smith returned to Far West, having evidently received word that Emma was about to give birth.[94] The next day, June 2, Emma gave birth to a son named Alexander Hale Smith.[95] Joseph left Emma the following day with Rigdon, Hyrum Smith, and others for Adam-ondi-Ahman, where he stayed overnight with Moses Dailey. In the morning, Smith and company went to Wight's house, where they began the work of building the city of Adam-ondi-Ahman, constructing houses and drafting a city plat.[96] George A. Smith reported that he helped his father, John, build "a two story log house on a lot in Adam-ondi-Ahman," and that he also "helped to raise twenty-five log houses in 25 days."[97]

Concerning the naming of Adam-ondi-Ahman, Swartzell wrote that on June 11, he, Smith, and Martin Harris dug a spring near Spring Hill, while Lyman Wight hauled stone to line it. When finished, they knelt and blessed it to be an "everlasting fountain" to the Saints, but in two or three days it began to fail and in a week became dry. After the blessing, Swartzell recalled, "I observed to Joseph Smith that this city should have a new name. Brother Joseph placed his back against a small shady tree near the spring and then said, 'We shall alter the name of this *stake*,' … and looking towards heaven for a short time, said, 'It does not take me long to get a revelation from heaven, and this stake, or city, shall be called Adam-on-Diammon.' He assigned as a reason for calling it so, that there was no place by that name under heaven."[98] According to John Corrill, Smith interpreted Adam-ondi-Ahman, often shortened to Diahman, to mean "the valley of God, in which Adam blessed his children."[99] Smith may have referred to this occasion when he later said: "I saw Adam in the valley of Ah-dam-ondi-ahman—he called together his children & blessed them with a Patriarchal blessing. The Lord appeared in their midst. & he (Adam) blessed them all & foretold what should befall them to the latest generation."[100] If the Saints could not

---

94. Smith, Journal, June 1, 1838 (*JSP*, J1:274).

95. Joseph Smith, Jr., Family Bible, private possession (*EMD*, 1:583).

96. Smith, Journal, June 4–5, 1838 (*JSP*, J1:275).

97. George A. Smith, Memoirs and Autobiography, 108.

98. Swartzell, *Mormonism Exposed*, 11–12. Martin Harris's presence in Missouri at this time is doubtful. Possibly in fleshing out his diary, Swartzell interpreted a reference to "Harris" to mean Martin Harris, when it was George W. Harris, a resident of Far West and who eventually owned land in Adam-ondi-Ahman (see *JSP*, J1:412).

99. Corrill, *A Brief History*, 28 (*JSP*, H2:163); see also Joseph Smith and Sidney Rigdon, Letter to Stephen Post, Sep. 17, 1838, [1] (*JSP*, D6:242).

100. Richards, "W. Richards Pocket Companion Written in England," 65 (*JSP*, D6:544); see also D&C 107:53–57.

possess Zion, the land where Jesus was to descend and reign a thousand years, then perhaps the valley where Adam would appear to bless his posterity would be a temporary substitute. Smith, Rigdon, and Robinson spent the sabbath at Adam-ondi-Ahman, but later in the day moved six miles farther north and set up camp.

Banishing Dissenters

Smith returned to Far West from Adam-ondi-Ahman about June 16, when John Smith and his family arrived from Ohio with six other families. Uncle John recorded in his journal that he had "met Joseph & Hyrum" at church services in Far West on June 17.[101] According to Smith's history, he "counseled them" to settle at Adam-ondi-Ahman.[102]

Prior to Smith's return to Far West, high councilor Jared Carter and Constable Dimick Huntington had called a secret meeting to discuss plans for removing dissenters from the town. Reed Peck, who attended the meeting and later left the church, claimed someone proposed that dissenters should be killed so "that they would not be capable of injuring the church," which was "strenuously opposed" by John Corrill and Thomas Marsh.[103] According to Corrill, when he later told Rigdon about the meeting and expressed reservations regarding some of the proposals, Rigdon told him that he should withdraw but that Carter, Huntington, and the others "would do as they pleased," which implied that Rigdon was aware of the meeting.[104] Smith also likely became aware of the meeting upon his return to Far West.

On Sunday, June 17, Joseph Smith attended a meeting at which he heard a fiery sermon delivered by Rigdon. Drawing on Jesus's words in Matthew 5:13, Rigdon railed against dissenters, likening them to salt that has lost its savor that was "henceforth good for nothing but to be cast out, and trodden under foot of men." According to Peck, Rigdon accused dissenters of seeking to "destroy the presidency laying plans to take their lives &c.," and "accused them of counterfeiting lying cheating and numerous other crimes and called on the people to rise en masse and rid the county of Such a nuisance." He further remarked, "When a country, or body of people have individuals among them with whom they do not wish to associate and a public expression is taken against their remaining among them and such

---

101. John Smith, Journal, June 16–17, 1838.
102. JS History, vol. B-1, Addenda, 6, Note V (DHC 3:38).
103. Reed Peck, Letter to "Dear Friends," Sep. 18, 1839, 22–23.
104. John Corrill, Testimony, in Transcript of Proceedings, Nov. 12–29, 1838, State of MO v. Joseph Smith et al. for Treason, [29] (*Document*, 110); hereafter Transcript.

individuals do not remove it is the principle of republicanism itself that gives that community a right to expel them forcibly." Ironically, Jackson Countians had cited this same principle when they expelled the Mormons from their community five years earlier. Rigdon's rhetoric became especially frightening when he said: "It is the duty of this people to trample them into the earth and if the county cannot be freed from them any other way I will assist to trample them down or to erect a gallows on the square of Far West and hang them up ... and it would be an act at which the angels would smile with approbation."[105]

According to Peck, "Joseph Smith in a short speech sanctioned what had been said by Rigdon, though said he I don't want the brethren to act unlawfully." However, he equivocated by adding that the story of Judas hanging himself in the New Testament was incorrect and that he had actually been hung by the apostle Peter. Peck interpreted this as a "hint" that, combined with Rigdon's remarks, "created a great excitement and prepared the people to execute anything that should be proposed."[106]

About this time, 83 Mormon men signed a letter accusing dissenters of such crimes as counterfeiting, stealing, and using vexatious lawsuits to persecute the Saints and warned Cowdery, David Whitmer, John Whitmer, Phelps, and Lyman Johnson to leave Caldwell County within three days "or else a more fatal calamity shall befall you."[107] Neither Smith nor Rigdon signed the document, and its authorship is uncertain. Ebenezer Robinson, who was one of the signers, recalled in 1890 that it was commonly understood that the letter "was gotten up in the office of the First Presidency."[108] Sampson Avard, who later testified in the November 1838 hearing, said

---

105. Peck, Letter to "Dear Friends," 24–25, 33.

106. Peck, 25–26.

107. Sidney Rigdon, Letter to Oliver Cowdery and Others, ca. June 17, 1838, in Transcript, [13]–[20] (*Document*, 103–106). Alexander Baugh places the forced expulsion of the dissenters from Far West in the larger context of "warning out" practiced both in Britain and early America. However, such warnings were typically directed at the poor to circumvent a community's obligation to care for them and were not accompanied by the threat of violence. Baugh also compares it to the extralegal activities of citizen committees such as the one that ordered Mormons to leave Jackson County in July 1833. While this is more relevant to the situation with the dissenters in Far West in June 1838, it too is fraught with irony and contradiction given the continual complaints of Joseph Smith and other Mormon leaders of being deprived of their constitutional right to own property and live wherever they pleased. Baugh, "'We Have a Company of Danites in These Times,'" 3–9. What the Mormons did to dissenters in Far West was more like what Puritans did to people they considered heretics like Roger Williams and Anne Hutchinson in seventeenth-century New England: banish them.

108. Ebenezer Robinson, "'Saints Herald,' Again," *Return*, Feb. 1890, 218–19.

that Rigdon had "drafted" the "paper against the dissenters."[109] The letter re-hearses many of the same charges Smith and Rigdon had made at the recent trials of Cowdery, Johnson, and the Whitmers. Regardless, the letter was apparently not delivered to the addressees, although they seem to have got-ten the message that their lives were in danger.[110] John Whitmer attributed his departure from Far West on June 19 to verbal threats.[111] George Rob-inson noted approvingly in Smith's journal that dissenters "took warning" from Rigdon's so-called Salt Sermon "and soon they were seen bounding over the prairie like the scape Goat to carry of[f] their own sins."[112] Phelps, however, reconciled with church leaders by agreeing to "conform to the rules of the church in all things" and was permitted to remain in the county.[113]

The editors of the Joseph Smith Papers observe that several of the accu-sations against dissenters were "overdrawn and unsubstantiated." Certainly, there is no evidence of counterfeiting. However, as these editors observe, Cowdery and Johnson had violated the "communitarian ethics" of the Mormons by initiating or threatening lawsuits to collect debts, and John Whitmer and Phelps were guilty of purchasing land with church funds and trying to profit from their sale.[114] According to John Whitmer, the Mor-mons soon began their own use of vexatious lawsuits to drive dissenters from Far West, stating in his history that the First Presidency directed Ebenezer Robinson to begin suing their enemies "by attachment for debts," and soon they seized most of their possessions.[115]

The letter also accused Cowdery of theft and John Whitmer and Phelps of receiving stolen goods: "After Oliver Cowdrey had been taken by a States warrent for stealing and the stolen property found concealed in the house of William W Phelps; in which nefarious transaction John Whitmier had also participated. Oliver Cowdry stole the property Conveyed it to John Whit-mier and John Whitmore to William W Phelps and there the officers of the law found it."[116] This probably refers to the printing press Cowdery had

---

109. Sampson Avard, in Transcript, [13] (*Document*, 102).
110. Cowdery later claimed that he was unaware of the letter's existence until after its publi-cation in 1841. Cowdery, Letter to Brigham Young and Others, Dec. 25, 1843.
111. Whitmer, History, 86–87 (*JSP*, H2:98).
112. Smith, Journal, July 4, 1838 (*JSP*, J1:278).
113. William W. Phelps, in Transcript, [87] (*Document*, 122).
114. *JSP*, J1:278n169.
115. Whitmer, History, 86–87 (*JSP*, H2:97–98); see also Corrill, *Brief History*, 30 (*JSP*, H2:165–66).
116. Sidney Rigdon, Letter to Oliver Cowdery and Others, ca. June 17, 1838, in Transcript, [15] (*Document*, 103).

purchased from Smith and Rigdon in the spring of 1837, which he brought with him to Far West and turned over to Whitmer and Phelps in exchange for "timbered land."[117] According to Rigdon, Cowdery had gone into the printing office in Kirtland and "took whatever he pleased & so completely stripped the office … that there was scarcely enough left to print the 'Elders Journal.'"[118] In an 1846 letter to brother-in-law Phineas Young, Cowdery denied having committed "crimes of theft, forgery, &c., … which all my former associates knew to be false."[119]

The signers were aware of the contradiction of tearing down the reputations of three of the Book of Mormon's witnesses, especially Cowdery and David Whitmer who claimed to have seen an angel with the plates, while at the same time relying on their word for the existence of the plates: "We wish to remind you that Oliver Cowdry and David Whitmier were among the principal of those who were the means of geathering us to this place by their testimony which they gave concerning the plates of the book of Mormon, that they were shown to them by an Angel which testimony we believe now as much as before you so scandalously disgraced it."[120] This apparent contradiction did not go unnoticed by Mormon critics.[121] "A religion whose principal use is to denounce the witnesses upon which it relies to establish its truth is of frail tenure indeed," one columnist observed in 1882. "After all that one would naturally think the belief in their testimony as to the truth of the Book of Mormon would be weakened, for surely the testimony of men known to be thieves, forgers, counterfeiters and liars could not have any weight, especially in heavenly things. … So much for the three witnesses; they fell by the way side, condemned even more heartily by their own dupes and confederates than by anybody else."[122]

Ironically, the authors of this threatening letter were appalled that dissenters had warned that they would defend themselves if attacked. "And to crown the whole you have had the audacity to threaten us that if we offered to disturb you—you would get up a mob from Clay and Ray Counties—for this insult if nothing else and your threatenings to shoot us if we offered to

---

117. John Whitmer, Letter to Oliver Cowdery and David Whitmer, Aug. 29, 1837.

118. Minutes, Apr. 12, 1838, Minute Book 2, 125 (*JSP*, D6:92).

119. Oliver Cowdery, Letter to Phineas Young, Mar. 23, 1846 (*EMD*, 2:491).

120. Sidney Rigdon, Letter to Oliver Cowdery and Others, ca. June 17, 1838, in Transcript, [16] (*Document*, 104).

121. Harris, *Mormonism Portrayed*, 5–7; "Mormonism," *Christian Secretary* (Hartford, CT), Dec. 24, 1841; "Mormonism," *Millennial Harbinger* (Bethany, WV), Nov. 1842, 502.

122. "The Quarrels of Rogues," *Salt Lake Daily Tribune*, June 3, 1882.

molest you We will put you from the County of Caldwell So help us God."[123] Dissenters believed that church leaders were beyond reason and determined to have their way.

Danites

About this time a clandestine group called the "Society of the Daughter of Zion" was formed among Mormons to enforce orthodoxy and facilitate the warning out of dissenters. The name was taken from Micah 4:13: "Arise and thresh, O daughter of Zion: for I will make thine horn iron, and I will make thy hoofs brass: and thou shalt beat in pieces many people: and I will consecrate their gain unto the Lord, and their substance unto the Lord of the whole earth."[124] This group was subsequently given the nickname Danites by Joseph Smith. Reflecting on this period in January 1844, Smith said the name "grew out of an expression I made use of when the brethren were preparing to defend themselves from the Missouri mob, in reference to the stealing of Macaiah's [Micah's] images" in Judges 18 about the tribe of Dan. "If the enemy comes," he said, "the Danites will be after them, meaning the brethren in self-defense."[125] By early August, Corrill estimated that there were about 300 Danites.[126] This number may have swelled to between 800 and 1,000 by November, according to the testimony of John N. Sapp, a former Mormon who might have assumed that all Mormon troops were Danites.[127]

Ebenezer Robinson, himself a Danite, said that the 83 men who signed the letter warning dissenters out of Caldwell County were Danites.[128] Sampson Avard, a leader and instigator of the Danite band, later testified that "the original object ... was to drive from the county of Caldwell all those who dissented from the Mormon church; in which they succeeded admirably and to the satisfaction of those concerned."[129] However, the secret organization quickly evolved into what the editors of the Joseph Smith Papers called "a private Mormon militia" and "the church's private militia," and LDS historian Alexander Baugh described as "a paramilitary organization" of

123. Sidney Rigdon, Letter to Oliver Cowdery and Others, ca. June 17, 1838, in Transcript, [20] (*Document*, 106).

124. See Corrill, *Brief History*, 32 (*JSP*, H2:168).

125. Nauvoo City Council Rough Minutes, Jan. 3, 1844, 36 (Dinger, *The Nauvoo City and High Council Minutes*, 204).

126. Corrill, *Brief History*, 32 (*JSP*, H2:169).

127. See John N. Sapp, in *Document*, 17. D. Michael Quinn, *Mormon Hierarchy*, 479, accepted Sapp's estimate, whereas Baugh, "'We Have a Company of Danites in These Times,'" 19–20, has questioned it.

128. Ebenezer Robinson, "Items of Personal History of the Editor," *Return*, Oct. 1889, 147.

129. Sampson Avard, in Transcript, [2] (*Document*, 97).

"ultra-loyalists."[130] Corrill said the Danites were organized into companies of tens and fifties with captains over each, and Danite Albert P. Rockwood said there were captains over tens, fifties, and hundreds, which was similar to the organizational structure in ancient Israel.[131]

Corrill described the goals of the Danites in his 1839 history: "Some time in June last, a few individuals began to form a society that should be agreed in all things. ... As this society began to increase they secretly entered into solemn covenants, before God, and bound themselves under oath to keep the secrets of the society, and covenanted to stand by one another in difficulty, whether right or wrong, but said they would correct each others wrongs among themselves. ... They therefore entered into a covenant, that the word of the presidency should be obeyed, and none should be suffered to raise his hand or voice against it; for, as they stood at the head of the church, it was considered no more than reasonable that they knew more of the will of God than any others did; consequently, all things must be in submission to them, and, moreover, all tattling, lying, and backbiting, must be put down, and he that would not submit willingly should be forced to it, or leave the county."[132] Strict and unquestioning obedience to church leaders, especially the prophet, will become an enduring Danite legacy.

Avard testified that Smith said that "it was necessary this band should be bound together by a covenant, that those who reveald the secrets of the society should be put to death." The members of the society were required to raise their right hand and state: "In the name of Jesus Christ the Son of God, I do solemnly obligate myself, ever to conceal & never to reveal the secret purposes of this Society called the daughter of Zion; Should I ever do the same I hold my life as the forfeiture." Avard also testified that "instruction was given to the danite band by Jos Smith Jr. that if any of them should get into a difficulty, the rest should help him out, and that they should stand by each other right or rong, &. that this instruction was given at a publick address, delivered at a danite meeting."[133]

These Masonic-like blood oaths, which included signs, countersigns, and passwords, were seen by some church members as a violation of the Book of Mormon's prohibition against such things (2 Ne. 26:22; Alma 37:26–31;

---

130. *JSP*, H1:474n39; *JSP*, H1:475n46; Baugh, "A Call to Arms," 79–80.

131. Corrill, *Brief History*, 31 (*JSP*, H2:167); Rockwood, Journal, 11. See Ex. 18:13–26.

132. Corrill, *Brief History*, 30–31 (*JSP*, H2:166–67). A similar oath of secrecy was imposed on the members of Smith's secret Council of Fifty in Nauvoo in 1844. Council of Fifty, "Record," vol. 1, [26] (*JSP*, CFM, 42, and n. 75).

133. Sampson Avard, in Transcript, [2]–[3] (*Document*, 97–98).

Hel. 3:23; 6:21–27; Morm. 8:27; Ether 8:14–26).[134] As Corrill noted, "Now this secret combination was directly opposed to the former revelation, and especially the book of Mormon, which declared that God worketh not in secret, and all such as did should be destroyed. Many were opposed to this society, but such was their determination and also their threatenings against them, that those opposed dare not speak their minds on the subject."[135] Corrill became troubled by these developments because, he wrote, "it was clearly evident to me that the leaders of this faction intended to set up a monarchical government, in which the presidency should tyranize and rule over all things. In fact there was so much tyranny and oppression exercised, that for several weeks many persons dare not speak their minds, nor let them be known."[136]

As the Danites became more concerned with protecting the Mormon community from external threats, Smith's appellation for the group took on prophetic significance. According to Rockwood, "Those companies are called Danites because the Prophet Daniel has said they shall take the kingdom and possess it for ever."[137] This alludes to Daniel's prophetic dream in the Old Testament, wherein he saw that a stone that was cut out of a mountain "without hands" shall roll forth in the last days and smash all the kingdoms of the earth and grow into a great mountain and fill the whole earth, representing the establishment of God's kingdom in the last days, "which shall never be destroyed" (Dan. 2:33–35, 44). Avard testified that Smith "compared the Mormon church to the little stone spoken of by the Prophet Daniel; and the dissenters first, and the State next, was part of the image that should be destroyed by this little stone."[138]

Avard presented the court with a copy of the Constitution of the Society of the Daughter of Zion, which he claimed had been drafted in late June 1838.[139] This highly sensitive document was kept so secret that anti-Danite church historian Corrill had not heard of it before the trial.[140] Authorship of

---

134. Luman Shurtliff, Autobiography, 120–21. Shurtliff remembered that "sighns and passwords [were] given" so that "each member could know the other where ever they met night or day." Luman Shurtliff, Autobiography, 120.

135. Corrill, *Brief History*, 31 (*JSP*, H2:167).

136. Corrill, 31–32 (*JSP*, H2:168).

137. Rockwood, Journal, 12.

138. Avard, in Transcript, [3] (*Document*, 99).

139. Constitution of the Society of the Daughter of Zion, ca. late June 1838, in Transcript, [10]–[12] (*Document*, 101–102).

140. Corrill, *Brief History*, 31–32 (*JSP*, H2:168); John Corrill, in Transcript, [34] (*Document*, 113). John Cleminson also said he had not heard of the Danite Constitution until the trial, but admitted he "did not attend the first meetings in which the danite band was formed." John Cleminson, in Transcript, [54] (*Document*, 116).

the document is unknown, although some suspected it was Rigdon.[141] Avard claimed that it had been "read to the first presidency" in Rigdon's home and that it "was approved" and "unanimously adopted by them, as their rule & guide in future." It was then read "article by article to the Danite band and unanimously adopted by them."[142]

The Danite constitution begins by announcing: "We the members of the society of the Daughter of Zion do agree to regulate ourselves under such laws as in righteousness shall be deemed necessary for the preservation of our holy religion and of our most sacred rights, and the rights of our wives and children." Among other things, it declares their intention to "resist tyrany whether it be in Kings, or in people, It is all alike unto us, our rights we must have, and our rights we will shall have, in the name of Israels God." Its second and third articles stipulate: "The executive power shall be vested in the President of the whole church and his counsellors," and that "the legislative powers shall reside in the president and his cousellors together, and with the generals and colonels of the Society. By them all Laws shall be made regulating the society."[143]

In a March 1839 petition to Missouri Judge George Thompson, Joseph Smith denied Avard's claims about a constitution, stating that "Doctor Avard also swore false concerning a constitution as he said was introduced among the danit[e]s."[144] Smith also claimed in 1844 that the "Danites system never had any [official] existence" in the church, but a passage in his journal, dated July 27, 1838, spoke of them favorably: "We have a company of Danites in these times, to put to rights physically that which is not righ[t], and to clense the Church of verry great evils which hath hitherto existed among us, inasmuch as they cannot be put to rights by teachings & persuaysons."[145] The extent of Smith's involvement in the Danite organization has been disputed, but he knew about them and their activities. According to Corrill, "The first

---

141. Elias Higbee reported in 1840 that a Mr. Corwin of St. Louis claimed Rigdon had authored the Danite Constitution. Elias Higbee, Letter to Joseph Smith, Feb. 22, 1840, JS Letterbook 2, 113 (*JSP*, D7:196). The editors of the Joseph Smith Papers, however, state that "there is no indication that Rigdon authored the constitution." *JSP*, D7:196n406.

142. Avard, in Transcript, [9]–[10] (*Document*, 101).

143. Constitution of the Society of the Daughter of Zion, ca. late June 1838, in Transcript, [10]–[12] (*Document*, 101–102). For a discussion of the Danite constitution in the context of nineteenth-century vigilantism, see Park, "The Danite Constitution."

144. Alanson Ripley et al., Petition to George Tompkins, ca. Mar. 9–15 1839, [5], JS Collection (*JSP*, D6:349).

145. Nauvoo City Council Rough Minutes, Jan. 3, 1844 (Dinger, *The Nauvoo City and High Council Minutes*, 204); Smith, Journal, July 27, 1838 (*JSP*, J1:293).

presidency did not seem to have much to do with it at first: they would, how-ever, go into their meetings occasionally, and sanction their doings." Corrill also believed that Avard was the tool of the First Presidency, who "stood as wire workers behind the curtain."[146] Reed Peck referred to Smith as "the most busy actor and sharpest tool of the presidency," although his ranking of brigadier general was below Jared Carter's rank of captain general, the highest rank.[147] At the subsequent trial of Smith and others for treason and other crimes, Avard asserted that Smith was "the prime mover and organizer of this Danite band" and that Smith later removed him from his position as brigadier general and appointed him as surgeon to the Danites.[148] Carter was also subsequently removed and replaced by Elias Higbee, a Caldwell County judge, not Avard, for criticizing one of Rigdon's sermons.[149] Yet Avard will become the archvillain in Smith's narrative—largely because of his key testimony at the November court hearing—and Smith's scapegoat.

George Robinson, a colonel in the Danite organization and also the keeper of Smith's journal, wrote that the Danite companies were "exibited" at the Fourth of July 1838 celebration at Far West, over which Smith pre-sided.[150] Robinson made another entry in Smith's journal about an August 1838 expedition from Caldwell County to Daviess County to investigate re-ported mob violence against the Mormons, and that the expedition was led by "all the first presidency," as well as Danite officers "General [Elias] Hig-bee," "Gen. [Sampson] Avard," and "Colonel" Robinson, "whose duty it is to command one regiment."[151] This passage demonstrates that Smith was not only familiar with the Danites but worked in coordination with them, mak-ing his subsequent attempt to distance himself from them unconvincing.

---

146. Corrill, *Brief History*, 31 (*JSP*, H2:167).

147. Peck, Letter to "Dear Friends," 47, 50. On Avard's rank, see Peck, 45, 48; Peck, in Tran-script, [55]–[56]; Avard, in Transcript, [6]; "Celebration of the 4th of July," *Elders' Journal*, Aug. 1838, 60.

148. Avard, in Transcript, [1], [6] (*Document*, 97, 99).

149. Peck, Letter to "Dear Friends," Sep. 18, 1839, 47–48.

150. Smith, Journal, July 27, 1838 (*JSP*, J1:293). Concerning Robinson's status in the Danite society, see Smith, Journal, Aug. 7–9, 1838 (*JSP*, J1:299); Peck, Letter to "Dear Friends," Sep. 18, 1839, 46.

151. Smith, Journal, Aug. 7–9, 1838 (*JSP*, J1:298–301).

Call to Arms

JUNE–SEPTEMBER 1838

*We take God and all the holy angels to witness this day, that we
warn all men in the name of Jesus Christ, to come on us no more
forever, for from this hour, … it shall be between us and them a war
of extermination …*
— *Sidney Rigdon, Discourse, July 4, 1838, in* Oration, *12*

On June 23, 1838, the high council appointed a committee to visit tavern
keepers John Burk and Joseph Smith, who owned the only two taverns in Far
West, to ensure that they keep "good orderly houses, and have no drinking,
swearing, gambling, and debauchery carried on therein."[1] Five days later, the
committee reported that "Mr J. Smith jr, Mr J Burke and families manifested
a perfect willingness to comply with the request of your Honorable body."[2]

Smith soon began making preparations to move his family from the tavern into the former home of George Hinkle, who was moving to De Witt,
Carroll County, Missouri. Lucy Mack Smith, who mistakenly believed the
tavern had been purchased from a "brother Gilbert," remembered that her
son proposed that she and Joseph Smith Sr. "take a large tavern house … and
keep a tavern."[3] Records suggest that the extended Smith family moved into
the tavern, formerly owned by Samuel Musick, sometime between June 23
and 28.[4] On July 6 the high council ordered Bishop Partridge to purchase

---

1. Minutes, June 23, 1838, Minute Book 2, 142 (Cannon and Cook, *Far West Record*, 189).

2. Minutes, June 28–29, 1838, Minute Book 2, 143 (Cannon and Cook, *Far West Record*,
191). Webster's *American Dictionary of the English Language* (1828) defines "TAVERN" as "A
house licensed to sell liquors in small quantities, to be drank on the spot. In some of the United
States, however, tavern is synonymous with *inn* or *hotel*, and denotes a house for the entertainment
of travelers, as well as for the sale of liquors, licensed for that purpose."

3. Lucy Mack Smith, History, 1844–45, bk. 15, [6] (Anderson, ed., *Lucy's Book*, 630).

4. See Samuel Musick, Receipt, Far West, Caldwell Co., MO, to Joseph Smith, July 14, 1838,
JS Collection (*JSP*, D6:206); and *JSP*, D6:205n211.

the Hinkle house for Smith.[5] The house, which had been built by Hinkle and sold to Partridge for $1,200, was located in the southwest quadrant of Far West.[6] It was described nearly forty years later, in 1877, as "a rude, old-fashioned, one-story frame building, with two rooms" and featured "an unusually large and clumsy" chimney.[7]

At the time, Smith's family consisted of "a wife, five children, hired servants &c."[8] Joseph and Emma were the parents of seven-year-old adopted daughter Julia Murdock and three sons: five-year-old Joseph III, two-year-old Frederick, and newborn Alexander Hale Smith. The fifth child was apparently thirteen-year-old Johanna Carter, an orphan girl, who may have been taken into the Smith household in January 1836.[9] According to Israel Barlow, his brother Jonathan was "apointed Steward in the hous of President Joseph Smith."[10] Jonathan Barlow said that he "did the feeding, wartering horses, cutting wood &c about the place of Joseph Smith Jr."[11]

Adam-ondi-Ahman Stake

Smith visited Adam-ondi-Ahman in late June and was present with his counselors on Sunday, June 24, when, according to resident William Swartzell, Lyman Wight delivered a disturbing sermon. "I cannot listen with ease to the preaching of Lyman White—his exhorting a war upon the peaceful citizens of Missouri," Swartzell wrote. "In one of his sermons he denounced the citizens of Missouri, because they would not embrace the Mormon faith, as 'hypocrites, long-faced dupes, devils, infernal hob-goblins, and ghosts, and that they ought to be damned, and sent to hell, where they properly belonged.'" Swartzell, who would soon leave the Mormons, responded unfavorably to such talk, writing: "My blood felt chilled while listening to such blasphemous discourses."[12]

---

5. Minutes, July 6, 1838, Minute Book 2, 150 (Cannon and Cook, *Far West Record*, 197). See also Murdock, Journal, June 23, 1838; Murdock, Affidavit, Jan. 10, 1840.

6. See "List of Names of the Church of Latter Day Saints Living in the S W Quarter of Far West," Mar. 25, 1838, [5], in Teachers Quorum Minutes; Higbee, Deposition, Apr. 22, 1842.

7. A sketch and description of the home appeared in Barns, *The Commonwealth of Missouri*, 242; see also *JSP*, D6:171.

8. Joseph Smith, Letter to Isaac Galland, Mar. 22, 1839, *Times and Seasons*, Feb. 1840, 53 (*JSP*, 6:382).

9. Joseph Smith, Letter to Emma Smith, Apr. 4, 1839, [2] (*JSP*, D6:404, and n. 817).

10. Israel Barlow, Autobiographical Statement. Barlow's memory necessarily dates prior to his departure from Far West with Brigham Young in October 1838.

11. Jonathan Barlow, in Transcript of Proceedings, Nov. 12–29, 1838, [118]; hereafter Transcript. See also Jonathan Barlow, Testimony, Feb. 12, 1839, State of Missouri v. Ripley et al., Justice of the Peace Court, Clay County Archives and Historical Library, Liberty, MO.

12. Swartzell, *Mormonism Exposed*, 13–14.

Four days later, on June 28, Smith presided over a conference to organize the Adam-ondi-Ahman stake. Swartzell described the location of the meeting as "a grove, in the woods, adjoining brother White's house," that was "situated between Grand River and a large prairie, well timbered and beautifully shaded" and that had several benches "made out of trees split in two."[13] John Smith was chosen as president of the stake with Reynolds Cahoon and Lyman Wight as counselors. Vinson Knight was appointed as bishop *pro tempore,* and high councilors were also chosen, many of whom had previously served in the Kirtland stake. "President J. Smith Jr. made remarks by way of charge to the Presidents and counsellors, instructing them in the duty of their callings, and the responsibility of their stations; exhorting them to be cautious and deliberate, in all their councils, and to be careful to act in righteousness in all things."[14]

Soon after this meeting, Smith returned to Far West. Peter H. Burnett, who later became the first governor of California, recounted that he first met Smith on a Sunday "in June or July, 1838," possibly July 1, when he and John McDaniel, a young merchant from Liberty, attended church with the Mormons at Far West. Unknown to Burnett, McDaniel had "openly ridiculed Smith's pretensions to the gift of prophecy, and his remarks had been reported to the prophet." The meeting was held in "a large frame building, with seats well arranged and a good pulpit." After listening to two sermons, which Burnett described as "simply plain, practical discourses, and created no emotion," Smith rose and spoke with "the most intense excitement." Burnett was taken by surprise when Smith "boldly denounced McDaniel in the most severe terms, saying, in substance, that no man should come to Far West and openly vilify and slander him, and that, if his brethren would not protect him, he would protect himself." Burnett said, "I watched him as he sat by my side, and he was as pale as a corpse, but did not stir or open his lips."

After the meeting, McDaniel wanted to speak privately with Smith and requested Burnett to accompany him. Burnett said little about the exchange, only that "an explanation was made on both sides, and the matter there terminated."[15] Given the fact that his repeated efforts to establish Zion in Missouri met with failure despite prophecies and revelations, Smith's prophetic gift was vulnerable to attack, from both within and without. His response to such

---

13. Swartzell, *Mormonism Exposed*, 14.

14. Minutes, June 28, 1838, *Elders' Journal*, Aug. 1838, 60–61 (*JSP*, D6:162–67).

15. Burnett, *Recollections*, 56–57. The previous Sunday in June, Smith was in Adam-ondi-Ahman, according to Swartzell, *Mormonism Exposed*, 13–14.

criticism was often to vilify and expel the dissenters. A visiting non-Mormon was left to express what was forbidden among believers. Smith's display of outrage and anger was less about McDaniel's comments than about his followers' tolerance of such talk and what he perceived as a lack of loyalty.

On July 3, according to Edward Stevenson, "There was a general meeting of the Saints in Far West, about 1500 met and had a grand time Ground was broken for A Temple 110 feet x 80 feet A House of The Lord to be reared in this our day, and on this Holy land once occupied by our Father Adam."[16]

Fourth of July

On July 4 Smith participated in a celebration on the public square at Far West, which was attended by many church officials, a military regiment of the state militia, and "several thousand spectators."[17] There was also a company of Danites in attendance, according to Smith's journal.[18] Ebenezer Robinson, who assisted with the publication of the *Elders' Journal*, recalled that "a stand was erected for the officers and orator of the day, large enough also to seat several distinguished visitors."[19] This stand was erected on the northeast corner of the public square near the temple site.

The celebration began at 10:00 a.m. with a parade in which the Caldwell County regiment of the state militia as well as a company of Danites marched around the square and then formed a line around the temple excavation, where Smith offered a prayer and the band played a musical number. Church officers and others participated in the ceremonial laying of the cornerstones for the temple. After that, the procession reassembled around the stand, where Sidney Rigdon delivered the oration. According to Smith's journal, Rigdon delivered the discourse "under the hoisted flagg representing the Liberty and independence of these United States of America," and used this occasion to declare Mormon "independence from all mobs and persecutions which have been inflicted upon them, time after time," which they would "bear ... no longer."[20]

Swartzell said Rigdon "read off his oration with considerable energy and eloquence."[21] It was quickly published at Liberty in the periodical *Far*

---

16. Stevenson, Autobiography, 64.

17. Smith, Journal, July 4, 1838 (*JSP*, J1:275–78).

18. Smith, Journal, July 27, 1838 (*JSP*, J1:293).

19. Ebenezer Robinson, "Items of Personal History of the Editor," *Return* (Davis City, IA), Oct. 1889, 148.

20. Smith, Journal, July 4, 1838 (*JSP*, J1:276).

21. Swartzell, *Mormonism Exposed*, 16.

West, and as an eleven-page pamphlet printed by the church at Far West the following month titled *Oration Delivered by Mr. S. Rigdon on the 4th of July, 1838, at Far West, Caldwell County, Missouri*.[22] Robinson wrote in his reminiscence that "Rigdon was not alone responsible for the sentiment expressed in his oration, as that was a carefully prepared document, previously written, and well understood by the First Presidency, but Elder Rigdon was the mouth piece to deliver it."[23] In an editorial published in the August 1838 issue of the *Elders' Journal*, Smith endorsed Rigdon's speech and recommended that church members obtain a copy of the pamphlet.[24]

In his sermon, Rigdon declared that the Mormons would no longer tolerate harassing lawsuits or mob violence but would aggressively defend themselves and pursue their constitutional right to establish Far West as a gathering center and to expand into neighboring counties. "We have not only when smitten on one cheek turned the other, but we have done it, again and again, until we are wearied of being smitten, and tired of being trampled upon," Rigdon proclaimed. "We have proved the world with kindness, we have suffered their abuse without cause, with patience, and have endured without resentment, until this day, and still their persecutions and violence does not cease. But from this day and this hour, we will suffer it no more." He then boldly declared:

> We take God and all the holy angels to witness this day, that we warn all men in the name of Jesus Christ, to come on us no more forever, for from this hour, we will bear it no more, our rights shall no more be trampled on with impunity. The man or the set of men, who attempts it, does it at the expense of their lives. And that mob that comes on us to disturb us; it shall be between us and them a war of extermination, for we will follow them, till the last drop of their blood is spilled, or else they will have to exterminate us: for we will carry the seat of war to their own houses, and their own families, and one party or the other shall be utterly destroyed. ... We this day then proclaim ourselves free, with a purpose and a determination, that never can be broken, "no never! *no never*!! NO NEVER."!!![25]

"At the conclusion of the oration," Robinson later reported, "the vast multitude shouted, Hosanna! Hosanna!! Hosanna!!! three times, in confirmation

---

22. See Smith, Journal, Aug. 1–3, 1838 (*JSP*, D6:296); Crawley, *A Descriptive Bibliography*, 1:80.

23. Ebenezer Robinson, "Items of Personal History of the Editor," *Return*, Nov. 1889, 170.

24. [Joseph Smith], Editorial, *Elders' Journal*, Aug. 1838, 54.

25. Rigdon, *Oration Delivered by Mr. S. Rigdon*, 12; compare covenants described in Smith, Journal, Sep. 24, 1835 and Mar. 30, 1836 (*JSP*, J1:64, 215).

of the declaration of independence made by the speaker."[26] The First Presidency descended from the stand and "marched to the south side of the public square," where the assembled troops "passed in review before them."[27] With this demonstration of military preparedness, the celebration came to a close.

According to Edward Stevenson, "Several Missourians Manifested their Indipendance by being Babtized into the Church of Jesus Christ of L.D. Saints,"[28] but most non-Mormons were angered by Rigdon's rhetoric. Rigdon's speech would prove to be one of the biggest blunders of the Mormon leadership, and publishing the speech amplified tensions between the Mormons and Missourians. Historian Marvin S. Hill called this speech "the turning point in Mormon-Gentile relations in western Missouri."[29] One resident of Liberty declared in the *Western Star*: "Until July 4th, we heard no threats being made against them in any quarters. The people had all become reconciled to let them remain where they are. ... But one Sidney Rigdon, in order to show himself a great man, collected them all together in the town of Far West, on the 4th of July, and there delivered a speech containing the essence of, if not treason itself."[30] On September 12 anti-Mormons in Daviess and Livingston Counties stated in a letter to Missouri governor Lilburn W. Boggs that "for several weeks past the Mormons have been making formidable preparation for a civil war—and one which they are pleased to call a war of extermination."[31] Six years later, Jedediah M. Grant asserted that Rigdon's 4th of July oration "was the main auxiliary that fanned into a flame the burning wrath of the mobocratic portion of the Missourians."[32] Samuel Miles, a convert from New York, later described Rigdon's "noble oration" as "'the beginning of the end' of our stay in Missouri."[33]

Ebenezer Robinson also reported that "a few days after" the raising of the flag pole "a thunderstorm arose, and passing over the place, a shaft of

---

26. Ebenezer Robinson, "Items of Personal History of the Editor," *Return*, Oct. 1889, 149. See also Swartzell, *Mormonism Exposed*, 16; Pratt, *History of the Late Persecution*, 26–27; "A History of the Persecution, of the Church of Jesus Christ, of Latter Day Saints in Missouri," *Times and Seasons*, Apr. 1840, 81 (*JSP*, H2:234).

27. Smith, Journal, July 4 and 27, 1838 (*JSP*, J1:275–78, 293).

28. Stevenson, Autobiography, 64, 67, 68, 69, 70.

29. Hill, *Quest for Refuge*, 79.

30. Quoted in "The Mormons," *Missouri Argus* (St. Louis), Sep. 27, 1838, [1].

31. "Citizens of Daviess and Livingston Counties," Letter to Lilburn W. Boggs, Sep. 12, 1838, [1], Mormon War Papers (*Document*, 18).

32. Grant, *A Collection of Facts*, 11. See also "Continuation of Elder Rigdon's Trial," *Times and Seasons*, Oct. 1, 1844, 667.

33. Samuel Miles, "Recollections of the Prophet Joseph Smith," *Juvenile Instructor*, Mar. 15, 1892, 174.

lightning struck the liberty pole and rived it into more than a thousand atoms," which "struck dismay into the hearts of some." Smith apparently felt compelled to respond to this bad omen. Robinson was not there, but soon after heard that Smith prophesied as he walked over the scattered splinters, "so we will trample our enemies under our feet," which "gave encouragement to the fearful and timid."[34] Mosiah Hancock remembered Smith said, "There goes the liberty of the people."[35] According to Philo Dibble, a lieutenant colonel in the Caldwell County regiment of the state militia and a Danite, "Joseph walked around on the splinters and said: 'As that pole was splintered, so shall the nations of the earth be!'"[36] Parley Pratt also wrote that the splintering of the liberty pole manifested "to many that there was an end to liberty and law in that state ... and seemed to portend the awful fate which awaited that devoted city, and the county and people around."[37]

Conference and Revelations

On July 6 Smith attended the first of a three-day conference, during which Bishop Partridge was granted authority to use church funds to purchase George Hinkle's house and furnish it with a new stove, and otherwise prepare it to be occupied by Smith and his family. On Sunday, July 8, the concluding day of the conference, Smith dictated five revelations relating to church organization and finances, three of which were read to the congregation at the worship meeting later in the afternoon.

One revelation, which "was read this day in the congregation of the saints," was given in answer to the question, "Show unto us thy will O Lord concerning the Twelve." Thomas Marsh, who was the only apostle at the meeting, was instructed to stay in Far West to publish God's word, and the Twelve were to return to England "next spring," departing from Far West at the temple lot on April 26, 1839. Former apostles William McLellin, Lyman Johnson, Luke Johnson, and John Boynton were to be replaced by John E. Page, who was still in Upper Canada, and John Taylor, Wilford Woodruff, and Willard Richards, who were already in England.[38]

Another revelation, which was subsequently read to the congregation but

---

34. Ebenezer Robinson, "Items of Personal History of the Editor," *Return*, Oct. 1889, 149.

35. Mosiah Lyman Hancock, Autobiography, 10.

36. Dibble, "Philo Dibble's Narrative," 88; Quinn, *Mormon Hierarchy*, 481.

37. Pratt, *History of the Late Persecution*, 27; see also "A History of the Persecution," *Times and Seasons*, Apr. 1840, 81 (*JSP*, H2:234).

38. Revelation, July 8, 1838-A, in Smith, Journal, Mar.–Sep. 1838, 54–55 [D&C 118] (*JSP*, J1:284–85).

was never canonized, demoted Frederick Williams, formerly a counselor to Smith, and Phelps, formerly a counselor to David Whitmer in the Missouri presidency, "in consequence of their transgressions." Thenceforth they were to be common elders.[39] Unlike other dissidents, Phelps and Williams repented and were allowed to remain in Far West.[40]

A third revelation, which later received a public reading, concerned church revenue, requiring that "all their surplus property be put into the hands of the Bishop. ... And after that, those who have thus been tithed, shall pay one-tenth of all their interest annually."[41] In a July 24, 1838, letter to Newel Whitney, Partridge explained that "the saints are required to give all their surplus property into the hands of the bishop of Zion, and after this first tithing they are to pay annually one tenth of all their interest. that is if a man is worth a $1000, the interest on that would be $60, and one/10. of the interest will be of course $6."[42] These funds were to be used for building the temple, laying the foundation of Zion, and paying the debts of the First Presidency.

A fourth revelation briefly directed that tithing funds be managed by a council consisting of the First Presidency, Bishop Partridge and his counselors, and the Zion high council.[43]

Finally, Smith dictated a revelation directing William Marks and Newel Whitney to settle their business and leave Kirtland before winter. The revelation waxed poetic in its reference to the Mormon expansion into Daviess County: "Is there not room enough upon the mountains of Adamondi awman, or upon the plains of Olea Shinihah, or the land where Adam dwelt. ... Therefore come up hither unto the land of my people even Zion." The revelation told Newel K. Whitney to "be ashamed of the Nicolitins, and of all their secret abominations ... and come up unto the land of Adam ondi awman and be a bishop unto my people saith the Lord, not in name but in deed."[44]

Both Mormons and their contemporaries associated the Nicolaitans of Revelation 2:6, 15, whose deeds and doctrines the Lord hates, with antinomianism, particularly with sexual sin, including belief in the "community of

---

39. Revelation, July 8, 1838-B, in Smith, Journal, Mar.–Sep. 1838, 55 [uncanonized] (*JSP*, J1:285–86).

40. In a letter, dated July 24, 1838, Edward Partridge mentioned that Phelps and Williams had been rebaptized "about 4 weeks since." Edward Partridge, Letter to Newel K. Whitney, July 24, 1838.

41. Revelation, July 8, 1838-C, in Smith, Journal, Mar.–Sep. 1838, 56 [D&C 119] (*JSP*, J1:288).

42. Edward Partridge, Letter to Newel K. Whitney, July 24, 1838.

43. Revelation, July 8, 1838-D, in Smith, Journal, Mar.–Sep. 1838, 57 [D&C 120] (*JSP*, J1:289).

44. Revelation, July 8, 1838-E, [1], Revelations Collection [D&C 117] (*JSP*, D6:196); see also Smith, Journal, Mar.–Sep. 1838, 57–59 (*JSP*, J1:289–90).

wives," polygamy, adultery, and fornication.[45] Only two days before dictating this revelation Smith received a letter from Orson Hyde and Heber Kimball that referred to the "Nicholatine Band of which you warned us," who deal in "sand stone & bogus," a possible reference to Warren Parrish and the dissenters.[46] Apparently, Smith's rhetoric concerning the "Nicholatine Band" began as early as his confrontation with dissidents and apostates in the summer of 1837 before Kimball and Hyde departed from Kirtland in mid-June.[47] In an editorial published in the August issue of the *Elders' Journal*, Smith told a story about Parrish going to Tinker's Creek, where there was a gang of swindlers, to buy a box of counterfeit coins with Kirtland Bank notes, but upon returning home and opening the box finding nothing but "sand and stones."[48] Smith was attempting to reverse Cowdery's accusations concerning his affair with Fanny Alger as well as Parrish's criticisms of his mismanaging the bank and misrepresenting and inflating its assets. The revelation also admonished Bishop Whitney, who was not directly implicated in any wrongdoing, to "be ashamed of the Nicolitins, and of all their secret abominations."

In the afternoon, Smith presided over the third day of the conference. The three revelations he dictated at Kirtland on January 12, 1838, one of which concerned changes in which a member of the presidency could be tried and removed from office, were read. This was followed by a presentation of three of the five revelations that Smith had dictated earlier the same day.[49]

Later, Presidents Smith, Rigdon, and Hyrum Smith wrote to William Marks and Newel Whitney in Kirtland instructing them to move to Missouri; their letter was to be delivered "by the hand of br O[liver] Granger." The presidency included a copy of the revelation concerning them, which had been "rec[eive]d this morning." They cautioned that although it was "wisdom for all the Saints that Come this Summer to come & make an effort to do so as it will be better for them," nevertheless it was important that "none think to get property whenever they Come here for there is

45. Bancroft, *Sermons*, 315; Clarke, *The Holy Bible*, Rev. 2:6; John Greenhow to editor, *Times and Seasons*, Mar. 15, 1843, 138; Zenas H. Gurley, "History of the Reorganization," *Saints' Herald*, Mar. 1860, 53; Whitmer, *An Address to All Believers in Christ*, 5.

46. Orson Hyde and Heber C. Kimball, Letter to Joseph Smith, May 22 and 28, 1838, in Smith, Journal, July 6, 1838 (*JSP*, J1:279–80; D6:147).

47. "Mission to England, or the First Foreign Mission of the Latter-Day Saints," *Millennial Star* (Liverpool, Eng.), Apr. 1841, 289. Cf. DHC 2:492.

48. [Joseph Smith], editorial, *Elders' Journal*, Aug. 1838, 58.

49. Smith, Journal, July 8, 1838 (*JSP*, J1:281–90).

none for them at present but there will be."[50] Smith and others had spent May and early June surveying and laying claim to large tracts of land in Daviess County; however, on July 24 Partridge wrote to Whitney that it was unclear when the government would sell the land.[51] Nevertheless, the presidency encouraged migration, insisting that "there need be no fear in the saints coming up here there are provisions or will be in great abundance of all kinds indeed there is a plenty now neither has there been a scarcity at any time since we come."[52]

Danite Meetings in Daviess County

Meanwhile, on July 8, Sunday services were also being held at Adam-ondi-Ahman. According to Swartzell, Wight sermonized about "the sons of thunder, and of war." He also said that "the Missourians were blind, and stank strongly of the Devil—and that Peter's having cut off the ear of the High Priest's (Caiphus) servant, was a strong argument for war."[53] About July 10 Smith left Far West with Rigdon, Hyrum Smith, and George Robinson to visit Adam-ondi-Ahman.[54]

Four days later Smith preached at a Danite meeting in a grove near Wight's house. Swartzell reported: "Sentinels, armed with pistols, swords, and guns, were posted on the outskirts of the grove." When Swartzell was asked if he could "eat strong meat," he answered that he could "if the meat had a good scent" and was not allowed to attend the meeting. Afterward Ezra Thayer said to Swartzell, "Ah! brother Swartzell, you should have been at the meeting; you should have heard all about the Daranite [Danite] business, for brother Joseph preached, and brother Hiram, and brother Rigdon. ... I dare not tell you what they said or preached; but never mind, next Saturday is another Darinite meeting, and then I will cause you to come in, too, to learn this mystery—provided no one objects to your being a Daranite, or a MAN of war!"[55]

On July 19 Swartzell wrote: "All things are going as briskly as ever. The brethren are getting lots, and raising houses on them—two or three every day." However, Swartzell noted that there was "much complaining among the poor

---

50. Joseph Smith, Sidney Rigdon, and Hyrum Smith, Revelation and Letter to William Marks and Newel K. Whitney, July 8, 1838, [1]–[2], JS Collection (*JSP*, D6:196–97).

51. Partridge, Letter to Newel K. Whitney, July 24, 1838.

52. Joseph Smith et al., Revelation and Letter to William Marks and Newel K. Whitney, Kirtland, July 8, 1838, [2], JS Collection (*JSP*, D6:197).

53. Swartzell, *Mormonism Exposed*, 17. See John 18:10.

54. JS History, vol. B-1, 804 (DHC 3:47).

55. Swartzell, *Mormonism Exposed*, 17–18.

for food and water," and that Wight, who was a counselor in the Adam-ondi-Ahman bishopric, "employed another brother to haul wheat, flour, and corn, with his team, to satisfy the craving appetites of the hungry brethren."[56]

On Saturday, July 21, Smith attended another Danite meeting. Swartzell, who attended and was initiated into the group's ranks, wrote: "The Daranites [Danites] were all armed; some had swords, some had pistols, and others had guns and cow-hides. ... A circle was formed, in the midst of which, the regular Daranites seated themselves, while sentinels, well armed, guarded the outposts, and secured the usual entrance to the place of meeting, so that no one could enter except a regular member, or those desirous of being initiated." Swartzell described the process of initiation in detail, stating that men were "initiated in companies of eleven at a time. So that each company, after initiation, should choose a Captain, and remain the even number, ten." The initiation ceremony was conducted by Wight, who had his hair cut in "a peculiar manner" and "held in his hand a cow-hide, on the end of which, was about a pound of lead, with a string to it, passed around his wrist; and he said that every Daranite should have such a weapon." Initiates were to have "no enmity against his follow" members but were required to settle all grievances immediately. After a short sermon by Smith, Wight administered a Masonic-like oath of secrecy, wherein initiates swore with uplifted hands to "conceal, and never reveal, at the peril of committing perjury, and the pains of death, and my body be given to the shot, and laid in the dust."[57] Wight then gave them a secret sign, "whereby ye may know each other anywhere," especially "if a brother be in distress." This sign, as Swartzell described it, was "to clap the right hand to the right thigh, and then raise it quick to the right temple, the thumb extending behind the ear." Wight then gave them the password, which was to be given while shaking hands in answer to the question *"Who be you?"* Answer: *"Anama."* Wight explained that the word *anama* "is, by interpretation, *a friend."*[58]

Swartzell remembered that Wight gave the following charge: "That every Daranite [Danite] must hold himself in readiness, at a moment's warning, by day or by night. Each one of you must be equipped with a gun, or a cow-skin, or a pistol, &c., according to your different stations; each one of you to have on hand, (when called upon to go at a moment's warning, asking no

---

56. Swartzell, 19.

57. Six years later, a similar oath of secrecy will be imposed on the members of Smith's secret Council of Fifty in Nauvoo. Council of Fifty, "Record," vol. 1, [26] (*JSP*, CFM, 42, and n. 75).

58. Swartzell, *Mormonism Exposed*, 20–23.

questions) one pound of powder, and one hundred bullets." Militant rhetoric ran high; one of the captains admonished his fellow Danites to be "true and faithful. I will be with you in life or death. I expect to be one in the great battle of Gog and Magog, until the blood shall come up to the horse-bridles."[59]

On Sunday, July 22, Smith probably attended church services in Adam-ondi-Ahman, where, according to Swartzell, "Brother [Lyman] White [Wight] preached to-day, on the *consecration* ... of property to the Church of the Latter-Day-Saints. He said that after the brethren had bought lots to suit themselves, with their own money, in the city of Adam-on-Diammon, ... then they should consecrate all their money and property to the Church, so that the Church can purchase the lands and locations within 12 miles from the centre of the *stake*, in every direction."[60] Soon after this meeting, Smith returned to Far West.

Danite Meeting in Far West

On July 26 Smith and his counselors in the First Presidency met with the high council and bishopric of Far West to discuss the management of property donated by church members in Caldwell County. "It was agreed that the first presidency keep all their properties, that they can dispose of to their advantage and support, and the remainder be put into the hands of the Bishop or Bishops, agreeably to the commandments, and revelations."[61]

During this meeting, seven propositions were passed: (1) that the traveling expense of the First Presidency is to be defrayed, with the bishops of Far West and Adam-ondi-Ahman each paying half when traveling the twenty-five miles between the two places; (2) that this is to become the general practice wherever they travel; (3) that the bishop is authorized to exchange the assets of emigrating Mormons for land in Missouri; (4) that this exchange is to be subject to control by the First Presidency; (5) that the bishop of Zion is to receive consecrations of those not belonging to a stake; (6) that the leadership is to use their influence to stop the sale of liquor at Far West and bring down the price of provisions; and (7) that Phelps is to "draw up a petition to remove the county seat [of Caldwell County] to Far West."[62] As Caldwell County would not have an official county seat until the spring of 1843, when Kingston was organized, Far West served as the de facto seat

---

59. Swartzell, 23.

60. Swartzell, 23–24.

61. Minutes, July 26, 1838, in Smith, Journal, Mar.–Sep. 1838, 59 (*JSP*, J1:291; D6:207).

62. Smith, Journal, Mar.–Sep. 1838, 59–60 (*JSP*, J1:291–93; D6:207–208).

because county justices Elias Higbee and Phelps, county clerk John Cleminson, and the circuit court all operated there.[63]

On the same day, Swartzell wrote: "Doing nothing today, except looking at the hands employed in getting out logs for brother Joseph Smith's house, in which he intends translating the hieroglyphics of the Egyptian mummies."[64] Smith was presently living in George Hinkle's old house, and, despite his possible intentions, there is no evidence that he occupied another residence in Far West or worked on his translation of the Egyptian papyri in Missouri.

Under July 27, George Robinson recorded in Smith's journal: "[For] some time past the brethren or saints have come up day after day to consecrate, and to bring their offerings into the store house of the lord, to prove him now herewith and se[e] if he will not pour us out a blessings that there will not be room enough to contain it."[65] On this day, the Danites came to the bishop's storehouse in companies of ten to consecrate the surplus of their property. "Shortly after the Danites became organized," wrote Corrill, "they set out to enforce the law of consecration; but this did not amount to much."[66] According to Reed Peck, "In July the law of consecration took effect which required every person to give up to the bishop all surplus property of every description, not necessary for their present support." Peck said that Danite leader Sampson Avard told him and Corrill that "all persons who attempted to deceive and retain property that should be given up would meet with the fate of Ananias and Saphira who were Killed by Peter," an interpolation of Acts 5:1–10, where Ananias and his wife, Sapphira, suddenly "gave up the ghost" as a divine punishment for withholding a portion of their consecration to the apostles.[67]

Danite Meetings in Daviess County

On July 28 Smith and Rigdon left Far West for Adam-ondi-Ahman to transact some business and make arrangements to settle some of the Canadian immigrants, who were expected to arrive imminently.[68] While there, the two men attended a meeting of the Danites, during which they were organized and integrated with the Danites at Far West. According to Swartzell,

---

63. See *History of Caldwell and Livingston Counties, Missouri*, 259; *JSP*, J1:293n204; *JSP*, D6:208n229.

64. Swartzell, *Mormonism Exposed*, 25.

65. Smith, Journal, July 27, 1838 (*JSP*, J1:293). Cf. Mal. 3:10.

66. Corrill, *Brief History*, 46 (*JSP*, H2:193).

67. Peck, Letter to "Dear Friends," Sep. 18, 1839, 51–52.

68. Smith, Journal, July 28, 1838 (*JSP*, J1:294).

"After considerable preaching, as usual"—suggesting that Smith may have addressed the Danites on this occasion—the Danites at Adam-ondi-Ahman were "organized into companies of tens, twenties, fifties, hundreds, &c.," and then placed under the command of a brigadier general and other officers. During the meeting, Wight "stood up in the middle of eleven men, and with their hands uplifted, administered the oath, and initiated them into the band of warriors, and sons of thunder."[69]

On Sunday, July 29, Smith attended church services in Wight's unfinished home at the foot of Tower Hill and delivered a discourse about the harassment and spiritual manifestations he had experienced.[70] Rigdon spoke first, taking Ephesians 4:4–13 as his text and, expounding on the theme of "one Lord, one faith, one baptism," criticized other Christian denominations for their lack of "those gifts which Jesus Christ gave to men when he ascended on high." Smith preached "on prophecy, and said that the Spirit of God had appeared to him, with wonderful *light* and *mystery*—in such a manner that we would not believe him, were he to tell us what he had seen." Smith also declared: "I know that all the world is threatening my life; but I regard it not, for I am willing to die at any time when God calls for me. I have been beaten, abused, stoned, persecuted, and have had to escape by day and by night. I have been sued at law, and have always proved myself innocent. I have had *twenty-one law-suits*. I am of age; and care not how long I live. Not my will be done, but thine, O Lord!"[71]

Election-Day Conflict

Smith and Rigdon returned to Far West on the evening of July 30. Despite his fatigue, Smith attended court with his brother Hyrum. The circuit court began sitting on this day with Judge Austin A. King presiding, along with his entourage of lawyers.[72] King was a judge in Missouri's fifth judicial circuit court, which included Caldwell, Daviess, Ray, Clay, Carroll, and Livingston Counties.[73] The next day, Smith returned to court and later had

---

69. Swartzell, *Mormonism Exposed*, 25–26. John Smith, president of the Adam-ondi-Ahman stake, noted that at least three Danite meetings had taken place by August 4, 1838. John Smith, Journal, Aug. 4, 1838.

70. On the location of the meeting, see Berrett, *Sacred Places*, 4:376, 399–402; for a photograph of Wight's home, see *JSP*, D6:211.

71. Swartzell, *Mormonism Exposed*, 26–27. John Smith noted in his journal the following week that Smith and Rigdon held a meeting in Adam-ondi-Ahman "last Sabbath." John Smith, Journal, Aug. 4, 1838.

72. Smith, Journal, July 30, 1838 (*JSP*, J1:294).

73. See *JSP*, J1:294n209.

a brief visit from King and one of the circuit attorneys, Thomas Burch, both of whom subsequently visited Rigdon and requested him to preach. Rigdon declined because he was still fatigued from his late arrival to Far West the previous night.[74]

Meanwhile, Daviess County was preparing for the upcoming August 6 state and county elections. "Missourians electioneering hard among the brethren to-day," Swartzell wrote.[75] At the same time, conflict between Missourians and Mormons over land was brewing, with, according to Swartzell, the Mormons being the aggressors: "Twenty of the Mormons drove off some of the Missourians from their improvements with cow-hides. The brethren are determined to have all the lands and property that they can lay their hands upon." Swartzell's use of an exact number likely reflects the operation of the Danites. Swartzell said to Ezra Thayer, "They will be friends with the brethren until the election is over, and then look out that they don't make them smoke, for driving the citizens off of their lands. This will be kept quiet until after the election: then will come hard times." The ever-faithful Thayer responded: "The land is ours, and we will either have actual settlers upon it, or we will take it by the sword."[76] Smith's journal mentions that "office seekers from without the Church who depend verry much on our help, begin to flatter us with smooth stories but we understand them verry well through the wisdom of God."[77]

On August 4 the Danites held a meeting of officers at Far West, which "appointed a committee, consisting of one man from each township in the county, who called upon the first presidency to assist them in making out a nomination." During the night they printed a ticket of candidates and in the morning distributed copies among church members. The result was that the Van Buren ticket got 351 votes in Caldwell County, the Whig only got 2. Corrill reported that many members believed that the Danite bill was "from head quarters, and that it was the will of God that all should go for it," but others saw it as "taking an undue advantage of the election, and were extremely dissatisfied; not so much with the ticket itself as with the principle in which it had been got up, for the ticket was democratic, and the Mormons, as individuals, are almost universally of that party."[78]

---

74. Smith, Journal, July 31, 1838 (*JSP*, J1:296).

75. Swartzell, *Mormonism Exposed*, 27.

76. Swartzell, 27–28.

77. Smith, Journal, Aug. 6, 1838 (*JSP*, J1:297).

78. Corrill, *Brief History*, 33 (*JSP*, H2:169–70); "Editorial Items," *Quincy (IL) Whig*, Aug. 25, 1838, [2].

On August 6—Election Day—a fight broke out between Mormons and non-Mormons at Gallatin, the county seat for Daviess County, with the intent of preventing the Mormons from voting. The instigator of the riot, William P. Peniston, was trying to get elected to the Missouri House of Representatives on the Whig ticket. Peniston had previously approached Lyman Wight to gain the crucial Mormon voting bloc, but the Mormons were predominantly Democrats and were aware of Peniston's involvement in a previous attempt to expel them from Clay County. On Election Day, in front of the store where the voting was taking place, Peniston climbed on top of a large whisky barrel and delivered a "flaming speech," telling the gathered crowd: "The leaders of the [Mormon] Church was a set of horse thieves liars counterfieters &c he s[ai]d. you know that they profess to heal the sick, cast out devils &c. & you all know it is a d—d lie— & appealed to the people if we suffer such men as those to vote, you will soon lose your suffrage."[79] Corrill wrote that the rapid growth of Adam-ondi-Ahman "stirred up the people of Davies," who believed "it would injure Gallatin, their county seat, and also that the Mormons would soon overrun Davis, and rule the county, and they did not like to live under the laws and administration of 'Joe Smith.'"[80]

When Mormon Samuel Brown attempted to vote, "one of the mob standing by, opposed his voting, contending that a Mormon had no more right to vote than a Negro."[81] A drunken Richard Weldon asked Brown if he believed in "healing the sick by the laying on of hands, speaking in tongues, and casting out devils?" When Brown answered in the affirmative, Weldon said, "You are a d—d liar. Joseph Smith is a d—d imposter."[82] An angry exchange of words quickly escalated to blows. Instantly, a free-for-all fight involving clubs, sticks, and boards ensued; about eight Mormons tried to resist a mob of about sixty non-Mormons.[83] Men on both sides were injured, some seriously, and the Mormons were forced to flee.

---

79. Corrill, *Brief History*, 33 (*JSP*, H2:170); John D. Lee and Levi Stewart, Statement, 1845. Vogel, *History of Joseph Smith*, 8:70–80. On the fight at the election poll and its aftermath, see Gentry, "A History of the Latter-day Saints in Northern Missouri," 170–73; Durham, "The Election Day Battle at Gallatin"; and LeSueur, "Mixing Politics with Religion."

80. Corrill, *Brief History*, 28 (*JSP*, H2:163).

81. Joseph Smith et al., Memorial to the United States Senate and House of Representatives, ca. Oct. 30, 1839–Jan. 27, 1840, 11 (*JSP*, D7:154–55).

82. Lee, *Mormonism Unveiled*, 58.

83. Lee reported that only eight Mormons took part in the fight. Lee, *Mormonism Unveiled*, 60. According to Joseph Smith, "about 150 Missourians faut against from 6 to 12 of our brethren." Smith, Journal, Aug. 7, 1838 (*JSP*, J1:299). Another source names ten Mormons who participated, six of whom, according to Gentry, were Danites. *Deseret News* (Salt Lake City), Sep. 10, 1904; Gentry, "A

Mormon John L. Butler remembered that when the fighting broke out, "the first thing that came to my mind was the covenants entered into by the Danites to the effect that they were to protect each other," so he yelled: "O yes, you Danites, here is a job for us."[84] John D. Lee said he and a few other Mormon men were lying on the grass nearby and saw Butler give the Danite signal of distress, to which they immediately responded. "Seeing the sign," wrote Lee, "I sprang to my feet and armed myself with one of the oak sticks, I did this because I was a Danite, and my oaths that I had taken required immediate action on my part, in support of the one giving the sign."[85] The result of the violence was that very few, if any, Mormons voted.[86] Nevertheless, Peniston lost to Democrat John Williams.

Meanwhile, at Far West, the First Presidency met at Smith's home to discuss the problem of some of the Canadian members settling at the forks of Grand River, located in Clinton County (now in Gentry County) about thirty miles northwest of Adam-ondi-Ahman, "contrary to council" given them on July 28.[87] Their actions were considered a violation of one of the revelations dictated on July 8, 1838, which designated Adam-ondi-Ahman as the place of settlement.[88]

In the afternoon, the citizens of Far West held a meeting at the schoolhouse with Elias Higbee as chair. It was decided that Rigdon should replace Phelps as postmaster. Smith spoke of the need for a weekly newspaper and suggested Rigdon as editor, which never occurred due to the outbreak of hostilities between the Mormons and Missourians. Smith also advocated for all brethren, including those running farms in rural areas, to reside in the cities. It was also decided to circulate a petition to designate Far West as the county seat for Caldwell County.[89]

Confrontation

On August 7—the day after the election-day skirmish—a false report was received at Far West that Mormons had been killed at Gallatin, that their

---

History of the Latter-day Saints in Northern Missouri," 93, 110n27. John D. Lee and Levi Stewart reported that the Mormons were outnumbered "about 8 to 1." Lee and Stewart, Statement, 1845, [1].

84. See Butler, Autobiography, in Journal History, Aug. 6, 1838.

85. Lee, *Mormonism Unveiled*, 59–60.

86. It is unclear if any of the Mormons succeeded in voting. Later in life, Lee claimed that "all the Mormons voted," whereas his earlier joint account with Levi Stewart stated that "very few Mormons voted that day." See Lee, *Mormonism Unveiled*, 58; and Lee and Stewart, Statement, 1845, [1].

87. Smith, Journal, July 28 and Aug. 6, 1838 (*JSP*, J1:294, 297).

88. Revelation, July 8, 1838-E, [1], Revelations Collection [D&C 117:8–9] (*JSP*, D6:193).

89. Smith, Journal, Aug. 6, 1838 (*JSP*, J1:297–98).

bodies still lay on the ground, and that the mob was intending to drive all Mormons from Daviess County. Alarmed by the news, Smith started immediately for Gallatin with Rigdon, Hyrum Smith, and about twenty armed men. Along the way, they were joined by others, including General Elias Higbee, General Sampson Avard, and Colonel George Robinson, all Danite officers.[90] According to Corrill, Avard, referred to in Smith's journal as a general, "called for volunteers, and raised about one hundred and fifty men, who went out to Davies under arms."[91] When they reached Wight's house, they learned the rumors were inaccurate, that no one had died, although several were severely wounded, but that a mob, headed by Judge Adam Black, had gathered at Millport, three miles east of Gallatin, and was planning to expel the Mormons from the county.[92]

Swartzell noted that as soon as news of the election-day fight reached Adam-ondi-Ahman, "an express was immediately sent to Far West, and 180 armed brethren assembled at Adam-on-Diammon, for the purpose of resisting an attack that was hourly expected." Women and children were gathered together and guarded in expectation of a siege. "All was in an uproar," Swartzell wrote. The next day, August 8, Swartzell recorded: "The morning has came, and no 'mobs' yet."[93]

The day began with military exercises. At 6:00 a.m., according to Swartzell, "we all marched out upon the prairie, where we formed a hollow square—the horsemen on one side, and the foot soldiers on the other." Inside the square stood Smith, Rigdon, and other officers, all in uniform. Rigdon drew his sword and, amidst a severe thunderstorm, said, "We have been imposed upon and persecuted, ever since the rising of this Church— have been driven from Kirtland, Ohio, to Jackson county, Missouri; from Jackson to Clay county; from Ray to Caldwell county, and now we are in Daviess county. We are the people of God: and the only people that believe in His word. We fear God, our Almighty Protector; and we will be no more driven from this blessed land. Now, we, as the people of God, do declare—do declare and decree, by the great Jehovah, the eternal and omnipotent God, that sits upon his vast and everlasting throne, beyond that etherial blue— [pointing his sword upwards]—*we* WILL *bathe our swords in the* VITAL BLOOD

---

90. Smith, Journal, Aug. 7, 1838 (*JSP*, J1: 298–300). See Sampson Avard, in Transcript, [3]–[4]; Smith, Affidavit, Caldwell Co., MO, Sep. 5, 1838, JS Collection (*JSP*, D6:222–25).

91. Corrill, *Brief History*, 34 (*JSP*, H2:171); Smith, Journal, Aug. 7, 1838 (*JSP*, J1:299).

92. Smith, Affidavit, Sep. 5, 1838, [1]–[2], JS Collection (*JSP*, D6:223).

93. Swartzell, *Mormonism Exposed*, 28–29.

of the Missourians, or die in the attempt!" In solidarity, the entire company joined in giving three cheers.[94]

Smith dispatched messengers to the home of Judge Black, located about 1.5 miles northeast of Adam-ondi-Ahman, to demand that he sign a document promising to keep the peace and not harass the Mormons. He refused.[95] "Upon the refusal of Mr. Black to sign the articles of agreement," Swartzell reported, "we all marched, in silence, to his house, which we immediately surrounded."[96] Avard and a few others dismounted, went into the cabin, and confronted Black about a rumor that he was intending to lead a mob against the Mormons at Adam-ondi-Ahman. After a few minutes, Smith was called into the house.[97] What happened would become the subject of a subsequent trial the following November during which conflicting accounts were presented before Judge Austin A. King.

Black testified that thirty minutes after the first committee left, about 154 armed Mormon men surrounded his house and "blocked up his doors." When Avard entered the house, he allegedly demanded that Black sign the agreement to uphold the law and threatened to shoot him if he refused. At Black's request, Smith then entered the house to discuss the matter. Although Smith did not use threatening language, Black said, "seeing the situation of his family," he agreed to write his own statement that he would "support the constitution of this State, and of the U[nited]. States, and will support no mob," and that he would "not molest the people called Mormons ... if they will not molest me."[98] The purpose of getting Black's statement, according to the memorial that Smith, Rigdon, and Elias Higbee sent to the US Senate and

---

94. Swartzell, 29. Brackets in original.

95. Smith, Affidavit, Sep. 5, 1838, [2], JS Collection (*JSP*, D6:223). On the location of Adam Black's cabin, see Berrett, *Sacred Places*, 4:452–53.

96. Swartzell, *Mormonism Exposed*, 30.

97. Smith, Journal, Aug. 7–9, 1838 (*JSP*, J1:300). Baugh has noted that the absence of Higbee, the commanding officer, in the arbitration with Black may indicate that Higbee "either stepped aside or resigned from his Danite post, opening the door for Avard to be in command." While this might have been the case, Baugh's assumption that Smith did not initially confront Black because he "was not in charge, nor was he even affiliated with the Danite organization," does not account for the fact that Smith, while not a field commander, nevertheless held executive and legislative power over the Danites, according to their constitution, and as such held supreme command over all Danite operations. Baugh, "'We Have a Company of Danites in These Times,'" 18. See also Articles 2 and 3 of the Constitution of the Society of the Daughter of Zion, ca. late June 1838, in Avard, in Transcript, [10]–[12] (*Document*, 102).

98. Adam Black, Testimony, Sep. 18, 1838, in Robert Wilson, Letter to James L. Minor, Mar. 18, 1841, *Document*, 161–62; see also Adam Black, Affidavit, Aug. 28, 1838, Mormon War Papers; [Rigdon], *An Appeal to the American People*, 24.

House of Representatives in 1840, was "to calm the public mind, and to allay the existing excitement."[99] Smith's action, however, had the opposite result.

According to Black, as Smith and his men were leaving his house, Avard said they were on their way to procure statements from Col. Peniston and Capt. Bowman, adding that "he could shoot a man who would not sign that obligation, or that would oppose him, or be in a mob against him, and drink his heart's blood." Black then asked Smith "if he protected Dr. Avard in his savage disposition, or if he possessed such a heart? he replied no."[100] Avard's aggressiveness may have led to his demotion shortly after Mormon forces returned to Far West.[101]

Later the same day, Black signed an affidavit accusing the Mormons of surrounding his home and threatening his life.[102] This confrontation was yet another mistake of the Mormon leadership, serving only to fuel hatred toward their people. Smith, who was not present when Avard threatened Black, later claimed that "no violence was offered to any individual, in his presence or within his knowledge, and that no insulting language was given by either party"—which was not exactly true.[103] Smith, Rigdon, and Higbee also accused Black of being motivated to drive the Mormons out of Daviess County by a desire to steal back the pre-emption rights to lands he had previously sold to them.[104]

Swartzell wrote that when they returned to Adam-ondi-Ahman, there was "a crowd of spectators … looking on, in idle curiosity, at these proceedings." In the crowd was "a young man by the name of Rigsby, a citizen of Missouri [who] could not subdue his indignation, and uttered some strong invective against the conduct of the Mormons." This so irritated Smith, according to Swartzell, that he commanded Rigsby to come to him as he stood in the center of a square that the soldiers had formed and then handed him

---

99. Smith et al., Memorial to the United States Senate and House of Representatives, ca. Oct. 30, 1839–Jan. 27, 1840, 12 (*JSP*, D7:155).

100. Adam Black, Affidavit, Sep. 18, 1838, in *Document*, 162. See also "The Mormon Difficulties," *Niles' National Register* (Washington DC), Oct. 13, 1838, 103.

101. Avard, in Transcript, [6] (*Document*, 99). Avard implied that he was relieved of his command before the Mormon vigilante raids in Daviess County in mid-October, during which he took no commanding role, even returning to Far West days before the Mormon troops. See also Nimer, "Treachery and False Swearing in Missouri," 45–46; Baugh, "'We Have a Company of Danites in These Times,'" 18.

102. Adam Black, Affidavit, Aug. 8, 1838, in "Public Meeting," *Missouri Republican* (St. Louis), Sep. 3, 1838, [2]; see also *Western Star* (Liberty, MO), in Swartzell, *Mormonism Exposed*, 43–44.

103. Smith, Affidavit, Sep. 5, 1838, [3], JS Collection (*JSP*, D6:224).

104. Smith et al., Memorial, to the United States Senate and House of Representatives, ca. Oct. 30, 1839–Jan. 27, 1840, 13 (*JSP*, D7:156–57).

a paper, demanding that he sign it. When Rigsby refused, Smith "ordered six men, all armed with cow-skins, from out of the square, observing, at the same time, to the young gentleman, that if did not sign the articles of peace, he should receive sixty lashes with the cow-skin. The young man hesitated for a moment, but seeing that the six men were ready, at a given signal, to obey the commands of the Prophet, very reluctantly signed the paper, and immediately made good his escape."[105]

In the evening, some citizens from Millport, the center of anti-Mormon activity in Daviess County, visited Smith and other Mormon leaders at Adam-ondi-Ahman and arranged to meet with them at noon the next day. The committee that arrived included Josiah Morin, senator-elect, John Williams, representative-elect, and James B. Turner, clerk of the circuit court. The Mormon committee consisted of Wight, Vinson Knight, John Smith, Reynolds Cahoon, and others. On August 9 both parties entered into "a covenant of peace."[106] Later that day, Swartzell wrote: "All quiet; nothing very material going on, except cooking and eating. Spies were sent out, and returned without making any discoveries."[107]

After breakfast, according to Swartzell, "they commenced wrestling before Lyman White's house, for exercise, which they kept up till near noon. One would act champion, until another, more active, would throw him; and carry off the palm of victory, Brothers Robinson and Smith, appeared to excel at this amusement." During the contest, the crowd was humorously entertained "when prophet Smith and orator Rigdon entered the arena," and "in the struggle the prophet gained an advantage, on account of the orator's sword becoming entangled between his legs, which brought him to the ground." After a dinner of beef and corn on the cob, one of the Danite leaders "made a very eloquent speech, in which he congratulated the band of warriors for their consummate bravery, and noble daring in their recent attack upon the house of Mr. Black."[108]

Soon after, Smith and company left Adam-ondi-Ahman, arriving in Far West about midnight.[109] Hyrum Smith remembered that they had "parted with the best of feelings and each man returned home to his own home."[110] Despite the peace agreement, hostilities would resume within days.

---

105. Swartzell, *Mormonism Exposed*, 30.
106. Smith, Journal, Aug. 9, 1838 (*JSP*, J1:301); "The Mormons," *Missouri Argus*, Sep. 6, 1838, [1].
107. Swartzell, *Mormonism Exposed*, 31.
108. Swartzell, 31.
109. Smith, Journal, Aug. 9, 1838 (*JSP*, J1:301).
110. Hyrum Smith, Testimony, July 1843, in *Times and Seasons*, July 1, 1843, 246.

Evading Arrest

At Richmond, in neighboring Ray County, citizens held a public meeting on August 9 and 10 to discuss the Mormon menace in Daviess County and to form a committee to investigate Adam Black's claims against the Mormons, whose actions were "of a highly illegal and dangerous character." On the first day, a committee of seven was appointed to investigate and report the following day. Their findings, which created alarm, read: "Upon an examination of the facts and circumstances appearing to and examined by us, consisting of certificates, documents, and other evidence, we are satisfied that there is an armed force now collected and embodied in Daviess county, of about 500 Mormons whose movements are highly insurrectionary and unlawful:—that they have already committed outrages on individuals who were old and respectable citizens of Daviess county, ... that they are still embodied, and are purchasing and collecting ammunition, and making all preparations for an insurrection,—or, at least, a great and enormous violation of the laws and the private rights of the citizens of Daviess county."[111] Seven resolutions were passed, which, "although not violent in their tone," according to the *Western Star,* published at Liberty, Clay County, "had evident reference to the prospect of a speedy and bloody conflict."[112] Nevertheless, the Ray County committee was determined to "deprecate any hasty or improper action on the part of the citizens of this county, and that they will do no act which is not justified by the laws of the land."[113] In one resolution, they urged Judge Austin King to bring the Mormons to justice, particularly Smith and Wight.[114]

Later, on August 10, King issued an arrest warrant for Smith and Wight, apparently on a charge of riot, and assigned Daviess County sheriff William Morgan to execute the warrant.[115] However, Morgan would not attempt to arrest the two men until August 16. Meanwhile, on August 11, Smith left Far West with his councilors and Almon Babbitt to visit the settlement of

---

111. "Public Meeting," *Missouri Republican*, Sep. 3, 1838, [2].

112. *Western Star*, in Swartzell, *Mormonism Exposed*, 44. The date of this issue of the *Star* is unknown, but it was quoted and summarized in "Mormon War," *Missouri Republican*, Sep. 3, 1838, [2].

113. "Mormon War," *Missouri Republican*, Sep. 3, 1838, [2]; "Public Meeting," *Missouri Republican*, Sep. 3, 1838, [2].

114. "Public Meeting," *Missouri Republican*, Sep. 3, 1838, [2].

115. State of Missouri, Austin A. King, Warrant for Joseph Smith and Lyman Wight, Ray Co., MO, Aug. 10, 1838. King's warrant did not identify a charge, but a Daviess County grand jury later indicted Smith, Wight, and other Mormon men for riot, stating that they did "unlawfully, riotously, and routously [noisily], assemble and meet together to disturb the peace" at "the dwelling house of one Adam Black." Indictment, Honey Creek Township, Daviess Co., MO, ca. Apr. 10, 1839, State of Missouri v. Joseph Smith et al. for Riot; see also *JSP*, D6:220n288.

Canadians at Three Forks of the Grand River. On their way, Smith and company stopped overnight at Adam-ondi-Ahman.[116]

While at Adam-ondi-Ahman, Smith held a meeting, during which he was approached by a committee of Clay County residents, who had come to investigate Black's complaint and, if possible, ease tensions between the Missourians and Mormons. When they urged the Mormons "to yield obedience to the laws," according to Swartzell, Wight addressed the committee, which included two judges, and declared that "he owed nothing to the laws—the laws had not protected him—he had been on the rack, and persecution had followed him these seven years—he had suffered enough—God did not require him to endure more—and that he would not yield to the laws of Missouri—he would sooner die and be buried." Despite this confrontational tone, the Clay County committee followed Smith and other Mormon leaders to Wight's house, where they discussed the matter for several hours. According to Swartzell, the refusal of Smith and Wight "to accede to the reasonable and just requirements of these laws, created much murmuring and dissatisfaction in the Mormon camp."[117]

At the same time, in Smith's absence, another committee from Ray County arrived at Far West to inquire about recent hostilities in Daviess County, having received a complaint from Black, Peniston, and others. A meeting was held at the city hall with Bishop Partridge presiding. It was resolved to investigate the matter and report back.[118]

On Sunday, August 12, church services were held at Adam-ondi-Ahman, where Smith spoke about the troubles between the Mormons and the Missourians. According to Swartzell, Smith exhorted his followers "to be of good cheer, and not to be 'scared at trifles,' that he would tell them when danger was near—that at present he did not even anticipate such a thing—for us to hold ourselves in readiness at a moment's warning well armed and equipped, to go down to Carroll county and rescue brother Hinkle, who is in a suffering condition; and that they must expect to endure trials there."[119]

Two months earlier, George Hinkle had sold his house to Smith and moved down the river to De Witt.[120] In late July, non-Mormons held a meeting at Carrollton and demanded that the Mormons leave the county

---

116. Smith, Journal, Aug. 10, 1838 (*JSP*, J1:302).

117. Swartzell, *Mormonism Exposed*, 32.

118. Smith, Journal, Aug. 11, 1838 (*JSP*, J1:302–303).

119. Joseph Smith, Discourse, Aug. 12, 1838, in Swartzell, *Mormonism Exposed*, 32–33 (*JSP*, D6:214–15).

120. See Minutes, July 6, 1838, Minute Book 2, 150 (Cannon and Cook, *Far West Record*, 197).

by August 7. After investigation, another meeting was held on August 7, when a committee reported that the Mormons were determined to stay and that "they would apply to the Far West for assistance" if needed. In response, non-Mormons in Carroll County began petitioning neighboring counties, requesting "aid to remove Mormons, abolitionists, and other disorderly persons" from their county.[121] The prospect of Smith's leading an armed conflict against the Missourians in Carroll County was sobering to Swartzell. "My eyes were opened; the scales dropped off; and I began to view things more correctly than ever," he wrote. "I concluded that ... the idea of such a band attacking a State ... was preposterous." According to Swartzell, "Several of the brethren felt as I did, at this time, but for fear of detection, we dared not converse with each other on the subject; and if we had been found guilty of rebellion against the commands of the Prophet and High Priest [Wight], death would have been the probable result."[122]

Later the same day, Smith and his counselors, Hyrum Smith and Rigdon, visited the Canadian Mormons in the Three Forks area.[123] Anson Call, who was already farming in the area before the arrival of the Canadians, remembered that Smith announced that he had come on a "special errand" and wished to speak to the leading brethren privately. After retiring to a nearby cornfield, according to Call, Smith "stated to us we must leave for there were going to be difficulties." Smith told them he did not know the source of the conflict, only that "the message he had received was for us to leave and go to Far West or Adam ondi Ahman." The unanimous decision was made to leave the area, but they asked Smith "whether it was necessary for us to go forthwith or whether we could stay and save our crops and sell our farms." He answered, "You need not sell your farms and he presumed we should have time to get away but how much time he knew not." After dinner, Smith and the others left.[124] Smith's followers at Adam-ondi-Ahman began immediately to prepare for the probable escalation of difficulties with their non-Mormon neighbors. On August 15 Swartzell wrote: "This morning the

---

121. "The Mormons in Carroll County," *Missouri Republican*, Aug. 18, 1838, [2]; "The Mormons," *Missouri Argus*, Sep. 6, 1838, [1].

122. Swartzell, *Mormonism Exposed*, 33.

123. Smith, Journal, Aug. 12, 1838 (*JSP*, J1:303).

124. Call, Autobiography and Journal, 10; Call, Statement, Dec. 30, 1885, 10–12. Call misdated Smith's visit to the Three Forks area to a Sunday in September. See *JSP*, J1:303n232. The Kirtland Revelation Book includes "Material facts left out the history of the church," compiled by Phelps and Willard Richards, which mentions: "1838. Aug 16 to 20. Joseph was att the 3 forks of grand river, with Rigdon Hyrum & [Almon] Babbit[t], to see the country, with Anson Call—mob tried to intercept him on his ret[u]rn." *JSP*, MRB:661.

brethren are gathering in from all quarters, anticipating difficulties of a serious nature with the citizens of Missouri."[125]

Meanwhile, Smith returned to Far West on Monday, August 13, having been chased by enemies for ten or twelve miles. Within about eight miles of Far West, Smith learned that King had issued a warrant for his and Wight's arrest.[126] Nevertheless, Smith spent the next two days quietly at home.[127]

On August 16 Sheriff Morgan went to Wight's house to arrest him, but when he arrived, he "found an armed force of from 80 to 100 men" and was told by Wight "that he would not be taken alive—that the law had never protected him, and he owed them no obedience—that the whole state of Missouri could not take him."[128] Morgan left without Wight and headed to Far West.

When Morgan and Judge Morin arrived at Smith's home and announced they were there to arrest him, Smith said he was willing to be tried, provided it took place in Caldwell County, not in Daviess. According to Smith's journal, the sheriff said he would go to Richmond and consult with King. When the sheriff returned, he informed Smith that Caldwell County was out of his jurisdiction and then left.[129] The newly-appointed Morgan may not have known that a change of venue was irrelevant to an arrest and could only be applied after an indictment.[130] Nevertheless, Morgan was required by Missouri statute to work with local authorities to arrest Smith, which he apparently did not do.[131]

In the memorial they sent to Congress in 1840, Smith, Rigdon, and Higbee misrepresented Smith's and Wight's encounters with the sheriff, stating that it was incorrectly reported that they "had refused to be taken" and that "the Sheriff had never made any effort either to take them or serve the process; and that Smith and Wight, so far from opposing resistance, did not know that a writ had been issued against them" until they heard rumors some days later.[132] Contrary to this, in mid-August 1838, Smith had Judge

125. Swartzell, *Mormonism Exposed*, 34.

126. Smith, Journal, Aug. 13, 1838 (*JSP*, J1:303).

127. Smith, Journal, Aug. 14–15, 1838 (*JSP*, J1:304).

128. "Mormon War," *Missouri Republican*, Sep. 3, 1838, [2].

129. Smith, Journal, Aug. 16, 1838 (*JSP*, J1:304–305); "Mormon War," *Missouri Republican*, Sep. 3, 1838, [2].

130. See *JSP*, J1:305n238; see also online introduction to Elias Higbee, Petition, Aug. 16, 1838 (josephsmithpapers.org).

131. An Act to Regulate Proceedings in Criminal Cases, *Revised Statutes of the State of Missouri*, 475, art. 2, sects. 4–5.

132. Joseph Smith et al., Memorial to the United States Senate and House of Representatives, ca. Oct. 30, 1839–Jan. 27, 1840, 12–13 (*JSP*, D7:156).

Elias Higbee prepare a petition for a writ of habeas corpus challenging his arrest should Morgan attempt to do so. The petition was never used, but dated August 1838, with a blank space to insert the day.[133] During the November 1838 hearings, Phelps testified against Smith and others, stating that they were prepared to take extreme measures to resist arrest.[134]

Meanwhile, the Mormons at Adam-ondi-Ahman continued to build their city, "cutting and hauling logs, and putting up houses."[135] On August 20 and 21, Smith participated in forming three agricultural companies at Far West. Two of the companies, the "Western Agricultural Company" and "Southern Agricultural Company," covered 7,680 acres each.[136] Reed Peck said a revelation made membership in the newly-formed companies compulsory and that all members were to consecrate all their property, but, according to Corrill, "Smith said every man must act his own feelings, whether to join or not, yet great exertions were used, and especially by Doctor Averd, to persuade all to join."[137] Peck said that "many were violently opposed to this new church order but after much *argument, preaching teaching* and *explaining* by S[ampson] Avard the excitement was allayed and all but a few consented to give up their property." One of those who refused to participate, according to Peck, was Corrill, who let it be known that "he did not 'think it his duty to unite with the firm and that he had no confidense in the revelation that required it.'" When Smith and Rigdon learned of Corrill's rebellion, they chastised him in the presence of several persons. According to Peck, Smith angrily shook his fists at Corrill and threatened that if he should ever go about the streets proclaiming he did "not believe this or that revelation. ... I will walk on your neck Sir." Peck said Smith "cited us to the case of Judas" and claimed that "Peter told him in a conversation a few days ago that [he] himself hung Judas for betraying Christ." Smith also promised Corrill that if he did not repent, "you shall never be admitted into the

---

133. Anticipating Smith's arrest, the petition declares: "Whereas Joseph Smith Junr. of the County of Caldwell and state aforesaid is now restrained of his liberty and in the custody of and detained by Mr. [William] Morgan Sheriff of Davis County ... your Petitioner verily believes said process is either not authorized by any provision of law or is not allowed by law under the circumstances ... and that in attempting to take the said Joseph Smith Junr. out of the County of Caldwell aforesaid would be to exceed the right or Jurisdiction of the said Sheriff Therefore your Petitioner requests that a writ of Habeas Corpus may be immediately Issued directed to said Sheriff to enquire in to the cause of such confinement or restraint August [*blank*] AD 1838." Elias Higbee [on behalf of Joseph Smith], Petition to Elias Higbee, ca. Aug. 16, 1838.

134. William W. Phelps, in Transcript, [89] (*Document*, 123).

135. Swartzell, *Mormonism Exposed*, 34 (Aug. 17, 1838).

136. Smith, Journal, Aug. 20 and 21, 1838 (*JSP*, J1:305).

137. Peck, Letter to "Dear Friends," Sep. 19, 1839, 51–53; Corrill, *Brief History*, 46 (*JSP*, H2:194).

Kingdom of Heaven." In fact, Smith said, "I will stand at the entrance myself and oppose you myself and will Keep you out." Corrill replied, "I may possibly get there first."[138]

The argument between Smith and Corrill was continued ten days later, when Corrill said he would not subordinate his judgment to that of the church, even if Smith claimed a revelation, stating that "he is a republican, and as such he will do, say, act, and believe, what he pleases." Smith responded that Corrill was putting his judgment ahead of God's. Rigdon joined the discussion, and, according to Smith's journal, Corrill eventually changed his mind.[139]

On August 22 Smith counseled the brethren on "different subjects" and observed that "Brethren continue to gather into Zion Daily."[140] Meanwhile, as far away as Huntsville, a little more than a hundred miles east of Far West, Warren Foote's migrating company from New York heard a rumor "that the troops have been called out against the Mormons, and having a permit from the Governor they were going to take 'Joe Smith,' and Sidney Rigdon, but they had run away."[141] As he was leaving Missouri, having lost his faith in Mormonism, Swartzell stopped at Lafayette, about sixty miles south of Far West, "where I was told that a reward of $3,000 was offered for the head of the Prophet."[142] Nevertheless, Smith spent the week in relative tranquility mostly at home.[143]

On August 28 Adam Black filed a second complaint before Daviess County justice William Dryden alleging that his life was threatened on August 8 by a mob of about 154 Mormons. Significantly, Smith was not included among the sixteen Mormon men named in Black's complaint.[144] In response, Dryden issued a warrant the next day ordering special deputy Nathaniel Blakely to arrest the sixteen men, but when he attempted to serve the warrant, he was purportedly "driven by force" from Adam-ondi-Ahman. This convinced Dryden that "the power of the County is wholy unable to execute any civil or Criminal process" against the Mormons. "They also declare that they are independent," Dryden reported, and they "hold in utter

---

138. Peck, 53–55.
139. Smith, Journal, Aug. 31, 1838 (*JSP*, J1:309–10).
140. Smith, Journal, Aug. 22, 1838 (*JSP*, J1:306).
141. Foote, Journal, Aug. 22, 1838.
142. Swartzell, *Mormonism Exposed*, 36 (Aug. 23, 1838).
143. Smith, Journal, Aug. 23–29, 1838 (*JSP*, J1:306).
144. Adam Black, Complaint, Daviess Co., Aug. 28, 1838, Mormon War Papers.

contempt the institutions of the Country in which they live."[145] According to George A. Smith, who was one of the sixteen men named in the warrant, there was no attempt to arrest him, but instead Sheriff Morgan "endeavored to excite the people of the State, by reporting we would not submit to the law."[146] However, Smith's not being approached by Dryden personally does not invalidate Blakely's report about Dryden's failure.

On August 29 Dryden, Peniston, and others belonging to a "Committee of Vigilance" met at Millport and reported that Smith and Wight "say they will not be taken, nor submit to the law of the land" and that "two or three ... attempts have been made to bring them to justice." They appointed another meeting for Friday, August 31, "at which time they will all be authorized by our Sheriff and held in readiness until we may get such assistance from other counties, as they may deem fit to render us, who will also be summoned by our Sheriff. ... That the laws may then be enforced."[147]

Atchison's Arrival

On August 30 Governor Lilburn W. Boggs issued an order to General David R. Atchison of the 3rd Division of the Missouri Militia in Liberty to organize his militia to be "held in readiness" only as a "precautionary measure" against Indian disturbances on the frontier, and "recent civil disturbances" in Caldwell, Daviess, and Carroll Counties, which is to be done with "as little excitement as possible."[148] A similar letter was sent to six other major generals.

On September 1 Smith, his councilors, Hyrum and Rigdon, and Judge Higbee, as surveyor, traveled about fifteen miles north to the half-way house run by Brother Waldo Littlefield to lay out a new city to be called Seth. Smith and the others may have believed the land they surveyed was located just inside Caldwell County, although it was actually in southern Daviess County. Smith evidently hoped Seth would provide some strategic advantage in defending Adam-ondi-Ahman, but events would prevent Seth's becoming more than an idea.[149]

Under this date in Smith's journal is a passage in George Robinson's handwriting that captured Smith's frustration with his enemies and determination

---

145. William Dryden, Petition, Daviess Co., MO, Sep. 15, 1838, Mormon War Papers (*Document*, 22).

146. George A. Smith, Autobiography, 110.

147. "Mormons Once More," *Hannibal (MO) Commercial Advertiser*, Sep. 25, 1838.

148. B. M. Lisle, Letter to General David. R. Atchison, Aug. 30, 1838, Mormon War Papers (*Document*, 20).

149. Smith, Journal, Sep. 1, 1838 (*JSP*, J1:311; see also 311n258; 312n264).

to defend his rights by force if necessary: "We have appealed to magistrates, to Sheriffs, to Judges, to governours and to the President of the United States, all in vain, yet we have yealded, peacibly to all these things. ... But in the name of Jesus Christ the Son of the Living God we will endure it no longer, if the Great God will arm us with courage, with strength and with power, to resist them in their persecutions. We will not act on the offensive but always on the defensive, our rights and our liberties shall not be taken from us, and we peacibly submit to it, as we have done heretofore, but we will avenge ourselves of our enemies, inasmuch as they will not let us alone."[150] The journal entry also complained that their enemies were "seeking if possible an occasion against us" and that "they are continually chafing us, and provoking us to anger if possible," but Smith had already been provoked and unwisely pressured Judge Black to sign a peace agreement, which gave their enemies all the pretext they needed.[151]

On Sunday, September 2, after attending church in the morning, Smith was visited by a man from Livingston County who warned him that men were gathering from the eleven counties in Upper Missouri to arrest him and Wight.[152] "Runners went into other counties to solicit assistance," wrote Corrill. "They requested the citizens to gather in by a day appointed, and be in readiness to assist the sheriff in taking Wight. Accordingly they gathered in to a considerable number. ... The citizens continued to gather, and news came to Smith that there would be four thousand together in a few days."[153] Robinson wrote in Smith's journal: "This looks a leettle to[o] much like mobocracy, it foretells some evil intentions, the whole uper Missouri is all in an uproar and confusion."[154]

That same evening, Smith sent word to General Atchison at Liberty to come with his division of militia to stop the collection of people and put an end to hostilities. Smith also sent a petition to King at Richmond to disperse the mob.[155] Philo Dibble, a lieutenant colonel in the state militia, later said he had advised Smith to send for Atchison, as "he was in command of the third division of the militia of the State of Missouri, and was a lawyer and friend to law," whereupon Smith sent one of the men on the "best horse" to

---

150. Smith (*JSP*, J1:311–12). The editors of the Joseph Smith Papers assign these "sentiments" to George Robinson, rather than to Smith, but that is not altogether clear (*JSP*, J1312n263).

151. Smith (*JSP*, J1:311).

152. Smith, Journal, Sep. 2, 1838 (*JSP*, J1:312).

153. Corrill, *Brief History*, 34 (*JSP*, H2:172–73).

154. Smith, Journal, Sep. 2, 1838 (*JSP*, J1:312–13).

155. Smith (*JSP*, J1:313).

Atchison.[156] However, Smith was unaware that Atchison had already been commissioned to raise a force of 400 men to keep the peace in Caldwell, Daviess, and Carroll Counties and would arrive in the area on September 3.[157]

About this time, some of the counties sent investigative committees that found no cause to be alarmed. Howard County representatives, for instance, said they were not concerned at that time because Smith and other Mormon leaders "have intimated their willingness to submit themselves to the legal authorities; hence we may infer that no serious difficulties will arise."[158] The committee from Chariton County reported that Smith and Wight said they had "at all times been willing to give themselves up to an officer, to administer law, but not willing to be taken by a mob who were threatening their lives daily, and who were endeavoring to drive them from the country."[159] Livingston and Jackson Counties, on the other hand, had already decided to send volunteers.[160]

Atchison arrived at Far West in the evening of September 3, and on the following day he consulted with Smith, promising to do all he could to disperse the mob. Smith was familiar with Atchison as well as another lawyer, Alexander Doniphan, who shared an office with Atchison in Liberty and was expected to arrive soon with a regiment of the state militia. Because Atchison and Doniphan had represented the Mormons during their expulsion from Jackson County in 1833 and petitioned the Missouri legislature to form Caldwell County in 1836, Smith hired them to represent him and Wight in the upcoming trial in the Adam Black case. At this time, it was decided that Smith and Wight would be tried by King on the 6th in Littlefield's half-way house near the border of Daviess and Caldwell Counties, perhaps as a precaution against being trapped by a mob.[161] On the same day, King wrote to Sheriff Morgan to say that he agreed to Atchison's request "for the sake of giving quiet to the country," and instructed him to "go to Mr. Wight who will submit to your process."[162]

---

156. Dibble, "Philo Dibble's Narrative," 88; Philo Dibble, "Recollections of the Prophet Joseph Smith," *Juvenile Instructor*, June 1, 1892, 345.

157. B. M. Lisle, Letter to David R. Atchison, Aug. 30, 1838, Mormon War Papers (*Document*, 20).

158. "The Mormons," *Missouri Argus*, Sep. 13, 1838, [3].

159. "The Mormon Difficulties," *Niles' National Register*, Oct. 13, 1838, 103.

160. Hiram Comstock, Letter to "the Citizens of Carroll County," Aug. 12, 1838, *Missouri Argus*, Sep. 6, 1838, [1]; "The Mormons—Public Meeting," *Jeffersonian Republican* (Jefferson City, MO), Sep. 22, 1838, [2].

161. Smith, Journal, Sep. 3, 1838 (*JSP*, J1:314).

162. King, Letter to William Morgan, Sep. 4, 1838.

On September 5, in preparation for the hearing, Smith appeared before Caldwell County Judge Elias Higbee and made an affidavit about the Adam Black incident, claiming that Black although "hostile" gave his statement voluntarily and that "no violence was offered to any individual in his presence, or within his knowledge."[163] Not long after Atchison left Far West, King arrived and stayed the night.[164] Meanwhile, at Adam-ondi-Ahman, Morgan served Wight a warrant and took him into custody.[165]

Preliminary Hearing

On September 6 Smith left Far West at 7:30 a.m. for Littlefield's halfway house with Hyrum Smith, Elias Higbee, and George Robinson. Black failed to appear, so the trial was postponed until 10:00 a.m. the next day and moved farther south to John Raglin's cabin, about a half-mile north of the Daviess-Caldwell county line.[166] This change concerned Smith because Raglin was not a Mormon but an active participant in the mob and the Daviess County Vigilance Committee had set September 7 as the date for the mob to seize Wight. It was just before dark when Smith and the others returned to Far West.[167]

About sunrise, Smith and a few others left for Raglin's cabin. A company of armed Mormons had been placed in the woods at the county line during the night in case there was a disturbance at the hearing.[168] William Moore Allred, who was in the company of volunteers, later said: "We heard that a mob was collecting to take him [Smith], so a company of us went out to lay in ambush near the court, in case we were needed. I lived eight miles from Far West, but I was in town when the company was made up, so I volunteered to go. ... We lay in ambush till night, and Joseph was discharged and we returned home."[169] When Smith arrived at Raglin's property, some Missourians who had gathered to witness the proceedings began to "curse and swear" at him, but Atchison warned them off, "If you fire the first gun there will not be one of you left."[170]

---

163. Joseph Smith, Affidavit, Sep. 5, 1838, JS Collection (*JSP*, D6:219–25); [Rigdon], *Appeal to the American People*, 26–28.

164. Smith, Journal, Sep. 5, 1838 (*JSP*, J1:316).

165. State of Missouri, Austin A. King, Warrant for Joseph Smith and Lyman Wight, Ray Co., MO, Aug. 10, 1838.

166. Berrett, *Sacred Places*, 4:496–98.

167. Smith, Journal, Sep. 6, 1838 (*JSP*, J1:316, 325).

168. Smith, Journal, Sep. 7, 1838 (*JSP*, J1:316, 325).

169. Allred, Reminiscences and Diary, 5.

170. Dibble, "Philo Dibble's Narrative," 88–89.

The preliminary hearing was held in a grove of trees near Raglin's cabin. The prosecutor was William Peniston and his only witness was Adam Black, who apparently had no specific complaint against Smith other than the implication that the men who threatened him had acted under the Mormon leader's direction. Witnesses for the defense were Dimick Huntington, Gideon Carter, George W. Robinson, who were all Danites and eyewitnesses, and Adam Lightner, who was not a church member but lived in Caldwell County. Nevertheless, King ruled that there was sufficient evidence that Smith and Wight had committed misdemeanor riot at Black's home on August 8 and held them over on a $500 bond to appear at the Daviess County circuit court on November 29, 1838.[171]

Smith and the others returned to Far West the same evening, accompanied by two men from Chariton County who were sent to investigate whether or not their county should send the militia. The next day, the First Presidency met with Chariton County residents Sterling Price, a member of the Missouri House of Representatives, and Edgar Flory, as well as Clay County attorney David R. Atchison. After hearing about "this whole matter, the present state of exitement and the cause of all this confusion," Price and Flory "expressed their fullest satisfaction upon this matter" that the Mormons "had been outrageously imposed upon."[172] After returning to Chariton County, they published their findings on September 22 in the *Columbia Patriot*, which included Smith and Rigdon's affidavit that denounced the charge that they were plotting with the Indians to "commit depredations" upon Missourians and affirmed their commitment to being law-abiding citizens. Their report included an interview with Black in which he conceded that "Mr. Smith may have said that he [Black] would not be forced to sign any instrument of writing but that he requested it as a favor."[173] The *Western Star* at Liberty also reported that the hearing had shown that "Black had misrepresented

---

171. Smith, Journal, Sep. 7, 1838 (*JSP*, J1:317–18); State of Missouri, Recognizance of Joseph Smith and Lyman Wight, Sep. 7, 1838 (*JSP*, D6:225–29).

172. Smith, Journal, Sep. 7–8, 1838 (*JSP*, J1:317–18).

173. Their report, dated September 10, was first published in the *Columbia Patriot*, Sep. 22, 1838; though not extant, it is available through a reprint in "The Mormon Difficulties," *Niles' National Register*, Oct. 13, 1838, 103. Smith and Rigdon were specifically responding to the claims of former Mormon Nathan Marsh, who had prepared a statement in Chariton County alleging that he had heard Mormon preachers declare that "the time had arrived, when the flying Angel should pass through the land accompanied by the Indians, to accomplish the work of destruction of all that are not mormons," and that Smith had publicly declared that he could call an army of fourteen thousand men if needed, "which was generally understood to mean Indians." Nathan Marsh, Statement, n.d., in Daniel Ashby et al., Letter to Lilburn W. Boggs, Sep. 1, 1838, Mormon War Papers (*Document*, 16); see also "The Mormons," *Hannibal Commercial Advertiser*, Sep. 18, 1838, [3]).

Mormon intentions."[174] An entry in Smith's journal in George Robinson's handwriting accuses Black of being paid by Peniston to lie about Smith, and, although "nothing was proven against" Smith and Wight, King ruled as he did "to pacify as much as possible the feelings of the mobers."[175]

If Black had exaggerated Smith's involvement, Smith misrepresented his and Wight's actions in this case. In their 1840 memorial to Congress, Smith, Rigdon, and Higbee asserted that as soon as Smith and Wight learned of the warrant against them, they "surrendered themselves accordingly to Judge King ... underwent a trial, and in the absence of any just accusations against them, were acquitted and dis-charged."[176] In fact, Smith and Wight initially evaded arrest and were eventually bound over to be tried in November, which trial was never held due to their incarceration for treason and other crimes allegedly committed during the conflict between the Mormons and other Missourians in October 1838.

---

174. Reprinted in the *Missouri Republican*, Sep. 22, 1838.

175. Smith, Journal, Sep. 7, 1838 (*JSP*, J1:316–17).

176. Joseph Smith et al., Memorial to the United States Senate and House of Representatives, Washington DC, ca. Oct. 30, 1839–Jan. 27, 1840, 13 (*JSP*, D7:157). The words "acquitted and" were inserted in different ink and hand. See also Joseph Smith et al., Petition Draft to United States Congress, ca. Nov. 29, 1839, 16, JS Collection.

30

War

The Mormons must be treated as enemies, and must be exterminated
or driven from the State if necessary for the public peace.
—*Lilburn W. Boggs to Gen. John B. Clark,*
Oct. 27, 1838, in Document, 61

On the evening of September 8, 1838, Joseph Smith learned that a mob might attack Adam-ondi-Ahman, and quickly sent a company of men to assist in the Saints' defense.[1] In the morning, Smith received word that a shipment of government guns had been illegally seized in Richmond and was being transported across county lines to Daviess County to aid anti-Mormon vigilantes. He immediately dispatched an additional company of ten mounted men, led by Captain William Allred of the Caldwell County militia, to intercept the weapons. Prior to their departure, Smith addressed them: "I want you to ride as fast as your horses can carry you," promising "and you will get those arms."[2] This company intercepted the stolen guns about a half-mile from Richmond and captured three men, taking them with a writ to Far West, where the guns were distributed among the Mormons. "This was a glorious day indeed," Smith wrote, "the plans of the mob were frustrated in losing their guns, and all their efforts appeared to be blasted."[3] Such action, which took place outside Caldwell County, was legally questionable, and the distribution of government arms was unethical and concerning to the authorities.[4]

---

1. Smith, Journal, Sep. 8, 1838 (*JSP*, J1:318).
2. Tyler, "Incidents of Experience," 33.
3. Smith, Journal, Sep. 9, 1838 (*JSP*, J1:318–19).
4. The editors of the Joseph Smith Papers argue that since Allred was a Caldwell County militia captain, he was therefore authorized to take volunteers and intercept the arms shipment. *JSP*, J1:318n288; see also Baugh, "A Call to Arms," 125. In an 1843 affidavit, Caldwell County sheriff George Pitkin defended the arrest of the three Missourians, claiming that he had "deputized William Allred to go with a company of men and to intercept" the gunrunners. *JSP*, D6:238; see Baugh, 127–32.

At this time, false reports were received at Far West that a mob was "torturing" Mormon "prisoners to death," but Smith and his followers understood that it was done to provoke them into making the "first act of violence."[5] In his September 10 letter to Smith and Rigdon, Austin King mentioned that the two Mormon prisoners, Umpstead and Owens, were unhurt.[6] Nevertheless, Hyrum Smith reported these rumors as fact in his testimony at Nauvoo in 1843.[7]

Doniphan's Arrival

On Monday, September 10, the three Missourian prisoners—John B. Comer of Ray County, and Allen Miller and William L. McHaney of Daviess County—were arraigned before justice of the peace Albert Petty for "abetting the mob" by "carying the guns and amunition to those murderers." They were denied bail and held over until Wednesday.[8] On the same day, Smith and Rigdon sent a letter to Judge King at Richmond asking what should be done with the prisoners and stolen weapons. King directed them later the same day to release the prisoners immediately, but as to the weapons he could not say if they were stolen and had no advice on what to do with them. "The guns belong to the Government," he wrote, and assured them that "they shall not through any agency of mine be taken from you to be converted & used for illegal purposes." He also indicated that he had sent a message to Atchison, "who I presume will do his duty. in reference to dispensing the armed force on grand river," and expressed his hope that armed conflict could be avoided.[9]

King sent Atchison orders "to send a force of 200 men, or more if necessary. Dispel the force in Daviess and all the assembled armed forces in Caldwell and while there to cause those Mormons who refuse to give up, to surrender and be recognized, for it will not do to compromise the law with them."[10] Acting on King's advice, Atchison ordered 400 men from Clay and Ray Counties to go to Daviess County to prevent violence between the Mormons and the vigilantes and to ensure that the Mormons

---

5. Smith, Journal, Sep. 9, 1838 (*JSP*, J1:319).

6. Austin A. King, Letter to Joseph Smith and Sidney Rigdon, Sep. 10, 1838, [2], JS Collection.

7. Hyrum Smith, Testimony, Nauvoo, IL, July 1843, in *Times and Seasons*, July 1, 1843, 246–47.

8. Smith, Journal, Sep. 10, 1838 (*JSP*, J1:319).

9. King, Letter to Joseph Smith and Sidney Rigdon, Sep. 10, 1838, JS Collection (*JSP*, D6:239–40).

10. Austin A. King, Letter to David R. Atchison, Sep. 10, 1838, [1] (*Document*, 28–29).

charged with riot related to the August 8 confrontation with Adam Black would be held responsible.[11]

On September 12 Adam Black, having filed a complaint in late August against sixteen Mormons who had assaulted him earlier that month, filed a parallel complaint before another Daviess County justice of the peace, Philip Covington.[12] As with the first warrant, the second was also returned without being served, with Deputy Elisha T. Denison reporting he was "Resisted by Rifles presnted at my breast."[13]

Later, the same day, Brigadier General Doniphan arrived at Far West with his aide, after having sent his troops to encamp on Crooked River. He immediately demanded that the prisoners be released into his custody and that the captured weapons be handed over to him.[14] Atchison later reported to Governor Boggs that the arms and prisoners were "given up, upon demand, with seeming cheerfulness."[15]

On September 13 Doniphan sent prisoner Comer and the confiscated weapons under guard to Atchison in Ray County; prisoners Miller and McHaney accompanied him to Daviess County, where they were set free.[16] When he arrived at the mob's camp near Millport, he found between 200 and 300 armed men from several surrounding counties and ordered them to disperse. Moving on to Adam-ondi-Ahman, where the Mormons had gathered more than 300 men from Daviess and Caldwell Counties, Doniphan met with Colonel Lyman Wight, whom Atchison described as "a bold, brave, skillful, and I may add, a desperate man."[17] Doniphan reported that Wight agreed to give up any Mormon accused of a crime and to disband. The general then withdrew and situated his troops between the two camps to prevent a confrontation and waited for them to disband on their own.[18]

---

11. See Austin A. King, Letter to David R. Atchison, Sep. 10, 1838; David R. Atchison, Letter to Lilburn W. Boggs, Sep. 12, 1838; and David R. Atchison, Letter to Lilburn W. Boggs, Sep. 17, 1838, Mormon War Papers.

12. State of Missouri, Adam Black, Complaint before Philip Covington, Daviess Co., MO, Sep. 12, 1838.

13. State of Missouri, Philip Covington, Warrant, to Daviess Co. Sheriff [William Morgan] or Constable, for Alanson Ripley et al., Daviess Co., MO, Sep. 12, 1838.

14. Alexander Doniphan, Letter to David R. Atchison, Sep. 15, 1838, [1]–[2], Mormon War Papers (*Document*, 24–25).

15. David R. Atchison, Letter to Lilburn W. Boggs, Sep. 20, 1838, [4], Mormon War Papers (*Document*, 28).

16. Alexander Doniphan, Letter to David R. Atchison, Richmond, MO, Sep. 15, 1838, [2]–[3], Mormon War Papers (*Document*, 25); see also [Rigdon], *An Appeal to the American People*, 25–26.

17. David R. Atchison, Letter to Lilburn W. Boggs, Sep. 20, 1838, [4], Mormon War Papers (*Documents*, 28).

18. Alexander Doniphan, Letter to David R. Atchison, Sep. 15, 1838, [3], Mormon War Papers (*Document*, 25).

Days would pass with little change. In their 1840 memorial to Congress, Smith, Rigdon, and Elias Higbee complained that although Doniphan had placed his troops between the Mormons and the mob, no action was taken to disperse the mob. "These officers"—Atchison, Doniphan, and Parks— "made no attempt to disperse the mob," they wrote, "and excused themselves by saying, 'that the sympathies of their men were in their [the mob's] favor.'"[19] However, an examination of the correspondence between the three generals and other militia leaders shows that between September 15 and 25 they made several attempts to disperse the mob.[20]

On September 15 Daviess County Justice of the Peace William Dryden reported to Boggs that he was unable to execute a warrant and arrest Alanson Ripley, George A. Smith, and others for assaulting and threatening Adam Black on August 8 because he was forcibly driven from town by well-armed Mormons.[21] Boggs immediately issued an order to Atchison to raise enough troops to aid the civil officers in Daviess County to execute all writs.[22] On the same day, Atchison arrived in Daviess County with troops from Ray County and was joined by Doniphan's troops near Gallatin. Two days later, Atchison reported that "the citizens of Daviess, or a large portion of them residing on each side of the Grand River, had left their farms and removed their families either to the adjoining counties or collected them together at a place called the Camp Ground. The whole County on the east side of Grand River appears to be deserted, with the exception of a few who are not so timid as their neighbors."[23] On September 20 Atchison reported to Boggs that Wight "gave up the offenders with a good deal of promptness."[24]

Conflict Averted

On September 18, while Smith was sick at home, Boggs ordered five of his officers, including General Samuel D. Lucas and his 400 troops, to march

---

19. Joseph Smith et al., Memorial to the United States Senate and House of Representatives, Washington DC, ca. Oct. 30, 1839–Jan. 27, 1840, 14 (*JSP*, D7:158).

20. See, for example, Alexander Doniphan, Letter to David Atchison, Sep. 15, 1838; David Atchison, Letter to Lilburn W. Boggs, Sep. 17, 1838; David Atchison, Letter to Lilburn W. Boggs, Sep. 23, 1838; and Hiram Parks, Letter to Lilburn W. Boggs, Sep. 25, 1838, Mormon War Papers.

21. William Dryden, Petition to Lilburn W. Boggs, Sep. 15, 1838, Mormon War Papers (*Document*, 21–22).

22. Lilburn W. Boggs, Letter to B. M. Lisle, Sep. 15, 1838; and B. M. Lisle, Letter to David R. Atchison, Sep. 15, 1838, Mormon War Papers (*Documents*, 22–23).

23. David R. Atchison, Letter to Lilburn W. Boggs, Sep. 17, 1838, [1], Mormon War Papers (*Documents*, 26).

24. David R. Atchison, Letter to Lilburn W. Boggs, Sep. 20, 1838, [4], Mormon War Papers (*Document*, 28).

immediately to Daviess County.[25] That same day, Atchison left the Gallatin area with his troops toward the south, leaving two companies of fifty men each from Ray County under the command of General Parks to keep the peace and help the constable of Daviess County execute warrants and bring the offending Mormons to justice.[26] Also, on this day, thirteen Mormon men appeared at a preliminary hearing before Daviess County justices of the peace Elijah Foley and John Wright on the charge of rioting, following which they voluntarily entered into a recognizance to appear before a grand jury at the next session of the circuit court in April 1839.[27] Six more Mormon men were charged with "misdemeanors" on September 29 and agreed to appear at the next term of the Daviess County Circuit Court.[28]

On September 20 Atchison wrote to Boggs from Liberty, informing him that he had left two companies under the command of Parks stationed in Daviess County and recommended that they remain for about twenty days. He also mentioned that all the warrants against the Mormons had been issued and that those individuals had been arraigned by prosecutor Thomas C. Birch and recognized to appear at the next circuit court. He said that the present crisis had passed, but there was ample reason to fear another conflict. He then described why the Mormon threat should be taken seriously: "From the best information I can get, there are about two hundred and fifty Mormon families in Daviess county, nearly one half of the population, and the whole of the Mormon forces, in Daviess, Caldwell and the adjoining counties, is estimated at from thirteen to fifteen hundred men, capable of bearing arms." In a passage silently deleted in Smith's official history, Atchison gave reason for alarm:

> If an attack is made upon the Mormons in Daviess county, to drive them from that county, it is very much to be feared that the Mormons, to a man, will assist the Mormons of that county; this will be the case I have no doubt. I will further inform your Excellency, that the Mormons are well armed, most of them being equipped with a good rifle or musket, a brace of

---

25. Smith, Journal, Sep. 18, 1838 (*JSP*, J1:328). See Lilburn W. Boggs via B. M. Lisle, Letter to Capt. Childs, Sep. 18, 1838; and Lilburn W. Boggs via B. M. Lisle, Letter to Samuel D. Lucas, Sep. 18, 1838, Mormon War Papers (*Documents*, 23–24).

26. See Hiram G. Parks, Letter to Lilburn W. Boggs, Sep. 25, 1838, Mormon War Papers (*Document*, 32–33).

27. Transcript of Proceedings, ca. Sep. 18, 1838, State of MO v. Joseph Smith et al. for Riot, in *Document*, 159.

28. Transcript, in *Document*, 158. The upcoming hearing was mentioned by Hiram G. Parks in his September 25, 1838, letter to Boggs, [2], Mormon War Papers (*Document*, 32).

large belt pistols, and a broad sword, so that from their position, and their fanaticism, and their unalterable determination not to be driven, much blood will be spilt, and much suffering endured, if a blow is once struck, without the interposition of your Excellency.[29]

Nevertheless, on September 24 Boggs, having received word that "the civil disturbances in the counties of Daviess and Caldwell have been quieted and order restored to the community," ordered his generals to discharge their troops immediately.[30] The cost of the state's September operation in Caldwell and Daviess Counties was an estimated $50,000–$60,000.[31]

On September 25 Parks, unaware that Boggs had rescinded his order to mobilize more troops, wrote to the governor from Millport informing him that Atchison had left the area with the body of the troops and advised him that additional troops were unnecessary, that his two companies were more than sufficient to handle the situation. "Whatever may have been the disposition of the people called Mormons, before our arrival here," wrote Parks, "since we have made our appearance they have shown no disposition to resist the laws, or of hostile intentions." In a portion left out of Smith's history, Parks expressed his opinion that "if the Maj. General [Atchison] had not taken the field with a sufficient force, as promptly as he did, there is every reason to fear a dreadful conflict would have ensued." According to Parks, "a large body of men" from the adjoining counties in response to an appeal of the non-Mormon citizens of Daviess County was gathered "without being called out by the proper authorities" with the intention "to drive the Mormons with powder and lead."[32]

The Mormon and non-Mormon committees met at Adam-ondi-Ahman on September 26, and the Mormons agreed to buy out anyone who desired to leave Daviess County. According to Rigdon, these negotiations resulted in the Missourians agreeing to sell their preemption rights to the Mormons, amounting to "some twenty-five thousand dollars worth of property … in improvements and crops."[33] In their 1840 memorial to Congress, Smith,

29. David R. Atchison, Letter to Lilburn W. Boggs, Sep. 20, 1838, [2]–[3], Mormon War Papers (*Document*, 27). Compare JS History, vol. B-1, 827 (DHC 3:82); and Vogel, *History of Joseph Smith*, 3:91.

30. Lilburn W. Boggs (via B. M. Lisle), Letter to John B. Clark, Sep. 24, 1838, [1], Mormon War Papers (*Document*, 31).

31. "The Mormon War," *Missouri Republican* (St. Louis, MO), Oct. 6, 1838. In today's money, this would be about $1,316,448–$1,579,738.

32. Hiram G. Parks, Letter to Lilburn W. Boggs, Sep. 25, 1838, [3], Mormon War Papers (*Document*, 32).

33. [Rigdon], *Appeal to the American People*, 34.

Rigdon, and Higbee claimed that while these purchases were being made, some of the Missourian sellers were heard to say "that as soon as they had sold out to the Mormons, and received their pay, they would drive them off, and keep both lands and the money."[34] Later the same day, the high council of Adam-ondi-Ahman assigned Don Smith, George A. Smith, Lorenzo Barnes, and Harrison Sagers to collect money from the churches in the south and east to buy out the non-Mormons, which Smith approved when this committee visited Far West the same evening.[35]

Writing to Boggs on September 27 from Liberty, Atchison repeated what Parks had previously communicated to him, that there was no need for additional troops in Daviess County and that the situation was not as dangerous as rumored; in fact, he said, "I have no doubt your Excellency has been deceived by the exaggerated statements of designing or half crazy men. I have found there is no cause of alarm on account of the Mormons; they are not to be feared."[36]

With negotiations underway and the vigilantes from other counties having left the area, it seemed the Mormons had prevailed. "We thought that the matter was settled and we all went about our business," remembered Vinson Knight, acting bishop of Adam-ondi-Ahman.[37] However, when William Austin, leader of the vigilante forces in Daviess County, returned home to Carroll County, he ignited another conflict with about seventy Mormon families residing in the town of De Witt, located along the Missouri River in the southeastern part of the county about seventy miles east of Far West.

Siege of De Witt

Mormons in Carroll County had long been in conflict with non-Mormons. Meetings were held in Carroll County on July 30 and August 7 to force the Mormons out of the county.[38] On September 20 William Austin and his band of about 150 vigilantes visited De Witt and spoke with Colonel George Hinkle, giving him and the Mormons who lived there an ultimatum

---

34. Joseph Smith et al., Memorial to the United States Senate and House of Representatives, ca. Oct. 30, 1839–Jan. 27, 1840, 14–15 (*JSP*, D7:158).

35. JS History, vol. B-1, Addenda, 7, Note W (DHC 3:84–85). This note was probably added under George A. Smith's direction before August 6, 1845. Vogel, *History of Joseph Smith*, 3:98n130.

36. David R. Atchison, Letter to Lilburn W. Boggs, Sep. 27, 1838, [1], Mormon War Papers (*Document*, 34).

37. Vinson Knight, Letter to William Cooper, Feb. 3, 1839, 2.

38. "The Mormons in Carroll County," *Missouri Republican*, Aug. 18, 1838, [2], daily edition.

to leave the county by October 1 or face extermination.[39] According to one account, Hinkle responded coolly that he would "be at his post and prepared to extend a hearty reception."[40]

Two days later the Mormons at De Witt petitioned Boggs for protection.[41] "The Mormons were informed that the Governor said they must take care of themselves," wrote John Corrill. "This the Governor has since told me was a mistake, for he was at St. Louis at the time."[42] Boggs later reported to the state legislature that he was absent from the capital when the petition was delivered and therefore did not respond.[43] This may have been true for the September appeal. However, A. L. Caldwell personally delivered a subsequent appeal to Boggs and returned to Carroll County on October 9 or 10 with the governor's reply, which, according to Rigdon, was "that the Mormons had got into a scrape, and they might fight it out; for he would have nothing to do with it."[44]

In late September, Smith traveled to southern Caldwell County "for the purpose of selecting a location for a Town." On his way, he was met by "one of our Friends with a message from Duet [De Witt] in Carrol[l] County stateing that our Brethren who had settled in that place were & had for some time been surrounded by a mob who had threatned their lives and had shot several times at them." In his June 1839 statement, Smith said: "Immediately on hearing theis strange Intelligence I made preparations to start" for DeWitt.[45]

Smith returned to Far West to raise a force to help the De Witt Saints, but he was delayed in this effort when the Kirtland Camp arrived at Far West on October 2 at about 5:00 p.m. and encamped on the public square around the excavation for the temple's basement. The next day the camp continued its journey to Adam-ondi-Ahman, and Smith, Rigdon, Hyrum

39. See Henry Root, Petition, Mar. 16, 1840, Quincy, IL, CHL, in Johnson, *Mormon Redress Petitions*, 332.

40. A. C. Blackwell, Reminiscence, in "History of Carroll County, Missouri," *An Illustrated Historical Atlas Map, Carroll County, MO*, 13. Blackwell served as a secretary at the Carroll County vigilante meetings.

41. Benjamin Kendrick et al., Petition to Lilburn W. Boggs, Sep. 22, 1838, Mormon War Papers; see also *Document*, 29–30.

42. Corrill, *Brief History*, 35–36 (*JSP*, H2:174–75).

43. Lilburn W. Boggs, Letter to the Missouri House of Representatives, Dec. 5, 1838, Mormon War Papers (*Document*, 14).

44. [Rigdon], *Appeal to the American People*, 29. See also John Murdock, Affidavit, Jan. 10, 1840 (Johnson, *Mormon Redress Petitions*, 504).

45. Joseph Smith, Bill of Damages, June 4, 1839, [2], JS Collection (*JSP*, D6:496); see also Joseph Smith, "Extract, from the Private Journal," *Times and Seasons*, July 1839, 3.

Smith, and Brigham Young rode with them one or two miles before returning to Far West.[46]

Word of the siege at De Witt arrived at Far West on October 4.[47] According to John Corrill, "When they got this news at Far West they turned
out about one hundred in number, and went to assist their brethren at Dewitt. Smith and Rigden went along."[48] In Smith's absence, Young attempted
to hold the third quarterly conference on October 5 in Caldwell County but
quickly adjourned due to an insufficient number of members.[49]

Smith and his volunteer force arrived at De Witt about October 6.[50] He
later said the Mormons were "only a handful, in comparison to the mob, by
which they were surrounded."[51] However, Parks reported to Atchison on the
7th: "On arriving in the vicinity of De Witt, I found a body of armed men,
under the command of Dr. [William] Austin, encamped near De Witt, be-
sieging that place, to the number of two or three hundred, with a piece of
Artillery ready to attack the town of De Witt. On the other side, Hinkle
has in that place three or four hundred Mormons to defend it, and says he
will die before he is driven from thence. ... The Mormons are at this time
too strong, and no attack is expected before Wednesday or Thursday next,
at which time Dr. Austin hopes his forces will amount to five hundred men
when he will make a second attempt on the town of De Witt."[52] Parks's
estimation of Mormon defenders may have relied on the inflated number
supplied to him by Hinkle, but the actual number after the arrival of the
Caldwell troops was probably around 130.[53]

Before Smith's arrival, non-Mormon A. L. Caldwell had left De Witt

46. Tyler, "A Journal of the traveling of the Camp of Latter-day Saints which sent out from
Kirtland for Zion July 6th 1838," July 6–Oct. 4, 1838, 74–75; Elias Smith, "Journal of the camp of
the Seventies during their journey from Kirtland to Far West 1838," Mar.–Oct. 1838, 58.

47. Rockwood, Journal, Oct. 14, 1838; see also Peck, Letter to "Dear Friends," Sep. 18, 1839, 73.

48. Corrill, *Brief History*, 35 (*JSP*, H2:174).

49. Minutes, Oct. 5, 1838, Minute Book 2, 160 (Cannon and Cook, *Far West Record*, 208).

50. "Extract, from the Private Journal of Joseph Smith Jr.," *Times and Seasons*, Nov. 1839,
3 (*JSP*, H1:472), states that Smith arrived at De Witt "about the first of October." His bill of
damages reads "on the [*blank*] day." Smith, Bill of Damages, June 4, 1839, [2], JS Collection (*JSP*,
D6:496). Smith was still in Far West around 10:00 a.m. on October 5 and could not have arrived in
De Witt, over fifty miles to the east, before October 6. Smith, Journal, Oct. 5, 1838 (*JSP*, J1:330).
According to Smith's history, recorded by Thomas Bullock in 1845, Smith arrived in De Witt on
October 6. JS History, vol. B-1, 833 (DHC 3:153); Vogel, *History of Joseph Smith*, 1:xci.

51. "Extract, from the Private Journal of Joseph Smith Jr.," *Times and Seasons*, Nov. 1839, 3
(*JSP*, H1:472).

52. Hiram Parks, Letter to David R. Atchison, Oct. 7, 1838, [1]–[2], Mormon War Papers
(*Document*, 37).

53. Baugh, "Call to Arms," 173; *JSP*, H1:472n28.

about October 2 or 3 to appeal to Boggs for help.[54] Meanwhile, an appeal for protection was made to Judge King, who presided over the Fifth Judicial District, which included Carroll County, as well as other judges in the area.[55] Accordingly, Parks and his two companies of militia arrived on October 4 and camped about five miles from De Witt. Mormon John Murdock reported that Parks told him that he "could do nothing because of the mob spirit in his men."[56] According to Smith, "General Parks informed us that the greater part of his men under Capt. [Samuel] Bogart had mutinied, and that he should be obliged to draw them off from the place, for fear they would [j]oin the mob; consequently he could afford us no assistance."[57] Parks reported to Atchison on the 7th that with only two companies he could "do nothing but negotiate between the parties until further aid is sent me." He requested ten additional companies but apparently received no reinforcements.[58]

On Sunday, October 7, Smith and Rigdon preached to their beleaguered De Witt followers. Recent arrival Christopher Merkley remembered that he "loaded his rifle and went to meeting, which was held but a short distance from our wagon. We formed a hollow square: I sat down with my gun on my lap. We listened to splendid sermons from the Prophet Joseph, and Sidney Rigdon, who had come down during the night with sixty men to help protect us."[59]

In his October 7 communication to Atchison, Parks neglected to mention his troubles with Bogart and his men and their sympathies with the mob. Bogart later complained to Boggs that Parks had prevented him and his men from intercepting Smith and his Mormon reinforcements from Caldwell County.[60] On October 9 Atchison reported to Boggs that he had ordered Parks to "disperse" both Mormon and anti-Mormon non-resident vigilantes and to

---

54. Murdock, Affidavit, Jan. 10, 1840; JS History, vol. B-1, 834–35. See [Rigdon], *Appeal to the American People*, 29–30, for name of messenger.

55. Smith, Bill of Damages, June 4, 1839, [2], JS Collection (*JSP*, D6:496–97). Mormon leaders may have also petitioned Carroll County judges William Crockett, Thomas Arnold, and John Standley. See *JSP*, H1:473n31.

56. Murdock, Letter to Sister Crocker and Others, July 21, 1839; see also Murdock, Journal, Oct. 1838, 102.

57. "Extract, from the Private Journal of Joseph Smith Jr.," *Times and Seasons*, Nov. 1839, 3 (*JSP*, H1:473).

58. Hiram Parks, Letter to David R. Atchison, Oct. 7, 1838, Mormon War Papers (*Document*, 37).

59. Merkley, *Biography of Christopher Merkley*, 4.

60. Samuel Bogart, Letter to Lilburn W. Boggs, Oct. 13, 1838, [1], Mormon War Papers (*Document*, 48).

suggest that De Witt Mormons sell out to local non-Mormons. Atchison also recommended that Boggs come personally to De Witt to "restore peace."[61]

A. L. Caldwell, who had left De Witt earlier in the month to appeal to Boggs personally, returned on October 9 or 10, reporting that the governor said "the quarrel was between the Mormons and the mob" and that the Mormons should "fight it out."[62] Without aid from either the governor or Parks, the situation for the Mormons in De Witt became desperate. "We had now, no hopes whatever, of successfully resisting the mob, who kept constantly increasing," Smith recalled. "Our provisions were entirely exhausted and we being wearied out, by continually standing on a guard, and watching the movements of our enemies; who, during the time I was there, fired at us a great many times. Some of the brethren died, for want of the common necessaries of life, and perished from starvation; and for once in my life, I had the pain of beholding some of my fellow creatures fall victims to the spirit of persecution."[63] In 1843 Rigdon noted that the Mormons in De Witt were "suffering for food and every comfort of life, in consequence of which there was much sickness and many died."[64] Smith said, "Seeing no prospect of relief ... the brethren came to the conclusion to leave that place, and seek a shelter elsewhere."[65] Murdock also reported that the Mormons agreed to leave De Witt on October 10. "After maintaining our ground and holding the place about 10 days, against a force 8–10 times our number," he wrote, "we were forced, contrary to the law of the land, or any just right, of either God or man, to surrender the place; although we had bought it with our own money."[66]

The Mormon evacuation from De Witt began on the afternoon of October 11.[67] According to Rigdon, Smith led about seventy families "about twelve miles, and encamped in a grove of timber, near the road."[68] In his June 1839 statement, Smith said "about 70 wagons left Duet [De Witt] for

---

61. David R. Atchison, Letter to Lilburn W. Boggs, Oct. 9, 1838, Mormon War Papers (*Document*, 38).

62. "Extract, from the Private Journal of Joseph Smith Jr.," *Times and Seasons*, Nov. 1839, 3 (*JSP*, H1:472–73). See also Smith History, vol. B-1, 834–35 (DHC 3:157); Murdock, Affidavit, Jan. 10, 1840; Corrill, *Brief History*, 36 (*JSP*, H2:176); and Sidney Rigdon, Testimony, July 1, 1843, in *Times and Seasons*, July 15, 1843, 270.

63. "Extract, from the Private Journal of Joseph Smith Jr.," *Times and Seasons*, Nov. 1839, 4 (*JSP*, H1:473); see also Smith, Bill of Damages, June 4, 1839, [2], JS Collection (*JSP*, D6:497).

64. Sidney Rigdon, Testimony, July 1, 1843, in *Times and Seasons*, July 15, 1843, 270.

65. "Extract, from the Private Journal of Joseph Smith Jr.," *Times and Seasons*, Nov. 1839, 4 (*JSP*, H1:473); see also Smith, Bill of Damages, June 4, 1839, [2], JS Collection (*JSP*, D6:497).

66. Murdock, Journal, Oct. 1838.

67. Murdock, Affidavit, Jan. 10, 1840; Baugh, "Call to Arms," 179–81.

68. [Rigdon], *Appeal to the American People*, 40.

Caldwell and duri[n]g their Journey were continually insulted by the mob who threatened to destroy us: in our Journey several of our Friends died and had to be interred withou[t] a Coffin & under such Circumstances, which were extremely distressing."[69] In their 1840 memorial to Congress, Smith, Rigdon, and Higbee wrote: "Many others were sick, from starvation and fatigue, and being deprived of medical aid and sustenance, died upon the road."[70] Rigdon specifically reported that "a woman, who had, some short time before, given birth to a child, in consequence of the exposure occasioned by the operations of the mob, and having to move her before her strength would admit, died, and was buried in the grove, without a coffin."[71] According to Morris Phelps, another woman also died due to "the infirmity of old age."[72] Rigdon added that "there were a considerable number sick, both grown persons and children, which was principally owing to their exposure, and to their having been obliged to live in their wagons and tents so long, and to being deprived of suitable food."[73] The refugees trudged their way toward the distant Mormon capital.

Mormon Offensive in Daviess County

On October 12 Smith and Rigdon arrived at Far West with some of the De Witt Mormons.[74] Others soon followed. According to Murdock: "On the 13th–15th of October, the brethren arrived in Caldwell County. There being from 40–50 families, for quite a number had come on from the eastern country."[75] The loss of De Witt was a serious blow to Mormon expansion outside Caldwell County as well as a humiliation Smith was eager not to repeat.

Upon his return to Far West, Smith later recalled, "I was informed by General Doniphan of Clay county, that a company of mobbers eight hundred strong, were marching towards a settlement of our people's in Daviess county."[76] However, Smith was already aware that mobbers planned to attack Mormons in Daviess County and had organized an armed expedition

---

69. Smith, Bill of Damages, June 4, 1839, [3], JS Collection (*JSP*, D6:497).

70. Joseph Smith et al., Memorial to the United States Senate and House of Representatives, ca. Oct. 30, 1839–Jan. 27, 1840, 15–16 (*JSP*, D7:159).

71. [Rigdon], *Appeal to the American People*, 40.

72. Morris Phelps, Reminiscences, [8].

73. [Rigdon], *Appeal to the American People*, 40; see also "A History of the Persecution, of the Church of Jesus Christ, of Latter Day Saints in Missouri," *Times and Seasons*, May 1840, 97 (*JSP*, H2:237).

74. JS History, vol. B-1, 836 (DHC 3:160).

75. Murdock, Journal, Oct. 1838.

76. "Extract, from the Private Journal of Joseph Smith Jr.," *Times and Seasons*, Nov. 1839, 4 (*JSP*, H1:474).

to Adam-ondi-Ahman, but he wished to give the impression that his defense of Daviess County was authorized by Doniphan.

Corrill reported a conversation he had with Smith on Sunday, October 14, before Smith delivered a memorable, militant sermon. Smith and others were discussing how government officials had failed them at De Witt and that "they must take care of themselves." When they expressed a determination to "expel the mob from Davies and then from Caldwell county," even if they had to "spill their [the mob's] blood in the streets," Corrill asked Smith "whether he thought they could hold out in that course and prosper in carrying it into effect. He answered they would, or die in the attempt." When Corrill responded that "they would have the whole state upon them," Smith replied: "No; they would not have the whole state on them, but only that party which was governed by a mob spirit, and they were not very numerous: and they, when they found they would have to fight, would not be so fond of gathering together against them."[77]

Later the same day, Smith preached from John 15:13—"Greater love hath no man than this, that a man lay down his life for his friends."[78] Corrill reported that "Smith preached that day pretty much from the same spirit" that he displayed during their previous conversation.[79] According to Apostle Thomas Marsh, Smith said "all the Mormons who refused to take up arms, if necessary, in difficulties with the citizens, should be shot, or otherwise put to death."[80] Smith then called on all the men who would stand by him to meet on the public square the next day.[81]

On the morning of October 15, a leadership meeting was held and resolutions passed, which, according to Corrill, instructed that "all the members of the church should take hold and help; those who had been backward in carrying on the warfare should now come forward, and their property should be consecrated, so far as might be necessary for the use of the army. If any man undertook to leave the place, and go to the enemy, he should be stopped and brought back, or loose his life."[82]

After this meeting adjourned, Smith and hundreds of armed Mormon men assembled on the public square. According to Reed Peck, Smith

77. Corrill, *Brief History*, 36, 37 (*JSP*, H2:176).

78. Sarah Head, Statement, 1845, Historian's Office, JS History Documents.

79. Corrill, *Brief History*, 37 (*JSP*, H2:176).

80. Thomas B. Marsh, Affidavit, Oct. 24, 1838, 1, Mormon War Papers (*Document*, 57).

81. Sarah Head, Statement, 1845, Historian's Office, JS History Documents; Corrill, *Brief History*, 37 (*JSP*, H2:176).

82. Corrill, 37 (*JSP*, H2:176–77).

addressed the men and informed them that the governor had refused to help the Mormons in De Witt and said they should defend themselves. "We will take our affairs into our own hands and manage for ourselves," he declared. "We have yielded to the mob in Dewitt and now they are preparing to strike a blow in Daviess, but I am determined that we will not give another foot and I care not how many come against us, 10 or 10000 God will send his angels to our deliverance and we can conquer 10000 as easily as 10." As the Mormons were ill-equipped to carry on such a large operation, Smith advised that they supply themselves from the spoils of war, that they hunt the vigilantes and seize their property. "Some may go from here and report that I taught you to steal," Smith reportedly said, "but I distinctly toll [told] you all not to steal when you can get plenty without." He then closed his comments by relating an anecdote about a colonel who had stationed his troops near an old Dutchman farmer who refused to sell them his potatoes. Later that night, when addressing his men, the colonel said, "Now don't let a *man* of you be *caught* stealing that old dutchmans potatoes. In the morning, there was not a potatoe in the old man's field."[83] This was interpreted as Smith's way of protecting himself while at the same time giving volunteers permission to steal from non-Mormons.

Peck testified at the November 1838 hearing that "in refference to stealing," Smith said that "in a general way he did not approve of it" but that under certain circumstances it was necessary, such as when the "Saviour & his disciples stole corn in passing thro' the corn fields for the reason that they could not otherwise procure anything to eat."[84] Phelps testified that Smith gave the speech because "when they went out to war it was necessary to take spoils to live on."[85]

According to Peck, Smith was followed by Rigdon, who declared that dissenters—those who remained at home crying "O don't! O don't! you are breaking the law you are bringing ruin on the [Mormon] Society &c."—should be the first to die, that "those traitors among them who had always opposed their doings should be slain and then the remainder could act in union." Perceiving little enthusiasm for such a measure, Rigdon urged that dissenters "be forced to take their arms and march with the band on the morrow to Daviess county and if they refused they should be pitched on

---

83. Peck, Letter to "Dear Friends," Sep. 18, 1839, 82.

84. Reed Peck, Testimony, in Transcript of Proceedings, Richmond, Ray Co., MO, Nov. 12–29, 1838, [57]; hereafter Transcript. See Matt. 12:1–8; Mark 2:23–28; Luke 6:1–5.

85. William W. Phelps, in Transcript, [89].

their horses with bayonets and placed in front of the battle." This proposition, Reed wrote, "was answered with a hearty *Amen* from the congregation." Nevertheless, it was understood that "should these traitors attempt to leave the county their lives should be the forfeit and their property confiscated for the use of the army."[86] Reflecting on the situation in Far West, Corrill wrote: "I now saw plainly that they had become desperate, and their career would soon end; for I knew that their doings would soon bring the people on them, and I dreaded the consequences. I would have been glad to have left the county with my family, but I could not get away; the decree was passed, and there was no other chance for me and the other dissenters but to pretend to take hold with the rest. I now understood that they meant to fall upon and scatter the mob wherever they could find them collected."[87]

At this time, a call was made for volunteers. According to Corrill, "About two hundred were raised to go to Davies county. Others were raised to guard Far West. A company, called the Fur Company, was raised, for the purpose of procuring provisions, for pressing teams, and even men sometimes, into the army in Caldwell."[88] Those who volunteered to march to Adam-ondi-Ahman were told to reassemble on the following day, and the meeting adjourned.

Later that evening, Doniphan arrived at Far West and told Smith that 800 vigilantes from Carroll County were marching to Adam-ondi-Ahman armed with a cannon.[89] In his June 1839 statement, Smith said Doniphan "advised that we should immediately go to protect our Brethren in Daviess County ... untill he should get the malitia to put them down." He said the militia under his command could not be relied on because of their sympathies with the mob and described them as "'damned' rotten hearted."[90] Rigdon reported that Doniphan said that "his troops were so mutinous, that there was but little reliance to be placed in them" and "advised the authorities of Caldwell county, to send out two or three hundred men to Daviess county, to defend the people against the violence intended by the mob; until such time, as effectual measures could be taken by the authorities, to put a stop to their operations."[91] In 1843 Rigdon testified that Doniphan advised that the

86. Peck, Letter to "Dear Friends," Sep. 18, 1839, 83–84.

87. Corrill, *Brief History*, 37 (*JSP*, H2:176–77).

88. Corrill, 37.

89. "Extract, from the Private Journal of Joseph Smith Jr.," *Times and Seasons*, Nov. 1839, 4 (*JSP*, H1:474).

90. Smith, Bill of Damages, June 4, 1839, [3], JS Collection (*JSP*, D6:498); Corrill, *Brief History*, 38 (*JSP*, H2:178).

91. [Rigdon], *Appeal to the American People*, 41–42; see also "A History of the Persecution," *Times and Seasons*, May 1840, 97–98 (*JSP*, H2:239–40).

Caldwell County men marching to Daviess County "should go in small parties, unarmed in which condition they were not subject to any arrest, from any authority whatever." [92]

Doniphan also informed Smith that vigilantes from Clinton and Platte Counties under the leadership of Cornelius Gilliam were camped about twenty miles northwest of Far West on Grindstone Creek and preparing to attack Mormons in Caldwell County. He said, according to Rigdon, "it was absolutely necessary, that there should be a strong guard kept at Far West, to defend the place. In accordance with his representation, the authorities of the County, had the militia regularly called out, and a number went to Daviess County as he had recommended, to await the movement and operations of the mob; and to act accordingly."[93] Despite the implication in Rigdon's account that those who went to Daviess County had authority from militia leaders in Caldwell County, who in turn had authority from Doniphan, those who marched to Adam-ondi-Ahman actually had no such authority and the general's instruction to travel in small unarmed groups was ignored. "Such an operation," historian Alexander Baugh noted, "could only be authorized through the circuit judge, Austin King, or by state military authorities."[94] Likewise, historian Stephen LeSueur observed that "the Caldwell County militia did not belong to Doniphan's brigade," and therefore "he did not have the authority—no one in Caldwell County had the authority—to order the Mormon troops to march to Daviess County." Moreover, "the Mormon soldiers were not organized strictly into their state militia units," which indicates that the argument given by Rigdon and other early Mormons was an after-the-fact justification.[95]

On October 16 Smith and approximately 150–300 Mormon men marched from Far West to Adam-ondi-Ahman, arriving in the evening and setting up camp.[96] Peck reported that among those who "had the honor of being enrolled in one of these companies and under the bayonet resolutions

---

92. Sidney Rigdon, Testimony, July 1, 1843, in *Times and Seasons*, Aug. 1, 1843, 273.

93. [Rigdon], *Appeal to the American People*, 41–42.

94. Baugh, "Call to Arms," 190.

95. LeSueur, *The 1838 Mormon War in Missouri*, 115–16. In their July 1, 1843, affidavits, Hyrum Smith, Parley P. Pratt, and Brigham Young also claimed that those who marched to Daviess County were authorized either by Doniphan or by Caldwell County Judge Elias Higbee. See *Times and Seasons*, July 1, 1843, 247; July 15, 1843, 257, 261; see also Greene, *Facts Relative to the Expulsion of the Mormons*, 20, 24.

96. Thomas B. Marsh, Affidavit, Oct. 24, 1838, 1, Mormon War Papers (*Document*, 57); Rockwood, Journal, Oct. 19, 1838; Foote, Journal, Oct. 21, 1838; John Smith, Journal, Oct. 16, 1838; Corrill, *Brief History*, 37 (*JSP*, H2:177).

marched to Daviess county" against their will were Corrill, Phelps, John Cleminson, himself, and "several other AntiDanites."[97] Smith remained in Daviess County over the next few days to oversee Mormon operations.[98]

A severe snow storm on October 17 prevented patrols from leaving the camp. "There was not much done," Corrill wrote, "except perhaps to lay some plans of operation."[99] Edward Stevenson remembered: "Joseph the Prophet ... cheering up the Chilly boys" by organizing a snowball fight. "Two lines were formed of about equal strength and a charge made and for a time the snow balls flew rapidly ... all in good humor and full of mirth." Stevenson said within two days the snow cleared and the weather became moderate.[100]

The vigilantes were primarily stationed in Gallatin and Millport and running raids on the scattered Mormon settlements in Daviess County, burning houses, scattering flocks, and whipping some Mormon men.[101] According to Thomas Marsh, "Scouting parties frequently went out, and brought in intelligence that they had seen from three to five hundred men."[102]

Mormon leaders decided to take the fight to their enemies. Sampson Avard later claimed he was present at a council meeting held in Daviess County on October 17, during which Smith instructed several church leaders that they should defend their rights "and that we should be free & independent. and that as the state of Missouri & the U[nited] states would not protect us. It was time then we should rise as the saints of the most high God & protect ourselves & take the Kingdom. ... He considered the U[nited] States rotten [and] he compared the Mormon church to the little stone spoken of by the Prop[he]t Daniel & that the dissenters first ... & the state next ... should be destroyed by this little stone." The council then voted unanimously to support Smith's proposal. During the meeting, Wight boasted that "before winter was over he thought we would be in St Louis & take it."[103]

The next day, Stevenson remembered an alarm was sounded because it was believed the mob was on its way to attack them. After the men assembled in

---

97. Peck, Letter to "Dear Friends," Sep. 18, 1839, 83–84. According to Corrill, however, Phelps did not arrive at Adam-ondi-Ahman until two days later. Corrill, *Brief History*, 38 (*JSP*, H2:178).

98. LeSueur, *1838 Mormon War in Missouri*, 112–28; Baugh, "Call to Arms," 185–210.

99. Corrill, *Brief History*, 37 (*JSP*, H2:177).

100. Stevenson, Autobiography, 92–93.

101. "Extract, from the Private Journal of Joseph Smith Jr.," *Times and Seasons*, Nov. 1839, 4–5 (*JSP*, H1:475–76); see also Smith, Bill of Damages, June 4, 1839, [3], JS Collection (*JSP*, D6:499).

102. Thomas B. Marsh, Affidavit, Oct. 24, 1838, 1, Mormon War Papers (*Document*, 57).

103. Sampson Avard, in Transcript, [6]–[7]. See Dan. 2:34–35.

the public square, "Lyman Wight rode through the ranks with his shirt sleeves roled up saying meny of them will be drunk and if they come against us we will hew them down like old Stumps." They then marched out and prepared for battle, but nothing happened.[104] Instead, Mormon forces launched preemptive raids on several towns where anti-Mormons were known to rendezvous. Marsh testified at the November 1838 hearing that a company of about 80 Mormons headed by Apostle Patten, whom Smith dubbed "Captain Fear-not," marched about seven miles south to Gallatin, burned a portion of the city and "hauled away all the goods from the store in Gallatin, and deposited them at the Bishop's storehouse at 'Diahmon.'"[105] Joseph McGee, who operated a tailor shop at Gallatin, reported that Patten and about 150 men drove him and sixteen other men out of the town, and, after looting the contents of his shop and Jacob Stollings's store, set fire to the buildings.[106] Oliver Huntington, a Mormon teenager in Adam-ondi-Ahman, remembered seeing smoke rising from the direction of Gallatin and the company of Mormon men returning with the plundered goods, which were placed in Bishop Vinson Knight's house.[107] Jeremiah Myers, who participated in the looting, testified that the goods removed from the Stollings store were "considered consecrated property & that they were to be dealt out by the bishop to those who stood in need."[108]

Marsh also testified that Wight and about 80 horsemen went to Millport but, seeing no one to fight and the houses empty, returned to Far West. According to Marsh, "The Prophet, on hearing the property was left" in Millport, began to say, "We had better see to it," but Wight stopped him, saying, "Never mind, we will have a private council." Smith replied, "Very well." In the evening, Marsh said, "a number of footmen came up from the direction of Millport, laden with property, which I was informed consisted of beds, clocks, and other household furniture." Later that night, three wagons were sent to Millport and returned in the morning with several beehives. Smith asked Wight if there were any slaves left in the town for them; Wight replied, "No." Marsh reported that "some one laughed, and said to Smith, 'You have lost your negro then.'"[109]

---

104. Stevenson, Autobiography, 79–80.

105. Thomas B. Marsh, Affidavit, Oct. 24, 1838, 1–[2], Mormon War Papers (*Document*, 57).

106. McGee, *Story of the Grand River Country*, 12. On the looting and burning of Stollings' store, see Agreement with Jacob Stollings, Apr. 12, 1839, JS Letterbook 2, 50 (*JSP*, D6:417–19); Baugh, "Call to Arms," 190–206; Patrick Lynch, in Transcript, [42].

107. Oliver Huntington, History, 25–26.

108. Jeremiah Myers, in Transcript, [69].

109. Thomas B. Marsh, Affidavit, Oct. 24, 1838, 3, Mormon War Papers (*Document*, 57–58). See also Lyman Wight, Affidavit, July 1, 1843, in *Times and Seasons*, July 15, 1843, 266.

In a late reminiscence, Edward Stevenson, who had participated in the raid on Millport, said that "Mill Port was burned and not a single house left. and to this day has not been built up again." However, Stevenson repeated Smith's claim that the mob had burned their own houses and blamed the Mormons, but he knew better.[110] On October 22 Josiah Morin, who lived nearby, and three others from Richmond found that all but two houses in Millport had been burned.[111]

Stevenson also reported the capture of the cannon, which was taken back to Adam-ondi-Ahman.[112] Daniel McArthur remembered that when the company returned to Adam-ondi-Ahman with the cannon, Smith directed that it be taken to the top of the hill overlooking the valley where he claimed Adam had blessed his posterity. "As soon as the sun rose in the morning," wrote McArthur, "the Saints collected on the spot and the cannon was prepared and loaded and fired three times, and every time it was discharged, the Saints took off their hats and shouted Hosannah to God and the Lamb. Three times the report was heard twenty-five miles distinctly."[113]

A third company of about twenty men led by Seymour Brunson, a Danite major, conducted raids against Cornelius Gilliam and other anti-Mormons in the Grindstone Forks area, ten to fifteen miles northwest of Adam-ondi-Ahman.[114] Corrill wrote that they "committed some little thefts" before returning to Adam-ondi-Ahman.[115] Finally, the Fur Company, consisting of about fifty men under the leadership of Jonathan Dunham, was also sent out on foot to procure provisions by randomly stealing among other things "fat hogs and cattle."[116]

Concerning these operations, Corrill remembered: "I heard nothing from the leaders, but in the camp it was said that they meant not only to scatter the mob, but also to destroy those places that harbored them; that Gallatin and Millport were of that number. ... They conjectured that mob after mob, as they termed it, would arise against them, which they would have

110. Stevenson, Autobiography, 96.

111. Charles Bleckley, in Transcript, [77]–[78]; C. R. Morehead et al., Statement, Oct. 24, 1838, Mormon War Papers.

112. Stevenson, Autobiography, 80–81.

113. McArthur, Autobiography, 7.

114. Lyman Wight, Affidavit, July 1, 1843, in *Times and Seasons*, July 15, 1843, 266. Peck estimated a force of about twenty men. Peck, Letter to "Dear Friends," Sep. 18, 1839, 87–88; see also Baugh, "Call to Arms," 195.

115. Corrill, *Brief History*, 37 (*JSP*, H2:177–78).

116. Thomas B. Marsh, Affidavit, Oct. 24, 1838, 3, Mormon War Papers (*Document*, 57–58); Corrill, *Brief History*, 37 (*JSP*, H2:178); Peck, Letter to "Dear Friends," Sep. 18, 1839, 86–87, 89–90.

to subdue, one after another, even till they should reach St. Louis, where [Lyman] Wight said he meant to winter." Corrill reported that many believed "the time had arrived for the riches of the gentiles to be consecrated to the house of Israel," which had been predicted in a February 1831 revelation. Although "they meant to confine themselves to the mob characters in their plunderings," he wrote, "it appeared to me also that the love of pillage grew upon them very fast, for they plundered every kind of property they could get hold of, and burnt many cabins in Davies, some say eighty, and some say one hundred and fifty."[117]

While Mormons like Marsh and Corrill denounced such acts as plundering and looting, others justified them as necessary for survival and permitted during times of war. Benjamin Johnson stated, "It should not be supposed because we sought to repel mob violence and were compelled to forage for food when hemmed in on all sides by a mob who had driven us from homes ... that we were common robbers because we took as by reprisal with which to keep from starvation our women and children. Ours was a struggle for our lives and homes; and a more conscientious, noble, and patriotic spirit never enthused man than that which animated our leaders in this just defense of our rights."[118] Similarly, Warren Foote wrote: "Now in order to sustain themselves, the mormons took their enimies corn, cattle, hogs etc. according to the usages of war."[119] Others gave a more theological justification according to John Whitmer, who noted that some Mormon participants "would Justify themselves by saying we are the people of God and all things are gods."[120]

While Mormon vigilantes burned twenty-five to fifty buildings in Daviess County, at this point the Mormons had lost only about ten cabins.[121] In Daviess County, "Mormon soldiers completely overwhelmed their foes," historian Stephen LeSueur observed. "Within a week after their arrival at Diahman, they had driven all enemy troops—and nearly all the non-Mormons—from the county."[122] Smith sent an express message to Far West containing news of the Mormon success in Daviess County and declaring

---

117. Corrill, *Brief History*, 38 (*JSP*, H2:178–79). Revelation, Feb. 9, 1831, "The Laws of the Church of Christ," [3], Revelations Collection [BC XLIV:32] (*JSP*, D1:252). Cf. Isa. 61:6.

118. Johnson, "A Life Review," 37.

119. Foote, Journal, Oct. 21, 1838.

120. Whitmer, History, 88 (*JSP*, H2:99).

121. Baugh, "Call to Arms," 215; LeSueur, *1838 Mormon War in Missouri*, 124.

122. LeSueur, 124.

"they had nothing to fear & that the enemy was in their hands," which Rigdon read to the troops.[123]

Mormon leaders subsequently tried to justify their actions in Daviess County by claiming they had been authorized by Parks. In their 1840 memorial to Congress, Smith, Rigdon, and Higbee represented Parks as telling Wight to "take a company of men and if necessary give the mob battle, and that he would be responsible for the consequences; saying, that they would have no peace with the mob until they had given them a scourging."[124] According to Rigdon, Parks told Wight "with an oath, 'go and give them a complete dressing, for you will never have any peace with them, until you do it; and I will stand between you and all difficulty.'"[125] In his 1843 petition, Wight claimed that Parks had given him authority to raise a force "and take such course as you may deem best in order to disperse the mob from this county." After receiving this charge, according to Wight, he went to Millport and ordered Patten to Gallatin.[126] However, as Baugh observes, Parks's October 21, 1838, letter to Atchison clearly indicates that he did not speak with Wight until *after* the raids on Gallatin, Millport, and Grindstone Fork.[127] Nevertheless, Baugh also argues that "since it was technically legal to form an independent militia company, Mormon leaders and Danite officers likely considered the creation of the Danite corps to be a division of the county militia and believed any operation undertaken by them would also be lawful"—an argument that no one made at the time. Baugh acknowledges that owing to the secret and clandestine nature of the Danites and their operating outside the official authorization and jurisdiction of the local militia, their existence and activities in Daviess County were, in fact, illegal.[128]

The situation in Daviess County left Smith and the Mormon leadership with few options. As Baugh notes, Mormon leaders could have acted in self-defense, which would have allowed anti-Mormon forces to gather strength and eventually force them from the county, as they had done in De Witt, or they could strike preemptively against their enemies and take

---

123. Nathaniel Carr, in Transcript, [47] (*Document*, 114).

124. Joseph Smith et al., Memorial to the United States Senate and House of Representatives, ca. Oct. 30, 1839–Jan. 27, 1840, 18 (*JSP*, D7:162).

125. [Rigdon], *Appeal to the American People*, 43–44; see also "A History of the Persecution," *Times and Seasons*, May 1840, 98 (*JSP*, H2:241).

126. Lyman Wight, Testimony, July 1, 1839, in *Times and Seasons*, July 15, 1843, 266; see also Hyrum Smith, Testimony, July 1, 1839, in *Times and Seasons*, July 1, 1843, 248.

127. Baugh, "Call to Arms," 203; Hiram Parks, Letter to David R. Atchison, Oct. 21, 1838, Mormon War Papers (*Document*, 47–48). See also LeSueur, *1838 Mormon War in Missouri*, 123.

128. Baugh, "'We Have a Company of Danites in These Times,'" 14.

control of the county, which is what they decided to do. However, it only succeeded in turning the public, who came to see them as the aggressors, against them.[129] On October 24 King wrote to Boggs: "Until lately I thought the Mormons wer[e] disposed to act on the defensive, but their recent conduct show that they are the aggressors, & that they intend to take the law into their own hands." King asked the governor to intervene. "The country is in great commotion and I can assure you that either with or without authority, something will shortly have to be done."[130]

Defectors in High Places

Smith and his company of vigilantes returned to Far West at about 7:00 p.m. on Monday, October 22.[131] Albert Rockwood wrote that when the cavalry of about 130 horsemen returned from Adam-ondi-Ahman, they rode into town "under the tune of Yanke Doudle." After assembling on the public square, "President Rigdon gave them a short address suited to the occation when all the people said Amen."[132] While this battle had been won, it would soon become apparent that the war was far from over.

When Smith returned, the town was preparing for battle. Two days earlier, Rigdon and Avard had called 50–100 "true men"—Danites—to meet in a well-guarded schoolhouse. This meeting was attended by Burr Riggs, who subsequently testified that Rigdon proposed that if any man attempted to escape Far West, "he should be pursued and brot back dead or alive"—which was unanimously accepted. Riggs also reported that "companies were chosen, some to procure wood for the town, and some to procure meal for the army at Far West, and also, for the families of those who were in the expedition to Daviess; and one company for spies ... to learn the movements of mobs."[133] On October 22, the day of Smith's return to Far West, Rockwood recorded in his journal: "A portion of each Day is set apart for drill, after which they go to their several stations (VIZ.) 2 Companies of 10.s are to provide the

---

129. Baugh, "Call to Arms," 217.
130. Austin A. King, Letter to Lilburn W. Boggs, Oct. 24, 1838, [1], [3], Mormon War Papers (*Document*, 53–54). King's letter was published in the Jefferson City *Missouri Watchman* on October 29, which is not extant but known through reprints in "Letter from Judge King," *Missouri Republican*, Nov. 2, 1838, [2]; and "Letter from Jud[g]e King," *Missouri Argus* (St. Louis), Nov. 8, 1838, [1].
131. Historian's Office, Joseph Smith History, Draft Notes, Manuscript 1, 27 (Oct. 22, 1838), which was created by Willard Richards about February 1845 with the date added by Richards above the line. Vogel, *History of Joseph Smith*, 7:xxxiii, 26.
132. Rockwood, Journal, Oct. 25, 1838.
133. Burr Riggs, in Transcript, [75] (*Document*, 135). See also the statements of W. W. Phelps, Benjamin Slade, and Addison F. Green in Transcript, [83]–[94], [105]–[108] (*Document*, 120–25, 143, 144).

famalies with meal[,] 2 provide wood[,] 2 or 3 Build cabbins, 1 company of 10.s collect & prepare armes, 1 company provide me[a]t, 1 Company are spies, one Company are for express, 1 for guard[,] 2 Companies are to gather the famalies that are scattered over the counties in the vicinity[,] 1 company to see to & provide for the sick, and the famalies of those that are off on duty[,] Others are employed gathering provisions into the city, &c &c."[134]

On October 24 Apostles Thomas Marsh and Orson Hyde went to Richmond and filed an affidavit criticizing the actions of Smith and Mormon vigilantes in Daviess County. The affidavit revealed the existence of the Danites, "who have taken an oath to support the heads of the Church in all things that they say to do, whether right or wrong," and the formation of a "Destruction Company, for the purpose of burning and destroying" in retaliation to the mob's actions. According to Marsh, "The Prophet inculcates the notion, and it is believed by every true Mormon, that Smith's prophecies are superior to the laws of the land. I have heard the Prophet say that he would yet tread down his enemies, and walk over their dead bodies; and if he was not let alone, he would be a second Mohammed to this generation, and that he would make it one gore of blood from the Rocky mountains to the Atlantic ocean; that like Mohammed, whose motto in treating for peace was, 'the Alcoran or the Sword.' So should it be eventually with us, 'Joseph Smith or the Sword.'"[135]

According to Corrill, while he was unable to contrive an excuse to leave Far West, "T. B. Marsh, O. Hyde, and some others, made their escape in the night, with their families, but were followed the next day by twenty horsemen from Far West without success."[136] In late October Marsh wrote to his brother-in-law and sister in Far West from his refuge in Richmond: "I have come to the full conclusion that he [Joseph Smith] is a very wicked man; ... I also am well convinced that he will not escape the just judgements of an offended God who pleads the cause of the innocent. I speak now of the innocent who are led by his deceitful tongue &c. ... The disposition manifested in J. Smith and S Rigdon to pillage, rob, plunder assassinate and murder, was never equalled, in my estimation, unless by some desperado Bandit. ... For the burning the Post office in Galeton, for pillaging goods &c in Davise, The Government will undoubtedly take notice, & I fear that many innocent

---

134. Rockwood, Journal, Oct. 22, 1838.

135. Thomas B. Marsh, Affidavit, Oct. 24, 1838, Mormon War Papers (*Document*, 57–59). Hyde's affidavit appends Marsh's.

136. Corrill, *Brief History*, 39 (*JSP*, H2:180–81).

among you will have to suffer. ... I know more about this matter than you. Be advised by your Brother, and escape for your lives, for I verily believe that God will destroy that place." In an appended letter, Hyde concurred: "I can say with him that I have left the Church called Latter Day Saints for con-science sake, fully believing that God is not with them, and is not the mover of their schemes and projects. ... I do really hope that my friends will hasten and get out of Caldwell County as <u>soon</u> as <u>possible</u>."[137]

Battle of Crooked River

Soon after his return to Far West, Smith learned of mob activity on Caldwell County's southern border. Responding to rumors that the Mormons intended to conduct raids in Ray County, Captain Samuel Bogart of the state militia sought and received authorization from Atchison on October 22 "to range the line between Caldwell & Ray County."[138] However, Bogart exceeded this authorization and on October 24 began harassing Mormons living near the border, burning at least one cabin and capturing three Mormon scouts.[139]

According to Smith, George Hinkle ordered David Patten to take his company of cavalry and "go against them, and stop their depredations, and drive them out of the county."[140] However, at the November 1838 hearing, Hinkle testified that he was at his home at the time and was not consult-ed.[141] Parley Pratt and Rigdon said Hinkle was not present when news of Bogart's actions reached Far West. Instead, Pratt reported that Patten and his men were ordered to go to Crooked River by John Killian, who he said commanded the Mormon troops in Hinkle's absence.[142]

During the night, Patten and about sixty men rode out of Far West for Bogart's vigilante encampment on the Crooked River.[143] When they arrived

---

137. Thomas B. Marsh and Orson Hyde, Letter to Lewis Abbott and Ann Marsh Abbott, Oct. 25–30, 1838, in JS Letterbook 2, 18, 19.

138. Samuel Bogart, Letter to David R. Atchison, Oct. 23, 1838, [1], Mormon War Papers (*Document*, 48); David R. Atchison, Letter to Samuel Bogart, Oct. 23, 1838, in Transcript, [26]. Rigdon later incorrectly asserted that Bogart only obtained permission after his October 25 skir-mish with Mormon forces. [Rigdon], *Appeal to the American People*, 48; see also "A History of the Persecution," *Times and Seasons*, July 1840, 129–30 (*JSP*, H2:254–56).

139. Rockwood, Journal, Oct. 25, 1838; see also Baugh, "Call to Arms," 219–25.

140. "Extract, from the Private Journal of Joseph Smith Jr.," *Times and Seasons*, Nov. 1839, 5 (*JSP*, H1:476); Smith, Bill of Damages, June 4, 1839, [4], JS Collection (*JSP*, D6:500).

141. George M. Hinkle, in Transcript, [40]–[41].

142. Pratt, *History of the Late Persecution*, 33; Sidney Rigdon, Testimony, June 1, 1843, in *Times and Seasons*, Aug. 1, 1843, 273–74.

143. Participant Charles C. Rich estimated that Patten's force consisted of "a bout seventy five men." Charles C. Rich, Statement, Historian's Office, JS History Documents, ca. 1839–56. Historian Alex Baugh has identified sixty-two possible participants. Baugh, "Call to Arms," appendix H.

near the southern border about dawn, they were ambushed. Five of Patten's men were immediately wounded, one fatally. Returning fire, Patten and his troops charged the gunmen. "The whole wilderness seemed for a few moments as if wrapped in a blaze of lightning; and overwhelmed with the sharp crack of peals of thunder," Pratt recalled.[144] In the charge, Patten was shot as the enemy fled across the creek, leaving their horses and baggage wagon in the camp. When the firing stopped, the Mormon troops yelled triumphantly, "God and Liberty!" As the smoke cleared, the Mormons discovered that they had killed one of the Ray County militiamen and at least seven lay wounded on the ground. They took one man prisoner temporarily. After loading the captured wagon with their wounded, Patten among the rest, the Mormon troops headed back to Far West, taking the abandoned horses with them and distributing them among the Mormons.[145]

"On the day after this affray," Smith wrote, "Capten Patten sent for me to pray for him which request I complied with."[146] Accordingly, Smith took his brother Hyrum and Amasa Lyman to Stephen Winchester's house, about three miles outside Far West. Avard testified that when he visited the dying Patten, he found Smith "laying hands on the wounds, and blessing them to heal them."[147] Morris Phelps similarly reported that Smith "went to the wounded and pronounced a blessing on them & prayed for them to be healed & saved."[148] Nevertheless, Patten died that night. Two days later, on October 27, prior to Patten's funeral and burial at Far West, Smith attended a viewing of the body with others and said, "There lies a man that has done just as he said he would—he has 'laid down his life for his friends.'"[149]

Defense of Far West

News of the Battle of Crooked River and other Mormon aggressions spread through northern Missouri faster than wildfire on the prairie. Smith, Rigdon,

---

144. Pratt, *History of the Late Persecution*, 35.

145. Rockwood, Journal, Oct. 25, 1838; Charles C. Rich, Statement, ca. Feb. 1845, Historian's Office, JS History Documents; Pratt, *History of the Late Persecution*, 35–36; Sidney Rigdon, Testimony, Nauvoo, IL, July 1, 1843, in *Times and Seasons*, Aug. 1, 1843, 274; Peck, Letter to "Dear Friends," Sep. 18, 1839, 95–101; Wyatt Cravens, in Transcript, [25]; Joseph Smith et al., Memorial to the United States Senate and House of Representatives, ca. Oct. 30, 1839–Jan. 27, 1840, 19–20 (*JSP*, D7:163–64); Corrill, *Brief History*, 39 (*JSP*, H2:180–81); *History of Caldwell and Livingston Counties,* 130; Baugh, "Call to Arms," 218–52.

146. Smith, Bill of Damages, June 4, 1839, [5], JS Collection (*JSP*, D6:501); Kimball, "History of Heber Chase Kimball by His Own Dictation," 86.

147. Sampson Avard, in Transcript, [21]–[22] (*Document*, 107).

148. Morris Phelps, in Transcript, [28] (*Document*, 110).

149. JS History, vol. B-1, 842 (DHC 3:175).

and Higbee wrote that report of the battle "created much excitement; and the citizens, through false and exaggerated statements, were made to believe that the Mormons were in rebellion against the laws of the country."[150] Amos Rees and Wiley Williams, residents of Ray County, sent a midnight dispatch to General John B. Clark stationed in Howard County, stating that "these wretched fanatics have thrown off all restraint and are destroying all before them." After briefly mentioning Mormon attacks on Gallatin and Millport and repeating a false rumor that "Capt Bogard and all his company amounting to between fifty and sixty were massacred by the Mormons" at Crooked River, Rees and Williams warned Clark: "They have determined to attack and burn Richmond to night And we have but little doubt but that they will attempt it[.] The women and children have all left Richmond and are leaving the County flying for protection to Livingston and elsewhere[.] These creatures will never Stop until they are stoped by the Strong hand of force."[151]

The escalation of conflict and spread of false information caused Mormons throughout Caldwell County to feel extremely vulnerable and to begin gathering in Far West. According to Peck, "Immediately after the battle of Crooked River nearly all Caldwell County were astir removing their families and effects to Far West as a place of Safety."[152] By this time, the population of Far West was already swelling well beyond capacity. "The City of Far West is literally crowded and the Brethren are gathering from all quarters," Rockwood wrote.[153] On September 17 Smith and Rigdon wrote to Stephen Post, a seventy in Crawford County, Pennsylvania, that "the road is full [of] companies of frequently 10, 20 & 30 wagons," which arrive at Far West "almost daily."[154]

On October 26 Boggs, via Adjutant-General B. M. Lisle, sent an order to General Clark to raise 2,000 men and assemble at Fayette on November 3, and from there march to Richmond, and then to Daviess County to protect and restore the citizens to their homes.[155] On the following day, at Jefferson City, Boggs issued his now-infamous "extermination order" to Clark concerning the Mormons: "The Mormons must be treated as enemies and must

---

150. Joseph Smith et al., Memorial to the United States Senate and House of Representatives, ca. Oct. 30, 1839–Jan. 27, 1840, 19–20 (*JSP*, D7:163–64).

151. Wiley C. Williams and Amos Rees, Letter to General John B. Clark, Oct. 25, 1838, [2], Mormon War Papers (*Document*, 59–60).

152. Peck, Letter to "Dear Friends," Sep. 18, 1839, [101]–[102].

153. Rockwood, Journal, Oct. 23, 1838.

154. Joseph Smith and Sidney Rigdon, Letter to Stephen Post, Sep. 17, 1838, [2] (*JSP*, D6:243).

155. B. M. Lisle, Letter to John B. Clark, Oct. 26, 1838, Mormon War Papers (*Document*, 62–63).

be exterminated or driven from the state if necessary for the public peace their outrages are beyond all description." Boggs was influenced by false reports from Rees and Williams, which Boggs said "places the Mormons in the attitude of an open and avowed defiance of the laws And of having made war upon the people of this State Your orders are therefore to hasten your operation with all possible speed." Boggs ordered Clark to take as many men as possible and join forces with Major General Wallock's 500, Brigadier General Doniphan's 500, and Brigadier General Parks's 400 in northern Daviess County and to "operate against the Mormons."[156]

Generals David Atchison and Samuel Lucas wrote Boggs on October 28 and requested his presence in Daviess County. "From late outrages committed by the *Mormons, civil war* is inevitable," they stated. "They have set the laws of the country at defiance, and are in open rebellion," they have therefore mobilized about two thousand troops to "keep them in check."[157]

On October 29 the state militia gathered about 1,800 men under the command of Lucas and Atchison and began their march toward Far West, arriving later the same day and setting up camp at Linville's Creek about sixteen miles from Far West, while Doniphan was encamped seven miles below Far West on Log Creek with a force of 500 men. On the following day, Lucas and Atchison rendezvoused at Log Creek with Doniphan and his troops. At this time, Boggs relieved Atchison of his command and ordered him to return to Liberty to resume his legislative duties.[158] Instead, he placed John B. Clark, stationed at Fayette, in command.[159] Rather than wait for Clark's arrival, Lucas assumed temporary command and continued the march of state troops toward Far West, a move for which Boggs would later criticize him.[160]

On the morning of October 30 Smith assembled the Mormon soldiers on the public square and declared his intention to defend Far West and Caldwell County. "They pretended to come out as militia, but ... they were all a damned set of mobs," Smith said of Bogart's troops. "God should damn

---

156. Lilburn W. Boggs, Letter to John B. Clark, Oct. 27, 1838, [1], Mormon War Papers (*Document*, 61). For a discussion of the historical background of Boggs' order, see Anderson, "Clarifications of Boggs's 'Order' and Joseph Smith's Constitutionalism."

157. David R. Atchison and Samuel D. Lucas, Letter to Lilburn W. Boggs, Oct. 28, 1838, [1], Mormon War Papers (*Document*, 76).

158. Samuel D. Lucas, Letter to Lilburn W. Boggs, Nov. 2, 1838; and Lilburn W. Boggs, Letter to John B. Clark, Nov. 6, 1838, Mormon War Papers (*Document*, 69–70, 72–75).

159. Lilburn W. Boggs, Letter to John B. Clark, Oct. 27, 1838, [1]–[2], Mormon War Papers (*Document*, 61).

160. Baugh, "Call to Arms," 303–308.

them."[161] Avard later testified that Smith promised that "the Lord would send angels, who would fight for us; and that we should be victorious."[162] Ebenezer Robinson remembered that Smith declared, "If the mob persisted in coming upon us, we will play hell with their applecart."[163]

Later the same day, Hinkle and about 150 horsemen left Far West to investigate the militia troops amassing on Caldwell's southern border but, upon arriving in the Crooked River area, learned that the militia had left and was making its way toward Far West. In attempting to return to the Mormon capital, Hinkle and his men were cut off by Lucas's troops about five miles below the city and nearly captured by a detachment of troops under Doniphan's command. Hinkle and his men eventually reached their destination by taking "a circuitous route, to Far West, passing [around] the rear of the enemy."[164] By the time Hinkle got within sight of the city, they found Doniphan's men and Mormon troops poised for a battle. As Corrill remembered, "We saw a line of battle drawn up by the militia, and the Mormons also arrayed to meet them, but the militia, for some cause, withdrew to their camp on Goose creek."[165] Not wishing a confrontation, Doniphan rejoined Lucas and the main encampment on Goose Creek about a mile south of Far West.[166]

While Hinkle and his troops were away, Pratt wrote that another "alarm came in to town that the whole county to the South of us was filled with hostile troops, who were murdering, plundering, and taking peaceable citizens prisoners, in their own houses, etc." These actions were being taken by Lucas's advance guard patrolling ahead of the main force of the militia. "On receiving this intelligence," Pratt remembered, "every man flew to arms, for the protection of our city." It was not long before "we discovered an army advancing on horse back, over the hills, at two miles distance from the town."[167] Someone exclaimed, "Retreat!" Smith responded, "Retreat! where in the name of God shall we retreat to?"[168] Pratt said the Mormon troops "marched

---

161. James C. Owens, in Transcript, [46] (*Document*, 113).

162. Sampson Avard, in Transcript, [9] (*Document*, 100).

163. Ebenezer Robinson, "Items of Personal History," *Return* (Davis City, IA), Jan. 1890, 206. See also George Hinkle and Samuel Kimball, in Transcript, [44], [83] (*Document*, 128, 138).

164. Amasa Lyman, "Amasa Lyman's History," *Millennia Star* (Liverpool, Eng.), Aug. 19, 1865, 520–21.

165. Corrill, *Brief History*, 40, (*JSP*, H2:182).

166. Baugh, "Call to Arms," 312–14.

167. Pratt, *History of the Late Persecution*, 38; see also "A History of the Persecution," *Times and Seasons*, June 1840, 115 (*JSP*, H2:249–50).

168. John Taylor, "The Dispensation of the Fulness of Times," Mar. 5, 1882, *Journal of Discourses*, 23:37.

out upon the plains on the South of the city, and formed in battle array, extending our line of foot [soldiers] something like a half mile, while a small company of horse[men] was posted on our right wing on a commanding eminence, and another small company in the rear of our main body, intended as a kind of reserve."[169] By stationing the men several feet apart, Ebenezer Robinson explained, "to an observer at a distance, we made a very formidable appearance."[170]

Despite the presence of Doniphan's troops south of the city, Hinkle and his men managed to enter the city. "Our company of a hundred and fifty soon returned," Pratt recalled, "informing us that they had been hemmed in through the day, and only escaped from their superior knowledge of the ground."[171] Safely home, Hinkle nevertheless tried immediately to diffuse the situation by ordering the front line to retreat." This angered Smith, who, as Hinkle later testified, "rode up, and upraided me for such an order and told me it should not be done." He then ordered the men to "stand still. & talked harshly to me charging me with cowerdice. I knew it would not do to oppose his wishes. and returned home." Smith took command of Hinkle's forces and "marched them down to the other line of mormons who were formed to recd [receive] the militia."[172]

It was near sunset when both sides sent out a few men bearing white flags, which met in the area between the two armies. The militia demanded the release of three non-Mormon residents of Far West "before they massacred the rest." Despite the danger, the non-Mormons, one of whom was married to a Mormon, subsequently informed militia officers that they wished to remain. Doniphan decided to end the standoff and set up an independent camp apart from Lucas's militia encampment on Goose Creek.[173]

With Smith's consent, Reed Peck rode into the enemy camp near dusk hoping to negotiate a compromise. "After delivering the message intrusted by Joseph," Peck reported, "I informed the Genl that there were many individuals among the Mormons who were as warmly opposed to the wicked transactions in Daviess County and the oppressive influence by which the church is led as any man in his army could be and that those men were now compelled to Stand in the Mormon rank where in the event of a battle their

169. Pratt, *History of the Late Persecution*, 38.

170. Ebenezer Robinson, "Items of Personal History," *Return*, Jan. 1890, 206.

171. Pratt, *History of the Late Persecution*, 39.

172. George M. Hinkle, in Transcript, [41] (*Document*, 127).

173. Pratt, *History of the Late Persecution*, 38–39; see also "A History of the Persecution," *Times and Seasons*, June 1840, 115 (*JSP*, H2:249–50).

blood would flow in defence of measures to which they had ever been ad-verse."[174] When Peck returned to the city, Corrill remembered, "he said that General Doniphan had appointed the next morning at eight o'clock to meet a committee of Mormons and make proposals of peace. He promised that no harm should befal us that night; he stated that their object was to bring the guilty to punishment, but the innocent should have an opportunity to escape before they would attack the place."[175]

The Mormons spent the night of October 30–31 fortifying the southern border of Far West. "That night," Corrill wrote, "the Mormons built a sort of breastwork of rails, house-logs, boards, &c. on that side of town next [to] the army, but it was about as good a defence as a common fence would be."[176] Pratt also mentioned building this breastwork: "Our people, being deter-mined, if attacked, to defend their homes, and wives and children to the last, spent the night in throwing up a temporary breastwork of building timber, logs, rails, &c., and by morning our south side of the city was fortified with a breastwork, and also a considerable part of the east and west sides; the whole line of fortification extending a mile and a half."[177]

On the morning of October 31 Doniphan and several officers rode into view of the city bearing a white flag. They were met by Hinkle, who had ap-parently resolved his dispute with Smith during the night, accompanied by Peck and Corrill. Doniphan informed them of the governor's extermination order and that General Lucas of Jackson County was in charge while they awaited the arrival of General Clark. Before departing, Hinkle requested a meeting with Lucas, which Doniphan promised to convey.[178]

During the day, Lucas remained busy with "receiving & encamping of fresh troops, who were hourly coming in."[179] Approximately 700 additional men arrived, including Neil Gilliam's vigilantes from Clinton and Platte Counties, swelling the militia forces to about 2,500.[180] He finally sent word

---

174. Peck, Letter to "Dear Friends," Sep. 18, 1839, 106; Corrill, *Brief History*, 40 (*JSP*, H2:182–83).

175. Corrill, *Brief History*, 40 (*JSP*, H2:182–83).

176. Corrill, 40.

177. Pratt, *History of the Late Persecution*, 39; see also Corrill, *Brief History*, 40 (*JSP*, H2:182–83); and "A History of the Persecution," *Times and Seasons*, June 1840, 116 (*JSP*, H2:250–51).

178. Baugh, "Call to Arms," 317–18.

179. Samuel D. Lucas, Letter to Lilburn W. Boggs, Nov. 2, 1838, [3], Mormon War Papers (*Document*, 73).

180. Samuel D. Lucas, Letter to Lilburn W. Boggs, Nov. 5, 1838, [3], Mormon War Papers (*Documents*, 71); Pratt, *History of the Late Persecution*, 39; see also "A History of the Persecution," *Times and Seasons*, June 1840, 116 (*JSP*, H2:250).

to Hinkle that he would meet with him at 2:00 p.m. on the "eminence" a little south of Far West.[181]

Prior to this meeting, the Mormons learned of the massacre of their people at Haun's Mill in Carroll County by a force of over 200 vigilantes on the previous afternoon. The attack that killed seventeen and wounded another fourteen Mormon men, women, and children was in retaliation for the recent Mormon "cleansing" of Daviess County as well as false reports that they had slaughtered Bogart's troops at Crooked River.[182] News of the tragedy was a sobering blow to the inhabitants of Far West—the "extermination order" was no longer simply a threat; it was chillingly real. Negotiations suddenly became more consequential as the Mormon leaders realized they had no option but to capitulate. Corrill, a member of the delegation, said Smith instructed him to "beg like a dog for peace."[183] The irony of Smith's instructions was not lost on Corrill, for he would subsequently remind the Mormon readers of his history: "Did not your prophet proclaim in your ears that the day was your own, and you should overcome; when in less than a week you were all made prisoners of war, and you would have been exterminated, had it not been for the exertions and influence of a few dissenters."[184] The three key negotiators for the Mormons—Hinkle, Peck, and Corrill—were subsequently maligned as traitors and became disaffected, resulting in the excommunications of Hinkle and Corrill.

---

181. Lucas, Letter to Boggs, Nov. 2, 1838, [3], Mormon War Papers (*Documents*, 73).
182. Baugh, "Call to Arms," 253–98.
183. Corrill, *Brief History*, 40–41 (*JSP*, H2:183).
184. Corrill, 48 (*JSP*, H2:197).

31

Arrest

OCTOBER–NOVEMBER 1838

I fear that a blast like that which has fallen on the devoted town of
Kirtland will come after time is sufficient to test the impropriety of
those plans advocated by some of this church.
                                    —*Oliver Cowdery to Warren Cowdery,*
                                    Feb. 24, 1838, Cowdery, Letterbook, 88

On the afternoon of October 31, 1838, according to arrangement, General
Lucas, accompanied by Brigadier Generals Wilson, Doniphan, and Gra-
ham, appeared on the "eminence" just outside Far West's southern border
bearing a flag of truce. They were soon met by Colonel Hinkle and a delegation consisting of Corrill, Peck, John Cleminson, and Phelps—all of whom
had become critical of the Danites and Joseph Smith's paramilitary operations in Daviess County.[1] Lucas reported to Boggs that Hinkle stated "the
object in asking me to meet him there was to know if there could not be
some compromise or settlement of the difficulty without a resort to arms."
Lucas read the governor's extermination order to Hinkle and the others,
who were shocked. "This order greatly agitated my mind," Corrill reflected.
"I expected we should be exterminated without fail. There lay three thousand
men, highly excited and full of vengeance, and it was as much as the officers
could do to keep them off from us any how; and they now had authority
from the executive to exterminate, with orders to cut off our retreat. ... So of
course there was no escape for any."[2] Lucas demanded compliance with the
following terms:

---

1. Corrill, *Brief History*, 40–41 (*JSP*, H2:183); Reed Peck, Letter to "Dear Friends," Sep. 18,
1839, 84, 108; George M. Hinkle, Letter to William W. Phelps, Aug. 14, 1844, in *Ensign* (Buffalo,
IA), Aug. 1844, 30–32. Accounts differ regarding whether Mormons Seymour Brunson and Arthur Morrison were part of the delegation (*JSP*, D6:270n20).
2. Corrill, *Brief History*, 42 (*JSP*, H2:185).

Deliver church leaders to be tried and punished;

Pay damages by signing over their property;

All Mormons must leave the state;

Surrender their arms (and receive a receipt for the same).[3]

According to Lucas, Hinkle "readily" agreed but "wished to postpone the matter until morning."[4] However, Hinkle later reminded Phelps that he had initially objected: "Did I not then and there oppose that part of the order requiring us to give up our arms and immediately leave the State, urging that if any had offended by breaking the law, we were willing and even anxious that such should be punished to the extent of justice, or the magnitude of the crime—but to give up our arms and leave the State, would be virtually throwing away our most sacred rites as citizens of a republican state; and that we would about as soon give up our lives?"[5] At this, Lucas, enraged, demanded that Hinkle surrender Smith, Rigdon, Wight, Parley Pratt, and George Robinson "as hostages for the faithful compliance with the terms" within the hour or he would order his troops to attack Far West. Nevertheless, Lucas agreed to let Hinkle confer with Mormon leaders and to think the matter over during the night, but warned that should the Mormon leadership reject the terms, the hostages would be returned in the morning and hostilities resumed, but if the decision was to comply, the hostages would be retained for trial.[6] With this ultimatum, there was little else Hinkle could do but to persuade Smith and the others to surrender to Lucas.

At the same time, according to Corrill, Lucas promised that if the Mormons complied that he "would be more mild than the order required; that if we would give up the heads of the church to be punished; surrender our arms; give up all our property, (those who had taken up arms,) to pay the debts of the whole church and the damages done in Davies[s] and elsewhere; and then all leave the State forthwith, except those retained to be punished, they would spare our lives, and protect us out of the State." Corrill said he and the others believed Lucas "had no authority, and his requirements were illegal; for he was out of the bounds of his division, and the Governor's order was to General Clark, and not to him: but there was no other way for the

---

3. Paraphrased from Samuel D. Lucas, Letter to Lilburn W. Boggs, Nov. 2, 1838, [4], Mormon War Papers (*Document*, 73).

4. Lucas, [4].

5. Hinkle to Phelps, Aug. 14, 1844, in *Ensign*, Aug. 1844, 31.

6. Lucas to Boggs, Nov. 2, 1838, [3]–[5], Mormon War Papers (*Document*, 73–74).

Mormons but to submit."[7] True, Lucas was outside his jurisdiction, but Boggs had ordered him to proceed to the territory that was under Atchison's jurisdiction, which included Far West and Adam-ondi-Ahman, and Lucas was given command over Atchison's troops.[8]

Arrest

Hinkle and the others returned to the city and reported the substance of their interview with Lucas to Smith, who, after consulting with Rigdon, Wight, Pratt, and Robinson, concluded to surrender. According to Peck, when Corrill announced that the "first term of the treaty" would be for the Mormons to leave the state, Smith replied "that he did not care," for "he would be glad to get out of the damnable state" of Missouri anyway. Confronted with Lucas's ultimatum, Smith "decided that they must give themselves up ... [and] that the church must comply with whatever the officers required."[9]

In an 1844 letter to Phelps, Hinkle mentioned another factor that encouraged Smith to surrender: "During this whole interview and transaction, were not thousands of troops drawn up near the city, ready to fall upon us, provided those demanded as hostages refused to go?"[10] After speaking with the Mormon delegation, Lucas returned to his camp near Goose Creek and prepared for a battle, ordering his men to surround Far West and to post a cannon on a nearby hill. The approach of the militia alarmed the Mormons "who rushed to their breastwork and bound up their heads in handkerchiefs in preparation for a coming fight," Peck remembered. "The drums beat, horns blew, men shouted and it seemed that nothing could prevent the effusion of blood should the Militia come within reach of the Mormon Rifles."[11]

As the sun set below the horizon, Hinkle and the peace delegation led Smith and the other hostages out of Far West on foot. When Lucas and his troops approached within 600 yards of Far West, he saw a white flag and the hostages coming toward him. Lucas and Doniphan left the body of troops and rode out with a small detail to meet the Mormons. Lucas said he "received the hostages, and placed a guard over them for their safety and protection."[12] As the guard closed their ranks around the hostages, Peck re-

---

7. Corrill, *Brief History*, 42 (*JSP*, H2:185).

8. Lilburn W. Boggs, Letter to John B. Clark, Nov. 6, 1838, Mormon War Papers (*Document*, 69–70); *JSP*, H2:185n209.

9. Peck to "Dear Friends," Sep. 18, 1838, 115–16.

10. Hinkle to Phelps, in *Ensign*, Aug. 14, 1844, 31.

11. Peck to "Dear Friends," Sep. 18, 1838, 116–17.

12. Lucas to Boggs, Nov. 2, 1838, [6], Mormon War Papers (*Document*, 74).

ported, the army shouted in triumph.[13] Their shouts were loud enough that Lucy Smith heard them from her porch near the town center, as well as gunshots, presumably into the air, which caused her and Joseph Sr. to fear that their son had been shot.[14] According to one member of the militia, the behavior of the troops frightened the captives, "except old Wright [Lyman Wight], who stood like a lion … without a sign of fear about him; but the Prophet Joe shook from head to foot, and his knees smote together as bad as Belshazzar's, who saw the hand-writing on the wall, and implored his friends to beg for him, for he looked on it as death to be taken to our camp."[15] According to Peck, Smith "plead with Genl Lucas for permission to remain over night with his family promising to comply with any terms he should name even if it were for the whole church to leave the state forthwith." Lucas rejected Smith's request and "told them that they must go to camp with him and bade them forward."[16]

Smith would later accuse Hinkle of tricking him and claim that he believed he was merely meeting Lucas for an "interview" and that his arrest was a complete "surprise."[17] Smith wrote a few days after his arrest that Hinkle "proved to be a traitor" and that he "decoyed us unawares."[18] In a December 1838 letter to the church, Smith called Hinkle "A wolf in sheep's clothing" and accused him, Peck, and Corrill of "leading us, as the savior was led, into the camp as a lamb prepared for the slaughter." He went so far as to insinuate that they, like Judas, were "greedy for a reward [and] sold us into the hands" of the enemy.[19] A petition dated March 15, 1839, and signed by five leading Mormons including Smith complained that Smith "was taken from his house by a fraude being practiced upon him by a man by the name of George M Hinkle and one or two others thereby your petitioner[s] respectfully show that he was forced contrary to his wishes and without knowing the cause into the camp which was commanded by General Lucas of Jackson County."[20]

---

13. Peck to "Dear Friends," Sep. 18, 1838, 118.

14. Lucy Mack Smith, History, 1844–45, bk. 16, [2] (Anderson, ed., *Lucy's Book*, 669).

15. Joseph Thorp, "Early Days in the Missouri," *Liberty (MO) Tribune*, Nov. 9, 1883.

16. Peck to "Dear Friends," Sep. 18, 1838, 117–18.

17. "Extract, from the Private Journal of Joseph Smith Jr.," *Times and Seasons*, Nov. 1839, 5 (*JSP*, H1:478).

18. Joseph Smith, Letter to Emma Smith, Nov. 4, 1838, [1] (*JSP*, D6:280).

19. Joseph Smith, Letter to the church in Caldwell County, MO, Dec. 16, 1838, [2], JS Collection (*JSP*, D6:300–301).

20. Alanson Ripley et al., Petition to George Tompkins, ca. Mar. 9–15, 1839, [1], JS Collection (*JSP*, D6:344).

Despite Smith's accusations, Hinkle maintained that the Mormon leader was fully informed of the alternatives: Smith and other church leaders were to be retained as prisoners to be tried for their crimes or returned to Far West for battle against the Missouri militia.[21] Both Corrill and Peck defended their roles in the negotiations, arguing that Smith fully understood Lucas's demands.[22] "Although the Mormons have accused us of giving up their leaders by intrigue," Corrill later wrote, "yet Smith himself was the first man that agreed to the proposals" and declared that "he had rather go to States-prison for twenty years, or had rather die himself than have the people exterminated."[23] Peck recalled that when he, Corrill, and Hinkle reported to Smith the substance of their negotiations with Lucas, Smith readily agreed to the terms, stating "that it would not do to resist the Militia of the state acting under the order of the Governor."[24] Hinkle later maintained that he left to Smith the decision whether or not to surrender and that Smith sent word to Far West the following morning from the militia's camp advising them to agree to the militia's terms for their surrender. In his 1844 letter, Hinkle reminded Phelps: "When the facts were laid before Joseph, did he not say, 'I will go;' and did not the others go with him, and that too *voluntarily*, so far as you and I were concerned?"[25] Smith's claim that he was unaware of the purpose of his surrender lacks credibility; Lucas had requested the surrender of specific men because they were wanted for crimes and would certainly be held for trial.

Smith himself gave contradictory accounts of his arrest. In 1839 in the *Times and Seasons*, he claimed that he voluntarily "went into the camp of the militia," where, to his "surprise," he and the others were "taken as prisoners of war."[26] In his previous 1839 "Bill of Damages," Smith said that he and the others went out to meet Lucas, "but instead of treating us with respect and as persons desiring [to] accommodate matters. we were to our astonishment ... delivered up as prisoners of war and taken into the camp as such."[27] The later claim that Smith and the others went into the camp on their own

---

21. Hinkle to Phelps, Aug. 14, 1844, in *Ensign*, Aug. 1844, 30–32.

22. Corrill, *Brief History*, 41–42 (*JSP*, H2:184–86); Peck to "Dear Friends," Sep. 18, 1839, 115–16.

23. Corrill, *Brief History*, 41 (*JSP*, H2:183–84).

24. Peck to "Dear Friends," Sep. 18, 1839, 116.

25. Hinkle to Phelps, in *Ensign*, Aug. 14, 1844, 31.

26. "Extract, from the Private Journal of Joseph Smith Jr.," *Times and Seasons*, Nov. 1839, 5 (*JSP*, H1:478).

27. Smith, Bill of Damages, June 4, 1839, [5], JS Collection (*JSP*, D6:500).

made it appear that they were more eager to cooperate than they were, a conclusion contradicted by Lucas's November 2, 1838, report to Boggs.[28]

The narrative of Hinkle's perfidy functioned as a cover story for why Smith did not stay and fight to the death, a theme of many speeches and sermons, beginning with Rigdon's "salt sermon." When faced with extermination, Smith's bravado quickly dissipated. Significantly, the betrayal narrative is missing from Smith's communications with government officials, because it was incompatible with the claim that the Mormons immediately complied with the governor's orders.

Pratt said that he and the other hostages "walked near a mile voluntarily, towards the camp of the enemy; who, when they saw us coming, came out to meet us by thousands, with general Lucas at their head. When the haughty General rode up to us, and scarcely passing a compliment, gave orders to his troops to surround us, which they did very abruptly, and we were marched into camp surrounded by thousands of savage looking beings, many of whom were painted like Indian warriors. These all set up a constant yell, like so many blood hounds let loose on their prey."[29] The painted men were Cornelius Gilliam's vigilantes, who had joined the militia's encampment on Goose Creek two days earlier.

Of his first night in custody, Wight wrote: "This proved to be a dismal night on account of the rain. The hideous screeches and screaming of this wretched, murderous band would have made a perfect dead silence with the damned in hell."[30] Smith said they had to sleep "on the cold ground surrounded by a Strong guard," who "utterly refused to hold any conversation with us." Despite his ill-treatment, which he said "was truly awfull and enough to appal the stoutest heart," Smith later wrote: "I felt perfectly calm, and resigned to the will of my heavenly Father. I knew my innocency, ... and notwithstanding that every avenue of escape seemed to be entirely closed, and death stared me in the face, and that my destruction was determined upon, as far as man was concerned; yet, from my first entrance into the camp, I felt an assurance, that I with my brethren and our families should be delivered. Yes, that still small voice, which has so often whispered consolation to

28. Lucas to Boggs, Nov. 2, 1838, [6], Mormon War Papers (*Document*, 74).
29. Pratt, *History of the Late Persecution*, 39–40; see also "A History of the Persecution, of the Church of Jesus Christ, of Latter Day Saints in Missouri," *Times and Seasons*, June 1840, 116 (*JSP*, H2:251).
30. Wight, Journal, 260 (Oct. 30, 1838).

my soul, in the depth of sorrow and distress, bade me be of good cheer, and promised deliverance, which gave me great comfort."[31]

Surrender of Far West

The next morning, November 1, Lucas awaited Hinkle's decision. The general's November 2 report to Boggs reveals that he intended to negotiate only with Hinkle as the military commander of the Mormon forces at Far West. Hinkle and other church leaders, on the other hand, probably wished for Smith to make the decision. In 1844 Hinkle reminded Phelps: "Were we not advised next day, by word sent expressly from Joseph Smith to us, to surrender?" Upon receiving Smith's instructions, Hinkle said he called together the Mormon troops at Far West and, after explaining to them the terms of the negotiated peace, asked those who were in favor of surrendering to make it known by taking three steps forward. "They made a very slow start," Hinkle said, "but finally all came forward."[32]

Lucas ordered his 2,500 troops to march to Far West at 9:30 a.m. When they were about 200 yards south of the town, they formed a hollow square with one side open, into which Hinkle marched his troops, which had been reduced to about 600 men by the flight of several dozen men during the night hoping to avoid capture for their involvement in the battle of Crooked River.[33] The Mormon troops grounded their weapons, and Hinkle rode up to Lucas and surrendered his sword and pistols, after which they were detained while the militia ransacked Far West looking for weapons and committing various depredations. "The rapacious soldiery went from house to house, plundering, pillaging, and destroying," Newel Knight recalled.[34] Hyrum Smith similarly testified in 1843: "The soldiers were permitted to patrol the streets, to abuse and insult the people at their leisure, and enter into houses and pillage them, and ravish the women, taking away every gun and every other kind of arms or military implements."[35] A committee of Caldwell County Mormons complained to the Missouri legislature in December 1838: "Much property was destroyed [by the troops] in town during their stay such as burning house logs corn cribs boards &c. the using of corn and hay the plundering of houses the killing of cattle sheep and hogs and also

---

31. Smith, Bill of Damages, June 4, 1839, [5], JS Collection (*JSP*, D6:501–502); "Extract, from the Private Journal of Joseph Smith Jr.," *Times and Seasons*, Nov. 1839, 8 (*JSP*, H1:485).

32. Hinkle to Phelps, in *Ensign*, Aug. 14, 1844, 31.

33. See Baugh, "Call to Arms," 326–29.

34. [Newel Knight], "Newel Knight's Journal," in *Scraps of Biography*, 99.

35. Hyrum Smith, Testimony, July 1843, in *Times and Seasons*, July 1, 1843, 251.

the taking off horses not their own and all this without regard to owners or asking any one for them. in the mean time men [were] insulted [and] women were abused or ravished, by the troops."[36] General John B. Clark, en route to Far West to take charge of the operation, later reported: "Hearing at Richmond that some of the guard left by Genl Lucas at Far West were killing prisoners and commiting other excesses I left my troops and went in advance riding all night in order to check such things." Although Clark concluded that such reports were exaggerated, he was unwilling to "vouch for the troops before [his] arrival" on November 4.[37]

Hinkle led the militia to Hyrum Smith's home, where the prophet's brother was arrested. Recounting his arrest in 1843, Hyrum said it was noon when "Colonel Hinkle came to my house with an armed force, opened the door and called me out of doors and delivered me up as a prisoner unto that force." Despite his illness, "They surrounded me and commanded me to march into the camp ... [and] forced me along with the point of the bayonet into the camp, and put me under the same guard with my brother Joseph—and within about half an hour afterwards, Amasa Lyman was also brought and placed under the same guard."[38] This brought the number of hostages to seven.

After parading his troops through the main streets of Far West in a show of force, Lucas set up a guard around the city and returned to camp, where he began disbanding his troops.[39] General Parks was sent to Adam-ondi-Ahman with a small force to subdue and confiscate the arms of about 150 Mormon troops stationed there.[40]

Court-Martial

Not knowing how Clark would handle the situation, Lucas held a hasty ad hoc court-martial during the evening of November 1, at which time Joseph Smith and the other prisoners were found guilty of treason—a capital offense—by a court composed of seventeen commissioned officers. However, the decision was not unanimous as five of the seventeen dissented.[41] Doniphan was the most vocal, stating that "there was not one of them, in

---

36. Partridge et al., Petition to the Missouri State Legislature, Dec. 10, 1838, 4.

37. John B. Clark, Letter to Lilburn W. Boggs, Nov. 29, 1838, [7], Mormon War Papers (*Document*, 90).

38. Hyrum Smith, Testimony, July 1843, in *Times and Seasons*, July 1, 1843, 251.

39. Lucas to Boggs, Nov. 2, 1838, [7]–[8], Mormon War Papers (*Document*, 75); Ebenezer Robinson, "Items of Personal History," *Return* (Davis City, IA), Feb. 1890, 210.

40. Corrill, *Brief History*, 42–43 (*JSP*, H2:187).

41. Josiah Butterfield, Letter to John Elden, June 17, 1839; Alanson Ripley, Letter to Editors, ca. Jan. 1840, in *Times and Seasons*, Jan. 1840, 37.

the least degree, acquainted with the Military law, and understood nothing about court Martials."[42] He argued that Smith and most of the prisoners were civilians and therefore a military court-martial had no legal jurisdiction over them, that they should be turned over to civil authorities to be tried, and that he would remove his troops rather than witness such an illegal execution.[43] Doniphan stomped out of the court in protest and returned to his camp, where he informed the prisoners of the unjust verdict. "I have washed my hands against such cool and deliberate murder," he said.[44]

Lucas quickly drafted an order and dispatched it to Doniphan, in whose camp the prisoners were being held: *Brigadier-General Doniphan.—*Sir: You will take Joseph Smith and the other prisoners into the public square of Far West, and shoot them at 9 o'clock to-morrow morning. [Signed] Samuel D. Lucas, *Major General Commanding.*"[45] The order may have been delivered to Doniphan by Brigadier-General Moses Wilson, who also took it upon himself to deliver the news to the prisoners personally. "I regret to tell you your die is cast; your doom is fixed," the Jackson County general announced. "You are sentenced to be shot tomorrow morning on the public square in Far West." Wight defiantly responded: "Shoot, and be d[amne]d."[46] Smith later claimed that he had a conversation with Wilson, a Democrat, in which he asked the general why he was being mistreated since "I had always been a supporter of the constitution and of Democracy," and that the general answered: "I know it, and that is the reason why I want to kill you or have you killed."[47]

Doniphan flat out refused to obey the order, sending Lucas an immediate reply: "It is cold-blooded murder. I will not obey your order. My brigade shall march for Liberty to-morrow morning, at 8 o'clock; and if you execute these men, I will hold you responsible before an earthly tribunal, so help me God! [Signed] A. W. Doniphan, *Brigadier-General.*"[48] Possible legal jeopardy and threat from Doniphan, a well-known and able attorney, caused Lucas to rethink his rash order.

---

42. [Rigdon], *An Appeal to the American People,* 51; see also "A History of the Persecution," *Times and Seasons,* July 1840, 130–31 (*JSP,* H2:258).

43. Sidney Rigdon, July 1843, in *Times and Seasons,* Aug. 1, 1843, 275; see also Launius, "Alexander William Doniphan and the 1838 Mormon War," 91.

44. Lyman Wight, Testimony, July 1, 1839, in *Times and Seasons,* July 15, 1843, 267.

45. *History of Caldwell and Livingston Counties,* 137.

46. Lyman Wight, Testimony, July 1, 1839, in *Times and Seasons,* July 15, 1843, 267.

47. "Extract, from the Private Journal of Joseph Smith Jr.," *Times and Seasons,* Nov. 1839, 5 (*JSP,* H1:479); see also Smith, Bill of Damages, June 4, 1839, [6], JS Collection (*JSP,* D6:502); *JSP,* D6:502n355.

48. *History of Caldwell and Livingston Counties,* 137.

Early in the morning of November 2 Doniphan visited the prisoners and remarked, "By God you have been sentenced by the court martial to be shot this morning; but I will be damned if I will have any of the honor of it, or any of the disgrace of it; therefore I have ordered my brigade to take up the line of march and to leave the camp, for I consider it to be cold blooded murder, and I bid you farewell."[49] He wished them well, shook their hands, and departed with the main body of his troops to another location about three miles away.[50] According to Wight, this move threw the remaining troops "into the utmost confusion and consternation." Soon the prisoners learned that Lucas had "revoked the decree" and that they were instead to be transported to his headquarters in Independence under Wilson's care.[51] Lucas's reports to Boggs did not mention a court-martial until November 11, when he denied one had been held. "I never had any idea of trying any of the prisoners by a Court martial," he wrote.[52] Smith credited his escape to "the kind providence of God," but knew he was indebted to Doniphan.[53]

Meanwhile, the sound of a drum beating summoned the Mormon men of Far West to the public square. Once assembled, they were compelled to step forward one by one to sign over their land to the state as reparation for damages done in Daviess County.[54] Meanwhile, a heavily guarded wagon drew into Far West carrying Smith and the other six prisoners to collect clothing and other items in preparation for a long confinement.[55] "We were taken to the town, into the public square; and before our departure from Far West, we, after much entreaties, were suffered to see our families, being attended all the while with a strong guard," Smith wrote. "When I entered my house," he recalled, "they clung to my garments, their eyes streaming with tears, while mingled emotions of joy and sorrow were manifest in their countenances." Smith requested a private interview with his family but was

---

49. Hyrum Smith, Testimony, July 1, 1843, in *Times and Seasons*, July 1, 1843, 251.

50. William Draper, Autobiography, 1881, 17; Baugh, "Call to Arms," 339.

51. Wight, Testimony, July 1, 1839, in *Times and Seasons*, July 15, 1843, 268; Lucas to Boggs, Nov. 2, 1838, [8], Mormon War Papers (*Document*, 75).

52. Samuel D. Lucas, Letter to Lilburn W. Boggs, Nov. 11, 1838, [2], Mormon War Papers (*Document*, 64).

53. Smith, Bill of Damages, June 4, 1839, [6], JS Collection (*JSP*, D6:502).

54. Samuel D. Lucas, Letter to Lilburn W. Boggs, Nov. 5, 1838, [4], Mormon War Papers (*Documents*, 71); Corrill, *Brief History*, 43 (*JSP*, H2:187–88); Ebenezer Robinson, "Items of Personal History," *Return*, Feb. 1890, 210; Greene, *Facts Relative to the Expulsion of the Mormons*, 13–14; [Rigdon], *Appeal to the American People*, 50; see also "A History of the Persecution," *Times and Seasons*, July 1840, 130 (*JSP*, H2:257).

55. Pratt, *Autobiography*, 207; Hyrum Smith, Testimony, July 1, 1843, in *Times and Seasons*, July 1, 1843, 251.

denied as the guards quickly pushed him out the door. "My partner wept, my children clung to me and were only thrust from me by the swords of the guard who guarded me," he remembered. "I felt overwhelmed while I witnessed the scene."[56] The soldiers marched him back to the public square where the wagon waited to rush him and the others to Jackson County. James Henry Bracken said that he and many of his brethren feared that they would never see their leader again and "tried to get to the wagon to shake hands with the Prophet but the mob would not allow that privilege, so the Prophet, raised the wagon cover and put out his hand toward the brethren and said, 'Good-bye,' and passed on in silence."[57]

Smith and the others were taken back to the camp, from which they would begin the fifty-mile trip to Independence with Lucas and Wilson and 300 state militiamen from Jackson County. Wight reported that prior to starting, Wilson said that "he would guarantee that we should be well treated; which promise he fulfilled to the very letter." The first day, they traveled seventeen miles to Crooked River, then camped for the night.[58]

On the morning of November 3 Smith told the other prisoners privately: "Be of good cheer, brethren; the word of the Lord came to me last night that our lives should be given us, and that whatever we may suffer during this captivity, not one of our lives shall be taken."[59] The next day Smith wrote to Emma describing the events of the previous day: "When we arrived at the river last night an express came to gene[r]al Willson from gene[r]al Clark of Howard County claiming the right of command ordering us back [to] where or what place God only knows, and there is some feelings betwen the offercers, I do not know where it will end, it is said by some that general Clark, is determined to exterminate [but] God has spared some of us thus far perhaps he will extend mercy in some degree toward us yet."[60]

Clark sent orders on November 3 for Lucas to bring the prisoners to him in Richmond.[61] Both Lucas and Wilson ignored Clark's order. On the same

---

56. "Extract, from the Private Journal of Joseph Smith Jr.," *Times and Seasons*, Nov. 1839, 6 (*JSP*, H1:479–80); Smith, Bill of Damages, June 4, 1839, [6], JS Collection (*JSP*, D6:502).

57. James Henry Bracken, "Recollections of the Prophet Joseph Smith," *Juvenile Instructor*, Apr. 1, 1892, 203.

58. Wight, Journal, 295 (Nov. 1, 1838).

59. Pratt, *Autobiography*, 210. Italics removed.

60. Joseph Smith, Letter to Emma Smith, Nov. 4, 1838, [2] (*JSP*, D6:281).

61. John B. Clark, Letter to Samuel D. Lucas, Nov. 3, 1838, [1], Mormon War Papers (*Document*, 85).

day, Clark wrote to Boggs to complain that Lucas had disobeyed his orders.[62] On November 5 Lucas wrote to Boggs, explaining that although he and Clark were both major generals, he believed that his "grade of Office" was superior to Clark's and therefore he "could not under any circumstance be commanded by a Junior Major Genl." Lucas believed he was the commanding officer in the field since he was given charge over Atchison's division, which included Far West, when he was relieved of duty. He said that at the time he transported the prisoners to Independence, he was unaware that Boggs had placed Clark over the entire operation, but that he had since been informed differently. "I received a copy of your Orders to him," Lucas wrote, "and I intend to start the prisoners and arms to Richmond in the morning when the whole will be subject to his order."[63] On November 11 Lucas claimed that he "only ordered them to my Head Quarters to await your further orders."[64]

Arrival of General Clark

Clark arrived at Far West on November 4 with a force of approximately 1,600 men.[65] As he later reported: "Hearing at Richmond that some of the guard left by Genl Lucas at Far West were killing prisoners and commiting other excesses, I left my troops and went in advance riding all night in order to check such things." After an investigation, he concluded that the reports were exaggerated.[66]

On the following day, November 5, Clark delivered a harsh and insulting speech to the Mormons of Far West and explained why it was essential that Smith be taken into custody. "Had your leader not been given up and the treaty complied with before this," he said, "you and your families would have been destroyed, and your houses in ashes." He identified the Mormon tendency to gather as the source of their inevitable troubles with their neighbors. He therefore encouraged them to "become as other citizens" and "to scatter abroad and never again organize with Bishops, Presidents, &c."[67] He

---

62. Clark's November 3, 1838, letter of complaint is mentioned in Lilburn W. Boggs, Letter to John B. Clark, Nov. 6, 1838, Mormon War Papers (*Document*, 69–70).

63. Samuel D. Lucas, Letter to Lilburn W. Boggs, Nov. 5, 1838, [2], Mormon War Papers (*Document*, 71).

64. Lucas to Boggs, Nov. 11, 1838, [2], Mormon War Papers (*Document*, 64).

65. John B. Clark, Letter to Lilburn W. Boggs, Nov. 10, 1838, [3], Mormon War Papers (*Document*, 65).

66. Clark to Boggs, Nov. 29, 1838, [3], Mormon War Papers (*Document*, 90).

67. [Rigdon], *Appeal to the American People*, 82; see also "A History of the Persecution," *Times and Seasons*, Oct. 1840, 177 (*JSP*, H2:284); Greene, *Facts relative to the Expulsion of the Mormons*, 27. Judge Austin King, before whom Smith and the other defendants would soon appear, shared this view. "If the Mormons would disperse and not gather into exclusive communities of their

then ordered them to "leave the State forthwith, and whatever your feelings concerning this affair,—whatever your innocence, it is nothing to me," and warned them against non-compliance: "You must not think of staying here another season or of putting in crops; for the moment you do, the citizens will be upon you. … If I have to come again, because the treaty which you have made here shall be broken, you need not expect any mercy, but extermination." Concerning Smith and the other leaders in custody, Clark coldly said, "Do not once think—do not imagine for a moment—do not let it enter your mind, that they will be delivered, or that you will see their faces again, for their fate is fixed, their die is cast—their doom is sealed."[68]

On November 6 Boggs wrote to Clark and among other things instructed that a military court of inquiry should be held in both Caldwell and Daviess Counties and that the whole matter should be resolved before he disbanded his troops. "The ringleaders of this rebellion, though, ought by no means be permitted to escape the punishment they merit," Boggs wrote.[69] On November 7 Clark ordered Wilson to go to Adam-ondi-Ahman, restore the citizens of Daviess County to their homes, ascertain which Mormons had committed crimes there, and transport them to Keytesville.[70] Meanwhile, Clark's investigations at Far West into those who participated in the battle of Crooked River and raids in Daviess County resulted in the arrest of about fifty Mormons. On November 9 he transported forty-six of them through the snow to Richmond, where they were held for more than two weeks in the unfinished brick courthouse while awaiting a court of inquiry.[71]

Four Days in Independence

On November 3, Smith and the others were taken across the Missouri River

---

own," he said, "I think with the exception of a few of their leaders, the people might be reconciled to them, but this they utterly refuse to do." Austin A. King, Letter to Lilburn W. Boggs, Dec. 23, 1838, [2], Mormon War Papers (*Document*, 95).

68. [Rigdon], *Appeal to the American People*, 82.

69. Lilburn W. Boggs, Letter to John B. Clark, Nov. 6, 1838, [2], Mormon War Papers (*Document*, 70).

70. John B. Clark, Letter to Robert Wilson, Nov. 7, 1838, [1], Mormon War Papers (*Document*, 86). Not much came of Wilson's investigations in Daviess County, as he later reported to Clark that most of the Mormons who could be identified as lawbreakers had absconded before he arrived in Adam-ondi-Ahman. Robert Wilson, Letter to John B. Clark, Nov. 12, 1838, [1], Mormon War Papers (*Document*, 77).

71. Edward Partridge et al., Petition to the Missouri State Legislature, Dec. 10, 1838, in "The Mormons," *Quincy (IL) Whig*, Mar. 16, 1839, [1]; see also Greene, *Facts Relative to the Expulsion of the Mormons*, 10–16; John B. Clark, Letter to Lilburn W. Boggs, Nov. 10, 1838, [3]–[4], Mormon War Papers (*Document*, 66); Pratt, *History of the Late Persecution*, 51–52; Corrill, *Brief History*, 43 (*JSP*, H2:188); and JS History, vol. C-1, 861–66 (DHC 3:205–15).

at Williams's Ferry into Jackson County and camped for the night.[72] The next morning, Sunday, November 4, Smith delivered an impromptu sermon on "faith in the Lord Jesus Christ, repentance towards God, reformation of life, immersion in water, in the name of Jesus Christ, for remission of sins, and the gift of the Holy Ghost by the laying on of hands."[73] About 10:00 a.m., they continued their march toward Independence. "Several times in the course of this day," Wight recorded, "we were exhibited as a public show" as they sat in "a covered wagon," and "with one exception we were treated in the most genteel manner."[74] This was surprising considering how callously the Mormons were chased from the county in 1833. Despite a severe rain storm, the soldiers and prisoners were greeted at Independence by a large crowd of citizens. "Hundreds crowded to witness the procession, and to gaze at us as we were paraded in martial triumph through the principal streets, the bugles sounding a blast of triumphant joy," Pratt remembered.[75] They were lodged in a large vacant "old log house" on Maple Street, north of Independence's public square and courthouse, with a few guards.[76] According to Wight, "We had many respectable visitors this evening, together with some few of the offscouring [outcasts] of the earth. We had food prepared for and brought to us."[77]

On his first day of confinement, Smith managed to write a letter to Emma. "My dear and beloved companion, of my bosam, in tribulation, and affliction," he began. "I woud inform you that I am well, and that we are all of us in good spirits." She was no doubt concerned about his safety in Jackson County, but he assured her that he and the others were being "protected by the Jackson County boys, in the most genteel manner," which was exhibited in the extraordinary fact that "instead of going to goal [jail] we have a good house provided for us and the kind[e]st treatment." Not everyone supported the governor's orders to exterminate or evacuate the Mormons, for Smith reported that "some of the people of this place have told me that some of the mormans may settle in this county as other men do," which made Smith hopeful that "something may turn out for good to the afflicted saints." Nevertheless, Smith expressed uncertainty about his future: "What God may do

---

72. Wight, Journal, 295 (Nov. 2 [3], 1838). Dates in Wight's journal appear to be a day off.
73. Pratt, *Autobiography*, 211.
74. Wight, Journal, 295 (Nov. [4], 1838).
75. Pratt, *Autobiography*, 212; see also Pratt, *History of the Late Persecution*, 46.
76. Parley P. Pratt, Letter to Mary Ann Frost Pratt, Nov. 4, 1838; Wight, Journal, Nov. [4], 1838, in Smith and Smith, *History of the Reorganized Church*, 2:295–97.
77. Wight, Journal, 295 (Nov. [4], 1838).

for us I do not know but I hope for the best always in all circumstances [and] although I go unto death, I will trust in God, what outrages may be committed by the mob I know not, but expect there will be but little or no restraint Oh may God have mercy on us."[78]

Smith had left his family and followers in a dangerous situation and was naturally worried about them: "I have great anxiety about you, and my lovely children, my heart morns and bleeds for the brotheren, and sisters, and for the slain of the people of God." He also feared that his inability to speak directly to his followers would lead to further defections and even expressed concerns about Emma's loyalty: "I hope you will be faithful and true to every trust, I cant write much in my situation. ... Oh Emma for God sake do not forsake me nor the truth but remember, if I do not meet you again in this life may God grant that we may meet in heaven, I cannot express my feelings, my heart is full, Farewell Oh my kind and affectionate Emma I am yours forever your Husband and true friend." He also wished Emma to tell his children that "father is yet alive, God grant that he may see them again."[79]

For the indefinite future Emma would have to manage family affairs on her own. "Conduct all matters as your circumstances and necesities require," Smith advised. "May God give you wisdom and prudance and sobriety, which I have every reason to believe you will."[80] By the time Emma received this letter, she and her children had been evicted from their home and were staying with George and Lucinda Harris in Far West. As Smith later learned, "The Malitia then went to my house and drove my Family out of Doors under sanction of General Clark and carried away all my property."[81] In a March 1839 petition to Judge George Tompkins, Smith complained that "imidiately after" he was taken into custody "his family was frightened and driven out of their house ... and plundered of their goods that the prisoner was rob[b]ed of a verry fine horse Saddle and bridle and other property of conciderable amount."[82] Smith's June 1839 "Bill of Damages" listed stolen horses, harnesses, cattle, hogs, books, and store goods.[83]

In a deposition Emma made for an 1842 lawsuit against Hinkle, she stated that immediately following her husband's arrest, Hinkle entered

78. Smith, Letter to Emma Smith, Nov. 4, 1838, [1] (*JSP*, D6:280–82).

79. Smith, [1]–[2].

80. Smith, [2] (*JSP*, D6:282).

81. Smith, Bill of Damages, June 4, 1839, [6], JS Collection (*JSP*, D6:502).

82. Alanson Ripley et al., Petition to George Tompkins, ca. Mar. 9–15, 1839, [4], JS Collection (*JSP*, D6:348).

83. Smith, Bill of Damages, June 4, 1839, [8], JS Collection (*JSP*, D6:505).

their home in Far West and stole "a Horse, Saddle, Bridle Martingales & two Horse Blankets," as well as dry goods, clothing, and furniture, valued at $400. She testified that Hinkle "used Coersive measures to drive Witness and her Family therefrom, the Premises & House," and that after she had left her home and moved in with the Harris family, Hinkle "came shortly afterwards upon the same day, & expressed much Surprize at my being there, & that I had not left the Country, & ordered me to do so."[84] In a deposition, Lucinda Harris corroborated Emma's testimony, stating that Emma came to her home "in Tears" with her "small Children"; that Hinkle came and ordered her to leave the country; that later the same day someone notified Emma that Hinkle was removing items from her home, and that Emma left to prevent Hinkle's actions.[85] The person who notified Emma that Hinkle was plundering her house was Caroline Clark, a young girl who had been living with Emma at the time and later married William D. Huntington. Caroline testified in 1842 that "about the first day of November [1838]" Hinkle "took possession of the House wherein Pltfs [Plaintiff's/Smith's] wife & family resided, & so took same against the will of Plaintiffs Wife, & Plaintiffs Wife fled with her Children to the House of George W. Harris for protection, at which place witness [Caroline Clark Huntington] afterwards notified Plaintiffs wife that Deft [defendant] was destroying or Converting to his own use the Property of Pltf."[86]

Wight and Robinson testified that Hinkle subsequently told them that he had taken the horse, saddle, and bridle and sold them to Captain Bogart. According to Wight, Hinkle believed he was safe from prosecution because he did not think Smith "would ever get out of the Hands of the Mob," and that he "had understood from the officers of the Mob that Plaintiff would never get away from them, but that he would be Shot."[87] John Scott similarly testified that Hinkle "informed Witness that Plaintiff never would get out of the Hands of the Mob, and that he Deft might as well take what Property he could get … and witness also saw Deft have a piece of Carpet, and some

---

84. Lee County, Iowa Territory, District Court, Emma Smith, Deposition, Apr. 22, 1842, Joseph Smith v. George M. Hinkle. Emma dated the event to "the 1 day of November 1838" and "between the 23rd day of Octr & second day of Nov. 1838."

85. Lee County, Iowa Territory, District Court, Lucinda Harris, Deposition, Apr. 22, 1842, Joseph Smith v. George M. Hinkle. Harris dated the event to "about the first day of November 1838."

86. Lee County, Iowa Territory, District Court, Caroline Huntington, Deposition, Apr. 22, 1842, Joseph Smith v. George M. Hinkle.

87. Lee County, Iowa Territory, District Court, Lyman Wight, Deposition, Apr. 22, 1842, Joseph Smith v. George M. Hinkle.

Books in his Arms at Pltfs House in Far West."[88] Robinson also testified that Hinkle "stated that he had taken the Plaintiffs Horse Saddle & Bridle & sold same to Captain Saml Bogart, and also heard said Bogart say he had bought the same from the Deft."[89]

Concern for his family and followers no doubt lingered on Smith's mind as he sealed his letter to Emma and settled in for the night with the other prisoners. Rigdon remarked that they slept "on some blankets we had with us."[90] According to Smith, "We had to sleep on the floor with nothing but a mantle for our coverings and a stick of wood for our pillow."[91] Nevertheless, Wight wrote, "we rested very comfortably through the night."[92]

On the following day, November 5, Smith and the others remained under light guard and received visitors, not all of whom were friendly. "While there," Hyrum Smith recalled, "I was subject to continual insult from the people who visited us."[93] According to Wight, the day after their arrival the prisoners "were at liberty to go where they pleased about through the town," including the place Smith had designated for the New Jerusalem temple in 1831.[94] Pratt wrote, "Were it not for the absence of Our families we Should forget that we were Prisoners."[95] The prisoners were so grateful for the kind treatment that they wrote a letter on this day thanking the citizens of Independence.[96]

On November 6 Wight noted in his journal that the prisoners "were invited to dine with General Wilson, by the request of his wife and family, where we were treated in the most genteel style. When the blessing was asked at the table his wife shed tears freely. We retired after dinner to our place of residence for the night."[97] The next morning, November 7, Wight recorded that "General Wilson ordered us to be moved to Knowlten's hotel,

88. Lee County, Iowa Territory, District Court, John Scott, Deposition, Apr. 22, 1842, Joseph Smith v. George M. Hinkle.

89. Lee County, Iowa Territory, District Court, George W. Robinson, Deposition, Apr. 22, 1842, Joseph Smith v. George M. Hinkle.

90. [Rigdon], *Appeal to the American People*, 62.

91. Smith, Bill of Damages, June 4, 1839, [6], JS Collection (*JSP*, D6:502–503).

92. Wight, Journal, 295 (Nov. 3 [4], 1838).

93. Hyrum Smith, Bill of Damages, ca. June 1839 (DHC 3:374).

94. Wight, Journal, 295–96 (Nov. 4 [5], 1838); Revelation, July 20, 1831, Revelation Book 1, 93 [D&C 57:3] (*JSP*, D2:8).

95. Pratt, Letter to Mary Ann Frost, Nov. 4, 1838; see also Pratt, *History of the Late Persecution*, 46–47.

96. Joseph Smith et al., Letter to the "citizens of Jackson County," MO, Nov. 5, 1838, in *Daily Commercial Bulletin* (St. Louis), Nov. 19, 1838, [2] (*JSP*, D6:282–84).

97. Lyman Wight, Journal, 295 (Nov. [6], 1838).

where we were treated in a genteel manner."[98] Wight apparently meant the inn operated by Smallwood Noland.[99] It was better than jail, but they were required to "pay the most extravagant price" to stay there.[100] Smith later complained that he and the others "had to pay for our own <u>board</u>," although they were Lucas's prisoners.[101] During their brief stay in Independence, the prisoners also incurred a debt with resident William Collins, who received payment during a subsequent visit to the jail in Liberty: "Recd of Lyman Wight & Joseph Smith an order for $93 25 cts in full for a Saddle and Board at Nolands and trade at Roberts in Jackson County. [Signed] Wm. Collins."[102] Wight noted that they "spent the day walking about through town, and also traded some, and returned to Knowlten's for the night."[103] They may have purchased the saddle from Collins for one of the two horses they were permitted to ride during their anticipated thirty-five-mile trip from Independence to Richmond, where they would face legal proceedings.[104]

According to Wight, after dining "at a hotel in the lower part of the town," they "returned to Knowlten's in the evening, and were introduced to Colonel Price, who gave us to understand that he had been sent by General Clark, who had just arrived in Richmond with five thousand troops, and who, by the order of the Governor, was commander in chief of all the mob militia in the State, ordered us forthwith to Richmond for a new trial, as he claims the highest authority of martial law on the occasion. ... We now retired to rest, and to wait the result of another day."[105]

Richmond

On November 8 Smith and the other prisoners at Independence prepared to move to Richmond. Lyman Wight recorded in his journal: "This morning we made every necessary preparation to repair to Richmond as quick as possible. Colonel Arnat and two other men attended us as guards. We started and crossed the Missouri River fifteen miles from this place about the setting of the sun, and camped in an old house on the opposite bank."[106]

---

98. Lyman Wight, Journal, 296 (Nov. [7], 1838).

99. See *JSP*, D6:325.

100. Wight, Testimony, July 1, 1839, in *Times and Seasons*, July 15, 1843, 268.

101. Smith, Bill of Damages, June 4, 1839, [6], JS Collection (*JSP*, D6:503).

102. William Collins, Receipt for Joseph Smith and Lyman Wight, Liberty, Clay Co., MO, Feb. 8, 1839, JS Collection (*JSP*, D6:325–26).

103. Wight, Journal, 296 (Nov. [7], 1838).

104. Hyrum Smith, Testimony, July 1, 1843, in *Times and Seasons*, July 1, 1843, 252.

105. Wight, Journal, 296 (Nov. 7, 1838). See also John B. Clark, Letter to Lilburn W. Boggs, Nov. 29, 1838, [3]–[4], Mormon War Papers (*Document*, 90).

106. Lyman Wight, Journal, 296 (Nov. 8, 1838).

Rigdon wrote that they were taken to Richmond by "three guards only, and they had been obtained with great difficulty, after laboring all the previous day to get them."[107] This difficulty arose because Price had evidently dismissed his troops before reaching Independence.

Smith later claimed that he and the others thought they were being returned to Far West, but instead they were unexpectedly taken to Richmond. In 1839 he wrote: "After remaining there [in Independence] a few days we were ordered by General Clark to return [to Far West]; we were accordingly taken back as far as Richmond, and there we were thrust into prison and our feet bound with fetters."[108] The same year, he also wrote: "While we were in Jackson General Clark with his troops arrived in Caldwell and sent an order for our return—holding out the inducement that we were to be reinstated to our former priviledges: but instead of being taken to Caldwell we were taken to Richmond w[h]ere we [were] immured in Prison and bound in—Chains."[109] Smith may have believed that Clark should have given such an order, but there is no chance that he did. Prior to arriving at Far West, Clark had twice sent orders for Lucas to incarcerate the prisoners in Richmond.[110] It makes no sense for him to have Smith and the others brought to Far West when he intended to escort a large number of prisoners to Richmond to be tried.

If Smith believed he was being taken to Far West to be reinstated, contrary to the governor's orders to leave the state or be exterminated, why did he and the others try to escape? Wight failed to record in his journal that between Independence and Roy's Ferry on the Missouri River Smith and the other prisoners temporarily escaped. Rigdon wrote that before reaching the river, the three guards "got drunk, and we got possession of their arms and horses. It was late in the afternoon, near the setting of the sun. We travelled about a half-mile after we crossed the river, and put up for the night."[111] In the morning, Smith and the other prisoners were discovered by a group of armed men. A messenger was sent to Richmond for more guards to escort the prisoners to the town. They had not traveled long before Colonel

---

107. [Rigdon], *Appeal to the American People*, 64–65; see also "A History of the Persecution," *Times and Seasons*, Sep. 1840, 162 (*JSP*, H2:274).

108. "Extract, from the Private Journal of Joseph Smith Jr.," *Times and Seasons*, Nov. 1839, 6 (*JSP*, H1:479).

109. Smith, Bill of Damages, June 4, 1839, [6]–[7], JS Collection (*JSP*, D6:503).

110. John B. Clark, Letter to Samuel D. Lucas, Nov. 3, 1838, [1], Mormon War Papers (*Document*, 85); John B. Clark, Letter to Lilburn W. Boggs, Nov. 29, 1838, [2]–[3], Mormon War Papers (*Document*, 90); [Rigdon], *Appeal to the American People*, 62–65.

111. [Rigdon], *Appeal to the American People*, 65; see also "A History of the Persecution," *Times and Seasons*, Sep. 1840, 162 (*JSP*, H2:274).

Price and about seventy-four men came and conducted them the remaining fifty miles.[112] The next year, Smith and others wrote that the prisoners were forced to march "from thence to Ray County sleeping on the ground and suffering many insults and inguries [injuries] and deprivations which were calculated in their nature to break down the spirits and constitution of the most robust and hardy of mankind."[113]

Upon arriving in Richmond, Smith and the others were put into a vacant log house near the unfinished courthouse, where Clark had also confined forty-six other Mormon men. "Sometime through the course of that day," Rigdon recalled, "General Clark came in and we were introduced to him. We enquired of him the reason why we had been thus carried from our homes and what were the charges against us. He said that he was not then able to determine, but would be in a short time, and with very little more conversation withdrew." Shortly, Price and several armed guards came into the room. They pointed their guns at the prisoners while another man with three chains and seven padlocks joined the seven prisoners together at their legs about two feet apart.[114] "We spent this day in chains for the first time, ruminating from present prospects what the future might be," Wight wrote. "You may well calculate the day passed off with gloomy aspect."[115]

As late as November 10 Clark was considering the possibility of a court-martial for Smith and other Mormon leaders. On this day he wrote to Boggs requesting him to solicit the opinion of Missouri's attorney general on whether the prisoners could be charged with "having mutinied in time of war."[116] According to Rigdon, "The troops said that he had p[r]omised when they left, that there were two or three that they should have the privilege of shooting before they returned."[117] Nevertheless, Clark informed Boggs: "I this day made out charges against the prisoners, and called on Judge King to

---

112. [Rigdon], *Appeal to the American People*, 65; see also "A History of the Persecution," *Times and Seasons*, Sep. 1840, 162 (*JSP*, H2:274).

113. Alanson Ripley et al., Petition to George Tompkins, ca. Mar. 9–15, 1839, [1], JS Collection (*JSP*, D6:345).

114. [Rigdon], *Appeal to the American People*, 65; see also "A History of the Persecution," *Times and Seasons*, Sep. 1840, 162 (*JSP*, H2:274); Wight, Journal, 296–97 (Nov. 9, 1838); Sidney Rigdon, Joseph Smith et al., Petition Draft ["To the Publick"], ca. Sep. 1838–Oct. 1839, 44[a], JS Collection; John B. Clark, Letter to Lilburn W. Boggs, Nov. 10, 1838, [5], Mormon War Papers (*Document*, 66–67); Berrett, *Sacred Places*, 4:243–49.

115. Lyman Wight, Journal, 297–98 (Nov. 10, 1838).

116. John B. Clark, Letter to Lilburn W. Boggs, Nov. 10, 1838, [7], Mormon War Papers (*Document*, 67).

117. [Rigdon], *Appeal to the American People*, 65; see also "A History of the Persecution," *Times and Seasons*, Sep. 1840, 162 (*JSP*, H2:275).

try them as a committing Court, and I am now busily engaged in procuring witnesses and submitting facts."[118] On the matter of the court-martial, Clark also sought information from military lawyers at Fort Leavenworth and was told that military law did not apply to civilians and that it would be murder if he executed the prisoners.[119] Boggs responded on November 19: "You will not attempt to try them by court martial, the civil law must govern."[120]

On the morning of November 12 Smith wrote to Emma, in his own hand, expressing his feelings for his family and determination in the face of adversity. "We are prisoners in chains, and under strong guards, for Christ sake and for no other causes," he began. Smith failed to recognize that his need to gather and build economic and political power disrupted the existing social order and attracted opposition. Nor could he acknowledge that his responses to persecution were extreme and dangerous. Instead, he blamed others, telling Emma: "Although there has been things that were unbeknown to us, and altogether beyond our controal, that might seem, to the mob to be a pretext, for them to persacute us, but on examination, I think that the authorities, will discover our inocence, and set us free, but if this blessing cannot be obtained, I have this consolation that I am an innocent man, let what will befall me."[121] In a subsequent letter to the church, dated December 16, he claimed he did not know about Sampson Avard's teachings or of the existence of the Danites and blamed dissenters for persecutions.[122]

Smith then turned to prayer: "Oh God grant that I may have the privaliege of seeing once more my lovely Family, in the injoyment, of the sweets of liberty, and sotiaial [social] life, to press them to my bosam and kissng their lovely cheeks would fill my heart with unspeakable great grattitude." He instructed Emma to "tell the chilldren that I am alive and trust I shall come and see them before long, comfort their hearts all you can, and try to be comforted yourself, all you can." He assured Emma, "There is no possible dainger but what we shall be set at Liberty if Justice can be done. … We are bound

118. John B. Clark, Letter to Lilburn W. Boggs, Nov. 10, 1838, [6], Mormon War Papers (*Document*, 67).

119. Hyrum Smith, Testimony, July 1, 1843, in *Times and Seasons*, July 1, 1843, 252; Lyman Wight, Journal, 297 (Nov. 10, 1838).

120. Lilburn W. Boggs, Letter to John B. Clark, Nov. 19, 1838, [1], Mormon War Papers (*Document*, 81).

121. Joseph Smith, Letter to Emma Smith, Nov. 12, 1838, 1 (*JSP*, D6:291). Emma's letter is no longer extant.

122. Joseph Smith, Letter to the church in Caldwell County, MO, Dec. 16, 1838, JS Collection (*JSP*, D6:294–310).

together in chains as well as the cords of everlasting love, we are in good spirits and rejoice that we are counted worthy to be persicuted for christ sake."

Smith closed: "Oh my affectionate Emma, I want you to remember that I am a true and faithful friend, to you and the chilldren, forever, my heart is intwined around you[r]s forever and ever, Oh may God bless you all amen I am your husband and am in bonds and tribulation &c. ... Write as often as you can, and if possible come and see me, and bring the chilldren if possible, act according to your own feelings and best Judgement, and indeavour to be comforted, if possible, and I trust that all will turn out for the bist [best]."[123] Despite such optimism, Smith knew that he was in peril and that things were probably going to turn out badly for him, especially since much of the testimony against him was from former high-ranking Mormons.

---

123. Smith, Letter to Emma, Nov. 12, 1838, [2] (*JSP*, D6:292–93).

32

Trial

NOVEMBER 1838

As to making any impression on [Judge] King, if a cohort of angels were to come down and declare we were clear, ... it would all be the same, for he (King) had determined from the beginning to cast us into prison.

—Sidney Rigdon, An Appeal to the American People
(Cincinnati: Glezen and Shepard, 1840), 66–67

It was still morning when Smith and his fellow prisoners were taken to the unfinished courthouse, where about forty-six men, including Edward Partridge, Isaac Morley, and Ebenezer Robinson were being kept. Speaking of this large gathering of prisoners, Wight wrote that General Clark had "placed them in the courthouse about twenty rods from where we now are, which has neither floor nor door-shutter, and the weather is very inclement."[1] Partridge added that they were "confined in a large open room, where the cold northern blast penetrated freely."[2] Robinson noted that "the courthouse ... was a new unfinished brick building, with no inside work done except a floor laid across one end, some 16 or 20 feet wide," with "two large fire places built in the wall where the floor was laid."[3]

On the first day of this court of inquiry or preliminary hearing, which lasted a little more than two weeks, Judge Austin King informed the prisoners that they were to be tried for the crimes of high treason, murder, burglary, arson, robbery, and larceny. He also ordered that the prisoners be represented and defended by Amos Rees, Alexander Doniphan, and John Williams. The court record indicates that "not being able to progress further in the cause

---

1. Wight, Journal, 297 (Nov. 9, 1838).
2. Edward Partridge, Jr., *Biography and Family Genealogy*, 52–53.
3. Ebenezer Robinson, "Items of Personal History," *Return* (Davis City, IA), Mar. 1890, 234.

the court adjourned until to-morrow morning 9 o'clock."[4] According to Wight, "Court was called and adjourned for want of testimony," after which "we retired to our chains and couches of straw and spent the night."[5]

The men remained under guard, whom Pratt described as "frequently composed of the most noisy, foul-mouthed, vulgar, disgraceful, indecent rabble that ever defiled the earth."[6] Smith said that Colonel Sterling Price "suffered us to be abused in every manner which the people thought propper: our situation at this time was truly painful."[7] One night during the hearing, as Pratt later reported, the prisoners "listened for hours to the obscene jests, the horrid oaths, the dreadful blasphemies and filthy language of our guards, Colonel Price at their head, as they recounted to each other their deeds of rapine, murder, robbery, etc.," committed against the Mormons in Caldwell County. Suddenly, when he could bear it no longer, Smith rose to his feet and faced down the guards and, as Pratt recounted, spoke in a loud dramatic tone: "*SILENCE, ye fiends of the infernal pit. In the name of Jesus Christ I rebuke you, and command you to be still; I will not live another minute and hear such language. Cease such talk, or you or I die THIS INSTANT!*" As he stood his ground, the guards, according to Pratt, cowered in the corner with their guns lowered begging forgiveness. Such courage commanded loyalty from the likes of Pratt, who remained in awe of Smith many decades after his death and who wrote that of the many dignitaries he had observed during his life, both in America and England, he had seen "dignity and majesty … but *once*, as it stood in chains, at midnight, in a dungeon in an obscure village of Missouri."[8]

Richmond Hearing

When the court reconvened in the morning, the prosecution began presenting its case.[9] In all, forty-two witnesses, twenty Missourians and twenty-two Mormons, many disaffected, testified that Smith and other church leaders began plotting an insurrection against the state of Missouri as early as spring 1838 and subsequently instigated preemptive raids on non-Mormon communities. Among the Mormons who testified against Smith were Hinkle,

---

4. Transcript of Proceedings, Nov. 12–29, 1838, [2].

5. Wight, Journal, 298 (Nov. [12], 1838).

6. Pratt, *History of the Late Persecution*, 52.

7. Smith, Bill of Damages, June 4, 1839, [7], JS Collection (*JSP*, D6:503).

8. Pratt, *Autobiography*, 227–30. Smith's actual words may not have been so grandiloquent.

9. The Richmond hearing has been reviewed in Baugh, "The Final Episode of Mormonism in Missouri in the 1830s"; and Marquardt, "Judge Austin A. King's Preliminary Hearing."

Corrill, Phelps, John Whitmer, and Peck. Smith was undoubtedly irked by the prospect of being held accountable by some of his own people.

As this was a preliminary hearing, at which the judge decides not the guilt or innocence of the defendants, but whether there is "probable cause to believe the prisoner guilty" of a crime and to proceed with a formal trial, King's focus was on the prosecuting attorney's witnesses. Thomas Burch, the state's attorney, needed only to present enough evidence to establish "probable cause" for believing Smith and the others were guilty of the alleged crimes.[10] Defense attorneys Alexander Doniphan and Amos Rees presented seven rebuttal witnesses, but their inclination would have been not to make an extended presentation since it would not change the outcome of the hearing.

As judge of the fifth judicial circuit, King's jurisdiction included all the counties where the alleged crimes had been committed. He could have recused himself based on the fact that he had a relative killed during the expulsion of the Mormons from Jackson County in 1833 and made no secret of his animosity towards Smith and his followers, but Doniphan and Rees did not object to his presence. In any case, given the situation in western Missouri, it would have been difficult to find an unbiased justice to replace King. Despite subsequent complaints by Smith and others about perceived irregularities in King's court, Rees reported that "Judge King ... heard all the evidence in a regular way and had it all reduced to writing as required by law, the mormons were then heard by their counsel in defence, &c. and after this the Judge proceeded to commit some of them for treason and murder, to discharge others, and to admit to bail the great majority of them."[11]

Of the charges facing Smith and the others, treason was the most controversial. Missouri law defined "treason against the state" as "levying war against the same, or by adhering to the enemies thereof, by giving them aid and comfort," and those convicted of this crime could "suffer death, or be sentenced to imprisonment in the penitentiary for a period not less than ten years."[12] The prosecution based this charge on testimony that church leaders, particularly Smith and Rigdon, declared that they were not subject to state authority and would resist any legal process against them; ordered Mormon soldiers to attack state troops at Crooked River, resulting in the murder of one of Bogart's men, and waged war by making pre-emptive raids on

10. *Revised Statutes of the State of Missouri, 1835*, Article II, sec. 22, 476–77, Practice and Proceedings in Criminal Cases.

11. Amos Rees, Letter to Abiel Leonard, Nov. 1, 1839.

12. *Revised Statutes of the State of Missouri*, Article I, sec. 1, 166, Crimes and Punishments.

communities in Daviess County, committing burglary, robbery, larceny, and arson; fostered the secret Danite organization to enforce the mandates of the First Presidency and violate the civil rights of the dissenters; and attempted to establish an independent government in western Missouri.

Avard was the prosecution's key witness.[13] For two days, he testified that the Society of the Daughter of Zion, later dubbed the Danites by Smith, was formed in June 1838 to drive dissenters out of Caldwell County and that he considered Smith "the prime mover and organizer of this Danite band." He said that soon after its organization, Smith and his counselors in the First Presidency, Rigdon and Hyrum Smith, attended a Danite meeting in the schoolhouse in Far West and that Smith "blessed them & prophesied over them, declaring that they should be the means in the hands of God of bringing forth the Milleniel Kingdom." At the same time, Smith instructed that the members of the band should bind themselves with a death-oath to keep the secrets of the organization. At another Danite meeting, Smith instructed that "if any of them should get into a difficulty the rest should help him out, and that they should stand by each other right or rong."

At a subsequent meeting held in Rigdon's home, according to Avard, a constitution was created and "adopted" by the First Presidency "as their rule & guide in future." This document was read "article by article to the Danite band and unanimously adopted by them."[14] Shortly after this meeting, Avard testified, he "was instructed by the council to destroy it, as, if it should be discovered, it would be considered treasonable." Avard understood that the order to destroy the Danite papers, which he ignored, was issued by the First Presidency. Later, when Avard was arrested, the constitution fell into Clark's hands and subsequently entered into the court record. Avard recounted the events surrounding the expulsion of the dissenters from Far West in June 1838, which was aided by the Danites, and provided the court with a copy of the threatening letter sent to each dissenter, of which he was the first of the eighty-three signers.

Avard testified that Smith was the commander of the force that surrounded Adam Black's house and that "if Black had not signed the paper he did. It was the common understanding & belief that he would have shared the fate of the dissenters." Prior to Mormon aggressions in Daviess County

---

13. The following summary is from Sampson Avard's testimony in Transcript of Proceedings, Nov. 12–29, 1838, [2]–[23] (*Document*, 97–108); hereafter Transcript.

14. Avard, in Transcript, [9]; see also Constitution of the Society of the Daughter of Zion, ca. late June 1838, at josephsmithpapers.org.

in October, Smith had delivered a speech in which he declared that it was "high time that we should take measure to defend our own rights," and proposed that the Mormon men organize themselves and go to Daviess County and "attack the mob," appointing David Patten and Seymour Brunson as "Generals" of the expedition. He also said it was permissible in times of war to steal from gentiles (non-Mormons), and that "the Children of God did not go to war at their own expense."

Avard added that after arriving at Adam-ondi-Ahman, he attended a leadership meeting on October 17, 1838, at which Smith declared that "we must in future stand up for our rights as citizens of the U[nited]. States & as saints of the most high God & that it was the will of God we should do so." At this time, Smith also declared that "he considered the U[nited]. States rotten," and that "it was time then [that] we should rise as the saints of the most high God & protect ourselves & take the Kingdom. ... He compared the Mormon church to the little stone spoken of by the Prop[he]t Daniel & that the dissenters first ... & the state next ... should be destroyed by this little stone" (Dan. 2:34–35, 44–45). During this meeting, Wight boasted that "before winter was over he thought we would be in St Louis & take it." A unanimous vote was made to take the fight to the mobbers and the state if necessary. The following day Patten led the raid on Gallatin, plundering and then burning Stollings's store, and Wight's men raided and plundered Millport. Avard said he observed the raiders returning and taking their plunder to the bishop's storehouse. According to Avard, "Jos Smith Jr was at Diahmon giving directions about things in general connected with the war."

Avard said he did not participate in the battle of Crooked River but witnessed Smith blessing Patten afterward. He also witnessed the militia's siege on Far West, and said that prior to their arrival, Smith assembled the troops and addressed them, declaring that "the Kingdom of God should be set up, & should never fall, and for every one that we lacked in number, in amount of those who came against us, the Lord would send angles, who would fight for us, & that we should be victorious." When the militia arrived and Smith determined resistance was futile, he advised his followers to "know nothing of what had happend to say nothing & to keep dark—that he Smith had forgotten more than he then knew."

Finally, Avard implicated Smith in the actions taken by the Danites, stating, "I was continualy in the society or company of the presidency, continually receiving instruction from them, as to the teachings of the danite band & I continually informed them of my teachings—and they were well apprised of my course & teachings in the Danite society."

Much of Avard's testimony was substantiated by other witnesses. Corrill testified that during the previous April, shortly after they arrived in Missouri, he heard Smith and Rigdon declare that "they would suffer vexatious law suits no longer. & that they would resist even an officer in the discharge of his duty." They also declared that they would tolerate dissension no longer and that the dissenters were to be expelled from the Mormon community. According to Corrill, the secret Danite society was organized not only to rid the community of the dissenters and enforce obedience to the First Presidency, but with the help of the Danites the church would become like "the little stone spoken of by Daniel, which should roll on and crush all opposition to it, and ultimately should be established as a temporal as well as a spiritual kingdom." Consequently, Corrill said, "the Danite band" was "organized into bands of tens fifties &c ready for war." The situation was such that "it was dangerous for any man to set up opposition to any thing that might be set on foot and I became afraid to speak my own mind." Besides, Corrill believed objection to the Danite band would be useless since it appeared to him that Smith "upheld" Avard "& would not allow any objections to him."

Corrill testified that during the previous June he had attended some meetings of the Danite society, but, he said, "there were some things I did not like." He particularly objected to the oath that obligated members to shield one another from the law, that "if one brother got into any kind of a difficulty, it was the duty of the rest to help him out right or rong." He also testified that he was present at one meeting that was attended by the First Presidency, and that Smith blessed each member and said among other things that "he wished to do nothing unlawful & if the people would let him alone they would preach the gospel & live in peace … but if they came on us to molest us, we would establish our religion by the sword & that he would become to this generation a second mahommet."

Corrill said he was present at a Sunday meeting previous to the Mormon raids in Daviess County in October when Smith addressed the congregation and gave tacit permission for Mormon troops to subsist on plunder. Corrill remembered that Smith "spoke of persons taking at some times, what at other times it would be rong to take, and gave as an example the case of David eating the Shew-bread, & also of the Saviour & his appostles plucking the ears of corn & eating as they passed thro. The corn-field." In speaking to the Mormon troops the following day, Smith suggested that "persons who would not engage" in the raids should have "their property … consecrated to the use of those who did engage." Smith was followed by Rigdon, who said that "those who were unwilling to go into the war, they ought to be put upon their horses with guns & bayonets, and forced into the front of the war." After the 400–500 Mormon troops arrived at Adam-ondi-Ahman, Corrill said he heard Lyman Wight state in public that "the earth was the Lord's and the fullness thereof, with the cattle upon a thousand hills," and on the next day he saw four or five cattle being driven through the town and was told jokingly that they had been consecrated by a Methodist priest.[15]

Robert Snodgrass, a dissenter who owned a mill near Far West, testified that he heard Smith declare at Far West "that the time had now come that the Saints should rise & take the kingdom, and they should do it by the sword of the Spirit, and if not, by the sword of power, and further said that they had been trampled on and abused as long as the Lord required it." He also testified that he heard Smith and Rigdon say that "their church was that kingdom spoken of by Daniel that should overcome all other kingdoms."[16] Snodgrass had fled Far West with the other dissenters, but with the arrival of Lucas and the militia, he returned to his mill only to find that the Mormon troops had helped themselves to a large quantity of his corn.[17]

Another dissenter, George Walter, testified that he heard Smith declare in Corrill's store that "he believed Mahommet was an inspired man, and had done a great deal of good, & that he intended to take the same cou[r]se Mohommad did. that if the people would let him alone he would after a while die a natural death, but if they did not. he would make it one gore of blood from the rocky Mountains to State of Maine." He said Smith compared the driving out of the dissenters to the papal Inquisition, an ecclesiastical tribunal used at various times and places in Medieval Europe responsible for the suppression, torture, and murder of people judged to be heretics. After he paid Lyman Johnson's bail, they were shot at while leaving town. When he returned to Far West, Rigdon reprimanded him for helping Johnson, a known dissenter. About a week before the arrival of Lucas and his troops, Walter said he was taken by force of arms to speak with Smith and other church leaders. According to Walter, "Jos Smith Jr accused me of lying, of harbouring the mob, of being too intimate with the dissenters & carrying

15. John Corrill, in Transcript, [29]–[34] (*Document*, 110–13).
16. Robert Snodgrass, in Transcript, [35].
17. John Murdock, Journal, 106–107 (Dec. 1838).

news to Richmond & other places. and said as to people leaving the county a stop must be put to it, that it was a time of war, and to permit persons who are right in among them to go out and carry news, would never do and it should be stoped, if not in any other way, they would do it by taking their lives." They let him go, but they kept his wagon and all except one of his horses.[18]

The next witness, George Hinkle, who commanded Mormon troops in defense of both De Witt and Far West, was careful not to implicate himself and testified that he "went down [to Daviess County] without being attached to any company, or without having any command." Instead, Wight was appointed "commander in chief of all the mormon forces in Daviess county," while Smith "seemed to give general directions." Hinkle said he had a conversation with Smith and "told him that this course of things of burning houses & plundering by the mormon troops would ruin us, that it could not be kept hid and would bring the force of the State upon us, that houses would be searched & stolen property found." According to Hinkle, Smith responded "in a pretty rough manner," and told him "to keep still, that I should say nothing about it, that it would discourage the men & he would not suffer me to say any thing about it." On another occasion, Hinkle again told Smith that he "thought things were running to a dangerous extreme & he ought to exercise his influence to stop it as this course of things would ruin his people." According to Hinkle, Smith said "I was mistaken & that I was scared, & that this was the only way to gain our liberty & our point, that the mob had begun it with us in Jackson c[oun]ty & had been kept up to this day, & told me to be cheered up & not oppose him, & pledged himself in some way that it would go on right." He also testified to seeing the troops deliver plunder, which they called consecrated property, to Bishop Vinson Knight to be "divided out among them as their wants might require." When he asked them if they were concerned about being prosecuted for theft, they answered that they could swear each other out of trouble in court, which Hinkle interpreted as alluding to their Danite oath. Hinkle said the raids on Gallatin and Millport "seemed to be done under Jos Smith Jr inspection," and reported that he "heard Smith find fault with Wight" for not being as tough on Millport as Patten was on Gallatin.[19]

After returning to Far West from Daviess County, Hinkle said that Judge Higbee ordered him to call out the Caldwell County militia but that he

---

18. George Walter, in Transcript, [35]–[38].

19. Hinkle's testimony here contradicts some writers who think Mormon troops carried out raids beyond what Smith intended. See Baugh, "Call to Arms," 210.

received little response because, as militia members explained, "they cared nothing for their commissions. that the organization of the Danite band had taken all power out of their hands." Hinkle testified concerning the time when the Missouri militia faced off with Mormon troops outside Far West, and, not wishing a confrontation, he commanded his men to retreat, which caused Smith to reprimand him, "charging me with cowerdice," and then he "took command of the forces." According to Hinkle, Smith did not care that it was the state militia he was challenging, for "it was a general understanding given out by Jos Smith Jr that he calculated that he would fight any forces that should come against them. whether militia or mob. & if they pushed them too tight, they would march thro Jefferson City." While in Daviess County he had heard Wight declare "that the sword had now been drawn & should not be sheathed, until he had marched to DeWit in Carroll county, into Jackson county & to many other places in the State. & swore that he was able to accomplish it." Hinkle noted that there had been a change in the church's teachings: "The general teachings of the presidency were that the kingdom they were setting up, was a temporal as well as a Spiritual kingdom. that it was the little stone spoken of by Daniel. Until lately the teachings of the church appeared to be peaceable & that the kingdom was to be set up peaceably. but lately a different idea has been advanced, that the time had come when this kingdom was to be set up by forcible means, if necessary."[20]

Loyal Mormon James C. Owens testified that he heard Smith in a speech to the Mormon troops say that "he did not care any thing about the comeing of the troops, nor about the laws ... & he did not intend to try to keep the law, or please them any longer. that they were a damned set, and God should damn them so help him Jesus Christ.—that he meant to ... take his own course & kill & destroy." Referring to the Mormon raids in Daviess County, Smith said that "they had commenced consecrating in Daviess c[oun]ty that he intended to have the surrounding counties consecrated to him, that the time had come, when the riches of the Gentiles should be consecrated to the saints."[21]

Another loyal Mormon Abner Scovel testified that in late June he heard Smith declare that "if the people would let him alone he would conquer them by the sword of the Spirit, but if they would not he would beat the plow shears into swords & their pruning hooks into spears & conquer them." Soon after this, Smith said, "What do we care for the laws of the

---

20. George M. Hinkle, in Transcript, [38]–[45] (*Document*, 125–29). On Hinkle's command of Mormon troops, see Baugh, "Call to Arms," 157–161, 309–314.

21. James C. Owens, in Transcript, [46]–[47] (*Document*, 113). BC XLIV:32.

land, so long as there is no person to put them in force." Shortly after Phelps and Frederick Williams were rebaptized in late July or early August, Scovel said he heard Rigdon say that "if Phelps or Williams apostatised again, or set up against the government or kingdom [of God], the Lord would kill them in half an hour, or would put it into the hearts of his saints to kill them."[22]

John Cleminson, a dissenting Mormon who served as clerk of the Caldwell County circuit court, testified that he attended two or three Danite meetings in June and that "it was taught there as part of the duty of that band, that they should support the presidency in all their designs right or rong.—that whatever they said was to be obeyed, and whoever opposed the presidency in what they said or desired done, should be expeled [from] the county, or have their lives taken." Although Avard was the "teacher and active agent of the Society," Cleminson said it was understood that "his teachings were approved of by the presidency." This was evident when the First Presidency attended one of the meetings and Avard, "to satisfy the people" that he was acting with their approval, called on Smith to speak. Smith then "gave them a pledge that if they led them into a difficulty, he would give them his head for a foot ball. and that it was the will of God these things should be so."

Cleminson further testified that when a legal process was filed in his office against Smith and others, Joseph and Hyrum Smith visited him and the former "told me not to issue that writ, that he did not intend to submit to it; that it was a vexatious thing & I had a right to Judge of it. and that he would see me out of it." Hyrum, who was not a defendant in that suit, made the same promise. Cleminson said, "I considered myself not a proper judge, as to whether it was a vexatious suit or not … and I felt myself intimidated and in danger if I issued it, knowing the regulation that had been entered into by the Danite band."

Cleminson also testified that he felt intimidated by the Danite enforcers into participating in the Mormon raid on Gallatin. Prior to the expedition to Daviess County, he heard Rigdon say that "those who had heretofore been backward in taking up arms in defending themselves ought to or should be put upon their horses with bayonets or pitchforks & Smith said forced into the front of the battle and that the property of those who would not go into the war, should be consecrated to the use of those who did." According to Cleminson, "It was generally understood that every movement made in Daviess was under the direction and supervision of the first Presidency."

---

22. Abner Scovel, in Transcript, [49].

Cleminson said that the object of marching to Diahmon was to drive out the mob, but when none was found they were ordered to "drive out all the citizens of Daviess & get possession of their property."[23]

Reed Peck, a former Danite and member of the Mormon delegation that negotiated with Lucas, testified that he attended a Danite meeting in late June, after Cowdery and other dissenters had been driven from Far West, at which time Avard explained that they were organizing to "defend ourselves against mobs. that we were all to be governd by the presidency, & do whatever they required. and uphold them that we were not to judge for ourselves whether it were right or rong that God had raised us a prophet who would judge for us, & that it was proper we should stand by each other in all cases ... whether the Danite was to blame or not." At this meeting, the Danite oath was administered to about thirty or forty men. Peck learned that the Danites were a quasi-military organization and that its leaders were designated by military rank, that Avard was a brigadier general, Cornelius Lott a major general, and Jared Carter a captain general, the highest rank. Peck reported that Avard said that he was following orders from the First Presidency and that "he had procured the presidency to come there to show the society that what he was doing was according to their direction or will." Sure enough, they came and "approved of Avards course, in the society." However, Peck added, Avard "did not explain to the presidency what his teaching had been in the society." Of course, that was something Peck could not have known but only surmised.

Nevertheless, Peck testified that he had heard Smith and Rigdon criticize those who did not wish to participate in unlawful acts, such as the raids on several towns in Daviess County, and call them traitors and "O don't men." Previous to the expedition to Daviess County, Peck heard Smith declare in a public address that "he had a reverence for the Constitution of the United States and of this State, but as for the laws of this state [of Missouri] he did not intend to regard them, nor care any thing about them, as they were made by lawyers and black legs." On the day before leaving for Daviess County, Peck testified that Smith spoke to the Mormon troops and "in refference to stealing, that in a general way he did not approve of it, but that on one occasion our Saviour & his disciples stole corn in passing thro' the corn fields for the reason that they could not otherwise procure any thing to eat. He told an anecdote of a Dutchmans potatoes, and said in substance that a colonel

---

23. John Cleminson, in Transcript, [49]–[54] (*Document*, 114–16).

or captain was quarterd near a Dutchman from whom he wished to pur-chase some potatoes, who refused to sell them. the officer then charged his men, not to be caught stealing the dutchmans potatoes but next morning he found his potatoes all dug." While stationed at Adam-ondi-Ahman, Peck saw raiding parties return with plunder, place it in the bishop's storehouse, and make their reports to the presidency.[24]

The state produced several witnesses to testify concerning the burning and looting of Gallatin. One witness, Thomas Odell, reported that he and his family were run out of their home by a company of Mormons, after which the house was looted and burned.[25] He named several men in the company, including James Henry Rollins, who happened to be among the prisoners standing behind Joseph and Hyrum Smith and their attorneys. When his name was mentioned, Rollins impulsively shouted that Odell was a "curly headed liar." Instantly, Joseph Smith "turned his head toward me," Rollins later recalled, "and said, 'Sh[hhh], Henry, don't say anything,'" which "caused some consternation in the court room."[26]

Another witness, Andrew Job, testified that he was taken prisoner by David Patten's men and taken to Adam-ondi-Ahman. Along the way, he said he "counted ten houses on fire." Job added that he and two other pris-oners were set free the next morning by Wight and told that they had four hours to leave Daviess County, after which they would be killed if found. Job testified that after the surrender of Far West, he and his step-mother, along with many other residents of Daviess County, went there to find their stolen property and recovered a feather bed and some knives and forks in Wight's home.[27] Jeremiah Myers testified that he saw "store goods at the bishop's store, and was informed by Mahlon Johnson, one of the company to Gall-atin, that the goods taken from the store in Gallatin were the goods I saw deposited in the bishops store, they were called and considered consecrated property & that they were to be dealt out by the bishop to those who stood in need."[28] Burr Riggs, a Danite, testified that he did not participate in the plundering, but when he arrived at Diahman, he saw "a great deal of plunder

---

24. Reed Peck, in Transcript, [54]–[63] (*Document*, 116–20). Several witnesses testified to hearing Smith's speech to those going to Daviess County when he related an anecdote about the Dutchman, which implied his approval of the Danite teaching that Mormon troops could subsist on the spoils of war by robbing and plundering. See also Morris Phelps, in Transcript, [28]–[29] (*Document*, 108–109).

25. Thomas M. Odell, in Transcript, [64]–[65] (*Document*, 130).

26. Rollins, Reminiscences, 12.

27. Andrew Job, in Transcript, [69]–[71] (*Document*, 132–33).

28. Jeremiah Myers, in Transcript, [68] (*Document*, 132).

brought in, consisting of beds. & bed cloths, I also saw one clock, and I saw 36 head of cattle drove up & put in a pen. ... I heard John L Butler, one of the mormons who was engaged in assisting to drive the cattle in, say that they had taken the cattle from the citizens of the Grindstone fork, and said he had made a valuable expedition."[29] Charles Bleckley testified that when one of the houses at Millport was burning, "I saw Joseph Smith Jr Lyman Wight, and Geo W. Robertson & two others sitting on their horses looking at the burning."[30]

Phelps, formerly David Whitmer's counselor in the Missouri presidency, testified Rigdon declared at a meeting in April that he had "bourne persecutions & law suits & other privations, and did not intend to bear them any longer. that they meant to resist the law, and if a sheriff came after them with writs they would kill him. and if any body opposed them they would take off their heads." Phelps said that Smith followed Rigdon and echoed his sentiments. Phelps said that both Rigdon and Smith at this time "observed that they meant to have the words of the presidency to be as good, and as undisputed as the words of God. and that no one should speak against what they said."

Phelps, who was one of the justices of the county court, further testified that Smith forbade him from "issuing any process against him." When Phelps learned from clerk John Cleminson that Smith also prohibited him from issuing a writ against him and Rigdon, Phelps confronted Smith, explaining that it was a small matter of not paying the clerk's fee. Smith replied that "he did not care for that, he did not intend to have any writ issued against him in the county." Nevertheless, Phelps observed, "these things together with many others alarmed me for the situation of our county. and at our next circuit court. I mentioned these things to the Judge & several members of the bar." Phelps said that when Patten told him that Rigdon was preparing a Fourth of July oration that would declare Mormon independence, he remarked that he "thought such a thing treasonable, to set up a government within a government."

Phelps also testified that prior to the Mormon purge of Daviess County Smith addressed about 200 or 300 troops and said that "they were then about to go to war in Daviess county, that those persons who had not turned out, their property should be taken to maintain the war." On the same

---

29. Burr Riggs, in Transcript, [73] (*Document*, 134).
30. Charles Bleckley, in Transcript, [77] (*Document*, 136).

occasion, Phelps said, Rigdon proposed that "the blood of those who were thus backward, should first be spilt in the streets of Far West." Some agreed, but Smith spoke up and said that "they [should] be taken out to Daviess & if they came to battle they should be put on their horses with bayonets & pitch forks, and put in front." This proposal was "passed without a dissenting voice," Phelps said. Smith then declared that "when they went out to war it was necessary to take spoils to live on … [and] told the anecdote of the dutch man's potatoes."

Phelps stated that he arrived at Adam-ondi-Ahman a few days after Smith and was present when plans were being made for conducting raids on several towns. On the night that he arrived, Phelps said he "heard a good deal of conversation about driving out the mob from Daviess." In the morning, "Wight asked Joseph Smith Jr twice if he had come to the point now to resist the law, that he wanted that matter now distinctly understood." Smith replied, "The time had come when he should resist all law … [and] a plan of opperations was agreed on." The plan was that Patten, who was present, "should take a company of 100 or more men, and go & take Gallatin that day, to take the goods out of the Store at Gallatin, bring them to Diahmon & burn the Store. Lyman Wight was to take a company & go to Mill Port, the same day, and Seymore Brunson was to take a company and go up on the Grindstone fork also on the same day." Phelps not only provided eyewitness testimony about Smith's involvement in planning the raids, but he also testified to seeing the Mormon troops return to Adam-ondi-Ahman with plunder.

Phelps said that when he returned to Far West, he attended a meeting of forty to fifty "true men" at the schoolhouse (October 20), during which Rigdon "commenced making covenants, with uplifted hands." The first was that anyone attempting to leave the county should be killed. If any man observed another packing or otherwise preparing to move, he "should kill him. and haul him aside into the brush. and that all the burial he should have, should be in a turkey-buzzards guts." After a vote was taken resulting in unanimous acceptance, Rigdon proposed that if a stranger was found walking around the town, "any one of that meeting was to kill him and throw him aside into the brush." This also passed unanimously. The third covenant Rigdon introduced was to "conceal all these things" on the penalty of death. He then organized several companies to provide security for the Mormons in Caldwell County. Amasa Lyman was appointed captain of a company "whose duty it was to watch the movements of the enemy, or mob in Buncombe [now Knoxville], and if they burnt one house in Caldwell, his company was to burn 4 of theirs." Rigdon then instructed all the companies that if "the inhabitants commenced burning houses in Caldwell, if they could not get clear of them in any other way they would poison them off."[31]

Next, John Whitmer, another former counselor to David Whitmer in the Missouri presidency, testified that in April Smith publicly declared that "he did not intend in future to have any process served on him and the officer who attempted it should die. that any person who spoke or acted against the presidency or the church should leave the county, or die. that he would suffer no such to remain there. that they should loose their head." At the same time, Rigdon also declared that "he would suffer no process of law to be served on him hereafter."[32]

Gallatin's postmaster, George W. Worthington, who lived a half-mile outside of town, testified that about fifty Mormons looted and burned his house and that subsequently, after the surrender of the Mormons, he retrieved some of his property at a vacant house in Adam-ondi-Ahman and Bishop Knight's storehouse.[33] Joseph H. McGee testified that he saw the Mormons robbing and setting fire to his tailor shop in Gallatin.[34] Resident Porter Yale testified that he saw Mormons plundering his father's house and that he followed them to Adam-ondi-Ahman, where during his three-day stay he observed "a great deal of plunder brought in."[35]

On November 23 Mormon dissenters and key witnesses for the prosecution Phelps, George Walter, John Cleminson, George Hinkle, and John Corrill signed a certificate attesting to General Clark's fair treatment of the Mormons following their surrender at Far West.[36] Clark had arrived on November 4, after the surrender and Lucas's men had terrorized the inhabitants of Far West. On November 24 Judge King dismissed twenty-three prisoners due to insufficient evidence.[37]

---

31. William W. Phelps, in Transcript, [83]–[94] (*Document*, 120–25). Benjamin Slade, a loyal Mormon from Colesville, New York, and Addison F. Green, also a loyal Mormon, gave testimony in support of Phelps's account of Rigdon's speech instructing the true-men to kill anyone attempting to leave the county. See Benjamin Slade and Addison F. Green, in Transcript, [105]–[108] (*Document*, 143, 144).

32. John Whitmer, in Transcript, [95]–[97] (*Document*, 138–39).

33. George W. Worthington, in Transcript, [98]–[100] (*Document*, 140–41).

34. Joseph H. McGee, in Transcript, [101]–[102] (*Document*, 141).

35. Porter Yale, in Transcript, [104]–[105] (*Document*, 142–43).

36. W. W. Phelps, George Walter, John Cleminson, George M. Hinkle, and John Corrill, Certificate, Nov. 23, 1838, in *Document*, 87.

37. Austin A. King, "Defendants against whom nothing is proven," Nov. 24, 1838, JS Collection (see also *Document*, 143; DHC 3:211).

When court resumed, Mormon Ezra Williams testified that he was in Patten's counpany when Stollings's store in Gallatin was robbed.[38] Another loyal Mormon, Timothy Lewis, testified to seeing Patten's men returning to Adam-ondi-Ahman with "a great deal of property and plunder." When Lewis questioned them about breaking the law, the men told him "there was no law in this state. but that a law was about to be established by a higher power. to be given by revelation."[39]

The final witness for the prosecution was Patrick Lynch, a clerk in Stollings's store, who testified that when he saw the Mormons coming, he fled into the brush after locking the door. From a distance of about 100–200 yards, Lynch saw them taking the goods out of the store and loading them onto their horses, and when he was about a half-mile away, he saw wagons traveling on the road loaded with goods taken from the store. After about three hours, he returned to find the store in ashes.[40]

At this point, according to the record, "the Court informed the prisoners that it would now proceed to take their examination, without oath in relation to the offences charged, and the said Defendants declined making any statement."[41] The defense then presented seven rebuttal witnesses.

Malinda Porter, a boarder at Lyman Wight's house, testified that Wight was not involved in the raids in Daviess County and that he was home the whole time. She also contradicted Andrew Job's testimony that he and his step-mother recovered stolen property, including a feather bed and some knives and forks, from Wight's home, stating that the items had been in the home for at least two years.[42] Another boarder at Wight's house, Delia F. Pine, and Ezra Chipman, who was convalescing at the residence, testified to the same.[43] King probably regarded this testimony as not credible since testimony had been given that Wight was assigned to lead the raid on Millport and had been seen on his horse watching a house burn. Before the hearing, Thomas Marsh had submitted an affidavit stating that Wight and about eighty horsemen went to Millport and then later in the evening returned to Diahman laden with property, which he was informed, consisted

---

38. Ezra Williams, in Transcript, [107] (*Document*, 144).

39. Timothy Lewis, in Transcript, [109] (*Document*, 145).

40. Patrick Lynch, in Transcript, [110]–[111] (*Document*, 145).

41. Transcript, [112] (*Document*, 146).

42. Andrew Job, in Transcript, [69]–[71] (*Document*, 132–33); Malinda Porter, in Transcript, [113] (*Document*, 146).

43. Delia F. Pine, in Transcript, [114]–[115] (*Document*, 146–47); Ezra Chipman, in Transcript, [118]–[119] (*Document*, 148).

of beds, clocks, and other household furniture.[44] In his July 1, 1843, affidavit, Wight confessed that he went to Millport but claimed that the inhabitants in a "diabolical scheme" against the Mormons had burnt their own houses after removing the contents.[45]

In an attempt to impeach Avard's testimony, Rigdon's sixteen-year-old daughter, Nancy, testified that she "heared Sampson Avard say that he would swear to a lie to accomplish an object. that he had told many a lie, and would do so again."[46] At the time he allegedly made this statement, Avard was a faithful Mormon and a leader of the Smith-approved Danite band, bound by an oath to help a brother Danite out of trouble, whether he was right or wrong. His willingness to lie to protect Smith and other Danites or to further the interests of the church was, to him, a sign of loyalty to the church. Ironically, his testifying at this trial was a violation of his Danite oath.

Early in the trial, Samuel Bogart and several of his men, including Wyatt Cravens who was wounded and taken by the Mormons as a prisoner, testified concerning the battle of Crooked River and the death of Moses Rowland.[47] Jonathan Barlow and Thorit Parsons testified for the defense that Smith was in Far West at the time of the battle.[48] While this testimony was meant to demonstrate Smith's innocence, it was irrelevant where he was when the crime was committed since they were acting on his orders.

At this point, both the prosecution and defense rested and awaited King's decision.

Mormon Objections

Smith and the other prisoners later complained that the hearing was a charade that made a mockery of the law. In March 1839 Smith and other prisoners petitioned Missouri Supreme Court Justice George Tompkins for a habeas corpus review of their cases in which Smith said he "underwent a long and tedious ... mock examination" and that "there was not the least shadow of honor or justice or law administered." At the same time, he complained that the examination was one-sided and that he was unable to present a defense.[49] The problem was that most of those who could testify

---

44. Thomas B. Marsh, Affidavit, Oct. 24, 1838, in *Document*, 57.

45. Lyman Wight, Affidavit, July 1, 1843, in *Times and Seasons*, July 15, 1843, 266.

46. Nancy Rigdon, in Transcript, [115] (*Document*, 147).

47. Transcript, [24]–[27], [102]–[104] (*Document*, 110, 142).

48. Jonathan W. Barlow, in Transcript, [116]–[117] (*Document*, 147–48); Jonathan W. Barlow, in Transcript, [117]–[118] (*Document*, 148).

49. Ripley et al., Petition to George Tompkins, ca. Mar. 9–15, 1839, [1], JS Collection (*JSP*, D6:345).

were either defendants themselves or witnesses for the prosecution. Hyrum Smith later testified that about sixty potential defense witnesses were brought from Far West by Bogart and his men and imprisoned to prevent them from testifying.[50] A more likely reason for their imprisonment was that in providing statements, they had implicated themselves in a crime. Nevertheless, seven witnesses did testify for the defense.[51]

The manner in which the testimony was recorded made it appear that there was little, if any, cross-examination of the witnesses. The Missouri legislature stated at the time of its publication of the court record in 1841 that "they consider the evidence adduced in the examination there held, in a great degree *ex parte* [one-sided], and not of the character which should be desired for the basis of a fair and candid investigation."[52] LDS attorney Gordon A. Madsen went so far as to assert that the court record contains "no testimony adduced from cross-examination and no questions from Judge King and answers thereto are in the record."[53] The court record is not a verbatim transcript of the hearing and does not contain the question-and-answer style of eliciting testimony, but is written in the form of statements. Nevertheless, the record includes three references to "upon cross examination" followed by additional testimony.[54] According to Parley Pratt,

> This Court of Inquisition inquired diligently into our belief in the seventh chapter of Daniel concerning the kingdom of God, which should subdue all other kingdoms and stand forever. And when told that we believed in that prophecy, the Court turned to the clerk and said: "*Write that down; it is a strong point for treason.*" Our lawyer observed as follows: "Judge, you had better make the Bible treason." The Court made no reply.[55]

Clay County attorney William T. Wood, who said he had been retained by Governor Boggs to assist circuit attorney Thomas Burch and "was present during the whole of the examining trial," denied hearing King tell the clerk to write down that the Mormon belief in Daniel 7 constituted treason.[56] Of course, King did not think that belief in Bible prophecy was treasonable. What was legally treasonable was attempting to fulfill prophecy through the

---

50. Hyrum Smith, Testimony, July 1, 1843, in *Times and Seasons*, July 1, 1843, 253.

51. See testimonies of Malinda Porter, Delia F. Pine, Nancy Rigdon, Jonathan Barlow, Thorit Parsons, and Ezra Chipman, in Transcript, [115]–[121].

52. "Legislative Proceedings," in *Document*, 2.

53. Madsen, "Joseph Smith and the Missouri Court of Inquiry," 97.

54. Transcript, [34], [116].

55. Pratt, *Autobiography*, 230. See Dan. 2:34–35, 44–45; 7:18, 27.

56. William T. Wood, "Mormon Memoirs," *Liberty (MO) Tribune*, Apr. 9, 1886, [1].

use of force, which no amount of quoting the Bible could justify. Several witnesses had testified that Smith referenced Daniel 7 to defend his call for the use of force in Daviess County.[57] Smith no doubt included this testimony in his 1839 petition, when he complained that "a long catalogue of garbled testimony was permitted by the Court perporting to be the religious sentiment of the said Joseph Smith Jr, which testimony was false," and contended that he could produce witnesses who were at the meeting who could testify that "Joseph Smith Jr did not promulg[at]e such ridiculas and absurd sentiments for his religion."[58] However, the sentiments being denied were published and promulgated in Rigdon's pamphlet of his Fourth of July oration, which, with Smith's approval, had declared that if a "mob ... comes on us to disturb us; it shall be between us and them a war of extermination, for we will follow them, till the last drop of their blood is spilled, or else they will have to exterminate us: for we will carry the seat of war to their own houses, and their own families, and one party or the other shall be utterly destroyed."[59] Smith's error in judgment was further complicated when he failed to distinguish between an anti-Mormon mob and the state militia.

As this was a preliminary hearing, at which the judge decides not the guilt or innocence of the defendants but whether or not there is enough evidence to proceed with a formal trial, the focus was on the prosecuting attorney's witnesses. This was made clear to Morris Phelps, a Mormon who testified for the prosecution, who later recounted: "I was soon called on [to be] a witness on the part of the mob. In giving testimony I was sworn in I was first stop[p]ed by the prosecuting At[t]orney then by the Judge saying to me we do not want to here [hear] any testimony on that side of the question (meaning in favor of Joseph & Hyrum and others of the prisoners)."[60]

Smith claimed "that the witnesses on the part of the State were taken by force of arms and threatned [threatened] with ... immediate Death and were brought without subpoena or warrant under this awful and glaring anticipation of being exterminated if they did not swear something against him to please the Mob."[61] However, Smith was incorrect about King's not

---

57. See the testimonies of Sampson Avard, John Corrill, Robert Snodgrass, George M. Hinkle, and John Whitmer, in Transcript, [7], [31], [35], [42], and [96].

58. Ripley et al., Petition to George Tompkins, ca. Mar. 9–15, 1839, [2]–[3], JS Collection (*JSP*, D6:346).

59. Rigdon, *Oration Delivered by Mr. S. Rigdon*, 12.

60. Morris Phelps, Reminiscences, 1.

61. Ripley et al., Petition to George Tompkins, ca. Mar. 9–15, 1839, [1], JS Collection (*JSP*, D6:345).

issuing subpoenas since some still exist.[62] Hyrum Smith later contradicted his brother on this point, testifying that subpoenas were issued for about forty witnesses for the defense.[63] Hinkle later denied accusations that he had turned state's evidence, stressing that he had been "legally subpoenaed."[64]

No doubt some Mormon witnesses were uncooperative and the court may have compelled them to testify, although Smith's description may have been exaggerated. This seems borne out in Rigdon's version, which gives more details: "If a witness did not swear to please the court, he or she would be threatened to be cast into prison. They never pleased the Court when their testimony was favorable to the defendants. ... When a witness did not swear to please the attorney, Birch, he would order them to be taken into custody, and they were immediately cast into prison, and the next morning they would be brought forward and tried again. ... By such means they got men to swear for them, and to swear to most unhallowed falsehoods. It was indeed suborning witnesses to swear, to promise a man's life if he would swear, and death or imprisonment if he did not swear, and not only to swear, but swear to please them."[65] Rigdon also seems to exaggerate what may have been the prosecuting attorney compelling uncooperative witnesses to testify by jailing some of them for contempt and plea bargaining with others. Reminding uncooperative witnesses that they could be charged with treason may have sounded like a death threat to some. Rigdon seemed to understand this, for he reported that Avard advised Oliver Olney that "if he wished to save himself, he must swear hard against the heads of the Church, as they were the ones, the court wanted to criminate."[66] Naturally, Avard chose to cooperate because he wished to escape punishment, but there was plenty to testify to without fabricating events. Besides, nearly everything Avard said was corroborated by other witnesses, both at the trial and afterward. As historian Stephen C. LeSueur has observed, "If you tossed out Avard's testimony, you still would come up with pretty much the same interpretation of the Danites."[67]

Smith also attempted to deny his involvement with the Danites and accused Avard of testifying falsely concerning his attending a certain meeting

---

62. See *JSP*, D6:345n429.

63. Hyrum Smith, Testimony, July 1, 1843, in *Times and Seasons*, July 1, 1843, 253.

64. George M. Hinkle, Letter to William W. Phelps, Aug. 14, 1844, in *Ensign*, Aug. 1844, 31.

65. [Rigdon], *Appeal to the American People*, 66–67; see also "A History of the Persecution, of the Church of Jesus Christ, of Latter Day Saints in Missouri," *Times and Seasons*, Sep. 1840, 163 (*JSP*, H2:276).

66. [Rigdon], *Appeal to the American People*, 66; see also "A History of the Persecution," *Times and Seasons*, Sep. 1840, 162–63 (*JSP*, H2:276).

67. LeSueur, "The Danites Reconsidered," 46.

on the night of October 17 at James Sloan's boarding house, where Smith stayed when visiting Adam-ondi-Ahman. In the March 1839 petition, Smith and his cosigners asserted that "there was no such councyl ... and there was no such vote nor conversastion as Doctor Avard swore too."[68] Smith's cosigners—Heber Kimball, William Huntington, Joseph Noble, and Alanson Ripley—vouched that they knew such was the case because they "were with the prisoner" in Adam-ondi-Ahman at the time. None of these men was named by Avard as being present. Ripley and Huntington were residents of Adam-ondi-Ahman, and so would not have necessarily been with Smith the entire day. Nevertheless, this council no doubt was the one mentioned by Hinkle as occurring "the evening after I arrived at Diahmon ... in which some officers were appointed." He was not in attendance but learned details from "Hyram Smith & others."[69] Hyrum was one of the men at the council meeting, according to Avard, but Hyrum later claimed "that he knew nothing of the Council spoken of by Doctor arverd [Sampson Avard] in Cald weld [Caldwell] County nor in Davis County at James Sloans."[70] While both Joseph and Hyrum mention Sloan's residence as the location of the meeting, the record of Avard's testimony does not mention a specific location in Adam-ondi-Ahman for the meeting, but it may have been held at Wight's residence, which was subsequently named the "council chamber."[71] At this meeting, according to Avard, Smith spoke and compared the Saints to the little stone in Daniel 7 that smashes the kingdoms of the earth and becomes a great mountain and declared it was time for the Saints to protect themselves, after which a unanimous vote was given in support.[72] This part of Avard's testimony demonstrated that Smith was responsible for initiating the Mormon offensive in Daviess County, which in turn led to the outbreak of armed conflict in Caldwell County and the battle at Crooked River. Little wonder Smith was anxious to deny his presence at this meeting. Regardless, denying that Smith attended a specific meeting is not the same as saying he was not in command of the Mormon forces.

In a carefully worded statement that was included in his December 16, 1838, letter to the church, Smith claimed that he did not know about Avard's "false and pernicious" activities until after his incarceration. Smith

---

68. Ripley et al., Petition to George Tompkins, ca. Mar. 9–15, 1839, [4]–[5], JS Collection (*JSP*, D6:349).

69. George M. Hinkle, in Transcript, [39] (*Document*, 126).

70. Hyrum Smith, Petition, Mar. 9, 1839.

71. George Walters, in Transcript, [37].

72. Sampson Avard, in Transcript, [6]–[7]. See Dan. 2:34–35, 44–45; 7:18, 27.

said these "frauds and secret abominations and evil works of darkness" were solely the responsibility of Avard, who was "palming it all the time upon the presidency while mean time the presidency were ignorant as well as innocent of these things."[73] However, John Corrill, John Cleminson, and Reed Peck had testified to attending a Danite meeting in Far West where members of the First Presidency were present, and William Swartzell mentioned Smith's presence at two, possibly three, Danite meetings in Adam-ondi-Ahman.[74] LDS historian Alexander Baugh has tried to reconcile Smith's denial by arguing that Smith "did not deny his knowledge or participation in Mormon/Danite military activities," only that "he indicated that he did not know about the 'pernicious things' being engaged in and taught by Avard and his cohorts."[75] LeSueur has similarly suggested that Smith may have had reference to the extreme measures Avard proposed "near the end of the Mormon War" such as indiscriminately plundering the Missourians and poisoning their crops. "It is possible," LeSueur argued, "that the prophet, who was away from Far West at the time and then was captured shortly after his return, did not learn about this and perhaps other radical measures proposed by Avard until the Richmond hearing."[76] However, no one was concerned about Avard's teachings or extreme proposals. That is not why Smith was in trouble with the law. Rather, Smith was taking advantage of the secrecy and attempting to blame responsibility for the insurrectionist raids in Daviess County ("evil works of darkness") on Avard, whom Smith had previously relieved of his command. While the documentary evidence demonstrates that the majority of those who took part in the confrontation with Judge Black in August, as well as the raids in Daviess County and the battle at Crooked River in October, were Danites, the Danites had been assimilated into the army of Israel and were operating under Smith's direction as commander-in-chief.[77] The debate over how much Smith knew about the

---

73. Smith, Letter to the church in Caldwell County, MO, Dec. 16, 1838, [5], JS Collection (*JSP*, D6:306).

74. Corrill, in Transcript, [30] (*Document*, 111); Cleminson, in Transcript, [50] (*Document*, 114); Peck, in Transcript, [55] (*Document*, 117); Swartzell, *Mormonism Exposed*, 17–18, 20–23.

75. Baugh, "'We Have a Company of Danites in These Times,'" 25.

76. LeSueur, "The Danites Reconsidered," 49–50.

77. On Smith's involvement with the Danites and raids in Daviess County, see LeSueur, "'High Treason and Murder,'" 16–17; LeSueur, *The 1838 Mormon War in Missouri*, 208–10. On the Danite participation, compare Appendix 3, "Danites in 1838: A Partial List," in Quinn, *The Mormon Hierarchy*, 479–90, with Appendix E, "Mormon Participants in the October Defense of Daviess County," and Appendix H, "Documented Caldwell Militia Participants in the Crooked River Expedition," in Baugh, "Call to Arms," 395–98, 407–13.

Danites or approved of Avard's activities is irrelevant. Smith—not Avard—was responsible for the raids.[78]

While Smith was "an active participant in the civil conflict," Baugh argues that he acted as a private citizen and not in any official military capacity. Baugh refers to Smith's public denials of belonging to the Caldwell County militia, and that Smith was exempt from such duty owing to his being a minister and having a post-surgical limp: "If Joseph Smith purposely and intentionally sought to excuse himself from militia service, it stands to reason he would have also endeavored to distance himself from the more militant Danite organization."[79] However, Baugh ignores the fact that Smith's involvement was as the commander-in-chief of the army of Israel, an office he held as early as 1834 when he led the march of Zion's Camp to Missouri, and that the Danites recognized him as such in their constitution. Hinkle testified that while Wight was in charge of the forces in Daviess County, Smith "seemed to give general directions" to Wight and Patten, who were apparently accountable to him, and that the raids on Gallatin and Millport "seemed to be done under Jos Smith Jr['s] inspection."[80] Phelps testified that he had heard Smith and other men planning the raids and Wight saying that he was waiting for Smith's order to act.[81] Cleminson testified that "it was generally understood that every movement made in Daviess was under the direction and supervision of the first Presidency."[82] Rockwood, a Danite living in Far West, wrote soon after that "Joseph Smith Jr & Lyman Wight were at the head of the army of Israel that went up to the relief of the Brethren in Davies County."[83]

Despite Smith's attempt to distance himself from Avard and the Danites, he was aware of them and their activities. Ironically, the earliest appearance of the word "Danite" in the historical record is in the journal that was kept for Smith by George Robinson, the First Presidency's scribe and a colonel in the Danite society. Robinson wrote that one purpose for forming the Danites was to "cleanse the Church of verry great evils," and that they, as

---

78. Baugh distances Smith from Avard and the Danites in "'We Have a Company of Danites in These Times,'" 21–25, while at the same time acknowledging that Smith was involved in the activities that Smith later tried to blame on them. He also acknowledges that shortly after the confrontation with Judge Black that Smith relieved Avard of his command and that he was appointed as surgeon to the Danite organization.

79. Baugh, "'We Have a Company of Danites in These Times,'" 25.

80. George M. Hinkle, in Transcript, [38]–[39] (*Document*, 126).

81. Phelps, in Transcript, [89] (*Document*, 123).

82. John Cleminson, in Transcript, [52] (*Document*, 115).

83. Rockwood, Journal, 2.

a paramilitary organization, were "exibited on the fourth day of July" at the church's 1838 Independence Day celebration at Far West, over which Smith presided.[84] Smith's journal also mentions that "Gen. Avard" accompanied the First Presidency to Adam-ondi-Ahman in early August, a rank Avard held only as a Danite.[85] Reed Peck testified that the First Presidency attended a meeting "to show the society that what he [Avard] was doing was according to their direction or will."[86] And Avard testified that the presidency directed his every move and that he "continually informed them of my teachings— and they were well apprised of my course & teachings in the Danite society."[87] Clearly, Smith was aware of Avard and the Danite society and used them during his defense of Mormon interests in Daviess and Caldwell Counties.

In his 1839 petition, Smith claimed that he "had nothing to do with burning in Davies County ... [and] made publick proclimation against such things."[88] In light of multiple testimonies regarding Smith's telling the story of the Dutchman's field of potatoes and the commander's instruction to his men not to get caught stealing, Smith's proclamations against certain actions were ambiguous and not necessarily what they seemed. Phelps testified that he heard Smith and Wight planning the raids in Daviess County, and that those plans included removing goods from Stollings's store and burning it. Phelps also said that following his return to Far West, Rigdon appointed Amasa Lyman to be a captain of a company, "whose duty it was to watch the movements of the enemy, or mob in Buncombe, and if they burnt one house in Caldwell, his company was to burn 4 of theirs."[89] Hinkle testified that Smith told him if he learned that "the citizens of Richmond & surrounding country rose" against the Mormons, "he would have men to slip in behind them, and lay waste the cou[n]try & burn their houses."[90] In addition to being indicted for treason, Smith was also the subject of an investigation that resulted in a Daviess County grand jury indicting him in April 1839 on two counts of arson in Gallatin and Millport.[91]

---

84. Smith, Journal, July 27, 1838 (*JSP*, J1:293).

85. Smith, Journal, Aug. 7–9, 1838 (*JSP*, J1:299). See also "Celebration of the 4th of July," *Elders' Journal*, Aug. 1838, 69.

86. Reed Peck, in Transcript, [55] (*Document*, 117).

87. Avard, in Transcript, [22] (*Document*, 107).

88. Ripley et al., Petition to George Tompkins, ca. Mar. 9–15, 1839, [5], JS Collection (*JSP*, D6:349–50).

89. Phelps, in Transcript, [90], [92] (*Document*, 123, 124).

90. Hinkle, in Transcript, [45] (*Document*, 129).

91. State of Missouri, Indictment, Honey Creek Township, Daviess Co., MO, ca. Apr. 10, 1839, State of Missouri v. Gates et al. (Including Joseph Smith) for Arson, Daviess Co. Circuit

Smith also denied complicity in the battle of Crooked River: "The prisoner did not have any thing to do with what is called Bogarts Battle for
he knew nothing of it untill it was all over that he was at home and in the
bosome of his own family during the time of that whole transaction."[92] True,
he did not know about the battle until it was over, but it is unlikely that
Smith was unaware of or was excluded from the decision to send Patten and
his men to confront the mob at the southern border of Caldwell County.
The Danite constitution recognized Smith as the commander-in-chief, a
position Smith had held for more than four years, and for three years Smith
stood at the head of the church's "war department, by Revelation."[93] Before Patten's departure, according to Avard, a council was held at Rigdon's
house where various officers received their commissions, with Hinkle being
in charge of the foot soldiers, Patten of the cavalry, and that Smith "should
be commander in chief of the whol[e] kingdom."[94] Previously, in Daviess
County, Wight deferred to Smith's judgment before carrying out the raids.[95]
There can be little doubt, as historian D. Michael Quinn has observed, that
"what the Danites did militarily during the summer and fall of 1838 was
by the general oversight and command of Joseph Smith."[96] Nevertheless,
Smith tried to shift blame for the Crooked River skirmish to Hinkle, stating
in 1839 that Hinkle ordered Captain Patten to take his company of cavalry
and "go against them, and stop their depredations, and drive them out of the
county."[97] However, Hinkle claimed in court that he was at his home at the
time and was not consulted.[98] Pratt and Rigdon confirmed that Hinkle was
not present.[99] Nevertheless, attempting to give Patten's company the appearance of having legal authority, Pratt claimed it was Captain John Killian who
ordered Patten and his men to go to the Crooked River area, while others
claimed that Patten had been called out by Caldwell County Judge Elias

Court, 1839; State of Missouri, Indictment, Honey Creek Township, MO, ca. Apr. 10, 1839, State
of Missouri v. Baldwin et al. (Including Joseph Smith) for Arson, Daviess Co. Cir. Ct 1839.

92. Ripley et al., Petition to George Tompkins, ca. Mar. 9–15, 1839, [5], JS Collection (*JSP*,
D6:350).

93. Avard, in Transcript, [12] (*Document*, 102); John Whitmer, History, 81 (*JSP*, H2:90).

94. Avard, in Transcript, [8] (*Document*, 100).

95. Charles Bleckley, in Transcript, [77] (*Document*, 136).

96. Quinn, *The Mormon Hierarchy*, 99.

97. "Extract, from the Private Journal of Joseph Smith Jr.," *Times and Seasons*, Nov. 1839, 5
(*JSP*, H1:476); Smith, Bill of Damages, June 4, 1839, [4], JS Collection (*JSP*, D6:500).

98. George M. Hinkle, in Transcript, [40]–[41].

99. Pratt, *History of the Late Persecution*, 33; Rigdon, Testimony, June 1, 1843, in *Times and
Seasons*, Aug. 1, 1843, 273–74.

Higbee as a militia.[100] In any case, it is implausible for Smith and others to claim that he was not involved with the decision to dispatch Patten and his men to confront anti-Mormon vigilantes in the Crooked River area.

King's Ruling

On November 29, after both the prosecution and defense had rested, Judge King dismissed seven more prisoners for lack of evidence. Another twenty-three men were released on bail to be tried in Daviess County on March 28, 1839, for arson, burglary, robbery, and larceny. King ruled that there was "probable cause" to believe Smith, Wight, Hyrum Smith, Alexander McRae, and Caleb Baldwin had committed "overt acts of treason" in Daviess County during the conflict in October, for which they were to be tried in that county beginning on March 7. King also ruled that Rigdon had committed the same offense in Caldwell County and that he was to be tried in that county beginning on April 1. Because treason was a nonbailable offense, he ordered the accused to be committed to jail to await their trials, specifically the Clay County jail in Liberty as neither Daviess nor Caldwell County had a jail. Finally, King ruled that there was probable cause to believe Parley Pratt, Morris Phelps, Luman Gibbs, Darwin Chase, and Norman Shearer were guilty of the murder of Moses Rowland in the Crooked River skirmish and, because murder was also nonbailable, King committed Pratt and the others to the Ray County jail to await trial, set to begin on March 11.[101]

In 1840 Smith wrote landowner Isaac Galland that he and the other prisoners "were committed to this jail, on a pretended charge of treason, against the State of Missouri, without the slightest evidence to that effect."[102] While a reasonable argument may be made that Smith and the others would have been acquitted of the charge of treason had it come to trial, as Mormon legal analyst Gordon A. Madsen has argued, considering the testimony presented, his knowledge of state law regarding treason, and the purpose of a preliminary hearing, King had little choice but to rule as he did. [103] Clay County attorney William T. Wood, who assisted prosecuting attorney Thomas Burch, denied Mormon claims that it was a "mock trial." In

---

100. Pratt; Greene, *Facts Relative to the Expulsion of the Mormons*, 21; George W. Pitkin, Affidavit, July 1, 1843, in *Times and Seasons*, July 15, 1843, 260.

101. Austin A. King, Ruling, in Transcript, [121] (*Document*, 150). Pratt was subsequently indicted in April 1839 for Rowland's murder. See Quinn, *The Mormon Hierarchy*, 99, 340n89; Baugh, "Call to Arms," 244.

102. Joseph Smith, Letter to Isaac Galland, Mar. 22, 1839, in *Times and Seasons*, Feb. 1840, 52.

103. Madsen, "Joseph Smith and the Missouri Court of Inquiry," 93–136.

an 1886 statement, he insisted that "Judge King presided in good faith and with fairness." Wood said that prior to his involvement he had "little faith that the prosecution could be made successful," because he "regarded them [Mormons] as harmless, and in no respect dangerous to law and order; but developements made on that trial by the evidence, worked a change in my opinion, and candor compels me now to say, that I believe them to be dangerously unfriendly to our Government and to the law of the land." Upon reflection, Wood concluded: "If Mormon evidence, given by such of them as Dr. Avery [Avard], W. W. Phelps, David [John] Whitmer and others, is entitled to credit, Judge King could not have ruled otherwise than he did."[104]

---

104. William T. Wood, "Mormon Memoirs," *Liberty (MO) Tribune*, Apr. 9, 1886, [1].

33

Imprisonment

DECEMBER 1838–MARCH 1839

Thy God shall stand by the[e] for ever and ever.
—Revelation in Joseph Smith and Others, Letter, Liberty Jail,
    to the Church, Mar. 1839, 3–4, Revelations Collection

Immediately after Judge King rendered his verdict on November 29, 1838, Captain Samuel Bogart and his men escorted Smith, his brother Hyrum, Rigdon, Wight, Caleb Baldwin, and Alexander McRae twenty-seven miles from Richmond to Liberty in Clay County. Smith was no doubt outraged to see Bogart sitting on the saddle Hinkle had taken from his property after his arrest.[1] Upon arriving at Liberty on December 1, the prisoners were promptly incarcerated in the county jail, a small two-level building constructed of four-foot-thick walls made of limestone and oak, with an inside measurement of 14 by 14.5 feet (203 square feet).[2]

Smith and the others would spend the rest of the winter primarily in the cold lower-level enclosure, which was ventilated and lighted by two very small grated openings. In his March 1839 letter to landowner Isaac Galland, Smith described his days in this dungeon: "We are kept under a strong guard, night and day, in a prison of double walls and doors. ... Our food is scant, uniform, and coarse; we have not the privilege of cooking for

---

1. See depositions of Hyrum Smith, Vinson Knight, Lyman Wight, Nauvoo, IL, Apr. 22, 1842, in Lee County, Iowa Territory, District Court, Joseph Smith v. George M. Hinkle. Joseph Smith wrote: "Captain Bogart ... stole a valuable horse, saddle and bridle from me; which cost two hundred dollars, and then sold the same to General Wilson. On understanding this I applied to General Wilson for the horse, who assured me, upon the honor of a gentleman, and an officer, that I should have the horse returned to me; but this promise has not been fulfilled." "Extract, from the Private Journal of Joseph Smith Jr.," *Times and Seasons*, Nov. 1839, 7 (*JSP*, H1:484).

2. "Clay County, Missouri," *Historical Record* (Salt Lake City), Dec. 1888, 7:670; Andrew Jenson, Edward Stevenson, and Joseph S. Black, "Liberty Jail," *Deseret News* (Salt Lake City), Oct. 3, 1888, 608; "Liberty Jail," *Liahona, the Elders' Journal*, Aug. 18, 1914, 122.

ourselves, we have been compelled to sleep on the floor with straw, and not blankets sufficient to keep us warm; and when we have a fire, we are obliged to have almost a constant smoke."[3] In a brief letter written on the same day of their arrival and sent by the hand of Captain Bogart, Smith notified Emma of their situation, stating that they were "in good spirits."[4]

Jailer Samuel Hadley and his deputy, Samuel Tillery, kept watch over the prisoners and occasionally permitted them to dine in the upper floor of the jail or meet with visitors.[5] "We were sometimes visited by our friends … but frequently we were not suffered to have that privilege," Smith remarked. "Their attention and affection to me, while in prison, will ever be remembered by me," but it pained him to see them "thrust away, and abused by the jailor and guard."[6] According to McRae, they were also visited by their enemies, some of whom "were angry with Brother Joseph, and accused him of killing a son, a brother, or some relative of theirs."[7]

Smith and the other prisoners were occasionally permitted to leave the jailhouse under the supervision of a guard. Sherriff Hadley, according to William T. Wood, a Liberty attorney who had aided the prosecution at the Richmond hearing, "was not only kind and humane, but generously indulgent to these prisoners." He remembered that Smith, his brother Hyrum, Wight, and others visited his office, four blocks from the jail, and remained there in conversation for an hour or two. Among other things, Smith asked him to help in their defense and promised to give him a "liberal fee." Wood responded, "I was through with my engagement with the State, but so far as the prosecution had secrets I [knew] them, and I could not appear in their defence without seeming to take a fee on both sides and, this, no fee could induce me to do." Before leaving, Smith borrowed a book of poetry.[8]

Reflecting on their time in prison in an 1840 memorial to Congress, Smith and Rigdon wrote that "the horrors of a prison for four long months,

---

3. Joseph Smith, Letter to Isaac Galland, Mar. 22, 1839, in *Times and Seasons*, Feb. 1840, 52 (*JSP*, D6:380).

4. Smith, Letter to Emma Smith, Dec. 1, 1838 (*JSP*, D6:294).

5. The jailers are named in State of Missouri, Mittimus, Richmond, Ray Co., MO, Nov. 29, 1838, State of MO v. Joseph Smith et al. for Treason and Other Crimes, MO 5th Judicial Circuit, JS Collection; Woodson, *History of Clay County, Missouri*, 333. On the prisoners being allowed into the upper floor of the prison, see Alexander McRae, "Incidents in the History of Joseph Smith," *Deseret News* (Salt Lake City), Nov. 2, 1854, [1]; George A. Smith, Memoirs and Autobiography, 123–25.

6. "Extract, from the Private Journal of Joseph Smith Jr.," *Times and Seasons*, Nov. 1839, 6, 8 (*JSP*, H1:486).

7. Alexander McRae, "Incidents in the History of Joseph Smith," *Deseret News*, Nov. 2, 1854, [1].

8. William T. Wood, "Mormon Memoirs, *Liberty (MO) Tribune*, Apr. 9, 1886, [1].

in darkness, in want, alone and during the cold of winter, can better be conceived than expressed."[9] Concerning his incarceration, Hyrum said: "I was confined for more than four months, and endured almost everything but death, from the nauseous cell, and the wretched food we were obliged to eat." Hyrum claimed in his 1839 bill of damages that owing to his long confinement and cruel treatment, his body is "broken down" and his health "very much impaired" so much so that he has been unable "to perform any labor."[10]

Hyrum later claimed that the prisoners were "subjected to the necessity of eating human flesh, for the space of five days, or go without food, except a little coffee, or a little corn bread, the latter I chose in preference to the former." The guard, according to Hyrum, taunted them, asking how they liked the "Mormon beef," implying the flesh was taken from one of their murdered brethren.[11] Wood challenged this story: "As to the 'Mormon beef,' 'human flesh,' 'the flesh of some of their brethren,' all bosh! No Mormon was even killed in Clay county [or] within many miles of Liberty [jail], and no Mormon near the date of their confinement in the Clay county jail."[12] Hyrum was sure it was real human flesh and not simply a cruel joke because he "described the appearance of this flesh to several experienced physicians, and they have decided that it was human flesh." However, Hyrum gave no details about what made this flesh distinctive or how these physicians knew what cooked human flesh looked like.

On December 8 Emma visited her husband with Rigdon's wife, Phebe, and stayed overnight.[13] Emma would return to the jail on December 20 and January 21. Six-year-old Joseph III accompanied her twice. On one visit, as he later remembered, Erastus Snow was also visiting and "sang two ditties or ballads characteristic of the times, which made an impression upon me." He also recounted another occasion when "my father with another, laid hands upon my head and blessed me, as his eldest son, to the blessings which had come down to him through the blessings of his progenitors."[14] On December 10 Wight's wife and four boys came to the jail, remained two nights,

9. Joseph Smith et al., Memorial, to the United States Senate and House of Representatives, Washington DC, ca. Oct. 30, 1839–Jan. 27, 1840, 23 (*JSP*, D7:168).

10. Hyrum Smith, Bill of Damages, ca. June 1839 (DHC 3:374).

11. Hyrum Smith, Testimony, July 1, 1843, in *Times and Seasons*, July 1, 1843, 254–55; George A. Smith, "Historical Address," Oct. 8–9, 1868, *Journal of Discourses*, 13:108.

12. William T. Wood, "Mormon Memoirs," *Liberty Tribune*, Apr. 9, 1886, [1].

13. Smith and Smith, *History of the Reorganized Church*, 2:309.

14. Anderson, *Joseph Smith III and the Restoration*, 13–14; *Saints' Herald* (Independence MO), Nov. 6, 1934; Smith and Smith, *History of the Reorganized Church*, 2:309, 315.

and left on the 12th. McRae's wife and two little boys came on the 13th and remained until the 15th.[15]

Leading the Church from Jail

Meanwhile, on December 10 Bishop Partridge and other church leaders petitioned the Missouri legislature, recounting the persecution of the Mormons in Missouri, appealing to them to rescind Boggs's extermination order, and requesting that they make an appropriation and pay for the losses of the Mormons in Jackson County.[16] The legislature briefly considered the petition but did not take action, mostly "on account of the upper Missouri members being so violently opposed to it, that they used their utmost exertions and finally succeeded in getting a majority against it."[17]

With their leader in jail and having been utterly defeated by Missouri troops, some Mormons began to question their faith in Smith. On December 13 Brigham Young presided at a meeting of the high council at Far West and cautioned them to act judiciously. He reaffirmed that "his faith ... was the same as ever." Apostle Heber Kimball also affirmed that "his faith was as good as ever" and vowed to "keep a straight forward course." Councilor Simeon Carter also reaffirmed his faith, declaring that "he did not think that Joseph was a fallen prophet, but he believed in every revelation that had come through him: still he thought that perhaps Joseph had not acted in all things according to the best wisdom; yet how far he had been unwise he could not say. He did not think that Joseph would be removed and another planted in his stead; but he believed he would still perform his work." Other leaders stated they would stand by the prophet. Solomon Hancock said he still believed in the Book of Mormon and Doctrine and Covenants, and declared that "Br. Joseph is not a fallen Prophet, but will yet be exalted and become very high."[18] Evidently the members of the council were reacting to others who were suggesting that Smith was a fallen prophet and it was time to appoint another in his place, possibly David Whitmer.

On the following day, Smith was visited by Isaac Morley, Reynolds Cahoon, and William Allred, who probably notified him about recent disaffections as

---

15. Smith and Smith, *History of the Reorganized Church*, 2:309.
16. Edward Partridge et al., Petition to the Missouri State Legislature, Dec. 10, 1838; see also Greene, *Facts Relative to the Expulsion of the Mormons*, 211–20.
17. *Journal of the House of Representatives, of the State of Missouri*, 128; Elias Higbee, Letter to Joseph Smith, en route to Nauvoo, IL, Feb. 21, 1840, JS Letterbook 2, 101 (*JSP*, D7:191).
18. Minutes, Dec. 13, 1838, Minute Book 2, 173–75 (Cannon and Cook, *Far West Record*, 221–23).

well as the affirmations of the leaders.[19] On the day after this visit, Smith dictated a long letter to the church that proclaimed his innocence and attacked his enemies.

After greetings, Smith mentioned that their persecutions have been "greatly augmented by the wickedness and corruption of false brethren." Indeed, he was in prison, not for any crime he may have committed, but because of "false witnesses," who have momentarily succeeded but will ultimately fail. "Know assuredly dear brethren that it is for the testimony of Jesus that we are in bonds and in prison. ... We glory in our tribulation because we know that God is with us, that he is our friend and that he will save our souls."[20]

Unable to conceal his anger, Smith attacked those who had testified against him at Richmond. "Look at Mr [George M.] Hinkle. A wolf in sheep's clothing. Look at his brother John Corrill Look at the beloved brother Reed Peck who aided him in leading us, as the savior was led, into the camp as a lamb prepared for the slaughter." He accused them without evidence of betraying him for bribe money: "These men like Balaam being greedy for a reward sold us into the hands of those who loved them, for the world loves his own" (see Num. 22).[21] Hinkle later denied this accusation.[22]

Smith next attacked Phelps, who by late July had joined the dissenters in opposing Smith and Rigdon's militancy and testified against them at Richmond the previous month.[23] Smith wrote, "I would remember W. W. Phelps, who comes up before us as one of Job's comforters," equating him with those who visited Job during his illness and told him that he had perhaps angered God by sinning in some way. "God suffered such kind of beings to afflict Job, but it never entered into their hearts that Job would get out of it all," he said, suggesting that he too would escape his current difficulties. "This poor man who professes to be much of a prophet has no other dumb ass to ride but David Whitmer," apparently referring to Phelps's support for Whitmer as Smith's successor. Speaking of Whitmer, Smith said, "This ass not being of

---

19. Smith and Smith, *History of the Reorganized Church*, 2:309 (Dec. 14, 1838).

20. Joseph Smith, Letter to the church in Caldwell County, Dec. 16, 1838, [1], JS Collection (*JSP*, D6:298–300).

21. Smith, 2 (*JSP*, D6:300–302).

22. George M. Hinkle, Letter to William W. Phelps, Aug. 14, 1844, in *Ensign*, Aug. 1844, 30–32.

23. According to Mormon Burr Riggs, Rigdon said in late July 1838 that Phelps, as well as Frederick Williams and John Corrill, "were using their influence against the presidency of the Church, and further said that Corrill and Phelps were men of great influence in the country, and their influence must be put down." Burr Riggs, Testimony, in Transcript of Proceedings, Nov. 12–29, 1838, [73]–[74].

the same kind of Balaams therefore the angel notwithstanding appeared unto him yet he could not penetrate his understanding sufficiently so but what he brays out cursings instead of blessings. Poor ass." He then predicted that "whoever lives to see it will see him and his rider perish like those who perished in the gainsaying of Core, or after the same condemnation."[24] Korah (Core in the New Testament) led a rebellion against Moses and Aaron until the ground opened up and swallowed them and fire came down from heaven and destroyed those who had escaped (see Num. 16:1–3, 31–35; Jude 11).

As Job had false accusers, so also Smith. Apparently alluding to Cowdery's accusations about Fanny Alger, Smith mentioned that the "dissenters are running through the world and spreading various foul and libelous reports against us," including the charge of "adultery." Calling the dissenters "base traitors and sycophants," Smith conflated the issue with the belief in a "community of wives," which he calls "an abomination in the sight of God." Smith insisted, "We have been misrepresented and misunderstood and belied and the purity of our hearts have not been known."[25]

Smith asserted that the persecution of his followers was due to a conspiracy between "certain priests and certain lawyers and certain judges who are the instigators aiders and abettors of a certain gang of murderers and robbers who have been carrying on a scheme of mobocracy to uphold their priestcraft against the saints." He proclaimed his innocence, denying that he and the other prisoners had committed treason or any unlawful acts. He likened the militia to a wolf in sheep's clothing because he believed it was the mob pretending to be a militia: "The mob-militia ... was a wolf in the first instance hide and Hair, teeth, and legs, and tail, who afterwards put on a militia sheepskin with the wool on, who can sally forth in the day time into the flock and snarl & show his teeth, and scatter and devour the flock and satiate himself upon his prey, and then sneak back into the brambles in order that he might conceal himself in his well tried skin with the wool on." The mob was attempting to "make the world believe that we had committed murder by making an attack upon this howling wolf" that they falsely claimed was a sheep. Nevertheless, Smith denied involvement because he was at home asleep at the time of the battle at Crooked River. "Therefore we say again unto you we are innocent of these things [and] they have represented us falsely."[26]

---

24. Joseph Smith, Letter to the church in Caldwell County, Dec. 16, 1838, 2, JS Collection (*JSP*, D6:300–302).

25. Smith, 4–6 (*JSP*, D6:305, 307).

26. Smith, 3–5 (*JSP*, D6:306).

The Mormons were not only victims of a Satan-inspired conspiracy from outsiders, but there was a secret society seeking to destroy them from within, which needed to be rooted out. Smith denied knowing about Avard's activities until he was imprisoned: "We have learned also since we have been in prison that many false and pernicious things which were calculated to lead the saints far astray and to do great injury have been taught by Dr. Avard as coming from the Presidency … which if they had known of, they would have spurned them and their authors from them as they would the gates of hell."[27] Smith's attempt to deny involvement with the Danites and shift blame to Avard was contradicted at Richmond by testimony from those of his followers who had become dissenters, and he did not hesitate to call them sinners and liars.

Of the dissenters, Smith said: "By a long face and sanctified [sanctimonious] prayers, and very pious sermons, had power to lead the minds of the ignorant and unwary, and thereby obtain such influence," an accusation they leveled at him as well. He then entered into a long diatribe attacking their characters in an attempt to diminish their influence—naming Hinkle, Corrill, Phelps, Avard, Peck, and John Cleminson, all of whom testified for the prosecution during the Richmond hearing, as "ill bred and … so very ignorant that they cannot appear respectable in any decent and civilized society, and whose eyes are full of adultery and cannot cease from sin." Apostle William McLellin, John Whitmer, David Whitmer, Oliver Cowdery, and Martin Harris, the last three being special witnesses to the Book of Mormon, were "too mean to mention," but Smith did anyway. Apostles Thomas Marsh and Orson Hyde, who had signed an affidavit describing the Danite society and the Mormon military operations in Daviess County, were "full of corruption" and "hypocrisy." Concerning such traitors, Smith declared: "Therefore we say unto you dear brethren in the name of the Lord Jesus Christ, we deliver these characters unto the buffetings of satan untill the day of redemption that they may be dealt with according to their works and from henceforth their works shall be made manifest."[28]

He closed by assuring the church that "the holy priesthood hath been conferred upon us, and the keys of the kingdom hath not been taken from us, for verily thus saith the Lord be of good cheer for the keys that I gave unto you are yet with you." He reminded them of the new and everlasting covenant and implored his followers to hold to the faith "even unto death,

---

27. Smith, 5 (*JSP*, D6:306).
28. Smith, 6–7 (*JSP*, D6:307–308).

for he that seeks to save his life shall lose it but he that loseth his life for my sake and the gospels, shall find it sayeth Jesus Christ" (Matt. 16:25). As the redemption of Zion in Jackson County appeared to be slipping farther away, Smith promised: "Zion shall yet live though she seemeth to be dead."[29]

How well Smith's letter was received by the church is unknown, but some leaders continued to criticize the actions that were taken in Daviess County. When the high council met on December 19, council member Harlow Redfield affirmed his faith, but said that "he did not feel to fellowship all the proceedings of the brethren in Daviess county; he thought they did not act as wisely as they might have done, &c." At the same meeting, John Page and John Taylor were ordained apostles by Brigham Young and Heber Kimball, and Edward Partridge and John Taylor were assigned to draft a petition to the US Congress.[30]

The prisoners continued to receive visitors almost daily. On December 20 Emma entered the cell and spent two days, along with the wives of Caleb Baldwin and Reynolds Cahoon. They were visited on Christmas Day by a Disciple of Christ preacher by the name of Howard Evert, on January 3 by Rigdon's wife, as well as Wight's wife and two daughters, and two days later by Cowdery's older brother, Lyman.[31]

Habeas Corpus

At some point, Smith and the other prisoners began working on a petition for a habeas corpus hearing, during which incarcerated individuals may challenge the legal grounds of their imprisonment. This process may have begun on January 8 when attorney Peter Burnett, a colleague of Alexander Doniphan, and Judge Joel Turnham, who later presided over the habeas corpus hearing, visited them.[32] This was apparently the occasion Smith wrote about in his 1839 bill of damages when he stated that immediately upon being committed to jail, they petitioned Turnham for a writ of habeas corpus but "owening [owing] to the prejudice of the Jailor all communication was entirely cut off however at lengthe we succeeded in getting a petition conveyed to the Judge but he neglected to pay any attention to it for Fourteen days and kept us in suspence: he then ordered us to appear before him."[33] On the following day, January 9, Burnett and Doniphan visited the jail, probably

---

29. Smith, 6, 7 (*JSP*, D6:309–10).

30. Minutes, Dec. 19, 1838, Minute Book 2, 175–76 (Cannon and Cook, *Far West Record*, 224).

31. Smith and Smith, *History of the Reorganized Church*, 2:315.

32. Smith and Smith, 315.

33. Smith, Bill of Damages, June 4, 1839, [7], JS Collection (*JSP*, D6:503).

to discuss the upcoming hearing before Turnham. This may have included a plan to present witnesses at the hearing, although that would have been beyond the scope of the habeas corpus hearing. Smith wrote that Turnham "utterly refused to hear any of our witnesses which we had been at great trouble in providing."[34] Burnett returned on the 12th and 13th.[35]

On January 16 Smith and his counselors, Rigdon and Hyrum, wrote to Heber Kimball and Brigham Young and appointed them, as senior apostles, to preside over the church in their absence. They were instructed to fill the vacancies in the Quorum of Twelve Apostles, nominating George A. Smith and Lyman Sherman to replace Orson Hyde and Thomas Marsh, leaving five other vacancies to fill.[36] The presidency reminded the two apostles that they must remain in Far West or return by April 26, 1839, to fulfill a July 8, 1838, revelation that instructed the Twelve to preach the gospel in lands "over the great waters" and to "take leave of my saints in the City of Far West on the 26th day of April next on the building spot of my house."[37] Sensitive to the fact that foreign converts could no longer gather to Zion, the letter states that "America will be a Zion to all that choose to come to it."[38]

The letter may have been carried to Far West by Bishop Partridge, who visited the jail on January 16 and 17.[39] Emma visited the jail for the last time on January 21, along with Rigdon's son-in-law George W. Robinson and church member John Daley.[40]

Responding to the petition for habeas corpus, Turnham held court in the second story of the Clay County courthouse in Liberty on January 22–30 before about 100 angry spectators. At this time, a trial date was set for the 25th. However, the case was continued on the 26th, and then adjourned until Monday, the 28th. On that day, William Wood presented the state's case, and on the following day attorneys Doniphan and Burnett argued for

---

34. Smith (*JSP*, D6:503–504).

35. Smith and Smith, *History of the Reorganized Church*, 2:315.

36. Due to death and apostasy, there were seven vacancies in the Quorum of Twelve Apostles at this time. John Boynton, Luke Johnson, Lyman Johnson, and William McLellin had been excommunicated; Thomas Marsh and Orson Hyde resigned; and David Patten was killed in the battle of Crocked River. George A. Smith would not be ordained until April 1839, and Lyman Sherman died eleven days after this letter was written.

37. Revelation, July 8, 1838, Brigham Young, Journal, May 4, 1837–Mar. 28, 1845, 106[a]–106[b] [D&C 118:4–5] (*JSP*, D6:179–80).

38. Sidney Rigdon, Joseph Smith, and Hyrum Smith, Letter to Heber C. Kimball and Brigham Young, Jan. 16, 1839 (*JSP*, D6:315).

39. Smith and Smith, *History of the Reorganized Church*, 2:315.

40. Smith and Smith, *History of the Reorganized Church*, 2:315; Smith, *Joseph Smith III and the Restoration*, 14.

the defendants, each of whom made a statement to the court. On January 30 Turnham decided that the evidence against Rigdon, who had remained in Caldwell County throughout the raids in Daviess County, was insufficient and released him on bail. The others, however, were sent back to jail.[41]

Turnham's decision to issue the writ of habeas corpus met considerable opposition in Clay County. "In conducting the proceedings before him there was imminent peril," Burnett recalled. Some contended that Turnham was a county judge and therefore did not have authority to review the ruling of King, who was a circuit judge. However, as Burnett observed, Missouri law permitted any court or justice to receive petitions for writs of habeas corpus, but there was an exception, which Burnett failed to mention: writs of habeas corpus did not apply to nonbailable cases like treason.[42] Still, Burnett wrote, "We apprehended that we should be mobbed, the prisoners forcibly seized, and most probably hung." Nevertheless, "all of us were intensely opposed to mobs. ... We therefore determined inflexibly to do our duty to our clients at all hazards. ... We rose above all fear, and felt impressed with the idea that we had a sublime and perilous but sacred duty to perform." They also felt it necessary to employ their friends as armed bodyguards for themselves and their clients. Burnett said he delivered the opening arguments, while the closing statement was given by Doniphan, who delivered "one of the most eloquent and withering speeches I ever heard."[43]

According to Wight, Doniphan subsequently informed the prisoners that "Judge Turnham did not think that we had committed treason, but the responsibility was too great for him; accordingly he remanded us for fear he should offend Judge King."[44] While a habeas corpus hearing is not intended to be an examination of the evidence or an attempt to retry the case, nevertheless it sometimes occurred in the nineteenth century.[45] Rigdon said that it was in Turnham's court that he had "for the first time, an opportunity of hearing the evidence, as it was all written and read before the court."[46]

---

41. None of the documents from this hearing are extant; see Sidney Rigdon, Testimony, Nauvoo, IL, July 1, 1843, in *Times and Seasons*, Aug. 1, 1843, 277; Burnett, *Recollections and Opinions*, 53–55; Smith and Smith, *History of the Reorganized Church*, 2:315–16; Joseph Smith, Letter to Isaac Galland, Mar. 22, 1839, *Times and Seasons*, Feb. 1840, 52 (*JSP*, D6:379); and Smith, Bill of Damages, June 4, 1839, [7], JS Collection (*JSP*, D6:503–504).

42. An Act to Regulate Proceedings on Writs of Habeas Corpus, *Revised Statutes of the State of Missouri*, 297, art. I, secs. 2 and 6.

43. Burnett, *Recollections and Opinions*, 54–55.

44. Wight, Journal, 323 (Mar. 23, 1839).

45. Walker, "Invoking Habeas Corpus in Missouri and Illinois," 372–75.

46. Rigdon, Testimony, July 1, 1843, in *Times and Seasons*, Aug. 1, 1843, 277.

Burnett indicated that Turnham "decided to release Sidney Rigdon, against whom there was no sufficient proof in the record of the evidence taken before Judge King."[47] One reason for the irregularities in Turnham's court was that he was not a lawyer, as Burnett explained. Another factor was mentioned by Meacham Curtis, Turnham's assistant, who remembered the judge stating that "he would have acquitted the prisoners" if not "for fear that they would be assassinated by a furious mob."[48] Rigdon verified that soon after their incarceration, "we heard nothing but threatenings, that if any Judge or Jury, or Court of any kind should clear any of us, that we should never get out of the state alive."[49] Yet, Turnham released Rigdon.

Smith blamed his failure to get released from jail on Turnham's prejudice, his inability to present witnesses, and inadequate representation.[50] In a March 1839 epistle, Smith complained that he and the others should have been liberated with Rigdon "had not our own lawyers interpreted the law contrary to what it reads against us, which prevented us from introducing our evidence before the mock court." He also claimed that Doniphan and Burnett "have of late acknoledged that the law was misconstrewed and tantalised our feelings with it and have intirally [entirely] forsaken us and have forfeited their oaths and their bonds … for they are co-workers with the mob."[51] Two days later, Smith told Isaac Galland: "The Judges have gravely told us from time to time that they knew we were innocent, and ought to be liberated, but they dare not administer the law unto us, for fear of the mob. But if we will deny our religion, we can be liberated. Our lawyers have gravely told us, that we are only held now by the influence of long faced Baptists; how far this is true, we are not able to say: but we are certain that our most vehement accusers, are the highest toned professors of religion."[52]

Fearing the mob, Rigdon remained in the jail until February 5, a week and a half after he was officially released. On the night that Rigdon was to exit the jail, he was so frightened that Sheriff Hadley had to drag him out to the street. Rigdon later wrote, "He took me by the hand and bade me farewell,

47. Burnett, *Recollections and Opinions*, 55.

48. Meacham Curtis, Affidavit, July 23, 1878, *Saints' Herald*, Aug. 15, 1878, 256.

49. [Rigdon], *Appeal to the American People*, 69–70; see also "A History of the Persecution, of the Church of Jesus Christ, of Latter Day Saints in Missouri," *Times and Seasons*, Sep. 1840, 164–65 (*JSP*, H2:280).

50. Smith, Bill of Damages, June 4, 1839, [7], JS Collection (*JSP*, D6:503–504).

51. Joseph Smith et al., Letter to the church and Edward Partridge, Mar. 20, 1839, 5, JS Collection (*JSP*, D6:363).

52. Joseph Smith, Letter to Isaac Galland, Mar. 22, 1839, *Times and Seasons*, Feb. 1840, 52 (*JSP*, D6:380).

telling me to make my escape, which I did with all possible speed." A carriage whisked him away, taking a circuitous route to Tinney's Grove, about twenty-five miles south from Far West in northeastern Ray County, where he was united with his family before continuing on to Quincy, Illinois.[53]

Attempted Escapes

While the prisoners pursued legal means to obtain their freedom, they also made several attempts to escape. Rigdon wrote that because of continual death threats, they became determined to "escape out of their hands as soon as we could, and by any means we could."[54] On January 29 Hyrum's wife, Mary Fielding Smith, visited the jail with her four-month-old infant and sister, Mercy R. Thompson.[55] Mercy, who referred to the dungeon as "a dark and dismal den," later remembered: "The night was spent in fearful forebodings, owing to a false rumor having gone out that the prisoners contemplated making an attempt to escape, which greatly enraged the jailor and the guards."[56]

On February 6 Hyrum suggested that Joseph inquire of the Lord for permission to escape. The answer came in the affirmative. The next evening, according to McRae, six brethren came to visit them: Alanson Ripley, David Holman, Watson Barlow, William Huntington, Erastus Snow, and Cyrus Daniels. Later, when the jailor opened the door to leave, Daniels followed him. Suddenly, Hyrum rushed to the door and tried to hold it open for the others to escape, but the jailor and a guard forced the door closed and locked everyone inside, except Daniels, who tried to flee but was captured.[57] The men were subsequently charged with being accessory to an attempted escape.[58]

News of the attempted jailbreak quickly spread; outraged townspeople surrounded the jail calling for the death of the prisoners. The prisoners were

---

53. Rigdon, Testimony, July 1, 1843, *Times and Seasons*, Aug. 1, 1843, 278; [Rigdon], *Appeal to the American People*, 69–70; Wight, Journal, 316 (Feb. 5, 1839); Editorial, *Quincy (IL) Whig*, Feb. 23, 1839.

54. [Rigdon], *Appeal to the American People*, 69–70; see also "A History of the Persecution," *Times and Seasons*, Sep. 1840, 164–65 (*JSP*, H2:280).

55. Smith and Smith, *History of the Reorganized Church*, 314.

56. Mercy R. Thompson, "Recollections of the Prophet Joseph Smith," *Juvenile Instructor*, July 1, 1892, 398. Mercy believed the visit occurred sometime in February.

57. Alexander McRae, "Incidents in the History of Joseph Smith," *Deseret News*, Nov. 2, 1854, [1]. McRae dated the attempted escape to February 8, 1839, but Clay County records date it to the 7th.

58. Samuel Tillery, Testimony, Liberty, MO, Feb. 8, 1839, in State of Missouri v. Alanson Ripley, Watson Barlow, William D. Huntington, David Holman, and Erastus Snow. See also Samuel Tillery, Testimony, Liberty, MO, Feb. 11, 1839; and Alanson Ripley, Testimony, Liberty, MO, Feb. 12, 1839, in State of Missouri v. Ripley et al. For copies and transcriptions of the documents, see Cottle and Cottle, *Liberty Jail and the Legacy of Joseph*, 88, 93–104.

terrified, but Smith assured them "not to fear, that not a hair of their heads should be hurt." Snow asked if he should hire a lawyer, but Smith advised him to represent himself: "go and plead for justice as hard as you can, and quote Blackstone and other authors now and then, and they will take it all for law." At the conclusion of the trial, according to McRae, the lawyers who were present complimented Snow and asked where he had studied law. Snow was eventually acquitted, but the other four men were released on bail on the 13th and soon after left the state.[59]

Following their failed effort to free themselves, the prisoners devised another desperate plan, which involved cutting through the one-foot square hardwood logs, removing the loose rock, and then pushing out one or more of the large limestone blocks of the outer wall. About March 1, the prisoners began drilling and chipping away at the timbers with an auger, a small hand drill used much like a corkscrew that had been handed to them through the small window by "a friend" whom Wight identified by the name of Shoemaker. In a March 16 letter to his wife, Hyrum described their escape plan, which by then had been discovered: "We made a hole through the logs in the lower room & through the stone wall all but the out side stone which was suffitiently large to pass out when it was pushed out but we were hindered for want of handles to the augurs[.] the logs were so hard that the handles would split & we had to make new ones with our fire wood[.] we had to bore the hole for the shank with my penknife which delayed time in spite of all we could do."[60]

On March 3 Wight recorded in his journal: "This morning hard at work for our deliverance. We expect to go to-day without fail. We have worked hard all day—we could not finish. We will do it to-morrow if the Lord will." On the following day, he wrote: "We expect to make our escape this afternoon without fail. We got all ready to go out, and Shoemaker felt so tickled to think that he was our assistant that he made a confidant of Doctor Moss. The thing leaked out, and there were ten guards called for."[61] In a March 20 letter, Smith and the other prisoners stated that "we applied to a friend and a verry slight uncautious act gave rise to some suspition and before we could fully succeed our plan was discovered. we had evry thing in readiness but the last stone and we could have made our escape in one minute and should have

59. Alexander McRae, "Incidents in the History of Joseph Smith," *Deseret News*, Nov. 2, 1854, [1].

60. Hyrum Smith, Letter to Mary Fielding, Mar. 16, 1839, [1].

61. Wight, Journal, 317 (Mar. 3–4, 1839). The identities of Shoemaker and Dr. Moss remain unknown.

succeeded admirably had it not been for a little imprudance or over anxiety on the part of our friend." In the same letter, the men made light of their attempted jailbreak: "The sheriff and jailor did not blame us for our attempt it was a fine breach and cost the county a round sum but publick oppinion says that we ought to have been permitted to have made our escape that then the disgrace would have been on us, but now it must come on the state."[62] A few days before, Hyrum wrote that "there apeared to be no hard feelings on the part of the Sheriff & Jailor but the old Baptists prisbiterians & methodists were verry mutch Excited they turned out in tens as volenteers to gard the Jail till it was mended. Since then there has been a gard day & Knight."[63]

Quincy

Meanwhile, the evacuation of 8,000–10,000 Mormons from Missouri had begun.[64] The plan was to travel about 200 miles east and gather in Quincy, Illinois, a town just over the Mississippi River.[65] A committee was formed on January 26 to oversee the migration and, especially, to assist the poor, and John Smith, former president of the Adam-ondi-Ahman stake, was chosen as chair.[66] On the first of February the committee resolved to prioritize the removal of the families of the presidency and other prisoners. On February 7 Emma Smith and the children left Far West and arrived at Quincy in mid-February.[67] The next week senior apostle Brigham Young, whom Smith had previously appointed with Heber Kimball to lead the church in his absence, fled Far West to escape enemies and headed for Illinois.[68] On the same day, February 14, Don Carlos Smith left for Quincy with his parents.[69] By this time Rigdon had already left Missouri with his wife and family, arriving at Quincy on February 16.[70]

The residents of Quincy were welcoming toward the refugees. Public meetings of Quincy's Democratic Association were held on February 27 and

---

62. Joseph Smith et al., Letter to the church and Edward Partridge, Mar. 20, 1839, 6, JS Collection (*JSP*, D6:364).

63. Hyrum Smith, Letter to Mary Fielding, Mar. 16, 1839, [2].

64. There were eight to ten thousand Mormons in Missouri in 1838, although Joseph Smith later said there were 15,000. See *JSP*, D6:383n678; D7:152n102, 170.

65. See Hartley, "'Almost Too Intolerable a Burthen'"; Hartley, "The Saints' Forced Exodus from Missouri, 1839"; and Bennett, "'Quincy the Home of Our Adoption.'"

66. See Far West Committee, Minutes, Jan.–Apr. 1839.

67. Far West Committee, Minutes, Feb. 7, 1839; Historian's Office, Joseph Smith History, Draft Notes, Feb. 6–7 and 15, 1839. Vogel, *History of Joseph Smith*, 7:40–41.

68. Arrington, *Brigham Young*, 70.

69. Alanson Ripley Statement, 1845, 2, in Historian's Office, JS History Documents; Anderson, *Lucy's Book*, 680.

70. *Quincy (IL) Whig*, Feb. 23, 1839, [1].

28 to solicit donations to assist poor Mormons in settling.[71] On March 5 Edward Partridge wrote to Smith and others in Liberty jail, giving an account of recent developments and the situation of members who had recently arrived in the Quincy area. "The people receive us kindly here," he wrote. "They have contributed near $100 cash besides other property for the relief of the suffering among our people." He mentioned that Emma was living with John Cleveland, whose wife, Sarah, would later become one of Smith's polyandrous wives.[72] He also mentioned that the wives of Hyrum Smith, Wight, and Alexander McRae were living nearby but that he had not seen Caleb Baldwin's family. "This place is full of our people," wrote Partridge, "yet they are scattering off nearly all the while." Partridge discussed land dealer Isaac Galland's offer to sell large tracts of land to the church, including in Commerce (later renamed Nauvoo), but that he, Rigdon, and Elias Higbee were "of opinion that it is not wisdom to make a trade with the Doctr. [Galland] at present." Partridge closed, "Br[ethre]n, I hope that you will bear patiently the privations that you are called to endure—the Lord will deliver in his own due time. ... We greatly desire to see you, and to have you enjoy your freedom. The Citizens here are willing that we should enjoy the privileges guaranteed to all civil people without molestation."[73]

On the following day, Don Carlos wrote to brothers Joseph and Hyrum announcing the safe arrival of their parents at Quincy. "Father's family have all arrived in this state, except you two," he wrote. "And could I but see your faces, this side of the Mississippi, and know and realize that you had been delivered from your enemies, it would certainly light up a new gleam of hope in our bosoms; nothing could be more satisfactory, nothing could give us more joy." He reported, "Emma and the children are well," and gave information about other members of the family, including that Mary Fielding Smith "has not got her health yet, but I think it increases slowly." He related a rumor: "We just heard that the Governor says that he is a going to set you all at liberty; I hope it's true." It was not. William Smith appended a note to this letter and apologized for not visiting them in jail and promised to take care of their families.[74]

On March 7 Emma wrote to Smith informing him of her departure and

---

71. *Quincy Whig*, Mar. 2, 1839, [2]; "The Mormons," *Quincy Whig*, Mar. 16, 1839, [1].

72. Compton, *In Sacred Loneliness*, 276–78.

73. Edward Partridge, Letter to Joseph Smith and Others, Mar. 5, 1839, JS Letterbook 2, 3–4 (*JSP*, D6:329–31).

74. Don Carlos Smith and William Smith, Letter to Joseph Smith and Hyrum Smith, Liberty, Mar. 6, 1839, JS Letterbook 2, 38–39 (*JSP*, D6:331–34).

arrival in Illinois: "I shall not attempt to write my feelings altogether, for the situation in which you are, the walls, bars, and bolts, rolling rivers, running streams, rising hills, sinking vallies and spreading prairies that separate us, and the cruel injustice that first cast you into prison and still holds you there, with many other considerations, places my feelings far beyond description. ... No one but God, knows the reflections of my mind and the feelings of my heart when I left our house and home, and allmost all of every thing that we possessed excepting our little Children, and took my journey out of the State of Missouri, leaving you shut up in that lonesome prison." In closing, she declared her loyalty to Smith and the church: "I still live and am yet willing to suffer more if it is the will of kind Heaven, that I should for your sake. ... But I hope there is better days to come to us yet."[75]

Second Habeas Corpus

On March 8 the committee on removal met in Far West with William Huntington as chair. Alanson Ripley reported on his visit to Liberty Jail, stating that Smith, reversing years of uncompromising policy, "counseled to sell all the Land in Jackson [County] and all other lands in the State whatsoever." Previously, on February 14, the committee discussed paying off debts in Clay County and appointed Ripley to negotiate with attorney Peter Burnett. Ripley drew up a power of attorney to authorize selling lands to pay off those debts, but the committee was reluctant to proceed. In the interim, Ripley apparently consulted with Smith.[76] At the March meeting, it was also resolved to obtain a power of attorney from Bishop Partridge in Quincy to sell lands in Jackson County.[77]

On March 15 Ripley, accompanied by Heber Kimball, William Huntington, Joseph Noble, and Presendia Buell, visited the prisoners. On this day, Hyrum wrote in his journal: "Many of our brethren & Sisters call to see us & to adminester to our necesities their reward is in Heaven." This was in contrast to those who "Call to see us out of curiosity to view us as they would an Elephant."[78] Buell asked to talk privately with the prisoners, but the apprehensive jailer would not permit it.[79]

About this time, Smith and the other prisoners wrote petitions of habeas

75. Emma Smith, Letter to Joseph Smith, Mar. 7, 1839, JS Letterbook 2, 37 (*JSP*, D6:339–40).

76. Far West Committee, Minutes, Feb. 14, 1839.

77. Minutes, Mar. 8, 1839.

78. Hyrum Smith, Diary, Mar. 15, 1839.

79. Joseph Smith, Letter to Presendia Huntington Buell, Mar. 15, 1839, [1], in JS History, vol. C-1, between 897 and 898 (*JSP*, D6:354).

corpus to "Judge Tompkins, or either of the Judges of the Supreme Court of the State of Missouri" in Jefferson City.[80] In a March 20 letter to the church at Quincy, Smith complained that they have "tryed for a long time to get our lawyers to draw us some petitions to the supream Judges of this state. but they uterly refused we have examined the law and drawn the petitions ourselvs and have obtained abundance of proof to counter act all the testimony that was against us, so that if the supream Judge dose [does] not grant us our liberty he has got to act without cause contrary to honor evidence law or justice."[81] Although Hyrum kept notes on the Missouri habeas corpus statute in the back of his diary, they apparently did not understand that habeas corpus did not apply to them because they had been incarcerated for treason, a nonbailable offense specifically excluded in the statute.[82]

In a letter to his wife, dated March 16, Hyrum mentioned that Ripley and Kimball had visited the jail the previous day and that "we have Sent them to the Judges of the Supreme Court of this State with a petition for a writ of Haebues Corpuss we Expect them back in ten Days. ... We hope that the writ of haebeas Corpuss will Snatch us out of their hands."[83] However, on March 18, the committee on removal appointed Theodore Turley and Kimball to carry the petitions to Jefferson City.[84] According to Turley, the justices of the Missouri Supreme Court rejected the petitions because they were not accompanied by Judge King's November 29, 1838, order of commitment. Turley complained that "Lawyer Doniphan deceived us," having "sent us to the Governor without proper documents."[85] On March 30 Turley and Kimball visited the jail to report their failure. On that day, Hyrum recorded: "In the morning brother Turley & brother H C Kimble came here from the Citty of Jefferson from the Supreme Judges (but did not obtain the writ of Habaes Corpus in consequence of a lack of the order of Committment."[86] When Erastus Snow returned to Jefferson City in early

80. Ripley et al., Petition to George Tompkins, ca. Mar. 9–15, 1839, JS Collection (*JSP*, D6:340–52).

81. Joseph Smith et al., Letter to the church and Edward Partridge, Mar. 20, 1839, 6–7, JS Collection (*JSP*, D6:364–65).

82. See Hyrum Smith, Diary, Mar.–Apr. 1839, Oct. 1840; An Act to Regulate Proceedings on Writs of Habeas Corpus, *Revised Statutes of the State of Missouri*, 297, art. I, sec. 6.

83. Hyrum Smith, Letter to Mary Fielding Smith, Mar. 16, 1839, [1]–[2]; see also Hyrum Smith, Diary, Mar. 15, 1839.

84. Far West Committee, Minutes, Mar. 17–18, 1839.

85. Turley, Memoranda, 1845, [1]; and Hyrum Smith, Diary, Mar. 30, 1839.

86. Hyrum Smith, Diary, Mar. 30, 1839.

April, presumably with a copy of the mittimus, he said "the Judges ... would do nothing about it."[87]

While the prisoners were waiting to hear from Kimball and Turley, the jailor came into their dungeon on March 17 and "found an augur handle he said nothing but went & soon after he came back with a bout 25 men and made search in the Jaul for tools[.] the Jailor apeard to be offended [and] thretned to put us in Chains [but] he soon calmd down and a greed to Call a gain and Settle the matter." The next day, Hyrum wrote: "All things seem calm & Serene the Spirit of persecution appears to be failing [and] the matters of difficulty betwen us & the Jailor is setled no harm done they seem to be more friendly than Ever."[88] On March 19 Hyrum wrote to his wife: "I have been q[u]ite out of hea[l]th to day have Kept my bed all day."[89]

Meanwhile, at Quincy, Brigham Young presided over a church conference on March 17 that excommunicated many of those who testified for the prosecution during the November 1838 court of inquiry, including George Hinkle, Sampson Avard, John Corrill, Reed Peck, Phelps, Frederick Williams, Thomas Marsh, and Burr Riggs.[90]

Letters

On March 19 Mormon David Rogers, on his way to negotiate land deals on behalf of the church in Jackson County with Charles Bird, visited the prisoners at the jail and delivered a packet of letters.[91] Rogers reported, "We visited the Prophet Joseph Smith in Liberty Jail, and then and there made my report of the up-river mission [in Commerce and Iowa] and delivered to him the documents and papers sent by the Authorities at Quincy. And having received his sanction and blessing, we crossed over the river into Jackson County."[92]

Smith spent the following day dictating a long epistle to the church and Partridge at Quincy.[93] As he tried to inspire his followers, Smith's rhetorical power and rough eloquence were on full display, often lapsing into revelatory vernacular and adopting the voice of deity.

---

87. Erastus Snow, Journal, 47–48.

88. Hyrum Smith, Diary, Mar. 17–18, 1839.

89. Hyrum Smith, Letter to Mary Fielding Smith, Mar. 19, 1839, [1].

90. Conference Minutes, Mar. 17, 1839, *Times and Seasons*, Nov. 1839, 15.

91. Hyrum Smith, Letter to Mary Fielding Smith, Mar. 19, 1839, [1]; David Rogers, Statement, Feb. 1, 1839, [1].

92. Rogers, [1].

93. Joseph Smith et al., Letter to the church and Edward Partridge, Mar. 20, 1839, JS Collection (*JSP*, D6:356–72). Parts of this letter were canonized in 1876 as D&C 121.

He began by protesting the unjust and cruel incarceration of himself and others. "Most of you are well acquainted with the rongs and the high toned injustice and cruelty that is practiced upon us," he wrote. "We have been taken prisoners charged falsly with evry kind of evil and thrown into prison inclosed with strong walls surrounded with a strong guard who continually watch day and knight." Then, acknowledging that his exiled followers were also suffering, he then said that their shared affliction had forged an unbreakable bond, writing that "evry species of wickedness and cruelty practised upon us will only tend to bind our harts together and seal them together in love."[94]

After describing recent persecutions in detail, Smith lapsed into an extended prayer filled with biblical allusions:

> O God where art thou and where is the pavilion that covereth thy hiding place[.] how long shall thy hand be stayed and thine eye yea thy pure eye behold from the eternal heavens the rongs of thy people and of thy servants ... o Lord how long shall they suffer these rongs and unlawfull oppressions before thine hart shall be softened towards them ... Streach forth thy hand ... let thine hart be softened and thy bowels moved with compassion toward us[.] let thine anger be kindle[d] against our enemi[e]s and in the fury of thine hart with thy sword avenge us of our rongs.[95]

Reminding his followers that their persecutions were the fulfillment of prophecy about the end times, Smith assured them that other predicted signs would appear, such as the sun being darkened and the moon turning blood red, and then "the time shall soon come when the son of man shall descend in the clouds of heaven." Take courage, for the time will soon come when "God will have our oppressors in derision that he will laugh at their calamity and mock when their fear comith." Follow the example of your leaders in prison, for "our harts do not shrink neither are our spirits altogether broken at the grievious yoak which is put upon us."[96]

Smith yearned for personal contact. "Oh that we could be with you Brethren and unbosome our feeling to you," he said. Nevertheless, he was cheered by recent communications. "We received some letters last evening ... all breathing a kind and consoling spirit," Smith wrote. "We had been a long time without information and when we read those letters they

---

94. Smith, 1–2 (*JSP*, D6:361). Cf. Rom. 8:35, 39; Col. 2:2.
95. Smith, 3–4 (*JSP*, D6:362–63). Cf. Ps. 18:11; 27:5; 89:16; 102:2; Ex. 20:11; Rev. 16–17.
96. Smith, 5 (*JSP*, D6:363). Cf. 2 Tim. 3:1; Joel 2:31; Matt. 24:30; Ps. 2:4; 59:8; Prov. 1:26.

were to our souls as the gentle air, is refreshing but our joy was mingled with greaf because of the suffering of the poor and much injured saints and we need not say to you that the flood gates of our harts were hoisted and our eyes were a fountain of tears."[97]

At this point, Smith seemed to channel God's voice: "When the hart is sufficiently contrite then the voice of inspiration steals along and whispers my son pease be unto thy soul thine advirsity and thy afflictions shall be but a small moment and then if thou indure it well God shall exalt the[e] on high." A few days prior, Smith had compared Phelps to Job's accusers; now, speaking in the voice of deity, he distinguishes the dissenters from his true friends who will not question him about the Danites or the Alger affair. "Thy friends do stand by the[e] and they shall hail the[e] again with warm harts and friendly hands thou art not yet as Job thy friends do not contend again[st] the[e] neither charge the[e] with transgretion as they did Job."[98] Continuing in God's voice, he rebuked the dissenters for testifying for the prosecution at the Richmond hearing, and for suggesting that he and other church leaders had transgressed and were fallen prophets:

> Cursed are all those that shall lift up the heel against mine anointed, saith the Lord and cry they have sin[n]ed when they have not sined before me saith the Lord but have done that which was meat in mine eyes and which I commanded them but those who cry transgresion do it becaus they are the servants of sin and are the children of disobediance themselvs and those who swear false against my servants that they might bring them unto bondage and death. Wo unto them. ... They shall be severed from the ordinances of mine house and ... they shall not have right to the priesthood nor their posterity after them from generation to generation. ... Wo unto all those that discomfort my people and drive and murder and testify against them saith the Lord of host.[99]

Church leaders are not in transgression because they followed the voice of revelation, but rather the dissenters, in being disobedient, are the ones who have sinned. They have been excommunicated for questioning the Lord's appointed leaders and testifying against them, and therefore have no access to saving ordinances. Smith implored his followers not to lose faith. "We think also that it will be a tryal of our faith equal to that of Abraham,"

---

97. Smith, 5, 7 (*JSP*, D6:363, 365).
98. Smith, 7 (*JSP*, D6:365–66).
99. Smith, 9 (*JSP*, D6:366–67). Cf. Ps. 41:9; John 8:34; 13:18; Rom. 6:17; Col. 3:6; Eph. 2:2; 5:6.

he wrote. Similar to Abraham, who at the last moment was prevented from sacrificing Isaac, Smith hoped his followers would trust "that a Ram may be caught in the thicket speedily to releave the sons and daughters of Abraham from their great anxiety."[100]

Smith advised church leaders to be more conservative and deliberative, cautioning them to be "awar[e] of an aspiring spirit which spirit has often-times urged men fowards to make foul speaches and influaance the church and to reject milder councils and has eventually been the means of bringing much death and sorrow upon the church"—a critique that could apply to the fiery speeches delivered by Rigdon, Wight, and Smith himself in previous months. As long as church leaders remain imprisoned, Smith advised that "the general affairs of the church ... s[h]ould be transacted by a general con-ferance of the most faithfull and the most respictible of the authorities of the church." Nevertheless, he instructed that the minutes of meetings be sent to him for review, and if there should be any corrections he would make them, but cautioned that anything coming from him should not be considered binding "ex[ce]pt by commandment or thus saith the Lord."[101]

He advised his followers to leave the mysteries alone and beware of "a fanciful and flowerly [flowery] and heated immagination," for "the things of God Are of deep import and time and expeariance and car[e]ful and pon-durous and solom though[ts] can only find them out. ... How much more dignifide and noble are the thoughts of God, than the vane immagination of the human heart." Be patient, for a time will come "in the which noth-ing shall be with held whither there be one god or many god's"—reflecting the words of the Apostle Paul in 1 Corinthians 8:5. Then, continuing on the theme of mysteries in language reminiscent of the cosmology in his Egyptian Grammar and Alphabet, he provided the earliest reference to his developing theology of a plurality of gods, no doubt sparked by his Hebrew lessons: "also if there be bounds set to the heavens or to the seas or to the dry land or to the sun moon or starrs all the times of their revolutions all their appointed days month and years and all the Days of their days, months and years and all their glories laws and set times shall be reveald in the days of the dispensation of the fullness of times according to that which was ordaind in the midst of the councyl of the eternal God of all other Gods before this world was." Smith was the one with the most experience of spiritual matters,

---

100. Smith, 10 (*JSP*, D6:367). See Gen. 22:13.
101. Smith, 10–11 (*JSP*, D6:367–68).

and he alone was capable of thinking deeply and solemnly enough to penetrate the mysteries of God. Those who stood with him would be rewarded with this knowledge. Near the close of his letter, Smith declared that Mormonism is true because "God is the author of it."[102]

In a letter written to Emma the next day, Smith said he sent his epistle to the church to her because he wanted her to have "the first reading of it and then I want Father and Mother to have a coppy of it [and] keep the original yourself as I dectated the matter myself."[103] On April 11 Mary Fielding Smith wrote to Hyrum and mentioned that she had read this and another epistle, which she said was "food to the hungrey."[104]

In his letter to Emma, Smith tried to console her: "My Dear Emma I very well know your toils and simpathise with you if God will spare my life once more to have the privelege of takeing care of you I will ease your care and indeavour to cumfort your heart." He asked if his dog "old major" was still alive, and what his children—"those little pratlers"—were saying about their father. He asked: "Do you tell them I am in prison that their lives might be saved"? This question was more in keeping with his voluntary surrender, than with the story he later told of being betrayed by Hinkle. He instructed that every member of the church "make out a bill of damages and apply to the united states Court as soon as possible. ... I b[e]lieve that there is a way to git redress for such things." He apologized for his shaky handwriting, saying "my nerve trembles from long confinement."[105]

On March 22 Smith wrote a long letter to landowner Isaac Galland, informing him of the church's desire to purchase land from him in Lee County, Iowa, and in Commerce, Illinois, which eventually occurred in April and June 1839. Smith also discussed the persecution of his people as well as church doctrine at length, which apparently led to Galland's baptism in July 1839.[106]

About this time, Smith continued his general epistle to the church began on March 20, containing reflections on persecution and various instructions

102. Smith, 12, 14, 16 (*JSP*, D6:368–71).

103. Joseph Smith, Letter to Emma Smith, Mar. 21, 1839, [1], JS Collection (*JSP*, D6:373).

104. Mary Fielding Smith, Letter to Hyrum Smith, Apr. 11, 1839, [3].

105. Joseph Smith, Letter to Emma Smith, Mar. 21, 1839, [1]–[3], JS Collection (*JSP*, D6:373–75).

106. Joseph Smith, Letter to Isaac Galland, Mar. 22, 1839, *Times and Seasons*, Feb. 1840, 51–56 (*JSP*, D6:376–88); see also Smith, Journal, Apr. 24–May 3, 1839 (*JSP*, J1:336); Minutes, Apr. 24, 1839, Historian's Office, General Church Minutes (*JSP*, D6:438); Robinson, Agreement, with Joseph Smith and Others, Apr. 30, 1839 (*JSP*, D6:441–42).

to priesthood leaders.[107] As with his first communication, this letter also exhibits Smith's charisma and invokes the divine voice. He begins by counseling Partridge and other leaders to "secure to themselves the contract of the Land which is proposed to them by Mr. Isaac Galland and to cultivate the friendly feelings of that gentleman," as well as with Iowa governor Robert Lucas and attorney-general Isaac Van Allen, and "to lay hold of evry door that shall seem to be opened."

Smith's letter quickly takes a poetic turn when it discusses the traits that priesthood leaders should both cultivate and avoid. "Behold there are ma[n]y called but few are chosen," he began. "And why are they not chosen?" The answer may be read as a criticism of his accusers or as a moment of introspection:

> When we undertake to cover our sins or to gratify our pride or vain ambition or to exercise controle or dominion or compulsion upon the souls of the children of men in any degree of unritiousness behold the heavens withdraw themselves the spirit of the Lord is grieved and when it has withdrawn Amen to the priesthood or the authority of that man. ... We have learned by sad experiance that it is the nature and disposition of almost all men as soon as they get a little authority as they suppose they will imediately begin to [e]xercise unritious dominion. hence ma[n]y [are] called but few are ch[osen. No power or in]f[luence] can or ought to be maintained by [vi]rt[ue] of the Priesthood only by persuasion by long-suffering by gentleness and meekness and by love unfaigned by kindness by pure knowledge which shall greatly enlarge the soul without hypocrisy and without guile.[108]

Smith may have thought he was describing dissenters, but the dissenters were the ones who were accusing Smith of covering up his sins and attempting to exercise unrighteous dominion over them in their economic and worldly affairs and enforcing it through the Danites. Where was his long suffering and gentleness in their cases? If he had listened to them, perhaps things would have turned out differently. The letter slips into the consoling voice of deity as Smith attempted to cast himself as the persecuted and ultimately triumphant hero and the dissenters as villains:

---

107. Joseph Smith et al., Letter to Edward Partridge and the church, ca. Mar. 22, 1839, Revelations Collection (*JSP*, 6:391–401). Parts of this letter were canonized in the Doctrine and Covenants in 1876 [D&C 121].

108. Smith, 1–3 (*JSP*, D6:391–94).

The ends of the Earth shall [enq]uire after thy na[me] and fools shall have thee in deri[s]ion and hell shall rage against thee while the pure in heart and the wise and the noble and the virtious shall seek counsel and authority and blessings constantly from under thy hand and thy people shall never be turned against thee by the testimony of traitors and although their influenance shall cast the[e] into trouble and into bars and walls thou shalt be had in honor and but for a small moment and thy voice shall be more terable in the midst of thine enemies than the fierce Lion because of thy righteousness and thy God shall stand by the[e] for ever and ever.

In a lyrical passage, deity reminds Smith that no matter how bad his situation seems, it pales in comparison to what Jesus endured, and that he should be comforted in the knowledge that he will be eternally rewarded for remaining faithful.

If thou art called to pass through tribulation. If thou art in perals among fals brethren. ... If thou art accused with all maner of fals accusations. If thine enimies fall upon the[e]. ... And if with a drawn sword thine enimies tear the[e] from the bosome of thy Wife and of thine offsprings ... and thou be draged to prison and thine enimies prowl around the[e] like wolves for blood of the Lamb and if thou shouldest be cast into the pit or into the hands of murderers and the sentantce of death pased upon thee. ... know thou my son that all these things shall give thee experiance and shall be for thy good. The son of man hath desended below them all art thou greater than he? Therefore hold on thy way and the priesthood shall remain with thee.[109]

These words of comfort and promise of ultimate triumph were not only intended to encourage Smith, but his followers as well. He must have had concerns about their loyalty. How strong was his hold on them? Could their confidence in him withstand such a severe trial? Indeed, this was the lowest point of his career since the failure of Zion's camp, having lost half of his apostles and many others in leadership positions and, most of all, having lost everything in Missouri, especially the holy land of Zion. His dream of establishing a New Jerusalem, of converting the Indians, of amassing a great army of holy warriors, and of saving the United States was virtually dead.

Smith gave no indication that he was willing to accept responsibility for running the church into the ditch. It was the dissenters' fault. He was following God's will; they were traitors. In truth, the dissenters tried to warn Smith and other church leaders that their increasing fascination with worldly

---

109. Smith, 3–4 (*JSP*, D6:394–95).

power and militancy risked leading the church to destruction. In his discussion of charismatic religious leaders, psychologist Len Oakes noted the need "to control others and to define reality in his terms, so as to always be right; and his refusal to compromise or accept criticisms or appear vulnerable."[110]

The remainder of Smith's letter contains various instructions about church governance, such as not forming communities of common stock or property, blaming the previous failures on corrupt and aspiring men; and for all the Saints to create a record of their suffering and losses and the names of their persecutors. Concerning these instructions, the editors of the Joseph Smith Papers observe: "As well as providing evidence for redress petitions and attempting to draw public sympathy for their plight, the community effort to create history served to strengthen the church's cohesion and solidify what it meant to be Mormon. History, then, became a means not only to share their story, but to forge a shared Latter-day Saint identity."[111] Smith also suggested the possibility of appointing a committee to gather up all slanderous and libelous publications about the Mormons. If any still considered themselves Danites, Smith advised them to renounce their oaths, stating that it was improper to form into "bands or companies by covenant or oaths by penalties or secrecies but let the time past of our experiance and sufferings by the wickedness of Doctor Avard suffise and let our covenant be that of the everlasting covenant as is contained in the Holy writ and the things that God hath revealed unto us. Pure friendship always becomes weakened the verry moment you undertake to make it stronger by penal oaths and secrecy."[112] He would soon violate his own advice with his 1842 initiation into Freemasonry and subsequent introduction of the secret temple endowment ceremony as well as his founding of the underground Council of Fifty in 1844.

---

110. Oakes, *Prophetic Charisma*, 83.
111. *JSP*, H1:xxiv.
112. Joseph Smith et al., Letter to Edward Partridge and the church, ca. Mar. 22, 1839, 5–7, Revelations Collection Smith (*JSP*, D6:396–99).

34

Escape

MARCH–APRIL 1839

Joseph Smith ... with Lyman Wright, Caleb Baldwin, Hiram Smith, and Alex'r M'Rae, escaped from the guard, who got drunk ... Considering the little justice they had reason to expect from a trial in the Boone Court, their escape was justifiable.
——Sangamo Journal (Springfield, IL), *May 3, 1839*

On January 24, the day before attorney Peter Burnett delivered his opening arguments at the habeas corpus hearing, Smith and the other prisoners wrote a memorial or petition to the Missouri legislature, with Burnett's help, requesting a change of venue.[1] This was their second attempt as it mentions having sent another petition "a few days since," which is no longer extant. In the postscript, Burnett requested Clay County representative James M. Hughes to present the petition to the legislature. However, because Hughes had taken a leave of absence, it was probably presented by Representative David R. Atchison.[2]

This petition argued that a change of venue was justified because they "believe that the state of excitement existing in most of the upper Counties is such that a jury would be improperly influenced by it." They also argued that Judge King was incapable of giving them a fair, impartial trial, having "written much upon the subject of our late difficulties, in which he has placed us in the wrong," and "these letters have been published to the world."[3] They

---

1. Joseph Smith et al., Memorial to Missouri Legislature, Jan. 24, 1839, JS Letterbook 2, 66–67 (*JSP*, D6:318–23).

2. See discussion in *JSP*, D6:422–26.

3. See Austin A. King, Letter to Lilburn W. Boggs, Oct. 24, 1838, Mormon War Papers (*Document*, 53–54). King's letter was first published in the *Missouri Watchman* in Jefferson City on October 29, which cannot be located, and reprinted in "Letter from Judge King," *Missouri Republican* (St. Louis), Nov. 2, 1838, [2]; "Letter from Jud[g]e King," *Missouri Argus* (St. Louis), Nov. 8, 1838, [1].

also mentioned that King presided at an anti-Mormon meeting in Ray County on December 26, 1838, "and no doubt sanctioned all the proceedings."[4] In their opinion, the origin of King's animosity against them may be traced to the 1833 Jackson County conflict, during which King's brother-in-law, Hugh L. Breazeale, was killed.[5] Owing to this unfortunate episode, it would only be "natural that the Judge should have some feeling against us, whether we were right or wrong in that controversy." Moreover, they argued, it would be unfair to have the same judge who had just presided at the preliminary hearing and condemned them to prison now to preside over their trial, especially for a capital offense. "We look upon Judge King as like all other mere men, liable to be influenced by his feelings, his prejudices, and his previously formed opinions. ... We believe that from the relation he bears to us, he would himself prefer that our trials should be had in a different circuit, and before a different court."[6] With such compelling reasoning, they would eventually prevail in getting a change of venue.

Last Days in Prison

On Sunday, March 31, Hyrum criticized the inhabitants of Liberty in his journal for not observing the Sabbath Day, writing that they "seem to have no regard for their souls Salvation," but instead "play Cards & ball" and allow "the Negroes [to] run at large." No doubt he was beginning to feel his long incarceration grinding on his soul. "We feel wearyed [wearied] of this prison our beds are worn out," he wrote. He complained of an earache and wrote that Joseph was sick and that jailor Samuel Tillery "seemd to be some what dissatisfied at what was said by us," but did not elaborate. The day was not completely miserable, for their lawyer, Burnett, visited them and while there "made some confessions [and] left us in a good Spirit." He probably informed them that they would soon be transported from Liberty to Gallatin, where they would appear before a grand jury hearing on April 8 and apply for a change of venue. "We Expect to leave next Saturday the 6th of April," Hyrum recorded.[7]

---

4. "Public Sentiment," *Jefferson Republican* (Jefferson City, MO), Jan. 19, 1839, [1]. In early January the Missouri legislature debated King's fitness to preside at the trials after having chaired an "anti-Mormon meeting," but no resolution was reached. *Daily Missouri Republican* (St. Louis), Jan. 8, 1839, [2]; "Letter from the Editor," *Daily Missouri Republican*, Jan. 10, 1839, [2].

5. Breazeale married King's sister, Amanda, in 1827 and was killed on November 4, 1833. *JSP*, D6:323n306.

6. Joseph Smith et al., Memorial to Missouri Legislature, Jan. 24, 1839, JS Letterbook 2, 66–67 (*JSP*, D6:321–23).

7. Hyrum Smith, Diary, Mar. 31, 1839.

On April 1 Hyrum recorded in his diary that "little Doctor King a Brother of Austin A King" came into their cell to abuse them. He told them that he was writing an account of the "Downfall of Mormonism," which they believed would probably be a "liebelious Record," if published, but "he got no Sattisfaction from us." Another prisoner joined them, Horace Corwin, who "was thrust in to this prison for debt" and remained there for three days. The next day, Hyrum recorded that Brother John Dawson passed a letter through the window to them from Jacob Scott, a convert from Canada living in Far West, which was "Insolent and Saucy." They wrote a response, which they gave to Dawson to deliver when he visited them with a Sister Walton on the following day. Hyrum wrote that these visitors were badly treated by the jailor, who "acted Mad and foulish." Hyrum also complained that early in the morning, they "are frequently Saluted at the Door by the Children of the Streets ban[g]ing against the Door saying Come out here damn ye Ill kill you God Dam you Pray god Dam ye Prophesy ye damd Rascals[.] this Is the spirit by which we are treated In this lonesome prison." Powerless to do anything about it, Hyrum consoled himself: "god will take cognsance of all these things and bring them to an awful acount At his comeing If not before that time." While eating dinner the same evening, an old man by the name of McCord, who was "drunk and foolish and disagreeable," was "put in to the Jail for Stabbing a man with a Chisel."[8] In a letter written to his wife the following day, Hyrum said McCord's neighbor was not expected to survive the "five deep and dangerous wounds In his body and … If he does not the old man will have to be hung or go to the penetentionry."[9]

On April 4 Heber Kimball and Theodore Turley came to the jail to report their failure to get a habeas corpus hearing in Jefferson City but had to speak with Joseph Smith from outside through the grate.[10] Smith told them, "Be of good cheer Brother Kimball and Brother Turley no arm can deliver us now but God, but we shall be delivered, tell the Brethren be of good cheer and get them away as fast as possible."[11] Hyrum recorded that Stephen

---

8. Smith, Apr. 1–3, 1839.

9. Hyrum Smith, Letter to Mary Fielding, ca. Apr. 5, 1839. The letter is undated but it was postmarked on April 5.

10. JS History, vol. C-1, 912. This information was added interlinearly by Thomas Bullock and incorporated in vol. C-2, 64, by Franklin D. Richards about August 21–25, 1845. Vogel, *History of Joseph Smith*, 3:281n6; DHC 3:306. This information was supplied by Heber Kimball, who was present on August 19, 1845, when this note was inserted. See Apostolic Review of Book C-1, in Vogel, 7:581. Cf. Heber C. Kimball, Autobiography, ca. 1856, 65, which gives the date March 30, 1839, rather than April 3 as printed in Thompson, *Journal of Heber C. Kimball*, 70.

11. Turley, Memoranda, 1845, [1].

Markham and William Huntington also visited but were not permitted into the jail. Reflecting on the increased security, Hyrum wrote: "This bringeth painfull sensations to our minds to think that our beloved Bretheren take pains to come to see us and then they are forbiden and have to go away grieved with their treatment they received from the Jailor[.] we Pray god that when we are taken from this place we shall fall in to better hands may god give us our liberty is our prair dayly."[12]

The sun was just setting when Joseph wrote to Emma: "With immotions known only to God, do I write this letter, the contemplations, of the mind under these circumstances, defies the pen, or tounge, or Angels, to discribe, or paint, to the human being, who never experiance[d] what we experience." Reflecting on that experience, he continued: "It is now about five months and six days since I have been under the <u>grimace</u>, of a guard night and day, and within the walls grates and screeking [squeaking] iron dors, of a lonesome dark durty prison." With some relief, he informed Emma: "This night we expect; is the last night we shall try our weary Joints and bones on our dirty straw couches in these walls … as we expect to start to morrow, for Davis Co, for our trial. We shall have a change of Venue to some of the lower counties, for the final <u>trial</u>, as our <u>Lawyers</u> generaly say, if law can be adheared to in Davis, as it grants us the privaliege."[13] Smith was anxious to leave and hoped that the petition for a change of venue would succeed where habeas corpus had failed.

Smith continued to cast himself and his people as innocent victims and thereby accepted no responsibility. "There is great thirsting for our blood, in this state," he wrote; "not because we are guilty of any thing: but because they say these men will give an account of what has been done to them; the wrongs they have sustain[ed] if it is known, it will ruin the State. So the mob party have sworn, to have our lives, at all hasards, but God will disappoint them we trust."[14] In other words, charging Smith and the others with treason was a conspiracy to cover up Missouri's mistreatment of the Mormons. But Missouri, by driving the Mormons from the state, actually made their mistreatment more widely known. Missouri was not trying to hide anything. Smith and the Mormons were not heroic victims. They lost the moral high ground when they chose to respond to the Missourians in kind, engage in

---

12. Hyrum Smith, Diary, Apr. 4, 1839.
13. Joseph Smith, Letter to Emma Smith, Apr. 4, 1839, [1] (*JSP*, D6:403–404).
14. Smith, [1] (*JSP*, D6:404).

armed confrontation, raid several communities, and maraud the countryside, burning, plundering, and terrorizing non-Mormon citizenry.

As a husband and father, Smith expressed his devotion to his family: "My Dear Emma I think of you and the children continually. ... I would gladly walk from here to you barefoot, and bareheaded, and half naked, to see you and think it great pleasure, and never count it toil. ... I want you should not let those little fellows, forgit me, tell them Father loves them with a perfect love, and he is doing all he can to git away from the mob to come to them. ... Tell them Father says they must be good children, and mind their mother."[15] No doubt the children were experiencing trauma during the long months of their father's incarceration.

Speaking directly to Emma, Smith said he could "find no fault" with her, but nevertheless seemed to fret about her loyalty: "For God sake, do not b[e] so foolish as to yield to the flattery of the Devel, faslshoods, and vainty, in this hour of trouble, that our affections be drawn, away from the right objects, those preasious things, God has given us will rise up in judgement against us if we do not mark well our steps, and ways. My heart has often been exceeding sorrowful when I have thought of these thing[s]." He then admonished her not to forsake him for his weaknesses: "Do not [be] self willed, neither harber a spirit of revevenge: and again remember that he who is my enemys, is yours also, and never give up an old tried friend, who has waded through all manner of toil, for your sake, and throw him away becaus fools may tell you he has some faults."[16]

Gallatin Hearing

On Saturday, April 6, Smith and the other prisoners were taken from Liberty and escorted about fifty-seven miles to Gallatin under a guard of about fifteen men, including Sheriff Samuel Hadley and jailor Samuel Tillery, whom Hyrum said were "friendly & good Nature[d]." The first day, they traveled about eighteen miles out of their way to avoid Far West and spent the night in Plattsburg. Continuing their journey on Sunday morning, April 7, they became "verry weary" and stopped at an unnamed location, where they spent the night at "a Mrs Tailors." They arrived at Gallatin on Monday, April 8, about noon. Hyrum wrote that they were greeted by "a large Concourse of people gazing & gaping Straining theirs Eyes to see us they Seem the most Ignorant of all Adams Race & more the most savage race that dwells on

15. Smith, [2] (*JSP*, D6:404–405).
16. Smith, [3] (*JSP*, D6:405–406).

the Earth may god grant that we may be delivered out of their hands." A short time later, the prisoners were turned over into the custody of William Morgan, sheriff of Daviess County, and deputies William Bowman, John Brassfield, and John Page, whom Wight described as "the most loathsome and despotic guard they could produce in that county of lawless mobs."[17]

Later the same day, the prisoners were taken to Elisha B. Creekmore's log house, about a mile southeast of Gallatin, because Daviess County's courthouse had been "burned the fall before by Lyman Wight's expedition."[18] Alexander McRae remembered that they were greeted by an angry crowd that rushed towards them, swearing, cursing, and threatening to kill them. Smith calmly addressed the mob. "We are in your hands," he exclaimed; "if we are guilty, we refuse not to be punished by the law." With this assurance, the crowd was mollified.[19] According to Hyrum, they "held council with the lawyers."[20] They were again represented by Peter Burnett, as well as by Amos Rees, an attorney with an office in Liberty. Burnett said the building was "a rough log school-house, about twenty-five feet square," and that "the floor was almost covered with mud," which had been tracked in from the soggy ground around the building.[21]

After spending the day mostly in consultation with their lawyers, the prisoners returned to their lodgings but got little rest, because, as Hyrum recorded, "the gard set up all knight & drank grog & played cards & blasphemed."[22] Burnett, who stayed in confinement with them, later wrote that Smith and the others were "fully aware of their extreme danger. ... The prisoners did not sleep any for several nights. Their situation was too perilous to admit of repose." Burnett also remembered that "Smith and Wight talked almost incessantly," and that at one point "Smith would send some one for a bottle of whisky; and, while he kept sober himself, Lyman Wight would become pretty drunk, and would kindly invite the guards ... to drink with him, which invitation was cordially accepted."[23]

---

17. Turley, Memoranda, 1845, [1]; Hyrum Smith, Diary, Apr. 6–8, 1839; JS History, vol. C-1, 914 (DHC 3:309), which is based on interview notes with Stephen Markham, located between pages 50 and 51 of Joseph Smith History Draft Notes, Manuscript 1. Vogel, *History of Joseph Smith*, 7:499; and Lyman Wight, Testimony, July 1, 1843, *Times and Seasons*, July 15, 1843, 269; see also Baugh, "We Took Our Change of Venue," 63–65.

18. See Leopard et al., *History of Daviess and Gentry Counties*, 75; and Berrett, *Sacred Places*, 4:485; *JSP*, D6:278n66.

19. Alexander McRae, "Incidents in the History of Joseph Smith," *Deseret News*, Nov. 9, 1854, 1.

20. Hyrum Smith, Diary, Apr. 8, 1839.

21. Burnett, *Recollections and Opinions*, 65.

22. Hyrum Smith, Diary, Apr. 8, 1839.

23. Burnett, *Recollections and Opinions*, 65.

On the following day, April 9, the hearing commenced before Judge Thomas C. Burch, who had previously prosecuted them before Judge King at the Richmond hearing in November and was now a judge in the newly formed eleventh judicial circuit.[24] Sheriff William Morgan impaneled twenty residents as a grand jury, and the case against the defendants was presented by circuit attorney James A. Clark.[25] Stephen Markham said "Jury all drunk & Judge, too," and Smith's official history states that Burch appeared to be "as drunk as the jury."[26] While the court was examining witnesses, Markham arrived from Far West with $100 from Heber Kimball and a copy of a statute that the Missouri legislature had just passed, which permitted changes of venue between circuits.[27] Although their January petition to the legislature had led to a revision in the statute, Burch would grant the prisoners a change of venue on different grounds. After court, Markham stayed with the prisoners, along with Josiah Morin, a sympathetic former judge from Millport, and one of the jurymen.[28] As on the previous night, the guards got drunk. Hyrum recorded that "the gard hooted & hollowed all Knight [and] no one slept at all."[29]

On April 10 the court again spent the day examining various witnesses, including Sampson Avard, who at the Richmond hearing had testified about the secret Danite band, but Burch would not permit Markham to testify.[30] On this night, Hyrum recorded, "The guard [was] quite Still & peacible," which allowed him to sleep "in a bed for the first time for five months."[31]

On April 11, the third and final day of the examination, Markham was allowed to testify for the defense, after which one of the guards, James Blakely, said he wanted to speak with him outside. Once outside, Blakely assaulted Markham with a club, but Markham took the club away from him and tossed it over a fence. Ten of the mob, including the captain of the

---

24. Bay, *Reminiscences of the Bench and Bar of Missouri*, 487. Smith's published history names Austin A. King as the presiding judge at the Gallatin hearing, but the court records indicate that it was Thomas C. Burch, who is also named in the July 1, 1843, testimonies of Hyrum Smith and Lyman Wight in *Times and Seasons*, July 1, 1843, 255; and July 15, 1843, 269.

25. Daviess Co., MO, Circuit Court Record, Apr. 1839, vol. A, 43.

26. Stephen Markham, Interview Notes, in Historian's Office, Joseph Smith History Draft Notes, Manuscript 1, between pages 50 and 51. Vogel, *History of Joseph Smith*, 7:499; JS History, vol. C-1, 914 (DHC 3:309); see also Smith, Bill of Damages, June 4, 1839, [7], JS Collection (*JSP*, D6:504).

27. An Act to Amend an Act concerning Criminal Proceedings, *Laws of the State of Missouri*, [1839], 98.

28. JS History, vol. C-1, 914 (DHC 3:309–10; Vogel, *History of Joseph Smith*, 7:499). See also Smith, Bill of Damages, June 4, 1839, [7], JS Collection (*JSP*, D6:504); and Stephen Markham, Interview Notes (Vogel, *History of Joseph Smith*, 7:499).

29. Hyrum Smith, Diary, Apr. 11, 1839.

30. Markham, Interview Notes (Vogel, *History of Joseph Smith*, 7:499).

31. Hyrum Smith, Diary, Apr. 11, 1839.

guard William Peniston, rushed towards Markham and threatened to kill him. Markham, apparently a man of some stature who subsequently became Smith's bodyguard in Nauvoo, warned them that he would kill them with one blow each and they ran off to get their guns. The incident was observed by the court through a window as it carried on with the business at hand.[32]

On this day, the grand jury indicted Smith, Rigdon, Hyrum Smith, Caleb Baldwin, and Alexander McRae for treason, riot, arson, larceny, and receiving stolen goods.[33] The defendants' requested a change of venue on the grounds that Judge Burch had served as the prosecuting attorney in the November 1838 hearing and was therefore not likely to be fair or impartial. This was granted.[34] However, Burch ordered Sheriff Morgan to transport the prisoners 100 miles to Columbia, Boone County, in the middle of the state, even though the defendants had requested to be sent to Palmyra, Marion County, which was about sixteen miles from their witnesses in Quincy, Illinois.[35] For additional security, Morgan hired William Bowman, Wilson McKinny, John Brassfield, and John Page to accompany him.[36]

During the night, Smith awoke Markham and told him that he had just had a vision of his own escape and warned Markham that he was in danger. Instead of leaving Gallatin with the lawyers and judge in the morning, as

---

32. Markham (Vogel, *History of Joseph Smith*, 7:499–500); Hyrum Smith.

33. An indictment was handed down for each charge as follows: Indictment, Honey Creek Township, Daviess Co., MO, ca. Apr. 10, 1839, State of MO v. Gates et al. for Treason, Daviess Co., MO, Circuit Court; Indictment, Honey Creek Township, Daviess Co., MO, ca. Apr. 10, 1839, State of MO v. Gates et al. for Arson [in Millport], Daviess Co., MO, Circuit Court; and Indictment, Honey Creek Township, Daviess Co., MO, ca. Apr. 10, 1839, State of MO v. Joseph Smith for Receiving Stolen Goods, Daviess Co., MO, Circuit Court. Photocopies of these indictments are located in Parkin, Collected Missouri Court Documents. The next two are in Historical Department, Nineteenth-Century Legal Documents Collection. Indictment, Honey Creek Township, Daviess Co., MO, ca. Apr. 10, 1839, State of MO v. Joseph Smith et al. for Riot, Daviess Co., MO, Circuit Court; and Indictment, Honey Creek Township, Daviess Co., MO, ca. Apr. 10, 1839, State of MO v. Baldwin et al. for Arson [in Gallatin], Daviess Co., MO, Circuit Court. Lastly, Indictment, Honey Creek Township, Daviess Co., MO, ca. Apr. 10, 1839, State of MO v. Worthington et al. for larceny, Daviess Co., MO, Circuit Court, Daviess County Courthouse, Gallatin, MO. Note that the Joseph Smith Papers editors have dated the indictments to ca. Apr. 10, 1839, although the docket entries for the indictments are dated Apr. 11, 1839 (Docket Entry, Indictment, Honey Creek Township, Daviess Co., MO, Apr. 11, 1839, in Daviess County Circuit Court Record, vol. A, 57–58).

34. Burch issued removal orders for each charge, which were recorded in Daviess County Circuit Court Record, vol. A, 66–70 (Apr. 11, 1839).

35. Elias Higbee, Letter to Joseph Smith, Feb. 21, 1840, JS Letterbook 2, 102 (*JSP*, D7:192).

36. Order of Commitment, Honey Creek Township, Daviess Co., MO, Apr. [11], 1839, partly copied in William. Affidavit, July 1, 1839, William Morgan Papers. Smith's history and Joseph Smith Papers misidentifies "John Page" as "John Pogue" (DHC 3:309; *JSP*, D6:424 and H2:280n271), although the online transcription of the Order of Commitment reads correctly (josephsmithpapers.com).

he had planned, Smith instructed him to rise early and depart quickly and, when he reached Far West, to tell church leaders that they must leave the state immediately. Leaving town at dawn, Markham was nevertheless pursued by the mob but succeeded in reaching Far West by 9:00 a.m.[37]

As Burnett was leaving Gallatin, he observed Smith "out among the crowd, conversing freely with every one, and seeming to be perfectly at ease." For Burnett, this was proof of Smith's ability to influence others. "In the short space of five days he had managed so to mollify his enemies that he could go unprotected among them without the slightest danger."[38] He recalled that when the court was not in session, some of the citizens would come into the room and converse with the prisoners for hours at a time about theological matters, including two preachers, but that Smith "invariably silenced them sooner or later." Burnett explained that those who attempted to engage Smith were "men of but ordinary capacity, and, being unacquainted with the grounds Smith would take, were not prepared to answer his positions; while Smith himself foresaw the objections they would raise against his theory, and was prepared accordingly."[39] He also reported that Smith won the respect of the guards by throwing their best wrestler, John Brassfield, "to the great amusement of the spectators."[40] Resident Joseph H. McGee said he saw "Joseph Smith throw John Brassfield, the champion wrestler of the county the first two falls out of three. He [Smith] was a powerful man."[41]

Having defended Smith more than once, Burnett was well positioned to give an outsider's view of the Mormon leader. In an 1880 autobiography, he remarked at length about Smith's charisma and leadership, stating that although one "could see at a glance that his education was very limited" and that he was "an awkward but vehement speaker," who "used too many words to express his ideas, and would not generally go directly to a point," Smith was nevertheless "much more than an ordinary man." Smith "possessed the most indomitable perseverance, was a good judge of men, and deemed himself born to command, and he did command. His views were so strange and striking, and his manner was so earnest, and apparently so candid, that you could not but be interested. ... He was very courteous in discussion, readily

---

37. JS History, vol. C-1, 919 (DHC 3:316); Markham, Interview Notes (Vogel, *History of Joseph Smith*, 7:500).
38. Burnett, *Recollections and Opinions*, 67.
39. Burnett, 65.
40. Burnett, 67–68.
41. "Special Correspondence," *Deseret News*, Sep. 10, 1904, 23; see also *History of Daviess County*, 169–70.

admitting what he did not intend to controvert, and would not oppose you abruptly, but had due deference to your feelings. He had the capacity for discussing a subject in different aspects, and for proposing many original views, even of ordinary matters. His illustrations were his own. He had great influence over others."[42]

Before leaving Gallatin on April 12, Smith entered into an agreement with merchant Jacob Stollings, whose Gallatin store had been looted and then burned down by the Danites. Stollings promised to forgive the debts Mormons had incurred at his store if Smith would assist in retrieving his missing account books, which Smith was never able to do.[43]

"Leg Bail"

About 2:00 p.m., Morgan and his four guards took Smith and the other prisoners to Adam-ondi-Ahman, five miles north, where they stayed two nights at William Bowman's home, which he had purchased from Lyman Wight.[44] "The purpose of the layover was probably so Morgan and Bowman could procure some belongings and get outfitted before starting on the journey," observed historian Alexander Baugh. "The officers probably intended to leave Diahman the next morning (13 April), but rain caused them to delay their departure until the following day."[45] Hyrum recorded that they were "treated Kindly," and that "it was with no ordinary feelings to look upon the spot where the Saints were once Dwelling in peace but now Scattered to the four winds of Heaven without a home or shelter & the place a ruined & desolate."[46]

Leaving Adam-ondi-Ahman on Sunday, April 14, Smith and the other prisoners were taken seven miles eastward to Millport, where they spent the night at the residence of ex-judge Josiah Morin, who had returned home from the Gallatin hearing. Hyrum was upbeat when he recorded: "All things tend to be favourable to us the gard verry lenient and Kind the weather fair & pleasant."[47]

The company left Morin's home on April 15, traveling eastward on the main road connecting Gallatin with Chillicothe, located in Livingston County

---

42. Burnett, *Recollections and Opinions*, 65–66.

43. Joseph Smith, Agreement with Jacob Stollings, Apr. 12, 1839, JS Letterbook 2, 50 (*JSP* D6:417–20).

44. Hyrum Smith, Diary, Apr. 12–14, 1839.

45. Baugh, "We Took Our Change of Venue," 66. Hyrum Smith recorded: "Stayed all day at Diaman raind In the Knight some thunder & lightning." Hyrum Smith, Diary, Apr. 13, 1839.

46. Hyrum Smith, Diary, Apr. 12, 1839.

47. Smith, Apr. 14, 1839.

about thirty miles southeast of Gallatin.[48] In his 1843 statement, Hyrum said that when they left Morin's, they "travelled on the road about twenty miles distance."[49] They stopped for the night at the home of a family named Cox, which must have been unpleasant since Hyrum recorded they were "mormon Eaters."[50] On the following morning, April 16, the company continued on the main road traveling directly east about nineteen miles, passing Chillicothe and then setting up camp near a stream that Wight called Yellow Creek, probably near Rothville.[51] They had traveled about seventy-five miles in three days.

Later the same evening, Smith and his companions escaped. "Our Guards getting intoxicated," Smith later wrote, "I thought it a favourable time to Effect our Escape from such men whose aim was only to destroy our lifes. ... Accordingly we took advantage of their situation and made our Escape."[52] There was more to this story. While passing through one of the towns, the prisoners, according to Hyrum, "bought a jug of whiskey, with which we treated the company." Hyrum also later testified that Morgan informed the prisoners that Burch privately instructed him not to deliver them to the authorities in Boone County, and showed them that the mittimus was without date or signature. Morgan said, "I shall take a good drink of grog and go to bed; and you may do as you have a mind to. Three others of the guard drank pretty freely of whiskey, sweetened with honey; they also went to bed, and were soon asleep." The one remaining guard, probably Brassfield, "helped to saddle the horses."[53] A note in Smith's 1843 journal states that "Mr. John Brassfield ... helped Joseph to escape from the Missourians."[54]

On the same day, April 16, Brassfield received a promissory note for $150 signed by Joseph Smith and possibly others.[55] Because the note mentions only that payment was "for value received," there has been speculation about

---

48. Baugh, "We Took Our Change of Venue," 66.

49. Hyrum Smith, Testimony, Nauvoo, IL, July 1, 1843, in *Times and Seasons*, July 1, 1843, 255.

50. Hyrum Smith, Diary, Apr. 15, 1839. Baugh notes that Hyrum made an obvious error in recording that Cox lived in Clinton County, which is southwest of Daviess County, and that he probably meant Livingston County. Baugh, "We Took Our Change of Venue," 79n36.

51. Hyrum Smith, Diary, Apr. 16, 1839; Lyman Wight, Testimony, July 1, 1843, *Times and Seasons*, July 15, 1843, 269; Berrett, *Sacred Places*, 4:490; Baugh, "We Took Our Change of Venue," 66, 79n39.

52. Smith, Bill of Damages, June 4, 1839, [8], JS Collection (*JSP*, D6:504); see also "Extract, from the Private Journal of Joseph Smith Jr.," *Times and Seasons*, Nov. 1839, 7 (*JSP*, H1:483).

53. Hyrum Smith, Testimony, July 1, 1843, in *Times and Seasons*, July 1, 1843, 255–56.

54. Smith, Journal, Feb. 28, 1843 (*JSP*, J2:279).

55. Joseph Smith, Promissory Note to John Brassfield, Apr. 16, 1839, JS Collection (*JSP*, D6:422–26). The note was written in the handwriting of Alexander McRae, but since fulfilled promissory notes were canceled by tearing off the signatures, only part of what appears to be a "J" is visible. The identity of the "we" is uncertain (*JSP*, D6:424).

the nature of the exchange, specifically whether it was for one of the two horses purchased by the prisoners, a bribe, or something else.[56] Hyrum later testified that while at Adam-ondi-Ahman, the prisoners "bought two horses of the guard, and paid for one of them in our clothing which we had with us, and for the other we gave our note."[57] Hyrum did not mention who sold them the horses or when the note was given, but they had stopped at Adam-ondi-Ahman on April 12–13, probably because Morgan and Bowman lived there. A later history of Daviess County names Bowman as the one who sold the horses to the prisoners, but it also claims the purchase took place on the road, forcing some of the guards to return to Gallatin on foot. This same history states that the sheriff and guards were met at Gallatin by an angry mob that "rode the sheriff on a rail and Bowman was dragged over the square by the hair of his head."[58] Less than a month later, Phelps, who at the time was estranged from the church, reported rumors that Smith and the other prisoners had "bribed the guard with six thousand dollars."[59] About the same time, a public meeting was held in Daviess County at which Morgan and his guards were censored for neglect of duty in allowing Smith and the other prisoners to escape. In response, Morgan made a certificate, dated July 1, 1839, stating that the Mormon prisoners "made there Escape without the conivance concent or negligence of myself or said guard."[60]

On June 4, shortly after Smith arrived in Illinois, Bishop Vinson Knight recorded in his account book a $150 debit for Smith for "cash p[ai]d Brass Field."[61] This was apparently unrelated to the $500 Heber Kimball, as the most senior apostle in Far West, said he paid to an unidentified man in late April 1839 who presented him with "an order drawn on me by Joseph Smith ... saying it was for horses furnished him."[62] If the promissory note to Brassfield was not related to one of the horses, it may have been for something else such as a saddle, bridle, or possibly a bribe. Historian Baugh has argued that if there was a payment to Brassfield in exchange for their freedom, it was not a bribe, since "the actions of Morgan, Bowman, and the other guards indicate they had no intention of delivering the Mormon prisoners to Boone County but had been instructed by Judge Burch, in fact, to

56. See *JSP*, D6:424–25.
57. Hyrum Smith, Testimony, July 1, 1843, *Times and Seasons*, July 1, 1843, 255.
58. *History of Daviess County*, 206.
59. William W. Phelps, Letter to Sally Phelps, May 1, 1839, 5.
60. William Morgan, Affidavit, July 1, 1839.
61. Vinson Knight, Account Book, 1839–42, 1, 3.
62. Kimball, "History," 102.

release them at some appropriate time and place," and therefore "it cannot be construed that the Mormon prisoners bribed the guard—but rather agreed to their terms."[63] However, Baugh proposes a distinction without much of a difference. Hyrum's account implies that only Morgan knew the plan, and therefore Brassfield may have been the one guard who remained awake and needed a financial incentive to let them escape. Payment of the bribe may have occurred when Brassfield came to Nauvoo to visit Smith on February 28, 1843, and "spent the day and night."[64] According to Joseph Smith III, who was ten years old at the time, Brassfield and another man came "for the purpose of collecting the amount of the bribe for which they [the guards] had allowed the prisoners to escape." He remembered the amount collected was $800, and said his father and others spent the day and evening "closeted" in a room with the men from Missouri and eventually gave one of the men a "cream-colored or 'clay-bank' horse" to replace the one used during the escape, which was "a fine saddle horse—a dark chestnut sorrel stallion, named Medley."[65]

According to Hyrum, "Two of us mounted the horses, and the other three started on foot," adding dryly, "and we took our change of venue for the State of Illinois."[66] In the nineteenth century, escaping custody was euphemistically referred to as taking "leg bail."[67] In this case, it was horse and leg bail. By taking turns riding the horses and resting, they were able to move quickly on the road in the dark. In this way, they covered the approximately 120 miles to Quincy faster than if all five were on foot. After traveling all night in this fashion, they stopped to water their horses. Reflecting on his flight to freedom, Smith said he was the "worst off" of the five fugitives. "When we escaped," he later remarked, "I jumped into the mud [and then] put on my boots without working [them on] and when I got to water after going over 15 miles [of] prairie my boots were full of blood."[68]

Continuing on the road until about noon, they saw a man coming toward them. Fearing detection, they left the road and traveled on the prairie about five miles without Baldwin, who had run into some hazel brush to hide. They sent McRae on horseback to look for Baldwin, but he returned without him. They continued in an eastern direction, being careful to avoid any

63. Baugh, "We Took Our Change of Venue," 71.
64. Smith, Journal Feb. 28, 1843 (*JSP*, J2:279).
65. "The Memoirs of President Joseph Smith," *Saints' Herald*, Nov. 13, 1934, 1454.
66. Hyrum Smith, Testimony, July 1, 1843, *Times and Seasons*, July 1, 1843, 255–56.
67. Partridge, *A Dictionary of Slang and Unconventional English*, 476.
68. Smith, Journal, Dec. 30, 1842 (*JSP*, J2:199).

inhabitants, until late in the night, when, according to Hyrum, "we lay down on the prarie to rest."[69]

The next morning, April 18, they continued towards the sound of a distant bell, which after traveling five or six miles led them to a plantation run by a family whose closest neighbor was several miles away. After a brief stop, they continued and found a family of Mormons by the name of Harris, who lived in Chariton or Macon County on the banks of the Chariton River, a tributary of the Missouri River to the south. After staying the night with the Harrises, "as we was setting by the fire," Hyrum wrote, "to our astonishment brother baldwin came in" the house. "He had traveled all Knight In the wilderness & providentialy came to us."[70]

At this point, they had traveled only approximately twenty-five miles since their escape, an average of about twelve miles per day, which was half the rate when they traveled with the guards. This was probably due to the loss of time looking for Baldwin. After leaving the Harrises on the morning of April 19, they nearly doubled that rate for the approximately 95 miles that remained. Little is known about the last leg of their trip. Two days later, on April 21, McRae left the group, because, according to Wight, he was "displeased with Joseph."[71]

On Monday, April 22, Smith and his fellow escapees arrived in the morning by ferry at Quincy, where he was reunited with Emma and his children. "After enduring considerable Fatigue & suffering hunger & weariness Expecting that our enemies would be in persuit," Smith later wrote, "we arrived in the Town of Quincy Illinois amidst the congratulations of our Friends & the Joy of our Familys."[72] Dimick Huntington, who had served as a constable in Caldwell County before fleeing the state, gave more details, recalling that Smith was "Drest in an old Pair of Boots full of Holes, Pants Torn, Tucked Inside of Boots, Blue Cloak with collar Turned up, wide Brimd Black hat Rim S[l]oped Down not been Shaved for Some time Looked Pale & Hag[g]ard." Smith, who did not want to be recognized for fear of being arrested, told a surprised Huntington not to reveal his presence. Huntington asked if he wanted to see his parents, who were in Quincy, but Smith declined because "it would be to[o] Great a Shock they are old & cannot bear it." Instead, he said: "Take me to my family as Quick as you can." When

---

69. Hyrum Smith, Diary, Apr. 17, 1839.

70. Smith, Apr. 18, 1839.

71. Wight, Journal, 330 (Apr. 21, 1839).

72. Smith, Bill of Damages, June 4, 1839, [8], JS Collection (*JSP*, D6:504–505).

they arrived at the residence of John and Sarah Cleveland, about four miles east of Quincy, "Emma Knew him as he was Dismounting from his Horse [and] She met him Half way to the Gate."[73] No doubt both were immensely relieved to have put Missouri behind them.

Smith's journal records that he "spent all next day greeting and receiving visits from his brethren and friends,"[74] who had come to welcome him. There was little time for celebration or rest, for he began immediately to make plans for the settlement of his people in Commerce (soon to be Nauvoo), Illinois, and across the river in Iowa. He had escaped Missouri, but there was no escaping the demands of his office and the needs of his followers.

---

73. Dimick B. Huntington, Statement, ca. 1854–56, Historian's Office, JS History Documents.
74. Smith, Journal, Apr. 22–23, 1839 (*JSP*, J1:336).

Epilogue

I have now resided in this neighborhood for several weeks ... but the authorities of Mo., knowing that they had no justice in their crusade against me, and the people with whom I was associated, have not yet to my knowledge, taken the first step towards having me arrested.

—*Joseph Smith,* Times and Seasons, *July/Nov. 1839, 7*

In the July 1839 issue of the *Times and Seasons*, Joseph Smith published an extract from what he called "The Private Journal of Joseph Smith," in which he asserted that although he was a fugitive from justice and living in the open in Illinois, the fact that Missouri officials had made no attempt to arrest him was evidence of their corruption and his innocence.[1] Smith spoke too soon, for Missouri officials had already begun the process of extraditing him and fellow escapees, although formal proceedings would not occur until the following year.[2] In fact, over the next several years, Missouri would make several attempts to arrest Smith and carry him back to Missouri to be tried, all of which he eluded.[3]

The first attempt began in September 1840, when Missouri's newly elected governor, Thomas Reynolds, initiated extradition proceedings against Smith and the other escapees. Smith was eventually arrested near Quincy on June 5, 1841. The case was heard by Judge Stephen A. Douglas, who would

---

1. Joseph Smith, "Extract, from the Private Journal of Joseph Smith Jr.," *Times and Seasons*, July/Nov. 1839, 7 (*JSP*, H1:484). The first issue of the *Times and Seasons* was printed twice. This "journal" was based on Smith, Bill of Damages, June 4, 1839, [8], JS Collection (*JSP*, D6:505).

2. Austin A. King, Letter to Lilburn W. Boggs, June 7, 1839, Mormon War Papers; Burch, Letter to James L. Minor, June 24, 1839.

3. Gayler, "The Attempts of the State of Missouri to Extradite Joseph Smith"; Thurston, "The Boggs Shooting and Attempted Extradition"; Walker, "Habeas Corpus in Early Nineteenth-Century Mormonism"; Walker, "Invoking Habeas Corpus in Missouri and Illinois." On Missouri's attempts to extradite Joseph Smith and the continuing conflict between Mormons and Missouri during the Nauvoo years, see Shepard and Marquardt, "Mortal Enemies."

become famous for running on the Democratic ticket against Republican candidate Abraham Lincoln in 1860. Douglas, however, ruled that the writ against Smith was illegal and discharged him on June 10.[4]

In July 1842 Reynolds issued another requisition to Illinois governor Thomas Carlin for the extradition of Smith and Orrin Porter Rockwell in connection with the attempted assassination of former Missouri governor Boggs, who had been shot through a window in his house and seriously injured on May 6, 1842. It was immediately suspected that Smith had sent Rockwell, who was in Independence at the time visiting relatives, to carry out the assassination. On August 8 Smith was arrested on a charge of being an accessory to an assault "with intent to kill" Boggs and brought before an Adams County judge, who granted Smith and Rockwell a habeas corpus hearing and placed them in the custody of the county sheriff, who turned them over to the Nauvoo city marshal, Dimick Huntington. For the next few months, Smith went into hiding.

On September 20 Carlin issued a "proclamation" declaring that Smith and Rockwell had "resisted the laws by refusing to go with the officers who had them in custody" and that he is issuing "executive warrants" and a reward of $200 for each of their apprehensions.[5] In early December, Smith sent a delegation to Springfield to petition new governor Thomas Ford on the possibility of dismissing the warrant for his arrest because Smith was in Illinois on May 6, the day of the attempt on Boggs's life. On December 17 Ford wrote to Smith refusing to interfere in the acts of the previous governor and inviting him to come to Springfield to have his extradition case heard. Accordingly, on December 26 Smith surrendered to Wilson Law, a general in the Nauvoo Legion, who conveyed him to Springfield, where on December 31 he appeared before Judge Nathaniel Pope of the US District Court. His attorney, Justin Butterfield, motioned for a new habeas corpus hearing, which was granted. Three days after Smith had prophesied in public that he would not be taken to Missouri, Pope dismissed the charges against Smith.[6]

There is little evidence, mostly circumstantial, pointing to Rockwell as the shooter, but Smith's culpability can only be surmised. Rockwell had rejoined

---

4. Walker, "Habeas Corpus in Early Nineteenth-Century Mormonism," 34–39; Walker, "Invoking Habeas Corpus in Missouri and Illinois," 377–80.

5. Proclamation of Thomas Carlin, Sep. 20, 1842, in "Four Hundred Dollars Reward!" *Sangamo Journal*, Sep. 30, 1842.

6. Thurston, "The Boggs Shooting and Attempted Extradition"; Walker, "Habeas Corpus in Early Nineteenth-Century Mormonism," 45–71; Walker, "Invoking Habeas Corpus in Missouri and Illinois," 384–96.

his pregnant wife at Independence nine days before the attempted assassination and was living with his in-laws while working as a stableman in town under an alias, perhaps to avoid persecution. The handgun that was found in a puddle outside Boggs's window was recognized by a shopkeeper as the one that had been stolen shortly after a stranger had come into his store to look at it. Moreover, the suspect had suddenly disappeared and could not be located, although he was subsequently identified as Rockwell. Eight days later, Rockwell appeared in Nauvoo. "If Rockwell was innocent, as the best evidence suggests," LDS historian Glen M. Leonard observed, "his efforts to care for the needs of his pregnant wife had put him in the wrong place at the wrong time."[7] After evading arrest, Rockwell returned to Independence in March 1843 to face charges; a grand jury acquitted him the following December for insufficient evidence.[8]

Boggs had not died, and Smith's reported prophecy that he would die a violent death remained unfulfilled. When the *Quincy Whig* misreported Boggs's death, it added that "Smith ... the Mormon Prophet, as we understand, prophesied, a year or so ago, his death by violent means."[9] After Smith denied making such a prediction in the Nauvoo *Wasp*, he received a letter from Quincy, signed "Hinkel," probably George Hinkle, stating that his denial "wont do, too many people have heard you myself among the rest."[10] On June 30, 1842, Illinois governor Carlin wrote Smith and remarked that he had heard a rumor of his prediction about Boggs as well as another that he (Carlin) should "die in a ditch," but regarded them as "idle boasting," that is, until the recent attempt on Boggs. Despite Smith's recent denial, Carlin told the Mormon prophet that "nothing has contributed more towards fixing the belief upon the public mind, that you had made such prediction, than the repeated statements of a portion of your followers, that the manner of his death had been revealed to you, and their exultation that it must [nee]ds be fulfilled."[11] Even if one were to conclude Rockwell was the shooter, it would remain unclear if he acted on his own or under Smith's direction.

Yet another attempt to arrest and extradite Smith to Missouri occurred

---

7. Leonard, *Nauvoo*, 280.

8. McLaws, "The Attempted Assassination of Missouri's Ex-Governor, Lilburn W. Boggs"; Schindler, *Orrin Porter Rockwell*, 74–82.

9. "Assassination of Ex-Governor Boggs of Missouri," *Quincy (IL) Whig*, May 21, 1842, [3].

10. *Wasp* (Nauvoo, IL), May 28, 1842, [2]; "Hinkle," Letter to Joseph Smith, June 12, 1842, JS Collection (*JSP*, D10:142).

11. Thomas Carlin, Letter to Joseph Smith, June 30, 1842, in JS Letterbook 2, 238–39 (*JSP*, D10:212–13).

in June 1843 while he was visiting relatives in Dixon, Illinois. On June 17 Governor Ford issued an arrest warrant for Smith in connection with the Missouri treason charge of June 10. When Stephen Markham and William Clayton arrived at Dixon from Nauvoo to warn him, Smith declared "he had no fear for he knew they could not hurt him."[12] On June 23 Joseph Reynolds, sheriff of Jackson County, and Constable Harmon Wilson of Carthage, Illinois, arrested Smith at his brother-in-law's. On the following day, Smith hired several attorneys, who obtained a writ of habeas corpus returnable before Judge John Caton at Ottowa, Illinois. On June 26, after learning Caton was unavailable, Smith secured a second writ of habeas corpus at Dixon, which was returnable before Judge Stephen Douglas in Quincy. On June 27, near Geneseo, Illinois, still in the custody of Reynolds and Wilson, Smith was joined by members of the Nauvoo Legion and, shedding tears of joy, said, "I am not going to Missouri this time. These are my boys." Smith convinced his lawyers that the nearest place where writs of habeas corpus could be heard was Nauvoo. The Municipal Court of Nauvoo held a habeas corpus hearing on July 1, during which testimony was given by Hyrum Smith, Parley Pratt, George Pitkin, Brigham Young, Lyman Wight, and Sidney Rigdon. On July 2 the court ordered Smith discharged "for want of substance in the warrant ... as well as upon the merits of the case."[13]

Anticipating his acquittal, Smith addressed a congregation of thousands on June 30 and defended Nauvoo's unusual charter and the city council's August 1842 ordinance granting the municipal court "power to go behind the writ [of habeas corpus]. & try the merits of the case." This broad interpretation of habeas corpus and city ordinance was controversial because it made it virtually impossible to extradite Smith, no matter the merits. Another ordinance that was passed the following November strengthened the previous one and included punishment for arresting officers who attempted to abuse the legal process to harass Nauvoo citizens.[14] Apostle Wilford Woodruff, who attended the meeting at Smith's home as a Nauvoo alderman, recorded that "after it was passed Joseph felt secure to stay at home as the law protected him as well as all other citizens."[15] Willard Richards captured Smith's hyperbolic style of oratory when he recorded

---

12. William Clayton, Journal, June 21, 1843, CHL, quoted in Allen, *No Toil nor Labor Fear*, 400.

13. "Missouri *vs* Joseph Smith," *Times and Seasons*, July 1, 1843, 241–56; "Trial of Joseph Smith," *Times and Seasons*, July 15, 1843, 257–72; and Aug. 1, 1843, 273–78. See also Leonard, *Nauvoo*, 282–84.

14. Dinger, *The Nauvoo City and High Council Minutes*, xxxiii–xxxv.

15. Woodruff, Journal, Nov. 12, 1842 (Vogel, *The Wilford Woodruff Journals*, 1:517).

in Smith's journal: "Deny me the right of H. Corpus & I will. fight with gu[n]s swo[r]d cann[on] behind & thunder till I am used up." Still, Smith declared his intention to fight extradition, even if his legal barriers failed: "Before I will be dragged again away among my enemies. for trial I will spill the la[s]t drop of blood in my veins. [and] see all my enemies to hell." He then asked his followers: "Shall we bear it any longer." The response was "one Universal NO. [which] ran through all th[e] va[s]t assembly like on[e] vast peal of thunder."[16] Scribe William Clayton recorded that Smith "also said that he had restrained the saints from using violence in self defense, but from henceforth he restrained them no more."[17] Smith believed that if he were ever taken to Missouri, he would be killed.

While Smith was eluding Missouri officials, he made repeated attempts to petition Washington for help in recovering financial losses suffered in the Mormon expulsion from Missouri. During his incarceration in Liberty jail, Smith had instructed that every member of the church "make out a bill of damages and apply to the united states Court as soon as possible. ... I b[e]lieve that there is a way to git redress for such things."[18] On May 4–5, 1839, Smith presided at a general church conference in Quincy, where it was decided that Rigdon should travel to Washington, DC, to appeal to the federal government to intervene in Missouri on behalf of the Mormon people.[19] Church members were asked to document their financial losses, and Smith produced his own bill of damages on June 4, claiming $100,000 in losses.[20] When Smith, Rigdon, Elias Higbee, and Orrin Rockwell left Commerce in a two-horse carriage for Washington, DC, on October 29, they carried with them a twenty-eight-page memorial and 481 bills seeking redress for Mormon losses in Missouri.[21] Smith and Higbee reported that during their November 29 visit with President Martin Van Buren, he claimed: "What can I do? I can do nothing for you! If I do anything, I shall come in contact with

16. Smith, Journal, June 30, 1843 (*JSP*, D12:420, 422; Ehat and Cook, *The Words of Joseph Smith*, 222–24). On Nauvoo's habeas corpus ordinance, see Dinger, *The Nauvoo City and High Council Minutes*, 89–90, 101–102, 104–105.

17. Clayton, Journal, June 30, 1843 (Ehat and Cook, *The Words of Joseph Smith*, 225).

18. Joseph Smith, Letter to Emma Smith, Mar. 21, 1839, [2], JS Collection (*JSP*, D6:374).

19. Minutes, Quincy, IL, 4–5 May 1839, [3], Historian's Office, General Church Minutes (*JSP*, D6:446).

20. Smith, Bill of Damages, June 4, 1839, JS Collection (*JSP*, D6:492–505).

21. JS History, vol. C-1, 972 (DHC 4:19); Joseph Smith et al., Memorial to the United States Senate and House of Representatives, ca. Oct. 30, 1839–Jan. 27, 1840 (*JSP*, D7:138–74); Johnson, "The Missouri Redress Petitions"; Johnson, ed., *Mormon Redress Petitions*.

the whole state of Missouri."[22] The petition was referred to the senate judiciary committee, which rejected it as beyond their authority and suggested that the petitioners seek relief in the courts.[23] Smith returned to Commerce in early March 1840 empty-handed.

The lack of response in Washington angered Smith and his followers. Historian Kenneth H. Winn has observed that Mormons "became obsessed with the wrongs they had suffered, and in their circumscribed world, their sense of injury remained ever fresh, reverberating from the pulpit to the flock and back again, coloring all of their subsequent thought and action."[24] A second delegation went to Washington in 1842, and yet another in 1844, both of which were equal failures.[25] "In all," writes historian Glen Leonard, "the financial claims against Missouri amounted to nearly $2.4 million in more than eight hundred petitions from nearly seven hundred individuals."[26] Apostle Orson Hyde wrote to Smith from Washington on June 11, 1844: "We are now thrown back upon our own resources. We have tried every department of government to obtain our rights, but we cannot find them."[27]

Meanwhile, in early 1841, Missouri's legislature reversed an earlier decision and approved the publication of the evidence, correspondence, and documents associated with the Mormon war. In December 1838 publication had been blocked for fear of embarrassing the state. However, when the Mormons began publishing their views on the Missouri conflict, the legislature felt a need to respond but not to investigate.[28] Nevertheless, they acknowledged that the publication was limited and that Judge King's preliminary hearing was a one-sided examination.[29]

On April 26, 1839, seven apostles, including newly ordained Wilford Woodruff and George A. Smith, met at Far West secretly in the middle of the night to lay a cornerstone of the temple and to fulfill Smith's April 26 and July 8, 1838, revelations commanding that the temple construction begin

---

22. Joseph Smith and Elias Higbee, Letter to Hyrum Smith, Dec. 5, 1839, JS Letterbook 2, 85–88 (*JSP*, D7:69); Johnson, *Mormon Redress Petitions*, 101–19.

23. Senate Judiciary Committee, Report on the Memorial of the Delegation of the Latter Day Saints, Mar. 4, 1840, Senate Doc. 247, 26th Cong., 1st Sess. (1840), Library of Congress; see also Sidney Rigdon, Letter to Joseph Smith, Apr. 3, 1840, JS Letterbook 2, 125–26 (*JSP*, D7:239–40).

24. Winn, *Exiles in a Land of Liberty*, 156.

25. Johnson, ed., *Mormon Redress Petitions*, xxi–xxii, 393–410, 563–614.

26. Leonard, *Nauvoo*, 276. In current dollars, this would be approximately $94,819,520.

27. Orson Hyde, Letter to Joseph Smith, June 11, 1844, JS Collection.

28. Gentry and Compton, *Fire and Sword*, 497–501.

29. "Legislative Proceedings," *Document*, 2.

on this day and predicting that on the same day the Twelve would leave on a mission to the British Isles starting at the temple site.[30] Within days of the event, Phelps, who was still out of the church at this time, wrote to his wife from Far West and scoffed that it was one of the "forcible tricks of the mormons ... undoubtedly done to strengthen the faith of weak members, and for effect abroad." While Smith was relocating his people and building anew in Illinois, Far West had nearly become a ghost town. "The inhabitants are gone," Phelps wrote. "The sound of the hammer, and the bustle of business have ceased; The grass is growing in the streets. ... The fences have disappeared, and nothing but empty houses, and the moaning of the spring breeze, tell what was in Zion (so revealed.) My love of it has vanished."[31]

Oliver Huntington, younger brother of Dimick, later remarked, "When the Saints were driven from the state of Missouri it was a very surprising circumstance that we could not understand. We naturally asked ourselves the question, 'Where can we find another Holy land? How or when shall we get back to the consecrated spot for the New Jerusalem, that is to be built?'" He then explained how some believers resolved this predicament: "Our only hope was that as God had given us a prophet he would certainly tell us how to manage and where to go, or what to do. Oh! what confidence we had in that man! What comfort we derived through our faith in God and Joseph Smith. How little we knew of the great future, and for that one thing I feel very thankful! Joseph finally led us to Nauvoo. Under his all-inspiring words, we quickly resolved, 'We will stay here as long as Joseph wants us to—he knows what is best.'"[32] Smith's charisma was such that he could inspire followers to continue to sacrifice despite clear evidence that his spiritual gift was fallible, much as he had done as a treasure seer in his youth. Whether treasure or the New Jerusalem, the more his followers were invested, the harder it was for them to abandon faith in obtaining the prize—which because of demonic forces kept slipping away.

Apostle Parley Pratt was less patient. Troubled by the loss of Zion and the non-fulfillment of Mormonism's central prophecy, Pratt sought "a word of encouragement" from the Mormon prophet. Writing from his mission field in Manchester, England, on December 4, 1841, after having escaped

---

30. Revelation, Apr. 26, 1838, in Smith, Journal, Mar.–Sep. 1838, 33, [D&C 115:11] (*JSP*, J1:258–60; D6:115–16); Revelation, Far West, MO, July 8, 1838–A, in Smith, Journal, Mar.–Sep. 1838, 55 [D&C 118:4–5] (*JSP*, J1:285).

31. William W. Phelps, Letter to Sally Phelps, May 1, 1839, 4.

32. Oliver B. Huntington, Letter to Editor, *Young Woman's Journal* (Salt Lake City), Apr. 1891, 314–15.

jail in Missouri, Pratt asked Smith: "When Will The *'purchased possesion'* be Redeemed and the temple and city commence in Jackson Co, Mo.[?] ... When Will the ungodly, lying, Gentiles begin to loose their Power and cease to Rule; and We who have now spent half our lives for them be privaledged to turn from the Gentiles and go in full power to the Remnants of joseph [Indians] and Israel?"[33] Pratt's petition apparently went unanswered.

However, Smith had previously answered such questions in sermons by expanding the definition of Zion and deemphasizing Zion as the only place of refuge. In the summer of 1839, he declared: "The time is soon coming when no man will have any peace but in Zion & her Stakes." He also spoke of the signs that should precede the Second Coming: "These things are at our doors," but "I know not how soon these things will take place."[34] In another sermon, delivered about July 19, 1840, Smith read the parable of the twelve olive trees from an 1833 revelation and then remarked: "The Land of Zion ... consists of all N. & S America but that any place where the Saints gather is Zion which every righteous man will build up for a place of safety for his children that The olive trees are 12 stakes which are yet to be built not the Temple in Jackson as some suppose for while the 12 olive stakes are being built we will be at peace but the Nations of the Earth will be at war." This was a major shift. Instead of fleeing to Jackson County for safety, Smith instructed the Saints to seek refuge in Zion's scattered stakes. "The redemption of Zion is the redemption of all N & S America," he explained, "and those 12 stake[s] must be built up before the redemption of Zion can take place." What had seemed imminent in the early 1830s, Smith now moved to an unspecified and more distant future: "Zion and Jerusalem ... must both be built up before the coming of Christ. ... How long will it take to do this 10 years yes more than 40 years will pass before this work will be accomplished and when these cities are built then shall the coming of the son of man be." Finally, he declared:

> I prophecy that the time shall be when these saints shall ride proudly over the mountains of Missouri and no Gentile dog nor Missouri dog Shall dare lift a tongue against them but will lick up the dust from beneath their feet and I pray the father that many here may realize this and see it with their eyes And if it should be (Stretching his hand towards the place and in a melancholly tone that made all hearts tremble) [the] will of God that I might

33. Parley P. Pratt, Letter to Joseph Smith, Dec. 4, 1841, [1], [2], JS Collection (*JSP*, D9:12, 13).
34. Joseph Smith, Discourse, ca. June 26–Aug. 4, 1839, in Willard Richards, "W. Richards Pocket Companion," 70–71 (*JSP*, D6:547).

live to behold that temple completed and finished from the foundation to the top stone I will say Oh Lord it is enough Lord let thy servant depart in peace which is my ernest prayer in the name of the L[ord] Jesus Amen.[35]

On January 19, 1841, Smith dictated a revelation that rescinded the "commandment ... to build up a city and a house unto my name, in Jackson county, Missouri" (D&C 124:49, 51).[36] By the time he received Pratt's questions, he was apparently receiving criticism for this revelation, responding publicly on December 19, 1841: "A man would Command his Son to dig potatoes, saddle his horse but before he had done either tell him to do sumthing els[e]. this is all considered right. But as soon as the Lord gives a commandment & revokes that decree & commands sumthing els[e] then the prophet is considerd fallen &c."[37]

Many of his followers continued to believe in the September 1832 prophecy that the temple "shall be reared in this generation" and that "this generation shall not all pass away until an house shall be built unto the Lord" in Jackson County, Missouri (D&C 84:4). Smith's Zion would be delayed, but not indefinitely. Mormon millennial expectations were reignited in the period of national calamity surrounding the Civil War.[38] Mormon leader George Q. Cannon declared in 1864 that "the day is near when a Temple shall be reared in the Center Stake of Zion, and the Lord has said his glory shall rest on that House in this generation in which the revelation was given, which is upwards of thirty years ago."[39] Apostle Orson Pratt said in 1870 that Mormons in Utah still had "confidence in returning to Jackson county and the building of a great central city. ... There are many of the old stock ... still living, whose faith in returning to Jackson county ... is as firm and fixed as the throne of the Almighty."[40] On August 23, 1862, Wilford Woodruff recorded in his journal that Brigham Young said the Saints "have to go back to Jackson County which [he] Expet[s] will be in 7 years."[41]

Historian John G. Gager has discussed the process by which millenarian movements survive failure and noted that Smith too responded to the

35. Joseph Smith, Discourse, ca. July 19, 1840, Martha Jane Coray, Notebook, [9]–[10], [15], [21]–[22] (*JSP*, D7:341, 343–45). For the parable, see D&C 101:43–62.

36. See *JSP*, D7:519.

37. Woodruff, Journal, Dec. 19, 1841 (Vogel, *The Wilford Woodruff Journals*, 1:486; *JSP*, D9:34).

38. Erickson, *As a Thief in the Night*, 163–77.

39. George Q. Cannon, "The Increase of Faith among the Saints," Oct. 23. 1864, *Journal of Discourses*, 10:344.

40. Orson Pratt, "The Latter-day Kingdom of God," Apr. 10, 1870, *Journal of Discourses*, 13:138.

41. Woodruff, Journal, Aug. 23, 1862 (Vogel, *The Wilford Woodruff Journals*, 3:519.

non-fulfillment of prophecy by blaming his followers' lack of faith. Smith employed various strategies to overcome the failure of charisma like redefining Zion, doubling down on prophecy, altering his revelations, and shifting the focus on unfulfilled pre-conditions such as establishing twelve stakes and preaching the Mormon gospel in every nation. Gager also noted that Smith predictably guided his followers away from preparing for the end of the world and redirected their energies toward missionary work and building the kingdom.[42] Another strategy was his repeated promises for greater and greater blessings and authority; most notably, the 1831 endowment of high priesthood, the 1836 spiritual endowment in the Kirtland Temple, and his 1842 temple endowment ceremony and reception of special keys in Nauvoo.

German sociologist Max Weber would not have been surprised to learn that Smith responded to challenges to his charisma by institutionalizing authority, expanding the church's hierarchy, and introducing a more legal concept of authority, aided by his and Oliver Cowdery's accounts of angelic ordinations.[43] By sharing and expanding authority Smith fostered group cohesion and created incentives for continued participation despite persecution and charismatic failings. The elaborate structure also helped to insulate Smith, especially as his weaknesses and indiscretions became public. As Weber observed, in the institutionalization of charisma, "the charismatic qualities and powers of the office are emancipated from the personal qualities of the priest."[44] Indeed, Smith was no longer a prophet-leader relying on his revelatory powers to outmaneuver challengers but had become president of the church with the authority of his office to lead and now could only be removed through a difficult and legalistic process. As Catholic sociologist Thomas O'Dea noted, "Even the overwhelming unpopularity that he [Smith] experienced after the Kirtland bank failure of 1837 could not upset what had been accomplished." By the time of Smith's death in mid-1844, continued O'Dea, "charisma had been successfully contained within the organized structure of the church and identified with the functions of church office."[45] After all, as Len Oakes noted in his study of charismatic prophets, "perhaps they do succeed, but in a different way" than they originally intended.[46]

---

42. Gager, "Early Mormonism and Early Christianity," 56–57. See also Gager, *Kingdom and Community*, esp. 37–49; L. Festinger et al., *When Prophecy Fails*.

43. Eisenstadt, *Max Weber on Charisma and Institution Building*, 54.

44. Eisenstadt, 57.

45. O'Dea, *The Mormons*, 159, 160.

46. Oakes, *Prophetic Charisma*, 183.

The road to and from Zion was littered with the bodies of those who tried to divert Smith from his quest for both temporal and ecclesiastical power. Smith never admitted the mistakes he made in Ohio and Missouri or accepted blame for what happened at Crooked River. It was always the fault of others: dissenters and anti-Mormons. His son, Joseph III, who became leader of the Reorganized Church of Jesus Christ of Latter Day Saints in 1860, said his father and others erred in becoming militaristic. "I believe it was a mistake to allow the spirit of militarism to take possession of the leading authorities of the church," he wrote in his memoirs. "Blame for some of the warlike disposition among the people has been visited upon the Prophet Joseph Smith, my father. But it must be remembered that from 1830 to the time of his death, he and his people were never safe from invasion and persecution from which the Saints were well worn out. ... Looking back along the pathway I feel it was a pity that such a spirit crept in among them, however, and a still greater one that the leading minds of the church partook of it."[47] The militarism of Missouri continued in Nauvoo, which had its own legion of up to 4,000 troops, with Smith holding the rank of Lieutenant General.

Smith's narcissism was present from the beginning, but the trauma of near execution and extended incarceration may have triggered the need to feel invulnerable, seeking power, protection, and control. This may have manifested itself in his attraction to the trappings of the military, and even his rapid escalation of plural (and polyandrous) marriages beginning in 1841 that placed him in a dominant role over first husbands. With Smith, it was about power most of all. He was not satisfied with secret affairs, but drew others into the unions as enablers and groomers and created a web of coercive connections, believing he would be insulated and protected by his extended family alliances. Those women who were cajoled and coerced into participating, despite strong religious, moral, and emotional barriers, sacrificed themselves in demonstration of their loyalty to their leader.

Whatever feelings of helplessness Smith may have felt during his Missouri incarceration were seemingly pushed aside as his sermons and teachings began to display increasing grandiosity, even megalomania. On Sunday, May 26, 1844, a month before his murder, Smith proclaimed that despite his enemies, whom he called liars, "I will come out on the top at last." Then he declared: "I have more to boast of than ever any man had. I am the only man that has ever been able to keep a whole church together since the days

---

47. Anderson, *Joseph Smith III and the Restoration*, 42–43.

of Adam—a large majority of the whole have stood by me:—neither Paul, John, Peter nor Jesus never did it. I boast that no man ever did such a work as me—the followers of Jesus ran away from him, the Latter Day Saints never ran away from me yet." Smith also boasted that he had "suffered more than Paul," adding: "I should be like a fish out of water if I were out of persecution; perhaps my brethren think it requires all this to keep me humble—the Lord has constituted me so curiously that I glory in persecution."[48]

In Nauvoo, Smith expanded his concept of the godhead to include a council of gods and implied that he was among them. When he published the second installment of his Book of Abraham in March 1842, it contained newly translated material about the pre-existence of humans as spirit intelligences and creation by a council of gods. Hebrew prophet Abraham was told that he was one of the great spirits over which the Son presided and that he had participated in the Creation and therefore was chosen before birth—and, by implication, so was Smith.[49] He believed it, but dared not speak it. An oft-told story handed down among his followers in early Utah was that Smith had once said: "Would to God, brethren, I could tell you who I am! Would to God I could tell you what I know! But you would call it blasphemy, and there are men upon this stand who would want to take my life."[50] He left his followers to puzzle and argue about his true identity.[51]

The protective bubble Smith created through a network of secret marriages and rituals and a coercive and corrupt hold on the machinery of government, administration of justice, and law enforcement in Nauvoo could not save him. It was bound to burst, sooner or later. And when it did, it was violent and final—or so it seemed to his enemies. They could not have anticipated what would happen next, for they had assumed Mormonism could not survive the death of its founder. They could not have been more wrong.

---

48. "Sermon of Joseph the Prophet May 26 1844," 1–2, JS Collection (Vogel, *History of Joseph Smith*, 7:424). Cf. DHC 6:408–409.

49. *Times and Seasons*, Mar. 15, 1842, 719–22. Cf. Abr. 3:21–24; 4:1.

50. Orson F. Whitney, *Life of Heber C. Kimball*, 332–33. Whitney introduces the quote by stating: "Had not Joseph said many times—are not men now living who heard him say."

51. Blythe, "'Would to God, Brethren, I Could Tell You Who I Am!'"

Maps and Illustrations

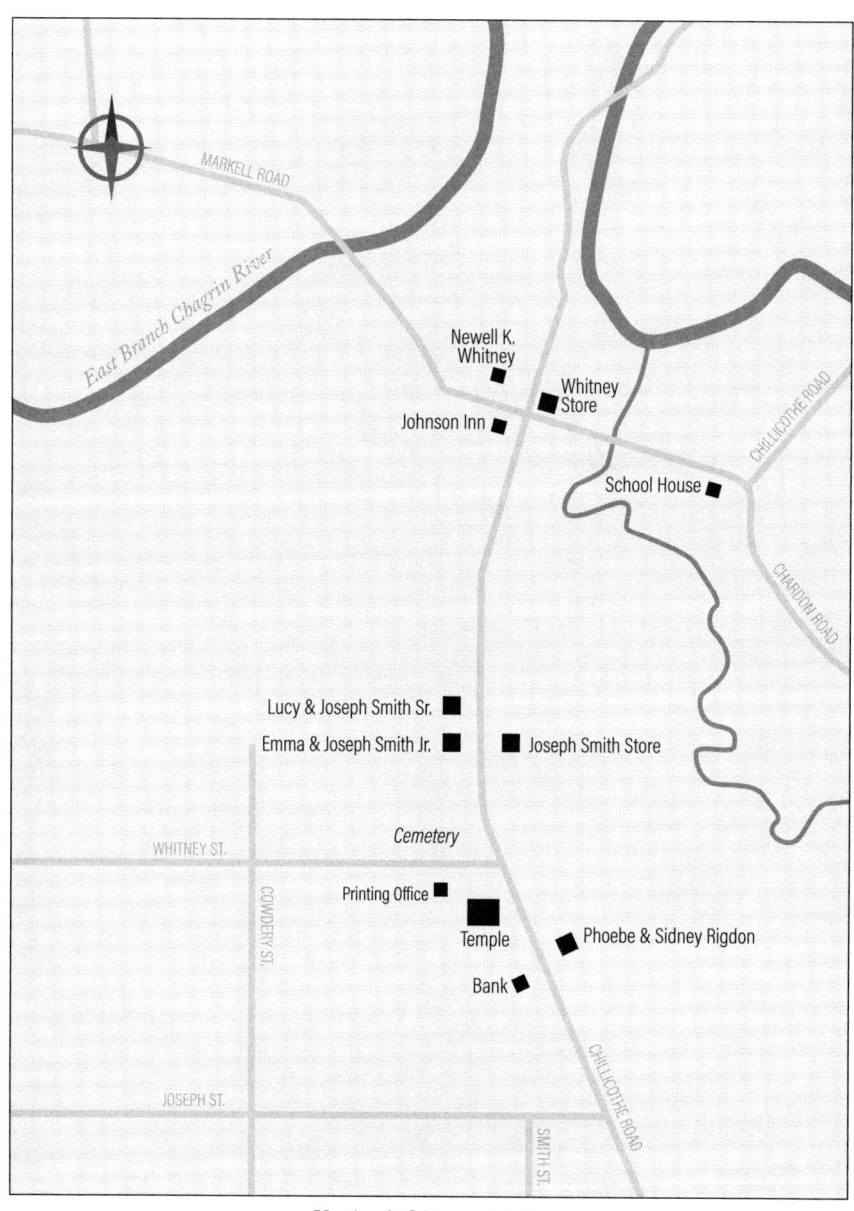

Kirtland, Ohio, ca. 1838

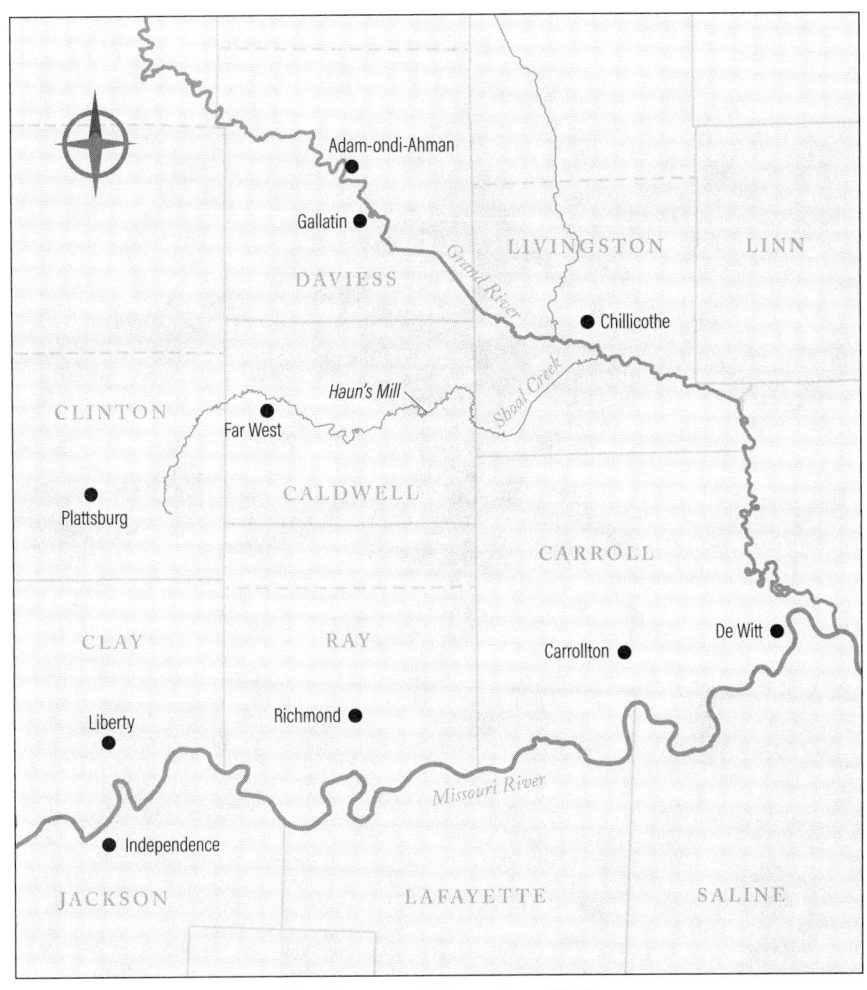

Northwestern Missouri, ca. 1838

Newel K. Whitney Store, Kirtland, Ohio, 1907

John Johnson Farm, Hiram, Ohio

Kirtland Temple, ca. 1870

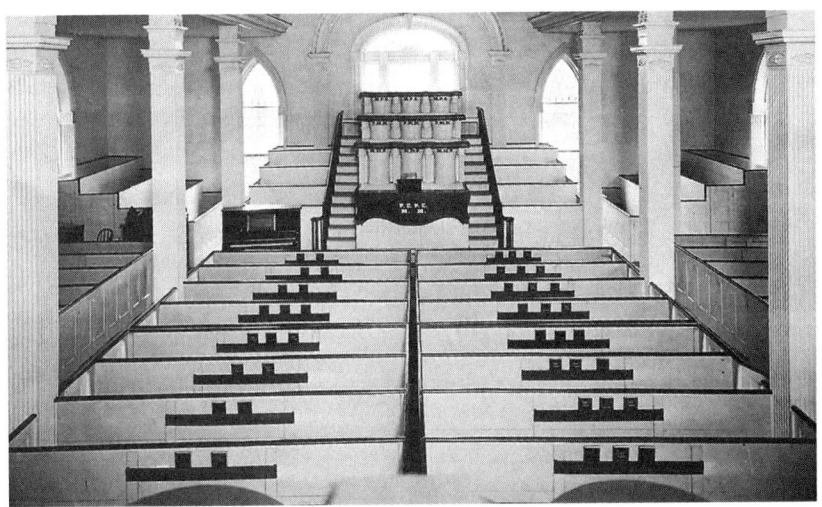

Kirtland Temple, lower court, 1920s

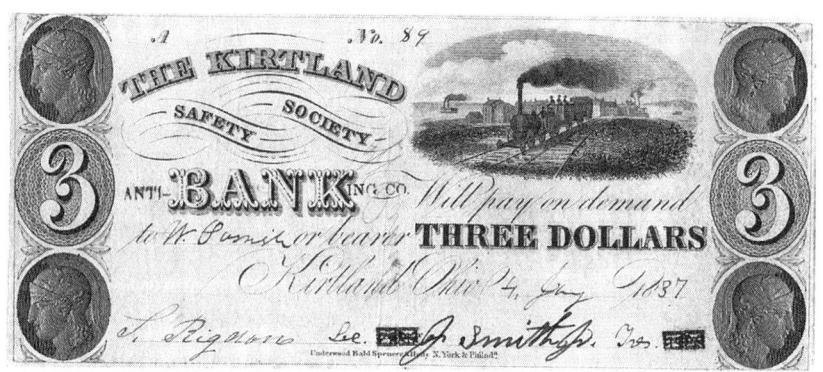

Kirtland Safety Society Notes

Joseph and Emma Smith home, Kirtland, Ohio, 1907

Emma Smith

Lucy Mack Smith

Hyrum Smith

Oliver Cowdery

Sidney Rigdon

Newel K. Whitney

Isaac Morley

Eber D. Howe

Tarring and Feathering of Joseph Smith

Joseph Smith Fragment I from the Hôr papyrus

Far West, Missouri, temple site, 1907

Liberty, Missouri, jail ruins

Edward Partridge

William W. Phelps

David Whitmer

John Whitmer

Lilburn W. Boggs

Alexander Doniphan

Austin A. King

Artist's depiction of Haun's Mill Massacre

Bibliography

Abbreviations

BC   *A Book of Commandments, for the Government of the Church of Christ, Organized according to Law, on the 6th of April, 1830.* Zion [Independence], MO: W. W. Phelps, 1833.

BYU   L. Tom Perry Special Collections, Harold B. Lee Library, Brigham Young University, Provo, UT.

CCLA   Community of Christ Library–Archives, Independence, MO.

CHL   Church History Library, The Church of Jesus Christ of Latter-day Saints, Salt Lake City.

D&C   [Joseph Smith Jr. et al.] *Doctrine and Covenants of the Church of Jesus Christ of Latter-day Saints: Containing Revelations Given to Joseph Smith the Prophet, with Some Additions by His Successors in the Presidency of the Church.* Salt Lake City: Deseret Book, for the Church, 1981.

DHC   Documentary History of the Church / Joseph Smith Jr. et al. *History of the Church of Jesus Christ of Latter-day Saints,* edited by B. H. Roberts, 2nd ed. rev. 7 vols. Salt Lake City: Deseret Book, 1977 printing.

EMD   Dan Vogel, *Early Mormon Documents.* 5 vols. Salt Lake City: Signature Books, 1996–2003.

FHL   Family History Library, The Church of Jesus Christ of Latter-day Saints, Salt Lake City.

GAEL   "Grammar & A[l]phabet of the Egyptian Language," ca. July–Nov. 1835. Kirtland Egyptian Papers. CHL.

I.V.   *Inspired Version. The Holy Scriptures, Containing the Old and New Testaments. An Inspired Revision of the Authorized Version.* By Joseph Smith, Junior. A New Corrected Edition. The Reorganized Church of Jesus Christ of Latter Day Saints. Independence, MO: Herald Publishing House, 1944.

***JSP*, CFM**   Matthew J. Grow, Ronald K. Esplin, Mark Ashurst-McGee, Gerrit J. Dirkmaat, and Jeffrey D. Mahas, eds. *The Joseph Smith Papers: Council of Fifty, Minutes, March 1844–January 1846.* Salt Lake City: Church Historian's Press, 2016.

905

JSP, D1   Michael Hubbard MacKay, Gerrit J. Dirkmaat, Grant Underwood, Robert J. Woodford, and William G. Hartley, eds. *The Joseph Smith Papers: Documents, Volume 1: July 1828–June 1831.* Salt Lake City: Church Historian's Press, 2013.

JSP, D2   Matthew C. Godfrey, Mark Ashurst-McGee, Grant Underwood, Robert J. Woodford, and William G. Hartley, eds. *The Joseph Smith Papers: Documents, Volume 2: July 1831–January 1833.* Salt Lake City: Church Historian's Press, 2013.

JSP, D3   Gerrit J. Dirkmaat, Brent M. Rogers, Grant Underwood, Robert J. Woodford, and William G. Hartley, eds. *The Joseph Smith Papers: Documents, Volume 3: February 1833–March 1834.* Salt Lake City: Church Historian's Press, 2014.

JSP, D4   Matthew C. Godfrey, Brenden W. Rensink, Alex D. Smith, Max H Parkin, and Alexander L. Baugh, eds. *The Joseph Smith Papers: Documents, Volume 4: April 1834–September 1835.* Salt Lake City: Church Historian's Press, 2016.

JSP, D5   Brent M. Rogers, Elizabeth A. Kuehn, Christian K. Heimburger, Max H Parkin, Alexander L. Baugh, and Steven C. Harper, eds. *The Joseph Smith Papers: Documents, Volume 5: October 1835–January 1838.* Salt Lake City: Church Historian's Press, 2017.

JSP, D6   Mark Ashurst-McGee, David W. Grua, Elizabeth Kuehn, Alexander L. Baugh, and Brenden W. Rensink, eds. *The Joseph Smith Papers: Documents, Volume 6: February 1838–August 1839.* Salt Lake City: Church Historian's Press, 2017.

JSP, D7   Matthew C. Godfrey, Spencer W. McBride, Alex D. Smith, and Christopher James Blythe, eds. *The Joseph Smith Papers: Documents, Volume 7: September 1839–January 1841.* Salt Lake City: Church Historian's Press, 2018.

JSP, D9   Alex D. Smith, Christian K. Heimburger, and Christopher James Blythe, eds. *The Joseph Smith Papers: Documents, Volume 9: December 1841–April 1842.* Salt Lake City: Church Historian's Press, 2019.

JSP, D10   Elizabeth A. Kuehn, Jordan T. Watkins, Matthew C. Godfrey, and Mason K. Allred, eds. *The Joseph Smith Papers: Documents, Volume 10: May–August 1842.* Salt Lake City: Church Historian's Press, 2020.

JSP, D11   Spencer W. McBride, Jeffrey D. Mahas, Brett D. Dowdle, and Tyson Reeder, eds. *The Joseph Smith Papers: Documents, Volume 11: September 1842–February 1843.* Salt Lake City: Church Historian's Press, 2020.

JSP, D12   David W. Grua, Brent M. Rogers, Matthew C. Godfrey, Robin Scott Jensen, Christopher James Blythe, and Jessica M. Nelson, eds. *The Joseph Smith Papers: Documents, Volume 12: March–July 1843.* Salt Lake City: Church Historian's Press, 2021.

JSP, H1   Karen Lynn Davidson, David J. Whittaker, Mark Ashurst-McGee, and Richard L. Jensen, eds. *The Joseph Smith Papers: Histories, Volume 1: Joseph Smith Histories, 1832–1844.* Salt Lake City: Church Historian's Press, 2012.

JSP, H2   Karen Lynn Davidson, Richard L. Jensen, and David J. Whittaker, eds. *The Joseph Smith Papers: Histories, Volume 2: Assigned Historical Writings, 1831–1847*. Salt Lake City: Church Historian's Press, 2012.

JSP, J1   Dean C. Jessee, Mark Ashurst-McGee, and Richard L. Jensen, eds. *The Joseph Smith Papers: Journals, Volume 1: 1832–1839*. Salt Lake City: Church Historian's Press, 2008.

JSP, J2   Andrew H. Hedges, Alex D. Smith, and Richard Lloyd Anderson, eds. *The Joseph Smith Papers: Journals, Volume 2: December 1841–April 1843*. Salt Lake City: Church Historian's Press, 2011.

JSP, J3   Andrew H. Hedges, Alex D. Smith, and Brent M. Rogers, eds. *The Joseph Smith Papers: Journals, Volume 3: May 1843–June 1844*. Salt Lake City: Church Historian's Press, 2015.

JSP, MRB   Robin Scott Jensen, Robert J. Woodford, and Steven C. Harper, eds. *The Joseph Smith Papers: Manuscript Revelation Books. Facsimile Edition*. Salt Lake City: Church Historian's Press, 2009.

JSP, R4   Robin Scott Jensen and Brian M. Hauglid, eds. *The Joseph Smith Papers: Revelations and Translations, Volume 4: Book of Abraham and Related Manuscripts*. Salt Lake City: Church Historian's Press, 2018.

JST   Joseph Smith Translation / See I.V.

Sources Cited

Adams, Dale W. "Chartering the Kirtland Bank." *BYU Studies* 23, no. 4 (1983): 467–82.

Addams, R. Jean. "The History and Acquisition of the Original Temple Lot Property in Independence, Jackson County, Missouri." *Mormon Historical Studies* 20, no. 1 (Spring 2019): 1–76.

An Address from the Berean Society of Universalists in Boston, to the Congregation of the First Church in Weymouth . . . Boston: Munroe, Francis & Parker, 1809.

Allen, James B. "Emergence of a Fundamental: The Expanding Role of Joseph Smith's First Vision in Mormon Religious Thought." *Journal of Mormon History* 7 (1980): 43–61.

———. *No Toil nor Labor Fear: The Story of William Clayton*. Provo, UT: Brigham Young University Press, 2002.

Allred, William Moore. Reminiscences and Diary, 1885–87. CHL.

Alper, Matthew. *The "God" Part of the Brain: A Scientific Interpretation of Human Spirituality and God*. Brooklyn: Rogue Press, 2001.

Ames, Ira. Autobiography and Journal, 1858. CHL.

Anderson, Lavina Fielding, ed. *Lucy's Book: A Critical Edition of Lucy Mack Smith's Family Memoir*. Salt Lake City: Signature Books, 2001.

Anderson, Mary Audentia Smith. *Joseph Smith III and the Restoration*. Independence, MO: Herald House, 1979.

Anderson, Richard Lloyd. "Clarifications of Boggs's 'Order' and Joseph Smith's Constitutionalism." In Garr and Johnson, eds., *Regional Studies in Latter-day Saint Church History: Missouri*, 27–83.

———. "The Mature Joseph Smith and Treasure Searching." *BYU Studies* 24, no. 4 (1984): 489–560.

Anderson, Robert D. *Inside the Mind of Joseph Smith: Psychobiography and the Book of Mormon*. Salt Lake City: Signature Books, 1999.

Angell, Truman O. Autobiography, 1884. CHL.

Anon. *An Enquiry into the Meaning of that text Genesis i. 26. Let us make Man in our Image, after our Likeness*. London: W. Owen, 1748.

———. *Reflections on the Character of Our Saviour. For Sunday Scholars*. Boston: Leonard C. Bowles, 1833.

Armstrong, Lebbeus. *Masonry Proved to Be a Work of Darkness, Repugnant to the Christian Religion; and Inimical to a Republican Government*. New York: Printed for the Author, 1830.

Arrington, Leonard J. *Brigham Young: American Moses*. New York: Knopf, 1985.

Ashbrook, James B., and Carol Rausch Albright. *The Humanizing Brain: Where Religion and Neuroscience Meet*. Cleveland: Pilgrim Press, 1997.

Austin, Emily M. *Mormonism; or, Life among the Mormons*. Madison, WI: M. J. Cantwell, 1882.

Backman, Milton V., Jr. "Flight from Kirtland." In Backman, ed., *Regional Studies in Latter-day Saint Church History: Ohio*, 139–53.

———. *The Heavens Resound: A History of the Latter-day Saints in Ohio, 1830–1838*. Salt Lake City: Deseret Book, 1983.

———, comp. *A Profile of Latter-day Saints of Kirtland, Ohio, and Members of Zion's Camp, 1830–1839: Vital Statistics and Sources*. 2nd ed. Provo, UT: Department of Church History and Doctrine, BYU, 1983.

———. *Regional Studies in Latter-day Saint Church History: Ohio*. Provo, Utah: Department of Church History and Doctrine, BYU, 1990.

Baer, Klaus. "The Breathing Permit of Hôr: A Translation of the Apparent Source of the Book of Abraham," *Dialogue: A Journal of Mormon Thought* 3, no. 3 (Autumn 1968): 107–34.

Baldwin, Nathan Bennett. Account of Zion's Camp, 1882. Typescript. CHL.

Ballou, Hosea. *A Treatise on Atonement*. Randolph, VT: Sereno Wright, 1805.

Bancroft, Aaron. *Sermons on Those Doctrines of the Gospel, and on Those Constituent Principles of the Church, which Christian Professors Have Made the Subject of Controversy*. Worcester: William Manning & Son, 1822.

Bank of Geauga Discount Book. 1832–38. Lake County Historical Society, Painesville, OH.

Banks, Richard. *Astronomy; or, The solar system explained on mechanical principles . . .* London: Simpkin and Marshall, 1829.

Barclay, James. *A Complete and Universal English Dictionary.* London: J. F. and C. Rivington, et. al., 1792.

Barlow, Israel. Autobiographical Statement, n.d. Barlow Family Collection, 1816–1969. CHL.

Barnes, Lorenzo D. Reminiscences and Diaries, 1834–39. 2 vols. CHL.

Barney, Kevin L. "The Joseph Smith Translation and Ancient Texts of the Bible." In Vogel, ed., *The Word of God,* 143–60.

Barney, Ronald O. "Joseph Smith and the Conspicuous Scarcity of Early Mormon Documentation," 372–401. In Mark Ashurst-McGee, Robin Scott Jensen, and Sharalyn D. Howcroft, eds., *Foundational Texts of Mormonism: Examining Major Early Sources.* New York, NY: Oxford University Press, 2018.

Barnouw, Erik. "The Benson Exodus of 1833: Mormon Converts and the Westward Movement." *Vermont History* 54, no. 3 (Summer 1986): 133–48.

Barns, C. R., ed. *The Commonwealth of Missouri: A Centennial Record.* St. Louis: Bryan, Brand, 1877.

Barrett, Deirdre. "Dissociaters, Fantasizers, and their Relation to Hypnotizability." In *Hypnosis and Hypnotherapy.* 2 vols., edited by D. L. Barrett, 1:15–36. New York, NY: Praeger/Greenwood, 2010.

Baugh, Alexander L. "A Call to Arms: The 1838 Mormon Defense of Northern Missouri." PhD diss., Brigham Young University, 1996.

———. "The Final Episode of Mormonism in Missouri in the 1830s: The Incarceration of the Mormon Prisoners at Richmond and Columbia Jails, 1838–1839." *John Whitmer Historical Association Journal* 28 (2008): 1–34.

———. "Joseph Smith's Dog, Old Major." *BYU Studies* 56, no. 4 (2017): 53–67.

———. "'We Have a Company of Danites in These Times': The Danites, Joseph Smith, and the 1838 Missouri Conflict." *Journal of Mormon History* 45, no. 3 (2019): 1–25.

———. "'We Took Our Change of Venue to the State of Illinois': The Gallatin Hearing and the Escape of Joseph Smith and the Mormon Prisoners from Missouri, April 1839." *Mormon Historical Studies* 2, no. 1 (2001): 59–82.

Bay, W. V. N. *Reminiscences of the Bench and Bar of Missouri.* St. Louis: F. H. Thomas, 1878.

Bayley, John. *The Book of Common Prayer . . . Together with Such of the Sunday Lessons, as are taken from the Old Testament, with Notes.* London: Joseph Butterworth & Son, 1824.

Becker, Ernest. *The Denial of Death.* New York: Free Press, 1973.

Belnap, Daniel L. "'Those Who Receive You Not': The Rite of Wiping Dust off the Feet." In *By Our Rites of Worship: Latter-day Saint Views on Ritual in Scripture,*

History, and Practice, edited by Daniel L. Belnap, 209–60. Provo, UT: Religious Studies Center, BYU; Salt Lake City: Deseret Book, 2013.

Belsham, Thomas. *A Calm Inquiry into the Scripture Doctrine Concerning the Person of Christ.* London: Unitarian Society, 1817.

Bennett, James Gordon. Diary, June–Aug. 1831. Rare Books and Manuscripts Division. New York Public Library. New York, NY.

Bennett, John C. *The History of the Saints; or, An Exposé of Joe Smith and Mormonism.* Boston: Leland & Whiting, 1842.

Bennett, Richard E. "'Quincy the Home of Our Adoption': A Study of the Mormons in Quincy, Illinois, 1838–1840." In *A City of Refuge: Quincy, Illinois,* edited by Susan Easton Black and Richard E. Bennett, 83–105. Salt Lake City: Millennial Press, 2000.

Benson, RoseAnn. "Alexander Campbell: Another Restorationist." *Journal of Mormon History* 41, no. 4 (2015): 1–42.

Benton, Josiah Henry. *Warning Out in New England, 1656–1817.* Boston: W. B. Clarke, 1911.

Berger, Peter L., and Thomas Luckmann. *The Social Construction of Reality: A Treatise in the Sociology of Knowledge.* Garden City, NY: Anchor Books, 1966.

Bergera, Gary James. "Joseph Smith and the Hazards of Charismatic Leadership." *John Whitmer Historical Association Journal* 6 (1986): 33–42.

———, ed. *Line Upon Line: Essays on Mormon Doctrine.* Salt Lake City: Signature Books, 1989.

Berrett, LaMar C., ed. *Sacred Places: A Comprehensive Guide to Early LDS Historical Sites.* 6 vols. Salt Lake City: Deseret Book, 1999–2007.

Bickmore, Barry R. "Does the Book of Mormon Teach Mainstream Trinitarianism or Modalism?" Felton, CA: FAIR, 2001.

Bidamon, Emma Smith. Letter to Emma Pilgrim, Mar. 27, 1870. Emma Smith Papers, CCLA. (*EMD*, 1:532–33.) Published in *Return*, July 15, 1895, 2.

Bingham, Ryan Stuart. "Curses and Marks: Racial Dispensations and Dispensations of Race in Joseph Smith's Bible Revision and the Book of Abraham." *Journal of Mormon History* 41, no. 3 (2015): 22–57.

Blake, J[ohn] L. *The Family Encyclopedia of Useful Knowledge and General Literature.* New York: Peter Hill, 1834.

———. *First Book in Astronomy, Adapted to the Use of Common Schools.* Boston: Lincoln and Edmands, 1831.

Blakeman, Elisha D. "A Mormon Interview. Copied from Brother Ashbel Kitchell's Pocket Journal," 1856. Shaker Museum and Library. Old Chatham, NY. Also available in Lawrence R. Flake, "A Shaker View of a Mormon Mission," *BYU Studies* 20, no. 1 (1979): 96–98.

Blasi, Anthony J. *Making Charisma: The Social Construction of Paul's Public Image.* New Brunswick, NJ: Transaction Publishers, 1991.

Blocker, Jack S. Jr., *American Temperance Movements: Cycles of Reform.* Boston: Twayne, 1989.

Blumell, Lincoln H., Matthew J. Grey, and Andrew H. Hedges, eds. *Approaching Antiquity: Joseph Smith and the Ancient World.* Provo, UT: Religious Studies Center, BYU; Salt Lake City: Deseret Book, 2015.

Blythe, Christopher James. "'Would to God, Brethren, I Could Tell You Who I Am!': Nineteenth-Century Mormonisms and the Apotheosis of Joseph Smith." *Nova Religio* 18, no. 2 (Nov. 2014): 5–27.

Book of Mormon, 1830 ed. / Joseph Smith. *The Book of Mormon: An Account Written by the Hand of Mormon, upon Plates Taken from the Plates of Nephi.* Palmyra, NY: E. B. Grandin, 1830.

Bowen, Brigham John. "Present in the World of Glory: Joseph Smith and Early Nineteenth-Century Views of Heaven." In *Archive of Restoration Culture: Summer Fellows' Papers, 2000–2002,* edited by Richard Lyman Bushman, 99–105. Provo, UT: Joseph Fielding Smith Institute for Latter-day Saint History, BYU, 2005.

Bowen, Walter D. "The Versatile W. W. Phelps." M.A. thesis, Brigham Young University, 1958.

Braden, Clark, and E. L. Kelley, *Public Discussion of the Issues Between the Reorganized Church of Jesus Christ of Latter Day Saints and the Church of Christ (Disciples) Held in Kirtland, Ohio, Beginning February 12, and Closing March 8, 1884 Between E. L. Kelley, of the Reorganized Church of Jesus Christ of Latter Day Saints and Clark Braden, of the Church of Christ.* St. Louis: Clark Braden, [1884].

Bradley, Don. "Mormon Polygamy before Nauvoo? The Relationship of Joseph Smith and Fanny Alger." In Bringhurst and Foster, eds., *The Persistence of Polygamy,* 14–58.

Bradley, James L. *Zion's Camp 1834: Prelude to the Civil War.* Logan, UT: printed by the author, 1990.

Bradshaw, M. Scott. "Joseph Smith's Performance of Marriages in Ohio." *BYU Studies* 39, no. 4 (2000): 23–69.

Bradstreet, Stephen I. *A Sermon on Future Punishment.* Cleveland, OH: Z. Willes, 1824.

Brewster, James Colin. *Very Important! To the Mormon Money Diggers, Why do the Mormons Rage, and the People Imagine a Vain Thing?* Springfield, IL: n.p., Mar. 20, 1843.

Bringhurst, Newell G., and Craig L. Foster, eds. *The Persistence of Polygamy: Joseph Smith and the Origins of Mormon Polygamy.* Independence, MO: John Whitmer Books, 2010.

Broadside. "Prayer, at the Dedication of the Lord's House in Kirtland, Ohio, March 27, 1836—by Joseph Smith, Jr. President of the Church of the Latter Day Saints." [Kirtland, OH: 1836]. CHL.

Brodie, Fawn M. *No Man Knows My History: The Life of Joseph Smith, the Mormon Prophet.* 2nd ed. New York: Knopf, 1975.

Brody, Howard. *Placebos and the Philosophy of Medicine.* Chicago: University of Chicago Press, 1980.

Brown, Benjamin. Letter to Sarah M. Brown, Mar. 1836 [ca. Apr. 1836]. Benjamin Brown Family Collection. CHL.

———. *Testimonies for the Truth.* Liverpool, Eng.: S. W. Richards, 1853.

Brown, Lorenzo. Diary and Autobiography, 1856–99. BYU.

Brown, Richard Maxwell. *Strain of Violence.* New York: Oxford University Press, 1975.

Brown, S. Kent, Donald Q. Cannon, and Richard H. Jackson, eds. *Historical Atlas of Mormonism.* New York: Simon and Schuster, 1994.

Brown, Samuel. "The Prophet Elias Puzzle." *Dialogue: A Journal of Mormon Thought* 39, no. 3 (Fall 2006): 1–17.

Bruening, Ari D., and David L. Paulsen. "The Development of the Mormon Understanding of God: Early Mormon Modalism and Other Myths." *FARMS Review of Books* 13, no. 2 (2001): 109–69.

Burch, Thomas C. Letter to James L. Minor, June 24, 1839. Mormon Collection. Missouri History Museum Archives. St. Louis.

Burgess, Harrison. Autobiography, ca. 1883. CHL.

Burnett, Peter H. *Recollections and Opinions of an Old Pioneer.* New York: D. Appleton, 1880.

Burton, Edward, ed. *An Inquiry into the Heresies of the Apostolic Age in Eight Sermons Preached before the University of Oxford, in the Year MDCCCXCXIX.* Oxford: Samuel Collingwood, 1829.

Bush, Lester E., Jr. "The Spalding Theory Then and Now." *Dialogue: A Journal of Mormon Thought* 10, no. 4 (Autumn 1977): 40–69.

———. "The Word of Wisdom in Early Nineteenth-Century Perspective." In Vogel, ed., *The Word of God,* 161–85.

Bushman, Richard Lyman. *Believing History: Latter-day Saint Essays.* Edited by Reid L. Neilson and Jed Woodworth. New York: Columbia University Press, 2004.

———. "The Character of Joseph Smith," *BYU Studies* 42, no. 2 (2003): 23–34.

———, ed. *The Great Awakening: Documents on the Revival of Religion, 1740–1745.* Chapel Hill: University of North Carolina Press, 1989.

———. *Joseph Smith: Rough Stone Rolling.* New York: Alfred A. Knopf, 2005.

Butler, John L. Autobiography. Typescript in Historical Department. Journal History, Aug. 6, 1838. CHL.

Butterfield, Josiah. Letter to John Elden, June 17, 1839. Josiah Butterfield Correspondence. Missouri Historical Society, St. Louis, MO.

Cahoon, Reynolds. Diaries, 1831–32. CHL.

Cahoon, William F. Autobiographical Sketch, 1878. CHL.

Call, Anson. Autobiography and Journal, ca. 1856–89. CHL.

———. "Copied from the Journal of Anson Call," Feb. 1879. CHL.

———. Reminiscences, ca. 1856. CHL.

———. Statement, Dec. 30, 1885. CHL.

Campbell, Alexander. *Delusions: An Analysis of the Book of Mormon … and a Refutation of Its Pretences to Divine Authority.* Boston: Benjamin H. Greene, 1832. Originally published in *Millennial Harbinger,* Feb. 7, 1831.

———. *Memoirs of Alexander Campbell Embracing a View of the Origin, Progress and Principles of the Religious Reformation Which He Advocated.* Edited by Robert Richardson. Philadelphia: J. B. Lippincott, 1868.

Cannon, Donald Q., and Lyndon W. Cook, eds. *Far West Record: Minutes of The Church of Jesus Christ of Latter-day Saints, 1830–44.* Salt Lake City: Deseret Book, 1983.

Carter, Jared. Journal, 1831–33. CHL.

Carter, John S. Journal, 1831–33. CHL.

Carter, K. Codell. *The Decline of Therapeutic Bloodletting and the Collapse of Traditional Medicine.* New Brunswick & London: Transaction Publishers, 2012.

Clarke, Adam. *The Holy Bible, Containing the Old and New Testaments . . . With a Commentary and Critical Notes.* 8 vols. Originally published, 1810–26, with many editions in America and England. Cited by passage.

Clater, Francis. *Every Man His Own Cattle Doctor; Containing the Causes, Symptoms, and Treatment of All the Diseases Incident to Oxen, Sheep, Swine, Poultry, and Rabbits.* 7th ed. London: Baldwin and Cradock, 1832.

Clayton, William. Journals, 1842–45. CHL.

Cleaveland, John. *An Attempt to Nip in the Bud, the Unscriptural Doctrine of Universal Salvation.* Salem, MA: E. Russell, 1776.

Coleman, Elihu. *A Testimony against that Anti-Christian Practice of Making Slaves of Men.* New Bedford, MA: Abraham Shearman, Jr., 1825. Originally published in 1733.

A Collection of Sacred Hymns, for the Church of the Latter Day Saints. Edited by Emma Smith. Kirtland, OH: F. G. Williams, 1835.

Collier, Fred C., and William S. Harwell, eds. *Kirtland Council Minute Book.* 2nd ed. Salt Lake City: Collier's Publishing, 2002.

Coltrin, Zebedee. Diaries, 1832–34. CHL.

Compton, Todd. *In Sacred Loneliness: The Plural Wives of Joseph Smith.* Salt Lake City: Signature Books, 1997.

———. "A Trajectory of Plurality: An Overview of Joseph Smith's Thirty-Three Plural Wives." *Dialogue: A Journal of Mormon Thought* 29, no. 2 (Summer 1996): 1–38.

Cook, Lyndon W. "'I Have Sinned Against Heaven, and Am Unworthy of Your Confidence, But I Cannot Live without a Reconciliation': Thomas B. Marsh Returns to the Church." *BYU Studies* 20, no. 4 (Summer 1980): 389–400.

———. *Joseph Smith and the Law of Consecration.* Provo, UT: Grandin Book, 1985.

————. *The Revelations of the Prophet Joseph Smith: A Historical and Biographical Commentary of the Doctrine and Covenants.* Provo, UT: Seventy's Mission Bookstore, 1981.

————, and Milton V. Backman, Jr., eds. *Kirtland Elders' Quorum Record, 1836–1841.* Provo, UT: Grandin Book, 1985.

Cooper, Rex Eugene. "The Promises Made to the Fathers: A Diachronic Analysis of Mormon Covenant Organization with Reference to Puritan Federal Theology." 2 vols. Ph.D. diss., University of Chicago, 1985.

Cooper, Robert. *The Infidel's Text-book: Being the Substance of Thirteen Lectures on the Bible.* London: H. R. Johnson, 1816.

Copyright for Doctrine and Covenants, Feb. 14, 1835. Copyright Records, OH, 1831–48 (Department of State), unnumbered vol. Rare Book and Special Collections Division, Library of Congress, Washington DC.

Coray, Howard. Letter to Martha Jane Lewis, Aug. 2, 1889. CHL.

Coray, Martha Jane. Notebook, ca. 1850. CHL.

Corrill, John. *A Brief History of the Church of Christ of Latter Day Saints.* St. Louis, MO: J. Corrill, 1839. (*JSP*, H2:121–201.)

Cottle, Thomas D., and Patricia C. Cottle. *Liberty Jail and the Legacy of Joseph.* 2nd ed. Portland, OR: Insight, 1999.

Council of Fifty / "Record of the Council of Fifty or Kingdom of God," Mar. 1844–Jan. 1846. CHL.

Courcey, K. "Medical Claims for Intercessory Prayer Remain Elusive." *Scientific Review of Alternative Medicine* 4, no. 2 (2000): 9–11.

Cowdery, Oliver. "Account Book of Writing," 1835–36. CHL.

————. Diary, Jan.–Mar. 1836. CHL.

————. Docket Book, June–Sep. 1837. Includes entries by Warren A. Cowdery, 1837–38. Henry E. Huntington Library. San Marino, CA.

————. Letter to "Our Brethren" [Joseph Smith and others], Nov. 12, 1830. Newel Knight, History, ca. 1871, 207–10. Private possession. (*JSP*, D1:211–14.)

————. Letter to William Clark, Feb. 14, 1831. U.S. Office of Indian Affairs, Central Superintendency, Records, vol. 6, 103. Kansas State Historical Society. Topeka. Transcribed in Leland H. Gentry, "Light on the 'Mission to the Lamanites,'" *BYU Studies* 36, no. 2 (1996–97): 233.

————. Letter, with postscript by Joseph Smith, to William W. Phelps, John Whitmer, Edward Partridge, Isaac Morley, John Corrill, and Sidney Gilbert, Aug. 10, 1833. CHL. (*JSP*, D3:238–43.)

————. Letter to Warren Cowdery and Lyman Cowdery, June 2, 1838. Lyman Cowdery Papers. CHL.

————. Letter to Brigham Young and Others, Dec. 25, 1843. Brigham Young Office Files, 1831–78. Brigham Young Collection. CHL.

———. Letter to Phineas Young, Mar. 23, 1846. CHL.

———. Letter to Brigham Young, Feb. 27, 1848. Brigham Young Office Files, 1832–78. CHL.

———. Letterbook, 1833–38. Henry E. Huntington Library, San Marino, CA.

———, and Elizabeth Ann Cowdery. Power of Attorney to Hyrum Smith, Sep. 5, 1837. Hyrum Smith papers. CHL.

Cox, Cordelia Morley. "Brief History of Patriarch Isaac Morley and Family," 1907. CHL.

Coxe, John Redman. *The American Dispensatory, Containing the Natural, Chemical, Pharmaceutical, and Medical History of the Different Substances Employed in Medicine.* Philadelphia: H. C. Carey & I. Lea, 1827.

Crary, Christopher. *Pioneer and Personal Reminiscences.* Marshalltown, IA: Marshall, 1893.

Crawley, Peter. *A Descriptive Bibliography of the Mormon Church.* 3 vols. Provo, UT: Religious Studies Center, BYU, 1997–2012.

Crawley, Peter, and Richard L. Anderson. "The Political and Social Realities of Zion's Camp." *BYU Studies* 14, no. 4 (1974): 406–20.

Crosby, Jonathan. Autobiographical Sketch, 1871–72. Jonathan Crosby Papers, 1871–72. CHL.

Crowley, Ariel L. *About the Book of Mormon.* Salt Lake City: Deseret Press, 1961.

D&C, 1835 ed. / [Joseph Smith et al.] *Doctrine and Covenants of the Church of the Latter Day Saints: Carefully Selected from the Revelations of God.* Kirtland, OH: F. G. Williams, 1835.

d'Aquili, Eugene G., and Andrew B. Newberg. *The Mystical Mind: Probing the Biology of Religious Experience.* Minneapolis: Fortress Press, 1999.

Darowski, Joseph F. "Schools of the Prophets: An Early American Tradition." *Mormon Historical Studies* 9, no. 1 (Spring 2008): 1–13.

Daviess County, Missouri. Circuit Court Record, vol. A, July 1837–Oct. 1843. Daviess County Courthouse, Gallatin, MO.

de Leon, Edwin. *Thirty Years of My Life on Three Continents.* London: Ward and Downey, 1890.

De Pillis, Mario S. "Christ Comes to Jackson County: The Mormon City of Zion and Its Consequences." *John Whitmer Historical Association Journal* 23 (2003): 21–44.

"Description of Far West Plat," 1837. State Historical Society of Missouri, Columbia.

Deseret News. Salt Lake City. 1850–.

DeZeng, Philip. Bill of Costs, 1826. Clerk of the Board of Supervisors, Chenango County Office Building, Norwich, NY. (*EMD*, 4:263–66.)

Diagnostic and Statistical Manual of Mental Disorders. 5th ed. Washington, DC: American Psychiatric Publishing, 2013.

Dibble, Philo. "Philo Dibble's Narrative." In *Early Scenes in Church History,* 74–96.

————. Reminiscences, n.d. Typescript. CHL.

Dick, Thomas. *Philosophy of a Future State*. New York: R. Schoyer, 1831.

Dickinson, Ellen E. *New Light on Mormonism*. New York: Funk & Wagnalls, 1885.

Dickinson, Jonathan. *Remarks upon Mr. Gales Reflections on Mr. Walls History of Infant Baptism*. New York: T. Wood, 1721.

Dinger, John S., ed. *The Nauvoo City and High Council Minutes*. Salt Lake City: Signature Books, 2011.

Dirkmaat, Gerrit J. "Searching for 'Happiness': Joseph Smith's Alleged Authorship of the 1842 Letter to Nancy Rigdon." *Journal of Mormon History* 42, no. 3 (July 2016): 94–119.

Divett, Robert T. "His Chastening Rod: Cholera Epidemics and the Mormons." *Dialogue: A Journal of Mormon Thought* 12, no. 3 (Fall 1979): 6–15.

Document Containing the Correspondence, Orders, &c., in Relation to the Disturbances with the Mormons; and the Evidence Given before the Hon. Austin A. King, Judge of the Fifth Judicial Circuit of the State of Missouri, at the Court-House in Richmond, in a Criminal Court of Inquiry, Begun November 12, 1838, on the Trial of Joseph Smith, Jr., and Others, for High Treason and Other Crimes against the State. Fayette, MO: Boon's Lick Democrat, 1841.

Dowen, John C. Statement, Jan. 2, 1885. Collection of Manuscripts about Mormons, 1832–1954, Chicago History Museum, Chicago, IL.

Doxey, Cynthia. "The Early Latter-day Saints in Livingston County, New York." In *Regional Studies in Latter-day Saint Church History: New York–Pennsylvania*, edited by Larry C. Porter, Milton V. Backman Jr., and Susan Easton Black, 69–89. Provo, UT: Department of Church History and Doctrine, BYU, 2002.

Draper, William. Autobiography, 1881. CHL.

Durham, Reed C., Jr. "The Election Day Battle at Gallatin." *BYU Studies* 13, no. 1 (1972): 36–61.

Early Scenes in Church History. Eighth Book of the Faith-Promoting Series. Salt Lake City: Juvenile Instructor Office, 1882.

East India Marine Society Records, 1799–1972. Phillips Library, Peabody Essex Museum, Salem, MA.

Eco, Umberto. *Serendipities: Language and Lunacy*. Translated by William Weaver. New York: Columbia University Press, 1998.

Edwards, Jonathan. *The Works of President Edwards*. 10 vols. New York: S. Converse, 1829.

Ehat, Andrew F., and Lyndon W. Cook. *The Words of Joseph Smith: The Contemporary Accounts of the Nauvoo Discourses of the Prophet Joseph*. Vol. 6 in the Religious Studies Monograph Series. Provo, UT: Religious Studies Center, BYU, 1980.

Ehrman, Bart D. *Forged: Writing in the Name of God—Why the Bible's Authors Are Not Who We Think They Are*. New York, NY: HarperCollins, 2012.

———. *Forgery and Counter-Forgery: The Use of Literary Deceit in Early Christian Polemics.* Oxford, NY: Oxford University Press, 2013.

———. *Misquoting Jesus: The Story Behind Who Changed the Bible and Why.* New York: Harper Collins, 2005.

Eisenstadt, S. N., ed. *Max Weber on Charisma and Institution Building: Selected Papers.* Chicago: University of Chicago Press, 1968.

Elders' Journal of the Church of Latter Day Saints. Kirtland, OH, Oct.–Nov. 1837; Far West, MO, July–Aug. 1838.

Erickson, Dan. *As a Thief in the Night: The Mormon Quest for Millennial Deliverance.* Salt Lake City: Signature Books, 2002.

———. "Joseph Smith's 1891 Millennial Prophecy: The Quest for Apocalyptic Deliverance." *Journal of Mormon History* 22, no. 2 (1996): 1–34.

Esplin, Scott C. "The Fall of Kirtland: The Doctrine and Covenants' Role in Reaffirming Joseph." *The Religious Educator: Perspectives on the Restored Gospel* 8, no. 1 (2007): 13–24.

The Evening and the Morning Star. Independence, MO, June 1832–July 1833; Kirtland, OH, Dec. 1833–Sept. 1834.

F. G. Williams & Co. Account Book, 1833–35. CHL.

Far West Committee. Minutes, Jan.–Apr. 1839. CHL.

Farnsworth, Kenneth W. "Lamanitish Arrows and Eagles with Lead Eyes: Tales of the First Recorded Explorations in an Illinois Valley Hopewell Mound." *Illinois Archaeology* 22, no. 1 (2010): 25–48.

Faulring, Scott H., Kent P. Jackson, and Robert J. Matthews, eds. *Joseph Smith's New Translation of the Bible: Original Manuscripts.* Provo, UT: Religious Studies Center, BYU, 2004.

Feldberg, Michael. *The Turbulent Era: Riot and Disorder in Jacksonian America.* New York: Oxford University Press, 1980.

Ferriss, Edwin. *The Plain Restitutionist.* Montrose, PA: C. R. Marsh, 1827.

Festinger, Leon, Henry W. Riecken, and Stanley Schachter. *When Prophecy Fails.* New York: Harper and Row, 1956.

Fielding, Mary. See under Smith, Mary Fielding

Fischer, David Hackett. *Historians' Fallacies: Toward a Logic of Historical Thought.* New York: Harper and Row, 1970.

Fisher, Josephine R. Affidavit, Feb. 24, 1915. Andrew Jenson Papers, ca. 1871–1942. CHL.

Foote, Warren. Journals, 1817–1903. CHL.

Ford, Clyde D. "The Book of Mormon, the Early Nineteenth-Century Debates over Universalism, and the Development of the Novel Mormon Doctrines of

Ultimate Rewards and Punishments." *Dialogue: A Journal of Mormon Thought* 47, no. 1 (Spring 2014): 1–23.

Foster, Lawrence. "The Psychology of Prophetic Charisma: New Approaches to Understanding Joseph Smith and the Development of Charismatic Leadership." *Dialogue: A Journal of Mormon Thought* 36, no. 4 (Winter 2003): 1–14.

———. *Religion and Sexuality: Three American Communal Experiments of the Nineteenth Century.* New York: Oxford University Press, 1981.

———. "Why the Prophet is a Puzzle: The Challenges of Using Psychological Perspectives to Understand the Character and Motivation of Joseph Smith, Jr." *Dialogue: A Journal of Mormon Thought* 53, no. 2 (2020):1–35.

Fullmer, Desdemona W. Autobiography, June 7, 1868. Desdemona W. Fullmer papers. CHL.

Gager, John G. "Early Mormonism and Early Christianity: Some Parallels and Their Consequences for the Study of New Religions." *Journal of Mormon History* 9 (1982): 53–60.

———. *Kingdom and Community: The Social World of Early Christianity.* Englewood Cliffs, NJ: Prentice-Hall, 1975.

Garr, Arnold K., and Clark V. Johnson, eds. *Regional Studies in Latter-day Saint Church History: Missouri.* Provo, UT: Department of Church History and Doctrine, BYU, 1994.

Gates, Susa Young [Homespun, pseud.]. *Lydia Knight's History.* Noble Women's Lives Series 1. Salt Lake City: Juvenile Instructor Office, 1883.

Gayler, George R. "The Attempts of the State of Missouri to Extradite Joseph Smith, 1841–1843." *Northwest Missouri State College Studies* 14 (June 1955): 3–18.

Geauga Co., OH, Court of Common Pleas. Court Records, 1807–1904. Geauga County Archives and Records Center, Chardon, OH. Also available on microfilm in U.S. and Canada Record Collection, FHL.

Geauga Co., OH, Deed Records, 1795–1921. Geauga County Archives and Records Center, Chardon, OH. Also available on microfilm in U.S. and Canada Record Collection, FHL.

Geauga Co., OH, Duplicate Tax Records, 1832–33. Geauga County Archives and Records Center, Chardon, OH. Also available on microfilm in U.S. and Canada Record Collection, FHL.

Geauga Co., OH, Marriage Records. Geauga County Archives and Records Center, Chardon, OH. Also available on microfilm in U.S. and Canada Record Collection, FHL.

Gentry, Leland H. "A History of the Latter-day Saints in Northern Missouri from 1836 to 1839." PhD diss., Brigham Young University, 1965.

———. "What of the Lectures on Faith?" *BYU Studies* 19, no. 1 (1978): 3–19.

———, and Todd M. Compton. *Fire and Sword: A History of the Latter-day Saints in Northern Missouri, 1836–39.* Salt Lake City: Greg Kofford Books, 2011.

Gilbert, Algernon Sidney. Notebook of Revelations, 1831–ca. 1833. Revelations Collection, 1831–ca. 1844, 1847, 1861, ca. 1876. CHL.

Gilje, Paul A. *Rioting in America.* Bloomington: Indiana University Press, 1996.

Givens, Terryl, with Brian M. Hauglid. *The Pearl of Greatest Price: Mormonism's Most Controversial Scripture.* New York: Oxford University Press, 2019.

Godfrey, Kenneth W. "The Zelph Story." *BYU Studies* 29, no. 2 (1989): 31–56.

Godfrey, Matthew C. "'Seeking after Monarchal Power and Authority': Joseph Smith and Leadership in the Church of Christ, 1831–1832." *Mormon Historical Studies* 13 (Spring/Fall 2012): 15–37.

Goldman, Shalom. "Joshua/James Seixas (1802–74): Jewish Apostasy and Christian Hebraism in Early Nineteenth-Century America." *Jewish History* 7, no. 1 (Spring 1993): 65–88.

Grant, Jedediah M. *Collection of Facts Relative to the Course Taken by Elder Sidney Rigdon in the States of Ohio, Illinois, and Pennsylvania.* Philadelphia: Brown, Bicking & Guilbert, 1844.

Green, Celia, and Charles McCreery. *Apparitions.* London: Hamish Hamilton, 1975.

Greene, John P. Diary, Sep.–Oct. 1833. CHL.

———. *Facts Relative to the Expulsion of the Mormons or Latter Day Saints, from the State of Missouri, under the "Exterminating Order." By John P. Greene, an Authorized Representative of the Mormons.* Cincinnati: R. P. Brooks, 1839.

Gregg, Josiah. *Commerce of the Prairies; or, The Journal of a Santa Fé Trader, during Eight Expeditions across the Great Western Prairies, and a Residence of Nearly Nine Years in Northern Mexico.* 2 vols. 2nd ed. New York: J. and H. G. Langley, 1845.

Grey, Matthew J. "Approaching Egyptian Papyri through Biblical Language: Joseph Smith's Use of Hebrew in His Translation of the Book of Abraham." In MacKay et al., eds., *Producing Ancient Scripture*, 390–451.

———. "'The Word of the Lord in the Original': Joseph Smith's Study of Hebrew in Kirtland." In Blumell et al., eds., *Approaching Antiquity*, 249–302.

Grimsted, David. *American Mobbing, 1828–1861: Toward Civil War.* New York: Oxford University Press, 1998.

Grow, Matthew J. "'Clean from the Blood of This Generation': The Washing of Feet and the Latter-day Saints." In *Archive of Restoration Culture Summer Fellows' Papers, 2000– 2002,* edited by Richard Lyman Bushman, 131–38. Provo, UT: Joseph Fielding Smith Institute for Latter-day Saint History, 2005.

Grua, David W. "Joseph Smith and the 1834 D. P. Hurlbut Case." *BYU Studies* 44, no. 1 (2005): 33–54.

Gurley, Zenas H., Jr. "Questions asked of David Whitmer at his home in Richmond Ray County Mo. Jan 14–1885." CHL.

Hacking, Ian. *The Social Construction of What?* Cambridge, MA: Harvard University Press, 1999.

Hales, Brian C. "Fanny Alger and Joseph Smith's Pre-Nauvoo Reputation." *Journal of Mormon History* 35, no. 4 (2009): 112–90.

———. "'Guilty of Such Folly?': Accusations of Adultery or Polygamy against Oliver Cowdery." In *Days Never to Be Forgotten: Oliver Cowdery,* edited by Alexander L. Baugh, 279–93. Provo, UT: Religious Studies Center, BYU, 2009.

———, with the assistance of Don Bradley. *Joseph Smith's Polygamy.* 3 vols. Salt Lake City: Greg Kofford Books, 2013.

Hales, Kenneth Glyn, comp. *Windows: A Mormon Family.* Tucson, AZ: Skyline Printing, 1985.

Hall, William. *The Abominations of Mormonism Exposed.* Cincinnati, OH: W. Hall, 1852.

Hamblin, William J. "'There Really is a God, and He Dwells in the Temporal Parietal Lobe of Joseph Smith's Brain.'" *Dialogue: A Journal of Mormon Thought* 36 (Winter 2003): 79–87.

Hancock, Levi W. Autobiographical Sketch, 1878. CHL.

———. Autobiography, ca. 1854. CHL.

———. Statement, ca. 1845. CHL.

Hancock, Mosiah Lyman. Autobiography, n.d. Typescript. CHL.

———. "Autobiography of Levi Ward Hancock," ca. 1896. CHL.

Harper, Steven C. "'Dictated by Christ': Joseph Smith and the Politics of Revelation." *Journal of the Early Republic* 26, no. 2 (Summer 2006): 275–304.

———. *Joseph Smith's First Vision: A Guide to the Historical Accounts.* Salt Lake City: Deseret Book, 2012.

Harrell, Charles R. *"This Is My Doctrine": The Development of Mormon Theology.* Salt Lake City: Greg Kofford Books, 2011.

Harris, William. *Mormonism Portrayed. Its Errors and Absurdities Exposed, and the Spirit and Designs of Its Authors Made Manifest.* Warsaw, IL: Sharp & Gamble, 1841.

Hartley, William G. "'Almost Too Intolerable a Burthen': The Winter Exodus from Missouri, 1838–39." *Journal of Mormon History* 18, no. 2 (Fall 1992): 6–40.

———. "Newel and Lydia Bailey Knight's Kirtland Love Story and Historic Wedding." *BYU Studies* 39, no. 4 (2000): 7–22.

———. "The Saints' Forced Exodus from Missouri, 1839." In *Joseph Smith: The Prophet and Seer,* edited by Richard Neitzel Holzapfel and Kent P. Jackson, 347–89. Provo, UT: Religious Studies Center, Brigham Young University; Salt Lake City: Deseret Book, 2010.

Hauglid, Brian. *A Textual History of the Book of Abraham: Manuscripts and Editions.* Provo, Utah: Neal A. Maxwell Institute for Religious Scholarship, BYU, 2010.

Haven, Charlotte. Letter to her mother, Feb. 19, 1843. In "A Girl's Letters from Nauvoo," *Overland Monthly* (San Francisco), Dec. 1890, 622–24.

Hawker, [Robert S.] *The Abba, Amen, and Corpus Christi Hymns.* London: A. A. Paris, 1818.

Haws, J. B. "Joseph Smith, Emanuel Swedenborg, and Section 76: Importance of the Bible in Latter-day Revelation." In *The Doctrine and Covenants, Revelations in Context: The 37th Annual Brigham Young University Sidney B. Sperry,* edited by Andrew H. Hedges, J. Spencer Fluhman, and Alonzo L. Gaskill, 142–67. Provo, UT: Religious Studies Center, BYU; Salt Lake City: Deseret Book, 2008.

Hayden, Amos S. *Early History of the Disciples in the Western Reserve, Ohio: With Biographical Sketches of the Principal Agents in Their Religious Movement.* Cincinnati: Chase and Hall, 1876.

Hedges, Andrew H. "A Wanderer in a Strange Land: Abraham in America, 1800–1850." In *Astronomy, Papyrus, and Covenant,* edited by John Gee and Brian M. Hauglid, 175–87. Provo, UT: FARMS, 2005.

Henry, Matthew. *An Exposition of the Old and New Testament.* 3 vols. London: Joseph Ogle Robinson, 1828.

———. *A New Family Bible, Containing the Old and New Testaments . . .* Vol. 2. Bungay, England: C. Brightly, 1804.

Hiatt, Alfred. *The Making of Medieval Forgeries: False Documents in Fifteenth-Century England.* London: The British Library, 2004.

Higbee, Elias. Deposition, Nauvoo, IL, Apr. 22, 1842. Joseph Smith v. George M. Hinkle, 1841–42. Lee Co. District Court, 1842. CHL.

———. Petition, Far West, Caldwell Co., MO, to Elias Higbee, ca. Aug. 16, 1838. George W. Robinson papers. CHL.

Hill, Marvin S. *Quest for Refuge: The Mormon Flight from American Pluralism.* Salt Lake City: Signature Books, 1989.

Hinsdale, Burke A. "Life and Character of Symonds Ryder: A Funeral Sermon Preached in Hiram, Ohio, August 3, 1870." Hiram College Library, Hiram, OH. Reprinted in Hayden, *Early History of the Disciples in the Western Reserve,* 245–66.

Historian's Office. Brigham Young History Drafts, 1856–58. Box 1, folder 5. CHL.

Historian's Office, General Church Minutes, 1839–77. CHL.

Historian's Office. Histories of the Twelve, 1856–58, 1861. CHL.

Historian's Office. "History of Luke Johnson." Histories of the Twelve, 1856–58, 1861. CHL.

Historian's Office. "History of William E. McLellin." Histories of the Twelve, 1856–58, 1861. CHL.

Historian's Office. JS History Documents, 1839–60. CHL.

Historian's Office. Joseph Smith History Draft Notes, ca. 1839–56. CHL.

Historical Department. Journal History of the Church, 1830–2008. CHL. Daily scrapbook; entries primarily contain newspaper clippings and typed extracts from other sources.

History of Caldwell and Livingston Counties, Missouri, Written and Compiled from the Most Authentic Official and Private Sources. . . . St. Louis: National Historical Co., 1886.

The History of Daviess County, Missouri. Kansas City, MO: Birdsall & Dean, 1882.

"History of Orson Hyde." Historian's Office, Histories of the Twelve, 1856–58, 1861. CHL.

"History of Orson Pratt." Historian's Office, Histories of the Twelve, 1856–58, 1861. CHL.

History of the Ohio Falls Cities and Their Counties. 2 vols. Cleveland, OH: L. A. Williams, 1882.

Holbrook, Joseph. Autobiography and Journal, ca. 1860–71. CHL.

Holifield, E. Brooks. *Theology in America: Christian Thought from the Age of the Puritans to the Civil War.* New Haven, CT: Yale University Press, 2003.

Holtzman, Nicholas S., and Michael J. Strube. "Narcissism and Attractiveness." *Journal of Research in Personality* 44 (2010): 133–36.

Hood, Ralph W., and William Paul Williamson. *Them That Believe: The Power and Meaning of the Christian Serpent-handling Tradition.* Berkeley, CA: University of California Press, 2008.

Hopkins, Samuel. *An Inquiry Concerning the Future State of those who die in their Sins.* Newport, RI: Solomon Southwick, 1783.

Howe, Eber D. Affidavit, Apr. 8, 1885. Arthur B. Deming Collection. Chicago History Museum, Chicago, IL.

———. *Autobiography and Recollections of a Pioneer Printer: Together with Sketches of the War of 1812 on the Niagara Frontier.* Painesville, OH: Telegraph Steam Printing House, 1878.

———. *Mormonism Unvailed: or, A Faithful Account of That Singular Imposition and Delusion, from Its Rise to the Present Time.* Painesville, OH: E. D. Howe, 1834. Also available in E. D. Howe, *Mormonism Unvailed.* Edited by Dan Vogel. Salt Lake City: Signature Books, 2015.

Humbert, Royal, ed. *A Compend of Alexander Campbell's Theology.* St. Louis: Bethany Press, 1961.

Huntington, Dimick B. Statement, ca. 1854–56. Historian's Office. JS History Documents. CHL.

Huntington, Oliver B. History, 1845–46. Oliver Boardman Huntington papers, 1843–1932. BYU.

Huntington, William. "A History of William Huntington Written by Himself and Transcribed by His Son O. B. Huntington," Jan. 1855. BYU.

Hutchinson, Anthony A. "A Mormon Midrash? LDS Creation Narratives Reconsidered." *Dialogue: A Journal of Mormon Thought* 21, no. 4 (Winter 1988): 11–74.

Hyde, John. *Mormonism: Its Leaders and Designs.* New York: W. P. Fetridge, 1857.

Hyde, Orson, and Orson Pratt. Notebook of Revelations, 1834. Revelations Collection, 1831–ca. 1844, 1847, 1861, ca. 1876. CHL.

Hyde, William. Autobiographical Sketch, n.d. CHL.

An Illustrated Historical Atlas Map, Carroll County, MO: Carefully Compiled from Personal Examinations and Surveys. N.p.: Brink, McDonough, 1876.

"Incidents of Joseph Smith's Journal," ca. 1845. Historian's Office. JS History Documents, 1839–60. CHL.

Jackson, Kent P. "Joseph Smith and the Bible." *Scottish Journal of Theology* 63, no. 1 (2010): 24–40.

———, ed. *Manuscript Found: The Complete Original "Spaulding Manuscript."* Provo, UT: Religious Studies Center, BYU, 1996.

———. "Some Notes on Joseph Smith and Adam Clarke." *Interpreter: A Journal of Latter-day Saint Faith and Scholarship* 40 (2020): 15–60. Available online at https://journal.interpreterfoundation.org.

Jackson, Richard H. "The Mormon Village: Genesis and Antecedents of the City of Zion Plan." *BYU Studies* 17, no. 2 (1977): 223–40.

Jackson Co., MO, Deed Records, 1827–1909. Jackson County Records Center, Independence, MO. Available on microfilm in U.S. and Canada Record Collection, FHL.

Jennings, Erin B. "The Consequential Counselor: Restoring the Root(s) of Jesse Gause." *Journal of Mormon History* 34, no. 2 (Spring 2008): 182–227.

Jennings, Warren A. "Factors in the Destruction of the Mormon Press in Missouri, 1833." *Utah Historical Quarterly* 35, no. 1 (Winter 1967): 57–76.

———. "Isaac McCoy and the Mormons." *Missouri Historical Review* 61, no. 1 (Oct. 1966): 62–82.

———. "Zion Is Fled: The Expulsion of the Mormons from Jackson County, Missouri." PhD diss. University of Florida, 1962.

Jessee, Dean C. "Priceless Words and Fallible Memories: Joseph Smith As Seen in the Effort to Preserve His Discourses." *BYU Studies* 31, no. 2 (1991): 19–40.

Johnson, Benjamin F. Letter to George S. Gibbs, Apr.–Oct. 1903. Benjamin F. Johnson Papers, 1852–1923. CHL.

———. "A Life Review," ca. 1885–94, 1923. Benjamin F. Johnson, Papers, 1852–1923. CHL.

Johnson, Clark V. "The Missouri Redress Petitions: A Reappraisal of Mormon Persecutions in Missouri." *BYU Studies* 26, no. 2 (1986): 31–44.

———, ed. *Mormon Redress Petitions: Documents of the 1833–1838 Missouri Conflict.* Vol. 16 in the Religious Studies Center Monograph Series. Provo, UT: Religious Studies Center, BYU, 1992.

Johnson, Joel Hills. Autobiographical Sketch and Journal, Aug. 1835–Dec. 1859. CHL.

―――. Notebook. Personal papers, ca. 1877–79. Joel Hills Johnson papers, ca. 1835–82. CHL.

Jones, Jacob. "Testimony of Jacob Jones," n.d. CHL.

Journal of Discourses. 26 vols. Liverpool: Latter-day Saints' Book Depot, 1854–86.

"Journal of the Branch of the Church of Christ in Pontiac," 1834. CHL.

Journal of the House of Representatives, of the State of Missouri, at the First Session of the Tenth General Assembly, Begun and Held at the City of Jefferson, on Monday, the Nineteenth Day of November, in the Year of Our Lord, One Thousand Eight Hundred and Thirty-Eight. Jefferson City, MO: Calvin Gunn, 1839.

Juster, Susan. *Doomsayers: Anglo-American Prophecies in the Age of Revolution.* Philadelphia: University of Pennsylvania Press, 2003.

Juvenile Instructor. Salt Lake City. 1866–1929.

JS Collection / Joseph Smith Collection, 1827–46. CHL.

JS History / Smith, Joseph, et al. History, 1838–56. Vols. A-1–F-1. Historian's Office, History of the Church, 1839–ca. 1882. CHL. (*JSP*, H1:204–463; Draft 2.) The period up to August 5, 1838, was composed during Joseph Smith's lifetime.

JS History, 1832 / Smith, Joseph. "A History of the Life of Joseph Smith Jr," ca. Summer 1832. In JS Letterbook 1, 1–[6] (earliest numbering). JS Collection. CHL. (*JSP*, H1:3–16.)

JS History, 1834–36 / Smith, Joseph, et al. History, 1834–36. In Joseph Smith et al., History, 1838–56, vol. A-1, back of book (earliest numbering), 9–20, 46–187. Historian's Office, History of the Church, 1839–ca. 1882. CHL. (*JSP*, H1:23–185.)

JS History, 1838–ca. 1841 (draft). CHL. (*JSP*, H1:204–463; Draft 1.)

JS History, ca. 1841. CHL. (*JSP*, H1:204–463; Draft 3.)

JS Letterbook 1. "Letter Book A," 1832–35. JS Collection. CHL.

JS Letterbook 2. "Copies of Letters, &c. &c.," 1839–43. JS Collection, 1827–46. CHL.

JS Office Papers / Joseph Smith Office Papers, ca. 1835–45. CHL.

Kanter, Rosabeth Moss. *Commitment and Community: Communes and Utopias in Sociological Perspective.* Cambridge, MA: Harvard University Press, 1972.

Kawaler, Steven, and J. Veverka. "The Habitable Sun: One of William Herschel's Stranger Ideas." *Journal of the Royal Astronomical Society of Canada* 75 (Jan. 1981): 46–55.

Kelley, William. Notebook, No. 5, Mar. 6, 1881. William H. Kelley Papers. CCLA. (*EMD*, 2:83–87.)

Kimball, Heber C. Autobiography, ca. 1842–58. Heber C. Kimball Papers, 1837–66. CHL.

―――. Autobiography, ca. 1856. Heber C. Kimball Papers, 1837–66. CHL.

————. "History of Heber Chase Kimball by His Own Dictation," ca. 1842–56. Heber C. Kimball Papers, 1837–66. CHL.

Kimball, Stanley B. *On the Potter's Wheel: The Diaries of Heber C. Kimball.* Salt Lake City: Signature Books, 1987.

Kimball, Vilate. Letter to Heber C. Kimball, Sep. 6, 1837. Private possession. Photocopy in Heber C. Kimball Correspondence. CHL.

————. Letter to Heber C. Kimball, ca. Sep. 11, 1837. Heber C. Kimball Collection. CHL.

————. Letter to Heber C Kimball, Jan. 19, 21, and 24, 1838. Heber C. Kimball Collection. CHL.

King, Austin A. Letter to William Morgan, Sep. 4, 1838. William Morgan Papers. CHL.

Kirtland Elders Certificates / Kirtland Elders Quorum. "Record of Certificates of Membership and Ordinations of the First Members and Elders of the Church of Jesus Christ of Latter Day Saints Dating from March 21st 1836 to June 18th 1838 Kirtland Geauga Co. Ohio," 1836–38. CHL.

Kirtland Elders Quorum. "A Record of the First Quorurum of Elders Belonging to the Church of Christ: In Kirtland Geauga Co. Ohio," 1836–38, 1840–41. CCLA.

Kirtland Safety Society. Account with Bank of Monroe, Painesville, Geauga Co., OH, Feb. 11–Apr. 4, 1837. CHL.

Kirtland Safety Society. Daybook, Kirtland Township, Geauga Co., OH, ca. Jan. 4–16, 1837. JS Office Papers. CHL.

Kirtland Safety Society. Stock Ledger, 1836–37. Collection of Manuscripts about Mormons, 1832–1954, Chicago History Museum, Chicago, IL. Copy at CHL.

Kirtland Township Trustees' Minutes and Poll Book, 1817–38. Lake County Historical Society, Painesville, OH.

Kling, David W. "New Divinity Schools of the Prophets, 1750–1825: A Case Study in Ministerial Education." *History of Education Quarterly* 37, no. 2 (Summer 1997): 185–206.

Knight, Anthony P. *A Guide to Poisonous House and Garden Plants.* Jackson, WY: Teton NewMedia, 2007.

Knight, Joseph, Jr. Autobiographical Sketch, 1862. CHL.

Knight, Joseph, Sr. Reminiscences, n.d. [ca. 1835–47]. CHL. (*EMD,* 4:11–24.)

Knight, LaFayette. Letter to James H. and Sharon Fellows, Dec. 21, 1843. CHL.

Knight, Newel. Autobiography and Journal, ca. 1846. CHL.

————. Journal, ca. 1846–47. CHL.

[Knight, Newel]. "Newel Knight Journal." In *Scraps of Biography. Tenth Book of the Faith-Promoting Series,* 46–104.

Knight, Vinson. Account Book, 1839–42. Microfilm. CHL.

————. Letter to William Cooper, Feb. 3, 1839. CHL.

Kohut, Heinz. *The Analysis of the Self: A Systematic Approach to the Psychoanalytic Treatment of Narcissistic Disorders*. New York: International Universities Press, 1971.

————. "Reflections on *Advances in Self-psychology*," in *Advances in Self-Psychology*. Edited by A. Goldberg. New York: International Universities Press, 1980.

————. *Self-psychology and the Humanities: Reflections on a New Psychoanalytic Approach*. Edited by C. Strozier. New York: W. W. Norton, 1985.

Kosslyn, S. M., G. Ganis, and W. L. Thompson. "Neural Foundations of Imagery." *Nature Reviews Neuroscience*, 2, no. 9 (2001): 635–42.

Lambert, Neal E., and Richard H. Cracroft. "Literary Form and Historical Understanding: Joseph Smith's First Vision." *Journal of Mormon History* 7 (1980): 31–42.

Lancaster, James E. "The Translation of the Book of Mormon." In Vogel, ed., *The Word of God*, 97–112.

Larson, Stan. "The Historicity of the Matthean Sermon on the Mount in 3 Nephi." In Metcalfe, ed., *New Approaches to the Book of Mormon*, 115–63.

————, and Samuel J. Passey, eds. *The William E. McLellin Papers, 1854–1880*. Salt Lake City: Signature Books, 2007.

Latrobe, Charles Joseph. *The Rambler in North America, MDCCCXXXII–MDCCCXXXIII*. Vol. 1. New York: Harper and Brothers, 1835.

Latter Day Saints' Messenger and Advocate. Kirtland, OH. Oct. 1834–Sept. 1837.

Latter-day Saints' Millennial Star. Manchester, England, 1840–42; Liverpool, 1842–1932; London, 1932–70.

Laub, George. Reminiscences and Journal, 1845–46. CHL.

Launius, Roger D. "Alexander William Doniphan and the 1838 Mormon War." *John Whitmer Historical Association Journal* 18 (1998): 63–110.

————, and Linda Thatcher, eds. *Differing Visions: Dissenters in Mormon History*. Urbana: University of Illinois Press, 1994.

Laws of the State of Missouri, Passed at the First Session of the Tenth General Assembly, Begun and Held at the City of Jefferson, on Monday, the Nineteenth Day of November, in the Year of Our Lord, One Thousand Eight Hundred and Thirty-Eight. Jefferson, MO: Calvin Gunn, 1838 [1839].

Laws of the State of New York, Revised and Passed at Thirty-Sixth Session of the Legislature. 2 vols. Albany, NY: H. C. Southwick, 1813.

Lee, E. G. *The Mormons, or, Knavery Exposed*. Philadelphia: George Webber and William Fenimore, 1841.

Lee, John D. *Mormonism Unveiled: The Life and Confessions of John D. Lee*. St. Louis: Bryan, Brand, 1877.

————, and Levi Stewart. Statement, 1845. Historian's Office. JS History Documents. CHL. (Vogel, *History of Joseph Smith*, 8:79–80.)

Lee County, Iowa Territory, District Court. Joseph Smith v. George M. Hinkle, 1841–42. CHL.

Leonard, Glen M. *Nauvoo: A Place of Peace, a People of Promise.* Salt Lake City: Deseret Book; Provo, UT: Brigham Young University Press, 2002.

Leopard, John C., Buel Leopard, R. M. McCammon, and Mary McCammon Hillman. *History of Daviess and Gentry Counties, Missouri.* Topeka, KS: Historical Publishing, 1922.

LeSueur, Stephen C. "The Danites Reconsidered: Were They Vigilantes or Just the Mormon's Version of the Elks Club?" *John Whitmer Historical Association Journal* 14 (1994): 35–51.

———. *The 1838 Mormon War in Missouri.* Columbia, MO: University of Missouri Press, 1987.

———. "'High Treason and Murder': The Examination of Mormon Prisoners at Richmond, Missouri, in November 1838." *BYU Studies* 26, no. 2 (1986): 2–30.

———. "Missouri's Failed Compromise: The Creation of Caldwell County for the Mormons." *Journal of Mormon History* 31, no. 3 (Fall 2005): 113–44.

———. "Mixing Politics with Religion: A Closer Look at Electioneering and Voting in Caldwell and Daviess Counties in 1838." *John Whitmer Historical Association Journal* 33, no. 1 (Spring/Summer 2013): 184–208.

License Record Book, Dec. 1837–May 1862. CHL.

Lightner, Mary Elizabeth Rollins. Address at Brigham Young University, Apr. 14, 1905. Typescript. BYU.

———. Reminiscences, ca. 1905. Mary Elizabeth Rollins Lightner Family Collection, 1833–1973. CHL.

———. "Statement," signed Feb. 8, 1902. Typescript in Vesta Crawford Papers, Marriott Library, University of Utah, Salt Lake City.

Loftus, Elizabeth F. "Memory Malleability: Constructivist and Fuzzy-Trace Explanations." *Learning and Individual Differences* 7, no. 2 (1995): 133–37.

———, and Jacqueline E. Pickrell. "The Formation of False Memories." *Psychiatric Annals* 25, no. 12 (Dec. 1995): 720–25.

Lyman, Eliza Maria Partridge. Journal, 1846–85. CHL.

Lyon, T. Edgar. "Independence, Missouri, and the Mormons, 1827–1833." *BYU Studies* 13, no. 1 (1972): 10–19.

Mace, Wandle. "Autobiography of Wandle Mace," n.d. Typescript. BYU.

MacKay, Michael Hubbard. *Prophetic Authority: Democratic Hierarchy and the Mormon Priesthood.* Urbana, IL: University of Illinois Press, 2020.

———. *Sacred Space: Exploring the Birthplace of Mormonism.* Provo: Religious Studies Center, BYU; Salt Lake City: Deseret Book, 2016.

————, Mark Ashurst-McGee, and Brian M. Hauglid, eds. *Producing Ancient Scripture: Joseph Smith's Translation Projects in the Development of Mormon Christianity*. Salt Lake City, UT: University of Utah Press, 2020.

————, and Nicholas J. Frederick. *Joseph Smith's Seer Stones*. Provo, UT: Religious Studies Center, BYU; and Salt Lake City: Deseret Book, 2016.

Madsen, Gordon A. "Joseph Smith and the Missouri Court of Inquiry: Austin A. King's Quest for Hostages." *BYU Studies* 43, no. 4 (2004): 92–136.

————. "Tabulating the Impact of Litigation on the Kirtland Economy." In Madsen et al., eds., *Sustaining the Law*, 227–46.

————, Jeffrey N. Walker, and John W. Welch, eds. *Sustaining the Law: Joseph Smith's Legal Encounters*. Provo, UT: BYU Studies, 2014.

Manscill, Craig K. "'Journal of the Branch of the Church of Christ in Pontiac, … 1834': Hyrum Smith's Division of Zion's Camp." *BYU Studies* 39, no. 1 (2000): 167–88.

Marchant, John, et al. *A New Complete English Dictionary . . .* London: J. Fuller, 1760.

Markham, Stephen. Interview Notes, ca. 1845. Historian's Office, Joseph Smith History Draft Notes, Manuscript 1, between pages 50 and 51. CHL. (Vogel, *History of Joseph Smith*, 7:499–500.)

Marquardt, H. Michael. *Early Patriarchal Blessings of The Church of Jesus Christ of Latter-day Saints*. Salt Lake City: Smith-Pettit Foundation, 2007.

————. *The Joseph Smith Revelations: Text and Commentary*. Salt Lake City: Signature Books, 1999.

————. "Judge Austin A. King's Preliminary Hearing: Joseph Smith and the Mormons on Trial." *John Whitmer Historical Association Journal* 24 (2004): 41–55.

Marsh, Thomas B. History and Autobiography, 1857. Historian's Office. Histories of the Twelve, 1856–58, 1861. CHL.

————. Letter to Wilford Woodruff, ca. June 18, 1838. Wilford Woodruff Collection. CHL.

[Mather, Frederick G.] "The Early Mormons. Joe Smith Operates at Susquehanna." *Binghamton Republican,* July 29, 1880. (*EMD*, 4:148–59.)

Mauss, Armand L. "The Fading of the Pharaohs' Curse: The Decline and Fall of the Priesthood Ban Against Blacks in the Mormon Church." *Dialogue: A Journal of Mormon Thought* 14, no. 3 (Autumn 1981): 10–35.

McArthur, Daniel D. Autobiography, ca. 1856. Typescript. BYU.

McBride, Reuben. Reminiscence, n.d. CHL.

McGee, Joseph H. *Story of the Grand River Country: Memoirs of Maj. Joseph H. McGee, 1821–1905*. Gallatin, MO: North Missourian Press, 1909.

McGrath, Alister E. *Christian Theology: An Introduction*. 6th ed. Chichester, Eng.: Wiley Blackwell, 2017.

McKiernan, F. Mark. "The Conversion of Sidney Rigdon to Mormonism." *Dialogue: A Journal of Mormon Thought* 5, no. 2 (Summer 1970): 71–78.

McLaws, Monte B. "The Attempted Assassination of Missouri's Ex-Governor, Lilburn W. Boggs." *Missouri Historical Review* 60, no. 1 (Oct. 1965): 50–62.

McLellin, William E. Journals, 1831–36. William E. McLellin Papers, 1831–78. CHL.

———. Letter to "Beloved Relatives," Aug. 4, 1832. Photocopy. CHL.

———. Letter to Orson Pratt, Apr. 29, 1854. CHL.

———. Letter to Joseph Smith III, Jan. 10, 1861. CCLA.

———. Letter to Joseph Smith III, July 1872. CCLA.

———. Letter to J. L. Traughber, Aug. 25, 1877. John L. Traughber Papers, 1854–1910. J. Willard Marriott Library, University of Utah, Salt Lake City.

———. Letter to John L. Traughber, Dec. 14, 1878. John L. Traughber Papers, 1854–1910. J. Willard Marriott Library, University of Utah. Salt Lake City.

———. Letter to John L. Traughber, Jan. 5, 1879. John L. Traughber Papers, 1854–1910. J. Willard Marriott Library, University of Utah. Salt Lake City.

———. Notebook [containing religious treatises and copies of revelations], 1877. In "W. E. Mc.Lellan Jan—1877," William E. McLellin Papers, 1831–78. CHL.

———. Notebook, ca. 1880. "Reasons Why I am Not a 'Mormon.'" William E. McLellin Papers, 1831–78. J. Willard Marriott Library, University of Utah Library, Salt Lake City. Available in "Reasons Why I am Not a 'Mormon,'" Larson and Passey, eds., *The William E. McLellin Papers*, 379–429.

The Mennonite Encyclopedia. Vol. 2, *D–H.* Scottsdale, PA: Mennonite Publishing House, 1956.

Merkley, Christopher. *Biography of Christopher Merkley: Written by Himself.* Salt Lake City: J. H. Parry, 1887.

Metcalfe, Brent Lee. "The Curious Textual History of 'Egyptus' the Wife of Ham." *John Whitmer Historical Association Journal* 34, no. 2 (Fall/Winter 2014): 1–11.

———, ed. *New Approaches to the Book of Mormon: Explorations in Critical Methodology.* Salt Lake City: Signature Books, 1993.

———. "The Priority of Mosiah: A Prelude to Book of Mormon Exegesis." In Metcalfe, ed., *New Approaches to the Book of Mormon*, 395–44.

Millard, David. *The True Messiah.* Union Mills, NY: Christian General Book Association, 1837.

Miller, Lewis. Docket Book. Henry E. Huntington Library, San Marino, CA.

Miller, Russell E. *The Larger Hope: The First Century of the Universalist Church in America, 1770–1870.* Boston: Unitarian Universalist Association, 1979.

Millet, Artemus. Reminiscences, ca. 1855. CHL.

Minute Book 1 / "Conference A," 1832–37. CHL.

Minute Book 2 / "The Conference Minutes and Record Book of Christ's Church of Latter Day Saints," 1838, 1842, 1844. CHL.

Missouri Republican. St. Louis. 1822–1919.

Missouri, State of. Adam Black, Complaint before Philip Covington, Daviess Co., MO, Sep. 12, 1838. State of MO v. Joseph Smith et al. for Riot, Daviess Co., MO, Justice of the Peace Court, 1838. Historical Department. Nineteenth-Century Legal Documents Collection. CHL.

Missouri, State of. Austin A. King, Warrant, Ray Co., MO, to Daviess Co. Sheriff [William Morgan], for Joseph Smith and Lyman Wight, Aug. 10, 1838. State of MO v. Joseph Smith et al. for Riot. Private possession. Copy in CHL. Includes endorsement by William Morgan, Aug. 12, 1838, and notation, Sep. 6, 1838. Microfilmed by the Utah Genealogical Society in 1974 at the Daviess Co. Court House, Gallatin, MO. See microfilm 959,084 (images 39–41), U.S. and Canada Record Collection, FHL.

Missouri, State of. Indictment, Honey Creek Township, Daviess Co., MO, ca. Apr. 10, 1839. State of MO v. Baldwin et al. (Including Joseph Smith) for Arson, Daviess Co. Circuit Court, 1839. Historical Department, Nineteenth-Century Legal Documents Collection, CHL.

Missouri, State of. Indictment, Honey Creek Township, Daviess Co., MO, ca. Apr. 10, 1839. State of MO v. Gates et al. (Including Joseph Smith) for Arson, Daviess Co. Circuit Court, 1839. Daviess County Courthouse, Gallatin, MO. Also available in microfilm 959,084, U.S. and Canada Record Collection, FHL.

Missouri, State of. Indictment, Honey Creek Township, Daviess Co., MO, ca. Apr. 10, 1839. State of MO v. Joseph Smith et al. for Riot, Daviess Co. Circuit Court, 1839. Historical Department, Nineteenth-Century Legal Documents Collection, CHL.

Missouri, State of. Indictment of Joseph Smith and Others for Riot, Daviess Co., MO, Apr. 1839. Boone Co., MO, Circuit Court Records. Western Historical Manuscript Collection, Ellis Library of Missouri, Columbia.

Missouri, State of. Philip Covington, Warrant to Daviess Co. Sheriff [William Morgan] or Constable, for Alanson Ripley, Ephraim Owen, Harvey Olmsted Cornelius P. Lott, George A. Smith, Hiram Nelson, Alanson Brown, John L. Butler John Woods, Harlow Redfield, Riley Stewart, James Whitaker, Ephraim Tubbs, James Nelson, and Joseph W. Younger, Sep. 12, 1838. State of MO v. Joseph Smith et al. for Riot, Daviess Co., MO, Justice of the Peace Court, 1838. Daviess County Courthouse, Gallatin, MO.

Missouri, State of. Recognizance of Joseph Smith and Lyman Wight, Sep. 7, 1838. State of MO v. Joseph Smith et al. for Riot, Daviess Co. Circuit Court, 1839. BYU. (*JSP*, D6:225–29.)

Miyahara, Kojiro. "Charisma: From Weber to Contemporary Sociology." *Sociological Inquiry* 53, no. 4 (Oct. 1983): 368–88.

Moore, Humphrey. *Treatise on the Divine Nature, Exhibiting the Distinction of Father, Son, and Holy Spirit.* Boston: Samuel T. Armstrong, 1824.

Moore, Patrick. *New Guide to the Moon*. New York: W. W. Norton, 1976.

Moore, Russell D. "Personal and Cosmic Eschatology." In *A Theology for the Church*, edited by Daniel L. Akin, David Paul Nelson, and Peter R. Schemm, 858–926. Nashville, TN: B & H Publishing, 2007.

Morgan, Joseph. *The Portsmouth disputation examined, being a brief answer to arguments used by the anti-Paedo-Baptists*. New York: William Bradford, 1713.

Morgan, William. *Illustrations of Masonry*. Batavia, NY: David C. Miller, 1826.

Morgan, William. Affidavit, July 1, 1839. William Morgan Papers, 1838–39. CHL.

Mormon War Papers, 1838–41. Missouri State Archives, Jefferson City, MO.

Morris, Larry E. "Oliver Cowdery's Vermont Years and the Origins of Mormonism." *BYU Studies* 39, no. 1 (2000): 106–29.

Moss, J. J. Letter to J. T. Cobb, Dec. 17, 1878. A. T. S. Schroeder Collection. Wisconsin State Historical Society, Madison, WI.

Mulder, William, and A. Russell Mortensen, eds. *Among the Mormons: Historic Accounts by Contemporary Observers*. Lincoln: University of Nebraska Press, 1958.

Murdock, John. Affidavit, Adams Col., IL, Jan. 10, 1840. Photocopy. Material relating to Mormon Expulsion from Missouri, 1839–43. CHL.

———. Autobiography, ca. 1859–67. John Murdock, Journal and Autobiography, ca. 1830–67. CHL.

———. Journal, ca. 1830–59. John Murdock, Journal and Autobiography, ca. 1830–67. CHL.

———. Letter to Sister Crocker and Others, July 21, 1839. CHL.

Murray, John. *Letters, and Sketches of Sermons*. 3 vols. Boston: Joshua Belcher, 1813.

Naked Truths about Mormonism: Also a Journal for Important, Newly Apprehended Truths, and Miscellany. Oakland, CA. Jan. and Apr. 1888.

Nauvoo City Council Rough Minute Books, 1841–45. Nauvoo, IL. Records, 1841–45. CHL.

Neely, Albert. Bill of Costs, 1826. Clerk of the Board of Supervisors, Chenango County Office Building, Norwich, NY. (*EMD*, 4:257–62.)

Nevin, J[ohn] W. *The Anxious Bench*. Chambersburg, PA: Office of the Weekly Messenger, 1843.

A New Conductor Generalis: Being a Summary of the Law Relative to the Duty and Office of Justice of the Peace, Sheriffs, Coroners, Constables, Jurymen, Overseers of the Poor, &c. &c. Albany, NY: E. R. Backus, 1819.

New Testament Revision 1. "A Translation of the New Testament Translated by the Power of God," 1831. CCLA. Also available in Faulring et al., eds., *Joseph Smith's New Translation of the Bible*, 153–228.

New Testament Revision 2, part 1, 1831. CCLA. Also available in Faulring et al., eds., *Joseph Smith's New Translation of the Bible*, 235–98.

Newberg, Andrew, Eugene d'Aquili, and Vince Rause. *Why God Won't Go Away: Brain Science and the Biology of Belief.* New York: Ballantine Books, 2001.

Nickell, Joe. *Looking For a Miracle: Weeping Icons, Relics, Stigmata, Visions, and Healing Cures.* Amherst, NY: Prometheus Books, 1993.

Nimer, Corwin L. "Treachery and False Swearing in Missouri: The Rise and Fall of Sampson Avard." *Mormon Historical Studies* 5, no. 2 (Fall 2004): 37–60.

Nineteenth-Century Legal Documents Collection, 1829–1973. CHL.

Noble, Joel K. Letter to Jonathan B. Turner, Mar. 8, 1842. Jonathan Baldwin Turner Papers. Illinois State Historical Library, Springfield, IL. (*EMD*, 4:106–111.)

Noble, Joseph B., and Mary Adeline Beaman Noble. Reminiscences, 1836–66. CHL.

Nuttall, L. John. Diary, 1876–84. L. John Nuttall Papers, 1857–1904. BYU.

Oakes, Len. *Prophetic Charisma: The Psychology of Revolutionary Religious Personalities.* Syracuse, New York: Syracuse University Press, 1997.

O'Dea, Thomas F. *The Mormons.* Chicago: University of Chicago Press, 1957.

Ogden, D. Kelly. "The Kirtland Hebrew School (1835–36)." In Backman, ed., *Regional Studies in Latter-day Saint Church History: Ohio,* 63–87.

Ohio Star. Ravenna. 1830–54.

Old Testament Revision 1. "A Revelation Given to Joseph the Revelator June 1830," 1830–31. CCLA. Also available in Faulring, et al., eds., *Joseph Smith's New Translation of the Bible,* 75–152.

Old Testament Revision 2, 1831–33. CCLA. Also available in Faulring, et al., eds., *Joseph Smith's New Translation of the Bible,* 591–851.

Ostler, Blake T. "The Book of Mormon as a Modern Expansion of an Ancient Source." *Dialogue: A Journal of Mormon Thought* 20, no. 1 (Spring 1987): 66–123.

———. "Earliest Pre-Existence Allusion?" Letter to the editor. *Dialogue: A Journal of Mormon Thought* 15, no. 3 (Autumn 1982): 6.

———. "The Idea of Pre-Existence in the Development of Mormon Thought." *Dialogue: A Journal of Mormon Thought* 15, no. 1 (Spring 1982): 59–78.

[Owen, Robert]. *Robert Owen's Opening Speech, and His Reply to the Rev. Alex. Campbell, in the Recent Public Discussion in Cincinnati, to Prove That the Principles of all Religions are erroneous, and that their Practice is injurious to the Human Race.* Cincinnati: Published by Robert Owen, 1829.

Paine, Thomas. *The Age of Reason. Part the First. Being An Investigation of True and Fabulous Theology.* London, 1795.

Painesville Telegraph. Painesville, OH. 1822–1986.

Palmer, James. Reminiscences, ca. 1884–98. CHL.

Paris, J. A. *Pharmacologia; Comprehending the Art of Prescribing upon Fixed and Scientific Principles.* 2 vols. 5th ed. London: W. Phillips, 1822.

Park, Benjamin E. Park, Benjamin E. "The Danite Constitution and Theories of Democratic Justice in Frontier America." *BYU Studies* 60, no. 1 (2021): 43–64.

———. "'Thou Wast Willing to Lay Down Thy Life for Thy Brethren': Zion's Blessings in the Early Church." *John Whitmer Historical Association Journal* 29 (2009): 27–37.

Parkin, Max H. Collected Missouri Court Documents, 1838–40. Photocopy. CHL.

———. "The Courthouse Mentioned in the Revelation on Zion." *BYU Studies* 14, no. 4 (1974): 451–57.

———. "A History of the Latter-day Saints in Clay County, Missouri, from 1833 to 1837." PhD diss., Brigham Young University, 1976.

———. "Joseph Smith and the United Firm: The Growth and Decline of the Church's First Master Plan of Business and Finance, Ohio and Missouri, 1832–34." *BYU Studies* 46, no. 3 (2007): 5–66.

———. "Mormon Political Involvement in Ohio." *BYU Studies* 9, no. 4 (1969): 484–502.

———. "Zion's Camp Cholera Victims Monument Dedication." *Missouri Mormon Frontier Foundation Newsletter* 15 (Fall 1997): 4–5.

Parkinson, R. B., Whitfield Diffie, Mary Fischer, and R. S. Simpson. *Cracking Codes: The Rosetta Stone and Decipherment.* Berkeley: University of California Press, 1999.

Parsons, Lucius Pomeroy. Letter to "Dear Sister" [Pamelia Parsons], Apr. 10, 1836. Western Reserve Historical Society. Cleveland, OH.

Partridge, Edward. Bonds, Far West, MO, to William W. Phelps and John Whitmer, May 17, 1837. John Whitmer Family Papers. CHL.

———. Diaries, 1818, 1835–36. Edward Partridge Papers, 1818–39. CHL.

———. History, Manuscript, ca. 1839. CHL.

———. Letter to Lydia Partridge, Aug. 5–7, 1831. Edward Partridge, Letters, 1831–35. CHL.

———. Letter to Lydia Partridge, Nov. 2–10, 1835. Edward Partridge, Letters, 1831–35. CHL.

———. Letter to Newel K. Whitney, July 24, 1838. In Reynolds Cahoon, Letter to Newel K. Whitney, July 23, 1838. CHL.

———. Proposal for Zion's City Center, Independence, Jackson Co., MO, ca. late Sep. 1833. Edward Partridge Collection. CHL. (*JSP*, D3:308–13.)

———. Report, Oct. 31, 1835. Missionary Reports, 1831–1900. CHL.

———. Scriptural Passages, ca. 1836. CHL.

———, and Lydia Partridge. Mortgage, Far West, MO, to William W. Phelps and John Whitmer, May 17, 1837. John Whitmer Family Papers, 1837–1912. CHL.

———, et al. Petition, Far West, MO, to the Missouri State Legislature, Dec. 10, 1838. Edward Partridge Papers, 1818–39. CHL.

Partridge, Edward, Jr. *Biography and Family Genealogy. Unpublished Journal.* Salt Lake City: n.p., 1878.

———. Genealogical Record, 1878. CHL.

Partridge, Eric. *A Dictionary of Slang and Unconventional English.* New York: Macmillan, 1967.

Partridge, Scott H. "Edward Partridge in Painesville, Ohio." *BYU Studies* 42, no. 1 (2003): 51–73.

Patriarchal Blessing Book, 1833–40. Vol. 1. CHL. Bound with Quorum of the Twelve Apostles Record, Feb.–Aug. 1835.

Patrides, C. A. "The Salvation of Satan." *Journal of the History of Ideas* 28 (Oct.–Dec. 1967): 467–78.

Patten, David W. Journal, 1832–34. CHL.

Patterson, Robert. *Who Wrote the Book of Mormon.* Philadelphia: L. H. Everts, 1882.

Paul, Erich Robert. "Joseph Smith and the Plurality of Worlds Idea." *Dialogue: A Journal of Mormon Thought* 19, no. 2 (Summer 1986): 12–36.

———. *Science, Religion, and Mormon Cosmology.* Urbana: University of Illinois Press, 1992.

Peck, Reed. Letter to "Dear Friends," Sep. 18, 1839. Henry E. Huntington Library, San Marino, CA.

Perego, Ugo. "Was Joseph Smith the biological father of Josephine Lyon? The genetic evidence." Mormon History Association Conference, 2016. Snowbird, UT.

Petersen, Lauritz G. "The Kirtland Temple." *BYU Studies* 12, no. 4 (1972): 400–409.

Peterson, H. Donl. *The Story of the Book of Abraham: Mummies, Manuscripts, and Mormons.* Salt Lake City: Deseret Book, 1995.

Peterson, Paul H. "An Historical Analysis of the Word of Wisdom." Master's thesis, Brigham Young University, 1972.

Pettegrew, David. "An History of David Pettegrew," n.d. David Pettegrew Papers, 1840–57. CHL.

———. Journal. David Pettegrew Family Collection, 1836–83, 1926–30. CHL.

Pettengill, Amos. *A View of the Heavens, or Familiar Lessons on Astronomy.* New Haven: Nathan Whiting, 1826.

Phelps, Morris. Reminiscences, n.d. CHL.

Phelps, William W. Collection of Missouri Documents, 1833–37. CHL.

———. Diary, Jan.–June 1835, 1864. CHL.

———. Diary and Notebook, ca. 1835–36, 1843, 1864. CHL.

———. Letter to Sally Phelps, May 26–27, 1835. William W. Phelps Papers, 1835–65. BYU.

————. Letter to Sally Phelps, July 19–20, 1835. Historical Department, Journal History of the Church, July 20, 1835, 1. CHL.

————. Letter to Sally Phelps, Sep. 11, 1835. William W. Phelps, letters, 1835–41. CHL.

————. Letter to Sally Phelps, Sep. 16, 1835. Private possession. Copy at CHL.

————. Letter to Sally Phelps, Jan. 1836. William W. Phelps Papers, 1835–65. BYU.

————. Letter to Sally Phelps, Apr. 1836. William W. Phelps Papers, 1835–65. BYU.

————. Letter to Sally Phelps, May 1, 1839. CHL.

————. Reminiscence ["A Short History of W. W. Phelps' Stay in Missouri"], 1864. CHL.

Pitman Shorthand Transcriptions, 1998–2013. CHL.

Plan of the House of the Lord, [Kirtland Township, Geauga Co., OH], ca. June 1–25, 1833. CHL. (*JSP*, D3:131–46.)

Plan of the House of the Lord in Kirtland, OH (four fragments), [Kirtland Township, Geauga Co., OH], ca. June 1833. Egyptian Papyri. CHL. (*JSP*, D3:91–102.)

Plat and Explanation of the City of Zion, [Kirtland Township, Geauga Co., OH], ca. early June–June 25, 1833. CHL. (*JSP*, D3:121–30.)

Plat of Kirtland, OH, ca. 1833. CHL. (*JSP*, D3:208–20.)

Porter, Larry C. "The Colesville Branch in Kaw Township, Jackson County, Missouri, 1831–1833." In Garr and Johnson, eds., *Regional Studies in Latter-day Saint Church History: Missouri,* 281–303.

————. "The Odyssey of William Earl McLellin: Man of Diversity, 1806–83." In Shipps and Welch, eds., *The Journals of William E. McLellin,* 323–32.

————. "A Study of the Origins of the Church of Jesus Christ of Latter-day Saints in the States of New York and Pennsylvania, 1816–1831." Ph.D. diss., Brigham Young University, 1971.

————. "'Ye Shall Go to the Ohio': Exodus of the New York Saints to Ohio, 1831." In Backman, ed., *Regional Studies in Latter-day Saint Church History: Ohio,* 1–25.

Post, Jerrold M. "Narcissism and the Charismatic Leader–Follower Relationship." *Political Psychology* 7 (Dec. 1986): 675–88.

Post, Stephen. Journals, 1835–79. Stephen Post Papers, 1835–1921. CHL.

Pratt, Orson. Journal, 1833–37. Orson Pratt, Autobiography and Journals, 1833–47. CHL.

————. Letter to Brigham Young, Nov. 20, 1852. Brigham Young Collection. CHL.

Pratt, Parley P. *The Autobiography of Parley Parker Pratt.* Edited by Parley P. Pratt, Jr. New York: Russell Brothers, 1874.

————. *History of the Late Persecution Inflicted by the State of Missouri Upon the Mormons, In Which Ten Thousand American Citizens were Robbed, Plundered, and Driven From the State, and Many Others Imprisoned, Martyred, &c. For Their Religion, and All This by Military Force, by Order of the Executive. By P. P. Pratt,*

Minister of the Gospel. Written During Eight Months Imprisonment in that State. Detroit: Dawson and Bates, 1839.

———. *Late Persecution of the Church of Jesus Christ of Latter Day Saints.* New York: J. W. Harrison, 1840.

———. Letter to Mary Ann Frost Pratt, Nov. 4, 1838. Parley P. Pratt, Letters, 1838–39. CHL.

———. *Mormonism Unveiled: Zion's Watchman Unmasked, and Its Editor, Mr. L. R. Sunderland, Exposed: Truth Vindicated: The Devil Mad, and Priestcraft in Danger!* New York: P. P. Pratt, 1838.

———. *A Short Account of a Shameful Outrage, Committed by a Part of the Inhabitants of the Town of Mentor upon the Person of Elder Parley P. Pratt.* Kirtland: Messenger and Advocate Press, 1835.

Prayer, at the Dedication of the Lord's House in Kirtland, Ohio, March 27, 1836—By Joseph Smith, Jr. President of the Church of the Latter Day Saints. Kirtland, OH, 1836.

Price, Robert M. "Joseph Smith: Inspired Author of the Book of Mormon." In Vogel and Metcalfe, eds., *American Apocrypha,* 321–66.

Prince, Gregory A. *Power from on High: The Development of Mormon Priesthood.* Salt Lake City: Signature Books, 1995.

The Proceedings of the United States Anti-Masonic Convention, Held at Philadelphia, September 11, 1830. Philadelphia: I. P. Trimble, 1830.

Proper, David B. "Joseph Smith and Salem." *Essex Institute Historical Collections* 100 (Apr. 1964): 88–98.

Quinn, D. Michael. *Early Mormonism and the Magic World View.* 2nd rev. ed. Salt Lake City: Signature Books, 1998.

———. *The Mormon Hierarchy: Origins of Power.* Salt Lake City: Signature Books, in association with Smith Research Associates, 1994.

Quorum of the Twelve Apostles. Minutes, 1840–44. CHL.

Radke, Andrea G. "We Also Marched: The Women and Children of Zion's Camp, 1834." *BYU Studies* 39, no. 1 (2000): 147–65.

Record of Seventies / First Council of the Seventy. "Book of Records," 1837–43. Vol. A. First Council of the Seventy, Records, 1837–85. CHL.

Record of the Twelve Apostles. "A Record of the Transactions of the Twelve Apostles of the Church of the Latter Day Saints from the Time of Their Call to the Apostleship Which Was on the 14th Day of Feby. AD 1835," Feb.–Aug. 1835. In Patriarchal Blessing Book, vol. 2. CHL.

Rees, Amos. Letter to Abiel Leonard, Nov. 1, 1839. Abiel Leonard Papers, 1792–1932. Manuscript Collection. State Historical Society of Missouri, Columbia, MO.

Rees, Thomas. *Todd's Johnson's Dictionary of the English Language, in Miniature.* London: Longman, Hurst, Reese, et. al, 1826.

Remini, Robert V. *The Election of Andrew Jackson.* Philadelphia: J. B. Lippincott, 1963.

Report of the Committee on the Abduction of William Morgan. Made to the Senate, Feb. 14, 1829. Albany, NY: Croswell and Van Benthuysen, 1829.

The Return. Davis City, IA, 1889–91; Richmond, MO, 1892–93; Davis City, 1895–96; Denver, 1898; Independence, MO, 1899–1900.

Revelation Book 1 / "A Book of Commandments and Revelations of the Lord Given to Joseph the Seer and Others by the Inspiration of God and Gift and Power of the Holy Ghost Which Beareth Re[c]ord of the Father and Son and Holy Ghost Which Is One God Infinite and Eternal World without End Amen," 1831–35. CHL. (*JSP*, MRB, 1–405.)

Revelation Book 2 / "Book of Revelations," 1832–34. Revelations Collection, 1831–ca. 1844, 1847, 1861, ca. 1876. CHL. (*JSP*, MRB, 407–665.)

Revelations Collection, 1831–ca. 1844, 1847, 1861, ca. 1876. CHL.

Revised Plan of the House of the Lord, Kirtland Township, OH, ca. Aug. 10–ca. Sep. 4, 1833. CHL. (*JSP*, D3:269–87.)

The Revised Statutes of the State of Missouri, Revised and Digested by the Eighth General Assembly during the Years One Thousand Eight Hundred and Thirty-Four, and One Thousand Eight Hundred and Thirty-Five. . . . St. Louis: Argus Office, 1835.

Reynolds, Noel B. "The Case for Sidney Rigdon as Author of the Lectures on Faith." *Journal of Mormon History* 31, no. 3 (Fall 2005): 1–41.

Rich, Charles C. Diaries, 1833–62. Charles C. Rich Collection, 1832–1908. CHL.

Richards, Hepzibah. Letter to Willard Richards, Jan. 18–19, 1838. Willard Richards Papers, 1821–54. CHL.

Richards, Jane S. "Reminiscences of Mrs. F. D. [Jane Snyder] Richards," San Francisco, 1880. Bancroft Library, University of California, Berkeley.

Richards, Willard. Journals, 1836–53. Willard Richards Papers, 1821–54. CHL.

———. Letter to Hepzibah Richards, Jan. 20, 1837. Levi Richards Family Correspondence, 1827–48. CHL.

———. Letter to John Whitmer, Feb. 23, 1844. Willard Richards Papers, 1821–54. CHL.

———. "W. Richards Pocket Companion Written in England." Willard Richards, Journals and Papers, 1821–54. CHL.

Richardson, Josiah. *The New-England Farrier, and Family Physician.* Exeter, NH: By the author, 1828.

Ridlon, G[ideon]. T[ibbetts]. *Saco Valley Settlements and Families: Historical, Biographical, Genealogical, Traditional, and Legendary.* Portland, ME: By the Author, 1895.

Rigdon, John Wickliff. "Life Story of Sidney Rigdon," n.d. CHL.

Rigdon, Sidney. *An Appeal to the American People: Being an Account of the Persecutions of the Church of Latter Day Saints; and of the Barbarities Inflicted on Them by the Inhabitants of the State of Missouri.* Cincinnati: Glezen and Shepard, 1840.

937

———. Letter to "the Saints," Aug. 31, 1831. Sidney Rigdon Collection, 1831–58. CHL.

———. *Oration Delivered by Mr. S. Rigdon on the 4th of July, 1838, at Far West, Caldwell County, Missouri.* Far West, MO: Journal Office, 1838.

———. Statement, 1842. Historian's Office. JS History Documents, 1839–60. CHL.

———, Jesse Gause, David Whitmer, Peter Whitmer Jr., Hyrum Smith, and Reynolds Cahoon. Charges against Missouri Conference Preferred to Joseph Smith, Hiram Township, Portage Co., OH, ca. Mar. 1832. General Ecclesiastical Court Trials, 1832–1963. CHL. (*JSP*, D2:222–29.)

———, Joseph Smith and Hyrum Smith. Letter to Heber C. Kimball and Brigham Young, Jan. 16, 1839. Kimball Family Correspondence, 1838–71. CHL. (*JSP*, D6:310–16.)

Riggs, Michael S., and John E. Thompson. "Joseph Smith, Jr., and 'The Notorious Case of Aaron Lyon': Evidence of Earlier Doctrinal Development of Salvation for the Dead and a Trigger for the Practice of Polyandry?" *John Whitmer Historical Association Journal* 26 (2006): 101–19.

Ritner, Robert K. *The Joseph Smith Egyptian Papyri: A Complete Edition.* Salt Lake City: Smith-Petit Foundation, 2011.

Robinson, George W. Agreement with Joseph Smith, Sidney Rigdon, and Hyrum Smith, Apr. 30, 1839. Newel K. Whitney Papers, 1825–1906. BYU. (*JSP*, D6:439–42.)

———. Letter to Thomas B. Marsh, Jan. 10, 1838. CHL.

Robinson, Joseph Lee. Autobiography and Journal, 1853–83. CHL.

Robison, Elwin C. *The First Mormon Temple: Design, Construction, and Historic Context of the Kirtland Temple.* Provo, UT: Brigham Young University Press, 1997.

Rockwood, Albert Perry. Journal Entries, Oct. 1838–Jan. 1839. Photocopy. CHL. Beinecke Rare Book and Manuscript Library. Yale University. New Haven, CT.

Roelofs, Karin, Kees A. L. Hoogduin, Ger P. J. Keijsers, Gerard W. B. Naring, Franny C. Moene and Pieter Sandijck. "Hypnotic Susceptibility in Patients with Conversion Disorder." *Journal of Abnormal Psychology* 3, no. 2 (2002): 390–95.

Rogers, David. Statement, Feb. 1, 1839. CHL.

Rollins, James Henry. "The History of James Henry Rollins," 1924. Typescript. Mary Elizabeth Rollins Lightner family collection, 1833–1973. CHL. Dictated by Rollins in 1896.

———. Reminiscences, 1896, 1898. CHL.

Romig, Ronald E. *Early Independence, Missouri: "Mormon" History Tour Guide.* Independence, MO: Missouri Mormon Frontier Foundation, 1994.

———, and Michael S. Riggs. "Reassessing Joseph Smith's 'Appointed Time for the Redemption of Zion.'" In Spencer, ed., *The Missouri Mormon Experience*, 27–49.

———, and John H. Siebert. "First Impressions: The Independence, Missouri, Printing Operation, 1832–33." *John Whitmer Historical Association Journal* 10 (1990): 51–66.

Roper, Matthew. "The Mythical 'Manuscript Found.'" *FARMS Review* 17, no.2 (2005): 7–140. Review of Wayne L. Cowdrey, Howard Davis, Hugh O'Neal, and Arthur Vanick, *Who Really Wrote the Book of Mormon? The Spalding Enigma* (St. Louis: Concordia Publishing House, 2005).

Rosenberg, Charles E. *The Cholera Years: The United States in 1832, 1849, and 1866.* Chicago: University of Chicago Press, 1962.

Rowley, William. Autobiography, ca. 1843. Special Collections, J. Willard Marriott Library, University of Utah Library, Salt Lake City.

Saints' Herald. Independence, MO. 1860–.

Sanborn, P[eter]. *Minutes of an Address, Delivered before the Anti-Masonic Convention of Reading, Mass. January 15, 1829.* Boston: The Free Press, 1829.

Saunders, Benjamin. Interview with William H. Kelley, ca. Sep. 1884. "Miscellany." CCLA. (*EMD,* 2:136–39.)

Saunders, Lorenzo. Interview with E. L. Kelley, Nov. 12, 1884. E. L. Kelley Papers. CCLA. (*EMD,* 2:146–64.)

———. Interview with William H. Kelley, Sep. 17, 1884. E. L. Kelley Papers. CCLA. (*EMD,* 2:125–35.)

Saunders, Richard LaVell. *A Transcription of "Zion's Messenger," by Francis Gladden Bishop, Council Bluffs, Iowa,* 1854. Logan, UT: n.p., 1986.

Schaffer, Simon. "'The Great Laboratories of the Universe': William Herschel on Matter Theory and Planetary Life." *Journal for the History of Astronomy* 11, no. 2 (June 1980): 81–111.

Schick, Theodore, Jr., and Lewis Vaughn. *How to Think about Weird Things: Critical Thinking for a New Age.* 2nd ed. Mountain View, CA: Mayfield Publishing, 1999.

Schindler, Harold. *Orrin Porter Rockwell: Man of God, Son of Thunder.* Salt Lake City, UT: University of Utah Press, 1966.

Schlesinger, Arthur M., Jr. *The Age of Jackson.* Boston: Little, Brown, and Company, 1945.

School of the Prophets Provo Records, 1868–72. CHL.

School of the Prophets Saint George Records, 1883, 1885. CHL.

School of the Prophets Salt Lake City Minutes, Apr.–Dec. 1883. CHL.

Scott, Thomas. *The Holy Bible, Containing the Old and New Testaments . . . Vol. 1.* Boston: Samuel T. Armstrong, 1827.

Scraps of Biography. Tenth Book of the Faith-Promoting Series. Salt Lake City: Juvenile Instructor Office, 1883.

Seixas, Joshua. Certificate to Joseph Smith, Kirtland Township, Geauga Co., OH, Mar. 30, 1836. JS Collection. CHL. (*JSP,* D5:214–16.)

———. *A Manual Hebrew Grammar for the Use of Beginners.* 2nd ed. Andover, MA: Gould and Newman, 1834.

Shafer, Robert Jones. *A Guide to Historical Method.* 3rd ed. Belmont, CA: Wadsworth Publishing, 1980.

Shepard, William, and H. Michael Marquardt. *Lost Apostles: Forgotten Members of Mormonism's Original Quorum of Twelve.* Salt Lake City: Signature Books, 2014.

———. "Mortal Enemies: Mormons and Missourians 1839–1844." *John Whitmer Historical Association Journal* 36, no. 1 (Spring/Summer 2016): 35–80.

———. "The Relationship of Oliver Cowdery with Joseph Smith." *John Whitmer Historical Association Journal* 38, no. 1 (Spring/Summer 2018): 95–130.

Shipps, Jan. "The Prophet Puzzle: Suggestions Leading toward a More Comprehensive Interpretation of Joseph Smith." In Waterman, ed., *The Prophet Puzzle,* 25–47. Originally published in *Journal of Mormon History* 1 (1974): 3–20.

———, and John W. Welch, eds. *The Journals of William E. McLellin, 1831–1836.* Provo, UT: BYU Studies; Urbana: University of Illinois Press, 1994.

Shurtliff, Luman A. Autobiography, ca. 1852–76. CHL.

Shook, Charles A. *The True Origin of the Book of Mormon.* Cincinnati, OH: Standard Publishing, [1914].

Shurtliff, Luman A. Autobiography, ca. 1852–76. CHL.

Smith, Elias. "Journal of the camp of the Seventies during their journey from Kirtland to Far West 1838," Mar.–Oct. 1838. CHL.

Smith, George A. History / "History of George A. Smith by Himself," ca. 1857–75. George A. Smith Papers, 1834–77. CHL. Rough draft of Memoirs.

———. Memoirs and Autobiography, ca. 1860–82. George Albert Smith Papers, 1834–77. CHL.

Smith, George D. *Nauvoo Polygamy: "…But We Called It Celestial Marriage."* Salt Lake City: Signature Books, 2008.

Smith, Hyrum. Bill of Damages, ca. June 1839. CHL.

———. Diary, Nov. 1832–Apr. 1833. Hyrum Smith Papers, ca. 1832–ca. 1911. BYU.

———. Diary and Account Book, Nov. 1831–Feb. 1835. Hyrum Smith Papers, ca. 1832–44. BYU.

———. Letter to Mary Fielding Smith, Mar. 16, 1839. Mary Fielding Smith Collection. CHL.

———. Letter to Mary Fielding Smith, Mar. 19, 1839. Mary Fielding Smith Collection. CHL.

———. Letter to Mary Fielding Smith, ca. Apr. 5, 1839. Mary Fielding Smith Collection. CHL.

———. Petition, Liberty, Clay Co., MO, Mar. 9, 1839. CHL.

Smith, Hyrum M., and Janne M. Sjodahl. *Doctrine and Covenants Commentary.* Salt Lake City: Deseret Book, 1978.

Smith, Job. "Diary of Job Smith, a Pioneer of Nauvoo, Ill., and Utah," n.d. Typescript. CHL.

Smith, John. Journal, 1833–41. John Smith Papers, 1833–54. CHL.

———. Letter to George A. Smith, Jan. 1, 1838. George A. Smith Papers. CHL.

———, and Marcellus Cowdery. Letter to George A. Smith, Sep. 26, 1837. George Albert Smith Papers. CHL.

———, and Clarissa Smith. Letter to George A. Smith, Jan. 15 and 17, 1838. With additional letter by Don Carlos Smith, Jan. 18, 1838. George Albert Smith Papers. CHL.

———, and Clarissa Smith. Letter to George A. Smith, Jan. 1, 1838. With additional letter by Samuel James, Jan. 17, 1838. George Albert Smith Papers. CHL.

Smith, John E., ed. *The Works of Jonathan Edwards.* 5 vols. New Haven and London: Yale University Press, 1972.

Smith, Joseph. Agreement, Kirtland Township, Geauga Co., OH, Jan. 4, 1838. CHL. (*JSP*, D5:489–92.)

———. Journal, Nov. 1832–Dec. 1834. JS Collection. CHL.

———. Journal, Sept. 1835–Apr. 1836. JS Collection. CHL.

———. Journal, Mar.–Sept. 1838. In "General," Record Book, 1838, verso of Patriarchal Blessings, vol. 5. CHL.

———. Journal, Apr.–Oct. 1839. JS Collection. CHL.

———. Journal, 4 vols., Dec. 1842–June 1844. JS Collection. CHL.

———. Letter to Emma Smith, June 6, 1832. Manuscripts about Mormons, 1832–1954. Chicago History Museum. Chicago, IL. (*JSP*, D2:246–57.)

———. Letter to Emma Smith, Oct. 13, 1832. CCLA. (*JSP*, D2:304–14.)

———. Letter to Emma Smith, May 18, 1834. Joseph Smith Materials. CCLA. (*JSP*, D4:48–52.)

———. Letter to Sally Phelps, July 20, 1835. Photograph of original. CHL. (*JSP*, D4:368–71.)

———. Letter to Emma Smith, Aug. 19, 1836. Charles Aldrich Autograph Collection. State Historical Society of Iowa, Des Moines. (*JSP*, D5:280–83.)

———. Letter and Revelation to Edward Partridge, Jan. 7, 1838. In Edward Partridge Jr., Genealogical Record, 52. CHL. (*JSP*, D5:492–94.)

———. Letter to Emma Smith, Nov. 4, 1838. JS Materials. CCLA. (*JSP*, D6:279–82.)

———. Letter to Emma Smith, Far West, MO, Nov. 12, 1838. JS Materials. CCLA. (*JSP*, D6:290–93.)

———. Letter to Emma Smith, Dec. 1, 1838. CHL. (*JSP*, D6:293–94.)

———. Letter to Emma Smith, Apr. 4, 1839. Joseph Smith Papers. Beinecke Rare Book and Manuscript Library. Yale University. New Haven, CT. (*JSP*, D6:401–406.)

———. Letter to Oliver Granger, May 4, 1841. Abraham Lincoln Presidential Library & Museum, Springfield, IL. (*JSP*, D8:135–38.)

———, Sidney Rigdon, and Hyrum Smith. Blessing to Alvin Winegar, Feb. 7, 1836. Alvin Winegar, Record Book, ca. 1850s. Private possession. Photocopy in Alvin Winegar Papers. CHL. (*JSP*, D5:165–68.)

———, and Sidney Rigdon. Letter to Stephen Post, Sep. 17, 1838. Stephen Post Papers. CHL. (*JSP*, D6:240–45.)

———, Sidney Rigdon, and Elias Higbee. Memorial to the United States Senate and House of Representatives, Washington DC, ca. Oct. 30, 1839–Jan. 27, 1840. Records of the U.S. Senate, Record Group 46, National Archives and Records Administration. Washington DC. (*JSP*, D7:138–74).

———, and Others. Mortgage for Property in Kirtland Township, Geauga Co., OH, to Mead, Stafford & Co., July 11, 1837. Hiram Kimball Collection. CHL. (*JSP*, D5:404–10.)

———, Sidney Rigdon, and Oliver Cowdery to Holbrook & Ferme. Promissory Note, Kirtland, OH, Sep. 1, 1837. Ohio Historical Society, Columbus, OH.

———, Sidney Rigdon, and Oliver Cowdery to Holbrook & Ferme. Promissory Note, Kirtland, OH, Sep. 1, 1837. BYU.

———, Reuben Hedlock, Sidney Rigdon, John Gould, and Vinson Knight. Promissory Notes (3), Kirtland Township, Geauga Co., OH, to Bailey, Keeler & Remsen, New York City, New York Co., NY, Sep. 26, 1837. Lake County Historical Society. Painesville, OH.

———, Sidney Rigdon, and Hyrum Smith. Recommendation for Heber C. Kimball, Kirtland Township, Geauga Co., OH, ca. June 2–13, 1837. CHL. (*JSP*, D5:397–401.)

Smith, Joseph, III. Notes of Interview with Emma Smith Bidamon, Feb. 1879. CCLA. (*EMD*, 1:536–40.)

———, and Heman C. Smith. *The History of The Reorganized Church of Jesus Christ of Latter Day Saints.* Vols. 1–4. Lamoni, Iowa, 1896–1903.

Smith, Joseph F. Journals, 1856–83, 1909, 1912. Joseph F. Smith Papers, 1854–1918. CHL.

Smith, Lucy Mack. *Biographical Sketches of Joseph Smith the Prophet and His Progenitors for Many Generations.* Liverpool: S. W. Richards, 1853.

———. History, 1844–45. 18 books. CHL.

———. History, 1845. CHL.

Smith, Mary Fielding. Letter to Mercy Fielding Thompson, ca. June 1837. Mary Fielding Smith Collection. CHL.

———. Letter to Mercy Thompson, July 8, 1837. Mary Fielding Smith Collection. CHL.

———. Letter to Mercy Fielding Thompson, ca. Sep. 1837. Mary Fielding Smith Collection. CHL.

———. Letter to Mercy Fielding Thompson and Robert Thompson, Churchville, Oct. 7, 1837. Mary Fielding Smith Collection. CHL.

———. Letter to Hyrum Smith, Apr. 11, 1839. Mary Fielding Smith Collection. CHL.

Smith, Samuel. Diary, Nov.–Dec. 1831. CHL.

Smith, William. *William Smith on Mormonism.* Lamoni, IA: Herald Steam Book and Job Office, 1883. (*EMD*, 1:493–502.)

Smith, William V. "Early Mormon Priesthood Revelations: Text, Impact, and Evolution." *Dialogue: A Journal of Mormon Thought* 46, no. 4 (Winter 2013): 1–84.

Snow, Eliza R. Interview, ca. 1887. Andrew Jenson, Notes. Andrew Jenson Papers. Joseph Smith polygamy folder, Document 10. CHL.

———. "Sketch of My Life," ca. 1885. Utah and Mormons Collection. Bancroft Library, University of California, Berkeley. Microfilm copy in CHL.

Snow, Erastus. Journal, 1838–41. CHL.

Speech of Orson Hyde, Delivered Before the High Priest's Quorum in Nauvoo, April 27th, 1845. Nauvoo, IL: John Taylor, 1845.

Spencer, Thomas M., ed. *The Missouri Mormon Experience.* Columbia: University of Missouri Press, 2010.

———. "'Persecution in the Most Odious Sense of the Word.'" In Spencer, ed., *The Missouri Mormon Experience,* 1–26.

Stackhouse, Thomas. *An History of the Holy Bible: From the Beginning of the World . . .* Vol. 1. London: I. Garner, 1787.

Staker, Mark L. *Hearken, O Ye People: The Historical Setting of Joseph Smith's Ohio Revelations.* Salt Lake City: Greg Kofford Books, 2009.

———. "'Thou Art the Man': Newel K. Whitney in Ohio." *BYU Studies* 42, no. 1 (2003): 75–138.

State of Missouri v. Alanson Ripley, Watson Barlow, William D. Huntington, David Holman, and Erastus Snow, Feb. 8–13, 1839. Liberty, Clay Co., MO, Justice of the Peace Court, 1839. Clay County Archives and Historical Library, Liberty, MO.

The Statutes of Ohio and of the Northwestern Territory, Adopted or Enacted from 1788 to 1833 Inclusive: Together with the Ordinance of 1787; the Constitutions of Ohio and of the United States, and Various Public Instruments and Acts of Congress: Illustrated by a Preliminary Sketch of the History of Ohio; Numerous References and Notes, and Copious Indexes. 3 vols. Edited by Salmon P. Chase. Cincinnati: Corey and Fairbank, 1833–35.

Stearns, John G. *An Inquiry Into the Nature and Tendency of Speculative Free-Masonry.* 3rd ed. Utica, NY: Northway & Bennett, 1827.

Stenhouse, T. B. H. *The Rocky Mountain Saints.* New York: D. Appleton, 1873.

Stevens, Walter B. *Centennial History of Missouri (The Center State): One Hundred Years in the Union, 1820–1921.* Vol. 2. Chicago: S. J. Clarke Publishing, 1921.

Stevenson, Edward. Autobiography, ca. 1891–93. Edward Stevenson Collection. CHL.

———. Letter to Franklin D. Richards, Feb. 12, 1886. First Presidency (John Taylor) Correspondence, 1877–87. CHL.

———. *Reminiscences of Joseph, the Prophet, and the Coming Forth of the Book of Mormon.* Salt Lake City: Edward Stevenson, 1893.

Stewart, Grace G. "A History of the Medicinal Use of Tobacco, 1492–1860." *Medical History* 11, no. 3 (July 1967): 228–268.

Stokes, Durward T., ed. "Wilson Letters, 1835–1849." *Missouri Historical Review* 60, no. 4 (July 1966): 495–517.

Stone, William L. *Matthews and His Impostures: Or, The Progress of Fanaticism. Illustrated in the Extraordinary Case of Robert Matthews, and Some of His Forerunners and Disciples.* New York: Harper and Brothers, 1835.

Stout, Allen J. Statement, n.d. In Lafayette C. Lee, Notebook, n.d. CHL.

Swartzell, William. *Mormonism Exposed.* Perkin, OH: By the Author, 1840.

[Tanner, John]. "Sketch of an Elder's Life." In *Scraps of Biography. Tenth Book of the Faith-Promoting Series,* 1–19.

Tanner, Nathan. Address, n.d. CHL.

———. "History of John Tanner," n.d. CHL.

Taves, Ann. *Fits, Trances, and Visions: Experiencing Religion and Explaining Experience from Wesley to James.* Princeton, NJ: Princeton University Press, 1999.

———. "History and the Claims of Revelation: Joseph Smith and the Materialization of the Golden Plates." *Numen: International Review for the History of Religions* 61, nos. 1/2 (2014): 182–207.

Taylor, Alan. "Rediscovering the Context of Joseph Smith's Treasure Seeking." *Dialogue: A Journal of Mormon Thought* 19, no. 4 (Winter 1986): 18–28.

Taylor, John. "History of John Taylor," 1858. Historian's Office. Histories of the Twelve, 1856–58, 1861. CHL.

Teachers Quorum. Minutes, 1834–45. CHL.

Thomas, Keith. *Religion and the Decline of Magic: Studies in Popular Beliefs in Sixteenth and Seventeenth Century England.* New York: Charles Scribner's Sons, 1971.

Thompson, R. B. *Journal of Heber C. Kimball, an Elder of the Church of Jesus Christ of Latter Day Saints.* Nauvoo, IL: Robinson & Smith, 1840.

Thurston, Morris A. "The Boggs Shooting and Attempted Extradition: Joseph Smith's Most Famous Case." *BYU Studies* 48, no. 1 (2009): 5–56.

Times and Seasons. Commerce/Nauvoo, IL. Nov. 1839–Feb. 1846.

Tippets, John H. Autobiography, ca. 1882. CHL.

Todd, Jay M. *The Saga of the Book of Abraham.* Salt Lake City: Deseret Book, 1969.

Toland, John. *Amyntor, or, A Defense of Milton's Life: Containing I. A General Apology for All Writing of that Kind, II. A Catalogue of Books Attributes in the Primitive Times to Jesus Christ . . .* London, 1699.

Townsend, Jesse. Letter to Phineas Stiles, Dec. 24, 1833. In Tucker, *Origin, Rise, and Progress of Mormonism*, 288–91. (*EMD*, 3:20–23.)

Townsend, John K. *Narrative of a Journey across the Rocky Mountains to the Columbia River, and a Visit to the Sandwich Islands, Chili, &c.* Philadelphia: Henry Perkins, 1839.

Transcript of Proceedings, Richmond, Ray Co., MO, Nov. 12–29, 1838. State of MO v. Joseph Smith et al. for Treason. Fifth Judicial Circuit of MO 1838. Eugene Morrow Violette Collection. State Historical Society of Missouri, Columbia, MO.

Tucker, Pomeroy. *Origin, Rise, and Progress of Mormonism.* New York: D. Appleton, 1867.

Tullidge, Edward. *The Women of Mormondom.* New York: [Tullidge & Crandall], 1877.

Turley, Theodore. Memoranda, 1845. Historian's Office, JS History Documents, 1839–60. CHL. (*EMD*, 5:240–41; Vogel, *History of Joseph Smith*, 103–106.)

Turner, O[rsamus]. *History of the Pioneer Settlement of Phelps and Gorham's Purchase.* Rochester, NY: William Alling, 1851.

Tyler, Daniel. "Incidents of Experience." In *Scraps of Biography. Tenth Book of the Faith-Promoting Series*, 20–46.

Tyler, Samuel D. "A Journal of the traveling of the Camp of Latter-day Saints which sent out from Kirtland for Zion July 6th 1838," July 6–Oct. 4, 1838. CHL.

Van Fossen, Anthony B. "How Do Movements Survive Failures of Prophecy?" In Stone, ed., *Expecting Armageddon*, 175–90.

Van Orden, Bruce. "Writing to Zion: The William W. Phelps Kirtland Letters (1835–36)." *BYU Studies* 33, no. 3 (1993): 543–91.

Van Wagoner, Richard S. *Mormon Polygamy: A History.* 2nd ed. Salt Lake City: Signature Books, 1989.

———. *Sidney Rigdon: A Portrait of Religious Excess.* Salt Lake City: Signature Books, 1994.

VanderMolen, Ronald J. "Providence as Mystery, Providence as Revelation: Puritan and Anglican Modifications of John Calvin's Doctrine of Providence." *Church History* 47, no. 1 (Mar. 1978): 27–47.

Vaughn, William Preston. *The Antimasonic Party in the United States, 1826–1843.* Lexington, KY: University Press of Kentucky, 1983.

Viner, Jacob. *The Role of Providence in the Social Order.* Philadelphia: American Philosophical Society, 1972.

Vogel, Dan. "Anti-Universalist Rhetoric in the Book of Mormon." In Metcalfe, ed., *New Approaches to the Book of Mormon*, 21–52.

———. *Book of Abraham Apologetics: A Review and Critique.* Salt Lake City: Signature Books, 2021.

———. "The Earliest Mormon Concept of God." In Bergera, ed., *Line Upon Line*, 17–33.

———, ed. *Early Mormon Documents.* 5 vols. Salt Lake City: Signature Books, 1996–2003. Available online at archive.org.

———. "Evolution of Early Mormon Priesthood Narratives." *John Whitmer Historical Association Journal* 34, no. 1 (Spring/Summer 2014): 58–80.

———. *History of Joseph Smith and The Church of Jesus Christ of Latter-day Saints: A Source- and Text-Critical Edition.* 8 vols. Salt Lake City: Smith–Pettit Foundation, 2015. Available online at archive.org.

———. *Indian Origins and the Book of Mormon: Religious Solutions from Columbus to Joseph Smith.* Salt Lake City: Signature Books, 1986. Available online at archive.org.

———. "James Colin Brewster: The Boy Prophet Who Challenged Mormon Authority." In *Differing Visions: Dissenters in Mormon History*, edited by Roger D. Launius and Linda Thatcher, 120–39. Urbana and Chicago: University of Illinois Press, 1994.

———. *Joseph Smith: The Making of a Prophet.* Salt Lake City: Signature Books, 2004.

———. "The Locations of Joseph Smith's Early Treasure Quests." *Dialogue: A Journal of Mormon Thought* 27, no. 3 (Fall 1994): 197–231.

———, ed. *Mormonism Unvailed.* Salt Lake City: Signature Books, 2015.

———. "Mormonism's 'Anti-Masonick Bible.'" *John Whitmer Historical Association Journal* 9 (1989): 17–30.

———. "'The Prophet Puzzle' Revisited." In Waterman, ed., *The Prophet Puzzle*, 49–67. Originally published in *Dialogue: A Journal of Mormon Thought* 31, no. 3 (Fall 1998): 125–40.

———. *Religious Seekers and the Advent of Mormonism.* Salt Lake City: Signature Books, 1988. Available online at archive.org.

———. "The Validity of the Witnesses' Testimonies." In Vogel and Metcalfe, eds., *American Apocrypha: Essays on the Book of Mormon*, 79–121.

———, ed. *The Wilford Woodruff Journals.* 6 vols. Salt Lake City: Benchmark Books, 2020.

———, ed. *The Word of God: Essays on Mormon Scripture.* Salt Lake City: Signature Books, 1990.

———, and Scott C. Dunn. "'The Tongue of Angels': Glossolalia among the Founding Mormons." *Journal of Mormon History* 19 (Fall 1993): 1–34.

————, and Brent Lee Metcalfe, eds. *American Apocrypha: Essays on the Book of Mormon*. Salt Lake City: Signature Books, 2002.

————, and Brent Lee Metcalfe. "Joseph Smith's Scriptural Cosmology." In Vogel, ed., *The Word of God*, 187–219.

Walker, Jeffrey N. "Habeas Corpus in Early Nineteenth-Century Mormonism: Joseph Smith's Legal Bulwark for Personal Freedom." *BYU Studies* 52, no. 1 (2013): 4–97.

————. "Invoking Habeas Corpus in Missouri and Illinois." In Madsen et al., eds., *Sustaining the Law*, 357–99.

————. "The Kirtland Safety Society and the Fraud of Grandison Newell: A Legal Examination." *BYU Studies* 54, no. 3 (2015): 33–147.

Walker, Ronald W. "The Persisting Idea of American Treasure Hunting." *BYU Studies* 24, no. 4 (1984): 429–59.

Wallis, Roy. "The Social Construction of Charisma." *Social Compass* 29, no. 1 (Feb. 1982): 25–39.

Walters, Wesley P. "New Light on Mormon Origins from the Palmyra Revival." *Dialogue: A Journal of Mormon Thought* 4, no.1 (Spring 1969): 60–81.

————. "A Reply to Dr. Bushman." *Dialogue: A Journal of Mormon Thought* 4, no. 1 (Spring 1969): 94–100.

Waterman, Bryan, ed. *The Prophet Puzzle: Interpretive Essays on Joseph Smith*. Salt Lake City: Signature Books, 1999.

Wayment, Thomas A. "Joseph Smith, Adam Clarke, and the Making of a Bible Revision." *Journal of Mormon History* 46, no. 3 (2020): 1–22.

————, and Haley Wilson-Lemmon. "A Recovered Resource: The Use of Adam Clarke's Bible Commentary in Joseph Smith's Bible Translation." In MacKay et al., *Producing Ancient Scripture*, 262–84.

Webb, Eliza Jane. Letter to Mary Bond, Apr. 24, 1876. Biographical Folder Collection. CCLA.

Weber, Max. *Economy and Society*. Translated by G. Roth and C. Wittich. Berkeley, CA: University of California Press, 1968. Originally published in 1922.

Weber, Samuel R. "'Shake Off the Dust of Thy Feet': The Rise and Fall of Mormon Ritual Cursing." *Dialogue: A Journal of Mormon Thought* 46, no. 1 (Spring 2013): 108–39.

Webster, Noah. *Compendious Dictionary of the English Language*. Hartford, CT: Hudson & Goodwin, 1806.

Weed, Harriet A. *Autobiography of Thurlow Weed*. Boston: Houghton, Mifflin, 1883.

West, William S. *A Few Interesting Facts Respecting the Rise Progress and Pretentions of the Mormons*. [Warren? OH]: Published by author, 1837.

Whiston, William, trans. *Josephus Complete Works*. Grand Rapids, MI: Kregel Publications, 1960.

White, Joseph W. "The Influence of Sidney Rigdon upon the Theology of Mormonism." Master's thesis, University of Southern California, 1947.

Whitmer, David. *An Address to All Believers in Christ.* Richmond, MO: D. Whitmer, 1887.

Whitmer, John. Daybook, 1832–78. CHL.

———. History, 1831–ca. 1847. CCLA. (*JSP*, H2:3–110.)

———. Letter to Oliver Cowdery and David Whitmer, Aug. 29, 1837. Western Americana Collection. Beinecke Rare Book and Manuscript Library, Yale University, New Haven CN.

Whitmer, Peter, Jr. Journal, Dec. 1831. CHL.

Whitney, Horace. Letter to Elizabeth Ann Whitney, Feb. 16, 1870. Newel K. Whitney Papers, 1825–1906. BYU.

Whitney, Newel K. Papers, 1825–1906. BYU.

———. Statement, 1842. Historian's Office. JS History Documents. CHL.

Whitney, Orson F. *Life of Heber C. Kimball.* Salt Lake City: The Kimball Family, 1888.

Whittaker, David J. "Mormons and Native Americans: A Historical and Biographical Introduction." *Dialogue: A Journal of Mormon Thought* 18, no. 4 (Winter 1985): 33–64.

Whittier, Charles H., and Stephen W. Stathis. "The Enigma of Solomon Spalding." *Dialogue: A Journal of Mormon Thought* 10, no. 4 (Autumn 1977): 70–73.

Wight, Lyman. Journal, 1837–39. In Smith and Smith, *The History of The Reorganized Church of Jesus Christ of Latter Day Saints*, vol. 1, 401–402, 443; vol. 2, 114, 155–56, 259–61, 295–98, 316–17, 323, 330.

———. Letter to Wilford Woodruff, Aug. 24, 1857. Historian's Office, Histories of the Twelve, ca. 1858–80. CHL.

Williams, Frederick G. "Account on Farm," n.d. Financial papers and statements, 1834–37. Frederick G. Williams Papers, 1834–42. CHL.

———. Statement, n.d. Financial papers and statements, 1837–42. Frederick G. Williams Papers, 1834–42. CHL.

———. "Statement of facts relative to J Smith & myself," n.d. Financial papers and statements, 1837–42. Frederick G. Williams Papers, 1834–42. CHL.

Williams, Frederick G., III. *The Life of Dr. Frederick G. Williams, Counselor to the Prophet Joseph Smith.* Provo, UT: BYU Studies, 2012.

Wilson, Haley, and Thomas Wayment. "A Recently Recovered Source: Rethinking Joseph Smith's Bible Translation." *Journal of Undergraduate Research* (Provo, UT: BYU, Mar. 16, 2017). Online at jur.byu.edu/?p=21296 (accessed Mar. 9, 2021).

Winchester, B[enjamin]. *The Origin of the Spaulding Story, concerning the Manuscript Found; with a Short Biography of Dr. P. Hulbert, the Originator of the Same; and Some Testimony Adduced, Showing It to Be a Sheer Fabrication, So Far as Its*

Connection with the Book of Mormon Is Concerned. Philadelphia: Brown, Bicking, and Guilbert, 1840.

Winchester, Benjamin. *Plain Facts, Shewing the Origin of the Spaulding Story, concerning the Manuscript Found, and Its Being Transformed into the Book of Mormon; with a Short History of Dr. P. Hulbert, the Author of the Said Story . . . Republished by George J. Adams, Minister of the Gospel, Bedford, England. To Which Is Added, a Letter from Elder S. Rigdon, Also, One from Elder O. Hyde, on the Above Subject.* Bedford, England: C. B. Merry, 1841.

Winn, Kenneth H. *Exiles in a Land of Liberty: Mormons in America, 1830–1846.* Chapel Hill: University of North Carolina Press, 1989.

———. "'Such Republicanism as This': John Corrill's Rejection of Prophetic Rule." In Launius and Thatcher, eds., *Differing Visions,* 45–75.

Winters, Mary Ann Stearns. "An Autobiographical Sketch of the Life of the Late Mary Ann Stearns Winters, Daughter of Mary Ann Sterns Pratt," n.d. Typescript. CHL.

Woodruff, Phebe. Letter to Wilford Woodruff, Mar. 1, 1838. Wilford Woodruff Collection, 1831–1905. CHL.

Woodruff, Wilford. "The History and Travels of Zion's Camp, Led by the Prophet Joseph Smith from Kirtland Ohio to Clay County Missoura in the Spring of 1834," 1882. CHL.

———. Journals, 1833–98. Wilford Woodruff, Journals and Papers, 1828–98. CHL.

Woodson, W. H. *History of Clay County, Missouri.* Topeka, KS: Historical Publishing, 1920.

Wright, David P. "Isaiah in the Book of Mormon: Or Joseph Smith in Isaiah." In Vogel and Metcalfe, eds., *American Apocrypha,* 157–234.

Wyl, Wilhelm. [pseud. Wilhelm Ritter von Wymetal]. *Mormon Portraits: or, The Truth about the Mormon Leaders from 1830 to 1886[,] Volume First[.] Joseph Smith, the Prophet, His Family and His Friends.* Salt Lake City: Tribune Printing and Publishing, 1886.

Young, Ann Eliza Webb. *Wife No. 19, or the Story of a Life in Bondage, being a Complete Expose of Mormonism, and Revealing the Sorrows, Sacrifices and Sufferings of Women in Polygamy.* Hartford, CN: Dustin, Gilman, 1875.

Young, Brigham. Journals, 1832–77. Brigham Young Office Files, 1832–78. CHL.

Young, Joseph, Sr. *History of the Organization of the Seventies: Names of First and Second Quorums. Items in Relation to the First Presidency of the Seventies. Also, a Brief Glance at Enoch and His City. Embellished with a Likeness of Joseph Smith, the Prophet, and a View of the Kirtland Temple.* Salt Lake City: Deseret News Steam Printing Establishment, 1878.

———. Letter to Lewis Harvey, Nov. 16, 1880. CHL.

Young, Lorenzo. "Lorenzo Dow Young's Narrative." In *Fragments of Experience: Sixth Book of the Faith-Promoting Series*, 22–54. Salt Lake City: Juvenile Instructor Office, 1882.

Young Woman's Journal. Salt Lake City. Oct. 1889–Oct. 1929.

Zaragoza, M. S., and K. J. Mitchell. "Repeated Exposure to Suggestion and the Creation of False Memories." *Psychological Science* 7, no. 5 (Sep. 1996): 294–300.

Zucker, Louis C. "Joseph Smith as a Student of Hebrew." *Dialogue: A Journal of Mormon Thought* 3, no. 2 (Summer 1968): 41–55.

Zusne, Leonard, and Warren H. Jones. *Anomalistic Psychology: A Study of Extraordinary Phenomena of Behavior and Experience.* Hillsdale, NJ: Lawrence Erlbaum Associates, 1982.

Zygmunt, Joseph F. "When Prophecies Fail: A Theoretical Perspective on the Comparative Evidence." In *Expecting Armageddon: Essential Readings in Failed Prophecy,* edited by Jon R. Stone, 87–105. New York: Routledge, 2000.

Index

writes description of Zion, 86–87, 102;
  wrestles with JS, 741, 744n124
Rigdon, Smith & Co., 581
Rigdon, Smith & Cowdery, 560, 577–78,
  596n111, 612, 623, 633
Riggs, Burr, 776, 820, 841n23, 854
Riggs, Michael S., 375, 685n108
Right, Dr., 48–49
Rigsby, Mr., 740–41
Ripley, Alanson, 682–83, 706, 758, 829, 848,
  852–53
Ritch, Abram, 639
Ritner, Robert K., 435, 490
Robbins, Lewis, 658
Roberts, Mr., 804
Robinson, Ebenezer, 471–72, 472n80, 507,
  573, 576, 580, 677, 706, 708, 711–13, 715,
  724–27, 782–83, 809
Robinson, George W., 640, 652, 674, 685, 689,
  713, 719, 730, 733, 738, 741, 749, 751, 752,
  788–89, 802–3, 831, 845
Robinson, Joseph Lee, xix
Robinson's Grove, 708
Rochester, New York, xxviii, 191, 591, 694
Rockford, Missouri, 570
Rockwell, Orrin Porter, 880–81, 883
Rockwood, Albert P., 624, 626, 716–17, 776,
  780, 831
Rocky Mountains, 77, 333–34, 345, 517, 777,
  815
Rogers, David, 854
Rogers, Isaac, 605
Rollins, James Henry, 4, 820
Romig, Ronald E., 375
Rosetta Stone, 430
Rothville, Missouri, 873
Rounds, Samuel D., 590, 648
Roundy, Shadrach, 507
Rowland, Moses, 825, 834, 834n101
Rowley, William, xx
Russell, Alpheus C., 305
Russell, Isaac, 609
Russell, Ohio, 590
Ryder, Mehitable, 48
Ryder, Simonds, 48, 105–8, 133–34, 149–50, 152
Ryland, John F., 266–67, 354, 359

Sabellianism, 171, 396–97
Sagers, Harrison, 761
Salem, Massachusetts, 572–74, 574n125, 576
Salem, Missouri, 708
Salisbury, Katharine, 188
Salisbury, Wilkins J., 559

Salt Lake City, 211
Salt Lake Tribune, 563
Salt River, 349–50
Sandusky County, Ohio, 322n104
Sandusky Plains, Ohio, 339
Sapham, Mr., 680
Sapp, John N., 715
Saxton, Noah C., 191–92
Scarborough, Canada, 626–27
Schenectady, New York, 572
School of the Elders, 196, 395, 403, 422, 466,
  476–77, 512, 523
School of the Prophets, 195, 201–2, 204–5,
  207–8, 210–11, 212n68, 213–14, 217, 219,
  221, 466, 477, 481
Scott, Jacob, 71, 865
Scott, John, 802
Scott, Walter, 75–76, 75n2
Scovel, Abner, 817–18
Scribner, Jonathan F., 560, 641–42
Scribner v. Rigdon, Smith & Cowdery, 642
seer stone, xxiv, 9, 21, 116, 116n5, 170, 224, 295,
  381, 383, 400, 467, 488, 566, 698
Seixas, Joshua, 519–20, 523, 529–31, 545
Seneca County, New York, 56
Sessions, Patty, 685
Sessions, Sylvia, *see* Sylvia Sessions Lyon
Shafer, Robert Jones, xiii
Shaker(s), 38n86, 54–56, 55n62, 59, 65, 69, 145
Shalersville, Ohio, 105–6, 118, 134–35, 150
Shearer, Norman, 834
Sherman, Lyman R., 410–11, 513, 566, 656,
  656n126, 845, 845n36
Sherwood, Henry G., 224
Sherwood, Jane, 224
Shipps, Jan, vii, 698
Shoal Creek, 569, 572, 642, 669
Shoemaker, Mr., 849
Shurtliff, Luman A., 137, 717n134
Silvers, William, 265
Sjodahl, Janne M., 292
Slade, Benjamin, 823n31
slavery, 39, 77, 191, 244–45, 244n38, 245n46,
  449, 492–95, 558–59, 572, 703
Sloan, James, 829
Smalling, Cyrus, 581, 601, 649, 700
Smith, Alexander Hale, 710, 722
Smith, Alvin, 296, 525, 691, 699
Smith, Asael, 559–60
Smith, Bathsheba W., xv
Smith, Don Carlos, 131, 281, 394, 458, 458n18,
  458n19, 472–73, 527, 533, 542, 560, 573,
  578, 578n5, 657, 850–51
Smith, Elias, 559

his mission, 541–42; blaming traitors for failure of Kirtland bank, 597; calling on God to witness injustice of Missourians, 351–52; denouncing dissenters, 591; denouncing non-Mormon in audience for making critical remarks about him, 723; denouncing Sidney Rigdon's claim church had lost keys of kingdom, 162–63; explaining power of high priesthood, 110; introducing high priesthood, 62–66; promising elders large congregations, 68; to Missouri delegation in power of God, 359; to recruits for Zion's Camp prior to leaving Kirtland, 335

appointments, blessings, callings, dedications, marriages, ordinations: approves fund-raising committee to buy out non-Mormons in Daviess County, 761; assigns W. W. Phelps to assist Cowdery as a printer in Kirtland, 369–70; assists in laying first log at the Colesville branch settlement in Kaw Township, 89–90; assesses characters of counselors Sidney Rigdon and Frederick G. Williams, then pronounces blessings on them, 280–81; attends church, 497; blesses children, 329, 476; fatally-wounded David Patten, 779; McLellin to have a witness of his apostleship, 550; saints who provided financial relief, 507; calls Edward Partridge and Newel K. Whitney as bishops, 5, 134; casts devil out of woman, 17; dedicates Independence temple lot, 90–91; dictates blessings on Oliver Cowdery and Smith family members, 291–93; expands and alters previous blessings, 458–62, 458n20; expands church hierarchy, 372; forms three agricultural companies in Adam-ondi-Ahman, 746–47; gives Zion blessing to Lorenzo Barnes, 517; heals Elsa Johnson's rheumatic arm, 48–50; William McLellin's ankle, 225; introduces washings and anointings of church leaders, 522–27; issues missionary licenses, 557; ordains David Whitmer as successor, 368; David Whitmer, W. W. Phelps, and John Whitmer presidents and twelve others composing the Missouri high council, 367; Frederick G. Williams as counselor, 210; Hyrum Smith as a president of the church, 394; Lyman Wight and Harvey Whitlock to high priesthood, 64; Oliver Cowdery as assistant president of the church, 392; Sidney Rigdon and Jesse

Gause as his counselors, 145; organizes Adam-ondi-Ahman stake, 723; school of the prophets and introduces washing of feet, 202–3; United Firm in Missouri, 157–58; performs marriages, 609–10, 685; of Ebenezer Robinson and Angeline Works, 507; of Newel Knight and Lydia Goldthwaite, 498–99; rebukes evil spirit during conference, 65; sends William McLellin to Florence, 387; sets Heber Kimball apart to preside over English mission, 608–9; unable to heal members of Zion's Camp of cholera, 365; two men at conference, 65; Warner Doty, 45–46

church appointments, priesthood: sustained as president of the high priesthood in Missouri, 66, 156; sustained as president of the high priesthood at Amherst conference, 136; receives blessing as leader of Zion's Camp, 327; receives blessing by his father, 394–95; acts as cashier/treasurer/secretary of the Kirtland bank, 579, 582; appointed with Rigdon to establish more stakes in Missouri, 640–41; misrepresents bank, 585

conferences, meetings: attends conferences/meetings in Amherst, 136; Avon, 317; Hiram, 108, 117–25, 127–28, 131–32; Kirtland, 6, 12, 61–66, 68, 134–35, 478, 483, 502, 517, 534; Missouri, 91–93, 156; New Portage, 380, 385, 450; Norton, 327; Orange, 108–14; two-day public debate in Huntsburg, 21–13; attends blessing meeting, 514, 17; conference of presidency, 531; dedication of temple, 536–37; Easter Sunday service in temple, 553; feast for poor at Bishop Whitney's, 520; funeral of Nathan Harris, 485; funeral of Polly Knight, 93–94; "Grand Council" in temple, 520–21; Hebrew school, 519, 527, 529–31; meeting with Presidency and Seventy, 534; prayer meetings and marriage ceremony, 472–73; priesthood meeting in association with temple dedication, 543–45; public debates, 485, 507–8; repeat of dedicatory service, 551; school of the prophets (elders), 210–12, 476, 477, 528; solemn assembly of the priesthood, 345–49; spirit-filled meeting of Seventy in temple, 527; United Firm, 143–44, 325; worship service in temple and is confronted by Parrish, 604; to bless those working on temple, 412; to call twelve apostles and members of the

Dan Vogel is the author of *Joseph Smith: The Making of a Prophet*, winner of the Mormon History Association's Best Biography Award and the John Whitmer Historical Association's Best Book Award. He also authored *Book of Abraham Apologetics: A Review and Critique*, *Indian Origins and the Book of Mormon*, and *Religious Seekers and the Advent of Mormonism*. He is the editor of the six-volume *The Wilford Woodruff Journals*, the eight-volume *History of Joseph Smith and The Church of Jesus Christ of Latter-day Saints: A Source- and Text-Critical Edition*, the award-winning five-volume series, *Early Mormon Documents*, and *The Word of God: Essays on Mormon Scripture*. He co-edited, with Brent Lee Metcalfe, *American Apocrypha: Essays on the Book of Mormon*. He lives in Ohio.

OTHER TITLES IN THIS TRILOGY

**Natural Born Seer: Joseph Smith,
American Prophet, 1805–1830**

Richard S. Van Wagoner

hardback | $29.00   ebook | $9.99

**Glorious in Persecution: Joseph Smith,
American Prophet, 1839–1844**

Martha Bradley-Evans

hardback | $29.00   ebook | $9.99

www.signaturebooks.com